Your Legal Environment: Essentials of Business Law

Haworth College of Business

Third Custom Edition

Authors: Jeffrey F. Beatty, Susan S. Samuelson, Patricia Sanchez Abril

D1362395

CENGAGE
Learning·

Australia • Brazil • Japan • Korea • Mexico • Singapore • Spain • United Kingdom • United States

Your Legal Environment: Essentials of Business Law: Haworth College of Business, Third Custom Edition

Business Law and the Legal Environment, Standard Edition
Jeffrey F. Beatty, Susan S. Samuelson, Patricia Sanchez Abril

For product information and technology assistance, contact us at
Cengage Learning Customer & Sales Support, 1-800-354-9706

For permission to use material from this text or product,
submit all requests online at **cengage.com/permissions**
Further permissions questions can be emailed to
permissionrequest@cengage.com

This book contains select works from existing Cengage Learning resources and was produced by Cengage Learning Custom Solutions for collegiate use. As such, those adopting and/or contributing to this work are responsible for editorial content accuracy, continuity and completeness.

Compilation © 2016 Cengage Learning

ISBN:978-1-337-03537-8

Cengage Learning

Cengage Learning is a leading provider of customized learning solutions with office locations around the globe, including Singapore, the United Kingdom, Australia, Mexico, Brazil, and Japan. Locate your local office at:
www.international.cengage.com/region.

Cengage Learning products are represented in Canada by Nelson Education, Ltd.

For your lifelong learning solutions, visit **www.cengage.com/custom.**

Visit our corporate website at **www.cengage.com.**

Table of Contents

Chapter 1

INTRODUCTION TO LAW

The Pagans were a motorcycle gang with a reputation for violence. Two of its rougher members, Rhino and Backdraft, entered a tavern called the Pub Zone, shoving their way past the bouncer. The pair wore gang insignia, in violation of the bar's rules. For a while, all was quiet, as the two sipped drinks at the bar. Then they followed an innocent patron toward the men's room, and things happened fast.

© Creative Travel Projects/Shutterstock.com

"Wait a moment," you may be thinking. "Are we reading a chapter on business law or one about biker crimes in a roadside tavern?" Both.

Law is powerful, essential, and fascinating. We hope this book will persuade you of all three ideas. Law can also be surprising. Later in the chapter, we will return to the Pub Zone (with armed guards) and follow Rhino and Backdraft to the back of the pub. Yes, the pair engaged in street crime, which is hardly a focus of this text. However, their criminal acts will enable us to explore one of the law's basic principles—negligence. Should a pub owner pay money damages to the victim of gang violence? The owner herself did nothing aggressive. Should she have prevented the harm? Does her failure to stop the assault make her liable?

> Should a pub owner pay money damages to the victim of gang violence?

We place great demands on our courts, asking them to make our large, complex, and sometimes violent society into a safer, fairer, more orderly place. The Pub Zone case is a good example of how judges reason their way through the convoluted issues involved. What began as a gang incident ends up as a matter of commercial liability. We will traipse after Rhino and Backdraft because they have a lesson to teach anyone who enters the world of business.

1-1 THE ROLE OF LAW IN SOCIETY

1-1a Power

The strong reach of the law touches nearly everything we do, especially at work. Consider a mid-level manager at Sublime Corp., which manufactures and distributes video games.

During the course of a day's work, she might negotiate a deal with a game developer (contract law). Before signing any deals, she might research whether similar games already exist, which might diminish her ability to market the proposed new game (intellectual property law). One of her subordinates might complain about being harassed by a coworker (employment law). Another worker may complain about being required to work long hours (administrative law). And she may consider investing her own money in her company's stock, but she may wonder whether she will get into trouble if she invests based on inside information (securities law).

It is not only as a corporate manager that you will confront the law. As a voter, investor, juror, entrepreneur, and community member, you will influence and be affected by the law. Whenever you take a stance about a legal issue, whether in the corporate office, in the voting booth, or as part of local community groups, you help to create the fabric of our nation. Your views are vital. This book will offer you knowledge and ideas from which to form and continually reassess your legal opinions and values.

1-1b Importance

Law is also essential. *Every* society of which we have any historical record has had some system of laws. For example, consider the Visigoths, a nomadic European people who overran much of present-day France and Spain during the fifth and sixth centuries A.D. Their code admirably required judges to be "quick of perception, clear in judgment, and lenient in the infliction of penalties." It detailed dozens of crimes.

Our legal system is largely based upon the English model, but many societies contributed ideas. The Iroquois Native Americans, for example, played a role in the creation of our own government. Five major nations made up the Iroquois group: the Mohawk, Cayuga, Oneida, Onondaga, and Seneca. Each nation governed its own domestic issues. But each nation also elected "sachems" to a League of the Iroquois. The league had authority over any matters that were common to all, such as relations with outsiders. Thus, by the fifteenth century, the Iroquois had solved the problem of *federalism*: how to have two levels of government, each with specified powers. Their system impressed Benjamin Franklin and others and influenced the drafting of our Constitution, with its powers divided between state and federal governments.[1]

1-1c Fascination

In 1835, the young French aristocrat Alexis de Tocqueville traveled through the United States, observing the newly democratic people and the qualities that made them unique. One of the things that struck de Tocqueville most forcefully was the American tendency to file suit: "Scarcely any political question arises in the United States that is not resolved, sooner or later, into a judicial question."[2] De Tocqueville got it right: For better or worse, we do expect courts to resolve many problems.

Not only do Americans litigate—they watch each other do it. Every television season offers at least one new courtroom drama to a national audience breathless for more

---

[1] Jack Weatherford, *Indian Givers* (New York: Fawcett Columbine, 1988), pp. 133–150.
[2] Alexis de Tocqueville, *Democracy in America* (1835), Vol. 1, Ch. 16.

cross-examination. Almost all of the states permit live television coverage of real trials. The most heavily viewed event in the history of the medium was the O. J. Simpson murder trial, in which a famous football star was accused of killing his wife. In most nations, coverage of judicial proceedings is not allowed.[3]

The law is a big part of our lives, and it is wise to know something about it. Within a few weeks, you will probably find yourself following legal events in the news with keener interest and deeper understanding. In this chapter, we develop the background for our study. We look at where law comes from: its history and its present-day institutions. In the section on jurisprudence, we examine different theories about what "law" really means. And finally we see how courts—and students—analyze a case.

1-2 ORIGINS OF OUR LAW

It would be nice if we could look up "the law" in one book, memorize it, and then apply it. But the law is not that simple, and *cannot* be that simple, because it reflects the complexity of contemporary life. In truth, there is no such thing as "the law." Principles and rules of law actually come from *many different* sources. This is so, in part, because we inherited a complex structure of laws from England.

Additionally, ours is a nation born in revolution, and created, in large part, to protect the rights of its people from the government. The Founding Fathers created a national government but insisted that the individual states maintain control in many areas. As a result, each state has its own government with exclusive power over many important areas of our lives. To top it off, the Founders guaranteed many rights to the people alone, ordering national *and* state governments to keep clear. This has worked, but it has caused a multilayered system, with 50 state governments and one federal government all creating and enforcing law.

1-2a English Roots

England in the tenth century was a rustic agricultural community with a tiny population and very little law or order. Vikings invaded repeatedly, terrorizing the Anglo-Saxon peoples. Criminals were hard to catch in the heavily forested, sparsely settled nation. The king used a primitive legal system to maintain a tenuous control over his people.

England was divided into shires, and daily administration was carried out by a "shire reeve," later called a sheriff. The shire reeve collected taxes and did what he could to keep peace, apprehending criminals and acting as mediator between feuding families. Two or three times a year, a shire court met; lower courts met more frequently. Today, this method of resolving disputes lives on as mediation, which we will discuss in Chapter 3.

Because there were so few officers to keep the peace, Anglo-Saxon society created an interesting method of ensuring public order. Every freeman belonged to a group of 10 freemen known as a "tithing," headed by a "tithingman." If anyone injured a person outside his tithing or interfered with the king's property, all 10 men of the tithing could be forced to pay. Today, we still use this idea of collective responsibility in business partnerships. All partners are personally responsible for the debts of the partnership. They could potentially lose their homes and all assets because of the irresponsible conduct of one partner. That liability has helped create new forms of business organization, including limited liability companies.

When cases did come before an Anglo-Saxon court, the parties would often be represented by a clergyman, by a nobleman, or by themselves. There were few professional lawyers. Each

---

[3]Regardless of whether we allow cameras, it is an undeniable benefit of the electronic age that we can obtain information quickly. From time to time, we will mention websites of interest. Some of these are for nonprofit groups, while others are commercial sites. We do not endorse or advocate on behalf of any group or company; we simply wish to alert you to what is available.

party produced "oath helpers," usually 12, who would swear that one version of events was correct. The Anglo-Saxon oath helpers were forerunners of our modern jury of 12 persons.

In 1066, the Normans conquered England. William the Conqueror made a claim never before made in England: that he owned all of the land. The king then granted sections of his lands to his favorite noblemen, as his tenants in chief, creating the system of feudalism. These tenants in chief then granted parts of their land to *tenants in demesne*, who actually occupied a particular estate. Each tenant in demesne owed fidelity to his lord (hence, "landlord"). So what? Just this: Land became the most valuable commodity in all of England, and our law still reflects that. One thousand years later, American law still regards land as special. The Statute of Frauds, which we study in the section on contracts, demands that contracts for the sale or lease of property be in writing. And landlord-tenant law, vital to students and many others, still reflects its ancient roots. Some of a landlord's rights are based on the 1,000-year-old tradition that land is uniquely valuable.

In 1250, Henry de Bracton (d. 1268) wrote a legal treatise that still influences us. *De Legibus et Consuetudinibus Angliae (On the Laws and Customs of England),* written in Latin, summarized many of the legal rulings in cases since the Norman Conquest. De Bracton was teaching judges to rule based on previous cases. He was helping to establish the idea of **precedent. The doctrine of precedent, which developed gradually over centuries, requires that judges decide current cases based on previous rulings.** This vital principle is the heart of American common law. Precedent ensures predictability. Suppose a 17-year-old student promises to lease an apartment from a landlord, but then changes her mind. The landlord sues to enforce the lease. The student claims that she cannot be held to the agreement because she is a minor. The judge will look for precedent, that is, older cases dealing with the same issue, and he will find many holding that a contract generally may not be enforced against a minor. That precedent is binding on this case, and the student wins. **The accumulation of precedent, based on case after case, makes up the common law.**

Today's society is dramatically different from that of medieval English society. But interestingly, legal disputes from hundreds of years ago are often quite recognizable today. Some things have changed but others never do.

Here is an actual case from more than six centuries ago, in the court's own language. The plaintiff claims that he asked the defendant to heal his eye with "herbs and other medicines." He says the defendant did it so badly that he blinded the plaintiff in that eye.

Medieval tenants in demesne harrowing, plowing and seeding a field.

North Wind/North Wind Picture Archives

Precedent
The tendency to decide current cases based on previous rulings.

Common law
Judge-made law

THE OCULIST'S CASE (1329)

LI MS. Hale 137 (1), fo. 150, Nottingham[4]

Attorney Launde [for defendant]: Sir, you plainly see how [the plaintiff claims] that he had submitted himself to [the defendant's] medicines and his care; and after that he can assign no trespass in his person, inasmuch as he submitted himself to his care: But this action, if he has any, sounds naturally in breach of covenant. We demand [that the case be dismissed].

---

[4]J. Baker and S. Milsom, *Sources of English Legal History* (London: Butterworth & Co., 1986).

Excerpts from Judge Denum's Decision: I saw a Newcastle man arraigned before my fellow justice and me for the death of a man. I asked the reason for the indictment, and it was said that he had slain a man under his care, who died within four days afterwards. And because I saw that he was a [doctor] and that he had not done the thing feloniously but [accidentally] I ordered him to be discharged. And suppose a blacksmith, who is a man of skill, injures your horse with a nail, whereby you lose your horse: You shall never have recovery against him. No more shall you here.

Afterwards the plaintiff did not wish to pursue his case any more.

This case from 1329 is an ancient medical malpractice action. Attorney Launde does not deny that his client blinded the plaintiff. He claims that the plaintiff has brought the wrong kind of lawsuit. Launde argues that the plaintiff should have brought a case of "covenant"; that is, a lawsuit about a contract.

Judge Denum decides the case on a different principle. He gives judgment to the defendant because the plaintiff voluntarily sought medical care. He implies that the defendant would lose only if he had attacked the plaintiff. As we will see when we study negligence law, this case might have a different outcome today. Note also the informality of the judge's ruling. He rather casually mentions that he came across a related case once before and that he would stand by that outcome. The idea of precedent is just beginning to take hold.

1-2b Law in the United States

The colonists brought with them a basic knowledge of English law, some of which they were content to adopt as their own. Other parts, such as religious restrictions, were abhorrent to them. Many had made the dangerous trip to America precisely to escape persecution, and they were not interested in recreating their difficulties in a new land. Finally, some laws were simply irrelevant or unworkable in a world that was socially and geographically so different. American law ever since has been a blend of the ancient principles of English common law and a zeal and determination for change.

During the nineteenth century, the United States changed from a weak, rural nation into one of vast size and potential power. Cities grew, factories appeared, and sweeping movements of social migration changed the population. Changing conditions raised new legal questions. Did workers have a right to form industrial unions? To what extent should a manufacturer be liable if its product injured someone? Could a state government invalidate an employment contract that required 16-hour workdays? Should one company be permitted to dominate an entire industry?

In the twentieth century, the rate of social and technological change increased, creating new legal puzzles. Were some products, such as automobiles, so inherently dangerous that the seller should be responsible for injuries even if no mistakes were made in manufacturing? Who should clean up toxic waste if the company that had caused the pollution no longer existed? If a consumer signed a contract with a billion-dollar corporation, should the agreement be enforced even if the consumer never understood it? New and startling questions arise with great regularity. Before we can begin to examine the answers, we need to understand the sources of contemporary law.

1-3 SOURCES OF CONTEMPORARY LAW

Throughout the text, we will examine countless legal ideas. But binding rules come from many different places. This section describes the significant categories of laws in the United States.

1-3a United States Constitution

America's greatest legal achievement was the writing of the United States Constitution in 1787. It is the supreme law of the land.[5] Any law that conflicts with it is void. This federal Constitution does three basic things. First, it establishes the national government of the United States, with its three branches. Second, it creates a system of checks and balances among the branches. And third, the Constitution guarantees many basic rights to the American people.

Branches of Government

The Founding Fathers sought a division of government power. They did not want all power centralized in a king or in anyone else. And so, the Constitution divides legal authority into three pieces: legislative, executive, and judicial power.

Legislative power gives the ability to create new laws. In Article I, the Constitution gives this power to the Congress, which is comprised of two chambers—a Senate and a House of Representatives. Voters in all 50 states elect representatives who go to Washington, D.C., to serve in the Congress and debate new legal ideas.

The House of Representatives has 435 voting members. A state's voting power is based on its population. Large states (Texas, California, and Florida) send dozens of representatives to the House. Some small states (Wyoming, North Dakota, and Delaware) send only one. The Senate has 100 voting members—two from each state.

Executive power is the authority to enforce laws. Article II of the Constitution establishes the president as commander in chief of the armed forces and the head of the executive branch of the federal government.

Judicial power gives the right to interpret laws and determine their validity. Article III places the Supreme Court at the head of the judicial branch of the federal government. Interpretive power is often underrated, but it is often every bit as important as the ability to create laws in the first place. For instance, the Supreme Court ruled that privacy provisions of the Constitution protect a woman's right to abortion, although neither the word "privacy" nor "abortion" appears in the text of the Constitution.[6]

At times, courts void laws altogether. For example, in 1995, the Supreme Court ruled that the Gun-Free School Zones Act of 1990 was unconstitutional because Congress did not have the authority to pass such a law.[7]

Checks and Balances

The authors of the Constitution were not content merely to divide government power three ways. They also wanted to give each part of the government some power over the other two branches. Many people complain about "gridlock" in Washington, but the government is slow and sluggish by design. The Founding Fathers wanted to create a system that, without broad agreement, would tend towards inaction.

The president can veto Congressional legislation. Congress can impeach the president. The Supreme Court can void laws passed by Congress. The president appoints judges to the federal courts, including the Supreme Court, but these nominees do not serve unless approved by the Senate. Congress (with help from the 50 states) can override the Supreme

---

[5]The Constitution took effect in 1788, when 9 of 13 colonies ratified it. Two more colonies ratified it that year, and the last of the 13 did so in 1789, after the government was already in operation. The complete text of the Constitution appears in Appendix A.

[6]Roe v. Wade, 410 U.S. 113 (1973).

[7]United States v. Alfonso Lopez, Jr., 514 U.S. 549 (1995).

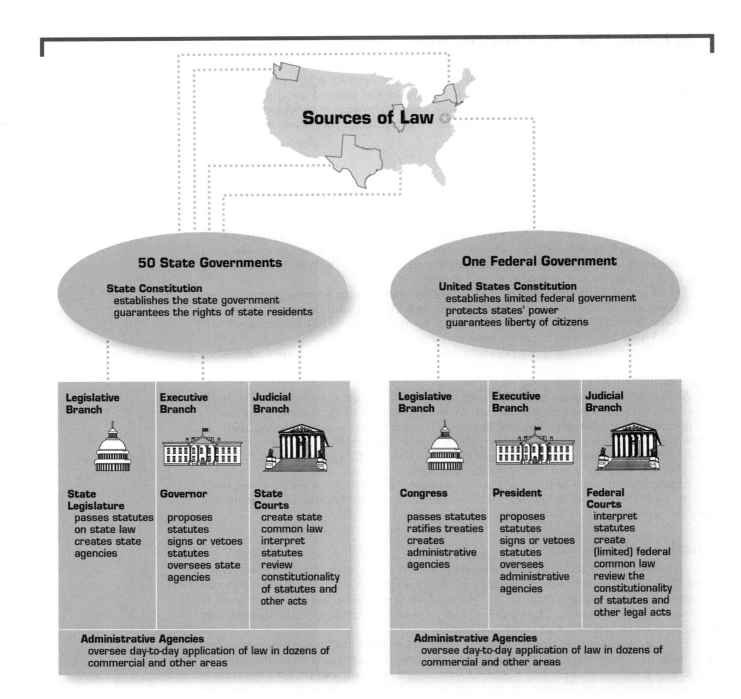

Federal Form of Government. Principles and rules of law come from many sources. The government in Washington creates and enforces law throughout the nation. But 50 state governments exercise great power in local affairs. And citizens enjoy constitutional protection from both state and federal government. The Founding Fathers wanted this balance of power and rights, but the overlapping authority creates legal complexity.

Court by amending the Constitution. The president and the Congress influence the Supreme Court by controlling who is placed on the court in the first place.

Many of these checks and balances will be examined in more detail later in this book, starting in Chapter 4.

Fundamental Rights

The Constitution also grants many of our most basic liberties. For the most part, they are found in the amendments to the Constitution. The First Amendment guarantees the rights of free speech, free press, and the free exercise of religion. The Fourth, Fifth, and Sixth Amendments protect the rights of any person accused of a crime. Other amendments ensure that the government treats all people equally and that it pays for any property it takes from a citizen.

By creating a limited government of three branches, and guaranteeing basic liberties to all citizens, the Constitution became one of the most important documents ever written.

1-3b Statutes

The second important source of law is statutory law. The Constitution gave to the United States Congress the power to pass laws on various subjects. These laws are called **statutes**, and they can cover absolutely any topic, so long as they do not violate the Constitution.

Statute
A law created by a legislature

Almost all statutes are created by the same method. An idea for a new law—on taxes, body. health care, texting while driving, or any other topic, big or small—is first proposed in the Congress. This idea is called a *bill*. The House and Senate then independently vote on the bill. To pass Congress, the bill must win a simple majority vote in each of these chambers.

If Congress passes a bill, it goes to the White House for the president's approval. If the president signs it, a new statute is created. It is no longer a mere idea; it is the law of the land. If the president refuses to approve, or *vetoes* a bill, it does not become a statute unless Congress overrides the veto. To do that, both the House and the Senate must approve the bill by a two-thirds majority. If this happens, it becomes a statute without the president's signature.

1-3c Common Law

Binding legal ideas often come from the courts. Judges generally follow *precedent*. When courts decide a case, they tend to apply the legal rules that other courts have used in similar cases.

The principle that precedent is binding on later cases is called *stare decisis*, which means "let the decision stand." *Stare decisis* makes the law predictable and this, in turn, enables businesses and private citizens to plan intelligently.

It is important to note that precedent is binding only on *lower* courts. For example, if the Supreme Court decided a case in one way in 1965, it is under no obligation to follow precedent if the same issue arises in 2015.

Sometimes, this is quite beneficial. In 1896, the Supreme Court decided (unbelievably) that segregation—separating people by race in schools, hotels, public transportation, and other public services—was legal under certain conditions.[8] In 1954, on the exact same issue, the court changed its mind.[9]

In other circumstances, it is more difficult to see the value in breaking with an established rule.

---

[8]Plessy v. Ferguson, 163 U.S. 537 (1896).
[9]Brown v. Board of Education of Topeka, 347 U.S. 483 (1954).

1-3d Court Orders

Judges have the authority to issue court orders that place binding obligations on specific people or companies. An injunction, for example, is a court order to stop doing something. A judge might order a stalker to stay more than 500 yards away from an ex-boyfriend or -girlfriend. An alcoholic might be ordered to stop drinking and enter rehab. Courts have the authority to imprison or fine those who violate their orders.

1-3e Administrative Law

In a society as large and diverse as ours, the executive and legislative branches of government cannot oversee all aspects of commerce. Congress passes statutes about air safety, but United States senators do not stand around air traffic towers, serving coffee to keep everyone awake. The executive branch establishes rules concerning how foreign nationals enter the United States, but presidents are reluctant to sit on the dock of the bay, watching the ships come in. Administrative agencies do this day-to-day work.

> **United States senators do not stand around air traffic towers, serving coffee to keep everyone awake.**

Most government agencies are created by Congress. Familiar examples are the Environmental Protection Agency (EPA), the Securities and Exchange Commission (SEC), and the Internal Revenue Service (IRS), whose feelings are hurt if it does not hear from you every April 15. Agencies have the power to create laws called *regulations*.

1-3f Treaties

The Constitution authorizes the president to make treaties with foreign nations. These must then be ratified by the United States Senate by a two-thirds vote. When they are ratified, they are as binding upon all citizens as any federal statute. In 1994, the Senate ratified the North American Free Trade Agreement (NAFTA) with Mexico and Canada. NAFTA was controversial then and remains so today—but it is the law of the land.

1-4 CLASSIFICATIONS

We have seen where law originated. Now we need to classify the various types of laws. First, we will distinguish between criminal and civil law. Then, we will take a look at the intersection between law and morality.

1-4a Criminal and Civil Law

Criminal law
Criminal law prohibits certain behavior for the benefit of society.

It is a crime to embezzle money from a bank, to steal a car, to sell cocaine. **Criminal law concerns behavior so threatening that society outlaws it altogether.** Most criminal laws are statutes, passed by Congress or a state legislature. The government itself prosecutes the wrongdoer, regardless of what the bank president or car owner wants. A district attorney, paid by the government, brings the case to court. The victim is not in charge of the case, although she may appear as a witness. The government will seek to punish the defendant with a prison sentence, a fine, or both. If there is a fine, the money goes to the state, not to the injured party.

Civil law
Civil law regulates the rights and duties between parties.

Civil law is different, and most of this book is about civil law. **The civil law regulates the rights and duties between parties.** Tracy agrees in writing to lease you a 30,000-square-foot store in her shopping mall. She now has a *legal duty* to make the space available. But then another tenant offers her more money, and she refuses to let you move in. Tracy has violated her duty, but she has not committed a crime. The government will not prosecute the case. It is up to you to file a civil lawsuit. Your case will be based on the common law of contract. You will also seek equitable relief, namely, an injunction ordering Tracy not to lease to anyone else. You should win the suit, and you will get your injunction and some monetary damages. But Tracy will not go to jail.

Some conduct involves both civil and criminal law. Suppose Tracy is so upset over losing the court case that she becomes drunk and causes a serious car accident. She has committed the crime of driving while intoxicated, and the state will prosecute. Tracy may be fined or imprisoned. She has also committed negligence, and the injured party will file a lawsuit against her, seeking money. We will again see civil and criminal law joined together in the *Pub Zone* case, later in the chapter.

1-4b Law and Morality

Law is different from morality, yet the two are obviously linked. There are many instances when the law duplicates what all of us would regard as a moral position. It is negligent to drive too fast in a school zone, and few would dispute the moral value of seeking to limit harm to students. And the same holds with contract law: If the owner of land agrees in writing to sell property to a buyer at a stated price, both the buyer and the seller must go through with the deal, and the legal outcome matches our moral expectations.

On the other hand, we have had laws that we now clearly regard as immoral. At the turn of the century, a factory owner could typically fire a worker for any reason at all—including, for example, his religious or political views. It is immoral to fire a worker because she is Jewish—and today the law prohibits it.

Finally, there are legal issues where the morality is less clear. You are walking down a country lane and notice a three-year-old child playing with matches near a barn filled with hay. Are you obligated to intervene? No, says the law, though many think that is preposterous. (See Chapter 4, on common law, for more about this topic.) A company buys property and then discovers, buried under the ground, toxic waste that will cost $300,000 to clean up. The original owner has gone bankrupt. Should the new owner be forced to pay for the cleanup? If the new owner fails to pay for the job, who will? (See Chapter 40, on environmental law, for more discussion on this issue.)

Chapter 2 will further examine the bond between law and morality, but our ethics discussion does not end there. Throughout the text, you will find ethics questions and features, like the one that follows, which ask you to grapple with the moral dimensions of legal questions.

Do we want to live in a world where no one ever pays attention in public places?

David Grossman/Alamy

Ethics It was a cold winter's day. In one of New York City's dank, dark subway stations, dozens of people waited for the next train, most of them engrossed in their smartphones. All of a sudden, a man was shoved onto the subway tracks. He screamed for help and struggled to climb up onto the platform. Because no one helped him, he was crushed to death by an oncoming train.[10]

---

[10]Christine Rosen, "The Gadget and the Bad Samaritan," *The Wall Street Journal*, Oct. 26–27, 2013.

Some of the bystanders were so busy peering at their smartphones, they did not even hear the man's screams for help. Use of technology has changed our awareness of our surroundings and our sense of civility and duty to those around us. Did these onlookers have an obligation to be more aware of their environment? Do we want to live in a world where no one ever pays attention in public places?

The second group saw what was happening, but still did not help. Sociologists call this the "bystander effect." Studies have shown that people in a group are much less likely to help others than are individuals on their own. In a crowd, responsibility is diffused. Everyone assumes that someone else will act.

A third group pulled out their phones to capture images and videos of the last minutes of the man's life. One man sold his picture of the episode to the *New York Post*, which published it on the cover the next day. Other witnesses shared their videos on YouTube. Some of these witnesses might argue that their images informed many people about the incident and brought awareness of it. Did they behave ethically?

What are the moral obligations of each of these groups of witnesses? Who has acted most unethically (if anyone)? Remember that the decision to help (or not) is one that is made in a split second. What would you have done?

1-5 JURISPRUDENCE

jurisprudence
The philosophy of law

We have had a glimpse of legal history and a summary of the present-day sources of American law. But what *is* law? That question is the basis of a field known as **jurisprudence**. What is the real nature of law? Can there be such a thing as an "illegal" law?

1-5a Legal Positivism

Sovereign
The recognized political power, whom citizens obey.

This philosophy can be simply stated: Law is what the sovereign says it is. The sovereign is the recognized political power whom citizens obey, so in the United States, both state and federal governments are sovereign. A legal positivist holds that whatever the sovereign declares to be the law *is* the law, whether it is right or wrong.

The primary criticism of legal positivism is that it seems to leave no room for questions of morality. A law permitting a factory owner to fire a worker because she is Catholic is surely different from a law prohibiting arson. Do citizens in a democracy have a duty to consider such differences? Consider the following example.

Most states allow citizens to pass laws directly at the ballot box, a process called voter referendum. California voters often do this, and during the 1990s, they passed one of the state's most controversial laws. Proposition 187 was designed to curb illegal immigration into the state by eliminating social spending for undocumented aliens. Citizens debated the measure fiercely but passed it by a large margin. One section of the new law forbade public schools from educating illegal immigrants. The law obligated a principal to inquire into the immigration status of all children enrolled in the school and to report undocumented students to immigration authorities. Several San Diego school principals rejected the new rules, stating that they would neither inquire into immigration status nor report undocumented aliens. Their statements produced a heated response. Some San Diego residents castigated the school officials as lawbreakers, claiming that:

- A school officer who knowingly disobeyed a law was setting a terrible example for students, who would assume they were free to do the same;

- The principals were advocating permanent residence and a free education for anyone able to evade our immigration laws; and

- The officials were scorning grass-roots democracy by disregarding a law passed by popular referendum.

Others applauded the principals' position, asserting that:

- The referendum's rules would transform school officials from educators into border police, forcing them to cross-examine young children and their parents;

- The new law was foolish because it punished innocent children for violations committed by their parents; and

- Our nation has long respected civil disobedience based on humanitarian ideals, and these officials were providing moral leadership to the whole community.

Ultimately, no one had to decide whether to obey Proposition 187. A federal court ruled that only Congress had the power to regulate immigration and that California's attempt was unconstitutional and void. The debate over immigration reform—and ethics—did not end, however. It continues to be a thorny issue.

1-5b Natural Law

St. Thomas Aquinas (1225–1274) answered the legal positivists even before they had spoken. In his *Summa Theologica*, he argued that an unjust law is no law at all and need not be obeyed. It is not enough that a sovereign makes a command. The law must have a moral basis.

Where do we find the moral basis that would justify a law? Aquinas says that "good is that which all things seek after." Therefore, the fundamental rule of all laws is that "good is to be done and promoted, and evil is to be avoided." This sounds appealing, but also vague. Exactly which laws promote good and which do not? Is it better to have a huge corporation dominate a market or many smaller companies competing? Did the huge company get that way by being better than its competitors? If Wal-Mart moves into a rural area, establishes a mammoth store, and sells inexpensive products, is that "good"? Yes, if you are a consumer who cares only about prices. No, if you are the owner of a Main Street store driven into bankruptcy. Maybe, if you are a resident who values small-town life but wants lower prices.

1-5c Legal Realism

Legal realists take a very different tack. They claim it does not matter what is written as law. What counts is who enforces that law and by what process it is enforced. All of us are biased by issues such as income, education, family background, race, religion, and many other factors. These personal characteristics, they say, determine which contracts will be enforced and which ignored, why some criminals receive harsh sentences while others get off lightly, and so on.

Judge Jones hears a multimillion dollar lawsuit involving an airplane crash. Was the airline negligent? The law is the same everywhere, but legal realists say that Jones's background will determine the outcome. If she spent 20 years representing insurance companies, she will tend to favor the airline. If her law practice consisted of helping the "little guy," she will favor the plaintiff.

Other legal realists argue, more aggressively, that those in power use the machinery of the law to perpetuate their control. The outcome of a given case will be determined by the needs of those with money and political clout. A court puts "window dressing" on a decision, they say, so that society thinks there are principles behind the law. A problem with legal realism, however, is its denial that any lawmaker can overcome personal bias. Yet clearly some do act unselfishly.

SUMMARY OF JURISPRUDENCE	
Legal Positivism	Law is what the sovereign says.
Natural Law	An unjust law is no law at all.
Legal Realism	Who enforces the law counts more than what is in writing.

No one school of jurisprudence is likely to seem perfect. We urge you to keep the different theories in mind as you read cases in the book. Ask yourself which school of thought is the best fit for you.

1-6 WORKING WITH THE BOOK'S FEATURES

In this section, we introduce a few of the book's features and discuss how you can use them effectively. We will start with *cases*.

1-6a Analyzing a Case

A law case is the decision a court has made in a civil lawsuit or criminal prosecution. Cases are the heart of the law and an important part of this book. Reading them effectively takes practice. This chapter's opening scenario is fictional, but the following real case involves a similar situation. Who can be held liable for the assault? Let's see.

KUEHN V. PUB ZONE

364 N. J. Super. 301
Superior Court of New Jersey, 2003

Facts: Maria Kerkoulas owned the Pub Zone bar. She knew that several motorcycle gangs frequented the tavern. From her own experience tending bar, and conversations with city police, she knew that some of the gangs, including the Pagans, were dangerous and prone to attack customers for no reason. Kerkoulas posted a sign prohibiting any motorcycle gangs from entering the bar while wearing "colors"; that is, insignia of their gangs. She believed that gangs without their colors were less prone to violence, and experience proved her right.

Rhino, Backdraft, and several other Pagans, all wearing colors, pushed their way past the tavern's bouncer and approached the bar. Although Kerkoulas saw their colors, she allowed them to stay for one drink. They later moved towards the back of the pub, and Kerkoulas believed they were departing. In fact, they followed a customer named Karl Kuehn to the men's room, where, without any provocation, they savagely beat him. Kuehn was knocked unconscious and suffered brain hemorrhaging, disc herniation, and numerous fractures of facial bones. He was forced to undergo various surgeries, including eye reconstruction.

Although the government prosecuted Rhino and Backdraft for their vicious assault, our case does not concern that prosecution. Kuehn sued the Pub Zone, and that is the case we will read. The jury awarded him $300,000 in damages. However, the trial court judge overruled the

jury's verdict. He granted a judgment for the Pub Zone, meaning that the tavern owed nothing. The judge ruled that the pub's owner could not have foreseen the attack on Kuehn, and had no duty to protect him from an outlaw motorcycle gang. Kuehn appealed, and the appeals court's decision follows:

Issue: *Did the Pub Zone have a duty to protect Kuehn from the Pagans' attack?*

Excerpts from Judge Payne's Decision: Whether a duty exists depends upon an evaluation of a number of factors including the nature of the underlying risk of harm, that is, its foreseeability and severity, the opportunity and ability to exercise care to prevent the harm, the comparative interests of and the relationships between or among the parties, and, ultimately, based on considerations of public policy and fairness, the societal interest in the proposed solution.

Since the possessor [of a business] is not an insurer of the visitor's safety, he is ordinarily under no duty to exercise any care until he knows or has reason to know that the acts of the third person are occurring, or are about to occur. He may, however, know or have reason to know, from past experience, that there is a likelihood of conduct on the part of third persons in general which is likely to endanger the safety of the visitor, even though he has no reason to expect it on the part of any particular individual.

We find the totality of the circumstances presented in this case give rise to a duty on the part of the Pub Zone to have taken reasonable precautions against the danger posed by the Pagans as a group. In this case, there was no reason to suspect any particular Pagan of violent conduct. However, the gang was collectively known to Kerkoulas to engage in random violence. Thus, Kerkoulas had knowledge as the result of past experience and from other sources that there was a likelihood of conduct on the part of third persons in general that was likely to endanger the safety of a patron at some unspecified future time. A duty to take precautions against the endangering conduct thus arose.

We do not regard our recognition of a duty in this case to give rise to either strict or absolute liability on the part of the Pub Zone. To fulfill its duty in this context, the Pub Zone was merely required to employ "reasonable" safety precautions. It already had in place a prohibition against bikers who were wearing their colors, and that prohibition, together with the practice of calling the police when a breach occurred, had been effective in greatly diminishing the occurrence of biker incidents on the premises. The evidence establishes that the prohibition was not enforced on the night at issue, that three Pagans were permitted entry while wearing their colors, and the police were not called. Once entry was achieved, the Pub Zone remained under a duty to exercise reasonable precautions against an attack.

The jury's verdict must therefore be reinstated.

Analysis

Let's take it from the top. The case is called *Kuehn v. Pub Zone*. Karl Kuehn is the **plaintiff**, the person who is suing. The Pub Zone is being sued, and is called the **defendant**. In this example, the plaintiff's name happens to appear first, but that is not always true. When a defendant loses a trial and files an appeal, *some* courts reverse the names of the parties.

The next line gives the legal citation, which indicates where to find the case in a law library. We explain in the footnote how to locate a book if you plan to do research.[11]

The *Facts* section provides a background to the lawsuit, written by the authors of this text. The court's own explanation of the facts is often many pages long, and may involve complex matters irrelevant to the subject covered in this book, so we relate only what is necessary. This section will usually include some mention of what happened at the trial court. Lawsuits always begin in a trial court. The losing party often appeals to a court of appeals, and it is usually an appeals court decision that we are reading. The trial judge ruled in favor of Pub Zone, but later, in the decision we are reading, Kuehn wins.

Plaintiff
The party who is suing

Defendant
The party being sued

---

[11]If you want to do legal research, you need to know where to find particular legal decisions. A citation is the case's "address," which guides you to the official book in which it is published. Look, for example at *Kuehn v. Pub Zone*, which has this citation: 364 N. J. Super. 301, Superior Court of New Jersey, 2003. The string of numbers identifies the volume and page of the official court reporter for the state of New Jersey (N. J. Super) in which you can find the full text of this decision. New Jersey, like most states, reports its law cases in a series of numbered volumes. This case appears in volume 364 of the New Jersey Superior Court reporters. If you go to a law library and find that book, you can then turn to page 301 and—*voila!*—you have the case. Because some of the cases in this text are so new, the official books that will eventually contain them have not yet been published, so their citations will be incomplete. In this event, we will also give you an alternate "address" where you can find the full case. For example, one citation for *National Federation of Independent Business v. Sebelius*, which examined whether Obamacare was constitutional, is 567 U.S. ___ (2012). Notice that it is missing a page number because it will not be published in the U.S. Reports for a few years. However, since we can also find that case in another reporter at 132 S. Ct. 2566 (2012), we will also provide this citation. Most cases are now available online. Your professor or librarian can show you how to find them electronically.

The *Issue* section is very important. It tells you what the court had to decide—and also why you are reading the case. In giving its decision, a court may digress. If you keep in mind the issue and relate the court's discussion to it, you will not get lost.

Excerpts from Judge Payne's Decision begins the court's discussion. This is called the *holding*, meaning a statement of who wins and who loses. The holding also includes the court's *rationale*, which is the reasoning behind the decision.

The holding that we provide is an edited version of the court's own language. Some judges write clear, forceful prose; others do not. Either way, their words give you an authentic feel for how judges think and rule, so we bring it to you in the original. Occasionally we use brackets [] to substitute our language for that of the court, either to condense or to clarify. Notice the brackets in the second paragraph of the Pub Zone decision. Judge Payne explains the point at much greater length, so we have condensed some of his writing into the phrase "of a business."

We omit a great deal. A court's opinion may be 3 pages, or it may be 75. We do not use ellipses (…) to indicate these deletions, because there is more taken out than kept in, and we want the text to be clean. When a court quotes an earlier decision verbatim but clearly adopts those words as its own, we generally delete the quotation marks, as well as the citation to the earlier case. If you are curious about the full holding, you can always look it up.

Let us look at a few of Judge Payne's points. The holding begins with a discussion of *duty*. The court explains that whether one person (or bar) owes a duty to protect another depends upon several factors, including whether the harm could be foreseen, how serious the injury could be, and whether there was an opportunity to prevent it.

Judge Payne then points out that the owner of a business is not an insurer of a visitor's safety. Typically, the owner has a duty to a visitor *only* if he has a reason to know that some harm is likely to occur. How would a merchant know that? Based on the character of the business, suggests the judge, or the owner's experience with particular people.

The judge then applies this general rule to the facts of this case. He concludes that the Pub Zone did in fact have a duty to protect Kuehn from the Pagans' attack. Based on Kerkoulas's experience, and warnings received from the police, she knew that the gang was dangerous and should have foreseen that admitting them in their "colors" greatly increased the chance of an attack.

Next, the court points out that it is not requiring the Pub Zone to *guarantee* everyone's safety. The bar was merely obligated to do a *reasonable* job. The prohibition on colors was a good idea, and calling the police had also proven effective. The problem of course was that in this case, Kerkoulas ignored her own rule about gang insignia and failed to call the police.

Based on all the evidence, the jury's finding of liability was reasonable, and its verdict must be reinstated. In other words, Kuehn, who lost at the trial, wins on appeal. What the court has done is to *reverse* the lower court's decision, meaning to turn the loser into the winner. In other cases, we will see an appellate court *remand* the case, meaning to send it back down to the lower court for additional steps. Or the appellate judges could *affirm* the lower court's decision, meaning to leave it unchanged.

1-6b Exam Strategy

This feature gives you practice analyzing cases the way lawyers do—and the way *you* must on tests. Law exams are different from most others because you must determine the issue from the facts provided. Too frequently, students faced with a law exam forget that the questions relate to the issues in the text and those discussed in class. Understandably, students new to law may focus on the wrong information in the problem or rely on material learned elsewhere. Exam Strategies teach you to figure out exactly what issue is at stake, and then analyze it in a logical, consistent manner. Here is an example, relating to the element of "duty," which the court discussed in the Pub Zone case.

EXAM Strategy

Question: The Big Red Traveling (BRT) Carnival is in town. Tony arrives at 8:00 p.m., parks in the lot—and is robbed at gunpoint by a man who beats him and escapes with his money. There are several police officers on the carnival grounds, but no officer is in the parking lot at the time of the robbery. Tony sues, claiming that brighter lighting and more police in the lot would have prevented the robbery. There has never before been any violent crime—robbery, beating, or otherwise—at any BRT carnival. BRT claims it had no duty to protect Tony from this harm. Who is likely to win?

Strategy: Begin by isolating the legal issue. What are the parties disputing? They are debating whether BRT had a duty to protect Tony from an armed robbery, committed by a stranger. Now ask yourself: How do courts decide whether a business has a duty to prevent this kind of harm? The *Pub Zone* case provides our answer. A business owner is not an ensurer of the visitor's safety. The owner generally has no duty to protect a customer from the criminal act of a third party, unless the owner knows the harm is occurring or could foresee it is about to happen. (In the Pub Zone case, the business owner knew of the gang's violent history, and could have foreseen the assault.) Now apply that rule to the facts of this case.

Result: There has never been a violent attack of any kind at a BRT carnival. BRT cannot foresee this robbery, and has no duty to protect against it. The carnival wins.

1-6c You Be the Judge

Many cases involve difficult decisions for juries and judges. Often both parties have legitimate, opposing arguments. Most chapters in this book will have a feature called "You Be the Judge," in which we present the facts of a case but not the court's holding.

We offer you two opposing arguments based on the kinds of claims the lawyers made in court. We leave it up to you to debate and decide which position is stronger or to add your own arguments to those given.

The following case is another negligence lawsuit, with issues that overlap those of the *Pub Zone* case. This time the court confronts a fight that resulted in a death. The victim's distraught family sued the owner of a bar, claiming that one of his employees was partly responsible for the death. Once again, the defendant asked the court to dismiss the case, claiming that he owed no duty to protect the victim—the same argument made by the *Pub Zone*.

But there is a difference here—this time the defendant owned the bar across the street, not the one where the fight took place. Could he be held legally responsible for the death? You be the judge.

You be the Judge

SOLDANO V. O'DANIELS
141 Cal. App. 3d 443
Court of Appeal of California, 1983

Facts: In the days before cell phones, a fight broke out at Happy Jack's Saloon. A good Samaritan ran across the street to the Circle Inn. He asked the bartender at the Circle Inn to let him use the telephone to call the police, but he refused.

Back at Happy Jack's Saloon, the fight escalated, and a man shot and killed Soldano's father. Soldano sued the owner of the Circle Inn for negligence. He argued that the bartender violated a legal duty when he refused to hand over the inn's telephone and that, as the employer of the bartender, O'Daniels was partially liable for Soldano's father's death.

The lower court dismissed the case, citing the principle that generally a person does not have a legal responsibility to help another unless he created the dangerous situation in the first place. Soldano appealed.

You Be the Judge: *Did the bartender have a duty to allow the use of the Circle Inn's telephone?*

Argument for the Defendant: Your honors, my client did not act wrongfully. He did nothing to create the danger. The fight was not even on his property. We sympathize with the plaintiff, but it is the shooter, and perhaps the bar where the fight took place, that are responsible for his father's death. Our client was not involved. Liability can be stretched only so far.

The court would place a great burden on the citizens of California by going against precedent. The Circle Inn is Mr. O'Daniel's private property. If the court imposes potential liability on him in this case, would citizens be forced to open the doors of their homes whenever a stranger claims that there is an emergency? Criminals would delight in their newfound ability to gain access to businesses and residences by simply demanding to use a phone to "call the police."

The law has developed sensibly. People are left to decide for themselves whether to help in a dangerous situation. They are not legally required to place themselves in harm's way.

Argument for the Plaintiff: Your honors, the Circle Inn's bartender had both a moral and a legal duty to allow the use of his establishment's telephone. The Circle Inn may be privately owned, but it is a business and is open to the public. Anyone in the world is invited to stop by and order a drink or a meal. The Good Samaritan had every right to be there.

We do not argue that the bartender had an obligation to break up the fight or endanger himself in any way. We simply argue he had a responsibility to stand aside and allow a free call on his restaurant's telephone. Any "burden" on him or on the Circle Inn was incredibly slight. The potential benefits were enormous. The trial court made a mistake in concluding that a person *never* has a duty to help another. Such an interpretation makes for poor public policy.

There is no need to radically change the common law. Residences can be excluded from this ruling. People need not be required to allow telephone-seeking strangers into their homes. This court can simply determine that businesses have a legal duty to allow the placement of emergency calls during normal business hours.

Chapter Conclusion

We depend upon the law to give us a stable nation and economy, a fair society, a safe place to live and work. These worthy goals have occupied ancient kings and twenty-first-century lawmakers alike. But while law is a vital tool for crafting the society we want, there are no easy answers about how to create it. In a democracy, we all participate in the crafting. Legal rules control us, yet *we* create *them*. A working knowledge of the law can help build a successful career—and a solid democracy.

EXAM REVIEW

1. **THE FEDERAL SYSTEM** Our federal system of government means that law comes from a national government in Washington, D.C., and from 50 state governments.

2. **LEGAL HISTORY** The history of law foreshadows many current legal issues, including mediation, partnership liability, the jury system, the role of witnesses, the special value placed on land, and the idea of precedent.

3. **PRIMARY SOURCES OF LAW** The primary sources of contemporary law are:

   - United States Constitution and state constitutions;

   - Statutes, which are drafted by legislatures;

   - Common law, which is the body of cases decided by judges, as they follow earlier cases, known as precedent;

   - Court orders, which place obligations on specific people or companies;

   - Administrative law, the rules and decisions made by federal and state administrative agencies; and

   - Treaties, agreements between the United States and foreign nations.

EXAM Strategy

Question: The stock market crash of 1929 and the Great Depression that followed were caused, in part, because so many investors blindly put their money into stocks they knew nothing about. During the 1920s, it was often impossible for an investor to find out what a corporation was planning to do with its money, who was running the corporation, and many other vital things. Congress responded by passing the Securities Act of 1933, which required a corporation to divulge more information about itself before it could seek money for a new stock issue. What kind of law did Congress create?

Strategy: What is the question seeking? The question asks you which *type* of law Congress created when it passed the 1933 Securities Act. What are the primary kinds of law? Administrative law consists of rules passed by agencies. Congress is not a federal agency. Common law is the body of cases decided by judges. Congress is not a judge. Statutes are laws passed by legislatures. Congress is a legislature. (See the "Result" at the end of this section.)

4. **CRIMINAL AND CIVIL LAW** Criminal law concerns behavior so threatening to society that it is outlawed altogether. Civil law deals with duties and disputes between parties, not with outlawed behavior.

Question: Bill and Diane are hiking in the woods. Diane walks down a hill to fetch fresh water. Bill meets a stranger, who introduces herself as Katrina. Bill sells a kilo of cocaine to Katrina, who then flashes a badge and mentions how much she enjoys her job at the Drug Enforcement Agency. Diane, heading back to camp with the water, meets Freddy, a motorist whose car has overheated. Freddy is late for a meeting where he expects to make a $30 million profit; he's desperate for water for his car. He promises to pay Diane $500 tomorrow if she will give him the pail of water, which she does. The next day, Bill is in jail and Freddy refuses to pay for Diane's water. Explain the criminal law/civil law distinction and what it means to Bill and Diane. Who will do what to whom, with what results?

Strategy: You are asked to distinguish between criminal and civil law. What is the difference? The criminal law concerns behavior that threatens society and is therefore outlawed. The government prosecutes the defendant. Civil law deals with the rights and duties between parties. One party files a suit against the other. Apply those different standards to these facts. (See the "Result" at the end of this section.)

5. **JURISPRUDENCE**   Jurisprudence is concerned with the basic nature of law. Three theories of jurisprudence are

- Legal positivism: The law is what the sovereign says it is.

- Natural law: An unjust law is no law at all.

- Legal realism: Who enforces the law is more important than what the law says.

---

3. Result: The Securities Act of 1933 is a statute.

4. Result: The government will prosecute Bill for dealing in drugs. If convicted, he will go to prison. The government will take no interest in Diane's dispute. However, if she chooses, she may sue Freddy for $500, the amount he promised her for the water. In that civil lawsuit, a court will decide whether Freddy must pay what he promised; however, even if Freddy loses, he will not go to jail.

MULTIPLE-CHOICE QUESTIONS

1. The United States Constitution is among the finest legal accomplishments in the history of the world. Which of the following influenced Ben Franklin, Thomas Jefferson, and the rest of the Founding Fathers?
   (a) English common-law principles
   (b) The Iroquois's system of federalism
   (c) Both A and B
   (d) None of the above

2. Which of the following parts of the modern legal system are "borrowed" from medieval England?

(a) Jury trials

(b) Special rules for selling land

(c) Following precedent

(d) All of the above

3. Union organizers at a hospital wanted to distribute leaflets to potential union members, but hospital rules prohibited leafleting in areas of patient care, hallways, cafeterias, and any areas open to the public. The National Labor Relations Board, a government agency, ruled that these restrictions violated the law and ordered the hospital to permit the activities in the cafeteria and coffee shop. What kind of law was it creating?

(a) A statute

(b) Common law

(c) A constitutional amendment

(d) Administrative regulation

4. If the Congress creates a new statute with the president's support, it must pass the idea by a _____ majority vote in the House and the Senate. If the president vetoes a proposed statute and the Congress wishes to pass it without his support, the idea must pass by a _____ majority vote in the House and Senate.

(a) simple; simple

(b) simple; two-thirds

(c) simple; three-fourths

(d) two-thirds; three-fourths

5. What part of the Constitution addresses the most basic liberties?

(a) Article I

(b) Article II

(c) Article III

(d) Amendments

CASE QUESTIONS

1. Burglar Bob breaks into Vince Victim's house. Bob steals a flat-screen television and laptop and does a significant amount of damage to the property before he leaves. Fortunately, Vince has a state-of-the-art security system. It captures excellent images of Bob, who is soon caught by police.

Assume that two legal actions follow, one civil and one criminal. Who will be responsible for bringing the civil case? What will be the outcome if the jury believes that Bob burgled Vince's house? Who will be responsible for bringing the criminal case? What will be the outcome if the jury believes that Bob burgled Vince's house?

2. As *The Oculist's Case* indicates, the medical profession has faced a large number of lawsuits for centuries. In Texas, a law provides that, so long as a doctor was not reckless and did not intentionally harm a patient, recovery for "pain and suffering" is limited to $750,000. In many other states, no such limit exists. If a patient will suffer a lifetime of pain after a botched operation, for example, he might recover millions in compensation. Which rule seems more sensible to you - the "Texas" rule or the alternative?

3. **YOU BE THE JUDGE WRITING PROBLEM** Should trials be televised? Here are a few arguments on both sides of the issue. You be the judge. **Arguments against live television coverage:** We have tried this experiment and it has failed. Trials fall into two categories: those that create great public interest and those that do not. No one watches dull trials, so we do not need to broadcast them. The few that are interesting have all become circuses. Judges and lawyers have shown that they cannot resist the temptation to play to the camera. Trials are supposed to be about justice, not entertainment. If a citizen seriously wants to follow a case, she can do it by reading the daily newspaper. **Arguments for live television coverage:** It is true that some televised trials have been unseemly affairs, but that is the fault of the presiding judges, not the media. Indeed, one of the virtues of television coverage is that millions of people now understand that we have a lot of incompetent people running our courtrooms. The proper response is to train judges to run a tight trial by prohibiting grandstanding by lawyers. Access to accurate information is the foundation on which a democracy is built, and we must not eliminate a source of valuable data just because some judges are ill-trained or otherwise incompetent.

4. Leslie Bergh and his two brothers, Milton and Raymond, formed a partnership to help build a fancy saloon and dance hall in Evanston, Wyoming. Later, Leslie met with his friend and drinking buddy, John Mills, and tricked Mills into investing in the saloon. Leslie did not tell Mills that no one else was investing cash or that the entire enterprise was already bankrupt. Mills mortgaged his home, invested $150,000 in the saloon—and lost every penny of it. Mills sued all three partners for fraud. Milton and Raymond defended on the grounds that they did not commit the fraud; only Leslie did. The defendants lost. Was that fair? By holding them liable, what general idea did the court rely on? What Anglo-Saxon legal custom did the ruling resemble?

5. *Kuehn v. Pub Zone* and *Soldano v. O'Daniels* both involve attacks in a bar. Should they have the same result? If so, in which way—in favor of the injured plaintiffs or owner-defendants? If not, why should they have different outcomes? What are the key facts that lead you to believe as you do?

Discussion Questions

1. In the 1980s, the Supreme Court ruled that it is legal for protesters to burn the American flag. This activity counts as free speech under the Constitution. If the Court hears a new flag-burning case in this decade, should it consider changing its ruling, or should it follow precedent? Is following past precedent something that seems sensible to you: always, usually, sometimes, rarely, or never?

2. When should a business be held legally responsible for customer safety? Consider the following statements, and consider the degree to which you agree or disagree:

- A business should keep customers safe from its own employees.

- A business should keep customers safe from other customers.

- A business should keep customers safe from themselves. (Example: an intoxicated customer who can no longer walk straight.)

- A business should keep people outside its own establishment safe if it is reasonable to do so.

3. In his most famous novel, *The Red and the Black,* the French author Stendhal (1783–1842) wrote: "There is no such thing as 'natural law': This expression is nothing but old nonsense. Prior to laws, what is natural is only the strength of the lion, or the need of the creature suffering from hunger or cold, in short, need." What do you think? Does legal positivism or legal realism seem more sensible to you?

4. Before becoming a Supreme Court justice, Sonia Sotomayor stated in a speech to students: "I would hope that a wise Latina woman with the richness of her experiences would more often than not reach a better conclusion than a white male who hasn't lived that life." During her Senate confirmation proceedings, this statement was heavily probed and criticized. One senator said that the focus of the hearings was to determine whether Judge Sotomayor would "decide cases based only on the law as made by the people and their elected representatives, not on personal feelings or politics." (Sotomayor convinced many of her critics, because the Senate confirmed her by a vote of 68–31.) Should judges ignore their life experiences and feelings when making judicial decisions?

5. Consider the following statements. To what extent do you agree or disagree with each?

- I believe that members of Congress usually try to do the right thing for America.

- I believe that presidents usually try to do the right thing for America.

- I believe that Supreme Court justices usually try to do the right thing for America.

ANSWERS TO SELECTED END OF CHAPTER QUESTIONS

MULTIPLE-CHOICE QUESTIONS

Presented are the answers for the ODD-numbered multiple-choice questions in the end-of-chapter material.

1. C
3. D
5. D

CASE QUESTIONS

Presented are the answers for all of the ODD-numbered case questions in the end-of-chapter material.

1. **Answer:** The civil case will be brought by Victim, and the outcome of a successful case against Bob would be some type of monetary award such as restitution. The criminal case would be brought by state prosecutors, and the outcome would be imprisonment for Bob.

3. **Answer:** For most of the "You Be the Judge" writing problems, we provide the case citation and holding. For this question, of course, there is no definitive answer.

5. **Answer:** Answers will vary.

Chapter 2

ETHICS AND CORPORATE SOCIAL RESPONSIBILITY

© Creative Travel Projects/Shutterstock.com

Eating is one of life's most fundamental needs and greatest pleasures. Yet all around the world many people go to bed hungry. Food companies have played an important role in reducing hunger by producing vast quantities of food cheaply. So much food, so cheaply that, in America, one in three adults and one in five children are obese. Some critics argue that food companies bear responsibility for this overeating because they make their products *too* alluring. Many processed food products are calorie bombs of fat (which is linked to heart disease), sugar (which leads to diabetes), and salt (which causes high blood pressure). What obligation do food producers and restaurants have to their customers? After all, no one is forcing anyone to eat. Do any of the following examples cross the line into unethical behavior?

> **Food with high levels of fat, sugar and salt not only taste better, they are also more addictive.**

1. Increasing Addiction. Food with high levels of fat, sugar, and salt not only taste better, they are also more addictive.[1] Food producers hire neuroscientists who perform MRIs on consumers to gauge the precise level of fat, sugar, and salt that will create the most powerful cravings, the so-called "bliss point." To take one example, in some Prego tomato sauces, sugar is the second most important ingredient after tomatoes.

---

[1] Researchers report that rats find Oreo cookies as addictive as cocaine. And they like the creamy middle best, too. *Connecticut College News*, "Student-faculty research shows Oreos are just as addictive as drugs in lab rats."

Did you know you were getting two heaping teaspoons of sugar in a small serving of pasta sauce?[2]

2. Increasing Quantity. Food companies also work hard to create new categories of products that increase the number of times a day that people eat and the amount of calories in each session. For example, they have created a new category of food that is meant to be more than a snack but less than a meal, such as Hot Pockets. But some versions of this product have more than 700 calories, which would be a lot for lunch, never mind for just a snack. And candy companies carefully package their products to encourage consumers to nibble all day. For example, when Hershey's learned that the wrappers on a Reese's Peanut Butter Cup act as a deterrent to nonstop eating, the company created Reese's minis, which are unwrapped candies in a resealable bag. Feel free to chow down!

Food executives argue that they are just providing what consumers want.

3. Increasing Calories. Uno Chicago Grill serves a macaroni and cheese dish that, by itself, provides more than two-thirds of the calories that a moderately active man should eat in one day, and almost three times the amount of saturated fat. But this dish is at least *food*. Dunkin, Donuts offers a Frozen Caramel Coffee Coolatta with more than one-third the calories that a male should have in a day and 50 percent more saturated fat. Of course, these items are even worse choices for women and children. Should restaurants serve items such as these? If they do, what disclosure should they make?

4. Targeting Children. Kraft Food developed Lunchables, packaged food designed for children to take to school. The first version contained bologna, cheese, crackers, and candy—all of which delivered unhealthy levels of fat, sugar, and salt. The company lured children by advertising on Saturday morning cartoons.

5. Targeting the Poor. Traditionally, Coca-Cola focused its marketing efforts on low-income areas in the United States. It then took this effort overseas, selling Coke in the slums of Brazil. One of its strategies is to provide small bottles that cost only 20 cents. Said Jeffrey Dunn, the former president and chief operating officer for Coca-Cola in North and South America, "These people need a lot of things, but they don't need a Coke.' I almost threw up."[3] When Dunn tried to develop more healthful strategies for Coke, he was fired.

---

[2]To find nutritional information on this or other products, search the Internet for the name of the product with the word "nutrition."

[3]Michael Moss, "The Extraordinary Science of Addictive Junk Food," *The New York Times*, Feb. 20, 2013.

2-4 THEORIES OF ETHICS

When making ethical decisions, people sometimes focus on the reason for the decision—they want to do what is right. Thus, if they think it is wrong to lie, then they will tell the truth no matter what the consequence. Other times, people think about the outcome of their actions. They will do whatever it takes to achieve the right result, no matter what. This choice—between doing right and getting the right result—has been the subject of much philosophical debate.

2-4a Utilitarian Ethics

In 1863, Englishman John Stuart Mill wrote *Utilitarianism*. **To Mill, a correct decision is one that maximizes overall happiness and minimizes overall pain, thereby producing the greatest net benefit.** As he put it, his goal was to produce the greatest good for the greatest number of people. Risk management and cost-benefit analyses are examples of utilitarian business practices.

Suppose that an automobile manufacturer could add a device to its cars that would reduce air pollution. As a result, the incidence of strokes and lung cancer would decline dramatically, saving society hundreds of millions of dollars over the life of the cars. But by charging a higher price to cover the cost of the device, the company would sell fewer cars and shareholders would earn lower returns. A utilitarian would argue that, despite the decline in profits, the company should install the device.

Consider this example that a student told us:

> During college, I used drugs—some cocaine, but mostly prescription painkillers. Things got pretty bad. At one point, I would wait outside emergency rooms hoping to buy drugs from people who were leaving. But that was three years ago. I went into rehab and have been clean ever since. I don't even drink. I've applied for a job, but the application asks if I have ever used drugs illegally. I am afraid that if I tell the truth, I will never get a job. What should I say on the application?

A utilitarian would ask: What harm will be caused if she tells the truth? She will be less likely to get that job, or maybe any job—a large and immediate harm. What if she lies? She might argue that no harm would result because she is now clean, and her past drug addiction will not have an adverse impact on her new employer.

Critics of utilitarian thought argue that it is very difficult to *measure* utility accurately, at least in the way that one would measure distance or the passage of time. The car company does not really know how many lives will be saved or how much its profits might decline if the device is installed. It is also difficult to *predict* benefit and harm accurately. The recovered drug addict may relapse, or her employer may find out about her lie.

A focus on outcome can justify some really terrible behavior. Among other things, it can be used to legitimize torture. After the 9/11 terrorist attacks, Americans debated the acceptability of torture. Is it ethical to torture a terrorist with the hope of obtaining the details of an upcoming attack?

Or suppose that wealthy old Ebenezer has several chronic illnesses that cause him great suffering and prevent him from doing any of the activities that once gave meaning to his life. Also, he is such a nasty piece of work that everyone who knows him hates him. If he were to die, all of his heirs would benefit tremendously from the money they inherited from him, including a disabled grandchild who then could afford medical care that would improve his life dramatically. Would it be ethical to kill Ebenezer?

2-4b Deontological Ethics

Deontological

From the Greek word for *obligation*. The duty to do the right thing, regardless of the result

The word **deontological** comes from the Greek word for *obligation*. **Proponents of deontological ethics believe that utilitarians have it all wrong and that the *results* of a decision are not as important as the *reason* for making it.** To a deontological thinker, the ends do not justify the means. Rather, it is important to do the right thing, no matter the result.

Did you know you were getting two heaping teaspoons of sugar in a small serving of pasta sauce?[2]

2. Increasing Quantity. Food companies also work hard to create new categories of products that increase the number of times a day that people eat and the amount of calories in each session. For example, they have created a new category of food that is meant to be more than a snack but less than a meal, such as Hot Pockets. But some versions of this product have more than 700 calories, which would be a lot for lunch, never mind for just a snack. And candy companies carefully package their products to encourage consumers to nibble all day. For example, when Hershey's learned that the wrappers on a Reese's Peanut Butter Cup act as a deterrent to nonstop eating, the company created Reese's minis, which are unwrapped candies in a resealable bag. Feel free to chow down!

   Food executives argue that they are just providing what consumers want.

3. Increasing Calories. Uno Chicago Grill serves a macaroni and cheese dish that, by itself, provides more than two-thirds of the calories that a moderately active man should eat in one day, and almost three times the amount of saturated fat. But this dish is at least *food*. Dunkin, Donuts offers a Frozen Caramel Coffee Coolatta with more than one-third the calories that a male should have in a day and 50 percent more saturated fat. Of course, these items are even worse choices for women and children. Should restaurants serve items such as these? If they do, what disclosure should they make?

4. Targeting Children. Kraft Food developed Lunchables, packaged food designed for children to take to school. The first version contained bologna, cheese, crackers, and candy—all of which delivered unhealthy levels of fat, sugar, and salt. The company lured children by advertising on Saturday morning cartoons.

5. Targeting the Poor. Traditionally, Coca-Cola focused its marketing efforts on low-income areas in the United States. It then took this effort overseas, selling Coke in the slums of Brazil. One of its strategies is to provide small bottles that cost only 20 cents. Said Jeffrey Dunn, the former president and chief operating officer for Coca-Cola in North and South America, "These people need a lot of things, but they don't need a Coke.' I almost threw up."[3] When Dunn tried to develop more healthful strategies for Coke, he was fired.

---

[2]To find nutritional information on this or other products, search the Internet for the name of the product with the word "nutrition."

[3]Michael Moss, "The Extraordinary Science of Addictive Junk Food," *The New York Times*, Feb. 20, 2013.

2-1 INTRODUCTION

Ethics
How people should behave.

Ethics decision
Any choice about how a person should behave that is based on a sense of right and wrong.

This text, for the most part, covers legal ideas. The law dictates how a person *must* behave. This chapter examines **ethics**, or how people *should* behave. Any choice about how a person should behave that is based on a sense of right and wrong is an **ethics decision**. This chapter will explore ethics dilemmas that commonly arise in workplaces, and present tools for making decisions when the law does not require or prohibit any particular choice.

If a person is intent on lying, cheating, and stealing his way through a career, then he is unlikely to be dissuaded by anything in this or any other course. But for the large majority of people who want to do the right thing, it is useful to study new ways of recognizing and dealing with difficult problems.

Laws represent society's view of basic ethics rules. And most people agree that certain activities such as murder, assault, and fraud are wrong. **However, laws may permit behavior that some feel is wrong and it may criminalize acts that some feel are right.** For example, assisted suicide is legal in a few states. Some people believe it is wrong under all circumstances, while others think it is the right thing to do for someone suffering horribly from a terminal illness. Likewise, many people feel it is ethical to record videos of farm animals being mistreated, although some states now prohibit secret videotaping on farms.

In this chapter, the usual legal cases are replaced by Ethics Cases with discussion questions. In some of these cases, reasonable people may disagree about the right thing to do. In others, the right answer is obvious, but actually doing it is difficult. These cases give you the opportunity to practice applying your values to the types of ethics issues you will face in your life. It is also important during class discussions for you to hear different points of view. In your career, you will work with and manage a variety of people, so it is useful to have insight into different perspectives on ethics.

Life principles
The rules by which you live your life

We also hope that hearing these various points of view will help you develop your own **Life Principles**. These principles are the rules by which you live your life. As we will see, **research shows that people who think about the right rules for living are less likely to do wrong.** Developing your own Life Principles, based on your values, may be the most important outcome of reading this chapter and studying ethics.

How do you go about preparing a list of Life Principles? Think first of important categories. A list of Life Principles should include your rules on:

- Lying

- Stealing

- Cheating

- Applying the same or different standards at home and at work

- Your responsibility as a bystander when you see other people doing wrong, or being harmed

Specific is better than general. Many people say, for example, that they will maintain a healthy work/life balance, but such a vow is not as effective as promising to set aside certain specific times each week for family activities. Many religions honor the sabbath for this reason. Another common Life Principle is: "I will always put my family first." But what does that mean? That you are willing to engage in unethical behavior at work to make sure that you keep your job? Increase your income by cheating everyone you can? Or live your life so that you serve as a good example?

Some Life Principles focus not so much on right versus wrong but, rather, serve as a general guide for living a happier, more engaged life: I will keep promises, forgive those who harm me, say I'm sorry, appreciate my blessings every day, understand the other person's point of view, try to say "yes" when asked for a favor.

Remember that, no matter what you *say*, every ethics decision you make illustrates your *actual* Life Principles. For example, one MBA student told the story of how his boss had ordered him to cheat on his expense report. The company did not require any receipts for meals that cost less than $25. He and his fellow salespeople habitually ate at fast food restaurants where it was almost impossible to spend $25. Everyone else was reporting a lot of $24 meals while he was submitting bills for $12. His boss told him he was making everyone else look bad and he needed to increase the amounts he claimed. What is your Life Principle in this case? Understand that if you fudge the expense report, your Life Principle is effectively: I am willing to cheat if I am unlikely to get caught or if my boss authorizes it. An alternative would be: I will not cheat even if my boss tells me to—I'll look for another job instead.

It is important to think through your Life Principles now, so that you will be prepared when facing ethics dilemmas in the future.

In this chapter, we will present eight topics:

1. The Role of Business in Society

2. Why Be Ethical?

3. Theories of Ethics

4. Ethics Traps

5. Lying

6. Applying the Principles

7. When the Going Gets Tough: Responding to Unethical Behavior

8. Corporate Social Responsibility

2-2 THE ROLE OF BUSINESS IN SOCIETY

Nobel Prize-winning economist Milton Friedman is famous for arguing that a corporate manager's primary responsibility is to the owners of the organization, that is, to shareholders. Unless the owners explicitly provide otherwise, managers should make the company as profitable as possible while also complying with the law.[4]

Others have argued that corporations should instead consider all company stakeholders, not just the shareholders. Stakeholders include employees, customers, and the communities and countries in which a company operates. This choice can create an obligation to such broad categories as "society" or "the environment." For example, after the shooting in Newtown, Connecticut, in which 20 first-graders and 6 educators were murdered, General Electric Co. stopped lending funds to shops that sell guns. GE headquarters are near Newtown. Many of its employees lived in the area and some had children in the Sandy Hook Elementary School where the shooting took place. In this case, GE was putting its employees ahead of its investors.

Every executive will treat employees well if she believes that doing so leads to increased profits. All executives are in favor of giving money to charity if the donation improves the company's image and thereby increases profits enough to pay for itself. But such win-win cases are not ethics dilemmas. In a true dilemma, a company considers an action that would not increase shareholder returns in any certain or measureable way, but would benefit other stakeholders.

---

[4]He also mentions that managers should comply with "ethical custom," but never explains what that means. Milton Friedman, *The New York Times Magazine*, September 13, 1970.

As we will see in this chapter, managers face many choices in which the most profitable option is not the most ethical choice. For example, Michael Mudd, a former executive vice president of global corporate affairs for Kraft Foods, had this to say about his fellow executives:

> In so many other ways, these are good people. But, little by little, they strayed from the honorable business of feeding people appropriately to the deplorable mission of "increasing shareholder value" by enticing people to consume more and more high-margin, low-nutrition branded products.[5]

Of course, when profitability increases and, with it, a company's stock price, managers benefit because their compensation is often tied to corporate results, either explicitly or through ownership of stock and options. Thus, managers who say that they are just acting in the best interest of shareholders are also conveniently benefiting themselves. That connection creates an incentive to ignore stakeholders.

Conversely, doing the right thing will sometimes lead to a loss of profits or even one's job. For example, Hugh Aaron worked for a company that sold plastic materials.[6] One of the firm's major clients hired a new purchasing agent who refused to buy any product unless he was provided with expensive gifts, paid vacations, and prostitutes. When Aaron refused to comply with these requests, the man bought from someone else. And that was that—the two companies never did business again. Aaron did not regret his choice. He believed that his and his employees' self-respect were as important as profits. But if your *only* concern is maximizing your company's profitability in the short run, you will find yourself in a position of making unethical choices.

2-3 WHY BE ETHICAL?

An ethical decision may not be the most profitable, but it does generate a range of benefits for employees, companies, and society.

2-3a Society as a Whole Benefits from Ethical Behavior

John Akers, the former chairman of IBM, argued that without ethical behavior, a society could not be economically competitive. He put it this way:

> Ethics and competitiveness are inseparable. We compete as a society. No society anywhere will compete very long or successfully with people stabbing each other in the back; with people trying to steal from each other; with everything requiring notarized confirmation because you can't trust the other fellow; with every little squabble ending in litigation; and with government writing reams of regulatory legislation, tying business hand and foot to keep it honest. That is a recipe not only for headaches in running a company, but for a nation to become wasteful, inefficient, and noncompetitive. There is no escaping this fact: The greater the measure of mutual trust and confidence in the ethics of a society, the greater its economic strength.[7]

In short, ethical behavior builds trust, which is important in all of our relationships. It is the ingredient that allows us to live and work together happily.

---

[5]Michael Moss, "How to Force Ethics on the Food Industry," *The New York Times*, March 16, 2013.
[6]Virtually all of the examples in this chapter are true events involving real people. Only their first names are used unless the individual has consented or the events are a matter of public record.
[7]David Grier, "Confronting Ethical Dilemmas," unpublished manuscript of remarks at the Royal Bank of Canada, Sept. 19, 1989.

2-3b People Feel Better When They Behave Ethically

Every businessperson has many opportunities to be dishonest. But each of us must ask ourselves: What kind of person do we want to be? In what kind of world do we want to live? You might think about how you would like people who know you to describe you to others.

Managers want to feel good about themselves and the decisions they have made; they want to sleep well at night. Their decisions—to lay off employees, install safety devices in cars, burn a cleaner fuel—affect people's lives. And their unethical decisions are painful to remember.

To take an example, an executive, whom we will call "Hank," told a story that still haunts him. His boss had refused to pay his tuition for an MBA program, so Hank went over his head and asked Sam, an executive several levels higher. Sam interceded immediately and personally approved the tuition reimbursement. He then took Hank under his wing, checking with him regularly to find out how the program and his work were going. Naturally, Hank felt grateful and indebted. Then one day, some other higher ups told him that they were planning a coup against Sam. They were trying to get him fired in a complete blindside. They offered Hank a big promotion in return for his help. All went according to plan and Sam was fired. When Sam found out about Hank's betrayal, he called to tell the younger man exactly what he thought of his character. Hank said that he will carry that phone call and his guilt forever. And because he was so untrustworthy, he finds it hard to trust others.

2-3c Unethical Behavior Can Be Very Costly

Unethical behavior is a risky business strategy—it can harm not only the bad actors but entire industries and even countries. For example, when VIPshop recently offered its shares publicly in the United States, they plummeted in price. This was the first Chinese company to go public in the United States in nine months, since a series of accounting frauds in other Chinese companies had caused billions of dollars in losses. Although VIPshop had done nothing wrong, investors were skeptical of *all* Chinese companies.

Although unethical decisions may increase short-term profits, they can create a lot of long-term harm. Johnson & Johnson manufactured a new artificial hip that had more metal parts than the old version. In theory, the hip would last longer and thereby let the patient avoid difficult replacement surgery. But the theory turned out to be wrong. The two parts ground together, releasing microscopic bits of metal that not only failed quickly but also irreparably damaged the patient's bone and tissue. Even when Johnson & Johnson had data from an English surgeon revealing these problems, it denied and stonewalled while continuing to sell the product. J&J subsequently faced more than 10,000 lawsuits. The company not only paid more than $4 billion to settle these cases, it also found its reputation sullied.

What is the cost of a lost reputation? **Research indicates that consumers are willing to pay more for a product that they believe to be ethically produced.** And much less if they believe it was made using shoddy ethical practices.[8]

Unethical behavior can also cause other, subtler damage. In one survey, a majority of those questioned said that they had witnessed unethical behavior in their workplace and that this behavior had reduced productivity, job stability, and profits. **Unethical behavior in an organization creates a cynical, resentful, and unproductive workforce.**

Although there is no *guarantee* that ethical behavior pays in the short or long run, there is evidence that the ethical company is more *likely* to win financially. Ethical companies tend to have a better reputation, more creative employees, and higher returns than those that engage in wrongdoing.[9]

But if we decide that we want to behave ethically, how do we know what ethical behavior is?

---

[8]Remi Trudel and June Cotte, "Does It Pay to Be Good?" *Sloan Management Review*," January 8, 2009.
[9]For sources, see "Ethics: A Basic Framework," Harvard Business School case 9-307-059.

2-4 THEORIES OF ETHICS

When making ethical decisions, people sometimes focus on the reason for the decision—they want to do what is right. Thus, if they think it is wrong to lie, then they will tell the truth no matter what the consequence. Other times, people think about the outcome of their actions. They will do whatever it takes to achieve the right result, no matter what. This choice—between doing right and getting the right result—has been the subject of much philosophical debate.

2-4a Utilitarian Ethics

In 1863, Englishman John Stuart Mill wrote *Utilitarianism*. **To Mill, a correct decision is one that maximizes overall happiness and minimizes overall pain, thereby producing the greatest net benefit.** As he put it, his goal was to produce the greatest good for the greatest number of people. Risk management and cost-benefit analyses are examples of utilitarian business practices.

Suppose that an automobile manufacturer could add a device to its cars that would reduce air pollution. As a result, the incidence of strokes and lung cancer would decline dramatically, saving society hundreds of millions of dollars over the life of the cars. But by charging a higher price to cover the cost of the device, the company would sell fewer cars and shareholders would earn lower returns. A utilitarian would argue that, despite the decline in profits, the company should install the device.

Consider this example that a student told us:

> During college, I used drugs—some cocaine, but mostly prescription painkillers. Things got pretty bad. At one point, I would wait outside emergency rooms hoping to buy drugs from people who were leaving. But that was three years ago. I went into rehab and have been clean ever since. I don't even drink. I've applied for a job, but the application asks if I have ever used drugs illegally. I am afraid that if I tell the truth, I will never get a job. What should I say on the application?

A utilitarian would ask: What harm will be caused if she tells the truth? She will be less likely to get that job, or maybe any job—a large and immediate harm. What if she lies? She might argue that no harm would result because she is now clean, and her past drug addiction will not have an adverse impact on her new employer.

Critics of utilitarian thought argue that it is very difficult to *measure* utility accurately, at least in the way that one would measure distance or the passage of time. The car company does not really know how many lives will be saved or how much its profits might decline if the device is installed. It is also difficult to *predict* benefit and harm accurately. The recovered drug addict may relapse, or her employer may find out about her lie.

A focus on outcome can justify some really terrible behavior. Among other things, it can be used to legitimize torture. After the 9/11 terrorist attacks, Americans debated the acceptability of torture. Is it ethical to torture a terrorist with the hope of obtaining the details of an upcoming attack?

Or suppose that wealthy old Ebenezer has several chronic illnesses that cause him great suffering and prevent him from doing any of the activities that once gave meaning to his life. Also, he is such a nasty piece of work that everyone who knows him hates him. If he were to die, all of his heirs would benefit tremendously from the money they inherited from him, including a disabled grandchild who then could afford medical care that would improve his life dramatically. Would it be ethical to kill Ebenezer?

2-4b Deontological Ethics

Deontological
From the Greek word for *obligation*. The duty to do the right thing, regardless of the result

The word **deontological** comes from the Greek word for *obligation*. **Proponents of deontological ethics believe that utilitarians have it all wrong and that the *results* of a decision are not as important as the *reason* for making it.** To a deontological thinker, the ends do not justify the means. Rather, it is important to do the right thing, no matter the result.

The best-known proponent of the deontological model was the eighteenth-century German philosopher Immanuel Kant. He believed in what he called the **categorical imperative**. He argued that you should not do something unless you would be willing to have everyone else do it, too. Applying this idea, he concluded that one should always tell the truth because if *everyone* lied, the world would become an awful place. Thus, Kant would say that the drug user should tell the truth on job applications, even if that meant she could not find work. The truth should be told, no matter the outcome.

Kant also believed that human beings possess a unique dignity and that no decision that treats people as commodities could be considered just, even if the decision tended to maximize overall happiness, or profit, or any other quantifiable measure. Thus, Kant would argue against killing Ebenezer, no matter how unpleasant the man was.

The problem with Kant is that the ends *do* matter. Yes, it is wrong to kill, but a country might not survive unless it is willing to fight wars. Although many people disagree with some of Kant's specific ideas, most people acknowledge that a utilitarian approach is incomplete, and that winning in the end does not automatically make a decision right.

2-4c Rawlsian Justice

How did you manage to get into college or graduate school? Presumably owing to some combination of talent, hard work, and support from family and friends. Imagine that you had been born into different circumstances—say, in a country where the literacy rate is only 25 percent and almost all of the population lives in desperate poverty. Would you be reading this book now? Most likely not. People are born with wildly different talents into very different circumstances, all of which dramatically affect their outcomes. Even for people born poor in the United States, circumstances matter hugely. For example, poor children in San Francisco are almost three times more likely to be prosperous as adults than are children from Atlanta.[10]

John Rawls (1921–2002) was an American philosopher who referred to these circumstances into which we are born as **life prospects**. In his view, hard work certainly matters, but so does luck. Rawls argued that we should think about what rules for society we would propose if we faced a "**veil of ignorance**." In other words, suppose that there is going to be a lottery tomorrow that would determine all our attributes. We could be a winner, ending up a hugely talented, healthy person in a loving family, or we could be poor and chronically ill from a broken, abusive family in a violent neighborhood with deplorable schools and social services.

What type of society would we establish now, if we did not know whether we would be one of life's winners or losers? First, we would design some form of a democratic system that provided equal liberty to all and important rights such as freedom of speech and religion. Second, we would apply the **difference principle**. Under this principle we would *not* plan a system in which everyone received an equal income. Society is better off if people have an incentive to work hard, so we would reward the type of work that provides the most benefit to the community as a whole. We might decide, for example, to pay doctors more than baseball players.

Kant's categorical imperative
An act is only ethical if it would be acceptable for everyone to do the same thing.

Life prospects
The opportunities one has at birth, based on one's natural attributes and initial place in society.

Veil of ignorance
The rules for society that we would propose if we did not know how lucky we would be in life's lottery.

Difference principle
Rawls' suggestion that society should reward behavior that provides the most benefit to the community as a whole.

Healthy, talented children born into a loving family are lucky to have such good life prospects.

© Creativa/Shutterstock.com

---

[10]David Leonhardt, "In Climbing Income Ladder, Location Matters," *The New York Times*, July 22, 2013.

But maybe not *all* doctors; perhaps just the ones who research cancer cures or provide care for the poor, not cosmetic surgeons operating on the affluent. Rawls argues that everyone should have the opportunity to earn great wealth so long as the tax system provides enough revenue to provide decent health, education, and welfare for all. In thinking about ethical decisions, it is worth remembering that many of us have been winners in life's lottery and that the unlucky are deserving of our compassion.

2-4d Front Page Test

There you are, trying to decide what to do in a difficult situation. How would you feel if your actions went viral—on YouTube, the Huffington Post, all over Facebook, or on the front page of a national newspaper? Would that help you decide what to do? Would such exposure have caused Hank to tell Sam about the planned coup? Make the Johnson & Johnson executives manage their hip implant differently?

The Front Page test is not completely foolproof—there are times you might want to do something private for legitimate reasons. You might, for example, think that having an abortion is completely ethical, but still not want everyone to know. Or, if you live in a state that prohibits the videotaping of mistreated farm animals, you would not want everyone to know that you had done so, even if you thought it the right thing to do.

2-4e Moral Universalism and Relativism

For many ethics dilemmas, reasonable people may well disagree about what is right. For example, we have seen that a Kantian approach may lead to a different decision than a utilitarian view. However, some people believe that particular acts are always right or always wrong, regardless of what others may think. This approach is called **moral universalism**. Alternatively, others believe that it is right to be tolerant of different viewpoints and customs. And, indeed, a decision may be acceptable even if it is not in keeping with one's own ethical standards. This approach is referred to as **moral relativism**. For example, Pope Benedict XVI wrote that homosexuality is "a strong tendency ordered toward an intrinsic moral evil," while his successor, Pope Francis, took a different approach, saying, "If someone is gay and he searches for the Lord and has good will, who am *I* to judge?"[11] Pope Benedict's view reflects a moral universalism—he believes that homosexuality is always wrong—while Pope Francis is taking a more relativistic approach—under certain circumstances, he will not judge.

There are at least two types of moral relativism: cultural and individual. To cultural relativists, what is right or wrong depends on the norms and practices in each society. For example, some societies permit men to have more than one wife, while others find that practice abhorrent. A cultural relativist would say that polygamy is an ethical choice in societies where such practice is long-standing and culturally significant. And, as outsiders to that society, who are we to judge? In short, culture defines what is right and wrong.

To individual relativists, people must develop their own ethical rules. And what is right for *me* might not be good for *you*. Thus, I might believe that monogamy is bad because it goes against human nature. Therefore, I might decide that it is right for me to have relationships with many partners while you believe that being faithful to one partner is the cornerstone of an ethical life. The danger of individual relativism is obvious: It can justify just about anything.

Like so much in ethics, none of these approaches will always be right or wrong. There are times when certain acts are just wrong, no matter what anyone says to the contrary. But, of course, truly ethical people may differ. It is, however, ethically lazy simply to default to moral relativism as an excuse for condoning any behavior.

Moral universalism
A belief that some acts are always right or always wrong

Moral relativism
A belief that a decision may be right even if it is not in keeping with our own ethical standards.

---

[11] Rachel Donadio, "On Gay Priests, Pope Francis Asks, 'Who Am I to Judge?" *The New York Times*, July 30, 2013.

2-4f Ethics Case: Lincoln at War

In 1865, toward the end of the American Civil War, President Abraham Lincoln had to choose between two rival goals: an immediate end to a devastating, bloody war or a change to the Constitution that would make slavery illegal. If he ended the war immediately, the Southern states would return to the Union and then be eligible to vote on the anti-slavery amendment. They would have enough votes to defeat it. He ultimately decided to delay peace with the South, a decision that cost thousands of lives.

To obtain the votes he needed, Lincoln did whatever it took. He figured out how to win over each individual Congressman, appealing to one man's sense of idealism, another's greed. He made threats and promises, handed out jobs and cash. And, in the end, he succeeded in ending the barbarous practice of slavery.[12]

Questions

- What would Mill, Kant, and Rawls have said about Lincoln's actions?

- What would have been the result if Lincoln had applied the Front Page test?

- Did Lincoln do the right thing?

- Lincoln risked people's lives for his principles and made decisions that affected millions. Can you think of a similar scenario in a business context?

2-5 ETHICS TRAPS

Very few people wake up one morning and think, "Today I'll do something unethical." Then why do so many unethical things happen? Sometimes our brains trick us into believing wrong is right. It is important to understand the ethics traps that create great temptation to do what we know to be wrong or fail to do what we know to be right.

2-5a Money

Money is a powerful lure because most people believe that they would be happier if only they had more. But that is not necessarily true. Good health, companionship, and enjoyable leisure activities all contribute more to happiness than money does. And, regardless of income, 85 percent of Americans feel happy on a day-to-day basis anyway.

Money *can*, of course, provide some protection against the inevitable bumps in the road of life. Being hungry is no fun. If you lose your winter coat, you will be happier if you can replace it. It is easier to maintain friendships if you can afford to go out together occasionally. So money can contribute to happiness, but research indicates that this impact disappears when household income exceeds $75,000. Above that level, income seems to have no impact on day-to-day happiness. Indeed, there is some evidence that higher income levels actually *reduce* the ability to appreciate small pleasures. Interestingly, too, people who come into a windfall are happier if they spend it on others or save it, rather than blowing it in a spree.[13]

Money is also a way of keeping score. If my company pays me more, that must mean I am a better employee. So, although an increase in income above $75,000 does not affect

---

[12]The Steven Spielberg movie *Lincoln* illustrates this process.
[13]Elizabeth Dunn and Michael Norton, "Don't Indulge, Be Happy," *The New York Times*, July 8, 2012, and Daniel Kahneman and Angus Deaton, "High Income Improves Evaluation of Life but not Emotional Well-Being," in the Proceedings of the National Academy of Sciences of the United States of America, August 4, 2010.

day-to-day happiness, higher pay can make people feel more satisfied with their lives. They consider themselves more successful and feel that their life is going better.

In short, the relationship between money and happiness is complicated. Above a certain level, more money does not make for more day-to-day happiness. Higher pay can increase general satisfaction with life, but when people work so hard or so dishonestly that their health, friendships, and leisure activities suffer, it has the reverse effect.

2-5b Competition

Humans are social animals who cannot help but compare themselves with other people. Deep down, we all want to be better than the other fellow. In one telling experiment, young children elected to get *fewer* prizes for themselves, as long as they still got more than other participants. For example, a child chose to get one prize for herself and zero for the other person, rather than two for herself and two for the other participant. For an adult example, consider Rajat Gupta, who retired as CEO of the consulting firm McKinsey, worth $100 million. As CEO, he had been top dog. But in retirement, he began spending time with far wealthier businesspeople, such as Bill Gates, who were *giving away* hundreds of millions of dollars. To keep up with the Gateses, Gupta began illegal insider trading. He was ultimately sentenced to two years in prison.

> Humans are social animals who cannot help but compare themselves with other people.

In a related phenomenon, researchers have found that the mere process of negotiating the price of a product reduces a person's sense of morality. Participants in an experiment were offered a payment of €10 but, in return, a young, healthy mouse would be euthanized. If they rejected the payment, the mouse would continue to live in a happy mouse environment to the end of its natural life, which was about two years. In a different version, two participants—a buyer and a seller—negotiated the payment for euthanizing the mouse. And in a third round, larger groups of buyers and sellers negotiated against each other. People in the multi-party negotiations were more likely to kill the mouse than were the pairs of two people, and those pairs were much more likely to choose death than individuals acting on their own. In short, being involved in a market reduced the players' sense of morality, at least when mice were involved.[14]

2-5c Rationalization

A recent study found that more creative people tend to be less ethical. The reason? They are better at rationalizing their bad behavior. Virtually any foul deed can be rationalized. Some common rationalizations:

- If I don't do it, someone else will.
- I deserve this because…
- They had it coming.
- I am not harming a *person*—it is just a big company.
- This is someone else's responsibility.
- Just this once.

---

[14]Armin Falk and Nora Szech, "Morals and Markets," *Science*, 340, 707 (2013).

For example, Duke professor Dan Ariely has found in his groundbreaking research that almost everyone is willing to cheat, at least on a small scale. We all want to get the greatest benefit, but we also want to think of ourselves as being honest. If we cheat—just a little—then we can tell ourselves it does not really count. Ariely did an experiment in which he paid people for solving math problems. Participants averaged four correct answers. But when people were allowed to grade the tests themselves without anyone checking up on them, all of a sudden they began averaging six correct answers.[15] You can imagine how they might have rationalized that behavior—"I was close on this one. I normally would have gotten that one right. Today was an off day for me." Surprisingly, when the participants were paid a lot for each correct answer ($10 as opposed to $0.50) they cheated *less*. Presumably, they would have felt worse about themselves if they stole a lot of money rather than a little.

To take a real example, mostly elderly volunteers ran the gift shop at the Kennedy Center for the Performing Arts in Washington, D.C.. The shop had revenues of $400,000 a year, but someone was stealing $150,000 of that. It turned out there was not one thief. Instead, dozens of volunteers were each stealing a little bit, which added up. These people felt good about themselves for being volunteers so they thought that stealing a little was fine.[16] When we do something wrong, we tend to be creative at explaining why it did not really count.

2-5d We Can't Be Objective About Ourselves

Do you do more than your fair share of work at home? On your team? In your study group? Of course you do! At least, that is what most people think. **In reality, people are not objective when comparing themselves to others.** Many studies looking at groups as various as married couples, athletes, MBA students, and organizational behavior professors have found a tendency for people to overestimate their own contribution to a group effort.[17] Even Nobel-prize winners fall prey to this trap. When Frederick Banting won the prize with John Macleod for discovering insulin, he boycotted the ceremony because he was outraged that Macleod had been given credit, too.[18]

Or, to take another example, participants in a study were put in the position of deciding whether they or someone else got an easy assignment. When asked in the abstract what would be a fair method for assigning tasks, everyone said that the computer should make the assignments randomly. But when another group of people was actually given the authority to decide, three-quarters ignored the computer option and just assigned themselves the easy jobs. And then they rated themselves high on a fairness scale.[19] In making a decision that affects you, it is important to remember that you are unlikely to be objective.

2-5e Conflicts of Interest

Suppose that your doctor is writing a prescription for you. Do you care that she does so with a pen given to her by a pharmaceutical company? You should. The evidence is that doctors are influenced by gifts and, indeed, small gifts are surprisingly influential

---

[15]Dan Ariely, "Why We Lie," *The Wall Street Journal*, May 26, 2012.

[16]David Brooks, "The Moral Diet," *The New York Times*, June 7, 2012.

[17]MBA students were asked what percentage of the work each had done in their study groups. The total credit claimed per group averaged 139%. Organizational behavior professors overestimated their own contribution by a similar amount. Mahzarin R. Banaji, Max H. Bazerman, and Dolly Chugh, "How (Un)Ethical Are You?", *Harvard Business Review*, December 2003.

[18]Eugene M. Caruso, Nicholas Epley, and Max H. Bazerman, "The Costs and Benefits of Undoing Egocentric Responsibility Assessments in Groups," *Journal of Personality and Social Psychology*, November 1, 2006.

[19]John Tierney, "Deep Down, We Can't Fool Even Ourselves," *The New York Times*, July 1, 2008.

Should Orlanda accept such a gift?

because the recipients do not make a conscious effort to overcome any bias these tokens may create. With larger gifts, the recipients are more aware and, therefore, take more effort in overcoming their biases. Doctors are not alone in their reaction. For everyone, the bias created by a conflict of interest tends to be unconscious and unintentionally self-serving. In short, if ethical decisions are your goal, it is better to avoid all conflicts of interest—both large and small. No one—including you—is good at overcoming the biases that these conflicts create.

2-5f Conformity

Famed investor Warren Buffett has been quoted as saying, "The five most dangerous words in business may be: 'Everybody else is doing it.'" Because humans are social animals, they are often willing to follow the leader, even to a place where they do not really want to go. If all the salespeople in a company cheat on their expense accounts, a new hire is much more likely to view this behavior as acceptable.

2-5g Ethics Case: Diamonds in the Rough

When Orlanda graduated from college, she got a job as a software engineer in Silicon Valley. After two years working in technical support, one of her customers offered her a job at his company. It turned out that her new firm was in shambles but, after months of killer hours, she managed to get the company on a better path. One of her biggest accomplishments was to help a major supplier solve its technical problems so that its product would work reliably. On her birthday, her contact at the supplier (who was a friend of her boss) gave her a diamond watch. Her company had no policy on accepting gifts, so she kept it. Afterward, she realized that she was spending even more time working on this supplier's issues. But, she said to herself, this was good for her company, too. Also, no one at her company had high ethical standards anyway.

Some months later, the same supplier offered to buy her a diamond necklace if she would make his company a preferred supplier. He said the necklace would look just like the one he had given her boss.

Questions

1. What ethics traps is Orlanda facing?

2. Is there anything wrong with accepting these gifts?

2-5h Following Orders

When someone in authority issues orders, even to do something clearly wrong, it is very tempting to comply. Fear of punishment, the belief in authority figures, and the ability to rationalize all play a role. In a true story (with the facts disguised), Amanda worked at a private school that was struggling to pay its bills. As a result, it kept the lights turned off in the hallways. On a particularly cloudy day, a visitor tripped and fell in one of these darkened passages. When the visitor sued, the principal told Amanda to lie on the witness stand and say that the lights had been on. The school's lawyer reinforced this advice. Amanda did as she was told. When asked why, she said, "I figured it must be the right thing to do if the lawyer said so. Also, if I hadn't lied, the principal would have fired me, and I might not have been able to get another job in teaching."

In your life, you are likely to face the dilemma of a boss who orders you to do something wrong. Executives have told us that they have been ordered to:

- Misrepresent data in a presentation to the board (so the boss could take on a project that was not as profitable as it should have been)

- Avoid hiring certain ethnic groups or pregnant women

- "Smooth" numbers, that is, report sales that had not, actually, taken place

- Support the boss's position, even if it was clearly wrong

Be aware, too, that setting goals for your subordinates carries risks, especially if the goals are too narrowly focused. A law firm partner once said, "If we tell associates they have to bill 2,000 hours a year, they will bill 2,000 hours. Whether they will *work* 2,000 hours is another matter." Research supports this view. Participants in an experiment were more likely to cheat if they had been assigned specific goals, whether or not they were actually being paid for meeting the targets.[20]

As you might expect, employees who work for firms with a culture of blind-obedience are twice as likely to report having seen unethical behavior as are workers at companies with a more collaborative environment.[21]

2-5i Euphemisms and Reframing

The term "friendly fire" has a cheerful ring to it, much better than "killing your own troops," which is what it really means. In a business setting, to "smooth earnings" sounds a lot better than to "cook the books" or "commit fraud." "Right-sizing" is more palatable than "firing a whole bunch of people." And "file sharing" sounds friendly and helpful, very different from "stealing intellectual property." In making ethical decisions, it is important to use accurate terminology. Anything else is just a variation on rationalization.

Aerospace engineer Roger Boisjoly (pronounced "Boh-zho-lay") tried to convince his superiors at Morton-Thiokol, Inc. to scrub the launch of the space shuttle *Challenger*. His superiors were engineers, too, so they were qualified to evaluate Boisjoly's concerns. But during the discussion, one of the bosses said, "We have to make a management decision." Once the issue was reframed as "management," not "engineering," their primary concern was to please their customer, NASA. The flight had already been postponed twice and, as managers, they felt they needed really clear data to justify another postponement. The Morton-Thiokol managers had to be convinced that it was *not* safe to fly. With that clear evidence lacking, these men approved the launch, which ended catastrophically when the space shuttle exploded 73 seconds after liftoff, killing all seven astronauts onboard. If they had asked an engineering question—"Is this spaceship definitely safe?"—they would have made a different decision. In answering a question, it is always a good idea to consider whether the frame is correct.

---

[20]Alina Tugend, "Experts' Advice to the Goal-Oriented: Don't Overdo It," *The New York Times*, October, 5, 2012.
[21]"The View from the Top and Bottom," *The Economist*, September 224, 2011.

2-5j Lost in a Crowd

After being struck by a car, a two-year-old child lies at the side of the road as people walk and ride by. No one stops to help, and the child dies. On a busy street, a man picks up a seven-year-old girl and carries her away while she screams, "You're not my dad—someone help me!" No one responds. The first incident was real; the second one was a test staged by a news station. It took hours and many repetitions before anyone tried to prevent the abduction.

When in a group, people are less likely to take responsibility, because they assume (hope?) that someone else will. They tend to check the reactions of others and, if everyone else seems calm, they assume that all is right. Bystanders are much more likely to react if they are alone and have to form an independent judgment.

Thus, in a business, if everyone is lying to customers, smoothing earnings, or sexually harassing the staff, it is tempting to go with the flow rather than protest the wrongdoing. In the example about food companies that began this chapter, one former executive says that producers shrug off responsibility for obesity in America by pointing to all the "other causes": a car culture; too much screen time; less outdoor play; fewer women at home to cook. And, Americans spend half of their food money outside the home anyway.

2-5k Ethics Case: Man Down

Wesley Autrey was standing on a train platform with his two young daughters and a man he did not know. Suddenly, this man had a seizure, causing him to fall on the tracks. Autrey could hear a train approaching so he knew he had only seconds to act. Leaping on to the track, he pulled the man between the rails and lay on top of him to protect him from the train. The train engineer tried to stop, but five cars passed over the two men. Both were unharmed.

Some years later in New York City, a homeless man pushed Ki-Suck Han onto subway tracks, in view of many people. No one reacted, except a photographer who took photos as Han was killed by a train.

Questions

- Why was Autrey more likely to act than the crowds watching Han?

- What are your ethical obligations to respond when someone needs help? Or you observe wrongdoing?

- Imagine that, at your work, you know that someone is:
  - Lying on an expense account
  - Wrongly booking sales that have not yet occurred
  - Sexually harassing staff members

What is your ethical obligation? What would you do, under what circumstances?

2-5l Short-Term Perspective

Many times, people make unethical decisions because they are thinking short-term. Your boss asks you to book sales in this quarter that actually will not happen until next. That "solution" would solve the immediate issue of low sales while potentially creating an enormous long-term problem that could lead to bankruptcy and prison-time. One manager told this story:

> A vice president from the customer service team told me that the company's largest customer was going to be conducting an on-site audit. In my area, the customer would be particularly interested in seeing the dedicated computing equipment that was part of their contract. As it turns out, we did not have any dedicated computing equipment. The VP was incredulous because the past director of my area had, on multiple occasions, told him that there was. As it turned out, the

former director had been lying. To survive the audit, the VP asked me to lie and also to put fake labels on some of the machines to show the customer. If I didn't agree, I knew the VP would be furious and we might lose this client.

In the short-run, lying is an appealing option in this case, as lying often is. But eventually the customer was likely to find out about the breach of contract, which could mean one client lost and one lawsuit acquired. The manager refused to lie and, in the end, was given the extra funds to comply with the contract.

2-5m Blind Spots

As Bob Dylan memorably sang, "How many times can a man turn his head and pretend that he just doesn't see?" The answer is: a whole lot. For example, Bernard Madoff will long be remembered for running one of the biggest frauds ever through his brokerage house. One of the mysteries yet unresolved is: Who else knew what was going on? His brother, Peter, was second in command at his brother's firm. He admitted that he had committed many crimes, including income tax evasion and filing false documents with regulators. But he has always insisted that he had no idea his brother was committing fraud.

And then there is the case of Barry Bonds, one of the greatest baseball players of all time. Although he quickly gained tremendous weight and muscle mass that was consistent with the illegal use of steroids, neither his team nor baseball executives took any action against him until the federal government began an investigation.[22]

Or a partner in a law firm who was consistently billing 2,000+ hours a year. Yet he seemed to have time to attend his children's school functions in the middle of the day and was rarely in the office early or late. Firm executives were shocked to discover that he had been overbilling clients.[23]

We all have a tendency to ignore even blatant evidence that we would rather not know. Just as tobacco manufacturers were very slow to learn that smoking caused cancer, officials at Pennsylvania State University overlooked compelling evidence that football coach Jerry Sandusky was molesting children.

2-5n Avoiding Ethics Traps

These ethics traps represent potential dangers for us all. But they are not, by any means, inevitable.

Three practices will help us avoid these pitfalls:

1. **Slow down.** We all make worse decisions when in a hurry. In one experiment, a group of students at Princeton Theological Seminary (that is, people in training to be ministers) were told to go to a location across campus to give a talk. On their walk over, they encountered a man lying in distress in a doorway. Only one-tenth of those participants who had been told they were late for their talk stopped to help the ill man, while almost two-thirds of those who thought they had plenty of time did stop.[24]

2. **Do not trust your first instinct.** You make many decisions without thinking. When sitting down for dinner, you do not ask yourself, "Which hand should I use to pick up the fork? How will I cut up my food?" You use System 1 thinking—an automatic, instinctual, sometimes emotional process. This approach is efficient but can also lead

---

[22]To see the drastic change in Bonds's physique, search the Internet for "steroids, Barry Bonds."

[23]For more on this topic, see Max Bazerman and Ann Tenbrunsel, *Blind Spots: Why We Fail To Do What's Right and What To Do About It*, Princeton University Press.

[24]John M. Darley and Daniel C. Batson, "From Jerusalem to Jericho: A Study of Situational and Dispositional Variables in Helping Behavior," *Journal of Personality and Social Psychology*, Vol. 27(1), July 1973, 100–108.

to more selfish and unethical decisions. When taking an exam, System 1 thinking would not get you far. For that, you need System 2 thoughts—those that are conscious and logical.

Being in a hurry, or in a crowd, being able to rationalize easily, using euphemisms, doing what every else does, receiving an order, being dazzled by money; these can all lead you to make a quick and wrong System 1 decision. Before making an important choice, bring in System 2 thinking.

3. **Remember your Life Principles.** In his research, Ariely found that participants were less likely to cheat if they were reminded of their school honor code or the Ten Commandments. This result was true even if the participants were atheists. Also, in the case of the seminary students, the topic of the talk mattered. Those who were speaking on the Parable of the Good Samaritan (in which a man offers aid to an injured person from a different clan) were twice as likely to provide help than those who were giving a talk on careers for seminarians. It is a good practice to remind yourself of your values. What about keeping a list of your Life Principles as wallpaper on your phone or computer?

2-6 LYING: A SPECIAL CASE

We are taught from an early age to tell the truth. Yet research shows that we tell between one and two lies a day.[25] Is honesty the best policy? The consequences of lying can be severe: Students are suspended, employees are fired, and witnesses are convicted of perjury. Sometimes the impact is subtler but still significant: a loss of trust or of opportunities.

When is lying acceptable? If poker players bluff their way through lousy hands, we consider them skilled because that is an accepted part of the game. What about white lies to make others feel better: I love your lasagna. You're not going bald. No, that sweater doesn't make you look fat. When Victoria McGrath suffered a terrible wound to her leg in the Boston Marathon bombing, Tyler Dodd comforted her at the scene by telling her that he had recovered from a shrapnel wound in Afghanistan. His story was not true—he had never been in combat or Afghanistan. McGrath was grateful to him for his lie because it gave her strength and hope. Was he right or wrong? What are your rules on lying?

Kant felt that any lie violated his principle of the categorical imperative. Because the world would be intolerable if everyone lied all the time, no one should lie ever. He gave the example of the murderer who knocks on your door and asks, "Where's Lukas?" You know Lukas is cowering just inside, but you might be tempted to lie and send the murderer off in the opposite direction. Kant preferred that you tell what is now called a **Kantian Evasion** or a **palter**. That is, you would make a truthful statement that is nonetheless misleading. So, you might say, truthfully, "I saw Lukas in the park just an hour ago." And off the murderer would go.

Kantian evasion or a palter
A truthful statement that is nonetheless misleading.

Is a Kantian Evasion really more ethical than a lie? For example, when a candidate for the presidency, Bill Clinton was asked if he had ever smoked marijuana. He answered that he "never broke the laws of my state or of the United States." Later, it was revealed that he had used marijuana while a student in England. So, although technically correct, his statement was misleading. Was that really better than lying about marijuana use?

One could argue that Clinton was at least honoring the importance of truth-telling. He went to some effort *not* to lie. However, some commentators argue that paltering is actually

---

[25]Bella M. DePaulo, Deborah A. Kashy, Susan E. Kirkendol, and Melissa M. Wyer, "Lying in Everyday Life," *Journal of Personality and Social Psychology*, 1996, Vol. 70, No. 5, 979–995.

worse than lying. Although the harm to the victim is the same, palterers are less likely to be caught and are, therefore, more likely to palter again.

What are your Life Principles on this issue? There may indeed be good reasons to lie but what are they? Would it be right to say that you would only lie to benefit other people? Hiding Lukas from the murderer? Deceiving children who believe in Santa Claus? It is useful to analyze this issue now rather than to rationalize later.

What about in business? Does the presence of *competition* make a difference? When do the ends justify the means?

2-6a Ethics Case: Truth (?) in Borrowing

Rob is in the business of buying dental practices. He finds solo practitioners, buys their assets, signs them to a long-term contract and then improves their management and billing processes so effectively that both he and the dentists are better off.

Rob has just found a great opportunity with a lot of potential profit. There is only *one* problem. The bank will not give him a loan to buy the practice without checking the dentist's financial record. Her credit rating is fine, but it turns out that she filed for bankruptcy 20 years ago. That event no longer appears on her credit record but, on the form it required her to sign, the bank asked about *all* bankruptcies. She is perfectly willing to lie. Rob refused to turn in the form with a lie. But when the bank learned about the bankruptcy, it denied his loan even though *her* bankruptcy in no way affects *his* ability to pay the loan. And the incident is ancient history—the dentist's current finances are strong. Subsequently four other banks also refused to make the loan.

Rob is feeling pretty frustrated. He figures the return on this deal would be 20 percent. Everyone would benefit—the dentist would earn more, her patients would have better technology, he could afford a house in a better school district, and the bank would make a profit. There is one more bank he could try.

Questions

1. Should Rob file loan documents with the bank, knowing the dentist has lied?

2. Who would be harmed by this lie?

3. What if Rob pays back the loan without incident? Was the lie still wrong? Do the ends justify the means?

4. What is your Life Principle about telling lies? When is making a misrepresentation acceptable? To protect someone's life or physical safety? To protect a job? To protect another person's feelings? To gain an advantage? When others are doing the same? When it makes sense from a cost-benefit perspective?

5. Do you have the same rule when lying to protect yourself, as opposed to benefiting others?

2-7 APPLYING THE PRINCIPLES

Having thought about ethics principles and traps, let's now practice applying them to situations that are similar to those you are likely to face in your life. Be aware that some of these ethical dilemmas illustrate the trade-off between shareholders and stakeholders. It is important to recognize explicitly the forces that push or pull you when making a decision. Unless you are aware of these factors, you cannot make a truly informed decision.

2-7a **Personal Ethics in the Workplace**

Should you behave in the workplace the way you do at home, or do you have a separate set of ethics for each part of your life? What if your employees behave badly outside of work—should that affect their employment? Consider the following case.

2-7b **Ethics Case: Weird Wierdsma**

Beatrix Szeremi immigrated to the United States from Hungary. But her American dream turned into a nightmare when she married Charles Wierdsma. He repeatedly beat her and threatened to suffocate and drown her. Ultimately, he pleaded guilty to one felony count and went to jail. Despite his son's guilt, Thomas Wierdsma pressured his daughter-in-law to drop the charges and delete photos of her injuries from her Facebook page. When she refused, he threatened her and her lawyer that he would report her to immigration officials. Father and son discussed how they could get her deported. Thomas also testified in a deposition that it was not wrong to lie to a federal agency. "It happens all the time," he said.[26] Thomas Wierdsma is the senior vice president at The GEO Group, Inc.

Research indicates that CEOs who break the law outside of the office are more likely to engage in workplace fraud. Although their legal infractions—driving under the influence, use of illegal drugs, domestic violence, even speeding tickets—were unrelated to their work, they seemed to indicate a disrespect for the rule of law and a lack of self-control.[27]

Questions

1. If you were the CEO of Thomas Wierdsma's company, would you fire him? Impose some other sanction?

2. Which is worse—threatening his daughter-in-law or stating that it is acceptable to lie to a federal agency?

3. Would you fire a warehouse worker who behaved this way? How high up in the hierarchy does an employee have to be for this behavior to be forgiven?

4. GEO runs prisons and immigration facilities for the government. Does that fact change any of your answers?

5. Wierdsma's woes were reported in major newspapers and his statement about lying to a federal agency is on YouTube (see footnote). Do these facts change any of your answers?

6. What would Kant and Mill say is the right thing to do in this case? What result under the Front Page Test?

7. What ethics traps might Wierdsma's boss face in this situation?

8. What is your Life Principle? What behavior are you willing to tolerate in the interest of profitability?

9. What would you say to someone who argues that the goal at work is to make as much money as possible, but at home it is to be a kind and honorable human being?

---

[26]Nancy Lofholm, "GEO Investigated in Son's Domestic Violence Case," *The Denver Post*, April 8, 2013. The YouTube video of his admission about lying to a federal agency is at http://www.youtube.com/watch?v=UTi9fbo202M.

[27]Robert Davidson, Aiyesha Dey, and Abbie Smith, "Executives' 'Off-the-Job' Behavior, Corporate Culture, and Financial Reporting Risk," Chicago Booth Paper No. 12-24.

2-7c **The Organization's Responsibility to Society**

Many products can potentially cause harm to customers or employees. Does it matter if they willingly accept exposure to these products? What constitutes informed agreement? What is the company's responsibility to those who are *unwittingly* harmed by its products?

2-7d **Ethics Case: Breathing the Fumes**

Every other year, the National Institutes of Health publish the Report on Carcinogens, which lists products that cause cancer. Among those in the most recent report was formaldehyde, found in furniture, cosmetics, building products, carpets, and fabric softeners. Unless we take heroic efforts to avoid this chemical, we are all exposed to it on a daily basis. Indeed, almost all homes have formaldehyde levels that exceed government safety rules. In an effort to shoot the messenger, the American Chemistry Council, which is an industry trade group, lobbied Congress to cut off funding for the Report on Carcinogens—not improve it, but defund it.

Questions

1. If you were one of the many companies using products that contain formaldehyde, what would you do? What would you be willing to pay to provide a safer product?

2. If you were an executive at Exxon, Dow, or DuPont, all members of the American Chemistry Council, how would you react to this effort to hide the facts on formaldehyde?

3. What would Mill and Kant recommend?

4. What ethics traps would you face in making a decision?

5. What Life Principle would you apply?

2-7e **The Organization's Responsibility to Its Employees**

Organizations cannot be successful without good workers. In many circumstances, the shareholder and stakeholder models agree that employees should be treated well. Disgruntled workers are likely to be unmotivated and unproductive. But sometimes doing what is best for employees may not lead to higher profits. In these cases, does an organization have a duty to take care of its workers? The shareholder model says no; the stakeholder model takes the opposite view.

Corporate leaders are often faced with difficult decisions when the issue of layoffs arises. Choices can be particularly difficult to navigate when outsourcing is an option. *Outsourcing* refers to cutting jobs at home and relocating operations to another country. That is the issue in the following scenario.

2-7f **Ethics Case: The Storm After the Storm**

Yanni is the CEO of Cloud Farm, a company that provides online data centers for Internet companies. Because these data centers are enormous, they are located in rural areas where they are often the main employer. A series of tornados has just destroyed a data center near Farmfield, Arkansas, a town with a population of roughly 5,000 people. Farmfield is a two-hour drive from the nearest city, Little Rock.

Here is the good news: The insurance payout will cover the full cost of rebuilding. Indeed, the payout will be so generous that Cloud Farm could build a bigger and better facility than the one destroyed. The bad news? Data centers are much more expensive to build and operate in the United States than in Africa, Asia, or Latin America. Yanni could take the money from the insurance company and build three data centers overseas. He has asked Adam and Zoe to present the pros and cons of relocating.

Adam says, "If we rebuild overseas, our employees will never find equivalent jobs. We pay $20 an hour, and the other jobs in town are mostly minimum wage. And remember how some of the guys worked right through Christmas to set up for that new client. They have been loyal to us—we owe them something in return. Going overseas is not just bad for Farmfield or Arkansas, it's bad for the country. We can't continue to ship jobs overseas."

Zoe responds, "That is the government's problem, not ours. We'll pay to retrain the workers, which, frankly, is a generous offer. Our investors get a return of 4 percent; the industry average is closer to 8 percent. If we act like a charity to support Farmfield, we could all lose our jobs. It is our obligation to do what's best for our shareholders—which, in this case, happens to be what's right for us, too."

Questions

1. Do you agree with Zoe's argument that it is the government's responsibility to create and protect American jobs, and that it is a CEO's job to increase shareholder wealth?

2. Imagine that you personally own shares in Cloud Farm. Would you be upset with a decision to rebuild the data center in the United States?

3. If you were in Yanni's position, would you rebuild the plant in Arkansas or relocate overseas?

4. If Cloud Farm decides to rebuild in Arkansas, should it pay the workers while the center is being rebuilt? If yes, should it pay all workers, or just the high-level ones who might leave if they were not paid?

5. What ethics traps does Yanni face in this situation?

6. What is your Life Principle on this issue? Would you be willing to risk your job to protect your employees?

2-7g An Organization's Responsibility to Its Customers

Customers are another group of essential stakeholders. A corporation must gain and retain loyal buyers if it is to stay in business for long. Treating customers well usually increases profits and helps shareholders.

But when, if ever, does an organization go too far? Is a leader acting appropriately when she puts customers first in a way that significantly diminishes the bottom line? The shareholder model says no. What do you say?

2-7h Ethics Case: Mickey Weighs In

As we have seen, many food companies manipulate products to maximize their appeal, without regard to the health of their customers. Disney is taking a different approach, announcing recently that only healthy foods can be advertised on its children's television channels, radio stations, and websites. Candy, fast food, and sugared cereals are banned from Mickey land.

Kicked to the curb are such childhood favorites as Lunchables and Capri Sun drinks. In addition, sodium must be reduced by one-quarter in food served at its theme parks. Nor does Disney permit its characters to associate with unhealthy foods. No more Mickey Pop-Tarts or Buzz Lightyear Happy Meals. Said Disney chairman, Robert Iger, "Companies in a position to help with solutions to childhood obesity should do just that."[28]

Disney will certainly lose advertising, but would not say how much. Food sales at its theme parks may decline if children find the options unappealing. Its licensing revenues are also affected by its decision to remove Disney characters from the likes of Pop-Tarts and Happy Meals.

On the other hand, this healthy initiative will enhance its reputation, at least with parents, who increasingly seek healthy food options for their children. Disney will profit from license fees it receives for the use of a Mickey Check logo on healthy food in grocery aisles and restaurants. This food initiative may also help forestall more onerous government regulation.

In contrast, the Nickelodeon television channel, home to SpongeBob SquarePants and Dora the Explorer, still allows ads for such nutritional failures as Trix and Cocoa Puffs cereals. It said that its goal is "to make the highest quality entertainment content in the world for kids … [while leaving] the science of nutrition to the experts." Food ads are the third highest source of advertising revenues for Nickelodeon. Also, it does not have as many other revenue streams as Disney does—no theme parks, for example.

Questions

1. What obligation do Disney and Nickelodeon have to their young customers? Do they owe anything other than entertainment?

2. How much advertising and licensing revenue would you be willing to give up to protect children from ads for unhealthy foods? Does your answer depend on how profitable the division is?

3. Does this information make you more likely to buy Disney products or allow your children to watch Disney TV? Less likely to watch Nickelodeon?

4. What would Mill or Kant have said? What result with the Front Page Test?

5. What ethics traps do Disney and Nickelodeon face?

6. What is your Life Principle? How much profitability (or income) would you be willing to give up to protect children you do not know?

2-7i Organization's Responsibility to Overseas Workers

What ethical duties does an American manager have overseas, to stakeholders in countries where the culture and economic circumstances are very different? Should American companies (and consumers) buy goods that are produced in sweatshop factories?

Industrialization has always been the first stepping-stone out of dire poverty—it was in England in centuries past, and it is now in the developing world. Eventually, higher productivity leads to higher wages. The results in

> Industrialization has always been the first stepping-stone out of dire poverty

---

[28]Brooks Barnes, "Promoting Nutrition, Disney to Restrict Junk-Food Ads," *The New York Times*, June 5, 2012.

China have been nothing short of remarkable. During the Industrial Revolution in England, per-capita output doubled in 58 years; in China, it took only 10 years.

During the past 50 years, Taiwan and South Korea welcomed sweatshops. During the same period, India resisted what it perceived to be foreign exploitation. Although all three countries started at the same economic level, Taiwan and South Korea today have much lower levels of infant mortality and much higher levels of education than India.[29]

In theory, then, sweatshops might not be all bad. But are there limits? Consider the following case.

2-7j Ethics Case: A Worm in the Apple

"Riots, Suicides and More," blares an Internet headline about a FoxConn factory where iPhones and other Apple products are assembled. Apple is not alone in facing supplier scandals. So have Nike, Coca-Cola, and Gap, among many others. Do companies have an obligation to the employees of their suppliers? If so, how can they, or anyone, be sure what is really going on in a factory on the other side of the world? Professor Richard Locke of MIT has studied supply chain issues.[30] His conclusions:

- The first step that many companies took to improve working conditions overseas was to establish a code of conduct and then conduct audits. Professor Locke found that these coercive practices do not work and that compliance is sporadic, at best. For example, despite Hewlett-Packard's best efforts, only a handful of its 276 overseas factories consistently met its standards.

- A more collaborative approach worked better—when the auditors sent by multinationals saw their role as less of a police officer and more as a partner, committed to problem solving and sharing of best practices.

- It can be hard to improve conditions without also changing a company's business model. One of the reasons that Apple uses Chinese manufacturers such as FoxConn is that its workers have fewer overtime restrictions. Just before the first iPhone was released, Steve Jobs decided that the screens had to be unscratchable glass instead of plastic. One Chinese company supplied a team of engineers that was housed in a dormitory and willing to work around the clock to design the right glass. When the glass arrived at FoxConn in the middle of the night, thousands of assemblers were put to work immediately.

What would you do if you were a manager in the following circumstances?

- In clothing factories, workers often remove the protective guards from their sewing machines, because the guards slow the flow of work. As a result, many workers suffer needle punctures. Factories resist the cost of buying new guards because the workers just take them off again. Is there a solution?

- In a factory in Central America, powerful chemicals were used to remove stains from clothing. The fumes from these chemicals were a health hazard but ventilation systems were too expensive. What could be done?

- Timberland, Nike, and Hewlett-Packard have recognized that selling large numbers of new products creates great variation in demand and therefore pressure on factory workers to work overtime. What can a company do to reduce this pressure?[31]

---

[29]The data in this and the preceding paragraph are from Nicholas D. Kristof and Sheryl Wu Dunn, "Two Cheers for Sweatshops," *New York Times Magazine*, Sept. 24, 2000, p. 70.

[30]"When the Jobs Inspector Calls," *The Economist*, March 31, 2012.

[31]These examples are from: Richard Locke, Matthew Amengual, and Akshay Mangla, "Virtue out of Necessity?: Compliance, Commitment and the Improvement of Labor Conditions in Global Supply Chains," available at Princeton.edu.

2-8 WHEN THE GOING GETS TOUGH: RESPONDING TO UNETHICAL BEHAVIOR

We have talked about the kinds of ethical issues that you are likely to face in your career. If you find yourself working for a company that tolerates an intolerable level of unethical behavior, you face three choices.

2-8a Loyalty

It is always important to pick one's battles. For example, a firm's accounting department must make many decisions about which reasonable people could disagree. Just because their judgment is different from yours does not mean that they are behaving unethically. Being a team player means allowing other people to make their own choices sometimes. However, the difference between being a team player and starting down the slippery slope can be very narrow. If you are carrying out a decision, or simply observing one, that makes you uncomfortable, then it is time to consult your Life Principles and review the section on ethics traps.

2-8b Exit

When faced with the unacceptable, one option is to walk out the door quietly. You resign "to spend more time with your family," "to explore other opportunities," or "to accept an offer that is too good to refuse." This approach may be the safest for you because you are not ruffling any feathers or making any enemies. It is a small world and you never know when someone you have offended will be in a position to do you harm. But a quiet exit leaves the bad guys in position to continue the unsavory behavior. For example, the CEO was sexually harassing Laura, but she left quietly for fear that if she reported him, he would harm her career. No one likes to hire a troublemaker. So the CEO proceeded to attack other women at the company until finally a senior man got wind of what was going on and confronted the chief. In short, the braver and better option may be to exit loudly—reporting the wrongdoing on the way out the door.

2-8c Voice

As we saw in our discussion of conformity, wrongdoing often occurs because everyone just goes along to get along. One valiant soul with the courage to say, "This is wrong," can be a powerful force for the good. But confrontation may not be the only, or even the best, use of your voice. Learning to persuade, cajole, or provide better options are all important leadership skills. For example, Keith felt that the CEO of his company was about to make a bad decision but he was unable to persuade the man to choose a different alternative. When Keith turned out to be correct, the CEO gave him no credit, saying, "You are equally responsible because your arguments weren't compelling enough." Keith thought the man had a point.

2-9 CORPORATE SOCIAL RESPONSIBILITY (CSR)

So far, we have largely been talking about a company's duty not to cause harm. But do companies have a **corporate social responsibility**—that is, an obligation to contribute positively to the world around them? Do businesses have an affirmative duty to do good?.

Corporate social responsibility
An organization's obligation to contribute positively to the world around it

You remember Milton Friedman's view that a manager's obligation is to make the company as profitable as possible while also complying with the law. Harvard Professor Michael Porter has written that CSR often benefits a company. For example, improving economic and social conditions overseas can create new customers with money to spend. Educational programs may provide a better workforce. However, in Porter's view, a company should not undertake a CSR project unless it is profitable for the company in its own right, regardless of any secondary benefits the company may receive from, say, an improved reputation.[32] Thus, for example, Yoplait has periodically run a "Save Lids to Save Lives" campaign. For every Yoplait lid mailed in, the company makes a donation to a breast cancer charity. During these campaigns, Yoplait gains market share. Should companies be willing to improve the world even if their efforts *reduce* profitability?

2-9a Ethics Case: The Beauty of a Well-Fed Child

Cosmetic companies often use gift-with-purchase offers to promote their products. For example, with any $45 Estee Lauder purchase at Bloomingdale's, you can choose a free seven-piece gift of creams and makeup valued at more than $165, plus a special-edition Lily Pulitzer cosmetic bag.

But Clarins has put a new spin on these offers with what it calls "gift with *purpose*." Buy two Clarins items at Macy's and you will receive six trial-size products *and* the company will pay the United Nations World Food Program enough for 10 school meals.

Because so many cosmetic companies do gift-with-purchase offers, it is difficult for any one business to stand out from the crowd. That is Clarins's goal with this offer. The company hopes that cosmetic buyers, many of whom are women with children, will find this opportunity to feed children particularly compelling. Says the Macy's vice president for national media relations and cause marketing, "With no energy or lift on the customers' part, they get this really feel-good element with the shopping experience."[33]

Questions

1. If you were an executive at Clarins or Macy's, what would you want to know before approving this promotion?

2. How important is it to improve the image of these two companies? Would this promotion do so?

3. Would you approve this promotion if it were not profitable on its own account? How much of a subsidy would you be willing to grant?

Chapter Conclusion

Many times in your life, you will be tempted to do something that you know in your heart of hearts is wrong. Referring to your own Life Principles, being aware of potential traps, will help you to make the right decisions. But it is also important that you be able to afford to do the right thing. Having a reserve fund to cover six months' living expenses makes it easier for you to leave a job that violates your personal ethics. Too many times, people make the wrong, and sometimes the illegal, decision for financial reasons.

---

[32]Michael E. Porter and Mark R. Kramer, "The Competitive Advantage of Corporate Philanthropy," *Harvard Business Review*, December 2002.

[33]Adam Andrew Newman, "A Cosmetic Freebie with a Cause," *The New York Times*, April 7, 2013.

Managers wonder what they can do to create an ethical environment in their companies. In the end, the surest way to infuse ethics throughout an organization is for top executives to behave ethically themselves. Few will bother to do the right thing unless they observe that their bosses value and support such behavior. Even employees who are ethical in their personal lives may find it difficult to uphold their standards at work if those around them behave differently. To ensure a more ethical world, managers must be an example for others, both within and outside their organizations.

EXAM REVIEW

1. **ETHICS** The law dictates how a person *must* behave. Ethics governs how people *should* behave.

2. **LIFE PRINCIPLES** Life Principles are the rules by which you live your life. If you develop these Life Principles now, you will be prepared when facing ethical dilemmas in the future.

3. **THE ROLE OF BUSINESS IN SOCIETY** An ongoing debate about whether managers should focus only on what is best for shareholders or whether they should consider the interests of other stakeholders as well.

4. **WHY BE ETHICAL?**

   - Society as a whole benefits from ethical behavior.

   - People feel better when they behave ethically.

   - Unethical behavior can be very costly.

5. **THEORIES OF ETHICS**

   - Utilitarian thinkers such as John Stuart Mill believe that the right decision maximizes overall happiness and minimizes overall pain.

   - Deontological thinkers such as Immanuel Kant believe that the ends do not justify the means. Rather, it is important to do the right thing, no matter the result.

   - With his categorical imperative, Kant argued that you should not do something unless you would be willing to have everyone else do it, too.

   - John Rawls asked us to consider what rules we would propose for society if we did not know how lucky we would be in life's lottery. He called this situation "the veil of ignorance."

   - Under the Front Page Test, you ask yourself what you would do if your actions were going to be reported publicly online or offline.

6. **ETHICS TRAPS**

   - Money

   - Competition

   - Rationalization

- We Can't Be Objective About Ourselves
- Conflicts of Interest
- Conformity
- Following Orders
- Euphemisms and Reframing
- Lost in a Crowd
- Short-Term Perspective
- Blind Spots

7. To avoid ethics traps:

- Slow down.
- Do not trust your first instinct.
- Remember your Life Principles.

8. **KANTIAN EVASION**   A truthful statement that is nonetheless misleading.

9. **WHEN THE GOING GETS TOUGH**   When faced with unethical behavior in your organization, you have three choices:

- Loyalty
- Exit (either quiet or noisy)
- Voice

10. **CORPORATE SOCIAL RESPONSIBILITY**   An organization's obligation to contribute positively to the world around it.

MULTIPLE-CHOICE QUESTIONS

1. Milton Friedman was a strong believer in the _____ model. He _____ argue that a corporate leader's sole obligation is to make money for the company's owners.
   (a) shareholder; did
   (b) shareholder; did not
   (c) stakeholder; did
   (d) stakeholder; did not

2. Which of the following wrote the book *Utilitarianism* and believed that ethical actions should "generate the greatest good for the greatest number"?
   (a) Milton Friedman
   (b) John Stuart Mill
   (c) Immanuel Kant
   (d) John Rawls

3. Which of the following believed that the dignity of human beings must be respected, and that the most ethical decisions are made out of a sense of obligation?

   (a) Milton Friedman

   (b) John Stuart Mill

   (c) Immanuel Kant

   (d) John Rawls

4. Kant believed that:

   (a) it is ethical to tell a lie if necessary to protect an innocent person from great harm.

   (b) it is ethical to tell a lie if the benefit of the lie outweighs the cost.

   (c) it is ethical to make a true, but misleading, statement.

   (d) it is wrong to tell an outright lie or to mislead.

5. The following statement is true:

   (a) Most people are completely honest most of the time.

   (b) Even people who do not believe in God are more likely to behave honestly after reading the Ten Commandments.

   (c) When confronted with the option of engaging in wrongdoing, most people accurately evaluate the ethics of these situations.

   (d) People make their best ethical decisions when in a hurry.

CASE QUESTIONS

1. The Senate recently released a report on wrongdoing at JPMorgan Chase & Co. It found that bank executives lied to investors and the public. Also, traders, with the knowledge of top management, changed risk limits to facilitate more trading and then violated even these higher limits. Executives revalued the bank's investment portfolio to reduce apparent losses. The bank's internal investigation failed to find this wrongdoing. Into what ethics traps did these JPMorgan employees fall? What options did the executives and traders have for dealing with this wrongdoing?

2. Located in Bath, Maine, Bath Iron Works builds high-tech warships for the Navy. Winning Navy contracts is crucial to the company's success—it means jobs for the community and profits for the shareholders. Navy officials held a meeting at Bath's offices with its executives and those of a competitor to review the specs for an upcoming bid. Both companies desperately wanted to win the contract. After the meeting, a Bath worker realized that one of the Navy officials had left a folder on a chair labeled: "Business Sensitive." It contained information about the competitors' bid that would be a huge advantage to Bath. William Haggett, the Bath CEO, was notified about the file just as he was walking out the door to give a luncheon speech. What should he do? What ethics traps did he face? What result if he considered Mill, Kant, or the Front Page test?

3. A group of medical schools conducted a study on very premature babies—those born between 24 and 27 weeks of gestation (instead of the normal 40 weeks). These children face a high risk of blindness and death. The goal of the study was to

determine which level of oxygen in a baby's incubator produced the best results. Before enrolling families in the study, the investigators did not tell them that being in the study could *increase* their child's risk of blindness or death. The study made some important discoveries about the best oxygen level. These results could benefit many children. What would Mill and Kant say about this decision *not* to tell the families?

4. I oversee the internal audit function at my company. Although we always use a Big Four accounting firm, we have no loyalty to any one particular firm. We hold periodic bid competitions to get the lowest price we can. At the moment, we are using Firm A. Recently, one of the partners at A offered me box seats to a Red Sox baseball game. I love the Red Sox, and even more important, I could have taken my father who, even though he has always been a big Sox fan, has never been to a game. However, I knew that we would soon be asking A to bid against the other Big Four firms for the right to do next year's audit. Needless to say, I was torn about what I should do.

What traps does this person face? Would something as minor as Red Sox tickets affect his decision about which audit firm to use?

5. Each year, the sale of Girl Scout cookies is the major fund-raiser for local troops. But because the organization was criticized for promoting such unhealthy food, it introduced a new cookie, Mango Cremes with Nutrifusion. It promotes this cookie as a vitamin-laden, natural whole food. "A delicious way to get your vitamins." But these vitamins are a minuscule part of the cookie. The rest has more bad saturated fat than an Oreo. The Girl Scouts do much good for many girls. And to do this good, they need to raise money. What would Kant and Mill say about Mango Cremes? What about the Front Page test? What do you say?

6. In Japan, automobile GPS systems come equipped with an option for converting them into televisions so that drivers can watch their favorite shows, yes, while driving. "We can't help but respond to our customers' needs," says a company spokesperson.[34] Although his company does not recommend the practice of watching while driving, he explained that it is the driver's responsibility to make this decision. Is it right to sell a product that could cause great harm to innocent bystanders? Where does the company's responsibility end and the consumer's begin? What would Mill and Kant say?

Discussion Questions

1. While waiting in line at a supermarket, you observe a woman trying to pay with food stamps. Under the law, food stamps cannot be used to pay for prepared items so the register would not accept the stamps in payment for a $6 container of chicken noodle soup from the deli counter. The woman explained that she was sick and did not have the energy to cook. She just wanted to go home and get in bed. In general, you agree that this law is reasonable—people on limited budgets should not be buying more expensive prepared food. But the woman is sick. Would it be ethical for you to buy her chicken soup if she agreed to buy $6 worth of your grocery items?

---

[34]Chester Dawson, "Drivers Use Navigation Systems to Tune In," *The Wall Street Journal*, April 23, 2013.

2. Because Raina processes payroll at her company, she knows how much everyone earns, including the top executives. This information could make for some good gossip, but she has kept it all completely confidential. She just found out, however, that it is against company policy for her to do payroll for C-level employees. And her boss knew it. Yesterday, the CEO went to her boss to confirm that he, the boss, was personally doing the processing for top management. Her boss lied to the CEO and said that he was. Then he begged Raina not to tell the truth if the CEO checked with her. Raina just got a message that the CEO wants to see her. What does she say if he asks about the payroll?

3. Darby has been working for 14 months at Holden Associates, a large management consulting firm. She is earning $85,000 a year, which *sounds* good but does not go very far in New York City. It turns out that her peers at competing firms are typically paid 20 percent more and receive larger annual bonuses. Darby works about 60 hours a week—more if she is traveling. A number of times, she has had to reschedule her vacation or cancel personal plans to meet client deadlines. She hopes to go to business school in a year and has already begun the application process.

   Holden has a policy that permits any employee who works as late as 8:00 p.m. to eat dinner at the company's expense. The employee can also take a taxi home. Darby is in the habit of staying until 8:00 p.m. every night, whether or not her workload requires it. Then she orders enough food for dinner, with leftovers for lunch the next day. She has managed to cut her grocery bill to virtually nothing. Sometimes she invites her boyfriend to join her for dinner. As a student, he is always hungry and broke. Darby often uses the Holden taxi to take them back to his apartment, although the cab fare is twice as high as to her own place.

   Sometimes Darby stays late to work on her business school applications. Naturally, she uses Holden equipment to print out and photocopy the finished applications. Darby has also been known to return online purchases through the Holden mailroom on the company dime. Many employees do that, and the mailroom workers do not seem to mind.

   Is Darby doing anything wrong? What ethics traps is she facing? What would your Life Principle be in this situation?

4. Steve supervises a team of account managers. One night at a company outing, Lawrence, a visiting account manager, made some wildly inappropriate sexual remarks to Maddie, who is on Steve's team. When she told Steve, he was uncertain what to do, so he asked his boss. She was concerned that if Steve took the matter further and Lawrence was fired or even disciplined, her whole area would suffer. Lawrence was one of the best account managers in the region, and everyone was overworked as it was. She told Steve to get Maddie to drop the matter. Just tell her that these things happen, and Lawrence did not mean anything by it.

   What should Steve do? What ethics traps does he face? What would be your Life Principle in this situation? What should Maddie do?

5. Many people enjoy rap music at least in part because of its edgy, troublemaking vibe. The problem is that some of this music could cause real trouble. Thus, Ice-T's song "Cop Killer" generated significant controversy when it was released. Among other things, its lyrics celebrated the idea of slitting a policeman's throat. Rick Ross rapped about drugging and raping a woman. Time Warner Inc. did not withdraw Ice-T's song but Reebok fired Ross over his lyrics. One difference: Time Warner was struggling with a $15 billion debt and a depressed stock price. Reebok at first refused to take

action but then singing group UltraViolet began circulating an online petition against the song and staged a protest at the main Reebok store in New York.

What obligation do companies have to their customers? What factors matter when making a decision about the content of entertainment.

6. You are negotiating a new labor contract with union officials. The contract covers a plant that has experienced operating losses over the past several years. You want to negotiate concessions from labor to reduce the losses. However, labor is refusing any compromises. You could tell them that, without concessions, the plant will be closed, although that is not true.

Is bluffing ethical? Under what circumstances? What would Kant and Mill say? What result under the Front Page test? What is your Life Principle?

7. When James Kilts became CEO of Gillette Co., the consumer products giant had been a mainstay of the Boston community for 100 years. But the organization was going through hard times: Its stock was trading at less than half its peak price, and some of its established brands of razors were suffering under intense competitive pressure. In four short years, Kilts turned Gillette around—strengthening its core brands, cutting jobs, and paying off debt. With the company's stock up 61 percent, Kilts had added $20 billion in shareholder value.

Then Kilts suddenly sold Gillette to Procter & Gamble (P&G) for $57 billion. So short was Kilts's stay in Boston that he never moved his family from their home in Rye, New York. The deal was sweet for Gillette shareholders—the company's stock price went up 13 percent in one day. And also for Kilts—his payoff was $153 million, including a $23.9 million reward from P&G for having made the deal and a "change in control" clause in his employment contract that was worth $12.6 million. In addition, P&G agreed to pay him $8 million a year to serve as vice chairman after the merger. When he retired, his pension would be $1.2 million per year. Moreover, two of his top lieutenants were offered payments totaling $57 million.

Was there any downside to this deal? Four percent of the Gillette workforce— 6,000 employees—were fired. If the payouts to the top three Gillette executives were divided among these 6,000, each unemployed worker would receive $35,000. The loss of this many employees (4,000 of whom lived in New England) had a ripple effect throughout the area's economy. Although Gillette shareholders certainly benefited in the short run from the sale, their profit would have been even greater without this $210 million payout to the executives. Moreover, about half the increase in Gillette revenues during the time that Kilts was running the show were attributable to currency fluctuations. A cheaper dollar increased revenue overseas. If the dollar had moved in the opposite direction, there might not have been any increase in revenue. Indeed, for the first two years after Kilts joined Gillette, the stock price declined. It was not until the dollar turned down that the stock price improved.

Do CEOs who receive incentives have too strong of a motivation to sell their companies? Should their incentives be based on factors that they do not control or even affect (such as the strength of the dollar)? Is it unseemly for them to be paid so much when many employees will lose their jobs?

8. Craig Newmark founded craigslist, the most popular website in the country for classified ads. Rather than maximizing its profits, craigslist instead focused on developing a community among its users. It was a place to find an apartment, a pet, a job, a couch, a date, a babysitter, and, it turned out, a prostitute. Most of the ads on

craigslist were free, but blatant ads for sex were not. Much of the company's revenue was from these illegal services. Many of the prostitutes available on craigslist were not independent entrepreneurs; they were women and girls bought and sold against their will. To fight sex trafficking, craigslist required credit cards and phone numbers, and it reported any suspicious ads. Law enforcement officials pressured craigslist to close the sex section of its website. But some people argued that blocking these ads was a violation of free speech and would just drive this business more underground where law enforcement officials were less likely to be able to find it. Others said that banning these ads made the business model of selling children for sex less profitable. Does it seem that trafficking women and children was in keeping with the founder's Life Principles? What were his options? Could he have had any real impact on this thriving industry? What traps did he face?

9. You are a president of a small, highly rated, liberal college in California. Many of the dining hall workers are Latino. Some of these workers are trying to organize a union, which would dramatically increase the college's costs at a time of budget pressure. One of your vice presidents suggests hiring a law firm to review the college's employment records to make sure all employees have the proper documentation showing that they are in the United States legally. It seems likely that some of the rabble rousers will turn out to be illegal and could be deported, thereby solving your union problem. What would you do?

10. Many socially responsible funds are now available to investors who want to make ethical choices. For example, the Appleseed Fund avoids tobacco products, alcoholic beverages, gambling, weapons systems, or pornography, while the TIAA-CREF Social Choice Equity Premier Fund invests in companies that are "strong stewards of the environment," devoted to serving local communities and committed to high labor standards. Are socially responsible funds attractive to you? Does it matter if they are less profitable than other alternatives? How much less profitable? Do you now, or will you in the future, use them in saving for your own retirement?

11. David has just spoken with a member of his sales team who has not met her sales goals for some months. She has also missed 30 days of work in the past six months. It turns out that she is in the process of getting a divorce, and her teenage children are reacting very badly. Some of the missed days have been for court; others because the children have refused to go to school. If David's team does not meet its sales goals, no one will get a bonus and his job may be at risk. What should he do?

ANSWERS TO SELECTED END OF CHAPTER QUESTIONS

MULTIPLE-CHOICE QUESTIONS

Presented are the answers for the ODD-numbered multiple-choice questions in the end-of-chapter material.

1. A
3. C
5. B

CASE QUESTIONS

Presented are the answers for all of the ODD-numbered case questions in the end-of-chapter material.

1. **Answer:** A) Money, rationalization, conformity, following orders, lost in a crowd; B) loyalty, exit, voice
3. **Answer:** Kant would say it was wrong. Mill would say that the study helped save the eyesight and lives of lots of other children.
5. **Answer:** Mill would say that the benefit of selling the cookie is greater than the harm. Kant would say that it is the wrong thing to do. The Girl Scouts would not want this information on the front page.

Chapter 4

© Creative Travel Projects/Shutterstock.com

COMMON LAW, STATUTORY LAW, AND ADMINISTRATIVE LAW

The finale of the *Seinfeld* TV series illustrated an important legal issue. After striking a deal with NBC to produce their pilot television show, New Yorkers Jerry, George, Elaine, and Kramer decided to celebrate by going to Paris on NBC's private jet. In-flight hijinks ensued, causing the plane to nosedive and make an emergency landing in Latham, Massachusetts.

While the four friends awaited repairs to their jet, they took a walk around the small town. There, they witnessed a crime in progress—a gunman carjacking a helpless man in a red subcompact car. Unmoved and unaffected, the bunch stood by—cracking insensitive jokes about the victim's weight, and laughing smugly.

The bunch stood by—cracking insensitive jokes about the victim's weight, and laughing smugly.

As the gunman jerked the man out of the driver's seat, Jerry quipped, "There goes the money for the lipo." Elaine observed that a large victim is easier to outrun. George supposed the thief was actually doing the victim a favor because "it's less money for him to buy food." As the thief drove away with the stolen car, Kramer proudly captured the crime on his video camera and bragged about selling the footage to a major television network.

4-1 COMMON LAW

Jerry, George, Elaine, and Kramer represent more than a classic television show. Their story also presents a classic legal puzzle: What, if anything, must a bystander do when he sees someone in danger? We will examine this issue to see how the common law works.

The *common law* is judge-made law. It is the sum total of all the cases decided by appellate courts. The common law of Pennsylvania consists of all cases decided by appellate courts in that state. The Illinois common law is made up of all of the cases decided by Illinois appellate courts. Two hundred years ago, almost all of the law was common law. Today, common law still predominates in tort, contract, and agency law, and it is very important in property, employment, and some other areas.

Common law
Judge-made law.

4-1a **Stare Decisis**

Nothing perks up a course like Latin. *Stare decisis* means "let the decision stand." It is the essence of the common law. **Once a court has decided a particular issue, it will generally apply the same rule in similar cases in the future.** Suppose the highest court of Arizona must decide whether a contract signed by a 16-year-old can be enforced against him. The court will look to see if there is **Precedent**, that is, whether the high court of Arizona has already decided a similar case. The Arizona court looks and finds several earlier cases, all holding that such contracts may not be enforced against a minor. The court will probably apply that precedent and refuse to enforce the contract in this case. Courts do not always follow precedent, but they generally do: *stare decisis*.

A desire for predictability created the doctrine of *stare decisis*. The value of predictability is apparent: People must know what the law is. If contract law changed daily, an entrepreneur who leased factory space and then started buying machinery would be uncertain if the factory would actually be available when she was ready to move in. Will the landlord slip out of the lease? Will the machinery be ready on time? The law must be knowable. Yet, there must also be flexibility in the law, some means to respond to new problems and a changing social climate. Sometimes, we are better off if we are not encumbered by ironclad rules established before electricity was discovered. These two ideas are in conflict: The more flexibility we permit, the less predictability we enjoy. We will watch the conflict play out in the bystander cases.

Stare decisis
"Let the decision stand," that is, the ruling from a previous case must be followed.

Precedent
An earlier case that decided the issue

4-1b **Bystander Cases**

This country inherited from England a simple rule about a **bystander's obligations: You have no duty to assist someone in peril unless you created the danger.** In *Union Pacific Railway Co. v. Cappier*,[1] through no fault of the railroad, a train struck a man. Railroad employees saw the incident happen but did nothing to assist him. By the time help arrived, the victim had died. The court held that the railroad had no duty to help the injured man:

> With the humane side of the question courts are not concerned. It is the omission or negligent discharge of legal duties only which come within the sphere of judicial cognizance. For withholding relief from the suffering, for failure to respond to the calls of worthy charity, or for faltering in the bestowment of brotherly love on the unfortunate, penalties are found not in the laws of men but in [the laws of God].

As harsh as this judgment might seem, it was an accurate statement of the law at that time in both England and the United States: Bystanders need do nothing. Contemporary writers found the rule inhumane and cruel, and even judges criticized it. But—*stare decisis*—they

---

[1] 66 Kan. 649 (1903).

followed it. With a rule this old and well established, no court was willing to scuttle it. What courts did do was seek openings for small changes.

Eighteen years after the Kansas case of *Cappier*, a court in nearby Iowa found the basis for one exception. Ed Carey was a farm laborer, working for Frank Davis. While in the fields, Carey fainted from sunstroke and remained unconscious. Davis simply hauled him to a nearby wagon and left him in the sun for an additional four hours, causing serious permanent injury. The court's response:

> It is unquestionably the well-settled rule that the master is under no legal duty to care for a sick or injured servant for whose illness or injury he is not at fault. Though not unjust in principle, this rule, if carried unflinchingly and without exception to its logical extreme, is sometimes productive of shocking results. To avoid this criticism [we hold that where] a servant suffers serious injury, or is suddenly stricken down in a manner indicating the immediate and emergent need of aid to save him from death or serious harm, the master, if present is in duty bound to take such reasonable measures as may be practicable to relieve him, even though such master be not chargeable with fault in bringing about the emergency. [2]

And this is how the common law often changes: bit by tiny bit. In Iowa, a bystander could now be liable *if* he was the employer and *if* the worker was suddenly stricken and *if* it was an emergency and *if* the employer was present. That is a small change but an important one.

For the next 50 years, changes in bystander law came very slowly. Consider *Osterlind v. Hill*, a case from 1928.[3] Osterlind rented a canoe from Hill's boatyard, paddled into the lake, and promptly fell into the water. For *30 minutes*, he clung to the side of the canoe and shouted for help. Hill heard the cries but did nothing; Osterlind drowned. Was Hill liable? No, said the court: A bystander has no liability. Not until a half-century later did the same court reverse its position and begin to require assistance in extreme cases. Fifty years is a long time for the unfortunate Osterlind to hold on.[4]

In the 1970s, changes came more quickly.

TARASOFF v. REGENTS OF THE UNIVERSITY OF CALIFORNIA

17 Cal. 3d 425
Supreme Court of California, 1976

Facts: On October 27, 1969, Prosenjit Poddar killed Tatiana Tarasoff. Tatiana's parents claimed that two months earlier, Poddar had confided his intention to kill Tatiana to Dr. Lawrence Moore, a psychologist employed by the University of California at Berkeley. They sued the university, claiming that Dr. Moore should have warned Tatiana and/or should have arranged for Poddar's confinement.

Issue: *Did Dr. Moore have a duty to Tatiana Tarasoff, and did he breach that duty?*

Excerpts from Justice Tobriner's Decision: Although under the common law, as a general rule, one person owed no duty to control the conduct of another, nor to warn those endangered by such conduct, the courts have carved out an exception to this rule in cases

---

[2]Carey v. Davis, 190 Iowa 720 (1921).
[3]263 Mass. 73 (1928).
[4]Pridgen v. Boston Housing Authority, 364 Mass. 696 (1974).

in which the defendant stands in some special relationship to either the person whose conduct needs to be controlled or in a relationship to the foreseeable victim of that conduct. Applying this exception to the present case, we note that a relationship of defendant therapists to either Tatiana or Poddar will suffice to establish a duty of care.

We recognize the difficulty that a therapist encounters in attempting to forecast whether a patient presents a serious danger of violence. Obviously we do not require that the therapist, in making that determination, render a perfect performance; the therapist need only exercise that reasonable degree of skill, knowledge, and care ordinarily possessed and exercised by members of [the field] under similar circumstances.

In the instant case, however, the pleadings do not raise any question as to failure of defendant therapists to predict that Poddar presented a serious danger of violence. On the contrary, the present complaints allege that defendant therapists did in fact predict that Poddar would kill, but were negligent in failing to warn.

In our view, once a therapist does in fact determine, or under applicable professional standards reasonably should have determined, that a patient poses a serious danger of violence to others, he bears a duty to exercise reasonable care to protect the foreseeable victim of that danger.

[The Tarasoffs have stated a legitimate claim against Dr. Moore.]

The *Tarasoff* exception applies when there is some special relationship, such as therapist–patient. What if there is no such relationship? Remember the *Soldano v. O'Daniels* case from Chapter 1, in which the bartender refused to call the police.

As in the earlier cases we have seen, this lawsuit presented an emergency. But the exception created in *Carey v. Davis* applied only if the bystander was an employer, and that in *Tarasoff* only for a doctor. In *Soldano*, the bystander was neither. Should the law require him to act, that is, should it carve a new exception? Here is what the California court decided:

> Many citizens simply "don't want to get involved." No rule should be adopted [requiring] a citizen to open up his or her house to a stranger so that the latter may use the telephone to call for emergency assistance. As Mrs. Alexander in Anthony Burgess' A *Clockwork Orange* learned to her horror, such an action may be fraught with danger. It does not follow, however, that use of a telephone in a public portion of a business should be refused for a legitimate emergency call.

> We conclude that the bartender owed a duty to [Soldano] to permit the patron from Happy Jack's to place a call to the police or to place the call himself. It bears emphasizing that the duty in this case does not require that one must go to the aid of another. That is not the issue here. The employee was not the Good Samaritan intent on aiding another. The patron was.

And so, courts have made several subtle changes to the common-law rule. Let's apply them to the opening scenario. If the carjacking victim sues Jerry and his friends, will he be successful? Probably not.

Jerry and his friends did not employ the victim, nor did they have any special relationship. The New Yorkers did not stand in the way of someone else trying to call the police. They may be morally culpable for refusing to help and making cruel jokes, but they will not be liable in a civil case unless the common law changes entirely.

The bystander rule, that hardy oak, is alive and well. Various initials have been carved into its bark—the exceptions we have seen and a variety of others—but the trunk is strong and the leaves green. Perhaps someday the proliferating exceptions will topple it, but the process of the common law is slow and that day is nowhere in sight.

EXAM Strategy

Question: While Rachel is walking her dog, Bozo, she watches a skydiver float to earth. He lands in an enormous tree, suspended 45 feet above ground. "Help!" the man shouts. Rachel hurries to the tree and sees the skydiver bleeding profusely. She takes out her cell phone to call 911 for help, but just then Bozo runs away. Rachel darts after the dog, afraid he will jump into a nearby pond and emerge smelling of mud. She forgets about the skydiver and takes Bozo home. Three hours later, the skydiver expires.

The victim's family sues Rachel. She defends by saying she feared that Bozo would have an allergic reaction to mud, and in any case she could not have climbed 45 feet up a tree to save the man. The family argues the dog is not allergic to mud, that even if he is, a pet's inconvenience pales compared to human life, and Rachel could have phoned for emergency help without climbing an inch. Please rule.

Strategy: The family's arguments might seem compelling, but are they relevant? Rachel is a bystander, someone who perceives another in danger. What is the rule concerning a bystander's obligation to act? Apply the rule to the facts of this case.

Result: A bystander has no duty to assist someone in peril unless she created the danger. Rachel did not create the skydiver's predicament. She had no obligation to do anything. Rachel wins.

4-2 STATUTORY LAW

If you are a *Seinfeld* fan, you may remember what happened to Jerry and his friends in the episode recounted in the introduction to this chapter. When the victim reported that Jerry's group did nothing to help him, the police officer promptly arrested them for failing to act. Arrested? Why, you might wonder. The Latham officer informed them that a recently enacted state *criminal statute* required bystanders to help anyone in danger. Jerry, George, Elaine, and Kramer were mercilessly thrown in jail for violating this criminal Good Samaritan statute. At trial, the four were found guilty and sentenced to one year in prison.

Although this was a fictional "made-for-TV" law, Massachusetts and nine other states *do* have versions of a "Duty to Rescue" statute based on the Good Samaritan common-law principles discussed earlier.[5] These criminal statutes require witnesses of certain violent crimes to *report* the crime as soon as they can, if they can do so without endangering themselves or others. (There is no obligation to try to *prevent* the crime or *go to the aid of* the victim.) These laws differ from the common law because they are enacted by a legislature, criminalize certain actions, and spell out their penalties. (In Massachusetts the penalty is a fine ranging from $500–$2,500, not a jail sentence.)

How are statutes different from common law? In fact, more law is created by statute than by the courts. Statutes affect each of us every day, in our business, professional, and personal lives. When the system works correctly, this is the one part of the law over which "we the people" have control. We elect the legislators who pass state statutes; we vote for the senators and representatives who create federal statutes.

---

[5]In addition to Massachusetts, California, Florida, Hawaii, Minnesota, Ohio, Rhode Island, Vermont, Washington, and Wisconsin have Good Samaritan statutes.

Every other November, voters in all 50 states cast ballots for members of Congress. The winners of congressional elections convene in Washington, D.C., and create statutes. In this section, we look at how Congress does its work creating statutes.[6] Using the Civil Rights Act as a backdrop, we will follow a bill as it makes its way through Congress and beyond.

4-2a Bills

Bill
A proposed statute, submitted to Congress or a state legislature.

Veto
The power of the president to reject legislation passed by Congress

Congress is organized into two houses, the House of Representatives and the Senate. Either house may originate a proposed statute, which is called a **bill**. **To become law, the bill must be voted on and approved by both houses.** Once both houses pass it, they will send it to the president. If the president signs the bill, it becomes law and is then a statute. If the president opposes the bill, he will **veto** it, in which case, it is not law.[7]

If you visit either house of Congress, you will probably find half a dozen legislators on the floor, with one person talking and no one listening. This is because most of the work is done in committees. Both houses are organized into dozens of committees, each with special functions. The House currently has about 25 committees (further divided into about 150 subcommittees) and the Senate has approximately 20 committees (with about 86 subcommittees). For example, the armed services committee of each house oversees the huge defense budget and the workings of the armed forces. Labor committees handle legislation concerning organized labor and working conditions. Banking committees develop expertise on financial institutions. Judiciary committees review nominees to the federal courts. There are dozens of other committees, some very powerful, because they control vast amounts of money, and some relatively weak. Few of us ever think about the House Agricultural Subcommittee on Specialty Crops. But if we owned a family peanut farm, we would pay close attention to the subcommittee's agenda, because those members of Congress would pay close attention to us.

When a bill is proposed in either house, it is referred to the committee specializing in that subject. Why are bills proposed in the first place? For any of several reasons:

- **New Issue, New Worry.** If society begins to focus on a new issue, Congress may respond with legislation. We consider in the next section, for example, the congressional response in the 1960s to employment discrimination.

- **Unpopular Judicial Ruling.** If Congress disagrees with a judicial interpretation of a statute, the legislators may pass a new statute to modify or "undo" the court decision. For example, if the Supreme Court misinterprets a statute about musical copyrights, Congress may pass a new law correcting the Court's error. However, the legislators have no such power to modify a court decision based on the Constitution. When the Supreme Court ruled lawyers had a right *under the First Amendment* to advertise their services, Congress lacked the power to change the decision.

- **Criminal Law.** Statutory law, unlike common law, is prospective. Legislators are hoping to control the future. And that is why almost all criminal law is statutory. A court cannot retroactively announce that it *has been* a crime for a retailer to accept kickbacks from a wholesaler. Everyone must know the rules in advance because the consequences—prison, a felony record—are so harsh.

4-2b Discrimination: Congress and the Courts

The civil rights movement of the 1950s and 1960s convinced most citizens that African Americans suffered significant and unacceptable discrimination in jobs, housing, voting, schools, and other basic areas of life. Demonstrations and boycotts, marches and

---

[6]State legislatures operate similarly in creating state laws.
[7]Congress may, however, attempt to override the veto. See the discussion following.

countermarches, church bombings, and killings persuaded the nation that the problem was vast and urgent.

In 1963, President Kennedy proposed legislation to guarantee equal rights in these areas. The bill went to the House Judiciary Committee, which heard testimony for weeks. Witness testimony indicated blacks were often unable to vote because of their race, landlords and home sellers adamantly refused to sell or rent to African Americans, education was grossly unequal, and blacks were routinely denied good jobs in many industries. Eventually, the Judiciary Committee approved the bill and sent it to the full House.

The bill was dozens of pages long and divided into "titles," with each title covering a major issue. Title VII concerned employment. We will consider the progress of Title VII in Congress and in the courts. Here is one section of Title VII, as reported to the House floor:[8]

A civil rights demonstrator being arrested by the police.

Sec. 703(a). It shall be an unlawful employment practice for an employer—

(1) to fail or refuse to hire or to discharge any individual, or otherwise to discriminate against any individual with respect to his compensation, terms, conditions, or privileges of employment, because of such individual's race, color, religion, or national origin; or

(2) to limit, segregate, or classify his employees in any way which would deprive or tend to deprive any individual of employment opportunities or otherwise adversely affect his status as an employee, because of such individual's race, color, religion, or national origin.

4-2c Debate

The proposed bill was intensely controversial and sparked argument throughout Congress. Here are some excerpts from one day's debate on the House floor, on February 8, 1964:[9]

MR. WAGGONNER. I speak to you in all sincerity and ask for the right to discriminate if I so choose because I think it is my right. I think it is my right to choose my social companions. I think it is my right if I am a businessman to run it as I please, to do with my own as I will. I think that is a right the Constitution gives to every man. I want the continued right to discriminate and I want the other man to have the right to continue to discriminate against me, because I am discriminated against every day. I do not feel inferior about it.

I ask you to forget about politics, forget about everything except the integrity of the individual, leaving to the people of this country the right to live their lives in the manner they choose to live. Do not destroy this democracy for a Socialist government. A vote for this bill is no less.

MR. CONTE. If the serious cleavage which pitted brother against brother and citizen against citizen during the tragedy of the Civil War is ever to be justified, it can be justified in this House and then in the other body with the passage of this legislation which can and must reaffirm the rights to all individuals which are inherent in our Constitution.

The distinguished poet Mark Van Doren has said that "equality is absolute or no, nothing between can stand," and nothing should now stand between us and the passage of strong and effective civil rights legislation. It is to this that we are united in a strong bipartisan coalition

---

[8]The section number in the House bill was actually 704(a); we use 703 here because that is the number of the section when the bill became law and the number to which the Supreme Court refers in later litigation.

[9]The order of speakers is rearranged, and the remarks are edited.

today, and when the laws of the land proclaim that the 88th Congress acted effectively, judiciously, and wisely, we can take pride in our accomplishments as free men.

Other debate was less rhetorical and aimed more at getting information. The following exchange anticipates a 30-year controversy on quotas:

MR. JOHANSEN. I have asked for this time to raise a question and I would ask particularly for the attention of the gentleman from New York [MR. GOODELL] because of a remark he made—and I am not quarreling with it. I understood him to say there is no plan for balanced employment or for quotas in this legislation … . I am raising a question as to whether in the effort to eliminate discrimination—and incidentally that is an undefined term in the bill—we may get to a situation in which employers and conceivably union leaders, will insist on legislation providing for a quota system as a matter of self-protection.

Now let us suppose this hypothetical situation exists with 100 jobs to be filled. Let us say 150 persons apply and suppose 75 of them are Negro and 75 of them are white. Supposing the employer … hires 75 white men. [Does anyone] have a right to claim they have been discriminated against on the basis of color?

MR. GOODELL. It is the intention of the legislation that if applicants are equal in all other respects there will be no restriction. One may choose from among equals. So long as there is no distinction on the basis of race, creed, or color it will not violate the act.

The debate on racial issues carried on. Later in the day, Congressman Smith of Virginia offered an amendment, which could scarcely have been smaller—or more important:

Amendment offered by MR. SMITH of Virginia: On page 68, line 23, after the word "religion," insert the word "sex."

In other words, Smith was asking that discrimination on the basis of sex also be outlawed, along with the existing grounds of race, color, national origin, and religion. Congressman Smith's proposal produced the following comments:

MR. CELLER. You know, the French have a phrase for it when they speak of women and men. They say "*vive la différence*." I think the French are right. Imagine the upheaval that would result from adoption of blanket language requiring total equality. Would male citizens be justified in insisting that women share with them the burdens of compulsory military service? What would become of traditional family relationships? What about alimony? What would become of the crimes of rape and statutory rape? I think the amendment seems illogical, ill timed, ill placed, and improper.

MRS. ST. GEORGE. Mr. Chairman, I was somewhat amazed when I came on the floor this afternoon to hear the very distinguished chairman of the Committee on the Judiciary [MR. CELLER] make the remark that he considered the amendment at this point illogical. I can think of nothing more logical than this amendment at this point.

There are still many States where women cannot serve on juries. There are still many States where women do not have equal educational opportunities. In most States and, in fact, I figure it would be safe to say, in all States—women do not get equal pay for equal work. That is a very well known fact. And to say that this is illogical. What is illogical about it? All you are doing is simply correcting something that goes back, frankly to the Dark Ages.

The debate continued. Some supported the "sex" amendment because they were determined to end sexual bias. But politics are complex. Some *opponents* of civil rights supported the amendment because they believed it would make the legislation less popular and cause Congress to defeat the entire Civil Rights bill.

That strategy did not work. The amendment passed, and sex was added as a protected trait. And, after more debate and several votes, the entire bill passed the House. It went to the Senate, where it followed a similar route from Judiciary Committee to full Senate. Much of the Senate debate was similar to what we have seen. But some senators raised a new issue, concerning §703(2), which prohibited *segregating or classifying* employees based on any of the protected categories (race, color, national origin, religion, or sex). Senator Tower was concerned that §703(2) meant that an employee in a protected category could never be given any sort of job test. So the Senate amended §703 to include a new subsection:

> Sec. 703(h). Notwithstanding any other provision of this title, it shall not be an unlawful employment practice for an employer ... to give and to act upon the results of any professionally developed ability test provided that such test ... is not designed, intended or used to discriminate because of race, color, religion, sex or national origin.

With that amendment, and many others, the bill passed the Senate.

Conference Committee

Civil rights legislation had now passed both houses, but the bills were no longer the same due to the many amendments. This is true with most legislation. The next step is for the two houses to send representatives to a House–Senate Conference Committee. This committee examines all of the differences between the two bills and tries to reach a compromise. With the Civil Rights bill, Senator Tower's amendment was left in; other Senate amendments were taken out. When the Conference Committee had settled every difference between the two versions, the new, modified bill was sent back to each house for a new vote.

The House of Representatives and the Senate again angrily debated the compromise language reported from the Conference Committee. Finally, after years of violent public demonstrations and months of debate, each house passed the same bill. President Johnson promptly signed it. The Civil Rights Act of 1964 was law. See Exhibit 4.1.

But the passing of a statute is not always the end of the story. Sometimes courts must interpret congressional language and intent.

4-2d **Statutory Interpretation**

Title VII of the Civil Rights Act obviously prohibited an employer from saying to a job applicant, "We don't hire minorities." In some parts of the country, sayings such as that had been common practice; after the Civil Rights Act passed, it became rare. Employers who routinely hired whites only, or promoted only whites, found themselves losing lawsuits. A new group of cases arose, those in which some job standard was set that appeared to be racially neutral, yet had a discriminatory effect. In North Carolina, the Duke Power Co. required that applicants for higher-paying, promotional positions meet two requirements: They must have a high school diploma, and they must pass a standardized written test. There was no evidence either requirement related to successful job performance. Blacks met the requirements in lower percentages than whites, and consequently whites obtained a disproportionate share of the good jobs.

Title VII did not precisely address this kind of case. It clearly outlawed overt discrimination. Was Duke Power's policy overt discrimination, or was it protected by Senator Tower's amendment, §703(h)? The case went all the way to the Supreme Court, where the Court had to interpret the new law.

Courts are often called upon to interpret a statute, that is, to explain precisely what the language means and how it applies in a given case. There are three primary steps in a court's statutory interpretation:

- **Plain Meaning Rule.** When a statute's words have ordinary, everyday significance, the court will simply apply those words. Section 703(a)(1) of the Civil Rights Act prohibits firing someone because of her religion. Could an employer who had fired a Catholic because of her religion argue that Catholicism is not really a religion, but more of a social group? No. The word "religion" has a plain meaning and courts apply its commonsense definition.

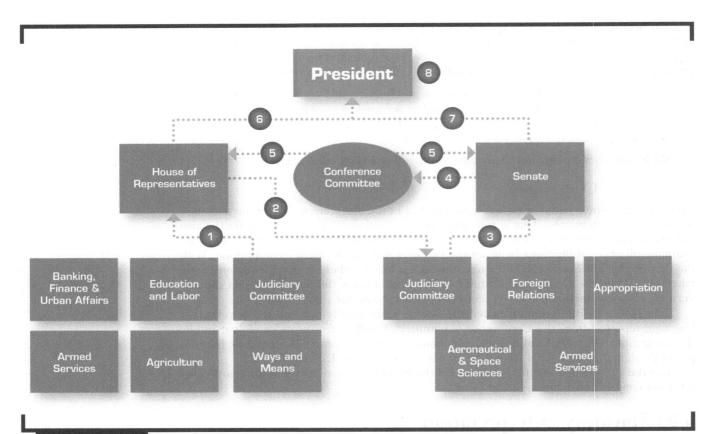

EXHIBIT 4.1 The two houses of Congress are organized into dozens of committees, a few of which are shown here. The path of the 1964 Civil Rights Act (somewhat simplified) was as follows: (1) The House Judiciary Committee approved the bill and sent it to the full House; (2) the full House passed the bill and sent it to the Senate, where it was assigned to the Senate Judiciary Committee; (3) the Senate Judiciary Committee passed an amended version of the bill and sent it to the full Senate; (4) the full Senate passed the bill with additional amendments. Because the Senate version was now different from the bill the House passed, the bill went to a Conference Committee. The Conference Committee (5) reached a compromise and sent the new version of the bill back to both houses. Each house passed the compromise bill (6 and 7) and sent it to the president, who signed it into law (8).

- **Legislative History and Intent.** If the language is unclear, the court must look deeper. Section 703(a)(2) prohibits classifying employees in discriminatory ways. Does that section prevent an employer from requiring high school diplomas, as Duke Power did? The explicit language of the statute does not answer the question. The court will look at the law's history to determine the intent of the legislature. The court will examine committee hearings, reports, and the floor debates we have seen.

- **Public Policy.** If the legislative history is unclear, courts will rely on general public policies, such as reducing crime, creating equal opportunity, and so forth. They may include in this examination some of their own prior decisions. Courts assume the legislature is aware of prior judicial decisions, and if the legislature did not change those decisions, the statute will be interpreted to incorporate them.

Here is how the Supreme Court interpreted the 1964 Civil Rights Act.

Landmark Case

GRIGGS V. DUKE POWER CO.
401 U.S. 424
United States Supreme Court, 1971

Facts: See the discussion of the Duke Power Co.'s job requirements in the earlier "Statutory Interpretation" section.

Issue: *Did Title VII of the 1964 Civil Rights Act require that employment tests be job-related?*

Excerpts from Chief Justice Burger's Decision: The objective of Congress in the enactment of Title VII is plain from the language of the statute. It was to achieve equality of employment opportunities and remove barriers that have operated in the past to favor an identifiable group of white employees over other employees. Under the Act, practices, procedures, or tests neutral on their face, and even neutral in terms of intent, cannot be maintained if they operate to "freeze" the status quo of prior discriminatory employment practices.

The Act proscribes not only overt discrimination but also practices that are fair in form, but discriminatory in operation. The touchstone is business necessity. If an employment practice which operates to exclude Negroes cannot be shown to be related to job performance, the practice is prohibited.

On the record before us, neither the high school completion requirement nor the general intelligence test is shown to bear a demonstrable relationship to successful performance of the jobs for which it was used.

Senator Tower offered an amendment which was adopted verbatim and is now the testing provision of section 703(h). Speaking for the supporters of Title VII, Senator Humphrey endorsed the amendment, stating: "Senators on both sides of the aisle who were deeply interested in Title VII have examined the text of this amendment and have found it to be in accord with the intent and purpose of that title." The amendment was then adopted. From the sum of the legislative history relevant in this case, the conclusion is inescapable that the ... requirement that employment tests be job related comports with congressional intent.

And so the highest Court ruled that if a job requirement had a discriminatory impact, the employer could use that requirement only if it was related to job performance. Many more cases arose. For almost two decades courts held that once workers showed a job requirement had a discriminatory effect, the employer had the burden to prove that the requirement was necessary for the business. The requirement had to be essential to achieve an important goal. If there was any way to achieve that goal without discriminatory impact, the employer had to use it.

4-2e Changing Times

But things changed. In 1989, a more conservative Supreme Court decided *Wards Cove Packing Co. v. Atonio.*[10] The plaintiffs were nonwhite workers in salmon canneries in Alaska. The canneries had two types of jobs, skilled and unskilled. Nonwhites (Filipinos and native Alaskans) invariably worked as low-paid, unskilled workers, canning the fish. The higher–paid, skilled positions were filled almost entirely with white workers, who were hired during the off-season in Washington and Oregon.

---

[10]490 U.S. 642 (1989).

There was no overt discrimination. But plaintiffs claimed that various practices led to the racial imbalances. The practices included failing to promote from within the company, hiring through separate channels (cannery jobs were done through a union hall, skilled positions were filled out of state), nepotism, and an English-language requirement. Once again the case reached the Supreme Court, where Justice White wrote the Court's opinion.

If the plaintiffs succeeded in showing that the job requirements led to racial imbalance, said the Court, the employer now only had to demonstrate that the requirement or practice "serves, in a significant way, the legitimate employment goals of the employer ... . [T]here is no requirement that the challenged practice be 'essential' or 'indispensable' to the employer's business." In other words, the Court removed the "business necessity" requirement of *Griggs* and replaced it with "legitimate employment goals."

4-2f Voters' Role

The response to *Wards Cove* was quick. Liberals decried it; conservatives hailed it. Everyone agreed it was a major change, which would make it substantially harder for plaintiffs to bring successful discrimination cases. Democrats introduced bills to reverse the interpretation of *Wards Cove*. President George H. W. Bush strongly opposed any new bill. He said it would lead to "quotas," that is, employers would feel obligated to hire a certain percentage of workers from all racial categories to protect themselves from suits. This was the issue that Congressman Johansen had raised in the original House debate in 1964.

Both houses passed bills restoring the "business necessity" holding of *Griggs*. Again there were differences, and a Conference Committee resolved them. After acrimonious debate, both houses passed the compromise bill in October 1990. Was it therefore law? No. President Bush immediately vetoed the bill. He said it would compel employers to adopt quotas.

4-2g Congressional Override

When the president vetoes a bill, Congress has one last chance to make it law: an override. If both houses repass the bill, each by a two-thirds margin, it becomes law over the president's veto. Congress attempted to pass the 1990 Civil Rights bill over the Bush veto, but it fell short in the Senate by one vote.

Civil rights advocates tried again, in January 1991, introducing a new bill to reverse the *Wards Cove* rule. Again, both houses debated and bargained. The new bill stated, that, once an employee proves a particular employment practice causes a discriminatory impact, the employer must "demonstrate that the challenged practice is job related for the position in question and consistent with business necessity."

Now the two sides fought over the exact meanings of two terms: "job related" and "business necessity." Each side offered definitions, but they could not reach agreement. It appeared the entire bill would founder over those terms. So Congress did what it often does when faced with a problem of definition: It dropped the issue. Liberals and conservatives agreed not to define the troublesome terms. They would leave that task to courts to perform through statutory interpretation.

With the definitions left out, the new bill passed both houses. In November 1991, President Bush signed the bill into law. The president stated that the new bill had been improved and no longer threatened to create racial quotas. His opponents charged he had reversed course for political reasons, anticipating the 1992 presidential election.

And so, the Congress restored the "business necessity" interpretation to its own 1964 Civil Rights Act. However, no one would say it had been a simple process.

EXAM Strategy

Question: Kelly Hackworth took a leave of absence from her job at Progressive Insurance to care for her ailing mother. When she offered to return, Progressive refused to give her the same job or one like it. She sued based on the Family Medical Leave Act (FMLA), a federal statute requiring firms to give workers returning from family leave their original job or an equivalent one. However, the statute excludes from its coverage workers whose company employs "fewer than 50 people within 75 miles" of the worker's job site. Between Ms. Hackworth's job site in Norman, Oklahoma, and the company's Oklahoma City workplace (less than 75 miles away), Progressive employed 47 people. At its Lawton, Oklahoma, facility, Progressive employed three more people—but Lawton was 75.6 miles (wouldn't you know it) away from Norman. Progressive argued that the job was not covered by the statute. Hackworth claimed that this distance should be considered "within 75 miles," thereby rendering her eligible for FMLA leave. Even if it were not, she urged, it would be absurd to disqualify her from important rights based on a disparity of six-tenths of a mile. Please rule.

Strategy: The question asks you to interpret a statute. How do courts do that? There are three steps: the plain meaning rule; legislative history; and public policy. Apply those steps to these facts.

Result: In this real case, the court ruled that the plain meaning of "within 75 miles" was *75 miles or less*. Lawton was not 75 miles or less from Norman. The statute did not apply and Ms. Hackworth lost.[11]

4-3 ADMINISTRATIVE LAW

Before beginning this section, please return your seat to its upright position. Stow the tray firmly in the seatback in front of you. Turn off any laptops, cell phones, or other electronic devices. Sound familiar? Administrative agencies affect each of us every day in hundreds of ways. They have become the fourth branch of government. Supporters believe they provide unique expertise in complex areas; detractors regard them as unelected government run amok.

Many administrative agencies are familiar. The Federal Aviation Administration, which requires all airlines to ensure your seats are upright before takeoff and landing, is an administrative agency. The Internal Revenue Service expects to receive our tax filings every April 15. The Environmental Protection Agency regulates the water quality of the river in your town. The Federal Trade Commission oversees the commercials shouting at you from your television set.

Other agencies are less familiar. You may never have heard of the Bureau of Land Management, but if you go into the oil and gas industry, you will learn that this powerful agency has more control over your land than you do. If you develop real estate in Palos Hills, Illinois, you will tremble every time the Appearance Commission of the City of Palos Hills speaks, because you cannot construct a new building without its approval. If your software corporation wants to hire an Argentine expert on databases, you will get to know the complex workings of Immigration and Customs Enforcement: No one lawfully enters this country without its nod of approval.

---

[11]Hackworth v. Progressive Casualty Ins. Co., 468 F.3d 722 (10th Cir. 2006).

4-3a **Background**

By the 1880s, trains crisscrossed America. But this technological miracle became an economic headache. Congress worried that the railroads' economic muscle enabled a few powerful corporations to reap unfair profits. The railroad industry needed closer regulation. Who would do it? **Courts decide individual cases; they do not regulate industries.** Congress itself passes statutes, but it has no personnel to oversee the day-to-day working of a huge industry. For example, Congress lacks the expertise to establish rates for freight passing from Kansas City to Chicago, and it has no personnel to enforce rates once they are set.

A new entity was needed. Congress passed the Interstate Commerce Act, creating the Interstate Commerce Commission (ICC), the first administrative agency. The ICC began regulating freight and passenger transportation over the growing rail system and continued to do so for more than 100 years. Congress gave the ICC power to regulate rates and investigate harmful practices, to hold hearings, issue orders, and punish railroads that did not comply.

The ICC was able to hire and develop a staff expert in the issues Congress wanted controlled. The agency had enough flexibility to deal with the problems in a variety of ways: by regulating, investigating, and punishing. And that is what has made administrative agencies an attractive solution for Congress: One entity, focusing on one industry, can combine expertise and flexibility. However, the ICC also developed great power, which voters could not reach, and thereby started the great and lasting conflict over the role of agencies.

During the Great Depression of the 1930s, the Roosevelt administration and Congress created dozens of new agencies. Many were based on social demands, such as the need of the elderly population for a secure income. Political and social conditions dominated again in the 1960s, as Congress created agencies, such as the Equal Employment Opportunity Commission, to combat discrimination.

Then during the 1980s the Reagan administration made an effort to decrease the number and strength of the agencies. For several years some agencies declined in influence, though others did not. Today, there is still controversy about how much power agencies should have.

4-3b **Classification of Agencies**

Agencies exist at the federal, state, and local level. We will focus on federal agencies because they have national impact and great power. Most of the principles discussed apply to state and local agencies as well. Virtually any business or profession you choose to work in will be regulated by at least one administrative agency, and it may be regulated by several.

Types of Agencies: Executive and Independent

Some federal agencies are part of the executive branch while others are independent agencies. This is a major distinction. The president has much greater control of executive agencies simply because he can fire the agency head at any time. An executive agency will seldom diverge far from the president's preferred policies. Some familiar executive agencies are the Internal Revenue Service (part of the Treasury Department); the Federal Bureau of Investigation (Department of Justice); the Food and Drug Administration (Department of Health and Human Services); and the Nuclear Regulatory Commission (Department of Energy).

The president has no such removal power over independent agencies. The Federal Communications Commission (FCC) is an independent agency. For many corporations involved in broadcasting, the FCC has more day-to-day influence on their business than Congress, the courts, and the president combined. Other powerful independent agencies are the Federal Trade Commission, the Securities and Exchange Commission, the National Labor Relations Board, and the Environmental Protection Agency.

Enabling Legislation

Congress creates a federal agency by passing **enabling legislation**. The Interstate Commerce Act was the enabling legislation that established the ICC. Typically, the enabling legislation describes the problems that Congress believes need regulation, establishes an agency to do it, and defines the agency's powers.

Critics argue Congress is delegating to another body powers that only the legislature or courts are supposed to exercise. This puts administrative agencies above the voters. But legal attacks on administrative agencies have consistently failed for several decades. Courts acknowledge that agencies have become an integral part of a complex economy, and so long as there are some limits on an agency's discretion, courts will generally uphold its powers.

4-4 POWER OF AGENCIES

Administrative agencies use three kinds of power to do the work assigned to them: They make rules, they investigate, and they adjudicate.

4-4a Rulemaking

One of the most important functions of an administrative agency is to make rules. In doing this, the agency attempts, prospectively, to establish fair and uniform behavior for all businesses in the affected area. **To create a new rule is to promulgate it.** Agencies promulgate two types of rules: legislative and interpretive.

Types of Rules: Legislative and Interpretive

Legislative rules are the most important agency rules, and they are much like statutes. Here, an agency creates law by requiring businesses or private citizens to act in a certain way. Suppose you operate a website for young shoppers, ages 10 to 18. Like most online merchants, you consider yourself free to collect as much data as possible about consumers. *Wrong.* The Federal Trade Commission, a federal agency, has promulgated detailed rules governing any site directed to young children. Before obtaining private data from these immature consumers, you must let them know exactly who you are, how to contact site operators, precisely what you are seeking, and how it will be used. You must also obtain verifiable parental consent before collecting, using, or disclosing any personal information. Failure to follow the rules can result in a substantial civil penalty. This modest legislative rule, in short, will be more important to your business than most statutes passed by Congress.

Interpretive rules do not change the law. They are the agency's interpretation of what the law already requires. But, they can still affect all of us. For example, in 1977 Congress amended the Clean Air Act in an attempt to reduce pollution from factories. The act required the Environmental Protection Agency (EPA) to impose emission standards on "stationary sources" of pollution. But what did "stationary source" mean? It was the EPA's job to define that term. Obscure work, to be sure, yet the results could be seen and even smelled, because the EPA's definition would determine the quality of air entering our lungs every time we breathe. Environmentalists wanted the term defined to include every smokestack in a factory so that the EPA could regulate each one. The EPA, however, developed the "bubble concept," ruling that "stationary source" meant an entire factory, but not the individual smokestacks. As a result, polluters could shift emission among smokestacks in a single factory to avoid EPA regulation. Environmentalists howled that this gutted the purpose of the statute, but to no avail. The agency had spoken, merely by interpreting a statute.[12]

How Rules Are Made

Corporations fight many a court battle over whether an agency has the right to issue a particular rule and whether it was promulgated properly. The critical issue is this: How much participation is the public entitled to before an agency issues a rule? There are two basic methods of rulemaking.[13]

Informal Rulemaking. On many issues, agencies may use a simple "notice and comment" method of rulemaking. The agency must publish a proposed rule in advance and permit the public a comment period. During this period, the public may submit any objections and arguments, with supporting data. The agency will make its decision and publish the final rule.

For example, the Department of Transportation may use the informal rulemaking procedure to require safety features for all new automobiles. The agency must listen to objections from interested parties, notably car manufacturers, and it must give a written response to the objections. The agency is required to have rational reasons for the final choices it makes. However, it is not obligated to satisfy all parties or do their bidding.

Formal Rulemaking. In the enabling legislation, Congress may require an agency to hold a hearing before promulgating rules. Congress does this to make the agency more accountable to the public. After the agency publishes its proposed rule, it must hold a public hearing. Opponents of the rule, typically affected businesses, may cross-examine the agency experts about the need for the rule and may testify against it. When the agency makes its final decision about the rule, it must prepare a formal, written response to everything that occurred at the hearing.

When used responsibly, these hearings give the public access to the agency and can help formulate sound policy. When used irresponsibly, hearings can be manipulated to stymie needed regulation. The most famous example concerns peanut butter. The Food and Drug Administration (FDA) began investigating peanut butter content in 1958. It found, for example, that Jif peanut butter, made by Procter & Gamble (P&G), had only 75 percent peanuts and 20 percent of a Crisco-type base. P&G fought the investigation, and any changes, for years. Finally, in 1965, the FDA proposed a minimum of 90 percent peanuts in peanut butter; P&G wanted 87 percent. The FDA wanted no more than 3 percent hydrogenated vegetable oil; P&G wanted no limit.

The hearings dragged on for months. One day, the P&G lawyer objected to the hearing going forward because he needed to vote that day. Another time, when an FDA official testified that consumer letters indicated the public wanted to know what was really in peanut butter, the P&G attorney demanded that the official bring in and identify the letters—all 20,000 of them. Finally, in 1968, a decade after beginning its investigation, the FDA promulgated final rules requiring 90 percent peanuts but eliminating the 3 percent cap on vegetable oil.[14] But delay does not end when the FDA issues final rules because, as we see in the following case, they can still be challenged in court. Should the FDA have the right to require tobacco companies to plaster cigarette packages with gross images? You be the judge.

---

[12]An agency's interpretation can be challenged in court, and this one was.

[13]Certain rules may be made with no public participation at all. For example, an agency's internal business affairs and procedures can be regulated without public comment, as can its general policy statements. None of these directly affect the public, and the public has no right to participate.

[14]For an excellent account of this high-fat hearing, see Mark J. Green, *The Other Government* (New York: W. W. Norton & Co., 1978), pp. 136–150.

You be the Judge

Facts: The Family Smoking Prevention and Tobacco Control Act (FSPTCA) instructed the FDA to issue regulations requiring cigarette packaging to contain images depicting the negative consequences of smoking. After holding hearings on its proposed regulation, the FDA issued final rules, which required the top half of all cigarette packs to depict the adverse effects of smoking. The FDA's chosen images were graphic and jarring: a corpse after

R. J. Reynolds Tobacco Co. v. Food and Drug Administration
696 F.3d 1205
District of Columbia Circuit Court of Appeals, 2012

an autopsy, a smoker's damaged lung, and a man exhaling smoke out of a hole in his neck, among others. The rule also required packages to include written warnings ("WARNING: Smoking causes cancer) and the phone number for an antismoking hotline, "1-800-QUIT-NOW."

Tobacco companies filed suit to challenge the FDA regulation, claiming the rule violated the First Amendment by requiring them to speak against their will. The FDA argued it was just educating the public with factual information.

You Be the Judge: *Could the FDA compel tobacco companies to put graphic and emotionally charged warning labels on their products?*

Argument for the FDA: Cigarettes are the deadliest product sold in America, and one of the most addictive. The tobacco industry has a history of deceiving customers —particularly the young and uneducated—about these risks. We are simply ending this history of deception by requiring companies to disclose factual and uncontroversial information. Smokers have obviously not been deterred by the current text-only warnings, so these powerful images are the obvious next step in trying to influence them. The fact that the warnings are powerful does not make them a violation of the First Amendment. Nor does the Constitution prohibit us from requiring that lethal and addictive products carry informative warning labels. Moreover, Congress instructed us to proceed with these requirements so we are obligated to do so.

Argument for Tobacco Companies: Your honors, look at these pictures. These awful images do not educate or protect consumers from deception—they just scare them into quitting. The FDA is treating every single pack of cigarettes as a mini-billboard for an emotionally charged anti-smoking agenda. The pictures are neither factual nor accurate: They *symbolize* the bad effects of smoking, which is something very different from providing factual information. Rather than educating and promoting informed choice, the FDA is simply trying to disgust consumers so that they will "QUIT NOW." *Advocating* that the public should not purchase a legal product is not the same as *educating* consumers. If it wants to promote an anti-smoking message, the government should do so through advertising or increased cigarette taxes, not by making tobacco companies speak.

The FDA required cigarette packaging to contain graphics and photos depicting the negative consequences of smoking, along with written warnings about cigarettes and an anti-smoking hotline number. The European Community has been dealing with this issue in a similar way. Shown is an example of one of the European Communities proposed warning labels.

4-4b Investigation

Agencies do a wide variety of work, but they all need broad factual knowledge of the field they govern. Some companies cooperate with an agency, furnishing information and even voluntarily accepting agency recommendations. For example, the U.S. Consumer Product Safety Commission investigates hundreds of consumer products every year and frequently urges companies to recall goods the agency considers defective. Many firms comply.

Other companies, however, jealously guard information, often because corporate officers believe disclosure would lead to adverse rules. To force disclosure, agencies use *subpoenas* and *searches*.

Subpoenas

Subpoena
An order to appear at a particular place and time. A subpoena *duces tecum* requires a person to produce certain documents or things.

A **subpoena** is an order to appear at a particular time and place to provide evidence. A **subpoena** *duces tecum* requires the person to appear and bring specified documents. Businesses and other organizations intensely dislike subpoenas and resent government agents plowing through records and questioning employees. What are the limits on an agency's investigation? The information sought:

- Must be *relevant* to a lawful agency investigation. The FCC is clearly empowered to investigate the safety of broadcasting towers, and any documents about tower construction are obviously relevant. Documents about employee racial statistics might indicate discrimination, but the FCC lacks jurisdiction on that issue and thus may not demand such documents.

- Must not be *unreasonably burdensome*. A court will compare the agency's need for the information with the intrusion on the corporation.

- Must not be *privileged*. The Fifth Amendment privilege against self-incrimination means that a corporate officer accused of criminal securities violations may not be compelled to testify about his behavior.

Search and Seizure

At times an agency will want to conduct a surprise **search** of an enterprise and **seize** any evidence of wrongdoing. May an agency do that? Yes, although there are limitations. When a particular industry is *comprehensively regulated*, courts will assume companies know they are subject to periodic, unannounced inspections. In those industries, an administrative agency may conduct a search without a warrant and seize evidence of violations. For example, the mining industry is minutely regulated, with strict rules covering equipment, mining depths, and air quality. Mining executives understand they are closely watched. Accordingly, the Bureau of Mines may make unannounced, warrantless searches to ensure safety. [15]

The following case established many of the principles just described.

---

[15]Donovan v. Dewey, 452 U.S. 594 (1981).

Landmark Case

UNITED STATES V. BISWELL

406 U.S. 311
United States Supreme Court, 1972

Facts: Biswell operated a pawnshop and had a license to sell "sporting weapons." Treasury agents demanded to inspect Biswell's locked storeroom. The officials claimed the Gun Control Act of 1968 gave them the right to search without a warrant.

That law says, in part, "the Secretary [of the Treasury] may enter during business hours the premises of any firearms dealer for the purpose of inspecting or examining (1) any records or documents required to be kept by such dealer, and (2) any firearms or ammunition kept or stored by such dealer."

Biswell voluntarily opened the storeroom, and the agent found two sawed-off rifles inside. The guns did not remotely meet the definition of "sporting weapons," and Biswell was convicted on firearms charges.

The appellate court found that because the search violated the Fourth Amendment, the rifles could not be admitted as evidence. It reversed the conviction, and the government appealed to the Supreme Court.

Issue: *Did the agent's warrantless search violate the Constitution?*

Excerpts from Justice White's Decision: When the officers asked to inspect respondent's locked storeroom, they were merely asserting their statutory right, and respondent was on notice as to their identity and the legal basis for their action. Respondent's submission to lawful authority and his decision to step aside and permit the inspection rather than face a criminal prosecution is analogous to a householder's acquiescence in a search pursuant to a warrant when the alternative is a possible criminal prosecution for refusing entry or a forcible entry. In neither case does the lawfulness of the search depend on consent; in both, there is lawful authority independent of the will of the householder who might, other things being equal, prefer no search at all.

In the context of a regulatory inspection system of business premises that is carefully limited in time, place, and scope, the legality of the search depends not on consent but on the authority of a valid statute.

Federal regulation of the interstate traffic in firearms is undeniably of central importance to federal efforts to prevent violent crime. Large interests are at stake, and inspection is a crucial part of the regulatory scheme.

Here, if inspection is to be effective and serve as a credible deterrent, unannounced, even frequent, inspections are essential. In this context, the prerequisite of a warrant could easily frustrate inspection; and if the necessary flexibility as to time, scope, and frequency is to be preserved, the protections afforded by a warrant would be negligible.

It is also plain that inspections for compliance with the Gun Control Act pose only limited threats to the dealer's justifiable expectations of privacy. When a dealer chooses to engage in this pervasively regulated business and to accept a federal license, he does so with the knowledge that his business records, firearms, and ammunition will be subject to effective inspection. Each licensee is annually furnished with a revised compilation of ordinances that describe his obligations. The dealer is not left to wonder about the purposes of the inspector or the limits of his task.

We have little difficulty in concluding that where, as here, regulatory inspections further urgent federal interest, and the possibilities of abuse and the threat to privacy are not of impressive dimensions, the inspection may proceed without a warrant where specifically authorized by statute. The seizure of respondent's sawed-off rifles was not unreasonable under the *Fourth Amendment*, the judgment of the Court of Appeals is reversed, and the case is remanded to that court.

Adjudication

Adjudicate
To hold a formal hearing about an issue and then decide it

To **adjudicate** a case is to hold a hearing about an issue and then decide it. Agencies adjudicate countless cases. The FCC adjudicates which applicant for a new television license is best qualified. The Occupational Safety and Health Administration (OSHA) holds adversarial hearings to determine whether a manufacturing plant is dangerous.

Administrative law judge
An agency employee who acts as an impartial decision maker

Most adjudications begin with a hearing before an **administrative law judge** (ALJ). There is no jury. An ALJ is an employee of the agency but is expected to be impartial in her rulings. All parties are represented by counsel. The rules of evidence are informal, and an ALJ may receive any testimony or documents that will help resolve the dispute.

After all evidence is taken, the ALJ makes a decision. The losing party has a right to appeal to an appellate board within the agency. The appellate board may ignore the ALJ's decision. If it does not, an unhappy party may appeal to federal court.

4-5 LIMITS ON AGENCY POWER

There are four primary methods of reining in these powerful creatures: statutory, political, judicial, and informational.

4-5a Statutory Control

As discussed, the enabling legislation of an agency provides some limits. It may require the agency to use formal rulemaking or investigate only certain issues. The Administrative Procedure Act imposes additional controls by requiring basic fairness in areas not regulated by the enabling legislation.

4-5b Political Control

The president's influence is greatest with executive agencies. Congress, though, "controls the purse." No agency, executive or independent, can spend money it does not have. An agency that angers Congress risks having a particular program defunded or its entire budget cut. Further, Congress may decide to defund an agency as a cost-cutting measure. In its effort to balance the budget, Congress abolished the Interstate Commerce Commission, transferring its functions to the Transportation Department.

Congress has additional control because it must approve presidential nominees to head agencies. Before approving a nominee, Congress will attempt to determine her intentions. And, finally, Congress may amend an agency's enabling legislation, limiting its power.

4-5c Judicial Review

An individual or corporation directly harmed by an administrative rule, investigation, or adjudication may generally have that action reviewed in federal court.[16] The party seeking review, for example, a corporation, must have suffered direct harm; the courts will not listen

---

[16]In two narrow groups of cases, a court may not review an agency action. In a few cases, courts hold that a decision is "committed to agency discretion," a formal way of saying courts will keep hands off. This happens only with politically sensitive issues, such as international air routes. In some cases, the enabling legislation makes it absolutely clear that Congress wanted no court to review certain decisions. Courts will honor that.

to theoretical complaints about an agency action.[17] And that party must first have taken all possible appeals within the agency itself.[18]

Standard on Review

Suppose OSHA promulgates a new rule limiting the noise level within steel mills. Certain mill operators are furious because they will have to retool their mills in order to comply. After exhausting their administrative appeals, they file suit seeking to force OSHA to withdraw the new rule. How does a court decide the case? Or, in legal terms, what standard does a court use in reviewing the case? Does it simply substitute its own opinion for that of the agency? No, it does not. The standard a court uses must take into account:

Facts. Courts generally defer to an agency's fact-finding. If OSHA finds that human hearing starts to suffer when decibels reach a particular level, a court will probably accept that as final. The agency is presumed to have expertise on such subjects. As long as there is *substantial evidence* to support the fact decision, it will be respected.

Law. Courts often—but not always—defer to an agency's interpretation of the law. This is due in part to the enormous range of subjects administrative agencies monitor. Consider the following example. "Chicken catchers" work in large poultry operations, entering coops, manually capturing broilers, loading them into cages, and driving them to a processing plant where they ... well, never mind. On one farm, the catchers wanted to organize a union, but the company objected, pointing out that *agricultural* workers had no right to do so. Were chicken catchers agricultural workers? The National Labor Relations Board, an administrative agency, declared that chicken catchers were in fact *ordinary* workers, entitled to organize. The Supreme Court ruled that courts were obligated to give deference to the agency's decision about chicken catchers. If the agency's interpretation was *reasonable* it was binding, even if the court itself might not have made the same analysis. The workers were permitted to form a union—though the chickens were not.

The following case contains vulgar language, so *please do not read it.*

FOX TELEVISION STATIONS, INC. v. FEDERAL COMMUNICATIONS COMMISSION

567 U.S. ___, 132 S.Ct. 2307
United States Supreme Court, 2012

Facts: U.S. law provides that "[w]hoever utters any obscene, indecent, or profane language by means of radio communication shall be fined ... or imprisoned not more than two years, or both." The Federal Communications Commission has been instructed by Congress to enforce this law between the hours of 6 a.m. and 10 p.m.

In the 2002 Billboard Music Awards, broadcast by Fox, the singer Cher exclaimed: "I've also had my critics

---

[17]The law describes this requirement by saying a party must have standing to bring a case. A college student who has a theoretical belief that the EPA should not interfere with the timber industry has no standing to challenge an EPA rule that prohibits logging in a national forest. A lumber company that was ready to log that area has suffered a direct economic injury: It has standing to sue.

[18]This is the doctrine of exhaustion of remedies. A lumber company may not go into court the day after the EPA publishes a proposed ban on logging. It must first exhaust its administrative remedies by participating in the administrative hearing and then pursuing appeals within the agency before venturing into court.

for the last 40 years saying that I was on my way out every year. Right. So f*** 'em." [During Fox's] Billboard Music Awards in 2003, Nicole Richie made the following unscripted remark while presenting an award: "Have you ever tried to get cow s*** out of a Prada purse? It's not so f ***ing simple." During [NBC's] 2003 Golden Globe Awards, the singer Bono exclaimed: "This is really, really, f ***ing brilliant. Really, really great,"upon winning the award for Best Original Song.

The Commission had long held that fleeting, or single and unscripted, expletives were not indecent. But after the first two incidents, involving Cher and Richie, the Commission changed its policy, holding that that even one-time use could be a violation. It then punished NBC for Bono's use of the F-word. Even though the Cher and Nicole Richie incidents took place before this policy change, the Commission retroactively applied its new policy to them and found Fox to be in violation of it.

Fox challenged the Commission's indecency regulations, claiming it did not have fair notice of what was forbidden. The Second Circuit found the policy was vague and, as a result, unconstitutional because it failed to give broadcasters sufficient notice of what would be considered indecent and because the Commission acted inconsistently. The Commission had on occasion found the fleeting use of the F-word and the S-word not indecent provided they occurred during a news interview or were "essential to an artistic or educational work." This standard left broadcasters guessing and led to a chill on protected speech. The FCC appealed and the Supreme Court granted *certiorari*.

Issue: *Did the Commission give broadcasters fair notice of its policies?*

Excerpts from Justice Kennedy's Opinion: A fundamental principle in our legal system is that laws which regulate persons or entities must give fair notice of conduct that is forbidden or required. This requirement of clarity in regulation is essential to the protections provided by the Due Process Clause of the Fifth Amendment. It requires the invalidation of laws that are impermissibly vague.

Even when speech is not at issue, the regulated parties should know what is required of them so they may act accordingly. Precision and guidance are necessary so that those enforcing the law do not act in an arbitrary or discriminatory way.

In 2001, the Commission stated that for material to be indecent it must depict sexual or excretory organs or activities and be patently offensive as measured by contemporary community standards. A key consideration was "whether the material dwell[ed] on or repeat[ed] at length." In 2004, the Commission changed course and held that fleeting expletives could be a statutory violation. Now the Commission determined fleeting expletives were actionably indecent.

This history makes it apparent that the Commission policy in place at the time of the broadcasts gave no notice to Fox that a fleeting expletive could be actionably indecent; yet Fox [was] found to be in violation. The Commission's standards were vague. The lack of notice and vague standards render the Commission's policy unconstitutional. The Commission's orders must be set aside.

4-5d **Informational Control and the Public**

We started this section describing the pervasiveness of administrative agencies. We should end it by noting one way in which all of us have some direct control over these ubiquitous authorities: information.

> A popular government, without popular information, or the means of acquiring it, is but a Prologue to a Farce or a Tragedy—or perhaps both. Knowledge will forever govern ignorance, and a people who mean to be their own Governors must arm themselves with the power which knowledge gives.

> *James Madison, President, 1809–1817*

Two federal statutes arm us with the power of knowledge.

Freedom of Information Act

Congress passed the landmark Freedom of Information Act (known as "FOIA") in 1966. It is designed to give all of us, citizens, businesses, and organizations alike, access to the information federal agencies are using. The idea is to avoid government by secrecy.

Any citizen or executive may make a "FOIA request" to any federal government agency. It is simply a written request for the agency to furnish whatever information it has on the subject specified. Two types of data are available under FOIA. Anyone is entitled to information about how the agency operates, how it spends its money, and what statistics and other information it has collected on a given subject. People routinely obtain records about agency policies, environmental hazards, consumer product safety, taxes and spending, purchasing decisions, and agency forays into foreign affairs. A corporation that believes that OSHA is making more inspections of its textile mills than it makes of the competition could demand all relevant information, including OSHA's documents on the mill itself, comparative statistics on different inspections, OSHA's policies on choosing inspection sites, and so forth.

Second, all citizens are entitled to any records the government has *about them.* You are entitled to information that the Internal Revenue Service, or the Federal Bureau of Investigation, has collected about you.

FOIA does not apply to Congress, the federal courts, or the executive staff at the White House. Note also that, since FOIA applies to federal government agencies, you may not use it to obtain information from state or local governments or private businesses.

Exemptions. An agency officially has Ten days to respond to the request. In reality, most agencies are unable to meet the deadline but are obligated to make good faith efforts. FOIA exempts altogether nine categories from disclosure. The most important exemptions permit an agency to keep confidential information relating to national security, criminal investigations, internal agency matters such as personnel or policy discussions, trade secrets or financial institutions, or an individual's private life.

Privacy Act

This 1974 statute prohibits federal agencies from giving information about an individual to other agencies or organizations without written consent. There are exceptions, but overall this act has reduced the government's exchange of information about us "behind our back." For more on privacy law, see Chapter 10 on Cyberlaw and Privacy.

EXAM Strategy

Question: Builder wants to develop 1,000 acres in rural Montana, land that is home to the Kite Owl. The EPA rules that the Kite Owl is an endangered species, and prohibits development of the property. The developer appeals to court. The EPA based its decision on five statistical studies, and the opinions of three out of seven experts. The court looks at the same evidence and acknowledges that the EPA decision to be carefully reasoned and fair. However, the judges believe the other four experts were right: The owl is *not* endangered. Should the court permit development?

Strategy: What is the legal standard for deciding whether a court should affirm or reverse an agency decision? As long as there is *substantial evidence* to support the factual conclusions, and a *reasonable basis* for the legal conclusion, the court should not impose its judgment. Agencies are presumed to have special expertise in their areas. As the *Fox Television* case tells us, an agency ruling should generally be affirmed unless it is arbitrary and capricious. Apply that standard here.

Result: The EPA made a careful, reasoned decision. The court may disagree, but it should not impose its views. The court must affirm the agency's ruling and prohibit development.

Chapter Conclusion

"Why can't they just fix the law?" They can, and sometimes they do—but it is a difficult and complex task. "They" includes a great many people and forces, from common law courts to members of Congress to campaign donors to administrative agencies. The courts have made the bystander rule slightly more humane, but it has been a long and bumpy road. Congress managed to restore the legal interpretation of its own 1964 Civil Rights Act, but it took months of debate and compromising. The FDA squeezed more peanuts into a jar of Jif, but it took nearly a decade to get the lid on.

A study of law is certain to create some frustrations. This chapter cannot prevent them all. However, an understanding of how law is made is the first step toward controlling that law.

EXAM REVIEW

1. **COMMON LAW** The common law evolves in awkward fits and starts because courts attempt to achieve two contradictory purposes: predictability and flexibility.

2. **STARE DECISIS** *Stare decisis* means "let the decision stand," indicating once a court has decided a particular issue, it will generally apply the same rule in future cases.

3. **BYSTANDER RULE** The common-law bystander rule holds, generally, no one has a duty to assist someone in peril unless the bystander himself created the danger. Courts have carved some exceptions during the last 100 years, but the basic rule still stands.

4. **LEGISLATION** Bills originate in congressional committees and go from there to the full House of Representatives or Senate. If both houses pass the bill, the legislation normally must go to a Conference Committee to resolve differences between the two versions. The compromise version then goes from the Conference Committee back to both houses, and if passed by both, to the president. If the president signs the bill, it becomes a statute; if he vetoes it, Congress can pass it over his veto with a two-thirds majority in each house.

5. **STATUTORY INTERPRETATION** Courts interpret a statute by using the plain meaning rule; then, if necessary, legislative history and intent; and finally, if necessary, public policy.

EXAM Strategy

Question: Whitfield, who was black, worked for Ohio Edison. Edison fired him, but then later offered to rehire him. Another employee argued Edison's original termination of Whitfield had been race discrimination. Edison rescinded its offer to rehire Whitfield. Whitfield sued Edison, claiming that the company was retaliating for the other employee's opposition to discrimination. Edison pointed out that Title VII of the 1964 Civil Rights Act did not explicitly apply in such cases. Among other things, Title VII prohibits an employer from retaliating against *an employee* who has opposed illegal discrimination. But it does not say anything about retaliation based on *another employee's* opposition to discrimination. Edison argued that the statute did not protect Whitfield.

Strategy: What three steps does a court use to interpret a statute? First, the plain meaning rule. Does that rule help us here? The statute neither allows nor prohibits Edison's conduct. The law does not mention this situation, and the plain meaning rule is of no help. Second step: legislative history and intent. What did Congress intend with Title VII generally? With the provision barring retaliation against a protesting employee? Resolving those issues should give you the answer to this question. (See the "Result" at the end of this section.)

6. **ADMINISTRATIVE AGENCIES**   Congress creates federal administrative agencies with enabling legislation. The Administrative Procedure Act controls how agencies do their work.

7. **RULEMAKING**   Agencies may promulgate legislative rules, which generally have the effect of statutes, or interpretive rules, which merely interpret existing statutes.

8. **INVESTIGATION**   Agencies have broad investigatory powers and may use subpoenas and, in some cases, warrantless searches to obtain information.

EXAM Strategy

Question: When Hiller Systems, Inc., was performing a safety inspection on board the M/V *Cape Diamond,* an oceangoing vessel, an accident killed two men. The Occupational Safety and Health Administration (OSHA), a federal agency, attempted to investigate, but Hiller refused to permit any of its employees to speak to OSHA investigators. What could OSHA do to pursue the investigation? What limits would there have been on OSHA's actions?

Strategy: Agencies make rules, investigate, and adjudicate. Which is involved here? Investigation. During an investigation, what power has an agency to force a company to produce data? What are the limits on that power? (See the "Result" at the end of this section.)

9. **ADJUDICATION**   Agencies adjudicate cases, meaning that they hold hearings and decide issues. Adjudication generally begins with a hearing before an administrative law judge and may involve an appeal to the full agency or ultimately to federal court.

10. **AGENCY LIMITATIONS**   The four most important limitations on the power of federal agencies are statutory control in the enabling legislation and the APA; political control by Congress and the president; judicial review; and the informational control created by the FOIA and the Privacy Act.

5. Result: Congress passed Title VII as a bold, aggressive move to end race discrimination in employment. Further, by specifically prohibiting retaliation against an employee, Congress indicated it was aware that companies might punish those who spoke in favor of the very goals of Title VII. Protecting an employee from anti-discrimination statements made by a *coworker* is a very slight step beyond that, and appears consistent with the goals of Title VII and the anti-retaliation provision. Whitfield should win, and in the real case, he did.[19]

8. Result: OSHA can issue a subpoena *duces tecum*, demanding those on board the ship, and their supervisors, appear for questioning, and bring with them all relevant documents. OSHA may ask for anything (1) relevant to the investigation, (2) not unduly burdensome, and (3) not privileged. Conversations between one of the ship inspectors and his supervisor are clearly relevant; a discussion between the supervisor and the company's lawyer is privileged.

MULTIPLE-CHOICE QUESTIONS

1. A bill is vetoed by ——————— .
   (a) the Speaker of the House
   (b) a majority of the voting members of the Senate
   (c) the president
   (d) the Supreme Court

2. If a bill is vetoed, it may still become law if it is approved by ——————— .
   (a) two-thirds of the Supreme Court
   (b) two-thirds of registered voters
   (c) two-thirds of the Congress
   (d) the president
   (e) an independent government agency

3. When courts interpret statutes, they ask ——————— .
   (a) what the words in the statute ordinarily mean
   (b) which political parties endorsed the law
   (c) what Congress intended the law to do
   (d) whether or not the law supports good public policy
   (e) all of the above, except (b)

4. Under FOIA, any citizen may demand information about ——————— .
   (a) how an agency operates
   (b) how an agency spends its money
   (c) files that an agency has collected on the citizen herself
   (d) all of the above

5. If information requested under FOIA is not exempt, an agency has ——————— to comply with the request.
   (a) 10 days
   (b) 30 days
   (c) 3 months
   (d) 6 months

---

[19]EEOC v. Ohio Edison, 7 F.3d 541 (6th Cir. 1993).

CASE QUESTIONS

1. Until recently, every state had a statute outlawing the burning of American flags. But in *Texas v. Johnson*,[20] the Supreme Court declared such statutes unconstitutional, saying that flag burning is symbolic speech protected by the First Amendment. Does Congress have the power to overrule the Court's decision?

2. In 1988, terrorists bombed Pan Am Flight 103 over Lockerbie, Scotland, killing all passengers on board. Congress sought to remedy security shortcomings by passing the Aviation Security Improvement Act of 1990, which, among other things, ordered the Federal Aviation Authority (FAA) to prescribe minimum training requirements and staffing levels for airport security. The FAA promulgated rules according to the informal rulemaking process. However, the FAA refused to disclose certain rules concerning training at specific airports. A public interest group called Public Citizen, Inc., along with family members of those who had died at Lockerbie, wanted to know the details of airport security. What steps should they take to obtain the information? Are they entitled to obtain it?

3. The Aviation Security Improvement Act (ASIA) states that the FAA can refuse to divulge information about airport security. The FAA interprets this to mean that it can withhold data in spite of the FOIA. Public Citizen and the Lockerbie family members interpret FOIA as being the controlling statute, requiring disclosure. Is the FAA interpretation binding?

4. An off-duty, out-of-uniform police officer and his son purchased some food from a 7-Eleven store and were still in the parking lot when a carload of teenagers became rowdy. The officer went to speak to them, and the teenagers assaulted him. The officer shouted to his son to get the 7-Eleven clerk to call for help. The son entered the store, told the clerk that a police officer needed help, and instructed the clerk to call the police. He returned 30 seconds later and repeated the request, urging the clerk to say it was a Code 13. The son claimed the clerk laughed at him and refused to do it. The policeman sued the store. **Argument for the Store:** We sympathize with the policeman and his family, but the store has no liability. A bystander is not obligated to come to the aid of anyone in distress unless the bystander created the peril, and obviously the store did not do so. The policeman should sue those who attacked him. **Argument for the Police Officer:** We agree that in general a bystander has no obligation to come to the aid of one in distress. However, when a business that is open to the public receives an urgent request to call the police, the business should either make the call or permit someone else to do it

5. Federal antitrust statutes are complex, but the basic goal is straightforward: to prevent a major industry from being so dominated by a small group of corporations that they destroy competition and injure consumers. Does Major League Baseball violate the antitrust laws? Many observers say it does. A small group of owners not only dominate the industry, but also actually *own* it, controlling the entry of new owners into the game. This issue went to the United States Supreme Court in 1922. Justice Holmes ruled, perhaps surprisingly, that baseball is exempt from the antitrust laws, holding baseball is not "trade or commerce." Suppose members of Congress dislike this ruling and the current condition of baseball. What can they do?

---

[20]491 U.S. 397 (1989).

DISCUSSION QUESTIONS

1. Courts generally follow precedent, but in the *Tarasoff* and *Soldano* cases discussed earlier in this chapter, they did not. Consider the opening scenario based on the *Seinfeld* season finale. *Should* Jerry and his friends bear any civil *legal* responsibility for the carjacking or should a court follow precedent and hold the smug bunch blameless?

2. Revisit the *Fox* case. Do you agree with the opinion? What would a sensible broadcast obscenity policy contain? When (if ever) should a network face fines for airing bad language?

3. This chapter presents various examples where the law intersects with ethics. Jerry and his friends were rude and refused to help. Cher and Nicole Richie uttered profanity on live national television at a time when children were watching. What are your Life Principles on these issues?

4. During live national coverage of a Super Bowl half-time show, Justin Timberlake tore off part of Janet Jackson's shirt, exposing her breast for nine-sixteenths of a second. Television network CBS called it a "wardrobe malfunction," but the "malfunction" coincidentally occurred just as Timberlake was singing the lyrics, "Gonna have you naked by the end of this song." The FCC fined CBS $550,000 but the network challenged the fine in court. The appeals court held CBS did not have to pay because the FCC did not have a clear policy on momentary displays of nudity. Do you agree with this conclusion? Do you think the incident was intentional or truly accidental? If it was intentional, should CBS have known better, regardless of FCC policies? If it was accidental, should CBS still be held accountable? Should it matter if it was intentional or accidental?

5. Suppose you were on a state supreme court and faced with a restaurant choking case. Should you require restaurant employees to know and employ the Heimlich maneuver to assist a choking victim? If they do a bad job, they could cause additional injury. Should you permit them to do nothing at all? Is there a compromise position? What social policies are most important?

ANSWERS TO SELECTED END OF CHAPTER QUESTIONS

MULTIPLE-CHOICE QUESTIONS

Presented are the answers for the ODD-numbered multiple-choice questions in the end-of-chapter material.

1. C
3. E
5. A

CASE QUESTIONS

Presented are the answers for all of the ODD-numbered case questions in the end-of-chapter material.

1. **Answer:** No. When the Supreme Court declares that the Constitution protects an activity, such as flag burning, that is the final word. This is different from the *Griggs-Wards Cove* dispute. There, the Court was simply interpreting a statute, the 1964 Civil Rights Act. Whenever Congress believes that the Court has misinterpreted a statute, it is free to pass a law correcting the interpretation. But Congress has no power to overrule the Court on a matter of Constitutional rights.

3. **Answer:** No. Pursuant to the *Chevron* case, a court will look to see if there is clear congressional intent. If there is, it must be followed. If there is not, then the agency's interpretation will be followed if it is "permissible," meaning reasonable. In *Public Citizen, Inc. v. FAA*, 988 F.2d 186, 1993 U.S. App. LEXIS 6024 (D.C. Cir. 1993), the court found that there was a clear congressional intent: to permit the ASIA to exempt additional information from public disclosure for purposes of airport security. The agency's view became irrelevant, but plaintiffs lost anyway.

5. **Answer:** The congressman could introduce a bill overruling the Supreme Court's interpretation of federal antitrust statutes. The bill would specify that baseball is part of trade and commerce and that Congress intends that it be subject to the antitrust laws, the same as any other nationwide industry.

Chapter 5

© Creative Travel Projects/Shutterstock.com

CONSTITUTIONAL LAW

TO MAJOR JOHN CARTWRIGHT.
MONTICELLO, June 5, 1824.

DEAR AND VENERABLE SIR,

I am much indebted for your kind letter…

Our Revolution presented us an album on which we were free to write what we pleased. We had no occasion to search into musty records, to hunt up royal parchments, or to investigate the laws and institutions of a semi-barbarous ancestry. We appealed to those of nature, and found them engraved on our hearts.

We had never been permitted to exercise self-government. When forced to assume it, we were novices in its science. Its principles and forms had entered little into our former education. We established, however, some, although not all, its important principles.

The constitutions of most of our States assert that all power is inherent in the people; that they may exercise it by themselves, or they may act by representatives, freely and equally chosen; that it is their right and duty to be at all times armed; that they are entitled to freedom of person, freedom of religion, freedom of property, and freedom of the press.

In the structure of our legislatures, we think experience has proved the benefit of subjecting questions to two separate bodies of deliberants. The wit of man cannot devise a more solid basis for a free, durable and well-administered republic.

[O]ur State and federal governments are coordinate departments of one simple and integral whole. To the State governments are reserved all legislation and administration, in affairs which concern their own citizens only, and to the federal government is given whatever concerns foreigners, or the citizens of other States.

You will perceive that we have not so far [made] our constitutions unchangeable. [W]e consider them not otherwise changeable than by the authority of the people.

Can one generation bind another, and all others, in succession forever? I think not. A generation may bind itself as long as its majority continues in life; when that has disappeared,

> **The wit of man cannot devise a more solid basis for a free, durable and well-administered republic.**

Congress wields tremendous power. Its members create statutes that influence our jobs, money, health care, military, communications, and virtually everything else. But can Congress create *any* kind of law it wishes? No.

Article I, section 8 is a critically important part of the Constitution. It lists the 18 types of statutes that Congress is allowed to pass, such as imposing taxes, declaring war, and coining money. Thus, only the national government may create currency. The state of Texas cannot print $20 bills with George W. Bush's profile.

States like Texas *are* supposed to create all other kinds of laws for themselves because the Tenth Amendment says, "All powers not delegated to the United States by the Constitution … are reserved to the States."

The **Commerce Clause** is the specific item in Article I, section 8, most important to your future as a businessperson. It calls upon Congress "to regulate commerce… among the several States," and its impact is described in the next section.

Commerce Clause
The part of Article I, Section 8, that gives Congress the power to regulate commerce with foreign nations and among states

Interstate Commerce

With the Commerce Clause, the Framers sought to accomplish several things in response to the commercial chaos that existed under the Articles of Confederation. They wanted the federal government to speak with one voice when regulating commercial relations with foreign governments. The Framers also wanted to give Congress the power to bring coordination and fairness to trade among the states, and to stop the states from imposing the taxes and regulations that were wrecking the nation's domestic trade.

Virtually all of the numerous statutes that affect businesses are passed under the Commerce Clause. But what does it mean to regulate interstate commerce? Are all business transactions "interstate commerce," or are there exceptions? In the end, the courts must interpret what the Constitution means.

Substantial Effect Rule

An important test of the Commerce Clause came in the Depression years of the 1930s, in *Wickard v. Filburn*.[1] The price of wheat and other grains had fluctuated wildly, severely harming farmers and the national food market. Congress sought to stabilize prices by limiting the bushels per acre that a farmer could grow. Filburn grew more wheat than federal law allowed and was fined. In defense, he claimed that Congress had no right to regulate him because none of his wheat went into *interstate* commerce. He sold some locally and used the rest on his own farm as food for livestock and as seed. The Commerce Clause, Filburn claimed, gave Congress no authority to limit what he could do.

The Supreme Court disagreed and held that **Congress may regulate any activity that has a substantial economic effect on interstate commerce.** Filburn's wheat *affected* interstate commerce because the more he grew for use on his own farm, the less he would need to buy in the open market of interstate commerce. In the end, "interstate commerce" does not require that things travel from one state to another.

In *United States v. Lopez*,[2] however, the Supreme Court ruled that Congress *had* exceeded its power under the Commerce Clause. Congress had passed a criminal statute called the "Gun-Free School Zones Act," which forbade any individual from possessing a firearm in a school zone. The goal of the statute was obvious: to keep schools safe. Lopez was convicted of violating the act and appealed his conviction all the way to the high Court, claiming that Congress had no power to pass such a law. The government argued that the Commerce Clause gave it the power to pass the law, but the Supreme Court was unpersuaded:

> The possession of a gun in a local school zone is in no sense an economic activity that might, through repetition elsewhere, substantially affect any sort of interstate commerce. [Lopez] was a local student at a local school; there is no indication that he had recently moved in interstate

---

[1]317 U.S. 111 (1942).
[2]514 U.S. 549 (1995).

commerce, and there is no requirement that his possession of the firearm have any concrete tie to interstate commerce. To uphold the Government's contentions here, we would have to pile inference upon inference in a manner that would bid fair to convert congressional authority under the Commerce Clause to a general police power of the sort retained by the States. [The statute was unconstitutional and void.]

In the following case, the Supreme Court was faced with a decision that would profoundly affect the health care and pocketbook of every American: Does the Commerce Clause allow Congress to *compel* people to enter into commerce?

NATIONAL FEDERATION OF INDEPENDENT BUSINESS v. SEBELIUS

576 U.S. ___, 132 S. Ct. 2566
United States Supreme Court, 2012

Facts: In 2010, Congress enacted the Patient Protection and Affordable Care Act (the Act), which aimed to increase the number of Americans covered by health insurance and decrease the cost of health care. The Act required most Americans either to maintain health insurance coverage, or pay a "penalty" to the IRS. This provision was commonly referred to as the "individual mandate." The logic was that, if everyone—even healthy young people—had health insurance, health care costs would go down for all.

On the day president Obama signed the Act into law, 13 states challenged it, alleging that neither the Constitution's Commerce provision nor its Taxing Clause gave Congress the authority to enact the individual mandate. Both the federal district court and the appeals court agreed. The Supreme Court granted *certiorari*.

Issue: *Did Congress have the power to make every American purchase health insurance?*

Excerpts from Chief Justice Roberts's Decision: In our federal system, the National Government possesses only limited powers; the States and the people retain the remainder. In this case we must determine whether the Constitution grants Congress power to enact the individual mandate under the Commerce Clause or as an exercise of its power to tax.

The Constitution authorizes Congress to regulate interstate commerce and activities that substantially affect interstate commerce. [The Government argues] Congress may order individuals to buy health insurance because the failure to do so affects interstate commerce.

[But] the individual mandate does not regulate existing commercial activity. It instead compels individuals to become active in commerce by purchasing a product, on the ground that their failure to do so affects interstate commerce.

Every day individuals do not do an infinite number of things. Allowing Congress to justify federal regulation by pointing to the effect of inaction on commerce would bring countless decisions within the scope of federal regulation, and empower Congress to make those decisions.

[This] logic would justify a mandatory purchase to solve almost any problem. Many Americans do not eat a balanced diet. The failure of that group to have a healthy diet increases health care costs to a greater extent than the failure of the uninsured to purchase insurance. Under the Government's theory, Congress could address the diet problem by ordering everyone to buy vegetables.

The Commerce Clause is not a general license to regulate an individual from cradle to grave, simply because he will predictably engage in particular transactions. Any police power to regulate individuals as such, as opposed to their activities, remains vested in the States.

The individual mandate forces individuals into commerce precisely because they elected to refrain from commercial activity. Such a law cannot be sustained under a clause authorizing Congress to "regulate Commerce."

Congress also has the power to "lay and collect Taxes." Even if Congress lacks the power to direct individuals to buy insurance, the only effect of the individual mandate is to raise taxes on those who do not do so, and thus the law may be upheld as a tax.

Under the mandate, if an individual does not maintain health insurance, the only consequence is that he must pay the IRS. The mandate is not a legal command to buy insurance. Rather, it makes going without insurance just another thing the Government taxes, like buying gasoline or earning income. And if the mandate is in effect just a tax hike on certain taxpayers who do not have health insurance, it [is] within Congress's constitutional power to tax.

The [Act's penalty] looks like a tax in many respects, regardless of labels. It is paid into the Treasury by reform, the bill can dominate the news—and Congress—for months or even years. The president, of course, also has the power to veto bills.[5]

Foreign Policy

The president conducts the nation's foreign affairs, coordinating international efforts, negotiating treaties, and so forth. The president is also the commander in chief of the armed forces, meaning that he heads the military. But Article II does not give him the right to declare war—only the Senate may do that. A continuing tension between the president and Congress has resulted from the president's use of troops overseas *without* a formal declaration of war.

5-3c Judicial Power

Article III of the Constitution creates the Supreme Court and permits Congress to establish lower courts within the federal court system.[6] Federal courts have two key functions: adjudication and judicial review.

Chief Justice John Marshall

North Wind Picture Archives/Alamy

Adjudicating Cases

The federal court system hears criminal and civil cases. Generally, prosecutions of federal crimes begin in United States District Court. That same court has limited jurisdiction to hear civil lawsuits, a subject discussed in Chapter 3, on dispute resolution.

Judicial Review

One of the greatest "constitutional" powers appears nowhere in the Constitution. In 1803, the Supreme Court decided *Marbury v. Madison*.[7] Congress had passed a relatively minor statute that gave certain powers to the Supreme Court, and Marbury wanted the Court to use those powers. The Court refused. In an opinion written by Chief Justice John Marshall, the Court held that the statute violated the Constitution because Article III of the Constitution did not grant the Court those powers. The details of the case were insignificant, but the ruling was profound: Because the statute violated the Constitution, said the Court, it was void. **Judicial review refers to the power of federal courts to declare a statute or governmental action unconstitutional and void.**

This formidable grab of power has produced two centuries of controversy. The Court was declaring that it alone had the right to evaluate acts of the other two branches of government—the legislative and the executive—and to decide which were valid and which void. The Constitution nowhere grants this power. Undaunted, Marshall declared that "[I]t is emphatically the province and duty of the

---

[5]For a discussion of the president's veto power and Congress's power to override a veto, see Chapter 4, on statutory law.
[6]For a discussion of the federal court system, see Chapter 3, on dispute resolution.
[7]5 U.S. 137(1803).

judicial department to say what the law is." In later cases, the Supreme Court expanded on the idea, holding that it could also nullify state statutes, rulings by state courts, and actions by federal and state officials. In this chapter, we have already encountered an example of judicial review in the *Lopez* case, where the justices declared that Congress lacked the power to pass local gun regulations.

Is judicial review good for the nation? Those who oppose it argue that federal court judges are all appointed, not elected, and that we should not permit judges to nullify a statute passed by elected officials because that diminishes the people's role in their government. Those who favor judicial review insist that there must be one cohesive interpretation of the Constitution and the judicial branch is the logical one to provide it. The following example of judicial review shows how immediate and emotional the issue can be. This is a criminal prosecution for a brutal crime. Cases like this force us to examine two questions about judicial review. What is the proper punishment for such a horrible crime? Just as important, *who should make that decision*—appointed judges, or elected legislators?

KENNEDY v. LOUISIANA

554 U.S. 407
United States Supreme Court, 2008

Facts: Patrick Kennedy raped his eight-year-old stepdaughter. Her injuries were the most severe that the forensic expert had ever seen. Kennedy was convicted of aggravated rape because the victim was under 12 years of age.

The jury voted to sentence Kennedy to death, which was permitted by the Louisiana statute. The state supreme court *affirmed* the death sentence, and Kennedy appealed to the United States Supreme Court. He argued that the Louisiana statute was unconstitutional. The Eighth Amendment prohibits cruel and unusual punishment, which includes penalties that are out of proportion to the crime. Kennedy claimed that capital punishment was out of proportion to rape and violated the Eighth Amendment.

Issues: *Did the Louisiana statute violate the Constitution by permitting the death penalty in a case of child rape? Is it proper for the Supreme Court to decide this issue?*

Excerpts from Justice Kennedy's Decision: The constitutional prohibition against excessive or cruel and unusual punishments mandates that the State's power to punish be exercised within the limits of civilized standards. Evolving standards of decency that mark the progress of a maturing society counsel us to be most hesitant before interpreting the Eighth Amendment to allow the extension of the death penalty, a hesitation that has special force where no life was taken in the commission of the crime.

Consistent with evolving standards of decency and the teachings of our precedents we conclude that, in determining whether the death penalty is excessive, there is a distinction between intentional first-degree murder on the one hand and nonhomicide crimes against individual persons, even including child rape, on the other. The latter crimes may be devastating in their harm, as here, but in terms of moral depravity and of the injury to the person and to the public, they cannot be compared to murder in their severity and irrevocability.

Louisiana reintroduced the death penalty for rape of a child in 1995. Five States have since followed Louisiana's lead: Georgia, Montana, Oklahoma, South Carolina, and Texas. By contrast, 44 states have not made child rape a capital offense. As for federal law, Congress in the Federal Death Penalty Act of 1994 expanded the number of federal crimes for which the death penalty is a permissible sentence, including certain nonhomicide offenses; but it did not do the same for child rape or abuse. [The court concludes that there is a national consensus against imposing the death penalty for rape, and strikes down the Louisiana statute.]

Justice Alito, dissenting: If anything can be inferred from state legislative developments, the message is very different from the one that the Court perceives. In just the past few years, five States have enacted targeted capital child-rape laws. Such a development would not be out of step with changes in our society's thinking. During that time, reported instances of child abuse have increased dramatically; and there are many indications of growing alarm about the sexual abuse of children.

Judicial Activism/Judicial Restraint. The power of judicial review is potentially dictatorial. The Supreme Court nullifies statutes passed by Congress (*Marbury v. Madison, United States v. Lopez*) and executive actions. May it strike down any law it dislikes? In theory, no—the Court should nullify only laws that violate the Constitution. But in practice, yes—the Constitution means whatever the majority of the current justices says it means, because it is the Court that tells us which laws are violative.

Judicial activism
A court's willingness to decide issues on constitutional grounds

Judicial restraint
A court's attitude that it should leave lawmaking to legislators

Judicial activism refers to a court's willingness, or even eagerness, to become involved in major issues and to decide cases on constitutional grounds. Activists are sometimes willing to "stretch" laws beyond their most obvious meaning. **Judicial restraint** is the opposite, an attitude that courts should leave lawmaking to legislators and nullify a law only when it unquestionably violates the Constitution. Some justices believe that the Founding Fathers never intended the judicial branch to take a prominent role in sculpting the nation's laws and its social vision. In certain high-profile political cases, the Court has reminded us of its role. Notice the last sentence in the earlier *Sebelius* case: "Because the Constitution permits [the law], it is not our role to forbid it, or to pass upon its wisdom or fairness."

From the 1950s through the 1970s, the Supreme Court took an activist role, deciding many major social issues on constitutional grounds. The landmark 1954 decision in *Brown v. Board of Education* ordered an end to racial segregation in public schools, not only changing the nation's educational systems, but also forever altering its expectations about race.[8] The Court also struck down many state laws that denied minorities the right to vote. Beginning with *Miranda v. Arizona*, the Court began a sweeping reappraisal of the police power of the state and the rights of criminal suspects during searches, interrogations, trials, and appeals.[9] And in *Roe v. Wade*, the Supreme Court established certain rights to abortion, most of which remain after nearly 40 years of continuous litigation.[10]

Beginning in the late 1970s, and lasting to the present, the Court has pulled back from its social activism. Exhibit 5.1 illustrates the balance among Congress, the president, and the Court.

5-4 PROTECTED RIGHTS

The amendments to the Constitution protect the people of this nation from the power of state and federal government. The First Amendment guarantees rights of free speech, free press, and religion; the Fourth Amendment protects against illegal searches; the Fifth Amendment ensures due process; the Sixth Amendment demands fair treatment for defendants in criminal prosecutions; and the Fourteenth Amendment guarantees equal protection of the law. We consider the First, Fifth, and Fourteenth Amendments in this chapter and the Fourth, Fifth, and Sixth Amendments in Chapter 7, on crime.

The "people" who are protected include citizens and, for most purposes, corporations. Corporations are considered persons and receive most of the same protections. The great majority of these rights also extend to citizens of other countries who are in the United States.

Constitutional rights generally protect only against governmental acts. The Constitution generally does not protect us from the conduct of private parties, such as corporations or other citizens.

---

[8]347 U.S. 483 (1954).
[9]384 U.S. 436 (1966).
[10]410 U.S. 113 (1973).

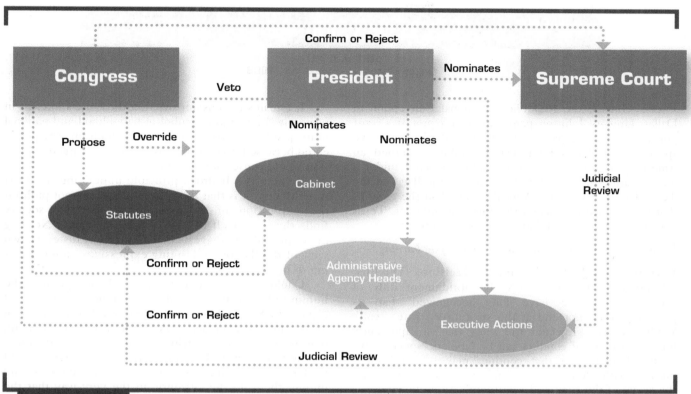

| EXHIBIT 5.1 | The Constitution established a federal government of checks and balances. Congress may propose statutes; the president may veto them; and Congress may override the veto. The president nominates cabinet officers, administrative heads, and Supreme Court justices, but the Senate must confirm his nominees. Finally, the Supreme Court (and lower federal courts) exercises judicial review over statutes and executive actions. Unlike the other checks and balances, judicial review is not provided for in the Constitution, but is a creation of the Court itself in *Marbury v. Madison*. |

5-4a Incorporation

A series of Supreme Court cases has extended virtually all of the important constitutional protections to *all levels* of national, state, and local government. This process is called **incorporation** because rights explicitly guaranteed at one level are incorporated into rights that apply at other levels.

5-4b First Amendment: Free Speech

The First Amendment states that "Congress shall make no law ... abridging the freedom of speech..." In general, we expect our government to let people speak and hear whatever they choose. The Founding Fathers believed democracy would work only if the members of the electorate were free to talk, argue, listen, and exchange viewpoints in any way they wanted. The people could only cast informed ballots if they were informed. "Speech" also includes symbolic conduct, as the following case flamingly illustrates.

TEXAS V. JOHNSON

491 U.S. 397
United States Supreme Court, 1989

Facts: Outside the Republican National Convention in Dallas, Gregory Johnson participated in a protest against policies of the Reagan administration. Participants gave speeches and handed out leaflets. Johnson burned an American flag. He was arrested and convicted under a Texas statute that prohibited desecrating the flag, but the Texas Court of Criminal Appeals *reversed* on the grounds that the conviction violated the First Amendment. Texas appealed to the United States Supreme Court.

Issue: *Does the First Amendment protect flag burning?*

Excerpts from Justice Brennan's Decision: The First Amendment literally forbids the abridgment only of "speech," but we have long recognized that its protection does not end at the spoken or written word. While we have rejected the view that an apparently limitless variety of conduct can be labeled "speech," we have acknowledged that conduct may be sufficiently imbued with elements of communication to fall within the scope of the First and Fourteenth Amendments.

In deciding whether particular conduct possesses sufficient communicative elements to bring the First Amendment into play, we have asked whether an intent to convey a particularized message was present, and [whether] the likelihood was great that the message would be understood by those who viewed it. Hence, we have recognized the expressive nature of students' wearing of black armbands to protest American military involvement in Vietnam; of a sit-in by blacks in a "whites only" area to protest segregation; of the wearing of American military uniforms in a dramatic presentation criticizing American involvement in Vietnam; and of picketing about a wide variety of causes.

[The Court concluded that burning the flag was in fact symbolic speech.]

It remains to consider whether the State's interest in reserving the flag as a symbol of nationhood and national unity justifies Johnson's conviction. Johnson was prosecuted because he knew that his politically charged expression would cause "serious offense."

If there is a bedrock principle underlying the First Amendment, it is that the Government may not prohibit the expression of an idea simply because society finds the idea itself offensive or disagreeable. Nothing in our precedents suggests that a State may foster its own view of the flag by prohibiting expressive conduct relating to it.

Could the Government, on this theory, prohibit the burning of state flags? Could it prohibit the burning of copies of the presidential seal? Or of the Constitution? In evaluating these choices under the First Amendment, how would we decide which symbols were sufficiently special to warrant this unique status? To do so, we would be forced to consult our own political preferences, and impose them on the citizenry, in the very way that the First Amendment forbids us to do.

The way to preserve the flag's special role is not to punish those who feel differently about these matters. It is to persuade them that they are wrong. We can imagine no more appropriate response to burning a flag than waving one's own, no better way to counter a flag-burner's message than by saluting the flag that burns, no surer means of preserving the dignity even of the flag that burned than by—as one witness here did—according its remains a respectful burial. We do not consecrate the flag by punishing its desecration, for in doing so we dilute the freedom that this cherished emblem represents.

The judgment of the Texas Court of Criminal Appeals is therefore *affirmed*.

Political Speech

Because the Framers were primarily concerned with enabling democracy to function, political speech has been given an especially high degree of protection. Such speech may not be barred even when it is offensive or outrageous. A speaker, for example, could accuse a U.S. senator of being insane and could use crude, violent language to describe him. The speech is still protected. **Political speech is protected unless it is intended and likely to create imminent lawless action.**[11] For example, suppose the speaker said, "The senator is

---

[11]Brandenburg v. Ohio, 395 U.S. 444 (1969).

inside that restaurant. Let's get some matches and burn the place down." Speech of this sort is not protected. The speaker could be arrested for attempted arson or attempted murder.

Time, Place, and Manner

Even when speech is protected, the government may regulate the *time*, *place*, and *manner* of such speech. A town may require a group to apply for a permit before using a public park for a political demonstration. The town may insist that the demonstration take place during daylight hours and that there be adequate police supervision and sanitation provided. However, the town may not prohibit such demonstrations outright.

Protected speech?

Many public universities have designated "free speech zones" located in high-traffic areas of campus that are not immediately adjacent to a large number of classrooms. The zones allow for debates to proceed and reach many students, but they minimize the chances that noisy demonstrations will interfere with lectures.

Morality and Obscenity

The regulation of morality and obscenity presents additional problems. Obscenity has never received constitutional protection. The Supreme Court has consistently held that obscenity does not play a valued role in our society and has refused to give protection to obscene works. That is well and good, but it merely forces the question: What is obscene?

In *Miller v. California*, the Court created a three-part test to determine if a creative work is obscene.[12] The basic guidelines for the fact finder are:

- Whether the average person, applying contemporary community standards, would find that the work, taken as a whole, appeals to the prurient interest;

- Whether the work depicts or describes, in a patently offensive way, sexual conduct specifically defined by the applicable state law; and

- Whether the work, taken as a whole, lacks serious literary, artistic, political, or scientific value.

If the trial court finds that the answer to all three of those questions is "yes," it may judge the material obscene; the state may then prohibit the work. If the state fails to prove any one of the three criteria, though, the work is not obscene. A United States District Court ruled that "As Nasty As They Wanna Be," recorded by 2 Live Crew, was obscene. The appeals court, however, *reversed*, finding that the state had failed to prove lack of artistic merit.[13]

Commercial Speech

This refers to speech that has a dominant theme to propose a commercial transaction. For example, most advertisements on television and in the newspapers are **commercial speech**. This sort of speech is protected by the First Amendment, but the government is permitted to regulate it more closely than other forms of speech. Commercial speech that is false or misleading may be outlawed altogether. **The government may regulate other commercial**

Commercial speech
Communication, such as advertisements, that has the dominant theme of proposing a business transaction

---

[12]413 U.S. 15 (1973).
[13]Luke Records, Inc. v. Navarro, 960 F. 2d 134, 1992 U.S. App. LEXIS 9592 (11th Cir. 1992).

of life, liberty, or property without due process of law; nor shall private property be taken for public use, without just compensation." These clauses prevent the government from arbitrarily taking the most valuable possessions of a citizen or corporation. The government has the right to take a person's liberty or property. But there are three important limitations:

- **Procedural Due Process.** Before depriving anyone of liberty or property, the government must go through certain steps, or procedures, to ensure that the result is fair.

- **The Takings Clause.** When the government takes property for public use, such as to build a new highway, it has to pay a fair price.

- **Substantive Due Process.** Some rights are so fundamental that the government may not take them from us at all. The substance of any law or government action may be challenged on fundamental fairness grounds.

Procedural Due Process

Takings Clause
A clause in the Fifth Amendment that ensures that when any governmental unit takes private property for public use, it must compensate the owner

The government deprives citizens or corporations of their property in a variety of ways. The Internal Revenue Service may fine a corporation for late payment of taxes. The Customs Service may seize goods at the border. As to liberty, the government may take it by confining someone in a mental institution or by taking a child out of the home because of parental neglect. The purpose of **procedural due process** is to ensure that before the government takes liberty or property, the affected person has a fair chance to oppose the action. There are two steps in analyzing a procedural due process case:

Procedural due process
The doctrine that ensures that before the government takes liberty or property, the affected person has a fair chance to oppose the action.

- Is the government attempting to take liberty or property?

- If so, how much process is due? (If the government is *not* attempting to take liberty or property, there is no due process issue.)

Is the Government Attempting to Take Liberty or Property? Liberty interests are generally easy to spot: Confining someone in a mental institution and taking a child from her home are both deprivations of liberty. A property interest may be obvious. Suppose that, during a civil lawsuit, the court **attaches** a defendant's house, meaning it bars the defendant from selling the property at least until the case is decided. This way, if the plaintiff wins, the defendant will have assets to pay the judgment. The court has clearly deprived the defendant of an important interest in his house, and the defendant is entitled to due process. However, a property interest may be subtler than that. A woman holding a job with a government agency has a "property interest" in that job, because her employer has agreed not to fire her without cause, and she can rely on it for income. If the government does fire her, it is taking away that property interest, and she is entitled to due process. A student attending any public school has a property interest in her education. If a public university suspends a student as described earlier, it is taking her property, and she, too, should receive due process.

How Much Process Is Due? Assuming that a liberty or property interest is affected, a court must decide how much process is due. Does the person get a formal trial, or an informal hearing, or merely a chance to reply in writing to the charges against her? If she gets a hearing, must it be held before the government deprives her of her property, or is it enough that she can be heard shortly thereafter? **What sort of hearing the government must offer depends upon how important the property or liberty interest is and on whether the government has a competing need for efficiency.** The more important the interest, the more formal the procedures must be.

Neutral Fact Finder. Regardless of how formal the hearing, one requirement is constant: The fact finder must be neutral. Whether it is a superior court judge deciding a multimillion-dollar contract suit or an employment supervisor deciding the fate of a government employee, the fact finder must have no personal interest in the outcome. In *Ward v. Monroeville*, the plaintiff was a motorist who had been stopped for traffic offenses in a small town.[14] He protested his innocence and received a judicial hearing. But the "judge" at the hearing was the town mayor. Traffic fines were a significant part of the town's budget. The motorist argued that the town was depriving him of procedural due process because the mayor had a financial interest in the outcome of the case. The United States Supreme Court agreed and *reversed* his conviction.

Attachment of Property. As described earlier, a plaintiff in a civil lawsuit often seeks to *attach* the defendant's property. This protects the plaintiff, but it may also harm the defendant if, for example, he is about to close a profitable real estate deal. Attachments used to be routine. In *Connecticut v. Doehr*, the Supreme Court required more caution.[15] Based on *Doehr*, when a plaintiff seeks to attach at the beginning of the trial, a court must look at the plaintiff's likelihood of winning. Generally, the court must grant the defendant a hearing *before* attaching the property. The defendant, represented by a lawyer, may offer evidence as to how attachment would harm him and why it should be denied.

Government Employment. A government employee must receive due process before being fired. Generally, this means some kind of hearing, but not necessarily a formal court hearing. The employee is entitled to know the charges against him, to hear the employer's evidence, and to have an opportunity to tell his side of the story. He is not entitled to have a lawyer present. The hearing "officer" need only be a neutral employee. Further, in an emergency, where the employee is a danger to the public or the organization, the government may suspend with pay, before holding a hearing. It then must provide a hearing before the decision becomes final.

Academic Suspension. There is still a property interest here, but it is the least important of those discussed. When a public school concludes that a student has failed to meet its normal academic standards, such as by failing too many courses, it may dismiss him without a hearing. Due process is served if the student receives notice of the reason and has some opportunity to respond, such as by writing a letter contradicting the school's claims.

In cases of disciplinary suspension or expulsion, courts generally require schools to provide a higher level of due process. In the hypothetical at the beginning of this section, the university has failed to provide adequate due process.[16] The school has accused the student of a serious infraction. The school must promptly provide details of the charge and cannot wait until the hearing to do so. The student should see the two papers and have a chance to rebut the charge. Moreover, Professor Holmes has demonstrated bias. He appears to have made up his mind in advance. He has placed the burden on the student to disprove the charges. And he probably feels obligated to support Watson's original conclusion, because Watson will be deciding his tenure case next year.

The Takings Clause

Florence Dolan ran a plumbing store in Tigard, Oregon. She and her husband wanted to enlarge it on land they already owned. But the city government said that they could expand only if they dedicated some of their own land for use as a public bicycle path and for other public use. Does the city have the right to make them do that? For an answer, we must look to a different part of the Fifth Amendment.

---

[14]409 U.S. 57 (1972).
[15]501 U.S. 1 (1991).
[16]See, e.g., University of Texas Medical School at Houston v. Than, (Tex. 1995).

Eminent domain
The power of the government to take private property for public use

The Takings Clause prohibits a state from taking private property for public use without just compensation. A town wishing to build a new football field may boot you out of your house. But the town must compensate you. The government takes your land through the power of **eminent domain**. Officials must notify you of their intentions and give you an opportunity to oppose the project and to challenge the amount the town offers to pay. But when the hearings are done, the town may write you a check and level your house, whether you like it or not.

More controversial issues arise when a local government does not physically take the property but passes regulations that restrict its use. Tigard is a city of 30,000 in Oregon. The city developed a comprehensive land use plan for its downtown area in order to preserve green space, to encourage transportation other than autos, and to reduce its flooding problems. Under the plan, when a property owner sought permission to build in the downtown section, the city could require some of her land to be used for public purposes. This has become a standard method of land use planning throughout the nation. States have used it to preserve coastline, urban green belts, and many environmental features.

When Florence Dolan applied for permission to expand, the city required that she dedicate a 15-foot strip of her property to the city as a bicycle pathway and that she preserve, as greenway, a portion of her land within a floodplain. She sued, and though she lost in the Oregon courts, she won in the United States Supreme Court. The Court held that Tigard City's method of routinely forcing all owners to dedicate land to public use violated the Takings Clause. The city was taking the land, even though title never changed hands.[17]

The Court did not outlaw all such requirements. What it required was that, **before a government may require an owner to dedicate land to a public use, it must show that this owner's proposed building requires this dedication of land.** In other words, it is not enough for Tigard to have a general plan, such as a bicycle pathway, and to make all owners participate in it. Tigard must show that it needs *Dolan's* land *specifically for a bike path and greenway*. This will be much harder for local governments to demonstrate than merely showing a citywide plan. A related issue arose in the following controversial case. A city used eminent domain to take property on behalf of *private developers*. Was this a valid public use?

The *Kelo* decision was controversial and, in response, some states passed statutes prohibiting eminent domain for private development.

KELO V. CITY OF NEW LONDON, CONNECTICUT

545 U.S. 469
United States Supreme Court, 2005

Facts: New London, Connecticut, was declining economically. The city's unemployment rate was double that of the state generally, and the population was at its lowest point in 75 years. In response, state and local officials targeted a section of the city, called Fort Trumbull, for revitalization. Located on the Thames River, Fort Trumbull comprised 115 privately owned properties and 32 additional acres of an abandoned naval facility. The development plan included one section for a waterfront conference hotel and stores; a second one for 80 private residences; and one for research facilities.

The state bought most of the properties from willing sellers. However, nine owners of 15 properties refused to sell, and filed suit. The owners claimed that the city was trying to take land for *private* use, not public, in violation of the Takings Clause. The case reached the United States Supreme Court.

Issue: *Did the city's plan violate the Takings Clause?*

Excerpts from Justice Stevens's Decision: It has long been accepted that the sovereign may not take the property of A for the sole purpose of transferring it to another private party B, even though A is paid just compensation. On the other hand, it is equally clear that a State may transfer property from one private party to another if future "use by the public" is the purpose of the

---

[17]Dolan v. City of Tigard, 512 U.S. 374 (1994).

taking; the condemnation of land for a railroad with common-carrier duties is a familiar example.

This is not a case in which the City is planning to open the condemned land—at least not in its entirety—to use by the general public. Nor will the private lessees of the land in any sense be required to operate like common carriers, making their services available to all comers. But this Court long ago rejected any literal requirement that condemned property be put into use for the general public, [embracing] the broader and more natural interpretation of public use as "public purpose." Thus, in a case upholding a mining company's use of an aerial bucket line to transport ore over property it did not own, Justice Holmes' opinion for the Court stressed "the inadequacy of use by the general public as a universal test."

The City has carefully formulated an economic development plan that it believes will provide appreciable benefits to the community, including—but by no means limited to—new jobs and increased tax revenue. As with other exercises in urban planning and development, the City is endeavoring to coordinate a variety of commercial, residential, and recreational uses of land, with the hope that they will form a whole greater than the sum of its parts. Because that plan unquestionably serves a public purpose, the takings challenged here satisfy the public use requirement of the Fifth Amendment.

To avoid this result, petitioners urge us to adopt a new bright-line rule that economic development does not qualify as a public use. [However, promoting] economic development is a traditional and long-accepted function of government. There is, moreover, no principled way of distinguishing economic development from the other public purposes that we have recognized. In our cases upholding takings that facilitated agriculture and mining, for example, we emphasized the importance of those industries to the welfare of the States in question. Clearly, there is no basis for exempting economic development from our traditionally broad understanding of public purpose.

The judgment of the Supreme Court of Connecticut is *affirmed*.

Justice O'Connor, dissenting: The Court today significantly expands the meaning of public use. It holds that the sovereign may take private property currently put to ordinary private use, and give it over for new, ordinary private use, so long as the new use is predicted to generate some secondary benefit for the public—such as increased tax revenue, more jobs, maybe even aesthetic pleasure. But nearly any lawful use of real private property can be said to generate some incidental benefit to the public. Thus, if predicted (or even guaranteed) positive side effects are enough to render transfer from one private party to another constitutional, then the words "for public use" do not realistically exclude *any* takings, and thus do not exert any constraint on the eminent domain power.

Any property may now be taken for the benefit of another private party, but the fallout from this decision will not be random. The beneficiaries are likely to be those citizens with disproportionate influence and power in the political process, including large corporations and development firms. As for the victims, the government now has license to transfer property from those with fewer resources to those with more.

Substantive Due Process

This doctrine is part of the Due Process Clause, but it is entirely different from procedural due process and from government taking. During the first third of the twentieth century, the Supreme Court frequently nullified state and federal laws, asserting that they interfered with basic rights. For example, in a famous 1905 case, *Lochner v. New York*, the Supreme Court invalidated a New York statute that had limited the number of hours that bakers could work in a week.[18] New York had passed the law to protect employee health. But the Court declared that private parties had a basic constitutional right to contract. In this case, the statute interfered with the rights of the employer and the baker to make any bargain they wished. Over the next three decades, the Court struck down dozens of state and federal laws that were aimed at working conditions, union rights, and social welfare generally. This was called **substantive due process** because the Court was looking at the underlying rights being affected, such as the right to contract, not at any procedures.[19]

substantive due process
A form of due process that holds that certain rights are so fundamental that the government may not eliminate them

[18]198 U.S. 45 (1905).

[19]Be the first on your block to pronounce this word correctly. The accent goes on the first syllable: substantive.

Critics complained that the Court was interfering with the desires of the voting public by nullifying laws that the justices personally disliked (judicial activism). During the Great Depression, however, things changed. Beginning in 1934, the Court completely *reversed* itself and began to uphold the types of laws it had struck down earlier.

The Supreme Court made an important substantive due process ruling in the case of *BMW v. Gore*.[20] A BMW dealership sold Gore a car that had sustained water damage. Instead of telling him of the damage, they simply repainted the car and sold it as new.

In Chapter 6, we will examine two different types of cash awards that juries may make in tort cases. For now, let's call them "ordinary" and "punitive" damages. When plaintiffs win tort cases, juries may always award ordinary damages to offset real, measureable losses. In addition, juries are sometimes allowed to add to an award to further punish a defendant for bad behavior.

In the BMW case, the jury awarded Gore $4,000 in ordinary damages as the difference in value between a flawless new car and a water-damaged car. The jury then awarded a delighted Gore $4 *million* in punitive damages. In the end, the Supreme Court decided that the punitive award was so disproportionate to the harm actually caused that it violated substantive due process rights.

5-4d Fourteenth Amendment: Equal Protection Clause

Shannon Faulkner wanted to attend The Citadel, a state-supported military college in South Carolina. She was a fine student who met every admission requirement that The Citadel set except one: She was not a man. The Citadel argued that its long and distinguished history demanded that it remain all male. Faulkner responded that she was a citizen of the state and ought to receive the benefits that others got, including the right to a military education. Could the school exclude her on the basis of gender?

Equal Protection Clause
A clause in the Fourteenth Amendment that generally requires the government to treat people equally

The Fourteenth Amendment provides that "No State shall … deny to any person within its jurisdiction the equal protection of the laws." This is the **Equal Protection Clause**, and it means that, generally speaking, **governments must treat people equally.** Unfair classifications among people or corporations will not be permitted. A notorious example of unfair classification would be race discrimination: Permitting only white children to attend a public school violates the Equal Protection Clause.

Yet clearly, governments do make classifications every day. People with high incomes pay a higher tax rate than those with low incomes; some corporations are permitted to deal in securities, while others are not. To determine which classifications are constitutionally permissible, we need to know what is being classified. There are three major groups of classifications. The outcome of a case can generally be predicted by knowing which group it is in.

- **Minimal Scrutiny: Economic and Social Relations.** Government actions that classify people or corporations on these bases are almost always upheld.

- **Intermediate Scrutiny: Gender.** Government classifications are sometimes upheld.

- **Strict Scrutiny: Race, Ethnicity, and Fundamental Rights.** Classifications based on any of these are almost never upheld.

Minimal Scrutiny: Economic and Social Regulation

Just as with the Due Process Clause, laws that regulate economic or social issues are presumed valid. They will be upheld if they are *rationally related to a legitimate goal.* This means a statute may classify corporations and/or people, and the classifications will be upheld if they make any sense at all. The New York City Transit Authority excluded all methadone users from any employment. The United States District Court concluded that this violated the Equal Protection Clause by unfairly excluding all those who were on

---

[20]517 U.S. 559 (1996).

methadone. The court noted that even those who tested free of any illegal drugs and were seeking non-safety-sensitive jobs, such as clerks, were turned away. That, said the district court, was irrational.

Not so, said the United States Supreme Court. The Court admitted that the policy might not be the wisest. It would probably make more sense to test individually for illegal drugs rather than automatically exclude methadone users. But, said the Court, it was not up to the justices to choose the best policy. They were only to decide if the policy was rational. Excluding methadone users related rationally to the safety of public transport and therefore did not violate the Equal Protection Clause.[21]

Intermediate Scrutiny: Gender

Classifications based on sex must meet a tougher test than those resulting from economic or social regulation. Such laws must *substantially relate to important government objectives.* Courts have increasingly nullified government sex classifications as societal concern with gender equality has grown.

At about the same time Shannon Faulkner began her campaign to enter The Citadel, another woman sought admission to the Virginia Military Institute (VMI), an all-male state school. The Supreme Court held that Virginia had violated the Equal Protection Clause by excluding women from VMI. The Court ruled that gender-based government discrimination requires an "exceedingly persuasive justification," and that Virginia had failed that standard of proof. The Citadel promptly opened its doors to women as well.[22]

Strict Scrutiny: Race, Ethnicity, and Fundamental Rights

Any government action that intentionally discriminates against racial or ethnic minorities, or interferes with a fundamental right, is presumed invalid. In such cases, courts will look at the statute or policy with *strict scrutiny;* that is, courts will examine it very closely to determine whether there is compelling justification for it. The law will be upheld only if it is *necessary to promote a compelling state interest.* Very few meet that test.

- **Racial and Ethnic Minorities.** Any government action that intentionally discriminates on the basis of race, or ethnicity, is presumed invalid. For example, in *Palmore v. Sidoti,* the state had refused to give child custody to a mother because her new spouse was racially different from the child.[23] The practice was declared unconstitutional. The state had made a racial classification, it was presumed invalid, and the government had no *compelling need* to make such a ruling.

- **Fundamental Rights.** A government action interfering with a fundamental right also receives strict scrutiny and will likely be declared void. For example, New York State gave an employment preference to any veteran who had been a state resident when he entered the military. Newcomers who were veterans were less likely to get jobs, and therefore this statute interfered with the right to travel, a fundamental right. The Supreme Court declared the law invalid.[24]

Fundamental rights
Rights so basic that any governmental interference with them is suspect and likely to be unconstitutional

---

[21]New York City Transit Authority v. Beazer, 440 U.S. 568 (1979).
[22]United States v. Virginia, 518 U.S. 515 (1996).
[23]466 U.S. 429 (1984).
[24]Attorney General of New York v. Soto-Lopez, 476 U.S. 898 (1986).

EXAM Strategy

Question: Megan is a freshman at her local public high school; her older sister Jenna attends a nearby private high school. Both girls are angry because their schools prohibit them from joining their respective wrestling teams, where only boys are allowed. The two girls sue based on the U.S. Constitution. Discuss the relevant law and predict the outcomes.

Strategy: One girl goes to private school and one to public school. Why does that matter? Now ask what provision of the Constitution is involved, and what legal standard it establishes.

Result: The Constitution offers protection from the *government*. A private high school is not part of the government, and Jenna has no constitutional case. Megan's suit is based on the Equal Protection Clause. This is gender discrimination, meaning that Megan's school must convince the court that keeping girls off the team *substantially relates to an important government objective.* The school will probably argue that wrestling with stronger boys will be dangerous for girls. However, courts are increasingly suspicious of any gender discrimination and are unlikely to find the school's argument persuasive.

Chapter Conclusion

The legal battle over power never stops. The obligation of a state to provide equal educational opportunity for both genders relates to whether Tigard, Oregon, may demand some of Ms. Dolan's store lot for public use. Both issues are governed by one amazing document. The same Constitution determines what tax preferences are permissible and even whether a state may require you to wear clothing. As social mores change in step with broad cultural developments, as the membership of the Supreme Court changes, the balance of power between federal government, state government, and citizens will continue to evolve. There are no easy answers to these constitutional questions because there has never been a democracy so large, so diverse, or so powerful.

EXAM REVIEW

1. **CONSTITUTION** The Constitution is a series of compromises about power.

2. **ARTICLES I, II, AND III** Article I of the Constitution creates the Congress and grants all legislative power to it. Article II establishes the office of president and defines executive powers. Article III creates the Supreme Court and permits lower federal courts; the article also outlines the powers of the federal judiciary.

3. **COMMERCE CLAUSE** Under the Commerce Clause, Congress may regulate any activity that has a substantial effect on interstate commerce.

4. **INTERSTATE COMMERCE** A state may not regulate commerce in any way that will interfere with interstate commerce.

EXAM Strategy

Question: Maine exempted many charitable institutions from real estate taxes but denied this benefit to a charity that primarily benefited out-of-state residents. Camp Newfound was a Christian Science organization, and 95 percent of its summer campers came from other states. Camp Newfound sued Maine. Discuss.

Strategy: The state was treating organizations differently depending on what states their campers came from. This raised Commerce Clause issues. Did the positive aspect or dormant aspect of that clause apply? The dormant aspect applied. What does it state? Apply that standard to these facts. (See the "Result" at the end of this section.)

5. **SUPREMACY CLAUSE** Under the Supremacy Clause, if there is a conflict between federal and state statutes, the federal law preempts the field. Even without a conflict, federal law preempts if Congress intended to exercise exclusive control.

6. **PRESIDENTIAL POWERS** The president's key powers include making agency appointments, proposing legislation, conducting foreign policy, and acting as commander in chief of the armed forces.

7. **FEDERAL COURTS** The federal courts adjudicate cases and also exercise judicial review, which is the right to declare a statute or governmental action unconstitutional and void.

8. **FREEDOM OF SPEECH** Freedom of speech includes symbolic acts. Political speech by both people and organizations is protected unless it is intended and likely to create imminent lawless action.

9. **REGULATION OF SPEECH** The government may regulate the time, place, and manner of speech.

10. **COMMERCIAL SPEECH** Commercial speech that is false or misleading may be outlawed; otherwise, regulations on this speech must be reasonable and directed to a legitimate goal.

EXAM Strategy

Question: A federal statute prohibits the broadcasting of lottery advertisements, except by stations that broadcast in states permitting lotteries. The purpose of the statute is to support efforts of states that outlaw lotteries. Truth Broadcasting operates a radio station in State A (a nonlottery state) but broadcasts primarily in State B (a lottery state). Truth wants to advertise State B's lottery but is barred by the statute. Does the federal statute violate Truth's constitutional rights?

Strategy: This case involves a particular kind of speech. What kind? What is the rule about that kind of speech? (See the "Result" at the end of this section.)

11. **PROCEDURAL DUE PROCESS** Procedural due process is required whenever the government attempts to take liberty or property. The amount of process that is due depends upon the importance of the liberty or property threatened.

EXAM Strategy

Question: Fox's Fine Furs claims that Ermine owes $68,000 for a mink coat on which she has stopped making payments. Fox files a complaint and also asks the court clerk to *garnish* Ermine's wages. A garnishment is a court order to an employer to withhold an employee's wages, or a portion of them, and pay the money into court so that there will be money for the plaintiff, if it wins. What constitutional issue does Fox's request for garnishment raise?

Strategy: Ermine is in danger of losing part of her income, which is property. The Due Process Clause prohibits the government (the court) from taking life, liberty, or property without due process. What process is Ermine entitled to? (See the "Result" at the end of this section.)

12. **TAKINGS CLAUSE** The Takings Clause prohibits a state from taking private property for public use without just compensation.

13. **SUBSTANTIVE DUE PROCESS** A substantive due process analysis presumes that any economic or social regulation is valid, and presumes invalid any law that infringes upon a fundamental right.

14. **EQUAL PROTECTION CLAUSE** The Equal Protection Clause generally requires the government to treat people equally. Courts apply strict scrutiny in any equal protection case involving race, ethnicity, or fundamental rights; intermediate scrutiny to any case involving gender; and minimal scrutiny to an economic or social regulation.

---

4. Result: The dormant aspect holds that a state statute that discriminates against interstate commerce is almost always invalid. Maine was subsidizing charities that served in-state residents and penalizing those that attracted campers from elsewhere. The tax rule violated the Commerce Clause and was void.[25]

10. Result: An advertisement is commercial speech. The government may regulate this speech so long as the rules are reasonable and directed to a legitimate goal. The goal of supporting nonlottery states is reasonable, and there is no violation of Truth's free speech rights.[26]

11. Result: Ermine is entitled to notice of Fox's claim and to a hearing before the court garnishes her wages.[27]

---

[25]Camps Newfound/Owatonna, Inc. v. Town of Harrison, Maine, 520 U.S. 564 (1997).
[26]United States v. Edge Broadcasting, 509 U.S. 418 (1993).
[27]Sniadach v. Family Finance Corp., 395 U.S. 337 (1969).

MULTIPLE-CHOICE QUESTIONS

1. Greenville College, a public community college, has a policy of admitting only male students. If the policy is challenged under the Fourteenth Amendment, ———————————— scrutiny will be applied.

   (a) strict

   (b) intermediate

   (c) rational

   (d) none of the above

2. You begin work at Everhappy Corp. at the beginning of November. On your second day at work, you wear a political button on your overcoat, supporting your choice for governor in the upcoming election. Your boss glances at it and says, "Get that stupid thing out of this office or you're history, chump." Your boss ———————————— violated your First Amendment rights. After work, you put the button back on and start walking home. You pass a police officer who blocks your path and says, "Take off that stupid button or you're going to jail, chump." The officer ———————————— violated your First Amendment rights.

   (a) has; has

   (b) has; has not

   (c) has not; has

   (d) has not; has not

3. Which of the following statements accurately describes statutes that Congress and the president may create?

   (a) Statutes must be related to a power listed in Article I, section 8, of the Constitution.

   (b) Statutes must not infringe on the liberties in the Bill of Rights.

   (c) Both A and B

   (d) none of the above

4. Which of the following is true of the origin of judicial review?

   (a) It was created by Article II of the Constitution.

   (b) It was created by Article III of the Constitution.

   (c) It was created in the *Marbury v. Madison* case.

   (d) It was created by the Fifth Amendment.

   (e) It was created by the Fourteenth Amendment.

5. Consider *Kelo v. City of New London*, in which a city with a revitalization plan squared off against property owners who did not wish to sell their property. The key constitutional provision was the Takings Clause in the ———————————— Amendment. The Supreme Court decided the city ———————————— use eminent domain and take the property from the landowners.

   (a) Fifth; could

   (b) Fifth; could not

   (c) Fourteenth; could

   (d) Fourteenth; could not

CASE QUESTIONS

1. In 1996, California legalized the medical use of marijuana, even though it was still illegal under federal law. Californians Angel Raich and Diane Monson used homegrown medical marijuana. When federal agents destroyed their plants, Monson and Raich sued, claiming, among other things, that the Commerce Clause did not permit the federal government to regulate activities that took place in their backyards and homes. The federal government argued that because consuming locally grown marijuana for medical purposes affects the interstate market for marijuana, the federal government may regulate—and prohibit—such consumption. Whose argument should prevail?

2. In the landmark 1965 case of *Griswold v. Connecticut*, the Supreme Court examined a Connecticut statute that made it a crime for any person to use contraception. The majority declared the law an unconstitutional violation of the right of privacy. Justice Black dissented, saying, "I do not to any extent whatever base my view that this Connecticut law is constitutional on a belief that the law is wise or that its policy is a good one. [It] is every bit as offensive to me as it is to the majority. [There is no criticism by the majority of this law] to which I cannot subscribe—except their conclusion that the evil qualities they see in the law make it unconstitutional." What legal doctrines are involved here? Why did Justice Black distinguish between his personal views on the statute and the power of the Court to overturn it?

3. Carter was an employee of the Sheriff's office in Hampton, Virginia. When his boss, Sheriff Roberts, was up for reelection against Adams, Carter "liked" the Adams campaign's Facebook page. Upon winning reelection, Sheriff Roberts fired Carter, who then sued on free speech grounds. Is a Facebook "like" protected under the First Amendment?

4. David Lucas paid $975,000 for two residential lots on the Isle of Palms near Charleston, South Carolina. He intended to build houses on them. Two years later, the South Carolina legislature passed a statute that prohibited building seaward of a certain line, and Lucas's property fell in the prohibited zone. Lucas claimed that his land was now useless and that South Carolina owed him its value. Explain his claim. Should he win?

5. The federal Defense of Marriage Act (DOMA) defined marriage as a union between a man and a woman. As a result, same-sex couples were not eligible for the federal marriage benefits given to heterosexual couples. Edith Windsor and Thea Spyer had been together for 40 years, and married for two, when Spyer died. Because of DOMA, the federal government did not treat Windsor as a surviving spouse for purposes of estate taxes, so she was presented with a tax bill of $363,000. If she had been married to a man, she would not have owed any taxes. Windsor challenged the statute, claiming the government had violated her right to equal protection. Should she win?

DISCUSSION QUESTIONS

1. What is the proper role of a judge in interpreting the Constitution? Do you believe in judicial activism or judicial restraint?

2. **ETHICS** Lawmakers have traditionally struggled when asked to define obscenity. Justice Potter Stewart simply defined it as "I know it when I see it." This chapter

discusses the guidelines that determine if speech is obscene for purposes of the First Amendment. In Chapter 4, you read about the FCC's vague guidelines on obscenity in *Fox Television Stations v. FCC*. Should obscenity ever be protected under the First Amendment? Where you do draw the line?

3. Consider the "tea party" movement. Do you believe that the federal government should be able to create whatever laws it deems to be in the country's best interests, or do you believe that individual states, like Florida and California, should have more control over the laws within their own borders?

4. This chapter is filled with examples of statutes that have been struck down by the courts. A Texas law banning flag burning was rejected by the Supreme Court, as was a Louisiana death penalty statute. The Affordable Healthcare Act was voided by multiple lower court judges before the Supreme Court ultimately upheld the law.

   Do you like the fact that courts can void laws which they determine to be in violation of the Constitution? Or is it wrong for appointed judges to overrule "the will of the majority," as expressed by elected members of Congress and state legislatures?

5. Gender discrimination currently receives "intermediate" Fourteenth Amendment scrutiny. Is this right? Should gender receive "strict" scrutiny as does race? Why or why not?

ANSWERS TO SELECTED END OF CHAPTER QUESTIONS

MULTIPLE-CHOICE QUESTIONS

Presented are the answers for the ODD-numbered multiple-choice questions in the end-of-chapter material.

1. B
3. C
5. A

CASE QUESTIONS

Presented are the answers for all of the ODD-numbered case questions in the end-of-chapter material.

1. **Answer:** Fane wins. The Court held that the Florida statute violates the First Amendment. Laws restricting commercial speech will only survive constitutional analysis if they are tailored in a reasonable manner to serve a substantial state interest. This statute fails on both tests. Florida has not demonstrated that the ban advances its goal of improving the quality of CPAs. Further, the state's approach greatly restricts free speech, and less intrusive means are available to achieve its goals. *Edenfield v. Fane*, 507 U.S. 761, 113 S.Ct. 1792, 1993 U.S. LEXIS 2985 (1993).

3. **Answer:** The right of privacy is nowhere stated in the Constitution, and its enforcement is an example of the Court applying substantive due process. Justice Black thought the law was terrible but he thought it was even worse for the Court to invent constitutional doctrine simply because it disliked a particular law. He would have preferred to practice judicial restraint—that is, to leave it up to the voters and the state legislature to decide the matter. Clearly a court should not go so far with judicial activism that it becomes a superlegislature. The Constitution makes it clear that courts should have a more limited role. Yet since *Marbury v. Madison*, federal courts have taken it upon themselves to say what the law is, and that frequently means overturning state and federal statutes. An activist court presents society with the danger of unelected judges, with lifetime tenure, foisting their own social agenda on an unwilling populace—but it also offers the potential for powerful officials, who do not have to worry about polls or reelections, to protect the people and the rights that are most vulnerable.

5. **Answer:** His claim is based on the Takings Clause of the Fifth Amendment. The Supreme Court was unable to make a final ruling because certain facts were unclear from the record. But the Court stated that when the owner of real property has been called upon to sacrifice all economically beneficial uses in the name of the common good, he has suffered a taking and is entitled to compensation. It appears very likely that Lucas's property has lost all beneficial uses. If South Carolina can demonstrate some unexpected common law right to prohibit Lucas from building, such as nuisance, it may prevail. In all likelihood, though, South Carolina will end up paying "just compensation" for Lucas's land. *Lucas v. South Carolina Coastal Council*, 505 U.S. 1003, 112 S. Ct. 2886, 1992 U.S. LEXIS 4537 (1992).

Chapter 6

DISPUTE RESOLUTION

Tony Caruso had not returned for dinner, and his wife, Karen, was nervous. She put on some sandals and hurried across the dunes, a half mile to the ocean shore. She soon came upon Tony's dog, Blue, tied to an old picket fence. Tony's shoes and clothing were piled neatly nearby. Karen and friends searched frantically throughout the evening.

© Creative Travel Projects/Shutterstock.com

A little past midnight, Tony's body washed ashore, his lungs filled with water. A local doctor concluded he had accidentally drowned.

Karen and her friends were not the only ones who were distraught. Tony had been partners with Beth Smiles in an environmental consulting business, Enviro-Vision. They were good friends, and Beth was emotionally devastated. When she was able to focus on business issues, Beth filed an insurance claim with the Coastal Insurance Group. Beth hated to think about Tony's death in financial terms, but she was relieved that the struggling business would receive $2 million on the life insurance policy.

> **A little past midnight, Tony's body washed ashore, his lungs filled with water.**

Several months after filing the claim, Beth received this reply from Coastal: "Under the policy issued to Enviro-Vision, we are conditionally liable in the amount of $1 million in the event of Mr. Caruso's death. If his death is accidental, we are conditionally liable to pay double indemnity of $2 million. But pursuant to section H(5), death by suicide is not covered.

"After a thorough investigation, we have concluded that Anthony Caruso's death was an act of suicide, as defined in section B(11) of the policy. Your claim is denied in its entirety." Beth was furious. She was convinced Tony was incapable of suicide. And her company could not afford the $2 million loss. She decided to consult her lawyer, Chris Pruitt.

6-1 THREE FUNDAMENTAL AREAS OF LAW

This case is a fictionalized version of several real cases based on double indemnity insurance policies. In this chapter, we follow Beth's dispute with Coastal from initial interview through appeal, using it to examine three fundamental areas of law: the structure of our court systems, civil lawsuits, and alternative dispute resolution.

When Beth Smiles meets with her lawyer, Chris Pruitt brings a second attorney from his firm, Janet Booker, who is an experienced **litigator**; that is, a lawyer who handles court cases. If they file a lawsuit, Janet will be in charge, so Chris wants her there for the first meeting. Janet probes about Tony's home life, the status of the business, his personal finances, everything. Beth becomes upset that Janet doesn't seem sympathetic, but Chris explains that Janet is doing her job: She needs all the information, good and bad.

6-1a Litigation versus Alternative Dispute Resolution

Janet starts thinking about the two methods of dispute resolution: litigation and alternative dispute resolution. **Litigation** refers to lawsuits, the process of filing claims in court, and ultimately going to trial. **Alternative dispute resolution** is any other formal or informal process used to settle disputes without resorting to a trial. It is increasingly popular with corporations and individuals alike because it is generally cheaper and faster than litigation, and we will focus on this topic in the last part of this chapter.

Litigation
The process of filing claims in court and ultimately going to trial.

Alternative dispute resolution
Any other formal or informal process used to settle disputes without resorting to a trial

6-2 COURT SYSTEMS

The United States has more than 50 *systems* of courts. One nationwide system of *federal* courts serves the entire country. In addition, each individual state has its court system. The state and federal courts are in different buildings, have different judges, and hear different kinds of cases. Each has special powers and certain limitations.

6-2a State Courts

The typical state court system forms a pyramid, as Exhibit 6.1 shows. Some states have minor variations on the exhibit. For example, Texas has two top courts: a Supreme Court for civil cases and a Court of Criminal Appeals for criminal cases.

Trial Courts

Almost all cases start in trial courts, which are endlessly portrayed on television and in film. There is one judge, and there will often (but not always) be a jury. This is the only court to hear testimony from witnesses and receive evidence. **Trial courts** determine the facts of a particular dispute and apply to those facts the law given by earlier appellate court decisions.

In the Enviro-Vision dispute, the trial court will decide all important facts that are in dispute. How did Tony Caruso die? Did he drown? Assuming he drowned, was his death accidental or suicide? Once the jury has decided the facts, it will apply the law to those facts. If Tony Caruso died accidentally, contract law provides that Beth Smiles is entitled to double indemnity benefits. If the jury decides he killed himself, Beth gets nothing.

Facts are critical. That may sound obvious, but in a course devoted to legal principles, it is easy to lose track of the key role that factual determinations play in the resolution of any dispute. In the Enviro-Vision case, we will see that one bit of factual evidence goes undetected, with costly consequences.

Jurisdiction refers to a court's power to hear a case. In state or federal court, a plaintiff may start a lawsuit only in a court that has jurisdiction over that kind of case. Some courts have very limited jurisdiction, while others have the power to hear almost any case.

Trial courts
Determine the facts of a particular dispute and apply to those facts the law given by earlier appellate court decisions

Jurisdiction
A court's power to hear a case

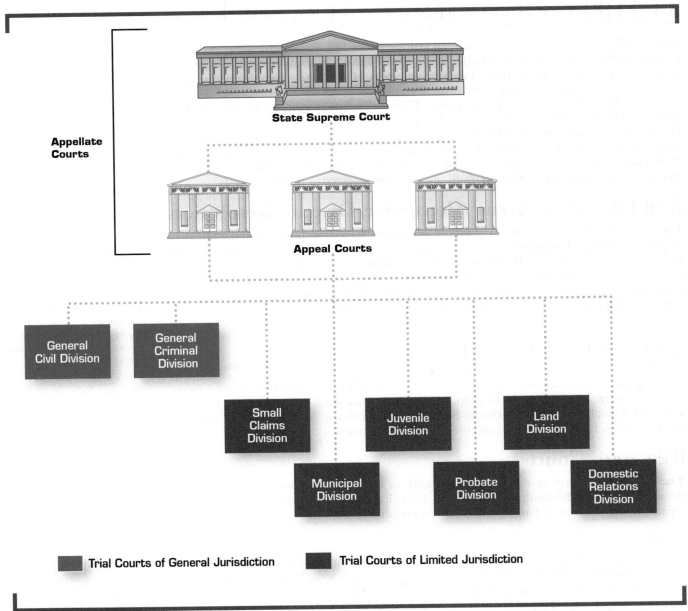

State Supreme Court

Appellate Courts

Appeal Courts

General Civil Division

General Criminal Division

Small Claims Division

Municipal Division

Juvenile Division

Probate Division

Land Division

Domestic Relations Division

■ Trial Courts of General Jurisdiction   ■ Trial Courts of Limited Jurisdiction

EXHIBIT 6.1   A trial court determines facts, while an appeals court ensures that the lower court correctly applied the law to those facts.

Subject Matter Jurisdiction

Subject matter jurisdiction
A court's authority to hear a particular type of case

Subject matter jurisdiction means that a court has the authority to hear a particular type of case.

Trial Courts of Limited Jurisdiction.   These courts may hear only certain types of cases. Small claims court has jurisdiction only over civil lawsuits involving a maximum of, say, $5,000 (the amount varies from state to state). A juvenile court hears only cases involving minors. Probate court is devoted to settling the estates of deceased persons, though in some states it will hear certain other cases as well.

Trial Courts of General Jurisdiction.   Trial courts of general jurisdiction, however, can hear a very broad range of cases. The most important court, for our purposes, is the general civil division. This court may hear virtually any civil lawsuit. In one day it might hear a $450 million shareholders' derivative lawsuit, an employment issue involving freedom of religion, and a foreclosure on a mortgage. Most of the cases we study start in this court.[1] If Enviro-Vision's case against Coastal goes to trial in a state court, it will begin in the trial court of general jurisdiction.

Personal Jurisdiction

In addition to subject matter jurisdiction, courts must also have **personal jurisdiction** over the defendant. Personal jurisdiction is the legal authority to require the defendant to stand trial, pay judgments, and the like. When plaintiffs file lawsuits, defendants sometimes make *a special appearance* to challenge a court's personal jurisdiction. If the court agrees with the defendant's argument, the lawsuit will be dismissed.

> **Personal jurisdiction**
> A court's authority to bind the defendant to its decisions

Personal jurisdiction generally exists, if:

1. For individuals, the defendant is a resident of the state in which a lawsuit is filed. For companies, the defendant is doing business in that state.

2. The defendant takes a formal step to defend a lawsuit. Most papers filed with a court count as formal steps, but special appearances do not.

3. A **summons** is *served* on a defendant. A summons is the court's written notice that a lawsuit has been filed against the defendant. The summons must be delivered to the defendant when she is physically within the state in which the lawsuit is filed.

> **Summons**
> The court's written notice that a lawsuit has been filed against the defendant

Corporations are required to hire a registered agent in any state in which they do business. If a registered agent receives a summons, then the corporation is served.

4. A **long-arm statute** applies. If all else fails—the defendant does not reside in the state, does not defend the lawsuit, and has not been served with a summons while in the state—a court still can obtain jurisdiction under long-arm statutes. These statutes typically claim jurisdiction over someone who commits a tort, signs a contract, or conducts "regular business activities" in the state.

> **Long-arm statute**
> A statute that gives a court jurisdiction over someone who commits a tort, signs a contract, or conducts "regular business activities" in the state

As a general rule, courts tend to apply long-arm statutes aggressively, hauling defendants into their courtrooms. However, the due process guarantees in the United States Constitution require fundamental fairness in the application of long-arm statutes. Therefore, courts can claim personal jurisdiction only if a defendant has had *minimum contacts* with a state. In other words, it is unfair to require a defendant to stand trial in another state if he has had no meaningful interaction with that state.

In the following Landmark Case, the Supreme Court established the "minimum contacts" rule.

---

[1]Note that the actual name of the court of general jurisdiction will vary from state to state. In many states, it is called *superior court* because it has power superior to the courts of limited jurisdiction. In New York, it is called *supreme court* (anything to confuse the layperson); in some states, it is called *court of common pleas*; in Oregon and other states, it is a *circuit court*. Within this branch, some states are beginning to establish specialized business and high-tech courts to hear complex commercial disputes.

Landmark Case

INTERNATIONAL SHOE CO. V. STATE OF WASHINGTON

326 U.S. 310
Supreme Court of the United States, 1945

Facts: Although International Shoe manufactured footwear only in St. Louis, Missouri, it sold its products nationwide. It did not have offices or warehouses in Washington State, but it did send about a dozen salespeople there. The salespeople rented space in hotels and businesses, displayed sample products, and took orders. They were not authorized to collect payments from customers.

When Washington State sought contributions to the state's unemployment fund, International Shoe refused to pay. Washington sued. The company argued that it was not engaged in business in the state, and, therefore, that Washington courts had no jurisdiction over it.

The Supreme Court of Washington ruled that International Shoe did have sufficient contacts with the state to justify a lawsuit there. International Shoe appealed to the United States Supreme Court.

Issue: *Did International Shoe have sufficient minimum contacts in Washington State to permit jurisdiction there?*

Excerpts from Chief Justice Stone's Decision: Appellant insists that its activities within the state were not sufficient to manifest its "presence" there and that in its absence, the state courts were without jurisdiction, that consequently, it was a denial of due process for the state to subject appellant to suit. Appellant [International Shoe] refers to those cases in which it was said that the mere solicitation of orders for the purchase of goods within a state, to be accepted without the state and filled by shipment of the purchased goods interstate, does not render the corporation seller amenable to suit within the state.

Historically the jurisdiction of courts to render judgment is grounded on their power over the defendant's person. Hence his presence within the territorial jurisdiction of a court was prerequisite to a judgment personally binding him. But now due process requires that [a defendant] have certain minimum contacts with it such that the maintenance of the suit does not offend "traditional notions of fair play and substantial justice."

Since the corporate personality is a fiction, its "presence" can be manifested only by those activities of the corporation's agent within the state which courts will deem to be sufficient to satisfy the demands of due process.

"Presence" in the state in this sense has never been doubted when the activities of the corporation there have not only been continuous and systematic, but also give rise to the liabilities sued on, even though no consent to be sued or authorization to an agent to accept service of process has been given. Conversely, it has been generally recognized that the casual presence of the corporate agent or even his conduct of single or isolated items of activities in a state in the corporation's behalf are not enough to subject it to suit on causes of action unconnected with the activities there. To require the corporation in such circumstances to defend the suit away from its home or other jurisdiction where it carries on more substantial activities has been thought to lay too great and unreasonable a burden on the corporation to comport with due process.

But to the extent that a corporation exercises the privilege of conducting activities within a state, it enjoys the benefits and protection of the laws of that state. The exercise of that privilege may give rise to obligations.

Applying these standards, the activities carried on in behalf of appellant in the State of Washington were neither irregular nor casual. They were systematic and continuous throughout the years in question. They resulted in a large volume of interstate business, in the course of which appellant received the benefits and protection of the laws of the state, including the right to resort to the courts for the enforcement of its rights. The obligation which is here sued upon arose out of those very activities. It is evident that these operations establish sufficient contacts or ties with the state of the forum to make it reasonable and just, according to our traditional conception of fair play and substantial justice, to permit the state to enforce the obligations which appellant has incurred there.

The state may maintain the present suit to collect the tax.

Affirmed.

Appellate Courts

Appellate courts are entirely different from trial courts. Three or more judges hear the case. There are no juries, ever. These courts do not hear witnesses or take new evidence. They hear appeals of cases already tried below. **Appeals courts** generally accept the facts given to them by trial courts and review the trial record to see if the court made errors of law.

Higher courts generally defer to lower courts on factual findings. Juries and trial court judges see all evidence as it is presented, and they are in the best position to evaluate it. An appeals court will accept a factual finding unless there was *no evidence at all* to support it. If the jury decides that Tony Caruso committed suicide, the appeals court will normally accept that fact, even if the appeals judges consider the jury's conclusion dubious. On the other hand, if a jury concluded that Tony had been murdered, an appeals court would overturn that finding if neither side had introduced any evidence of murder during the trial.

An appeals court reviews the trial record to make sure that the lower court correctly applied the law to the facts. If the trial court made an **error of law**, the appeals court may require a new trial. Suppose the jury concludes that Tony Caruso committed suicide but votes to award Enviro-Vision $1 million because it feels sorry for Beth Smiles. That is an error of law: If Tony committed suicide, Beth is entitled to nothing. An appellate court will reverse the decision. Or suppose that the trial judge permitted a friend of Tony's to state that he was certain Tony would never commit suicide. Normally, such opinions are not permissible in trial, and it was a legal error for the judge to allow the jury to hear it.

Court of Appeals. The party that loses at the trial court may appeal to the intermediate court of appeals. The party filing the appeal is the **appellant**. The party opposing the appeal (because it won at trial) is the **appellee**.

This court allows both sides to submit written arguments on the case, called **briefs**. Each side then appears for oral argument, usually before a panel of three judges. The appellant's lawyer has about 15 minutes to convince the judges that the trial court made serious errors of law, and that the decision should be **reversed**; that is, nullified. The appellee's lawyer has the same time to persuade the court that the trial court acted correctly, and that the result should be **affirmed**; that is, permitted to stand

State Supreme Court. This is the highest court in the state, and it accepts some appeals from the court of appeals. In most states, there is no absolute right to appeal to the Supreme Court. If the high court regards a legal issue as important, it accepts the case. It then takes briefs and hears oral argument just as the appeals court did. If it considers the matter unimportant, it refuses to hear the case, meaning that the court of appeals' ruling is the final word on the case.[2]

In most states, seven judges, often called *justices,* sit on the Supreme Court. They have the final word on state law.

6-2b **Federal Courts**

As discussed in Chapter 1, federal courts are established by the U.S. Constitution, which limits what kinds of cases can be brought in any federal court. See Exhibit 6.2. For our purposes, two kinds of civil lawsuits are permitted in federal court: federal question cases and diversity cases.

Appeals courts
Higher courts that review the trial record to see if the court made errors of law

Error of law
Because of this, the appeals court may require a new trial.

Appellant
The party filing the appeal

Appellee
The party opposing the appeal

Briefs
Written arguments on the case

Reversed
Nullified

Affirmed
Permitted to stand

---

[2]In some states with smaller populations, there is no intermediate appeals court. All appeals from trial courts go directly to the state supreme court.

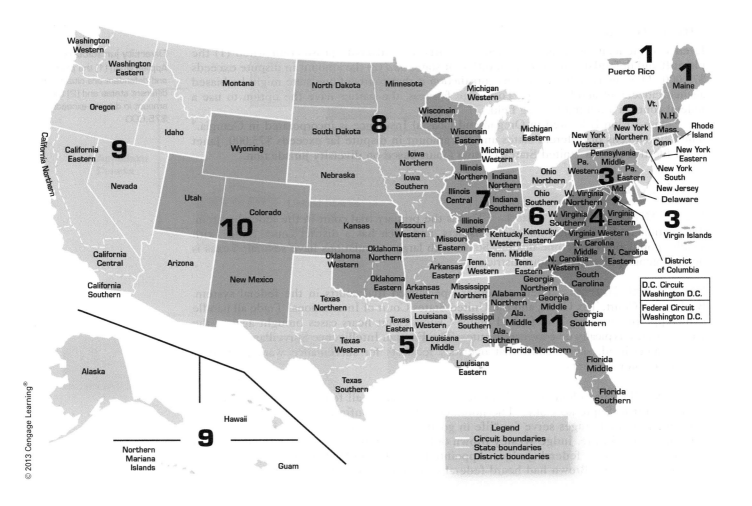

United States Supreme Court. This is the highest court in the country. There are nine justices on the Court. One justice is the chief justice and the other eight are associate justices. When they decide a case, each justice casts an equal vote. The chief justice's special power comes from his authority to assign opinions to a given justice. The justice assigned to write an opinion has an opportunity to control the precise language and thus to influence the voting by other justices.

The Supreme Court has the power to hear appeals in any federal case, and in certain cases that began in state courts. Generally, it is up to the Court whether or not it will accept a case. A party that wants the Supreme Court to review a lower court ruling must file a petition for a **writ of *certiorari***, asking the Court to hear the case. Four of the nine justices must vote in favor of hearing a case before a writ will be granted. The Court receives several thousand requests every year but usually accepts fewer than 100. Most cases accepted involve either an important issue of constitutional law or an interpretation of a major federal statute.

Writ of *certiorari*

A petition asking the Supreme Court to hear a case

EXAM Strategy

Question: Mark has sued Janelle, based on the state common law of negligence. He is testifying in court, explaining how Janelle backed a rented truck out of her driveway and slammed into his Lamborghini, causing $82,000 in damages. Where would this take place?

(a) State appeals court

(b) United States Court of Appeals

(c) State trial court

(d) federal district court

(e) Either state trial court or federal district court

Strategy: The question asks about trial and appellate courts, and also about state versus federal courts. One issue at a time, please. What are the different functions of trial and appellate courts? *Trial* courts use witnesses, and often juries, to resolve factual disputes. *Appellate* courts never hear witnesses and never have juries. Applying that distinction to these facts tells us whether we are in a trial or appeals court.

Next Issue: *State* trial courts may hear lawsuits on virtually any issue. *Federal District Courts* may only hear two kinds of cases: federal question (those involving a statute or constitutional provision), or diversity (where the parties are from different states *and* the amount at issue is $75,000 or higher). Apply what we know to the facts here.

Result: We are in a trial court because Mark is testifying. Could we be in Federal District Court? No. The suit is based on state common law. This is not a diversity case because the parties live in the same state. We are in a state trial court.

6-3 LITIGATION

Janet Booker decides to file the Enviro-Vision suit in the Oregon trial court. She thinks that a state court judge may take the issue more seriously than a federal district court judge.

6-3a Pleadings

The documents that begin a lawsuit are called the **pleadings**. These consist of the complaint, the answer, and sometimes a reply.

Complaint

The plaintiff files in court a **complaint**, which is a short, plain statement of the facts she is alleging and the legal claims she is making. The purpose of the complaint is to inform the defendant of the general nature of the claims and the need to come into court and protect his interests.

Janet Booker files the complaint, as shown below. Since Enviro-Vision is a partnership, she files the suit on behalf of Beth personally.

Pleadings
The documents that begin a lawsuit, consisting of the complaint, the answer, and sometimes a reply

Complaint
A short, plain statement of the facts alleged and the legal claims made

```
STATE OF OREGON
CIRCUIT COURT

Multnomah County                              Civil Action No. _____
_____
Elizabeth Smiles,
Plaintiff                                      JURY TRIAL DEMANDED

v.
Coastal Insurance Company, Inc.,
Defendant
_____

                           COMPLAINT

Plaintiff Elizabeth Smiles states that:
   1. She is a citizen of Multnomah County, Oregon.
   2. Defendant Coastal Insurance Company, Inc., is incorporated under the laws of Georgia and
      has as its usual place of business 148 Thrift Street, Savannah, Georgia.
   3. On or about July 5, 2015, plaintiff Smiles ("Smiles"), Defendant Coastal Insurance Co, Inc.
      ("Coastal") and Anthony Caruso entered into an insurance contract ("the contract"), a copy of
      which is annexed hereto as Exhibit "A." This contract was signed by all parties or their
      authorized agents, in Multnomah County, Oregon.
   4. The contract obligates Coastal to pay to Smiles the sum of two million dollars ($2 million) if
      Anthony Caruso should die accidentally.
   5. On or about September 20, 2015, Anthony Caruso accidentally drowned and died while
      swimming.
   6. Coastal has refused to pay any sum pursuant to the contract.
   7. Coastal has knowingly, willingly and unreasonably refused to honor its obligations under the
      contract.

WHEREFORE, plaintiff Elizabeth Smiles demands judgment against defendant Coastal for all monies
due under the contract; demands triple damages for Coastal's knowing, willing, and unreasonable
refusal to honor its obligations; and demands all costs and attorney's fees, with interest.
ELIZABETH SMILES,
By her attorney,
[Signed]
Janet Booker
Pruitt, Booker & Bother
983 Joy Avenue
Portland, OR
October 18, 2015
```

Service

When she files the complaint in court, Janet gets a summons, which is a paper ordering the defendant to answer the complaint within 20 days. A sheriff or constable then *serves* the two papers by delivering them to the defendant. Coastal's headquarters are in Georgia, so the state of Oregon has required Coastal to specify someone as its agent for receipt of service in Oregon.

Answer

Once the complaint and summons are served, Coastal has 20 days in which to file an answer. Coastal's answer, shown below, is a brief reply to each of the allegations in the complaint. The answer tells the court and the plaintiff exactly what issues are in dispute. Because Coastal admits that the parties entered into the contract that Beth claims they did, there is no need for her to prove that in court. The court can focus its attention on the disputed issue: whether Tony Caruso died accidentally.

STATE OF OREGON
CIRCUIT COURT

Multnomah County   Civil Action No. 09-5626

_____
Elizabeth Smiles,
Plaintiff
v.
Coastal Insurance Company, Inc.,
Defendant
_____

ANSWER

Defendant Coastal Insurance Company, Inc., answers the complaint as follows:

1. Admit.
2. Admit.
3. Admit.
4. Admit.
5. Deny.
6. Admit.
7. Deny.

COASTAL INSURANCE COMPANY, INC.,
By its attorney,
[Signed]
Richard B. Stewart
Kiley, Robbins, Stewart & Glote
333 Victory Boulevard
Portland, OR
October 30, 2015

If the defendant fails to answer in time, the plaintiff will ask for a **default judgment**. In granting a default judgment, the judge accepts every allegation in the complaint as true and renders a decision that the plaintiff wins without a trial.

Recently, two men sued PepsiCo, claiming that the company stole the idea for Aquafina water from them. They argued that they should receive a portion of the profits for every bottle of Aquafina ever sold.

PepsiCo failed to file a timely answer, and the judge entered a default judgment in the amount of $1.26 billion. On appeal, the default judgment was overturned and PepsiCo was able to escape paying the massive sum, but other defendants are sometimes not so lucky.

It is important to respond to courts on time.

Counterclaim

Sometimes a defendant does more than merely answer a complaint and files a **counterclaim**, meaning a second lawsuit by the defendant against the plaintiff. Suppose that after her complaint was filed in court, Beth had written a letter to the newspaper, calling Coastal a bunch of "thieves and scoundrels who spend their days mired in fraud and larceny." Coastal would not have found that amusing. The company's answer would have included a counter-claim against Beth for libel, claiming that she falsely accused the insurer of serious criminal acts. Coastal would have demanded money damages.

If Coastal counterclaimed, Beth would have to file a **reply**, which is simply an answer to a counterclaim. Beth's reply would be similar to Coastal's answer, admitting or denying the various allegations.

Default judgment
A decision that the plaintiff wins without trial because the defendant failed to answer in time

Counterclaim
A second lawsuit by the defendant against the plaintiff

Reply
An answer to a counterclaim

Before Beth's deposition date arrives, Rich sends Coastal's answers to Enviro-Vision's interrogatories. The answers contain no useful information whatsoever. For example, Interrogatory No. 10 asked, "If you claim that Anthony Caruso committed suicide, describe every fact upon which you rely in reaching that conclusion." Coastal's answer simply says, "His state of mind, his poor business affairs, and the circumstances of his death all indicate suicide."

Janet calls Rich and complains that the interrogatory answers are a bad joke. Rich disagrees, saying that it is the best information they have so early in the case. After they debate it for 20 minutes, Rich offers to settle the case for $100,000. Janet refuses and makes no counteroffer.

Janet files a **motion to compel answers to interrogatories**, in other words, a formal request that the court order Coastal to supply more complete answers. Janet submits a **memorandum** with the motion, which is a supporting argument. Although it is only a few pages long, the memorandum takes several hours of online research and writing to prepare—more costs. Janet also informs Rich Stewart that Beth will not appear for the deposition because Coastal's interrogatory answers are inadequate.

Rich now files *his* motion to compel, asking the court to order Beth Smiles to appear for her deposition. The court hears all of the motions together. Janet argues that Coastal's interrogatory answers are hopelessly uninformative and defeat the whole purpose of discovery. She claims that Coastal's large number of depositions creates a huge and unfair expense for a small firm.

Rich claims that the interrogatory answers are the best that Coastal can do thus far and that Coastal will supplement the answers when more information becomes available. He argues against Interrogatory No. 18, the one in which Janet asked for the names of other policyholders whom Coastal considered suicides. He claims that Janet is engaging in a fishing expedition that would violate the privacy of Coastal's insurance customers and provide no information relevant to this case. He demands that Janet make Beth available for a deposition.

These discovery rulings are critical because they will color the entire lawsuit. A trial judge has to make many discovery decisions before a case reaches trial. At times, the judge must weigh the need of one party to see documents against the other side's need for privacy. One device a judge can use in reaching a discovery ruling is an **in camera inspection**, meaning that the judge views the requested documents alone, with no lawyers present, and decides whether the other side is entitled to view them.

E-Discovery. The biggest change in litigation in the last decade is the explosive rise of electronic discovery. Companies send hundreds, or thousands, or millions of emails—every day. Businesses large and small have vast amounts of data stored electronically. And many people post volumes of personal information on social media sites. All of this information is potentially subject to discovery.

It is enormously time-consuming and expensive for companies to locate all of the relevant material, separate it from irrelevant or confidential matter, and furnish it. A firm may be obligated to furnish *millions* of emails to the opposing party. In one case, a defendant had to pay 31 lawyers full-time, for six months, just to wade through the e-ocean of documents and figure out which had to be supplied and how to produce them. Not surprisingly, this data eruption has created a new industry: high-tech companies that assist law firms in finding, sorting, and delivering electronic data.

Who is to say what must be supplied? What if an email string contains individual emails that are clearly privileged (meaning a party need not divulge them), but others that are not privileged? May a company refuse to furnish the entire string? Many will try. However, some courts have ruled that companies seeking to protect email strings must create a log describing every individual email and allow the court to determine which ones are privileged.[5]

Social media further complicates discovery. When a Facebook profile or Twitter account is public, opposing parties are free to rummage through the treasure trove of personal information. One recent study found that the word "Facebook" occurred in one-third of all U.S. divorce filings—and more than 80 percent of divorce lawyers have used social media evidence in court. Likewise, many plaintiffs have lost their tort cases because of incriminating online photos of them engaged in activities that undermine their claims. (What, you claim you can never work at a desk again, but you can still waterski?)

But what about access to a *private* social media profile? To protect people's privacy, courts require parties to show that the discovery request is reasonably calculated to lead to relevant and admissible evidence. For example, one court denied a company's request that an employee supply a list of all of his time-stamped social media postings during a four-year period because the request was unreasonably burdensome and unlikely to show whether the worker had taken lunch breaks.[6]

Another court found that limited discovery of a plaintiff's Twitter and Facebook accounts was proper because her online activity would likely reveal information about whether or not she was experiencing the emotional distress her lawsuit claimed.[7]

Both sides in litigation sometimes use gamesmanship during discovery. For example, if an individual sues a large corporation, the company may deliberately make discovery so expensive that the plaintiff cannot afford the legal fees. And if a plaintiff has a bad case, he might intentionally try to make the discovery process more expensive for the defendant than his settlement offer.

In the following case, it was not just legends that were forever—discovery was, too. Was the plaintiff's failure to cooperate part of a calculated plan to tire Nike into settling or just a costly decision?

LEGENDS ARE FOREVER, INC. v. NIKE, INC.

2013 WL 6086461, 2013 U.S. Dist. LEXIS 164091
U.S. District Court, Northern District, New York, 2013

Facts: Legends are Forever, Inc. (Legends) trademarked the slogan "Legends are Forever." When Nike used the slogan in an ad campaign featuring basketball player Kobe Bryant, Legends sued Nike.

But, during discovery, Legends repeatedly failed to comply with Nike's reasonable requests. Ultimately, Nike was forced to file a motion to compel Legends to produce the requested documents and witnesses. So, Nike requested more than just discovery: It also asked the court for recovery of all of the costs and fees it incurred in litigating the motion to compel, totaling $25,186.91. This sum included Nike's attorney's fees (ranging from $250 to $450 per hour) and all the travel expenses incurred by the two Nike attorneys who attended the hearing on the motion to compel.

The court agreed with Nike, granting it both discovery and its fees. Legends challenged the order, arguing that a small company should not have to pay for Nike's high-priced attorneys.

---

[5]Universal Service Fund Telephone Billing Practices Litigation, 232 F.R.D. 669 (D. Kan. 2005).
[6]Jewell v. Aaron's Inc., 2013 WL 3770837 (N.D. Ga. 2013).
[7]Kear v. Kohl's Department Stores, Inc., 2013 WL 3088922 (D. Kan. 2013).

Issue: *What is a reasonable penalty for unacceptable behavior during discovery?*

Excerpts from Magistrate Judge Peebles's Decision:

Discovery in this case has proceeded at an unacceptably slow pace, and Nike has experienced considerable difficulties in obtaining compliance by plaintiff with legitimate discovery demands. An award of costs and attorney's fees is warranted.

Now the task of the court shifts to determining the appropriate amount to award. Fee awards are awarded by determining a reasonable fee, reached by multiplying a reasonable hourly rate by the number of reasonably expended hours.

When establishing a reasonable rate, courts consider the time and labor required, the novelty of the questions, and the level of skill required to perform the legal service properly [among other factors]. Attorney's fees awarded as sanctions are not intended only as compensation of reimbursement for legal services, but also serve to deter abusive litigation practices and, as such, district courts have discretion in determining the amount of an attorney's fee awarded as sanctions. I conclude that the court should apply the following rates: $350 to $250 per hour.

I have reduced the number of hours upon which fees will be awarded for two reasons. First, it appears that several of the entries are excessive, given the description of the work performed. As one example, Nike chose to send two attorneys to the hearing, apparently as a result of a strategic decision. The motion, however, was relatively straightforward and not particularly complex. While Nike certainly retains the prerogative to send multiple attorneys to such a hearing, I decline to award costs and attorney's fees based upon that duplication of effort. Based upon the foregoing, I am awarding attorney's fees in the amount of $11,146.25,

In addition to attorney's fees, Nike has also sought recovery of costs representing travel expenses incurred for the hearing. It is appropriate to award the expense associated with [only one of Nike's attorneys] travel to the hearing, in the amount of $1,186.57.

Plaintiff Legends now complains that, as a small corporation, it would be economically disadvantaged by the award. Nike, however, despite its size and prominence, having been sued, is entitled to the same discovery as any other litigant. When discovery is sought but not provided, it is fair and appropriate to award costs and attorney's fees, notwithstanding the disparity in size of the two parties involved.

Nike, Inc., is hereby awarded the sum of $12,332.82, representing reasonable costs and attorney's fees associated with having to bring and argue the recent motion to compel discovery.

In the Enviro-Vision case, the judge rules that Coastal must furnish more complete answers to the interrogatories, especially as to why the company denied the claim. However, he rules against Interrogatory No. 18, the one concerning other claims Coastal has denied. This simple ruling kills Janet's hope of making a class action of the case. He orders Beth to appear for the deposition. As to future depositions, Coastal may take any 10 but then may take additional depositions only by demonstrating to the court that the deponents have useful information.

Rich proceeds to take Beth's deposition. It takes two full days. He asks about Enviro-Vision's past and present. He learns that Tony appeared to have won their biggest contract ever from Rapid City, Oregon, but that he then lost it when he had a fight with Rapid City's mayor. He inquires into Tony's mood, learns that he was depressed, and probes in every direction he can to find evidence of suicidal motivation. Janet and Rich argue frequently over questions and whether Beth should have to answer them. At times, Janet is persuaded and permits Beth to answer; other times, she instructs Beth not to answer. For example, toward the end of the second day, Rich asks Beth whether she and Tony had been sexually involved. Janet instructs Beth not to answer. This fight necessitates another trip into court to determine whether Beth must answer. The judge rules that Beth must discuss Tony's romantic life only if Coastal has some evidence that he was involved with someone outside his marriage. The company lacks any such evidence.

Now limited to 10 depositions, Rich selects his nine other deponents carefully. For example, he decides to depose only one of the two nurses; he chooses to question Jerry Johnson, the tennis partner, but not Craig Bergson, the former roommate; and so forth. When we look at the many legal issues this case raises, his choices seem minor. In fact,

PEREDA V. PARAJON

957 So.2d 1194
Florida Court of Appeals, 2007

Facts: Maria Parajon sued Diana Pereda for injuring her in a car accident. During voir dire, Parajon's lawyer asked the panel of prospective jurors these questions: "Is there anybody sitting on this panel now that has ever been under the care of a physician for personal injuries, whether you had a lawsuit or not? In other words, you may not have had any sort of lawsuit, but you slipped and fell—you had any accidents?"

Several of the prospective jurors raised their hands, allowing the lawyers to question more deeply into possible bias. However, Lisa Berg, a prospective juror who happened to be a lawyer, did not respond. Berg and others were seated as jurors, and ultimately awarded Parajon $450,000 for medical damages and pain and suffering.

After the trial, questioned in court by the judge, Berg admitted that three years earlier she had been injured in a car accident, hired a lawyer to sue, and settled out of court for $4,000. Asked about the settlement, Berg replied, "I think everyone always wants more money."

Parajon moved for a new trial but the judge denied the motion. Parajon appealed.

Issue: *Is Parajon entitled to a new trial based on Berg's failure to disclose her own personal injury lawsuit?*

Excerpts from Judge Rothenberg's Decision: To determine whether a juror's nondisclosure warrants a new trial, the complaining party must show that (1) the information is relevant and material to jury service in the case; (2) the juror concealed the information during questioning; and (3) the failure to disclose the information was not attributable to the complaining party's lack of diligence.

Both Parajon's and Pereda's respective counsels may indeed have been influenced to challenge Berg peremptorily had the facts of her personal injury litigation history been known. Berg's personal injury claim was not remote in time. Berg settled out of court at the urging of her parents in order to put the matter behind her. Her involvement in this matter may have affected her point of view in [this case]. Her nondisclosure, which precluded counsel's ability to question Berg about the experience and to fairly evaluate her as a prospective juror, was material.

It is clear from the record that Berg concealed her personal injury litigation history. She is a lawyer and an officer of the court. It is, therefore, difficult to imagine that she did not think the questions posed by Parajon's counsel applied to her.

The record evidence demonstrates that other prospective jurors, none of whom were lawyers, clearly understood what type of information Parajon's counsel was asking them to disclose. We find that Parajon's counsel made a diligent inquiry.

Reversed and remanded for a new trial.

6-4d Opening Statements

The next day, each attorney makes an opening statement to the jury, summarizing the proof he or she expects to offer, with the plaintiff going first. Janet focuses on Tony's successful life, his business and strong marriage, and the tragedy of his accidental death. [9]

Rich works hard to establish a friendly rapport with the jury. If members of the jury like him, they will tend to pay more attention to his presentation of evidence. He expresses regret about the death. Nonetheless, suicide is a clear exclusion from the policy. If insurance companies are forced to pay claims never bargained for, everyone's insurance rates will go up.

---

[9]Janet Booker has dropped her claim for triple damages against Coastal. To have any hope of such a verdict, she would have to show that Coastal had no legitimate reason at all for denying the claim. Discovery has convinced her that Coastal will demonstrate some rational reasons for what it did.

6-4e **Burden of Proof**

In civil cases, the plaintiff has the burden of proof. That means that the plaintiff must convince the jury that its version of the case is correct; the defendant is not obligated to disprove the allegations.

The plaintiff's burden in a civil lawsuit is to prove its case by a **preponderance of the evidence**. It must convince the jury that its version of the facts is at least *slightly more likely* than the defendant's version. Some courts describe this as a "51–49" persuasion; that is, that plaintiff's proof must "just tip" credibility in its favor. By contrast, in a criminal case, the prosecution must demonstrate **beyond a reasonable doubt** that the defendant is guilty. The burden of proof in a criminal case is much tougher because the likely consequences are, too. See Exhibit 6.3.

Preponderance of the evidence
The plaintiff's burden of proof in a civil lawsuit

Beyond a reasonable doubt
The government's burden of proof in a criminal prosecution

6-4f **Plaintiff's Case**

Because the plaintiff has the burden of proof, Janet puts in her case first. She wants to prove two things. First, that Tony died. That is easy because the death certificate clearly demonstrates it and Coastal does not seriously contest it. Second, in order to win double indemnity damages, she must show that the death was accidental. She will do this with the testimony of the witnesses she calls, one after the other. Her first witness is Beth. When a lawyer asks questions of her own witness, it is **direct examination**. Janet brings out all the evidence she wants the jury to hear: that the business was basically sound, though temporarily troubled, that Tony was a hard worker, why the company took out life insurance policies, and so forth.

Then Rich has a chance to **cross-examine** Beth, which means to ask questions of an opposing witness. He will try to create doubt in the jury's mind. He asks Beth only questions for which he is certain of the answers, based on discovery. Rich gets Beth to admit that the firm was not doing well the year of Tony's death; that Tony had lost the best client the firm ever had; that Beth had reduced salaries; and that Tony had been depressed about business.

Cross-examine
To ask questions of an opposing witness

6-4g **Rules of Evidence**

The lawyers are not free simply to ask any question they want. The **law of evidence** determines what questions a lawyer may ask and how the questions are to be phrased, what answers a witness may give, and what documents may be introduced. The goal is to

| EXHIBIT 6.3 | *Burden of Proof.* In a civil lawsuit, a plaintiff wins with a mere preponderance of the evidence. But the prosecution must persuade a jury beyond a reasonable doubt in order to win a criminal conviction. |

get the best evidence possible before the jurors so they can decide what really happened. In general, witnesses may only testify about things they saw or heard.

These rules are complex, and a thorough look at them is beyond the scope of this chapter. However, they can be just as important in resolving a dispute as the underlying substantive law. Suppose that a plaintiff's case depends upon the jury hearing about a certain conversation, but the rules of evidence prevent the lawyer from asking about it. That conversation might just as well never have occurred.

Janet calls an expert witness, a marine geologist, who testifies about the tides and currents in the area where Tony's body was found. The expert testifies that even experienced swimmers can be overwhelmed by a sudden shift in currents.

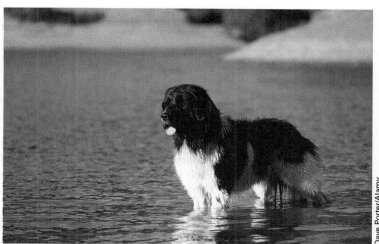

Dave Porter/Alamy

Rich objects strenuously that this is irrelevant, because there is no testimony that there *was* such a current at the time of Tony's death. The judge permits the testimony.

Karen Caruso testifies that Tony was in "reasonably good" spirits the day of his death, and that he often took Blue for walks along the beach. Karen testifies that Blue was part Newfoundland. Rich objects that testimony about Blue's pedigree is irrelevant, but Janet insists it will show why Blue was tied up. The judge allows the testimony. Karen says that whenever Blue saw them swim, he would instinctively go into the water and pull them to shore. Does that explain why Blue was tied up? Only the jury can answer.

Cross-examination is grim for Karen. Rich slowly but methodically questions her about Tony's state of mind and brings out the problems with the company, his depression, and tension within the marriage. Janet's other witnesses testify essentially as they did during their depositions.

6-4h Motion for Directed Verdict

At the close of the plaintiff's case, Rich moves for a directed verdict; that is, a ruling that the plaintiff has entirely failed to prove some aspect of her case. Rich is seeking to win without even putting in his own case. He argues that it was Beth's burden to prove that Tony died accidentally and that she has entirely failed to do that.

A directed verdict is permissible only if the evidence so clearly favors the defendant that reasonable minds could not disagree on it. If reasonable minds could disagree, the motion must be denied. Here, Judge Rowland rules that the plaintiff has put in enough evidence of accidental death that a reasonable person could find in Beth's favor. The motion is denied.

Directed verdict
A ruling that the plaintiff has entirely failed to prove some aspect of her case

There is no downside for Rich to ask for a directed verdict. The trial continues as if he had never made such a motion.

6-4i Defendant's Case

Rich now puts in his case, exactly as Janet did, except that he happens to have fewer witnesses. He calls the examining doctor, who admits that Tony could have committed suicide by swimming out too far. On cross-examination, Janet gets the doctor to acknowledge that he has no idea whether Tony intentionally drowned. Rich also questions several neighbors as to how depressed Tony had seemed and how unusual it was that Blue was tied up. Some of the witnesses Rich deposed, such as the tennis partner Jerry Johnson, have nothing that will help Coastal's case, so he does not call them.

Craig Bergson, sitting in the back of the courtroom, thinks how different the trial would have been had he been called as a witness. When he and Tony had the fateful drink, Tony had been distraught: Business was terrible, he was involved in an extramarital affair that he could not end, and he saw no way out of his problems. He had no one to talk to and had been hugely relieved to speak with Craig. Several times Tony had said, "I just can't go on like this. I don't want to, anymore." Craig thought Tony seemed suicidal and urged him to see a therapist Craig knew and trusted. Tony had said that it was good advice, but Craig is unsure whether Tony sought any help.

This evidence would have affected the case. Had Rich Stewart known of the conversation, he would have deposed Craig and the therapist. Coastal's case would have been far stronger, perhaps overwhelming. But Craig's evidence will never be heard. Facts are critical. Rich's decision to depose other witnesses and omit Craig may influence the verdict more than any rule of law.

6-4j Closing Arguments

Both lawyers sum up their case to the jury, explaining how they hope the jury will interpret what they have heard. Janet summarizes the plaintiff's version of the facts, claiming that Blue was tied up so that Tony could swim without worrying about him. Rich claims that business and personal pressures had overwhelmed Tony. He tied up his dog, neatly folded his clothes, and took his own life.

6-4k Jury Instructions

Judge Rowland instructs the jury as to its duty. He tells them that they are to evaluate the case based only on the evidence they heard at trial, relying on their own experience and common sense.

He explains the law and the burden of proof, telling the jury that it is Beth's obligation to prove that Tony died. If Beth has proven that Tony died, she is entitled to $1 million; if she has proven that his death was accidental, she is entitled to $2 million. However, if Coastal has proven suicide, Beth receives nothing. Finally, he states that if they are unable to decide between accidental death and suicide, there is a legal presumption that it was accidental. Rich asks Judge Rowland to rephrase the "legal presumption" part, but the judge declines.

6-4l Verdict

The jury deliberates informally, with all jurors entitled to voice their opinion. Some deliberations take two hours; some take two weeks. Many states require a unanimous verdict; others require only, for example, a 10–2 vote in civil cases.

This case presents a close call. No one saw Tony die. Yet even though they cannot know with certainty, the jury's decision will probably be the final word on whether he took his own life. After a day and a half of deliberating, the jury notifies the judge that it has reached a verdict. Rich Stewart quickly makes a new offer: $350,000. (The two sides have the right to settle a case until the moment when the last appeal is decided.) Beth hesitates but turns it down.

The judge summons the lawyers to court, and Beth goes as well. The judge asks the foreman if the jury has reached a decision. He states that it has: The jury finds that Tony Caruso drowned accidentally, and awards Beth Smiles $2 million.

6-4m Motions after the Verdict

Judgment *non obstante veredicto*

A judgment notwithstanding the jury's verdict

Rich immediately moves for a **judgment *non obstante veredicto*** (JNOV), meaning a judgment notwithstanding the jury's verdict. He is asking the judge to overturn the jury's verdict. Rich argues that the jury's decision went against all of the evidence. He also claims that the judge's instructions were wrong and misled the jury.

Judge Rowland denies the JNOV. Rich immediately moves for a new trial, making the same claim, and the judge denies the motion. Beth is elated that the case is finally over—until Janet says she expects an appeal. Craig Bergson, leaving the courtroom, wonders if he did the right thing. He felt sympathy for Beth and none for Coastal. Yet now he is neither happy nor proud.

6-5 APPEALS

Two days later, Rich files an appeal to the court of appeals. The same day, he phones Janet and increases his settlement offer to $425,000. Beth is tempted but wants Janet's advice. Janet says the risks of an appeal are that the court will order a new trial, and they would start all over. But to accept this offer is to forfeit over $1.5 million. Beth is unsure what to do. The firm desperately needs cash now, and appeals may take years. Janet suggests they wait until oral argument, another eight months.

Rich files a brief arguing that there were two basic errors at the trial: first, that the jury's verdict is clearly contrary to the evidence; and second, that the judge gave the wrong instructions to the jury. Janet files a reply brief, opposing Rich on both issues. In her brief, Janet cites many cases that she claims are **precedent**: earlier decisions by the state appellate courts on similar or identical issues

Eight months later, the lawyers representing Coastal and Enviro-Vision appear in the court of appeals to argue their case. Rich, the appellant, goes first. The judges frequently interrupt his argument with questions. They show little sympathy for his claim that the verdict was against the facts. They seem more sympathetic with his second point, that the instructions were wrong.

When Janet argues, all of their questions concern the judge's instructions. It appears they believe the instructions were in error. The judges take the case under advisement, meaning they will decide some time in the future—maybe in two weeks, maybe in five months.

6-5a Appeals Court Options

The court of appeals can **affirm** the trial court, allowing the decision to stand. The court may **modify** the decision, for example, by affirming that the plaintiff wins but decreasing the size of the award. (That is unlikely here; Beth is entitled to $2 million or nothing.) The court might **reverse and remand**, nullifying the lower court's decision and returning the case to the lower court for a new trial. Or it could simply **reverse**, turning the loser (Coastal) into the winner, with no new trial.

What will it do here? On the factual issue, it will probably rule in Beth's favor. There *was* evidence from which a jury could conclude that Tony died accidentally. It is true that there was also considerable evidence to support Coastal's position, but that is probably not enough to overturn the verdict. If reasonable people could disagree on what the evidence proves, an appellate court generally refuses to change the jury's factual findings. The court of appeals is likely to rule that a reasonable jury *could* have found accidental death, even if the appellate judges personally suspect that Tony may have killed himself.

The judge's instructions raise a more difficult problem. Some states would require a more complex statement about "presumptions."[10]

Precedent
Earlier decisions by the state appellate courts on similar or identical issues

Affirm
To allow the decision to stand

Modify
To affirm the outcome but with changes

Reverse and remand
To nullify the lower decision and return the case for reconsideration or retrial

---

[10]Judge Rowland probably should have said, "The law presumes that death is accidental, not suicide. So if there were no evidence either way, the plaintiff would win because we presume accident. But if there is competing evidence, the presumption becomes irrelevant. If you think that Coastal Insurance has introduced some evidence of suicide, then forget the legal presumption. You must then decide what happened based on what you have seen and heard in court, and on any inferences you choose to draw." Note that the judge's instructions were different, though similar.

harmless error

A mistake by the trial judge that was too minor to affect the outcome.

What does a court of appeals do if it decides the trial court's instructions were wrong? If it believes the error rendered the trial and verdict unfair, it will remand the case; that is, send it back to the lower court for a new trial. However, the court may conclude that the mistake was **harmless error**. A trial judge cannot do a perfect job, and not every error is fatal. The court may decide the verdict was fair in spite of the mistake.

Janet and Beth talk. Beth is very anxious and wants to settle. She does not want to wait four or five months, only to learn that they must start all over. Janet urges that they wait a few weeks to hear from Rich: They don't want to seem too eager.

A week later, Rich telephones and offers $500,000. Janet turns it down, but says she will ask Beth if she wants to make a counteroffer. She and Beth talk. They agree that they will settle for $1 million. Janet then calls Rich and offers to settle for $1.7 million. Rich and Janet debate the merits of the case. Rich later calls back and offers $750,000, saying he doubts that he can go any higher. Janet counters with $1.4 million, saying she doubts she can go any lower. They argue, both predicting that they will win on appeal.

Rich calls, offers $900,000, and says, "That's it. No more." Janet argues for $1.2 million, expecting to nudge Rich up to $1 million. He doesn't nudge, instead saying, "Take it or leave it." Janet and Beth talk it over. Janet telephones Rich and accepts $900,000 to settle the case.

If they had waited for the court of appeals decision, would Beth have won? It is impossible to know. It is certain, though, that whoever lost would have appealed. Months would have passed waiting to learn if the state supreme court would accept the case. If that court had agreed to hear the appeal, Beth would have endured another year of waiting, brief writing, oral argument, and tense hoping. The high court has all of the options discussed: to affirm, modify, reverse and remand, or simply reverse.

6-6 ALTERNATIVE DISPUTE RESOLUTION

As we have seen in the previous section, trials can be trying. Lawsuits can cause prolonged periods of stress, significant legal bills, and general unpleasantness. Many people and companies prefer to settle cases out of court. Alternative dispute resolution (ADR) provides several semiformal methods of resolving conflicts. We will look at different types of ADR and analyze their strengths and weaknesses.

6-6a Negotiation

In most cases, the parties negotiate, whether personally or through lawyers. Fortunately, the great majority of disputes are resolved this way. Negotiation often begins as soon as a dispute arises and may last a few days or several years.

6-6b Mediation

Mediation is the fastest-growing method of dispute resolution in the United States. Here, a neutral person, called a *mediator*, attempts to guide the two disputing parties toward a voluntary settlement. (In some cases, there may be two or more mediators, but we will use the singular.) Generally, the two disputants voluntarily enter mediation, although some judges order the parties to try this form of ADR before allowing a case to go to trial.

A mediator does not render a decision in the dispute, but uses a variety of skills to move the parties toward agreement. Often a mediator will shuttle between the antagonists, hearing their arguments, sorting out the serious issues from the less important, prompting the parties and lawyers alike to consider new perspectives, and looking for areas of agreement. Mediators must earn the trust of both parties, listen closely, try to diffuse anger and fear, and build the will to settle. Good mediators do not need a law degree, but they must have a sense of humor and low blood pressure.

Mediation has several major advantages. Because the parties maintain control of the process, the two antagonists can speak freely. They need not fear conceding too much, because no settlement takes effect until both parties sign. All discussions are confidential, further encouraging candid talk. This is particularly helpful in cases involving proprietary information that might be revealed during a trial.

Of all forms of dispute resolution, mediation probably offers the strongest "win–win" potential. Because the goal is voluntary settlement, neither party needs to fear that it will end up the loser. This is in sharp contrast to litigation, where one party will lose. Removing the fear of defeat often encourages thinking and talking that are more open and realistic than negotiations held in the midst of a lawsuit. Studies show that more than 75 percent of mediated cases do reach a voluntary settlement. Such an agreement is particularly valuable to parties that wish to preserve a long-term relationship. Consider two companies that have done business successfully for 10 years but now are in the midst of a million-dollar trade dispute. A lawsuit could last three or more years and destroy any chance of future trade. However, if the parties mediate the disagreement, they might reach an amicable settlement within a month or two and could quickly resume their mutually profitable business.

6-6c Arbitration

In this form of ADR, the parties agree to bring in a neutral third party, but with a major difference: The arbitrator has the power to impose an award. The arbitrator allows each side equal time to present its case and, after deliberation, issues a binding decision, generally without giving reasons. Unlike mediation, arbitration ensures that there will be a final result, although the parties lose control of the outcome.

Judge Judy and similar TV court shows are examples of arbitration. Before the shows are taped, people involved in a real dispute sign a contract in which they give up the right to go to court over the incident and agree to be bound by the judge's decision.

Parties in arbitration give up many additional rights that litigants retain, including discovery and class action. In arbitration, as already discussed as applied to trials, *discovery* allows the two sides in a lawsuit to obtain documentary and other evidence from the opponent before the dispute is decided. Arbitration permits both sides to keep secret many files that would have to be divulged in a court case, potentially depriving the opposing side of valuable evidence. A party may have a stronger case than it realizes, and the absence of discovery may permanently deny it that knowledge. As discussed earlier in this chapter, a *class action* is a suit in which one injured party represents a large group of people who have suffered similar harm. Arbitration eliminates this possibility because injured employees face the employer one at a time. Finally, the fact that an arbitrator may not provide a written, public decision bars other plaintiffs, and society generally, from learning what happened.

Traditionally, parties sign arbitration agreements *after* some incident took place. A car accident would happen first, and the drivers would agree to arbitration second. But today, many parties agree *in advance* to arbitrate any disputes that may arise in the future. For example, a new employee may sign an agreement requiring arbitration of any future disputes with his employer; a customer opening an account with a stockbroker or bank— or health plan—may sign a similar form, often without realizing it. The good news is fewer lawsuits; the bad news is you might be the person kept out of court.

Assume that you live in Miami. Using the Internet, you order a $2,000 ThinkLite laptop computer, which arrives in a carton loaded with six fat instructional manuals and many small leaflets. You read some of the documents and ignore others. For four weeks, you struggle to make your computer work, to no avail. Finally, you call ThinkLite and demand a refund, but the company refuses. You file suit in your local court, at which time the company points out that buried among the hundreds of pages it mailed you was a *mandatory arbitration form*. This document prohibits you from filing suit against the company and states that if you have any complaint with the company, you must fly to Chicago, pay a $2,000 arbitrator's fee, plead your case before an arbitrator selected by the Laptop Trade Association of America, and, should you lose, pay ThinkLite's attorneys' fees, which could be several thousand dollars. Is that mandatory arbitration provision valid? The majority of the courts that have faced such clauses have enforced them.[11]

Chapter Conclusion

No one will ever know for sure whether Tony Caruso took his own life. Craig Bergson's evidence might have tipped the scales in favor of Coastal. But even that is uncertain, since the jury could have found him unpersuasive. After two years, the case ends with a settlement and uncertainty—both typical lawsuit results. The missing witness is less common but not extraordinary. The vaguely unsatisfying feeling about it all is only too common and indicates why most parties settle out of court.

EXAM REVIEW

1. **COURT SYSTEMS** There are many *systems* of courts, one federal and one in each state. A federal court will hear a case only if it involves a federal question or diversity jurisdiction.

2. **TRIAL AND APPELLATE COURTS** Trial courts determine facts and apply the law to the facts; appeals courts generally accept the facts found by the trial court and review the trial record for errors of law.

EXAM Strategy

Question: Jade sued Kim, claiming that Kim promised to hire her as an in-store model for $1,000 per week for eight weeks. Kim denied making the promise, and the jury was persuaded: Kim won. Jade has appealed, and now she offers Steve as a witness. Steve will testify to the appeals court that he saw Kim hire Jade as a model, exactly as Jade claimed. Will Jade win on appeal?

Strategy: Before you answer, make sure you know the difference between trial and appellate courts. What is the difference? Apply that distinction here. (See the "Result" at the end of this section.)

---

3. **PLEADINGS** A complaint and an answer are the two most important pleadings; that is, documents that start a lawsuit.

---

[11]See, e.g., Hill v. Gateway 2000, 105 F.3d 1147 (7th Cir. 1997), upholding a similar clause.

4. DISCOVERY Discovery is the critical pre-trial opportunity for both parties to learn the strengths and weaknesses of the opponent's case. Important forms of discovery include interrogatories, depositions, production of documents and objects, physical and mental examinations, and requests for admission.

5. MOTIONS A motion is a formal request to the court.

6. SUMMARY JUDGMENT Summary judgment is a ruling by the court that no trial is necessary because there are no essential facts in dispute.

7. JURY TRIALS Generally, both plaintiff and defendant may demand a jury in any lawsuit for money damages.

8. VOIR DIRE Voir dire is the process of selecting jurors in order to obtain an impartial panel.

EXAM Strategy

Question: You are a lawyer, representing the plaintiff in a case of alleged employment discrimination. The court is selecting a jury. Based on questions you have asked, you believe that juror number 3 is biased against your client. You explain this to the judge, but she disagrees. Is there anything you can do?

Strategy: The question focuses on your rights during voir dire. If you believe that a juror will not be fair, you may make two different types of challenge. What are they? (See the "Result" at the end of this section.)

9. BURDEN OF PROOF The plaintiff's burden of proof in a civil lawsuit is preponderance of the evidence, meaning that its version of the facts must be at least slightly more persuasive than the defendant's. In a criminal prosecution, the government must offer proof beyond a reasonable doubt in order to win a conviction.

10. RULES OF EVIDENCE The rules of evidence determine what questions may be asked during trial, what testimony may be given, and what documents may be introduced.

11. VERDICTS The verdict is the jury's decision in a case. The losing party may ask the trial judge to overturn the verdict, seeking a JNOV or a new trial. Judges seldom grant either.

12. APPEALS An appeals court has many options. The court may affirm, upholding the lower court's decision; modify, changing the verdict but leaving the same party victorious; reverse, transforming the loser into the winner; and/or remand, sending the case back to the lower court.

13. ADR Alternative dispute resolution is any formal or informal process to settle disputes without a trial. Mediation, arbitration, and other forms of ADR have grown in popularity.

> **2. Result:** Trial courts use witnesses to help resolve fact disputes. Appellate courts review the record to see if there have been errors of law. Appellate courts never hear witnesses, and they will not hear Steve. Jade will lose her appeal.
>
> **8. Result:** You have already made a *challenge for cause*, claiming bias, but the judge has rejected your challenge. If you have not used up all of your *peremptory challenges*, you may use one to excuse this juror, without giving any reason.

MULTIPLE-CHOICE QUESTIONS

1. The burden of proof in a civil trial is to prove a case _____ .
   The burden of proof rests with the _____ .
   (a) beyond a reasonable doubt; plaintiff
   (b) by a preponderance of the evidence; plaintiff
   (c) beyond a reasonable doubt; defendant
   (d) by a preponderance of the evidence; defendant

2. Alice is suing Betty. After the discovery process, Alice believes that no relevant facts are in dispute, and that there is no need for a trial. She should move for _____ .
   (a) a judgment on the pleadings
   (b) a directed verdict
   (c) a summary judgment
   (d) a JNOV

3. Glen lives in Illinois. He applies for a job with a Missouri company, and he is told, amazingly, that the job is open only to white applicants. He will now sue the Missouri company under the Civil Rights Act, a federal statute. Can Glen sue in federal court?
   (a) Yes, absolutely.
   (b) Yes, but only if he seeks damages of at least $75,000. Otherwise, he must sue in a state court.
   (c) Yes, but only if the Missouri company agrees. Otherwise, he must sue in a state court.
   (d) No, absolutely not. He must sue in a state court.

4. A default judgment can be entered if which of the following is true?
   (a) A plaintiff presents her evidence at trial and clearly fails to meet her burden of proof.
   (b) A defendant loses a lawsuit and does not pay a judgment within 180 days.
   (c) A defendant fails to file an answer to a plaintiff's complaint on time.
   (d) A citizen fails to obey an order to appear for jury duty.

5. Barry and Carl are next-door neighbors. Barry's dog digs under Carl's fence and does $500 worth of damage to Carl's garden. Barry refuses to pay for the damage, claiming that Carl's cats "have been digging up my yard for years."

   The two argue repeatedly, and the relationship turns frosty. Of the following choices, which has no outside decision maker and is most likely to allow the neighbors to peacefully coexist after working out the dispute?

   (a) Trial

   (b) Arbitration

   (c) Mediation

CASE QUESTIONS

1. You plan to open a store in Chicago, specializing in rugs imported from Turkey. You will work with a native Turk who will purchase and ship the rugs to your store. You are wise enough to insist on a contract establishing the rights and obligations of both parties and would prefer an ADR clause. But you do not want a clause that will alienate your overseas partner. What kind of ADR clause should you include, and why?

2. Which court(s) have jurisdiction over each of these lawsuits—state or federal? Explain your reasoning for each answer.

   • Pat wants to sue his next-door neighbor, Dorothy, claiming that Dorothy promised to sell him the house next door.

   • Paula, who lives in New York City, wants to sue Dizzy Movie Theatres, whose principal place of business is Dallas. She claims that while she was in Texas on holiday, she was injured by their negligent maintenance of a stairway. She claims damages of $30,000.

   • Phil lives in Tennessee. He wants to sue Dick, who lives in Ohio. Phil claims that Dick agreed to sell him 3,000 acres of farmland in Ohio, worth more than $2 million.

   • Pete, incarcerated in a federal prison in Kansas, wants to sue the United States government. He claims that his treatment by prison authorities violates three federal statutes.

3. British discovery practice differs from that in the United States. Most discovery in Britain concerns documents. The lawyers for the two sides, called *solicitors,* must deliver to the opposing side a list of all relevant documents in their possession. Each side may then request to look at and copy those it wishes. Depositions are rare. What advantages and disadvantages are there to the British practice?

4. Trial practice also is dramatically different in Britain. The parties' solicitors do not go into court. Courtroom work is done by different lawyers, called barristers. The barristers have very limited rights to interview witnesses before trial. They know the substance of what each witness intends to say but do not rehearse questions and answers, as in the United States. Which approach do you consider more effective? More ethical? What is the purpose of a trial? Of pre-trial preparation?

5. Claus Scherer worked for Rockwell International and was paid more than $300,000 per year. Rockwell fired Scherer for alleged sexual harassment of several workers, including his secretary, Terry Pendy. Scherer sued in United States District Court, alleging that Rockwell's real motive in firing him was his high salary.

   Rockwell moved for summary judgment, offering deposition transcripts of various employees. Pendy's deposition detailed instances of harassment, including comments about her body, instances of unwelcome touching, and discussions of extramarital affairs. Another deposition, from a Rockwell employee who investigated the allegations, included complaints by other employees as to Scherer's harassment. In his own deposition, which he offered to oppose summary judgment, Scherer testified that he could not recall the incidents alleged by Pendy and others. He denied generally that he had sexually harassed anyone. The district court granted summary judgment for Rockwell. Was its ruling correct?

DISCUSSION QUESTIONS

1. In the Tony Caruso case described throughout this chapter, the defendant offers to settle the case at several stages. Knowing what you do now about litigation, would you have accepted any of the offers? If so, which one(s)? If not, why not?

2. The burden of proof in civil cases is fairly low. A plaintiff wins a lawsuit if he is 51 percent convincing, and then he collects 100 percent of his damages. Is this result reasonable? Should a plaintiff in a civil case be required to prove his case beyond a reasonable doubt? Or, if a plaintiff is only 51 percent convincing, should he get only 51 percent of his damages?

3. Large numbers of employees have signed mandatory arbitration agreements in employment contracts. Courts usually uphold these clauses. Imagine that you signed a contract with an arbitration agreement, that the company later mistreated you, and that you could not sue in court. Would you be upset? Or would you be relieved to go through the faster and cheaper process of arbitration?

4. Imagine a state law that allows for residents to sue "spammers"—those who send uninvited commercial messages through email—for $30. One particularly prolific spammer sends messages to hundreds of thousands of people.

   John Smith, a lawyer, signs up 100,000 people to participate in a class-action lawsuit. According to the agreements with his many clients, Smith will keep one-third of any winnings. In the end, Smith wins a $3 million verdict and pockets $1 million. Each individual plaintiff receives a check for $20.

   Is this lawsuit a reasonable use of the court's resources? Why or why not?

5. Higher courts are reluctant to review a lower court's *factual* findings. Should this be so? Would appeals be fairer if appellate courts reviewed *everything*?

ANSWERS TO SELECTED END OF CHAPTER QUESTIONS

MULTIPLE-CHOICE QUESTIONS

Presented are the answers for the ODD-numbered multiple-choice questions in the end-of-chapter material.

1. B
3. A
5. C

CASE QUESTIONS

Presented are the answers for all of the ODD-numbered case questions in the end-of-chapter material.

1. **Answer:** Yes. Try blending ADR mechanisms. Have the ADR clause state that in the event of a dispute, the parties will negotiate it in good faith, and take no further steps for 30 days. If negotiation fails, an additional 30-day cooling-off period follows. The next step could be a mini-trial in front of three people, two of whom represent the parties, respectively, and the third who acts as a neutral mediator. Finally, if the mini-trial fails to produce a settlement, the parties will hire an arbitrator. You might require that the arbitrator be a national of neither Turkey nor the United States. You must specify the law to be applied and where the arbitration will take place. List any claims that are not arbitrable, such as antitrust or securities claims. This should preserve a working relationship while ensuring that disputes will be settled rapidly.

3. **Answer:** Discovery is more efficient in Britain, since the solicitors are honor-bound to notify the opposing side of relevant documents. The fighting over discovery motions that drains time and money in the United States is uncommon there. However, the absence of depositions means that the parties go into court with less information about the opponent's case, making trials more open to surprise.

5. **Answer:** Yes. The court of appeals affirmed. *Scherer v. Rockwell International Corp.*, 975 F.2d 356, 1992 U.S. App. LEXIS 22080 (7th Cir. 1992). "When questioned about the specific instances of sexual harassment, he did not deny that the incidents occurred, but instead stated that he could not recall. In other sections of his deposition, he stated that he generally denied having sexually harassed any coworker.... Scherer may not defeat Rockwell's properly supported summary judgment motion without offering any evidence from which a jury could determine that the alleged sexual harassment did not actually occur and by merely asserting that the jury might disbelieve Rockwell's witness because of Rockwell's motive and desire to get out of the contract."

Chapter 7

CRIME

© Creative Travel Projects/Shutterstock.com

Crime can take us by surprise. Stacey tucks her nine-year-old daughter, Beth, into bed. Promising her husband, Mark, that she will be home by 11:00 p.m., she jumps into her car and heads back to Be Patient, Inc. She connects her iPhone to the Bluetooth device in her $100,000 sedan and tries to relax by listening to music. Be Patient is a healthcare organization that owns five geriatric hospitals. Most of its patients use Medicare, and Stacey supervises all billing to their largest client, the federal government.

She parks in a well-lighted spot on the street and walks to her building, failing to notice two men, collars turned up, watching from a parked truck. Once in her office, she goes straight to her computer and works on billing issues. Tonight's work goes more quickly than she expected, thanks to new software she helped develop. At 10:30 p.m. she emerges from the building with a quick step and a light heart, walks to her car—and finds it missing.

A major crime has occurred during the 90 minutes Stacey was at her desk, but she will never report it to the police.

A major crime has occurred during the 90 minutes Stacey was at her desk, but she will never report it to the police. It is a crime that costs Americans countless dollars each year, yet Stacey will not even mention it to friends or family. Stacey is the criminal.

When we think of crime, we imagine the drug dealers and bank robbers endlessly portrayed on television. We do not picture corporate executives sitting at polished desks. "Street crimes" are indeed serious threats to our security and happiness. They deservedly receive the attention of the public and the law. But when measured only in dollars, street crime takes second place to white-collar crime, which costs society *tens of billions* of dollars annually.

The hypothetical about Stacey is based on many real cases and is used to illustrate that crime does not always dress the way we expect. Her car was never stolen; it was simply towed. Two parking lot employees, watching from their truck, saw Stacey park illegally, and did their job. It is Stacey who committed a crime—Medicare fraud. Every month, she has billed the government about $10 million for work that her company has not performed. Stacey's scheme was quick and profitable—and a distressingly common crime.

Crime, whether violent or white-collar, is detrimental to all society. It imposes a huge cost on everyone. Just the *fear* of crime is expensive—homeowners buy alarm systems and businesses hire security guards. But the anger and fear that crime engenders sometimes tempt us to forget that not all accused people are guilty. Everyone suspected of a crime should have the protections that you would want in that situation. As the English jurist William Blackstone said, "Better that ten guilty persons escape than that one innocent suffer."

Thus, criminal law is a balancing act—between making society safe and protecting us all from false accusations and unfair punishment.

This chapter has four parts:

- The differences between a civil and criminal case;
- **Criminal procedure**—the *process* by which criminals are investigated, accused, tried, and sentenced;
- Crimes that *harm* businesses;
- Crimes committed *by* businesses.

Criminal procedure
The process by which criminals are investigated, accused, tried, and sentenced

7-1 A CIVIL VERSUS A CRIMINAL CASE

Most of this book focuses on civil law, so we begin with a discussion of the differences between a civil and criminal case.

Civil law involves the rights and liabilities that exist between private parties. As we have seen, if one person claims that another has caused her a civil injury, she bears the burden of filing a lawsuit and convincing a court of her damages.

Criminal law is different. **Conduct is criminal when *society* outlaws it.** When a state legislature or Congress concludes that certain behavior threatens public safety and welfare, it passes a statute forbidding that behavior; in other words, declaring it criminal. Medicare fraud, which Stacey committed, is a crime because Congress has outlawed it. Murder, on the other hand, is generally a state crime, although some particular murders are both state and federal offenses. It is, for example, a violation of a federal statute to murder the president (at any time) or a federal egg inspector (while performing his duties).[1]

Criminal law
Prohibits and punishes conduct that threatens public safety and welfare

7-1a Prosecution

Suppose the police arrest Roger and accuse him of breaking into a store and stealing 50 computers. The owner of the store has been harmed, so he has the right to sue the thief in civil court to recover money damages. **But only the government can prosecute a crime and punish Roger by sending him to prison.** The local prosecutor has total discretion in deciding whether to bring Roger to trial on criminal charges.

---

[1] 18 U.S.C. §1751 and 21 U.S.C. §1041, respectively.

7-1b Burden of Proof

In a civil case, the plaintiff must prove her case only by a preponderance of the evidence.[2] But because the penalties for conviction in a criminal case are so serious, **the government must prove its case beyond a reasonable doubt.** Also, the stigma of a criminal conviction would stay with Roger forever, making it more difficult to obtain work and housing. Therefore, in all criminal cases, if the jury has any significant doubt that Roger stole the computers, it *must* acquit him.

7-1c Right to a Jury

A judge or jury decides the facts of a case. **A criminal defendant has a right to a trial by jury for any charge that could result in a sentence of six months or longer.** The defendant may choose not to have a jury trial, in which case, the judge decides the verdict. When the judge is the fact finder, the proceeding is called a **bench trial.**

7-1d Felonies and Misdemeanors

A **felony** is a serious crime, for which a defendant can be sentenced to one year or more in prison. Murder, robbery, rape, drug dealing, money laundering, wire fraud, and embezzlement are felonies. A **misdemeanor** is a less serious crime, often punishable by a year or less in a county jail. Public drunkenness, driving without a license, and shoplifting are considered misdemeanors in most states.

Prison time is not the only penalty for a crime. A court can also impose a fine, which the government keeps and does not share with the victim. It can order **restitution**, meaning that the defendant reimburses the victim for harm suffered. The government can also limit the rights of convicted criminals in a surprisingly broad manner. Some states limit the right of felons to vote or the right to apply for a license. For example, someone convicted of a minor drug crime may not be able to obtain a hairdresser's license in some states.[3]

Beyond a reasonable doubt
The very high burden of proof in a criminal trial, demanding much more certainty than required in a civil trial

Bench Trial
There is no jury; the judge reaches a verdict

Felony
A serious crime, for which a defendant can be sentenced to one year or more in prison

Misdemeanor
A less serious crime, often punishable by less than a year in a county jail

Restitution
A court order that a guilty defendant reimburse the victim for the harm suffered

7-2 CRIMINAL PROCEDURE

The title of a criminal case is usually the government versus someone: *The United States of America v. Simpson* or *The State of Illinois v. Simpson*, for example. This name illustrates a daunting thought—if you are Simpson, the vast power of the government is against you. Moreover, a criminal defendant is often engaged in an uphill climb from the beginning because people often assume that anyone accused of a crime must be guilty. Because of these factors, criminal procedure is designed to protect the accused and ensure that criminal trials are fair. Many of the protections for those accused of a crime are found in the first ten amendments to the United States Constitution, known as the Bill of Rights.

7-2a Conduct Outlawed

Crimes are created by statute. To win a conviction, the prosecution must demonstrate to the court that a statute has outlawed the defendant's conduct. The Fifth and Fourteenth Amendments to the Constitution require **that the language of criminal statutes be clear and definite** enough that (1) ordinary people can understand what conduct is prohibited and (2) enforcement cannot be arbitrary and discriminatory. Returning to Roger, the alleged computer thief, the state charged that he stole computer equipment from a store, a crime clearly defined by statute as larceny. On the other hand, the Supreme Court ruled that a

---

[2]See the earlier discussion in Chapter 3, on dispute resolution.
[3]To learn more about the consequence of committing a crime, google "aba collateral consequences."

statute prohibiting the crime of loitering was unconstitutionally vague because it did not clarify exactly what behavior was prohibited and it tended to be enforced arbitrarily.[4]

The Supreme Court recently took on this issue again but, this time, the case did not involve a vagrant wandering the streets but, rather, a high-level corporate executive. Federal prosecutors had charged Jeffrey Skilling with "theft of honest services."[5] You might ask yourself: What does that mean? The fact that you have to ask is one indication that the law may be too vague.

SKILLING V. UNITED STATES

561 U.S. 358, 130 S. Ct. 2896
United States Supreme Court, 2010

Facts: Jeffrey Skilling was president and chief operating officer of Enron Corporation, the seventh-largest company in America in terms of revenue. At least, that is what everyone thought. Ten months into Skilling's term of office, Enron filed for bankruptcy protection. Its stock, which had been trading at $90 per share, became virtually worthless. A government investigation discovered that company executives had conducted an elaborate conspiracy to prop up Enron's stock price by overstating the company's finances.

Skilling was charged with the theft of honest services. Traditionally, this federal statute had been used to prosecute public officials who took bribes or kickbacks. But then prosecutors began to charge employees under this statute for having generally breached their duty to their employer—and that is what they decided to do with Skilling. They alleged that his financial shenanigans constituted a theft of honest services. He was convicted, sentenced to more than 24 years in prison, and ordered to pay $45 million in restitution. Skilling appealed, arguing that the honest services statute was unconstitutionally vague. The Fifth Circuit disagreed and affirmed his conviction. The Supreme Court granted *certiorari*.

Issue: *Was the honest services statute unconstitutionally vague?*

Excerpts from Justice Ginsburg's Decision: To satisfy due process, a penal statute must define the criminal offense [1] with sufficient definiteness that ordinary people can understand what conduct is prohibited and [2] in a manner that does not encourage arbitrary and discriminatory enforcement. According to Skilling, [the honest services statute] meets neither of the two due process essentials. First, the phrase "the right of honest services," he contends, does not adequately define what behavior it bars. Second, he alleges, [the honest services statute's] standardless sweep allows policemen, prosecutors, and juries to pursue their personal predilections, thereby facilitating opportunistic and arbitrary prosecutions.

In the main, prosecutions under this statute involved fraudulent schemes to deprive another of honest services through bribes or kickbacks. Confined to these paramount applications, [the honest services statute] presents no vagueness problem. The Government urges us to go further by locating within [this statute's] compass another category of proscribed conduct: "undisclosed self-dealing by a public official or private employee"—i.e., the taking of official action by the employee that furthers his own undisclosed financial interests while purporting to act in the interests of those to whom he owes a fiduciary duty.

Reading the statute to proscribe a wider range of offensive conduct, we acknowledge, would raise the due process concerns underlying the vagueness doctrine. To preserve the statute without transgressing constitutional limitations, we now hold that [the honest services statute] criminalizes only the bribe-and-kickback core.

The Government did not, at any time, allege that Skilling solicited or accepted side payments from a third party in exchange for making these misrepresentations. It is, therefore, clear that Skilling did not commit honest-services fraud.[6]

---

[4]Kolender v. Lawson, 461 U.S. 352 (S. Ct. 1983).

[5]18 U.S.C. § 1346.

[6]Skilling had originally been convicted of three crimes: honest services fraud, wire fraud, and securities fraud. When the Supreme Court cleared him of charges under the honest services statute, it remanded the case to the appeals court to determine if the other two convictions were independent enough to stand on their own. If not, he would have had to be retried. Ultimately, Skilling reached a settlement with the government under which he forfeited $42 million to pay back Enron victims and was resentenced to 14 years in prison (a reduction from the original 24). He could be released as early as 2017.

Although Skilling was not a sympathetic defendant—his misdeeds had cost thousands of people billions of dollars—commentators feared that if the Court upheld the government's broad interpretation of the honest services statute, it could even be used to prosecute a parent who called in sick to attend his child's school play.

Although we sometimes think that the criminal law protections in the Constitution serve only to help the down-and-outs of society, this case demonstrates that these protections are important to all of us, no matter where we reside on the income scale.

7-2b State of Mind

Voluntary Act

A defendant is not guilty of a crime if she was forced to commit it. In other words, she is not guilty if she acted under duress. However, the defendant bears the burden of proving by *a preponderance of the evidence* that she did act under duress. In 1974, a terrorist group kidnapped heiress Patricia Hearst from her apartment near the University of California at Berkeley. After being tortured for two months, she participated in a bank robbery with the group. Despite opportunities to escape, she stayed with the criminals until her capture by the police a year later. The State of California put on her on trial for bank robbery. One question for the jury was whether she had voluntarily participated in the crime. This was an issue on which many people had strong opinions. Ultimately, Hearst was convicted, sent to prison, and then later pardoned.

Guilty

A judge or jury's finding that a defendant has committed a crime

Patty Hearst, before she was kidnapped.

Entrapment

When the government induces the defendant to break the law, the prosecution must prove beyond a reasonable doubt that the defendant was predisposed to commit the crime. The goal is to separate the cases where the defendant was innocent before the government tempted him from those where the defendant was only too eager to break the law.

Kalchinian and Sherman met in the waiting room of a doctor's office where they were both being treated for drug addiction. After several more meetings, Kalchinian told Sherman that the treatment was not working for him and he was desperate to buy drugs. Could Sherman help him? Sherman repeatedly refused, but ultimately agreed to help end Kalchinian's suffering by providing him with drugs. Little did Sherman know that Kalchinian was a police informant. Sherman sold drugs to Kalchinian a number of times. Kalchinian rewarded this act of friendship by getting Sherman hooked again and then turning him in to the police. A jury convicted Sherman of drug dealing, but the Supreme Court overturned the conviction on the grounds that Sherman had been entrapped.[7] The court felt there was no evidence that Sherman was predisposed to commit the crime.

Conspiracy

Jeen and Sunny Han were 22-year-old identical twin sisters. But their relationship was far from sunny; they hated each other. The sisters had a long history of physical and verbal fights. Jeen had even threatened to kill Sunny. One day, Jeen and two teenage boys purchased gloves, twine, tape, Pine Sol, and garbage bags. While Jeen waited outside

---

[7]Sherman v. United States, 356 U.S. 369 (S. Ct. 1958).

Sunny's apartment, the boys forced their way in, tied up Sunny and her roommate, and put them in the bathtub. Luckily, Sunny had had a chance to dial 911 as she heard the boys breaking in. When the police arrived, the two boys fled. This case raises several questions: Has Jeen committed a crime? Are the boys guilty of anything more than breaking into Sunny's apartment? How did this family go so terribly wrong? (Because this is a business law text, we can only answer the first two questions.)

If the police discover a plot to commit a crime, they can arrest the defendants before any harm has been done. And if bad guys try to commit a crime, but fail, the police can arrest them without giving them a chance to try again. It is illegal to *conspire* to commit a crime, even if that crime never actually occurs. **A defendant can be convicted of taking part in a conspiracy if:**

- a conspiracy existed,

- the defendants knew about it, and

- some member of the conspiracy voluntarily took a step toward implementing it.

In the Han case, the jury convicted Jeen and the two boys of a conspiracy to murder her sister. As the court asked: What was she planning to do with the Pine Sol and plastic bags, given that she did not have a home?[8] She was sentenced to 26 years to life in prison. The two boys got lesser (but still substantial) sentences because the judge believed Jeen had masterminded the crime.

7-2c Gathering Evidence: The Fourth Amendment

If the police suspect that a crime has been committed, they will need to obtain evidence. **The Fourth Amendment to the Constitution prohibits the government from making illegal searches and seizures of individuals, corporations, partnerships, and other organizations.** The goal of the Fourth Amendment is to protect individuals and businesses from the powerful state.

Warrant

Warrant
Written permission from a neutral officer to conduct a search

Probable cause
It is likely that evidence of crime will be found in the place to be searched.

As a general rule, the police must obtain a warrant before conducting a search. A **warrant** is written permission from a neutral official, such as a judge or magistrate, to conduct a search.[9] The magistrate will issue a warrant only if there is probable cause. **Probable cause** means that, based on all the information presented, **it is likely that evidence of a crime will be found in the place to be searched.** Often, the police base their applications for a warrant on data provided by an informant. The magistrate will want evidence to support the informant's reliability. If it turns out that this informant has been wrong the last three times he gave evidence to the police, the magistrate will probably refuse the request for a warrant.

If the police search without a warrant, they have, in most cases, violated the Fourth Amendment. But even a search conducted with a warrant violates the Fourth Amendment if:

- there was no probable cause to issue the warrant;

- the warrant does not specify with reasonable precision the place to be searched and the things sought; or

- the search extends beyond what is specified in the warrant.

---

[8]The People v. Han, 78 Cal. App. 4th 797 (Ct. Appeal, CA 2000).

[9]A magistrate is a judge who tries minor criminal cases or undertakes primarily administrative responsibilities.

Thus, if the police say they have reason to believe that they will find bloody clothes in the suspect's car in his garage, they cannot also look through his house and confiscate file folders. In one case, the police had a warrant to search a ground floor apartment for child pornography. But when they arrived at the building, they realized the suspect lived upstairs. The court ruled that the search of the upstairs apartment had violated the Fourth Amendment.[10]

Searches Without a Warrant

There are seven circumstances under which police may search without a warrant:

Plain View. When Rashad Walker opened his door in response to a police officer's knock, he was holding a marijuana joint in his hand. The court held that the police did not need a warrant to make an arrest because evidence of the crime was in plain view.[11]

Stop and Frisk. None of us wants to live in a world in which police can randomly stop and frisk us on the street anytime they feel like it. The police do have the right to stop and frisk, but *only if* they have a clear and specific reason to suspect that criminal activity may be afoot and that the person may be armed and dangerous.[12]

The case of *Floyd v. New York City* illustrates how complicated stop and frisk issues can be.[13] In the course of a decade, major crime in New York City fell to historic lows. During this time, police engaged in an aggressive stop and frisk policy, halting hundreds of thousands of people on the street each year. More than 80 percent of the stops were of black and Hispanic men, although these two groups made up just slightly more than 50 percent of the population. Once stopped, the suspects were often pushed against the wall and thoroughly searched. Only about 10 percent of the stops yielded evidence of crime. It is worth noting that crime also fell in cities that did not have such an aggressive stop and frisk policy. To stop this practice in New York, the Center for Constitutional Rights sued the city. At trial, people of color testified about a relentless police presence in their neighborhoods. A judge ultimately ruled this practice unconstitutional and ordered the city to stop. What is the appropriate trade-off between a lower crime rate and intrusive police stops? What would you be willing to tolerate personally?

Emergencies. If the police believe that evidence is about to be destroyed, they can search without a warrant. For example, officers in Lexington, Kentucky, followed a crack dealer into an apartment building. They were not sure if he had entered the apartment on the left or on the right, but they smelled marijuana coming from the one on the right. When they banged on that door and shouted "Police" they heard noises coming from the apartment of "things being moved." After kicking in the door, they found a man with illegal drugs. They arrested him for drug trafficking. It turned out, however, that the dealer they had been following had gone into the apartment on the left. The Supreme Court held that their search was legal.[14]

---

[10]United States v. Voustianiouk, 685 F.3d 206 (2d Cir. 2012).
[11]State v. Walker, 213 N.J. 281 (N.J. 2013).
[12]Terry v. Ohio, 392 U.S. 1 (S. Ct. 1968).
[13]Floyd v. City of New York, 959 F. Supp. 2d 668 (S.D.N.Y. 2013).
[14]Kentucky v. King, 131 S. Ct. 1849 (U.S. 2011).

What about measuring the blood alcohol level in a suspected drunk driver? Is that an emergency? After all, alcohol in the blood dissipates over time. In a 5-4 decision, the Supreme Court ruled that the police cannot routinely force drunk drivers to give blood samples. Whether a warrantless blood test is reasonable must be determined on a case-by-case basis.[15]

Automobiles. If police have lawfully stopped a car and then observe evidence of other crimes in the car, such as burglary tools, they may search.

Lawful Arrest. Police may always search a suspect they have arrested. The goal is to protect the officers and preserve evidence.

Consent. Anyone lawfully living in a dwelling can allow the police in to search without a warrant. If your roommate gives the police permission to search your house, that search is legal.[16]

No Expectation of Privacy. The police have a right to search any area in which the defendant does not have a reasonable expectation of privacy. For example, Rolando Crowder was staying at his friend Bobo's apartment. Hearing the police in the hallway, he ran down to the basement. The police found Crowder in the basement with drugs nearby. Crowder argued that the police should have obtained a warrant, but the court ruled that he had no expectation of privacy in Bobo's basement.[17]

Technology and social media have created new challenges for the courts in determining what is a reasonable expectation of privacy. For example:

- **DNA Tests.** Alonso King was arrested for assault. During the booking process, the police used a cotton swab to take a DNA sample from the inside of his mouth. Because that DNA matched genetic material found on a rape victim in another case, King was convicted of that additional crime. In a 5-4 decision, the Supreme Court held that a cheek swab was not much more intrusive than fingerprinting and, therefore, did not violate King's rights under the Fourth Amendment (provided the swab had been done after an arrest for a "serious" offense).[18] Now, 28 states and the federal government collect DNA after an arrest for such offenses.

- **Heat-Seeking Devices.** In another 5-4 decision, the Supreme Court ruled that police officers need a warrant before pointing a heat-seeking device at a house.[19] These devices are used to detect heat lamps used in growing marijuana plants. Some states, however, will not permit police to use these devices even with a warrant.[20]

- **Digital Cameras.** After arresting a juvenile, the police searched him and discovered a digital camera. Without obtaining a warrant, they looked at the photos on the camera and found a photo of him with a sawed-off shotgun. The court held that the police officers were not required to obtain a warrant before looking at the pictures.[21]

- **Cellphones.** The Supreme Court has ruled that the police must obtain a warrant before listening in on a telephone conversation or searching the digital contents of a cellphone.[22] But, the courts are divided over whether they need one to obtain the

---

[15]Missouri v. McNeely, 133 S. Ct. 1552 (U.S. 2013).
[16]United States v. Matlock, 415 U.S. 164 (U.S. 1974).
[17]Ohio v. Crowder, 2010 Ohio 3766 (Ohio Ct. Appeals 2010).
[18]Maryland v. King, 133 S. Ct. 1958 (U.S. 2013).
[19]Kyllo v. United States, 533 U.S. 27 (U.S. 2001).
[20]Brundige v. State, 291 Ga. 677 (Ga. 2012).
[21]In re Alfredo C., 2011 Cal. App. Unpub. LEXIS 7626 (Cal. App. 2d Dist. 2011).
[22]Riley v. California, 2014 U.S. LEXIS 4497 (U.S. 2014).

phone's location or a list of numbers called. One federal appeals court has ruled, for example, that police must acquire a warrant before obtaining a list of the locations where a cellphone has been used, while a different appeals court set a lower standard.[23]

- **Computers.** People generally have a reasonable expectation of privacy for data stored on their own computer, in their possession. Thus, the police would have to obtain a warrant before searching it.[24] It is not clear now whether this protection applies to the same information stored in the cloud. Can your documents, photos, calendars, and financial data stored online be accessed without a warrant? Stay tuned.

- **Email.** Police generally do not need a warrant to find out *address information*, such as whom you have emailed. Under the Electronic Communications Privacy Act, police do need a warrant to intercept email in transit, but not to search opened email or messages sent more than six months prior.[25]

- **Websites.** In general, police do not need a warrant to find out what websites you have visited. Google says that it complies with many government requests for account information (and you agreed to those terms if you have a Gmail account).

- **Chats.** Laurence Bode sent chat messages to other users of a child pornography website. A court upheld the right of Homeland Security agents to access his chats without a warrant.[26]

- **Social Media.** Before James Holmes went into a movie theatre in Aurora, Colorado, and allegedly began shooting, he posted this phrase in his profile on two dating websites, "Will you visit me in prison?" A judge ruled that he did not have a reasonable expectation of privacy in those postings.[27] Similarly, a court in New York ruled that Twitter users do not have a reasonable expectation of privacy in their tweets.[28] Twitter has also generally been willing to grant government requests for account information. However, the police generally need a warrant to access a *private* Facebook profile. But if a "friend" of the accountholder allows them access, no warrant is necessary.[29]

- **GPS Tracking.** In the following case, the United States Supreme Court dealt with the issue of GPS tracking by the police. Although this technology is new, Justice Scalia based his decision on what eighteenth century people would have considered to be an unreasonable search.

---

[23]United States v. Davis, 754 F.3d 1205 (11th Cir. 2014), In re Application of the United States for Historical Cell Site Data, 724 F.3d 600 (5th Cir. 2013). 201201.

[24]Searching and Seizing Computers and Obtaining Electronic Evidence in Criminal Investigations, Published by Office of Legal Education Executive Office for United States Attorneys, 2009.

[25]18 U.S.C. §§ 2510-2522. This statute was passed at a time when email providers strictly limited how much email any one user could store. So recipients would download emails onto their computers and then erase them from the server. Thus, for all practical purposes, once an email was opened, it was not available to the police without a warrant because it only lived on an individual's computer. One of Gmail's innovations was to allow users to keep (and search) an unlimited amount of email on its servers.

[26]United States v. Bode, 2013 U.S. Dist. LEXIS 118627 (D. Md., 2013).

[27]People of the State of Colorado v. James Eagan Holmes, Case Number 12CR1522 (Dt. Ct. Col. 2013).

[28]People v. Harris, 36 Misc. 3d 613 (N.Y. City Crim. Ct. 2012).

[29]United States v. Meregildo, 883 F. Supp. 2d 523 (S.D.N.Y. 2012).

UNITED STATES V. JONES

132 S. Ct. 945
United States Supreme Court, 2012

Facts: The Washington, D.C., police suspected Antoine Jones of being a drug dealer. Without a valid search warrant, they attached a GPS tracking device to his car. For 28 days, they used the GPS to determine his whereabouts. Based on this evidence, Jones was convicted of a conspiracy to deal cocaine and was sentenced to life in prison. The appellate court reversed his conviction on the grounds that the police should have obtained a warrant before attaching the GPS. The Supreme Court granted *certiorari*.

Issue: *Was the warrantless use of a GPS an illegal search under the Fourth Amendment?*

Excerpts from Justice Scalia's Decision: The Fourth Amendment provides in relevant part that "[t]he right of the people to be secure in their persons, houses, papers, and effects, against unreasonable searches and seizures, shall not be violated." It is beyond dispute that a vehicle is an "effect" as that term is used in the Amendment.

The Government physically occupied private property for the purpose of obtaining information. We have no doubt that such a physical intrusion would have been considered a "search" within the meaning of the Fourth Amendment when it was adopted. [F]or most of our history the Fourth Amendment was understood to embody a particular concern for government trespass upon the areas ("persons, houses, papers, and effects") it enumerates.

The judgment of the Court of Appeals for the D. C. Circuit is affirmed.

Exclusionary Rule

Under the exclusionary rule, any evidence the government acquires illegally (or any information obtained as a result of this illegal behavior) may not be used at trial. (Information resulting from an illegal search is referred to as "the fruit of the poisonous tree.") Thus, for example, in the *Jones* case, the location evidence against the alleged drug dealer was thrown out because it had been illegally obtained. Without this evidence, his conviction was overturned. Suppose that the police put a GPS on Alice's car, without first obtaining a warrant. From that data, they discover that she has been going to Beau's house. They then see Beau dealing drugs. When they arrest him, he tells them that Caitlyn is his dealer and, indeed, the police find drugs in Caitlyn's apartment. None of this evidence—neither the confessions nor the drugs—is admissible in court because it all stemmed from an illegal search of Alice's car.

The Supreme Court created the exclusionary rule to prevent governmental misconduct. The theory is simple: If police and prosecutors know that illegally obtained evidence cannot be used in court, they will not be tempted to make improper searches or engage in other illegal behavior. Is the exclusionary rule a good idea?

Opponents of the rule argue that a guilty person may go free because one police officer bungled. They are outraged by cases like *Coolidge v. New Hampshire*.[30] Pamela Mason, a 14-year-old babysitter, was brutally murdered. Citizens of New Hampshire were furious, and the state's attorney general personally led the investigation. Police found strong evidence that Edward Coolidge had committed this terrible crime. They took the evidence to the attorney general, who personally issued a search warrant. After a search of Coolidge's car uncovered incriminating evidence, he was found guilty of murder and sentenced to life in prison. But the United States Supreme Court reversed the conviction. The warrant had not been issued by a neutral magistrate. A law officer may not lead an investigation and simultaneously decide what searches are permissible. Ultimately, Coolidge pleaded guilty to second degree murder and served many years in prison.

---

[30]403 U.S. 443 (S. Ct. 1971).

In fact, very few people do go free because of the exclusionary rule. One study showed that this rule led to the release of a defendant in only 0.7 percent of all prosecutions.[31]

There are three exceptions to the exclusionary rule:

- **Inevitable Discovery.** A court will admit any evidence that would have been discovered even without the illegal behavior on the part of the police. For example, when the police unlawfully questioned a suspect, he revealed the location of the body of a child he had murdered. His conviction was upheld because, the court ruled, the body would eventually have been discovered in the ditch where he had left it.[32]

- **Independent Source.** If the police find the tainted evidence from a different source, then they can use it. For example, the police lied to get a search warrant for Jerome Roberts's cellphone records. They told the magistrate that he was a murder suspect when, in fact, they knew that he had not committed the crime. However, his phone records revealed that he had spoken many times with Andre Bellinger, who turned out to be the real murderer. The police also had arrested someone else who happened to be in possession of the murder weapon. The court ruled that, although the phone records were not admissible, the police would have found Bellinger through the murder weapon. So it refused to overturn the murder conviction.[33]

- **Good Faith Exception.** Suppose the police use a search warrant believing it to be proper, but it later proves to have been defective. The search is legal so long as the police *reasonably believed* the warrant was valid.[34]

EXAM Strategy

Question: Police bang down the door of Mary Beth's apartment, enter without her permission, and search the apartment. They had no warrant. When the officers discover a meth lab, they arrest her. What motion will the defense lawyer make before trial? Please rule on the defendant's motion. Are there any facts that would make you change your ruling?

Strategy: The defendant's motion is based on the police conduct. What was wrong with that conduct, and what are the consequences?

Result: The defense lawyer will argue that the police violated the Fourth Amendment because they lacked a warrant for the search. He will ask that the court suppress the drug evidence. Ordinarily, the court would grant that motion unless there was other evidence—for example, an informant had just told other officers that Mary Beth was his meth supplier.

---

[31]See the discussion in United States v. Leon, 468 U.S. 897 (S. Ct. 1984) (Justice Brennan, *dissenting*).
[32]Nix v. Williams, 467 U.S. 431 (U.S. 1984).
[33]State v. Smith, 212 N.J. 365 (N.J. S. Ct. 2012).
[34]Ibid.

7-2d **After Arrest**

The Fifth Amendment

The Fifth Amendment to the Constitution protects criminal defendants—both the innocent and the guilty—in several ways.

Due process
Requires fundamental fairness at all stages of the case

Due Process. **Due Process** requires fundamental fairness at all stages of the case. The basic elements of due process are discussed in Chapter 5, on constitutional law. In the context of criminal law, due process sets additional limits. The requirement that the prosecution disclose evidence favorable to the defendant is a due process rule. Similarly, if a witness says that a tall white male robbed the liquor store, it would violate due process for the police to place the male suspect in a lineup with four short women of color.

Self-Incrimination. **The Fifth Amendment bars the government from forcing any person to provide evidence against himself.** In other words, the police may not use mental or physical coercion to force a confession or any other information out of someone. Society does not want a government that engages in torture. Such abuse might occasionally catch a criminal, but it would grievously injure innocent people and make all citizens fearful of the government that is supposed to represent them. Also, coerced confessions are inherently unreliable. The defendant may confess simply to end the torture. (The protection against self-incrimination applies only to people; corporations and other organizations are not protected and may be required to provide incriminating information.)

Miranda Rights.   The police cannot legally force a suspect to provide evidence against himself. But sometimes, under forceful interrogation, he might forget his constitutional rights. In the following landmark case, the Supreme Court established the requirement that police remind suspects of their rights—with the very same warning that we have all heard so many times on television shows.

Landmark Case

MIRANDA V. ARIZONA
384 U.S. 436
United States Supreme Court, 1966

Facts: Ernesto Miranda was a mentally ill, indigent citizen of Mexico. At a Phoenix police station, a rape victim identified him as her assailant. Two police officers took him to an interrogation room but did not tell him that he had a right to have a lawyer present during the questioning. Two hours later, the officers emerged with a written confession signed by Miranda. At the top of the statement was a typed paragraph stating that the confession was made voluntarily "with full knowledge of my legal rights, understanding any statement I make may be used against me."

At Miranda's trial, the judge admitted this written confession into evidence. The officers testified that Miranda had also made an oral confession during the interrogation. The jury found Miranda guilty of kidnapping and rape. He was sentenced to 20 to 30 years imprisonment. On appeal, the Supreme Court of Arizona affirmed the conviction. In reaching its decision, the court relied heavily on the fact that Miranda did not specifically request a lawyer. The Supreme Court of the United States granted *certiorari*.

Issues: *Was Miranda's confession admissible at trial? Should his conviction be upheld?*

Excerpts from Chief Justice Warren's Decision: Our holding briefly stated is this: the prosecution may not use statements, whether exculpatory or inculpatory, stemming from custodial interrogation of the defendant unless it demonstrates the use of procedural safeguards effective to secure the privilege against self-incrimination. By custodial interrogation, we mean questioning initiated by law enforcement officers after a person has been taken into custody or otherwise deprived of his freedom of action in any significant way. As for the procedural safeguards to be employed, the following measures are required. Prior to any questioning, the person must be warned that he has a right to remain silent, that any statement he does make may be used as evidence against him, and that he has a right to the presence of an attorney, either retained or appointed.

The defendant may waive these rights, provided the waiver is made voluntarily, knowingly, and intelligently. If, however, he indicates in any manner and at any stage of the process that he wishes to consult with an attorney before speaking, there can be no questioning. Likewise, if the individual is alone and indicates in any manner that he does not wish to be interrogated, the police may not question him. The mere fact that he may have answered some questions or volunteered some statements on his own does not deprive him of the right to refrain from answering any further inquiries until he has consulted with an attorney and thereafter consents to be questioned.

In a series of cases decided by this Court, the police resorted to physical brutality—beating, hanging, whipping—and to sustained and protracted questioning 'incommunicado' in order to extort confessions. Unless a proper limitation upon custodial interrogation is achieved, there can be no assurance that practices of this nature will be eradicated in the foreseeable future. Not only does the use of the third degree involve a flagrant violation of law by the officers of the law, but it involves also the dangers of false confessions, and it tends to make police and prosecutors less zealous in the search for objective evidence. As [an official] remarked: "If you use your fists, you are not so likely to use your wits."

[C]oercion can be mental as well as physical, and the blood of the accused is not the only hallmark of an unconstitutional inquisition. In a serious case, the interrogation may continue for days, with the required intervals for food and sleep, but with no respite from the atmosphere of domination. It is possible in this way to induce the subject to talk without resorting to duress or coercion.

Even without employing brutality, the very fact of custodial interrogation exacts a heavy toll on individual liberty and trades on the weakness of individuals. In [this case before the Court], the defendant was thrust into an unfamiliar atmosphere and run through menacing police interrogation procedures. It is obvious that such an interrogation environment is created for no purpose other than to subjugate the individual to the will of his examiner. This atmosphere carries its own badge of intimidation. To be sure, this is not physical intimidation, but it is equally destructive of human dignity. The current practice of 'incommunicado' interrogation is at odds with one of our Nation's most cherished principles—that the individual may not be compelled to incriminate himself.

All these policies point to one overriding thought: the constitutional foundation underlying the privilege is the respect a government—state or federal—must accord to the dignity and integrity of its citizens. To maintain a fair state-individual balance, to respect the inviolability of the human personality, our accusatory system of criminal justice demands that the government seeking to punish an individual produce the evidence against him by its own independent labors, rather than by the cruel, simple expedient of compelling it from his own mouth.

Miranda was not in any way apprised of his right to consult with an attorney and to have one present during the interrogation, nor was his right not to be compelled to incriminate himself effectively protected in any other manner. Without these warnings, the statements were inadmissible. The mere fact that he signed a statement which contained a typed-in clause stating that he had "full knowledge" of his "legal rights" does not approach the knowing and intelligent waiver required to relinquish constitutional rights.

Right to a Lawyer

As *Miranda* made clear, a criminal defendant has the right to a lawyer before being interrogated by the police. The Sixth Amendment guarantees the **right to a lawyer at all important stages of the criminal process.** Because of this right, the government must **appoint a lawyer** to represent, free of charge, any defendant who cannot afford one.

Indictment

Grand jury

A group of ordinary citizens who decides whether there is probable cause the defendant committed the crime with which she is charged

Once the police provide the local prosecutor with evidence, he presents this evidence to a **grand jury** and asks its members to indict the defendant. The grand jury is a group of ordinary citizens, like a trial jury, but the grand jury holds hearings for several weeks at a time, on many different cases. At the hearing in front of the grand jury, only the prosecutor presents evidence, not the defense attorney, because it is better for the defendant to save her evidence for the trial jury.

Indictment

The government's formal charge that the defendant has committed a crime and must stand trial

If the grand jury determines that there is probable cause that the defendant committed the crime with which she is charged, an **indictment** is issued. An indictment is the government's formal charge that the defendant has committed a crime and must stand trial. Because the grand jury never hears the defendant's evidence, it is relatively easy for prosecutors to obtain an indictment. In short, an indictment is not the same thing as a guilty verdict.

Arraignment

At an arraignment, a clerk reads the formal charges of the indictment. The defendant must enter a plea to the charges. At this stage, most defendants plead not guilty.

Plea Bargaining

Plea bargain

An agreement in which the defendant pleads guilty to a reduced charge, and the prosecution recommends to the judge a relatively lenient sentence

A **plea bargain** is an agreement between prosecution and defense that the defendant will plead guilty to a reduced charge, and the prosecution will recommend to the judge a relatively lenient sentence. In the federal court system, about 97 percent of all prosecutions end in a plea bargain. Such a high percentage has led to some concern that innocent people may be pleading guilty to avoid the risk of tough mandatory sentences. A judge need not accept the bargain but usually does.

Discovery

If the defendant does not plead guilty, the prosecution is obligated to hand over any evidence favorable to the defense that the defense attorney requests. The defense has a more limited obligation to inform the prosecution of its evidence. In most states, for example, if the defense will be based on an alibi, counsel must reveal the alibi to the government before trial.

Trial and Appeal

When there is no plea bargain, the case must go to trial. The mechanics of a criminal trial and appeal are similar to those for a civil trial, described in Chapter 6, on dispute resolution.

Double Jeopardy

Double jeopardy

A criminal defendant may be prosecuted only once for a particular criminal offense.

The prohibition against **double jeopardy** means that a defendant may be prosecuted only once for a particular criminal offense. The purpose is to prevent the government from destroying the lives of innocent citizens with repetitive prosecutions.

Punishment

The Eighth Amendment prohibits cruel and unusual punishment. Courts are generally unsympathetic to claims under this provision. For example, the Supreme Court has ruled that the death penalty is not cruel and unusual as long as it is not imposed in an arbitrary or capricious manner.[35]

Another important case under the Eighth Amendment involved California's "three strikes" law, which dramatically increases sentences for repeat offenders. Gary Ewing, on parole from a nine-year prison term, was prosecuted for stealing three golf clubs worth $399 each. Because he had prior convictions, his crime, normally a misdemeanor, was treated as a felony. Ewing was convicted and sentenced to 25 years to life. The Supreme Court ruled

---

[35]Gregg v. Georgia, 428 U.S. 153 (S. Ct. 1976).

that this sentence was not cruel and unusual and that the three strikes law was a rational response to a legitimate concern about crime.[36]

The Eighth Amendment also outlaws excessive fines. Forfeiture is the most controversial topic under this clause. **Forfeiture** is a *civil* law proceeding that is permitted by many different *criminal* statutes. Once a court has convicted a defendant under certain criminal statutes—such as a controlled substance law—the government may seek forfeiture of property associated with the criminal act. *How much* property can the government take? To determine if forfeiture is fair, courts generally look at three factors:

- whether the property was used in committing the crime
- whether it was purchased with proceeds from illegal acts, and
- whether the punishment is disproportionate to the defendant's wrongdoing.

Neal Brunk pleaded guilty to selling 2.5 ounces of marijuana, and the government promptly sought forfeiture of his house on 90 acres, worth about $99,000. The court found that forfeiture was legitimate because Brunk had used drug money to buy the land and then sold narcotics from the property.[37] By contrast, Hosep Bajakajian attempted to leave the United States without reporting $375,000 in cash to customs officials, as the law requires. The government demanded forfeiture of the full sum, but the Supreme Court ruled that seizure of the entire amount was grossly disproportionate to the minor crime of failing to report cash movement.[38]

7-3 CRIMES THAT HARM BUSINESSES (AND THEIR CUSTOMERS)

Businesses must deal with four major crimes: larceny, fraud, arson, and embezzlement.

7-3a **Larceny**

It is holiday season at the mall, the period of greatest profits—and the most crime. At the Foot Forum, a teenager limps in wearing ragged sneakers and sneaks out wearing Super Sneakers, valued at $145. Down the aisle at a home furnishing store, a man is so taken by a $375 power saw that he takes it. Sweethearts swipe sweaters; pensioners pocket produce. All are committing larceny.

Larceny is the trespassory taking of personal property with the intent to steal it. "Trespassory taking" means that someone else originally has the property. The Super Sneakers are personal property (not real estate), they were in the possession of the Foot Forum, and the teenager deliberately left without paying, intending never to return the goods. That is larceny. Each year, more than $34 billion in merchandise is stolen from retail stores in the United States.

Larceny
The trespassory taking of personal property with the intent to steal it

7-3b **Fraud**

Robert Dorsey owned Bob's Chrysler in Highland, Illinois. When he bought cars, the First National Bank of Highland paid Chrysler, and Dorsey—supposedly—repaid the bank as he sold the autos. Dorsey, though, began to suffer financial problems, and the bank suspected he was selling cars without repaying his loans. A state investigator notified Dorsey that he planned to review all dealership records. One week later, a fire engulfed the dealership. An arson investigator discovered that an electric iron, connected to a timer, had been placed on a pile of financial papers doused with accelerant.

---

[36]Ewing v. California, 538 U.S. 11 (S. Ct. 2003).
[37]United States v. Brunk, 11 Fed. Appx. 147 (4th Cir. Va. 2001).
[38]United States v. Bajakajian, 524 U.S. 321 (S. Ct. 1998).

The saddest part of this true story is that it is all too common. Some experts suggest that 1 percent of corporate revenues are wasted on fraud alone. Dorsey was convicted and imprisoned for committing two crimes that cost business billions of dollars annually—fraud (for taking money from the bank even after he knew he could not pay it back) and arson (for burning down the dealership).[39]

Fraud

Deception for the purpose of obtaining money or property

Fraud refers to various crimes, all of which have a common element: **the deception of another person for the purpose of obtaining money or property from him.** Robert Dorsey's precise violation was bank fraud, a federal crime.[40] It is bank fraud to use deceit to obtain money, assets, securities, or other property under the control of any financial institution.

Wire Fraud and Mail Fraud

Wire and mail fraud are additional federal crimes, involving the use of interstate mail, telegram, telephone, radio, or television to obtain property by deceit.[41] For example, if Marsha makes an interstate phone call to sell land that she does not own, that is wire fraud.

Insurance Fraud

Insurance fraud is another common crime. A Ford suddenly swerves in front of a Toyota, causing it to brake hard. A Mercedes, unable to stop, slams into the Toyota, as the Ford races away. Regrettable accident? No: a "swoop and squat" fraud scheme. The Ford and Toyota drivers were working together, hoping to cause an accident with someone else. The "injured" Toyota driver now goes to a third member of the fraud team—a dishonest doctor—who diagnoses serious back and neck injuries and predicts long-term pain and disability. The driver files a claim against the Mercedes's driver, whose insurer may be forced to pay tens or even hundreds of thousands of dollars for an accident that was no accident. Insurance companies investigate countless cases like this each year, trying to distinguish the honest victim from the criminal.

Internet Fraud

The Internet's anonymity and speed facilitate fraud. Common scams include advance fee scams,[42] the sale of merchandise that is either defective or nonexistent, the so-called Nigerian letter scam,[43] billing for services that are touted as "free," fake scholarship search services, romance fraud (you meet someone online who wants to visit you but needs money for travel expenses), and credit card scams (for a fee, you can get a credit card, even with a poor credit rating). One of the new scams involves *over*payment. You are renting out a house, selling a pet, or accepting a job, and "by accident," you are sent too much money. You wire the excess back, only to find out that the initial check or funds transfer was no good. Fraud on the Internet can be prosecuted under state law, the Computer Fraud and Abuse Act (discussed later in this chapter), and mail and wire fraud statutes.

Other common forms of Internet fraud include the following.

---

[39]United States v. Dorsey, 27 F.3d 285 (7th Cir. 1994).

[40]18 U.S.C. §1344.

[41]18 U.S.C. §§1341–1346.

[42]As in, "If you are willing to pay a fee in advance, then you will have access to (pick your choice) favorable financing, lottery winnings from overseas, fabulous investment opportunities."

[43]Victims receive an email from someone alleging to be a Nigerian government official who has stolen money from the government. He needs some place safe to park the money for a short time. The official promises that, if the victim will permit her account to be used for this purpose, she will be allowed to keep a percentage of the stolen money. Instead, of course, once the "official" has the victim's bank information, he cleans out the account.

Auctions. Internet auctions are the number one source of consumer complaints about online fraud. Wrongdoers either sell goods they do not own, provide defective goods, or offer fakes. In one case that seemed a defeat for consumers, a court held that eBay, the Internet auction site, was not liable to Tiffany & Company for the counterfeit Tiffany products sold on the site. The jewelry company had sued after discovering that most items advertised on eBay as Tiffany products were, in fact, fakes. The court held that eBay's only legal obligation was to remove products once told that they were counterfeit.[44]

Shilling is an increasingly popular online auction fraud. **Shilling means that a seller either bids on his own goods or agrees to cross-bid with a group of other sellers.** Shilling is prohibited because the owner drives up the price of his own item by bidding on it. Kenneth Walton, a San Francisco lawyer, auctioned on eBay a painting purportedly by artist Richard Diebenkorn. A bidder offered $135,805 before eBay withdrew the item in response to charges that Walton had placed a bid on the painting himself and had also engaged in cross-bidding with a group of other eBay users. Walton pleaded guilty to charges of federal wire and mail fraud. He was sentenced to almost four years in prison and paid almost $100,000 in restitution to the victims.

Shillers are also subject to suit under general anti-fraud statutes. In addition, some states explicitly prohibit shilling.[45]

Identity Theft. Identity theft is one of the scariest crimes against property. Thieves steal the victim's social security number and other personal information such as bank account numbers and mother's maiden name, which they use to obtain loans and credit cards. Victims have the difficult task of proving that they were not responsible for the debts and they may even find themselves unable to obtain a credit card, loan, or job. One victim spent several nights in jail after he was arrested for a crime that his identity thief had committed. Identity theft is broadly defined. For example, a court has ruled that creating a fake Facebook page in someone else's name constituted identity theft.

Although identity fraud existed before computers, the Internet has made it much easier. For example, consumer activists were able to purchase the social security numbers of the director of the CIA, the Attorney General of the United States, and other top administration officials. The cost was only $26 each. No surprise then that this crime is so common.

Is this the real deal, or a cheap imitation?

The Identity Theft and Assumption Deterrence Act of 1998 prohibits the use of false identification to commit fraud or other crime and it also permits the victim to seek restitution in court.[46] In addition, the Aggravated Identity Theft statute imposes a mandatory additional sentence of two years on anyone who engages in identity theft during the commission of certain crimes.[47] Also, many states have their own identity theft statutes.

Phishing. Have you ever received an instant message from a Facebook friend saying, "Hey, what's up?" with a link to an IQ test? This message is not from a friend, but rather from a fraudster hoping to lure you into revealing your personal information. In this case,

---

[44]Tiffany Inc. v. eBay, Inc., 600 F.3d 93 (2d Cir. 2010) and, *on remand,* 2010 U.S. Dist. LEXIS 96596 (S.D.N.Y. 2010).

[45]For example, New Mexico law provides that "It shall be unlawful to employ shills or puffers at any such auction sale or to offer or to make or to procure to be offered or made any false bid or offer any false bid to buy or pretend to buy any article sold or offered for sale." N.M. Stat. Section 61-16-14.

[46]18 U.S.C. §1028.

[47]18 U.S.C. §1028A.

people who clicked on the link were told that they had to provide their cell phone number to get the test results. Next thing they knew, they had been signed up for some expensive cell phone service. This scam is part of one of the most rapidly growing areas of Internet fraud: **phishing. In this crime, a fraudster sends a message directing the recipient to enter personal information on a website that is an illegal imitation of a legitimate site.**

In a traditional phishing scam, large numbers of generic emails are sprayed over the Internet asking millions of people to log on to, say, a fake bank site. But the latest development—called **spear phishing**—involves personalized messages sent from someone the victim knows. For example, your sister asks for your social security number so she can add you as a beneficiary to her life insurance policy. In reality, this email has come from a fraudster who hacked into her Facebook account to gain access to her lists of friends and family.[48] Even "Like" buttons can be "clickjacked" to take unwary users to bogus sites. Prosecutors can bring criminal charges against phishers for fraud.

EXAM Strategy

Question: Eric mails glossy brochures to 25,000 people, offering to sell them a one-month time-share in a stylish apartment in Las Vegas. The brochure depicts an imposing building, an opulent apartment, and spectacular pools. To reserve a space, customers need only send in a $2,000 deposit. Three hundred people send in the money. In fact, there is no such building. Eric, planning to flee with the cash, is arrested and prosecuted. His sentence could be as long as 20 years. (1) With what crime is he charged? (2) Is this a felony or misdemeanor prosecution? (3) Does Eric have a right to a jury trial? (4) What is the government's burden of proof?

Strategy: (1) Eric is deceiving people, and that should tell you the *type* of crime. (2) The potential 20-year sentence determines whether Eric's crime is a misdemeanor or felony, and whether or not he is entitled to a jury trial. (3) We know that the government has the burden of proof in criminal prosecutions—but *how much* evidence must it offer?

Result: Eric has committed fraud. A felony is one in which the sentence could be a year or more. The potential penalty here is 20 years, so the crime is a felony. Eric has a right to a jury, as does any defendant whose sentence could be six months or longer. The prosecution must prove its case beyond a reasonable doubt, a much higher burden than that in a civil case.

7-3c Arson

Arson
The malicious use of fire or explosives to damage or destroy real estate or personal property

Robert Dorsey, the Chrysler dealer, committed a second serious crime. **Arson is the malicious use of fire or explosives to damage or destroy any real estate or personal property.** It is both a federal and a state crime. Dorsey used arson to conceal his bank fraud. Most arsonists hope to collect on insurance policies. Every year thousands of buildings burn, as owners try to make a quick kill or extricate themselves from financial difficulties. Everyone who purchases insurance ends up paying higher premiums because of this wrongdoing.

---

[48]To prevent your Facebook account from being hijacked, be careful when accessing it over a public network (such as in a hotel or airport), where fraudsters might be able to capture your password. If you text "otp" to 32665, you will receive a password that can be used only once (a "one-time password"). Fraudsters thus cannot use this password to access your account.

7-3d **Embezzlement**

This crime also involves illegally obtaining property, but with one big difference: The culprit begins with legal possession. **Embezzlement** is the fraudulent conversion of property already in the defendant's possession.

There is no romance in this story: For 15 years, Kristy Watts worked part-time as a bookkeeper for romance writer Danielle Steele, handling payroll and accounting. During that time, Watts stole $768,000, despite earning a salary of $200,000 a year. Watts said that she had been motivated by envy and jealousy. She was sentenced to three years in prison and agreed to pay her former boss almost $1 million.

Embezzlement
The fraudulent conversion of property already in the defendant's possession

7-3e **Hacking**

During the 2008 presidential campaign, college student David Kernell guessed vice presidential candidate Sarah Palin's email password, accessed her personal Yahoo account, and published the content of some of her emails. To some, his actions seemed like an amusing prank. The joke turned out not to be so funny when Kernell was sentenced to one year in prison.

Gaining unauthorized access to a computer system is called **hacking**. It is a major crime. The FBI ranks cybercrime as its third-highest priority, right behind terrorism and spying. The goal of hackers is varied; some do it for little more than the thrill of the challenge. The objective for other hackers may be industrial espionage, extortion, theft of credit card information, plundering bank accounts, or revenge for perceived slights. Kernell hoped to prevent Palin from being elected vice president. Many governments engage in hacking for national security reasons or to steal intellectual property.

Hacking is a crime under the federal Computer Fraud and Abuse Act of 1986 (CFAA).[49] This statute applies to any computer, cell phone, or other gadget attached to the Internet. **The CFAA prohibits:**

- Accessing a computer without authorization and obtaining information from it,
- Computer espionage,
- Theft of financial information,
- Theft of information from the U.S. government,
- Theft from a computer,
- Computer fraud,
- Intentional, reckless, and negligent damage to a computer,
- Trafficking in computer passwords, and
- Computer extortion.

The CFAA also provides for civil remedies so that someone who has been harmed by a hacker can personally recover damages from the wrongdoer.

Courts are now in the process of figuring out how to interpret the CFAA. In the following case, a former employee clearly violated his company's policies, but did he commit a crime? You be the judge.

Hacking
Gaining unauthorized access to a computer system

---

[49]18 U.S.C. §1030.

UNITED STATES V. NOSAL

676 F.3d 854
United States Court of Appeals for the Ninth Circuit, 2012

Facts: David Nosal worked for an executive search firm, Korn/Ferry (K/F). Shortly after he left the company to start a competing business, he convinced some of his former colleagues to log into the company's confidential database and give him customer names and contact information. K/F had authorized the employees to access the database, but not to disclose confidential client information to outsiders.

The government charged Nosal with aiding and abetting his former colleagues in violating a provision of the CFAA that prohibits employees from exceeding their authorized access to a computer with intent to defraud. The trial court granted Nosal's motion to dismiss. The government appealed.

You Be the Judge: *Did Nosal commit a crime when he aided and abetted others in violating a workplace policy on computer use?*

Argument for the Defendant: This provision of the CFAA can mean one of two things: (1) either it is a crime to access unauthorized data or, (2) in a more expansive view, it can apply to anyone who is legally entitled to access data, but who then uses this data in an unauthorized manner. That is what happened here. The K/F employees were authorized to access the confidential database, but they were not permitted to send it to Nosal.

Congress enacted the CFAA primarily to address the growing problem of computer hacking, i.e., "intentionally trespassing into someone else's computer files." But, under the government's view, everyone who uses a computer in violation of company policy, which may well include everyone who uses a computer, would be a criminal. According to the government, if an employer keeps certain information in a separate database that can be viewed on a computer screen, but not copied or downloaded and an employee copies the information to a thumb drive, he could be charged with a crime.

The computer gives employees new ways to procrastinate, by g-chatting with friends, playing games, shopping, or watching sports highlights. Such activities are routinely prohibited by many computer-use policies. Under the broad interpretation of the CFAA, such minor violations would become federal crimes. While it is unlikely that you will be prosecuted for watching cat videos on your work computer, you could be. How will an employee know the difference between a minor personal use and a criminal act?

Employees who call family members from their work phones will become criminals if they send an email instead. They can read the sports section of *USA Today* at work, but they had better not visit ESPN.com. And Sudoku enthusiasts should stick to printed puzzles, because visiting www.dailysudoku.com from their work computers might give them more than enough time to hone their Sudoku skills behind bars.

Facebook prohibits its users from sharing login information. Are we going to cart every violator off to prison? The terms of service on dating websites prohibit inaccurate or misleading information. If you describe yourself as "tall, dark and handsome," when you are actually short and homely, could you end up wearing a handsome orange prison jumpsuit?

Argument for the Government: This statute explicitly requires an intent to commit fraud. Therefore, it has nothing to do with reading ESPN.com, playing Sudoku, checking email, or fibbing on dating sites. Instead, the K/F employees knowingly exceeded their access to a protected company computer and they did so with intent to defraud.

This distinction is not complicated. A bank teller is entitled to access money for legitimate banking purposes, but not to take the bank's money for himself. A new car buyer may be entitled to take a vehicle around the block on a test drive but not to drive it to Mexico on a drug run.

7-4 CRIMES COMMITTED BY BUSINESS

BP, the oil company formerly known as British Petroleum, pleaded guilty to criminal charges arising out of an oil rig explosion that caused 11 deaths and a tremendous oil spill in the Gulf of Mexico. It paid a fine of $4.5 *billion*. After pleading guilty to five felony charges of insider trading, SAC Capital paid a fine of $1.2 *billion*. But can a company commit a crime? Yes, under federal law. A corporation can be found guilty of a crime based on the conduct of any of its agents, who include anyone undertaking work on behalf of the corporation. An agent can be a corporate officer, an accountant hired to audit financial statements, a sales clerk, or almost any other person performing a job at the company's request. In the case of SAC, a number of its traders were convicted of insider trading. It is now suspected that the firm's impressive investment track record may be largely based on a systematic insider trading scheme.

If an agent commits a criminal act within the scope of his employment and with the intent to benefit the corporation, the company is liable.[50] This means that the agent himself must first be guilty. If the agent is guilty, the corporation is, too.

Some critics believe that the criminal law has gone too far. It is unfair, they argue, to impose *criminal* liability on a corporation, and thus penalize employees and shareholders, unless high-ranking officers were directly involved in the illegal conduct. Others argue that subjecting companies to criminal liability protects the public, deters wrongdoing, and publicizes the importance of complying with the law. Indeed, they argue that corporation fines are too small, that they should be large enough to take all the profitability out of criminal acts.

7-4a Making False Statements

It is illegal to make false statements or engage in a cover-up during any dealings with the United States government.[51] Sometimes this provision has been used to charge someone who is suspected of committing a complex crime that may itself be difficult to prove. In the most famous case, the government accused Martha Stewart, the celebrity homemaker and entrepreneur, of engaging in insider trading. At trial, that charge was thrown out but the jury nevertheless convicted her of lying to the officers who had investigated the alleged insider trading. Stewart ultimately served five months in prison. However, the Justice Department recently announced that it would only use this statute against defendants who knew their conduct was illegal.

7-4b Workplace Crimes

The workplace can be dangerous. Working on an assembly line exposes factory employees to fast-moving machinery. For a roofer, the first slip may be the last. The invisible radiation in a nuclear power plant can be deadlier than a bullet. The most important statute regulating the workplace is the federal **Occupational Safety and Health Act of 1970 (OSHA)**,[52] which sets safety standards for many industries.[53] May a state government go beyond standards set by OSHA and use the criminal law to punish dangerous conditions? In *People v. O'Neill*, the courts of Illinois answered that question with a potent "yes," permitting a *murder prosecution* against corporate executives themselves.[54]

Film Recovery Systems was an Illinois corporation in the business of extracting silver from used X-ray film. Workers at the factory soaked the film in large, open, bubbling vats of sodium cyanide. When one of the workers died of cyanide poisoning caused by inhaling the fumes, Illinois indicted Film Recovery and several of its managers for murder. The indictment charged that the officers had committed murder by not disclosing to the workers that

---

[50]New York Central & Hudson River R.R. Co. v. United States, 212 U.S. 481 (S. Ct. 1909). Note that what counts is the intention to benefit, not actual benefit. A corporation will not escape liability by showing that the scheme failed.

[51]18 U.S.C.S. §1001.

[52]29 U.S.C. §§651 *et seq.*

[53]See Chapter 29 on employment and labor law.

[54]23194 Ill. App. 3d 79 (Ill. App. Ct. 1990).

they were using cyanide and by failing to provide them with necessary safety equipment. The officers ultimately pleaded guilty to involuntary manslaughter and received sentences of between four months and three years.

7-4c RICO

Racketeer Influenced and Corrupt Organizations Act (RICO)

A powerful federal statute, originally aimed at organized crime, now used in many criminal prosecutions and civil lawsuits

The **Racketeer Influenced and Corrupt Organizations Act (RICO)** is one of the most powerful and controversial statutes ever written.[55] Congress passed the law primarily to prevent gangsters from taking money they earned illegally and investing it in legitimate businesses. But RICO has expanded far beyond the original intentions of Congress and is now used more often against ordinary businesses than against organized criminals. Some regard this wide application as a tremendous advance in law enforcement, but others view it as an oppressive weapon used to club ethical companies into settlements they should never have to make.

RICO prohibits using two or more racketeering acts to accomplish any of these goals: (1) investing in or acquiring legitimate businesses with criminal money; (2) maintaining or acquiring businesses through criminal activity; or (3) operating businesses through criminal activity.

What does that mean in English? It is a two-step process to prove that a person or an organization has violated RICO.

Racketeering acts

Any of a long list of specified crimes, such as embezzlement, arson, mail fraud, wire fraud, and so forth

- The prosecutor must show that the defendant committed two or more **racketeering acts**, which are any of a long list of specified crimes: embezzlement, arson, mail fraud, wire fraud, and so forth. Thus, if a gangster ordered a building torched in January and then burned a second building in October, that would be two racketeering acts. If a stockbroker told two customers that Bronx Gold Mines was a promising stock, when she knew that it was worthless, that would be two racketeering acts.

- The prosecutor must then show that the defendant used these racketeering acts to accomplish one of the three *purposes* listed earlier. If the gangster committed two arsons and then used the insurance payments to buy a dry cleaning business, that would violate RICO. If the stockbroker gave fraudulent advice and used the commissions to buy advertising for her firm, that would also violate RICO.

The government may prosecute both individuals and organizations for violating RICO. For example, the government prosecuted financier Michael Milken for manipulating stock prices. It also threatened to prosecute his employer, Drexel Burnham Lambert. If the government proves its case, the defendant can be hit with large fines and a prison sentence of up to 20 years. RICO also permits the government to seek forfeiture of the defendant's property. A court may order a convicted defendant to hand over any property or money used in the criminal acts or derived from them. Courts often freeze a defendant's assets once charges are brought to ensure that he will not hide the assets. If all his assets are frozen, he will have a hard time paying his defense lawyer, so a freeze often encourages a defendant to plea bargain on a lesser charge. Both Milken and Drexel entered into plea agreements with the government, rather than face a freeze on their assets, or in Milken's case, a long prison sentence.

In addition to criminal penalties, RICO also creates civil law liabilities. The government, organizations, and individuals all have the right to file civil lawsuits, seeking damages and, if necessary, injunctions. For example, a physician sued State Farm Insurance, alleging that the company had hired doctors to produce false medical reports that the company used to cut off claims by injured policy holders. As a result of these fake reports, the company refused to pay the plaintiff for legitimate services he performed on the policy holders. RICO is powerful (and for defendants, frightening) in part because a civil plaintiff can recover treble damages; that is, a judgment for three times the harm actually suffered, as well as attorney's fees.

---

[55] 18 U.S.C. §§1961-1968.

7-4d **Money Laundering**

Money laundering consists of taking the proceeds of certain criminal acts and either (1) using the money to promote crime, or (2) attempting to conceal the source of the money.[56]

Money laundering is an important part of major criminal enterprises. Successful criminals earn enormous sums, which they must filter back into the flow of commerce in a way that allows their crimes to go undetected. Laundering is an essential part of the corrosive traffic in drugs. Profits, all in cash, may mount so swiftly that dealers struggle to use the money without attracting the government's attention. For example, Colombian drug cartels set up a sophisticated system in which they shipped money to countries such as Dubai that do not keep records on cash transactions. This money was then transferred to the United States disguised as offshore loans. Prosecution by the U.S. government led to the demise of some of the banks involved.

But drug money is not the only or even major component of so-called flight capital. Criminals also try to hide the vast sums they earn from arms dealing and tax evasion. Some of this money is used to support terrorist organizations.

Money laundering
Using the proceeds of criminal acts either to promote crime or conceal the source of the money

---

EXAM Strategy

Question: Explain the difference between embezzlement and money laundering. Give an example of each.

Strategy: Both crimes involve money illegally obtained, but they are very different. In embezzlement the important question is: How did the criminal obtain the funds? In a laundering case, ask: To what use is the criminal trying to put the cash?

Result: Embezzlement refers to fraudulently taking money that is already in the defendant's possession. For example, if a financial advisor, *lawfully entrusted* with his client's funds for investing, uses some of the cash to buy himself a luxurious yacht, he has embezzled the client's money. Money laundering consists of taking *illegally obtained* money and either using the funds to promote additional crimes or attempting to *conceal* the source of the cash. Thus, an arms dealer might launder money so that he can use it to finance a terrorist organization.

7-4e **Hiring Illegal Workers**

It is illegal to knowingly employ unauthorized workers. Thus, employers are required to verify their workers' eligibility for employment in the United States. Within three days of hiring a worker, the employer must complete an I-9 form, documenting each worker's eligibility. The government has the right to arrest employees working illegally, and to bring charges against the business that hired them.

7-4f **Foreign Corrupt Practices Act**

Under the Foreign Corrupt Practices Act (FCPA), it is illegal for any employee or agent of a U.S. company (and some foreign companies) to give anything of value to any foreign official for purposes of influencing an official decision (unless the payment was merely intended to facilitate a routine governmental action.)[57]

---

[56]18 U.S.C. §§1956 *et seq.*
[57]15 U.S.C.S. §78dd-1.

Ethics In many countries, bribery is common and widely accepted. What is wrong with bribery, anyway? Many businesspeople think it is relatively harmless—just a cost of doing business, like New York City's high taxes or Germany's steep labor costs. But, corruption is not a victimless crime. Poor people in poor countries are the losers when officials are on the take; corruption means that good projects are squeezed out by bad ones. And corruption can reduce a country's entire administration to a state of decay. Honest officials give up. Bribes grow ever bigger and more ubiquitous. The trough becomes less well stocked; the snouts plunge deeper. The anticorruption czar in Mexico estimated that bribes reduce Mexico's gross domestic product annually by 9.5 percent, twice the country's education budget. Bribes also distort competition among American companies for foreign contracts, interfere with the free market system, and undermine confidence in business.[58]

The FCPA has two principal requirements:

- **Bribes.** The statute makes it illegal for U.S. companies and citizens (and some foreign companies) to bribe foreign officials to influence a governmental decision. The statute prohibits giving anything of value and also bars using third parties as a conduit for such payments. Note that the bribe need not be actually paid. A *promise* to pay bribes violates the FCPA. Also, the bribe need not be successful. If an American company makes an unauthorized payment but never gains any benefit, the company has still violated the law.

- **Recordkeeping.** All publicly traded companies—whether they engage in international trade or not—must keep accurate and detailed records to prevent hiding or disguising bribes. These records must be available for inspection by U.S. officials.

Not all payments violate the FCPA. While it is clearly illegal to bribe the high-level decision makers who award contracts in the first place, **a grease or facilitating payment for a routine governmental action is permitted.** Examples of routine governmental action include processing visas, or supplying utilities such as phone, power, or water. **To be legal, these payments must simply be hastening an inevitable result that does not involve discretionary action.** Thus, for example, "paying an official a small amount to have the power turned on at a factory might be a facilitating payment; paying an inspector to ignore the fact that the company does not have a valid permit to operate the factory would not be."[59]

This provision can be tricky to interpret. *The New York Times* reported that Wal-Mart had paid bribes to obtain building permits in Mexico. But were those payments simply speeding up a process that would inevitably have resulted in the permits being issued? As is often the case with bribery, what may have started as simple facilitating payments ultimately became clear wrongdoing. Among other offenses, Wal-Mart is alleged to have paid bribes to avoid compliance with zoning laws, or the requirement for construction licenses, and environmental permits.[60] These payments would be illegal.

A payment does not violate the FCPA if it was legal under the written laws of the country in which it was made. Because few countries establish written codes *permitting* officials to receive bribes, this defense is unlikely to help many Americans who hand out gifts.

---

[58]Adapted from, Who Will Listen to Mr. Clean?" *The Economist*, August 2, 1997, p. 52.

[59]U.S. Department of Justice and the U.S. Securities Exchange Commission, "A Resource Guide to the U.S. Foreign Corrupt Practices Act," http://www.justice.gov/criminal/fraud/fcpa/guide.pdf.

[60]David Barstow and Alejandra Xanic von Bertrab, "The Bribery Aisle: How Wal-Mart Got Its Way in Mexico," *The New York Times*, Dec. 17, 2012.

Punishments can be severe. A company may face large fines and the loss of profits earned as a result of illegal bribes. In 2011, Johnson & Johnson agreed to pay $77 million to settle an FCPA action. In addition to financial penalties, individuals who violate the FCPA can face up to five years in prison. However, the Justice Department has been lenient with companies that report their own wrongdoing. Thus, it did not prosecute Ralph Lauren Corporation after the company self-reported that one its officers had paid bribes to Argentine customs officials. The Justice Department seems likely to take a harder line with Wal-Mart. *The New York Times* reported that, after Wal-Mart discovered a widespread bribery campaign in Mexico, the company not only failed to report the wrongdoing, it actually promoted the man who had masterminded it.[61]

American executives long complained that the FCPA put their companies at a competitive disadvantage because everyone else was paying bribes. But that is no longer the case. As business has become more globalized, so has the fight against corruption. Members of the OECD (that is, most developed countries) have agreed to prohibit bribery and the United Nations approved a Convention Against Corruption.

7-4g Other Crimes

Additional crimes that affect business appear elsewhere in the text. An increasing number of federal and state statutes are designed to punish those who harm the environment. (See Chapter 40, on environmental law.) Antitrust violations, in which a corporation fixes prices, can lead to criminal prosecutions. (See Chapter 38, on antitrust law.) Finally, securities fraud is a crime and can lead to severe prison sentences. (See Chapter 37, on securities regulation.)

7-4h Punishing a Corporation

Fines

The most common punishment for a corporation is a fine. This makes sense in that a major purpose of a business is to earn a profit, and a fine, theoretically, hurts. But most fines are modest by the standards of corporate wealth. For example, BP was found guilty of two serious legal violations. In Alaska, company pipelines spilled 200,000 gallons of crude oil onto the tundra. In Texas, a catastrophic explosion at a refinery killed 15 people and injured 170 more. The total fine for both criminal violations was $62 million, which sounds like a large number.[62] But it was not enough, evidently, to change BP's practices. As we have seen, the company pleaded guilty to criminal charges in connection with the 2010 oil rig explosion in the Gulf of Mexico, which caused the largest marine oil spill ever. The rig that exploded had many safety violations. Will the $4.5 billion fine in that case change BP's business practices?

Compliance Programs

The **Federal Sentencing Guidelines** are the detailed rules that judges must follow when sentencing defendants convicted of crimes in federal court. The guidelines instruct judges to determine whether, at the time of the crime, the corporation had in place a serious **compliance program**; that is, a plan to prevent and detect criminal conduct at all levels of the company. A company that can point to a detailed, functioning compliance program may benefit from a dramatic reduction in the fine or other punishment meted out. Indeed, a tough compliance program may even convince federal investigators to curtail an investigation

Federal Sentencing Guidelines
The detailed rules that judges must follow when sentencing defendants convicted of crimes in federal court

Compliance program
A plan to prevent and detect improper conduct at all levels of the company

---

[61]David Barstow, "At Wal-Mart in Mexico, a Bribe Inquiry Silenced," *The New York Times*, April 21, 2012.
[62]Source: http://epa.gov/.

and to limit any prosecution to those directly involved, rather than attempting to convict high-ranking officers or the company itself.

For a compliance plan to be deemed effective:

- The program must be reasonably capable of reducing the prospect of criminal conduct.

- Specific, high-level officers must be responsible for overseeing the program.

- The company must not place in charge any officers it knows or should have known, from past experience, are likely to engage in illegal conduct.

- The company must effectively communicate the program to all employees and agents.

- The company must ensure compliance by monitoring employees in a position to cheat and by promptly disciplining any who break the law.

Chapter Conclusion

Crime has an enormous impact on business. Companies are victims of crimes, and sometimes they also commit criminal actions. Successful business leaders are ever-vigilant to protect their company from those who wish to harm it, whether from inside or out.

EXAM REVIEW

1. **BURDEN OF PROOF** In all prosecutions, the government must prove its case beyond a reasonable doubt.

EXAM Strategy

Question: A fire breaks out in Arnie's house, destroying the building and causing $150,000 in damage to an adjacent store. The state charges Arnie with arson. Simultaneously, Vickie, the store owner, sues Arnie for the damage to her property. Both cases are tried to juries, and the two juries hear identical evidence of Arnie's actions. But the criminal jury acquits Arnie, while the civil jury awards Vickie $150,000. How did that happen?

Strategy: The opposite outcomes are probably due to the different burdens of proof in a civil and criminal case. Make sure you know that distinction. (See the "Result" at the end of this section.)

2. **RIGHT TO A JURY** A criminal defendant has a right to a trial by jury for any charge that could result in a sentence of six months or longer.

3. **FELONY** A felony is a serious crime for which a defendant can be sentenced to one year or more in prison.

4. **CONDUCT OUTLAWED**   The language of criminal statutes must be clear and definite.

5. **VOLUNTARY ACT**   A defendant is not guilty of a crime if she committed it under duress. However, the defendant bears the burden of proving by a preponderance of the evidence that she acted under duress.

6. **ENTRAPMENT**   When the government induces the defendant to break the law, the prosecution must prove beyond a reasonable doubt that the defendant was predisposed to commit the crime.

7. **CONSPIRACY**   It is illegal to conspire to commit a crime, even if that crime never actually occurs.

8. **FOURTH AMENDMENT**   The Fourth Amendment to the Constitution prohibits the government from making illegal searches and seizures of individuals, corporations, partnerships, and other organizations.

9. **WARRANT**   As a general rule, the police must obtain a warrant before conducting a search, but there are seven circumstances under which the police may search without a warrant: plain view, stop and frisk, emergencies, automobiles, lawful arrest, consent, no expectation of privacy.

10. **PROBABLE CAUSE**   The magistrate will issue a warrant only if there is probable cause. Probable cause means that it is likely that evidence of a crime will be found in the place to be searched.

11. **THE EXCLUSIONARY RULE**   Under the exclusionary rule, any evidence the government acquires illegally (or any information obtained as a result of this illegal behavior) may not be used at trial.

12. **FIFTH AMENDMENT**   The Fifth Amendment requires due process in all criminal procedures and prohibits double jeopardy and self-incrimination.

13. **SIXTH AMENDMENT**   The Sixth Amendment guarantees criminal defendants the right to a lawyer.

14. **DOUBLE JEOPARDY**   A defendant may be prosecuted only once for a particular criminal offense.

15. **EIGHTH AMENDMENT**   The Eighth Amendment prohibits excessive fines and cruel and unusual punishments.

16. **LARCENY**   Larceny is the trespassory taking of personal property with the intent to steal.

17. **FRAUD**   Fraud refers to a variety of crimes, all of which involve the deception of another person for the purpose of obtaining money or property.

18. **IDENTITY THEFT**   The Identity Theft and Assumption Deterrence Act of 1998 prohibits the use of false identification to commit fraud or other crime and it also permits the victim to seek restitution in court. The Aggravated Identity Theft statute

imposes a mandatory additional sentence of two years on anyone who engages in identity theft during the commission of certain crimes.

19. **ARSON**   Arson is the malicious use of fire or explosives to damage or destroy real estate or personal property.

20. **EMBEZZLEMENT**   Embezzlement is the fraudulent conversion of property already in the defendant's possession.

21. **HACKING**   The federal Computer Fraud and Abuse Act of 1986 prohibits hacking. It is illegal, among other things, to access a computer without authorization and obtain information from it.

22. **CORPORATE LIABILITY**   If a company's agent commits a criminal act within the scope of her employment and with the intent to benefit the corporation, the company is liable.

23. **MAKING FALSE STATEMENTS**   It is illegal to make false statements or engage in a cover-up during any dealings with the United States government.

24. **RICO**   RICO prohibits using two or more racketeering acts to accomplish any of these goals: (1) investing in or acquiring legitimate businesses with criminal money; (2) maintaining or acquiring businesses through criminal activity; or (3) operating businesses through criminal activity.

EXAM Strategy

Question: Cheryl is a bank teller. She figures out a way to steal $99.99 per day in cash without getting caught. She takes the money daily for eight months and invests it in a catering business she is starting with Floyd, another teller. When Floyd learns what she is doing, he tries it, but is caught in his first attempt. He and Cheryl are both prosecuted.

(a) Both are guilty only of larceny.

(b) Both are guilty of larceny and violating RICO.

(c) Both are guilty of embezzlement; Cheryl is also guilty of violating RICO.

(d) Both are guilty of embezzlement and violating RICO.

Strategy: You need to know the difference between larceny and embezzlement. What is it? Once you have that figured out, focus on RICO. The government must prove two things: First, that the defendant committed crimes more than once—how many times? Second, that the defendant used the criminal proceeds for a specific purpose—what? (See the "Result" at the end of this section.)

25. **MONEY LAUNDERING**   Money laundering consists of taking profits from a criminal act and either using them to promote crime or attempting to conceal their source.

26. **IMMIGRATION LAW**   It is illegal to knowingly employ unauthorized workers.

27. **FOREIGN CORRUPT PRACTICES ACT**   Under the Foreign Corrupt Practices Act, it is illegal for any employee or agent of a U.S. company (and some foreign companies) to give anything of value to any foreign official for purposes of influencing an official decision (unless the payment was merely intended to facilitate a routine governmental action.)

Question: Splash is a California corporation that develops resorts. Lawrence, a Splash executive, is hoping to land a $700 million contract with a country in Southeast Asia. He seeks your advice. "I own a fabulous beach house in Australia. What if I allow a government official and his family to stay there for two weeks? That might be enough to close the resort deal. Would that be wrong? Should I do it?" Please advise him.

Strategy: What law governs Lawrence's proposed conduct? Is Lawrence legally safe, given that the land is foreign and the contract will be signed overseas? Are there any circumstances under which this house loan would be legal? (See the result at the end of this section.)

1. Result: The plaintiff offered enough proof to convince a jury by a preponderance of the evidence that Arnie had committed arson. However that same evidence, offered in a criminal prosecution, was not enough to persuade the jury beyond a reasonable doubt that Arnie had lit the fire.

24. Result: Cheryl and Floyd both committed embezzlement, which refers to fraudulently taking money that was properly in their possession. Floyd did it once, but a RICO conviction requires two or more racketeering acts—Floyd has not violated RICO. Cheryl embezzled dozens of times and invested the money in a legitimate business. She is guilty of embezzlement and RICO; the correct answer is C.

27. Result: If Lawrence gives anything of value (such as rent-free use of his house) to secure a government contract, he has violated the FCPA. It makes no difference where the property is located or the deal signed. He could go to jail, and his company could be harshly penalized. Ethically, his gift would exacerbate corruption in a developing nation and mean that the agreement was determined by a bribe, not the merits of Splash. Other companies might do a superior job employing local workers, constructing an enduring resort, and protecting the environment, all for less money. The loan of the house would be legal if the official was simply in charge of turning on utilities in the area where the resort would be built.

MULTIPLE-CHOICE QUESTIONS

1. In a criminal case, which statement is true?

(a) The prosecution must prove the government's case by a preponderance of the evidence.

(b) The criminal defendant is entitled to a lawyer even if she cannot afford to pay for it herself.

(c) The police are never allowed to question the accused without a lawyer present.

(d) All federal crimes are felonies.

2. The police are not required to obtain a warrant before conducting a search if:
   (a) a reliable informant has told them they will find evidence of a crime in a particular location.
   (b) they have a warrant for part of a property and another section of the property is in plain view.
   (c) they see someone on the street who could possibly have committed a criminal act.
   (d) someone living on the property has consented to the search.

3. Under the exclusionary rule, which statement is true?
   (a) Evidence must be excluded from trial if the search warrant is defective, even if the police believed at the time of the search that it was valid.
   (b) The prosecution cannot use any evidence the police found at the site of the illegal search, but it can use any evidence the police discover elsewhere as a result of the illegal search.
   (c) Any statements a defendant makes after arrest are inadmissible if the police do not read him his Miranda rights.
   (d) If a conviction is overturned because of the exclusionary rule, the prosecution is not allowed to retry the defendant.

4. Henry asks his girlfriend, Alina, to drive his car to the repair shop. She drives his car all right—to Las Vegas, where she hits the slots. Alina has committed:
   (a) fraud
   (b) embezzlement
   (c) larceny
   (d) a RICO violation

5. Which of the following elements is *required* for a RICO conviction?
   (a) Investment in a legitimate business
   (b) Two or more criminal acts
   (c) Maintaining or acquiring businesses through criminal activity
   (d) Operating a business through criminal activity

CASE QUESTIONS

1. *YOU BE THE JUDGE* **WRITING PROBLEM** An undercover drug informant learned from a mutual friend that Philip Friedman "knew where to get marijuana." The informant asked Friedman three times to get him some marijuana, and Friedman agreed after the third request. Shortly thereafter, Friedman sold the informant a small amount of the drug. The informant later offered to sell Friedman three pounds of marijuana. They negotiated the price and then made the sale. Friedman was tried for trafficking in drugs. He argued entrapment. Was Friedman entrapped? **Argument for Friedman:** The undercover agent had to ask three times before Friedman sold him a small amount of drugs. A real drug dealer, predisposed to commit the crime, leaps at an opportunity to sell. If the government spends time and money luring innocent

people into the commission of crimes, all of us are the losers. **Argument for the Government:** Government officials suspected Friedman of being a sophisticated drug dealer, and they were right. When he had a chance to buy three pounds, a quantity only a dealer would purchase, he not only did so, but he bargained with skill, showing a working knowledge of the business. Friedman was not entrapped—he was caught.

2. Conley owned video poker machines. Although they are outlawed in Pennsylvania, he placed them in bars and clubs. He used profits from the machines to buy more machines. Is he guilty of money laundering?

3. Karin made illegal firearm purchases at a gun show. At her trial, she alleged that she had committed this crime because her boyfriend had threatened to harm her and her two daughters if she did not. Her lawyer asked the judge to instruct the jury that the prosecution had an obligation to prove beyond a reasonable doubt that Karin had acted freely. Instead, the judge told the jury that Karin had the burden of proving duress by a preponderance of the evidence. Who is correct?

4. Shawn was caught stealing letters from mailboxes. After pleading guilty, he was sentenced to two months in prison and three years' supervised release. One of the supervised release conditions required him to stand outside a post office for eight hours wearing a signboard stating, "I stole mail. This is my punishment." He appealed this requirement on the grounds that it constituted cruel and unusual punishment. Do you agree?

5. While driving his SUV, George struck and killed a pedestrian. He then fled the scene of the crime. A year later, the police downloaded information from his car's onboard computer which they were able to use to convict him of the crime. Should this information have been admissible at trial?

6. While conducting a valid search of a computer for evidence of a murder, a police officer discovered child pornography. Is that evidence admissible, even though the warrant was limited to a search relating to the murder?

7. Police arrested Hank on a warrant issued in a neighboring county. When they searched him, the police found drugs and a gun. Only later did the police discover that when they had used the warrant, it was not valid because it had been recalled months earlier. The notice of recall had not been entered into the database. Should the evidence of drugs and a gun be suppressed under the exclusionary rule?

DISCUSSION QUESTIONS

1. Under British law, a police officer must now say the following to a suspect placed under arrest: "You do not have to say anything. But if you do not mention now something which you later use in your defense, the court may decide that your failure to mention it now strengthens the case against you. A record will be made of anything you say and it may be given in evidence if you are brought to trial." What is the goal of this British law? What does a police officer in the United States have to say, and what difference does it make at the time of an arrest? Which approach is better?

2. **ETHICS** You are a prosecutor who thinks it is possible that Nonnie, in her role as CEO of a brokerage firm, has stolen money from her customers, many of whom are not well off. If you charge her and her company with RICO violations, you know that she is likely to plea bargain because otherwise her assets and those of the company may be frozen by the court. As part of the plea bargain, you might be able to get her to disclose evidence about other people who might have taken part in this criminal activity. But you do not have any hard evidence at this point. Would such an indictment be ethical? Do the ends justify the means? Is it worth it to harm Nonnie for the chance of protecting thousands of innocent investors?

3. An informant bought drugs from Dorian. The police obtained a search warrant to search Dorian's house. But before they acted on the warrant, they sent the informant back to try again. This time, Dorian said he did not have any drugs. The police then acted on the warrant and searched his house. Did the police have probable cause?

4. Van is brought to the police station for questioning about a shooting at a mall. The police read him his Miranda rights. For the rest of the three-hour interrogation, he remains silent except for a few one-word responses. Has he waived his right to remain silent? Can those few words be used against him in court?

5. Officer Trottier stopped Marie for driving 20 miles over the speed limit. He then became suspicious because her son would not make eye contact and she was eating a Powerbar in a "hurried manner." The officer asked for and Marie granted him permission to search her car. During the search, he found a letter, which he read. Has he committed an illegal search?

6. Mickle pleaded guilty to rape. The judge sentenced him to prison for five years and also ordered that he undergo a vasectomy. Was this cruel and unusual punishment?

7. Ramona was indicted on charges of real estate fraud. During a legal search of her home, the police found a computer with encrypted files. Would it be a violation of her Fifth Amendment right against self-incrimination to force her to unencrypt these files?

8. Suppose two people are living together: the suspect and a tenant. If the tenant consents to a police search of the premises, then the police are not required to first obtain a warrant. What if the suspect and the tenant disagree, with the tenant granting permission while the suspect forbids the police to enter? Should the police be required to obtain a warrant before searching? Or what if the suspect denies permission to enter but the police go back later and the tenant consents?

9. Hiring relatives of foreign officials for no-show jobs is a violation of the FCPA. But what about hiring children of government officials into real jobs? Is that also a violation? The U.S. government is investigating JPMorgan Chase & Co.'s practice of hiring the children of top Chinese officials in Hong Kong. What are the rules in this situation? What should they be?

ANSWERS TO SELECTED END OF CHAPTER QUESTIONS

MULTIPLE-CHOICE QUESTIONS

Presented are the answers for the ODD-numbered multiple-choice questions in the end-of-chapter material.

1. B
3. C
5. B

CASE QUESTIONS

Presented are the answers for all of the ODD-numbered case questions in the end-of-chapter material.

1. **Answer:** Friedman argued entrapment, claiming that there was no evidence of his predisposition to traffic in drugs. The Alabama Supreme Court ruled against him. The court noted that Friedman admitted to occasional use of marijuana, that he had been able quickly to locate marijuana to resell to the agent, and that he showed a sophisticated knowledge of the drug when bargaining over the price of three pounds. The court held that there was no evidence of entrapment. *Friedman v. State*, 654 So.2d 50, 1994 Ala. Crim. App. LEXIS 179 (1994).

3. **Answer:** The Supreme Court sided with the trial judge. *Dixon v. United States*, 548 U.S. 1.

5. **Answer:** A California court ruled that Xinos did have a reasonable expectation of privacy and the data was not admissible in court because the computer had simply been recording his movements on a public road. *People v. Xinos*, 192 Cal. App. 4th 637 (Cal. App. 6th Dist. 2011).

Chapter 8

Intentional Torts and Business Torts

© biletskiy/Shutterstock.com

They say politics can get ugly. *Doubt it?* Just ask John Vogel and Paul Grannis. Both men started off as candidates for public office in California—and then learned about defamation the hard way. They had no defense when mean and nasty statements were posted about them online. Here is their story.

Joseph Felice ran a website that listed "Top Ten Dumb Asses." Vogel and Grannis earned the honor of being number 1 and 2 on the list, respectively. The site also claimed that Vogel was "WANTED as a Dead Beat Dad" because he was behind on his child support payments. When users clicked on Vogel's name, they were led to another website—www.satan.com—that included a picture of him altered to look like a devil.

Grannis did not fare any better. Felice's site declared him "Bankrupt, Drunk & Chewin' Tobaccy." It stated that Grannis had "bankrupted many businesses throughout California." His name was hyperlinked to a website with the address www.olddrunk.com that accused him of criminal, fraudulent, and immoral conduct.

Understandably offended, Vogel and Grannis sued Felice for libel.[1] But they soon learned that filing such a lawsuit is easier than winning it.

> **They had no defense when mean and nasty statements were posted about them online.**

---

[1]Vogel v. Felice, 127 Cal. App. 4th 1006 (2005).

The odd word *tort* is borrowed from the French, meaning "wrong." And that is what it means in law: a wrong. More precisely, a **tort** is a violation of a duty imposed by the civil law. When a person breaks one of those duties and injures another, it is a tort. The injury could be to a person or her property. Libel, which the politicians in the opening scenario alleged, is one example of a tort. A surgeon who removes the wrong kidney from a patient commits a different kind of tort, called *negligence.* A business executive who deliberately steals a client away from a competitor, interfering with a valid contract, commits a tort called *interference with a contract.* A con artist who tricks you out of your money with a phony offer to sell you a boat commits *fraud,* yet another tort.

Because tort law is so broad, it takes a while—and two chapters—to understand its boundaries. To start with, we must distinguish torts from two other areas of law: criminal law and contract law.

It is a *crime* to steal a car, to embezzle money from a bank, to sell cocaine. As discussed in Chapter 1, society considers such behavior so threatening that the government itself will prosecute the wrongdoer, whether or not the car owner or bank president wants the case to go forward. A district attorney, who is paid by the government, will bring the case to court, seeking to send the defendant to prison, fine him, or both. If there is a fine, the money goes to the state, not to the victim.

In a tort case, it is up to the injured party to seek compensation. She must hire her own lawyer, who will file a lawsuit. Her lawyer must convince the court that the defendant breached some legal duty and ought to pay money damages to the plaintiff. The plaintiff has no power to send the defendant to jail. Bear in mind that a defendant's action might be both a crime and a tort. A man who punches you in the face for no reason commits the tort of battery. You may file a civil suit against him and will collect money damages if you can prove your case. He has also committed a crime, and the state may prosecute, seeking to imprison and fine him.

Tort
A violation of a duty imposed by the civil law

Differences between Contract, Tort, and Criminal Law

Type of Obligation	Contract	Tort	Criminal Law
How the obligation is created	The parties agree on a contract, which creates duties for both	The civil law imposes duties of conduct on all persons	The criminal law prohibits certain conduct
How the obligation is enforced	Suit by plaintiff	Suit by plaintiff	Prosecution by government
Possible result	Money damages for plaintiff	Money damages for plaintiff	Punishment for defendant, including prison and/or fine
Example	Raul contracts to sell Deirdre 5,000 pairs of sneakers at $50 per pair, but fails to deliver them. Deirdre buys the sneakers elsewhere for $60 per pair and receives $50,000, her extra expense	A newspaper falsely accuses a private citizen of being an alcoholic. The plaintiff sues and wins money damages to compensate for her injured reputation	Leo steals Kelly's car. The government prosecutes Leo for grand theft, and the judge sentences him to two years in prison. Kelly gets nothing

A tort is also different from a contract dispute. A contract case is based on an agreement two people have already made. For example, Deirdre claims that Raul promised to sell her 10,000 pairs of sneakers at a good price but has failed to deliver them. She files a contract lawsuit. In a tort case, there is usually no "deal" between the parties. John Vogel and Paul Grannis had never made any kind of contract with their online critic. The plaintiff in a tort case claims that the law itself creates a duty that the defendant has breached.

Intentional torts
Harm caused by a deliberate action

Tort law is divided into categories. In this chapter, we consider **intentional torts**, that is, harm caused by a deliberate action. When Paula hits Paul, she has committed the intentional tort of battery. In the next chapter, we examine negligence, strict liability, and product liability, which involve injuries and losses caused by neglect and oversight rather than by deliberate conduct.

A final introductory point: When we speak of intentional torts, we do not necessarily mean that the defendant intended to harm the plaintiff. If the defendant does something deliberately and it ends up injuring somebody, she is probably liable even if she meant no harm. For example, intentionally throwing a snowball at a friend is a deliberate act. If the snowball permanently damages his eye, the *harm* is unintended, but the defendant is liable for the intentional tort of battery because the *act* was intentional.

We look first at the most common intentional torts and then at the most important intentional torts that are related to business.

8-1 INTENTIONAL TORTS

8-1a Defamation

The First Amendment guarantees the right to free speech, a vital freedom that enables us to protect other rights. But that freedom is not absolute.

Libel
Written defamation

Slander
Oral defamation

The law of defamation concerns false statements that harm someone's reputation. Defamatory statements can be written or spoken. Written defamation is called **libel**. Suppose a newspaper accuses a local retail store of programming its cash registers to overcharge customers when the store has never done so. That is libel. Oral defamation is **slander**. If Professor Wisdom, in class, refers to Sally Student as a drug dealer although she has never sold drugs, he has slandered her.

There are four elements to a defamation case. An element is something that a plaintiff must prove to win a lawsuit. The plaintiff in any kind of lawsuit must prove *all* of the elements to prevail. The elements in a defamation case are:

- **Defamatory statement.** This is a factual statement that is likely to harm another person's reputation. Because opinions are not factual, they do not generally count as defamatory statements. In the case from the opening scenario, the judge found that "dumb ass" was not a defamatory statement. The court interpreted that slang phrase as a general expression of contempt, not a fact. On the other hand, the accusations that Vogel owed child support payments and Grannis was bankrupt *were* defamatory statements because they were facts that could be proven true or false.

- **Falsity.** The statement must be false. Felice, the website's author, was ultimately successful in his defense because he proved that Vogel did in fact fail to pay child support and Grannis had filed for bankruptcy. Making a true statement, no matter how mean, is not defamation.

- **Communicated.** The statement must be communicated to at least one person *other than the plaintiff.* It stands to reason: If no one else receives the defamatory message, there is no harm done. Defamation protects against injury to reputation, not hurt feelings.

- **Injury.** The plaintiff must show some injury, unless the case involves false statements about sexual behavior, crimes, contagious diseases, and professional abilities. In these cases, the law is willing to *assume* injury without requiring the plaintiff to prove it. Lies in these four categories amount to **slander per se** when they are spoken and **libel per se** when they are published.[2]

The following case involves libel per se, *The New York Times*, and alleged police brutality. Set in Alabama during the racially charged Sixties, this landmark Supreme Court decision changed the rules of the defamation game for all public personalities.

Slander per se

When oral statements relate to criminal or sexual conduct, contagious diseases, or professional abilities, they are assumed to be harmful to the subject's reputation.

Libel per se

When written statements relate to criminal or sexual conduct, contagious diseases, or professional abilities, they are assumed to be harmful to the subject's reputation.

---

[2]The courts consider defamation on radio and television to be libel, not slander, because of their vast audiences. As a result, plaintiffs in broadcasting cases generally do not have to prove damages.

Landmark Case

NEW YORK TIMES CO. V. SULLIVAN
376 U.S. 254
United States Supreme Court, 1964

Facts: In 1960, *The New York Times* ran a full-page advertisement paid for by civil rights activists. The ad described an "unprecedented wave of terror" by the police of Montgomery, Alabama, against civil rights protesters. It stated that the police had assaulted nonviolent protesters with shotguns and tear gas and had padlocked a dining hall to starve them into submission. The ad also accused the Montgomery police of bombing the home of Dr. Martin Luther King, Jr., and unjustly arresting him seven times. Most of the ad's statements were true, but a few were not.

L.B. Sullivan was Montgomery's police commissioner. Although the ad did not mention him by name, Sullivan argued that the accusations hurt his reputation because he was head of the police. He sued *The New York Times* under Alabama's law on libel per se.

An Alabama court agreed with Sullivan, awarding him damages of $500,000. The Supreme Court of Alabama affirmed. *The New York Times* appealed to the U.S. Supreme Court, arguing that the ad was protected by the First Amendment and the evidence did not support such an award.

Issue: *Does the First Amendment protect those who criticize public officials?*

Excerpts from Justice Brennan's Decision: We consider this case against the background of a profound national commitment to the principle that debate on public issues should be uninhibited, robust, and wide-open, and that it may well include vehement, caustic, and sometimes unpleasantly sharp attacks on government and public officials. The present advertisement, as an expression of grievance and protest on one of the major public issues of our time, would seem clearly to qualify for the constitutional protection. The question is whether it forfeits that protection by the falsity of some of its factual statements and by its alleged defamation of respondent.

First Amendment protection does not turn upon the truth, popularity, or social utility of the ideas and beliefs which are offered. Erroneous statement [are] inevitable in free debate, and must be protected. Whatever is added to the field of libel is taken from the field of free debate. Criticism of official conduct does not lose its constitutional protection merely because it diminishes official reputations.

A rule compelling the critic of official conduct to guarantee the truth of all his factual assertions leads to self-censorship. Under such a rule, would-be critics of official conduct may be deterred from voicing their criticism. The rule thus dampens the vigor and limits the variety of public debate. It is inconsistent with the First Amendment.

The constitutional guarantees require a federal rule that prohibits a public official from recovering damages for a defamatory falsehood relating to his official conduct unless he proves that the statement was made with "actual malice"—that is, with knowledge that it was false or with reckless disregard of whether it was false or not.

Applying these standards, we consider that the facts do not support a finding of actual malice as to the *Times*. The *Times* published the advertisement without checking its accuracy. We think the evidence against the *Times* supports at most a finding of negligence in failing to discover the misstatements, and is constitutionally insufficient to show the recklessness that is required for a finding of actual malice.

The judgment of the Supreme Court of Alabama is reversed and the case is remanded.

Now we see another reason why the politicians from our chapter opener lost their defamation case. **The rule from *The New York Times* case is that a public official can win a defamation case only by proving the defendant's actual malice, that is, that the defendant knew the statement was false or acted with reckless disregard of the truth.** As candidates for public office, the politicians had to prove their critic's malice—and they could not do so. The *New York Times* rule has been extended to all public figures, like actors, business leaders, and anyone else who assumes an influential and visible role in society.[3]

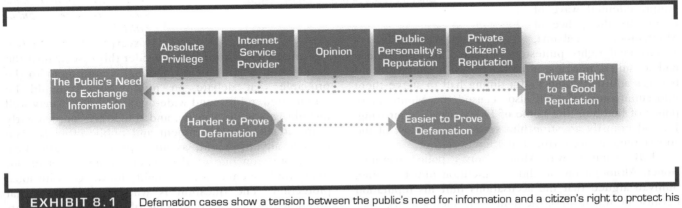

EXHIBIT 8.1 Defamation cases show a tension between the public's need for information and a citizen's right to protect his reputation.

---

[3]Curtis Publishing Co. v. Butts, 388 U.S. 130 (1967); Associated Press v. Walker, 388 U.S. 130 (1967).

Privilege

Defendants receive additional protection from defamation cases when it is important for them to speak freely. **Absolute privilege** exists in courtrooms and legislative hearings. Anyone speaking there, such as a witness in court, can say anything at all and never be sued for defamation. (Deliberately false testimony would be *perjury*, but still not *slander*.)

Absolute privilege
A witness testifying in a court or legislature may never be sued for defamation.

8-1b False Imprisonment

False imprisonment is the intentional restraint of another person without reasonable cause and without consent. Suppose that a bank teller becomes seriously ill and wants to go to the doctor, but the bank will not permit her to leave until she makes a final tally of her accounts. Against her wishes, company officials physically bar her from leaving the bank. That is false imprisonment. The restraint was unreasonable because her accounts could have been verified later.[4]

False imprisonment
The intentional restraint of another person without reasonable cause and without consent

False imprisonment cases most commonly arise in retail stores, which sometimes detain employees or customers for suspected theft. Most states now have statutes governing the detention of suspected shoplifters. **Generally, a store may detain a customer or worker for alleged shoplifting provided there is a reasonable basis for the suspicion and the detention is done reasonably.** To detain a customer in the manager's office for 20 minutes and question him about where he got an item is lawful. To chain that customer to a display counter for three hours and humiliate him in front of other customers is unreasonable and constitutes false imprisonment.

8-1c Intentional Infliction of Emotional Distress

What should happen when a defendant's conduct hurts a plaintiff emotionally but not physically? Historically, not much did happen. Courts once refused to allow recovery, assuming that if they awarded damages for mere emotional injury, they would be inviting a floodgate of dubious claims. But gradually judges reexamined their thinking and reversed this tendency. Today, most courts allow a plaintiff to recover for emotional injury that a defendant intentionally caused.

The **intentional infliction of emotional distress** results from extreme and outrageous conduct that causes serious emotional harm. A credit officer was struggling vainly to locate Sheehan, who owed money on his car. The officer phoned Sheehan's mother, falsely identified herself as a hospital employee, and said she needed to find Sheehan because his children had been in a serious auto accident. The mother provided Sheehan's whereabouts, which enabled the company to seize his car. But Sheehan spent seven hours frantically trying to locate his supposedly injured children, who in fact were fine. The credit company was liable for the intentional infliction of emotional distress.[5]

Intentional infliction of emotional distress
An intentional tort in which the harm results from extreme and outrageous conduct that causes serious emotional harm

By contrast, a muffler shop, trying to collect a debt from a customer, made six phone calls over three months, using abusive language. The customer testified that this caused her to be upset, to cry, and to have difficulty sleeping. The court ruled that the muffler shop's conduct was neither extreme nor outrageous.[6]

The following case arose in a setting that guarantees controversy—an abortion clinic.

---

[4]Kanner v. First National Bank of South Miami, 287 So.2d 715 (Fla. Dist. Ct. App. 1974).
[5]Ford Motor Credit Co. v. Sheehan, 373 So.2d 956 (Fla. Dist. Ct. App. 1979).
[6]Midas Muffler Shop v. Ellison, 133 Ariz. 194 (Ariz. Ct. App. 1982).

JANE DOE AND NANCY ROE V. LYNN MILLS

212 Mich. App. 73
Michigan Court of Appeals, 1995

Facts: Late one night, an anti-abortion protestor named Robert Thomas climbed into a dumpster located behind the Women's Advisory Center, an abortion clinic. He found documents indicating that the plaintiffs were soon to have abortions at the clinic. Thomas gave the information to Lynn Mills. The next day, Mills and Sister Lois Mitoraj created signs, using the women's names, indicating that they were about to undergo abortions, and urging them not to "kill their babies."

Doe and Roe (not their real names) sued, claiming intentional infliction of emotional distress (as well as breach of privacy, discussed later in this chapter). The trial court dismissed the lawsuit, ruling that the defendants' conduct was not extreme and outrageous. The plaintiffs appealed.

Issue: *Have the plaintiffs made a valid claim of intentional infliction of emotional distress?*

Excerpts from the Court's *Per Curiam* Decision: Liability for the intentional infliction of emotional distress has been found only where the conduct complained of has been so outrageous in character, and so extreme in degree, as to go beyond all possible bounds of decency, and to be regarded as atrocious and utterly intolerable in a civilized community. Liability does not extend to mere insults, indignities, threats, annoyances, petty oppressions, or other trivialities. It has been said that the case is generally one in which the recitation of the facts to an average member of the community would arouse his resentment against the actor, and lead him to exclaim, "Outrageous!"

The conduct in this case involved defendants identifying plaintiffs by name and publicizing the fact of their abortions by displaying such information on large signs that were held up for public view. In ruling that defendants' conduct was not sufficiently extreme and outrageous so as to permit recovery, the trial court was influenced in part by its conclusion that the information disclosed did not concern a private matter, inasmuch as it was obtained from a document that had been discarded into the trash. [But the plaintiffs themselves never placed their names on the discarded papers, and even if they had, such an act would not have indicated consent to such publicity.] The trial court also observed that defendants have a constitutional right to "protest peaceably against abortion." However, the objectionable aspect of defendants' conduct does not relate to their views on abortion or their right to express those views, but, rather, to the fact that defendants gave unreasonable or unnecessary publicity to purely private matters involving plaintiffs. Finally, the trial court observed that there is no statute prohibiting the kind of activity engaged in by defendants. It is not necessary, however, that a defendant's conduct constitute a statutory violation in order for it to be found extreme and outrageous.

We are of the opinion that the trial court erred in granting the defendants' motion for summary disposition of plaintiffs' claim of intentional infliction of emotional distress. Defendants' conduct involved more than mere insults, indignities, threats, annoyances, or petty oppressions. We believe this is the type of case that might cause an average member of the community, upon learning of defendants' conduct, to exclaim, "Outrageous!" Because reasonable men may differ with regard to whether defendants' conduct may be considered sufficiently outrageous and extreme so as to subject them to liability for intentional infliction of emotional distress, this matter should be determined by the trier of fact.

Summary judgment for the defendants is reversed, and the case is remanded for trial.

8-1d Battery and Assault

Battery

An intentional touching of another person in a way that is harmful or offensive

Assault and battery are related, but not identical. **Battery** is an intentional touching of another person in a way that is harmful or offensive.

If an irate parent throws a chair at a referee during his daughter's basketball game, breaking the man's jaw, he has committed battery. But a parent who cheerfully slaps the winning coach on the back has not committed battery because a reasonable coach would not be offended.

As mentioned earlier, there need be no intention to hurt the plaintiff. If the defendant intended to do the physical act, and a reasonable plaintiff would be offended by it, battery has occurred. An executive who gives an unwanted sexual caress to a secretary also commits this tort, even if he assumed that any normal female would be ecstatic over his attentions. (This is also sexual harassment, discussed in Chapter 29, on employment law.)

Assault occurs when a defendant does some act that makes a plaintiff *fear* an imminent battery. This tort is based on apprehension—it does not matter whether a battery ever occurs. Suppose Ms. Wilson shouts "Think fast!" at her husband and hurls a toaster at him. He turns and sees it flying at him. His fear of being struck is enough to win a case of assault, even if the toaster misses. If the toaster happens to strike him, Ms. Wilson has also committed battery.

Recall the shoplifting problem. Assume that a store guard pulls an unloaded pistol on Sandra Shopper, suspecting her of theft. Sandra faints and strikes her head on a counter. When sued for assault, the store defends by claiming the guard never touched her and the gun was unloaded. Obviously, the store did not have the benefit of this law course. A reasonable shopper would have feared imminent battery, and the store is liable for assault.

Assault
An act that makes a person reasonably fear an imminent battery

---

EXAM Strategy

Question: Mark is furious because his girlfriend, Denise, just told him she is leaving him. He never saw it coming. On the sidewalk, he picks up a rock and hurls it at Denise's head. She *does* see it coming, and she ducks. The rock misses Denise but hits Terrance (who never saw it coming) in the back of his head. Denise and Terrance both sue Mark for assault and for battery. Outcomes?

Strategy: Separate the two plaintiffs. What injury did Denise suffer? She saw a rock flying at her and thought she would be struck. Now recall the elements of the two torts. Battery is an intentional touching that is offensive. Assault is an act that makes another person *fear* an imminent battery.

Result: Was Denise touched? No. Did she fear an imminent battery? Yes. Denise wins a suit for assault but loses one for battery. Now Terrance: Was he touched? Yes. Did he fear an imminent battery? No. Terrance wins a suit for battery but loses one for assault.

8-1e Trespass, Conversion, and Fraud

Trespass

Trespass is intentionally entering land that belongs to someone else or remaining on the land after being asked to leave. It is also trespass if you have some object, let's say a car, on someone else's property and refuse to remove it. "Intentionally" means that you deliberately walk onto the land. If you walk through a meadow, believing it to be a public park, and it belongs to a private owner, you have trespassed.

Trespass
Intentionally entering land that belongs to someone else or remaining on the land after being asked to leave

Conversion

Conversion
Taking or using someone's personal property without consent

Conversion is taking or using someone's personal property without consent. Personal property is any possession other than land or structures permanently attached to land, such as houses. Priceless jewels, ratty sneakers, and sailboats are all personal property. If Stormy sails away in Jib's sailboat and keeps it all summer, that is conversion. Stormy owes Jib the full value of the boat. This, of course, is similar to the crime of theft. The tort of conversion enables a plaintiff to pursue the case herself, without awaiting a criminal prosecution, and to obtain compensation.

Fraud

Fraud
Injuring another person by deliberate deception

Fraud is injuring another person by deliberate deception. Later in this chapter, a plaintiff claims that for many years a cigarette manufacturer fraudulently suggested its product was safe, knowing its assurances were deadly lies. Fraud is a tort, but it typically occurs during the negotiation or performance of a contract, and it is discussed in detail in Unit 3, on contracts.

8-2 DAMAGES

8-2a Compensatory Damages

> Bien becomes frantic, writing a dozen notes, begging to leave, threatening to call the police.

Mitchel Bien, who is deaf and mute, enters the George Grubbs Nissan dealership, where folks sell cars aggressively. Very aggressively. Maturelli, a salesman, and Bien communicate by writing messages back and forth. Maturelli takes Bien's own car keys, and the two then test-drive a 300ZX. Bien says he does not want the car, but Maturelli escorts him back inside and fills out a sales sheet. Bien repeatedly asks for his keys, but Maturelli only laughs, pressuring him to buy the new car. Minutes pass. Hours pass. Bien becomes frantic, writing a dozen notes, begging to leave, threatening to call the police. Maturelli mocks Bien and his physical disabilities. Finally, after four hours, the customer escapes.

Bien sues for the intentional infliction of emotional distress. Two former salesmen from Grubbs testify they have witnessed customers cry, yell, and curse as a result of the aggressive tactics. Doctors state that the incident has traumatized Bien, dramatically reducing his confidence and self-esteem and preventing his return to work even three years later.

The jury awards Bien damages. But how does a jury calculate the money? For that matter, why should a jury even try? Money can never erase pain or undo a permanent injury. The answer is simple: Money, however inexact, is often the only thing a court has to give.

Compensatory damages
Money intended to restore a plaintiff to the position he was in before the injury

A successful plaintiff generally receives **compensatory damages**, meaning an amount of money that the court believes will restore him to the position he was in before the defendant's conduct caused injury. Here is how damages are calculated.

Single recovery principle
Requires a court to settle the matter once and for all by awarding a lump sum for past and future expenses

First, a plaintiff receives money for medical expenses that he has proven by producing bills from doctors, hospitals, physical therapists, and psychotherapists. Bien receives all the money he has paid. If a doctor testifies that he needs future treatment, Bien will offer evidence of how much that will cost. The **single recovery principle** requires a court to settle the matter once and for all, by awarding a lump sum for past *and future* expenses, if there will be any. A plaintiff may not return in a year and say, "Oh, by the way, there are some new bills."

Second, the defendants are liable for lost wages. The court takes the number of days or months that Bien missed work and multiplies that number times his salary. If Bien is currently unable to work, a doctor estimates how many more months he will miss work, and the court adds that to his damages.

Third, a plaintiff is paid for pain and suffering. Bien testifies about how traumatic the four hours were and how the experience has affected his life. He may state that he now fears shopping, suffers nightmares, and seldom socializes. To bolster the case, a plaintiff uses expert testimony, such as the psychiatrists who testified for Bien. Awards for pain and suffering vary enormously, from a few dollars to many millions, depending on the injury and depending on the jury. In some lawsuits, physical and psychological pains are momentary and insignificant; in other cases, the pain is the biggest part of the verdict. In this case, the jury awarded Bien $573,815, calculated as in the following table.[7]

Past medical	$ 70.00
Future medical	6,000.00
Past rehabilitation	3,205.00
Past lost earning capacity	112,910.00
Future lost earning capacity	34,650.00
Past physical symptoms and discomfort	50,000.00
Future physical symptoms and discomfort	50,000.00
Past emotional injury and mental anguish	101,980.00
Future emotional injury and mental anguish	200,000.00
Past loss of society and reduced ability to socially interact with family, former fiancée, friends, and hearing (i.e., nondeaf) people in general	10,000.00
Future loss of society and reduced ability to socially interact with family, former fiancée, friends, and hearing people	5,000.00
TOTAL	**$573,815.00**

---

[7]The compensatory damages are described in George Grubbs Enterprises v. Bien, 881 S.W.2d 843 (Tex. Ct. App. 1994). In addition to the compensatory damages described, the jury awarded $5 million in punitive damages. The Texas Supreme Court reversed the award of punitive damages, but not the compensatory. Id., 900 S.W.2d 337 (Tex. 1995). The high court did not dispute the appropriateness of punitive damages, but reversed because the trial court failed to instruct the jury properly as to how it should determine the assets actually under the defendants' control, an issue essential to punitive damages but not compensatory.

Awards for future harm (such as future pain and suffering) involve the court making its best estimate of the plaintiff's hardship in the years to come. This is not an exact science. If the judgment is reasonable, it will rarely be overturned. Ethel Flanzraich, age 78, fell on stairs that had been badly maintained. In addition to her medical expense, the court awarded her $150,000 for future pain and suffering. The day after the court gave its award, Ms. Flanzraich died of other causes. Did that mean her family must forfeit that money? No. The award was reasonable when made and had to be paid.[8]

8-2b Punitive Damages

Punitive damages

Damages that are intended to punish the defendant for conduct that is extreme and outrageous

Here we look at a different kind of award, one that is more controversial and potentially more powerful: punitive damages. The purpose is not to compensate the plaintiff for harm, because compensatory damages will have done that. **Punitive damages** are intended to punish the defendant for conduct that is extreme and outrageous. Courts award these damages in relatively few cases. The idea behind punitive damages is that certain behavior is so unacceptable that society must make an example of it. A large award of money should deter the defendant from repeating the mistake and others from ever making it. Some believe punitive damages represent the law at its most avaricious, while others attribute to them great social benefit.

Although a jury has wide discretion in awarding punitive damages, the Supreme Court has ruled that a verdict must be reasonable. Ira Gore purchased a new BMW automobile from an Alabama dealer and then discovered that the car had been repainted. He sued. At trial, BMW acknowledged a nationwide policy of not informing customers of predelivery repairs when the cost was less than 3 percent of the retail price. The company had sold about 1,000 repainted cars nationwide. The jury concluded that BMW had engaged in gross, malicious fraud and awarded Gore $4,000 in compensatory damages and $4 million in punitive damages. The Alabama Supreme Court reduced the award to $2 million, but the United States Supreme Court ruled that even that amount was grossly excessive. The Court held that in awarding punitive damages, a court must consider three "guideposts":

- The reprehensibility of the defendant's conduct;

- The ratio between the harm suffered and the award; and

- The difference between the punitive award and any civil penalties used in similar cases.

The Court concluded that BMW had shown no evil intent and that Gore's harm had been purely economic (as opposed to physical). Further, the Court found the ratio of 500 to 1, between punitive and compensatory damages, to be excessive, although it offered no definitive rule about a proper ratio. On remand, the Alabama Supreme Court reduced the punitive damages award to $50,000.[9]

The U.S. Supreme Court gave additional guidance on punitive damages in the following landmark case.

---

[8]Stinton v. Robin's Wood, 842 N.Y.S.2d 477 (N.Y. App. Div. 2007).
[9]BMW of North America, Inc. v. Gore, 517 U.S. 559 (1996).

Landmark Case

STATE FARM V. CAMPBELL
538 U.S. 408
Supreme Court of the United States, 2003

Facts: While attempting to pass several cars on a two-lane road, Campbell drove into oncoming traffic. An innocent driver swerved to avoid Campbell and died in a collision with a third driver. The family of the deceased driver and the surviving third driver both sued Campbell.

As Campbell's insurer, State Farm represented him in the lawsuit. It turned down an offer to settle the case for $50,000, the limit of Campbell's policy. The company had nothing to gain by settling because even if Campbell lost big at trial, State Farm's liability was capped at $50,000.

A jury returned a judgment against Campbell for $185,000. He was responsible for the $135,000 that exceeded his policy limit. He argued with State Farm, claiming that it should have settled the case. Eventually, State Farm paid the entire $185,000, but Campbell still sued the company, alleging fraud and intentional infliction of emotional distress.

His lawyers presented evidence that State Farm had deliberately acted in its own best interests rather than his. The jury was convinced, and in the end, Campbell won an award of $1 million in compensatory damages and $145 million in punitive damages. State Farm appealed.

Issue: *What is the limit on punitive damages?*

Excerpts from Justice Kennedy's Decision: We address whether an award of $145 million in punitive damages, where full compensatory damages are $1 million, is excessive and in violation of the Due Process Clause. The Utah Supreme Court relied upon testimony indicating that State Farm's actions, because of their clandestine nature, will be punished at most in 1 out of every 50,000 cases as a matter of statistical probability, and concluded that the ratio between punitive and compensatory damages was not unwarranted.

Compensatory damages are intended to redress the concrete loss that the plaintiff has suffered by reason of the defendant's wrongful conduct. By contrast, punitive damages serve a broader function; they are aimed at deterrence and retribution.

The Due Process Clause prohibits the imposition of grossly excessive or arbitrary punishments. The reason is

that elementary notions of fairness dictate that a person receive fair notice not only of the conduct that will subject him to punishment, but also of the severity of the penalty that a State may impose. To the extent an award is grossly excessive, it furthers no legitimate purpose and constitutes an arbitrary deprivation of property. A defendant should be punished for the conduct that harmed the plaintiff, not for being an unsavory.

We decline to impose a bright-line ratio which a punitive damages award cannot exceed. Our jurisprudence and the principles it has now established demonstrate, however, that, in practice, few awards exceeding a single-digit ratio between punitive and compensatory damages, to a significant degree, will satisfy due process. Single-digit multipliers are more likely to comport with due process, while still achieving the State's goals of deterrence and retribution, than awards with ratios in the range of 145 to 1.

Nonetheless, because there are no rigid benchmarks that a punitive damages award may not surpass, ratios greater than those we have previously upheld may comport with due process where a particularly egregious act has resulted in only a small amount of economic damages. The precise award in any case must be based upon the facts and circumstances of the defendant's conduct and the harm to the plaintiff.

In sum, courts must ensure that the measure of punishment is both reasonable and proportionate to the amount of harm to the plaintiff and to the general damages recovered. In the context of this case, we have no doubt that there is a presumption against an award that has a 145-to-1 ratio. The compensatory award in this case was substantial; the Campbells were awarded $1 million for a year and a half of emotional distress. This was complete compensation. The harm arose from a transaction in the economic realm, not from some physical assault or trauma; there were no physical injuries; and State Farm paid the excess verdict before the complaint was filed, so the Campbells suffered only minor economic injuries.

The judgment of the Utah Supreme Court is reversed, and the case is remanded for proceedings not inconsistent with this opinion.

Dramatic cases may *still* lead to very large awards.

And so, the Supreme Court seeks to limit, but not completely prohibit, enormous punitive damages. A California Court of Appeals decided the following case two years after *State Farm v. Campbell*. How should it implement the Supreme Court's guidelines? You be the judge.

You be the Judge

BOEKEN V. PHILIP MORRIS, INCORPORATED

127 Cal. App.4th 1640
California Court of Appeals, 2005

Facts: In the mid-1950s, Richard Boeken began smoking Marlboro cigarettes at the age of 10. Countless advertisements, targeted at boys ages 10 to 18, convinced him and his friends that the "Marlboro man" was powerful, healthy, and manly. Eventually, Richard changed to "Marlboro Lite" cigarettes but continued smoking into the 1990s, when he was diagnosed with lung cancer. He filed suit against Philip Morris, the cigarette manufacturer, for fraud and other torts. He died of cancer before the case was concluded.

Evidence at trial demonstrated that by the mid-1950s, scientists uniformly accepted that cigarette smoking caused lung cancer. However, at about the same time, Philip Morris and other tobacco companies began a decades-long campaign to convince the public that there was substantial doubt about any link between smoking and illness. The plaintiffs also demonstrated that tobacco was physically addictive, and that Philip Morris added ingredients such as urea to its cigarettes to increase their addictive power. Boeken testified that in the late 1960s he saw the Surgeon General warnings about the risk of smoking but trusted the cigarette company's statements that smoking was safe. By the 1970s he tried many times, and many cures, to stop smoking but always failed. He finally quit just before surgery to remove part of his lung but resumed after the operation.

The jury found Philip Morris liable for fraudulently concealing that cigarettes were addictive and carcinogenic. It awarded Boeken $5.5 million in compensatory damages, and also assessed punitive damages—of $3 *billion*. The trial judge reduced the punitive award to $100 million. Philip Morris appealed.

You Be the Judge: *Was the punitive damage award too high, too low, or just right?*

Argument for Philip Morris: The court should substantially reduce the $100 million punitive award because it constitutes an "arbitrary deprivation of property." The Supreme Court has indicated that punitive awards should not exceed compensatory damages by more than a factor of nine. The jury awarded Mr. Boeken $5.5 million in compensatory damages, which means that punitive damages should absolutely not exceed $49.5 million. We argue that they should be even lower.

Cigarettes are a legal product, and our packages have displayed the Surgeon General's health warnings for decades. Mr. Boeken's death is tragic, but his cancer was not necessarily caused by Marlboro cigarettes. And even if cigarettes did contribute to his failing health, Mr. Boeken chose to smoke throughout his life, even after major surgery on one of his lungs.

Argument for Boeken: The Supreme Court says that "few" cases may exceed the 9-to-1 ratio, but that "the precise award in any case must be based upon the facts and circumstances of the defendant's conduct and the harm to the plaintiff." Phillip Morris created ads that targeted children, challenged clear scientific data that its products caused cancer, and added substances to its cigarettes to make them more addictive. Does it get worse than that?

As for harm to the plaintiff, he died a terrible death from cancer. Philip Morris cigarettes kill 200,000 American customers each year. The defendant's conduct could not be more reprehensible. Philip Morris's weekly profit is roughly $100 million. At a minimum, the court should keep the punitive award at that figure. But we ask that the court reinstate the jury's original $3 billion award.

8-2c Tort Reform and the *Exxon Valdez*

Some people believe that jury awards are excessive and need statutory reform, while others argue that the evidence demonstrates excessive awards are rare and modest in size. About one-half of the states have passed limits. The laws vary, but many distinguish between **economic damage** and **noneconomic damages**. In such a state, a jury is permitted to award any amount for economic damages, meaning lost wages, medical expenses, and other measureable losses. However, noneconomic damages-pain and suffering and other losses that are difficult to measure—are capped at some level, such as $500,000. In some states, punitive awards have similar caps. These restrictions can drastically lower the total verdict.

In the famous *Exxon Valdez* case, the Supreme Court placed a severe limit on a certain type of punitive award. It is unclear how influential the decision will be because the case arises in the isolated area of maritime law, which governs ships at sea. Nonetheless, the justices wrote at length about punitive awards, and the decision may reverberate in future holdings. This is what happened.

Captain Joseph Hazelwood's negligence caused the *Exxon Valdez* to run aground off the coast of Alaska. The ship dumped 11 million gallons of oil into the sea, damaging 3,000 square miles of vulnerable ecosystem. The oil spill forced fishermen into bankruptcy, disrupted entire communities, and killed hundreds of thousands of birds and marine animals. A decade later, many of the damaged species had not recovered. The jury decided that Exxon had been reckless by allowing Hazelwood to pilot the ship when the company knew he was an alcoholic. The jury awarded compensatory damages to the plaintiffs, and punitive damages of $5 *billion*. Exxon appealed.

Almost two decades after the accident, the Supreme Court ruled. The justices discussed punitive damages in general, noting that much of the criticism of punitive awards appeared overstated. The court declared there had been no major increase in how frequently juries gave punitive damages. In the unusual cases where jurors made such awards, the sums were modest. The problem, declared the justices, was the unpredictability of punitive damages.

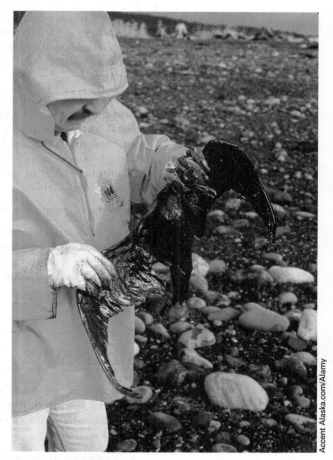

Until the 2010 Deepwater Horizon Oil Spill, the Exxon Valdez was the largest ever oil spill in U.S. waters.

Accent Alaska.com/Alamy

The court ruled that *in maritime cases*, the ratio should be no higher than 1:1. The court approved the jury's compensatory award of $507 million, and then reduced the punitive award from $5 billion to $507 million. Supporters of the court's decision stated that it would allow businesses to make plans based on predictable outcomes. Opponents said that the justices ignored the jury's finding of reckless behavior and calamitous environmental harm.[10]

---

[10]Exxon Shipping Co. v. Baker, 554 U.S. 471 (2008).

EXAM Strategy

Question: Patrick owns a fast-food restaurant, which is repeatedly painted with graffiti. He is convinced that 15-year-old John, a frequent customer, is the culprit. The next time John comes to the restaurant, Patrick locks the men's room door while John is inside. Patrick calls the police, but because of a misunderstanding, the police are very slow to arrive. John shouts and cries for help, banging on the door, but Patrick does not release him for two hours. John sues. He claims that he has suffered great psychological harm because of the incident; his psychiatrist asserts that John may have unpredictable suffering in the future. John sues for assault, battery, and false imprisonment. Will he win? May John return to court in the future to seek further damages?

Strategy: The question focuses on two issues: first, the distinction between several intentional torts; second, damages. Analyze one issue at a time. As to the intentional torts, what injury has John suffered? He was locked in the men's room and suffered psychological harm. Recall the elements of the three possible torts. Battery concerns an offensive touching. A defendant commits assault by causing an imminent fear of battery. False imprisonment: A store may detain someone if it does so reasonably.

As to damages, review the *single recovery principle*.

Result: Locking John up for two hours, based on an unproven suspicion, was clearly unreasonable. Patrick has committed false imprisonment. The single recovery principle forces John to recover now for all past and future harm. He may not return to court later and seek additional damages.

8-3 BUSINESS TORTS

In this section, we look at several intentional torts that occur almost exclusively in a commercial setting: interference with a contract, interference with a prospective advantage, and Lanham Act violations. Note that several business torts are discussed elsewhere in the book:

- Violations of the rights to privacy and publicity are examined in Chapter 10, on cyberlaw and privacy.

- Patents, copyrights, and trademarks are discussed in Chapter 41, on intellectual property.

- False advertising and other consumer issues are considered more broadly in Chapter 39, on consumer law.

8-3a Tortious Interference with Business Relations

Competition is the essence of business. Successful corporations compete aggressively, and the law permits and expects them to. But there are times when healthy competition becomes illegal interference. This is called *tortious interference with business relations*. It can take one of two closely related forms—interference with a contract or interference with a prospective advantage.

8-3b Tortious Interference with a Contract

Tortious interference with a contract exists if the plaintiff can establish the following four elements:

- There was a contract between the plaintiff and a third party;

- The defendant knew of the contract;

- The defendant improperly *induced* the third party to breach the contract or made performance of the contract impossible; and

- There was injury to the plaintiff.

Because businesses routinely compete for customers, employees, and market share, it is not always easy to identify tortious interference. There is nothing wrong with two companies bidding against each other to buy a parcel of land, and nothing wrong with one corporation doing everything possible to convince the seller to ignore all competitors. But once a company has signed a contract to buy the land, it is improper to induce the seller to break the deal. The most commonly disputed issues in these cases concern elements one and three: Was there a contract between the plaintiff and another party? Did the defendant improperly induce a party to breach it? Defendants will try to show that the plaintiff had no contract.

A defendant may also rely on the defense of **justification**, that is, a claim that special circumstances made its conduct fair. To establish justification, a defendant must show that:

- It was acting to protect an existing economic interest, such as its own contract with the third party;

- It was acting in the public interest, for example, by reporting to a government agency that a corporation was overbilling for government services; or

- The existing contract could be terminated at will by either party, meaning that although the plaintiff had a contract, the plaintiff had no long-term assurances because the other side could end it at any time.

> **Tortious interference with a contract**
>
> An intentional tort in which the defendant improperly induced a third party to breach a contract with the plaintiff

Texaco v. Pennzoil

The jury returned an enormous verdict in a famous case of contract interference. *Texaco, Inc. v. Pennzoil Co.* illustrates the two key issues: Did a contract exist, and was the defendant's behavior improper? Pennzoil made an unsolicited bid to buy 20 percent of Getty Oil at $100 per share. This offer was too low to satisfy the Getty board of directors, but it got the parties talking. The price increased to $110 per share, and the two sides began to put together pieces of a complicated deal: Gordon Getty would control four-sevenths of the Getty Oil stock, and Pennzoil would control three-sevenths. The J. Paul Getty Museum, which owned 11.8 percent of Getty stock, agreed to sell its shares provided it was paid immediately. Talks continued, the price moved up to $112.50 a share, and finally the Getty board voted to approve the deal. A press release announced an agreement in principle between Pennzoil and Getty.

Before the lawyers for both sides could complete the paperwork for the deal, Texaco appeared and offered Getty stockholders $125 per share for the entire company and later upped that offer to $128 per share. Getty turned its attention to Texaco, leaving Pennzoil the jilted lover. This lover, though, decided to sue. In Texas state court, Pennzoil claimed that Texaco had maliciously interfered with a Pennzoil–Getty contract, costing Pennzoil vast amounts of money.

Texaco argued that it had acted in good faith, asserting that there was no binding contract between the other two. But the jury bought Pennzoil's argument, and they bought

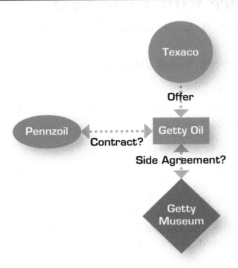

The $10 *billion* question. Texaco offered to pay $125 per share for Getty stock. The key issue was this: when Texaco made the offer, did a contract exist between Pennzoil and Getty? If, as the jury decided, there was a binding agreement, then Texaco committed tortious interference with a contract. If, however, Getty Corp. had a side agreement with the Getty Museum (one of its owners), then arguably there could be no contract between Getty and Pennzoil, and Texaco would have committed no tort at all.

it big: $7.53 billion in actual damages, plus $3 billion more in punitive damages. Texaco did not happen to have $10 billion it could spare, and the verdict threatened to destroy the oil company. Texaco appealed, but Texas appeals courts require a bond, in this case a $10 billion bond, meaning that the money must be paid into court while the appeal goes forward. Texaco filed for bankruptcy.

At the state supreme court, Texaco based its argument on an obscure rule of the Securities and Exchange Commission (SEC), Rule 10B-13. This rule prevents the parties in a takeover negotiation from arranging a "side deal" while an offer is pending. Texaco's argument thus became: Pennzoil's original $100 per share offer was still pending when the two sides came up with their $112.50 per share, "three-sevenths/four-sevenths" deal. That deal involved a side arrangement with the Getty Museum, which would get its money faster than any other shareholders would. Because it would get about $1 billion, early receipt was a major financial advantage. The deal violated Rule 10B-13 and was therefore invalid. There was no contract, and Texaco could not legally have interfered.

A $10 billion case would be decided on the classic "interference" issue of whether a contract existed. Then the SEC entered the case, filing a brief that appeared strongly to support Texaco's interpretation of the law. Pennzoil could sense that the tide was turning, and the companies settled: Texaco agreed to pay Pennzoil $3 billion as settlement for having wrongfully interfered with Pennzoil's agreement to buy Getty.

8-3c Tortious Interference with a Prospective Advantage

Tortious interference with a prospective advantage
Malicious interference with a developing economic relationship

Tortious interference with a prospective advantage is an awkward name for a tort that is simply a variation on interference with a contract. The difference is that, for this tort, there need be no contract; the plaintiff is claiming outside interference with an expected economic relationship. Obviously, the plaintiff must show more than just the hope of a profit. **A plaintiff who has a definite and reasonable expectation of obtaining an economic advantage may sue a corporation that maliciously interferes and prevents the relationship from developing.**

The defense of justification, discussed earlier, applies here as well. A typical example of justification is that the defendant is simply competing for the same business that the plaintiff seeks. There is nothing wrong with that.

To demonstrate interference with a prospective advantage, most courts require a plaintiff to show that the defendant's conduct was independently unlawful. Suppose Pink manufactures valves used in heart surgery. Pink is about to sign a deal for Rabbit to distribute the products. Zebra then says to Pink, "I want that deal. If you sign with Rabbit, I'll spread false rumors that the valves are unreliable." Pink gives in and signs a contract with Zebra. Zebra has committed interference with a prospective advantage because slander is independently illegal.[11]

The ice cream fight that follows demonstrates why plaintiffs often file but seldom win these cases.

CARVEL V. NOONAN

3 N.Y.3d 182
New York Court of Appeals, 2004

Facts: For decades, Carvel sold its ice cream only through franchised stores. However, a decline in revenues caused the company to begin selling its product in supermarkets. That effort expanded quickly, but many of the franchised stores (franchisees) went out of business. Franchisees filed suit, claiming tortious interference with a prospective advantage. In particular, the plaintiffs argued that Carvel undersold them in supermarkets and issued coupons only redeemable there. The case reached New York's highest court.

Issue: *Had Carvel committed tortious interference with a prospective advantage?*

Excerpts from Justice Smith's Decision: The franchisees' tort claim is that Carvel unlawfully interfered with the relationships between the franchisees and their customers. The franchisees do not claim that the customers had binding contracts that Carvel induced them to breach; they allege only that, by implementing its supermarket program, Carvel induced the customers not to buy Carvel products from the franchisees. The juries have found that Carvel did so induce customers, and the question for us is whether that inducement was tortious interference under New York law.

We have recognized that inducing breach of a binding agreement and interfering with a nonbinding "economic relation" can both be torts, but that the elements of the two torts are not the same. Where there has been no breach of an existing contract, but only interference with prospective contract rights, however, plaintiff must show more culpable conduct on the part of the defendant. The implication is that, as a general rule, the defendant's conduct must amount to a crime or an independent tort.

The franchisees claim that Carvel did use wrongful "economic pressure" but that argument is ill-founded for two independent reasons. First, it is ill-founded because the economic pressure that must be shown is not, as the franchisees assume, pressure on the franchisees, but on the franchisees' customers. Conduct constituting tortious interference with business relations is, by definition, conduct directed not at the plaintiff itself, but at the party with which the plaintiff has or seeks to have a relationship.

Here, all Carvel did to the franchisees' customers was to make Carvel goods available in supermarkets at attractive prices; this was not "pressure" on these third parties but

---

[11]For a more detailed explanation, see Wal-Mart Stores, Inc. v. Sturges, 52 S.W.3d 711 (Tex. 2001).

legitimate "persuasion," and thus tortious interference with economic relations was not established.

The franchisees' argument is also ill-founded because the Carvel activities they complain of do not amount to the sort of extreme and unfair "economic pressure" that might be "wrongful." The crux of the franchisees' complaint is that Carvel distributed its products through competitive channels, to an extent and in a way that was inconsistent with the franchisor–franchisee relationship. But the relationship between franchisors and franchisees is a complex one; while cooperative, it does not preclude all competition; and the extent to which competition is allowed should be determined by the contracts between the parties, not by courts or juries seeking after the fact to devise a code of conduct.

Apart from attacking the supermarket program in general as excessively and destructively competitive, the franchisees also attack the coupon-redemption element of that program as excessive "economic pressure." The essence of the coupon program was to give customers who used coupons a better price when they shopped in supermarkets. The mere institution of a coupon program was not "economic pressure" rising to the level of "wrongful" or "culpable" conduct.

Carvel's conduct was not tortious interference with a prospective advantage.

The Lanham Act

The Lanham Act provides broad protection against false statements intended to hurt another business. In order to win a case, a plaintiff must prove three things:

- That the defendants made false or misleading fact statements about the plaintiff's business. This could be a false comparative ad, showing the plaintiff's product to be worse than it is, or it could be a misleading ad, which, though literally accurate, is misleading about the defendant's own product.

- That the defendants used the statements in commercial advertising or promotion. In order to protect First Amendment rights of free speech, particularly political and social commentary, this act covers only commercial speech. A radio ad for beer could violate the Lanham Act; however, a radio ad urging that smoking be abolished in public places is not a commercial statement and cannot violate the act.

- That statements created the likelihood of harm to the plaintiff.[12]

"Knock It Off brand food supplement will help you lose weight and gain muscle faster than any competing supplement," shrieks the television commercial, offering an independent study as proof. However, a competitor sues and demonstrates that during the study, users of Knock It Off received free health club memberships and low-fat gourmet meals, distorting the results. Knock It Off has violated the Lanham Act. The court will order the company to knock it off and stop showing the commercial, and also to pay damages to the injured competitor.

Chapter Conclusion

This chapter has been a potpourri of misdeeds, a bubbling cauldron of conduct best avoided. Although tortious acts and their consequences are diverse, two generalities apply. First, the boundaries of intentional torts are imprecise, the outcome of a particular case depending to a considerable extent upon the factfinder who analyzes it. Second, thoughtful executives and careful citizens, aware of the shifting standards and potentially vast liability, will strive to ensure that their conduct never provides that factfinder an opportunity to give judgment.

---

[12]18 U.S.C §2511.

EXAM REVIEW

1. **TORT** A tort is a violation of a duty imposed by the civil law.

Question: Keith is driving while intoxicated. He swerves into the wrong lane and causes an accident, seriously injuring Caroline. Which statement is true?

a. Caroline could sue Keith, who might be found guilty in her suit.

b. Caroline and the state could start separate criminal cases against Keith.

c. Caroline could sue Keith, and the state could prosecute Keith for drunk driving.

d. The state could sue Keith but only with Caroline's consent.

e. The state could prosecute Keith and sue him at the same time for drunk driving.

Strategy: What party prosecutes a criminal case? The government does, not the injured party. What is the result in a criminal case? Guilt or innocence. What about a tort lawsuit? The injured party brings a tort suit. The defendant may be found liable but never guilty. (See the "Result" at the end of this section.)

2. **DEFAMATION** Defamation involves a defamatory statement that is false, uttered to a third person, and causes an injury. Opinion and privilege are valid defenses.

Question: Benzaquin had a radio talk show. On the program, he complained about an incident in which state trooper Fleming had stopped his car, apparently for lack of a proper license plate and safety sticker. Benzaquin explained that the license plate had been stolen and the sticker fallen onto the dashboard, but Fleming refused to let him drive away. Benzaquin and two young grandsons had to find other transportation. On the show, Benzaquin angrily recounted the incident, and then described Fleming and troopers generally: "we're not paying them to be dictators and Nazis"; "this man is an absolute barbarian, a lunkhead, a meathead." Fleming sued Benzaquin for defamation. Comment.

Strategy: Review the elements of defamation. Can these statements be proven true or false? If not, what is the result? Look at the defenses. Does one apply? (See the "Result" at the end of this section.)

3. **MALICE** Public personalities can win a defamation suit only by proving actual malice.

4. **FALSE IMPRISONMENT** False imprisonment is the intentional restraint of another person without reasonable cause and without consent.

5. **EMOTIONAL DISTRESS** The intentional infliction of emotional distress involves extreme and outrageous conduct that causes serious emotional harm.

6. **BATTERY** Battery is an intentional touching of another person in a way that is unwanted or offensive. Assault involves an act that makes the plaintiff fear an imminent battery.

Question: Caudle worked at Betts Lincoln-Mercury dealer. During an office party, many of the employees, including president Betts, were playing with an electric auto condenser, which gave a slight shock when touched. Some employees played catch with it. Betts shocked Caudle on the back of his neck, and chased him around. The shock later caused Caudle to suffer headaches, pass out, feel numbness, and eventually to require nerve surgery. He sued Betts for battery. Betts defended by saying that it was all horseplay and that he had intended no harm. Please rule.

Strategy: Betts argues he intended no harm. Is intent to harm an element? (See the "Result" at the end of this section.)

7. **DAMAGES** Compensatory damages are the normal remedy in a tort case. In unusual cases, the court may award punitive damages, not to compensate the plaintiff but to punish the defendant.

8. **TORTIOUS INTERFERENCE** Tortious interference with business relations involves the defendant harming an existing contract or a prospective relationship that has a definite expectation of success.

9. **LANHAM ACT** The Lanham Act prohibits false statements in commercial advertising or promotion.

---

1. Result: Choice (a) is wrong because a defendant cannot be found guilty in a civil suit. (b) is wrong because a private party has no power to prosecute a criminal case. (c) is correct. (d) is wrong because the state will prosecute Keith, not sue him. (e) is wrong for the same reason.

2. Result: The court ruled in favor of Benzaquin because a reasonable person would understand the words to be opinion and ridicule. They are not statements of fact because most of them could not be proven true or false. A statement like "dictators and Nazis" is not taken literally by anyone.[13]

6. Result: The court held that it was irrelevant that Betts had shown no malice toward Caudle nor intended to hurt him. Betts *intended the physical contact* with Caudle, and even though he could not foresee everything that would happen, he is liable for all consequences of his intended physical action.[14]

MULTIPLE-CHOICE QUESTIONS

1. Jane writes an article for a newspaper reporting that Ann was arrested for stealing a car. The story is entirely false. Ann is not a public figure. Which of the following torts has Jane committed?

   (a) Ordinary slander

   (b) Slander per se

   (c) Libel

   (d) None of the above

---

[13]Fleming v. Benzaquin, 390 Mass. 175, 454 N.E.2d 95 (1983).
[14]Caudle v. Betts, 512 So.2d 389 (La. 1987).

2. Refer to question 1. If Ann decides to sue, she _____ have to show evidence that she suffered an injury. If she ultimately wins her case, a jury _____ have the option to award punitive damages.

(a) will; will

(b) will; will not

(c) will not; will

(d) will not; will not

3. Sam sneaks up on Tom, hits him with a baseball bat, and knocks him unconscious. Tom never saw Sam coming. He wakes up with a horrible headache. Which of the following torts has Sam committed?

(a) Assault

(b) Battery

(c) Both A and B

(d) None of the above

4. Imagine a case in which a jury awards compensatory damages of $1 million. In most cases, a jury would rarely be allowed to award more than _____ in punitive damages.

(a) $1 million

(b) $3 million

(c) $9 million

(d) $10 million

(e) $25 million

5. Al runs a red light and hits Carol's car. She later sues, claiming the following losses:

$10,000—car repairs

$10,000—medical expenses

$10,000—lost wages (she could not work for two months after the accident)

$10,000—pain and suffering

If the jury believes all of Carol's evidence and she wins her case, how much will she receive in *compensatory* damages?

(a) $40,000

(b) $30,000

(c) $20,000

(d) $10,000

(e) $0

CASE QUESTIONS

1. Lou DiBella was an executive responsible for programming boxing shows on HBO cable network. DiBella signed Bernard Hopkins, the then–middleweight world boxing champion, to participate in a fight televised by HBO. After DiBella's departure from the network, he and Hopkins entered into an agreement in which Hopkins paid $50,000 for DiBella's promotional services. Months later, Hopkins publicly accused DiBella of taking bribes and "selling" spots in HBO fights, calling him greedy, filthy, and unethical. DiBella sued Hopkins for libel. What did DiBella have to prove to be successful in his claim?

2. You are a vice-president in charge of personnel at a large manufacturing company. In-house detectives inform you that Gates, an employee, was seen stealing valuable computer equipment. Gates denies the theft, but you believe the detectives and fire him. The detectives suggest that you post notices around the company, informing all employees what happened to Gates and why, because it will discourage others from stealing. While you are considering that, a phone call from another company's personnel officer asks for a recommendation for Gates. Should you post the notices? What should you say to the other officer?

3. Caldwell was shopping in a K-Mart store, carrying a large purse. A security guard observed her looking at various small items such as stain, hinges, and antenna wire. On occasion, she bent down out of sight of the guard. The guard thought he saw Caldwell put something in her purse. Caldwell removed her glasses from her purse and returned them a few times. After she left, the guard approached her in the parking lot and said that he believed she had store merchandise in her pocketbook, but he could not say what he thought was put there. Caldwell opened the purse, and the guard testified that he saw no K-Mart merchandise in it. The guard then told Caldwell to return to the store with him. They walked around the store for approximately 15 minutes, while the guard said six or seven times that he saw her put something in her purse. Caldwell left the store after another store employee indicated she could go. Caldwell sued. What kind of suit did she file, and what should the outcome be?

4. Tata Consultancy of Bombay, India, is an international computer consulting firm. It spends considerable time and effort recruiting the best personnel from India's leading technical schools. Tata employees sign an initial three-year employment commitment, often work overseas, and agree to work for a specified additional time when they return to India. Desai worked for Tata, but then he quit and formed a competing company, which he called Syntel. His new company contacted Tata employees by phone, offering higher salaries, bonuses, and assistance in obtaining permanent resident visas in the United States if they would come work for Syntel. At least 16 former Tata employees left their jobs without completing their contractual obligations and went to work for Syntel. Tata sued. What did it claim, and what should be the result?

5. Pacific Express began operating as an airline in 1982. It had routes connecting western cities with Los Angeles and San Francisco, and by the summer of 1983, it was beginning to show a profit. In 1983, United Airlines tried to enter into a cooperative arrangement with Pacific in which United would provide Pacific with passengers for some routes so that United could concentrate on its longer routes. Negotiations failed. Later that year, United expanded its routes to include cities that only Pacific had

served. United also increased its service to cities in which the two airlines were already competing. By early 1984, Pacific Express was unable to compete and sought protection under bankruptcy laws. It also sued United, claiming interference with a prospective advantage. United moved for summary judgment. Comment.

DISCUSSION QUESTIONS

1. The Supreme Court limits punitive damages in most cases to nine times the compensatory damages awarded in the same case. Is this a sensible guideline? If not, should it be higher or lower?

2. You have most likely heard of the *Liebeck v. McDonalds* case. Liebeck spilled hot McDonald's coffee in her lap and suffered third-degree burns. At trial, evidence showed that her cup of coffee was brewed at 190 degrees, and that, more typically, a restaurant's "hot coffee" is in the range of 140 to 160 degrees.

   A jury awarded Liebeck $160,000 in compensatory damages and $2.7 million in punitive damages. The judge reduced the punitive award to $480,000, or three times the compensatory award.

   Comment on the case and whether the result was reasonable.

3. With a national debt in the trillions, people are desensitized to "mere" billions. Stop for a moment and consider $1 billion. If you had that sum, invested it conservatively, and got a 5 percent return, you could spend roughly $1 million *a week* for the rest of your life *without reducing your principal*.

   This chapter described three lawsuits with jackpot punitive damage awards. The jury award was $10 billion in *Texaco v. Pennzoil*, $5 billion in the *Exxon Valdez* case, and $3 billion in *Boeken v. Philip Morris*. Is there any point at which the raw number of dollars awarded is just too large? Was the original jury award excessive in any of these cases? If so, which one(s)?

4. Many retailers have policies that instruct employees *not* to attempt to stop shoplifters. Some store owners fear false imprisonment lawsuits and possible injuries to workers more than losses related to stolen merchandise.

   Are these "don't be a hero" policies reasonable? Would you put one in place if you owned a retail store?

5. The Supreme Court has defined public figures as those who have "voluntarily exposed themselves to increased risk of injury by assuming an influential role in ordering society." When deciding whether someone is a public figure, courts look at whether this person has received press coverage, sought the public spotlight, and has the opportunity to publicly rebut the accusations. Some have argued that social media makes anyone with a public Facebook profile or a certain number of Twitter followers a public figure. Do you agree? Should the Court revisit the definition of "public figure" in light of social media?

ANSWERS TO SELECTED END OF CHAPTER QUESTIONS

MULTIPLE-CHOICE QUESTIONS

Presented are the answers for the ODD-numbered multiple-choice questions in the end-of-chapter material.

1. C
3. B
5. A

CASE QUESTIONS

Presented are the answers for all of the ODD-numbered case questions in the end-of-chapter material.

1. **Answer:** The district court found for DiBella. It found he was a public figure by virtue of his success in boxing, but that the statements had been made with malice. The court also found that Hopkins had made a defamatory statement that was false and communicated to others. The Second Circuit affirmed and the Supreme Court denied cert.

3. **Answer:** Caldwell sued for false imprisonment. The jury found in her favor, and the Court of Appeals affirmed. *Caldwell v. K Mart*, 306 S.C. 27, 410 S.E.2d 21, 1991 S.C. App. LEXIS 135 (S.C. Ct. App. 1991). From this evidence, a finder of fact could draw various inferences about whether K Mart's actions in investigating were conducted for a reasonable time and in a reasonable manner. The initial stop in the parking lot was probably justified, but the actions of the guard in walking Caldwell through the store and continuing to accuse her of taking merchandise were not justified as part of a reasonable investigation.

5. **Answer:** The U.S. District Court gave summary judgment for United, and the Court of Appeals affirmed. *Pacific Express, Inc. v. United Airlines, Inc.*, 959 F.2d 814, 1992 U.S. App. LEXIS 5139 (9th Cir. 1992). The primary issue was whether United was genuinely trying to compete, which it had the right to do, or was simply out to destroy Pacific, which would be interference with a prospective advantage (as well as an antitrust violation). United officials testified that the expanded routes would generate new connecting traffic for other San Francisco flights. That is a competitive purpose, which is legitimate, and enough to defeat Pacific's claim.

Chapter 9

NEGLIGENCE, STRICT LIABILITY, AND PRODUCT LIABILITY

© biletskiy/Shutterstock.com

The story you are about to read is true; not even the names have been changed. The participants were the plaintiff and defendant in a tort case. Do not try this at home.

Connie was very depressed. She felt so "overburdened," she decided to end her life by locking herself inside the trunk of her 1973 Ford LTD.

Fortunately, Connie decided against committing suicide. Unfortunately, her decision occurred after she had already closed the trunk. The LTD did not have an internal release latch or other emergency opening mechanism. And these were the days before cell phones. Result? Connie was trapped in her trunk for *nine* days awaiting rescue.

> Unfortunately, her decision occurred after she had already closed the trunk.

This awful episode caused Connie serious psychological and physical injuries. She sued Ford for damages under negligence and strict liability. According to Connie, Ford was negligent because it had a duty to warn her that there was no latch; and the missing latch was a design defect for which Ford should pay.[1]

But whose fault was it? Was Ford's design defective? Was the car unreasonably dangerous? Or was Connie just unreasonable?

These are all practical questions and moral ones, as well. They are also typical issues in the law of negligence, strict liability, and product liability. In these contentious areas, courts continually face one question: *When someone is injured, who is responsible?*

---

[1]Based on Daniell v. Ford Motor Co., 581 F. Supp. 728 (D. Ct. N.M. 1984).

9-1 NEGLIGENCE

We might call negligence the "unintentional" tort because it concerns harm that arises by accident. Should a court impose liability?

Things go wrong all the time, and people are hurt in large ways and small. Society needs a means of analyzing negligence cases consistently and fairly. We cannot have each court that hears such a lawsuit extend or limit liability based on an emotional response to the facts. One of America's greatest judges, Benjamin Cardozo, offered an analysis more than 85 years ago. In a case called *Palsgraf v. Long Island Railroad*, he made a decision that still influences negligence thinking today.

Landmark Case

PALSGRAF V. LONG ISLAND RAILROAD

248 N.Y. 339
Court of Appeals of New York, 1928

Facts: Helen Palsgraf was waiting on a railroad platform. As a train began to leave the station, a man carrying a package ran to catch it. He jumped aboard but looked unsteady, so a guard on the car reached out to help him as another guard, on the platform, pushed from behind. The man dropped the package, which struck the tracks and exploded—because it was packed with fireworks. The shock knocked over some heavy scales at the far end of the platform, and one of them struck Palsgraf, who was injured as a result. She sued the railroad.

Issue: *Was the railroad liable for Palsgraf's injuries?*

Excerpts from Judge Cardozo's Decision: The conduct of the defendant's guard was not a wrong in its relation to the plaintiff, standing far away. Relatively to her, it was not negligence at all. Nothing in the situation gave notice that the falling package had in it the potency of peril to persons thus removed. Negligence is not actionable unless it involves the invasion of a legally protected interest, the violation of a right. Negligence is the absence of care, according to the circumstances.

If no hazard was apparent to the eye of ordinary vigilance, an act innocent and harmless, at least to outward seeming, with reference to her, did not take to itself the quality of a tort because it happened to be a wrong with reference to some one else. In every instance, before negligence can be predicated of a given act, back of the act must be sought and found a duty to the individual complaining."

What the plaintiff must show is "a wrong" to herself and not merely a wrong to someone else. We are told that one who drives at reckless speed through a crowded city street is guilty of a negligent act because the eye of vigilance perceives the risk of damage. The risk reasonably to be perceived defines the duty to be obeyed.

Here, by concession, there was nothing in the situation to suggest to the most cautious mind that the parcel wrapped in newspaper would spread wreckage through the station.

The law of causation, remote or proximate, is thus foreign to the case before us. If there is no tort to be redressed, there is no occasion to consider what damage might be recovered if there were a finding of a tort. The consequences to be followed must first be rooted in a wrong.

Judge Cardozo ruled that the guard's conduct might have been a wrong as to the passenger, but not as to Ms. Palsgraf, standing far away. Her negligence case failed. "Proof of negligence in the air, so to speak, will not do," declared the judge. Courts are still guided by Judge Cardozo's ruling.

To win a negligence case, a plaintiff must prove five elements. Much of the remainder of the chapter will examine them in detail. They are:

- *Duty of Due Care.* The defendant had a legal responsibility *to the plaintiff*. This is the point from the *Palsgraf* case.

- *Breach.* The defendant breached her duty of care or failed to meet her legal obligations.

- *Factual Cause.* The defendant's conduct actually caused the injury.

- *Proximate Cause.* It was *foreseeable* that conduct like the defendant's might cause *this type of harm*.

- *Damages.* The plaintiff has actually been hurt or has actually suffered a measureable loss.

To win a case, a plaintiff must prove all the elements listed previously. If a defendant eliminates only one item on the list, there is no liability.

9-1a Duty of Due Care

Each of us has a duty to behave as a reasonable person would under the circumstances. If you are driving a car, you have a duty to all the other people near you to drive like a reasonable person. If you drive while drunk, or send text messages while behind the wheel, then you fail to live up to your duty of care.

But how *far* does your duty extend? Most courts accept Cardozo's viewpoint in the *Palsgraf* case. Judges draw an imaginary line around the defendant and say that she owes a duty to the people within the circle, but not to those outside it. The test is generally "foreseeability." If the defendant could have foreseen injury to a particular person, she has a duty to him. Suppose that one of your friends posts a YouTube video of you texting behind the wheel and her father is so upset from watching it that he falls down the stairs. You would not be liable for the father's downfall because it was not foreseeable that he would be harmed by your texting.

Let us apply these principles to a case involving a fraternity party.

HERNANDEZ V. ARIZONA BOARD OF REGENTS

177 Ariz. 244
Arizona Supreme Court, 1994

Facts: At the University of Arizona, the Epsilon Epsilon chapter of Delta Tau Delta fraternity gave a welcoming party for new members. The fraternity's officers knew that the majority of its members were under the legal drinking age, but they permitted everyone to consume alcohol. John Rayner, who was under 21 years of age, left the party. He drove negligently and caused a collision with an auto driven by Ruben Hernandez. At the time of the accident, Rayner's blood alcohol level was .15, exceeding the legal limit. The crash left Hernandez blind and paralyzed.

Hernandez sued Rayner, who settled the case based on the amount of his insurance coverage. The victim also sued the fraternity, its officers and national organization, all fraternity members who contributed money to buy alcohol, the university, and others. The trial court granted summary judgment for all defendants and the court of appeals affirmed. Hernandez appealed to the Arizona Supreme Court.

Issue: *Did the fraternity and the other defendants have a duty of due care to Hernandez?*

Excerpts from Justice Feldman's Decision: Before 1983, this court arguably recognized the common-law rule of non-liability for tavern owners and, presumably, for social hosts. Traditional authority held that when "an able-bodied man" caused harm because of his intoxication, the act from which liability arose was the consuming not the furnishing of alcohol.

However, the common law also provides that:

One who supplies [a thing] for the use of another whom the supplier knows or has reason to know to be likely because of his youth, inexperience, or otherwise to use it in a manner involving unreasonable risk of physical harm to himself and others is subject to liability for physical harm resulting to them.

We perceive little difference in principle between liability for giving a car to an intoxicated youth and liability for giving drinks to a youth with a car. A growing number of cases have recognized that one of the very hazards that makes it negligent to furnish liquor to a minor is the foreseeable prospect that the [youthful] patron will become drunk and injure himself or others.

Accordingly, modern authority has increasingly recognized that one who furnishes liquor to a minor breaches a common-law duty owed to innocent third parties who may be injured.

Furnishing alcohol to underaged drinkers violates numerous statutes. The conduct in question violates well-established common-law principles that recognize a duty to avoid furnishing dangerous items to those known to have diminished capacity to use them safely. We join the majority of other states and conclude that as to Plaintiffs and the public in general, Defendants had a duty of care to avoid furnishing alcohol to underage consumers.

Arizona courts, therefore, will entertain an action for damages against [one] who negligently furnishes alcohol to those under the legal drinking age when that act is a cause of injury to a third person. [Reversed and remanded.]

In several circumstances, people have special duties to others. Three of them are outlined here.

Special Duty: Landowners

The common law applies special rules to a landowner for injuries occurring on her property. In most states, the owner's duty depends on the type of person injured.

Lowest Liability: Trespassing Adults. A **trespasser** is anyone on the property without consent. A landowner is liable to a trespasser only for intentionally injuring him or for some other gross misconduct. The landowner has no liability to a trespasser for mere negligence. Jake is not liable if a vagrant wanders onto his land and is burned by defective electrical wires.

> **Trespasser**
> A person on another's property without consent

Mid-level Liability: Trespassing Children. The law makes exceptions when the trespassers are **children**. If there is some manmade thing on the land *that may be reasonably expected to attract children*, the landowner is probably liable for any harm. Daphne lives next door to a day-care center and builds a treehouse on her property. Unless she has fenced off the dangerous area, she is probably liable if a small child wanders onto her property and injures himself when he falls from the rope ladder to the treehouse.

Higher Liability: Licensee. A **licensee** is anyone on the land for her own purposes but with the owner's permission. A social guest is a typical licensee. A licensee is entitled to a warning of hidden dangers that the owner knows about. If Juliet invites Romeo for a late supper on the balcony and fails to mention that the wooden railing is rotted, she is liable when her hero plunges to the courtyard.

> **Licensee**
> A person on another's land for her own purposes but with the owner's permission

But Juliet is liable only for injuries caused by *hidden* dangers—she has no duty to warn guests of obvious dangers. She need not say, "Romeo, oh Romeo, don't place thy hand in the toaster, Romeo."

Highest Liability: Invitee. An **invitee** is someone who has a right to be on the property because it is a public place or a business open to the public. The owner has a duty of reasonable care to an invitee. Perry is an invitee when he goes to the town beach.

> **Invitee**
> A person who has a right to enter another's property because it is a public place or a business open to the public

Can the owner of this trampoline be liable?

If riptides have existed for years and the town fails to post a warning, it is liable if Perry drowns. Perry is also an invitee when he goes to Dana's coffee shop. Dana is liable if she ignores spilled coffee that causes Perry to slip.

With social guests, you must have *actual knowledge* of some specific hidden danger to be liable. Not so with invitees. You are liable even if you had *no idea* that something on your property posed a hidden danger. Therefore, if you own a business, you must conduct inspections of your property on a regular basis to make sure that nothing is becoming dangerous.

However, you generally do not have an obligation to protect against the wrongdoing of a third person. When a gunman went on a shooting spree at Virginia Tech, students Erin Peterson and Julia Pryde were among the 32 killed. The victims' families sued the university for wrongful death, claiming that it should have warned its students that a killer was on the loose. The Virginia Supreme Court disagreed. It held that the university had no duty to warn its students about this third-party criminal act because it was not reasonably foreseeable that the gunman would continue on and kill others. At the time of the initial shootings, the university believed it was an isolated incident and that gunman had left the university grounds.[2]

Special Duty: Professionals

A person at work has a heightened duty of care. While on the job, she must act as a reasonable person *in her profession*. A taxi driver must drive as a reasonable taxi driver would. A heart surgeon must perform bypass surgery with the care of a trained specialist in that field.

Two medical cases illustrate the reasonable person standard. A doctor prescribes a powerful drug without asking his patient about other medicines she is currently taking. The patient suffers a serious drug reaction from the combined medications. The physician is liable for the harm. A reasonable doctor *always* checks current medicines before prescribing new ones.

On the other hand, assume that a patient dies on the operating table in an emergency room. The physician followed normal medical procedures at every step of the procedure and acted with reasonable speed. In fact, the man had a fatal stroke. The surgeon is not liable. A doctor must do a reasonable professional job, but she cannot guarantee a happy outcome.

9-1b Breach of Duty

The second element of a plaintiff's negligence case is **breach of duty**. If a legal duty of care exists, then a plaintiff must show that the defendant did not meet it. Did the defendant act as a reasonable person, or as a reasonable professional? Did he warn social guests of hidden dangers he knew to exist in her apartment?

Normally, a plaintiff proves this part of a negligence case by convincing a jury that they would not have behaved as the defendant did—indeed, that no reasonable person would.

---

[2]Commonwealth of Virginia v. Peterson, __S.E.2d __ (S. Ct. Va. 2013).

Negligence Per Se

In certain areas of life, courts are not free to decide what a "reasonable" person would have done because the state legislature has made the decision for them. **When a legislature sets a minimum standard of care for a particular activity, in order to protect a certain group of people, and a violation of the statute injures a member of that group, the defendant has committed negligence per se.** A plaintiff who can show negligence per se need not prove breach of duty.

In Minnesota, the state legislature became alarmed about children sniffing glue, which they could easily purchase in stores. The legislature passed a statute prohibiting the sale to a minor of any glue containing toluene or benzene. About one month later, 14-year-old Steven Zerby purchased Weldwood Contact Cement from the Coast-to-Coast Store in his hometown. The glue contained toluene. Steven inhaled the glue and died from injury to his central nervous system.

The store clerk had not realized that the glue was dangerous. Irrelevant: He was negligent per se because he violated the statute. Perhaps a reasonable person would have made the same error. Irrelevant. The legislature had passed the statute to protect children, the sale of the glue violated the law, and a child was injured. The store was automatically liable.

9-1c Causation

We have seen that a plaintiff must show that the defendant owed him a duty of care and that the defendant breached the duty. To win, the plaintiff must also show that the defendant's breach of duty *caused* the plaintiff's harm. Courts look at two separate causation issues: Was the defendant's behavior the *factual cause* of the harm? Was it the *proximate cause?*

Factual Cause

If the defendant's breach led to the ultimate harm, it is the factual cause. Suppose that Dom's Brake Shop tells a customer his brakes are now working fine, even though Dom knows that is false. The customer drives out of the shop, cannot stop at a red light, and hits a bicyclist crossing the intersection. Dom is liable to the cyclist. Dom's unreasonable behavior was the factual cause of the harm. Think of it as a row of dominoes. The first domino (Dom's behavior) knocked over the next one (failing brakes), which toppled the last one (the cyclist's injury).

Suppose, alternatively, that just as the customer is exiting the repair shop, the cyclist hits a pothole and tumbles off her cycle. Dom has breached his duty to his customer, but he is not liable to the cyclist—she would have been hurt anyway. This is a row of dominoes that veers off to the side, leaving the last domino (the cyclist's injury) untouched. No factual causation.

Proximate Cause

For the defendant to be liable, the *type of harm* must have been reasonably *foreseeable*. In the example just discussed, Dom could easily foresee that bad brakes would cause an automobile accident. He need not have foreseen *exactly* what happened. He did not know there would be a cyclist nearby. What he could foresee was this *general type* of harm involving defective brakes. Because the accident that occurred was of the type he could foresee, he is liable.

By contrast, assume the collision of car and bicycle produces a loud crash. Two blocks away, a pet pig, asleep on the window ledge of a twelfth-story apartment, is startled by the noise, awakens with a start, and plunges to the sidewalk, killing a veterinarian who was making a house call. If the vet's family sues Dom, should it win? Dom's negligence was the factual cause: It led to the collision, which startled the pig, which flattened the vet. Most courts would rule, though, that Dom is not liable. The type of harm is too bizarre. Dom could not reasonably foresee such an extraordinary chain of events, and it would be unfair to make him pay for it. See Exhibit 9.1. Another way of stating that Dom is not liable to the vet's family is by calling the falling pig a *superseding cause*. When one of the "dominoes" in

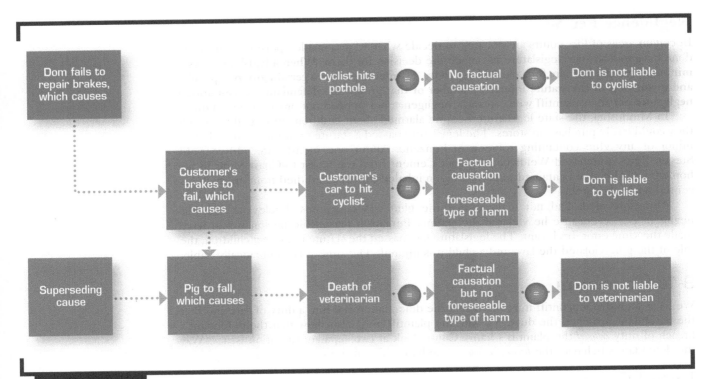

EXHIBIT 9.1

the row is entirely unforeseeable, courts will call that event a superseding cause, letting the defendant off the hook.

EXAM Strategy

Question: Jenny asked a neighbor, Tom, to water her flowers while she was on vacation. For three days, Tom did this without incident, but on the fourth day, when he touched the outside faucet, he received a violent electric shock that shot him through the air, melted his sneakers and glasses, set his clothes on fire, and seriously burned him. Tom sued, claiming that Jenny had caused his injuries by negligently repairing a second-floor toilet. Water from the steady leak had flooded through the walls, soaking wires and eventually causing the faucet to become electrified. You are Jenny's lawyer. Use one (and only one) element of negligence law to move for summary judgment.

Strategy: The four elements of negligence we have examined thus far are: duty to this plaintiff, breach, factual cause, and proximate cause. Which element seems to be most helpful to Jenny's defense? Why?

Result: Jenny is entitled to summary judgment because this was not a foreseeable type of injury. Even if she did a bad job of fixing the toilet, she could not reasonably have anticipated that her poor workmanship could cause *electrical* injuries to anyone.[3]

---

[3]Based on Hebert v. Enos, 60 Mass. App. Ct. 817 (Mass. Ct. App. 2004).

Res Ipsa Loquitur

Normally, a plaintiff must prove factual cause and foreseeable type of harm in order to establish negligence. But in a few cases, a court may be willing to *infer* that the defendant caused the harm under the doctrine of **res ipsa loquitur** ("the thing speaks for itself"). Suppose a pedestrian is walking along a sidewalk when an air conditioning unit falls on his head from a third-story window. The defendant, who owns the third-story apartment, denies any wrongdoing, and it may be difficult or impossible for the plaintiff to prove why the air conditioner fell. In such cases, many courts will apply *res ipsa loquitur* and declare that **the facts imply that the defendant's negligence caused the accident**. If a court uses this doctrine, then the defendant must come forward with evidence establishing that it did *not* cause the harm.

res ipsa loquitur
The facts *imply* that the defendant's negligence caused the accident.

Because *res ipsa loquitur* dramatically shifts the burden of proof from plaintiff to defendant, it applies only when (1) the defendant had exclusive control of the thing that caused the harm, (2) the harm normally would not have occurred without negligence, and (3) the plaintiff had no role in causing the harm. In the air conditioner example, most states would apply the doctrine and force the defendant to prove she did nothing wrong. The following case applies *res ipsa loquitur* to a prickly problem.

BRUMBERG V. CIPRIANI USA, INC.

2013 NY Slip Op 06759
Supreme Court of New York, 2013

Facts: Cornell professor Joan Jacobs Brumberg attended a university fundraiser catered by Cipriani. During the event, she feasted on fancy appetizers. About 30 minutes later, she felt intense abdominal pain, which did not go away. Weeks later, her doctors removed a 1 1/2-inch piece of wood from her digestive tract. The shard caused internal injuries, which took two surgeries to repair.

Brumberg's physician believed that her injuries were the result of eating wood at Cornell's cocktail party. On that day, she had eaten little else and had experienced no pain until the event, where she ate many appetizers, including shrimp on wood skewers. The doctor supposed that the wood moved through her digestive system for 30 minutes before becoming caught and causing the pain. But when experts compared Brumberg's shard with the wood in Cipriani's toothpicks and skewers, they found that the two were not the same material, eliminating direct evidence of causation.

Brumberg sued Cipriani USA, Inc. for negligence. A lower court dismissed her case on a motion for summary judgment, concluding there was not enough proof that Cipriani caused Brumberg's injury. The professor appealed, relying on the doctrine of *res ipsa loquitur*.

Issue: *Does* res ipsa loquitur *apply here?*

Excerpts from Judge Lahtinen's Decision: *Res ipsa loquitur* is neither a theory of liability nor a presumption of liability, but instead is simply a permitted inference— that the trier of fact may accept or reject—reflecting a common-sense application of the probative value of circumstantial evidence.

Criteria for *res ipsa loquitur* to apply are that (1) "the event must be of a kind which ordinarily does not occur in the absence of someone's negligence; (2) it must be caused by an agency or instrumentality within the exclusive control of the defendant; and (3) it must not have been due to any voluntary action or contribution on the part of the plaintiff."

The parties dispute the exclusive control element. Here, the event occurred at a banquet hall operated by Cipriani. Cipriani prepared and provided all of the food. Attendees were not permitted to bring food onto the premises. Individuals under Cipriani's control acted as captains, servers and bartenders. Cipriani thus exclusively prepared, provided, and served the food.

Although the shard possibly could have been present when the ingredients were purchased from suppliers, it was not so small as to have been concealed and not visible upon careful preparation.

Defendants point to the fact that other attendees had access to the hors d'oeuvres as reflecting a lack of exclusive control. Cipriani's personnel were present in the room serving the food both butler style and at stations, thus reducing the likelihood of some third party placing the shard unseen in food. There is sufficient proof under these circumstances to find ample control by defendants for purposes of *res ipsa loquitur*.

Defendants' further contention that *res ipsa loquitur* is foreclosed by their allegation of contributory negligence by plaintiff in not seeing the shard or discerning it while chewing the food in which it was located is without merit.

Plaintiffs' set forth ample proof to avoid summary judgment.

9-1d Damages

Finally, a plaintiff must prove that he has been injured, or that he has had some kind of measureable losses. In some cases, injury is obvious. For example, Ruben Hernandez suffered grievous harm when struck by the drunk driver. But in other cases, injury is unclear. **The plaintiff must persuade the court that he has suffered harm that is genuine, not speculative.**

Some cases raise tough questions. Among the most vexing are suits involving *future* harm. Exposure to toxins or trauma may lead to serious medical problems down the road—or it may not. A woman's knee is damaged in an auto accident, causing severe pain for two years. She is clearly entitled to compensation for her suffering. After two years, all pain may cease for a decade—or forever. Yet there is also a chance that in 15 or 20 years, the trauma will lead to painful arthritis. A court must decide today the full extent of present *and future* damages; the single recovery principle, discussed in Chapter 8, prevents a plaintiff from returning to court years later and demanding compensation for newly arisen ailments. The challenge to our courts is to weigh the possibilities and percentages of future suffering and decide whether to compensate a plaintiff for something that might never happen.

9-2 DEFENSES

9-2a Contributory and Comparative Negligence

Sixteen-year-old Michelle Wightman was out driving at night, with her friend Karrie Wieber in the passenger seat. They came to a railroad crossing, where the mechanical arm had descended and warning bells were sounding. They had been sounding for a long time. A Conrail train had suffered mechanical problems and was stopped 200 feet from the crossing, where it had stalled for roughly an hour. Michelle and Karrie saw several cars ahead of them go around the barrier and cross the tracks. Michelle had to decide whether she would do the same.

Long before Michelle made her decision, the train's engineer had seen the heavy Saturday night traffic crossing the tracks and realized the danger. The conductor and brakeman also understood the peril, but rather than posting a flagman, who could have stopped traffic when a train approached, they walked to the far end of their train to repair the mechanical problem. A police officer had come upon the scene, told his dispatcher to notify the train's parent company Conrail of the danger, and left.

Michelle decided to cross the tracks. She slowly followed the cars ahead of her. Seconds later, both girls were dead. A freight train traveling at 60 miles per hour struck the car broadside, killing both girls instantly.

Michelle's mother sued Conrail for negligence. The company claimed that it was Michelle's foolish risk that led to her death. Who wins when both parties are partly responsible? It depends on whether the state uses a legal theory called contributory negligence. Under contributory negligence, if the plaintiff is even slightly negligent, she recovers nothing. If Michelle's death occurred in a contributory negligence state, and the jury considered her even minimally responsible, her estate would receive no money.

Critics attacked this rule as unreasonable. A plaintiff who was 1 percent negligent could not recover from a defendant who was 99 percent responsible. So most states threw out the contributory negligence rule, replacing it with comparative negligence. In a comparative negligence state, a plaintiff may generally recover even if she is partially responsible. The jury will be asked to assess the relative negligence of the two parties.

Michelle died in Ohio, which is a comparative negligence state. The jury concluded that reasonable compensatory damages were $1 million. It also concluded that Conrail was 60 percent responsible for the tragedy and Michelle 40 percent. See Exhibit 9.2. The girl's mother received $600,000 in compensatory damages.

Today, most, but not all, states have adopted some form of comparative negligence. Critics claim that this principle rewards a careless plaintiff. If Michelle had obeyed the law, she would still be alive. In response to this complaint, many comparative negligence states do *not* permit a plaintiff to recover anything if he was more than 50 percent responsible for his own injury.

In the Conrail case, the jury decided that the rail company was extraordinarily negligent. Expert witnesses testified that similar tragedies occurred every year around the nation and the company knew it. Conrail could easily have prevented the loss of life by posting a flagman on the road. The jury awarded the estate $25 million in punitive damages. The trial judge reduced the verdict by 40 percent to $15 million. The state supreme court affirmed the award.[4]

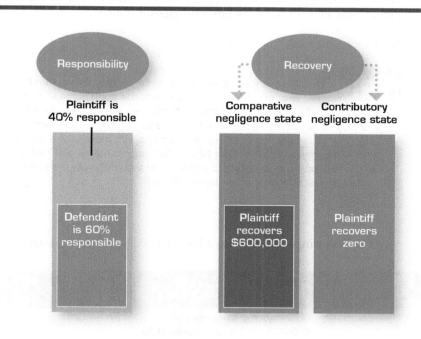

EXHIBIT 9.2   Defendant's negligence injures plaintiff, who suffers $1 million in damages.

[4]Wightman v. Consolidated Rail Corporation, 86 Ohio St. 3d 431(Ohio 1999).

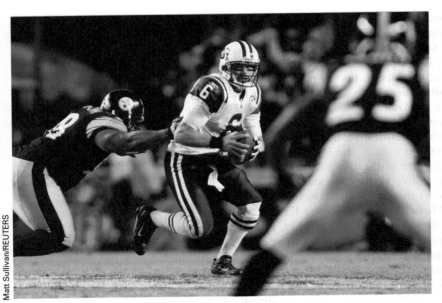

Do NFL players assume the risk of all on-field injuries?

Matt Sullivan/REUTERS

9-2b Assumption of the Risk

Good Guys, a restaurant, holds an ice-fishing contest on a frozen lake to raise money for accident victims. Margie grabs a can full of worms and strolls to the middle of the lake to try her luck, but slips on the ice and suffers a concussion. If she sues Good Guys, how will she fare? She will fall a second time. Wherever there is an obvious hazard, a special rule applies. **Assumption of the risk: A person who voluntarily enters a situation that has an obvious danger cannot complain if she is injured.** Ice is slippery and we all know it. If you venture onto a frozen lake, any falls are your own tough luck.

However, the doctrine does not apply if someone is injured in a way that is not an inherent part of the dangerous activity. NFL players assume substantial risks each time they take the field, but some injuries fall outside the rule. In a game between the Jets and the Dolphins, a Jets assistant coach standing on the sideline tripped a Dolphins player during a punt return. The trip was not a "normal" part of a football game, and the "assumption of the risk" doctrine would not prevent the player from recovering damages if injured.

Ethics Anyone who has watched an NFL game knows that football is a rough sport. But, did the NFL hide some of the sport's risks? In a negligence lawsuit, 4,500 football players with neurological injuries claimed that the NFL had decades of scientific evidence linking blows to the head to long-term brain damage, but it chose to bury these risks to make more money. A rougher sport makes for a better show—and more profit—the players argued. (The NFL makes approximately $10 billion in revenue per year.) Did the NFL owe a legal duty to the players or should the players just know better? What are the NFL's ethical duties to its players, if any?

The following case involves a lake, Jet Skis, and a great tragedy.

TRUONG V. NGUYEN

67 Cal. Rptr.3d 675
California Court of Appeals, 2007

Facts: On a warm California day, there were about 30 personal watercraft (Jet Skis) operating on Coyote Lake. The weather was fair and visibility good. Anthony Nguyen and Rachael Truong went for a ride on Anthony's Polaris watercraft. Cu Van Nguyen and Chuong Nguyen (neither of whom were related to Anthony) were both riding a Yamaha Waverunner. Both jet skis permitted a driver and passenger, each seated. The two watercraft collided near the middle of the lake. Rachael was killed, and the others all injured.

Rachael's parents sued Anthony, Cu Van, and Chuong, alleging that negligent operation of their watercraft caused their daughter's death. The defendants moved for summary judgment, claiming that assumption of the risk applies to jet skiing. The parents appealed, arguing that jet skiing was not a sport and Rachael never assumed any risk.

Issue: *Does assumption of the risk apply to jet skiing?*

Excerpts from Judge McAdams's Decision: In a sports context, [assumption of the risk] bars liability because the plaintiff is said to have assumed the particular risks inherent in a sport by choosing to participate. Thus, a court need not ask what risks a particular plaintiff subjectively knew of and chose to encounter, but instead must evaluate the fundamental nature of the sport and the defendant's role in or relationship to that sport.

In baseball, a batter is not supposed to carelessly throw the bat after getting a hit and starting to run to first base. However, assumption of risk recognizes that vigorous bat deployment is an integral part of the sport and a risk players assume when they choose to participate. A batter does not have a duty to another player to avoid carelessly throwing the bat after getting a hit.

Even when a participant's conduct violates a rule of the game and may subject the violator to internal sanctions prescribed by the sport itself, imposition of legal liability for such conduct might well alter fundamentally the nature of the sport by deterring participants from vigorously engaging in activity. Coparticipants' limited duty of care is to refrain from intentionally injuring one another or engaging in conduct that is so reckless as to be totally outside the range of the ordinary activity involved in the sport.

It appears that an activity falls within the meaning of 'sport' if the activity is done for enjoyment or thrill, requires physical exertion as well as elements of skill, and involves a challenge containing a potential risk of injury.

As a matter of common knowledge, jet skiing is an active sport involving physical skill and challenges that pose a significant risk of injury, particularly when it is done—as it often is—together with other jet skiers in order to add to the exhilaration of the sport by racing, jumping the wakes of the other jet skis or nearby boats, or in other respects making the sporting activity more challenging and entertaining. In response to the plaintiff's complaint that the trial court erroneously assumed that the litigants were contestants in some sort of consensual competition event and/or spectator sport, [we conclude] that the doctrine applies equally to competitive and non-competitive but active sports.

Plaintiffs urge [that] Rachael was merely a passenger on the Polaris and was not actively involved in the sport. The record supports the conclusion that riding as a passenger on a personal watercraft [is participating in a sport], because it is done for enjoyment or thrill, requires physical exertion as well as elements of skill, and involves a challenge containing a potential risk of injury. The vessel is open to the elements, with no hull or cabin. It is designed for high performance, speed, and quick turning maneuvers. The thrill of riding the vessel is shared by both the operator and the passenger. Obstacles in the environment such as spraying water, wakes to be crossed, and other watercraft are part of the thrill of the sport, both for the operator and the passenger.

The summary judgment is *affirmed*.

9-3 STRICT LIABILITY

Some activities are so naturally dangerous that the law places an especially high burden on anyone who engages in them. A corporation that produces toxic waste can foresee dire consequences from its business that a stationery store cannot. This higher burden is **strict liability**. There are two main areas of business that incur strict liability: *ultrahazardous activity* and *defective products*. Defective products are discussed in the following section, in the section on product liability.

Strict liability
A branch of tort law that imposes a much higher level of liability when harm results from ultrahazardous acts or defective products

9-3a Ultrahazardous Activity

Ultrahazardous activities include using harmful chemicals, operating explosives, keeping wild animals, bringing dangerous substances onto property, and a few similar activities where the danger to the general public is especially great. **A defendant engaging in an**

ultrahazardous activity is almost always liable for any harm that results. Plaintiffs do not have to prove duty or breach or foreseeable harm. Recall the deliberately bizarre case we posed earlier of the pig falling from a window ledge and killing a veterinarian. Dom, the mechanic whose negligence caused the car crash, could not be liable for the veterinarian's death because the plunging pig was a superseding cause.

But now imagine that the pig is jolted off the window ledge by a company engaged in an ultrahazardous activity. Sam's Blasting Co. sets off a perfectly lawful blast to clear ground for a new building down the street. When the pig is startled and falls, the blasting company is liable. Even if Sam took extraordinary care, it will do him no good at trial. The "reasonable person" rule is irrelevant in a strict liability case.

Because "strict liability" translates into "defendant is liable," parties in tort cases often fight over whether the defendant was engaged in an ultrahazardous activity. If the court rules that the activity was ultrahazardous, the plaintiff is assured of winning. If the court rules that it was not ultrahazardous, the plaintiff must prove all elements of negligence.

The line is often hazy. A lawful fireworks display does not incur strict liability, but crop dusting does. Cutting timber is generally not abnormally dangerous, but hauling logs might be. The enormous diversity of business activities in our nation ensures continual disputes over this important principle.

NEW JERSEY DEPARTMENT OF ENVIRONMENTAL PROTECTION v. ALDEN LEEDS, INC.

153 N.J. 272
Supreme Court of New Jersey, 1998

Facts: The Alden Leeds Company packages, stores, and ships swimming pool chemicals. The firm does most of its work at its facility in Kearns, New Jersey. At any given time, about 21 different hazardous chemicals are present.

The day before Easter, a fire of unknown origin broke out in "Building One" of the company's site, releasing chlorine gas and other potentially dangerous by-products into the air. There were no guards or other personnel on duty. The fire caused $9 million in damage to company property. Because of the potentially dangerous gas, the Department of Environmental Protection (DEP) closed the New Jersey Turnpike along with half a dozen other major highways, halted all commuter rail and train service in the area, and urged residents to stay indoors with windows closed. An unspecified number of residents went to local hospitals with respiratory problems.

Based on New Jersey's Air Pollution Control Act (APCA), the DEP imposed a civil fine on Alden Leeds for releasing the toxic chemicals. The appellate court reversed, finding that there was no evidence the company had caused the fire or the harm, and the case reached the state's high court.

Issue: *Did the company cause the harm?*

Excerpts from Justice Coleman's Decision: In 1962, this Court adopted the proposition that "an ultrahazardous activity which introduces an unusual danger into the community should pay its own way in the event it actually causes damage to others." In 1983, the Court expressly recognized "that the law of liability has evolved so that a landowner is strictly liable to others for harm caused by toxic wastes that are stored on his property and flow onto the property of others." The Court explained "that those who use, or permit others to use, land for the conduct of abnormally dangerous activities are strictly liable for resultant damages." The same rationale applies to pollution that is released into the air from chemicals stored at a chemical facility.

An actor who chooses to store dangerous chemicals should be responsible for the release of those chemicals into the air. That Alden Leeds lawfully and properly stored chemicals does not alter that conclusion. The risks attendant to the storage of dangerous substances counsel in favor of precautions to prevent their release. Alden Leeds took no such precautions. On the day of the fire, there was no one stationed at the plant to alert the authorities as soon as a fire or other unforeseen calamity erupted. Nor was there any other early warning system in place. A burglar or smoke alarm sounded, but there was no response to that alarm. The law imposes a duty upon those who store hazardous substances to ensure that the substances on their property do not escape in a manner harmful to the public. Alden Leeds failed to meet that burden.

Although Alden Leeds was not found responsible for the fire, the company's facility caused a release of air pollutants. The required nexus is satisfied by the knowing storage of hazardous chemicals. Regardless of what started the fire, it was the knowing storage of chemicals by Alden Leeds that caused the release of air contaminants once the fire reached the chemicals.

[Affirmed that the APCA is a strict liability statute and that there must be a causal nexus between the defendant and the harm. Reversed that the storing of hazardous chemicals by Alden Leeds does not satisfy that nexus. The DEP does *not* have to prove that the chemical operator started the fire.]

EXAM Strategy

Question: Ahmed plans to transport a 25-foot boa constrictor from one zoo to another. The snake is locked in a special cage in Ahmed's truck, approved by the American Zoo Society. Experts check the cage to be sure it is locked and entirely secure. Then Ahmed himself checks the cage. During the transport, his engine begins to fail. He pulls into the breakdown lane and sets up four flares, warning motorists of the stalled vehicle. Katy drives off the road and slams into Ahmed's truck. She is badly injured. Somehow the snake escapes and eats a champion show dog, worth $35,000. Katy and the dog's owner both sue Ahmed. What will be the result in each case?

Strategy: Ahmed's behavior seems reasonable throughout this incident. However, the two suits against him are governed by different rules: negligence in one case, strict liability in the other. Apply each rule to the correct case.

Result: The dog was killed by a dangerous snake. Transporting wild animals is an ultrahazardous activity, and Ahmed is strictly liable. His reasonable behavior will not save him. However, when he parked his truck in the breakdown lane, he did a reasonable job. Katy cannot prove that he breached his duty to her, and she loses.

9-4 PRODUCT LIABILITY

So far in this chapter, we have discussed how two tort theories—negligence and strict liability—apply when someone's action or inaction harms another. But sometimes products, not people, cause harm. When an exploding cola bottle, a flammable pajama, or a toxic cookie injures, who pays? Someone who is injured by a defective product may have claims in both negligence and strict liability.

9-4a Negligence

In negligence cases concerning goods, plaintiffs typically raise one or more of these claims:

- **Negligent design.** The buyer claims that the product injured her because the manufacturer designed it poorly. For example, company engineers placed the Ford Pinto's fuel tank behind the axle, making the car more likely to explode in a rear-end collision. Negligence law requires a manufacturer to design a product free of *unreasonable* risks. The product does not have to be absolutely safe. An automobile that nearly guaranteed a driver's safety could be made, in theory, but it would be prohibitively expensive. Reasonable safety features must be built in, if they can be included at a tolerable cost.

- **Negligent manufacture.** The buyer claims that the design was adequate but that failure to inspect or some other careless conduct caused a dangerous product to leave the plant. Peter Vamos got sick after gulping his Diet Coke—only to discover that there were two AA batteries in the bottle. Because he was able to prove that the batteries were in the bottle when it left the plant, Vamos recovered from the bottler for his injuries.[5]

- **Failure to warn.** A manufacturer is liable for failing to warn the purchaser or users about the dangers of normal use and also foreseeable misuse. However, there is no duty to warn about obvious dangers, a point evidently lost on some manufacturers. A Batman costume came with this statement: "For play only: cape does not enable user to fly."

In the following case, the plaintiffs raise issues of negligent design and failure to warn concerning a disposable lighter. Did the manufacturer breach its duty? You decide.

---

[5]Vamos v. The Coca-Cola Bottling Co. of New York, Inc., 627 N.Y.S.2d 265 (1995).
[6]198 Mich. App. 1 (Mich. Ct. App. 1993).

You be the Judge

BOUMELHEM V. BIC CORP.
211 Mich. App. 175
Michigan Court of Appeals, 1995

Facts: Ibrahim Boumelhem, aged four, began playing with a Bic disposable lighter that his parents had purchased. He started a fire that burned his legs and severely burned his six-month-old brother over 85 percent of his body. Ibrahim's father sued Bic, claiming that the lighter was negligently designed because it could have been childproof. He also claimed failure to warn because the lighter did not clearly warn of the danger to children.

The *Boumelhem* court considered evidence and analyses from several other cases against Bic. The court noted that consumers use over 500 million disposable lighters annually in the United States. Each lighter provides 1,000 to 2,000 lights. During one three-year period, children playing with disposable lighters started 8,100 fires annually, causing an average of 180 people to die every year, of whom 140 were children under five. Another 990 people were injured. The average annual cost of deaths, injuries, and property damage from child-play fires was estimated at $310 to $375 million, or 60 to 75 cents per lighter sold. Bic had acknowledged in earlier litigation that it was foreseeable lighters would get into children's hands and injure them. Bic had also agreed that it was feasible to make a more child-resistant lighter.

The trial court relied on a Michigan case. In *Adams v. Perry Furniture Co.*,[6] four minor children had died in a fire started when one of them was playing with a Bic lighter. The *Adams* court had found no negligent design and no failure to warn, and it dismissed all claims. The trial court in the present case followed *Adams* and dismissed Boumelhem's claims. He appealed.

You Be the Judge: *Did Bic negligently design its disposable lighter? Did Bic negligently fail to warn of the lighter's dangers?*

Argument for Boumelhem: Your honors, the Adams court decided the issues wrongly. There is a reason that new plaintiffs are back in this court, the year after Adams, raising related issues against Bic: The company is killing hundreds of children every year. In its efforts to maximize corporate profits, it is literally burning these children to death and injuring hundreds more. That's wrong.

Bic has acknowledged that its disposable lighters can and will get into the hands of children. Bic knows full well that its product will injure or kill a certain percentage of these children—very young children. Bic has admitted that it could design a childproof lighter, and it knows perfectly well how to include effective warnings on its lighters. But rather than improve product design and give effective warnings, Bic prefers to do business as usual and litigate liability for injured children.

We ask this court to rule that Bic breached its duty to design and manufacture a lighter that will keep our kids safe, and breached its duty to warn.

Argument for Bic: Your honors, the Bic Corp. is as horrified as anyone over the injuries to these children and the deaths of other kids. But Bic is not responsible. The children's parents are responsible. We sympathize with their grief, but not with their attempt to pass parental responsibility onto the shoulders of a corporation. There are several reasons Bic is not liable in this case.

First, the *Adams* court decided the matter, and that precedent is binding.

Second, Bic has no duty to design a different lighter. The test in design defect cases is whether the risks are unreasonable in light of the foreseeable injuries. Young children can hurt themselves in countless ways, from falls to poisonings to automobile injuries. There is one answer to these dangers, and it is called good parenting. The parents who bought this lighter purchased it because it could start a fire. The moment they purchased it, they assumed the obligation to keep it away from their children. These are useful products, which is why Bic sells hundreds of millions per year. Other consumers should not be forced to pay an outrageously high price for a simple tool, just because some parents fail to do their job.

The failure to warn argument is even weaker. The law imposes no failure to warn when the danger is obvious. Every adult knows that lighters are *potentially* dangerous, if misused, or if passed on to children. No one would be helped by a warning that said, "This lighter starts fires. Don't give it to children."

9-4b Strict Liability for Defective Products

The other tort claim that an injured person can bring against the manufacturer or seller of a product is strict liability. Like negligence, strict liability is a burden created by the law rather than by the parties. And, as with all torts, strict liability concerns claims of physical harm. But there is a key distinction between negligence and strict liability: in a negligence case, the injured buyer must demonstrate that the seller's conduct was unreasonable. Not so in strict liability.

In strict liability, the injured person need not prove that the defendant's conduct was unreasonable. The injured person must show only that the defendant manufactured or sold a product that was defective and that the defect caused harm. Almost all states permit such lawsuits, and most of them have adopted the following model:

1. One who sells any product in a defective condition unreasonably dangerous to the user or consumer or to his property is subject to liability for physical harm thereby caused to the ultimate user or consumer, or to his property, if

   a. the seller is engaged in the business of selling such a product, and

   b. it is expected to and does reach the user or consumer without substantial change in the condition in which it is sold.

2. The rule stated in Subsection (1) applies although

   a. the seller has exercised all possible care in the preparation and sale of his product, and

   b. the user or consumer has not bought the product from or entered into any contractual relation with the seller.[7]

---

[7]Restatement (Second) of Torts § 402A.

These are the key terms in subsection (1):

- **_Defective condition unreasonably dangerous to the user._** The defendant is liable only if the product is defective when it leaves his hands. There must be something wrong with the goods. If they are reasonably safe and the buyer's mishandling of the goods causes the harm, there is no strict liability. If you attempt to open a soda bottle by knocking the cap against a counter, and the glass shatters and cuts you, the manufacturer owes nothing. A carving knife can produce a lethal wound, but everyone knows that, and a sharp knife is not unreasonably dangerous. On the other hand, prescription drugs may harm in ways that neither a layperson nor a doctor would anticipate. The manufacturer _must provide adequate warnings_ of any dangers that are not apparent.

- **_In the business of selling._** The seller is liable only if she normally sells this kind of product. Suppose your roommate makes you a peanut butter sandwich and, while eating it, you cut your mouth on a sliver of glass that was in the jar. The peanut butter manufacturer faces strict liability, as does the grocery store where your roommate bought the goods. But your roommate is not strictly liable because he is not in the food business.

- **_Reaches the user without substantial change._** Obviously, if your roommate put the glass in the peanut butter thinking it was funny, neither the manufacturer nor the store is liable.

And here are the important phrases in subsection (2):

- **_Has exercised all possible care._** This is the heart of strict liability, which makes it a potent claim for consumers. _It is no defense that the seller used reasonable care._ If the product is dangerously defective and injures the user, the seller is liable even if it took every precaution to design and manufacture the product safely. Suppose the peanut butter jar did in fact contain a glass sliver when it left the factory. The manufacturer proves that it uses extraordinary care in keeping foreign particles out of the jars and thoroughly inspects each container before it is shipped. The evidence is irrelevant. The manufacturer has shown that it was not _negligent_ in packaging the food, but reasonable care is irrelevant in strict liability cases.

- **_No contractual relation._** When two parties contract, they are in privity. Note that privity only exists between the user and the person from whom she actually bought the goods, but in strict liability cases, _privity is not required._ Suppose the manufacturer that made the peanut butter sold it to a distributor, which sold it to a wholesaler, which sold it to a grocery store, which sold it to your roommate. You may sue the manufacturer, distributor, wholesaler, and store, even though you had no privity with any of them.

As we have seen, an injured plaintiff may sue a manufacturer for both negligence and strict liability. Remember Connie from the chapter opener? Let's see how her story ended.

DANIELL V. FORD

581 F. Supp. 728
U.S. District Court, New Mexico 1984

Facts: See the chapter opener. Connie Daniell argued that Ford was both (1) negligent because it did not warn her that there was no opening mechanism in the trunk and (2) strictly liable for this design defect. Ford sought summary judgment.

Issue: _Was Ford negligent in failing to warn Connie of the missing latch? Was Ford strictly liable for a design defect?_

Excerpts from Judge Baldock's Decision: Under strict products liability or negligence, a manufacturer has a duty to consider only those risks of injury which are foreseeable. A risk is not foreseeable by a manufacturer where a product is used in a manner which could not reasonably be anticipated by the manufacturer and that use is the cause of the plaintiff's injury. The plaintiff's injury would not be foreseeable by the manufacturer.

The purposes of an automobile trunk are to transport, stow, and secure the automobile spare tire, luggage, and other goods and to protect those items from elements of the weather. The design features of an automobile trunk make it well near impossible that an adult intentionally would enter the trunk and close the lid. The dimensions of a trunk, the height of its sill and its load floor are among the design features which encourage closing and latching the trunk lid while standing outside the vehicle. The plaintiff's use of the trunk compartment as a means to attempt suicide was an unforeseeable use. Therefore, the manufacturer had no duty to design an internal release or opening mechanism that might have prevented this occurrence.

Nor did the manufacturer have a duty to warn the plaintiff of the danger of her conduct, given the plaintiff's unforeseeable use of the product. The risk is obvious. There is no duty to warn of known dangers in strict products liability or tort. Moreover, the potential efficacy of any warning, given the plaintiff's use of the automobile trunk compartment for a deliberate suicide attempt, is questionable.

The automobile trunk was not defective under these circumstances. The automobile trunk was not unreasonably dangerous within the contemplation of the ordinary consumer or user of such a trunk when used in the ordinary ways and for the ordinary purposes for which such a trunk is used.

The defendant's Motion for Summary Judgment is granted.

Contemporary Trends

If the steering wheel on a brand new car falls off, and the driver is injured, that is a clear case of defective manufacturing, and the company will be strictly liable. Those are the easy cases. But defective design cases have been more contentious. Suppose a vaccine that prevents serious childhood illnesses inevitably causes brain damage in a very small number of children because of the nature of the drug. Is the manufacturer liable? What if a racing sailboat, designed only for speed, is dangerously unstable in the hands of a less-experienced sailor? Is the boat's maker responsible for fatalities? Suppose an automobile made of lightweight metal uses less fuel but exposes its occupants to more serious injuries in an accident. How is a court to decide whether the design was defective? Often, these design cases also involve issues of warnings: Did the drug designer diligently detail dangers to doctors? Should a sailboat seller sell speedy sailboats solely to seasoned sailors?

Over the years, most courts have adopted one of two tests for design and warning cases. The first is *consumer expectation*. Here, a court finds the manufacturer liable for defective design if the product is less safe than a reasonable consumer would expect. If a smoke detector has a 3 percent failure rate and the average consumer has no way of anticipating that danger, effective cautions must be included, though the design may be defective anyway.

Many other states use a *risk-utility test*. Here, a court must weigh the benefits for society against the dangers that the product poses. Principal factors in the risk-utility test include:

- The *value* of the product,

- The *gravity*, or seriousness, of the danger,

- The *likelihood* that such danger will occur,

- The mechanical feasibility of a *safer alternative* design, and

- The *adverse consequences* of an alternative design.

9-4c Tort Reform

Some people believe that jury awards are excessive and need statutory reform. About two-thirds of the states have passed at least some limits on damages in tort actions. About one-third of states have created new rules for particular kinds of product liability. *Unavoidably unsafe* prescription drugs are an example. Suppose that a plaintiff proves that a prescription medicine caused her grievous, permanent harm, and that 1 percent of all users will suffer similar damage. If the pharmaceutical company can demonstrate that it is impossible to manufacture the drug to eliminate all danger, many states will deny the plaintiff any damages. These states have essentially decided that the benefits of that prescription medicine outweigh its risks. If the medicine is unavoidably unsafe—that is, it cannot be made safer—the company should not be held liable; large verdicts might drive pharmaceutical firms out of a business that has great social value.

Opponents consider tort reform dangerous to society. They argue that the real goal of the so-called reform is to free irresponsible corporations from any potential liability, enabling them to save money while injuring innocent people. They insist that giving the 12 average members of society on a jury a say in product safety benefits everyone.

9-4d Time Limits: Statutes of Limitations and Statutes of Repose

In tort cases, the passage of time provides a seller with two possible defenses: statutes of limitations and statutes of repose.

The statute of limitations requires that a lawsuit be brought within a specified period. These time limits vary from state to state, ranging from one year to five years, beginning when the defect is discovered or should have been discovered.

A statute of repose places an absolute limit on when a lawsuit may be filed, regardless of when the defect is discovered. Jeffrey Oats was riding in the back seat of a Nissan sports car when it was involved in an accident. Tragically, Oats suffered spinal cord injuries that left him a quadriplegic. Oats sued Nissan, based on defective design, claiming that the rear seat lacked adequate head and leg room and that the car's body panels lacked sufficient strength. He argued that these defects only became apparent in an accident. But the Idaho Supreme Court dismissed his claims because the car was 11 years old at the time of the accident. The Idaho statute of repose prohibits most product liability suits filed more than 10 years after the goods were sold, regardless of when the defects were discoverable.[8]

EXAM Strategy

Question: Stuart lives in a state that sets a three-year statute of limitations on tort claims. His state also has an eight-year statute of repose. Stuart bought a television on June 1, 2010. On July 1, 2017, a manufacturing defect causes the television to malfunction and cause an electrical fire. Stuart waits for a year and then files a lawsuit on July 1, 2018. Will he win, or will his case be dismissed?

Strategy: Because Stuart is a consumer, the court will not apply either the economic loss doctrine or the UCC's four-year statute of limitations. When does the state's three-year statute of limitations begin to run? What effect will the state's statute of repose have on Stuart's case?

---

[8]Oats v. Nissan Motor Corp., 126 Idaho 162 (1994).

Result: The statute of limitations' three-year period starts to run only when Stuart discovers the defect. Because he filed one year from the fire, the statute of limitations does not bar his recovery. But unfortunately, Stuart's lawsuit will fail because of the statute of repose. That eight-year limit begins to expire when Stuart buys the TV, and the lawsuit is not filed for eight years and one month from the time of the sale. Stuart loses.

Chapter Conclusion

Tort issues necessarily remain in flux, based on changing social values and concerns. There is no final word on what is an ultrahazardous activity, or whether a social host can be liable for the destruction caused by a guest. What is clear is that a working knowledge of these issues and pitfalls can help everyone—business executive and ordinary citizen alike.

EXAM REVIEW

1. **ELEMENTS**   The five elements of negligence are duty of due care, breach, factual causation, proximate causation, and damage.

2. **DUTY**   If the defendant could foresee that misconduct would injure a particular person, he probably has a duty to her. Special duties exist for people on the job, landowners, and employers.

EXAM Strategy

Question: A supervisor reprimanded an employee for eating in a restaurant when he should have been at work. Later, the employee showed up at the supervisor's office and shot him. Although the employee previously had been violent, management withheld this information from supervisory personnel. Is the company liable for the supervisor's injury?

Strategy: An employer must do a *reasonable* job of hiring and retaining employees. (See the "Result" at the end of this section.)

3. **BREACH OF DUTY**   A defendant breaches his duty of due care by failing to meet his duty of care.

4. **NEGLIGENCE PER SE**   If a legislature sets a minimum standard of care for a particular activity in order to protect a certain group of people, and a violation of the statute injures a member of that group, the defendant has committed negligence per se.

5. **FACTUAL CAUSE**   If one event directly led to the ultimate harm, it is the factual cause.

6. **PROXIMATE CAUSE**   For the defendant to be liable, the type of harm must have been reasonably foreseeable.

7. **DAMAGE**   The plaintiff must persuade the court that he has suffered a harm that is genuine, not speculative. Damages for emotional distress, without a physical injury, are awarded only in select cases.

8. **CONTRIBUTORY AND COMPARATIVE NEGLIGENCE**   In a contributory negligence state, a plaintiff who is even slightly responsible for his own injury recovers nothing; in a comparative negligence state, the jury may apportion liability between plaintiff and defendant.

EXAM Strategy

Question: There is a collision between cars driven by Candy and Zeke. The evidence is that Candy is about 25 percent responsible, for failing to stop quickly enough, and Zeke about 75 percent responsible, for making a dangerous turn. Candy is most likely to win:

(a) A lawsuit for battery

(b) A lawsuit for negligence in a comparative negligence state

(c) A lawsuit for negligence in a contributory negligence state

(d) A lawsuit for strict liability

(e) A lawsuit for assault

Strategy: Battery and assault are intentional torts, irrelevant in a typical car accident. Are such collisions strict liability cases? No; therefore, the answer must be either (b) or (c). Apply the distinction between comparative and contributory negligence to the evidence here. (See the "Result" at the end of this section.)

---

9. **STRICT LIABILITY**   A defendant is strictly liable for harm caused by an ultrahazardous activity or a defective product. Strict liability means that if the defendant's conduct led to the harm, the defendant is liable, even if she exercises extraordinary care.

EXAM Strategy

Question: Marko owned a cat and allowed it to roam freely outside. In the three years he had owned the pet, the animal had never bitten anyone. The cat entered Romi's garage. When Romi attempted to move it outside, the cat bit her. Romi underwent four surgeries, was fitted with a plastic finger joint, and spent more than $39,000 in medical bills. She sued Marko, claiming both strict liability and ordinary negligence. Assume that state law allows a domestic cat to roam freely. Evaluate both of Romi's claims.

Strategy: Negligence requires proof that the defendant breached a duty to the plaintiff by behaving unreasonably, and that the resulting harm was foreseeable.

Was it? When would harm by a domestic cat be foreseeable? A defendant can be strictly liable for keeping a wild animal. Apply that rule as well. (See the "Result" at the end of this section.)

---

2. Result: This employer *may* have been liable for negligently hiring a previously violent employee, and it *certainly* did an unreasonable job in retaining him without advising his supervisor of the earlier violence. The assault was easily foreseeable, and the employer is liable.[9]

8. Result. In a contributory negligence state, a plaintiff even 1 percent responsible for the harm loses. Candy was 25 percent responsible. She can win *only* in a comparative negligence state.

9. Result: If Marko's cat had bitten or attacked people in the past, this harm was foreseeable and Marko is liable. If the cat had never done so, and state law allows domestic animals to roam, Romi probably loses her suit for negligence. Her strict liability case definitely fails: a housecat is not a wild animal.

MULTIPLE-CHOICE QUESTIONS

1. Two cars, driven by Fred and Barney, collide. At trial, the jury determines that the accident was 90 percent Fred's fault and 10 percent Barney's fault. Barney's losses total $100,000. If he lives in a state that uses contributory negligence, Barney will recover _____.

    (a) $0

    (b) $10,000

    (c) $50,000

    (d) $90,000

    (e) $100,000

2. Assume the same facts as in Question 1, except now Barney lives in a state that follows comparative negligence. Now Barney will recover _____.

    (a) $0

    (b) $10,000

    (c) $50,000

    (d) $90,000

    (e) $100,000

3. Zack lives in a state that prohibits factory laborers from working more than 12 hours in any 24-hour period. The state legislature passed the law to cut down on accidents caused by fatigued workers.

---

[9]Based on Smith v. National R.R. Passenger Corp., 856 F.2d 467 (2d Cir. 1988).

Ignoring the law, Zack makes his factory employees put in 14-hour days. Eventually, a worker at the end of a long shift makes a mistake and severely injures a coworker. The injured worker sues Zack.

Which of the following terms will be most relevant to the case?

(a) *Res ipsa loquitur*

(b) Assumption of the risk

(c) Negligence per se

(d) Strict liability

4. Randy works for a vending machine company. One morning, he fills up an empty vending machine that is on the third floor of an office building. Later that day, Mark buys a can of Pepsi from that machine. He takes the full can to a nearby balcony and drops it three floors onto Carl, a coworker who recently started dating Mark's ex-girlfriend. Carl falls unconscious. Which of the following can be considered a factual cause of Carl's injuries?

(a) Randy

(b) Mark

(c) Both Randy and Mark

(d) None of the above

5. For this question, assume the same facts as in Question 4. Now determine which of the following can be considered a proximate cause of Carl's injuries.

(a) Randy

(b) Mark

(c) Both Randy and Mark

(d) None of the above

6. *CPA QUESTION* Which of the following factors is least important in determining whether a manufacturer is strictly liable in tort for a defective product?

(a) The negligence of the manufacturer

(b) The contributory negligence of the plaintiff

(c) Modifications to the product by the wholesaler

(d) Whether the product caused injuries

CASE QUESTIONS

1. At approximately 7:50 p.m, bells at the train station rang and red lights flashed, signaling an express train's approach. David Harris walked onto the tracks, ignoring a yellow line painted on the platform instructing people to stand back. Two men shouted to Harris, warning him to get off the tracks. The train's engineer saw him too late to stop the train, which was traveling at approximately 55 mph. The train struck and killed Harris as it passed through the station. Harris's widow sued the railroad, arguing that the railroad's negligence caused her husband's death. Evaluate her argument.

2. Ryder leased a truck to Florida Food Service; Powers, an employee, drove it to make deliveries. He noticed that the strap used to close the rear door was frayed, and he asked Ryder to fix it. Ryder failed to do so in spite of numerous requests. The strap broke, and Powers replaced it with a nylon rope. Later, when Powers was attempting to close the rear door, the nylon rope broke and he fell, sustaining severe injuries to his neck and back. He sued Ryder. The trial court found that Powers's attachment of the replacement rope was a superseding cause, relieving Ryder of any liability, and granted summary judgment for Ryder. Powers appealed. How should the appellate court rule?

3. A new truck, manufactured by General Motors Corp. (GMC), stalled in rush hour traffic on a busy interstate highway because of a defective alternator, which caused a complete failure of the truck's electrical system. The driver stood nearby and waved traffic around his stalled truck. A panel truck approached the GMC truck, and immediately behind the panel truck, Davis was driving a Volkswagen fastback. Because of the panel truck, Davis was unable to see the stalled GMC truck. The panel truck swerved out of the way of the GMC truck, and Davis drove straight into it. The accident killed him. Davis's widow sued GMC. GMC moved for summary judgment, alleging (1) no duty to Davis, (2) no factual causation, and (3) no foreseeable harm. Comment.

4. *YOU BE THE JUDGE* WRITING PROBLEM   When Thomas and Susan Tamplin were shopping at Star Lumber with their six-year-old daughter Ann Marie, a 150-pound roll of vinyl flooring fell on the girl, seriously injuring her head and pituitary gland. Ann was clearly entitled to recover for the physical harm, such as her fractured skull. The plaintiffs also sought recovery for potential future harm. Their medical expert was prepared to testify that although Ann would probably develop normally, he could not rule out the slight possibility that her pituitary injury might prevent her from sexually maturing. Is Ann entitled to damages for future harm? **Argument for Ann:** This was a major trauma, and it is impossible to know the full extent of the future harm. Sexual maturation is a fundamental part of life; if there is a possibility that Ann will not develop normally, she is entitled to present her case to a jury and receive damages. **Argument for Star Lumber:** A plaintiff may not recover for speculative harm. The "slight possibility" that Ann could fail to develop is not enough for her to take her case to the jury.

5. Texaco, Inc., and other oil companies sold mineral spirits in bulk to distributors, which then resold to retailers. Mineral spirits are used for cleaning. Texaco allegedly knew that the retailers, such as hardware stores, frequently packaged the mineral spirits (illegally) in used half-gallon milk containers and sold them to consumers, often with no warnings on the packages. Mineral spirits are harmful or fatal if swallowed. David Hunnings, aged 21 months, found a milk container in his home, swallowed the mineral spirits, and died. The Hunnings sued Texaco for negligence. The trial court dismissed the complaint, and the Hunnings appealed. What is the legal standard in a negligence case? Have the plaintiffs made out a valid case of negligence? Remember that at this stage, a court is not deciding who wins, but what standard a plaintiff must meet in order to take its case to a jury. Assume that Texaco knew about the repackaging and the grave risk but continued to sell in bulk because doing so was profitable. (If the plaintiffs cannot prove those facts, they will lose even if they *do* get to a jury.) Would that make you angry? Does that mean such a case should go to a jury? Or would you conclude that the fault still lies with the retailer, the parents, or both?

6. Boboli Co. wanted to promote its "California-style" pizza, which it sold in supermarkets. The company contracted with Highland Group, Inc., to produce 2 million recipe brochures, which would be inserted in the carton when the freshly baked pizza was still very hot. Highland contracted with Comark Merchandising to print the brochures. But when Comark asked for details concerning the pizza, the carton, and so forth, Highland refused to supply the information. Comark printed the first lot of 72,000 brochures, which Highland delivered to Boboli. Unfortunately, the hot bread caused the ink to run, and customers opening the carton often found red or blue splotches on their pizzas. Highland refused to accept additional brochures, and Comark sued for breach of contract. Highland defended by claiming that Comark had breached its warranty of merchantability. Please comment.

DISCUSSION QUESTIONS

1. Imagine an undefeated high school football team on which the average lineman weighs 300 pounds. Also, imagine an 0–10 team on which the average lineman weighs 170 pounds. The undefeated team sets out to hit as hard as they can on every play and to run up the score as much as possible. Before the game is over, 11 players from the lesser team have been carried off the field with significant injuries. All injuries were the result of "clean hits"—none of the plays resulted in a penalty. Even late in the game, when the score is 70–0, the undefeated team continues to deliver devastating hits that are far beyond what would be required to tackle and block. The assumption of the risk doctrine exempts the undefeated team from liability. Is this reasonable?

2. Should the law hold landowners to different standards of care for trespassers, social guests, and invitees? Or do the few states that say, "Just always be reasonable," have a better rule?

3. Are strict liability rules fair? Someone has to dispose of chemicals. Someone has to use dynamite if road projects are to be completed. Is it fair to say to those companies, "You are responsible for all harm caused by your activities, even if you are as careful as you can possibly be?"

4. People who serve alcohol to others take a risk. In some circumstances, they can be held legally responsible for the actions of the people they serve. Is this fair? Should an intoxicated person be the only one liable if harm results? If not, in what specific circumstances is it fair to stretch liability to other people?

5. In the near future, we will rely increasingly on robots in daily life. Honda has predicted that by the year 2020, it will sell as many personal robots as it does cars. It is likely that these robots will be capable of many household tasks, such as folding laundry and tidying rooms. How do these automated beings fit into existing tort law? When a robot malfunctions unforeseeably and causes harm, who should be at fault?

ANSWERS TO SELECTED END OF CHAPTER QUESTIONS

MULTIPLE-CHOICE QUESTIONS

Presented are the answers for the ODD-numbered multiple-choice questions in the end-of-chapter material.

1. A
3. C
5. B

CASE QUESTIONS

Presented are the answers for all of the ODD-numbered case questions in the end-of-chapter material.

1. **Answer:** Harris was a trespasser and as a result the railroad had no duty of due care to him. The railroad would be liable only if it caused Harris's death by reckless or intentional conduct. There was no evidence of either. The widow was not permitted to introduce evidence of negligence, because even if the railroad had been negligent, it would be not be liable. *Harris v. Mass. Bay Transit Authority* (D. Mass. 1994), *Mass. Lawyer's Weekly*, Feb. 7, 1994, p.15.

3. **Answer:** Summary judgment for GMC denied. *General Motors Corp. v. Davis*, 141 Ga. App. 495, 233 S.E.2d 825 (Ga. Ct. App. 1977). GMC owes a duty to everyone on the highway since the possibility of an accident is apparent. There was factual causation: had it not been for the faulty alternator the truck would never have stalled. And this chain of events is entirely foreseeable. GMC need not foresee precisely what happened; only that something like this could happen.

5. **Answer:** The standard is whether the defendant acted as a "reasonable person" would have. The appeals court reversed, holding that the plaintiffs had made out a valid negligence claim and were entitled to take their evidence to a jury. Plaintiffs could argue, for example, that Texaco should have provided warnings of the danger, should have discouraged distributors from selling to retailers who illegally packaged the goods in used milk containers, and should have refused to sell to distributors who didn't cooperate. *Hunnings v. Texaco, Inc.*, 29 F.3d 1480, 1994 U.S. LEXIS 21833 (11th Cir. 1994).

Chapter 11

INTRODUCTION TO CONTRACTS

Chris always planned to propose to his girlfriend, Alissa, at Chez Luc, their favorite ritzy restaurant. When he was ready to pop the question, Chris went on Chez Luc's website to reserve a special table. But the website would not grant him a seating time unless he clicked the box that said: "No one in my party will use a cell phone at Chez Luc." Chris agreed and was issued a booking at his waterfront table of choice.

After Alissa's exuberant "yes" during the appetizer course, the newly engaged couple could not contain their excitement. First they posted selfies on both their Facebook pages. Then they called their parents to share the good news ... only to be confronted by the angry maître d', who escorted the couple out of the dining room for breaching their contract with the restaurant.

© Honza Krej/Shutterstock.com

> **The angry maitre d' escorted the couple out of the dining room.**

We make promises and agreements all the time—from the casual "I'll call you later" to more formal business contracts. These agreements may be long or short, written or oral, negotiable or not. But they are not necessarily enforceable through the legal system. One of the aims of contract law is to determine which agreements are "worthy" of legal enforcement. How do we know if an agreement is "worthy"?

Contract law is based on the notion that you are the best judge of your own welfare. By and large, you are free to make whatever agreements you want, subject to whatever rules you choose, and the law will support you. However, this freedom is not limitless: The law does impose seven requirements, which we will analyze in detail in upcoming chapters.

Contract law is a story of freedom and power, rules and relationships—with drama to spare. It is important to study this story to avoid your own contract drama. Let's start with an introduction to contracts.

11-1 CONTRACTS

11-1a Elements of a Contract

A contract is a legally enforceable agreement. People regularly make promises, but only some of them are enforceable. For a contract to be enforceable, seven key characteristics *must* be present. We will study this "checklist" at length in the next several chapters.

Contracts Checklist
- [ ] Offer
- [ ] Acceptance
- [ ] Consideration
- [ ] Legality
- [ ] Capacity
- [ ] Consent
- [ ] Writing

- *Offer.* All contracts begin when a person or a company proposes a deal. It might involve buying something, selling something, doing a job, or anything else. But only proposals made in certain ways amount to a legally recognized offer.

- *Acceptance.* Once a party receives an offer, he must respond to it in a certain way. We will examine the requirements of both offers and acceptances in the next chapter.

- *Consideration.* There has to be bargaining that leads to an *exchange* between the parties. Contracts cannot be a one-way street; both sides must receive some measureable benefit.

- *Legality.* The contract must be for a lawful purpose. Courts will not enforce agreements to sell cocaine, for example.

- *Capacity.* The parties must be adults of sound mind.

- *Consent.* Certain kinds of trickery and force can prevent the formation of a contract.

- *Writing.* While verbal agreements are often contracts, some types of contracts must be in writing to be enforceable.

11-1b Other Important Issues

Once we have examined the essential parts of contracts, the unit will turn to other important issues:

- *Third-Party Interests.* If Jerome and Tara have a contract, and if the deal falls apart, can Kevin sue to enforce the agreement? It depends.

- *Performance and Discharge.* If a party fully accomplishes what the contract requires, his duties are discharged. But what if his obligations are performed poorly, or not at all?

- *Remedies.* A court will award money or other relief to a party injured by a breach of contract.

Let's apply these principles to the opening scenario.

Is the "contract" between Chris and Chez Luc legally binding? Can Chez Luc kick out—or even *sue*—Chris for using his phone? In deciding this issue, a judge would consider whether the parties intentionally made an agreement, which included:

- A *valid offer and acceptance*. The restaurant's website set forth its terms, which was an offer. Chris accepted when he clicked the box.

- *Consideration*. A judge would then carefully examine whether the parties exchanged something of value that proved that they both meant to be bound by this agreement. And there was. The restaurant gave up a coveted reservation time in exchange for Chris's promise to stay away from his phone.

- *Capacity and Legality*. A judge would also verify that the parties were adults of sound mind and that the subject matter of the contract was legal. It seems that Chris understood what he was doing and was of legal age (we certainly hope so, since he was getting engaged).

- *Consent*. There was no fraud or trickery on the part of the restaurant (the terms were clear, not buried so that Chris was unaware of them).

- *Writing*. The terms were in writing (although they did not have to be.)

Therefore, the agreement was valid and enforceable. Whether kicking out a newly engaged couple is good business practice for a restaurant ... now, that's a different story!

11-1c All Shapes and Sizes

Some contracts—like those in the opener—are small. But contracts can also be large. Lockheed Martin and Boeing spent years of work and millions of dollars competing for a U.S. Defense Department aircraft contract. Why the fierce effort? The deal was potentially good for 25 years and *$200 billion*. Lockheed won. The company earned the right to build the next generation of fighter jets—3,000 planes, with different varieties of the aircraft to be used by each of the American defense services and some allied forces as well.

Many contracts involve public issues. The Lockheed agreement concerns government agencies deciding how to spend taxpayer money for national defense. Other contracts concern intensely private matters. Mary Beth Whitehead signed a contract with William and Elizabeth Stern of New Jersey. For a fee of $10,000, Whitehead agreed to act as a surrogate mother, and then deliver the baby to the Sterns for adoption after she carried it to term. But when little Melissa was born, Whitehead changed her mind and fled to Florida with the baby. The Sterns sued for breach of contract. Surrogacy contracts now lead to hundreds of births per year. Are the contracts immoral? Should they be illegal? Are there limits to what one person may pay another to do? The New Jersey Supreme Court, the first to rule on the issue, declared the contract illegal and void. The court nonetheless awarded Melissa to the Sterns, saying that it was in the child's best interest to live with them. Inevitably, legislators disagree about this emotional issue. Some states have passed statutes permitting surrogacy, while others prohibit it.

At times, we even enter contracts without knowing it. We make contracts each time we download an app, purchase software, and order from a restaurant menu. We even form legally enforceable agreements when we buy a bag of chips from a vending machine.

11-1d Contracts Defined

Contract
A legally enforceable agreement

We have seen that a **contract** is a promise that the law will enforce. As we look more closely at the elements of contract law, we will encounter some intricate issues. This is partly because we live in a complex society, which conducts its business in a wide variety of ways.

Remember, though, that we are usually interested in answering three basic questions, all relating to promises:

- Is it certain that the defendant promised to do something?

- If she did promise, is it fair to make her honor her word?

- If she did not promise, are there unusual reasons to hold her liable anyway?

11-1e Development of Contract Law

Courts have not always assumed that promises are legally significant. In the twelfth and thirteenth centuries, promises were not binding unless a person made them *in writing and affixed a seal* to the document. This was seldom done, and therefore most promises were unenforceable.

The common law changed very slowly, but by the fifteenth century, courts began to allow some suits based on a broken promise. There were still major limitations. Suppose a merchant hired a carpenter to build a new shop, and the carpenter failed to start the job on time. Now courts would permit the suit, but only if the merchant had paid some money to the carpenter. If the merchant made a 10 percent down payment, the contract would be enforceable. But if the merchant merely *promised* to pay when the building was done, and the carpenter never began work, the merchant could recover nothing.

In 1602, English courts began to enforce mutual *promises;* that is, deals in which neither party gave anything to the other but both promised to do something in the future. Thus, if a farmer promised to deliver a certain quantity of wheat to a merchant and the merchant agreed on the price, both parties were now bound by their promise, even though there had been no down payment. This was a huge step forward in the development of contract law, but many issues remained. Consider the following employment case from 1792, which raises issues of public policy that still challenge courts today.

Davis v. Mason

Michaelmas Term, 33d George III, p. 118
Court of King's Bench, 1792

Facts: Mason was a surgeon/apothecary in the English town of Thetford. Davis wished to apprentice himself to Mason. The two agreed that Davis would work for Mason and learn his profession. They further agreed that if Davis left Mason's practice, he would not set up a competing establishment within 10 miles of Thetford at any time within 14 years. Davis promised to pay £200 if he violated the agreement not to compete.

Davis began working for Mason in July 1789. In August 1791, Mason dismissed Davis, claiming misconduct, although Davis denied it. Davis then established his own practice within 10 miles of Thetford. Mason sued for the £200.

Davis admitted promising to pay the money. But he claimed that the agreement should be declared illegal and unenforceable. He argued that 14 years was unreasonably long to restrict him from the town of Thetford and that 10 miles was too great a distance. (In those days, 10 miles might take the better part of a day to travel.) He added an additional policy argument, saying that it was harmful to the public health to restrict a doctor from practicing his profession: If the people needed his service, they should have it. Finally, he said that his "consideration" was too great for this deal. In other words, it was unfair that he should pay £200 because he did not receive anything of that value from Mason.

Issue: *Was the contract too unreasonable to enforce?*

Excerpts from Lord Kenyon's Decision: Here, the plaintiff being established in business as a surgeon at

Thetford, the defendant wished to act as his assistant with a view of deriving a degree of credit from that situation; on which the former stipulated that the defendant should not come to live there under his auspices and steal away his patients: this seems to be a fair consideration. Then it was objected that the limits within which the defendant engaged not to practise are unreasonable: but I do not see that they are necessarily unreasonable, nor do I know how to draw the line. Neither are the public likely to be injured by an agreement of this kind, since every other person is at liberty to practise as a surgeon in this town.

Judgment for the Plaintiff.

Noncompetition agreement

A contract in which one party agrees not to compete with another

The contract between Davis and Mason is called a **noncompetition agreement**. Today they are more common than ever, and frequently litigated. The policy issues that Davis raised have never gone away. You may well be asked to sign a noncompetition agreement sometime in your professional life. We look at the issue in detail in Chapter 13, on consideration. That outcome was typical of contract cases for the next 100 years. Courts took a *laissez-faire* approach, declaring that parties had *freedom to contract* and would have to live with the consequences. Lord Kenyon saw Davis and Mason as equals, entering a bargain that made basic sense, and he had no intention of rewriting it. After 500 years of evolution, courts had come to regard promises as almost sacred. The law had gone from ignoring most promises to enforcing nearly all.

By the early twentieth century, bargaining power in business deals had changed dramatically. Farms and small businesses were yielding place to huge corporations in a trend that accelerated throughout the century. In the twenty-first century, multinational corporations span many continents, wielding larger budgets and more power than many of the nations in which they do business. When such a corporation contracts with a small company or an individual consumer, the latter may have little or no leverage. Courts increasingly looked at the basic fairness of contracts. Noncompetition agreements are no longer automatically enforced. Courts may alter them or ignore them entirely because the parties have such unequal power and because the public may have an interest in letting the employee go on to compete. Davis's argument—that the public is entitled to as many doctors as it needs—is frequently more successful in court today than it was in the days of Lord Kenyon.

Legislatures and the courts limit the effect of promises in other ways. Suppose you purchase a lawn mower with an attached tag, warning you that the manufacturer is not responsible in the event of any malfunction or injury. You are required to sign a form acknowledging that the manufacturer has no liability of any kind. That agreement is clear enough—but a court will not enforce it. The law holds that the manufacturer *has* warranted the product to be good for normal purposes, regardless of any language included in the sales agreement. If the blade flies off and injures a child, the manufacturer is liable. This is socially responsible, even though it interferes with a private agreement.

The law has not come full circle back to the early days of the common law. Courts still enforce the great majority of contracts. But the possibility that a court will ignore an agreement means that any contract is a little less certain than it would have been a century ago.

11-2 Types of Contracts

Before undertaking a study of contracts, you need to familiarize yourself with some important vocabulary. This section will present five sets of terms.

11-2a Bilateral and Unilateral Contracts

Bilateral contract

A promise made in exchange for another promise

In a **bilateral contract**, both parties make a promise. A producer says to Gloria, "I'll pay you $2 million to star in my new romantic comedy, which we are shooting three months from now in Santa Fe." Gloria says, "It's a deal." That is a bilateral contract. Each party has made a promise to do something. The producer is now bound to pay Gloria $2 million, and Gloria is obligated to show up on time and act in the movie. The vast majority of contracts are bilateral contracts. They can be for services, such as this acting contract; they can be for the sale of goods, such as 1,000 tons of steel, or for almost any other purpose. When the bargain is a promise for a promise, it is a bilateral agreement.

In a unilateral contract, one party makes a promise that the other party can accept only by *actually doing* **something.** These contracts are less common. Suppose the movie producer tacks a sign to a community bulletin board. It has a picture of a dog with a phone number, and it reads, "I'll pay $100 to anyone who returns my lost dog." If Leo sees the sign, finds the producer, and merely promises to find the dog, he has not created a contract. Because of the terms on the sign, Leo must actually find and return the dog to stake a claim to the $100.

11-2b Executory and Executed Contracts

A contract is **executory** when it has been made, but one or more parties has not yet fulfilled its obligations. Recall Gloria, who agrees to act in the producer's film beginning in three months. The moment Gloria and the producer strike their bargain, they have an executory bilateral express contract.

A contract is **executed** when all parties have fulfilled their obligations. When Gloria finishes acting in the movie and the producer pays her final fee, their contract will be fully executed.

> **Executory contract**
> An agreement in which one or more parties has not yet fulfilled its obligations
>
> **Executed contract**
> An agreement in which all parties have fulfilled their obligations

---

EXAM Strategy

Question: Abby has long coveted Nicola's designer handbag because she saw one of them in a movie. Finally, Nicola offers to sell her friend the bag for $350 in cash. "I don't have the money right now," Abby replies, "but I'll have it a week from Friday. Is it a deal?" Nicola agrees to sell the bag. Use two terms to describe the contract.

Strategy: In a bilateral contract, both parties make a promise, but in a unilateral agreement, only one side does so. An executory contract is one with unfulfilled obligations, while an executed agreement is one with nothing left to be done.

Result: Nicola promised to sell the bag for $350 cash, and Abby agreed to pay. Because both parties made a promise, a bilateral agreement resulted. The deal is not yet completed, meaning that they have an executory contract.

11-2c Valid, Unenforceable, Voidable, and Void Agreements

A **valid contract** is one that satisfies all of the law's requirements. It has no problems in any of the seven areas listed at the beginning of this chapter, and a court will enforce it. The contract between Gloria and the producer is a valid contract, and if the producer fails to pay Gloria, she will win a lawsuit to collect the unpaid fee.

An **unenforceable agreement** occurs when the parties intend to form a valid bargain, but a court declares that some rule of law prevents enforcing it. Suppose Gloria and the producer orally agree that she will star in his movie, which he will start filming in 18 months. The law, as we will see in Chapter 16, requires that this contract be in writing because it cannot be completed within one year. If the producer signs up another actress two months later, Gloria has no claim against him.

A **voidable contract** occurs when the law permits one party to terminate the agreement. This happens, for example, when an agreement is signed under duress or a party commits

> **Voidable contract**
> An agreement that may be terminated by one of the parties

fraud. Suppose that, during negotiations, the producer lies to Gloria, telling her that Steven Spielberg has signed on to be the film's director. That is a major reason why she accepts the contract. As we will learn in Chapter 14, this fraudulent agreement is voidable at Gloria's option. If she later decides that another director is acceptable, she may choose to stay in the contract. But if she wants to cancel the agreement and sue, she can do that as well.

A **void agreement** is one that neither party can enforce, usually because the purpose of the deal is illegal or because one of the parties had no legal authority to make a contract.

The following case illustrates the difference between voidable and void agreements.

Void agreement

A contract that neither party can enforce, because the bargain is illegal or one of the parties had no legal authority to make it

MR. W FIREWORKS, INC. V. OZUNA

No. 04-08-00820-CV Court of Appeals of Texas, San Antonio, 2009

Facts: Mr. W sells fireworks. Under Texas law, retailers may sell fireworks to the public only during the two weeks immediately before the Fourth of July and during two weeks immediately before New Year's Day. And so, fireworks sellers like Mr. W tend to lease property.

Mr. W leased a portion of Ozuna's land. The lease contract contained two key terms:

"In the event the sale of fireworks on the aforementioned property is or shall become unlawful during the period of this lease and the term granted, this lease shall become void.

"Lessor(s) agree not to sell or lease any part of said property, including any adjoining, adjacent, or contiguous property, to any person(s) or corporation for the purpose of selling fireworks in competition to the Lessee during the term of this lease, *and for a period of ten years after lease is terminated.*" (Emphasis added.)

A longstanding San Antonio city ordinance bans the sale of fireworks inside city limits, and also within 5,000 feet of city limits. Like all growing cities, San Antonio sometimes annexes new land, and its city limits change. One annexation caused the Ozuna property to fall within 5,000 feet of the new city limits, and it became illegal to sell fireworks from the property. Mr. W stopped selling fireworks and paying rent on Ozuna's land.

Two years later, San Antonio's border shifted again. This time, the city *disannexed* some property and *shrank.* The new city limits placed Ozuna's property just beyond the 5,000-foot no-fireworks zone. Ozuna then leased a part of his land to Alamo Fireworks, a competitor of Mr. W.

Mr. W sued for breach of contract, arguing that Ozuna had no right to lease to a competitor for a period of 10 years. The trial court granted Ozuna's motion for summary judgment. Mr. W appealed.

Issue: *Did Ozuna breach his contract with Mr. W by leasing his land to a competitor?*

Excerpts from Judge Angelini's Decision: The property owners [argue] that when the city ordinance made the sale of fireworks illegal on the subject properties, the leases became void, resulting in the property owners and Mr. W no longer having an enforceable agreement. Mr. W argues that the provision restricting the property owners from leasing to competitors survived the agreement. This is inconsistent with the meaning of "voidable" contracts. For example, when a minor enters into a contract, that contract is not void, but is voidable at the election of the minor. This means that the minor may set aside the entire contract at his option, but he *is not entitled to enforce portions that are favorable to him and at the same time disaffirm other provisions that he finds burdensome.* He is not permitted to retain the benefits of a contract while repudiating its obligations.

Could Ozuna declare independence from contractual obligations?

Here, while Mr. W is arguing that the illegalization of the sale of fireworks made the contract "voidable," it is still seeking to enforce the provision of the contract prohibiting the property owners from leasing to competitors. We decline to adopt such an interpretation.

Further, contracts requiring an illegal act are void. We therefore hold that the illegalization of the sale of the fireworks on the respective properties did not trigger the provision in the leases prohibiting the property owners from leasing to competitors of Mr. W.

We affirm the judgment of the trial court.

11-2d Express and Implied Contracts

In an **express contract**, the two parties explicitly state all the important terms of their agreement. The vast majority of contracts are express contracts. The contract between the producer and Gloria is an express contract because the parties explicitly state what Gloria will do, where and when she will do it, and how much she will be paid. Some express contracts are oral, as that one was, and some are written. They might be bilateral express contracts, as Gloria's was, or unilateral express contracts, as Leo's was. Obviously, it is wise to make express contracts, and to put them in writing. We emphasize, however, that many oral contracts are fully enforceable.

In an implied contract, the words and conduct of the parties indicate that they intended an agreement. Suppose every Friday, for two months, the producer asks Lance to mow his lawn, and loyal Lance does so each weekend. Then, for three more weekends, Lance simply shows up without the producer asking, and the producer continues to pay for the work done. But on the 12th weekend, when Lance rings the doorbell to collect, the producer suddenly says, "I never asked you to mow it. Scram." The producer is correct that there was no express contract because the parties had not spoken for several weeks. But a court will probably rule that the conduct of the parties has *implied* a contract. Not only did Lance mow the lawn every weekend, but the producer even paid on three weekends when they had not spoken. It was reasonable for Lance to assume that he had a weekly deal to mow and be paid.

Today, the hottest disputes about implied contracts continue to arise in the employment setting. Many corporate employees have at-will relationships with their companies. This means that the employees are free to quit at any time and the company has the right to fire them, for virtually any reason. But often a company provides its workers with personnel manuals that lay out certain rights. Does a handbook create a contract guaranteeing those rights? What is your opinion?

Express contract
An agreement with all the important terms explicitly stated

You be the Judge

DEMASSE V. ITT CORPORATION
194 Ariz. 500
Supreme Court of Arizona, 1999

Facts: Roger DeMasse and five others were employees-at-will at ITT Corporation, where they started working at various times between 1960 and 1979. Each was paid an hourly wage.

ITT issued an employee handbook, which it revised four times over two decades.

The first four editions of the handbook stated that within each job classification, any layoffs would be made in reverse order of seniority. The fifth handbook made two important changes. First, the document stated that "nothing contained herein shall be construed as a guarantee of continued employment. ITT does not guarantee continued employment to employees and retains the right to terminate or lay off employees."

Second, the handbook stated that "ITT reserves the right to amend, modify, or cancel this handbook, as well as any or all of the various policies [or rules] outlined in it." Four years later, ITT notified its hourly employees that layoff guidelines for hourly employees would be based not on seniority, but on ability and performance. About 10 days later, the six employees were laid off, though less senior employees kept their jobs. The six employees sued.

You Be The Judge: *Did ITT have the right to unilaterally change the layoff policy?*

Argument for the workers: It is true that all of the plaintiffs were originally employees-at-will, subject to termination at the company's whim. However, things changed when the company issued the first handbook. ITT chose to include a promise that layoffs would be based on seniority. Long-term workers and new employees all understood the promise and relied on it. The company put it there to attract and retain good workers. The policy worked. Responsible employees understood that the longer they remained at ITT, the safer their job was. Company and employees worked together for many years with a common understanding, and that is a textbook definition of an implied contract.

Once a contract is formed, whether express or implied, it is binding on both sides. That is the whole point of a contract. If one side could simply change the terms of an agreement on its own, what value would any contract have? The company's legal argument is a perfect symbol of its arrogance: It believes that because these workers are mere hourly workers, they have no rights, even under contract law. The company is mistaken. Implied contracts are binding, and ITT should not make promises it does not intend to keep.

Argument for ITT: Once an at-will employee, always one. ITT had the right to fire any of its employees at any time—just as the workers had the right to quit whenever they wished. That never changed, and in case any workers forgot it, the company reiterated the point in its most recent handbook. If the plaintiffs thought layoffs would happen in any particular order, that is their error, not ours.

All workers were bound by the terms of whichever handbook was then in place. For many years, the company had made a seniority-[based]-layoff promise. Had we fired a senior worker during that period, he or she would have had a legitimate complaint—and that is why we did not do it. Instead, we gave everyone four years' notice that things would change. Any workers unhappy with the new policies should have left to find more congenial work.

Why should an employee be allowed to say, "I prefer to rely on the old, outdated handbooks, not the new one"? The plaintiffs' position would mean that no company is ever free to change its general work policies and rules. Since when does an at-will employee have the right to dictate company policy? That would be disastrous for the whole economy—but fortunately it is not the law.

11-2e Promissory Estoppel and Quasi-Contracts

Now we turn away from "true" contracts and consider two unusual circumstances. Sometimes, courts will enforce agreements even if they fail to meet the usual requirement of a contract. We emphasize that these remedies are uncommon exceptions to the general rules. Most of the agreements that courts enforce are the express contracts that we have already studied. Nonetheless, the next two remedies are still pivotal in some lawsuits. In each case, a sympathetic plaintiff can demonstrate an injury but *there is no contract*. The plaintiff cannot claim that the defendant breached a contract, because none ever existed. The plaintiff must hope for more "creative" relief.

The two remedies can be confusingly similar. The best way to distinguish them is this:

- In promissory estoppel cases, the defendant made a promise that the plaintiff relied on.

- In quasi-contract cases, the defendant received a *benefit* from the plaintiff.

Promissory Estoppel

A fierce fire swept through Dana and Derek Andreason's house in Utah, seriously damaging it. The good news was that agents for Aetna Casualty promptly visited the Andreasons and helped them through the crisis. The agents reassured the couple that all of the damage was covered by their insurance, instructed them on which things to throw out and replace, and helped them choose materials for repairing other items. The bad news was that the agents were wrong: The Andreasons' policy had expired six weeks before the fire. When Derek Andreason presented a bill for $41,957 worth of meticulously itemized work that he had done under the agents' supervision, Aetna refused to pay.

The Andreasons sued—but not for breach of contract. There *was* no contract—they allowed their policy to expire. They sued Aetna under the legal theory of promissory estoppel: even when there is no contract, a plaintiff may use **promissory estoppel** to enforce the defendant's promise if he can show that:

- The defendant made a promise knowing that the plaintiff would likely rely on it;

- The plaintiff did rely on the promise; and

- The only way to avoid injustice is to enforce the promise.

> **Promissory estoppel**
>
> A *possible* remedy for an injured plaintiff in a case with no valid contract, when the plaintiff can show a promise, reasonable reliance, and injustice.

Aetna made a promise to the Andreasons—namely, its assurance that all of the damage was covered by insurance. The company knew that the Andreasons would rely on that promise, which they did by ripping up a floor that might have been salvaged, throwing out some furniture, and buying materials to repair the house. Is enforcing the promise the only way to avoid injustice? Yes, ruled the Utah Court of Appeals.[1] The Andreasons' conduct was reasonable and based entirely on what the Aetna agents told them. Under promissory estoppel, the Andreasons received virtually the same amount they would have obtained had the insurance contract been valid.

> ## Is enforcing the promise the only way to avoid injustice?

Many promissory estoppel cases involve employment law—bosses make promises that they fail to keep. The following case illustrates what can happen when you bet on the wrong promise.

DONALD L. HARMON V. DELAWARE HARNESS RACING COMMISSION

62 A.3d 1198
Supreme Court of Delaware, 2013

Facts: The Delaware Harness Racing Commission hired Donald Harmon to be the Presiding Judge of harness racing (charged with enforcing racetrack rules). After years on the job, Harmon was arrested for improperly changing a judging sheet to favor a horse. The Commission suspended him without pay pending the outcome of the criminal case.

Quasi-contract may require compensation even when no contract exists.

John Wayne (yes, his name was John Wayne) was the executive officer of the Commission. During his suspension, Harmon asked Wayne to find out from the Commission whether it would reinstate him he if he was acquitted. When Wayne asked the commissioners this question they looked at each other and then said "Yes." The commissioners told Wayne he could relay that message to Harmon. Based on this promise, Harmon decided not to look for other jobs.

Immediately after his acquittal, Harmon asked for his job back. After some time, the Commission refused to reinstate him as promised. Harmon sued the Commission, claiming promissory estoppel. A trial court sided with Harmon and awarded him $102,273, representing the wages he would have earned if the Commission had kept its promise. But the Superior Court reversed the decision, so Harmon appealed to the Supreme Court of Delaware.

Issue: *Was the commissioners' promise to Harmon enforceable?*

Excerpts from Justice Berger's Decision: To prevail on a promissory estoppel claim, a plaintiff must establish

---

[1] Andreason v. Aetna Casualty & Surety Co.,1993 Utah App. (1993).

that: (i) a promise was made; (ii) it was the reasonable expectation of the promisor to induce action or forbearance on the part of the promisee; (iii) the promisee reasonably relied on the promise and took action to his detriment; and (iv) such promise is binding because injustice can be avoided only by enforcement of the promise.

The first element is a promise. The trial court reasoned that [because] no [formal] vote was taken before the members said "Yes," Wayne could not have reasonably believed that the Commission wanted him to commit to reinstate Harmon. But the fact that the Commission members all looked at each other before answering Wayne's question could be construed as a vote, albeit an informal one. Second, the Commission did not address all matters by vote. It was not hiring or reinstating Harmon at the time Wayne conveyed its position to Harmon. The Commission was only promising to take action in the future. In short, there was evidence that the promise was made.

The second element is that the Commission reasonably expected Harmon to rely on Wayne's representations. Wayne had authority to transmit the Commission's decision to Harmon. If Wayne's testimony is credited, there is no real dispute about this point.

The third element is that Harmon reasonably relied on the Commission's promise and took action to his detriment. But for the Commission's promise to reinstate him, [Harmon] would have looked for other work. He was offered several horse training opportunities, but he could not pursue them because, if he did, he would not be allowed to return to his position as a judge. This testimony satisfies Harmon's burden of showing reliance to his detriment.

The final element of a promissory estoppel claim is a finding that the promise must be enforced to avoid injustice. That is another way of saying that it would be unjust not to enforce the Commission's promise because Harmon suffered damages by relying on it. During the time that he was waiting to be reinstated, Harmon could not accept another job, and suffered lost income as a result. That lost income constitutes damages.

Based on the foregoing, the judgment of the Superior Court is reversed.

Why have we chosen to illustrate an important point of law—promissory estoppel—with a case that fails? Because that is the typical outcome. Plaintiffs allege promissory estoppel very frequently, but seldom succeed. They do occasionally win, as the Andreasons demonstrated earlier, but courts are skeptical of these claims. The lesson is clear: Before you rely on a promise, negotiate a binding contract.

Quasi-Contract

Don Easterwood leased over 5,000 acres of farmland in Jackson County, Texas, from PIC Realty for one year. The next year, he obtained a second one-year lease. During each year, Easterwood farmed the land, harvested the crops, and prepared the land for the following year's planting. Toward the end of the second lease, after Easterwood had harvested his crop, he and PIC began discussing the terms of another lease. While they negotiated, Easterwood prepared the land for the following year, cutting and plowing the soil. But the negotiations for a new lease failed, and Easterwood moved off the land. He sued PIC Realty for the value of his work preparing the soil.

Easterwood had neither an express nor an implied contract for the value of his work. How could he make any legal claim? By relying on the legal theory of a quasi-contract: Even when there is no contract, a court may use **quasi-contract** to compensate a plaintiff who can show that:

Quasi-contract
A *possible* remedy for an injured plaintiff in a case with no valid contract, when the plaintiff can show benefit to the defendant, reasonable expectation of payment, and unjust enrichment.

- The plaintiff gave some benefit to the defendant;

- The plaintiff reasonably expected to be paid for the benefit and the defendant knew this; and

- The defendant would be unjustly enriched if he did not pay.

If a court finds all of these elements present, it will generally award the value of the goods or services that the plaintiff has conferred. The damages awarded are called *quantum meruit*, meaning that the plaintiff gets "as much as he deserves." The court is awarding money that it believes the plaintiff *morally ought to have*, even though there was no valid contract entitling her to it. This again is judicial activism, with the courts inventing a "quasi" contract where no true contract exists. The purpose is justice, the term is contradictory.

Don Easterwood testified that in Jackson County, it was quite common for a tenant farmer to prepare the soil for the following year but then be unable to farm the land. In those cases, he claimed, the landowner compensated the farmer for the work done. Other witnesses agreed that this was the local custom. The court ruled that indeed there was no contract, but that all elements of quasi-contract had been satisfied. Easterwood gave a benefit to PIC because the land was ready for planting. Jackson County custom caused Easterwood to assume he would be paid, and PIC Realty knew it. Finally, said the court, it would be unjust to let PIC benefit without paying anything. The court ordered PIC to pay the fair market value of Easterwood's labors.

Quantum meruit

"As much as he deserves"—the damages awarded in a quasi-contract case

FOUR THEORIES OF RECOVERY

Theory	Did the Defendant Make a Promise?	Is There a Contract?	Description
Express Contract	Yes	Yes	The parties intend to contract and agree on explicit terms.
Implied Contract	Not explicitly	Yes	The parties do not formally agree, but their words and conduct indicate an intention to create a contract.
Promissory Estoppel	Yes	No	There is no contract, but the defendant makes a promise that she can foresee will induce reliance; the plaintiff relies on it; and it would be unjust not to enforce the promise.
Quasi-Contract	No	No	There is no intention to contract, but the plaintiff gives some benefit to the defendant, who knows that the plaintiff expects compensation; it would be unjust not to award the plaintiff damages.

EXAM Strategy

Question: The preceding table lists the different theories a plaintiff may use to recover damages in a contract dispute. In the following examples, which one will each plaintiff use in trying to win the case?

1. Company pays all employees 10 percent commission on new business they develop. Company compensates each employee when the new customer pays its first bill. After Leandro obtains three new clients, Company fires him. When the new customers pay their bill, Company refuses to pay Leandro a commission because he is no longer an employee. Leandro sues.

2. Burt agrees in writing to sell Red 100 lobsters for $15 each, payable by credit card, in exactly 30 days. When the lobsters fail to arrive, Red sues.

3. Company handbook, given to all new hires, states that no employee will be fired without a hearing and an appeal. Company fires Delores without a hearing or appeal. She sues.

Strategy: In (1), the Company never promised to pay a commission to nonemployees, so there is no contract. However, the Company *benefited* from Leandro's work. In (2), the parties have *clearly stated all terms* to a simple sales agreement. In (3), the Company and Delores never negotiated termination, but *the handbook suggests* that all employees have certain rights.

Result: (1) is a case of quasi-contract because the company benefited and should reasonably expect to pay. (2) is an express contract because all terms are clearly stated. (3) is an implied contract, similar to the *DeMasse* case, based on the handbook.

11-3 SOURCES OF CONTRACT LAW

11-3a Common Law

We have seen the evolution of contract law from the twelfth century to the present. Express and implied contracts, promissory estoppel, and quasi-contract were all crafted, over centuries, by courts deciding one contract lawsuit at a time. Many contract lawsuits continue to be decided using common-law principles developed by courts.

11-3b Uniform Commercial Code

Business methods changed quickly during the first half of the last century. Transportation speeded up. Corporations routinely conducted business across state borders and around the world. These developments presented a problem. Common-law principles, whether related to contracts, torts, or anything else, sometimes vary from one state to another. New York and California courts often reach similar conclusions when presented with similar cases, but they are under no obligation to do so. Business leaders became frustrated that, to do business across the country, their companies had to deal with many different sets of common-law rules.

Executives, lawyers, and judges wanted a body of law for business transactions that reflected modern commercial methods and provided uniformity throughout the United States. It would be much easier, they thought, if some parts of contract law were the same in every state. That desire gave birth to the Uniform Commercial Code (UCC), created in 1952. The drafters intended the UCC to facilitate the easy formation and enforcement of contracts in a fast-paced world. The Code governs many aspects of commerce, including the sale and leasing of goods, negotiable instruments, bank deposits, letters of credit, investment securities, secured transactions, and other commercial matters. Every state has adopted at least part of the UCC to govern commercial transactions within that state. For our purposes in studying contracts, the most important part of the Code is Article 2, which governs the sale of goods. **"Goods" means anything movable, except for money, securities, and certain legal rights.** Goods include pencils, commercial aircraft, books, and Christmas trees. Goods do not include land or a house because neither is movable, nor do they include a stock certificate. A contract for the sale of 10,000 sneakers is governed by the UCC; a contract for the sale of a condominium in Marina del Rey is governed by the California common law.

When analyzing any contract problem as a student or businessperson, you must note whether the agreement concerns the sale of goods. For many issues, the common law and the UCC are reasonably similar. But sometimes, the law is quite different under the two sets of rules.

And so, the UCC governs contracts for a sale of goods, while common-law principles govern contracts for sales of services and everything else. Most of the time, it will be clear whether the UCC or the common law applies. But what if a contract involves both goods and services? When you get your oil changed, you are paying in part for the new oil and oil filter (goods) and in part for the labor required to do the job (services). In a mixed contract, Article 2 governs only if the *primary purpose* was the sale of goods. In the following case, the court had to decide the primary purpose.

FALLSVIEW GLATT KOSHER CATERERS, INC. v. ROSENFELD

794 N.Y.S. 2d 790
Civil Court, City of New York, 2005

Facts: During the Jewish holidays, Fallsview Glatt Kosher Caterers organized programs at Kutcher's Country Club, where it provided all accommodations, food, and entertainment.

Fallsview sued Willie Rosenfeld, alleging that he had requested accommodations for 15 members of his family, agreeing to pay $24,050, and then failed to appear or pay.

Rosenfeld moved to dismiss, claiming that even if there had been an agreement, it was never put in writing. Under UCC §2-201, any contract for the sale of goods worth $500 or more can be enforced only if it is in writing and signed. Fallsview argued that the agreement was not for the sale of goods, but for services. The company claimed that because the contract was not governed by the UCC, it should be enforced even with no writing.

Issue: *Was the agreement one for the sale of goods, requiring a writing, or for services, enforceable with no writing?*

Excerpts from Judge Battaglia's Decision: Mr. Rosenfeld contends that the "predominant purpose" and "main objective" of the agreement alleged by Fallsview was the "service of Kosher food," while the hotel accommodations and entertainment were merely "incidental or collateral" services.

Defendant's contention that the "predominant purpose" of the alleged agreement is the sale of food is said to be compelled by the very nature of the Passover holiday. [He argues that] "the essential religious obligation during this eight-day period and the principal reason why people attend events similar to the Program sponsored by plaintiff is in order to facilitate their fulfillment of the requirement to eat only food which is prepared in strict accordance with the mandate of Jewish law for Passover, i.e., food which is 'Kosher for Passover.' It is the desire to obtain these 'goods' and not the urge for 'entertainment' or 'accommodations' that motivates customers to subscribe to such 'Programs.' "

[Fallsview submitted] ten sheets, designated "Kutcher's Country Club Daily Activities" for Sunday, April 4, through Tuesday, April 13, 2004. The activities possible include tennis, racquetball, swimming, Swedish massage, "make over face lift show," "trivia time," aerobics, bingo, ice skating, dancing, "showtime," "power walk," arts and crafts, day camp, ping-pong, Yiddish theater, board games, horse racing, horseback riding, wine tasting, and indoor baci and that is only through Wednesday. These activities are provided, together with accommodations and food, for an "all inclusive" price that is apparently determined by the size and location of the room(s) and the numbers and ages of the persons in each party.

A review of the characteristics of the "program," which is the subject matter of the alleged agreement, leads the Court to conclude that the "essence" of the family and communal "experience" is defined primarily by "services" and not by "goods."

The intended scope of UCC section 2-201 is also indicated by its provision that "[a]writing is not insufficient because it omits or incorrectly states a term agreed upon but the contract is not enforceable under this paragraph beyond the quantity of goods shown in the writing." For the Code, quantity is even more important than price.

A contract of the type involved here would rarely, if ever, specify the "quantity" of the "goods" to be provided. Nor would, for example, a contract for a week's stay at a weight-loss spa, or a zen-vegetarian retreat, or a cruise of the islands.

Plaintiff argues that "Defendant's proposition that a hotel reservation is a sale of goods would render all reservations made via telephone or the Internet unenforceable and would leave hotels in a precarious economic position." That may or may not be true, but the argument does highlight the importance of ensuring that a Statute of Frauds structured and outfitted by the Legislature for a particular transactional context not be casually applied to a very different commercial segment and model. The structure and terms of section 2-201 tell us that it was not intended to cover the agreement alleged in this Complaint.

Defendant's motion to dismiss is denied.

EXAM Strategy

Question: Leila agrees to pay Kendrick $35,000 to repair windmills. Confident of this cash, Kendrick contracts to buy Derrick's used Porsche for $33,000. Then Leila informs Kendrick she does not need his help and will not pay him. Kendrick tells Derrick that he no longer wants the Porsche. Derrick sues Kendrick, and Kendrick files suit against Leila. What law or laws govern these lawsuits?

Strategy: Always be conscious of whether a contract is for services or the sale of goods. Different laws govern. To make that distinction, you must understand the term "goods." If you are clear about that, the question is answered easily.

Result: *Goods* means anything movable, and a Porsche is movable—one might say "super-movable." The UCC will control Derrick's suit. Repairing windmills is primarily a service. Kendrick's lawsuit is governed by the common law of contracts.

Chapter Conclusion

Contracts govern countless areas of our lives, from intimate family issues to multibillion-dollar corporate deals. Understanding contract principles is essential for a successful business or professional career and is invaluable in private life. This knowledge is especially important because courts no longer rubber-stamp any agreement that two parties have made. If we know the issues that courts scrutinize, the agreement we draft is likelier to be enforced. We thus achieve greater control over our affairs—the very purpose of a contract.

EXAM REVIEW

1. **CONTRACTS: DEFINITION AND ELEMENTS** A contract is a legally enforceable promise. Analyzing whether a contract exists involves inquiring into these issues: offer, acceptance, consideration, capacity, legal purpose, consent, and sometimes, whether the deal is in writing.

2. **DEVELOPMENT** The development of contract law stretches into the distant past. Before the fifteenth century, courts rarely enforced promises at all. By the 1600s, courts enforced many mutual promises, and by 1900, most promises containing the seven elements of a contract were strictly enforced.

3. **UNILATERAL AND BILATERAL CONTRACTS** In bilateral contracts, the parties exchange promises. In a unilateral contract, only one party makes a promise, and the other must take some action—his return promise is insufficient to form a contract.

4. **EXECUTORY AND EXECUTED CONTRACTS** In an executory contract, one or both of the parties have not yet have not done everything that they promised to do. In an executed contract, all parties have fully performed.

5. **ENFORCEABILITY**

   - Valid contracts are fully enforceable.

   - An unenforceable agreement is one with a legal defect.

   - A voidable contract occurs when one party has an option to cancel the agreement.

   - A void agreement means that the law will ignore the deal regardless of what the parties want.

EXAM Strategy

Question: Yasmine is negotiating to buy Stewart's house. She asks him what condition the roof is in.

"Excellent," he replies. "It is only 2 years old, and should last 25 more." In fact, Stewart knows that the roof is 26 years old and has had a series of leaks. The parties sign a sales contract for $600,000. A week before Yasmine is to pay for the house and take possession, she discovers the leaks and learns that the mandatory new roof will cost $35,000. At the same time, she learns that the house has increased in value by $60,000 since she signed the agreement. What options does Yasmine have?

Strategy: You know intuitively that Stewart's conduct is as shabby as his roof. What is the legal term for his deception? Fraud. Does fraud make an agreement void or voidable? Does it matter? (See the "Result" at the end of this section.)

6. **EXPRESS AND IMPLIED CONTRACTS** If the parties formally agreed and stated explicit terms, there is probably an express contract. If the parties did not formally agree but their conduct, words, or past dealings indicate they intended a binding agreement, there may be an implied contract.

7. **OTHER REMEDIES**   If there is no contract, are there other reasons to give the plaintiff damages?

- A claim of promissory estoppel requires that the defendant made a promise knowing that the plaintiff would likely *rely*, and the plaintiff did so. It would be wrong to deny recovery.

- A claim of quasi-contract requires that the defendant received a benefit, knowing that the plaintiff would expect compensation, and it would be unjust not to grant it.

EXAM Strategy

Question: The Hoffmans owned and operated a successful small bakery and grocery store. They spoke with Lukowitz, an agent of Red Owl Stores, who told them that for $18,000, Red Owl would build a store and fully stock it for them. The Hoffmans sold their bakery and grocery store and purchased a lot on which Red Owl was to build the store. Lukowitz then told Hoffman that the price had gone up to $26,000. The Hoffmans borrowed the extra money from relatives, but then Lukowitz informed them that the cost would be $34,000. Negotiations broke off, and the Hoffmans sued. The court determined that there was no contract because too many details had not been worked out—the size of the store, its design, and the cost of constructing it. Can the Hoffmans recover any money?

Strategy: Because there is no contract, the Hoffmans must rely on either promissory estoppel or quasi-contract. Promissory estoppel focuses on the defendant's promise and the plaintiff's reliance. Those suing in quasi-contract must show that the defendant received a benefit for which it should reasonably expect to pay. Does either fit here? (See the "Result" at the end of this section.)

8. **SOURCES OF CONTRACT LAW**   If a contract is for the sale of goods, the UCC is the relevant body of law. For anything else, the common law governs. If a contract involves both goods and services, a court will determine the agreement's primary purpose.

EXAM Strategy

Question: Honeywell, Inc., and Minolta Camera Co. had a contract providing that Honeywell would give to Minolta various technical information on the design of a specialized camera lens. Minolta would have the right to use the information in its cameras, provided that Minolta also used certain Honeywell parts in its cameras. Honeywell delivered to Minolta numerous technical documents, computer software, and test equipment, and Honeywell engineers met with Minolta engineers at least 20 times to discuss the equipment. Several years later, Honeywell sued, claiming that Minolta had taken the design information but failed to use Honeywell parts in its cameras. Minolta moved to dismiss, claiming that the UCC required lawsuits concerning the sale of goods to be filed within four years of the breach and that this lawsuit was too late. Honeywell answered that the UCC did not apply, and that therefore, Minnesota's six-year statute of limitations governed. Who is right?

Strategy: Like many contracts, this one involves both goods, which are governed by the UCC, and services, controlled by the common law. We decide which of those two laws governs by using the predominant purpose test. Was this contract primarily about selling goods or about providing services? (See the "Result" at the end of this section.)

---

5. Result: Indeed, it does matter. Stewart's fraud makes the contract voidable by Yasmine. She has the right to terminate the agreement and pay nothing. However, she may go through with the contract if she prefers. The choice is hers—but not Stewart's.

7. Result: Red Owl received no benefit from the Hoffmans' sale of their store or purchase of the lot. However, Red Owl did make a promise and expected the Hoffmans to rely on it, which they did. The Hoffmans won their claim of promissory estoppel.

8. Result: The primary purpose of this agreement was not the sale of goods, but rather the exchange of technical data, ideas, designs, and so forth. The common law governs the contract, and Honeywell's suit may go forward.

MULTIPLE-CHOICE QUESTIONS

1. A sitcom actor, exhausted after his 10-hour workweek, agrees to buy a briefcase full of cocaine from Lewis for $12,000. Lewis and the actor have a(n) _____ contract.

   (a) valid

   (b) unenforceable

   (c) voidable

   (d) void

2. Carol says, "Pam, you're my best friend in the world. I just inherited a million bucks, and I want you to have some of it. Come with me to the bank tomorrow, and I'll give you $10,000." "Sweet!" Pam replies. Later that day, Carol has a change of heart. She is allowed to do so. Examine the list of the elements of a contract, and cite the correct reason.

   (a) The agreement was not put into writing.

   (b) The agreement lacks a legal purpose.

   (c) Pam did not give consideration.

   (d) Pam does not have the capacity to make a contract.

3. On the first day of the baseball season, Dean orders a new Cardinals hat from Amazon. At the moment he submits his order, Dean and Amazon have an _____ contract. Two days later, Amazon delivers the hat to Dean's house. At this point, Dean and Amazon have an _____ contract.

   (a) executory; executory

   (b) executory; executed

   (c) executed; executory

   (d) executed; executed

4. Linda goes to an electronics store and buys a high-definition TV. Lauren hires a company to clean her swimming pool once a week. The _____ governs Linda's contract with the store, and the _____ governs Lauren's contract with the cleaning company.

   (a) common law; common law

   (b) common law; UCC

   (c) UCC; common law

   (d) UCC; UCC

5. Consider the following scenarios:

I. Madison says to a group of students, "I'll pay $35 to the first one of you who shows up at my house and mows my lawn."

II. Lea posts a flyer around town that reads, "Reward: $500 for information about the person who keyed my truck last Saturday night in the Wag-a-Bag parking lot. Call Lea at 555-5309."

   Which of these proposes a *unilateral* contract?

   (a) I only

   (b) II only

   (c) Both I and II

   (d) None of the above

CASE QUESTIONS

1. Gail Norton began dating Russell Hoyt under the mistaken impression that he was single. She later learned that he was married, but he repeatedly assured her he was getting a divorce. Six years later, Hoyt convinced Norton to quit her job so that they could travel together. He promised that he would "take care of her for life." The couple lived lavishly all over the world. Hoyt rented Norton an apartment, bought her cars, and repeated his promises to divorce his wife and marry her. He did neither. After 23 years, Hoyt ended the relationship with Norton. On what theory could Norton sue Hoyt? Is she likely to win?

2. Central Maine Power Co. made a promotional offer in which it promised to pay a substantial sum to any homeowner or builder who constructed new housing heated with electricity. Motel Services, Inc., which was building a small housing project for the city of Waterville, Maine, decided to install electrical heat in the units in order to

qualify for the offer. It built the units and requested payment for the full amount of the promotional offer. Is Central Maine obligated to pay? Why or why not?

3. Interactive Data Corp. hired Daniel Foley as an assistant product manager at a starting salary of $18,500. Over the next six years, Interactive steadily promoted Foley until he became Los Angeles branch manager at a salary of $56,116. Interactive's officers repeatedly told Foley that he would have his job as long as his performance was adequate. In addition, Interactive distributed an employee handbook that specified "termination guidelines," including a mandatory seven-step pre-termination procedure. Two years later, Foley learned that his recently hired supervisor, Robert Kuhne, was under investigation by the FBI for embezzlement at his previous job. Foley reported this to Interactive officers. Shortly thereafter, Interactive fired Foley. He sued, claiming that Interactive could fire him only for good cause, after the seven-step procedure. What kind of a claim is he making? Should he succeed?

4. **ETHICS** You want to lease your automobile to a friend for the summer but do not want to pay a lawyer to draw up the lease. Joanna, a neighbor, is in law school. She is not licensed to practice law. She offers to draft a lease for you for $100, and you unwisely accept. Later, you refuse to pay her fee, and she sues to collect. Who will win the lawsuit, and why? Apart from the law, was it morally right for the law student to try to help you by drafting the lease? Was she acting helpfully or foolishly or fraudulently? Is it just for you to agree to her fee and then refuse to pay it? What is society's interest in this dispute? Should a court be more concerned with the ethical issue raised by the conduct of the two parties or with the social consequences of this agreement?

5. *YOU BE THE JUDGE* **WRITING PROBLEM** John Stevens owned a dilapidated apartment that he rented to James and Cora Chesney for a low rent. The Chesneys began to remodel and rehabilitate the unit. Over a four-year period, they installed two new bathrooms, carpeted the floors, installed new septic and heating systems, and rewired, replumbed, and painted the apartment. Stevens periodically stopped by and saw the work in progress. The Chesneys transformed the unit into a respectable apartment. Three years after their work was done, Stevens served the Chesneys with an eviction notice. The Chesneys counterclaimed, seeking the value of the work they had done. Are they entitled to it? **Argument for Stevens:** Mr. Stevens is willing to pay the Chesneys exactly the amount he agreed to pay: nothing. The parties never contracted for the Chesneys to fix up the apartment. In fact, they never even discussed such an agreement. The Chesneys are making the absurd argument that anyone who chooses to perform certain work, without ever discussing it with another party, can finish the job and then charge it to the other person. If the Chesneys expected to get paid, obviously they should have said so. If the court were to allow this claim, it would be inviting other tenants to make improvements and then bill the landlord. The law has never been so foolish. **Argument for the Chesneys:** The law of quasi-contract was crafted for cases exactly like this. The Chesneys have given an enormous benefit to Stevens by transforming the apartment and enabling him to rent it at greater profit for many years to come. Stevens saw the work being done and understood that the Chesneys expected some compensation for these major renovations. If Stevens never intended to pay the fair value of the work, he should have stopped the couple from doing the work or notified them that there would be no compensation. It would be unjust to allow the landlord to seize the value of the work, evict the tenants who did it, and pay nothing.

DISCUSSION QUESTIONS

1. Have you ever made an agreement that mattered to you, only to have the other person refuse to follow through on the deal? Looking at the list of elements in the chapter, did your agreement amount to a contract? If not, which element did it lack?

2. Consider promissory estoppel and quasi-contracts. Do you like the fact that these doctrines exist? Should courts have "wiggle room" to enforce deals that fail to meet formal contract requirements? Or, should the rule be "If it's not an actual contract, too bad. No deal."

3. Is it sensible to have two different sets of contract rules—one for sales of goods and another for everything else? Would it be better to have a single set of rules for all contracts?

4. Have you read your apartment lease lately? How about your cellular service agreement? One study found that 67% of consumers do not read the contracts they sign. But notice that a contract is still enforceable, whether or not you read it. Which contracts should you read? iTunes terms and conditions? Your mortgage? An employment agreement?

5. Some states give consumers the right to cancel certain contracts for any reason within a short period of time after entering into them. For example, consumers in California can get out of gym membership contracts by sending the gym a cancellation notice within five business days of joining. Similar statutes cover insurance, weight loss services, door-to-door sales, and home repair contracts. If these agreements meet all of the requirements for a contract, why would a state allow people to get out of them so easily? Is this good policy? Alternatively, if consumers can cancel these contracts, why not allow everyone to cancel any contract within a few days?

Answers to Selected End of Chapter Questions

MULTIPLE-CHOICE QUESTIONS

Presented are the answers for the ODD-numbered multiple-choice questions in the end-of-chapter material.

1. D
3. B
5. C

CASE QUESTIONS

Presented are the answers for all of the ODD-numbered case questions in the end-of-chapter material.

1. **Answer:** Norton could try to make a claim for promissory estoppel, since her only argument is that she justifiably relied on Hoyt's reasonable promise. However, her claim is weak. First, there was no definite promise. Taking care of someone for life could have many meanings—social, emotional, or financial. Second, Hoyt had proved himself a liar over the past 23 years. The man never did what he said he was going to do, so it would be unreasonable to place trust on any representation he made.

3. **Answer:** Foley is arguing that he has an implied contract with Interactive based on the informal discussions concerning his future and the employee handbook. His argument convinced the California Supreme Court. *Foley v. Interactive Data Corp.*, 47 Cal. 3d 654, 765 P.2d 373, 1988 Cal. LEXIS 269 (1988). Foley had no express contract for any period, and thus he started work as an employee-at-will. But the company's repeated assurances, plus the handbook, created an implied contract.

5. **Answer:** Yes, they are entitled to the value of their work, said the court in *Chesney v. Stevens*, 435 Pa. Super. 71, 644 A.2d 124.0, 1994 Pa. Super. LEXIS 2388 (Pa. Super. Ct. 1994). They have neither an express nor an implied contract for the work. Stevens did nothing to create either. But he was aware of the work they were doing, and he should know that they would reasonably expect compensation. It would be unjust, said the court, to permit him to keep the benefit without paying anything, and so the Chesneys won their case of quasi-contract, receiving *quantum meruit* damages for the value of their work.

Chapter 12

© Honza Krej/Shutterstock.com

THE AGREEMENT: OFFERS AND ACCEPTANCES

Interior. A glitzy café, New York. Evening. Bob, a famous director, and Katrina, a glamorous actress, sit at a table, near a wall of glass looking onto a New York sidewalk that is filled with life and motion. Bob sips a margarita while carefully eyeing Katrina. Katrina stares at her wineglass.

BOB *(smiling confidently)*: *Body Work* is going to be huge—for the right actress. I know a film that's gonna gross a hundred million when I'm holding one. I'm holding one.

KATRINA *(perking up at the mention of money)*: It is quirky. It's fun. And she's very strong, very real.

BOB: She's you. That's why we're sitting here. We start shooting in seven months.

KATRINA *(edging away from the table)*: I have a few questions. That nude scene.

BOB: The one on the toboggan run?

KATRINA: *That* one was OK. But the one in the poultry factory—very explicit. I don't work nude.

BOB: It's not really nude. Think of all those feathers fluttering around.

KATRINA: It's nude.

BOB: We'll work it out. This is a romantic comedy, not tawdry exploitation. Katrina, we're talking $2.5 million. A little accommodation, please. We'll give you $600,000 up front, and the rest deferred, the usual percentages.

KATRINA: Bob, my fee is $3 million. As you know. That hasn't changed.

> I should talk with my agent. I'd need something in writing about the nude scene...

Katrina picks up her drink, doesn't sip it, places it on the coaster, using both hands to center it perfectly. He waits, as she stares silently at her glass.

BOB: We're shooting in Santa Fe, the weather will be perfect. You have a suite at the Excelsior, plus a trailer on location.

KATRINA: I should talk with my agent. I'd need something in writing about the nude scene, the fee, percentages—all the business stuff. I never sign without talking to her.

BOB: Shrugs and sits back.

KATRINA: *(made anxious by the silence)*: I love the character, I really do.

BOB: You and several others love her. *(That jolts her.)* Agents can wait. I have to put this together fast. We can get you the details you want in writing. *Body Work* is going to be bigger than *Game of Thrones*.

That one hooks her. She looks at Bob. He nods reassuringly. Bob sticks out his hand, smiling. Katrina hesitates, lets go of her drink, and SHAKES HANDS, looking unsure. Bob signals for the check.

Do Bob and Katrina have a deal? *They* seem to think so. But is her fee $2.5 million or $3 million? What if Katrina demands that all nude scenes be taken out, and Bob refuses? Must she still act in the film? Or suppose her agent convinces her that *Body Work* is no good even with changes. Has Katrina committed herself? What if Bob auditions another actress the next day, likes her, and signs her? Does he owe Katrina her fee? Or suppose Bob learns that the funding has fallen apart and there will be no film. Is Katrina entitled to her money?

Bob and Katrina have acted out a classic problem in *agreement*, one of the basic issues in contract law. Their lack of clarity means that disputes are likely and lawsuits possible. Similar bargaining goes on every day around the country and around the world, and the problems created are too frequently resolved in court. Some negotiating is done in person; more is done over the phone, by fax, by email—or all of them combined. This chapter highlights the most common sources of misunderstanding and litigation so that you can avoid making contracts you never intended—or deals that you cannot enforce.

There almost certainly is no contract between Bob and Katrina. Bob's offer was unclear. Even if it was valid, Katrina counteroffered. When they shook hands, it is impossible to know what terms each had in mind.

> **Contracts Checklist**
> - ☑ Offer
> - ☑ Acceptance
> - ☐ Consideration
> - ☐ Legality
> - ☐ Capacity
> - ☐ Consent
> - ☐ Writing

12-1 MEETING OF THE MINDS

Remember from the last chapter that contracts have seven key characteristics. Agreements that have a problem in any of the areas do not amount to valid contracts. In this chapter, we examine the first two items on the checklist.

Parties form a contract only if they have a meeting of the minds. For this to happen, one side must make an **offer** and the other must make an **acceptance**. An offer proposes definite terms, and an acceptance unconditionally agrees to them.

Throughout the chapter, keep in mind that courts make *objective* assessments when evaluating offers and acceptances. A court will not try to get inside Katrina's head and decide what she was thinking as she shook hands. It will look at the handshake *objectively*, deciding how a reasonable person would interpret her words and conduct. Katrina may honestly have meant to conclude a deal for $3 million with no nude scenes, while Bob might in good faith have believed he was committing himself to $2.5 million and absolute control of the script. Neither belief will control the outcome.

Offer

An act or statement that proposes definite terms and permits the other party to create a contract by accepting those terms

12-2 OFFER

Bargaining begins with an offer. The person who makes an offer is the **offeror**. The person to whom he makes that offer is the **offeree**. The terms are annoying but inescapable because, like handcuffs, all courts use them.

Offeror

The person who makes an offer

Two questions determine whether a statement is an offer:

- Do the offeror's words and actions indicate an *intention* to make a bargain?

- Are the terms of the offer reasonably definite?

Offeree

The person to whom an offer is made

Zachary says to Sharon, "Come work in my English language center as a teacher. I'll pay you $800 per week for a 35-hour week, for six months starting Monday." This is a valid offer. Zachary's words seem to indicate that he intends to make a bargain and his offer is definite. If Sharon accepts, the parties have a contract that either one can enforce.

In the following section, we present several categories of statements that are generally *not* valid offers.

12-2a Statements that Usually Do Not Amount to Offers

Invitations to Bargain

An invitation to bargain is not an offer. Suppose Martha telephones Joe and leaves a message on his answering machine, asking if Joe would consider selling his vacation condo on Lake Michigan. Joe faxes a signed letter to Martha saying, "There is no way I could sell the condo for less than $150,000." Martha promptly sends Joe a cashier's check for that amount. Does she own the condo? No. Joe's fax was not an offer. It is merely an invitation to negotiate. Joe is indicating that he might well be happy to receive an offer from Martha, but he is not promising to sell the condo for $150,000 or for any amount.

Price Quotes

A price quote is generally not an offer. If Imperial Textile sends a list of fabric prices for the new year to its regular customers, the list is not an offer. Once again, the law regards it merely as a solicitation of offers. Suppose Ralph orders 1,000 yards of fabric, quoted in the list at $40 per yard. *Ralph* is making the offer, and Imperial may decline to sell at $40, or at any price, for that matter.

This can be an expensive point to learn. Leviton Manufacturing makes electrical fixtures and switches. Litton Microwave manufactures ovens. Leviton sent a price list to Litton, stating what it would charge for specially modified switches for use in Litton's microwaves. The price letter included a statement greatly limiting Leviton's liability in the event of any problem with the switches. Litton purchased thousands of the switches and used them in manufacturing its microwaves. But consumers reported fires due to defects in the switches. Leviton claimed that under the contract it had no liability. But the court held that the price letter was not an offer.

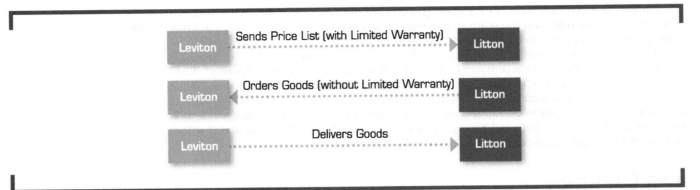

EXHIBIT 12.1 The Litton case demonstrates why it is important to distinguish a valid offer from a mere price quote. Leviton's price list (including a limited warranty) was *not* an offer. When Litton ordered goods (with no limit to the warranty), it was making an offer, which Leviton accepted by delivering the goods. The resulting contract did not contain the limited warranty that Leviton wanted, costing that company a $4 million judgment.

It was a request to receive an offer. Thus, the contract ultimately formed did not include Leviton's liability exclusion. Litton won over $4 million.[1] See Exhibit 12.1.

Letters of Intent

In complex business negotiations, the parties may spend months bargaining over dozens of interrelated issues. Because each party wants to protect itself during the discussions, ensuring that the other side is serious without binding itself to premature commitments, it may be tempting during the negotiations to draft a **letter of intent**. The letter *might* help distinguish a serious party from one with a casual interest, summarize the progress made thus far, and assist the parties in securing necessary financing. Usually, letters of intent do not create any legal obligation. They merely state what the parties are considering, not what they have actually agreed to. But note that is possible for a letter of intent to bind the parties if its language indicates that the parties *intended* to be bound.

Letter of intent
A letter that summarizes negotiating progress

Advertisements

Mary Mesaros received a notice from the United States Bureau of the Mint, announcing a new $5 gold coin to commemorate the Statue of Liberty. The notice contained an order form stating:

> VERY IMPORTANT—PLEASE READ: YES, Please accept my order for the U.S. Liberty Coins I have indicated. I understand that all sales are final and not subject to refund. Verification of my order will be made by the Department of the Treasury, U.S. Mint. If my order is received by December 31, I will be entitled to purchase the coins at the Pre-Issue Discount price shown.

Mesaros ordered almost $2,000 worth of the coins. But the Mint was inundated with so many requests for the coin that the supply was soon exhausted. Mesaros and thousands of others never got their coins. This was particularly disappointing because the market value of the coins doubled shortly after their issue. Mesaros sued on behalf of the entire class of disappointed purchasers. Like most who sue based on an advertisement, she lost.[2] **An advertisement is generally not an offer.** An advertisement is merely a request for offers. The consumer makes the offer, whether by mail, like Mesaros, or by arriving at a merchant's

---

[1]Litton Microwave Cooking Products v. Leviton Manufacturing Co., Inc., 15 F.3d 790 (8th Cir. 1994).
[2]Mesaros v. United States, 845 F.2d 1576 (Fed. Cir. 1988).

store ready to buy. The seller is free to reject the offer. Advertisers should be careful, however, not to be too specific in their ads. Some ads do count as offers, as the following case illustrates.

Landmark Case

CARLILL V. CARBOLIC SMOKE BALL COMPANY
1 QB 256 Court of Appeal, 1892

Facts: In the early 1890s, English citizens greatly feared the Russian flu. The Carbolic Smoke Ball Company ran a newspaper ad that contained two key passages:

"£100 reward will be paid by the Carbolic Smoke Ball Company to any person who contracts the influenza after having used the ball three times daily for two weeks according to the printed directions supplied with each ball.

"£1000 is deposited with the Alliance Bank, shewing our sincerity in the matter."

The product was a ball that contained carbolic acid. Users would inhale vapors from the ball through a long tube.

Carlill purchased a smoke ball and used it as directed for two months. She then caught the flu. She sued, arguing that because her response to the ad had created a contract with the company, she was entitled to £100.

The trial court agreed, awarding Carlill the money. The company appealed.

Issues: *Did the advertisement amount to an offer? If so, was the offer accepted?*

Excerpts from Lord Justice Lindley's Decision: The first observation I will make is that we are dealing with an express promise to pay £100 in certain events. Read the advertisement how you will, and twist it about as you will, here is a distinct promise expressed in language which is perfectly unmistakable.

We must first consider whether this was intended to be a promise at all. The deposit is called by the advertiser as proof of his sincerity in the matter—that is, the sincerity of his promise to pay this £100 in the event which he has specified. I say there is the promise, as plain as words can make it.

Then it is contended that it is not binding. In the first place, the performance of the conditions is the acceptance of the offer. Unquestionably, as a general proposition, when an offer is made, it is necessary that the acceptance should be notified. But is that so in cases of this kind? I think that in a case of this kind that the person who makes the [offer] shews by his language and from the nature of the transaction that he does not expect and does not require notice of the acceptance apart from notice of the performance.

We, therefore, find here all the elements which are necessary to form a binding contract enforceable in point of law.

It appears to me, therefore, that the defendants must perform their promise, and, if they have been so unwary as to expose themselves to a great many actions, so much the worse for them. Appeal dismissed.

Carlill lived 50 years more, dying at the age of 96—of the flu.

This case serves as a cautionary tale. Running a "normal" ad, which describes a product, its features, and its price, does not amount to an offer. But, if a company proposes to take an action—such as pay $100 to customers who take certain, specific actions—then it may find itself contractually obligated to follow through on its promises. The acceptance of the offer makes a unilateral contract.

Note also that, regardless of whether an ad counts as an offer, consumers have protection from those shopkeepers who are intent upon deceit. Almost every state has some form of **consumer protection statute**, which outlaws false advertising. For example, an automobile dealer who advertises a remarkably low price but then has only one automobile at that price has probably violated a consumer protection statute because the ad was published in bad faith, to trick consumers into coming to the dealership. In the *Mesaros* case, the United

Consumer protection statute
Laws protecting consumers from fraud

You have the high bid—but you may not win.

AP Images/Seth Wenig

States Mint did not violate any consumer protection statute because it acted in good faith and simply ran out of coins.

Auctions

It is the property you have always dreamed of owning—and it is up for auction! You arrive bright and early, stand in front, bid early, bid often, bid higher, bid highest of all—it's yours! For five seconds. Then, to your horror, the auctioneer announces that none of the bids were juicy enough and he is withdrawing the property. Robbery! Surely he cannot do that? But he can. Auctions are exciting and useful, but you must understand the rules.

Every day, auctions are used to sell exquisite works of art, real estate, and many other things. **Placing an item up for auction is *not* an offer—it is merely a request for an offer.** The *bids* are the offers. If and when the hammer falls, the auctioneer has accepted the offer.

The important thing to know about a particular auction is whether it is conducted with or without reserve. Most auctions are *with reserve,* meaning that the items for sale have a minimum price. The law assumes that an auction is with reserve unless the auctioneer clearly states otherwise. The auctioneer will not sell anything for less than its reserve (minimum price). So when the bidding for your property failed to reach the reserve, the auctioneer was free to withdraw it.

The rules are different in an auction *without reserve.* Here, there is no minimum. Once the first bid is received, the auctioneer *must* sell the merchandise to the highest bidder.

EXAM Strategy

Question: Ahn and Chet are both unhappy. (1) Ahn, an interior designer, is working on a hotel project. In the annual catalog of a furniture wholesaler, she sees that sofa beds cost $3,000. Based on the catalog, she sends an order for 100 sofa beds to the wholesaler. The wholesaler notifies Ahn that the price has gone up to $4,000. (2) At an estate auction, held without reserve, Chet is high bidder on a rare violin. The seller considers Chet's bid too low and refuses to sell. Both Ahn and Chet sue, but only one will win. Which plaintiff will win, and why?

Strategy: (1) A contract requires an offer and an acceptance. When the furniture wholesaler sent out its catalog, did it make an offer that Ahn could accept? (2) Chet was high bidder. At some auctions, the high bidder is merely making an offer, but at others, he wins the item. Which kind of auction was this?

Result: (1) A price quote is generally not an offer. Ahn's order for 100 sofas was the offer, and the company was free to reject it. Ahn loses. (2) Most auctions are with reserve, meaning that the high bidder is merely making an offer. However, this one was without reserve. Chet gets the violin.

12-2b Problems with Definiteness

It is not enough that the offeror indicates that she intends to enter into an agreement. **The terms of the offer must also be definite.** If they are vague, then even if the offeree agrees to the deal, a court does not have enough information to enforce it and there is no contract.

You want a friend to work in your store for the holiday season. This is a definite offer: "I offer you a job as a sales clerk in the store from November 1 through December 29, 40 hours per week at $10 per hour." But suppose, by contrast, you say: "I offer you a job as a sales clerk in the store during the holiday season. We will work out a fair wage once we see how busy things get." Your friend replies, "That's fine with me." This offer is indefinite, and there is no contract. What is a fair wage? $15 per hour? Or $20 per hour? What is the "holiday season"? How will the determinations be made? There is no binding agreement.

The following case, which concerns a famous television show, presents a problem with definiteness.

BAER V. CHASE

392 F.3d 609
Third Circuit Court of Appeals, 2004

Facts: David Chase was a television writer-producer with many credits, including a detective series called *The Rockford Files*. He became interested in a new program, set in New Jersey, about a "mob boss in therapy," a concept he eventually developed into *The Sopranos*. Robert Baer was a prosecutor in New Jersey who wanted to write for television. He submitted a *Rockford Files* script to Chase, who agreed to meet with Baer.

When they met, Baer pitched a different idea, concerning "a film or television series about the New Jersey Mafia." He did not realize Chase was already working on such an idea. Later that year, Chase visited New Jersey. Baer arranged meetings for Chase with local detectives and prosecutors, who provided the producer with information, material, and personal stories about their experiences with organized crime. Detective Thomas Koczur drove Chase and Baer to various New Jersey locations and introduced Chase to Tony Spirito. Spirito shared stories about loan sharking, power struggles between family members connected with the mob, and two colorful individuals known as Big Pussy and Little Pussy, both of whom later became characters on the show.

Back in Los Angeles, Chase wrote and sent to Baer a draft of the first *Sopranos* teleplay. Baer called Chase and commented on the script. The two spoke at least four times that year, and Baer sent Chase a letter about the script.

When *The Sopranos* became a hit television show, Baer sued Chase. He alleged that on three separate occasions Chase had agreed that if the program succeeded, Chase would "take care of" Baer, and would "remunerate Baer in a manner commensurate to the true value of his services." This happened twice on the phone, Baer claimed, and once during Chase's visit to New Jersey. The understanding was that if the show failed, Chase would owe nothing. Chase never paid Baer anything.

The district court dismissed the case, holding that the alleged promises were too vague to be enforced. Baer appealed.

Issue: *Was Chase's promise definite enough to be enforced?*

Excerpts from Judge Greenberg's Decision: A contract arises from offer and acceptance, and must be sufficiently definite so that the performance to be rendered by each party can be ascertained with reasonable certainty. Therefore parties create an enforceable contract when they agree on its essential terms and manifest an intent that the terms bind them. If parties to an agreement do not agree on one or more essential terms of the purported agreement courts generally hold it to be unenforceable.

New Jersey law deems the price term, that is, the amount of compensation, an essential term of any contract. An agreement lacking definiteness of price, however, is not unenforceable if the parties specify a

307

practicable method by which they can determine the amount. However, in the absence of an agreement as to the manner or method of determining compensation the purported agreement is invalid. Additionally, the duration of the contract is deemed an essential term and therefore any agreement must be sufficiently definitive to allow a court to determine the agreed upon length of the contractual relationship.

Baer premises his argument on his view that New Jersey should disregard the well-established requirement of definiteness in its contract law when the subject-matter of the contract is an "idea submission." [However,] New Jersey precedent does not support Baer's attempt to carve out an exception to traditional principles of contract law for submission-of-idea cases. The New Jersey courts have not provided even the slightest indication that they intend to depart from their well-established

requirement that enforceability of a contract requires definiteness with respect to the essential terms of that contract.

Nothing in the record indicates that the parties agreed on how, how much, where, or for what period Chase would compensate Baer. The parties did not discuss who would determine the "true value" of Baer's services, when the "true value" would be calculated, or what variables would go into such a calculation. There was no discussion or agreement as to the meaning of "success" of *The Sopranos*. There was no discussion how "profits" were to be defined. There was no contemplation of dates of commencement or termination of the contract. And again, nothing in Baer's or Chase's conduct, or the surrounding circumstances of the relationship, shed light on, or answers, any of these questions.

Affirmed.

"I'll take care of you." You probably have a sense of what this statement meant to Baer when he heard it from Chase: a reliable assurance that he would be paid. However, it was not enough to be a legally enforceable promise. Recall that courts only make *objective* assessments when evaluating offers and acceptances. Judges cannot—and will not—guess what the parties *meant to do* or analyze what was in their heads.

In the following case, the court asked whether a reasonable person would consider a syllabus to be a contract. You be the (objective) judge.

You be the Judge

GABRIEL V. ALBANY COLLEGE OF PHARMACY AND HEALTH SERVICES

No. 2:12-cv 14
United States District Court for
the District of Vermont, 2013

Facts: Matthew Gabriel was a student in Professor Pumo's immunology class. Professor Pumo's syllabus outlined course requirements and stated that "plagiarism will not be tolerated." After grading the first assignment, Professor Pumo realized that many papers had sentences copied from other sources without citations. Instead of reporting everyone for plagiarism, Professor Pumo said she would give students a *"free pass"* on one copied sentence. But Gabriel's paper contained many plagiarized sentences, so he received a failing grade for the assignment.

Gabriel sued the professor for breach of contract. He argued that the syllabus was a contract and that the "free pass" policy broke it—because that term was not part of their original agreement. According to Gabriel, since the professor breached the contract, he was no longer obligated to refrain from plagiarizing, and so should not be punished.

You Be the Judge: *Was the professor's syllabus an offer whose acceptance formed an enforceable contract?*

Argument for Gabriel: A syllabus is a contract. On the first day of class, the professor presents the syllabus as an offer and students agree by staying in the course. Who has not chosen a class because of its particular workload or assignments? The terms in the syllabus are promises upon which students rely. Professor Pumo unilaterally changed the written "rules of the game." Once she broke her promise, there was no longer a "deal." Students should not be held to her arbitrary rules.

Argument for Professor: Professors do not intend to make an offer when they hand out a syllabus—much less be legally bound! The syllabus is merely an announcement that provides general information about course requirements, grading policies, and behavior guidelines. Reasonable people do not expect a syllabus to be enforceable in court. It was not a contract—Professor Pumo had the right to change the class rules, make additional assignments, or even kick Gabriel out at any time. Even if the syllabus were a contract, the phrase "plagiarism will not be tolerated" is too indefinite to be a valid offer. Gabriel is not immune from the plagiarism rules.

12-2c The UCC and Open Terms

In the last chapter, we introduced the Uniform Commercial Code (UCC). Article 2 of the UCC governs contracts when the primary purpose is a sale of goods. Remember that goods are moveable, tangible objects. Usually, UCC provisions are not significantly different from common-law rules. But on occasion, the UCC modifies the common-law rule in some major way. In such cases, we will present a separate description of the key UCC provision. The UCC as a whole is covered in Unit 3. Depending on the class time available, some instructors prefer to discuss the UCC separately, while others like to include it in the general discussion of contracts. This book is designed to work with either approach.

We have just seen that, under the common law, the terms of an offer must be definite. But under the UCC, many indefinite contracts are allowed to stand. Throughout this unit, we witness how the Uniform Commercial Code makes the law of sales more flexible. There are several areas of contract law where imperfect negotiations may still create a binding agreement under the Code, even though the same negotiations under the common law would have yielded no contract. "Open terms" is one such area.

Yuma County Corp. produced natural gas. Yuma wanted a long-term contract to sell its gas so that it could be certain of recouping the expenses of exploration and drilling. Northwest Central Pipeline, which operated an interstate pipeline, also wanted a deal for 10 or more years so it could make its own distribution contracts, knowing it would have a steady supply of natural gas in a competitive market. But neither Yuma nor Northwest wanted to make a long-term *price* commitment, because over a period of years the price of natural gas could double—or crash. Each party wanted a binding agreement without a definitive price. If their negotiations had been governed by the common law, they would have run smack into the requirement of definiteness—no price, no contract. But because this was a sale of goods, it was governed by the UCC.

Under UCC §2-204(3), even though one or more terms are left open, a contract does not fail for indefiniteness if the parties have intended to make a contract and there is a reasonably certain basis for giving an appropriate remedy. Thus, a contract for the sale of goods may be enforced when a key term is missing. Business executives may have many reasons to leave open a delivery date, a price, or some other term. But note that the parties must still have *intended* to create a contract. The UCC will not create a contract where the parties never intended one.

In some cases, the contract will state how the missing term is to be determined. Yuma County and Northwest drafted a contract with alternative methods of determining the price. In the event that the price of natural gas was regulated by the Federal Energy Regulatory Commission (FERC), the price would be the highest allowed by the FERC. If the FERC deregulated the price (as it ultimately did), the contract price would be the average of the two highest prices paid by different gas producers in a specified geographic area.

Gap-Filler Provisions

Even if a UCC contract lacks a specific method for determining missing terms, the Code itself contains **gap-filler provisions**, which are rules for *supplying* missing terms. Some of the most important gap-filler provisions of the Code follow.

Gap-filler provisions
UCC rules for supplying missing terms

Open Price.   In general, if the parties do not settle on a price, the Code establishes that the goods will be sold for a reasonable price. This will usually be the market value or a price established by a neutral expert or agency.[3]

Output and Requirements Provisions.   An **output contract** obligates the seller to sell all of his output to the buyer, who agrees to accept it. For example, a cotton grower might agree to sell all of his next crop to a textile firm. A **requirements contract** obligates a buyer to obtain all of his needed goods from the seller. A vineyard might agree to buy all of its wine bottles from one supplier. Output and requirements contracts are by definition incomplete, since the exact quantity of the goods is unspecified. The Code requires that in carrying out such contracts, both parties act in good faith. Neither party may suddenly demand a quantity of goods (or offer a quantity of goods) that is disproportionate to their past dealings or their reasonable estimates.[4]

Output contract
Obligates the seller to sell all of his output to the buyer, who agrees to accept it

Requirements contract
Obligates a buyer to obtain all of his needed goods from the seller

12-2d Termination of Offers

Once an offer has been made, it faces only two possible fates—it can be terminated or accepted. If an offer is terminated, it can never be accepted. If it is accepted, and if there are no problems with any of the five remaining elements on the Contracts Checklist, then a valid contract is created. Offers can be terminated in four ways: revocation, rejection, expiration, and by operation of law.

Termination by Revocation

An offer is **revoked** when the offeror "takes it back" before the offeree accepts. In general, the offeror may revoke the offer any time before it has been accepted. Imagine that I call you and say, "I'm going out of town this weekend. I'll sell you my ticket to this weekend's football game for $75." You tell me that you'll think it over and call me back. An hour later, my plans change. I call you a second time and say, "Sorry, but the deal's off—I'm going to the game after all." I have revoked my offer, and you can no longer accept it.

Making Contracts Temporarily Irrevocable

Some offers cannot be revoked, at least for a time. Often, people and businesses need time to evaluate offers. If a car dealer offers you a green sedan for $25,000, you may want to shop around for a few days to try to find a better price. In the meantime, you may want to make sure that the green sedan is still available if you decide to return. Can you legally prevent the car dealer from selling the car to anyone else while you ponder the offer? In some circumstances, yes.

Option Contract (All types of contracts).   With an option contract, an interested purchaser *buys* the right to have the offer held open. **The offeror may not revoke an offer during the option period.** Suppose you pay the car dealer $250 to hold open its offer until February 2. Later that day, the dealership notifies you that it is selling to someone else. Result? You can enforce *your* contract. The car dealer had no power to revoke because you purchased an option.

---

[3]UCC §2-305
[4]UCC §2-306

Firm Offers (UCC contracts only). Once again, the UCC has changed the law on the sale of goods. If a promise made in writing is signed by a *merchant*, and if it agrees to hold open an offer for a stated period, then an offer may not be revoked. The open period may not exceed three months. So, if the car dealer gives you a piece of paper that reads, "The offer on the green sedan is open at $25,000 until Friday at noon," he cannot revoke the offer before Friday at noon, even though you have not paid him anything.[5]

Termination by Rejection

If an offeree clearly indicates that he does not want to take the offer, then he has **rejected** it. **If an offeree rejects an offer, the rejection immediately terminates the offer.** Suppose a major accounting firm telephones you and offers a job, starting at $80,000. You respond, "Nah. I'm gonna work on my surfing for a year or two." The next day, you come to your senses and write the firm, accepting its offer. No contract. Your rejection terminated the offer and ended your power to accept it.

Counteroffer. A party makes a **counteroffer** when it responds to an offer with a new and different proposal. Frederick faxes Kim, offering to sell a 50 percent interest in the Fab Hotel in New York for only $135 million. Kim faxes back and says, "That's too much, but I'll pay $115 million." Moments later, Kim's business partner convinces her that Frederick's offer was a bargain, and she faxes an acceptance of his $135 million offer. Does Kim have a binding deal? No. **A counteroffer is a rejection.** When Kim offered $115 million, she rejected Frederick's offer. Her original fax created a new offer, for $115 million, which Frederick never accepted. The parties have no contract at any price.

Counteroffer
A different proposal made in response to an original offer

Termination by Expiration

An offeror may set a time limit. Quentin calls you and offers you a job in his next motion picture. He tells you, "I've got to know by tomorrow night." If you call him in three days to accept, you are out of the picture. **When an offer specifies a time limit for acceptance, that period is binding.**

If the offer specifies no time limit, the offeree has a *reasonable* period in which to accept. A reasonable period varies, depending upon the type of offer, previous dealings between the parties, and any normal trade usage or customary practices in a particular industry.

Termination by Operation of Law

In some circumstances, the law itself terminates an offer. **If an offeror dies or becomes mentally incapacitated, the offer terminates automatically and immediately.** Arnie offers you a job as an assistant in his hot-air balloon business. Before you can even accept, Arnie tumbles out of a balloon at 3,000 feet. The offer terminates along with Arnie.

Destruction of the subject matter terminates the offer. A car dealer offers to sell you a rare 1938 Bugatti for $7,500,000 if you bring cash the next day. You arrive, suitcase stuffed with cash, just in time to see Arnie drop 3,000 feet through the air and crush the Bugatti. The dealer's offer is terminated.

12-3 ACCEPTANCE

As we have seen, when there is a valid offer outstanding, it remains effective until it is terminated or accepted. An offeree accepts by saying or doing something that a reasonable person would understand to mean that he definitely wants to take the offer. Assume that

---

[5]UCC §2-205

Ellie offers to sell Gene her old iPod for $50. If Gene says, "I accept your offer," then he has indeed accepted, but there is no need to be so formal. He can accept the offer by saying, "It's a deal," or, "I'll take it," or any number of things. He need not even speak. If he hands her a $50 bill, he also accepts the offer.

It is worth noting that **the offeree must say or do *something* to accept.** Marge telephones Vick and leaves a message on his answering machine: "I'll pay $75 for your business law textbook from last semester. I'm desperate to get a copy, so I will assume you agree unless I hear from you by 6:00 tonight." Marge hears nothing by the deadline and assumes she has a deal. She is mistaken. Vick neither said nor did anything to indicate that he accepted.

> **Was it sensible to deny the professor a job over a mere 14-day difference? Sensible or not, that is the law.**

12-3a Mirror Image Rule

If only he had known! A splendid university, an excellent position as department chair—gone. And all because of the mirror image rule.

Ohio State University wrote to Philip Foster offering him an appointment as a professor and chair of the art history department. His position was to begin July 1, and he had until June 2 to accept the job. On June 2, Foster telephoned the dean and left a message accepting the position, *effective July 15.* Later, Foster thought better of it and wrote the university, accepting the school's starting date of July 1. Too late! Professor Foster never did occupy that chair at Ohio State. The court held that since his acceptance varied the starting date, it was a counteroffer. And a counteroffer, as we know, is a rejection.[6]

Was it sensible to deny the professor a job over a mere 14-day difference? Sensible or not, that is the law. The common-law **mirror image rule** requires that acceptance be on *precisely* the same terms as the offer. If the acceptance contains terms that add or contradict the offer, even in minor ways, courts generally consider it a counteroffer. The rule worked reasonably well in the nineteenth century, when parties would write an original contract and exchange it, penciling in any changes. But now that businesses use standardized forms to purchase most goods and services, the rule creates enormous difficulties. Sellers use forms they have prepared, with all conditions stated to their advantage, and buyers employ their own forms, with terms they prefer. The forms are exchanged in the mail or electronically, with neither side clearly agreeing to the other party's terms.

The problem is known as the "battle of forms." Once again, the UCC has entered the fray, attempting to provide flexibility and common sense for those contracts involving the sale of goods. But for contracts governed by the common law, such as Professor Foster's, the mirror image rule is still the law.

Mirror image rule
Requires that acceptance be on precisely the same terms as the offer

12-3b UCC and the Battle of Forms

UCC §2-207 dramatically modifies the mirror image rule for the sale of goods. Under this provision, an acceptance that adds additional or different terms often will create a contract.

Additional or Different Terms

One basic principle of the common law of contracts remains unchanged: the key to creation of a contract is a valid offer that the offeree *intends* to accept. If there is no intent to accept, there is no contract. The big change brought about by UCC §2-207 is this: **An offeree who**

---

[6]Foster v. Ohio State University, 41 Ohio App. 3d 86 (1987).

accepts may include in the acceptance terms that are additional to or different from those in the offer. Thus, even with additional or different terms, the acceptance may well create a contract.

> *Example A.* Wholesaler writes to Manufacturer, offering to buy "10,000 wheelbarrows at $50 per unit. Payable on delivery, 30 days from today's date." Manufacturer writes back, "We accept your offer of 10,000 wheelbarrows at $50 per unit, payable on delivery. *Interest at normal trade rates for unpaid balances.*" Manufacturer clearly intends to form a contract. The company has added a new term, but there is still a valid contract.

However, if the offeree states that her acceptance is *conditioned on the offeror's assent* to the new terms, there is no contract.

> *Example B.* Same offer as above. Manufacturer adds the interest rate clause and states, "Our acceptance is conditional upon your agreement to this interest rate." Manufacturer has made a counteroffer. There is no contract, yet. If Wholesaler accepts the counteroffer, there is a contract; if Wholesaler does not accept it, there is no contract.

Additional terms are those that bring up *new* issues, such as interest rates, not contained in the original offer. Additional terms in the acceptance are considered proposals to add to the contract. Assuming that both parties are merchants, the additional terms *will generally become part of the contract.* Thus, in Example A, the interest rate will become a part of the binding deal. If Wholesaler is late in paying, it must pay whatever interest rate is current.

In three circumstances, the additional terms in the acceptance *do not* become part of the contract:

- If the original offeror *insisted on its own terms*. In other words, if Wholesaler wrote, "I offer to buy them on the following terms and *no other terms*," then Manufacturer is not free to make additions.

- If the additional terms *materially alter* the original offer. Suppose Manufacturer wrote back, "We accept your offer for 10,000 wheelbarrows. Delivery will be made within 180 days, unless we notify you of late delivery." Manufacturer has changed the time from 30 days to 180 days, with a possible extension beyond that. That is a material alteration, and it will not become part of the contract. By contrast, Manufacturer's new language concerning "interest at normal trade rates" was not a material alteration, and therefore that interest rate becomes part of the contract.

- If the offeror receives the additional terms and *promptly objects* to them.

Different terms are those that contradict terms in the offer. For example, if the seller's form clearly states that no warranty is included, and the buyer's form says the seller warrants all goods for three years, the acceptance contains different terms. An acceptance may contain different terms and still create a contract. But in these cases, courts have struggled to decide what the terms of the contract are. **The majority of states hold that different (contradictory) terms cancel each other out.** Neither term is included in the contract. Instead, the neutral terms from the Code itself are "read into" the contract. These are the gap-filler terms discussed earlier. If, for example, the forms had contradictory warranty clauses (as they almost always do), the different terms would cancel each other out, and the warranty clauses from the UCC would be substituted.[7]

---

[7]Not all states follow this rule, however. Some courts have held that when the acceptance contains terms that contradict those in the offer, the language in the offer should be final. A few courts have ruled that the terms in the acceptance should control.

EXAM Strategy

Question: Elaine faxes an offer to Raoul. Raoul writes, "I accept. Please note, I will charge 2 percent interest per month for any unpaid money." He signs the document and faxes it back to Elaine. Do the two have a binding contract?

Strategy: Slow down, this is trickier than it seems. Raoul has added a term to Elaine's offer. We must take two steps to decide whether there is a contract. In a contract for services, acceptance must mirror the offer, but not so in an agreement for the sale of goods.

Result: If this is an agreement for services, there is no contract. However, if this agreement is for goods, the additional term *may* become part of an enforceable contract.

Question: Assume that Elaine's offer concerns goods. Is there an agreement?

Strategy: Under UCC §2-207, an additional term will become part of a binding agreement for goods except in three instances. What are the three exceptions?

Result: Raoul's extra term will be incorporated in a binding contract unless (1) Elaine's offer made clear she would accept no other terms, (2) Raoul's interest rate is a material alteration of the offer (almost never the case for interest rates), or (3) Elaine promptly rejects the interest rate.

12-3c Clickwraps and Shrinkwraps

You want to purchase Attila brand software and download it to your computer. You type in your credit card number and other information, agreeing to pay $99. Attila also requires that you "read and agree to" all of the company's terms. You click "I agree," without having read one word of the terms. Three frustrating weeks later, tired of trying to operate defective Attilaware, you demand a refund and threaten to sue. The company replies that you are barred from suing because the terms you agreed to included an arbitration clause. To resolve any disputes, you must travel to Attila's hometown, halfway across the nation, use an arbitrator that the company chooses, pay one-half the arbitrator's fee, and also pay Attila's legal bills if you should lose. The agreement makes it financially impossible for you to get your money back. Is that contract enforceable?

You have entered into a "clickwrap" agreement. Similar agreements, called "shrinkwraps," are packaged inside many electronic products. A shrinkwrap notice might require that before inserting a purchased CD into your computer, you must read and agree to all terms in the brochure. Clickwraps and shrinkwraps often include arbitration clauses. They frequently limit the seller's liability if anything goes wrong, saying that the manufacturer's maximum responsibility is to refund the purchase price (even if the software destroys your hard drive).

Many courts that have analyzed these issues have ruled that clickwrap and shrinkwrap agreements are indeed binding, even against consumers. The courts have emphasized that sellers are entitled to offer a product on any terms they wish, and that shrinkwrap and clickwrap are the most efficient methods of including complicated terms in a small space. Think before you click![8]

---

[8]ProCD, Inc. v. Zeidenberg, 86 F.3d 1447 (7th Cir. 1996), is the leading case to enforce shrinkwrap agreements (and, by extension, clickwraps).

However, some courts have *refused* to enforce such contracts against a consumer, stating that the buyer never understood or agreed to the shrinkwrapped terms. The court in the following case works hard to balance the competing interests, and in the process demonstrates that this new area of law is very much in flux.

SPECHT V. NETSCAPE COMMUNICATIONS CORPORATION

306 F.3d 17
Second Circuit Court of Appeals, 2002

Facts: A group of plaintiffs sued Netscape, claiming that two of the company's products illegally captured private information about files that they downloaded from the Internet. The plaintiffs alleged that this was electronic eavesdropping, in violation of two federal statutes.

From Netscape's web page, the plaintiffs had downloaded SmartDownload, a software plug-in that enabled them to download the company's Communicator software. The Web page advertised the benefits of SmartDownload, and near the bottom of the screen was a tinted button labeled "Download." The plaintiffs clicked to download. If, instead of downloading, they had scrolled further down, they would have seen an invitation to "review and agree to the terms of the Netscape SmartDownload software license agreement." By clicking the appropriate button, they would have been sent to a series of linked pages, and finally arrived at a license agreement. Among the terms was an agreement to arbitrate any dispute. In other words, a consumer downloading SmartDownload was in theory giving up the right to file suit if anything went wrong, and agreeing to settle the dispute by arbitration. However, the plaintiffs never reviewed the license terms.

In the district court, Netscape moved to dismiss the case and compel arbitration. Netscape claimed that the plaintiffs had forfeited any right to sue based on the license agreement. The district court denied the company's motion, ruling that the plaintiffs had not agreed to the terms of the license. Netscape appealed.

Issue: *Had the plaintiffs agreed to arbitrate their claims?*

Excerpts from Judge Sotomayor's Decision: Defendants argue that plaintiffs must be held to a standard of reasonable prudence and that, because notice of the existence of SmartDownload license terms was on the next scrollable screen, plaintiffs were on "inquiry notice" of those terms. We disagree with the proposition that a reasonably prudent offeree in plaintiffs' position would necessarily have known or learned of the existence of the SmartDownload license agreement prior to acting, so that plaintiffs may be held to

have assented to that agreement with constructive notice of its terms.

Receipt of a physical document containing contract terms or notice thereof is frequently deemed, in the world of paper transactions, a sufficient circumstance to place the offeree on inquiry notice of those terms. These principles apply equally to the emergent world of online product delivery, pop-up screens, hyperlinked pages, clickwrap licensing, scrollable documents, and urgent admonitions to "Download Now!" What plaintiffs saw when they were being invited by defendants to download this fast, free plug-in called SmartDownload was a screen containing praise for the product and, at the very bottom of the screen, a "Download" button. Defendants argue that a fair and prudent person using ordinary care would have been on inquiry notice of SmartDownload's license terms.

We are not persuaded that a reasonably prudent offeree in these circumstances would have known of the existence of license terms. Plaintiffs were responding to an offer that did not carry an immediately visible notice of the existence of license terms or require unambiguous manifestation of assent to those terms. Thus, plaintiffs' apparent manifestation of consent was to terms contained in a document whose contractual nature was not obvious. Moreover, the fact that, given the position of the scroll bar on their computer screens, plaintiffs may have been aware that an unexplored portion of the Netscape Web page remained below the download button does not mean that they reasonably should have concluded that this portion contained a notice of license terms.

We conclude that in circumstances such as these, where consumers are urged to download free software at the immediate click of a button, a reference to the existence of license terms on a submerged screen is not sufficient to place consumers on inquiry or constructive notice of those terms. There is no reason to assume that viewers will scroll down to subsequent screens simply because screens are there.

For the foregoing reasons, we affirm the district court's denial of defendants' motion to compel arbitration and to stay court proceedings.

The plaintiffs in *Specht* won because they knew nothing about the arbitration clause and were unlikely to discover it on the company's website. Notice what happens when a user *does* know about terms posted online. Register.com was a registrar of Internet domain names, meaning that it issued domain names to people and companies establishing a new website. The company was legally obligated to make available to the public, for free, the names and contact information of its customers. Register was also in the business of assisting owners, for a fee, to develop their websites.

Verio, Inc. competed in the site development business. Verio's automated software program (robot) would search Register.com daily, seeking information about new sites. *After* Verio obtained contact information, a notice would appear on the Register site, stating:

> By submitting a query, you agree that under no circumstances will you use this data to support the transmission of mass unsolicited, commercial advertising or solicitation via email.

In fact, though, Verio used the contact information for exactly that purpose, sending mass emailings to owners of new websites, soliciting their development business. Register sued. Verio defended by stating it was not bound by the notice because the notice did not appear until after it had obtained the information. Verio argued that when it sent the queries, it was unaware of any restrictions on use of the data. The court was unpersuaded, and explained its reasoning with a simple but telling metaphor:

> The situation might be compared to one in which plaintiff P maintains a roadside fruit stand displaying bins of apples. A visitor, defendant D, takes an apple and bites into it. As D turns to leave, D sees a sign, visible only as one turns to exit, which says "Apples—50 cents apiece." D does not pay for the apple. D believes he has no obligation to pay because he had no notice when he bit into the apple that 50 cents was expected in return. D's view is that he never agreed to pay for the apple. Thereafter, each day, several times a day, D revisits the stand, takes an apple, and eats it. D never leaves money.
>
> P sues D in contract for the price of the apples taken. D defends on the ground that on no occasion did he see P's price notice until after he had bitten into the apples. D may well prevail as to the first apple taken. D had no reason to understand upon taking it that P was demanding the payment. In our view, however, D cannot continue on a daily basis to take apples for free, knowing full well that P is offering them only in exchange for 50 cents in compensation, merely because the sign demanding payment is so placed that on each occasion D does not see it until he has bitten into the apple.

Register.com won its case. Verio was prohibited from using the contact information for mass emailings because it had actual knowledge of the restrictions placed on its use.[9]

Ethics Imagine browsing for an airline ticket online, only to discover that the first class fare from New York to India is $1, round trip. Would you rush to purchase it? Airlines regularly make programming mistakes resulting in mispriced online fares. Brian Kelly found a United Airlines first class ticket from New York to Hong Kong—which usually costs about $11,000—for $43 and immediately bought it on the company's online ticketing system.[10] Kelly, who runs a website for frequent flyers, advised his readers to take advantage of the glitch before United discovered it. And many did.

Are these "mistake fares"—which are obviously "too good to be true"—enforceable as contracts? Is there a valid offer and acceptance? Ethically speaking, would you take advantage of this deal? Why or why not?

---

[9]Register.Com v. Verio, Inc., 353 F.3d 393 (2d Cir. 2004).
[10]Tim Hume, *Too good to be true: New York to Hong Kong for $43*, CNN.com (July 23, 2012).

12-3d Communication of Acceptance

The offeree must communicate his acceptance for it to be effective. The questions that typically arise concern the method, the manner, and the time of acceptance.

Method and Manner of Acceptance

The term *method* refers to whether acceptance is done in person or by mail, telephone, email, or fax. The term *manner* refers to whether the offeree accepts by promising, by making a down payment, by performing, and so forth. **If an offer demands acceptance in a particular method or manner, the offeree must follow those requirements.** An offer might specify that it be accepted in writing, or in person, or before midnight on June 23. An offeror can set any requirements she wishes. Omri might say to Oliver, "I'll sell you my bike for $200. You must accept my offer by standing on a chair in the lunchroom tomorrow and reciting a poem about a cow." Oliver can only accept the offer in the exact manner specified if he wants to form a contract.

If the offer does not specify a type of acceptance, the offeree may accept in any reasonable manner and method. An offer generally may be accepted by performance or by a promise, unless it specifies a particular method. The same freedom applies to the method. If Masako faxes Eric an offer to sell 1,000 acres in Montana for $800,000, Eric may accept by mail or fax. Both are routinely used in real estate transactions, and either is reasonable.

Time of Acceptance: The Mailbox Rule

An acceptance is generally effective upon dispatch, meaning the moment it is out of the offeree's control. Terminations, on the other hand, are effective when received. When Masako faxes her offer to sell land to Eric, and he mails his acceptance, the contract is binding the moment he puts the letter into the mail. In most cases, this **mailbox rule** is just a detail. But it becomes important when the offeror revokes her offer at about the same time the offeree accepts. Who wins? Suppose Masako's offer has one twist:

> **Mailbox rule**
> Acceptance is generally effective upon dispatch. Terminations are effective when received.

- On Monday morning, Masako faxes her offer to Eric.

- On Monday afternoon, Eric writes, "I accept" on the fax, and Masako mails a revocation of her offer.

- On Tuesday morning, Eric mails his acceptance.

- On Thursday morning, Masako's revocation arrives at Eric's office.

- On Friday morning, Eric's acceptance arrives at Masako's office.

Outcome? Eric has an enforceable contract. Masako's offer was effective when it reached Eric. His acceptance was effective on Tuesday morning, when he mailed it. Nothing that happens later can "undo" the contract.

SOLDAU v. ORGANON, INC.

860 F.2d 355
United States Court of Appeals for the Ninth Circuit, 1988

Facts: Organon fired John Soldau. Then the company sent to him a letter offering to pay him double the normal severance pay, provided Soldau would sign a full release, that is, a document giving up any and all claims he might have against Organon. The release was included with the letter. Soldau signed it, dated it, and took it to the nearest post office, where he deposited it in the mailbox. When he returned home, Soldau discovered in the mail a check from Organon for the double severance pay. He hustled back to the post office, where he persuaded a postal clerk to open the mailbox and retrieve the release he had posted. He then cashed Organon's check and finally filed a suit against the company, alleging that his firing was age discrimination.

The federal district court gave summary judgment for Organon, ruling that Soldau's acceptance of the proposed release was effective when he mailed it, creating a contract. He appealed.

Issue: *Did Soldau create a contract by mailing the release?*

Excerpts from the *Per Curiam* Decision: The district court was clearly correct under California law. Soldau does not argue to the contrary. Instead, he contends that the formation and validity of the release are governed by federal law, and would not have been effective unless and until it had been received by Organon. We need not decide which body of law controls. Under federal as well as California law, Soldau's acceptance was effective when it was mailed.

The so-called mailbox or effective when mailed rule was adopted and followed as federal common law by the Supreme Court [at the beginning of the 20th century]. We

could not change the rule, and there is no reason to believe the Supreme Court would be inclined to do so. It is almost universally accepted in the common law world. It is enshrined in the Restatement (Second) of Contracts and endorsed by the major contract treatises.

Commentators are also virtually unanimous in [supporting the "effective upon dispatch" rule,] pointing to the long history of the rule; its importance in creating certainty for contracting parties; its essential soundness, on balance, as a means of allocating the risk during the period between the making of the offer and the communication of the acceptance or rejection to the offeror; and the inadequacy of the rationale offered by the Court of Claims for the change.

Since Soldau's contractual obligation to release Organon in return for Organon's obligation to make the enhanced severance payment arose when Soldau deposited his acceptance in the post office mailbox, his subsequent withdrawal of the acceptance was ineffectual. *Affirmed.*

Chapter Conclusion

The law of offer and acceptance can be complex. Yet for all its faults, the law is not the principal source of dispute between parties unhappy with negotiations. Most litigation concerning offer and acceptance comes from *lack of clarity* on the part of the people negotiating. The many examples discussed are all understandable given the speed and fluidity of the real world of business. But the executive who insists on clarity is likelier in the long run to spend more time doing business and less time in court.

EXAM REVIEW

1. **MEETING OF THE MINDS** The parties can form a contract only if they have a meeting of the minds, which requires that they understand each other and show that they intend to reach an agreement.

EXAM Strategy

Question: Norv owned a Ford dealership and wanted to expand by obtaining a BMW outlet. He spoke with Jackson and other BMW executives on several occasions. Norv now claims that those discussions resulted in an oral contract that requires BMW to grant him a franchise, but the company disagrees. Norv's strongest evidence of a contract is the fact that Jackson gave him forms on which to order BMWs. Jackson answered that it was his standard practice to give such forms to prospective dealers, so that if the franchise were approved, car orders could be processed quickly. Norv states that he was "shocked" when BMW refused to go through with the deal. Is there a contract?

Strategy: A court makes an *objective* assessment of what the parties did and said to determine whether they had a meeting of the minds and intended to form a contract. Norv's "shock" is irrelevant. Do the order forms indicate a meeting of the minds? Was there additional evidence that the parties had reached an agreement? (See the "Result" at the end of this section.)

2. **OFFER**   An offer is an act or statement that proposes definite terms and permits the other party to create a contract by accepting those terms.

3. **OTHER STATEMENTS**   Invitations to bargain, price quotes, letters of intent, and advertisements are generally not offers. However, an ad in which a company proposes to take a specific action when a customer takes a specific action can amount to an offer. And letters of intent that indicate the parties intended to be bound can also count as offers.

Question: "Huge selection of Guernsey sweaters," reads a newspaper ad from Stuffed Shirt, a clothing retailer. "Regularly $135, today only $65." Waldo arrives at Stuffed Shirt at 4:00 that afternoon, but the shop clerk says there are no more sweaters. He shows Waldo a newly arrived Shetland sweater that sells for $145. Waldo sues, claiming breach of contract and violation of a consumer protection statute. Who will prevail?

(a)   Waldo will win the breach of contract suit and the consumer protection suit.

(b)   Waldo will lose the breach of contract suit but might win the consumer protection suit.

(c)   Waldo will lose the consumer protection suit but should win the breach of contract suit.

(d)   Waldo will win the consumer protection suit only if he wins the contract case.

(e)   Waldo will lose both the breach of contract suit and the consumer protection suit.

Strategy: Waldo assumes that he is accepting the store's offer. But did Stuffed Shirt make an offer? If not, there cannot be a contract. Does the consumer protection statute help him? (See the "Result" at the end of this section.)

4. **DEFINITENESS**   The terms of the offer must be definite, although under the UCC the parties may create a contract that has open terms.

5. **TERMINATION**   An offer may be terminated by revocation, rejection, expiration, or operation of law.

EXAM Strategy

EXAM Strategy

Question: Rick is selling his Espresso Coffee Maker. He sends Tamara an email, offering to sell the machine for $350. Tamara promptly emails back, offering to buy the item for $300. She hears nothing from Rick, so an hour later Tamara stops by his apartment, where she learns that he just sold the machine to his roommate for $250. She sues Rick. Outcome?

(a) Tamara will win because her offer was higher than the roommate's.

(b) Tamara will win because Rick never responded to her offer.

(c) Tamara will win because both parties made clear offers, in writing.

(d) Tamara will lose because she rejected Rick's offer.

(e) Tamara will lose because her offer was not definite.

Strategy: A valid contract requires a definite offer and acceptance. Rick made a valid offer. When Tamara said she would buy the machine for a lower amount, was that acceptance? If not, what was it? (See the "Result" at the end of this section.)

6. **MIRROR IMAGE RULE AND UCC §2-207** The common-law mirror image rule requires acceptance on precisely the same terms as the offer. Under the UCC, an offeree may often create a contract even when the acceptance includes terms that are additional to or different from those in the offer.

7. **CLICKWRAP AGREEMENTS** Clickwrap and shrinkwrap agreements are generally enforceable.

8. **MANNER OF ACCEPTANCE** If an offer demands acceptance in a particular method or manner, the offeree must follow those requirements. If the offer does not specify a type of acceptance, the offeree may accept in any reasonable manner and medium.

9. **MAILBOX RULE** An acceptance is generally effective upon dispatch, meaning from the moment it is out of the offeree's control. Terminations usually are not effective until received.

1. Result: The order forms are neither an offer nor an acceptance. Norv has offered no evidence that the parties agreed on price, date of performance, or any other key terms. There is no contract. Norv allowed eagerness and optimism to replace common sense.

3. Result: An advertisement is usually not an offer, but merely a solicitation of one. It is Waldo who is making the offer, which the store may reject. Waldo loses his contract case, but he may win under the consumer protection statute. The correct answer is B. If Stuffed Shirt proclaimed "huge selection" when there were only five sweaters, the store was deliberately misleading consumers, and Waldo wins. However, if there was indeed a large selection, and Waldo arrived too late, he is out of luck.

5. Result: Tamara made a counteroffer of $300. A counteroffer is a rejection. Tamara rejected Rick's offer and simultaneously offered to buy the coffee maker at a lower price. Rick was under no obligation to sell to Tamara at any price. He will win Tamara's suit.

MULTIPLE-CHOICE QUESTIONS

1. Rebecca, in Honolulu, faxes a job offer to Spike, in Pittsburgh, saying, "We can pay you $55,000 per year, starting June 1." Spike faxes a reply, saying, "Thank you! I accept your generous offer, though I will also need $3,000 in relocation money. See you June 1. Can't wait!" On June 1, Spike arrives, to find that his position is filled by Gus. He sues Rebecca.

   (a) Spike wins $55,000.

   (b) Spike wins $58,000.

   (c) Spike wins $3,000.

   (d) Spike wins restitution.

   (e) Spike wins nothing.

2. Arturo hires Kate to work in his new sporting goods store. "Look," he explains, "I can only pay you $9.00 an hour. But if business is good a year from now, and you're still here, I'm sure I can pay you a healthy bonus." Four months later, Arturo terminates Kate. She sues.

   (a) Kate will win her job back, plus the year's pay and the bonus.

   (b) Kate will win the year's pay and the bonus.

   (c) Kate will win only the bonus.

   (d) Kate will win only her job back.

   (e) Kate will win nothing.

3. Manny offers to sell Gina his TV for $100 on January 1. On January 2, Gina writes out a letter of acceptance. On January 3, Gina drops the letter in a mailbox. On January 4, a postal worker gets the letter out of the mailbox and takes it to the post office. On January 5, the letter arrives in Manny's mailbox. When (if ever) was a contract formed?

   (a) January 2

   (b) January 3

   (c) January 4

   (d) January 5

   (e) None of the above—a contract has not been formed.

4. Frank, an accountant, says to Missy, "I'll sell you my laptop for $100." Missy asks, "Will you give me until tomorrow to make up my mind?" "Sure," Frank replies. Which of the following is true?

   (a) Frank cannot revoke his offer, no matter what.

   (b) Frank cannot revoke his offer, but only if Missy pays him to keep the offer open until tomorrow.

   (c) Frank can revoke his offer no matter what, because he is not a merchant.

   (d) Frank can revoke his offer no matter what, because he did not promise Missy anything in writing.

5. Which of the following amounts to an offer?
   (a) Ed says to Carmen, "I offer to sell you my pen for $1."
   (b) Ed says to Carmen, "I'll sell you my pen for $1."
   (c) Ed writes, "I'll sell you my pen for $1," and gives the note to Carmen.
   (d) All of the above
   (e) A and C only

CASE QUESTIONS

1. The town of Sanford, Maine, decided to auction off a lot it owned. The town advertised that it would accept bids through the mail, up to a specified date. Arthur and Arline Chevalier mailed in a bid that turned out to be the highest. When the town refused to sell them the lot, they sued. Result?

2. The Tufte family leased a 260-acre farm from the Travelers Insurance Co. Toward the end of the lease, Travelers mailed the Tuftes an option to renew the lease. The option arrived at the Tuftes' house on March 30, and gave them until April 14 to accept. On April 13, the Tuftes signed and mailed their acceptance, which Travelers received on April 19. Travelers claimed there was no lease and attempted to evict the Tuftes from the farm. May they stay?

3. Consolidated Edison Co. of New York (Con Ed) sought bids from General Electric Co. (GE) and others to supply it with two huge transformers. Con Ed required that the bids be held open for 90 days. GE submitted a written bid and included a clause holding the bid open for 90 days. During that period, Con Ed accepted GE's bid, but GE refused to honor it. Is there a contract?

4. Niels owned three adjoining parcels of land in Arizona. Hannah wanted to buy one. Over dinner, the two sketched and signed this agreement: "Binding Contract: Niels agrees to sell one of his three Arizona lots to Hannah. Within 14 days, the parties will meet on the land, decide which lot Hannah is buying, and settle on a price. If they cannot agree on a price, they will decide a fair method of doing so. Both parties agree to be bound by this contract." Later, Niels refused to sell any land, and Hannah sued. What will happen?

5. When a Tom Cat Bakery delivery van struck Elizabeth Nadel, she suffered significant injuries, Nadel filed suit. Before the trial, Tom Cat's attorney offered a $100,000 settlement, which Nadel refused. While the jury was deliberating, the bakery's lawyer again offered Nadel the $100,000 settlement. She decided to think about it during lunch. Later that day, the jury sent a note to the judge. The bakery owner told her lawyer that if the note indicated the jury had reached a verdict, he should revoke the settlement offer. Back in the courtroom, the bakery's lawyer said, "If the note is a verdict, my client wants to take the verdict." Nadel's lawyer then said, "My client will take the settlement." The trial court judge allowed the forewoman to read the verdict, which awarded Nadel—nothing. Did Nadel's lawyer accept the settlement offer in time?

Discussion Questions

1. Each time employees at BizCorp enter their work computers, the following alert appears: "You are attempting to access the BizCorp network. By logging in, you agree to BizCorp's Computer Usage Policy and certify that your use of this computer is strictly for business purposes. Any activities conducted on this system may be monitored for any reason at the discretion of BizCorp." Once an employee has logged in, have the parties formed a valid contract? Discuss.

2. Case law tells us that a course syllabus is not a binding contract—but how about your school's honor code? Under what conditions could an honor code be a contract?

3. The day after Thanksgiving, known as Black Friday, is the biggest shopping day of the year. One major retailer advertised a "Black Friday only" laptop for $150. On Thanksgiving night, hundreds of people waited for the store to open to take advantage of the laptop deal—only to learn that the store only had two units for sale at the discounted price. Did the retailer breach its contract with the hundreds of consumers who sought the deal? What obligation, if any, does the retailer have to its consumers?

4. Someone offers to sell you a concert ticket for $50, and you reply, "I'll give you $40," The seller refuses to sell at the lower price, and you say, "OK, OK, I'll pay you $50." Clearly, no contract has been formed, because you made a counteroffer. If the seller has changed her mind and no longer wants to sell for $50, she doesn't have to. But is this fair? If it is all part of the same conversation, should you be able to accept the $50 offer and get the ticket?

5. If you click an "I agree" box, odds are that its terms are binding on you, even if the box contains dozens or even hundreds of lines of dense text. Is this fair? Should the law change to limit the enforceability of clickwraps?

6. Courts stick to objective (reasonable person) standards when evaluating offers and acceptances. Juries are not asked to "get inside someone's head," they are instructed to determine what a reasonable person would think of offerors' and offereees' statements. Is this practice reasonable? Would it be better if the law directly considered whether people *wanted* to make contracts?

ANSWERS TO SELECTED END OF CHAPTER QUESTIONS

MULTIPLE-CHOICE QUESTIONS

Presented are the answers for the ODD-numbered multiple-choice questions in the end-of-chapter material.

1. E
3. B
5. D

CASE QUESTIONS

Presented are the answers for all of the ODD-numbered case questions in the end-of-chapter material.

1. **Answer:** No contract, no sale. An auction is with reserve unless stated otherwise. The ad was silent on the subject, so this auction was with reserve. That means that all of the bids, including the highest, are merely offers. The auctioneer, in this case the town, has the right to reject all of the offers, and the Chevaliers have no right to the lot. *Chevalier v. Town of Sanford*, 475 A.2d 1148 (Me. 1984).

3. **Answer:** Yes. GE made a "firm offer," governed by UCC §2-205. When a merchant signs a written firm offer, the offer may not be revoked within that period or three months, whichever is less. Here the offer was for three months, so it is irrevocable. *Consolidated Edison Co. v. General Electric*, 555 N.Y.S.2d 355, 1990 N.Y. App. LEXIS 5774 (N.Y. App. Div. 1990).

5. **Answer:** Excerpt from Judge's decision: Plaintiff's motion to enforce "the settlement" has generated considerable debate between the parties. Plaintiff asserts that the defendant is bound to a settlement. Plaintiff's problem is that there was no "agreement" to speak of. To be sure, there was an offer from defendant. During the quoted colloquy, clearly there were also words of acceptance from plaintiff. But when the words, "my client will take the settlement" were uttered, it was too late for them to be effective. By that time, defense counsel had made it clear that if the jury had already come to a verdict, the offer was off the table. That condition could not be ignored, as the verdict that would mean all bets were off had already been reached. For the foregoing reasons, plaintiff's motion is denied.

CONSIDERATION

© Honza Krej/Shutterstock.com

Have you ever rented a movie that you did not want every one of your friends to know about? Cathryn Harris did. Imagine her shock when she rented a movie online from Blockbuster, only to find out that this news was automatically transmitted to her Facebook page and then broadcast to all her "friends." Just think how bad that could be.

Harris sued Blockbuster for this violation of her privacy, only to find out she had clicked away her right to sue. To rent the movie, she clicked that little box saying she agreed to all the terms and conditions. And one of those terms and conditions was an agreement to arbitrate, not litigate. Can Blockbuster get away with this?

It turns out that this movie has a happy ending. The court ruled that the contract between Harris and Blockbuster was unenforceable because there was no *consideration*.

> **To rent the movie, she had to click that little box saying she agreed to all the terms and conditions.**

Consideration is our next step on the road to understanding contracts. In the Chapter 12, we learned what it takes to create an agreement. But an agreement is not necessarily a legally enforceable contract.

This is the first of four chapters that will examine problems that can prevent an agreement from becoming a contract. A lack of consideration is one of them. Without it, a promise is "just a promise" and nothing more.

13-1 WHAT IS CONSIDERATION?

Contracts Checklist
- ☐ Offer
- ☐ Acceptance
- ✔ Consideration
- ☐ Legality
- ☐ Capacity
- ☐ Consent
- ☐ Writing

In early English law, courts would not enforce contracts unless they were under formal seal.[1]

It soon became evident that many other types of mutual promises should be recognized as contracts, regardless of their form. But how would judges know which promises were worth enforcing? How would they distinguish between mere gifts and legally binding commitments?

The answer is **consideration. Consideration is the inducement, price, or promise that causes a person to enter into a contract and forms the basis for the parties' exchange.** The central idea of consideration is simple: Contracts must be a two-way street. If one side gets all the benefit and the other side gets nothing, then an agreement lacks consideration and is not an enforceable contract. Consideration is proof that the parties intended to be bound to their promises.

Consideration
The inducement, price, or promise that causes a person to enter into a contract and forms the basis for the parties' exchange.

There are two basic elements of consideration:

1. **Value** Consideration requires legal benefit to the promisor or legal detriment to the promisee. Legal benefit means receiving something of *measureable value*. That thing can be money, groceries, insurance, a promise not to sue, or anything else of value to the promisee.

2. **Bargained-for Exchange** According to Supreme Court Justice Oliver Wendell Holmes, Jr., the essence of consideration is that "the promise must induce the detriment and the detriment must induce the promise."[2] Consideration involves reciprocity. The parties must have *bargained for* whatever was exchanged and struck a deal: "If you do this, I'll do that." If you just decide to deliver a cake to your neighbor's house without her knowing, that may be something of value, but since you two did not bargain for it, there is no contract and she does not owe you the price of the cake.

For Holmes, consideration required a reciprocal bargain.

Let's take an example: Sally's Shoe Store and Baker Boots agree that Sally's will pay $20,000 for 100 pairs of boots. As to the $20,000, Sally's is the promisor (because it has committed to paying) and Baker the promisee (because it is the recipient). Regarding the boots, Baker is the promisor, and Sally's the promisee. Both parties get a legal benefit that is of value—Sally gets the boots, Baker gets the money. Also, each incurs a detriment—Sally gives up the money, Baker parts with the boots. Note that a contract is

---

[1]It was once common to authenticate contracts with a seal, an instrument that creates an impression on paper or wax. This practice is rare today.
[2]Wisconsin & Michigan Ry. v. Powers, 191 U.S. 379 (1903).

formed at the moment when the promises are made because a promise to give something of value counts. The two have bargained for this deal, so there is valid consideration.

Now for an example where there is no consideration. Marvin works at Sally's. At 9 a.m., he is in a good mood and promises to buy his coworker a Starbucks latte during the lunch hour. The delighted coworker agrees. Later that morning, the coworker is rude to Marvin, who then changes his mind about buying the coffee. He is free to do so. His promise was a one-way street: The coworker stood to receive all the benefit of the agreement, while Marvin got nothing. Because Marvin received no value, there is no contract.

13-1a What Is Value?

As we have seen, an essential part of consideration is that both parties must get something of value. That item of value can be either an "act," a "forbearance," or a promise to do either of these.

Act

Act

Any action that a party was not legally required to take in the first place

A party commits an **act** when she does something she was not legally required to do in the first place. She might do a job, deliver an item, or pay money, for example. An act does not count if the party was simply complying with the law or fulfilling her obligations under an existing contract. Suppose that your professor tells the university that she will not post final grades unless she is paid an extra $5,000. Even if the university agrees to this outrageous demand, that agreement is not a valid contract because the professor is already under an obligation to post final grades.

Forbearance

Forbearance

Refraining from doing something that one has a legal right to do

A **forbearance** is, in essence, the opposite of an act. A person forbears if he agrees *not* to do something he had a legal right to do. An entrepreneur might promise a competitor *not* to open a competing business, or an elderly driver (with a valid driver's license) might promise concerned family members that he will not drive at night.

Promise to Act or Forbear

A promise to do (or not do) something in the future counts as consideration. When evaluating whether consideration exists, the *promise* to mow someone's lawn next week is the equivalent of actually *doing* the yardwork.

Let's apply these ideas to the most famous of all consideration lawsuits. Our story begins in 1869, when a well-meaning uncle made a promise to his nephew. Ever since *Hamer v. Sidway* appeared, generations of U.S. law students have dutifully inhaled the facts and sworn by its wisdom; now you, too, may drink it in.

Landmark Case

HAMER V. SIDWAY
124 N.Y. 538
New York Court of Appeals, 1891

Facts: This is a story with two Stories. William Story wanted his nephew to grow up healthy and prosperous. In 1869, he promised the 15-year-old boy (who was also named William Story) $5,000 if the lad would refrain from drinking liquor, using tobacco, swearing, and playing cards or billiards for money until his twenty-first birthday. (In that wild era—can you believe it?—the nephew had a legal right to do all those things.) The nephew agreed and, what is more, he kept his word. When he reached his twenty-first birthday, the nephew notified his uncle that he had honored the agreement. The uncle congratulated the young man and promised to give him the money but said he would wait a few more years before handing over the cash, until the nephew was mature enough to handle such a large sum. The uncle died in 1887 without having paid, and his estate refused to honor the promise. Because the nephew had transferred his rights in the money, it was a man named Hamer who eventually sought to collect from the uncle's estate. The estate argued that since the nephew had given no consideration for the uncle's promise, there was no enforceable contract. The trial court found for the plaintiff, and the uncle's estate appealed.

Issue: *Did the nephew give consideration for the uncle's promise?*

Excerpts from Justice Parker's Decision: The defendant contends that the contract was without consideration to support it, and therefore invalid. He asserts that the promisee, by refraining from the use of liquor and tobacco, was not harmed, but benefited; that that which he did was best for him to do, independently of his uncle's promise, and insists that it follows that, unless the promisor was benefited, the contract was without consideration, a contention which, if well founded, would seem to leave open for controversy in many cases whether that which the promisee did or

omitted to do was in fact of such benefit to him as to leave no consideration to support the enforcement of the promisor's agreement. Such a rule could not be tolerated, and is without foundation in the law. Courts will not ask whether the thing which forms the consideration does in fact benefit the promisee or a third party, or is of any substantial value to anyone. It is enough that something is promised, done, forborne, or suffered by the party to whom the promise is made as consideration for the promise made to him.

Now applying this rule to the facts before us, the promisee used tobacco, occasionally drank liquor, and he had a legal right to do so. That right he abandoned for a period of years upon the strength of the promise of the testator [that is, the uncle] that for such forbearance he would give him $5,000. We need not speculate on the effort which may have been required to give up the use of those stimulants. It is sufficient that he restricted his lawful freedom of action within certain prescribed limits upon the faith of his uncle's agreement, and now, having fully performed the conditions imposed, it is of no moment whether such performance actually proved a benefit to the promisor, and the court will not inquire into it.

The issue of value in a contract is an important one, so let's look at another case. In the movies, when a character wants to get serious about keeping a promise—*really* serious—he sometimes signs an agreement in blood. As it turns out, this kind of thing actually happens in real life. In the following case, did the promise of forbearance have value? Did a contract signed in blood count? You be the judge.

You be the Judge

KIM V. SON
2009 Cal. App. LEXIS 2011, 2009 WL 597232
Court of Appeal of California, 2009

Facts: Stephen Son was a part owner and operator of two corporations. Because the businesses were corporations, Son was not personally liable for the debts of either one.

Jinsoo Kim invested a total of about $170,000 in the companies. Eventually, both of them failed, and Kim lost his investment. Son felt guilty over Kim's losses.

Later, Son and Kim met in a sushi restaurant and drank heroic quantities of alcohol. At one point, Son pricked his finger with a safety pin and wrote the following in his own blood: "Sir, please forgive me. Because of my deeds, you have suffered financially. I will repay you to the best of my ability." In return, Kim agreed not to sue him for the money owed.

Son later refused to honor the bloody document and pay Kim the money. Kim filed suit to enforce their contract.

The judge determined that the promise did not create a contract because there had been no consideration.

You Be the Judge: *Was there consideration?*

Argument for Kim: As a part of the deal made at the sushi restaurant, Kim agreed not to sue Son. What could be more of a forbearance than that? Kim had a right to sue at any time, and he gave the right up. Even if Kim was unlikely to win, Son would still prefer not to be sued.

Besides, the fact that Son signed the agreement in blood indicates how seriously he took the obligation to repay his loyal investor. At a minimum, Son eased his guilty conscience by making the agreement, and surely that is worth something.

Argument for Son: Who among you has not at one point or another become intoxicated, experienced emotions more powerful than usual, and regretted them the next morning? Whether calling an ex-girlfriend and professing endless love or writing out an agreement in your own blood, it is all the same.

A promise not to file a meritless lawsuit has no value at all. It did not matter to Son whether or not Kim filed suit because Kim could not possibly win. If this promise counts as value, then the concept of consideration is meaningless because anyone can promise not to sue anytime. Son had no obligation to pay Kim. And the bloody napkin does not change that fact because it was made without consideration of any kind. It is an ordinary promise, not a contract that creates any legal obligation.

13-1b What Is a Bargained-for Exchange?

Bargained for

When something is sought by the promisor and given by the promise in exchange for their promises

The parties must bargain for the consideration. Something is **Bargained for** if it is sought by the promisor and given by the promisee in exchange for their respective promises. Eliza hires Joe to be her public relations manager for $15,000 a year. Both Eliza and Joe have made promises to induce the other's action. But what if the going rate for a PR manager with Joe's experience is $65,000?

Joe made a bad deal, but that does not mean it lacked consideration. **Courts do not analyze the economic terms of an exchange to determine whether consideration was adequate.** For consideration to be adequate in the eyes of the law, it must provide some benefit to the promisor or some detriment to the promisee, but these need not amount to much. Law professors often call this the "peppercorn rule," a reference to a Civil War–era case in which a judge mused, "What is a valuable consideration? A peppercorn."[3] Here, both Eliza and Joe are promisor and promisee; each receives a benefit and incurs a detriment.

Gold can make people crazy. At the turn of the 20th century, John Tuppela joined the gold rush to Alaska. He bought a mine, but sadly, his prospecting proved futile. In 1914, a court declared him insane and locked him in an institution. Four years later, Tuppela emerged and learned to his ecstasy that gold had been discovered in his mine, now valued at over half a million dollars. Then the bad news hit: A court-appointed guardian had sold the mine for pennies while Tuppela was institutionalized. Destitute and forlorn, Tuppela turned to his lifelong friend, Embola, saying, "If you will give me $50 so I can go to Alaska and get my property back, I will pay you $10,000 when I win my property." After Tuppela won back his mine, his court-appointed guardian refused to pay Embola, arguing that $50 was not enough consideration to support Tuppela's $10,000 promise. The court disagreed. Embola and Tuppela freely bargained for those terms.

Although the difference between Embola's $50 and Tuppela's $10,000 was staggering, it was not for the court to judge whether it was an intelligent bargain. Both parties knew what they were doing, Embola undertook a risk, and his $50 was valid consideration. The question of adequacy is for the parties as they bargain, not for the courts.

---

[3]Hobbs v. Duff, 23 Cal. 596 (1863).

EXAM Strategy

Question: 50 Cent has been rapping all day, and he is very thirsty. He pulls his Ferrari into the parking lot of a convenience store. The store turns out to be closed, but luckily for him, a soda machine sits outside. While walking over to it, he realizes that he has left his wallet at home. Frustrated, he whistles to a 10-year-old kid who is walking by. "Hey kid!" he shouts. "I need to borrow fifty cents!" "I know you are!" the kid replies. Fiddy tries again. "No, no, I need to *borrow* fifty cents!" The kid walks over. "Well, I'm not going to just give you my last fifty cents. But maybe you can sell me something." 50 Cent cannot believe it, but he really is very thirsty. He takes off a Rolex, which is his least expensive bling. "How about this?" "Deal," the kid says, handing over two quarters. Is the kid entitled to keep the luxury watch?

Strategy: Even in extreme cases, courts rarely take an interest in *how much* consideration is given, or whether everyone got a "good deal." Even though the Rolex is worth thousands of times more than the quarters, the quarters still count under the peppercorn rule.

Result: After this transaction, 50 Cent may have second thoughts, but they will be too late. The kid committed an act by handing over his money—he was under no legal obligation to do so. And 50 Cent received something of small but measureable value. So there is consideration to support this deal, and 50 Cent would not get his watch back.

13-2 WHAT CONSIDERATION IS NOT

For centuries, scholars and judges have tried unsuccessfully to craft a single, simple rule of consideration but a rigid application of these rules would sometimes interfere with legitimate business goals or, in the worst case, lead to an unfair outcome. As a result, **courts have created three exceptions to the basic rule of consideration: illusory promises, preexisting duties, and past consideration.** Of course, exceptions are the spice of law, and these consideration rules provide us with a rackful. Why, in some cases, we have exceptions to the exception.

> Of course, exceptions are the spice of law, and these consideration rules provide us with a rackful.

13-2a Illusory Promises

Annabel calls Jim and says, "I'll sell you my bicycle for 325 bucks. Interested?" Jim says, "I'll look at it tonight in the bike rack. If I like what I see, I'll pay you in the morning." At sunrise, Jim shows up with the $325, but Annabel refuses to sell. Can Jim enforce their deal? No. He said he would buy the bicycle *if he liked it*, keeping for himself the power to get out of the agreement for any reason at all. He is not *committing* himself to do anything, and the law considers his promise illusory—that is, not really a promise at all. **An illusory promise is not consideration.** Because he has given no consideration, there is no contract, and *neither party* can enforce the deal.

Let's revisit the Blockbuster case from the opening scenario. Blockbuster's clickwrap box read, in part:

> "Blockbuster may at any time, and at its sole discretion, modify these Terms and Conditions of Use, including without limitation the Privacy Policy, with or without notice. Such modifications will be effective immediately upon posting."

Because Blockbuster had the ability to change the rules at any time for any reason, the court determined that the contract was illusory and that Harris was not bound by Blockbuster's arbitration clause.[4]

Exception: Requirements and Output Contracts under the UCC

In a **requirements contract**, the buyer agrees to purchase 100 percent of her goods from one seller. The seller agrees to sell the buyer whatever quantity she reasonably needs. The quantity is not stated in the contract, though it may be estimated based on previous years or best calculations. In an **output contract**, the seller guarantees to sell 100 percent of its output to one buyer, and the buyer agrees to accept the entire quantity. For example, a vineyard might agree to sell all of its wine to a chain restaurant.

The common law frowned on requirements and output contracts because the promisors are making no real commitment, and hence are giving no consideration. In the view of common-law courts, these were illusory contracts.

The problem with the common-law rule was that many merchants valued these contracts. Consider the utility of requirements contracts. From the buyer's viewpoint, a requirements contract provides flexibility. The buyer can adjust purchases based on consumer demands. The agreement also guarantees her a source of goods in a competitive market. For a seller, the requirements agreement will ensure him at least this one outlet and will prevent competitors from selling to this buyer. The contract should enable the seller to spend less on marketing and may enable him to predict sales more accurately. Output contracts have similar value.

The UCC responded in a forthright fashion: **Section 2-306 expressly allows output and requirements contracts in the sale of goods.**[5] However, the Code places one limitation on how much the buyer may demand (or the seller may offer):

> A term which measures the quantity by the output of the seller or the requirements of the buyer means such actual output or requirements as may occur *in good faith,* ...

The "good faith" phrase is critical. In requirements contracts, courts have ruled that it is the "good faith" that a buyer brings to the deal that represents her consideration.[6] In other words, by agreeing to act in good faith, she actually is limiting her options. Because she is obligating herself, the deal becomes binding. Beware that this is not just wordplay. A buyer *must make its requirement demands in good faith,* based on the expectations the parties had when they signed the deal.

Suppose that you operate a T-shirt business. You and a wholesaler agree on a two-year requirements contract with a fixed price of $3 per T-shirt and an estimate of 150 T-shirts per

---

[4]Harris v. Blockbuster Inc., 622 F. Supp. 2d 396 (N.D. Tex. 2009).

[5]UCC §2-306(2) permits a related type of contract, the exclusive dealing agreement. Here, either a buyer or a seller of goods agrees to deal exclusively with the other party. The results are similar to an output or requirements agreement. Once again, one party is receiving a guarantee in exchange for a promise that the common law would have considered illusory. Under the Code, such a deal is enforceable.

[6]Famous Brands, Inc. v. David Sherman Corp., 814 F.2d 517 (8th Cir. 1987).

week. If business is slow the first two months, you are permitted to purchase only 25 T-shirts per week if that is all you are selling. Should sales suddenly boom and you need 200 per week, you may also require that many. Both of those demands are made in good faith. But suppose the price of cotton skyrockets and the wholesale cost of T-shirts everywhere suddenly doubles. You have a two-year guaranteed price of $3 per T-shirt. Could you demand 2,000 T-shirts per week, knowing that you will be able to resell the shirts to other retailers for a big profit? No. That is not acting in good faith based on the original expectations of the parties. The wholesaler is free to ignore your exorbitant demand. The legal requirement has come full circle: Your good faith is valid consideration and makes the deal enforceable—but it is binding on you, too.

EXAM Strategy

Question: Will bought simple wood furniture and custom-painted it for sale to interior designers. He entered into a written agreement to buy all the furniture he needed, for two years, from Wood Knot, Inc. Wood Knot agreed to supply Will with all the furniture he requested. During the second year, Will's business grew, and he requested 28 percent more furniture than in the first year. Wood Knot would not deliver unless Will would pay a higher price per unit, which Will would not. Will sued. What kind of a contract was this? Will Will win? Why or why not?

Strategy: Because this agreement did not specify the quantity of goods being sold, we know that it was either a requirements contract or an output contract. Review the difference between the two. Which was this agreement? These contracts are now legal, with one major limitation. What is that limitation? Apply it here.

Result: This was a requirements contract because Will agreed to purchase all his furniture from Wood Knot. Under the UCC, requirements contracts are enforceable, provided the buyer makes his demands in good faith. Will's increased order was a result of his booming business. Indeed, he entered into this agreement to protect his ability to grow his company. He made the request in good faith, the contract is enforceable, and yes—Will will win.

13-2b Preexisting Duty

Imagine yourself at the beach right now (in our dreams). Into the water you go, where an undertow grabs you and carries you out into deep water. The lifeguard leaps from her chair and runs to the water's edge. But instead of jumping in, she yells to you, "I won't get my hair wet unless you pay me $100." Helplessly, you signal your assent. Once you are safely back on shore, do you owe the lifeguard anything?

You may be relieved to hear that the answer is no. **If someone provides a service that she is already obligated to do, that act does not count as consideration.** A lifeguard who saves people cannot receive additional money for her rescues because, well, that is what lifeguards are supposed to do. A police officer who apprehends a criminal in the line of duty cannot collect the posted reward. A banker cannot get a bonus for upholding the law. In these cases, consideration does not induce their actions, duty does. Since they already have the duty to perform, they suffer no legal detriment when they do their job.

In the following Landmark Case, many fishy things occurred. There was a catch. But was it sufficient consideration?

Landmark Case

ALASKA PACKERS' ASS'N V. DOMENICO

117 F. 99
United States Court of Appeals for the Ninth Circuit,
1902

Facts: Twenty-one seamen entered into a written contract with the Alaska Packer's Association (APA) to sail from San Francisco to Pyramid Harbor, Alaska, where they would work as fisherman and sailors during the salmon-fishing season. The workers agreed to perform "regular ship's duty, both up and down, discharging and loading; and to do any other work whatsoever when requested to do so by the captain." In return, the APA was to pay each worker $50 for the season, and two cents for each red salmon he caught.

A few days after arriving at Pyramid Harbor, the men collectively stopped working and demanded an additional $50—or else they would return to San Francisco. At that point, it was impossible for the APA to replace them, so after several days of unproductive negotiations, the APA's superintendent in Alaska yielded to their demands—and agreed to double their pay.

When they returned to San Francisco at the close of the fishing season, the seamen demanded their $100, but the APA refused, claiming that the Alaska agreement failed for lack of consideration. The lower court agreed with the seamen, but the APA appealed.

Issue: *Was there consideration for the promise to pay more money?*

Excerpts from Judge Ross's Decision:[7] The seamen agreed in writing, for certain stated compensation, to render their services to the APA in remote waters where the season for conducting fishing operations is extremely short, and in which enterprise the APA had a large amount of money invested; and, after having entered upon the discharge of their contract, and at a time when it was impossible for APA to secure other men in their places, the seamen, without any valid cause, absolutely refused to continue the services they were under contract to perform unless the APA would consent to pay them more money.

Consent to such a demand, under such circumstances, if given, was, in our opinion, without consideration, for the reason that it was based solely upon the seamen's agreement to render the exact services, and none other, that they were already under contract to render. The case shows that they willfully and arbitrarily broke that obligation.

No astute reasoning can change the plain fact that the party who refuses to perform, and thereby coerces a promise from the other party to the contract to pay him an increased compensation for doing that which he is legally bound to do, takes an unjustifiable advantage of the necessities of the other party. Surely it would be a travesty on justice to hold that the party so making the promise for extra pay was estopped from asserting that the promise was without consideration. A party cannot lay the foundation of an estoppel by his own wrong, where the promise is simply a repetition of a subsisting legal promise.

There can be no consideration for the promise of the other party, and there is no warrant for inferring that the parties have voluntarily rescinded or modified their contract. The promise cannot be legally enforced, although the other party has completed his contract in reliance upon it.

The judgment must be reversed. It is so ordered.

Exception: Additional Work

When a party agrees to do something above and beyond what he is obligated to do, his promise is generally valid consideration. If the seamen had agreed to work overtime or commit to a longer fishing season in exchange for the increased pay, the court would have upheld their second contract. The APA would have been obligated to pay because the seamen's extra work would have been valid consideration.

---

[7]For readability, the authors have inserted "APA" and "seamen" instead of "appellant" and "libelants."

Exception: Modification

Under the common law, additional consideration is necessary for a modification of contract terms because it is unfair for one party to get something more, while the other does not. As we saw in the *Alaska Packers* case, if one side unfairly coerces the other into the changes, the modification is invalid.

Once again, the UCC has changed the common law, making it easier for merchants to modify agreements for the sale of goods. **UCC §2-209 provides:**

- An agreement modifying a contract within this Article needs no consideration to be binding.

- A signed agreement which excludes modification or rescission except by a signed writing cannot be otherwise modified or rescinded.

Here is how these two provisions work together. Mike's Magic Mania (MMM) agrees to deliver 500 rabbits and 500 top hats to State University for the school's Sleight of Hand 101 course. The goods, including 100 cages and 1,000 pounds of rabbit food, are to arrive no later than September 1, in time for the new semester, with payment on delivery. By September 20, no rabbits have appeared, in or out of hats. The university buys similar products from another supply house at a 25 percent steeper price and sues MMM for the difference. Mike claims that in early September, the dean had orally agreed to permit delivery in October. The dean is on sabbatical in Tahiti and cannot be reached for comment. Is the alleged modification valid?

Under the common law, the modification would have been void because MMM gave no consideration for the extended delivery date. However, this is a sale of goods, and under UCC §2-209, an oral modification may be valid even without consideration. Unfortunately for Mike, though, the original agreement included a clause forbidding oral modification. Any changes had to be in writing, signed by both parties. Mike never obtained such a document. Even if the dean did make the oral agreement, the university wins.

If both parties agree that a modification is necessary, the surest way to accomplish that result is to rescind the original contract and draft a new one. To **rescind** means to cancel. Thus, if neither party has completed its obligations, the agreement to rescind will terminate each party's rights and obligations under the old contract. This should be done in writing. Then the parties sign the new agreement. Courts will *generally* enforce a rescission and modification provided both parties voluntarily entered into it, in good faith.

Rescind
To cancel

EXAM Strategy

Question: Star Struck, a Hollywood talent agency, employs Puneet as one of its young agents and Max as a part-time delivery boy. Puneet's contract is for one year. She earns $5,000 per month, payable on the last day of each month. After she has worked at the firm for four months, a Star Struck executive says to her, "We are having cash flow problems. We cannot pay you this month, and will probably fall about two months behind. However, if you will agree to do Max's job for the next few months, we can pay you on time." Puneet cheerfully agrees to the deal. However, after a few weeks of the extra labor, Puneet confesses that she is overwhelmed and can no longer do Max's job. Star Struck fires her. Puneet sues. Was there a binding agreement for Puneet to do Max's work?

Strategy: Star Struck made an offer to Puneet and she accepted it. But a contract needs more than offer and acceptance. Both parties must give consideration. Had they done more than they were required to do under their preexisting duty?

Result: A promise to do what a party is already obligated to do is not consideration. Star Struck was required to pay Puneet every month, so its "offer" included no consideration. Without consideration, there can be no agreement. Puneet was not obligated to do Max's job, and she will win this lawsuit.

Exception: Unforeseen Circumstances

Hugo has a deal to repair major highways. Hugo hires Hal's Hauling to cart soil and debris. Hal's trucks begin work, but after crossing the work site several times, they sink to their axles in sinister, sucking slime. Hal demands an additional 35 percent payment from Hugo to complete the job, pointing out that the surface was dry and cracked and that neither Hal nor Hugo was aware of the subsurface water. Hal howls that he must use different trucks with different tires and work more slowly to permit the soil to dry. Hugo hems and haws and finally agrees. But when the hauling is finished, Hugo refuses to pay the extra money. Is Hugo liable?

Yes. When unforeseen circumstances cause a party to make a promise regarding an unfinished project, that promise is generally valid consideration. Even though Hal is only promising to finish what he was already obligated to do, his promise is valid consideration because neither party knew of the subsoil mud. Hal was facing a situation quite different from what the parties anticipated. It is almost as though he were undertaking a new project. Hal has given consideration, and Hugo is bound by his promise to pay extra money

13-2c Past Consideration

A completed act cannot be the basis for consideration. When they learn that their son earned an "A" in Advanced Business Law, Pablo's doting parents promise to buy him a car. This star student will surely know that the generous promise is unenforceable in court. It lacks consideration because it is based on something Pablo has already done. However, if early in the semester, Pablo's parents make the same promise, consideration is present. Pablo's detriment is his future work, which is induced by the promise of a reward.

Exception: Parties Agree in Advance

Moore was psychic. She foresaw that Elmer was going to die before a certain date. In gratitude and amazement, Elmer gave her a signed letter stating that if what she said proved true, he would pay off her mortgage. Apparently, Moore was clairvoyant: Elmer died before her predicted date. What happened next is not difficult to predict. Moore's heirs refused to pay her, claiming his promise lacked consideration.

The court agreed. Although Moore argued that the promise was payment for her services, she had voluntarily offered the information and after that, Elmer gave her the note. Had the parties agreed in advance that he would pay her if her predictions proved true, the court would have foreseen a different outcome: **Past consideration is valid consideration when the parties agree that it will be** *in advance.*

Exception: Promissory Estoppel

As we saw in Chapter 11, promissory estoppel is a theory courts use to enforce promises that are not contracts. It applies when a defendant makes a promise, which the plaintiff reasonably relied on, and enforcing that promise is the only way to avoid injustice.

Courts sometimes use promissory estoppel to validate promises based on past consideration. Feinberg had been a loyal employee for 37 years. She was so beloved that, in gratitude for her service, her employer's board of directors elected to pay her $200 a month for the rest of her life, once she retired. Two years later, she retired in reliance on her monthly pension, which she enjoyed—until new management decided to revoke it. By this time, she was ill, unemployable, and wholly dependent on the pension. The court held for Feinberg, even though the promise was based on past consideration. Because she justifiably relied on the board's offer, Feinberg's pension was upheld under promissory estoppel.

13-3 SPECIAL CONSIDERATION CASES

We have seen what consideration is and what it is not. Now we will look at some special cases that involve two very familiar four-letter words: debt and work.

13-3a Settlement of Debts

You claim that your friend Felicity owes you $90,000, but she refuses to pay. Finally, when you are desperate, Felicity offers you a cashier's check for $60,000—provided you accept it as full settlement. To get your hands on some money, you agree and cash the check. The next day, you sue Felicity for $30,000. Who wins? It will depend principally upon one major issue: Was Felicity's debt liquidated or unliquidated?

Liquidated Debt

A **liquidated debt** is one in which there is no dispute about the amount owed. A loan is a typical example. If a bank lends you $10,000, and the note obligates you to repay that amount on June 1 of the following year, you clearly owe that sum. The debt is liquidated.

Liquidated debt
A debt in which there is no dispute about the amount owed

One famous jurist commented that a creditor may accept anything—"a horse, hawk, or robe"—in satisfaction of a liquidated debt.[8]

But the one thing he may not accept? Less than one hundred cents on the dollar. **In cases of liquidated debt, if the creditor agrees to take less than the full amount as full payment, her agreement is not binding.** The debtor has given no consideration to support the creditor's promise to accept a reduced payment, and therefore the creditor is not bound by her word. The reasoning is simply that the debtor is already obligated to pay the full amount, so no bargaining could reasonably cause the creditor to accept less. If Felicity's debt to you is liquidated, your agreement to accept $60,000 is not binding, and you will successfully sue for the balance.

> But the one thing he may not accept? Less than one hundred cents on the dollar.

Exception: Different Performance. There is one important exception to this rule. If the debtor offers a *different performance* to settle the liquidated debt, and the creditor agrees to take it as full settlement, the agreement is binding. Suppose that Felicity, instead of paying $60,000, offers you five acres in Alaska, and you accept. When you accept the deed to the land, you have given up your entire claim, regardless of the land's precise value.

Unliquidated Debt: Accord and Satisfaction

A debt is **unliquidated** for either of two reasons: (1) The parties dispute whether any money is owed, or (2) the parties agree that some money is owed but dispute how much. When a debt is unliquidated for either reason, the parties may enter into a binding agreement to settle for less than what the creditor demands.

Unliquidated
A debt that is disputed because the parties disagree over its existence or amount

---

[8]Birdsall v. Saucier, 1992 WL 33731 (Conn. Super. Ct. 1992).

If there is no doubt about the amount owed, that debt is liquidated.

Such a compromise will be enforced if:

- The debt is unliquidated;

- The parties agree that the creditor will accept as full payment a sum less than she has claimed; and

- The debtor pays the amount agreed upon.

This agreement is called an **accord and satisfaction**. The accord is the agreement to settle for less than the creditor claims. The satisfaction is the actual payment of that compromised sum. An accord and satisfaction is valid consideration to support the creditor's agreement to drop all claims. Each party is giving up something: the creditor gives up her full claim, and the debtor gives up his assertion that he owed little or nothing.

Accord and satisfaction
A completed agreement to settle a debt for less than the sum claimed

Accord and Satisfaction by Check. Most accord and satisfaction agreements involve payment by check. UCC §3-311 governs these agreements, using the same common-law rules described earlier.[9] The Code specifies that when the debtor writes "full settlement" on the check, a creditor who cashes the check generally has entered into an accord and satisfaction. If Felicity's debt is unliquidated, and she gives you a check with "full payment of all debts" written on the face in bold letters, the moment you deposit the check, you lose any claim to more money. What happens if the debtor makes such a notation but the creditor changes it? A massage therapist learned the answer and felt sore for days.

HENCHES V. TAYLOR

138 Wash. App. 1026
Washington Court of Appeals, 2007

Facts: Jim Henches, a licensed massage therapist, treated Benjamin Taylor after he was injured in a car accident. When all treatments were finished, Henches billed Taylor for more than $7,000. Taylor's insurance company claimed the bill was exorbitant and paid only $2,625, for 24 massage treatments.

Henches continued to send bills to Taylor, not only for the balance due but for additional time spent consulting with Taylor's other health care providers, preparing to testify in

Taylor's personal injury lawsuit, and attempting to collect his debts. In response to a bill for $11,945.86, Taylor's lawyer, James Harris, sent Henches a letter, stating:

I have reviewed your billing statements and am having a difficult time understanding a number of charges you included. By my calculations, the amount owed to you is approximately $5,243.45. I have enclosed a check for that amount as payment in full to settle Mr. Taylor's account with you.

---

[9]A check is legally an instrument, which is why this section comes from Article 3 of the Code. For a full discussion of instruments, see Chapters 25–26.

The letter was accompanied by a check with "final payment" written on the notation line. Henches filed suit, seeking the full balance. Then he wrote "attorney/fee" on the check, over the word "final," and deposited the check.

The trial court gave summary judgment to Taylor, ruling that deposit of the check constituted accord and satisfaction. Henches appealed.

Issue: *Was there an accord and satisfaction, discharging the debt?*

Excerpts from Judge Ellington's Decision: A debt is discharged by accord and satisfaction when the debtor and creditor agree to settle a claim by some performance other than that which is claimed due, and the creditor accepts the substituted performance as full satisfaction of the claim. Accord and satisfaction requires a bona fide dispute, an agreement to settle the dispute for a certain sum, and performance of the agreement.

Taylor easily satisfied the first element of accord and satisfaction. The parties' contracts did not establish a liquidated amount for the services provided, and the letter that accompanied Taylor's check to Henches demonstrates a good faith dispute over the amount owed.

As with any contract, an accord and satisfaction cannot be formed without a meeting of the minds. But the required intent is shown when payment is offered in full satisfaction and is accompanied by conduct from which the creditor cannot fail to understand that payment is tendered on condition its acceptance constitutes satisfaction.

Given the undisputed facts here, Henches could not fail to understand that the check was offered on condition of full settlement. Henches' alteration of the "final payment" language is further demonstration that he read and understood the notation. Taylor tendered a check in final payment and Henches deposited the check, thereby accepting that payment.

A creditor can accept payment and avoid formation of an accord only where both parties understand before payment is accepted that the payment will not settle the claim. Henches contends his alteration of the check prevents accord and satisfaction. But a creditor cannot prevent formation of an accord by making a unilateral change to a draft tendered in full payment, even if the creditor endorses the check with the words accepted as partial payment and not as payment in full and not as an accord and satisfaction of the known full amount legally due and owing.

Where the amount due is in dispute, and the debtor sends cash or check for less than the amount claimed, clearly expressing his intention that it is sent as a settlement in full, and not on account or in part payment, the retention and use of the money or the cashing of the check is almost always held to be an acceptance of the offer operating as full satisfaction, even though the creditor may assert or send word to the debtor that the sum is received only in part payment.

Henches' alteration of the check was a unilateral act not communicated to Taylor. Accord and satisfaction discharged Taylor's debts to Henches. We affirm the trial court's summary judgment dismissal of Henches' suit.

UCC Exceptions. The Code creates two exceptions for accord and satisfaction cases involving checks. The first exception concerns "organizations," which typically are businesses. The general rule of §3-311 is potentially calamitous to them because a company that receives thousands of checks every day is unlikely to inspect all notations. A consumer who owes $12,000 on a credit card might write "full settlement" on a $200 check, potentially extinguishing the entire debt through accord and satisfaction. Under the exception, if an organization notifies a debtor that any offers to settle for less than the debt claimed must be made to a particular official, and the check is sent to anyone else in the organization, depositing the check generally does *not* create an accord and satisfaction. Thus, a clerk who deposits 900 checks daily for payment of MasterCard debts will not have inadvertently entered into dozens of accord and satisfaction agreements.

The second exception allows a way out to most creditors who have inadvertently created an accord and satisfaction. If, within 90 days of cashing a "full payment" check, the creditor offers repayment of the same amount to the debtor, there is no accord and satisfaction. Homer claims that Virgil owes him $7 million but foolishly cashes Virgil's check for $3 million, without understanding that "paid in full" means just what it says. Homer has created an accord and satisfaction. But if he promptly sends Virgil a check for $3 million, he has undone the agreement and may sue for the full amount.

13-3b Employment Agreements

In a noncompete agreement, an employee promises not to work for a competitor for some time after leaving the company. It used to be that these covenants were rare and reserved for top officers, but they have now become commonplace throughout many organizations. We will talk about them more in the next chapter, but often these covenants raise an issue of consideration: What consideration does the employee receive for signing a covenant not to compete? After all, the company is already under an obligation to pay the employee for working. What additional value does the employee receive in return for signing the agreement?

The following case reflects the current majority view. Sometimes consideration issues can drive you nuts.

SNIDER BOLT & SCREW v. QUALITY SCREW & NUT

2009 U.S. Dist. LEXIS 50797, 2009 WL 1657549
United States District Court for the Western District of Kentucky, 2009

Facts: James Scott signed a covenant not to compete when he went to work for Snider Bolt & Screw. The agreement prohibited him from taking a job with a competitor for one year after leaving Snider. Three years later, Scott quit his job at Snider and immediately went to work for Quality Screw & Nut (QSN).

Snider obtained a temporary restraining order that banned Scott from working at his new job. QSN argued that the covenant not to compete was void for lack of consideration. It asked the court to lift the temporary restraining order.

Issue: *Did the covenant not to compete lack consideration?*

Excerpt from Judge Heyburn's Decision: Snider says that when Scott signed his covenant not to compete, he did so based upon an implied promise that Snider would continue his employment. Indeed, Snider did maintain Scott's employment until Scott himself left his job. Kentucky courts have found quite specifically that "where an employer has fulfilled an implied promise to continue the employee's employment, that promise is sufficient consideration [to] support enforcement of the employee's promise not to compete." The Kentucky Supreme Court subsequently held that even continued at-will employment would be sufficient consideration. Here, Scott worked for another three years and left on his own accord to join QSN. These circumstances fit within the rule and the Court finds that the Covenant is supported by adequate consideration.

Consequently, the Court has no basis for sustaining QSN's motion.

13-4 MORAL CONSIDERATION

Some promises should not be broken. No one wants to live in a society where donors to charity go back on their word or promises to widows and orphans are ignored. These are commitments whose obligation is moral, not necessarily legal, in nature. Under some circumstances, courts will uphold agreements with "moral consideration."

Consider a pledge to charity. If Dave promises to give $25,000 to "Save the Mexican Spotted Owl" and then fails to make the donation, there is no consideration because he has received nothing in return. If the nonprofit sues to enforce the promise, it cannot show that it gave anything up in return for Dave's promise, so there is no consideration.[10]

Nevertheless, some courts will force donors like Dave to make good on their pledges anyway. If, based on Dave's promise, the charity funded a bird-watching program or began construction on a sanctuary, it can prove reliance. As we have seen, judges can use the doctrine of promissory estoppel to enforce promises if there has been reliance and a great injustice would otherwise result.

Other courts have dispensed with the reliance requirement, requiring promisors to pay if breaching would simply be unjust. Especially in the case of large donations, courts will often cite the "grave injustices" that can follow from breaking a promise. "If you don't give 'Save the Mexican Spotted Owl' the $25,000 you've pledged, then the bird will become extinct," a judge might say.

It is unwise to make charitable pledges, especially large pledges, unless you intend to follow through.

Ethics What is a "moral obligation" and when should it be enforced? Courts are divided on this issue. Two cases illustrate the leading schools of thought:

In an Alabama case, Webb saved McGowin's life by preventing a 75 lb. block of wood from falling on his head. Webb was permanently disabled in the accident and was never able to work again. Later, McGowin promised to give Webb money every two weeks for the rest of his life. McGowin made the payments for a while but then stopped. Webb sued. The court found that "moral consideration" was present because McGowin received a material benefit. Webb was entitled to the payments to prevent substantial injustice.[11]

A famous Massachusetts case reaches the opposite conclusion. Twenty-five-year-old Levi Wyman contracted an illness while at sea. Mills nursed Wyman during his sickness. After Wyman's death, his parents promised to repay Mills for the expenses incurred in caring for their son. Later, Wyman refused to pay, so Mills filed suit. The court sided with Wyman, holding that a moral obligation was not enough to constitute consideration.[12]

Mills v. Wyman is the majority rule; *Webb v. McGowin* is the minority rule. But some commentators have argued that this discrepancy serves another moral purpose: It allows judges the leeway to enforce promises when they feel enforcement is just. Do you agree? How else can these cases be reconciled? Is it possible to formulate a single rule applying to every case of moral obligation?

It is important to note that applications of promissory estoppel and similar doctrines are rare. Ordinarily, if there is no consideration, then there is no contract. However, in extreme cases, it is possible for a court to enforce a deal even without consideration. But this is not something you can count on.

---

[10]An exception to this, of course, would be if the charity agreed to give Dave something at the time he made the pledge. As a "fix" for consideration problems, many charities send donors something of trivial value when pledges are made—maybe a water bottle or a tote bag. Under the peppercorn rule, even something of small value counts as a legal act, and it converts a mere promise of a donation into an enforceable contract.

[11]Webb v. McGowin, 168 So. 196 (Ala. 1935).

[12]Mills v. Wyman 20 Mass. (3 Pick.) 207 (Mass. Sup. Jud. Ct. 1825).

Chapter Conclusion

This ancient doctrine of consideration is simple to state but subtle to apply. The parties must bargain and enter into an exchange of promises or actions. If they do not, there is no consideration and the courts are unlikely to enforce any promise made. A variety of exceptions modify the law, but a party wishing to render its future more predictable—the purpose of a contract—will rely on a solid bargain and exchange.

EXAM REVIEW

1. **CONSIDERATION** There are two basic rules of consideration:

   - Value: Both parties must get something of *measureable value* from the contract.
   - Bargained for Exchange: The two parties must have *bargained for* whatever was exchanged.

2. **ACT, FORBEARANCE, OR PROMISE** The item of value can be either an act or a forbearance.

EXAM Strategy

Question: An aunt saw her eight-year-old nephew enter the room, remarked what a nice boy he was, and said, "I would like to take care of him now." She promptly wrote a note, promising to pay the boy $3,000 upon her death. Her estate refused to pay. Is it obligated to do so?

Strategy: A contract is enforceable only if the parties have given consideration. The consideration might be an act or a forbearance. Did the nephew give consideration? (See the "Result" at the end of this section.)

3. **ADEQUACY** The courts examine whether consideration exists, but will seldom inquire if it was enough consideration or a smart financial deal. This is the "peppercorn rule."

4. **ILLUSORY PROMISES** An illusory promise is not consideration.

EXAM Strategy

Question: Eagle ran convenience stores. He entered into an agreement with Commercial Movie in which Commercial would provide Eagle with DVDs for rental. Eagle would pay Commercial 50 percent of the rental revenues. If Eagle stopped using Commercial's service, Eagle could not use a competitor's services for 18 months. The agreement also provided: "Commercial shall not be liable for compensation or damages of any kind, whether on account of the loss by Eagle of profits, sales or expenditures, or on account of any other event or cause whatsoever." Eagle complied with the agreement for two years but then began using a competitor's service, and Commercial sued. Eagle claimed that the agreement was unenforceable for lack of consideration. Please rule.

Strategy: In this case, both parties seem to have given consideration. But there is a flaw in the "promise" that Commercial made. Commercial can never be liable to Eagle—no matter what happens. (See the "Result" at the end of this section.)

5. **REQUIREMENT AND OUTPUT CONTRACTS** Under sales law, requirement and output contracts are valid. Although one side controls the quantity, its agreement to make demands *in good faith* is consideration.

6. **PREEXISTING DUTY** Under the doctrine of preexisting duty, a promise to do something that the party is already legally obligated to perform is generally not consideration.

7. **LIQUIDATED DEBT** A liquidated debt is one in which there is no dispute about the amount owed. For a liquidated debt, a creditor's promise to accept less than the full amount is not binding.

8. **UNLIQUIDATED DEBT** For an unliquidated debt, if the parties agree that the creditor will accept less than the full amount claimed and the debtor performs, there is an accord and satisfaction and the creditor may not claim any balance.

9. **"FULL PAYMENT" NOTATIONS** In most states, payment by a check that has a "full payment" notation will create an accord and satisfaction unless the creditor is an organization that has notified the debtor that full payment offers must go to a certain officer.

Question: When White's wife died, he filed a claim with Boston Mutual for $10,000 death benefits under her insurance policy. The insurer rejected the claim, saying that his wife had misrepresented her medical condition in the application form. The company sent White a check for $478.75, which it said represented "a full refund of all applicable premiums paid" for the coverage. White deposited the check. Had the parties reached an accord and satisfaction?

Strategy: The UCC permits parties to enter into an accord and satisfaction by check. The debtor must make clear that the check is offered in full payment of a disputed debt. Debtors generally do that by writing "Final Settlement," "Accepted as Full Payment of All Debts," or some similar notation on the check. Had the insurance company complied with that requirement? (See the "Result" at the end of this section.)

EXAM Strategy

341

10. PROMISSORY ESTOPPEL Sometimes, to prevent injustice, courts will enforce agreements even if no consideration is present. These deals are still not formal contracts, but the courts will enforce a promise nonetheless.

EXAM Strategy

Question: Phil Philanthropist called PBS during a fund drive and pledged to donate $100,000. PBS then planned and began to produce a Fourth of July *Sesame Street* special, counting on the large donation to fund it. Later, Phil changed his mind and said he had decided not to donate the money after all. PBS sued because without the money, it would not be able to complete the show. Will PBS win the lawsuit?

Strategy: Analyze the promise to donate the $100,000. Does it contain consideration? If not, is there any other legal possibility? (See the "Result" at the end of this section.)

2. Result: The nephew gave no consideration. He did not promise to do anything. He committed no act or forbearance. Without consideration, there is no enforceable contract. The estate wins.

4. Result: Commercial's promise was illusory. The company was free to walk away from the deal at any time. Commercial could never be held liable. Commercial gave no consideration, and there was no binding contract for either party to enforce.

9. Result: The insurer merely stated that its check was a refund of premiums. Nowhere did the company indicate that the check was full payment of its disputed obligation. The company should have made it clear that it would not pay any benefits and that this payment was all that it would offer. There was no accord and satisfaction.

10. Result: There is no "regular" consideration here because Phil received no measureable benefit and PBS did not act or forbear. But PBS can likely make a strong case that a great injustice will be done if the money is not paid. A judge might well decide to apply the doctrine of promissory estoppel and require Phil to make the donation.

MULTIPLE-CHOICE QUESTIONS

1. For consideration to exist, there must be:
   (a) A bargained-for exchange
   (b) A manifestation of mutual assent
   (c) Genuineness of assent
   (d) Substantially equal economic benefits to both parties

2. Which of the following requires consideration in order to be binding on the parties?

   (a) Modification of a contract involving the sale of real estate

   (b) Modification of a sale of goods contract under the UCC

   (c) Both A and B

   (d) None of the above

3. Ted's wallet is as empty as his bank account, and he needs $3,500 immediately. Fortunately, he has three gold coins that he inherited from his grandfather. Each is worth $2,500, but it is Sunday, and the local rare coins store is closed. When approached, Ted's neighbor Andrea agrees to buy the first coin for $2,300. Another neighbor, Cami, agrees to buy the second for $1,100. A final neighbor, Lorne, offers "all the money I have on me"—$100—for the last coin. Desperate, Ted agrees to the proposal. Which of the deals is supported by consideration?

   (a) Ted's agreement with Andrea only

   (b) Ted's agreements with Andrea and Cami only

   (c) All three of the agreements

   (d) None of the agreements

4. In a(n) _____ contract, the seller guarantees to sell 100 percent of its output to one buyer, and the buyer agrees to accept the entire quantity. This kind of arrangement _____ acceptable under the UCC.

   (a) output; is

   (b) output; is not

   (c) requirements; is

   (d) requirements; is not

5. Noncompete agreements are common features of employment contracts. Currently, courts _____ enforce these clauses.

   (a) always

   (b) usually

   (c) rarely

   (d) never

CASE QUESTIONS

1. American Bakeries had a fleet of over 3,000 delivery trucks. Because of the increasing cost of gasoline, the company was interested in converting the trucks to propane fuel. It signed a requirements contract with Empire Gas, in which Empire would convert "approximately 3,000" trucks to propane fuel, as American Bakeries requested, and would then sell all the required propane fuel to run the trucks. But American Bakeries changed its mind and never requested a single conversion. Empire sued for lost profits. Who won?

2. CeCe Hylton and Edward Meztista, partners in a small advertising firm, agreed to terminate the business and split assets evenly. Meztista gave Hylton a two-page document showing assets, liabilities, and a bottom line of $35,235.67, with half due to each partner. Hylton questioned the accounting and asked to see the books. Meztista did not permit Hylton to see any records and refused to answer her phone calls. Instead, he gave her a check in the amount of $17,617.83, on which he wrote "Final payment/payment in full." Hylton cashed the check, but she wrote on it, "Under protest—cashing this check does not constitute my acceptance of this amount as payment in full." Hylton then filed suit, demanding additional monies. Meztista claimed that the parties had made an accord and satisfaction. What is the best argument for each party? Who should win?

3. **ETHICS** Melnick built a house for Gintzler, but the foundation was defective. Gintzler agreed to accept the foundation if Melnick guaranteed to make future repairs caused by the defects. Melnick agreed but later refused to make any repairs. Melnick argued that his promise to make future repairs was unsupported by consideration. Who will win the suit? Is either party acting unethically? Which one, and why?

4. Sami walks into a restaurant. She is given a menu, which indicates that lobster is $30. Sami orders the lobster. It arrives, and Sami thinks it is very tasty. When the bill arrives, Sami tries to execute a clever ploy she learned about in her business law class. She writes a check to the restaurant for $20 and writes "full settlement" across the top. The waiter accepts the check without looking at it, and the restaurant manager later deposits it in the restaurant's bank account. Is this a liquidated or an unliquidated debt? Is Sami off the hook for the last $10?

5. In the bleachers …

> "You're a prince, George!" Mike exclaimed. "Who else would give me a ticket to the big game?"
>
> "No one, Mike, no one."
>
> "Let me offer my thanks. I'll buy you a beer!"
>
> "Ah," George said. "A large beer would hit the spot right now."
>
> "Small. Let me buy you a small beer."
>
> "Ah, well, good enough."
>
> Mike stood and took his wallet from his pocket. He was distressed to find a very small number of bills inside. "There's bad news, George!" he said.
>
> "What's that?"
>
> "I can't buy you the beer, George."
>
> George considered that for a moment. "I'll tell you what, Mike," he said. "If you march to the concession stand right this minute and get me my beer, I won't punch you in the face."
>
> "It's a deal!" Mike said.

Discuss the consideration issues raised by this exchange.

6. Jack Tallas came to the United States from Greece in 1914. He lived in Salt Lake City for nearly 70 years, achieving great success in insurance and real estate. During the last 14 years of his life, his friend Peter Dementas helped him with numerous personal and business chores. Two months before his death, Tallas dictated a memorandum to Dementas, in Greek, stating:

PETER K. DEMENTAS is my best friend I have in this country, and since he came to the United States, he treats me like a father and I think of him as my own son. He takes me in his car grocery shopping. He drives me to the doctor and also takes me every week to Bingham to pick up my mail, collect the rents, and manage my properties. For all the services Peter has given me all these years, I owe to him the amount of $50,000 (Fifty Thousand Dollars). I will shortly change my will to include him as my heir.

Tallas signed the memorandum, but he did not in fact alter his will to include Dementas. The estate refused to pay, and Dementas sued. Was there consideration? Please rule.

DISCUSSION QUESTIONS

Apply the following material to the next two questions.

Some view consideration as a technicality that allows people to make promises and then back out of them. Perhaps all promises should be enforced. In Japan, for example, promises to give gifts are enforceable without consideration.[13]

In the United States, if I promise to give you a gift merely because I feel like being nice, I can freely change my mind as far as contract law is concerned. A court will not make me follow through because there is no consideration.

In Japan, I would be obligated to buy the gift if all other elements of a contract were present—an offer, an acceptance, and so forth.

1. When it comes to giving gifts, which is better—the Japanese or American rule?

2. Are there any specific types of agreements (perhaps high-value, long-term, extremely time-consuming ones) that should definitely require consideration?

3. Albert and Luis, lifelong friends, had a tradition. Every Friday, they took turns going to the corner store and buying what they called a "package"—some vodka and a lottery ticket. One lucky Friday, Albert purchased the package, but Luis scratched off the lottery ticket, only to learn that it was a $20,000 winner. Luis refused to share. Albert sued, claiming the former friends had an enforceable contract supported by valid consideration. Rule.

4. The consideration doctrine is controversial. Critics argue that it is a remnant of a bygone era, lacking any reasonable modern purpose and that it undermines the purpose of contract law, which is to enforce the intention of the parties to an agreement. Should consideration be abolished?

5. Amber Williams and Frederick Ormsby were lovers, embroiled in a turbulent romantic relationship. After knowing each other for a short time, Frederick moved into Amber's house and paid off her $310,000 mortgage. She then gave him title to the house. But their happiness was not to last. The couple canceled their plans to marry and Amber moved out of the house. Two months later, Frederick sought reconciliation. Amber refused to get back together unless Frederick gave her half ownership of the house. Frederick agreed. After the couple split up for the last time, Amber sued for her half of the house. Frederick argued that his promise was not supported by adequate consideration. Was it?

---

[13]See Japan's Civil Code, Article 549.

ANSWERS TO SELECTED END OF CHAPTER QUESTIONS

MULTIPLE-CHOICE QUESTIONS

Presented are the answers for the ODD-numbered multiple-choice questions in the end-of-chapter material.

1. A
3. C
5. B

CASE QUESTIONS

Presented are the answers for all of the ODD-numbered case questions in the end-of-chapter material.

1. **Answer:** Empire won over $3.2 million dollars, and the appeals court affirmed. *Empire Gas Corp. v. American Bakeries Co.*, 840 F.2d 1333, 1988 U.S. App. LEXIS 2482 (7th Cir. 1988). Since this was a requirements contract for the sale of goods (the conversion units and the propane gas were the goods), it was governed by UCC §2-306. American Bakeries did have the right to reduce the number of conversions from the estimated 3,000. It could potentially reduce them even to zero, but any reduction had to be done *in good faith*, meaning that changed circumstances made a reduction important. Here, American Bakeries never offered any reason at all, and the jury verdict was reasonable.

3. **Answer:** Gintzler should, and did. The consideration to support Melnick's promise of repairs was Gintzler's acceptance of the defective foundation. He was under no obligation to accept a house in that condition. *Gintzler v. Melnick*, 116 N.H. 566,364 A.2d 637 (1976).

5. **Answer:** Mike's initial promise to buy the beer is a gratuitous promise. He did receive a ticket from George, but the ticket was not given to induce Mike to promise to buy the beer.

   In the second half of the dialogue, George does not commit a forbearance when he agrees not to punch Mike, because he has no legal right to hit him. And so, Mike is under no contractual obligation to buy the beer.

LEGALITY

Soheil Sadri, a California resident, did some serious gambling at Caesar's Tahoe casino in Nevada. And lost. To keep gambling, he wrote checks to Caesar's and then signed two memoranda pledging to repay all money advanced. After two days, with his losses totaling more than $22,000, he went home. Back in California, Sadri stopped payment on the checks and refused to pay any of the money he owed Caesar's. The casino sued. In defense, Sadri claimed that California law considered his agreements illegal and unenforceable. He was unquestionably correct about one thing: A contract that is illegal is void and unenforceable.

© Honza Krej/Shutterstock.com

> **A contract that is illegal is void and unenforceable.**

14-1 CONTRACTS THAT VIOLATE A STATUTE

In this chapter, we examine a variety of contracts that may be void, or unenforceable. Illegal agreements fall into two groups: those that violate a statute, and those that violate public policy.

14-1a Wagers

Gambling is big business. Almost all states now permit some form of wagering, from casinos to racetracks to lotteries, and they eagerly collect the billions of dollars in revenue generated. Supporters urge that casinos create jobs and steady income, boost state coffers, and take business away from organized crime. Critics argue that naive citizens inevitably lose money they can ill afford to forfeit, and that addicted gamblers destroy their families and weaken the fabric of communities. With citizens and states divided over the ethics of gambling, it is inevitable that we have conflicts such as the dispute between Sadri and Caesar's. The basic rule, however, is clear: **A gambling contract is illegal unless it is a type of wagering** *specifically authorized* by state statute.

In California, as in many states, gambling on credit is not allowed. In other words, it is illegal to lend money to help someone wager. But in Nevada, gambling on credit is legal, and debt memoranda such as Sadri's are enforceable contracts. Caesar's sued Sadri in California (where he lived). The result? The court admitted that California's attitude toward gambling had changed, and that bingo, poker clubs, and lotteries were common. Nonetheless, the court denied that the new tolerance extended to wagering on credit:

> There is a special reason for treating gambling on credit differently from gambling itself. Having lost his or her cash, the pathological gambler will continue to play on credit, if extended, in an attempt to win back the losses. This is why enforcement of gambling debts has always been against public policy in California and should remain so, regardless of shifting public attitudes about gambling itself. If Californians want to play, so be it. But the law should not invite them to play themselves into debt. The judiciary cannot protect pathological gamblers from themselves, but we can refuse to participate in their financial ruin.[1]

Caesar's lost and Sadri kept his money. However, do not become too excited at the prospect of risk-free wagering. Casinos responded to cases like *Sadri* by changing their practices. Most now extend credit only to a gambler who agrees that disputes about repayment will be settled in *Nevada* courts. Because such contracts are legal in that state, the casino is able to obtain a judgment against a defaulting debtor and—yes— enforce that judgment in the gambler's home state.

Despite these more restrictive casino practices, Sadri's dispute is a useful starting place from which to examine contract legality because it illustrates two important themes.

First, morality is a significant part of contract legality. In refusing to enforce an obligation that Sadri undeniably had made, the California court relied on the human and social consequences of gambling and on the ethics of judicial enforcement of gambling debts. Second, "void" really means just that: A court will not intercede to assist either party to an illegal agreement, even if its refusal leaves one party shortchanged.

The gambling may be legal—but what about a gambling contract?

[1]Metropolitan Creditors Service of Sacramento v. Sadri, 15 Cal. App. 4th 1821 (Cal. Ct. App. 1993).

14-1b **Insurance**

Another market in which "wagering" unexpectedly pops up is that of insurance. You may certainly insure your own life for any sum you choose. But may you insure someone else's life? **Anyone taking out a policy on the life of another must have an insurable interest in that person.** The most common insurable interest is family connection, such as spouses or parents. Other valid interests include creditor-debtor status (the creditor wants payment if the debtor dies) and business association (an executive in the company is so valuable that the firm will need compensation if something happens to him). If there is no insurable interest, there is generally no contract.

EXAM Strategy

Question: Jimenez sold Breton a used motorcycle for $5,500, payable in weekly installments. Jimenez then purchased an insurance policy on Breton's life, worth $320,000 if Breton died in an accident. Breton promptly died in a collision with an automobile. The insurance company offered only $5,500, representing the balance due on the motorcycle. Jimenez sued, demanding $320,000. Make an argument that the insurance company should win.

Strategy: The issue is whether Jimenez had an insurable interest in Breton's life. If he had no interest, he cannot collect on an insurance policy. If he had an interest, what was it? For how much money?

Result: Jimenez had an interest in Breton's life to insure payment of the motorcycle debt—$5,500. Beyond that, this policy represented a wager by Jimenez that Breton was going to die. Contracts for such wagers are unenforceable. Jimenez is entitled only to $5,500.[2]

14-2 LICENSING STATUTES

You sue your next-door neighbor in small claims court, charging that he keeps a kangaroo in his backyard and that the beast has disrupted your family barbecues by leaping over the fence, demanding salad, and even kicking your cousin in the ear. Your friend Foster, a graduate student from Melbourne, offers to help you prepare the case, and you agree to pay him 10 percent of anything you recover. Foster proves surprisingly adept at organizing documents and arguments. You win $1,200, and Foster demands $120. Must you pay? The answer is determined by the law of licensing.

States require licenses for anyone who practices a profession, such as law or medicine, works as a contractor or plumber, and for many other kinds of work. These licenses are required in order to protect the public. States demand that an electrician be licensed because the work is potentially dangerous to a homeowner: The person doing the work must know an amp from a watt. **When a licensing requirement is designed to protect the public, any contract made by an unlicensed worker is unenforceable.** Your friend Foster is unlicensed to practice law. Even though Foster did a fine job with your small claims case, he cannot enforce his contract for $120.

---

[2]Jimenez v. Protective Life Insurance Co., 8 Cal. App. 4th 528 (Cal. App. 1992).

States use other licenses simply to raise money. For example, most states require a license to open certain kinds of retail stores. This requirement does not protect the public because the state will not investigate the store owner the way it will examine a prospective lawyer or electrician. The state is simply raising money. **When a licensing requirement is designed merely to raise revenue, a contract made by an unlicensed person is generally enforceable.** Thus, if you open a stationery store and forget to pay the state's licensing fee, you can still enforce a contract to buy 10,000 envelopes from a wholesaler at a bargain price.

Many cases, such as the following one, involve contractors seeking to recover money for work they did without a license.

AUTHENTIC HOME IMPROVEMENTS V. MAYO

2006 WL 2687533
District of Columbia Superior Court, 2006

Facts: Authentic Home Improvements (Authentic) performed work on Diane Mayo's home, but she sued for return of the money she had paid. In court, Authentic's owner acknowledged that he had no contractor's license when it began the work, but he expected to obtain it soon. The court ordered Authentic to refund Mayo the entire sum she had paid, and the company agreed. Later, however, Authentic returned to court, stating that things had changed. The license had in fact been issued soon after work began. Authentic argued that it should not be obligated to return Mayo's money and was in fact entitled to its full fee for the work accomplished.

Issue: *Did the new license entitle Authentic to its home improvement fee?*

Excerpts from Judge Goodbread's Decision: This is not a matter of a trial judge doggedly cleaving to his original ruling—one that he frankly wishes he could modify under these circumstances. To use the words of Proteus, "My duty pricks me on to utter that which else no worldly good should draw from me." Shakespeare, "The Two Gentlemen of Verona." Not that it makes any difference to anyone, but the undersigned, a carpenter's son dwelling at this end of the Judicial Food Chain, disagrees with the harsh general rule in these cases and [believes that exceptions to the licensing requirement should be made in deserving cases]. Nevertheless, the undersigned is bound by the repeated rulings of the Court of Appeals.

As early as 1974, our Court of Appeals noted the high incidence of complaints emanating from the home improvement industry, noting that, even then, it was estimated that fraudulent practices in the industry cost consumers from 500 million to 1 billion dollars annually (this would amount to over $4.3 billion in today's dollars). A simple search of the Internet for the term "home improvement fraud" brings up over two million sites.

Not only is it immaterial that the parties may be in equal fault in the home improvement contract matter, but it has also been held that the unlicensed contractor may not recover even in instances wherein the home-owner *already knew* at all times relevant that the contractor was not licensed and impliedly or expressly "waived" that requirement in return for the work being done promptly. Moreover—turning the purpose of the rule inside out—even where it was the contractor who was the "victim" and the home owner herself who knew in advance that the contract would be invalid and unenforceable, yet still benefitted unfairly from the contractor's good work, the homeowner was allowed to prevail, despite what might be termed "malice aforethought."

The unique defense of a "retroactive" license presented in this case does not vitiate the rule. [Authentic's owner argues that he] had every reasonable *expectation* of receiving a license and that, in fact, he *did* receive the license within a reasonable time of beginning work. Yet the requirement to have *already* had issued, and in hand, a license or permit to conduct or perform the act at issue is not a difficult concept to grasp and one need go no further than the common driver's permit or license tags to understand it. No one could legally drive a vehicle in *anticipation* of the license and the plates that had already been approved, on the premise that they would eventually arrive in the mail in due course, and that it would be all right to drive until they do.

The Court's original ruling in this case must stand.

14-2a Usury

It pays to understand usury.

Henry Paper and Anthony Pugliese were real estate developers. They bought property in Florida, intending to erect an office building. Walter Gross, another developer, agreed to lend them $200,000 at 15 percent interest. Gross knew the partners were desperate for the money, so at the loan closing, he demanded 15 percent equity (ownership) in the partnership, in addition to the interest. Paper and Pugliese had no choice but to sign the agreement. The two partners never repaid the loan, and when Gross sued, the court ruled that they need never pay a cent.

Usury laws prohibit charging excess interest on loans. Some states, such as New York, set very strict limits. Others, like Utah, allow for virtually any rate. A lender who charges a usurious rate of interest may forfeit the illegal interest, all interest, or, in some states, the entire loan.

Florida law requires a lender who exceeds 25 percent interest to forfeit the entire debt. Where was the usury in Gross's case? Just here: When Gross insisted on a 15 percent share of the partnership, he was simply extracting additional interest and disguising it as partnership equity. The Paper-Pugliese partnership had equity assets of $600,000. A 15 percent equity, plus interest payments of 15 percent over 18 months, was the equivalent of a per annum interest rate of 45 percent. Gross probably thought he had made a deal that was too good to be true. And in the state of Florida, it was. He lost the entire debt.[3]

Credit Card Debt

Many consumers are desperate to obtain credit cards on any terms. When First Premier Bank launched a credit card with a 79.9 percent rate of interest, 700,000 people applied for it within the next two years. How can such a rate exist?

Even if a state's usury statute applies to credit cards, savvy lenders can often avoid limits on interest rates. The Supreme Court has ruled that when national banks issue a credit card, they can use the rate of their own state or of that of the consumer, whichever is higher. Also, many card issuers require borrowers to sign contracts that say the laws of a lender-friendly state will be applied to all future disputes. New York customers might agree to live by Utah laws, for example.

Most courts continue to enforce these contracts that impose high out-of-state rates. But since the financial meltdown of 2008, some courts have started to express distaste for this practice. In the following case, a New York court addressed the issue.

AMERICAN EXPRESS TRAVEL RELATED SERVICES COMPANY, INC. v. ASSIH

893 N.Y.S.2d 438
Civil Court of the City of New York, Richmond County, 2009

Facts: American Express Travel Related Services (American Express) alleged that New York resident Titus Assih missed a credit card payment. His interest rate ballooned from 12.24 percent to 21 percent, and eventually to 27.99 percent. Assih made small payments for a time, but soon he stopped paying altogether.

American Express sued Assih. The company sought to enforce this provision of its agreement: "This Agreement is governed by Utah law and applicable federal law." The agreement's only connection to Utah was that American Express assigned its interest to a one-branch bank in Utah.

---

[3]Jersey Palm-Gross, Inc. v. Paper, 639 So.2d 664 (Fla. Ct. App. 1994).

Assih argued that New York law, which sets strict limits on maximum rates of credit card interest, should apply instead.

Issues: *Should New York or Utah law apply? Did the increased rates violate usury statutes?*

Excerpts from Judge Straniere's Opinion: Having dealt with thousands of consumer credit cases over the years, the court is sometimes caused to wonder if the regulations governing this industry originated in the Wonderful Land of Oz. For example, the scene where Dorothy and friends approach the gates of the Emerald City and ring the bell seeking entrance seems to present a number of the issues arising in debt collection litigation.

> Guardian: Well, that's more like it! Now state your business!
> Dorothy and Friends: We want to see the Wizard!
> Guardian: The Wizard? But nobody can see the Great Oz! Nobody's ever seen the Great Oz! Even I've never seen him!
> Dorothy: Well, then how do you know there is one?

Like the Land of Oz, run by a Wizard who no one has ever seen, the Land of Credit Cards permits consumers to be bound by agreements they never sign, agreements they may have never received, subject to change without notice and the laws of a state other than those existing where they reside.

The Utah usury statute provides: The parties to a lawful contract may agree upon any rate of interest for the loan that is the subject of their contract.

Is it any wonder that credit card issuers, such as plaintiff, make their agreements subject to Utah law? An interest rate is not usurious so long as the parties "agree upon any rate of interest." If Nathan Detroit had known he could make loans charging 100 percent interest a day by reducing them to writing, signed and subject to Utah law, he would not have had to seek a living running the "oldest, established, permanent floating crap game in New York." Incredibly, courts are expected to enforce these agreements against unsophisticated, unrepresented consumers who reside in states such as New York, which does not have similar statutes, and who have no idea that their agreement is subject to Utah law.

Is New York required to apply the Utah usury statute to credit card interest charges that far exceed the legal rate in New York? New York follows the "substantial relationship" approach, which provides:

> The law of the state chosen by the parties to govern their contractual rights and duties will be applied.... unless the chosen state has no substantial relationship to the parties.

The corporate plaintiff is incorporated in New York and its principal place of business is in New York. Defendant resides in New York. Most of the transactions charged to the credit card took place in New York. Payments on the credit card are mailed to a New York address. Utah has no substantial relationship to the parties.

Taking all of the above into account, it is clear that New York has the most significant contacts to the parties and New York law will apply to the Agreement.

The legal rate of interest in New York in general obligations [is] sixteen per cent. New York still retains a criminal usury statute for interest rates which exceed twenty-five per cent. Except for the initial interest rate charged on defendant's account by plaintiff of 12.24%, all other interest charges assessed by plaintiff violated the New York civil usury statutes. The last billings on this account in fact exceeded the criminal usury rate of 25% when they reached 27.99%.

Under New York law, all usurious contracts are void and the lender forfeits both principal and interest.

The Wizard in *The Wizard of Oz* warned Dorothy and friends, "Do not arouse the wrath of the great and powerful Oz." I am sure the court will likewise be arousing the wrath of the plaintiff.

Plaintiff's cause of action is dismissed.

14-3 CONTRACTS THAT VIOLATE PUBLIC POLICY

A judge may declare a contract void even if it does not violate a statute. Contracts that promote immorality or illegality are unenforceable. One court refused to enforce a contract for the sale of a company because its main business was the manufacture of marijuana bongs.[4] It reasoned that hearing about such a contract would have a negative

---

[4]Bovard v. American Horse Enterprises, Inc. 201 Cal. App. 3d 832 (1988).

impact on society. In this section, we examine cases in which a *public policy* prohibits certain contracts. In other words, we focus primarily on common law rules.

14-3a Restraint of Trade: Noncompete Agreements

Free trade is the basis of the U.S. economy, and any bargain that restricts it is suspect. Most restraint of free trade is barred by antitrust law. But it is the common law that still regulates one restriction on trade: agreements to refrain from competition. Some of these agreements are legal, and some are void.

Recall that a noncompete agreement is a contract in which one party agrees not to compete with another in a stated type of business. For example, an anchorwoman for an NBC news affiliate in Miami might agree that she will not anchor any other Miami station's news for one year after she leaves her present employer. Noncompetes are often valid, but the common law places some restrictions on them.

To be valid, an agreement not to compete must be ancillary to a legitimate bargain. "Ancillary" means that the noncompetition agreement must be part of a larger agreement. Suppose Cliff sells his gasoline station to Mina, and the two agree that Cliff will not open a competing gas station within 5 miles anytime during the next two years. Cliff's agreement not to compete is ancillary to the sale of his service station. His noncompetition promise is enforceable. But suppose that Cliff and Mina already had the only two gas stations within 35 miles. They agree between themselves not to hire each other's workers. Their agreement might be profitable to them because each could now keep wages artificially low. But their deal is ancillary to no legitimate bargain, and it is therefore void. Mina is free to hire Cliff's mechanic despite her agreement with Cliff.

The two most common settings for legitimate noncompetition agreements are the sale of a business and an employment relationship.

Sale of a Business

Kory has operated a real estate office, Hearth Attack, in a small city for 35 years, building an excellent reputation and many ties with the community. She offers to sell you the business and its goodwill for $300,000. But you need assurance that Kory will not take your money and promptly open a competing office across the street. With her reputation and connections, she would ruin your chances of success. You insist on a noncompete clause in the sale contract. In this clause, Kory promises that for one year, she will not open a new real estate office or go to work for a competing company within a 10-mile radius of Hearth Attack. Suppose, six months after selling you the business, Kory goes to work for a competing real estate agency two blocks away. You seek an injunction to prevent her from working. Who wins?

> With her reputation and connections, she would ruin your chances of success.

When a noncompete agreement is ancillary to the sale of a business, it is enforceable if reasonable in time, geographic area, and scope of activity. In other words, a court will not enforce a noncompete agreement that lasts an unreasonably long time, covers an unfairly large area, or prohibits the seller of the business from doing a type of work that she never had done before. Measured by this test, Kory is almost certainly bound by her agreement. One year is a reasonable time to allow you to get your new business started. A 10-mile radius is probably about the area that Hearth Attack covers, and realty is obviously a fair business from which to prohibit Kory. A court will probably grant the injunction, barring Kory from her new job.

If, on the other hand, the noncompetition agreement had prevented Kory from working anywhere within 200 miles of Hearth Attack, and she started working 50 miles away, a court would refuse to enforce the contract. That geographic restriction would be unreasonable since Kory never previously did business 50 miles away, and Hearth Attack is unlikely to be affected if she works there now. An overly broad restriction would make for bad public policy, and it would lack a legal purpose.

Employment

When you sign an employment contract, the document may well contain a noncompete clause. Employers have legitimate worries that employees might go to a competitor and take with them trade secrets or other proprietary information. Some employers, though, attempt to place harsh restrictions on their employees, perhaps demanding a blanket agreement that the employee will never go to work for a competitor.

Noncompetes limit an individual's right to make a living and choose their work. For this reason, about one-third of states have restrictions on the enforceability of employment-related noncompetes. California prohibits them altogether, except when they are tied to the sale of a business or a verifiable trade secret.[5] In other states, employment restrictions are highly scrutinized for fairness. **Generally, a noncompete clause in an employment contract is enforceable only if it is essential to the employer, fair to the employee, and harmless to the general public.**

Judges usually enforce these agreements to protect trade secrets and confidential information. They may protect customer lists that have been expensive to produce. Courts rarely restrain an employee simply because he wants to work for a competitor, and they disfavor agreements that last too long or apply in a very wide area. The following chart summarizes the factors that courts look at in all types of noncompetition agreements.

The Legality of Noncompetition Clauses (Noncompetes)

Type of Noncompetition Agreement	When Enforceable	
Not ancillary to a sale of business or employment	Never	
Ancillary to a sale of business	If reasonable in time, geography, and scope of activity	
Ancillary to employment	Contract is *more* likely to be enforced when it involves:	Contract is *less* likely to be enforced when it involves:
	• Trade secrets or confidential information: these are almost always protected	• Employee who already had the skills when he arrived, or merely developed general skills on the job
	• Customer lists developed over extended period of time and carefully protected	• Customer lists that can be derived from public sources
	• Limited time and geographical scope	• Excessive time or geographical scope
	• Terms essential to protect the employer's business	• Terms that are unduly harsh on the employee or contrary to public interest

---

[5]Edwards v. Arthur Andersen LLP, 44 Cal,.4th 937 (S. Ct. Cal. 2008).

Suppose that Gina, an engineer, goes to work for Fission Chips, a silicon chip manufacturer that specializes in defense work. She signs a noncompete agreement promising never to work for a competitor. Over a period of three years, Gina learns some of Fission's proprietary methods of etching information onto the chips. She acquires a great deal of new expertise about chips generally. Also, she periodically deals with Fission Chip's customers, all of whom are well-known software and hardware manufacturers. Gina accepts an offer from WriteSmall, a competitor. Fission Chips races to court, seeking an injunction that would prevent Gina from (1) working for WriteSmall, (2) working for any other competitor, (3) revealing any of Fission's trade secrets, (4) using any of the general expertise she acquired at Fission Chips, and (5) contacting any of Fission's customers.

This injunction threatens Gina's career. If she cannot work for a competitor or use her general engineering skills, what *will* she do? And for exactly that reason, no court will grant such a broad order. The court will allow Gina to work for competitors, including WriteSmall. It will order her not to use or reveal any trade secrets belonging to Fission. She will, however, be permitted to use the general expertise she has acquired, and she may contact former customers since anyone could get their names from the yellow pages.

Was the noncompete in the following case styled fairly, or was the employee clipped?

KING V. HEAD START FAMILY HAIR SALONS, INC.

886 So.2d 769
Supreme Court of Alabama, 2004

Facts: Kathy King was a single mother supporting a college-age daughter. For 25 years, she had worked as a hair stylist. For the most recent 16 years, she had worked at Head Start, which provided haircuts, coloring, and styling for men and women. King was primarily a stylist, though she had also managed one of the Head Start facilities.

King quit Head Start and began working as manager of a Sport Clips shop, located in the same mall as the store she just left. Sport Clips offered only haircuts and primarily served men and boys. Head Start filed suit, claiming that King was violating the noncompetition agreement that she had signed. The agreement prohibited King from working at a competing business within a 2-mile radius of any Head Start facility for 12 months after leaving the company. The trial court issued an injunction enforcing the noncompete. King appealed.

Issue: *Was the noncompetition agreement valid?*

Excerpts from Justice Lyons's Decision: King's most persuasive argument is that the geographic restriction contained in the noncompetition agreement imposes an undue hardship on her. King has been in the hair-care industry for 25 years, and it is the only industry in which she is skilled and the only industry in which she can find employment. Head Start has 30 locations throughout the Jefferson County and Shelby County area, making it virtually impossible for her to find employment in the hair-care industry at a facility that does not violate the terms of the noncompetition agreement. According to

King, the geographic restriction constitutes a blanket prohibition on practicing her trade.

It cannot reasonably be argued that King, at the age of 40 and having spent more than half of her life as a hair stylist, can learn a new job skill that would allow her to be gainfully employed and meet her needs and the needs of her daughter. Under the circumstances presented here, enforcement of the noncompetition agreement works an undue hardship upon King. The noncompetition agreement cannot so burden King that it would result in her impoverishment.

Head Start is nevertheless entitled to some of the protection it sought in the noncompetition agreement. Head Start has a valid concern that King would be able to attract many of her former Head Start customers if she is allowed to provide hair-care services unencumbered by any limitations. To prevent an undue burden on King and to afford some protection to Head Start, the trial court should enforce a more reasonable geographic restriction—such as one prohibiting King from providing hair-care services within a 2-mile radius of the location of the Head Start facility at which she was formerly employed or imposing some other limitation that does not unreasonably interfere with King's right to gainful employment while, at the same time, protecting Head Start's interest in preventing King from unreasonably competing with it during the one-year period following her resignation.

Reversed and remanded.

EXAM Strategy

Question: Caf-Fiend is an expanding chain of coffeehouses. The company offers to buy Bessie's Coffee Shop, in St. Louis, on these terms: Bessie will manage the store, as Caf-Fiend's employee, for one year after the sale. For four years after the sale, Bessie will not open a competing restaurant anywhere within 12 miles. For the same four years, she will not work anywhere in the United States for a competing coffee retailer. Are the last two terms enforceable against Bessie?

Strategy: This contract includes two noncompete clauses. In the first, Bessie agrees not to open a competing business. Courts generally enforce such clauses if they are reasonable in time, geography, and scope of activity. Is this clause reasonable? The second clause involves employment. Courts take a dimmer view of these agreements. Is this clause essential to protect the company's business? Is it unduly harsh for Bessie?

Result: The first restriction is reasonable. Caf-Fiend is entitled to prevent Bessie from opening her own coffeehouse around the corner and drawing her old customers. The second clause is unfair to Bessie. If she wants to move from St. Louis to San Diego and work as a store manager, she is prohibited. It is impossible to see how such employment would harm Caf-Fiend—but it certainly takes away Bessie's career options. The first restriction is valid, the second one unenforceable.

14-3b Exculpatory Clauses

You decide to capitalize on your expert ability as a skier and open a ski and snowboarding school in Colorado, "Pike's Pique." But you realize that skiing and snowboarding sometimes cause injuries, so you require anyone signing up for lessons to sign this form:

> I agree to hold Pike's Pique and its employees entirely harmless in the event that I am injured in any way or for any reason or cause, including but not limited to any acts, whether negligent or otherwise, of Pike's Pique or any employee or agent thereof.

The day your school opens, Sara Beth, an instructor, deliberately pushes Toby over a cliff because Toby criticized her clothes. Eddie, a beginning student, "blows out" his knee attempting an advanced racing turn, and Maureen, another student, reaches the bottom of a steep run and slams into a snowmobile that Sara Beth parked there. Maureen, Eddie, and Toby's families all sue Pike's Pique. You defend based on the form you had them sign. Does it save the day?

The form on which you are relying is an **exculpatory clause**, that is, one that attempts to release you from liability in the event of injury to another party. Exculpatory clauses are common. Ski and snowboarding schools use them, and so do parking lots, landlords, warehouses, sports franchises, fitness centers, and day-care centers. All manner of businesses hope to avoid large tort judgments by requiring their customers to give up any right to recover. Is such a clause valid? Sometimes. Courts frequently—but do not always—ignore exculpatory clauses, finding that one party was forcing the other party to give up legal rights that no one should be forced to surrender.

An exculpatory clause is generally unenforceable when it attempts to exclude an intentional tort or gross negligence. When Sara Beth pushes Toby over a cliff, that is the intentional tort of battery. A court will not enforce the exculpatory clause. Sara Beth is clearly liable.[6] As to the

Exculpatory clause
A contract provision that attempts to release one party from liability in the event the other is injured

---

[6]Note that Pike's Pique is probably not liable under agency law principles that preclude an employer's liability for an employee's intentional tort.

Exculpatory clauses are important to the operators of businesses that involve some risk, such as ski and snowboarding resorts.

snowmobile at the bottom of the run, if a court determines that was gross negligence (carelessness far greater than ordinary negligence), then the exculpatory clause will again be ignored. If, however, it was ordinary negligence, then we must continue the analysis.

An exculpatory clause is usually unenforceable when the affected activity is in the public interest, such as medical care, public transportation, or some essential service. Suppose Eddie goes to a doctor for surgery on his damaged knee, and the doctor requires him to sign an exculpatory clause. The doctor negligently performs the surgery, accidentally leaving his cuff links in Eddie's left knee. The exculpatory clause will not protect the doctor. Medical care is an essential service, and the public cannot give up its right to demand reasonable work.

But what about Eddie's suit against Pike's Pique? Eddie claims that he should never have been allowed to attempt an advanced maneuver. His suit is for ordinary negligence, and the exculpatory clause probably *does* bar him from recovery. Skiing and snowboarding are recreational activities. No one is obligated to do them, and there is no strong public interest in ensuring that we have access to ski slopes.

An exculpatory clause is generally unenforceable when the parties have greatly unequal bargaining power. When Maureen flies to Colorado, suppose that the airline requires her to sign a form contract with an exculpatory clause. Because the airline almost certainly has much greater bargaining power, it can afford to offer a "take it or leave it" contract. The bargaining power is so unequal, though, that the clause is probably unenforceable. Does Pike's Pique have a similar advantage? Probably not. Ski and snowboarding schools are not essential and are much smaller enterprises. A dissatisfied customer might refuse to sign such an agreement and take her business elsewhere. A court probably will not see the parties as *grossly* unequal.

An exculpatory clause is generally unenforceable unless the clause is clearly written and readily visible. If Pike's Pique gave all ski and snowboarding students an eight-page contract, and the exculpatory clause was at the bottom of page seven in small print, the average customer would never notice it. The clause would be void.

In the following case, the court focused on the public policy concerns of exculpatory clauses used in a very common setting. Should the exculpatory clause stop the tenant from suing the landlord? You be the judge.

You be the Judge

Facts: Barbara Richards leased an apartment at Twin Lakes, a complex owned by Lenna Ransburg. The written lease declared that:

- Twin Lakes would "gratuitously" maintain the common areas.

RANSBURG V. RICHARDS
770 N.E.2d 393
Indiana Court of Appeals, 2002

- Richards's use of the facilities would be "at her own risk."

- Twin Lakes was not responsible for any harm to the tenant or her guests, anywhere on the property (including the parking lot), even if the damage was caused by Twin Lakes' negligence.

It snowed. As Richards walked across the parking lot to her car, she slipped and fell on snow-covered ice. Richards sued Ransburg, who moved for summary judgment based on the exculpatory clause. The trial court denied Ransburg's motion, and she appealed.

You Be the Judge: *Was the exculpatory clause valid?*

Argument for Tenant: An exculpatory clause in a contract for an essential service violates public policy. When an ill person seeks medical care, his doctor cannot require him to sign an exculpatory clause. In the same way, a person has to live somewhere. Her landlord cannot force her to sign a waiver.

Landlords tend to be wealthy and powerful. There is generally no equality of bargaining power between them. The tenants are not freely agreeing to the exculpatory language.

Moreover, if a landlord fails to maintain property, not just the tenant is at risk. Visitors, the mail carrier, and the general public could all walk through the Twin Lakes parking lot. The public's interest is served when landlords maintain their properties. They must be held liable when they negligently fail to maintain common areas and injuries result.

Argument for Landlord: Ms. Richards does indeed have to live somewhere, but she does not have to live on the plaintiff's property. Surely there are many dozens of properties nearby. If Richards had been dissatisfied with any part of the proposed lease—excessive rent, strict rules, or an exculpatory clause—she was free to take her business to another landlord.

Landlords may generally be wealthier than their tenants, but that fact alone does not mean that a landlord is so powerful that leases are offered on a "take it or leave it" basis. Here, the landlord stated the exculpatory clause plainly. This is a clear contract between adults, and it should stand in its entirety.

Bailment Cases

Exculpatory clauses are very common in bailment cases. **Bailment** means giving possession and control of personal property to another person. The person giving up possession is the **bailor**, and the one accepting possession is the **bailee**. When you leave your laptop computer with a dealer to be repaired, you create a bailment. The same is true when you check your coat at a restaurant or lend your Matisse to a museum. Bailees often try to limit their liability for damage to property by using an exculpatory clause.

Judges are slightly more apt to enforce an exculpatory clause in a bailment case because any harm is to *property* and not persons. But courts will still look at many of the same criteria we have just examined to decide whether a bailment contract is enforceable. In particular, when the bailee is engaged in an important public service, a court is once again likely to ignore the exculpatory clause. The following contrasting cases illustrate this.

In *Weiss v. Freeman*,[7] Weiss stored personal goods in Freeman's self-storage facility. Freeman's contract included an exculpatory clause relieving it of any and all liability. Weiss's goods were damaged by mildew, and she sued. The court held the exculpatory clause valid. The court considered self-storage to be a significant business, but not as vital as medical care or housing. It pointed out that a storage facility would not know what each customer stored and therefore could not anticipate the harm that might occur. Freedom of contract should prevail, the clause was enforceable, and Weiss got no money.

Bailment
Giving possession and control of personal property to another person

Bailor
One who creates a bailment by delivering goods to another

Bailee
A person who rightfully possesses goods belonging to another

---

[7] 1994 Tenn. App. LEXIS 393 (Tenn. Ct. App. 1993).

But in *Gardner v. Downtown Porsche Audi*,[8] Gardner left his Porsche 911 at Downtown for repairs. He signed an exculpatory clause saying that Downtown was "Not Responsible for Loss or Damage to Cars or Articles Left in Cars in Case of Fire, Theft, or Any Other Cause Beyond Our Control." Due to Downtown's negligence, Gardner's Porsche was stolen. The court held the exculpatory clause void. It ruled that contemporary society is utterly dependent upon automobile transportation and Downtown was therefore in a business of great public importance. No repair shop should be able to contract away liability, and Gardner won. (This case also illustrates that using seventeen capitalized words in one sentence does not guarantee legal victory.)

EXAM Strategy

Facts: Shauna flew a World War II fighter aircraft as a member of an exhibition flight team. While the team was performing in a delta formation, another plane collided with Shauna's aircraft, causing her to crash-land and leaving her permanently disabled. Shauna sued the other pilot and the team. The defendants moved to dismiss based on an exculpatory clause that Shauna had signed. The clause was one paragraph long, and it stated that Shauna knew team flying was inherently dangerous and could result in injury or death. She agreed not to hold the team or any members liable in case of an accident. Shauna argued that the clause should not be enforced against her if she could prove the other pilot was negligent. Please rule.

Strategy: The issue is whether the exculpatory clause is valid. Courts are likely to declare such clauses void if they concern vital activities like medical care, exclude an intentional tort or gross negligence, or if the parties had unequal bargaining power.

Result: This is a clear, short clause, between parties with equal bargaining power, and does not exclude an intentional tort or gross negligence. The activity is unimportant to the public welfare. The clause is valid. Even if the other pilot was negligent, Shauna will lose, meaning the court should dismiss her lawsuit.

14-3c Unconscionable Contracts

An unconscionable contract is one that a court refuses to enforce because of fundamental unfairness. Even if a contract does not violate any specific statute or public policy, it may still be void if it "shocks the conscience" of the court.

Historically, a contract was considered unconscionable if it was "such as no man in his senses and not under delusion would make on the one hand, and as no honest and fair man would accept on the other."[9]

But that standard was unhelpfully vague. Further, anytime a court rejects a contract as unconscionable, it diminishes freedom of contract. If one party can escape a deal based on something as hard to define as unconscionability, then no one can rely as confidently on any agreement. As an English jurist said in 1824, "public policy is a very unruly horse, and when once you get astride it, you never know where it will carry you."[10]

The following historic case provides a classic example of unconscionability.

---

[8]180 Cal. App. 3d 713 (Cal. Ct. App. 1986).
[9]Hume v. United States, 132 U.S. 406 (1889), quoting Earl of Chesterfield v. Janssen, 38 Eng. Rep. 82, 100 (Ch. 1750).
[10]Richardson v. Mellish, 2 Bing. 229 (1824).

Landmark Case

WILLIAMS V. WALKER-THOMAS FURNITURE CO.

350 F.2d 445
United States Court of Appeals for the DC Circuit, 1965

Facts: Walker-Thomas Furniture Company operated a retail furniture store in an economically disadvantaged DC neighborhood. The store's standard boilerplate contract provided, in fine print, that when a purchaser bought more than one item, any payment she made would be applied equally to everything she had purchased. In this way, the purchaser would not actually own any item until she had paid for everything in full. As a result, when customers missed a payment, Walker-Thomas would repossess every item they ever bought.

Ora Williams was a single mother raising seven children on a $218 monthly welfare check. Despite this knowledge, Walker-Thomas sold Williams fourteen household items totaling $1,800 from 1957 to 1962. Williams dutifully made her monthly payments. In 1962, Williams bought a stereo valued at $514.95. At the time of this purchase, she still owed $164 from her prior purchases. When Williams defaulted on her payment, Walker-Thomas sought to repossess every item she had ever purchased.

With the help of a legal aid society, Williams and other Walker-Thomas customers sued the company, arguing the contract was void for unconscionability. Lower courts sided with Walker-Thomas, and the customers appealed.

Issue: *Is an unconscionable contract unenforceable?*

Excerpts from Judge Skelly Wright's Decision:
Unconscionability has generally been recognized to include an absence of meaningful choice on the part of one of the parties together with contract terms which are unreasonably favorable to the other party. Whether a meaningful choice is present in a particular case can only be determined by consideration of all the circumstances surrounding the transaction. In many cases the meaningfulness of the choice is negated by a gross inequality of bargaining power.

The manner in which the contract was entered is also relevant to this consideration. Did each party to the contract, considering his obvious education or lack of it, have a reasonable opportunity to understand the terms of the contract, or were the important terms hidden in a maze of fine print and minimized by deceptive sales practices? Ordinarily, one who signs an agreement without full knowledge of its terms might be held to assume the risk that he has entered a one-sided bargain. But when a party of little bargaining power, and hence little real choice, signs a commercially unreasonable contract with little or no knowledge of its terms, it is hardly likely that his consent, or even an objective manifestation of his consent, was ever given to all the terms. In such a case the usual rule that the terms of the agreement are not to be questioned should be abandoned and the court should consider whether the terms of the contract are so unfair that enforcement should be withheld.

The test [of unconscionability] is not simple, nor can it be mechanically applied. The terms are to be considered in the light of the general commercial background and the commercial needs of the particular trade or case. The test [is] whether the terms are 'so extreme as to appear unconscionable according to the mores and business practices of the time and place.'

[Now that this court has established the test for determining "unconscionability" the case is remanded to the trial court to decide if this contract meets the test.]

Today, plaintiffs claiming unconscionability must prove two elements: procedural and substantive unconscionability:

- **Procedural unconscionability** focuses on oppression or unfair surprise. Oppression exists when the stronger party forces an unfavorable contract on the weaker one, often by taking advantage of their lack of education. Unfair surprise means the

Procedural Unconscionability
One party uses its superior power to force a contract on the weaker party.

weaker part did not fully understand the consequences of the agreement because the terms were hidden in the fine print.

Substantive Unconscionability

A contract with extremely one-sided and unfair terms

- **Substantive unconscionability** refers to contract terms that are overly harsh or unfairly one-sided.

Paula desperately needed a job. When her prospective employer asked her to sign an employment contract, she did not hesitate. (After all, she thought, it would not bode well for her career if she haggled over the fine print.) The agreement contained an arbitration clause, which provided that Paula would give up her right to litigate in the event of breach. Although such clauses are generally favored as fair and efficient, this one contained a twist: If Paula wanted to arbitrate, she would have to pay $10,000 to bring a claim, a requirement that did not apply to her employer. This sneaky term made it difficult (if not impossible) for an employee to bring a claim, but easy for an employer to do so.[11] Courts have found that disparity in bargaining power, together with fine print and unequal terms, render a contract void for unconscionability.

Adhesion Contracts

Adhesion contracts

Standard form contracts prepared by one party and presented to the other on a "take it or leave it" basis

A related issue concerns **adhesion contracts**, which are standard form contracts prepared by one party and given to the other on a "take it or leave it" basis. We have all encountered them many times when purchasing goods or services. Adhesion contracts are generally enforced, but they are subject to greater scrutiny and unconscionability challenges.

The UCC: Unconscionability and Sales Law

With the creation of the Uniform Commercial Code (UCC), the law of unconscionability got a boost. The Code explicitly adopts unconscionability as a reason to reject a contract.[12] Although the Code directly applies only to the sale of goods, its unconscionability section has proven to be influential in other cases as well, and courts today are more receptive than they were 100 years ago to a contract defense of fundamental unfairness.

The drafters of the UCC reinforced the principle of unconscionability by including it in §2-302:

> If the court as a matter of law finds the contract or any clause of the contract to have been unconscionable at the time it was made the court may refuse to enforce the contract, or it may enforce the remainder of the contract without the unconscionable clause, or it may so limit the application of any unconscionable clause as to avoid any unconscionable result.

In Code cases, the issue of unconscionability often arises when a company attempts to limit the normal contract law remedies. Yet the Code itself allows such limitations, provided they are reasonable.

Section 2-719 provides in part:

> [A contract] may provide for remedies in addition to or in substitution for those provided [by the Code itself] *and may limit or alter the measure of damages recoverable* ... as by limiting the buyer's remedies to return of the goods and repayment of the price....

In other words, the Code includes two potentially competing sections: §2-719 permits a seller to insist that the buyer's only remedy for defective goods is return of the purchase price, but §2-302 says that *any unconscionable* provision is unenforceable. In lawsuits concerning defective goods, the seller often argues that the buyer's only remedies are those stated in the agreement, and the buyer responds that the contract limitation is unconscionable.

---

[11]See Sonic-Calabasas A Inc. v. Moreno, 57 Cal. 4th 1109 (S. Ct. Cal. 2013).
[12]UCC §2-302.

Electronic Data Systems (EDS) agreed to create complex software for Chubb Life America at a cost of $21 million. Chubb agreed to make staggered payments over many months as the work proceeded. The contract included a limitation on remedies, stating that if EDS became liable to Chubb, its maximum liability would be equal to two monthly payments.

EDS's work was woefully late and unusable, forcing Chubb to obtain its software elsewhere. Chubb sued, claiming $40 million in damages based on the money paid to EDS and additional funds spent purchasing alternative goods. EDS argued that the contract limited its liability to two monthly payments, a fraction of Chubb's damage. Chubb, of course, responded that the limitation was unconscionable.

The court noted that both parties were large, sophisticated corporations. As they negotiated the agreement, the companies both used experienced attorneys and independent consultants. This was no contract of adhesion presented to a meek consumer, but an allocation of risk resulting from hard bargaining. The court declared that the clause was valid, and EDS owed no more than two monthly payments.[13]

Chapter Conclusion

It is not enough to bargain effectively and obtain a contract that gives you exactly what you want. You must also be sure that the contract is legal. What appears to be an insurance contract might legally be an invalid wager. Unintentionally forgetting to obtain a state license to perform a certain job could mean you will never be paid for it. Bargaining a contract with a noncompete or exculpatory clause that is too one-sided may lead a court to ignore it. Legality is multifaceted, sometimes nuanced, and always important.

EXAM REVIEW

Illegal contracts are void and unenforceable. Illegality most often arises in these settings:

1. **WAGERING** A purely speculative contract—whether for gambling or insurance—is likely to be unenforceable.

2. **LICENSING** When the licensing statute is designed to protect the public, a contract by an unlicensed plaintiff is generally unenforceable. When such a statute is designed merely to raise revenue, a contract by an unlicensed plaintiff is generally enforceable.

EXAM Strategy

Question: James Wagner agreed to build a house for Nancy Graham. Wagner was not licensed as a contractor, and Graham knew it. When the house was finished, Graham refused to pay the final $23,000, and Wagner sued. Who will prevail?

---

[13]Colonial Life Insurance Co. v. Electronic Data Systems Corp., 817 F. Supp. 235 (D.N.H. 1993).

Strategy: A licensing statute designed to protect the public is strictly enforced, but that is not true for one intended only to raise revenue. What was the purpose of this statute? (See the "Result" at the end of this section.)

3. **USURY** Excessive interest is generally unenforceable and may be fatal to the entire debt. Credit card debt is often exempt from usury laws.

Question: McElroy owned 104 acres worth about $230,000. He got into financial difficulties and approached Grisham, asking to borrow $100,000. Grisham refused, but ultimately the two reached this agreement: McElroy would sell Grisham his property for $80,000, and the contract would include a clause allowing McElroy to repurchase the land within two years for $120,000. McElroy later claimed the contract was void. Is he right?

Strategy: Loans involving usury do not always include a clearly visible interest rate. You may have to do some simple math to see the interest being charged. McElroy wanted to borrow $100,000, but instead sold his property, with the right to repurchase. If he did repurchase, how much interest would he have effectively paid? (See the "Result" at the end of this section.)

4. **NONCOMPETE** A noncompete clause in the sale of a business must be limited to a reasonable time, geographic area, and scope of activity. In an employment contract, such a clause is considered reasonable—and enforceable—only to protect trade secrets, confidential information, and customer lists.

Question: The purchaser of a business insisted on putting this clause in the sales contract: The seller would not compete, for five years, "anywhere in the United States, the continent of North America, or anywhere else on Earth." What danger does that contract represent *to the purchaser?*

Strategy: This is a noncompete clause based on the sale of a business. Such clauses are valid if reasonable. Is this clause reasonable? If it is unreasonable, what might a court do? (See the "Result" at the end of this section.)

5. **EXCULPATORY CLAUSES** These clauses are generally void if the activity involved is in the public interest, the parties are greatly unequal in bargaining power, or the clause is unclear. In other cases, they are generally enforced.

6. **PROCEDURAL UNCONSCIONABILITY** Oppression and surprise may create an unconscionable bargain. An adhesion contract is especially suspect when it is imposed by a corporation on a consumer or small company. Under the UCC, a limitation of liability is less likely to be unconscionable when both parties are sophisticated corporations.

7. **SUBSTANTIVE UNCONSIONABILITY** When contract terms are unfairly one-sided at the time of contracting, the contract may be substantively unconscionable.

---

2. Result: This statute was designed to protect the public. Wagner was unlicensed and cannot enforce the contract. Graham wins.

3. Result: By selling at $80,000 and repurchasing at $120,000, McElroy would be paying $40,000 in interest on an $80,000 loan. The 50 percent rate is usurious. The court prohibited Graham from collecting the interest.

4. Result: "Anywhere else on Earth"? This is almost certainly unreasonable. It is hard to imagine a purchaser who would legitimately need such wide-ranging protection. In some states, a court might rewrite the clause, limiting the effect to the seller's state, or some reasonable area. However, in other states, a court finding a clause unreasonable will declare it void in its entirety—enabling the seller to open a competing business next door.

MULTIPLE-CHOICE QUESTIONS

1. At a fraternity party, George mentions that he is going to learn to hang glide during spring break. Vicki, a casual friend, overhears him, and the next day she purchases a $100,000 life insurance policy on George's life. George has a happy week of hang gliding. But on the way home, he is bitten by a parrot and dies of a rare tropical illness. Vicki files a claim for $100,000. The insurance company refuses to pay.
   (a) Vicki will win $100,000, but only if she mentioned animal bites to the insurance agent.
   (b) Vicki will win $100,000 regardless of whether she mentioned animal bites to the insurance agent.
   (c) Vicki will win $50,000.
   (d) Vicki will win nothing.

2. Now assume that Vicki has loaned George $50,000. George again mentions that he is going to learn to hang glide during spring break, so Vicki purchases the $100,000 life insurance policy on George's life. If George dies and the insurance company refuses to pay …
   (a) Vicki will win $100,000, but only if she mentioned animal bites to the insurance agent.
   (b) Vicki will win $100,000 regardless of whether she mentioned animal bites to the insurance agent.
   (c) Vicki will win $50,000.
   (d) Vicki will win nothing.

3. KwikFix, a Fortune 500 company, contracts with Allied Rocket, another huge company, to provide the software for Allied's new Jupiter Probe rocket for $14 million. The software is negligently designed, and when the rocket blasts off from Cape Kennedy, it travels only as far as Fort Lauderdale before crashing to Earth. Allied Rocket sues for $200 million and proves that as a result of the disaster, it lost a huge government contract, worth at least that much, which KwikFix was aware of. KwikFix responds that its contract with Allied included a clause limiting its liability to the value of the contract. Is the contract clause valid?

    (a) The clause is unenforceable because it is unconscionable.

    (b) The clause is unenforceable because it is exculpatory.

    (c) The clause is enforceable because both parties are sophisticated corporations.

    (d) The clause is enforceable because $200 million is an unconscionable claim.

4. Ricki goes to a baseball game. The back of her ticket clearly reads: "Fan agrees to hold team blameless for all injuries—pay attention to the game at all times for your own safety!" In the first inning, a foul ball hits Ricki in the elbow. She _____ sue the team over the foul ball. Ricki spends the next several innings riding the opposing team's first baseman. The *nicest* thing she says to him is, "You suck, Franklin!" In the eighth inning, Franklin has had enough. He grabs the ballboy's chair and throws it into the stands, injuring Ricki's other elbow.
    Ricki _____ sue the team over the thrown chair.

    (a) can; can

    (b) can; cannot

    (c) cannot; can

    (d) cannot; cannot

5. Jim, about to start a pickup soccer game, asks Desiree if she will hold his wallet while he plays. Desiree, a law student, says, "Sure, if you'll sign this exculpatory clause holding me blameless for negligence." Jim is very surprised, but he signs the paper that Desiree holds out for him. A bailment _____ been created. If Desiree is careless and loses the wallet, she _____ be liable to Jim.

    (a) has; will

    (b) has; will not

    (c) has not; will

    (d) has not; will not

CASE QUESTIONS

1. For 20 years, Art's Flower Shop relied almost exclusively on advertising in the yellow pages to bring business to its shop in a small West Virginia town. One year, the yellow pages printer accidentally did not print Art's ad, and Art's suffered an enormous drop in business. Art's sued for negligence and won a judgment of $50,000 from the jury, but the printing company appealed, claiming that under an exculpatory clause in the contract, the company could not be liable to Art's for more than the cost of the ad, about $910. Art's claimed that the exculpatory clause was unconscionable. Please rule.

2. Brockwell left his boat to be repaired at Lake Gaston Sales. The boat contained electronic equipment and other personal items. Brockwell signed a form stating that Lake Gaston had no responsibility for any loss to any property in or on the boat. Brockwell's electronic equipment was stolen and other personal items were damaged, and he sued. Is the exculpatory clause enforceable?

3. Guyan Machinery, a West Virginia manufacturing corporation, hired Albert Voorhees as a salesman and required him to sign a contract stating that if he left Guyan, he would not work for a competing corporation anywhere within 250 miles of West Virginia for a two-year period. Later, Voorhees left Guyan and began working at Polydeck Corp., another West Virginia manufacturer. The only product Polydeck made was urethane screens, which comprised half of 1 percent of Guyan's business. Is Guyan entitled to enforce its noncompete clause?

4. 810 Associates owned a 42-story skyscraper in midtown Manhattan. The building had a central station fire alarm system, which was monitored by Holmes Protection. A fire broke out and Holmes received the signal. But Holmes's inexperienced dispatcher misunderstood the signal and failed to summon the fire department for about nine minutes, permitting tremendous damage. 810 sued Holmes, which defended based on an exculpatory clause that relieved Holmes of any liability caused in any way. Holmes's dispatcher was negligent. Does it matter *how* negligent he was?

5. *YOU BE THE JUDGE* **WRITING PROBLEM** Oasis Waterpark, located in Palm Springs, California, sought out Hydrotech Systems, Inc., a New York corporation, to design and construct a surfing pool. Hydrotech replied that it could design the pool and sell all the necessary equipment to Oasis, but it could not build the pool because it was not licensed in California. Oasis insisted that Hydrotech do the construction work because Hydrotech had unique expertise in these pools. Oasis promised to arrange for a licensed California contractor to "work with" Hydrotech on the construction; Oasis also assured Hydrotech that it would pay the full contract price of $850,000, regardless of any licensing issues. Hydrotech designed and installed the pool as ordered. But Oasis failed to make the final payment of $110,000. Hydrotech sued. Can Hydrotech sue for either breach of contract or fraud (trickery)? **Argument for Oasis:** The licensing law protects the public from incompetence and dishonesty. The legislature made the section strict: no license, no payment. If the court were to start picking and choosing which unlicensed contractors could win a suit, it would be inviting incompetent workers to endanger the public and then come into court and try their luck. That is precisely the danger the legislature seeks to avoid. **Argument for Hydrotech:** This is not the kind of case the legislature was worried about. Hydrotech has never solicited work in California. Hydrotech went out of its way to avoid doing any contracting work, informing Oasis that it was unlicensed in the state. Oasis insisted on bringing Hydrotech into the state to do work. If Oasis has its way, word will go out that any owner can get free work done by hiring an *unlicensed* builder. Make any promises you want, get the work done to your satisfaction, and then stiff the contractor—you'll never have to pay.

DISCUSSION QUESTIONS

1. **ETHICS** Richard and Michelle Kommit traveled to New Jersey to have fun in the casinos. While in Atlantic City, they used their MasterCard to withdraw cash from an ATM conveniently located in the "pit"—the gambling area of a casino. They ran up debts of $5,500 on the credit card and did not pay. The Connecticut National Bank sued for the money. Law aside, who has the moral high ground? Is it acceptable for the casino to offer ATM services in the gambling pit? If a credit card company allows customers to withdraw cash in a casino, is it encouraging them to lose money? Do the Kommits have any ethical right to use the ATM, attempt to win money by gambling, and then seek to avoid liability?

2. The Justice Department shut down three of the most popular online poker websites (Poker Stars, Absolute Poker, and Full Tilt Poker). State agencies take countless actions each year to stop illegal gaming operations. Do you believe that gambling by adults *should* be regulated? If so, which types? Rate the following types of gambling from most acceptable to least acceptable:

– online poker	– state lotteries	– horse racing
– casino gambling	– bets on pro sports	– bets on college sports

3. Van hires Terri to add an electrical outlet to his living room for his new HDTV. Terri does an excellent job, and the new outlet works perfectly. She presents Van with a bill for $200. But Terri is not a licensed electrician. Her state sets licensing standards in the profession to protect the public. And so, Van can refuse to pay Terri's bill. Is this reasonable? *Should* he be able to avoid payment?

4. Imagine that you are starting your own company in your hyper-competitive industry: You are putting your life savings, your professional contacts, and your innovative ideas on the line. As you begin to hire a sales force, you consider binding new employees to noncompete agreements. Outline the ideal terms of your employees' noncompetes. What is its duration? What is its geographical radius? Are these terms appropriate for your industry? When you are done, pass your proposed terms to classmates and discuss its enforceability.

5. When Ruth Klopp was injured in a serious accident with an uninsured motorist, she filed a claim under her own policy with Worldwide Insurance. Her policy contained an arbitration provision, stating that if the arbitrators awarded more than $15,000, either side could appeal to the courts, but a low award could not be appealed. The arbitrators awarded Klopp $90,000, and Worldwide demanded a full trial. Klopp claimed that the appeal provision was unconscionable. What was the result?

6. **ETHICS** Some commentators argue that Walker-Thomas Furniture was providing a valuable service to Mrs. Williams and that the litigation ultimately harmed her community. No other business of the time was willing to offer credit to people of such limited means, much less to African Americans. As a result of that landmark case, Walker-Thomas went out of business and an entire group of people lost access to essential household items. Comment.

ANSWERS TO SELECTED END OF CHAPTER QUESTIONS

MULTIPLE-CHOICE QUESTIONS

Presented are the answers for the ODD-numbered multiple-choice questions in the end-of-chapter material.

1. D
3. C
5. B

CASE QUESTIONS

Presented are the answers for all of the ODD-numbered case questions in the end-of-chapter material.

1. **Answer:** The West Virginia Supreme Court gave judgment for Art's, holding that the clause was indeed unconscionable. The yellow pages were a monopoly in this part of West Virginia, there was essentially no other advertising available to Art's, and the contract was an adhesion contract presented to Art's on a take it or leave it basis. The clause was unenforceable. *Art's Flower Shop v. Chesapeake & Potomac Tel. Co. of West Virginia*, 186 W. Va. 613, 413 S.E.2d 670, 1991 W. Va. LEXIS 216 (1991).

3. **Answer:** No. The noncompete clause is unenforceable here because the two companies are not really in competition and Guyan therefore has no confidential information or customer lists to protect. *Voorhees v. Guyan Machinery Co.*, 191 W. Va. 450, 446 S.E.2d 672, 1994 W.Va. LEXIS 27 (1994).

5. **Answer:** Oasis Waterpark won, and Hydrotech's case was dismissed. The court was not persuaded that many owners would seek out unlicensed builders and then trick them into working, with the intention of denying payment. The judges believed that awarding damages would encourage unlicensed builders to ignore the statute's requirement; in the long run, homeowners and others who rely on licensed workers would suffer. *Hydrotech Systems, Ltd. v. Oasis Waterpark*, 52 Cal.3d 988, 803 P.2d 370, 1991 Cal. LEXIS 139 (Sup. Ct. Cal. 1991).

Chapter 15

© Honza Krej/Shutterstock.com

VOIDABLE CONTRACTS: CAPACITY AND CONSENT

As the sole heiress to a copper fortune, Mrs. Clark knew unimaginable luxury—a palatial 42-room home on Fifth Avenue and a vast collection of rare art, antiques, and expensive dolls with custom clothes by the House of Dior. But Mrs. Clark was also a recluse: For 40 years, she lived alone, malnourished, and dehydrated amidst her opulence and her dolls, whom she considered her closest friends.

At 85, she was admitted to Beth Israel Medical Center for routine surgery. And there she stayed for 20 years, despite being in reasonably good health. She passed her days watching *The Smurfs* cartoons and tending to her dolls. Finally, she died at the hospital, aged 105.

After her death, peculiar tales surfaced. Over the years, she had given her doctor over $900,000. The hospital aggressively courted her for money. Memos from the hospital's president revealed that he was only too happy to house his wealthy (but healthy) tenant. Ultimately, in addition to the $1,200 per day charged for her stay, Mrs. Clark gave a prized Manet painting and many millions of dollars to Beth Israel.[1]

> **Huguette Clark had no family or human friends, but she *did* have over $300 million to her name—which tended to draw people to her.**

---

[1]Bill Dedman, *Empty Mansions* (Ballantine Books, 2013); Anemona Hartocollis, "Hospital Caring for an Heiress Pressed Her to Give Lavishly," *The New York Times*, May 29, 2013.

Clark's estate sued Beth Israel and her doctor, claiming they took advantage of the heiress to extract lavish gifts. Although this case is still pending as of this writing, this true story leads us to examine two issues that interfere with valid contract formation: capacity and consent.

Capacity means the legal ability of a party to enter a contract in the first place. Someone may lack capacity because of youth or mental infirmity. **Consent** refers to whether a contracting party truly understood the terms of the contract and whether she made the agreement voluntarily. Consent issues arise in cases of fraud, mistake, duress, and undue influence.

Problems with capacity and consent make a contract **voidable**. When a contract is voidable, one party has the option either to enforce or terminate the agreement. If her estate can prove that Clark did not understand her promises or was defrauded, mistaken, or coerced, it can terminate the contracts.

Voidable contract
When a contract is voidable, the injured party may choose to terminate it.

15-1 CAPACITY

Capacity is the legal ability to enter into a contract. An adult of sound mind has capacity. Generally, any deal she enters into will be enforced if all elements on the Contracts Checklist—agreement, consideration, and so forth—are present. But two groups of people usually lack legal capacity: minors and those with a mental impairment.

Contracts Checklist
- ☐ Offer
- ☐ Acceptance
- ☐ Consideration
- ☐ Legality
- ☑ Capacity
- ☐ Consent
- ☐ Writing

15-1a **Minors**

In contract law, a minor is someone under the age of 18. **Because a minor lacks legal capacity, she normally can create only a voidable contract.** A voidable contract may be canceled by the party who lacks capacity. Notice that *only the party lacking capacity* may cancel the agreement. So a minor who enters into a contract generally may choose between enforcing the agreement or negating it. The other party—an adult, or perhaps a store—has no such right. Voidable contracts are very different from those that are void, which we examined in Chapter 14, on legality. A *void* contract is illegal from the beginning and may not be enforced by either party. A *voidable* contract is legal but permits one party to escape, if she so wishes.

Disaffirmance

A minor who wishes to escape from a contract generally may **disaffirm** it; that is, he may notify the other party that he refuses to be bound by the agreement. There are several ways a minor may disaffirm a contract. He may simply tell the other party, orally or in writing, that he will not honor the deal. Or he may disaffirm a contract by refusing to perform his obligations under it. A minor may go further—he can undo a contract that has already been completed by filing a suit to **rescind** the contract; that is, to have a court formally cancel it.

Kevin Green was 16 when he signed a contract with Star Chevrolet to buy a used Camaro. Because he was a minor, the deal was voidable. When the Camaro blew a gasket and Kevin informed Star Chevrolet that he wanted his money back, he was disaffirming the contract. He happened to do it because the car suddenly seemed a poor buy, but he could have disaffirmed for any reason at all, such as deciding that he no longer liked Camaros. When Kevin disaffirmed the contract, he was entitled to his money back.

Disaffirm
To give notice of refusal to be bound by an agreement

Rescind
To cancel a contract

Restitution

A minor who disaffirms a contract must return the consideration he has received, to the extent he is able. Restoring the other party to its original position is called **restitution**. The consideration that Kevin Green received in the contract was, of course, the Camaro.

What happens if the minor is not able to return the consideration because he no longer has it or it has been destroyed? Most states hold that the minor is *still* entitled to his money back. A

Restitution
Restoring an injured party to its original position

minority of states follow the status quo rule, which provides that, if a minor cannot return the consideration, the adult or store is only required to return its *profit margin* to the minor.

Assume that Kevin's Camaro was totaled, not just in need of repair. He had originally bought the Camaro for $7,000. Star Chevrolet had paid $5,000 for the used car at auction and then marked it up $2,000.

In most states, Kevin would be entitled to the full $7,000 purchase price, even though the car is now worthless. The dealer would simply have to absorb the loss. But, if Kevin lives in a state with the status quo rule, then the dealer would have to refund only $2,000 to Kevin. It is permitted to keep the other $5,000 so that it breaks even on the transaction, or is "returned to the status quo."

Ethics The rule permitting a minor to disaffirm a contract is designed to discourage adults from making deals with innocent children, and it is centuries old. Is this rule still workable in our modern consumer society? There are entire industries devoted to (and dependent upon) minors. Think of children's films, breakfast cereal, and gaming apps. Does this rule imperil retailers? Is it *right* to give a 17-year-old high school senior so much power to cancel agreements? Is it *right* for a 17-year-old high school senior to take advantage of this rule?

Timing of Disaffirmance/Ratification

A minor may disaffirm a contract anytime before she reaches age 18. She also may disaffirm within a reasonable time *after* turning 18. Suppose that 17-year-old Bret signs a contract to buy a $3,000 3-D television. The following week, he picks up the TV and pays for it in full. Four months later, he turns 18, and two months after that—after his Super Bowl party—he disaffirms the contract. His disaffirmance is effective. In most states, he gets 100 percent of his money back. In some cases, minors have been entitled to disaffirm a contract several *years* after turning 18. But the minor's right to disaffirm ends if he ratifies the contract.

Ratification is made by any words or action indicating an intention to be bound by the contract. Suppose Bret, age 17, buys his TV on credit, promising to pay $150 per month. He has made only four payments by the time he turns 18, but after reaching his majority, he continues to pay every month for six more months. He then attempts to disaffirm the contract. Too late. His actions—payment of the monthly bill for six months as an adult—ratified the contract he entered into as a minor. He is now fully obligated to pay the entire $3,000, on the agreed-upon schedule. Hope the party was worth it.

Ratification
Words or actions indicating an intention to be bound by a contract

Exception: Necessaries

A necessary is something essential to a minor's life and welfare. Food, clothing, housing, and medical care are necessaries. In some circumstances, courts have considered less essential items, like legal advice, automobiles, and tuition, to be necessaries.

On a contract for necessaries, a minor must pay for the value of the benefit received. In other words, the minor may still disaffirm the contract and return whatever is unused. But he is liable to pay for whatever benefit he obtained from the goods while he had them. Thus, the 16-year-old who buys and eats a 99-cent cheeseburger and later disaffirms his contract with Burger Central is only liable for what the burger is *reasonably* worth, which is less than the 99-cent purchase price. (And, no, he does not have to return the burger.)

> In some circumstances, courts have considered less essential items, like legal advice, automobiles, and tuition, to be necessaries.

Exception: Misrepresentation of Age

The rules change somewhat if a minor lies about his age. Sixteen-year-old Dan is delighted to learn from his friend Bret that a minor can buy a fancy TV, use it for a year or so, and then get his money back. Dan drops into SoundBlast and asks to buy a $4,000 surround-sound system. The store clerk says that the store no longer sells expensive systems to underage customers. Dan produces a fake driver's license indicating that he is 18, and the gullible clerk sells him the system. A year later, Dan drives up to SoundBlast and unloads the system, now in shambles. He asks for his $4,000 back. Is he still permitted to disaffirm?

States have been troubled by this problem, and there is no clear rule. A few states will still permit Dan to disaffirm the contract entirely. The theory is that a minor must be saved from his own poor judgment, including his foolish lie. Many states, though, will prohibit Dan from disaffirming the contract. They take the reasonable position that the law was intended to protect childhood innocence, not calculated deceit.

15-1b Mentally Impaired Persons

You are a trial court judge. Don wants you to rule that his father, Cedric, is mentally incompetent and, on behalf of Cedric, to terminate a contract he signed. Here is the evidence:

Cedric is a 75-year-old millionaire who keeps $300,000 stuffed in pillow cases in the attic. He lives in a filthy house with a parrot whom he calls the Bishop, an iguana named Orlando, and a tortoise known as Mrs. Sedgely. All of the pets have small beds in Cedric's grungy bedroom, and each one eats at the dining table with its master. Cedric pays college students $50 an hour to read poetry to the animals, but he forbids the reading of sonnets, which he regards as "the devil's handiwork."

Don has been worried about Cedric's bizarre behavior for several years and has urged his father to enter a nursing home. Last week, when Don stopped in to visit, Cedric became angry at him, accusing his son of disrespecting the Bishop and Mrs. Sedgely, who were enjoying a fifteenth-century Castilian poem that Jane, a college student, was reading. Don then blurted out that Cedric was no longer able to take care of himself. Cedric snapped back, "I'll show you how capable I am." On the back of a 40-year-old menu, he scratched out a contract promising to give Jane "$100,000 today and $200,000 one year from today if she agrees to feed, house, and care for the Bishop, Orlando, and Mrs. Sedgely for the rest of their long lives." Jane *quickly* signed the agreement. Don urges that the court, on Cedric's behalf, declare the contract void. How will you rule? Courts often struggle when deciding cases of mental competence.

A person suffers from a mental impairment if, by reason of mental illness or defect, he is unable to understand the nature and consequences of the transaction.[2] The mental impairment can be due to some mental illness, such as schizophrenia, or to mental retardation, brain injury, senility, or any other cause that renders the person unable to understand the nature and consequences of the contract.

A party suffering a mental impairment usually creates only a voidable contract. The impaired person has the right to disaffirm the contract just as a minor does. But again, the contract is voidable, not void. The mentally impaired party generally has the right to full performance if she wishes.

The law creates an exception: If a person has been adjudicated incompetent, then all of his future agreements are void. "Adjudicated incompetent" means that a judge has made a formal finding that a person is mentally incompetent and has assigned the person a guardian by court order.

---

[2]For a similar case, see Harwell v. Garrett, 239 Ark. 551 (1965).

How will a court evaluate Cedric's mental status? Of course, if there had already been a judicial determination that he was insane, any contract he signed would be void. Since no judge has issued such a ruling about Cedric, the court will listen to doctors or therapists who have evaluated him and to anyone else who can testify about Cedric's recent conduct. The court may also choose to look at the contract itself, to see if it is so lopsided that no competent person would agree to it.

How will Don fare in seeking to preserve Cedric's wealth? Poorly. Unless Don has more evidence than we have heard thus far, he is destined to eat canned tuna while Jane and the Bishop dine on caviar. Cedric is decidedly eccentric, and perhaps unwise. But those characteristics do not prove mental impairment. Neither does leaving a fortune to a poetry reader. If Don could produce evidence from a psychiatrist that Cedric, for example, was generally delusional or could not distinguish a parrot from a religious leader, that would persuade a court of mental impairment. But on the evidence presented thus far, Mrs. Sedgely and friends will be living well.[3]

Intoxication

Similar rules apply in cases of drug or alcohol intoxication. **When one party is so intoxicated that he cannot understand the nature and consequences of the transaction, the contract is voidable.**

We wish to stress that courts are *highly* skeptical of intoxication arguments. If you go out drinking and make a foolish agreement, you are probably stuck with it. Even if you are too drunk to drive, you are probably not nearly too drunk to make a contract. If your blood alcohol level is, say, .08, your coordination and judgment are poor. Driving in such a condition is dangerous, but you probably have a fairly clear awareness of what is going on around you.

To back out of a contract on the grounds of intoxication, you must be able to provide evidence that you did not understand the "nature of the agreement," or the basic deal that you made.

The following Landmark Case is a rare exception, where the defendant was able to escape the deal.

Landmark Case

BABCOCK V. ENGEL

58 Mont. 597
Supreme Court of Montana, 1920

Facts: While Charles Engel's wife was out of town, he sat home alone, drinking mightily. During this period, he made an agreement with G. M. Babcock to trade a 320-acre farm and $2,000 worth of personal property for a hotel. Engel's property was worth approximately twice the value of the hotel. Engel later refused to honor the deal on the grounds that he had been intoxicated when he made the agreement.

Babcock sued, but the jury sided with Engel and dismissed the complaint. Babcock appealed.

Issue: *Was Engel so intoxicated that his agreement with Babcock became voidable?*

Excerpts from Justice Holloway's Decision: If, as a matter of fact, Engel was so far under the influence of intoxicating liquor when he signed the contract that he was incapable of giving his assent, it would be

---

[3]Barbara's Sales, Inc. v. Intel Corp., 879 N.E.2d 910 (Ill. 2007).

voidable at the election of Engel when he became sober.

[T]he jury answered that on November 22, Engel was "so under the influence of intoxicating liquors as to deprive him of his powers of reasoning and render him unable to comprehend the consequences of his act in executing said agreement."

Engel himself testified to the effect that, availing himself of his wife's absence from home, he had been indulging greatly to excess and had been drunk on November 21; that he drank heavily of whisky which he had at his home on the morning of November 22; that immediately upon his arrival in the town, he had four or five drinks of whisky and blackberry before he entered upon the negotiations with Babcock.

Four other witnesses, each apparently disinterested, testified that at the time in question, Engel was intoxicated, could not comprehend the nature of his acts, in other words, that he was not qualified to transact business. The jury determined upon the credibility of the witnesses.

Intoxication is not made a defense by the Codes, and there was a time in the history of our jurisprudence when courts refused to lend their aid to relieve one from the consequences of his own voluntary intemperance, but the doctrine has long since been abandoned. The courts do not now concern themselves so much with the question of intoxication as with the question of contractual capacity, and if in fact either party is not mentally capable of giving his free consent to the terms disclosed by the writing, it is altogether immaterial by what cause his incapacity was produced. The courts have simply recognized the fact that intoxication, among other things, may render a person incapable of making a binding contract.

The test approved by the great majority of the decisions is the same which is applied in other forms of mental derangement, namely, that the deed or contract will be voidable if the person, at the time of its execution, was so far under the influence of intoxicants as to be unable to understand the nature and consequences of his act, and unable to bring to bear upon the business in hand any degree of intelligent choice and purpose.

Affirmed.

Restitution

A mentally infirm party who seeks to void a contract must make restitution. If a party succeeds with a claim of mental impairment, the court will normally void the contract but will require the impaired party to give back whatever she got. Suppose that Danielle buys a Rolls-Royce and promises in writing to pay $5,000 per month for five years. Three weeks later, she seeks to void the contract on the grounds of mental impairment. She must return the Rolls. If the car has depreciated, Danielle normally will have to pay for the decrease in value. What happens if restitution is impossible? Generally, courts require a mentally infirm person to make full restitution if the contract is to be rescinded. If restitution is impossible, the court will not rescind the agreement unless the infirm party can show bad faith by the other party. This is because, unlike minority, which is generally easy to establish, mental competence may not be apparent to the other person negotiating.

Contracts Checklist
- [ ] Offer
- [ ] Acceptance
- [ ] Consideration
- [ ] Legality
- [ ] Capacity
- [✓] Consent
- [ ] Writing

15-2 REALITY OF CONSENT

Smiley offers to sell you his house for $300,000, and you agree in writing to buy it. After you move in, you discover that the house is sinking into the earth at the rate of 6 inches per week. In twelve months, your only access to the house may be through the chimney. You sue, seeking to rescind. You argue that when you signed the contract, you did not truly consent because you lacked essential information. In this section, we look at four claims that parties make in an effort to rescind a contract based on lack of valid consent: (1) fraud, (2) mistake, (3) duress, and (4) undue influence.

15-2a Fraud

Fraud begins when a party to a contract represents something that is factually wrong. "This house has no termites," says a homeowner to a prospective buyer. If the house is swarming with the nasty pests, the statement is a misrepresentation. But does it amount to fraud? An injured person must show the following:

1. The defendant knew that his statement was false, or that he made the statement recklessly and without knowledge of whether it was false;

2. The false statement was material; and

3. The injured party justifiably relied on the statement.

Element One: Intentional or Reckless Misrepresentation of Fact

The injured party must show a false statement of fact. Notice that this does not mean the statement was a necessarily a "lie." If a homeowner says that the famous architect Stanford White designed her house, but Bozo Loco actually did the work, it is a false statement.

Now, if the owner knows that Loco designed the house, she has committed the first element of fraud. If she has no idea who designed the house, her assertion that it was "Stanford White" also meets the first element.

But the owner might have a good reason for the error. Perhaps a local history book identifies the house as a Stanford White. If she makes the statement with a reasonable belief that she is telling the truth, she has made an innocent misrepresentation (discussed in the next section) and not fraud.

Opinions and "puffery" do not amount to fraud. An opinion is not a statement of fact. A seller says, "I think land values around here will be going up 20 or 30 percent for the foreseeable future." That statement is pretty enticing to a buyer, but it is not a false statement of fact. The maker is clearly stating her own opinion, and the buyer who relies on it does so at his peril. A close relative of opinion is something called "puffery."

Get ready for one of the most astonishing experiences you've ever had! This section on puffery is going to be the finest section of any textbook you have ever read! You're going to find the issue intriguing, the writing dazzling, and the legal summary unforgettable!

"But what happens," you might wonder, "if this section fails to astonish? What if I find the issue dull, the writing mediocre, and the legal summary incomprehensible? Can I sue for fraud?" No. The promises we made were mere puffery. A statement is puffery when a reasonable person would realize that it is a sales pitch, representing the exaggerated opinion of the seller. Puffery is not a statement of fact. Because puffery is not factual, it is never a basis for rescission.

Consumers filed a class action against Intel Corporation, claiming fraud. They asserted that Intel advertised its Pentium 4 computer chip as the "best" in the market when in fact it was no faster than the Pentium III chip. The Illinois Supreme Court dismissed the claims, asserting that no reasonable consumer would make a purchase relying solely on the name Pentium 4. Even if the consumers could show that Intel plotted to persuade the market that the Pentium 4 was the finest processor, they are demonstrating nothing but puffery because "best" could mean the chip is anything from the cheapest to the newest compared to other processors.[4]

Courts have found many similar phrases to be puffery, including "high-quality," "expert workmanship," and "you're in good hands with us."

---

[4]Laidlaw v. Organ, 15 U.S. 178 (1817).

Element Two: Materiality

The injured party must demonstrate that the statement was material, or important. A minor misstatement does not meet this second element of fraud. Was the misstatement likely to influence the decision of the misled party significantly? If so, it was material.

Imagine a farmer selling a piece of his land. He measures the acres himself and calculates a total of 200 acres. If the actual acreage is 199, he has almost certainly not made a *material* misstatement. But if the actual acreage is 150, he has.

Element Three: Justifiable Reliance

The injured party also must show that she actually did rely on the false statement and that her reliance was reasonable. Suppose the seller of a gas station lies through his teeth about the structural soundness of the building. The buyer believes what he hears but does not much care because he plans to demolish the building and construct a day-care center. There was a material misstatement but no reliance, and the buyer may not rescind.

The reliance must be justifiable—that is, reasonable. If the seller of wilderness land tells Lewis that the area is untouched by pollution, but Lewis can see a large lake on the property covered with 6 inches of oily red scum, Lewis is not justified in relying on the seller's statements. If he goes forward with the purchase, he may not rescind.

No Duty to Investigate. In the previous example, Lewis must act reasonably and keep his eyes open if he walks around the "wilderness" property. But he has no duty to undertake an investigation of what he is told. In other words, if the seller states that the countryside is pure and the lake looks crystal clear, Lewis is not obligated to take water samples and have them tested by a laboratory. A party to a contract has no obligation to investigate the other party's factual statements.

Plaintiff's Remedies for Fraud

In the case of fraud, the injured party generally has a choice of rescinding the contract or suing for damages or, in some cases, doing both. The contract is voidable, which means that injured party is not *forced* to rescind the deal but may if he wants. Fraud *permits* the injured party to cancel. Alternatively, the injured party can sue for damages—the difference between what the contract promised and what it delivered.

Nancy learns that the building she bought has a terrible heating system. A new one will cost $12,000. If the seller told her the system was "like new," Nancy may rescind the deal, but it may be economically harmful for her to do so. She might have sold her old house, hired a mover, taken a new job, and so forth. What are her other remedies? She could move into the new house and sue for the difference between what she got and what was promised, which is $12,000, the cost of replacing the heating system.

In some states, a party injured by fraud may both rescind *and* sue for damages. In these states, Nancy could rescind her contract, get her deposit back, and then sue the seller for any damages she has suffered. Her damages might be, for example, a lost opportunity to buy another house or wasted moving expenses.

In fact, this last option—rescinding and still suing for damages—is available in all states when a contract is for the sale of goods. **UCC §2-721 permits a party to rescind a contract and then sue for damages when fraud is committed.**

Innocent Misrepresentation

If all elements of fraud are present except the misrepresentation of fact was not made intentionally or recklessly, then **innocent misrepresentation** has occurred. So, if a person misstates a material fact and induces reliance, but he had good reason to believe that his statement was true, then he has not committed fraud. Most states allow rescission of a contract, but not damages, in such a case.

Special Problem: Silence

We know that a party negotiating a contract may not misrepresent a material fact. The house seller may not say that "the roof is in great shape" when she sleeps under an umbrella to avoid rain. But what about silence? Suppose that the seller knows the roof is in dreadful condition but the buyer never asks. Does the seller have an affirmative legal obligation to disclose what she knows?

In 1817, the United States Supreme Court laid down the general rule that a party had no duty to disclose, even when he knew that the other person was negotiating under a mistake.[5] In other words, the Court was reinforcing the old rule of *caveat emptor*, "let the buyer beware." But social attitudes about fairness have changed. Today, a seller who knows something that the buyer does not know is often required to divulge it.

Nondisclosure of a fact amounts to misrepresentation in these four cases: (1) where disclosure is necessary to *correct a previous assertion*, (2) where disclosure would correct a *basic mistaken assumption* that the other party is relying on, (3) where disclosure would correct the other party's *mistaken understanding about a writing*, or (4) where there is a *relationship of trust* between the two parties.[5]

To Correct a Previous Assertion.

During the course of negotiations, one party's perception of the facts may change. When an earlier statement later appears inaccurate, the change generally must be reported.

W. R. Grace & Co. wanted to buy a natural-gas field in Mississippi. An engineer's report indicated the presence of large gas reserves. On the basis of the engineering report, the Continental Illinois National Bank committed to a $75 million nonrecourse production loan. A "nonrecourse loan" meant that Continental would be repaid only with revenues from the gas field. After Continental committed, but before it had closed on the loan, Grace had an exploratory well drilled and struck it rich—with water. The land would never produce any gas. Without informing Continental of the news, Grace closed the $75 million loan. When Grace failed to repay, Continental sued and won. A party who learns new information indicating that a previous statement is inaccurate must disclose the bad news.[6]

To Correct a Basic Mistaken Assumption.

When one party knows that the other is negotiating with a mistaken assumption about an important fact, the party who knows of the error must correct it. Jeffrey Stambovsky agreed to buy Helen Ackley's house in Nyack, New York, for $650,000. Stambovsky signed a contract and made a $32,500 down payment. Before completing the deal, he learned that in several newspaper articles, Ackley had publicized the house as being haunted. Ackley had also permitted the house to be featured in a walking tour of the neighborhood as "a riverfront Victorian (*with ghost*)." Stambovsky refused to go through with the deal and sued to rescind. He won. The court ruled that Ackley sold the house knowing Stambovsky was ignorant of the alleged ghosts. She also knew that a reasonable buyer might avoid a haunted house, fearing grisly events—or diminished resale value. Stambovsky could not have discovered the apparitions himself, and Ackley's failure to warn permitted him to rescind the deal.[7]

What if the defect is … a ghost?

---

[5]Restatement (Second) of Contracts §161.
[6]FDIC v. W.R. Grace & Co., 877 F.2d 614 (7th Cir. 1989).
[7]Stambovsky v. Ackley, 169 A.D.2d 254 (N.Y. App. Div. 1991).

A seller generally must report any latent defect he knows about that the buyer should not be expected to discover himself. As social awareness of the environment increases, a buyer potentially worries about more and more problems. We now know that underground toxic waste, carelessly dumped in earlier decades, can be dangerous or even lethal. Accordingly, any property seller who realizes that there is toxic waste underground, or any other hidden hazard, must reveal that fact.

To Correct a Mistaken Understanding about a Writing.
Suppose the potential buyer of a vacation property has a town map showing that the land he wants to buy has a legal right of way to a beautiful lake. If the seller of the land knows that the town map is out of date and that there is no such right of way, she must disclose her information.

A Relationship of Trust.
Maria is planning to sell her restaurant to her brother Ricardo. Maria has a greater duty to reveal problems in the business because Ricardo assumes she will be honest. **When one party naturally expects openness and honesty, based on a close relationship, the other party must act accordingly.** If the building's owner has told Maria he will not renew her lease, she must pass that information on to Ricardo.

What happens if an owner, rather than disclosing hidden defects, sells the property "as is"? The following case provides insight.

HESS V. CHASE MANHATTAN BANK, USA, N.A.

220 S.W.3d 758
Missouri Supreme Court, 2007

Facts: Billy Stevens owned a paint company. On several occasions, he ordered employees to load a trailer with 55-gallon paint drums and pallets of old paint cans and then dump them on property he owned. This illegal dumping saved Stevens the cost of proper disposal. Later, employees notified the Environmental Protection Agency (EPA) of what Stevens had done, and the EPA began an investigation. (Stevens later served time for environmental crimes.)

Stevens defaulted on his mortgage to the land. While Chase Manhattan Bank was in the process of foreclosing, it learned that the EPA was investigating the property for contamination. Chase foreclosed and put the property up for sale "as is." Several buyers expressed interest. The bank did not inform any of them of the ongoing EPA investigation. Dennis Hess bought the property for $52,000.

After Hess bought the land, he discovered the illegal waste and sued Chase for failing to disclose the EPA's investigation. The jury awarded Hess $52,000 and Chase appealed.

Issue: *Did Chase have a duty to disclose to Hess the ongoing investigation?*

Excerpts from Judge Stith's Decision: The buyer has a right to rely on the seller to disclose where the undisclosed material information would not be discoverable through ordinary diligence. Chase learned that the EPA was investigating the property before Chase completed its foreclosure of the mortgage. Even with superior knowledge, a duty to disclose will be imposed only if the material facts would not be discovered through the exercise of ordinary diligence. Chase asserts that a reasonable inspection of the property by Hess would have disclosed the presence of the paint cans near the old barn foundation. Chase's argument misapprehends the factual basis of Hess's fraudulent nondisclosure claim. It is the *EPA investigation* into hazardous waste dumping on the property that is the material fact that Hess asserts Chase had a duty to disclose, not the presence (or absence) of paint cans.

Hess presented evidence that two potential buyers who did discover the paint cans each still made an offer to purchase the property. Both testified that the presence of paint cans did not give them notice that the EPA was investigating and that, had they known of its investigation, they would not have made offers for the property. From this evidence, the jury could have found that even had Hess further inspected the property and discovered the paint cans, this would not have put him on notice that the EPA had an ongoing investigation into hazardous waste dumping on the property.

Chase asserts that in spite of the evidence of its knowledge and Hess's inability to discover the EPA investigation, a duty to disclose should not be imposed because the contract specified that Chase was making "no representations, guaranties, or warranties, either written or implied, regarding the property" and that "the property is being sold in AS-IS condition with no express or implied representations or warranties by the seller or its agents." It claims that through these provisions, it bargained for the right to remain silent and no duty to speak ever arose.

What Chase misapprehends is that Hess alleges *fraud in the inducement* to contract, not fraud in the terms of the contract. Missouri law holds that a party may not, by disclaimer or otherwise, contractually exclude liability for fraud in inducing that contract. Each of the individuals who made an offer to purchase this property did so without knowledge that it was under EPA investigation. They all testified that, had they known, they would not have made an offer to purchase this property and would not, therefore, have "bargained for" Chase's silence. Chase's duty to speak arose from its superior knowledge prior to the execution of this contract. The presence of a clause disclaiming warranties in a contract does not negate a pre-contractual duty to speak.

Affirmed.

EXAM Strategy

Question: Mako is selling his country house for $400,000. Guppy, an interested buyer, asks whether there is sufficient water from the property's well. Mako replies, "Are you kidding? Watch this." He turns on the tap, and the water flows bountifully. Mako then shows Guppy the well, which is full. Guppy buys the property, but two weeks later, the well runs dry. In fact, Mako knew the water supply was inadequate, and he had the well filled by a tanker truck while the property was being sold. A hydrologist tells Guppy it will cost $100,000 to dig a better well, with no guarantee of success. Guppy sues Mako. What remedy should Guppy seek? Who will win?

Strategy: Is this a case of innocent misrepresentation or fraud? Fraud. Therefore, Guppy may seek two remedies: damages or rescission. Make sure that you understand the difference. To win, Guppy must show he relied on a fact that was both false and material.

Result: When Mako responded to Guppy's question by demonstrating the apparent abundance of water, he made a false statement. This was fraud (not innocent misrepresentation), because Mako knew the well was inadequate. That was a material fact. Guppy reasonably relied on the demonstration. Guppy will win. He can elect to rescind the contract (return the property to Mako and get his money back) or choose damages (the cost of digging a proper well). Given the uncertain nature of well digging, he would be wise to rescind.

15-2b Mistake

When she heard she was going to lose her job, Laura became very upset, so of course, she went shopping. She bought a pair of $1,345 orange stiletto heels, on final sale for $941.50. The shoes consoled Laura for about two hours, after which she realized she had made a big mistake: She could neither return the impractical shoes nor pay her credit card bill. Despite Laura's retail regret, contract law will not fix her mistake. Nor does it excuse her when she signs a contract without reading it. Generally, contract law forces parties to suffer the consequences of their folly. But in some cases, such as when one party seeks to profit unreasonably from another's error, rescission may be warranted on the grounds of mistake.

Not all mistakes are created equal: Some mistakes lead to voidable contracts; others create enforceable (if unfortunate) deals. How can we know the difference? First, we must ask who was mistaken because different rules apply to unilateral and **mutual mistakes**. We must also examine the character of the mistake to see if its circumstances warrant rescission.

Unilateral Mistake

Unilateral mistake
Occurs when only one party enters a contract under a mistaken assumption

A **unilateral mistake** occurs when one party enters a contract under a mistaken assumption; the other is not mistaken. It is not easy for the mistaken party to rescind a contract—the more astute party may simply have made a better bargain. So, to rescind a contract, a mistaken party must show something more than just a regrettable deal.

To rescind for unilateral mistake, the mistaken party must demonstrate that he entered the contract because of a basic factual error and that:

- the nonmistaken party knew or had reason to know of the error, or
- the mistake is mathematical or mechanical alone, or
- enforcing the contract would be unconscionable.

Knowledge of the Error. Every market has information asymmetries. That is, some contracting parties know more than others, which helps them secure favorable deals. The law of unilateral mistake draws the line where one party takes *unfair* advantage of what he knows to be another's error. **If the nonmistaken party knows or has reason to know of the other party's error, courts will not allow him to profit by snapping it up.**

Fernando is an art dealer who specializes in nineteenth-century French painting. At Fiona's flea market stall, he sees a painting that he suspects is by Gustave Courbet. Knowing the painting could be worth millions, Fernando offers Fiona $10 for it. She accepts his offer because she thinks the painting is, at best, by one of Courbet's students. Fernando then does further research, which confirms his guess. He ultimately auctions the masterpiece for $2.4 million. For Fiona to be able to rescind the contract, she must show that Fernando's hunch was much more than a lucky guess, that he had known certainly that the painting was by Courbet. Practically speaking, cases like these are difficult for plaintiffs to win because they must prove that the nonmistaken party knew and that the parties had not assumed the risk of the error.

Mathematical and Mechanical Errors. Two plus two is four; but what happens when it is accidentally forty? Whether the mistake is due to bad math or a typographical error, courts generally allow the nonmistaken party to undo the faulty agreement, if there is clear and convincing evidence that the term was a mistake. A town obtains five bids for construction of a new municipal swimming pool. Four are between $100,000 and $111,000. Fred's bid is for $82,000. His offer includes a figure of $2,000 for excavation work, while all the others have allotted about $20,000 for that work. It is obvious that Fred has inadvertently dropped a zero, resulting in a bid that is $18,000 too low. Town officials are quick to accept Fred's offer. When he sues to rescind, Fred wins. Town

AP Images/Art Institue of Chicago

What would you do if you saw this painting in a flea market for $6?

officials knew that the work could not be done that cheaply, and it would be unfair to hold Fred to a mathematical error.[8]

Unconscionability. When enforcing the contract would result in exploitation or unfairness, contracts are voidable. St. Mary's School conducts an annual fundraising raffle, whose grand prize is free school tuition for a year. Accidentally, a machine prints multiple raffle tickets with the same number. As a result, ten people hold winning tickets and claim the tuition award. Since enforcing these ten agreements would likely bankrupt the school, a court will look kindly upon St. Mary's (even though the ten winners might not).

In the following case, an automobile dealer made a mistake in the customer's favor—how often does this happen?

DONOVAN V. RRL CORPORATION

26 Cal.4th 261
Supreme Court of California, 2001

Facts: Brian Donovan was in the market for a used car. As he scanned the Costa Mesa *Daily Pilot*, he came upon a "Pre-Owned Coup-A-Rama Sale!" at Lexus of Westminster. Of the 16 cars listed in the ad (with vehicle identification numbers), one was a sapphire-blue Jaguar XJ6 Vanden Plas, priced at $25,995.

Brian drove to a Jaguar dealership to do some comparison shopping. Jaguars of the same year and mileage cost about $8,000 to $10,000 more than the auto at the Lexus agency. The next day, Brian and his wife hurried over to the Coup-A-Rama event, spotted the Jaguar and asked a salesperson why it had such a good price. The salesperson responded that, as a Lexus dealership, it could offer better prices than Jaguar and suggested that the Donovans test drive it. Pleased with the ride, Brian said to the salesman, "O.K. We will take it at your price, $26,000." This figure startled the sales representative, who glanced at the newspaper ad Brian showed him, and responded, "That's a mistake."

As indeed it was. The Lexus agency had paid $35,000 for the Jaguar and intended to sell it for about $37,000. Brian was adamant. "No, I want to buy it at your advertised price, and I will write you a check right now." The sales manager was called in, and he refused to sell the car for less than $37,000.

It turned out that the *Daily Pilot*'s typographical and proofreading errors had caused the mistake, although the Lexus dealership had failed to review the proof sheet, which would have revealed the error before the ad went to press.

Brian sued. The trial court found that unilateral mistake prevented enforcement of the contract. The appellate court

reversed the decision, and Donovan appealed to the state's highest court.

The state supreme court first ruled that there *was* in fact a contract between the parties. (Generally, a newspaper advertisement is merely a solicitation for an offer, but a California statute generally holds *automobile dealers* to the terms of their offers.) The court then went on to examine the mistake to determine if the contract was enforceable.

Issue: *Did the Lexus dealer's mistake entitle it to rescind the contract?*

Excerpts from Justice George's Decision: A significant error in the price term of a contract constitutes a mistake regarding a basic assumption upon which the contract is made, and such a mistake ordinarily has a material effect adverse to the mistaken party. The defendant must show that the resulting imbalance in the agreed exchange is so severe that it would be unfair to require the defendant to perform.

Measured against this standard, defendant's mistake in the contract for the sale of the Jaguar automobile constitutes a material mistake regarding a basic assumption upon which it made the contract. Enforcing the contract with the mistaken price of $25,995 would require defendant to sell the vehicle to plaintiff for $12,000 less than the intended advertised price of $37,995—an error amounting to 32 percent of the price defendant intended. The exchange of performances would be substantially less desirable for defendant and more desirable for plaintiff.

The mere fact that a mistaken party could have avoided the mistake by the exercise of reasonable care

---

[8]Restatement (Second) of Contracts §153.

does not preclude avoidance on the ground of mistake. Indeed, since a party can often avoid a mistake by the exercise of such care, the availability of relief would be severely circumscribed if he were to be barred by his negligence. Nevertheless, in *extreme cases,* the mistaken party's fault is a proper ground for denying him relief for a mistake that he otherwise could have avoided.

If we were to accept plaintiff's position that that the dealer always must be held to the strict terms of a contract arising from an advertisement, we would be holding that the dealer intended to assume the risk of all typographical errors in advertisements, no matter how serious the error and regardless of the circumstances in which the error was made. For example, if an automobile dealer proofread an advertisement but, through carelessness, failed to detect a typographical error listing a $75,000 automobile for sale at $75, the defense of mistake would be unavailable to the dealer.

No evidence presented at trial suggested that defendant knew of the mistake before plaintiff attempted to purchase the automobile, that defendant intended to mislead customers, or that it had adopted a practice of deliberate indifference regarding errors in advertisements. The uncontradicted evidence established that the *Daily Pilot* made the proofreading error resulting in defendant's mistake.

We conclude that the municipal court correctly entered judgment in defendant's favor.

Mutual Mistake

A mutual mistake occurs when both contracting parties share the same mistake. If the contract is based on a fundamental factual error by both parties, the contract is voidable by either one.

But what types of errors are important enough to warrant rescission? Generally, when the parties are mistaken as to the existence or the identity of the contract's subject matter, the contract is voidable. Believing himself the rightful owner, Arthur contracts to sell a parcel of land to James. When it is later discovered that the land never belonged to Arthur, James can rescind the contract. Both parties were mistaken as to the existence of Arthur's land.

Farnsworth believes he is selling Corbin a topaz, and Corbin thinks he is buying a topaz. In fact, both are wrong: The stone turns out to be a diamond. Since the parties made a material error as to the subject of their contract, there was no valid assent and either one can rescind.

The following case is read by every U.S. law student. It illustrates a basic factual mistake as to the subject matter of a contract. When is a cow more than a cow? Answer: When it is two.

Landmark Case

SHERWOOD V. WALKER

66 Mich. 568
Supreme Court of Michigan, 1887

Facts: Rose 2d of Aberlone was a gentle, 1,420 lb. cow that lived in Michigan in 1886. Rose's owner, Hiram Walker & Sons, was a cattle breeder who bought her for $850. After a few years, Walker concluded that Rose could have no calves. As a barren cow, she was worth much less than $850, so Walker agreed to sell her for beef to T. C. Sherwood. Walker told Sherwood that Rose was "probably barren, and would not breed." After some negotiation, Walker agreed to sell Rose for "five and one-half cents per pound, live weight, fifty pounds shrinkage," or $80.

But when Sherwood came to collect Rose, the parties realized that (surprise!) she was pregnant. As a confirmed breeder, Rose was now worth about $1,000. Walker refused to part with the happy mother, and Sherwood sued for breach of contract. Walker defended, claiming that both parties had made a *mistake* and that the contract was voidable. After the lower court ruled the contract was enforceable, Walker appealed.

Issue: *Does a mutual mistake of fact render a contract voidable?*

Excerpts from Justice Morse's Decision: A party who has given an apparent consent to a contract of sale may refuse to execute it, or he may avoid it after it has been completed, if the assent was founded, or the contract made, upon the mistake of a material fact—such as the subject matter of the sale, the price, or some collateral fact materially inducing the agreement; and this can be done when the mistake is mutual.

If there is a difference as to the substance of the thing bargained for, then there is no contract; but if it be only a difference in some quality or accident, the contract remains binding.

The mistake of the parties went to the whole substance of the agreement. The parties would not have made the contract of sale except upon the understanding and belief that she was incapable of breeding, and of no use as a cow. A barren cow is substantially a different creature than a breeding one. There is as much difference between them for all purposes of use as there is between an ox and a cow that is capable of breeding and giving milk. The mistake affected the character of the animal for all time, and for its present and ultimate use. She was not in fact the animal, or the kind of animal, the defendants intended to sell or the plaintiff to buy.

The mistake affected the substance of the whole consideration, and it must be considered that there was no contract to sell or sale of the cow as she actually was. The thing sold and bought had in fact no existence. Defendants had a right to rescind, and to refuse to deliver, and the verdict should be in their favor.

The defense of mistake is not a cure-all for all bad deals. Courts will not rescind contracts on the basis of a prediction error, a mistaken value, or where the parties assume the risk of error.

Prediction Error. Sherwood and Walker were both wrong about Rose's reproductive ability, and the error was basic enough to cause a tenfold difference in price. Walker, the injured party, was entitled to rescind the contract. Note that the error must be *factual*. Suppose Walker sold Rose thinking that the price of beef was going to drop, when in fact the price rose 60 percent in five months. That would be simply a *prediction* that proved wrong, and Walker would have no right to rescind.

Mistake of Value. Here is one case in which it pays to know less. Suppose that Fiona the flea market vendor sold the nineteenth-century masterpiece for $100 to Marguerite, a financial analyst with no inkling of its real worth. Both Fiona and Marguerite shared the same mistake in their estimate of the painting's market value. Sadly for Fiona, Marguerite will reap the benefit of her bargain, because a mistaken value alone is not enough to take back a deal.

Conscious Uncertainty. No rescission is permitted where one of the parties knows he is taking on a risk; that is, he realizes there is uncertainty about the quality of the thing being exchanged. Rufus offers 10 acres of mountainous land to Priscilla. "I can't promise you anything about this land," he says, "but they've found gold on every adjoining parcel." Priscilla, eager for gold, buys the land, digs long and hard, and discovers—mud. She may not rescind the contract. She understood the risk she was assuming, and there was no mutual mistake.

15-2c Duress

True consent is also lacking when one party agrees to a contract under **duress**. If kindly Uncle Hugo signs over the deed to the ranch because Niece Nelly is holding a gun to his head, Hugo has not consented in any real sense, and he will have the right to rescind the contract.

Duress
An improper threat made to force another party to enter into a contract

If one party makes an improper threat that causes the victim to enter into a contract, and the victim had no reasonable alternative, the contract is voidable.

On a Sunday morning, Bancroft Hall drove to pick up his daughter Sandra, who had slept at a friend's house. The Halls are black and the neighborhood was white. A suspicious neighbor called the police, who arrived, aggressively prevented the Halls from getting into their own car, and arrested the father. The Halls had not violated any law or otherwise done anything wrong. Later an officer told Hall that he could leave immediately if he signed a release relinquishing his right to sue the police, but that if he refused to sign it, he would be detained for a bail hearing. Hall signed the release but later filed suit. The police defended based on the release.

The court held that the release was voidable because Hall had signed it under duress. The threat to detain Hall for a bail hearing was clearly improper because he had committed no crime. He also had no reasonable alternative to signing. A jury awarded the Halls over half a million dollars.[9]

Can "improper threats" take other forms? Does *economic* intimidation count? Many plaintiffs have posed that question over the last half century, and courts have grudgingly yielded.

Today, in most states, economic duress *can* also be used to void a contract. But economic duress sounds perilously close to hard bargaining—in other words, business. The free market system is expected to produce tough competition. A smart, aggressive executive may bargain fiercely. How do we distinguish economic duress from legal, successful business tactics? Courts have created no single rule to answer the question, but they do focus on certain issues.

In analyzing a claim of economic duress, courts look at these factors:

- Acts that have no legitimate business purpose
- Greatly unequal bargaining power
- An unnaturally large gain for one party
- Financial distress to one party

Is the following case one of duress or hard bargaining?

---

[9]Halls v. Ochs, 817 F.2d 920 (1st Cir. 1987).

You be the Judge

Facts: Amy Maida sued her employer, RLS Legal Solutions, for various claims relating to her job. RLS asked that the case be dismissed because Maida had signed an arbitration agreement. Maida had in fact signed the contract while already working at RLS. However, she responded that the agreement should not be enforced because she had signed it under economic duress. At trial, she was asked whether she had found the agreement acceptable:

In Re RLS Legal Solutions, L.L.C.
221 S.W.3d 629
Supreme Court of Texas, 2007

"I did not. The arbitration clause was going to allow me not to be able to be in a position that I needed to be in now, and that is, to have someone represent me to help me where I feel like the company did me wrong.

After I refused to agree to this arbitration clause, I was told that my payroll checks would not be direct deposited into my account until I signed the agreement and that I would not be paid until I signed the agreement. I had received my paychecks by direct deposit for three years. [RLS did in fact stop the direct deposit payment of Maida's salary.]

I needed my paycheck to meet my financial responsibilities since I am a single family income household provider. I had no way to pay my mortgage, vehicle note, car and homeowner's insurance as well as any household bills."

Maida testified that after signing and returning the agreement, she received a manual check. Maida said that when she asked why she had not been paid by direct deposit as usual, she was told her paycheck would be held until she signed the agreement.

RLS argued that Maida had eventually received every paycheck to which she was entitled, had suffered no losses, and was free to leave RLS at any time if she found her employment terms unacceptable.

The trial court refused to dismiss the case or order arbitration, and RLS appealed.

You Be the Judge: *Did Maida sign the arbitration under economic duress?*

Argument for RLS: Your honors, it is hard to take seriously a claim of economic duress when the plaintiff has not lost one cent and was never forced to sign anything. RLS runs a business, not a community center.

To stay competitive, we constantly revise our commercial practices, and this was one such change. We did not ask for a bizarre or inappropriate change: Arbitration is a widely favored method of settling disputes, quicker and cheaper *for all parties*. Maida signed. Yes, we stopped direct deposit of her check, but in the end, we paid her all she was due. We were not obligated to pay her in any particular fashion, or even to continue her employment. If she wanted to stay with us, she had to play by our rules.

Argument for Maida: The company could offer an arbitration contract to all workers. But that is distinct from forcing such agreements down employee throats, which is what they did here. RLS knows that its workers depend on prompt payment of payroll checks to avoid falling quickly into debt. The company offered Maida the arbitration agreement, she rejected it, and they responded by stopping direct deposit of her check. Knowing that she was the sole provider for her family, the firm intended to subject her to intolerable economic pressure. It worked. However, the court should have no part of this coercion. The two sides had hugely differing bargaining power, and RLS attempted to use financial distress to obtain what it could not by persuasion.

15-2d Undue Influence

Recall the hospital-bound Huguette Clark, who had penchants for the Smurfs and million-dollar gifts. If her estate can prove that Beth Israel and her physician preyed upon her vulnerability to get her money, it can rescind her agreements based on *undue influence*. Where one party has used undue influence, the contract is voidable at the option of the injured party. There are two elements to the plaintiff's case. **To prove undue influence, the injured party must demonstrate:**

- A relationship between the two parties either of trust or of domination, and

- Improper persuasion by the stronger party.[10]

Heiresses are not the only victims of undue influence. Eighty-year-old Agnes Seals owned a small building in New York City, but she was homebound and unable to care for herself or the property. A 35-year-old neighbor, David Aviles, seemingly came to her rescue. Promising to take care of her for the rest of her life, he earned her trust by bringing her groceries and ultimately convinced her to sell him her building at a deep discount. At the

---

[10]Restatement (Second) of Contracts §177.

closing, Mrs. Seals was represented by an attorney of David's choosing whom she had never met. The court ruled that David exploited Mrs. Seals for his own financial gain and that undue influence rendered the transactions voidable.[11]

Chapter Conclusion

Agreement alone may not be enough to make a contract enforceable. A minor or a mentally impaired person may generally disaffirm contracts. Even if both parties are adults of sound mind, courts will insist that consent be genuine. Misrepresentation, mistake, duress, and undue influence all indicate that at least one party did not truly consent. As the law evolves, it imposes an increasingly greater burden of *good faith negotiating* on the party in the stronger position.

EXAM REVIEW

1. **VOIDABLE CONTRACT** Capacity and consent are different contract issues that can lead to the same result: a voidable contract. A voidable agreement is one that can be canceled by a party who lacks legal capacity or who did not give true consent.

2. **MINORS** A minor (someone under the age of 18) generally may disaffirm any contract while she is still a minor or within a reasonable time after reaching age 18.

EXAM Strategy

Question: John Marshall and Kirsten Fletcher decided to live together. They leased an apartment, each agreeing to pay one-half of the rent. When he signed the lease, Marshall was 17. Shortly after signing the lease, Marshall turned 18, and two weeks later, he moved into the apartment. He paid his half of the rent for two months and then moved out because he and Fletcher were not getting along. Fletcher sued Marshall for one-half of the monthly rent for the remainder of the lease. Who wins?

Strategy: Marshall was clearly a minor when he signed the lease, and he could have rescinded the agreement at that time. However, after he turned 18, he moved in and began to pay rent. What effect did that have on his contract obligation? (See the "Result" at the end of this section.)

3. **MENTAL IMPAIRMENT** A mentally impaired person may generally disaffirm a contract. In such a case, though, he generally must make restitution.

---

[11]Sepulveda v. Aviles, 762 N.Y.S.2d 358 (NY S. Ct. 2003).

4. **INTOXICATION** A person who is so intoxicated that he fails to understand the nature of an agreement may disaffirm a contract.

5. **FRAUD** Fraud is grounds for rescinding a contract. The injured party must prove all of the following:

a. A false statement of fact made intentionally or recklessly

b. Materiality

c. Justifiable reliance

6. **INNOCENT MISREPRESENTATION** Innocent misrepresentation also allows an injured party to rescind a contract, but it does not allow a plaintiff to sue for damages. It has the same elements as fraud, but it does not require intent or recklessness.

EXAM Strategy

Question: Ron buys 1,000 "Smudgy Dolls" for his toy store. Karen, the seller, tells him the dolls are in perfect condition, even though she knows their heads are defectively attached. Ron sells all of the products, but then he has to face 1,000 angry customers with headless dolls. Ron sues Karen seeking recission. What is the likely outcome?

a. This is fraud, and Ron will be able to rescind.

b. This is an innocent misrepresentation, and Ron will be able to rescind.

c. This is fraud, but Ron will not be able to rescind.

d. This is an innocent misrepresentation, but Ron will not be able to rescind.

e. This is neither fraud nor an innocent misrepresentation.

Strategy: Karen knew her statement was false, so this is a case of fraud if all elements can be met. Ron must prove a false statement of fact, materiality, and reliance. Can he do so? (See the "Result" at the end of this section.)

7. **SILENCE** Silence amounts to misrepresentation only in four instances:

- When disclosure is necessary to correct a previous assertion
- When disclosure would correct a basic mistaken assumption on which the other party is relying
- When disclosure would correct the other party's mistaken understanding about a writing
- Where there is a relationship of trust between the two parties.

8. **UNILATERAL MISTAKE** In a case of unilateral mistake, the injured party may rescind only upon a showing that the other party knew or had reason to know of the mistake, the mistake was solely mathematical or mechanical, or that enforcement would be unconscionable.

9. **MUTUAL MISTAKE.** When both parties to a contract make the same fundamental factual error as to the existence or the identity of the contract's subject matter, either party may rescind.

10. **DURESS** If one party makes an improper threat that causes the victim to enter into a contract, and the victim had no reasonable alternative, the contract is voidable.

EXAM Strategy

Question: Andreini's nerve problem diminished the use of his hands. Dr. Beck operated, but the problem grew worse. A nurse told the patient that Beck might have committed a serious error that exacerbated the problem. Andreini returned for a second operation, which Beck assured him would correct the problem. But after Andreini had been placed in a surgical gown, shaved, and prepared for surgery, the doctor insisted that he sign a release relieving Beck of liability for the first operation. Andreini did not want to sign it, but Beck refused to operate until he did. Later, Andreini sued Beck for malpractice. A trial court dismissed Andreini's suit based on the release. You are on the appeals court. Will you affirm the dismissal or reverse?

Strategy: Andreini is claiming physical duress. Did Beck act *improperly* in demanding a release? Did Andreini have a *realistic alternative?* (See the "Result" at the end of this section.)

11. **UNDUE INFLUENCE** Once again the injured party may rescind a contract, but only upon a showing of a special relationship of trust and improper persuasion.

2. Result: A minor can disaffirm a contract. However, if he turns 18 and then ratifies the agreement, he is fully liable. When he paid the rent, Marshall ratified the contract, and thus he is fully liable.

6. Result: Karen made a false statement of fact, knowing it was wrong. It was material, and Ron reasonably relied on her. Karen has committed fraud. Ron is entitled to rescind the agreement. The correct answer is "a."

10. Result: The Utah Supreme Court reversed the trial court, so you probably should as well. Beck forced Andreini to sign under duress. The threat to withhold surgery was improper, and Andreini had no reasonable alternative.

MULTIPLE-CHOICE QUESTIONS

1. Kerry finds a big green ring in the street. She shows it to Leroy, who says, "Wow. That could be valuable." Neither Kerry nor Leroy knows what the ring is made of or whether it is valuable. Kerry sells the ring to Leroy for $100, saying, "Don't come griping if it turns out to be worth two dollars." Leroy takes the ring to a jeweler who

tells him it is an unusually perfect emerald, worth at least $75,000. Kerry sues to rescind.

(a) Kerry will win based on fraud.

(b) Kerry will win based on mutual mistake.

(c) Kerry will win based on unilateral mistake.

(d) Kerry will lose.

2. Veronica has a beer and then makes a contract. She continues drinking, and her blood alcohol level eventually rises to .09, which is just above her state's threshold for drunk driving. She makes a second contract while in this condition. Veronica's first contract is _____ , and her second contract is _____ .

(a) valid; valid

(b) valid; voidable

(c) voidable; voidable

(d) voidable; void

3. Jerry is so mentally ill that he is unable to understand the nature and consequences of his transactions, but he has not been adjudicated insane. Penny has been adjudicated insane, and has a court-appointed a guardian. Jerry's contracts are _____ , and Penny's contracts are _____ .

(a) valid; valid

(b) valid; voidable

(c) valid; void

(d) voidable; voidable

(e) voidable; void

4. Angela makes a material misstatement of fact to Lance, which he relies on when he signs Angela's contract. Fraud exists if Angela made the misstatement _____ .

(a) intentionally

(b) recklessly

(c) carelessly

(d) a and b only

(e) a, b, and c

5. Scarborough's Department Store opens for business on a busy shopping day just before Christmas. A hurried clerk places a sign in the middle of a table piled high with red cashmere sweaters. The sign reads, "SALE—100% Cashmere—$0.99 Each." The sign, of course, was supposed to read "$99 each."

This is a _____ mistake, and customers _____ be able to demand that Scarborough's sell the sweaters for 99 cents.

(a) unilateral; will

(b) unilateral; will not

(c) mutual; will

(d) mutual; will not

CASE QUESTIONS

1. Raymond Barrows owned a 17-acre parcel of undeveloped land in Seaford, Delaware. For most of his life, Mr. Barrows had been an astute and successful businessman, but by the time he was 85 years old, he had been diagnosed as "very senile and confused 90 percent of the time." Glenn Bowen offered to buy the land. Barrows had no idea of its value, so Bowen had it appraised by a friend, who said it was worth $50,000. Bowen drew up a contract, which Barrows signed. In the contract, Barrows agreed to sell the land for $45,000, of which Bowen would pay $100 at the time of closing; the remaining $44,900 was due whenever Bowen developed the land and sold it. There was no time limit on Bowen's right to develop the land nor any interest due on the second payment. Comment.

2. On television and in magazines, Maurine and Mamie Mason saw numerous advertisements for Chrysler Fifth Avenue automobiles. The ads described the car as "luxurious," "quality-engineered," and "reliable." When they went to inspect the car, the salesman told them the warranty was "the best ... comparable to Cadillacs and Lincolns." After the Masons bought a Fifth Avenue, they began to have many problems with it. Even after numerous repairs, the car was unsatisfactory and required more work. The Masons sued, seeking to rescind the contract based on the ads and the dealer's statement. Will they win?

3. The McAllisters had several serious problems with their house, including leaks in the ceiling, a buckling wall, and dampness throughout. They repaired the buckling wall by installing I-beams to support it. They never resolved the leaks and the dampness. When they decided to sell the house, they said nothing to prospective buyers about the problems. They stated that the I-beam had been added for reinforcement. The Silvas bought the house for $60,000. Soon afterward, they began to have problems with leaks, mildew, and dampness. Are the Silvas entitled to any money damages? Why or why not?

4. Roy Newburn borrowed money and bought a $49,000 truck from Treadwell Ford. A few months later, the truck developed transmission problems. Newburn learned that the truck had 170,000 more miles on it than the odometer indicated. The company admitted the mileage error and promised to install a new transmission for free. Treadwell did install the new transmission, but when Newburn came to pick up the truck, Treadwell demanded that he sign a general release absolving the dealership of any claims based on the inaccurate mileage. Treadwell refused to turn over the truck until Newburn finally signed. The truck broke down again, and delays cost Newburn so much income that he fell behind on his loan payments and lost the truck. He sued Treadwell, which defended based on the release. Is the release valid?

5. Morell bought a security guard business from Conley, including the property on which the business was located. Neither party knew that underground storage tanks were leaking and contaminating the property. After the sale, Morell discovered the tanks and sought to rescind the contract. Should he be allowed to do so?

DISCUSSION QUESTIONS

1. Sixteen-year-old Travis Mitchell brought his Pontiac GTO into M&M Precision Body and Paint for body work and a paint job. M&M did the work and charged $1,900, which Travis paid. When Travis later complained about the quality of the work, M&M did some touching up, but Travis was still dissatisfied. He demanded his $1,900 back, but M&M refused to refund it because all of the work was "in" the car and Travis could not return it to the shop. The state of Nebraska, where this occurred, follows the majority rule on this issue. Does Travis get his money? Is this a *fair* result?

2. Contract law gives minors substantial legal protection. But does a modern high school student *need* so much protection? Older teens may have been naive in the 1700s, but today, they are quite savvy. Should the law change so that only younger children—perhaps those aged 14 and under—have the ability to undo agreements? Or is the law reasonable the way it currently exists?

3. Ball-Mart, a baseball card store, had a 1968 Nolan Ryan rookie card in almost perfect condition for sale. Any baseball collector would have known that the card was worth at least $1,000; the published monthly price guide listed its market value at $1,200. Bryan was a twelve-year-old boy with a collection of over 40,000 baseball cards. When Bryan went to Ball-Mart, Kathleen, who knew nothing about cards, was filling in for the owner. The Ryan card was marked "1200," so Bryan asked Kathleen if this meant twelve dollars. She said yes and sold it to him for that amount. When Ball-Mart's owner realized the mix-up, he sued to rescind the contract. Who wins?

4. Paula was alone, pregnant, and confused. She needed help and support, which she found at Methodist Mission Home of Texas. In the days following her child's birth, representatives of Methodist Mission forcefully told her that she had no moral or legal right to keep her child: She had to place her baby for adoption. Paula signed the adoption papers, but days later, she decided she wanted to keep the baby after all. Was there any ground to rescind?

5. Do you have sympathy for intoxicated people who make agreements? Should the law ever let them back out of deals when they sober up? After all, no one forced them to get drunk. Should the law be more lenient, or is it reasonable as it currently exists?

6. When Steven Simkin and Laura Blank divorced in 2006, they agreed to split their $13.5 million fortune evenly. Two years later, it became evident that Simkin had a problem: His half was invested in Bernard Madoff's giant Ponzi scheme and he lost millions. Simkin asked Blank to revise their deal and she refused, so he sued to rescind their 2006 settlement based on mutual mistake of fact. He argued that the fatal mistake was that neither party knew that his half was invested in a fraud. Should a court invalidate the settlement for this mistake?

ANSWERS TO SELECTED END OF CHAPTER QUESTIONS

MULTIPLE-CHOICE QUESTIONS

Presented are the answers for the ODD-numbered multiple-choice questions in the end-of-chapter material.

1. D
3. E
5. B

CASE QUESTIONS

Presented are the answers for all of the ODD-numbered case questions in the end-of-chapter material.

1. **Answer:** The contract is voidable by Barrows's family. Barrows suffered from a mental impairment, senility. The contract is completely one-sided, with almost no money as a down payment and no interest. This reinforces the impression that Barrows was impaired. The family was permitted to rescind. *Barrows v. Bowen*, 1994 Del. Ch. LEXIS 63 (Del. Ch. 1994).

3. **Answer:** The Silvas are entitled to damages for fraud (saying the I-beams had been added merely for reinforcement) and nondisclosure (not mentioning the problems). The jury awarded $21,000 damages and $15,000 punitive damages, and the state supreme court affirmed the verdict. *Silva v. Stevens*, 156 Vt. 94, 589 A.2d 852, 1991 Vt. LEXIS 42 (1991).

5. **Answer:** Yes. There was no fraud or misrepresentation because Conley knew nothing of the tanks. But there is mutual mistake: The parties were both in error about an important factual assumption—namely, the ground's condition. Morell was permitted to rescind. *Morell v. Conley Detective and Security Guard Agency, Inc., Michigan Lawyers Weekly*, No. 18079, Nov. 28, 1994 (Mich. Ct. App. 1994).

WRITTEN CONTRACTS

> Perry moved out of their dorm room into a suite at the Ritz and refused to give Oliver one cent.

Chapter 16

WRITTEN CONTRACTS

© Honza Krej/Shutterstock.com

Oliver and Perry were college roommates, two sophomores with contrasting personalities. They were sitting in the cafeteria with some friends, Oliver chatting away, Perry slumped on a plastic bench. Oliver suggested that they buy a lottery ticket, as the prize for that week's drawing was $13 million. Perry muttered, "Nah. You never win if you buy just one ticket." Oliver bubbled up, "OK, we'll buy a ticket every week. We'll keep buying them from now until we graduate. Come on, it'll be fun. This month, I'll buy the tickets. Next month, you will, and so on." Other students urged Perry to do it and, finally, he agreed.

The two friends carefully reviewed their deal. Each party was providing consideration—namely, the responsibility for purchasing tickets during his month. The amount of each purchase was clearly defined at one dollar. They would start that week and continue until graduation day, two and a half years down the road.

> **Perry moved out of their dorm room into a suite at the Ritz and refused to give Oliver one red cent.**

Finally, they would share equally any money won. As three witnesses looked on, they shook hands on the bargain. That month, Oliver bought a ticket every week, randomly choosing numbers, and won nothing. The next month, Perry bought a ticket with equally random numbers—and won $52 million. Perry moved out of their dorm room into a suite at the Ritz and refused to give Oliver one red cent. Oliver sued, seeking $26 million, and the return of his blue fleece hoodie. If the former friends had understood the Statute of Frauds, they would never have gotten into this mess.[1]

---

[1] Based loosely on Lydon v. Beauregard (Middlesex Sup. Ct., Mass., 1989), reported in Paul Langher, "Couple Lose Suit to Share $2.8M Prize," *Boston Globe*, December 23, 1989, p. 21.

The rule we examine in this chapter is not exactly news. Originally passed by the British Parliament in 1677, the Statute of Frauds has changed little over the centuries. The purpose was to prevent lying (fraud) in civil lawsuits. Jury trials of that era invited perjury. Neither the plaintiff nor the defendant was permitted to testify, meaning that the jury never heard from the people who really knew what had happened. Instead, the court heard testimony from people who claimed to have witnessed the contract being created. Knowing that he would never be subjected to aggressive cross-examination, a plaintiff might easily allege that a fake contract was real and then bribe witnesses to support his case. A powerful earl, seeking to acquire 300 acres of valuable land owned by a neighboring commoner, might claim that the neighbor had orally promised to sell his land. Although the claim was utterly false, the earl would win if he could bribe enough "reputable" witnesses to persuade the jury.

To provide juries with more reliable evidence that a contract did or did not exist, Parliament passed the Statute of Frauds. It required that in several types of cases, a contract would be enforced only if it were in writing. Contracts involving interests in land were first on the list.

In the days before the Revolutionary War, when Pennsylvania was still a British possession, the colony's supreme court heard the following case, which centered on the Statute of Frauds. Notice the case citation. This is very nearly the first case reported in U.S. history. Back then, rulings were expressed quite differently (and everything was capitalized), but you will be able to see Judge Coleman's point.

Landmark Case

THE LESSEE OF RICHARDSON V. CAMPBELL
1 U.S. 10
Supreme Court of Pennsylvania, 1764

Facts: A tenant had rented land from Richardson. However, Campbell claimed the leased property was really his. Unless the tenant could prove that Richardson owned the land, he would have no right to stay there.

Richardson's tenant offered a deed (which was then called a *patent*) to support his claim; Campbell provided receipts as evidence that he had bought the property.

To prove that the receipts were for the disputed property, Campbell wanted to introduce statements from an important person—Thomas Penn, whose father, William, had founded the Pennsylvania colony. Obviously, the tenant did not want that evidence admitted in court.

Issue: *Was oral evidence about the ownership of land admissible in court?*

Excerpts from Justice Coleman's Decision: PLAINTIFF supported his Title by a Patent. The Defendant produced Receipts several Years prior to Plaintiff's Patent; but the Plaintiff contend[ed] that the Receipts were only for Money paid on an adjacent Tract; the Defendant produced a Witness to prove a parol Declaration of Mr. Thomas Penn that the Land in dispute was sold to Defendant.

This piece of Evidence was opposed by the Plaintiff, and refused BY THE COURT.

Almost all states of the United States have passed their own version of the Statute of Frauds. It is important to remember, as we examine the rules and exceptions, that Parliament and the state legislatures all had a commendable, straightforward purpose in passing their respective Statutes of Frauds: *to provide a court with the best possible evidence of whether the parties intended to make a contract.* Ironically, the British government has repealed the writing requirement for most contracts. Parliament concluded that the old statute, far from preventing wrongdoing, was helping people commit fraud. A wily negotiator could orally agree to terms and then, if the deal turned unprofitable, walk away from the contract, knowing it was unenforceable without written evidence.

Thus far, no state has entirely repealed its Statute of Frauds. Instead, courts have carved exceptions into the original statute to prevent unfairness. Some scholars have urged state legislatures to go further and repeal the law altogether. Other commentators defend the Statute of Frauds as a valuable tool for justice. They argue that, among other benefits, the requirement of a writing cautions people to be careful before making—or relying on—a promise. For now, the Statute of Frauds is a vital part of law. Sadly, Oliver from the opening scenario will learn this the hard way.

The Statute of Frauds: A plaintiff may not enforce any of the following agreements unless the agreement, or some memorandum of it, is in writing and signed by the defendant. The agreements that must be in writing are those:

- For any interest in **land;**

- That **cannot be performed within one year;**

- To pay the **debt of another;**

- Made by an **executor of an estate to pay the debt of the estate;**

- Made **in consideration of marriage;** and

- For the **sale of goods of $500 or more.**

In other words, when two parties make an agreement covered by any one of these six topics, it must be in writing to be enforceable. Oliver and Perry made a definite agreement to purchase lottery tickets during alternate months and share the proceeds of any winning ticket. But their agreement was to last two and a half years. As the second item on the list indicates, a contract must be in writing if it cannot be performed within one year. The good news is that Oliver gets back his fleece jacket. The bad news is he gets none of the lottery money. Even though three witnesses saw the deal made, it is unlikely to be enforced in any state. Perry will walk away with all $52 million.

Note that although the Oliver–Perry agreement is unenforceable, it is not void. Suppose that Perry does the right thing, agreeing to share the winnings with Oliver. Over the next 20 years, as he receives the winnings, Perry gives one-half to his friend. But then, having squandered his own fortune, Perry demands the money back from Oliver, claiming that the original contract violated the Statute of Frauds. Perry loses. **Once a contract is fully executed, it makes no difference that it was unwritten.** The Statute of Frauds prevents the enforcement of an executory contract; that is, one in which the parties have not fulfilled their obligations. But the contract is not *illegal.* Once both parties have fully performed, neither party may demand rescission. The Statute of Frauds allows a party to cancel future obligations but not to undo past actions.

Ethics The *law* permits Perry to keep all of the lottery money. But does Perry have a *moral* right to deny Oliver his half-share? Is the Statute of Frauds serving a useful purpose here? Remember that Parliament passed the original Statute of Frauds believing that a written document would be more reliable than the testimony of alleged witnesses. If we permitted Oliver to enforce the oral contract, based on his testimony and that of the witnesses, would we simply be inviting other plaintiffs to invent lottery "contracts" that had never been made?

16-1 COMMON LAW STATUTE OF FRAUDS: CONTRACTS THAT MUST BE IN WRITING

16-1a Agreements for an Interest in Land

A contract for the sale of any interest in land must be in writing to be enforceable. Notice the phrase "interest in land." This means *any legal right* regarding land. A house on a lot is an interest in land. A mortgage, an easement, and a leased apartment are all interests in land. As a general rule, leases must therefore be in writing, although most states have created an exception for short-term leases. A short-term lease is often one for a year or less, although the length varies from state to state.

Kary Presten and Ken Sailer were roommates in a rental apartment in New Jersey that had a view of the Manhattan skyline. The lease was in Sailer's name, but the two split all expenses. The building became a "cooperative," meaning that each tenant would have the option of buying the apartment.[2] Sailer learned he could buy his unit for only $55,800 if he promptly paid a $1,000 fee to maintain his rights. He mentioned to Presten that he planned to buy the unit, and Presten asked if he could become half-owner. Sailer agreed and borrowed the $1,000 from Presten to pay his initial fee. But as the time for closing on the purchase came nearer, Sailer realized that he could sell the apartment for a substantial profit. He placed an ad in a paper and promptly received a firm offer for $125,000. Sailer then told Presten that their deal was off, and that he, Sailer, would be buying the unit alone. He did exactly that, and Presten filed suit. Regrettably, the outcome of Presten's suit was only too easy to predict.

"Any interest in land" may sound obscure, but those who understand it are better off than those who do not.

A cooperative apartment is an interest in land, said the court. This agreement could be enforced only if put in writing and signed by Sailer. The parties had put nothing in writing, and therefore Presten was out of luck. He was entitled to his $1,000 back but nothing more. The apartment belonged to Sailer, who could live in it or sell it for a large, quick profit.[3]

Suppose that you are interested in buying five expensive acres in a fast-growing rural area. There is no water on the property, and the only way to bring public water to it is through land owned by the neighbor, Joanne, who agrees to sell you an easement through her property. An *easement* is a legal right that an owner gives to another person to make some use of the owner's land. In other words, Joanne will permit you to dig a 200-foot trench through her land and lay a water pipe there in exchange for $15,000. May you now safely purchase the 5 acres? Not until Joanne has signed the written easement. You might ignore this "technicality," since Joanne seems friendly and honest. But you could then

---

[2]Technically, the residents of a "co-op" do not own their apartments. They own a share of the corporation that owns the building. Along with their ownership shares, residents have a right to lease their unit for a modest fee.

[3]Presten v. Sailer, 225 N.J. Super. 178, 542 A.2d 7 (N.J. Super. Ct. App. Div. 1988).

spend $300,000 buying your property only to learn that Joanne has changed her mind. She might refuse to go through with the deal unless you pay $150,000 for the easement. Without her permission to lay the pipe, your new land is worthless. Avoid such nightmares: Get it in writing.

Exception: Full Performance by the Seller

If the seller completely performs her side of a contract for an interest in land, a court is likely to enforce the agreement even if it was oral. Adam orally agrees to sell his condominium to Maggie for $150,000. Adam delivers the deed to Maggie and expects his money a week later, but Maggie fails to pay. Most courts will allow Adam to enforce the oral contract and collect the full purchase price from Maggie.

Exception: Part Performance by the Buyer

The buyer of land may be able to enforce an oral contract if she paid part of the purchase price *and either* entered upon the land *or* made improvements to it. Suppose that Eloise sues Grover to enforce an alleged oral contract to sell a lot in Happydale. She claims they struck a bargain in January. Grover defends based on the Statute of Frauds, saying that, even if the two did reach an oral agreement, it is unenforceable. Eloise proves that she paid 10 percent of the purchase price, that she began excavating on the lot in February to build a house, and that Grover knew of the work. Eloise has established part performance and will be allowed to enforce her contract.

This exception makes sense if we recall the purpose of the Statute of Frauds: to provide the best possible evidence of the parties' intentions. The fact that Grover permitted Eloise to enter upon the land and begin building on it is compelling evidence that the two parties had reached an agreement. But be aware that most claims of part performance fail. Merely paying a deposit on a house is not part performance. A plaintiff seeking to rely on part performance must show partial payment *and* either entrance onto the land *or* physical improvements to it.

Exception: Promissory Estoppel

The other exception to the writing requirement is our old friend promissory estoppel. **If a promisor makes an oral promise that should reasonably cause the promisee to rely on it, and the promisee does rely, the promisee may be able to enforce the promise,** despite the Statute of Frauds, if that is the only way to avoid injustice. This exception potentially applies to any contract that must be written, such as those for land, those that cannot be performed within one year, and so forth.

Maureen Sullivan and James Rooney lived together for seven years, although they never married. They decided to buy a house. The two agreed that they would be equal owners, but Rooney told Sullivan that in order to obtain Veterans Administration financing, he would have to be the sole owner on the deed. They each contributed to the purchase and maintenance of the house, and Rooney repeatedly told Sullivan that he would change the deed to joint ownership. He never did. When the couple split up, Sullivan sued, seeking a 50 percent interest in the house. She won. The agreement was for an interest in land and should have been in writing, said the court. But Rooney had clearly promised Sullivan that she would be a half-owner, and she had relied by contributing to the purchase and maintenance. The Statute of Frauds was passed to *prevent* fraud, not to enable one person to mislead another and benefit at her expense.[4]

---

[4]Sullivan v. Rooney, 404 Mass. 160, 533 N.E.2d 1372 (1989).

EXAM Strategy

Question: Aditi and Danielle, MBA students, need an apartment for next September. They find a lovely two-bedroom unit that the owner is rehabbing. The students can see that the owner is honest, his workmanship excellent. The owner agrees to rent them the apartment beginning September 1, for $1,200 per month for one year. "Come back at the end of August. By then, my work will be done and I'll have the papers to sign." Aditi asks, "Should we sign something now, to be sure?" The landlord laughs and replies, "I trust you. You don't trust me?" They both trust him, and they shake hands on the deal. When the students return in August, the landlord has rented it to Danielle's former boyfriend for $1,400 per month. Aditi and Danielle sue. Who wins?

Strategy: Under the Statute of Frauds, a contract for the sale of any interest in land must be in writing to be enforceable. What does "any interest" mean? Does the Statute of Frauds apply to this case?

Result: An "interest" means any legal right. A lease is an interest in land, meaning that the students cannot enforce this agreement unless it is in writing, signed by the owner—and it is not. The students need to look for a different apartment.

16-1b Agreements That Cannot Be Performed within One Year

Contracts that cannot be performed within one year are unenforceable unless they are in writing. This one-year period begins on the date the parties make the agreement. The critical word here is "cannot." If a contract *could possibly* be completed within one year, it need not be in writing. Betty gets a job at Burger Brain, throwing fries in oil. Her boss tells her she can have Fridays off for as long as she works there. That oral contract is enforceable whether Betty stays one week or twenty years. "As long as she works there" *could* last for less than one year. Betty might quit the job after six months. Therefore, it does not need to be in writing.[5]

If an agreement will *necessarily* take longer than one year to finish, it must be in writing to be enforceable. If Betty is hired for a term of three years as manager of Burger Brain, the agreement is unenforceable unless put in writing. She cannot perform three years of work in one year.

Or, if you hire a band to play at your wedding 15 months from today, the agreement must be in writing. The gig may take only a single day, but that day will definitely not fall in the next 12 months.

The following case is not quite as old as the Statute of Frauds, but it is set in what now seems a distant time—the dark days before corporate executives knew about the Internet. Did the right to develop mtv.com need to be in writing?

---

[5]This is the majority rule. In most states, for example, if a company hires an employee "for life," the contract need not be in writing because the employee could die within one year. "Contracts of uncertain duration are simply excluded [from the Statute of Frauds]; the provision covers only those contracts whose performance cannot possibly be completed within a year." Restatement (Second) of Contracts §130, Comment a, at 328 (1981). See, e.g., Mackay v. Four Rivers Packing Co., 2008 WL 427789 (Id. 2008). However, a few states disagree. The Illinois Supreme Court ruled that a contract for lifetime employment is enforceable only if written. McInerney v. Charter Golf, Inc., 176 Ill. 2d 482 (Ill. 1997).

You be the Judge

<table>
<tr>
<td>

Facts: Adam Curry was an MTV video disc jockey ("VJ") and host of the popular *Headbanger's Ball* and *MTV Top 20 Video Countdown*. In the early days of the Internet, when VJs had big hair

</td>
<td>

MTV NETWORKS V. CURRY

867 F.Supp. 202
District Court for the Southern District of New York,
1994

</td>
<td>

Argument for MTV: According to Curry, his contract with MTV provided that he would promote MTV programming on his mtv.com site in return for MTV's promise to give up its web

</td>
</tr>
</table>

and many major companies (including MTV) were not yet online, Curry dreamed up the idea of a website with the address "mtv.com."

In June, 1993, Curry met with MTV vice president Matthew Farber to discuss his idea and ask if MTV would become his partner. Farber told Curry that MTV was not interested in mtv.com, but that Curry was free to register and develop the site at his own expense. And he did. Many MTV employees, including senior executives, encouraged Curry's efforts, even giving him materials to upload to the site. Curry and other VJs advertised mtv.com on air.

In late 1993, MTV began exploring its own online presence. It formally requested that Curry cease use of the mtv.com address. But Curry continued his site, which had already been accessed by millions.

MTV sued Curry for trademark infringement, and Curry counterclaimed for breach of oral contract. MTV moved to dismiss Curry's contract suit, claiming that the promise between MTV and Curry required a writing because it could not be fully executed within one year.

You Be the Judge: *Did an agreement for rights to a web address require a writing?*

address. Two problems. One, no executives in their right mind would give away a web address in such a casual way. Two, there is absolutely no possibility that this "contract" could be performed within one year. Curry was free to terminate his website at will, but MTV was giving up its rights to "mtv.com" forever. Curry's duties could be completed within a year, but MTV's obligations continue indefinitely. For this reason, this promise had to be in writing. The verbal assurances of MTV executives did not form a binding contract.

Argument for Curry: Your honor, we can all see what happened here. In 1993, MTV executives were blind to the commercial potential of the Internet, so they let Curry test the waters to see if mtv.com would be successful. And now that they have got with the program, they want mtv.com back. But they are too late—they have already contracted away mtv.com to Curry. The Statute of Frauds does not require this agreement to be in writing. Both parties' performances could have been completed within one year: Curry could have canceled development of the website at any time, which also means that MTV's promise to allow Curry to use mtv.com might have ended any time, too. The contract was enforceable and MTV has to pay Curry for its breach.

16-1c Promise to Pay the Debt of Another

When one person agrees to pay the debt of another as a favor to that debtor, it is called a collateral promise, and it must be in writing to be enforceable. D. R. Kemp was a young entrepreneur who wanted to build housing in Tuscaloosa, Alabama. He needed $25,000 to complete a project he was working on, so he went to his old college professor, Jim Hanks, for help. The professor said he would see what he could do about getting Kemp a loan. Professor Hanks spoke with his good friend Travis Chandler, telling him that Kemp was highly responsible and would be certain to repay any money loaned. Chandler trusted Professor Hanks but wanted to be sure of his money. Professor Hanks assured Chandler that if for any reason Kemp did not repay the loan, he, Hanks, would pay Chandler in full. With that assurance, Chandler wrote out a check for $25,000, payable to Kemp, never having met the young man.

Kemp, of course, never repaid the loan. (Thank goodness he did not; this textbook has no use for people who do what they are supposed to do.) Kemp exhausted the cash trying to sustain his business, which failed anyway, so he had nothing to give his creditor. Chandler approached Professor Hanks, who refused to pay, and Chandler sued. The outcome was easy to predict. Professor Hanks had agreed to repay Kemp's debt *as a favor to Kemp*, making it a collateral promise. Chandler had nothing in writing, and that is exactly what he got from his lawsuit—nothing.

Exception: The Leading Object Rule

There is one major exception to the collateral promise rule. **When the promisor guarantees to pay the debt of another and** *the leading object of the promise is some benefit to the promisor himself*, **then the contract will be enforceable even if unwritten.** In other words, if the promisor makes the guarantee not as a favor to the debtor, but primarily out of *self-interest*, the Statute of Frauds does not apply.

Robert Perry was a hog farmer in Ohio. He owed $26,000 to Sunrise Cooperative, a supplier of feed. Because Perry was in debt, Sunrise stopped giving him feed on credit and began selling him feed on a cash-only basis. Perry also owed money to Farm Credit Services, a loan agency. Perry promised Farm Credit he would repay his loans as soon as his hogs were big enough to sell. But Perry couldn't raise hogs without feed, which he lacked the money to purchase. Farm Credit was determined to bring home the bacon, so it asked Sunrise Cooperative to give Perry the feed on credit. Farm Credit orally promised to pay any debt that Perry did not take care of. When Perry defaulted on his payments to Sunrise, the feed supplier sued Farm Credit based on its oral guarantee. Farm Credit claimed the promise was unenforceable, based on the Statute of Frauds. But the court found in favor of Sunrise. The *leading object* of Farm Credit's promise to Sunrise was self-interest, and the oral promise was fully enforceable.[6]

16-1d Promise Made by an Executor of an Estate

This rule is merely a special application of the previous one, concerning the debt of another person. An executor is the person who is in charge of an estate after someone dies. The executor's job is to pay debts of the deceased, obtain money owed to him, and disburse the assets according to the will. In most cases, the executor will use only the estate's assets to pay those debts. The Statute of Frauds comes into play when an executor promises to pay an estate's debts with her own funds. **An executor's promise to use her own funds to pay a debt of the deceased must be in writing to be enforceable.**

Suppose Esmeralda dies penniless, owing Tina $35,000. Esmeralda's daughter, Sapphire, is the executor of her estate. Tina comes to Sapphire and demands her $35,000. Sapphire responds, "There is no money in mamma's estate, but don't worry, I'll make it up to you with my own money." Sapphire's oral promise is unenforceable. Tina should get it in writing while Sapphire is feeling generous.

16-1e Promise Made in Consideration of Marriage

This is not the stuff of fairy tales: Barney is a multimillionaire with the integrity of a gangster and the charm of a tax collector. He proposes to Li-Tsing, who promptly rejects him. Barney then pleads that if Li-Tsing will be his bride, he will give her an island he owns off the coast of California. Li-Tsing begins to see his good qualities and accepts. After they are married, Barney refuses to deliver the deed. Li-Tsing will get nothing from a court either, because **a promise made in consideration of marriage must be in writing to be enforceable.**

---

[6]Sunrise Cooperative v. Robert Perry, 1992 Ohio App. LEXIS 3913 (Ohio Ct. App. 1992).

16-2 THE COMMON LAW STATUTE OF FRAUDS: WHAT THE WRITING MUST CONTAIN

Each of the types of contract just described must be in writing in order to be enforceable. What must the writing contain? It may be a carefully typed contract, using precise legal terminology, or an informal memo scrawled on the back of a paper napkin at a business lunch. The writing may consist of more than one document, written at different times, with each document making a piece of the puzzle. But there are some general requirements: the writing

- **Must be signed by the defendant, and**
- **Must state with reasonable certainty the name of each party, the subject matter of the agreement, and all of the essential terms and promises.**[7]

16-2a Signature

A state's Statute of Frauds typically requires that the writing be "signed by the party to be charged therewith"; that is, the party who is resisting enforcement of the contract. Throughout this chapter, we refer to that person as the defendant, because when these cases go to court, it is the defendant who is disputing the existence of a contract.

Judges define "signature" very broadly. Using a pen to write one's name certainly counts, but it is not required. A secretary who stamps an executive's signature on a letter fulfills this requirement. In fact, any mark or logo placed on a document to indicate acceptance, even an "X," will generally satisfy the Statute of Frauds. And electronic commerce, as we discuss in the next section, creates new methods of signing.

16-2b Reasonable Certainty

Suppose Garfield and Hayes are having lunch, discussing the sale of Garfield's vacation condominium. They agree on a price and want to make some notation of the agreement even before their lawyers work out a detailed purchase and sales agreement. A perfectly adequate memorandum might say, "Garfield agrees to sell Hayes his condominium at 234 Baron Boulevard, Apartment 18, for $350,000 cash, payable on June 18, 2015, and Hayes promises to pay the sum on that day." They should make two copies of their agreement and sign both. Notice that although Garfield's memo is short, it is *certain* and *complete*. This is critical because problems of vagueness and incompleteness often doom informal memoranda.

Vagueness

Ella Hayden owned valuable commercial property on a highway called Route 9. She wrote a series of letters to her stepson Mark, promising that several of the children, including Mark, would share the property. One letter said: "We four shall fairly divide on the Route 9 property. [sic]" Other letters said: "When the Route 9 Plaza is sold, you can take a long vacation," and "The property will be sold. You and Dennis shall receive the same amount." Ella Hayden died without leaving Mark anything. He sued, but got nothing. The court ruled:

> The above passages written by Ms. Hayden do not recite the essential elements of the alleged contract with reasonable certainty. The writings do not state unequivocally or with sufficient

---

[7]Restatement (Second) of Contracts §131.

particularity the subject matter to which the writings relate, nor do they provide the terms and conditions of alleged promises made which constitute a contract. The alleged oral contract between Ms. Hayden and Mr. Hayden cannot be identified from the passages from Ms. Hayden's letters quoted above when applied to existing facts. In sum, Mr. Hayden's cause of action seeking an interest in the Route 9 property is foreclosed by the Statute of Frauds.[8]

Incompleteness

During Ronald McCoy's second interview with Spelman Memorial Hospital, the board of directors orally offered him a three-year job as assistant hospital administrator. McCoy accepted. Spelman's CEO, Gene Meyer, sent a letter confirming the offer, which said:

> To reconfirm the offer, it is as follows: 1. We will pay for your moving expenses. 2. I would like you to pursue your Master's Degree at an area program. We will pay 100 percent tuition reimbursement. 3. Effective September 26, you will be eligible for all benefits. 4. A starting salary of $48,000 annually with reviews and eligibility for increases at 6 months, 12 months, and annually thereafter. 5. We will pay for the expenses of 3 trips, if necessary, in order for you to find housing. 6. Vacation will be for 3 weeks a year after one year; however, we do allow for this to be taken earlier. [Signed] Gene Meyer.

Spelman Hospital fired McCoy less than a year after he started work, and McCoy sued. The hospital's letter seems clear, and it is signed by an authorized official. The problem is, it is incomplete. Can you spot the fatal omission? The court did.

McCoy wanted to hold the hospital's board to its spoken promise that he would have a job for a term of three years. To be enforceable, a contract for a term of over one year must be in writing under the Statute of Frauds.

To satisfy the Statute of Frauds, an employment contract—[or] its memorandum or note—must contain *all* essential terms, including *duration of the employment relationship*. Without a statement of duration, an employment-at-will arrangement is created, which is terminable at any time by either party with no liability for breach of contract. McCoy's argument that the letter constituted a memorandum of an oral contract fails because the letter does not state an essential element: duration. The letter did not state that Spelman was granting McCoy employment for any term—only that his salary would be reviewed at 6 months, 12 months, and "annually thereafter."[9]

The lawsuits in this section demonstrate the continuing force of the Statute of Frauds. If the promisor had truly wanted to make a binding commitment, he or she could have written the appropriate contract or memorandum in a matter of minutes. Great formality and expense are unnecessary. But the written document *must be clear and complete*, or it will fail.

EXAM Strategy

Question: Major Retailer and Owner negotiated a lease of a strip mall, the tenancy to begin August 1. Retailer's lawyer then drafted a lease accurately reflecting all terms agreed to, including the parties, exact premises, condition of the store, dates of the lease, and monthly rent of $18,000. Retailer signed the lease and delivered it to Owner on July 1. On July 20, Owner leased the same space to a different tenant for $23,000 per month. Retailer sued, claiming that the parties had a binding deal, and the Owner had breached his agreement in order to obtain higher rent. Who will win?

---

[8]Hayden v. Hayden, Mass. Lawyers Weekly No. 12-299-93 (Middlesex Sup. Ct. 1994).
[9]McCoy v. Spelman Memorial Hospital, 845 S.W.2d 727 (Mo. Ct. App. 1993).

Strategy: To comply with the Statute of Frauds, a writing must state all essential terms. This lease appears to do that. However, the writing must contain one other thing. What is it?

Result: The writing must be *signed* by the party claiming that there is no contract; that is, by the defendant. Owner never signed the lease. This lease does not comply with the Statute of Frauds, and the Retailer will lose his case.

16-2c Electronic Contracts and Signatures

Modern life has moved online: We can now buy everything from toothpaste to cars with the click of a mouse. What happens to the writing requirement, though, when there is no paper? The Statute of Frauds requires some sort of "signature" to prove that the defendant committed to the deal. Today, an "electronic signature" could mean a name typed (or automatically included) at the bottom of an email message, a retinal or vocal scan, or a name signed by electronic pen on a writing tablet, among others.

E-signatures are valid in all 50 states. Almost every state has adopted the Uniform Electronic Transactions Act (UETA), which makes *electronic* contracts and signatures as enforceable as those on paper.[10] In other words, the normal rules of contract formation apply, and neither party can avoid a deal merely because it originated electronically. A federal statute, the **Electronic Signatures in Global and National Commerce Act (E-SIGN)** extends UETA's principles to interstate and foreign commerce.

UETA and E-SIGN also require courts, when in doubt, to favor the validity of email contracts. This requirement means that parties must be careful to avoid entering into contracts *unintentionally*. Stevens was renegotiating his employment contract with his boss through several conversational rounds of email. At one point, Stevens wrote "I accept your proposal" on an email with his signature block. Before a formal contract was inked, Stevens changed his mind. But it was too late. A court ruled that the contract was enforceable the moment Stevens pressed "send" with an acceptance and a signature block. Stevens might have considered email to be an informal conversation, but in fact, it created a final, binding contract.[11]

Note that, in many states, certain documents still require a traditional (non-electronic) signature. Wills, adoptions, court orders, and notice of foreclosure are common exceptions. If in doubt, get a hard copy, signed in ink.

16-3 THE UCC'S STATUTE OF FRAUDS

We have reached another section dedicated to the Uniform Commercial Code. Remember that UCC rules govern only contracts involving a sale of goods. Because merchants can make many verbal contracts every day, the drafters of the UCC wanted to make the writing requirement less onerous for the sale of goods.

The UCC requires a writing for the sale of goods priced $500 or more. The Code's requirements are easier to meet than those of the common law. **UCC §2-201**, the Statute of Frauds section, has three important elements:

1. The basic rule

2. The merchants' exception

3. Special circumstances

---

[10]Note that while Illinois, New York, and Washington have not adopted UETA, they have adopted their own similar versions of it.

[11]Stevens v. Publicis, S.A. 50 AD3d 253 (N.Y. Sup. Ct. 2008).

16-3a UCC §2-201(1)—The Basic Rule

A contract for the sale of goods of $500 or more is not enforceable unless there is some writing, signed by the defendant, indicating that the parties reached an agreement. The key difference between the common-law rule and the UCC rule is that the Code does *not* require *all* of the terms of the agreement to be in writing. The Code looks for something simpler: *an indication that the parties reached an agreement.* Only two things are required: the signature of the defendant and the quantity of goods being sold. Suppose a short memorandum between textile dealers indicates that Seller will sell to Buyer "grade AA 100 percent cotton, white athletic socks." If the writing does not state the price, the parties can testify at court about what the market price was at the time of the deal. If the writing says nothing about the delivery date, the court will assume a reasonable delivery date, say, 60 days. But how many socks were to be delivered? 100 pairs or 100,000? The court will have no objective evidence, and so, the quantity must be written.

> The key difference between the common-law rule and the UCC rule is that the Code does *not* require *all* of the terms of the agreement to be in writing.

Writing	Result
"Confirming phone conversation today, I will send you 1,000 reams of paper for laser printing, usual quality & price. [Signed,] Seller."	This memorandum satisfies UCC §2-201(1), and the contract may be enforced against the seller. The buyer may testify as to the "usual" quality and price between the two parties, and both sides may rely on normal trade usage.
"Confirming phone conversation today, I will send you best quality paper for laser printing, $3.25 per ream, delivery date next Thursday. [Signed,] Seller."	This memorandum is not enforceable because it states no quantity.

The UCC's purpose is to make sales easier while still preventing fraud. Ultimately, courts seek to balance the formality of the writing requirement with their own common sense. They examine the situation as a whole to determine if there is enough evidence to show that the parties contracted. The following case involved an art auction, a wily buyer, and a precious Russian box worth, well, we do not know what it was worth, but definitely more than $500. The one thing lacking? A single document signed by the defendant.

WILLIAM J. JENACK ESTATE APPRAISERS AND AUCTIONEERS, INC. v. ALBERT RABIZADEH

2013 NY Slip Op 08373
Court of Appeals of New York, 2013

Facts: William J. Jenack Estate Appraisers and Auctioneers, Inc. sold fine art and antiques at public auctions. Albert Rabizadeh wanted to buy a nineteenth-century Russian silver and enamel box, with an estimated value of $4,000, that was to be sold at one of Jenack's auctions. Rabizadeh could not attend the auction, so he submitted an "absentee

This rare Russian box measured only 1½ by 3⅝ inches, but was worth a fortune.

bidder form," in accordance with Jenack's online and telephone bidder policy. Rabizadeh signed the form and listed his name, email address, telephone numbers, fax number, address, credit card number, and the items that he intended to bid on. Jenack assigned Rabizadeh bidder number 305.

The rare Russian box garnered much excitement from collectors who believed it was worth much more than its initially appraised value of $4,000. During the frenzied auction, Rabizadeh beat out many other bidders with a telephone bid of $400,000. (Yes, that is two zeros more than $4,000—it was quite a box.) Jenack recorded Rabizadeh's winning bid on an official "clerking sheet," along with the item, its description, and bidder number 305. When he received Jenack's invoice, Rabizadeh decided he did not want it anymore and refused to pay.

Jenack sued Rabizadeh for breach of contract. Rabizadeh claimed that there was no contract because the sale was not in a signed writing, as required by the UCC for goods over $500. Jenack argued that the clerking sheet and related documents satisfied the writing requirement, because they contained all the necessary terms. The trial court agreed with Jenack and awarded it $402,398. A New York appeals court reversed the decision. Jenack appealed to New York's highest court.

Issue: *Did the clerking sheet and the absentee bidder form satisfy the Statute of Frauds?*

Excerpts from Judge Rivera's Decision: In general, a contract for the sale of goods at a price of $500 or more must comply with the signed writing requirement of the UCC. In the case of a public auction, a bid may satisfy the [UCC's] Statute of Frauds where there exists an appropriate writing "signed by the party against whom enforcement is sought to be charged" (*see* UCC 2-201). [New York law also permits] a memorandum specifying the nature and price of the item, the terms of sale, and the names of the parties.

It is well established that the writing need not be contained in one single document, but rather may be furnished by piecing together other, related writings. Therefore, a court may look to documents relevant to the bidding and the auction.

The clerking sheet, in isolation, does not satisfy the New York law because it requires the disclosure of the name of the buyer. We are unpersuaded by Jenack's arguments that this requirement can be satisfied by Jenack's insertion of numbers in place of those names. To allow for numbers, rather than names, would undermine the purpose of the Statute by increasing the possibility of fraud.

We must consider whether there are "related writings" that supply the required names, and which may be read, along with the clerking sheet, to provide the information necessary to constitute a memorandum. The absentee bidder form, along with the clerking sheet, provide the necessary information to establish the name of Rabizadeh as the buyer. This conclusion is inescapable given that each of the documents contained information pertaining to the terms of the sale. Both contain the item number, the bidder number, the auctioneer, and a detailed description of the item.

The Statute of Frauds was not enacted to afford persons a means of evading just obligations. [That] is precisely what Rabizadeh attempts to do here, but the law and the facts foreclose him from doing so. Rabizadeh took affirmative steps to participate in Jenack's auction, including executing an absentee bidder form with the required personal information. He then successfully won the bidding, closing out other interested bidders, with his $400,000 bid. He cannot seek to avoid the consequences of his actions by ignoring the existence of a documentary trail leading to him.

16-3b UCC §2-201(2)—The Merchants' Exception

When both parties are "merchants," that is, businesspeople who routinely deal in the goods being sold, the Code will accept an even more informal writing. **Within a reasonable time of making an oral contract, if a merchant sends a written confirmation to another, and if the confirmation is definite enough to bind the *sender herself*, then the merchant who receives the confirmation will *also* be bound by it unless he objects in writing within 10 days.** This exception dramatically changes the rules from the common law, but it applies only between two merchants. The UCC's drafters assumed that experienced merchants are able to take care of themselves in fast-moving negotiations. The critical difference is this: A writing may create a binding contract *even when it is not signed by the defendant.*

Madge manufactures "beanies," that is, silly caps with plastic propellers on top. Rachel, a retailer, telephones her, and they discuss the price of the beanies, shipping time, and other details. Madge then faxes Rachel a memo: "This confirms your order for 2,500 beanies at $12.25 per beanie. Colors: blue, green, black, orange, red. Delivery date: 10 days. [Signed] Madge." Rachel receives the fax, reads it while negotiating with another manufacturer, and throws it in the wastebasket. Rachel buys her beanies elsewhere, and Madge sues. Rachel defends, claiming there is no written contract because she, Rachel, never signed anything. Madge wins under UCC §2-201(2). Both parties were merchants because they routinely dealt in these goods. Madge signed and sent a confirming memo that could have been used to hold her, Madge, to the deal. When Rachel read it, she was not free to disregard it. Obviously, the intelligent business practice would have been to promptly fax a reply saying, "I disagree. We do not have any deal for beanies." Since Rachel failed to respond within 10 days, Madge has an enforceable contract.

16-3c UCC §2-201(3)—Special Circumstances

An oral contract *may* be enforceable, even without a written memorandum, if:

- **The seller is specially manufacturing the goods for the buyer, *or***
- **The defendant admits in court proceedings that there was a contract, *or***
- **The goods have been delivered or they have been paid for.**

Specially Manufactured Goods

If a seller, specially manufacturing goods for the buyer, begins work on them before the buyer cancels, and the goods cannot be sold elsewhere, the oral contract is binding. Bernice manufactures solar heating systems. She phones Jason and orders 75 special electrical converter units designed for her heating system, at $150 per unit. Jason begins manufacturing the units, but then Bernice phones again and says she no longer needs them. Bernice is bound by the contract. The goods are being manufactured for her and cannot be sold elsewhere. Jason had already begun work when she attempted to cancel. If the case goes to court, Jason will win.

Admissions in Court

When the defendant admits in court proceedings that the parties made an oral contract, the agreement is binding. Rex sues Sophie, alleging that she orally agreed to sell him five boa constrictors that have been trained to stand in a line and pass a full wineglass from one snake to the next. Sophie defends the lawsuit, but during a deposition, she says, "OK, we agreed verbally, but nothing was ever put in writing, and I knew I didn't have to go through with it. When I went home, the snakes made me feel really guilty, and I decided not to sell." Sophie's admission under oath dooms her defense.

Goods Delivered or Paid For

If the seller has delivered the goods, or the buyer has paid for them, the contract may be enforced even with nothing in writing. Malik orally agrees to sell 500 plastic chairs to a university for use in its cafeteria. Malik delivers 300 of the chairs, but then the university notifies him that it will not honor the deal. Malik is entitled to payment for the 300 chairs, although not for the other 200. Conversely, if the university had sent a check for one-half of the chairs, it would be entitled to 250 chairs.

EXAM Strategy

Question: Beasley is a commercial honey farmer. He orally agrees to sell 500,000 pounds of honey to Grizzly at $1 per pound. Grizzly immediately faxes Beasley a signed confirmation, summarizing the deal. Beasley receives the fax but ignores it, and he never responds to Grizzly. Five days later, Beasley sells his honey to Brown for $1.15 per pound. Grizzly sues Beasley for breach of contract. Beasley claims that he signed nothing and was free to sell his honey anywhere he wanted. Who will win?

Strategy: Honey is a movable thing, meaning that this contract is governed by the UCC. Under the Code, contracts for the sale of goods worth $500 or more must be in writing. However, the merchant exception changes things when both parties are merchants. Beasley and Grizzly are both merchants. Apply the merchant exception.

Result: Beasley breached the contract. Within a reasonable time after making the agreement, Grizzly sent a memo to Beasley confirming it. Beasley had 10 days either to object in writing or be held to the agreement. Beasley will lose this lawsuit because he ignored the faxed confirmation.

16-4 PAROL EVIDENCE

Tyrone agrees to buy Martha's house for $800,000. The contract obligates Tyrone to make a 10 percent down payment immediately and pay the remaining $720,000 in 45 days. As the two parties sign the deal, Tyrone discusses his need for financing. Unfortunately, at the end of 45 days, he has been unable to get a mortgage for the full amount. He claims that the parties orally agreed that he would get his deposit back if he could not obtain financing, but the written agreement says no such thing, and Martha disputes the claim. Who will win? Probably Martha, because of the parol evidence rule.

Parol evidence refers to anything (apart from the written contract itself) that was said, done, or written *before* the parties signed the agreement or *as they signed it*. Martha's conversation with Tyrone about financing the house was parol evidence because it occurred as they were signing the contract. Another important term is **integrated contract**, which means a writing that the parties intend as the final, complete expression of their agreement. Now for the rule.

The parol evidence rule: When two parties make an integrated contract, neither one may use parol evidence to contradict, vary, or add to its terms. Negotiations may last for hours, weeks, or even months. Almost no contract includes everything that the parties said. When parties consider their agreement integrated, any statements they made before or while signing are irrelevant. If a court determines that Martha and Tyrone intended their agreement to be integrated, it will prohibit testimony about Martha's oral promises. One

Integrated contract
A writing that the parties intend as the final, complete expression of their agreement

way to avoid parol evidence disputes is to include an *integration clause.* That is a statement clearly proclaiming that this writing is the "full and final expression" of the parties' agreement, and that anything said before signing or while signing is irrelevant. In the following case, learned people learned about parol evidence the hard way.

Mayo v. North Carolina State University

168 N.C.App. 503
North Carolina Court of Appeals, 2005

Facts: Dr. Robert Mayo was a tenured faculty member of the engineering department at North Carolina State University (NCSU), and director of the school's nuclear engineering program. In July, he informed his department chair, Dr. Paul Turinsky, that he was leaving NCSU effective September 1. Turinsky accepted the resignation.

In October, after Mayo had departed, Phyllis Jennette, the university's payroll coordinator, informed him that he had been overpaid. She explained that for employees who worked 9 months but were paid over 12 months, the salary checks for July and August were in fact prepayments for the period beginning that September. Because Mayo had not worked after September 1, the checks for July and August were overpayment. When he refused to refund the money, NCSU sought to claim it in legal proceedings. The first step was a hearing before an administrative agency.

At the hearing, Turinsky and Brian Simet, the university's payroll director, explained that the "prepayment" rule was a basic part of every employee's contract. However, both acknowledged that the prepayment rule was not included in any of the documents that formed Mayo's contract, including his appointment letter, annual salary letter, and policies adopted by the university's trustees. The university officials used other evidence, outside the written documents, to establish the prepayment policy.

Based on the additional evidence, the agency ruled that NCSU was entitled to its money. However, Mayo appealed to court, and the trial judge declared that he owed nothing, ruling that the university was not permitted to rely on parol evidence to establish its policy. NCSU appealed.

Issue: *May NCSU rely on parol evidence to establish its prepayment rule?*

Excerpts from Judge Bryant's Decision: Here, the language of the employment agreement is clear and unambiguous—petitioner is to be paid in twelve monthly installments for his service as a nine-month, academic year, tenured faculty member.

The terms relied upon by NCSU were not expressly included in the employment agreement. Dr. Turinsky testified that petitioner's written employment agreement is comprised of terms found in petitioner's appointment letter, annual salary letter, and written policies adopted and amended by the UNC Board of Governors and the NCSU Board of Trustees. However, none of these documents forming the employment agreement set forth the compensation policies upon which NCSU bases its claim. Simet, Director of NCSU's Payroll Department, admitted at the agency hearing that the policies were "not stated anywhere specifically." Further, Dr. Turinsky testified he did not know of the existence of the terms until September, after petitioner left his employment with NCSU. NCSU, however, attempts to offer parol evidence to explain that payments made in July and August were prepayments for the following academic year.

The parol evidence rule prohibits the admission of parol evidence to vary, add to, or contradict a written instrument intended to be the final integration of the transaction. The rule is otherwise where it is shown that the writing is not a full integration of the terms of the contract, or when a contract is ambiguous, parol evidence is admissible to show and make certain the intention behind the contract.

Here Dr. Turinsky testified that petitioner's employment agreement consisted only of petitioner's appointment letter, his annual salary letter, and the policies adopted and amended by the UNC Board of Governors and by the NCSU Board of Trustees. It therefore appears the parties intended the above documents to be the final integration of the employment agreement. Additionally, we have already noted the language contained in the documents are unambiguous; thus, parol evidence may not be introduced to explain the terms of the agreement.

We hold petitioner does not owe a debt to NCSU as result of an alleged overpayment of salary.

[Affirmed.]

16-4a Exception: An Incomplete or Ambiguous Contract

If a court determines that a written contract is incomplete or ambiguous, it will permit parol evidence. Suppose that an employment contract states that the company will provide "full health coverage for Robert Watson and his family," but does not define *family*. Three years later, Watson divorces and remarries, acquiring three stepchildren, and a year later, his second wife has a baby. Watson now has two children by his first marriage and four by the second. The company refuses to insure Watson's first wife or his stepchildren. A court will probably find a key clause in his health care contract—"coverage for ... *his family*"—is ambiguous. A judge cannot determine exactly what the clause means from the contract itself, so the parties will be permitted to introduce parol evidence to prove whether or not the company must insure Watson's extended family.[12]

16-4b Fraud, Misrepresentation, or Duress

A court will permit parol evidence of fraud, misrepresentation, or duress. To encourage Annette to buy his house, Will assures her that no floodwaters from the nearby river have ever come within 2 miles of the house. Annette signs a contract that is silent about flooding and includes an integration clause stating that neither party is relying on any oral statements made during negotiations. When Annette moves in, she discovers that the foundation is collapsing due to earlier flooding and that Will knew of the flooding and the damage. Despite the integration clause, a court will probably allow Annette to testify about Will's misrepresentations.[13]

Chapter Conclusion

Some contracts must be in writing to be enforceable, and the writing must be clear and unambiguous. Drafting the contract need not be arduous. The disputes illustrated in this chapter could all have been prevented with a few carefully crafted sentences. It is worth the time and effort to write them.

EXAM REVIEW

1. **THE STATUTE OF FRAUDS** Several types of contract are enforceable only if written:

   - **LAND** The sale of any interest in land.

   - **ONE YEAR** An agreement that *cannot* be performed within one year.

---

[12]See, for example, Eure v. Norfolk Shipbuilding & Drydock Corp., Inc., 561 S.E.2d 663 (Va. 2002).
[13]Lindberg v. Roseth, 137 Idaho 222 (Idaho 2002).

CPA Question: Able hired Carr to restore Able's antique car for $800. The terms of their oral agreement provided that Carr had 18 months to complete the work. Actually, the work could be completed within one year. The agreement is:

(a) Unenforceable because it covers services with a value in excess of $500

(b) Unenforceable because it covers a time period in excess of one year

(c) Enforceable because personal service contracts are exempt from the Statute of Frauds

(d) Enforceable because the work could be completed within one year

Strategy: This is a subtle question. Notice that the contract is for a sum greater than $500. But that is a red herring. Why? The contract also might take 18 months to perform. But it *could* be finished in less than a year. (See the "Result" at the end of this section.)

- **DEBT OF ANOTHER** A promise to pay the debt of another, including promises made by executors to pay an estate's debts.

Question: Donald Waide had a contracting business. He bought most of his supplies from Paul Bingham's supply center. Waide fell behind on his bills, and Bingham told Waide that he would extend no more credit to him. That same day, Donald's father, Elmer Waide, came to Bingham's store, and said to Bingham that he would "stand good" for any sales to Donald made on credit. Based on Elmer's statement, Bingham again gave Donald credit, and Donald ran up $10,000 in goods before Bingham sued Donald and Elmer. What defense did Elmer make, and what was the outcome?

Strategy: This was an oral agreement, so the issue is whether the promise had to be in writing to be enforceable. Review the list of six contracts that must be in writing. Is this agreement there? (See the "Result" at the end of this section.)

- **EXECUTORS** A promise made by an executor of an estate to pay for the estate's debts.

- **MARRIAGE** A promise made in consideration of marriage.

- **GOODS** The sale of goods of $500 or more.

Question: James River-Norwalk, Inc., was a paper and textile company that needed a constant supply of wood. James River orally contracted with Gary Futch to supply wood for the company, and Futch did so for several years. The deal was worth many thousands of dollars, but nothing was put in writing. Futch actually purchased the wood for his own account and then resold it to James River. After a few years, James River refused to do more business with Futch. Did the parties have a binding contract?

Strategy: If this is a contract for services, it is enforceable without anything in writing. However, if it is one for the sale of goods, it must be in writing. Clearly what James River wanted was the wood, and it did not care where Futch found it. (See the "Result" at the end of this section.)

2. **CONTENTS** The writing must be signed by the defendant and must state the name of all parties, the subject matter of the agreement, and all essential terms and promises. Electronic signatures usually are valid.

3. **UNIFORM COMMERCIAL CODE (UCC)** A contract or memorandum for the sale of goods may be less complete than those required by the common law.

   - The basic UCC rule requires only a memorandum signed by the defendant, indicating that the parties reached an agreement and specifying the quantity of goods.

   - Between merchants, even less is required. If one merchant sends written confirmation of a contract, the merchant who receives the document must object within 10 days or be bound by the writing.

   - In the following special circumstances, no writing may be required: the goods are specially manufactured, one party admits in litigation that there was a contract, or one party pays for part of the goods or delivers some of the goods.

4. **PAROL EVIDENCE** When an integrated contract exists, neither party may generally use parol evidence to contradict, vary, or add to its terms. Parol evidence refers to anything (apart from the written contract itself) that was said, done, or written before the parties signed the agreement or as they signed it.

---

1. "One Year" Result: (d) A contract for the sale of goods worth $500 or more must be in writing—but this is a contract for *services*, not the sale of goods, so the $800 price is irrelevant. The contract *can* be completed within one year, and thus it falls outside the Statute of Frauds. This is an enforceable agreement.

1. "Debt of Another" Result: Elmer made a promise to pay the debt of another. He did so as a favor to his son. This is a collateral promise. Elmer never signed any such promise, and the agreement cannot be enforced against him.

1. "Goods" Result: James River was buying wood, and this is a contract for the sale of goods. With nothing in writing, signed by James River, Futch has no enforceable agreement.

MULTIPLE-CHOICE QUESTIONS

1. *CPA QUESTION* Two individuals signed a contract that was intended to be their entire agreement. The parol evidence rule will prevent the admission of evidence offered to:

   (a) Explain the meaning of an ambiguity in the written contract.

   (b) Establish that fraud had been committed in the formation of the contract.

(c) Prove the existence of a contemporaneous oral agreement modifying the contract.

(d) Prove the existence of a subsequent oral agreement modifying the contract.

2. Rafaella wants to plant a garden, and she agrees to buy a small piece of land for $300. Later, she agrees to buy a table for $300. Neither agreement is put in writing. The agreement to buy the land _____ enforceable, and the agreement to buy the table _____ enforceable.

   (a) is; is

   (b) is; is not

   (c) is not; is

   (d) is not; is not

3. The common-law Statute of Frauds requires that to be "in writing," an agreement must be signed by:

   (a) the plaintiff

   (b) the defendant

   (c) both a and b

   (d) none of the above

4. Mandy verbally tells a motorcycle dealer that she will make her son's motorcycle payments if he falls behind on them. Will Mandy be legally required to live up to this agreement?

   (a) Yes, absolutely.

   (b) Yes, if her son is under 18.

   (c) Yes, if Mandy will be the primary driver of the motorcycle.

   (d) Yes, if the motorcycle is worth less than $500.

   (e) No, absolutely not.

5. In December 2012, Eric hires a band to play at a huge graduation party he is planning to hold in May, 2014. The deal is never put into writing. In January 2014, if he wanted to cancel the job, Eric _____ be able to do so. If he does not cancel, and if the band shows up and plays at the party in May 2014, Eric _____ have to pay them.

   (a) will; will

   (b) will; will not

   (c) will not; will

   (d) will not; will not

CASE QUESTIONS

1. Richard Griffin and three other men owned a grain company, called Bearhouse, Inc., which needed to borrow money. First National Bank was willing to loan $490,000, but it insisted that the four men sign personal guarantees on the loan, committing themselves to repaying up to 25 percent of the loan each if Bearhouse defaulted. Bearhouse went bankrupt. The bank was able to collect some of its money from

Bearhouse's assets, but it sued Griffin for the balance. At trial, Griffin wanted to testify that before he signed his guaranty, a bank officer assured him that he would only owe 25 percent of *whatever balance was unpaid,* not 25 percent of the total loan. How will the court decide whether Griffin is entitled to testify about the conversation?

2. When Deana Byers married Steven Byers, she was pregnant with another man's child. Shortly after the marriage, Deana gave birth. The marriage lasted only two months, and the couple separated. In divorce proceedings, Deana sought child support. She claimed that Steven had orally promised to support the child if Deana would marry him. Steven claims he never made the promise. Comment on the outcome.

3. Lonnie Hippen moved to Long Island, Kansas, to work in an insurance company owned by Griffiths. After he moved there, Griffiths offered to sell Hippen a house he owned, and Hippen agreed in writing to buy it. He did buy the house and moved in, but two years later, Hippen left the insurance company. He then claimed that at the time of the sale, Griffiths had orally promised to buy back his house at the selling price if Hippen should happen to leave the company. Griffiths defended based on the Statute of Frauds. Hippen argued that the Statute of Frauds did not apply because the repurchase of the house was essentially part of his employment with Griffiths. Comment.

4. Landlord owned a clothing store and agreed in writing to lease the store's basement to another retailer. The written lease, which both parties signed, (1) described the premises exactly, (2) identified the parties, and (3) stated the monthly rent clearly. But an appeals court held that the lease did not satisfy the Statute of Frauds. Why not?

5. *YOU BE THE JUDGE* **WRITING PROBLEM**   Because of his success in a big case, a lawyer named Melbourne promised his assistant, Barbara, a large bonus. After the case settled, Melbourne met with Barbara to discuss when and how much he would pay her. In the conversation that she secretly recorded, Melbourne agreed to pay Barbara $1 million, plus $65,000 for a luxury automobile. Payments were to be made in monthly installments of $10,000, for 10 years. Melbourne also agreed to sign a document confirming his promise. Barbara's lawyer drafted the writing, but Melbourne never signed it. He did pay nine monthly installments, along with an extra payment of $100,000. Did Melbourne and Barbara have a valid contract? Argument for Barbara: The Statute of Frauds exists to prevent fraud. The fear that a plaintiff would lie about a contract is not an issue here. We know what Melbourne agreed to do because we *heard* him. Argument for Melbourne: If there was an agreement, it could not have been performed in one year because it had ten years' worth of installment payments.

DISCUSSION QUESTIONS

1. **ETHICS** Jacob Deutsch owned commercial property. He orally agreed to rent it for six years to Budget Rent A Car. Budget took possession, began paying monthly rent, and, over a period of several months, expended about $6,000 in upgrading the property. Deutsch was aware of the repairs. After a year, Deutsch attempted to evict Budget. Budget claimed it had a six-year oral lease, but Deutsch claimed that such a lease was worthless. Please rule. Is it ethical for Deutsch to use the Statute of Frauds

in attempting to defeat the lease? Assume that, as landlord, you had orally agreed to rent premises to a tenant, but then for business reasons, you preferred not to carry out the deal. Would you evict a tenant if you thought the Statute of Frauds would enable you to do so? How should you analyze the problem? What values are most important to you?

2. Mast Industries and Bazak International were two textile firms. Mast verbally offered to sell certain textiles to Bazak for $103,000. Mast promised to send documents confirming the agreement, but it never did. Finally, Bazak sent a memorandum to Mast confirming the agreement, describing the goods, and specifying their quantity and the price. Bazak's officer signed the memo. Mast received the memo but never agreed to it in writing. When Mast failed to deliver the goods, Bazak sued. Who will win? Why?

3. A disc jockey named Z-Trip made a remix of a Beastie Boys song with the hip-hop group's permission. Monster Energy (ME), an energy drink company, wanted to use the remix as part of a video promotion. ME sent an email asking Z-Trip to approve the video. In an email, Z-Trip responded "Dope!" When the Beastie Boys sued ME for copyright infringement, ME claimed that Z-Trip's reply was a contract granting it approval to use the remix. Is there an enforceable contract between Z-Trip and ME?

4. Does the coverage of the Statute of Frauds make sense as it currently stands? Would it be better to expand the law and require that all contracts be in writing? Or should the law be done away with altogether?

5. Compare the common-law Statute of Frauds to the UCC version. What are the specific differences? Which is more reasonable? Why?

ANSWERS TO SELECTED END OF CHAPTER QUESTIONS

MULTIPLE-CHOICE QUESTIONS

Presented are the answers for the ODD-numbered multiple-choice questions in the end-of-chapter material.

1. C
3. B
5. A

CASE QUESTIONS

Presented are the answers for all of the ODD-numbered case questions in the end-of-chapter material.

1. **Answer:** Under the parol evidence rule, if the parties intended the guaranty to be integrated, which they almost certainly did, Griffin may testify only if the writing is ambiguous or incomplete. The state supreme court ruled that the document was complete and unambiguous, and Griffin owed the entire remaining balance. *First National Bank v. Griffin*, 310 Ark. 164, 832 S.W.2d 816, 1992 Ark. LEXIS 439 (1992).

3. **Answer:** Hippen's claim fails. The purchase—or repurchase—of a house is the classic interest in land, and any such promise must be written to be enforceable. *Hippen v. First National Bank*, 1992 U.S. Dist. LEXIS 6029 (D. Kan. 1992).

5. **Answer:** At trial, jurors heard the tape recording, which confirmed the oral agreement. The jury concluded that the parties had reached a binding agreement and awarded Sawyer $900,000. However, the court granted a judgment notwithstanding the verdict for Mills because the agreement was barred by the Statute of Frauds. Sawyer appealed. Does the Statute of Frauds prevent enforcement of Mills's promise? Argument for Sawyer: The Statute of Frauds exists to prevent fraud. The fear of a plaintiff making up a false contract is legitimate, but obviously it does not apply in this case. We know that Mills agreed to pay a million dollars because we heard him. His own words verify the exact terms of the agreement and his promise to sign his name to it. What more evidence do you need? Argument for Mills: This is a simple case. If there was an agreement, it could not have been performed in one year because it had 10 years' worth of installment payments. Under the Statute of Frauds, an agreement that cannot be performed within one year is unenforceable unless written and signed.

Chapter 17

THIRD PARTIES

First, Ronald Schmalfeldt got his teeth knocked out … and then he got his wind knocked out by his dental bills. Here is what happened.

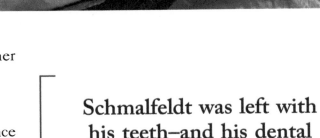

Schmalfeldt was at the Elite Bar playing a pick-up game of pool with another bar patron, whom he did not know. A heated argument ensued. Schmalfeldt tried to walk away but was struck in the face by the other player, who then fled—never to be heard from again. The brawl caused Schmalfeldt extensive dental damage, to the tune of $1,921. He asked the owner of the Elite Bar to pay his dental expenses, but the owner refused. Schmalfeldt was left with his teeth—and his dental bills—in his hands.

Schmalfeldt sought payment directly from North Pointe, which had issued a commercial liability insurance policy to the owner of the Elite Bar. He claimed that, as a pool-playing bar patron, he had a right to medical benefits under the policy. In its contract with Elite, North Pointe had agreed to pay up to $5,000 for medical expenses for a bodily injury caused by an accident occurring on Elite's premises, regardless of fault. When North Pointe refused to pay, Schmalfeldt sued. Could Schmalfeldt enforce the bar's contract rights, or did he have to put his money where his mouth was?[1]

> **Schmalfeldt was left with his teeth–and his dental bills–in his hands.**

---

[1]Schmalfeldt v. North Pointe Ins. Co. 469 Mich. 422 (2003).

Chapters 13 through 16 examined the Contracts Checklist, so you now know all the elements that must be present for a valid contract to exist. In this chapter and Chapters 18 and 19, we turn our attention to other contract issues.

17-1 THIRD-PARTY BENEFICIARY

The two parties who make a contract always intend to gain some benefit for themselves. Often, though, their bargain will also benefit *someone else*. **A third-party beneficiary is someone who was not a party to the contract but stands to benefit from it.** Many contracts are clear in their intent to create third-party beneficiaries—and some even mention these lucky people by name. Sometimes, however, unnamed third parties want to enforce others' contracts. In that case, courts must analyze the particulars of the deal to see who is entitled to recover. In the case from the opening scenario, the Michigan Supreme Court held that since the insurance contract was intended to benefit the insured (the bar) and made no mention of patrons, Schmalfeldt was not a third-party beneficiary and, therefore, could not recover his damages.

As another example, suppose a major league baseball team contracts to purchase from Seller 20 acres of an abandoned industrial site to be used for a new stadium. The owner of a pizza parlor on the edge of Seller's land might benefit enormously, since 40,000 hungry fans in the neighborhood for 81 home games every season could turn her once-marginal operation into a gold mine of cheese and pepperoni.

But what if the contract falls apart? What if the team backs out of the land deal? Seller can certainly sue because it is a party to the contract. But what about the pizza parlor owner? Can she sue to enforce the deal and recover lost profits for unsold sausage and green pepper?

The outcome in cases like these depends upon the intentions of the two contracting parties. If they *intended* to benefit the third party, she will probably be permitted to enforce their contract. If they did not intend to benefit her, she probably has no power to enforce the agreement.

17-1a Intended Beneficiaries

A person is an **intended beneficiary** and may enforce a contract if the parties intended her to benefit and if either (a) enforcing the promise will satisfy a *duty* of the promisee to the beneficiary, or (b) the promisee intended to make a *gift* to the beneficiary. (The **promisor** is the one who makes the promise that the third-party beneficiary is seeking to enforce. The **promisee** is the other party to the contract.)

In other words, a third-party beneficiary must show two things in order to enforce a contract that two other people created. First, she must show that the two contracting parties were aware of her situation and knew that she would receive something of value from their deal. Second, she must show that the promisee wanted to benefit her for one of two reasons: either to satisfy some duty owed or to make her a gift.

If the promisee is fulfilling some duty, the third-party beneficiary is called a **creditor beneficiary**. Most often, the duty that a promisee will be fulfilling is a debt already owed to the beneficiary. If the promisee is making a gift, the third party is a **donee beneficiary**.[2] As long as the third party is either a creditor or a donee beneficiary, she may enforce the contract. If she is only an incidental beneficiary, she may not.

John's father, Clarence, has an overgrown lawn. So, John enters into a contract with Billy Goat Landscapers for it to mow Clarence's lawn every week. Billy Goat is the promisor and John, the promisee. Although Clarence was not a party to the contract, he is the beneficiary—it is his lawn being cut. John did not owe his father a legal duty but simply

Intended beneficiary
Someone who may enforce a contract made between two other parties

Promisor
Makes the promise that a third party seeks to enforce

Promisee
The contract party *to whom* a promise is made

---

[2] "Donee" comes from the word *donate*.

intended to make him a gift, so, Clarence is an intended, donee beneficiary, and he can sue the landscaping company to enforce the contract himself.

By contrast, the pizza parlor owner will surely lose. A stadium is a multimillion-dollar investment, and it is most unlikely that the baseball team and the seller of the land were even aware of the owner's existence, let alone that they intended to benefit her. She probably cannot prove either the first element or the second element, and certainly not both.

In the following case, an unlikely plaintiff sues for breach of a state contract. Was the prison inmate an intended beneficiary or was his argument just smoke in mirrors? Who is entitled to sue?

RATHKE v. CORRECTIONS CORPORATION OF AMERICA, INC.

153 P.3d 303
Supreme Court of Alaska, 2007

Facts: The state of Alaska entered into a contract with Corrections Corporation of America (CCA), a private company, to house Alaska's inmates. The contract required CCA to abide by the terms of a settlement agreement between the state and its inmates known as the Cleary FSA. This agreement listed Alaska's duties to its prisoners and also provided a list of permissible disciplinary procedures.

Gus Rathke was an Alaska inmate at a CCA prison located in Arizona. A routine drug test revealed marijuana in his system. Rathke's level of marijuana was within the limit allowed by the Cleary FSA (50 ng/ml) but exceeded Arizona's limit (20 ng/ml). CCA applied the more stringent Arizona standard. As a result, Rathke spent thirty days in punitive segregation and lost his prison job.

Rathke sued CCA, seeking lost wages and an apology. He claimed that CCA breached its contract with Alaska when it punished him according to the stricter marijuana standard. Rathke argued that as an Alaska inmate, he was an intended third-party beneficiary of the contract between Alaska and CCA.

The trial court disagreed with Rathke. It held that, even though he was entitled to certain rights under the Cleary FSA, he was not a third-party beneficiary of the CCA/Alaska contract. It reasoned that the Clearly FSA duties were only between Alaska and the inmates, while the duties in the CCA/Alaska contract were only between CCA and the state. Rathke appealed to Alaska's Supreme Court.

Issue: *Was Rathke an intended beneficiary of the contract between the state of Alaska and CCA?*

Excerpts from Justice Carpeneti's Decision: In determining whether a third party is an intended beneficiary of a contract, we refer to the Restatement (Second) of Contracts. According to §302, "a beneficiary of a promise is an intended beneficiary if the circumstances indicate that the promisee intends to give the beneficiary the benefit of the promised performance."

When applying these provisions, the motives of the parties in executing a contract—especially the promisee—are determinative. As a general rule, if the promised performance is rendered directly to the beneficiary, the intent to benefit the third party will be clearly manifested.

The state owes legal duties to all Alaska inmates, including those housed like Rathke at the CCA's Arizona facility. These duties are detailed in the Cleary FSA, which is an enforceable contract between Alaska inmates and the state.

We disagree with the [lower] court's analysis. First, the Cleary settlement is incorporated by reference into the state/CCA contract. Even more, many of its provisions are repeated virtually word for word in the contract. For example, portions of the discipline section of the state/CCA contract, allegedly breached in Rathke's case are virtually identical to the Cleary FSA.

Given this identity of provisions between the FSA and the state/CCA contract, we conclude that the prisoners are intended third-party beneficiaries of the portions of the contract which are taken directly from the FSA.

Accordingly, we hold that inmates have the right to sue CCA for violations of the Cleary FSA provisions contained in the CCA's contract with the state.

EXAM Strategy

Question: Mr. Inspector examines houses and gives its reports to potential buyers. Mr. Inspector contracts with Greenlawn, a real estate agent, to furnish reports on houses that Greenlawn is selling. The agreement allows the agent to give the reports to potential buyers. Greenlawn gives Molly one of Mr. Inspector's reports and, relying upon it, she buys a house. Although the report states that the house is structurally sound, it turns out that chronic roof leaks have caused water to seep into the walls. Molly sues Mr. Inspector. The inspector requests summary judgment, claiming that he had no contract with Molly.

Strategy: Mr. Inspector is right in saying he had no agreement with Molly. To prevail, Molly must demonstrate she is a third-party beneficiary of the contract between the other two. A third-party beneficiary may enforce a contract if the parties intended to benefit her and either (a) enforcing the promise will satisfy a duty of the promisee to the beneficiary or (b) the promisee intended to make a gift to the beneficiary.

Result: Greenlawn used the inspection summaries as sales tools. When Greenlawn assured a potential buyer that she could rely upon a report, the real estate agent took on a duty to deliver reliable information. Mr. Inspector understood that. The two parties intended to benefit Greenlawn's buyers. Molly may sue Mr. Inspector for breach of his contract with the agent. Mr. Inspector's motion for summary judgment is denied.

17-1b Incidental Beneficiaries

A person who fails to qualify as a donee beneficiary or a creditor beneficiary is merely an **incidental beneficiary** and may not enforce the contract. The pizza parlor owner is an incidental beneficiary.

In an effort to persuade courts, many plaintiffs make creative arguments that they are intended beneficiaries with enforcement rights. Is every taxpayer an intended beneficiary of a government contract? Do labor unions have rights if a contract refers to them in general terms? Or are these plaintiffs incidental beneficiaries? The following case answers these questions.

> **Incidental beneficiary**
> Someone who might have benefited from a contract between two others but has no right to enforce that agreement

UNITE HERE LOCAL 30 v. CALIFORNIA DEPARTMENT OF PARKS AND RECREATION

2011 Cal. App. LEXIS 510
Court of Appeal of California, 2011

Facts: The California Department of Parks and Recreation (DPR) and Delaware North Companies (DNC) entered into a contract giving DNC the right to operate a concession stand at a state park in San Diego for 10 years. Four years into the contract, DNC assigned its rights to operate the stand to another company.

DNC fired many of its employees, and the new operator did not rehire them. Some of these workers were members of the union Unite Here Local 30. Local 30 sued to block the assignment. It was joined in the suit by Bridgette Browning, who lived in the area and seemed to care who provided her hot dogs.

The trial court rejected the plaintiff's claims, and the plaintiffs appealed.

Issue: *Were the plaintiffs incidental or donee beneficiaries?*

Excerpts from Judge Hull's Decision: Paragraph 37(a) of the contract limits assignments and reads: "No assignment shall be made unless first consented to in writing by State." Before State considers such assignment, the proposed assignment must comply with applicable law. DPR reviewed the evidence submitted by Delaware North and determined that the proposed assignment met the requirements under paragraph 37(a).

Plaintiffs contend a third party who is within the class of those for whose benefit a contract is made have standing to sue for breach of that contract. They further argue, Local 30 and the employees it represents are clearly intended beneficiaries of the original contract.

The test for determining whether a contract was made for the benefit of a third person is whether an intent to benefit a third person appears from the terms of the contract. Under the intent test, it is not enough that the third party would incidentally have benefited from performance. On the other hand, the third person need not be named or identified individually. A third party may enforce a contract where he shows that he is a member of a class of persons for whose benefit it was made.

Plaintiffs contend Bridgette Browning has a right to sue as a taxpayer of California. They point out that paragraph 37 procedures are intended to eliminate favoritism, fraud, corruption, and misuse of public funds. Thus, plaintiffs argue, can be said to have the intent to benefit the general public

and the taxpayer. Of course, any contract entered into by the state would presumably be for the benefit of the state's residents and taxpayers, just as a contract entered into by a corporation would presumably be for the benefit of the corporation's shareholders. However, the fact that members of the public derive a benefit from the contract does not make them intended beneficiaries. A person is a donee beneficiary only if the promisee's contractual intent is to make a gift to him. Browning is no more than an incidental beneficiary who benefits merely because the state as a whole benefits.

Likewise, Local 30 is no more than an incidental beneficiary. Plaintiffs argue that because the Concession Contract contains a neutrality agreement regarding union organizing, Local 30 and the employees it represents are clearly intended beneficiaries of the original contract. The neutrality agreement states, in part, "Concessionaire shall not use the Premises to hold a meeting if the purpose is to promote or deter union organizing." This provision hardly reveals an intent to confer a benefit on Local 30, or any union for that matter. At best, it shows an intent not to provide either a benefit or a detriment to union organizing.

We conclude the trial court correctly determined plaintiffs are not third party beneficiaries and therefore lack standing to sue on that basis.

The judgment is affirmed.

17-2 ASSIGNMENT AND DELEGATION

After a contract is made, one or both parties may wish to substitute someone else for themselves. Six months before Maria's lease expires, an out-of-town company offers her a new job at a substantial increase in pay. After taking the job, she wants to sublease her apartment to her friend Sarah.

Assignment
Transferring contract *rights*

Delegation
Transferring contract *duties*

A contracting party may transfer his rights under the contract, which is called an **assignment** of rights. Or a party may transfer her obligations under the contract, which is a **delegation** of duties. Frequently, a party will make an assignment and delegation simultaneously, transferring both rights (such as the right to inhabit an apartment) and duties (like the obligation to pay monthly rent) to a third party.

17-2a Assignment

Lydia needs 500 bottles of champagne. Bruno agrees to sell them to her for $10,000, payable 30 days after delivery. He transports the wine to her.

Bruno owes Doug $8,000 from a previous deal. He says to Doug, "I don't have your money, but I'll give you my claim to Lydia's $10,000." Doug agrees. Bruno then *assigns* to Doug his rights to Lydia's money, and in exchange Doug gives up his claim against Bruno for $8,000. Bruno is the assignor, the one making an assignment, and Doug is the assignee, the one receiving an assignment.

Why would Bruno offer $10,000 when he owed Doug only $8,000? Because all he has is a *claim* to Lydia's money. Cash in hand is often more valuable. Doug, however, is willing to assume some risk for a potential $2,000 gain.

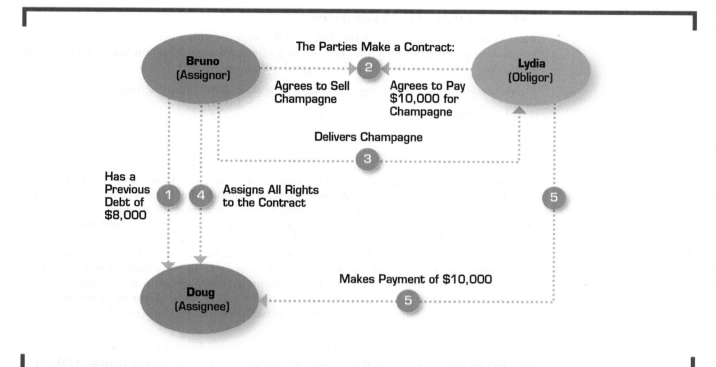

EXHIBIT 17.1

Bruno notifies Lydia of the assignment. Lydia, who owes the money, is called the **obligor**; that is, the one obligated to do something. At the end of 30 days, Doug arrives at Lydia's doorstep, asks for his money, and gets it, since Lydia is obligated to him. Bruno has no claim to any payment. See Exhibit 17.1.

Obligor
The party obligated to do something

EXAM Strategy

Question: Hasannah, an art dealer, signs a contract with Jason. Hasannah will deliver a David Hockney painting to Jason's house. Jason may keep it for 30 days and then either return it or pay Hasannah $2 million. Hasannah delivers the painting. Hasannah finds a better building to house her gallery and agrees to buy it from Shannon. She and Shannon sign a contract allowing Shannon to receive Jason's payment if he keeps the picture. Hasannah then notifies Jason to pay Shannon the $2 million. Identify the obligor, the assignor, and the assignee.

Strategy: The obligor is the one obligated to do something. The assignor makes an assignment and the assignee receives it.

Result: Jason is obligated either to return the picture or pay $2 million for it. He is the obligor. Hasannah is entitled to the money, but she assigns her right to Shannon. Hasannah is the assignor and Shannon the assignee.

What Rights Are Assignable?

Most contract rights are assignable, but not all. Disputes sometimes arise between the two contracting parties about whether one of the parties could legally assign her rights to a third party. Any **contractual right may be assigned unless assignment**

    (a) would substantially change the obligor's rights or duties under the contract;

    (b) is forbidden by law or public policy; or

    (c) is validly precluded by the contract itself.[3]

Substantial Change. An assignment is prohibited if it would substantially change the obligor's situation. For example, Bruno is permitted to assign to Doug his rights to payment from Lydia because it makes no difference to Lydia whether she writes a check to one person or another. But suppose that, before delivery, Lydia had wanted to assign her rights to the shipment of 500 bottles of champagne to a business in another country. In this example, Bruno would be the obligor, and his duties would substantially change. Shipping heavy items over long distances adds substantial costs, so Lydia would not be able to make the assignment.

Assignment is also prohibited when the obligor is agreeing to perform personal services. The close working relationship in such agreements makes it unfair to expect the obligor to work with a stranger. Warner, a candidate for public office, hires Mayer to be his campaign manager. Warner may not assign his right to Mayer's work to another candidate.

Public Policy. Some assignments are prohibited by public policy. For example, someone who has suffered a personal injury may not assign her claim to a third person. Vladimir is playing the piano on his roof deck when the instrument rolls over the balustrade and drops 35 stories before smashing Wanda's foot. Wanda has a valid tort claim against Vladimir, but she may not assign the claim to anyone else. As a matter of public policy, all states have decided that the sale of personal injury claims could create an unseemly and unethical marketplace.

Contract Prohibition. Finally, one of the contracting parties may try to prohibit assignment in the agreement itself. For example, most landlords include in the written lease a clause prohibiting the tenant from assigning the tenancy without the landlord's written permission.

Subleasing disputes between landlord and tenant are common. How much leeway does a landlord have in rejecting a proposed assignment? The following case provides the answer.

TENET HEALTHSYSTEM SURGICAL, L.L.C. V. JEFFERSON PARISH HOSPITAL SERVICE DISTRICT NO. 1

426 F.3d 738
Fifth Circuit Court of Appeals, 2005

Facts: MSC, Inc. owned the Marrero Shopping Center, and leased space to Tenet Healthsystem for use in outpatient surgery and general medical practice. The lease allowed Tenet to assign the lease with MSC's consent, and stated that consent would not be unreasonably withheld.

Two years later, MSC sold the shopping center to West Jefferson Medical Center, which owned an adjacent hospital and wanted the space for expansion. A few months after that, Tenet requested permission from West Jefferson to assign its lease to Pelican Medical, which

---

[3]Restatement (Second) of Contracts §317(2). And note that UCC §2-210 is, for our purposes, nearly identical.

intended to use the space for an occupational medical clinic. West Jefferson denied permission, stating that Pelican would be performing work not permitted under the original lease, and also because Pelican would compete with West Jefferson.

Tenet sued, claiming that West Jefferson was unreasonably withholding permission to assign. The trial court granted summary judgment for West Jefferson. Tenet appealed.

Issue: *Did West Jefferson unreasonably withhold permission to assign the lease?*

Excerpts from Judge Davis's Decision: West Jefferson asserts that Pelican's contemplated uses of the facility exceed those permitted under the lease [and also argues] that its refusal was reasonable because the proposed use of the facility poses more competition to its adjacent hospital.

Tenet used the facility for an outpatient surgery center. Pelican planned to use the facility for an occupational medical clinic. The services offered by an occupational medicine practice are quite comprehensive, from physical examinations and drug screening to low acuity emergencies. The clinic can treat patients with depression, lacerations, broken bones [and] pneumonia, and provides related lab and x-ray services. Nothing in this description takes the proposed practice outside the limits of a "general medical and physician's offices, including related uses," a permitted use under the lease.

West Jefferson also opposes the lease assignment from Tenet to Pelican on the basis that Pelican's broadened scope of operations would include new areas of competition with its hospital. When determining the reasonableness of a landlord's refusal to consent to an assignment of a lease, the standard is that of a reasonable prudent man.

In determining whether a landlord's refusal to consent was reasonable in a commercial context, only factors that relate to the landlord's interest in preserving the leased property or in having the terms of prime lease performed should be considered. Among factors a landlord can consider are the financial responsibility of the proposed subtenant, the legality and suitability of proposed use and nature of the occupancy. A landlord's personal taste or convenience is not properly considered. Rather the landlord's objection must relate to ownership and operation of leased property, not lessor's general economic interest. Under this standard, West Jefferson's refusal to consent to the assignment of the Tenet lease because Pelican would be a new competitor relates not to the ownership and operation of the leased property, but to West Jefferson's general economic interest.

West Jefferson's reason for denying consent to the assignment to Pelican based on increased competition is wholly personal to West Jefferson and does not relate in any way to an objective evaluation of Pelican as a tenant. Further, allowing West Jefferson to deny consent on a basis personal to it, a successor owner who took subject to the existing lease, would expand West Jefferson's rights under the lease to the detriment of the lessee in a manner not bargained for in the lease itself. Accordingly, we conclude that West Jefferson's refusal of consent to the assignment of the lease on the basis of increased competition was unreasonable.

Reversed and remanded.

How Rights Are Assigned

Writing.   In general, an assignment may be written or oral, and no particular formalities are required. However, when someone wants to assign rights governed by the Statute of Frauds, she must do it in writing. Suppose City contracts with Seller to buy Seller's land and then brings in Investor to complete the project. If City wants to assign to Investor its rights to the land, it must do so in writing.

Consideration.   An assignment can be valid with or without consideration, but the lack of consideration may have consequences. Two examples should clarify this. Recall Bruno, who sells champagne to Lydia and then assigns to Doug his right to payment. In that case, there *is* consideration for the assignment. Bruno assigns his rights only because Doug cancels the old debt, and his agreement to do that is valid consideration. **An assignment for consideration is irrevocable.** Once the two men agree, Bruno may not telephone Doug and say, "I've changed my mind, I want Lydia to pay me after all." Lydia's $10,000 now belongs to Doug.

But suppose that Bruno assigns his contract rights to his sister Brunhilde as a birthday present. This is a **gratuitous assignment**; that is, one made as a gift, for no consideration. **A gratuitous assignment is generally revocable if it is oral and generally irrevocable if it is written.** If Bruno verbally assigns his rights to Brunhilde, but then changes his mind, telephones Lydia, and says, "I want you to pay me after all," that revocation is effective and Brunhilde gets nothing. But if Bruno puts his assignment in writing and Brunhilde receives it, Bruno has given up his right to receive Lydia's payment.

Gratuitous assignment
One made as a gift, for no consideration

If you assign your rights under a contract, inform the obligor immediately.

Notice to Obligor. The assignment is valid from the moment it is made, regardless of whether the assignor notifies the obligor. But an assignor with common sense will immediately inform the obligor of the assignment. Suppose that Maude has a contract with Nelson, who is obligated to deliver 700 live frogs to her shop. If Maude (assignor) assigns her rights to Obie (assignee), Maude should notify Nelson (obligor) the same day. If she fails to inform Nelson, he may deliver the frogs to Maude. Nelson will have no further obligations under the contract, and Maude will owe Obie 700 frogs.

Rights of the Parties after Assignment

Once the assignment is made and the obligor notified, the assignee may enforce her contractual rights against the obligor. If Lydia fails to pay Doug for the champagne she gets from Bruno, Doug may sue to enforce the agreement. The law will treat Doug as though he had entered into the contract with Lydia.

But if a lawsuit arises, the reverse is also true. **The obligor may generally raise all defenses against the assignee that she could have raised against the assignor.** Suppose that Lydia opens the first bottle of champagne—silently. "Where's the pop?" she wonders. There is no pop because all 500 bottles have gone flat. Bruno has failed to perform his part of the contract, and Lydia may use Bruno's nonperformance as a defense against Doug. If the champagne was indeed worthless, Lydia owes Doug nothing.

Assignor's Warranty. The law implies certain warranties, or assurances, on the part of the assignor. Unless the parties expressly agree to exclude them, the assignor warrants that (1) the rights he is assigning actually do exist, and (2) there are no defenses to the rights other than those that would be obvious, such as nonperformance. But the assignor *does not* warrant that the obligor is solvent. Bruno is by implication warranting to Doug that Lydia has no defenses to the contract, but he is not guaranteeing Doug that she has the money to pay, or that she will pay.

Special Issue: The Uniform Commercial Code and Assignments of Security Interests

The provisions of the Uniform Commercial Code regarding assignments in contracts for the sale of goods are very similar to common-law rules.[4] However, Article 9 of the UCC has special rules about the assignment of **security interests**, which are the legal rights in personal property that ensure payment. When an automobile dealer sells you a new car on credit, the

Security interests
Rights in personal property that assure payment or the performance of some obligation

---

[4]UCC §2-210.

dealer will keep a security interest in your car. If you do not make your monthly payments, the dealer retains a right to repossess the vehicle. That authority is called a *security interest*. (See Chapter 25 for a full discussion.)

Companies that sell goods often prefer to assign their security interests to some other firm, such as a bank or finance company. The bank is the assignee. Just as we saw with the common law, the assignee of a security interest generally has all of the rights that the assignor had. And the obligor (the buyer) may also raise all of the defenses against the assignee that she could have raised against the assignor.

Under UCC §9-404, the obligor on a sales contract may generally assert any defenses against the assignee that arise from the contract, and any other defenses that arose before notice of assignment. The Code's reference to any defenses that arise from the contract means that if the assignor breached his part of the deal, the obligor may raise that as a defense. Suppose that a dealer sells you a new Porsche on credit, retaining a security interest. He assigns the security interest to the bank. The car is great for the first few weeks, but then the roof slides onto the street and both doors fall off. You refuse to make any more monthly payments. When the bank sues you, you may raise the automobile's defects as a defense, just as you could have raised them against the dealer itself. Where the Code talks about other defenses that arose before notice of assignment, it refers, for example, to fraud. Suppose that the dealer knew that before you bought the Porsche, it had been smashed up and rebuilt. If the dealer told you it was brand new, that was fraud, and you could raise the defense against the bank.

A contract may prohibit an obligor from raising certain defenses against an assignee. Sometimes a seller of goods will require the buyer to sign a contract that permits the seller to assign *and* prohibits the buyer from raising defenses against the assignee that he could have raised against the seller. University wants to buy a computer system on credit from Leland for $85,000. Leland agrees to the deal but insists that the contract permit him to assign his rights to anyone he chooses. He also wants this clause: "University agrees that it will not raise against an assignee any defenses that it may have had against Leland." This clause is sometimes called a *waiver clause* because the obligor is waiving (giving up) rights. Courts may also refer to it as an *exclusion clause* since the parties are excluding potential defenses. Leland wants a waiver clause because it makes his contract more valuable. As soon as University signs the agreement, Leland can take his contract to Krushem Collections, a finance company. Krushem might offer Leland $70,000 cash for the contract. Leland can argue, "You have to pay $85,000 for this. You are guaranteed payment by University since they cannot raise any defenses against you, even if the computer system collapses in the first half-hour." Leland gets cash and need not worry about collecting payments. Krushem receives the full value of the contract, with interest, spread out over several years.

Under UCC §9-403, an agreement by a buyer (or lessee) that he will not assert against an assignee any claim or defense that he may have against the seller (or lessor) is generally enforceable by the assignee if he took the assignment in good faith, for value, without notice of the potential defenses. In other words, Leland's waiver clause with University is enforceable. If Leland assigns the contract to Krushem Collections and the system proves worthless, Krushem is still entitled to its monthly payments from University. The school must seek its damages against Leland—a far more arduous step than simply withholding payment.

These waiver clauses are generally *not* valid in consumer contracts. If Leland sold a computer system to a consumer (an individual purchasing it for her personal use), the waiver would generally be unenforceable.

In the following case, one side pushes the waiver rule to its extreme. Can an assignee recover for money advanced … when the money was never advanced? You be the judge.

You be the Judge

Facts: Michael Brooks desperately needed financing for his company, BrooksAmerica, so he agreed to a sale-leaseback agreement with Terminal Marketing Company. Terminal would pay Brooks America $250,000, and in exchange it would obtain

WELLS FARGO BANK MINNESOTA V. BROOKSAMERICA MORTGAGE CORPORATION

419 F.3d 107
Second Circuit Court of Appeals, 2005

title to BrooksAmerica's computers and office equipment. BrooksAmerica would then lease the equipment for three years, for $353,000. The equipment would never leave BrooksAmerica's offices.

The contract included a "hell or high water clause" stating that BrooksAmerica's obligation to pay was "absolute and unconditional." Another clause permitted Terminal to assign its rights without notice to BrooksAmerica and stated that the assignee took its rights "free from all defenses, setoffs, or counterclaims."

Brooks also signed a "Delivery and Acceptance Certificate" stating that BrooksAmerica had received the $250,000 (even though no money had yet changed hands) and reaffirming BrooksAmerica's absolute obligation to pay an assignee, despite any defenses BrooksAmerica might have.

Terminal assigned its rights to Wells Fargo, which had taken about 2,000 other equipment leases from Terminal. Terminal never paid any portion of the promised $250,000. Brooks refused to make the required payments (about $10,000 per month) and Wells Fargo sued. Brooks acknowledged that Wells Fargo paid Terminal for the assignment.

Both parties moved for summary judgment. The trial court ruled in favor of Wells Fargo, and Brooks appealed.

You Be the Judge: *Is Wells Fargo entitled to its monthly lease payments despite the fact that BrooksAmerica never received financing?*

Argument for BrooksAmerica: We acknowledge the general validity of UCC §9-403. However, in this case, Wells Fargo makes an absurd argument. Neither Terminal nor any assignee has a right to enforce a financing contract when Terminal failed to deliver the financing. There is no valid contract to enforce here because Terminal never paid the $250,000 owed to BrooksAmerica. "Good faith" required Wells Fargo to make sure that Terminal had performed. A simple inquiry would have informed Wells Fargo that Terminal was entitled to no money. This entire transaction is a sham, and §9-403 was never drafted to encourage financial swindles.

The trial court *penalized* BrooksAmerica for acting in good faith. Mr. Brooks signed the Delivery Certificate assuming that any reasonable company would promptly deliver the money it had promised. Unfortunately, Terminal does not operate at the same ethical level—a fact that Wells Fargo should know from its earlier assignments.

Argument for Wells Fargo: Under UCC §9-403, an assignee such as Wells Fargo may enforce a waiver of defenses clause if the assignment was taken in good faith, for value, and free of knowledge of any claims or defenses. Wells Fargo meets that test.

The "simple inquiry" argument has two flaws. First, §9-403 does not require one. The UCC requires good faith, not an investigation. Second, Wells Fargo *did* investigate by checking the contract and the Delivery Certificate. We have done more than required. We have taken thousands of equipment leases as assignees. In this case, we examined the contract and the Delivery Certificate, and assumed that BrooksAmerica had received its money. If Terminal had not paid, why did Mr. Brooks sign a certificate stating he had received his cash? We are entitled to payment. Any dispute between BrooksAmerica and Terminal is for those parties to resolve.

17-2b Delegation of Duties

Garret has always dreamed of racing stock cars. He borrows $250,000 from his sister, Maybelle, in order to buy a car and begin racing. He signs a promissory note, which is a document guaranteeing that he will repay Maybelle the full amount, plus interest, on a monthly basis over 10 years. Regrettably, during his first race, Garret discovers that he has a speed phobia and quits the business. Garret transfers the car and all of his equipment to Brady, who agrees in writing to pay all money owed to Maybelle. Brady sends a check for a few months, but then the payments stop. Maybelle sues Garret, who defends based on the transfer to Brady. Will his defense work?

Garret has assigned his rights in the car and business to Brady, and that is entirely legal. But more important, he has *delegated his duties* to Brady. Garret was the **delegator** and Brady was the **delegatee**. In other words, the promissory note he signed was a contract, and the agreement imposed certain *duties* on Garret, primarily the obligation to pay Maybelle $250,000 plus interest. Garret had a right to delegate his duties to Brady, but delegating those duties did not relieve Garret of *his own* obligation to perform them. When Maybelle sues, she will win. Garret, like many debtors, would have preferred to wash his hands of his debt, but the law is not so obliging.

Most duties are delegable. But delegation does not by itself relieve the delegator of his own liability to perform the contract.

Garret's delegation to Brady was typical in that it included an assignment at the same time. If he had merely transferred ownership, that would have been only an assignment. If he had convinced Brady to pay off the loan without getting the car, that would have been merely a delegation. He did both at once. See Exhibit 17.2.

What Duties Are Delegable?

The rules concerning what duties may be delegated mirror those about the assignment of rights. And once again, the common law agrees with the UCC. An obligor may delegate his duties unless

1. delegation would violate public policy, or

2. the original contract prohibits delegation, or

3. the obligee has a substantial interest in personal performance by the obligor.[5]

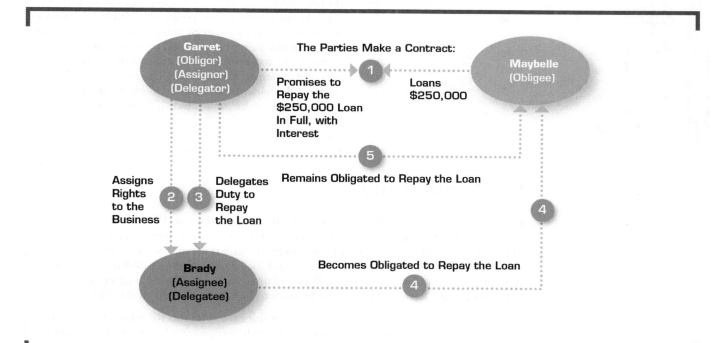

EXHIBIT 17.2

---

[5]Restatement (Second) of Contracts §318. And see UCC §2-210, establishing similar limits.

One may delegate and one may not.

Public Policy. Delegation may violate public policy, such as in a public works contract. If City hires Builder to construct a subway system, state law may prohibit Builder from delegating his duties to Beginner. The theory is that a public agency should not have to work with parties that it never agreed to hire.

Contract Prohibition. It is very common for a contract to prohibit delegation. We saw in the "Assignment" section that courts may refuse to enforce a clause that limits one party's ability to assign its contract rights. That does not hold true with delegation. The parties may forbid almost any delegation, and the courts will enforce the agreement. Hammer, a contractor, is building a house and hires Spot as his painter, including in his contract a clause prohibiting delegation. Just before the house is ready for painting, Spot gets a better job elsewhere and wants to delegate his duties to Brush. Hammer may refuse the delegation, even if Brush is equally qualified.

Substantial Interest in Personal Performance. Suppose Hammer had omitted the "nondelegation" clause from his contract with Spot. Could Hammer still refuse the delegation on the grounds that he has a substantial interest in having Spot do the work? No. Most duties are delegable, as long as they do not violate public policy or a clause in a contract. There is nothing so special about painting a house that one particular painter is required to do it. But some kinds of work do require personal performance, and obligors may not delegate these tasks. The services of lawyers, doctors, dentists, artists, and performers are considered too personal to be delegated. There is no single test that will perfectly define this group, but generally when the work will test the *character, skill, discretion, and good faith of the obligor*, she may *not* delegate her job.

EXAM Strategy

Question: Parker is a well-known actress. She agrees to act in Will's play for four weeks, for $30,000 per week. A week before rehearsals are to begin, Parker notifies Will that she cannot appear because a film producer has offered her over $1 million to start shooting immediately. She has arranged for Claire, another well-known actress, to appear in her place. Will objects. Parker claims, correctly, that their agreement does not prohibit her from making this substitution. Is Parker allowed to do this?

Strategy: Parker is attempting to delegate her duties. Under the Restatement, delegation is allowed unless (1) it would violate public policy, (2) it is prohibited by the contract, or (3) the obligee has a substantial interest in the obligor's personal performance.

Result: This is hardly a matter of public concern, and the contract does not speak to the issue. However, acting is a very personal kind of work. The actor must be right for the part, interact smoothly with other cast members, work well with the director, and help draw the audience. Will is entitled to have Parker perform the work, and she may not delegate her role.

Improper Delegation and Repudiation. Sometimes parties delegate duties they should not. Suppose Spot, having agreed not to delegate his painting job, is so tempted by the higher offer from another contractor that he delegates the work anyway. Hammer informs Spot he will not allow Brush on the job site. If Spot still refuses to work, he has **repudiated** the agreement; in other words, he has formally notified the other side that he will not perform his side of the contract. Hammer will probably sue him. On the other hand, if Hammer allows Brush up the ladder and Brush completes the job, Hammer has no claim against anybody.

Novation

As we have seen, a delegator does not automatically get rid of his duties merely by delegating them. But there is one way a delegator *can* do so. A **novation** is a three-way agreement in which the obligor transfers all rights and duties to a third party. The obligee agrees to look only to that third party for performance.

Recall Garret, the forlorn race car driver. When he wanted to get out of his obligations to Maybelle, he should have proposed a novation. Were one created, he would assign all rights and delegate all duties to Brady, and Maybelle would agree that *only Brady* was obligated by the promissory note, releasing Garret from his responsibility to repay. Why would Maybelle do this? She might conclude that Brady was a better bet than Garret and that this was the best way to get her money. Maybelle would prefer to have both people liable. But Garret might refuse to bring Brady into the deal until Maybelle permits a novation. In the example given, Garret failed to obtain a novation, and hence he and Brady were *both* liable on the promissory note.

Since a novation has the critical effect of releasing the obligor from liability, you will not be surprised to learn that two parties to a contract sometimes fight over whether some event was a simple delegation of duties or a novation. Here is one such contest.

It appears that Mary Pratt, moving to Arizona, honestly thought she was not only out of the ice cream business but relieved of any debt to the Rosenbergs. This lawsuit undoubtedly came as a cold shock. What should she have done to avoid the dispute?

Novation
A three-way agreement in which the obligor transfers all rights and duties to a third party

ROSENBERG V. SON, INC.

491 N.W.2d 71
Supreme Court of North Dakota, 1992

Facts: The Rosenbergs owned a Dairy Queen in Grand Forks, North Dakota. They agreed in writing to sell the Dairy Queen to Mary Pratt. The contract required her to pay $10,000 down and $52,000 over 15 years, at 10 percent interest. Two years later, Pratt assigned her rights and delegated her duties under the sales contract to Son, Inc. The agreement between Pratt and Son contained a "Consent to Assignment" clause, which the Rosenbergs signed. Pratt then moved to Arizona and had nothing further to do with the Dairy Queen. The Rosenbergs never received full payment for the Dairy Queen. They sued Mary Pratt.

The trial court gave summary judgment for Pratt, finding that she was no longer obligated on the original contract. The Rosenbergs appealed.

Issue: *Did Pratt obtain a novation relieving her of her duties under the original sales contract?*

Excerpts from Chief Justice Erickstad's Decision: It is a well-established principle in the law of contracts that a contracting party cannot escape its liability on the contract by merely assigning its duties and rights under the contract to a third party.

It is evident from the express language of the assignment agreement between Pratt and Son, Inc., that only an assignment was intended, not a novation. The agreement made no mention of discharging Pratt from any further liability on the contract.

Furthermore, the agreement was between Pratt and Son, Inc.; they were the parties signing the agreement, not the Rosenbergs. An agreement between Pratt and Son, Inc., cannot unilaterally affect the Rosenbergs' rights under the contract. As mentioned earlier, the Rosenbergs did sign a consent to the assignment at the bottom of the agreement. However, by merely consenting to the assignment, the Rosenbergs did not consent to a discharge of the principal obligor—Pratt. Nothing in the language of the consent clause supports such an allegation. A creditor is free to consent to an assignment without releasing the original obligor.

We *reverse* the summary judgment and *remand* for further proceedings.

Chapter Conclusion

A moment's caution! It is important to remember that the parties to a contract may not have the right to substitute someone else into the contract. The parties to a contract always have legal rights themselves, but when outsiders enter the picture, subtle differences in key areas determine whether additional rights exist.

EXAM REVIEW

1. **THIRD-PARTY BENEFICIARY** A third-party beneficiary may enforce a contract if the parties intended her to benefit from the agreement and if either (1) enforcing the promise will satisfy a debt of the promisee to the beneficiary, or (2) the promisee intended to make a gift to the beneficiary. The intended beneficiary described in (1) is a creditor beneficiary, while (2) describes a donee beneficiary. Any beneficiary who meets neither description is an incidental beneficiary and has no right to enforce the contract.

2. **ASSIGNMENT AND DELEGATION** An assignment transfers the assignor's contract rights to the assignee. A delegation transfers the delegator's duties to the delegatee.

3. **RIGHTS ASSIGNABLE** A party generally may assign contract rights unless doing so would substantially change the obligor's rights or duties, is forbidden by law, or is validly precluded by the contract.

EXAM Strategy

Question: Angelo Zavarella and Yvette Rodrigues were injured in an automobile accident allegedly caused by a vehicle belonging to Truck Equipment of Boston. Travelers Insurance Co. paid insurance benefits to Zavarella and Rodrigues, who then assigned to Travelers their claims against Truck Equipment. Travelers sued Truck Equipment, which moved to dismiss. What is Truck Equipment's claim that the case should be dismissed, and how would you rule?

Strategy: Travelers is claiming to be the assignee of the plaintiffs' claims. Any contractual right may be assigned except in the three instances listed. Does one of those prohibitions apply? (See the "Result" at the end of this section.)

4. ENFORCEMENT Once the assignment is made and the obligor notified, the assignee may enforce her contractual rights against the obligor. The obligor, in turn, may generally raise all defenses against the assignee that she could have raised against the assignor.

5. THE UCC AND SECURITY INTERESTS: Article 9 of the UCC governs security interests, which are the legal rights to personal property that assure payment of a debt. Under Article 9, obligors may assert defenses against assignees that arise from contracts, and agreements not to enforce such defenses are generally valid.

6. DUTIES DELEGABLE Duties are delegable unless delegation would violate public policy, the contract prohibits delegation, or the obligee has a substantial interest in personal performance by the obligor.

EXAM Strategy

Question: Pizza of Gaithersburg, Maryland, owned five pizza shops. Pizza arranged with Virginia Coffee Service to install soft drink machines in each of its stores and maintain them. The contract made no mention of the rights of either party to delegate. Virginia Coffee delegated its duties to the Macke Co., leading to litigation between Pizza and Macke. Pizza claimed that Virginia Coffee was barred from delegating because Pizza had a close working relationship with the president of Virginia Coffee, who personally kept the machines in working order. Was the delegation legal?

Strategy: Any contractual duty may be delegated except in the three instances listed. Does one of those prohibitions apply? (See the "Result" at the end of this section.)

7. DISCHARGE Unless the obligee agrees otherwise, delegation does not discharge the delegator's duty to perform.

8. NOVATION A novation is a three-way agreement in which the obligor delegates all duties to the delegatee and the obligee agrees to hold only the delegatee responsible.

EXAM Strategy

Question: Mardy, a general contractor, is building a house. He contracts with Plumbco to do all plumbing work for $120,000. Before Plumbco begins the work, it notifies Mardy in writing that Leo will be doing the work instead. Mardy does not respond. When Leo fails to perform, Mardy sues Plumbco. Plumbco is

(a) Liable

(b) Liable only if Plumbco agreed to remain responsible for the job

(c) Not liable because Mardy failed to repudiate the delegation

(d) Not liable because Plumbco validly delegated its duties

(e) Not liable because the parties entered into a novation

Strategy: Delegation does not by itself relieve the delegator of his own liability to perform the contract. In a novation, the obligee agrees to look only to the third party for performance. Was this a delegation or a novation? (See the "Result" at the end of this section.)

3. Result: Truck Equipment's winning argument was one sentence long: Claims for personal injury may not be assigned. Such assignments would transform accident claims into commercial commodities and encourage assignees to exaggerate the gravity of the harm.

6. Result: There is no public policy issue involved. The contract is silent as to delegation. And Pizza's only legitimate interest was in seeing that installation and maintenance were adequate. There is no reason to believe that Virginia Coffee would perform the work better than others. The duty was delegable, and Virginia Coffee wins.

8. Result: When Plumbco announced that Leo would do the work, Mardy did not respond. Mardy certainly did not agree to look exclusively to Leo for performance. There has not been a novation, and Plumbco remains liable on the contract. The correct answer is (a).

MULTIPLE-CHOICE QUESTIONS

1. *CPA QUESTION* Yost contracted with Egan for Yost to buy certain real property. If the contract is otherwise silent, Yost's rights under the contract are:
   (a) Assignable only with Egan's consent
   (b) Nonassignable because they are personal to Yost
   (c) Nonassignable as a matter of law
   (d) Generally assignable

2. *CPA QUESTION* One of the criteria for a valid assignment of a sales contract to a third party is that the assignment must:
   (a) Not materially increase the other party's risk or duty
   (b) Not be revocable by the assignor
   (c) Be supported by adequate consideration from the assignee
   (d) Be in writing and signed by the assignor

3. Amanda agrees to pay Jennifer $300 for a pair of tickets to see Jerry Seinfeld. "Seinfeld is my boyfriend Octavio's favorite comedian, and the tickets will be a great birthday present for him," she tells Jennifer. Amanda pays up and tells a delighted Octavio about the tickets, but Jennifer never delivers them. Octavio is a (n) ——————— beneficiary of the agreement, and as such, he ——————— have a right to enforce the contract himself.

(a) donee; does

(b) donee; does not

(c) incidental; does

(d) incidental; does not

4. A novation completely releases an ——————— from any further liability. To be effective, it ——————— require the agreement of both the obligor and obligee.

(a) obligor; does

(b) obligor; does not

(c) obligee; does

(d) obligee; does not

5. Will misses three straight payments on his SUV, and his bank repossesses it. The right to repossess ——————— a security interest. Security interests are governed by Article ——————— of the Uniform Commercial Code.

(a) is; 2

(b) is; 9

(c) is not; 2

(d) is not; 9

CASE QUESTIONS

1. Intercontinental Metals Corp. (IMC) contracted with the accounting firm of Cherry, Bekaert, & Holland to perform an audit. Cherry issued its opinion about IMC, giving all copies of its report directly to the company. IMC later permitted Dun & Bradstreet to examine the statements, and Raritan River Steel Co. saw a report published by Dun & Bradstreet. Relying on the audit, Raritan sold IMC $2.2 million worth of steel on credit, but IMC promptly went bankrupt. Raritan sued Cherry, claiming that IMC was not as sound as Cherry had reported and that the accounting firm had breached its contract with IMC. Comment on Raritan's suit.

2. Woodson Walker and Associates leased computer equipment from Park Ryan Leasing. The lease said nothing about assignment. Park Ryan then assigned the lease to TCB as security for a loan. Park Ryan defaulted on its loan, and Walker failed to make several payments on the lease. TCB sued Walker for the lease payments. Was the assignment valid, given the fact that the original lease made no mention of it? If the assignment was valid, may Walker raise defenses against TCB that it could have raised against Park Ryan?

3. Darin bought his fiancée Sarah a 3-carat diamond ring for $43,121 from Mandarin Gems. Later, Mandarin supplied Erstad with a written appraisal valuing the engagement ring at $45,500. Years later, the couple divorced and Sarah kept the ring. When she had the ring reappraised, another gemologist assessed its value at only $20,000. Sarah sued Mandarin for breach of contract, but the jeweller defended by saying that it had never made a contract with her. Does Sarah have contract rights against Mandarin?

4. *YOU BE THE JUDGE* **WRITING PROBLEM** David Ricupero suspected his wife Polly of having an affair, so he taped her phone conversations and, based on what he heard, sued for divorce. David's lawyer, William Wuliger, had the recorded conversations transcribed for use at trial. The parties settled the divorce out of court and signed an agreement that included this clause:

> Except as herein otherwise provided, each party hereto completely and forever releases the other and his attorneys from any and all rights each has or may have … to any property, privileges, or benefits accruing to either by virtue of their marriage, or conferred by the Statutory or Common Law of Ohio or the United States of America.

After the divorce was final, Polly sued William Wuliger for invasion of privacy and violation of federal wiretapping law. Wuliger moved to dismiss the case based on the clause quoted. Polly argued that Wuliger was not a party to the divorce settlement and had no right to enforce it. May Wuliger enforce the waiver clause from the Ricuperos' divorce settlement? **Argument for Wuliger:** The contract language demonstrates that the parties intended to release one another and their attorneys from any claims. That makes Wuliger an intended third-party beneficiary, and he is entitled to enforce the agreement. If Polly did not want to release Wuliger from such claims, she was free not to sign the agreement. **Argument for Polly Ricupero:** A divorce agreement settles the affairs between the couple. That is all it is ever intended to do, and the parties here never intended to benefit a lawyer. Wuliger is only an incidental beneficiary and cannot use this contract to paper over his violation of federal wiretapping law.

5. Judith and John Brooks hired Wayne Hayes to build a house. The contract required Hayes to "provide all necessary labor and materials and perform all work of every nature whatsoever to be done in the erection of the residence." Hayes hired subcontractors to do all of the work. One of Hayes's employees checked on the work site daily, but neither Hayes nor any of his employees actively supervised the building. The Brookses were aware of this working arrangement and consented to it. The mason negligently installed the fireplace, ultimately leading to a serious fire. The Brookses sued Hayes for breach of contract. Hayes contended that, when the Brookses approved of his hiring of subcontractors to do all work, that created a novation relieving him of any liability. Discuss.

DISCUSSION QUESTIONS

1. A century and a half ago, an English judge stated: "All painters do not paint portraits like Sir Joshua Reynolds, nor landscapes like Claude Lorraine, nor do all writers write dramas like Shakespeare or fiction like Dickens. Rare genius and extraordinary skill are not transferable." What legal doctrine is the judge describing? What is the ethical basis of this rule?

2. Nationwide Discount Furniture hired Rampart Security to install an alarm in its warehouse. A fire would set off an alarm in Rampart's office, and the security company was then supposed to notify Nationwide immediately. A fire did break out, but Rampart allegedly failed to notify Nationwide, causing the fire to spread next door and damage a building owned by Gasket Materials Corp. Gasket sued Rampart for breach of contract, and Rampart moved for summary judgment. Comment.

3. If a person promises to give you a gift, there is usually no consideration. The person can change his mind and decide not to give you the present, and there is nothing you can do about it. But if a person makes a contract with *someone else* and intends that you will receive a gift under the agreement, you are a donee beneficiary and you *do* have rights to enforce the deal. Are these rules unacceptably inconsistent? If so, which rule should change?

4. In response to the subprime mortgage crisis, the federal government created the Home Affordable Modification Program (HAMP) to help struggling homeowners refinance their mortgage debt, thereby reducing the foreclosure rate. HAMP facilitates contracts between the U.S. Treasury and mortgage lenders, who modify eligible homeowners' mortgage loans in return for incentive payments. The Mackenzies applied for a HAMP modification of their home. Although they were eligible, Flagstar bank foreclosed on their Massachusetts home. The Mackenzies sued Flagstar for breach of contract, claiming they were intended third-party beneficiaries of the lender's contract with the government. Will the Mackenzies succeed on this theory?

5. In our society, a person can buy and sell almost anything. But as this chapter describes, you cannot sell personal injury claims. Should you be able to? Imagine that you are injured in a car wreck. You are told that you might win $100,000 in a lawsuit eventually, but that you might not receive payment for years, and you might also lose the case and recover nothing. If someone is willing to pay you $20,000 cash-on-the-barrelhead today for the rights to your claim, is it fair that public policy concerns prohibit you from taking the money?

ANSWERS TO SELECTED END OF CHAPTER QUESTIONS

MULTIPLE-CHOICE QUESTIONS

Presented are the answers for the ODD-numbered multiple-choice questions in the end-of-chapter material.

1. D
3. A
5. B

CASE QUESTIONS

Presented are the answers for all of the ODD-numbered case questions in the end-of-chapter material.

1. **Answer:** Raritan was hoping to be a third-party beneficiary of the contract between IMC and Cherry, Bekaert. But the court was unpersuaded. It found that the accountants had no intention of benefiting anyone other than IMC, that they had no knowledge at all of Raritan, and that Raritan had never even seen the original audit, but merely a report of the audit. The court declared that Raritan was an incidental beneficiary and hence a loser. *Raritan River Steel Co. v. Cherry, Bekaert & Holland*, 329 N.C. 646, 407 S.E.2d 178, 1991 N.C. LEXIS 519 (1991).

3. **Answer:** The court held that Sarah was an intended done beneficiary. At the time of purchasing the ring, Darin had made clear to Mandarin that its purpose was as an engagement right for Sarah. Even though Sarah was not a party to the contract between Darin and Mandarin, she had a right to enforce it.

5. **Answer:** Hayes loses. He has indeed delegated his duties, but that in itself does not remove his own contractual liability. To establish a novation he had to demonstrate that the Brookses had explicitly agreed to look only to the subcontractors for performance. There was no such evidence, and no novation. Hayes remained liable. *Brooks v. Hayes*, 133 Wis. 2d 228, 395 N.W.2d 167 (1986).

Chapter 18

PERFORMANCE, BREACH, AND DISCHARGE

© Honza Krej/Shutterstock.com

Polly was elated. It was the grand opening of her new restaurant, Polly's Folly, and everything was bubbling. The waitstaff hustled, and Caesar, the chef, churned out succulent dishes. Polly had signed a contract promising him $1,500 per week for one year, "provided Polly is personally satisfied with his cooking." Polly was determined that her restaurant would be glorious. Her three-year lease would cost $6,000 per month, and she had signed an advertising deal with Billboard Bonanza for the same period. Polly had also promised Eddie, a publicity agent, a substantial monthly fee, to begin as soon as the restaurant was 80 percent booked for one month. Tonight, with candles flickering at packed tables, Polly beamed.

> **Polly disliked a veal dish and gagged on one of Caesar's soups. She fired her chef.**

After a week, Polly's smiles were a bit forced. Some of Caesar's new dishes had been failures, including a grilled swordfish that was hard to pierce and shrimp jambalaya that was too spicy. The restaurant was only 60 percent full, and the publicity agent yelled at Caesar for costing him money. Later that month, Polly disliked a veal dish and gagged on one of Caesar's soups. She fired her chef.

Then troubles gushed forth—literally. A water main burst in front of Polly's restaurant, flooding the street. The city embarked on a two-month repair job that ultimately took four times that long. The street was closed to traffic, and no one could park within blocks of Polly's restaurant. Patronage dropped steadily as hungry customers refused to deal with the bad parking and construction noise. After several months, behind on the rent and in debt to everyone, Polly closed her doors for good.

Shortly, the court doors swung open, offering a full menu of litigation. Polly's landlord sued for three years' rent, and Billboard Bonanza demanded its money for the same period. Caesar claimed his year's pay. Eddie, the agent, insisted on some money for his hard work. Polly defended vigorously, seeking to be *discharged* from her various contracts.

If a party is **discharged**, she is "finished," and has no more duties under a contract. In each lawsuit, Polly asked a court to declare that her obligations were terminated and that she owed no money.

Most contracts are discharged by full performance. In other words, the parties generally do what they promise. Suppose, before the restaurant opened, Walter had promised to deliver 100 sets of cutlery to Polly and she had promised to pay $20 per set. Walter delivered the goods on time, and Polly paid $2,000 on delivery. The parties got what they expected, and that contract was fully discharged.

Sometimes the parties discharge a contract by agreement. For example, the parties may agree to **rescind** their contract, meaning that they terminate it by mutual agreement.[1] If Polly's landlord believed he could get more rent from a new tenant, he might agree to rescind her lease. But he was dubious about the rental market and refused to rescind.

At times, a court may discharge a party who has not performed. When things have gone amiss, a judge must interpret the contract and issues of public policy to determine who in fairness should suffer the loss. In the lawsuits brought by the landlord and Billboard Bonanza, Polly argued a defense called "commercial impracticability," claiming that she should not be forced to rent space that was useless to her or buy advertising for a restaurant that had closed. From Polly's point of view, the claim was understandable. But we can also respect the arguments made by the landlord and the advertiser, that they did not cause the burst water main. Claims of commercial impracticability are difficult to win, and Polly lost against both of these opponents. Though she was making no money at all from the restaurant, the court found her liable in full for the lease and the advertising contract.[2]

Polly's argument against Caesar raised another issue of discharge. Caesar claimed that his cooking was good professional work and that all chefs have occasional disasters, especially in a new restaurant. But Polly responded that they had a "personal satisfaction" contract. Under such contracts, "good" work may not suffice if it fails to please the promisee. Polly won this argument, and Caesar recovered nothing.

As to Eddie's suit, Polly raised a defense called "condition precedent," meaning that some event had to occur before she was obligated to pay. Polly claimed that she owed Eddie money only if and when the restaurant was 80 percent full for a month, and that had never happened. The court agreed and discharged Polly on Eddie's claim.

We will analyze each of these issues, and begin with a look at conditions.

18-1 CONDITIONS

Parties often put conditions in a contract. A **condition** is an event that must occur before a party becomes obligated under a contract. "I'll agree to do something, but only if something else happens first." Polly agreed to pay Eddie, the agent, a percentage of her profits, but with an important condition: 80 percent of the tables had to be booked for a month. Unless and until those tables were occupied, Polly owed Eddie nothing. That never happened, or, in contract language, the *condition failed*, and so Polly was discharged.

---

[1]The parties could also decide that one party's duties will be performed by someone else, a modification called a novation. Alternatively, they could create an accord and satisfaction, in which they agree that one party will substitute a new kind of performance in place of his contract obligations. See Chapter 17, on third parties, and Chapter 13, on consideration.

[2]Based on Luminous Neon v. Parscale, 17 Kan. App. 2d 241 (Kan. Ct. App. 1992).

Discharge
A party is discharged when she has no more duties under the contract.

Rescind
To terminate a contract by mutual agreement

Condition
An event that must occur before a party becomes obligated under a contract

Conditions can take many forms. Alex would like to buy Kevin's empty lot and build a movie theater on it, but the city's zoning law will not permit that kind of business in that location. Alex signs a contract to buy Kevin's empty lot in 120 days, *provided that* within 100 days, the city rezones the area to permit a movie theater. If the city fails to rezone the area by day 100, Alex is discharged and need not complete the deal.

Another example: Friendly Insurance issues a policy covering Vivian's house, promising to pay for any loss due to fire, but only if Vivian furnishes proof of her losses within 60 days of the damage. If the house burns down, Friendly becomes liable to pay. But if Vivian arrives with her proof 70 days after the fire, she collects nothing. Friendly, though it briefly had a duty to pay, was discharged when Vivian failed to furnish the necessary information on time.

18-1a How Conditions Are Created

Express Conditions

The parties may expressly state a condition. Alex's contract with Kevin expressly discharged all obligations if the city failed to rezone within the stated period. Notice that **no special language is necessary to create the condition**. Phrases such as "provided that" frequently indicate a condition, but neither those nor any other specific words are essential. As long as the contract's language indicates that the parties *intended* to create a condition, a court will enforce it.

Because informal language can create a condition, the parties may dispute whether they intended one or not. Sand Creek Country Club, in Indiana, was eager to expand its clubhouse facilities and awarded the design work to CSO Architects. The club wanted the work done quickly but had not secured financing. The architects sent a letter confirming their agreement:

> It was our intent to allow Mr. Dan Moriarty of our office to start work on your project as early as possible in order to allow you to meet the goals that you have set for next fall. Also, it was the intent of CSO to begin work on your project and delay any billings to you until your financing is in place. As I explained to you earlier, we will continue on this course until we reach a point where we can no longer continue without receiving some payment.

The club gave CSO the go-ahead to begin design work, and the architects did their work and billed Sand Creek for $33,000. But the club, unable to obtain financing, refused to pay. Sand Creek claimed that CSO's letter created a *condition* in their agreement, namely, that the club would have to pay only if and when it obtained financing. The court was unpersuaded and ruled that the parties had never intended to create an express condition. The architects were merely delaying their billing as a convenience to the club. It would be absurd, said the court, to assume that CSO intended to perform $33,000 worth of work for free.[3]

Professional sports contracts are often full of conditions. Assume that the San Francisco Giants want to sign Tony Fleet to play center field. The club considers him a fine defensive player but a dubious offensive performer. The many conditional clauses in his contract reflect hard bargaining over an athlete who may or may not become a star. The Giants guarantee Fleet only $500,000, a very modest salary by Major League Baseball standards.

---

[3]Sand Creek Country Club, Ltd. v. CSO Architects, Inc., 582 N.E.2d 872 (Ind. Ct. App. 1991).

If the speedy outfielder appears in at least 120 games, his pay increases to $1 million. Winning a Gold Glove award is worth an extra $200,000 to him. The Giants insist on a team option to re-sign Fleet for the following season at a salary of $800,000, but if the center fielder plays in fewer than 100 games, the team loses that right, leaving Fleet free to negotiate for higher pay with other teams.

Implied Conditions

At other times, the parties say nothing about a condition, but it is clear from their agreement that they have implied one. Charlotte orally rents an apartment to Hakan for one year and promises to fix any problems in the unit. It is an implied condition that Hakan will promptly notify Charlotte of anything needing repair. Although the parties have not said anything about notice, it is only common sense that Hakan must inform his landlord of defects since she will have no other way to learn of them.

18-1b Types of Conditions

Courts divide conditional clauses into three categories: (1) condition precedent, (2) condition subsequent, and (3) concurrent conditions.[4] But what they have in common is more important than any of their differences. The key to all conditional clauses is this: **If the condition does not occur, one party will probably be discharged without having to perform his obligations under a contract.**

Condition Precedent

In this kind of condition, an event must occur *before* a duty arises. Polly's contract with Eddie concerned a condition precedent. Polly had no obligation to pay Eddie anything *unless and until* the restaurant was 80 percent full for a month. Since that never happened, she was discharged. If the parties agreed to a condition precedent, the *plaintiff* has the burden to prove that the condition happened and that the defendant was obligated to perform.

Contracts for the sale of real estate often have conditions precedent. Buyers commonly make purchase offers contingent on events like obtaining a mortgage or an acceptable property inspection. In these cases, the buyer has no duty to pay until the conditions are met.

Condition Subsequent

This type of condition must occur *after* a particular duty arises. If the condition does not occur, the duty is discharged. Vivian's policy with Friendly Insurance contains a condition subsequent. As soon as the fire broke out, Friendly became obligated to pay for the damage. But if Vivian failed to produce her proof of loss on time, Friendly's obligation ended—it was discharged. Note that, with a condition subsequent, it is the *defendant* who must prove that the condition occurred, relieving him of any obligation.

---

[4]The Restatement (Second) of Contracts has officially abandoned the terms *condition precedent* and *condition subsequent*. See Restatement §§224 et seq. But courts routinely use the terms, so it is difficult to avoid the old distinctions.

CONDITION PRECEDENT AND CONDITION SUBSEQUENT COMPARED

	Condition Created	Does Condition Occur?	Duty Is Determined	Result
Condition Precedent	"Fee to be paid when restaurant is filled to 80% capacity for one month."	Condition DOES occur: restaurant is packed.	Duty arises: Polly owes Eddie his fee.	Polly pays the fee.
		Condition DOES NOT occur: restaurant is empty.	Duty never arises: Polly is discharged.	Polly pays nothing.

	Condition Created	Duty Is Determined	Does Condition Occur?	Result
Condition Subsequent	"Vivian must give proof of loss within 60 days."	Fire damages property, and Friendly Insurance becomes obligated to pay Vivian.	Condition DOES occur: Vivian proves her losses within 60 days.	Friendly pays Vivian for her losses.
			Condition DOES NOT occur: Vivian fails to prove her losses within 60 days.	Friendly is discharged and owes nothing.

Concurrent Conditions

Here, both parties have a duty to perform *simultaneously*. Renee agrees to sell her condominium to Tim on July 5. Renee agrees to furnish a valid deed and clear title to the property on that date, and Tim promises to present a cashier's check for $200,000. The parties have agreed to concurrent conditions. Each performance is the condition for the other's performance. If Renee arrives at the Registry of Deeds and can say only, "Don't worry. I'm totally sure I own this property," Tim need not present his check; similarly, if Tim arrives with only an "IOU" scribbled on the back of a candy wrapper, Renee has no duty to hand over a valid deed.

EXAM Strategy

Question: Roberto wants to buy Naomi's house for $350,000 and is willing to make a 20 percent down payment, which satisfies Naomi. However, he needs a $280,000 mortgage in order to complete the purchase, and he is not certain he can obtain one. Naomi is worried that Roberto might change his mind about buying the house and then use alleged financing problems to skip out of the deal. How can the two parties protect themselves?

Strategy: Both parties should use conditional clauses in the sales agreement. Naomi must force Roberto to do his best to obtain a mortgage. How? Roberto's clause should protect him if he cannot obtain a sufficient mortgage. How?

Result: Naomi should demand the 20 percent down payment. Further, her conditional clause should state that Roberto forfeits the down payment unless he demonstrates that, within two weeks, he has applied in good faith for a mortgage to at least three banks. Roberto should insist that if he promptly and fully applies to three banks but fails to obtain a mortgage, his down payment is refunded.

Public Policy

At times, a court will refuse to enforce an express condition on the grounds that it is unfair and harmful to the general public. In other words, a court might agree that the parties created a conditional clause but conclude that permitting its enforcement would hurt society. Did the insurance contract in the following case harm society? You be the judge.

You be the Judge

ANDERSON V. COUNTRY LIFE INSURANCE CO.
180 Ariz. 625
Arizona Court of Appeals, 1994

Facts: On November 26, a Country Life Insurance agent went to the house of Donald and Anna Mae Anderson. He persuaded the Andersons to buy a life insurance policy and accepted a check for $1,600. He gave the Andersons a "conditional receipt for medical policy," dated that day. The form stated that the Andersons would have a valid life insurance policy with Country Life, effective November 26, but only when all conditions were met. The most important of these conditions was that the Country Life home office accepts the Andersons as medical risks. The Andersons were pleased with the new policy and glad that it was effective that same day.

It was not. Donald Anderson died of a heart attack a few weeks later. Country Life declined the Andersons as medical risks and refused to issue a policy. Anna Mae Anderson sued. Country Life pointed out that medical approval was a condition precedent. In other words, the company argued that the policy would be effective as of November 26, but only if it later decided to make the policy effective. Based on this argument, the trial court gave summary judgment for Country Life. Ms. Anderson appealed, claiming that the conditional clause was a violation of public policy.

You Be the Judge: *Did the conditional clause violate public policy?*

Argument for Ms. Anderson: Your honors, this policy is a scam. This so-called "conditional receipt for medical policy" is designed to trick customers and then steal their money. The company leads people to believe they are covered as of the day they write the check. But they aren't covered until *much later*, when the insurer gets around to deciding the applicant's medical status.

The company gets the customer's money right away and gives nothing in exchange. If the company, after taking its time, decides the applicant is not medically fit, it returns the money, having used it for weeks or even months to earn interest. If, on the other hand, the insurance company decides the applicant is a good bet, it then issues the policy effective for weeks or months *in the past, when coverage is of no use*. No one can die retroactively, your honors. The company is being paid for a period during which it had no risk. This is a fraud and a disgrace, and the company should pay the benefits it owes.

Argument for Country Life: Your honors, is Country Life supposed to issue life insurance policies without doing a medical check? That is the road to bankruptcy and would mean that no one could obtain this valuable coverage. Of course, we do a medical inquiry, as quickly as possible. It's in our interest to get the policy decided one way or the other.

The policy clearly stated that coverage was effective *only when approved by the home office*, after all inquiries were made. The Andersons knew that as well as the agent. If they were covered immediately, why would the company do a medical check? Country Life resents suggestions that this policy is a scam, when in reality it is Ms. Anderson who is trying to profit from a tragedy that the company had nothing to do with.

The facts of this case are unusual. Obviously, most insureds do not die between application and acceptance. It would be disastrous for society to rewrite every insurance policy in this state based on one very sad fact pattern. The contract was clear and it should be enforced as written.

18-2 PERFORMANCE

Caitlin has an architect draw up plans for a monumental new house, and Daniel agrees to build it by September 1. Caitlin promises to pay $900,000 on that date. The house is ready on time, but Caitlin has some complaints. The living room was supposed to be 18 feet high, but it is only 17 feet; the pool was to be azure, yet it is aquamarine; the maid's room was not supposed to be wired for cable television, but it is. Caitlin refuses to pay anything for the house. Is she justified? Of course not, it would be absurd to give her a magnificent house for free when it has only tiny defects. But in this easy answer lurks a danger. Technically, Daniel did breach the contract, and yet the law allows him to recover the full contract price, or virtually all of it. Once that principle is established, how far will a court stretch it? Suppose the living room is only 14 feet high, or 12 feet, or 5 feet? What if the foundation has a small crack? A vast and dangerous split? What if Daniel finishes the house a month late? Six months late? Three years late? At some point, a court will conclude that Daniel has so thoroughly botched the job that he deserves little or no money. But where, exactly, is that point? This is a question that businesses—and judges—face often.

The more complex a contract, the more certain that at least one party will perform imperfectly. Nearly every house ever built has at least some small defects. A delivery of a thousand bushels of apples is sure to include a few rotten ones. A custom-designed computer system for a huge airline is likely to have some glitches. The cases raise several related doctrines, all concerning *how well* a party performed its contractual obligations.

18-2a Strict Performance and Substantial Performance

Strict Performance

When Daniel built Caitlin's house with three minor defects, she refused to pay, arguing that he had not *strictly performed* his obligations. Her assertion was correct, yet she lost anyway. Courts dislike strict performance because it enables one party to benefit without paying and sends the other one home empty-handed. A party is generally not required to render **strict performance** unless the contract expressly demands it *and* such a demand is reasonable. Caitlin's contract never suggested that Daniel would forfeit all payment if there were minor problems. Even if Caitlin had insisted on such a clause, few courts would have enforced it because the requirement would be unreasonable for a project as complicated as the construction of a $900,000 home.

There are some cases where strict performance does make sense. Marshall agrees to deliver 500 sweaters to Leo's store, and Leo promises to pay $20,000 cash on delivery. If Leo has only $19,000 cash and a promissory note for $1,000, he has failed to perform, and Marshall need not give him the sweaters. Leo's payment represents 95 percent of what he promised, but there is a big difference between getting the last $1,000 in cash and receiving a promissory note for that amount.

Strict performance
Requires one party to perform its obligations precisely, with no deviation from the contract terms

Substantial Performance

Daniel, the house builder, won his case against Caitlin because he fulfilled *most* of his obligations, even though he did an imperfect job. Courts often rely on the substantial performance doctrine, especially in cases involving services as opposed to those concerning the sale of goods or land. In a contract for services, a party that **substantially performs** its obligations will generally receive the full contract price, minus the value of any defects. Daniel receives $900,000, the contract price, minus the value of a ceiling that is 1 foot too low, a pool the wrong color, and so forth. It will be for the trial court to decide how much those defects are worth. If the court decides the low ceiling is a $10,000 defect, the pool color is worth $5,000, and the cable television wiring error is worth $500, then Daniel receives $884,500.

Substantial performance
Occurs when one party fulfills enough of its contract obligations to warrant payment

On the other hand, a **party that fails to perform substantially receives nothing on the contract itself and will recover only the value of the work, if any.** If the foundation cracks in Caitlin's house and the walls collapse, Daniel will not receive his $900,000. In such a case, he collects only the market value of the work he has done, which, since the house is a pile of rubble, is probably zero.

When is performance substantial? There is no perfect test, but courts look at these issues:

Substantial performance is vital, unless you enjoy working for free.

- How much benefit has the promisee received?

- If it is a construction contract, can the owner use the thing for its intended purpose?

- Can the promisee be compensated with money damages for any defects?

- Did the promisor act in good faith?

EXAM Strategy

Question: Jade owns a straight track used for drag racing. She hires Trevor to resurface it, for $180,000, paying $90,000 down. When the project is completed, Jade refuses to pay the balance and sues Trevor for her down payment. He counterclaims for the $90,000 still due. At trial, Trevor proves that all of the required materials were applied by trained workers in an expert fashion, the dimensions were perfect, and his profit margin very modest. The head of the national drag racing association testifies that his group considers the strip unsafe. He noticed puddles in both asphalt lanes, found the concrete starting pads unsafe, and believed the racing surface needed to be ground off and reapplied. His organization refuses to sanction races at the track until repairs are made. Who wins the suit?

Strategy: When one party has performed imperfectly, we have an issue of substantial performance. To decide whether Trevor is entitled to his money, we apply four factors: (1) How much benefit did Jade receive? (2) Can she use the racing strip for its intended purpose? (3) Can Jade be compensated for defects? (4) Did Trevor act in good faith?

Result: Jade has received no benefit whatsoever. She cannot use her drag strip for racing. Compensation will not help Jade—she needs a new strip. Trevor's work must be ripped up and replaced. Trevor may have acted in good faith, but he failed to deliver what Jade bargained for. Jade wins all of the money she paid. (As we will see in the Chapter 19, she may also win additional sums for her lost profits.)

18-2b **Personal Satisfaction Contracts**

Sujata, president of a public relations firm, hires Ben to design a huge multimedia project for her company, involving computer software, music, and live actors, all designed to sell frozen bologna sandwiches to supermarkets. His contract guarantees him two years' employment, provided all of his work "is acceptable in the sole judgment of Sujata." Ben's immediate supervisor is delighted with his work and his colleagues are impressed, but Sujata is not. Three months later, she fires him, claiming that his work is "uninspired." Does she have the right to do that?

This is a **personal satisfaction contract**, in which the promisee makes a personal, subjective evaluation of the promisor's performance. Employment contracts may require personal satisfaction of the employer; agreements for the sale of goods may demand that the buyer be personally satisfied with the product; and deals involving a credit analysis of one party may insist that his finances be satisfactory to the other party. In resolving disputes like Ben and Sujata's, judges must decide: When is it *fair* for the promisee to claim that she is not satisfied? May she make that decision for any reason at all, even on a whim?

Personal Satisfaction Clauses

A court applies a subjective standard only if assessing the work involves personal feelings, taste, or judgment and the contract explicitly demanded personal satisfaction. A "subjective standard" means that the promisee's personal views will greatly influence her judgment, even if her decision is foolish and unfair. Artistic or creative work, or highly specialized tasks designed for a particular employer, may involve subtle issues of quality and personal preference. Ben's work combines several media and revolves around his judgment. Accordingly, the law applies a subjective standard to Sujata's decision. Since she concludes that his work is uninspired, she may legally fire him, even if her decision is irrational.

Personal satisfaction contract

Permit the promisee to make subjective evaluations of the promisor's performance

A woman offered to restore this mural for a church in Spain. The original mural is seen on the left. The mural before restoration is shown in the middle. The result of the restoration was the painting on the right. What would happen if the parties did not have a personal satisfaction clause?

Note that the promisee, Sujata, has to show two things: that assessing Ben's work involves her personal judgment *and* that their contract explicitly demands personal satisfaction. If the contract were vague on this point, Sujata would lose. Had the agreement merely said, "Ben will at all times make his best efforts," Sujata could not fire him.

In all other cases, a court applies an *objective* standard to the promisee's decision. In other words, the objective standard will be used if assessing the work does not involve personal judgment *or* if the contract failed to explicitly demand personal satisfaction. An objective standard means that the promisee's judgment of the work must be reasonable. Suppose Sujata hires Leila to install an alarm system for her company, and the contract requires that Sujata be "personally satisfied." Leila's system passes all tests, but Sujata claims, "It just doesn't make me feel secure. I know that someday it's going to break down." May Sujata refuse to pay? No.

Even though the contract used the phrase "personally satisfied," a mechanical alarm system does not involve personal judgment and taste. Either the system works or it does not. A reasonable person would find that Leila's system is just fine and, therefore, under the objective standard, Sujata must pay. The law strongly favors the objective standard because the subjective standard gives unlimited power to the promisee.

> **Either the system works or it does not.**

18-2c Good Faith

The parties to a contract must carry out their obligations in good faith. The difficulty, of course, is applying this general rule to the wide variety of problems that may arise when people or companies do business. How far must one side go to meet its good faith burden? Marvin Shuster was a physician in Florida. Three patients sued him for alleged malpractice. Shuster denied any wrongdoing and asked his insurer to defend the claims. But the insurance company settled all three claims without defending and with a minimum of investigation. Shuster paid nothing out of his own pocket, but he sued the insurance company, claiming that it acted in bad faith. The doctor argued that the company's failure to defend him caused emotional suffering and meant that it would be impossible for him to obtain new malpractice insurance. The Florida Supreme Court found that the insurer acted in good faith. The contract clearly gave all control of malpractice cases to the company. It could settle or defend as it saw fit. Here, the company considered it more economical to settle quickly, and Shuster should have known, from the contract language, that the insurer might choose to do so.[5]

In the following case, one party to a contract played its cards very close to its chest. Too close?

BRUNSWICK HILLS RACQUET CLUB INC. V. ROUTE 18 SHOPPING CENTER ASSOCIATES

182 N.J. 210
Supreme Court of New Jersey, 2005

Facts: Brunswick Hills Racquet Club (Brunswick) owned a tennis club on property that it leased from Route 18 Shopping Center Associates (Route 18). The lease ran for 25 years, and Brunswick had spent about $1 million in capital improvements. The lease expired, and Brunswick had the option of either buying the property or purchasing a 99-year lease, both on very favorable terms. To exercise its option, Brunswick had to notify Route 18 no later than September 30 and had to pay the option price of $150,000. If Brunswick failed to exercise its options, the existing lease automatically renewed as of September 30, for 25 more years, but at more than triple the current rent.

Brunswick's lawyer wrote to Rosen Associates, the company that managed Route 18, nineteen months before the option deadline, stating that Brunswick intended to exercise the option for a 99-year lease. He requested that the lease be sent well in advance so that he could review it. He did not make the required payment of $150,000. Rosen replied that it had forwarded Spector's letter to its attorney, who would be in touch. In April, Spector again wrote, asking for a reply from Rosen or its lawyer.

Over the next six months, the lawyer continually asked for a copy of the lease or further information, but neither Route 18's lawyer nor anyone else provided any data. Eventually, the September deadline passed.

Route 18's lawyer notified Brunswick that it could not exercise its option to lease because it had failed to pay the $150,000 by September 30.

Brunswick sued, claiming that Route 18 had breached its duty of good faith and fair dealing. The trial court found that Route 18 had no duty to notify Brunswick of impending deadlines, and it gave summary judgment for

---

[5]Shuster v. South Broward Hospital Dist. Physicians' Prof. Liability Ins. Trust, 591 So. 2d 174 (Fla. 1992).

Route 18. The appellate court affirmed, and Brunswick appealed to the state supreme court.

Issue: *Did Route 18 breach its duty of good faith and fair dealing?*

Excerpts from Justice Albin's Decision: Courts generally should not tinker with a finely drawn and precise contract entered into by experienced business people that regulates their financial affairs. [However,] every party to a contract is bound by a duty of good faith and fair dealing in both the performance and enforcement of the contract. Good faith is a concept that defies precise definition. Good faith conduct is conduct that does not violate community standards of decency, fairness, or reasonableness. The covenant of good faith and fair dealing calls for parties to a contract to refrain from doing anything which will have the effect of destroying or injuring the right of the other party to receive the benefits of the contract.

Our review of the undisputed facts of this case leads us to the inescapable conclusion that defendant breached the covenant of good faith and fair dealing. Nineteen months in advance of the option deadline, plaintiff notified defendant in writing of its intent to exercise the option to purchase the 99-year lease. Plaintiff mistakenly believed that the purchase price was not due until the time of closing.

During a 19-month period, defendant, through its agents, engaged in a pattern of evasion, sidestepping every request by plaintiff to discuss the option and ignoring plaintiff's repeated written and verbal entreaties to move forward on closing the 99-year lease despite the impending option deadline and obvious potential harm to plaintiff.

Defendant never requested the purchase price of the lease. Indeed, as defendant's attorney candidly admitted at oral argument, defendant did not want the purchase price because the successful exercise of the option was not in defendant's economic interest.

Ordinarily, we are content to let experienced commercial parties fend for themselves and do not seek to introduce intolerable uncertainty into a carefully structured contractual relationship by balancing equities. But there are ethical norms that apply even to the harsh and sometimes cutthroat world of commercial transactions. We do not expect a landlord or even an attorney to act as his brother's keeper in a commercial transaction. We do expect, however, that they will act in good faith and deal fairly with an opposing party. Plaintiff's repeated letters and telephone calls to defendant concerning the exercise of the option and the closing of the 99-year lease obliged defendant to respond, and to respond truthfully.

[Plaintiff is entitled to exercise the 99-year lease.]

EXAM Strategy

Question: Sun operates an upscale sandwich shop in New Jersey, in a storefront that she leases from Ricky for $18,000 per month. The lease, which expires soon, allows Sun to renew for five years at $22,000 per month. Ricky knows, but Sun does not, that in a year, Prada will open a store on the same block. The dramatic increase in pedestrian traffic will render Sun's space more valuable. Ricky says nothing about Prada, Sun declines to renew, and Ricky leases the space for $40,000 a month. Sun sues Ricky, claiming he breached his duty of good faith and fair dealing. Based on the *Brunswick Hills* case, how would the New Jersey Supreme Court rule?

Strategy: In the *Brunswick Hills* case, the court, on the one hand, criticized the defendant for cynically evading the plaintiff's efforts to renew. However, the court also said, "We do not expect a landlord or even an attorney to act as his brother's keeper in a commercial transaction." Using those opposing themes as guidelines, examine the court's decision and predict the ruling in Sun's suit.

Result: *Brunswick Hills* begins: "Courts generally should not tinker with a finely drawn and precise contract entered into by experienced business people." Sun's lease imposes no responsibility on Ricky to report on neighborhood changes or forecast profitability. Further, Sun made no requests to Ricky about the area's future. Sun is asking Ricky to be "her brother's keeper," and neither this court nor any other will do that. She loses.

18-2d Time of the Essence Clauses

Go, sir, gallop, and don't forget that the world was made in six days. You can ask me for anything you like, except time.

Napoleon, to an aide, 1803

Generals are not the only ones who place a premium on time. Ask Gene LaSalle. The Seabreeze Restaurant agreed to sell him all of its assets. The parties signed a contract stating the price and closing date. Seabreeze insisted on a clause saying, "Seabreeze considers that time is of the essence in consummating the proposed transaction." Such clauses are common in real estate transactions and in any other agreement where a delay would cause serious damage to one party. LaSalle was unable to close on the date specified and asked for an extension. Seabreeze refused and sold its assets elsewhere. A Florida court affirmed that Seabreeze acted legally.

A **time is of the essence clause** will generally make contract deadlines strictly enforceable. Seabreeze regarded a timely sale as important, and LaSalle agreed to the provision. There was nothing unreasonable about the clause, and LaSalle suffered the consequences of his delay.[6]

Suppose that the contract had named a closing date but included no time of the essence clause. If LaSalle offered to close three days late, could Seabreeze sell elsewhere? No. **Merely including a date for performance does not make time of the essence.** Courts dislike time of the essence arguments because even a short delay may mean that one party forfeits everything it expected to gain from the bargain. If the parties do not *clearly* state that prompt performance is essential, then both are entitled to reasonable delays.

Time is of the essence clause

Generally make contract dates strictly enforceable

18-3 BREACH

When one party breaches a contract, the other party is discharged. The discharged party has no obligation to perform and may sue for damages. Edwin promises that on July 1, he will deliver 20 tuxedos, tailored to fit male chimpanzees, to Bubba's circus for $300 per suit. After weeks of delay, Edwin concedes he hasn't a cummerbund to his name. Bubba is discharged and owes nothing. In addition, he may sue Edwin for damages.

18-3a Material Breach

As we know, parties frequently perform their contract duties imperfectly, which is why courts accept substantial performance rather than strict performance, particularly in contracts involving services. In a more general sense, **courts will discharge a contract only if a party committed a *material* breach.** A material breach is one that substantially harms the innocent party and for which it would be hard to compensate without discharging the contract. Suppose Edwin fails to show up with the tuxedos on June 1 but calls to say they will arrive under the big top the next day. He has breached the agreement. Is his breach material? No. This is a trivial breach, and Bubba is not discharged. When the tuxedos arrive, he must pay.

The following case raises the issue in the context of a major college sports program.

---

[6]Seabreeze Restaurant, Inc. v. Paumgardhen, 639 So.2d 69 (Fla. Dist. Ct. App. 1994).

O'BRIEN v. OHIO STATE UNIVERSITY

2007-Ohio-4833
Court of Appeals of Ohio, 2007

Facts: Ohio State University (OSU), experiencing a drought in its men's basketball program, brought in Coach Jim O'Brien to turn things around. The plan was successful. In only his second year, he guided the team to its best record ever. The team advanced to the Final Four, and O'Brien was named national coach of the year. OSU's athletic director promptly offered the coach a new, multiyear contract worth about $800,000 per year.

Section 5.1 of the contract included termination provisions. The university could fire O'Brien *for cause* if (a) there was a material breach of the contract by the coach or (b) O'Brien's conduct subjected the school to NCAA sanctions. OSU could also terminate O'Brien *without cause,* but in that case, it had to pay him the full salary owed.

O'Brien began recruiting a talented 21-year-old Serbian player named Alex Radojevic. While getting to know the young man, O'Brien discovered two things. First, it appeared that Radojevic had been paid to play briefly for a Yugoslavian team, meaning that he was ineligible to play college basketball. Second, it was clear that Radojevic's family had suffered terribly during the strife in his homeland.

O'Brien concluded that Radojevic would never play for OSU or any major college. He also decided to loan Radojevic's mother some money. Any such loan would violate an NCAA rule if done to recruit a player, but O'Brien believed the loan was legal since Radojevic could not play in the NCAA anyway. Several years later, the university learned of the loan and realized that O'Brien had never reported it. Hoping to avoid trouble with the NCAA, OSU imposed sanctions on itself. The university also fired the coach, claiming he had lied, destroyed the possibility of postseason play, and harmed the school's reputation.

O'Brien sued, claiming he had not materially breached the contract. The trial court awarded the coach $2.5 million, and the university appealed.

Issue: *Did O'Brien materially breach the contract?*

Excerpts from Judge Tyack's Decision: OSU argued that it was substantially injured by the self-imposed sanctions, which included a ban from post-season and NCAA tournament play [during the current season],

and relinquishing two basketball scholarships from the [next] recruiting class. Contrary to OSU's argument, however, the trial court found these sanctions to be insubstantial. [Athletic Director] Geiger announced the one-year post-season ban in December, and it appears from the timing of that announcement that Geiger made the decision based on the fact that the team was unlikely to be invited to a post-season tournament in the first place.

The second alleged harm was harm to OSU's reputation. The trial court found that any reputational harm was similarly exaggerated, at least as it specifically related to the Radojevic matter. Radojevic never enrolled at OSU, and never played a single second for OSU's basketball team.

NCAA violations happen all the time. It's the nature of the beast. Also relevant to the issue of OSU's allegedly damaged reputation is the fact that almost immediately after firing O'Brien, OSU was able to lure one of the nation's top coaching prospects, [Thad Matta], to assume O'Brien's former position. Shortly thereafter, Matta successfully recruited possibly the best recruiting class ever. Based on this evidence, the trial court could reasonably find the Radojevic loan did not cause serious harm to OSU.

OSU argues that O'Brien acted in bad faith by covering up his misconduct for several years. In the words of OSU's counsel at oral argument: *"If lying to your employer for four years is not a material breach, it's hard to imagine what would be!"* Although the premise for counsel's argument is sound, it is unsound in application because it assumes facts not in evidence. Counsel for OSU assumes for the purposes of the argument that O'Brien systematically either denied allegations about the Radojevic loan, or took affirmative steps to conceal it from OSU. The evidence does not support such a conclusion. After Radojevic was drafted by the NBA, there is not a single inference that can be drawn from the record to suggest that O'Brien even thought about the loan. In O'Brien's own mind, he did not believe he had done anything wrong; thus, he would not have had a motive to conceal what he had done.

[There was no material breach.]

Affirmed.

18-3b Anticipatory Breach

Sally will receive her bachelor's degree in May and already has a job lined up for September. She has signed a two-year contract to work as window display designer for Surebet Department Store. The morning of graduation, she reads in the paper that Surebet is going out of business that very day. Surebet has told Sally nothing about her status. Sally need not wait until September to learn her fate. Surebet has committed an **anticipatory breach by making it unmistakably clear that it will not honor the contract.** Sometimes a promisor will actually inform the promisee that it will not perform its duties. At other times, as here, the promisor takes some step that makes the breach evident. Sally is discharged and may immediately seek other work. She is also entitled to file suit for breach of contract. The court will treat Surebet's anticipatory breach just as though the store had actually refused to perform on September 1.

18-3c Statute of Limitations

A party injured by a breach of contract should act promptly. A **statute of limitations** begins to run at the time of injury and will limit the time within which the injured party may file suit. These laws set time limits for filing lawsuits. Statutes of limitation vary from state to state and from issue to issue within a state. Failure to file suit within the time limits discharges the party who breached the contract. Always consult a lawyer promptly in the case of a legal injury.

Statute of limitations
A statutory time limit within which an injured party must file suit

18-4 IMPOSSIBILITY

"Your honor, my client wanted to honor the contract. He just couldn't. *Honest.*" This plea often echoes around courtrooms as one party seeks discharge without fulfilling his contract obligations. Does the argument work? It depends. If performing a contract was truly impossible, a court will discharge the agreement. But if honoring the deal merely imposed a financial burden, the law will generally enforce the contract.

18-4a True Impossibility

These cases are easy—and rare. **True impossibility means that something has happened making it literally impossible to do what the promisor said he would do.** Francoise owns a vineyard that produces Beaujolais Nouveau wine. She agrees to ship 1,000 cases of her wine to Tyrone, a New York importer, as soon as this year's vintage is ready. Tyrone will pay $50 per case. But a fungus wipes out her entire vineyard. Francoise is discharged. It is theoretically impossible for Francoise to deliver wine from her vineyard, and she owes Tyrone nothing.

Meanwhile, though, Tyrone has a contract with Jackson, a retailer, to sell 1,000 cases of Beaujolais Nouveau wine at $70 per case. Tyrone has no wine from Francoise, and the only other Beaujolais Nouveau available will cost him $85 per case. Instead of earning $20 per case, Tyrone will lose $15. Does this discharge Tyrone's contract with Jackson? No. It is possible for him to perform—it's just more expensive. He must fulfill his agreement.

True impossibility is generally limited to these three causes:

- *Destruction of the Subject Matter.* This is what happened with Francoise's vineyard.

- *Death of the Promisor in a Personal Services Contract.* When the promisor agrees personally to render a service that cannot be transferred to someone else, her death discharges the contract. Producer hires Josephine to write the lyrics for a new Broadway musical, but Josephine dies after writing only two words: "Act One."

The contract was personal to Josephine and is now discharged. Neither Josephine's estate nor Producer has any obligation to the other. But notice that most contracts are not for personal services. Suppose that Tyrone, the wine importer, dies. His contract to sell wine to Jackson is not discharged because anyone can deliver the required wine. Tyrone's estate remains liable on the deal with Jackson.

- *Illegality.* Chet, a Silicon Valley entrepreneur, wants to capitalize on his computer expertise. He contracts with Construction Co. to build a factory in Iran that will manufacture computers for sale in that country. Construction Co. fails to build the factory on time, and Chet sues. Construction Co. defends by pointing out that the president of the United States has issued an executive order barring trade between the United States and Iran. Construction Co. wins; the executive order discharged the contract.

18-4b Commercial Impracticability and Frustration of Purpose

It is rare for contract performance to be truly impossible but very common for it to become a financial burden to one party. Suppose Bradshaw Steel in Pittsburgh agrees to deliver 1,000 tons of steel beams to Rice Construction in Saudi Arabia at a given price, but a week later, the cost of raw ore increases 30 percent. A contract once lucrative to the manufacturer is suddenly a major liability. Does that change discharge Bradshaw? Absolutely not. Rice signed the deal *precisely to protect itself against price increases.* As we have seen, the primary purpose of contracts is to enable the parties to control their future.

Yet there may be times when a change in circumstances is so extreme that it would be unfair to enforce a deal. What if a strike made it impossible for Bradshaw to ship the steel to Saudi Arabia, and the only way to deliver would be by air, at *five times* the sea cost? Must Bradshaw fulfill its deal? What if a new war meant that any ships or planes delivering the goods might be fired upon? Other changes could make the contract undesirable for *Rice.* Suppose the builder wanted steel for a major public building in Riyadh, but the Saudi government decided not to go forward with the construction. The steel would then be worthless to Rice. Must the company still accept it?

None of these hypotheticals involves true impossibility. It is physically possible for Bradshaw to deliver the goods and for Rice to receive. But in some cases, it may be so dangerous, costly, or pointless to enforce a bargain that a court will discharge it instead. Courts use the related doctrines of commercial impracticability and frustration of purpose to decide when a change in circumstances should permit one side to escape its duties.

Commercial impracticability means some event has occurred that neither party anticipated and *fulfilling the contract would now be extraordinarily difficult and unfair to one party.* If a shipping strike forces Bradshaw to ship by air, the company will argue that neither side expected the strike and that Bradshaw should not suffer a fivefold increase in shipping costs. Bradshaw will probably win the argument.

Frustration of purpose means some event has occurred that neither party anticipated and *the contract now has no value for one party.* If Rice's building project is canceled, Rice will argue that the steel now is useless to the company. Frustration cases are hard to predict. Some states would agree with Rice, but others would hold that it was Rice's obligation to protect itself with a government guarantee that the project would be completed. Courts consider the following factors in deciding impracticability and frustration claims:

- *Mere financial difficulties will never suffice to discharge a contract.* Barbara and Michael Luber divorced, and Michael agreed to pay alimony. He stopped making payments and claimed that it was impracticable for him to do so because he had hit hard times and simply did not have the money. The court dismissed his argument, noting that commercial impracticability requires some objective event that neither party anticipated, not merely the financial deterioration of one party.[7]

- *The event must have been truly unexpected.* Wayne Carpenter bought land from the state of Alaska, intending to farm it and agreeing to make monthly payments. The sales contract stated that Alaska did not guarantee the land for agriculture or any other purpose. Carpenter struggled to farm the land but failed; as soon as the ground thawed, the water table rose too high for crops. Carpenter abandoned the land and stopped making payments. Alaska sued and won. The high court rejected Carpenter's claim of impracticability since the "event"—bad soil—was not unexpected. Alaska had warned that the land might prove unworkable, and Carpenter had no claim for commercial impracticability.[8]

- *If the promisor must use a different means to accomplish her task, at a greatly increased cost, she probably does have a valid claim of impracticability.* If a shipping strike forces Bradshaw to use a different means of delivery—say, air—and this multiplies its costs several times, the company is probably discharged. But a mere increase in the cost of raw materials, such as a 30 percent rise in the price of ore, will almost never discharge the promisor.

- *A force majeure* clause is significant but not necessarily dispositive. To protect themselves from unexpected events, companies sometimes include a *force majeure* clause, allowing cancellation of the agreement in case of certain listed extraordinary and unexpected events. A typical clause might permit the seller of goods to delay or cancel delivery in the event of "acts of God, fire, labor disputes, accidents, or transportation difficulties." A court will always consider a *force majeure* clause, but it may not enforce it if one party is trying to escape from routine financial problems.

The following case involves risky business, complex financial instruments, and a lot of excuses. Does a global credit meltdown excuse a party's duty to pay?

HOOSIER ENERGY RURAL ELECTRIC COOPERATIVE, INC. V. JOHN HANCOCK LIFE INSURANCE CO.

582 F.3d 721
United States Court of Appeals for Seventh Circuit, 2009

Facts: John Hancock Life Insurance Co. receives lots of cash in premium payments, which it then invests so that it will have enough funds to pay claims from its policy holders. To this end, it entered into a leveraged lease with Hoosier Energy. This transaction was highly complex and only profitable because of convoluted provisions of the tax code. (You definitely do not want to try this at home.) In short, Hancock paid Hoosier $300 million to lease a power plant for 63 years, which Hoosier then leased back for 30 years.

But Hancock foresaw some risks: What if the power station became unprofitable? What if Hoosier stopped paying rent? (What would Hancock do if it was stuck with a power plant?) To mitigate these risks, it asked to Hoosier to

---

[7]Luber v. Luber, 418 Pa. Super. 542, 614 A.2d 771 (Pa. Super. Ct. 1992).
[8]State v. Carpenter, 869 P.2d 1181 (Alaska 1994).

secure a credit-default swap (CDS). A CDS is a financial contract that acts as insurance against a loan default and other contingencies. Ambac Assurance Corporation, the CDS provider, agreed to pay Hancock if certain events occurred. One of those triggering events was a decline in Ambac's own credit rating below a certain level. In that case, Hoosier had to find a replacement swap partner. If Hoosier was unsuccessful, Ambac would pay Hancock $120 million.

And then came 2008—and a global financial crisis. Ambac's credit rating plummeted, along with pretty much everyone else's. Hancock demanded that Hoosier find a replacement, but Hoosier stalled. If it replaced Ambac, it would have to pay big money—enough to send Hoosier into bankruptcy. So Hoosier sued, requesting an injunction to suspend its duty to find a swap partner. It claimed that the global financial crisis rendered its performance impossible—or at the very least, "temporarily impracticable" until the economy improved. The lower court sympathized with Hoosier and granted the injunction. Hancock appealed.

Issue: *Did the global credit crisis render performance impossible?*

Excerpts from Judge Easterbrook's Decision: Like other states, New York recognizes the doctrine of impossibility—but even then only the kind of impossibility that the parties could not have anticipated. Here, the parties anticipated the possibility that Hoosier, Ambac, or both might get into financial distress and provided what was to happen.

Suppose that Hoosier had an in-the-money option to purchase the Indianapolis Colts, and that as a result of the reduced availability of credit it was unable to find a lender to finance the transaction. That would not make performance "impossible." The "impossibility" doctrine never justifies failure to make a payment, because financial distress differs from impossibility.

It is hard to see why Hoosier should be able to stiff John Hancock, just because the very risk specified in the contract has occurred. Hoosier did not expect an economic downturn. Downturns are types of things that happen, and against which contracts can be designed. When they do happen, the contractual risk allocation must be enforced rather than set aside.

The district court called the credit crunch of 2008 a "once-in-a-century" event. That's an overstatement (the Great Depression occurred within the last 100 years, and the 20th Century also saw financial crunches in 1973 and 1987), and also irrelevant. An insurer that sells hurricane or flood insurance against a "once in a century" catastrophe, or earthquake insurance in a city that rarely experiences tremblors, can't refuse to pay on the ground that, when a natural event devastates a city, its very improbability makes the contract unenforceable.

The defense works only if some unexpected event upsets all parties' expectations; it is not enough that the unexpected event puts one side in a bind. Financial distress could be and was foreseen; that's what the credit-default swap is all about.

Chapter Conclusion

Negotiate carefully. A casually written letter may imply a condition precedent that the author never intended. The term *personal satisfaction* should be defined so that both parties know whether one party may fire the other on a whim. Never assume that mere inconvenience, financial distress—or even a global recession—will discharge contractual duties.

EXAM REVIEW

1. **CONDITION** A condition is an event that must occur before a party becomes obligated. It may be stated expressly or implied, and no formal language is necessary to create one.

Question: Stephen Krogness, a real estate broker, agreed to act as an agent for Best Buy Co., which wanted to sell several of its stores. The contract provided that Best Buy would pay Krogness a commission of 2 percent for "a sale to any prospect submitted directly to Best Buy by Krogness." Krogness introduced Corporate Realty Capital (CRC) to Best Buy, and the parties negotiated but could not reach agreement. CRC then introduced Best Buy to BB Properties (BB). Best Buy sold several properties to BB for $46 million. CRC acted as the broker. Krogness sought a commission of $528,000. Is he entitled to it?

Strategy: This contract contains a conditional clause. What is it? What must occur before Best Buy is obligated to pay Krogness? Did that event happen? (See the "Result" at the end of this section.)

2. **SUBSTANTIAL PERFORMANCE** Strict performance, which requires one party to fulfill its duties perfectly, is unusual. In construction and service contracts, substantial performance is generally sufficient to entitle the promisor to the contract price, minus the cost of defects in the work.

3. **PERSONAL SATISFACTION** Personal satisfaction contracts are interpreted under an objective standard, requiring reasonable ground for dissatisfaction, unless the work involves personal judgment *and* the parties intended a subjective standard.

4. **GOOD FAITH** Good faith performance is required in all contracts.

5. **TIME OF THE ESSENCE** Time of the essence clauses result in strict enforcement of contract deadlines.

Question: Colony Park Associates signed a contract to buy 44 acres of residential land from John Gall. The contract stated that closing would take place exactly one year later. The delay was to enable Colony Park to obtain building permits to develop condominiums. Colony Park worked diligently to obtain all permits, but delays in sewer permits forced Colony Park to notify Gall it could not close on the agreed date. Colony Park suggested a date exactly one month later. Gall refused the new date and declined to sell. Colony Park sued. Gall argued that since the parties specified a date, time was of the essence and Colony Park's failure to buy on time discharged Gall. Please rule.

Strategy: A time of the essence clause generally makes a contract date strictly enforceable. Was there one in this agreement? (See the "Result" at the end of this section.)

6. **MATERIAL BREACH** A material breach is the only kind that will discharge a contract; a trivial breach will not.

7. **IMPOSSIBILITY** True impossibility means that some event has made it impossible to perform an agreement. It is typically caused by destruction of the subject matter, the death of an essential promisor, or intervening illegality.

Question: Omega Concrete had a gravel pit and factory. Access was difficult, so Omega contracted with Union Pacific Railroad (UP) for the right to use a private road that crossed UP property and tracks. The contract stated that use of the road was solely for Omega employees and that Omega would be responsible for closing a gate that UP planned to build where the private road joined a public highway. In fact, UP never constructed the gate; Omega had no authority to construct the gate. Mathew Rogers, an Omega employee, was killed by a train while using the private road. Rogers's family sued Omega, claiming that Omega failed to keep the gate closed as the contract required. Is Omega liable?

Strategy: True impossibility means that the promisor cannot do what he promised to do. Is this such a case? (See the "Result" at the end of this section.)

8. **COMMERCIAL IMPRACTICABILITY** Commercial impracticability means that some unexpected event has made it extraordinarily difficult and unfair for one party to perform its obligations.

9. **FRUSTRATION OF PURPOSE** Frustration of purpose may occur when an unexpected event renders a contract completely useless to one party.

---

1. Result: The conditional clause requires Best Buy to pay a commission for "a sale to any prospect submitted directly to Best Buy by Krogness." Krogness did not in fact introduce BB Properties to Best Buy. The condition has not occurred, and Best Buy is under no obligation to pay.

5. Result: Merely including a date for performance does not make time of the essence. A party that considers a date critical must make that clear. This contract did not indicate that the closing date was vital to either party, so a short delay was reasonable. Gail was ordered to convey the land to Colony Park.

7. Result: There was no gate, and Omega had no right to build one. This is a case of true impossibility. Omega was not liable.

MULTIPLE-CHOICE QUESTIONS

1. *CPA QUESTION* Nagel and Fields entered into a contract in which Nagel was obligated to deliver certain goods by September 10. On September 3, Nagel told Fields that he had no intention of delivering the goods. Prior to September 10, Fields may successfully sue Nagel under the doctrine of:

   (a) promissory estoppel

   (b) accord and satisfaction

   (c) anticipatory breach

   (d) substantial performance

2. Most contracts are discharged by:

   (a) agreement of the parties

   (b) full performance

   (c) failure of conditions

   (d) commercial impracticability

   (e) a material breach

3. If a contract contains a condition precedent, the _____ has the burden of proving that the condition actually happened. If a condition subsequent exists, the _____ has the burden of showing that the condition occurred.

   (a) plaintiff; plaintiff

   (b) plaintiff; defendant

   (c) defendant; plaintiff

   (d) defendant; defendant

4. Big Co., a construction company, builds a grocery store. The contract calls for a final price of $5 million. Big Co. incurred $4.5 million in costs and stands to make a profit of $500,000. On a final inspection, the grocery store owner is upset. His blueprints called for 24 skylights, but the finished building has only 12. Installing the additional skylights would cost $100,000. Big Co. made no other errors. How much must the grocery store owner pay Big Co.?

   (a) $5,000,000

   (b) $4,900,000

   (c) $4,500,000

   (d) $0

5. Lenny makes K2, a synthetic form of marijuana, in his basement. He signs an agreement with the Super Smoke Shop to deliver 1,000 cans of K2 for $10,000. After the contract is signed, but before the delivery, Super Smoke Shop's state legislature makes the sale of K2 illegal. Lenny's contract will be discharged because of _____ .

   (a) true impossibility

   (b) commercial impracticability

   (c) frustration of purpose

   (d) none of the above

CASE QUESTIONS

1. **ETHICS** Commercial Union Insurance Co. (CU) insured Redux, Ltd. The contract made CU liable for fire damage but stated that the insurer would not pay for harm caused by criminal acts of any Redux employees. Fire destroyed Redux's property. CU claimed that the "criminal acts" clause was a condition precedent, but Redux asserted it was a condition subsequent. What difference does it make, and who is legally right? Does the insurance company's position raise any ethical issues? Who drafted the contract? How clear were its terms?

2. Stephen Muka owned U.S. Robotics. He hired his brother Chris to work in the company. His letter promised Chris $1 million worth of Robotics stock at the end of one year, "provided you work reasonably hard & smart at things in the next year." (We should all have such brothers.) Chris arrived at Robotics and worked the full year, but toward the end of the year, Stephen died. His estate refused to give Chris the stock, claiming their agreement was a personal satisfaction contract and only Stephen could decide whether Chris had earned the reward. Comment.

3. Ken Ward was an Illinois farmer who worked land owned by his father-in-law, Frank Ruda. To finance his operation, he frequently borrowed money from Watseka First National Bank, paying back the loans with farming profits. But Ward fell deeper and deeper into debt, and Watseka became concerned. When Ward sought additional loans, Watseka insisted that Ruda become a guarantor on all of the outstanding debt, and the father-in-law agreed. The new loans had an acceleration clause, permitting the bank to demand payment of the entire debt if it believed itself "insecure"; that is, at risk of a default. Unfortunately, just as Ward's debts reached more than $120,000, Illinois suffered a severe drought, and Ward's crops failed. Watseka asked Ruda to sell some of the land he owned to pay back part of the indebtedness. Ruda reluctantly agreed but never did so. Meanwhile, Ward decreased his payments to the bank because of the terrible crop. Watseka then "accelerated" the loan, demanding that Ruda pay off the entire debt. Ruda defended by claiming that Watseka's acceleration at such a difficult time was bad faith. Who should win?

4. Loehmann's clothing stores, a nationwide chain with headquarters in New York, was the anchor tenant in the Lincoln View Plaza Shopping Center in Phoenix, Arizona, with a 20-year lease from the landlord, Foundation Development, beginning in 1978. Loehmann's was obligated to pay rent the first of every month and to pay common-area charges four times a year. The lease stated that if Loehmann's failed to pay on time, Foundation could send a notice of default, and that if the store failed to pay all money due within 10 days, Foundation could evict. On February 23, 1987, Foundation sent to Loehmann's the common-area charges for the quarter ending January 31, 1987. The balance due was $3,500. Loehmann's believed the bill was in error and sent an inquiry on March 18, 1987. On April 10, 1987, Foundation insisted on payment of the full amount within 10 days. Foundation sent the letter to the Loehmann's store in Phoenix. On April 13, 1987, the Loehmann's store received the bill and, since it was not responsible for payments, forwarded it to the New York office. Because the company had moved offices in New York, a Loehmann's officer did not see the bill until April 20. Loehmann's issued a check for the full amount on April 24 and mailed it the following day. On April 28, Foundation sued to evict; on April 29, the company received Loehmann's check. Please rule.

5. *YOU BE THE JUDGE* **WRITING PROBLEM** Kuhn Farm Machinery, a European company, signed an agreement with Scottsdale Plaza Resort, of Arizona, to use the resort for its North American dealers' convention during March 1991. Kuhn agreed to rent 190 guest rooms and spend several thousand dollars on food and beverages. Kuhn invited its top 200 independent dealers from the United States and Canada and about 25 of its own employees from the United States, Europe, and Australia, although it never mentioned those plans to Scottsdale.

On August 2, 1990, Iraq invaded Kuwait, and on January 16, 1991, the United States and allied forces were at war with Iraq. Saddam Hussein and other Iraqi leaders threatened terrorist acts against the United States and its allies. Kuhn became concerned about the safety of those traveling to Arizona, especially its European employees. By mid-February, 11 of the top 50 dealers with expense-paid trips had either canceled their plans to attend or failed to sign up. Kuhn postponed the convention. The resort sued. The trial court discharged the contract under the doctrines of commercial impracticability and frustration of purpose. The resort appealed. Did commercial impracticability or frustration of purpose discharge the contract? **Argument for Scottsdale Plaza Resort:** The resort had no way of knowing that Kuhn anticipated bringing executives from Europe, and even less reason to expect that if anything interfered with their travel, the entire convention would become pointless. Most of the dealers could have attended the convention, and the resort stood ready to serve them. **Argument for Kuhn:** The parties never anticipated the threat of terrorism. Kuhn wanted this convention so that its European executives, among others, could meet top North American dealers. That is now impossible. No company would risk employee lives for a meeting. As a result, the contract has no value at all to Kuhn, and its obligations should be discharged by law.

DISCUSSION QUESTIONS

1. Evans built a house for Sandra Dyer, but the house had some problems. The garage ceiling was too low. Load-bearing beams in the "great room" cracked and appeared to be steadily weakening. The patio did not drain properly. Pipes froze. Evans wanted the money promised for the job, but Dyer refused to pay. Comment.

2. Krug International, an Ohio corporation, had a contract with Iraqi Airways to build aeromedical equipment for training pilots. Krug then contracted for Power Engineering, an Iowa corporation, to build the specialized gearbox to be used in the training equipment for $150,000. Power did not know that Krug planned to resell the gearbox to Iraqi Airways. When Power had almost completed the gearbox, the Gulf War broke out and the United Nations declared an embargo on all shipments to Iraq. Krug notified Power that it no longer wanted the gearbox. Power sued. Please rule.

3. Westinghouse sold uranium in long-term contracts at fixed prices, betting that market prices would be stable or fall (as they had been). But this was a bad bet: Uranium prices skyrocketed as a result of a cartel. Faced with large losses if it had to fulfill its contracts, Westinghouse argued that the unanticipated spike in uranium prices made its performance impossible. Should Westinghouse be freed of its contractual duties to sell uranium at a loss?

4. Jacobs Builders entered into a contract with Kent to build him a home. The agreement stated that Jacobs would use only certain brand-name materials. Upon completion of the home, Kent discovered that Jacobs had installed high-quality, but not brand-name, pipes throughout the house. This was an oversight, which even the architect failed to catch. Kent asked Jacobs to replace all the pipes, but this meant destroying all of the floors and walls in the house. Should Kent have to rebuild the house to get paid?

5. Franklin J. Moneypenny hires Angela to paint his portrait. She is to be paid $50,000 if the painting is acceptable "in Franklin's sole judgment." At the big unveiling, 99 of 100 attendees think that Angela has done a masterful job. Franklin disagrees. He thinks the painting makes him look like a toad. (He does in fact look like a toad, but he does not like to contemplate this fact.) Franklin refuses to pay, and, because he signed a personal satisfaction contract, Angela gets nothing. Is this fair? Should the law allow personal satisfaction contracts?

ANSWERS TO SELECTED END OF CHAPTER QUESTIONS

MULTIPLE-CHOICE QUESTIONS

Presented are the answers for the ODD-numbered multiple-choice questions in the end-of-chapter material.

1. C
3. B
5. A

CASE QUESTIONS

Presented are the answers for all of the ODD-numbered case questions in the end-of-chapter material.

1. **Answer:** The type of condition determines who must prove the source of the fire. CU claimed that the clause was a condition precedent, meaning that Redux had the burden of proving the fire was not arson. Redux argued that the clause was a condition subsequent, meaning that CU became liable to pay benefits as soon as the fire started, and could escape its duty only if the insurer proved Redux had committed arson. The court agreed with Redux, held that the clause was a condition subsequent, and placed the burden on CU to prove arson. *Redux, Ltd. v. Commercial Union Ins. Co.*, 1995 U.S. Dist. LEXIS 2545 (D. Kan. 1995). The most obvious ethical issues arise around the language of the contract and the sale of the policy. The contract says that the insurer is not liable for harm caused by criminal acts of employees. However, the contract says nothing about who must prove whether the harm was caused by such crimes. Further, it is very unlikely that the insurance agent explained, when selling the policy, that in the event of fire the insured company would have to prove the harm was not caused by employee arson. Some would say, as this court did, that the company is attempting to sneak one by its policyholders, using ambiguous language to help sell the policy, then sandbagging the insured once a loss occurs, claiming a contract interpretation that it had never before mentioned. Many would argue that the company that drafts a contract has an ethical obligation to make its terms clear. It is hard to believe that the insurance company would desire to be treated this way—for example, by reinsurers upon whom it depends.

3. **Answer:** The bank won. Good faith in this setting requires that the bank honestly believe itself to be insecure, and that there be *some basis* for the belief. The bank honestly did consider itself at risk of a default, and the combination of the drought and Ruda's refusal to sell land provided a basis for the belief. *Watseka First Natl. Bank v. Ruda*, 135 Ill. 2d 140, 552 N.E.2d 775, 1990 Ill. LEXIS 20 (1990).

5. **Answer:** Reversed. Summary judgment granted for Scottsdale Plaza, with the case remanded to the trial court to assess damages. Kuhn has no legitimate claim for impossibility or impracticability. Kuhn does not and cannot allege that it was impossible for it to perform, but rather that the *resort's* performance had been rendered worthless. That is a claim of frustration of purpose. To win on such a claim, Kuhn must show that the principal purpose in entering the contract was a convention at which the European employees would appear. That was not a principal purpose of the contract. Further, the majority of dealers were still prepared to attend. There has been no frustration of purpose. *7200 Scottsdale Road v. Kuhn Farm Machinery, Inc.*, 909 P.2d 408, 1995 Ariz. App. LEXIS 108 (Ariz. Ct. App. 1995).

Chapter 19

© Honza Krej/Shutterstock.com

REMEDIES

Margot had great expectations—the dating service, that is. She signed a contract in which she paid $3,790 to Great Expectations dating service. For this fee, the service promised to introduce her to at least 12 eligible bachelors who matched her requirements. Great Expectations would also provide high-quality photo shoots, dating advice, and invitations to members-only events. Representatives assured Margot that she would feel like "a kid in a candy store," with online access to over 175,000 Great Expectation members nationwide. They also told her that their location alone had had over 300 marriages in the last year.

As it turned out, Margot's experience was far from great. The company did not introduce her to anyone. (One man approached her after seeing her profile, but he was no prize.) Her photos were terrible, and the dating advice she received was useless because she had no dates. In fact, Great Expectations had greatly exaggerated their numbers of members and matches.[1]

Forlorn and angry, Margot sued the dating service. What did she *really* want? Margot did not want her money back: She wanted a date—many dates with many handsome, intelligent, and well-adjusted men of her age. She wanted them to swoon over her picture and tend to her every need. She wanted to get married. And she wanted to take back the three years she wasted with Great Expectations. But what could a court give her?

> **Margot sued the dating service. What did she really want? Margot did not want her money back: She wanted a date.**

---

[1]Adapted from Doe v. Great Expectations 10 Misc.3d 618 (N.Y. City Civ. Ct. 2005) and various states' attorneys general complaints against the company.

19-1 IDENTIFYING THE "INTEREST" TO BE PROTECTED

Someone breaches a contract when he fails to perform a duty without a valid excuse. Great Expectations breached its contract with Margot when it failed to deliver 12 dates. But what can Margot do about this breach? In other words, what is her *remedy?* **A remedy is the method a court uses to compensate an injured party.**

The first step that a court takes in choosing a remedy is to decide what interest it is trying to protect. An **interest** is a legal right in something. Someone can have an interest in property, for example, by owning it, or renting it to a tenant, or lending money so someone else may buy it. He can have an interest in a *contract* if the agreement gives him some benefit. There are four principal contract interests that a court may seek to protect:

- *Expectation interest.* This interest is what the injured party reasonably thought she would get from the contract. The goal is to put her in the position she would have been in if both parties had fully performed their obligations. Margot's great expectation was to find a mate, but a court cannot require the defendant to produce a husband. Typically, an expectation interest is the profit the plaintiff would have earned under a contract.

- *Reliance interest.* Even if the injured party has not shown an expectation interest, he can still recover damages if he proves that he *spent money* in reliance on the agreement and that, in fairness, he should receive compensation. If Margot had spent money flying to another city to meet a date who, it turned out, was a serial killer just released after 30 years in prison, she might have a reliance interest.

- *Restitution interest.* The injured party may be unable to show an expectation interest or reliance. But perhaps she has conferred a benefit *on the other party.* Here, the objective is to restore to the injured party the benefit she has provided. Margot provided the service with a benefit—money. Her best argument is in restitution. A court will not get her a date, but it can return her money.

- *Equitable interest.* In some cases, money damages will not suffice to help the injured party. Something more is needed, such as an order for the breaching party to perform (specific performance) or an order forcing it to stop doing something (an injunction). If a party who has promised to sell land ultimately refuses to do so, a court may order specific performance or may injoin the defendant from selling the property to someone else. As we will see, these actions are not always available to injured plaintiffs like Margot.

In this chapter, we look at all four interests.

Remedy
A court's compensation to the injured party

Interest
A legal right in something

> ## Ethics
>
> Although a court may have several alternative remedies available, it is important to note that most have one thing in common: The focus is on compensating the injured party rather than punishing the party in breach.
>
> Some critics argue that someone who willfully breaches a contract should pay a penalty. Margot and other Great Expectations members were duped by its false promises and inflated numbers. Should a remedy reflect morality? In this chapter, we will see very few instances in which a court *punishes* unethical conduct. Is this right? Should contract law exact a price for bad behavior? Should it try to prevent the same thing from happening to others? What would Kant and Mill say?

19-2 EXPECTATION INTEREST

This is the most common remedy that the law provides for a party injured by a breach of contract. **The expectation interest is designed to put the injured party in the position she would have been in had both sides fully performed their obligations.** A court tries to give the injured party the money she would have made from the contract. If accurately calculated, this should take into account all the gains she reasonably expected and all the expenses and losses she would have incurred. The injured party should not end up better off than she would have been under the agreement, nor should she suffer a loss.

If you ever go to law school, you will almost certainly encounter the following case during your first week of classes. It has been used to introduce the concept of damages in contract lawsuits for generations. Enjoy the famous "case of the hairy hand."

Landmark Case

HAWKINS V. MCGEE

84 N.H. 114
Supreme Court of New Hampshire, 1929

Facts: Hawkins suffered a severe electrical burn on the palm of his right hand. After years of living with disfiguring scars, he went to visit Dr. McGee, who was well known for his early attempts at skin-grafting surgery. The doctor told Hawkins "I will guarantee to make the hand a hundred percent perfect." Hawkins hired him to perform the operation.

McGee cut a patch of healthy skin from Hawkins's chest and grafted it over the scar tissue on Hawkins' palm. Unfortunately, the chest hair on the skin graft was very thick, and it continued to grow after the surgery. The operation resulted in a hairy palm for Hawkins. Feeling rather … embarrassed … Hawkins sued Dr. McGee.

The trial court judge instructed the jury to calculate damages in this way: "If you find the plaintiff entitled to anything, he is entitled to recover for what pain and suffering he has been made to endure and what injury he has sustained over and above the injury that he had before."

The jury awarded Hawkins $3,000, but the court reduced the award to $500. Dissatisfied, Hawkins appealed.

Issue: *How should Hawkins' damages be calculated?*

Excerpts from Justice Branch's Decision: The jury was permitted to consider two elements of damage, (1) pain and suffering due to the operation, and (2) positive ill effects of the operation upon the plaintiff's hand. [T]he foregoing instruction was erroneous.

By damages as that term is used in the law of contracts, is intended compensation to put the plaintiff in as good a position as he would have been in had the defendant kept his contract. The measure of recovery is what the defendant should have given the plaintiff, not what the plaintiff has given defendant or otherwise expended.

We conclude that the true measure of the plaintiff's damage in the present case is the difference between the value to him of a perfect hand and the value of his hand in its present condition, including any incidental consequences fairly within the contemplation of the parties when they made their contract.

The extent of the plaintiff's suffering does not measure this difference in value. The pain necessarily incident to a serious surgical operation was a part of the contribution which the plaintiff was willing to make to his joint undertaking with the defendant to produce a good hand. It furnished no test of the difference between the value of the hand which the defendant promised and the one which resulted from the operation.

[Remanded for a] new trial.

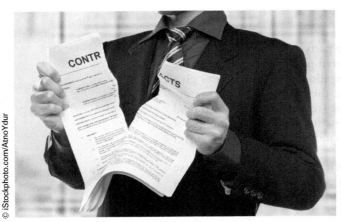
When a contract is broken, what kind of interest is harmed?

Now let's consider a more modern example.

William Colby was a former director of the CIA. He wanted to write a book about his 15 years in Vietnam. He paid James McCarger $5,000 for help in writing an early draft and promised McCarger another $5,000 if the book was published. He then hired Alexander Burnham to co-write the book. Colby's agent secured a contract with Contemporary Books, which included a $100,000 advance. But Burnham was hopelessly late with the manuscript and Colby missed his publication date. Colby fired Burnham and finished the book without him. Contemporary published *Lost Victory* several years late, and the book flopped, earning no significant revenue. Because the book was so late, Contemporary paid Colby a total of only $17,000. Colby sued Burnham for his lost expectation interest. The court awarded him $23,000, calculated as follows:

	$100,000	Advance, the only money Colby was promised
	–10,000	Agent's fee
	= 90,000	Fee for the two authors, combined
Divided by 2	= 45,000	Colby's fee (The other half went to the coauthor.)
	– 5,000	Owed to McCarger under the earlier agreement
	= 40,000	Colby's expectation interest
	– 17,000	Fee Colby eventually received from Contemporary
	= 23,000	Colby's **expectation damages**; that is, the additional amount he would have received had Burnham finished on time

Expectation damages
The money required to put one party in the position she would have been in had the other side performed the contract

The *Colby* case presented a relatively easy calculation of damages.[2] Other contracts are complex. Courts typically divide the expectation damages into three parts: (1) direct (or "compensatory") damages, which represent harm that flowed directly from the contract's breach; (2) consequential (or "special") damages, which represent harm caused by the injured party's unique situation; and (3) incidental damages, which are minor costs such as storing or returning defective goods, advertising for alternative goods, and so forth. The first two, direct and consequential, are the important ones.

Note that punitive damages are absent from our list. The golden rule in contracts cases is to give successful plaintiffs "the benefit of the bargain" and not to punish defendants. Punitive damages are occasionally awarded in lawsuits that involve both a contract *and* either an intentional tort (such as fraud) or a breach of fiduciary duty, but they are not available in "simple" cases involving only a breach of contract.

19-2a Direct Damages

Direct damages are those that flow directly from the contract. They are the most common monetary award for the expectation interest. These are the damages that inevitably result from the breach. Suppose that Ace Productions hires Reina to star in its new movie, *Inside Straight*. Ace promises Reina $3 million, providing she shows up June 1 and works until the film is finished. But in late May, Joker Entertainment offers Reina $6 million to star in its

---

[2]Colby v. Burnham, 31 Conn. App. 707 (Conn. App. Ct. 1993).

new feature, and on June 1, Reina informs Ace that she will not appear. Reina has breached her contract, and Ace should recover direct damages.

What are the damages that flow directly from the contract? Ace has to replace Reina. If Ace hires Kayla as its star and pays her a fee of $4 million, Ace is entitled to the difference between what it expected to pay ($3 million) and what the breach forced it to pay ($4 million), or $1 million in direct damages.

19-2b Consequential Damages

In addition to direct damages, the injured party may seek **consequential damages** or, as they are also known, "special damages." Consequential damages reimburse for harm that results from the *particular* circumstances of the plaintiff. These damages are only available if they are a *foreseeable consequence* of the breach. Suppose, for example, that Raould breaches two contracts—he is late picking both Sharon and Paul up for a taxi ride. His breach is the same for both parties, but the consequences are very different. Sharon misses her flight to San Francisco and incurs a substantial fee to rebook the flight. Paul is simply late for the barber, who manages to fit him in anyway. Thus, Raould's damages would be different for these two contracts. The rule concerning this remedy comes from a famous 1854 case, *Hadley v. Baxendale*. This is another case that all American law students read. Now it is your turn.

Consequential damages
Are those resulting from the unique circumstances of this injured party

Landmark Case

HADLEY V. BAXENDALE
9 Ex. 341
Court of Exchequer, 1854

Facts: The Hadleys operated a flour mill in Gloucester. The crankshaft broke, causing the mill to grind to a halt. The Hadleys employed Baxendale to cart the damaged part to a foundry in Greenwich, where a new one could be manufactured. Baxendale promised to make the delivery in one day, but he was late transporting the shaft, and as a result, the Hadleys' mill was shut for five extra days. They sued, and the jury awarded damages based in part on their lost profits. Baxendale appealed.

Issue: *Should the defendant be liable for profits lost because of his delay in delivering the shaft?*

Excerpts from Judge Alderson's Decision: Where two parties have made a contract which one of them has broken, the damages which the other party ought to receive in respect of such breach of contract should be such as may fairly and reasonably be considered either arising naturally, i.e. according to the usual course of things, from such breach of contract itself, or such as may reasonably be supposed to have been in the contemplation of both parties, at the time they made the contract, as the probable result of the breach of it. Now, if the special circumstances under which the contract was actually made were communicated by the plaintiffs to the defendants, and thus known to both parties, the damages resulting from the breach of such a contract, which they would reasonably contemplate, would be the amount of injury which would ordinarily follow from a breach of contract under these special circumstances so known and communicated. But, on the other hand, if these special circumstances were wholly unknown to the party breaking the contract, he, at the most, could only be supposed to have had in his contemplation the amount of injury which would arise generally, and in the great multitude of cases not affected by any special circumstances, from such a breach of contract.

Now, in the present case, if we are to apply the principles above laid down, we find that the only circumstances here communicated by the plaintiffs to the defendants at the time the contract was made, were that the article to be carried was the broken shaft of a mill, and that the plaintiffs were the millers of that mill. But how do these circumstances show reasonably that the profits of the mill must be stopped by an unreasonable delay in the delivery of the broken shaft by the carrier to the third person? Suppose the plaintiffs had another shaft in their possession put up or putting up at the time, and that they only wished to send back the broken shaft to the engineer who made it; it is clear that this would be quite consistent with the above circumstances, and yet the unreasonable delay in the delivery would have no effect upon the intermediate profits of the mill. It follows, therefore, that the loss of profits here cannot reasonably be considered such a consequence of the breach of contract as could have been fairly and reasonably contemplated by both the parties when they made this contract.

[The court ordered a new trial, in which the jury would *not* be allowed to consider the plaintiffs' lost profits.]

The rule from *Hadley v. Baxendale* has been unchanged ever since: **The injured party may recover consequential damages only if the *breaching party* should have *foreseen* them when the two sides formed the contract.**

Let us return briefly to *Inside Straight*. Suppose that, long before shooting began, Ace had sold the film's soundtrack rights to Spinem Sound for $2 million. Spinem believed it would make a profit only if Reina appeared in the film, so it demanded the right to discharge the agreement if Reina dropped out. When Reina quit, Spinem terminated the contract. Now, when Ace sues Reina, it will also seek $2 million in consequential damages for the lost music revenue.

The $2 million is not a direct damage. The contract between Reina and Act has nothing directly to do with selling soundtrack rights. But the loss is nonetheless a consequence of Reina bailing out on the project. So, if Reina knew about Ace's contract with Spinem when she signed to do the film, the loss would be foreseeable to her, and she would be liable for $2 million. If she never realized she was an essential part of the music contract, and if a jury determines that she had no reason to expect the $2 million loss, she owes nothing for the lost soundtrack profits.

Injured plaintiffs often try to recover lost profits. Courts will generally award these damages if (1) the lost profits were foreseeable and (2) the plaintiff provides enough information so that the factfinder can reasonably estimate a fair amount. The calculation need not be done with mathematical precision. In the following case, the plaintiffs lost not only profits—but their entire business. Can they recover for harm that is so extensive? You decide.

You be the Judge

BI-ECONOMY MARKET, INC. v. HARLEYSVILLE INS. CO. OF NEW YORK
2008 N.Y. Slip Op. 01418
New York Court of Appeals, 2008

Facts: Bi-Economy Market was a family-owned meat market in Rochester, New York. The company was insured by Harleysville Insurance. The "Deluxe Business Owner's" policy provided replacement cost for damage to buildings and inventory. Coverage also included "business interruption insurance" for one year, meaning the loss of pretax profit plus normal operating expenses, including payroll.

The company suffered a disastrous fire, which destroyed its building and all inventory. Bi-Economy immediately filed a claim with Harleysville, but the insurer responded slowly. Harleysville eventually offered a settlement of $163,000. A year later, an arbitrator awarded the Market $407,000. During that year, Harleysville paid for seven months of lost income but declined to pay more. The company never recovered or reopened.

Bi-Economy sued, claiming that Harleysville's slow, inadequate payments destroyed the company. The company also sought consequential damages for the permanent destruction of its business. Harleysville claimed that it was only responsible for damages specified in the contract: the building, inventory, and lost income. The trial court granted summary judgment for Harleysville. The appellate court affirmed, claiming that when they entered into the contract, the parties did not contemplate damages for termination of the business. Bi-Economy appealed to the state's highest court.

You Be the Judge: *Is Bi-Economy entitled to consequential damages for the destruction of its business?*

Argument for Bi-Economy: Bi-Economy is a small, family business. We paid for business interruption insurance for an obvious reason: In the event of a disaster, we lacked the resources to keep going while buildings were constructed and inventory purchased. We knew that in such a calamity, we would need prompt reimbursement—compensation covering the immediate damage and our ongoing lost income. Why else would we pay the premiums?

At the time we entered into the contract, Harleysville could easily foresee that if it responded slowly, with insufficient payments, we could not survive. They knew that is what we wanted to avoid—and it is just what happened. The insurer's bad faith offer of a low figure, and its payment of only seven months' lost income, ruined a fine family business. When the insurance company agreed to business interruption coverage, it was declaring that it would act fast and fairly to sustain a small firm in crisis. The insurer should now pay for the full harm it has wrought.

Argument for Harleysville: We contracted to insure the Market for three losses: its building, inventory, and lost income. After the fire, we performed a reasonable, careful evaluation and made an offer we considered fair. An arbitrator later awarded Bi-Market additional money, which we paid. However it is absurd to suggest that in addition to that, we are liable for an open-ended commitment for permanent destruction of the business.

Consequential damages are appropriate in cases where a plaintiff suffers a loss that was not covered in the contract. In this case, though, the parties bargained over exactly what Harleysville would pay in the event of a major fire. If the insurer has underpaid for lost income, let the court award a fair sum. However, the parties never contemplated an additional, enormous payment for cessation of the business. There is almost no limit as to what that obligation could be. If Bi-Market was concerned that a fire might put the company permanently out of business, it should have said so at the time of negotiating for insurance. The premium would have been dramatically higher.

Neither Bi-Market nor Harleysville ever imagined such an open-ended insurance obligation, and the insurer should not pay an extra cent.

19-2c Incidental Damages

Incidental damages are the relatively minor costs that the injured party suffers when *responding to* the breach. When Reina, the actress, breaches the film contract, the producers may have to leave the set and fly back to Los Angeles to hire a new actress. The travel cost is an incidental damage. In another setting, suppose Maud, a manufacturer, has produced 5,000 pairs of running shoes for Foot The Bill, a retail chain, but Foot The Bill breaches the agreement and refuses to accept the goods. Maud will have to store the shoes and advertise for alternate buyers. The storage and advertising costs are incidental expenses, and Maud will recover them.

> **Incidental damages**
> Relatively minor costs that the injured party suffers when responding to the breach

19-2d The UCC and Damages

Under the Uniform Commercial Code (UCC), remedies for breach of contract in the sale of goods are similar to the general rules discussed throughout this chapter. UCC §§2-703 through 2-715 govern the remedies available to buyers and sellers.[3]

---

[3]We discuss these remedies in greater detail in Unit 3, on commercial transactions.

Seller's Remedies

If a buyer breaches a sale of goods contract, the seller generally has at least two remedies. She may resell the goods elsewhere. If she acts in good faith, she will be awarded **the difference between the original contract price and the price she was able to obtain in the open market.** Assume that Maud, the manufacturer, had a contract to sell her shoes to Foot The Bill for $55 per pair and Foot The Bill's breach forces her to sell them on the open market, where she gets only $48 per pair. Maud will win $7 per pair times 5,000 pairs, or $35,000, from Foot The Bill.

Alternatively, the buyer may choose not to resell and settle for the difference between the contract price and the market value of the goods. Maud, in other words, may choose to keep the shoes. If she can prove that their market value is $48 per pair, for example, by showing what other retailers would have paid her for them, she will still get her $7 each, representing the difference between what the contract promised her and what the market would support. In either case, the money represents direct damages. Maud is also entitled to incidental damages, such as the storage and advertising expenses described. But there is one significant difference under the UCC: **Most courts hold that the seller of goods is *not* entitled to consequential damages.** Suppose Maud hired two extra workers to inspect, pack, and ship the shoes for Foot The Bill. Those are consequential damages, but Maud will not recover them because she is the seller and the contract is for the sale of goods.

Buyer's Remedies

The buyer's remedies in sale of goods contracts (which are, as always, governed by the UCC) are similar to those we have already considered. She typically has two options. First, the buyer can "cover" by purchasing substitute goods. To **cover** means to make a good faith purchase of goods similar to those in the contract. The buyer may then obtain **the difference between the original contract price and her cover price.** Alternatively, if the buyer chooses not to cover, she is entitled to the difference between the original contract price and the market value of the goods.

Suppose Mary has contracted to buy one thousand 6-foot Christmas trees at $25 per tree from Elmo. The market suddenly rises, and not feeling the spirit of the season, Elmo breaches his deal and sells the trees elsewhere. If Mary makes a good faith effort to cover but is forced to pay $40 per tree, she may recover the difference from Elmo, meaning $15 per tree times 1,000 trees, or $15,000. Similarly, if she chooses not to cover but can prove that $40 is now the market value of the trees, she is entitled to her $15 per tree.

Under the UCC, **the buyer *is* entitled to consequential damages, provided that the seller could reasonably have foreseen them.** If Mary tells Elmo, when they sign their deal, that she has a dozen contracts to resell the trees for an average price of $50 per tree, she may recover $25 per tree, representing the difference between her contract price with Elmo and the value of the tree *to her*, based on her other contracts.[4] If she failed to inform Elmo of the other contracts, she would not receive any money based on them. The buyer is also entitled to whatever incidental damages may have accrued.

Cover
To make a good faith purchase of goods similar to those in the contract

---

EXAM Strategy

Question: Chloe is a fashion designer. Her recent collection of silk-velvet evening gowns was gobbled up by high-end retailers, who now clamor for more. Chloe needs 300 yards of the same fabric by August 15. Mill House, which has supplied fabric to Chloe for many years, agrees to sell her 300 yards at $100 per yard, delivered on August 15. The market value of the fabric is $125, but Mill House gives Chloe a break because she is a major customer.

---

[4]As we discuss in the section on mitigation later in the chapter, Mary will get only her consequential damages if she attempts to cover.

Chloe contracts with high-end retailers Barneys and Neiman Marcus to sell a total of 50 dresses, at an *additional* profit to Chloe of $800 per dress. On August 15, Mill House delivers defective fabric. Chloe cannot make her dresses in time, and the retailers cancel their orders. Chloe sues Mill House and wins—but what are her damages?

Strategy: To determine damages, first ask whether the contract is governed by the common law or the UCC. This agreement concerns goods, so the Code applies. The UCC permits a buyer to recover damages for the difference between the contract price and the market value of the goods. The Code also allows consequential damages if the seller could have foreseen them. Apply those standards.

Result: Because Chloe's contract enabled her to save $25 per yard for 300 yards, she is entitled to $7,500. Chloe has also lost profits of $40,000. Mill House could easily have foreseen those losses because the supplier knew that Chloe was a designer who fabricated and sold dresses. Chloe is entitled to $47,500.

We turn now to cases where the injured party cannot prove expectation damages.

19-3 RELIANCE INTEREST

To win expectation damages, the injured party must prove the breach of contract caused damages that can be *quantified with reasonable certainty*. This rule sometimes presents plaintiffs with a problem.

George plans to manufacture and sell silk scarves during the holiday season. In the summer, he contracts with Cecily, the owner of a shopping mall, to rent a high-visibility stall for $100 per day. George then buys hundreds of yards of costly silk and gets to work cutting and sewing. But in September, Cecily refuses to honor the contract. George sues and proves Cecily breached a valid contract. But what is his remedy?

George cannot establish an expectation interest in his scarf business. He *hoped* to sell each scarf for a $40 gross profit. He *planned* on making $2,000 per day. But how much would he *actually* have earned? Enough to retire on? Enough to buy a salami sandwich for lunch? He has no way of proving his profits, and a court cannot give him his expectation interest.

Instead, George will ask for *reliance damages*. The **reliance interest** is designed to put an injured party in the position he would have been in had the parties never entered into a contract. This remedy focuses on the time and money the injured party spent performing his part of the agreement.

> **Reliance interest**
> Puts the injured party in the position he would have been in had the parties never entered into a contract

George should be able to recover reliance damages from Cecily. Assuming he is unable to sell the scarves to a retail store, which is probable since retailers will have made purchases long ago, George should be able to recover the cost of the silk fabric he bought and perhaps something for the hours of labor he spent cutting and sewing. But reliance damages can be difficult to win because *they are harder to quantify*. Courts prefer to compute damages using the numbers provided in a contract. If a contract states a price of $25 per Christmas tree and one party breaches, the arithmetic is easy. Judges can become uncomfortable when asked to base damages on vague calculations. How much was George's time worth in making the scarves? How good was his work? How likely were the scarves to sell? If George has a track record in the industry, he will be able to show a market price for his services. Without such a record, his reliance claim becomes a tough battle.

19-3a Promissory Estoppel

We have seen in earlier chapters that a plaintiff may sometimes recover damages based on promissory estoppel even when there is no valid contract. The plaintiff must show that the defendant made a promise knowing that the plaintiff would likely rely on it, that the plaintiff did rely, and that the only way to avoid injustice is to enforce the promise. **In promissory estoppel cases, a court will generally award** *reliance damages.* It would be unfair to give expectation damages for the full benefit of the bargain when, legally speaking, there has been no bargain.

In the following case, the victorious plaintiff demonstrates how unreliable reliance damages are and how winning can be hard to distinguish from losing.

Toscano v. Greene Music

124 Ca. App. 4th 685
Court of Appeal of California, 2004

Facts: Joseph Toscano was the general manager of Fields Pianos (Fields) in Santa Ana, California. He was unhappy with his job and decided to seek other employment. Toscano contacted Michael Greene, who owned similar stores. In July, Greene offered Toscano a sales management job starting September 1. Relying on that offer, Toscano resigned from Fields on August 1. However, in mid-August, Greene withdrew his employment offer. Toscano later found lower-paying jobs in other cities.

Toscano sued Greene for breach of contract and promissory estoppel. Greene argued that Toscano was not entitled to any expectation damages because his employment with Greene would have been at will, meaning he could lose the job at any time. Greene also urged that because Toscano was an at-will employee at Fields, he could recover at most one month's lost wage.

The trial court ruled that Toscano was entitled to reliance damages for all lost wages at Fields, starting from the day he resigned, going forward until his anticipated retirement in 2017. Toscano's expert accountant calculated his past losses (until the time of trial) at $119,061, and his future lost earnings at $417,772. The trial court awarded Toscano $536,833, and Greene appealed.

Issue: *Was Toscano entitled to reliance damages?*

Excerpts from Judge O'Rourke's Decision: Given the equitable underpinnings of the promissory estoppel doctrine, we hold that a plaintiff such as Toscano, who relinquished his job in reliance on an unfulfilled promise of employment, may on an appropriate showing recover the lost wages he would have expected to earn from his former employer but for the defendant's promise. Such a damage measure is in keeping with the equitable nature of promissory estoppel. The object of equity is to do right and justice.

Our holding necessarily rejects the notion that the at-will nature of Toscano's former employment with Fields (undisputed by the parties here) is a strict impediment to recovery of future wages that Toscano would have earned at Fields had he not relied on Greene's promise.

[However,] we conclude that even drawing all inferences in Toscano's favor, the evidence was too speculative to lend support to the trial court's award of Toscano's lost future earnings from September 1 to his retirement.

Roberta Spoon, Toscano's damages expert, testified that in calculating Toscano's lost wages for the remainder of his career, "[a]ll I have done is arithmetic. I have simply analyzed the numbers." She testified she was not aware that Toscano's employment with Fields called for any specific tenure. Indeed, Spoon admitted Toscano could have quit or been fired from that job from the time he resigned to the present. She simply assumed Toscano would have continued employment with Fields or another employer at a comparable salary, observing that he had never in the past changed employers for anything other than a pay increase.

Spoon's testimony does not establish Toscano had a definite expectation of continued employment with Fields for any particular period of time. It is evident her supposition was based only on Toscano's history of remaining with his employers until offered new employment. However, *Toscano's* intentions or practices are not relevant to whether he could expect to remain with Fields until his retirement. Evidence of Toscano's intentions does not establish with any reasonable certainty that Fields, an at-will employer who had the right to terminate Toscano at any time for any reason, had some different understanding of the terms of Toscano's employment, or that it would have continued to employ him until the end of his career. Neither party presented testimony from Jerry Goldman, Toscano's boss at Fields. An expert's opinion must not be based upon speculative or conjectural data.

The award of future earnings calculated from [the day he quit] to the date of Toscano's retirement in 2017 is vacated and the matter remanded for a new trial on the issue of damages only. The judgment is otherwise affirmed.

Notice that the court never even mentions that Toscano acted in good faith, relying on Greene's promise, while the latter offered no excuse for suddenly withdrawing his offer. Is it fair to permit Greene to escape all liability? This court, like most, simply will not award significant damages where there is no contract permitting a clear calculation of losses.

The judges, though, have not entirely closed the door on Toscano. What is the purpose of the remand? What might Toscano demonstrate on remand? What practical difficulties will he encounter?

19-4 RESTITUTION INTEREST

Restitution means giving back. The **restitution interest** is designed to return to the injured party a benefit that he has conferred on the other party, which it would be unjust to leave with that person. In the opening scenario, Margot suffered many damages. Unfortunately for her, the only remedy a court will afford her is restitution. Great Expectations misrepresented its network of singles and breached the contract. But Margot cannot prove expectation damages (no matter how *Great*) or reliance damages, so she will have to settle for getting her money back.

Restitution is awarded in three types of cases. First, the law allows restitution when a contract is breached or discharged. As you will recall, a contract is breached when one party fails to perform. A contract is said to be discharged when it is terminated by the nonoccurrence of a condition, impossibility, or another excuse. In such cases, a court may choose restitution because no other remedy is available or because no other remedy would be as fair. Second, judges allow restitution when the injured party to a voidable contract rescinds the agreement. Third, courts may award restitution in cases of quasi-contract, which we examined in Chapter 11. In quasi-contract cases, the parties never made a contract, but one side did benefit the other. We consider each kind of restitution interest in turn.

Restitution interest
Designed to return to the injured party a benefit he has conferred on the other party

19-4a **Restitution in Cases of Contract Breach or Discharge**

When one party breaches a contract, the other may be entitled to recoup what he put in. Lillian and Harold Toews signed a contract to sell 1,500 acres of Idaho farmland to Elmer Funk. (No, not him—the Bugs Bunny character you are thinking of is Elmer Fudd.) He was to take possession immediately, but he would not receive the deed until he finished paying for the property, in 10 years. This arrangement enabled him to enroll in a government program that would pay him "set-asides" for *not* farming. Funk kept most aspects of his agreement. He did move onto the land and did receive $76,000 from the government for a year's worth of inactivity. (Nice work if you can get it.) The only part of the bargain Funk did not keep was his promise to pay. The Toews sued. Funk had clearly breached the deal. But what was the remedy?

The couple still owned the land, so they did not need to recover it. Funk had no money to pay for the farm, so they would never get their expectation interest. And they had expended almost no money complying with the deal, so they had no reliance interest. What they had done, though, was to *confer a benefit* on Funk. They had enabled him to obtain $76,000 in government money. The Toews wanted restitution. They argued that they had bestowed a $76,000 benefit on Funk and that it was unfair for him to keep it. The Idaho Court of Appeals agreed. It ruled that the couple had a restitution interest in the government set-aside and ordered Funk to pay them the money.[5]

> He did move onto the land and did receive $76,000 from the government for a year's worth of inactivity. (Nice work if you can get it.)

---

[5]Toews v. Funk, 129 Idaho 316 (Idaho Ct. App. 1994).

In the following case, both parties breached the contract. Could the famous football player get restitution even if he dropped the ball?

ADDIE AND TAYLOR V. KJAER

737 F.3d 854
United States Court of Appeals for the Third Circuit, 2013

Facts: Christian Kjaer and his relatives (Sellers) owned a small island off the coast of St. Thomas, U.S. Virgin Islands. Some investors, led by Miami Dolphins football player Jason Taylor agreed to buy it for $21 million.

Marc Serota/Getty Images

Under the contract, Taylor paid a $1 million deposit and promised to close within 60 days. The contract allowed him to extend the closing date by paying an additional $500,000 nonrefundable deposit, which he did. The buyers' only other duty was to pay the remaining purchase price at closing. The Sellers committed to delivering clear title to the property, along with all of the island's permits.

According to the contract, if Taylor breached the contract, he would forfeit the deposits; if the Sellers breached, they would return the deposits. The contract did not say what would happen to the deposit it both parties breached.

On the closing date, the sale was not consummated; the Sellers delivered expired permits and did not convey clear title. Taylor and his partners did not pay. But the Sellers refused to return Taylor's deposit.

Taylor sued for restitution. The Sellers asserted they were entitled to the $1.5 million because Taylor breached the contract. Taylor argued that the Buyer's failure to deliver valid title discharged his obligation to close—and that allowing the Sellers to keep the money would

unjustly enrich them. The district court found that since Taylor breached the valid contract, he could not recoup the deposit. Taylor challenged the lower court's call.

Issue: *Was Taylor entitled to restitution?*

Excerpts from Judge Roth's Decision: Agreements concerning an exchange of promises require performance to be exchanged simultaneously whenever possible, unless the agreement indicates otherwise. This simultaneous exchange of performances creates concurrent conditions, under which performance by one party creates a condition precedent for performance by the other party.

Here, the Sellers were required to convey Clear and Marketable title and assignments of all permits, leases, and licenses necessary. Because the Contract of Sale did not indicate otherwise, the performance of each obligation was to occur simultaneously. Therefore, fulfillment of each obligation was a concurrent condition to the other.

With regard to awarding restitution in cases involving valid contracts, we look to the Restatement (Second) of Contracts:

> A party whose duty of performance does not arise or is discharged as a result of nonoccurrence of a condition is entitled to restitution for any benefit that he has conferred on the other party by way of part performance or reliance.[6]

For example, the Restatement illustrates: "A contracts to sell a tract of land to B for $100,000. After B has made a part payment of $20,000, A wrongfully refuses to transfer title. B can recover the $20,000 in restitution."

In applying the Restatement (Second) of Contracts, it is clear that restitution is in order. Taylor provided a deposit of $1.5 million to the Sellers with the intent to purchase the property. However, all of the parties failed to perform within the timeframe specified in the contracts, and their respective duties were discharged. Thus, as the Restatement instructs, Taylor is entitled to restitution for the benefit of the deposit that he conferred to the Sellers.

For the foregoing reasons, we will reverse the District Court and order the return of the deposit to Taylor.

---

[6]Restatement (Second) of Contracts § 377 (1981).

Ethics Imagine that you are in charge of negotiating the island's sale for the seller. You learn that several powerful voices in the government oppose the development of the island and realize that if the buyers learn this, they will lower their offer or reject the deal altogether. Your boss insists you tell the buyers that the island is ready for development. What will you do? What Life Principles will you apply?

19-4b Restitution in Cases of a Voidable Contract

Restitution is a common remedy in contracts involving fraud, misrepresentation, mistake, and duress. In these cases, restitution often goes hand in hand with **rescission**, which means to undo a contract and put the parties where they were before they made the agreement. Courtney sells her favorite sculpture to Adam for $95,000, both parties believing the work to be a valuable original by Barbara Hepworth. Two months later, Adam learns that the sculpture is a mere copy, worth very little. A court will permit Adam to rescind the contract on the ground of mutual mistake. At the same time, Adam is entitled to restitution of the purchase price. Courtney gets the worthless carving, and Adam receives his money back.

> **Rescission**
> To "undo" a contract and put the parties where they were before they made the agreement

19-4c Restitution in Cases of a Quasi-Contract

George Anderson owned a valuable 1936 Plymouth. He took it to Ronald Schwegel's repair shop, and the two orally agreed that Schwegel would restore the car for $6,000. Unfortunately, they never agreed on the meaning of the word *restore*. Anderson thought the term meant complete restoration, including body work and engine repairs, whereas Schwegel intended body work but no engine repairs. After doing some of the work, Schwegel told Anderson that the car needed substantial engine work, and he asked for Anderson's permission to allow an engine shop to do it. Anderson agreed, believing the cost was included in the original estimate. When the car was finished and running smoothly, Schwegel demanded $9,800. Anderson refused to pay more than the $6,000 agreed price, and Schwegel sued.

The court held that there was no valid contract between the parties. A contract requires a meeting of the minds. Here, said the court, there was no meeting of the minds on what *restore* included, and hence Schwegel could not recover either his expectation or his reliance interest since both require an enforceable agreement. Schwegel then argued that a quasi-contract existed. In other words, he claimed that even if there had been no valid agreement, he had performed a service for Anderson and that it would be unjust for Anderson to keep it without paying. **A court may award restitution, even in the absence of a contract, when one party has conferred a benefit on another and it would be unjust for the other party to retain the benefit.** The court ruled that Schwegel was entitled to the full $3,800 above and beyond the agreed price because that was the fair market value of the additional work. Anderson had asked for the repairs and now had an auto that was substantially improved. It would be unjust, ruled the court, to permit him to keep that benefit for free.[7]

19-5 OTHER REMEDIES

In contract lawsuits, plaintiffs are occasionally awarded the remedies of **specific performance**, injunction, and reformation.

> **Specific performance**
> Forces both parties to complete the deal

---

[7]Anderson v. Schwegel, 118 Idaho 362 (Idaho Ct. App. 1990).

19-5a Specific Performance

Leona Claussen owned Iowa farmland. She sold some of it to her sister-in-law, Evelyn Claussen, and, along with the land, granted Evelyn an option to buy additional property at $800 per acre. Evelyn could exercise her option anytime during Leona's lifetime or within six months of Leona's death. When Leona died, Evelyn informed the estate's executor that she was exercising her option. But other relatives wanted the property, and the executor refused to sell. Evelyn sued and asked for *specific performance*. She did not want an award of damages; she wanted *the land itself*. The remedy of specific performance forces the two parties to perform their contract.

A court will award specific performance, ordering the parties to perform the contract, only in cases involving the sale of land or some other asset that is considered "unique." Courts use this remedy when money damages would be inadequate to compensate an injured party. If the subject is unique and irreplaceable, money damages will not put the injured party in the same position she would have been in had the agreement been kept. So a court will order the seller to convey the rare object and the buyer to pay for it.

Historically, every parcel of land has been regarded as unique, and therefore **specific performance is always available in real estate contracts.** Family heirlooms and works of art are also often considered unique. Evelyn Claussen won specific performance. The Iowa Supreme Court ordered Leona's estate to convey the land to Evelyn for $800 per acre.[8] Generally, either the seller or the buyer may be granted specific performance. One limitation in land sales is that a buyer may obtain specific performance only if she was ready, willing, and able to purchase the property on time. If Evelyn had lacked the money to buy Leona's property for $800 per acre within the six-month time limit, the court would have declined to order the sale.

EXAM Strategy

Question: The Monroes, a retired couple who live in Illinois, want to move to Arizona to escape the northern winter. In May, the Monroes contract in writing to sell their house to the Temples for $450,000. Closing is to take place June 30. The Temples pay a deposit of $90,000. However, in early June, the Monroes travel through Arizona and discover it is too hot for them. They promptly notify the Temples they are no longer willing to sell, and return the $90,000, with interest. The Temples sue, seeking the house. In response, the Monroes offer evidence that the value of the house has dropped from about $450,000 to about $400,000. They claim that the Temples have suffered no loss. Who will win?

Strategy: Most contract lawsuits are for money damages, but not this one. The Temples want the house. Because they want the house itself, and not money damages, the drop in value is irrelevant. What legal remedy are the Temples seeking? They are suing for specific performance. When will a court grant specific performance? Should it do so here?

Result: In cases involving the sale of land or some other unique asset, a court will grant specific performance, ordering the parties to perform the agreement. All houses are regarded as unique. The court will force the Monroes to sell their house, provided the Temples have sufficient money to pay for it.

Other unique items, for which a court will order specific performance, include such things as secret formulas, patents, and shares in a closely held corporation. Money damages would be inadequate for all these things since the injured party, even if she got the cash,

---

[8] In re Estate of Claussen, 482 N.W.2d 381 (Iowa 1992).

could not go out and buy a substitute item. By contrast, a contract for a new Cadillac Escalade is not enforceable by specific performance. If the seller breaches, the buyer is entitled to the difference between the contract price and the market value of the car. The buyer can take his money elsewhere and purchase a virtually identical SUV.

19-5b Injunction

An **injunction** is a court order that requires someone to refrain from doing something.

In the increasingly litigious world of professional sports, injunctions are commonplace. In the following basketball case, the trial court issued a **preliminary injunction**; that is, an order issued early in a lawsuit prohibiting a party from doing something *during the course of the lawsuit.* The court attempts to protect the interests of the plaintiff immediately. If, after trial, it appears that the plaintiff has been injured and is entitled to an injunction, the trial court will make its order a **permanent injunction**. If it appears that the preliminary injunction should never have been issued, the court will terminate the order.

> **Injunction**
>
> A court order that requires someone to do something or refrain from doing something

MILICIC V. BASKETBALL MARKETING COMPANY, INC.

2004 Pa.A Super. 333
Superior Court of Pennsylvania, 2004

Facts: The Basketball Marketing Company (BMC) markets, distributes, and sells basketball apparel and related products. BMC signed a long-term endorsement contract with a 16-year-old Serbian player, Darko Milicic, who was virtually unknown in the United States. Two years later, Milicic became the second pick in the National Basketball Association draft, making him an immensely marketable athlete.

Four days after his 18th birthday, Milicic made a buyout offer to BMC, seeking release from his contract so that he could arrange a more lucrative one elsewhere. BMC refused to release him. A week later, Milicic notified BMC in writing that he was disaffirming the contract, and he returned all money and goods he had received from the company. BMC again refused to release Milicic.

Believing that Milicic was negotiating an endorsement deal with either Reebok or Adidas, BMC sent both companies letters informing them it had an enforceable endorsement deal with Milicic that was valid for several more years. Because of BMC's letter, Adidas ceased negotiating with Milicic just short of signing a contract. Milicic sued BMC, seeking a preliminary injunction that would prohibit BMC from sending such letters to competitors. The trial court granted the preliminary injunction, and BMC appealed.

Issue: *Is Milicic entitled to a preliminary injunction?*

Excerpts from Judge McCaffery's Decision:[9] BMC argues that the trial court erred by concluding that Milicic had proven the four essential prerequisites necessary for injunctive relief. However, Milicic did meet these four requirements.

1. Milicic had a strong likelihood of success on the merits.

   Pennsylvania law recognizes, except as to necessities, the contract of a minor is voidable if the minor disaffirms it at any reasonable time after the minor attains majority. Just 11 days after his 18th birthday, Milicic sent BMC a letter withdrawing from the agreement. This letter was sent within a reasonable time after Milicic's reaching the age of majority and stated his unequivocal revocation and voidance of the agreement. There exists more than a reasonable probability that Milicic will succeed in [nullifying the contract with BMC].

2. Injunctive relief was necessary to prevent immediate and irreparable harm that could not be adequately compensated by the awarding of monetary damages.

   Top N.B.A. draft picks generally solicit, negotiate, and secure endorsement contracts within a short time after the draft to take advantage of the

---

[9]The authors have substituted "BMC" for "appellant" and "Milicic" for "appellee."

publicity, excitement, and attendant marketability associated with the promotion. BMC blocked Milicic's efforts to enter into such an endorsement agreement. After being contacted by BMC, advanced negotiations between Milicic and Adidas were suspended. These business opportunity and market advantage losses may aptly be characterized as irreparable injury for purposes of equitable relief.

3. Greater injury would have occurred from denying the injunction than from granting the injunction.

BMC's refusal to acknowledge Milicic's ability to disaffirm the contract is at odds with public policy. Because infants are not competent to contract, the ability to disaffirm protects them from their own immaturity and lack of discretion. It is established practice in Pennsylvania to petition the court to appoint a guardian for the child, to protect the interests of both parties. It confounds the Court that BMC, a corporation of great magnitude, whose business may be said to be based in contract law, failed to have a guardian appointed for Milicic. Harm to the public is an additional consideration. The public policy consideration underlying the rule which allows a child to disaffirm a contract within a reasonable time after reaching the age of majority is that minors should not be bound by mistakes resulting from their immaturity or the overbearance of unscrupulous adults.

4. The preliminary injunction restored the parties to the status quo that existed prior to the wrongful conduct:

Enjoining BMC from further interfering with Milicic's ability to contract will place the parties where they were prior to BMC's wrongful conduct. As all four of the essential prerequisites have been satisfied in this case, the Court properly granted injunctive relief.

Order affirmed.

Was Darko Milicic entitled to a preliminary injunction against BMC?

19-5c Reformation

Reformation
A court may partially rewrite a contract to fix a mistake or cure an unenforceable provision.

The final remedy, and perhaps the least common, is **reformation**, a process in which a court will partially rewrite a contract. Courts seldom do this because the whole point of a contract is to enable the parties to control their own futures. But a court may reform a contract if it believes a written agreement includes a simple mistake. Suppose that Roger orally agrees to sell 35 acres to Hannah for $600,000. The parties then draw up a written agreement, accidentally describing the land as including 50 additional acres that neither party considered part of the deal. Roger refuses to sell. Hannah sues for specific performance but asks the court to *reform* the written contract to reflect the true agreement. Most but not all courts would reform the agreement and enforce it.

A court may also reform a contract to save it. If Natasha sells her advertising business to Joseph and agrees not to open a competing agency in the same city anytime in the next 10 years, a court may decide that it is unfair to force her to wait a decade. It could reform the agreement and permit Natasha to compete, say, 3 years after the sale. But some courts are reluctant to reform contracts and would throw out the entire noncompetition agreement rather than reform it. Parties should never settle for a contract that is sloppy or overbroad, assuming that a court will later reform errors. They may find themselves stuck with a bargain they dislike, or with no contract at all.

19-6 SPECIAL ISSUES

Finally, we consider some special issues of damages, beginning with a party's obligation to minimize its losses.

19-6a Mitigation of Damages

A party injured by a breach of contract may not recover for damages that he could have avoided with reasonable efforts. In other words, when one party perceives that the other has breached or will breach the contract, the injured party must try to prevent unnecessary loss. A party is expected to **mitigate** his damages; that is, to keep damages as low as he reasonably can.

Malcolm agrees to rent space in his mall to Zena, for a major department store. As part of the lease, Malcolm agrees to redesign the interior to meet her specifications. After Malcolm has spent $20,000 in architect and design fees, Zena informs Malcolm that she is renting other space and will not occupy his mall. Malcolm nonetheless continues the renovation work, spending an additional $50,000 on materials and labor. Malcolm will recover the lost rental payments and the $20,000 expended in reliance on the deal. He will *not* recover the extra $50,000. He should have stopped work when he learned of Zena's breach.

Mitigate
To keep damages as low as reasonable

19-6b Nominal Damages

Nominal damages are a token sum, such as one dollar, given to a plaintiff who demonstrates that the defendant breached the contract but cannot prove serious injury. A school board unfairly fires Gemma, a teacher. If she obtains a teaching job at a better school for identical pay the very next day, she probably can show no damages at all. Nonetheless, the school wrongfully terminated her, and a court may award nominal damages. Nominal damages provide plaintiff with a "moral victory."

Nominal damages
A token sum, such as one dollar, given to a plaintiff who demonstrates a breach but no serious injury

19-6c Liquidated Damages

It can be difficult or even impossible to prove how much damage the injured party has suffered. So lawyers and executives negotiating a deal may include in the contract a **liquidated damages clause**, a provision stating in advance how much a party must pay if it breaches. Assume that Laurie has hired Bruce to build a five-unit apartment building for $800,000. Bruce promises to complete construction by May 15. Laurie insists on a liquidated damages clause providing that if Bruce finishes late, Laurie's final price is reduced by $3,000 for each week of delay. Bruce finishes the apartment building June 30, and Laurie reduces her payment by $18,000. Is that fair? The answer depends on two factors: **A court will generally enforce a liquidated damages clause if** (1) **at the time of creating the contract, it was very difficult to estimate actual damages, and** (2) **the liquidated amount is reasonable.** In any other case, the liquidated damage will be considered a mere penalty and will prove unenforceable.

Liquidated damages
A clause stating in advance how much a party must pay if it breaches

We will apply the two factors to Laurie's case. When the parties made their agreement, would it have been difficult to estimate actual damages caused by delay? Yes. Laurie could not prove that all five units would have been occupied or how much rent the tenants would have agreed to pay. Was the $3,000 per week reasonable? Probably. To finance an $800,000 building, Laurie will have to pay at least $6,000 interest per month. She must also pay taxes on the land and may have other expenses. Laurie does not have to prove that every penny of the liquidated damages clause is justified, but only that the figure is reasonable. A court will probably enforce her liquidated damages clause.

On the other hand, suppose Laurie's clause demanded $3,000 per day. There is no basis for such a figure, and a court will declare it a penalty clause and refuse to enforce it. Laurie will be back to square one, forced to prove in court any damages she claims to have suffered from Bruce's delay.

EXAM Strategy

Question: In March, James was accepted into the September ninth-grade class at the Brookstone Academy, a highly competitive private school. To reserve his spot, James's father, Rex, sent in a deposit of $2,000 and agreed in writing to pay the balance due, $19,000. If James withdrew in writing from the school by August 1, Rex owed nothing more to Brookstone. However, once that date passed, Rex was obliged to pay the full $19,000, whether or not James attended. On August 5, Rex hand-delivered to Brookstone a letter stating that James would not attend. Brookstone demanded the full tuition and, when Rex refused to pay, sued for $19,000. Analyze the case.

Strategy: When one party seeks contract damages that are specified in the agreement, it is relying on a liquidated damages clause. A court will generally enforce a liquidated damages clause provided the plaintiff can prove two things. What are those two things? Can this plaintiff meet that standard?

Result: Brookstone must prove that at the time of creating the contract it was difficult to estimate actual damages and that the liquidated amount is reasonable. Rex will probably argue that the liquidated amount is unreasonable, contending that a competitive school can quickly fill a vacancy with another eager applicant. Brookstone will counter that budgeting, which begins in January, is difficult and imprecise. Tuition money goes toward staff salaries, maintenance, utilities, and many other expenses. If the school cannot not rely in January on a certain income, the calculation becomes impossible. Rex had four months to make up his mind, and by August 1, the school was firmly committed to its class size and budget. In a similar case, the court awarded the full tuition to the school, concluding that the sum was a reasonable estimate of the damages.

Chapter Conclusion

The powers of a court are broad and flexible and may suffice to give an injured party what it deserves. But problems of proof and the uncertainty of remedies demonstrate that the best solution is a carefully drafted contract and socially responsible behavior.

EXAM REVIEW

1. **BREACH** Someone breaches a contract when he fails to perform a duty without a valid excuse.

2. **REMEDY** A remedy is the method a court uses to compensate an injured party.

3. INTEREST An interest is a legal right in something, such as a contract. The first step that a court takes in choosing a remedy is to decide what interest it is protecting.

4. EXPECTATION The expectation interest puts the injured party in the position she would have been in had both sides fully performed. It has three components:

(a) Direct damages, which flow directly from the contract.
(b) Consequential damages, which result from the unique circumstances of the particular injured party. The injured party may recover consequential damages only if the breaching party should have foreseen them.
(c) Incidental damages, which are the minor costs an injured party incurs responding to a breach.

Question: Mr. and Ms. Beard contracted for Builder to construct a house on property he owned and sell it to the Beards for $785,000. The house was to be completed by a certain date, and Builder knew that the Beards were selling their own home in reliance on the completion date. Builder was late with construction, forcing the Beards to spend $32,000 in rent. Ultimately, Builder never finished the house, and the Beards moved elsewhere. They sued. At trial, expert testimony indicated the market value of the house as promised would have been $885,000. How much money are the Beards entitled to, and why?

Strategy: Normally, in cases of property, an injured plaintiff may use specific performance to obtain the land or house. However, there *is* no house, so there will be no specific performance. The Beards will seek their expectation interest. Under the contract, what did they reasonably expect? They anticipated a finished house, on a particular date, worth $885,000. They did not expect to pay rent while waiting. Calculate their losses. (See the "Result" at the end of this section.)

EXAM Strategy

5. RELIANCE The reliance interest puts the injured party in the position he would have been in had the parties never entered into a contract. It focuses on the time and money that the injured party spent performing his part of the agreement. If there was no valid contract, a court might still award reliance damages under a theory of promissory estoppel.

EXAM Strategy

Question: Bingo is emerging as a rock star. His last five concerts have all sold out. Lucia signs a deal with Bingo to perform two concerts in one evening in Big City for a fee of $50,000 for both shows. Lucia then rents the Auditorium for that evening, guaranteeing to pay $50,000. Bingo promptly breaks the deal before any tickets are sold. Lucia sues, pointing out that the Auditorium seats 3,000 and she anticipated selling all tickets for an average of $40 each, for a total gross of $120,000. How much will Lucia recover, if anything?

> **Strategy:** The parties created a valid contract, and Lucia relied on it. She claims two losses: the payment to rent the hall and her lost profits. A court may award reliance damages if the plaintiff can quantify them, provided the damages are not speculative. Can Lucia quantify either of those losses? Both of them? Were they speculative? (See the "Result" at the end of this section.)

6. **RESTITUTION** The restitution interest returns to the injured party a benefit that she has conferred on the other party which would be unjust to leave with that person. Restitution can be awarded in the case of a contract created, for example, by fraud, or in a case of quasi-contract, where the parties never created a binding agreement.

7. **SPECIFIC PERFORMANCE** Specific performance, ordered only in cases of land or a unique asset, requires both parties to perform the contract.

8. **INJUNCTION** An injunction is a court order that requires someone to do something or refrain from doing something.

9. **REFORMATION** Reformation is the process by which a court will—occasionally—rewrite a contract to ensure that it accurately reflects the parties' agreement and/or to maintain the contract's viability.

10. **MITIGATION** The duty to mitigate means that a party injured by a breach of contract may not recover for damages that he could have avoided with reasonable efforts.

EXAM Strategy

> **Question:** Ambrose hires Bierce for $25,000 to supervise the production of Ambrose's crop, but then breaks the contract by firing Bierce at the beginning of the season. A nearby grower offers Bierce $23,000 for the same growing season, but Bierce refuses to take such a pay cut. He stays home and sues Ambrose. How much money, if any, will Bierce recover from Ambrose, and why?
>
> **Strategy:** Ambrose has certainly breached the contract. The injured party normally receives the difference between his expectation interest and what he actually received. Bierce expected $25,000 and received nothing. However, Bierce made no effort to minimize his losses. How much would Bierce have lost had he mitigated? (See the "Result" at the end of this section.)

11. **NOMINAL DAMAGES** Nominal damages are a token sum, such as one dollar, given to an injured plaintiff who cannot prove damages.

12. **LIQUIDATED DAMAGES** A liquidated damages clause will be enforced if and only if, at the time of creating the contract, it was very difficult to estimate actual damages and the liquidated amount is reasonable.

> **4. Result:** The Beards' direct damages represent the difference between the market value of the house and the contract price. They expected a house worth $100,000 more than their contract price, and they are entitled to that sum. They also suffered consequential damages. Builder knew they needed the house as of the contract date, and he could foresee that his breach would force them to pay rent. He is liable for a total of $132,000.
>
> **5. Result:** Lucia can easily demonstrate that Bingo's breach cost her $50,000—the cost of the hall. However, it is uncertain how many tickets she would have sold. Unless Lucia has a strong track record selling tickets to concerts featuring Bingo, a court is likely to conclude that her anticipated profits were speculative. She will probably receive nothing for that claim.
>
> **10. Result:** Even if he had mitigated, Bierce would have lost $2,000. He is entitled to that sum. However, he cannot recover the remaining $23,000. After Ambrose breached, Bierce had identical work available to him, but he failed to take it. His failure to mitigate is fatal.

MULTIPLE-CHOICE QUESTIONS

1. *CPA QUESTION* Master Mfg., Inc. contracted with Accur Computer Repair Corp. to maintain Master's computer system. Master's manufacturing process depends on its computer system operating properly at all times. A liquidated damages clause in the contract provided that Accur would pay $1,000 to Master for each day that Accur was late responding to a service request. On January 12, Accur was notified that Master's computer system had failed. Accur did not respond to Master's service request until January 15. If Master sues Accur under the liquidated damage provision of the contract, Master will:

   (a) Win, unless the liquidated damages provision is determined to be a penalty
   (b) Win, because under all circumstances liquidated damage provisions are enforceable
   (c) Lose, because Accur's breach was not material
   (d) Lose, because liquidated damage provisions violate public policy

2. *CPA QUESTION* Kaye contracted to sell Hodges a building for $310,000. The contract required Hodges to pay the entire amount at closing. Kaye refused to close the sale of the building. Hodges sued Kaye. To what relief is Hodges entitled?

   (a) Punitive damages and direct damages
   (b) Specific performance and direct damages
   (c) Consequential damages or punitive damages
   (d) Direct damages or specific performance

3. A manufacturer delivers a new tractor to Farmer Ted on the first day of the harvest season. But, the tractor will not start. It takes two weeks for the right parts to be delivered and installed. The repair bill comes to $1,000. During the two weeks, some acres of Farmer Ted's crops die. He argues in court that his lost profit on those acres is $60,000. If a jury awards $1,000 for tractor repairs, it will be in the form

of _____ damages. If it awards $60,000 for the lost crops, it will be in the form of _____ damages.

(a) direct; direct

(b) direct; consequential

(c) consequential; direct

(d) consequential; consequential

(e) direct; incidental

4. Julie signs a contract to buy Nick's 2012 Mustang GT for $20,000. Later, Nick changes his mind and refuses to sell his car. Julie soon buys a similar 2012 Mustang GT for $21,500. She then sues Nick and wins $1,500. The $1,500 represents her _____.

(a) expectation interest

(b) reliance interest

(c) restitution interest

(d) none of the above

5. Under the Uniform Commercial Code, a seller _____ generally entitled to recover consequential damages, and a buyer _____ generally entitled to recover consequential damages.

(a) is; is

(b) is; is not

(c) is not; is

(d) is not; is not

CASE QUESTIONS

1. Lewis signed a contract for the rights to all timber located on Nine-Mile Mine. He agreed to pay $70 per thousand board feet ($70/mbf). As he began work, Nine-Mile became convinced that Lewis lacked sufficient equipment to do the job well and forbade him to enter the land. Lewis sued. Nine-Mile moved for summary judgment. The mine offered proof that the market value of the timber was exactly $70/mbf, and Lewis had no evidence to contradict Nine-Mile. The evidence about market value proved decisive. Why? Please rule on the summary judgment motion.

2. Twin Creeks Entertainment signed a deal with U.S. JVC Corp. in which JVC would buy 60,000 feature-film videocassettes from Twin Creeks over a three-year period. JVC intended to distribute the cassettes nationwide. Relying on its deal with JVC, Twin Creeks signed an agreement with Paramount Pictures, agreeing to purchase a minimum of $600,000 worth of Paramount cassettes over a two-year period. JVC breached its deal with Twin Creeks and refused to accept the cassettes it had agreed upon. Twin Creeks sued and claimed, among other damages, the money it owed to Paramount. JVC moved to dismiss the claim based on the Paramount contract, on the ground that Twin Creeks, the seller of goods, was not entitled to such damages. What kind of damages is Twin Creeks seeking? Please rule on the motion to dismiss.

3. Racicky was in the process of buying 320 acres of ranchland. While that sale was being negotiated, Racicky signed a contract to sell the land to Simon. Simon paid $144,000, the full price of the land. But Racicky went bankrupt before he could complete the *purchase* of the land, let alone its sale. Which of these remedies should Simon seek: expectation, restitution, specific performance, or reformation?

4. Parkinson was injured in an auto accident by a driver who had no insurance. Parkinson filed a claim with her insurer, Liberty Mutual, for $2,000 under her "uninsured motorist" coverage. Liberty Mutual told her that if she sought that money, her premiums would go "sky high," so Parkinson dropped the claim. Later, after she had spoken with an attorney, Parkinson sued. What additional claim was her attorney likely to make?

5. *YOU BE THE JUDGE* **WRITING PROBLEM** John and Susan Verba sold a Vermont lakeshore lot to Shane and Deborah Rancourt for $115,000. The Rancourts intended to build a house on the property, but after preparing the land for construction, they learned that a wetland protection law prevented building near the lake. They sued, seeking rescission of the contract. The trial court concluded that the parties had reached their agreement under a "mutual, but innocent, misunderstanding." The trial judge gave the Verbas a choice: they could rescind the contract and refund the purchase price, or they could give the Rancourts $55,000, the difference between the sales price and the actual market value of the land. The Rancourts appealed. Were the Rancourts entitled to rescission of the contract? **Argument for the Rancourts:** When the parties have made a mutual mistake about an important factual issue, either party is entitled to rescind the contract. The land is of no use to us and we want our money back. **Argument for the Verbas:** Both sides were acting in good faith and both sides made an honest mistake. We are willing to acknowledge that the land is worth somewhat less than we all thought, and we are willing to refund $55,000. The buyers shouldn't complain—they are getting the property at about half the original price, and the error was as much their fault as ours.

DISCUSSION QUESTIONS

1. **ETHICS** The National Football League owns the copyright to the broadcasts of its games. It licenses local television stations to telecast certain games and maintains a "blackout rule," which prohibits stations from broadcasting home games that are not sold out 72 hours before the game starts. Certain home games of the Cleveland Browns team were not sold out, and the NFL blocked local broadcast. But several bars in the Cleveland area were able to pick up the game's signal by using special antennas. The NFL wanted the bars to stop showing the games. What did it do? Was it unethical of the bars to broadcast the games that they were able to pick up? Apart from the NFL's legal rights, do you think it had the moral right to stop the bars from broadcasting the games?

2. Consequential damages can be many times higher than direct damages. Consider the "Farmer Ted" scenario raised in multiple-choice question 3, which is based on a real case.[10] Is it fair for consequential damages to be 60 times higher than direct damages?

---

[10]Prutch v. Ford, 574 P.2d 102 (Colo. 1977).

The Supreme Court is skeptical that *punitive* damages should be more than 9 times compensatory damages in a tort case. Should a similar "soft limit" apply to consequential damages in contract cases?

3. PepsiCo entered into a contract to sell its corporate jet to Klein for $4.6 million. Before the deal closed, the plane was sent to pick up PepsiCo's chairman of the board, who was stranded at Dulles airport. The chairman then decided that the company should not part with the plane. Klein sued PepsiCo for specific performance, arguing that he could not find a similar jet on the market for that price. Should a court force PepsiCo to sell its plane?

4. Walgreens operated a pharmacy in the Sara Creek mall. As part of this long-term lease, Sara Creek agreed not to lease mall space to another pharmacy. During an economic recession, Sara Creek's largest tenant left and the landlord informed Walgreens that it intended to rent that space out to a "deep discount" store that would contain a pharmacy. It was the only way to remain profitable, according to Sara Creek. Walgreens sued for an injunction against Sara Creek until its contract expired in 10 years. Should a court hold Sara Creek to its contract, even if this decision means bankrupting it?

5. Is it reasonable to require the mitigation of damages? If a person is wronged because the other side breached a contract, should she have any obligations at all? For example, suppose that a tenant breaches a lease by leaving early. Should the landlord have an obligation to try to find another tenant before the end of the lease?

ANSWERS TO SELECTED END OF CHAPTER QUESTIONS

MULTIPLE-CHOICE QUESTIONS

Presented are the answers for the ODD-numbered multiple-choice questions in the end-of-chapter material.

1. A
3. B
5. C

CASE QUESTIONS

Presented are the answers for all of the ODD-numbered case questions in the end-of-chapter material.

1. **Answer:** Motion granted. Nine Mile may have breached the agreement, but there is no evidence that Lewis lost money. To win he must demonstrate a difference between the contract price and the market value of the timber. There was no difference, and he recovers nothing. *Lewis v. Nine Mile Mines, Inc.*, 886 P.2d 912, 1994 Mont. LEXIS 283 (Mont. 1994).

3. **Answer:** He should, and did, seek restitution. Expectation damages will be unavailable since Racicky is bankrupt. Specific performance is impossible because Racicky does not own the land. Reformation is irrelevant. Simon gets restitution, since he has conferred a benefit on Racicky and it would be unjust for the defendant to keep it. *Racicky v. Simon*, 831 P.2d 241, 1992 Wyo. LEXIS 60 (Wyo. 1992).

5. **Answer:** The Rancourts win, and are entitled to rescission. Both parties clearly intended that the Rancourts would build a house near the lake. They cannot do so. That is a basic error of fact, and the Rancourts get their money back. The judge has no power to reshape the contract to express expectations that neither party ever held.

Chapter 20

© Honza Krej/Shutterstock.com

PRACTICAL CONTRACTS

Two true stories:

One

Holly (on the phone to her client, Judd): Harry's lawyer just emailed me a letter that Harry says he got from you last year. I'm reading from the letter now: "Each year that you meet your revenue goals, you'll get a 1 percent equity interest." Is it possible you sent that letter?

Judd: I don't remember the exact wording, but probably something like that.

Holly: You told me, absolutely, positively, you had never promised Harry any stock. That he was making the whole thing up.

Judd: He was threatening to leave unless I gave him some equity, so I said what he wanted to hear. But that letter didn't *mean* anything. This is a family business, and no one but my children will ever get stock.

Two

Grace (on the phone with her lawyer): Providential has raised its price to $12 a pound. I can't afford to pay that! We had a deal that the price would never go higher than 10 bucks. I've talked to Buddy over there, but he is refusing to back down. We need to do something!

Lawyer: Let me look at the contract.

Grace (her voice rising): I don't know what the *contract* says—that's just the legal stuff. Our *business* deal was no more than $10 a pound!

> **I don't know what the *contract* says—that's just the legal stuff.**

You have been studying the theory of contract law. This chapter is different: Its purpose is to demonstrate how that theory operates in *practice* and help you determine if the legal agreement reflects your business deal. We will look at the structure and content of a standard agreement and answer questions such as: Do you need a written agreement? What do all these legal terms mean? Are any important provisions missing? By the end of the chapter, you will have a road map for understanding a written contract.[1] (Note that we do not repeat here what you have learned in prior chapters about the *substantive* law of contracts.) This chapter has another goal, too: We will look at the relationship between lawyers and their clients and their different roles in creating a contract.

Businesspeople, not surprisingly, tend to focus more on business than on the technicalities of contract law. However, *ignoring* the role of a written agreement can lead to serious trouble. Both of the clients in the opening scenario ended up in contracts they did not want.

To illustrate our discussion of specific contract provisions, we will use a real movie contract between an actor and a producer. For reasons of confidentiality, however, we have changed the names.

Before we begin our discussion of written contracts, it is important to ask: **Do you need a written agreement at all?** Some years ago, this author was with a group of lawyers, all of whom had done a major home renovation and *none of whom* had signed a contract with the builder. All of the projects had turned out well. The lawyers had not prepared a written contract because they trusted their builders, who all had good recommendations from prior clients. Also, a building project by its very nature requires regular negotiations because it is impossible to predict all the potential changes: How much would it cost to move that door? How much do we save if we use Caesarstone instead of granite?

These cases worked out well without a written contract, but **there are times when you should *definitely* sign a written agreement:**

1. The Statute of Frauds requires it.

2. The deal is crucial to your life or the life of your business.

3. The terms are complex.

4. You do not have an ongoing relationship of trust with the other party.

Once you decide you need a written contract, then what?

20-1 THE LAWYER

The American Bar Association commissioned a study to find out what people think of lawyers. Survey participants responded with these words: greedy, corrupt, manipulative, snakes, and sharks.[2] Businesspeople sometimes refer to their lawyers with terms like "business prevention department." They are reluctant to ask an attorney to draft a contract for fear of the time and expense that lawyers can inject into the process. And they worry that the lawyers will interfere in the business deal itself, at best causing unnecessary hindrance, at worst killing the deal. Part of the problem is that lawyers and clients have different views of the future.

---

[1]For further reading on practical contracts, see Scott Burnham, *Drafting and Analyzing Contracts*, Lexis/Nexis, 2003; Charles M. Fox, *Working with Contracts*, Practical Law Institute, 2008; George W. Kuney, *The Elements of Contract Drafting*, Thomson/West, 2006.
[2]Robert Clifford, *Opening Statement: Now More than Ever*, 28 Litigation 1, Spring 2002.

20-1a Lawyers and Clients

Businesspeople are optimists—they believe that they have negotiated a great deal and everything is going to go well—sales will boom, the company will prosper. Lawyers have a different perspective—their primary goal is to protect their clients by avoiding litigation, now and in the future or, if litigation does occur, making sure their client wins. **For this reason, lawyers are trained to be pessimists—they try to foresee and protect against everything that can possibly go wrong.**

Businesspeople sometimes view this lawyering as a waste of time and a potential deal-killer. What if the two parties cannot agree about what to do in the event of a very unlikely circumstance? The deal might just collapse.

To take one example of this lawyerly perspective, a couple happily married for 40 years went to see a lawyer about changes in their will. The husband wanted to transfer some assets to his wife. The lawyer advised against it—after all, the couple might divorce. They became angry and indignant because *they would never get divorced*. And they may very well be right. However, just that week, the lawyer had seen another couple who did divorce after 41 years of marriage. He thought it better to be on the safe side and consider the possibility that such events might happen.

Lawyers also prefer to negotiate touchy subjects at the beginning of a relationship, when everyone is on friendly terms and eager to make a deal, rather than waiting until trouble strikes. In the long run, nothing harms a relationship more than unpleasant surprises. For example, the Artist in the movie contract we will refer to throughout this chapter did not know in advance how tough conditions on the set would be, how grueling the shooting schedule, or how many friends and family would visit him. So his lawyer negotiated a deal in which the Producer agreed to provide a driver, a "first-class star trailer (which shall be a double pop-out)," a luxury hotel suite, and an adjacent room for visitors. In the end, because the role called for the Artist to live in the wilderness, he ultimately slept in a tent on the set to experience his part more fully, so he did not need the double pop-out trailer or the luxury suite. He also dispensed with the driver. But, under different circumstances, he might have wanted those luxuries, and his lawyer's goal was to protect his interests. It is a lot easier to forgo an expense than to add one to a movie budget.

One advantage of using lawyers to conduct these negotiations is that they can serve as the bad guys. Instead of the client raising tough issues, the lawyers do. Many a client has said, "but my lawyer insists …" If the lawyer takes the blame, the client is able to maintain a better relationship with the other party. And hiring a lawyer communicates to the other parties that you are taking the deal seriously, and they will not be able to take advantage of you.

Of course, this lawyerly protection comes at a cost—legal fees, time spent bargaining, the hours used to read complex provisions, and the potential for good will to erode during negotiations.

Do you need a lawyer? The answer largely depends on the complexity and importance of the deal. Most people do not hire a lawyer to review an apartment lease—the language is standard, and the prospective tenant has little power to change the terms of the deal. On the other hand, you should not undertake a significant purchase agreement on your own.

20-1b Hiring a Lawyer

If you do hire a lawyer, be aware of certain warning signs. Although the lawyer's goal is to protect you, a good attorney should be a dealmaker, not a deal-breaker. She should help you achieve your goals and, therefore, should never (or, at least, hardly ever) say, "You cannot do this." Instead, she should say, "Here are the risks to this approach" or "Here is another way to accomplish your goal."

Moreover, your lawyer's goal should not be to annihilate the other side. In the end, the contract will be more beneficial to everyone if the parties' relationship is harmonious.

Trying to exact every last ounce of flesh, using whatever power you have to an abusive extreme, is not a sound long-term strategy. In the end, the best deals are those in which all the parties' incentives are aligned. Success for one means success for all—or at least, success for one party does not *prohibit* a positive outcome for the other side. If either side in the movie contract behaved unreasonably, word would quickly spread in the insular Hollywood world, damaging the troublemaker's ability to make other deals.

Now either you have a lawyer or you do not. The next step is to think about developing the contract.

20-2 THE CONTRACT

In this section, we discuss how a contract is prepared and what provisions it should include.

20-2a Who Drafts It?

Once businesspeople have agreed to the terms of the deal, it is time to prepare a draft of the contract. Generally, both sides would prefer to *control the pen* (that is, to prepare the first draft of the contract) because the drafter has the right to choose a structure and wording that best represents his interests. Typically, the party with the most bargaining power prepares the drafts. In the movie contract, Producer's lawyer was in charge of the first draft. The contract then went to Artist's lawyer, who added the provisions that mattered to his client.

20-2b How to Read a Contract

Reading a contract is not like cracking open a novel. Instead, it should be a focused, multistep process:

- **Pre-reading.** Before you begin reading the first draft of a contract, spend some time thinking about the provisions that are important to you. If you skip this step, you may find that, as you read, your attention is so focused on the specific language of the contract that you lose sight of the larger picture.

- **The first read.** Read through once, just to get the basic idea of the contract—its structure and major provisions.

- **What-ifs.** This is the time to think about various outcomes, good and bad. Under the terms of the contract, what happens if all goes according to your plan? Also consider worst-case scenarios. In both situations, does the contract produce the result that you want? What happens if sales are higher than you expect, or if the product causes unexpected harm?

- **The second read.** Now read the contract to make sure that it handles the what-ifs in a manner that is satisfactory to you. Think about the relationship between various provisions—does it make sense?

Following this approach will help you avoid mistakes.

20-2c Mistakes

This author once worked with a lawyer who made a mistake in a contract. "No problem," he said. "I can win that one in court." Not a helpful attitude, given that one purpose of a contract is to *avoid* litigation. In this section, we look at the most common types of mistakes and how to avoid them.

Vagueness

Vagueness means that the parties to a contract deliberately include a provision that is unclear. Why would anyone do that? It may be that they are not sure what they can get from the other side, or in some cases, even what they really want. One party may be trying to get a commitment from the other party without obligating itself. Or one side may feel *almost* ready to commit and yet still have reservations. It wants the *other* party to make a commitment so that planning can go forward. So they create a contract that keeps their options open. They hope that they can decide later what the provision really meant. This approach is understandable but dangerous. As the following case illustrates: **Vagueness is your enemy.**

Vagueness

When a provision in a contract is deliberately left unclear.

You be the Judge

QUAKE CONSTRUCTION, INC. v. AMERICAN AIRLINES, INC.
141 Ill. 2d 281
Supreme Court of Illinois, 1990

Facts: Jones Brothers Construction was the general contractor on a job to expand American Airlines' facilities at O'Hare International Airport. Jones verbally accepted Quake's bid to work on the project and promised that Quake would receive a written contract soon. Jones wanted the license numbers of the subcontractors that Quake would be using, but Quake could not furnish those numbers until it had assured its subcontractors that they had the job. Quake did not want to give that assurance until *it* was certain of its own work. So Jones sent a letter of intent that stated, among other things:

We have elected to award the contract for the subject project to your firm as we discussed on April 15. A contract agreement outlining the detailed terms and conditions is being prepared and will be available for your signature shortly.

Your scope of work includes the complete installation of expanded lunchroom, restaurant, and locker facilities for American Airlines employees, as well as an expansion of American Airlines' existing Automotive Maintenance Shop. A sixty (60) calendar day period shall be allowed for the construction of the locker room, lunchroom, and restaurant area beginning the week of April 22. The entire project shall be completed by August 15.

This notice of award authorizes the work set forth in the attached documents at a lump sum price of $1,060,568.00.

Jones Brothers Construction Corporation reserves the right to cancel this letter of intent if the parties cannot agree on a fully executed subcontract agreement.

The parties never signed a more detailed written contract, and ultimately Jones hired another company. Quake sued, seeking to recover the money it spent in preparation and its loss of anticipated profit.

You Be the Judge: *Was the letter of intent a valid contract?*

Argument for Quake: This letter was a valid contract. It explicitly stated that Jones awarded the contract to Quake. It also said, "This notice of award authorizes the work." The letter included significant detail about the scope of the contract, including the specific facilities Quake would be working on. Furthermore, the work was to commence approximately 4 to 11 days after the letter was written. This short period of time indicates that the parties intended to be bound by the letter so that work could begin quickly. And, the letter contained a cancellation clause. If it was not a contract, why would anyone need to cancel it?

Argument for Jones: This letter was not a contract. It referred several times to the execution of a formal contract by the parties, thus indicating that they did not intend to be bound by the letter. Look at the cancellation clause carefully: It could also be interpreted to mean that the parties did not intend to be bound by any agreement until they entered into a formal contract.

Litigating the meaning of this letter of intent was a disaster for both parties. If you were negotiating for Jones and wanted to clarify negotiations without committing your company, how could you do it? State in the letter that it is *not a contract*, and that *neither side is bound by it*. State that it is a memorandum summarizing negotiations thus far, but that neither party will be bound until a full written contract is signed.

But what if Quake cannot get a commitment from its subcontractors until they are certain that it has the job? Quake should take the initiative and present Jones with its own letter of intent, stating that the parties *do* have a binding agreement for $1 million of work. Jones would then be forced to decide whether it is willing to make a binding commitment. If it is not willing to commit, let it openly say so. At least both parties would know where they stood.

The movie contract provides another example of vagueness. In these contracts, nudity is always a contentious issue. Producers believe that nudity sells movie tickets; actors are afraid that it will tarnish their reputation. Artist's lawyer wanted to include this provision:

> Artist may not be photographed and shall not be required to render any services nude below the waist or in simulated sex scenes without Artist's prior written consent.

(This clause also applied to any double depicting Artist.) However, the script called for a scene in which Artist was swimming nude and the director wanted the option of showing him below the waist from the back. Ultimately, the nudity clause read as follows:

> Producer has informed Artist that Artist's role in the Picture might require Artist to appear and be photographed (a) nude, which nudity may include only above-the-waist nudity and rear below-the-waist nudity, but shall exclude frontal below-the-waist nudity; and (b) in simulated sex scenes. Artist acknowledges and agrees that Artist has accepted such employment in the Picture with full knowledge of Artist's required participation in nude scenes and/or in simulated sex scenes and Artist's execution of the Agreement constitutes written consent by Artist to appear in the nude scenes and simulated sex scenes and to perform therein as reasonably required by Producer. A copy of the scenes from the screenplay requiring Artist's nudity and/or simulated sex are attached hereto. Artist shall have a right of meaningful prior consultation with the director of the Picture regarding the manner of photography of any scenes in which Artist appears nude or engaged in simulated sex acts.
>
> Artist may wear pants or other covering that does not interfere with the shooting of the nude scenes or simulated sex scenes. Artist's buttocks and/or genitalia shall not be shown, depicted, or otherwise visible without Artist's prior written consent. Artist shall have the absolute right to change his mind and not perform in any nude scene or simulated sex scene, notwithstanding that Artist had prior thereto agreed to perform in such scene.

What does this provision mean? Has Artist agreed to perform in nude scenes or not? He has acknowledged that the script calls for nude scenes and he has agreed, in principle, that he would appear in them. However, since he had never worked with this director, he did not want to promise that he would definitely appear in nude scenes. So the contract states that Actor could refuse to shoot nude scenes altogether, or he could shoot them and then, after viewing them, decide not to allow them in the movie. Because of this clause, the director shot different versions of these scenes—some with nudity and some without—so that if Artist rejected a nude scene, the director still had options.

The true test of whether a vague clause belongs in a contract is this: Would you sign the contract if you knew that the other side's interpretation would prevail in litigation? In this example, each side was staking out its position, and deferring a final negotiation until there was an actual disagreement about a nude scene. If the other side's position is acceptable to you, the vague clause simply defers a fight that you can afford to lose. But if the point is really important, it may be wiser to resolve the issue before you sign the contract.

EXAM Strategy

Question: The nudity provision in the movie contract is vague. Rewrite it so that it accurately reflects the agreement between the parties.

Strategy: This is easy! Just say what the parties intended the deal to be.

Result: "The script for the Picture includes scenes showing Artist (a) with frontal nudity from the waist up and with rear below-the-waist nudity (but no frontal below-the-waist nudity); and (b) in simulated sex scenes. The Artist will give good faith consideration to appearing in these scenes, however, no scenes shall be shot in which Artist's buttocks and/or genitalia are shown, depicted, or otherwise visible without Artist's prior written consent. Artist shall have the absolute right not to perform in any nude scene or simulated sex scene. If shot, no nude or sex scenes may appear in the Picture without Artist's prior written consent."

Ambiguity

Vagueness occurs when the parties do not want the contract to be clear. **Ambiguity** is different—it means that the provision is *accidentally* unclear. It occurs in contracts when the parties think only about what *they* want a provision to mean, without considering the literal meaning or the other side's perspective. When reading a contract, try to imagine all the different ways a clause can be interpreted. Because you think it means one thing does not mean that the other side will share your view. For example, suppose that an employment contract says, "Employee agrees not to work for a competitor for a period of three years from employment." Does that mean three years from the date of hiring or the date of termination? Unclear, so who knows?

Many ambiguity cases arise in the context of insurance contracts. If you have ever read one of your insurance policies, you understand why. The following case provides an example of two provisions over which reasonable people could disagree.

Ambiguity
When a provision in a contract is unclear by accident

MINKLER V. SAFECO INS. CO. OF AMERICA

49 Cal. 4th 315
Supreme Court of California, 2010

Facts: Scott Minkler alleged that when he was a child, his Little League baseball coach, David Schwartz, had molested him. During the period when these terrible events occurred, David was living at the home of his mother, Betty Schwartz, and some of the episodes had taken place at her house. Scott sued Betty, alleging that she had been negligent in supervising events in her own home.

Betty had a homeowners' policy with Safeco Insurance Company, which covered any harm caused by the *unintentional* acts of the home's residents, including David. Since David's acts were *intentional*, Safeco was not responsible for the claims against him. But Safeco also argued that it was not responsible for claims against Betty because the wrongdoing that had caused the harm (that is, David's acts) had been intentional. Safeco's interpretation of this provision was valid under California law. However, Betty's policy had an additional provision that stated, "This insurance applies separately to each insured."

In short, Betty's policy was ambiguous. Safeco said the policy did not provide coverage if *any* insured had engaged in intentional wrongdoing while Betty argued that it did cover her if her own actions had been merely negligent.

Issue: *How should the court interpret ambiguous provisions in a contract?*

Excerpts from Justice Saxe's Decision: Our goal in construing insurance contracts, as with contracts generally, is to give effect to the parties' mutual intentions. If contractual language is clear and explicit, it governs. If the terms are ambiguous i.e., susceptible of more than one reasonable interpretation, we interpret them to protect the objectively reasonable expectations of the insured.

Only if these rules do not resolve a claimed ambiguity do we resort to the rule that ambiguities are to be resolved against the insurer. The "tie-breaker" rule of construction against the insurer stems from the recognition that the insurer generally drafted the policy and received premiums to provide the agreed protection.

Safeco could easily have removed any uncertainty. Safeco's intent was not clearly expressed, and the ambiguity must be resolved in a way that preserves the objectively reasonable coverage expectations of the insured seeking coverage. Betty had no reason to expect that David's residence in her home, and his consequent status as an additional insured on her homeowners policies, would narrow her own coverage, and the protection of her separate assets, against claims arising from his intentional acts. Betty's coverage must be analyzed on the basis of whether she herself committed an act or acts that fell within the intentional act exclusion.

This case illustrates an important rule of contract drafting: **Any ambiguity is interpreted against the drafter of the contract.** (The *Schwartz* policy is a good example of how complicated insurance policies can be. This complexity tends to erode judicial sympathy for the perpetrator.) Although both sides need to be careful in reading a contract—litigation benefits no one—the side that prepares the documents bears a special burden. This rule is meant to:

1. Protect laypeople from the dangers of form contracts that they have little power to change. Even if the insured in this case had read the contract carefully, it is unlikely that an insurance company would change its form contract for her.

2. Protect people who are unlikely to be represented by a lawyer. Most people do not hire a lawyer to read insurance contracts (or any form contract). And without an experienced lawyer, it is highly unlikely that an insured would ask, "If my son commits a crime in my house, will my insurance policy cover me?"

3. Encourage those who prepare contracts to do so carefully.

Because of a tiny typo, purchasers of condominiums in this building were able to back out of their deals.

Typos

The bane of a lawyer's existence! This author worked on a securities offering in which the sales document almost went out with part of the company's name spelled *Pertoleum* instead of *Petroleum*. (And legend has it that a United Airlines securities offering once featured "Untied Airlines.") Although clients tend not to have a sense of humor about such errors, at least there would be no adverse legal result. That is not always the case with typos.

A group of condominium buyers ended up in litigation over a tiny typo in their purchase agreements: an "8" instead of a "9." What difference could that possibly make? A lot, it turns out. Extell Development Corporation built the Rushmore, a luxury condominium complex in Manhattan. When Extell began selling the units, it agreed to refund any buyer's down payment if the first closing did not occur by September 1, 2009. (The goal was to protect buyers who might not have any place to live if the building was not finished on time.) In the end, the first closing occurred in February 2009. No problem, right? No problem except that the purchase contract had a typo: It said September 1, *2008* rather than *2009*. In the meantime, the Manhattan real estate market tumbled, and many purchasers of Rushmore condominiums wanted to back out. After litigation all the way to the Federal Court of Appeals, purchasers were allowed to cancel their contracts and obtain a refund of their deposits.

What is the law of typos? First of all, the law has a fancier word than *typo*—it is **scrivener's error.** (A scrivener is a clerk who copies documents.) **In the case of a scrivener's error, a court will reform a contract if there is clear and convincing evidence that the alleged mistake does not actually reflect the true intent of the parties.** In the Rushmore case, an arbitrator refused to reform the contract, ruling that there was no clear and convincing evidence that the parties intended something other than the contract term as written.

In the following case, even more money was at stake. What would you do if you were the judge?

Scrivener's error

A typo

You be the Judge

HERITAGE TECHNOLOGIES, L.L.C. v. PHIBRO-TECH, INC.

2008 U.S. Dist. LEXIS 329, 2008 WL 45380
United States District Court for the Southern District of Indiana, 2008

Facts: Heritage wanted to buy a substance called tribasic copper chloride (TBCC) from Phibro, but because of uncertainty in the industry, the two companies could not agree on a price for future years. It turned out, though, that the price of TBCC tended to rise and fall with that of copper sulfate, so Heritage proposed that the amount it paid for TBCC would increase an additional $15 per ton for each $0.01 increase in the cost of copper sulfate over $0.38 per pound.

Two top officers of Heritage and Phibro met in the Delta Crown Room at LaGuardia Airport to negotiate the purchase contract. At the end of their meeting, the Phibro officer hand wrote a document stating the terms of their deal and agreeing to the Heritage pricing proposal.

Negotiations between the two companies continued, leading to some changes and additions to their Crown Room agreement. In a draft prepared by Phibro, the $.01 number was changed to $0.1—that is, from 1 cent to 10 cents. In other words, in the original draft, Heritage agreed to an increase in price if copper sulfate went above 39 cents per pound, an additional price rise at 40 cents, and so on. But in the Phibro draft, Heritage's first increase would not occur until the price of copper sulfate went above 48 cents a pound, with a second rise at 58 cents. In short, the Phibro draft was much more favorable to Heritage than the Heritage proposal had been.

At some point during the negotiations, the lawyer for Heritage asked his client if the $0.1 figure was accurate. The Heritage officer said that the increase in this amount was meant to offset other provisions that favored Phibro. There is no evidence that this statement was true. The contract went through eight drafts and numerous changes, but after the Crown Room meeting, the two sides never again discussed the $0.1 figure.

After the execution of the agreement, Heritage discovered a different mistake. When Heritage brought the error to Phibro's attention, Phibro agreed to make the change even though it was to Phibro's disadvantage to do so.

All was peaceful until the price of copper sulfate went to $0.478 per pound. Phibro believed that because the price was above $0.38 per pound, it was entitled to an increased payment. Heritage responded that the increase would not occur until the price went above $0.48. Phibro then looked at the agreement and noticed the $0.1 term for the first time. Phibro contacted Heritage to say that the $0.1 term was a typo and not what the two parties had originally agreed in the Crown Room. Heritage refused to amend the agreement and Phibro filed suit.

You Be the Judge: *Should the court enforce the contract as written, or as the parties agreed in their Crown Room meeting? Which number is correct—$0.10 or $0.01?*

Argument for Phibro: In the Crown Room, the two negotiators agreed to a $15 per ton increase in the price of TBCC for each 1-cent increase in copper sulfate price. Then, by mistake, the contract said 10 cents. After the Crown Room meeting, the two parties never even discussed the 1-cent provision, much less agreed to change it. The court should revise this contract to be consistent with the parties' agreement, which was 1 cent.

Also, the 10-cent figure makes no economic sense. The point of the provision was that the price of TBCC would go up at the same rate as copper sulfate, and 1 cent for each ton is a much more accurate reflection of the relationship between these two commodities than 10 cents per ton.

Argument for Heritage: The Delta Crown Room agreement was nothing more than a draft. The parties then conducted negotiations by sending drafts back and forth rather than by talking on the phone. Each party was represented by a team of lawyers. Ultimately, the contract went through eight rounds of changes, and this pricing term was never altered despite several other changes and additions. Moreover, the change in price was in return for other terms that benefited Phibro.

Certainly, there is no clear and convincing evidence that both parties were mistaken about what the document actually said. Ultimately, the parties agreed to 10 cents, and that is what the court should enforce.

Ethics When Heritage found a different mistake in the contract, Phibro agreed to correct it, even though the correction was unfavorable to Phibro. But when a mistake occurred in Heritage's favor, it refused to honor the intended terms of the agreement. Is Heritage behaving ethically? Does Heritage have an obligation to treat Phibro as well as Phibro behaved toward Heritage? Is it right to take advantage of other people's mistakes? What Life Principle would you apply in this situation?

Preventing Mistakes

Here are ways to prevent mistakes in a contract.

> As a general rule, your lawyer is less likely to make mistakes than you are.

Let your lawyer draft the contract. As a general rule, your lawyer is less likely to make mistakes than you are. Of all the players in the Heritage case, only one person noticed the error—Heritage's lawyer.

Resist overlawyering. Yes, your lawyer should draft the contract, but that does not mean she should have free rein, no matter what. This author once worked with a real estate attorney who had developed his own standard mortgage contract, of which he was immensely proud. Whenever he saw a provision in another contract that was missing from his own, he immediately added it. His standard form contract soon topped 100 pages. That contract was painful to read and did no service to his clients.

Read the important terms carefully. Before signing a contract, check carefully and thoughtfully the names of the parties, the dates, dollar amounts, and interest rates. If all these elements are correct, you are unlikely to go too far wrong. And, of course, having read this chapter, you will never mistake $0.10 for $0.01.

Finally, when your lawyer presents you with a written contract, you should follow these rules:

1. Complain if your lawyer gives you a contract with provisions that are irrelevant to your situation.

2. If you do not know what a provision means, ask. If you still do not know (or if your lawyer does not know), ask her to take it out. Lawyers rarely draft from scratch; they tend to use other contracts as templates. Just because a provision was in another agreement does not mean that it is appropriate for you.

3. Remember that a contract is also a reference document. During the course of your relationship with the other party, you may need to refer to the contract regularly. That will be difficult if you do not understand portions of it, or if the contract is so disorganized you cannot find a provision when you need it.

Which brings us to our next topic—the structure of a contract. Once you understand the standard outline of a contract, it will be much easier to find your way through the thicket of provisions.

20-2d The Structure of a Contract

Traditional contracts tended to use archaic words—*whereas* and *heretofore* were common. Modern contracts are more straightforward, without as many linguistic flourishes. Our movie contract takes the modern approach.

Title

Contracts have a title, which generally is in capital letters, underlined, and centered at the top of the page. **The title should be as descriptive as possible**—a generic title such as AGREEMENT does not distinguish one contract from another. Much better to entitle it EMPLOYMENT AGREEMENT or CONFIDENTIALITY AGREEMENT. The title of our movie contract is MEMORANDUM OF AGREEMENT (not a particularly useful name), but in the upper-right-hand corner, there is space for the date of the contract and the subject. Let's say the subject is "Dawn Rising/Clay Parker." It would have been even better if the title of the movie had been: AGREEMENT BETWEEN CLAY PARKER AND WINTERFIELD PRODUCTIONS FOR DAWN RISING.

Introductory Paragraph

The introductory paragraph includes the date, the names of the parties, and the nature of the contract. The names of the parties and the movie are defined terms, e.g., Clay Parker ("Artist"). By defining the names, the actual names do not have to be repeated throughout the agreement. In this way, a standard form contract can be used in different deals without worrying about whether the names of the parties are correct throughout the document.

The introductory paragraph must also include specific language indicating that the parties entered into an agreement. In our contract, the opening paragraph states:

This shall confirm the agreement ("Agreement") between WINTERFIELD PRODUCTIONS ("Producer") and CLAY PARKER ("Artist") regarding the acting services of Artist in connection with the theatrical motion picture tentatively entitled "DAWN RISING" (the "Picture")[3] as follows:

This introductory paragraph is not numbered.

---

[3]These are not the parties' real names but are offered to illustrate the concepts.

It is here that traditional contracts included their "Whereas" provisions. Thus, for example, a traditional movie contract might say the following:

WHEREAS, Producer desires to retain the services of Artist for the purpose of making a theatrical motion picture; and

WHEREAS, Artist desires to work for Producer on the terms and subject to the conditions set forth herein;

NOW, THEREFORE, in consideration of the mutual covenants contained herein, and for other good and valuable consideration, the receipt and adequacy of which are hereby acknowledged, the parties agree as follows:

None of these flourishes are necessary, but some people prefer them.

Definitions

Most contracts have some definitions. As we have seen in the movie contract, *Artist*, *Producer*, and *Picture* were defined in the introductory paragraph. Sometimes, definitions are included in a separate section. Alternatively, they can appear throughout the contract. The movie contract does not have a definitions section, but many terms, such as *fixed compensation* and *teaser*, are defined in the body of the agreement.

Covenants

Now we get to the heart of the contract: What are the parties agreeing to do? Failure to perform these obligations constitutes a breach of the contract and will require the payment of damages. **Covenant** is a legal term that means a promise in a contract.

Covenant
A promise in a contract

At this stage, the relationship between lawyer and client is particularly important. They will obtain the best result if they work well together. And to achieve a successful outcome, both need to contribute. Clients should figure out what they need for the agreement to be successful. An hour or two of careful thought now could save months or even years of aggravation and expense later. It is at this point that clients have the most control over the deal, and they should exercise it. *It is a mistake to assume that everything will work itself out.* Lawyers can help in this negotiation and drafting process because they have worked on other similar deals and they know what can go wrong. Listen to them—they are on your side.

Imagine you are an actor about to sign a contract to make a movie. What provisions would you want? Begin by asking what your goals are for the project. Certainly, to make a movie that that critics like and the public wants to see. So you will ask for as much control over the process and product as you can get—selection of the director and costars, for instance. Maybe influence on the editing process. But you also want to make sure that the movie does not hurt your career. What provisions would you need to achieve that goal? And shooting a movie can be grueling work, so you want to ensure that your physical and emotional needs are met, particularly when you are on location away from home. Try to think of all the different events that could happen and how they would affect you. The contract should make provisions for these occurrences.

Now take the other side and imagine what you would want if you were the producer. The producer's goal is to make money—which means creating a high-quality movie while spending as little as possible and maintaining control over the process and final product. As you can see, some of the goals conflict—both Artist and Producer want control over the final product. Who will win that battle?

Here are the terms of the contract that Actor and Producer ultimately signed. The Artist negotiated:

1. a fixed fee of $1,800,000, to be paid in equal installments at the end of each week of filming

2. extra payment if the filming takes longer than 10 weeks

3. 7.5 percent of the gross receipts of the movie

4. a royalty on any product merchandising, the rate to be negotiated in good faith

5. approval over (but approval shall not be unreasonably withheld):

   a. the director, costars, hairdresser, makeup person, costume designer, stand-ins, and the look of his role (although he lists one director and costar whom he has preapproved);

   b. any changes in the script that materially affect his role;

   c. all product placements, but he preapproves the placement of Snickers candy bars;

   d. locations where the filming takes place;

   e. all videos, photos, and interviews of him;

   f. the translation of the script for French subtitles (he is fluent in French).

6. approval (at his sole discretion) over the release of any blooper videos

7. his name to be listed first in the movie credits, on a separate card (i.e., alone on the screen)

8. that the producer not give any photographs from the set to a tabloid (such as the *National Enquirer* or *Star)*.

9. at least 12 hours off duty from the end of each day of filming to the start of the next day

10. first-class airplane tickets to any locations outside Los Angeles

11. 10 first-class airline tickets for his friends to visit him on location

12. a luxury hotel suite for himself and a room for his friends

13. a driver and four-wheel-drive SUV to transport him to the set

14. the right to keep some wardrobe items

The Producer negotiated:

1. all intellectual property rights to the movie

2. the right not to make the movie, although he would still have to pay Artist the fixed fee

3. control over the final cut of the movie

4. that the Artist will show up on a certain date and work in good faith for

   a. 2 weeks in pre-production (wardrobe and rehearsals)

   b. 10 weeks shooting the movie

   c. 2 free weeks after the shooting ends, in case the director wants to reshoot some scenes. The Artist must in good faith make himself available whenever the director needs him.

5. the right to fire Artist if his appearance or voice materially changes before or during the filming of the movie

6. that the Artist help promote the movie on dates subject to Artist's approval, which shall not be unreasonably withheld

Language of the Covenants.   To clarify who exactly is doing what, covenants in a contract should use the active, not passive voice. In other words, a contract should say "Producer shall pay Artist $1.8 million," not "Artist shall be paid $1.8 million."

For important issues where disputes are likely to arise, the language should be precise, detailed, and complete. The movie contract uses 453 words to define the Artist's services just for shooting the movie, not including promotional efforts once the film is released. These acting services include "dubbing, retakes, reshoots, and added scenes."

Breach. So now we have the covenants in the movie contract. What happens if one of the parties breaches a covenant? Throughout the life of a contract, there could be many small breaches. Say, Artist shows up one day late for filming or he gains five pounds. Maybe Producer deposits Artist's paycheck a few days late. Perhaps a pop-out trailer is not available. Although these events may technically be violations, a court would not impose sanctions over such minor issues. **To constitute a violation of the contract, the breach must be material. A material breach** is important enough to defeat an essential purpose of the contract. Although a court would probably not consider one missed day to be a material breach, if Artist repeatedly failed to show up, that would be material.

Given that one goal of a contract is to avoid litigation, it is can be useful to define in the contract itself what a breach is. The movie contract uses this definition:

> Artist fails or refuses to perform in accordance with Producer's instructions or is otherwise in material breach or material default hereof," and "Artist's use of drugs [other than prescribed by a medical doctor]."

The contract goes on, however, to give Artist one free pass:

> It being agreed that with regard to one instance of default only, Artist shall have 24 hours after receipt of notice during principal photography, or 48 hours at all other times, to cure any alleged breach or default hereof.

Sometimes, you will recall, contracts state the consequences of a breach, such as the amount of damages. (You remember from prior chapters that these are called *liquidated damages*.) A damages clause can specify a certain amount, a limitation on the total, or other variations. In other words, the contract could say, "If Artist breaches, Producer is entitled to $1 million in damages." Alternatively, a damage clause could say, "Damages will not exceed $1 million." But the vast majority of contracts have neither liquidated damages nor damage caps.

Good Faith. Note that the covenants in the movie contract use three different standards of behavior: reasonably, in good faith or with sole discretion. **Reasonably** means ordinary or usual under the circumstances. **Good faith** means an honest effort to meet both the spirit and letter of the contract. A party with **sole discretion** has the *absolute* right to make any decision on that issue. Sole discretion clauses are not entered into lightly.

The following case involves a contract that did not specify which standard of behavior applied. What should the default standard be?

Material breach
A violation of a contract that defeats an essential purpose of the agreement

Reasonably
Ordinary or usual under the circumstances

Good faith
An honest effort to meet both the spirit and letter of the contract

Sole discretion
The *absolute* right to make any decision on an issue

DICK BROADCASTING CO. V. OAK RIDGE FM, INC.

395 S.W.3d 653
Supreme Court of Tennessee, 2013

Facts: Oak Ridge FM, Inc. and Dick Broadcasting Company (DBC) entered into a contract that gave DBC a right of first refusal to purchase all the assets of Oak Ridge's radio station WOKI-FM. The agreement also provided that:

> No party may assign its rights, interests or obligations here-under without the prior written consent of the other party,

and any purported assignment without such consent shall be null and void and of no legal force or effect.

When DBC asked permission to assign its rights to Citadel Broadcasting Company, Oak Ridge refused because it wanted to make its own deal directly with Citadel.

DBC sued Oak Ridge, alleging that it had breached the contract's *implied* covenant of good faith and fair dealing. The trial court dismissed the suit on a motion for summary judgment but the Court of Appeals overturned that decision. The Supreme Court of Tennessee agreed to hear the case.

Issues: *Is a covenant of good faith and fair dealing implied in this contract? In all contracts?*

Excerpts from Justice Lee's Decision: It is well-established that in Tennessee, the common law imposes a duty of good faith in the performance of contracts. These decisions are in accord with section 205 of the Restatement (Second) of Contracts, which provides that "every contract imposes upon each party a duty of good faith and fair dealing in its performance and its enforcement." In some cases, the courts have expressed this principle as allowing the qualifying word "reasonable"

and its equivalent "reasonably" to be read into every contract.

The Defendants argue that the trial court was correct in finding that the Right-of-First-Refusal Agreement was unambiguous and complete and holding that to interpret the contract in accordance with the implied covenant of good faith and fair dealing would be in effect to add a new provision to the contract which the parties were free to add themselves.

We disagree. The implied covenant of good faith and fair dealing does not create new contractual rights or obligations, it protects the parties' reasonable expectations as well as their right to receive the benefits of their agreement. To avoid the imposition of the implied covenant of good faith and fair dealing, the parties must explicitly state their intention to do so.

This case reflects the standard in Tennessee and in the Restatement (Second) of Contracts. Note, however, that about half the states disagree and do not imply a standard of good faith and fair dealing in contracts.

Reciprocal Promises and Conditions.   If one party to a contract breaches it, the other parties want to make sure that they can walk away without any further obligation to keep performing their covenants. To ensure this result, the terms of the contract must be *conditional* not *reciprocal*. Suppose that a contract states:

1. Actor shall take part in the principal photography of Movie for 10 weeks, commencing on March 1

2. Producer shall pay Artist $180,000 per week

In this case, even if Artist does not show up for shooting, Producer must still pay him. These provisions are **reciprocal promises, which means that they are each enforceable independently.** Producer must make payment and then sue Artist, hoping to recover damages in court.

> **Reciprocal promises**
> Promises that are each enforceable independently

The better approach is for the covenants to be **conditional**—a party agrees to perform them only if the other side has first done what it promised. In the real movie contract, Producer promises to pay Artist "On the condition that Artist fully performs all of Artist's services and obligations and agreements hereunder and is not in material breach or otherwise in material default hereof." For his part, Artist has the right to attend any premieres of the movie and invite three friends, "On the condition that Artist fully performs all services and material obligations hereunder."

> **Conditional promises**
> Promises that a party agrees to perform only if the other side has first done what it promised

In short, if you do not expect to perform under the contract until the other side has met its obligations, be sure to say so.

Representations and Warranties

Covenants are the promises the parties make about what they will do in the future. Representations and warranties are statements of fact about the past or present; they are true when the contract is signed (or at some other specific, designated time).[4]

> **Representations and warranties**
> Statements of fact about the past or present

---

[4]Although, technically, there is a slight difference between a representation and a warranty, many lawyers confuse the two terms, and the distinction is not important. We will treat them as synonyms, as many lawyers do.

Representations and warranties are important—without them, the other party might not have agreed to the contract. In the movie contract, Artist warrants that he is a member of the Screen Actors Guild. This provision is important because, if it was not true, Producer would either have to obtain a waiver or pay a substantial penalty.

In a contract between two companies, each side will generally represent and warrant facts such as: They legally exist, they have the authority to enter into the contract, their financial statements are accurate, they have revealed all material litigation, and they own all relevant assets. In a contract for the sale of goods, the contract will include warranties about the condition of the goods being sold.

EXAM Strategy

Question: Producer does not want Artist to pilot an airplane during the term of the contract. Would that provision be a warranty and representation or a covenant? How would you phrase it?

Strategy: Warranties and representations are about events in the past or present. A covenant is a promise for the future. If, for example, Producer wanted to know that Artist had never used drugs in the past, that provision would be a warranty and representation.

Result: A promise not to pilot an airplane is a covenant. The contract could say, "Until Artist completes all services required hereunder, he shall not pilot an airplane."

Boilerplate

These standard previsions are typically placed in a section entitled *Miscellaneous*. Many people think that *boilerplate* is a synonym for *boring and irrelevant,* but it is worth remembering that the term comes from the iron or steel that protects the hull of a ship—something that shipbuilders ignore to the passengers' peril. A contract without boilerplate is valid and enforceable, but these provisions do play an important protective role. In essence, boilerplate creates a private law that governs disputes between the parties. Courts can also play this role and, indeed, in the absence of boilerplate they will. But remember that an important goal of a contract is to avoid court involvement.

Here are some standard, and important, boilerplate provisions.

Choice of law provisions
Determine which state's laws will be used to interpret the contract.

Choice of forum provisions
Determine the state in which any litigation would take place.

Choice of Law and Forum. **Choice of law provisions** determine which state's laws will be used to interpret the contract. **Choice of forum** determines the state in which any litigation would take place. (One state's courts can apply another state's laws.) Lawyers often view these two provisions as the most important boilerplate. Particular states might have dramatically different laws. Even the so-called uniform statutes, such as the Uniform Commercial Code, can vary widely from state to state. Variations are even more pronounced in other areas of the law, in particular in the common law, which is created by state courts. As for forum, it is a lot more convenient and cheaper to litigate a case in one's home courts. The Supreme Court recently ruled that trial courts must enforce these forum selection clauses even if the result is highly inconvenient for one of the parties.[5]

---

[5]Atl. Marine Constr. Co. v. United States Dist. Court, 134 S. Ct. 568 (S. Ct. 2013).

When resolving a dispute, the choice of law and forum can strongly influence the outcome. For this reason, parties are sometimes reluctant to negotiate the provision and instead decide just to take their chances in the event of a lawsuit. Or they may choose a neutral, equally inconvenient forum such as Delaware. Without a choice of forum clause, the parties may well end up litigating where to litigate, or they may find themselves even worse off—with parallel cases filed by each party in its preferred forum.

The movie contract states: "This Agreement shall be deemed to have been made in the State of California and shall be construed and enforced in accordance with the law of the State of California." The contract did not, but might have, also specified the forum—that any litigation would be conducted in California.

Modification. Contracts should contain a provision governing modification. The movie contract states: "This Agreement may not be amended or modified except by an instrument in writing signed by the party to be charged with such amendment or modification."

"Charged with such amendment" means the party who is adversely affected by the change. For example, if Producer agrees to pay Artist more, then Producer must sign the amendment. Without this provision, a conversation over beers between Producer and Artist about a change in pay might turn out to be an enforceable amendment.

The original version of the movie contract said that Artist would be photographed nude only above the waist. He ultimately agreed to rear-below-the-waist photography. That amendment (which the parties called a **rider**—another term for amendment or addition) took the form of a letter from Artist agreeing to the change. Producer then signed the letter, acknowledging receipt and acceptance. The amendment would have been valid even without Producer's signature because Artist was "charged with such Amendment."

If a contract has a provision requiring that amendments be in writing, there are three ways to amend it:

1. Signing an amendment (or rider)

2. Crossing out the wrong language and replacing it by hand with the correct terms. It is good practice for both parties to initial such changes. This method is typically used at the last minute, say if a mistake is first noticed at the closing.

3. Rewriting the entire contract to include the changed provisions. In this case, the contract is typically renamed: The Amended and Restated Agreement. This method is most appropriate if there are many complex alterations.

Rider
An amendment or addition to a contract

Most commercial contracts provide that any amendment or modification must be in writing. The failure to comply *precisely* with this provision can lead to unfortunate consequences. In a recent case, Plaintiff agreed to buy real estate from Defendant for $56 million, with a $5 million down payment. The contract stated that all amendments had to be in writing. However, many times the parties agreed orally to extend the closing date but then did not sign the written amendment until afterward. Ultimately, this casual attitude backfired. They agreed to close at 12:00 noon on September 25 but Plaintiff did not arrive until 3 p.m. and, at that point, the two parties did not sign a modification.

Defendant then declared that, because Plaintiff had breached the agreement, Defendant could keep the $5 million deposit. Plaintiff sued, arguing that (a) it had complied with the contract by appearing at 3 p.m. and (b) the parties had orally agreed to postpone the closing (as they had done many times before). The court disagreed, ruling that Plaintiff had violated the contract by appearing three hours late, and that the oral modification was invalid because the contract provided that all amendments had to be in writing. Plaintiff learned a $5 million lesson (much, much more than the cost of this textbook).[6]

Also note that amending a contract may raise issues of consideration, a topic discussed in Chapter 13.

Assignment of Rights and Delegation of Duties.

Assignment of rights

A transfer of benefits under a contract to another person

Delegation of duties

A transfer of obligations under a contract

An **assignment of rights** is a transfer of the benefits under a contract to another person. Artist might, for example, want to assign his right to receive payment under the contract to his ex-wife. **Delegation of duties** is a transfer of the obligations under a contract. Suppose Artist received an offer to make another movie at the same time. He might want to assign his obligation to act in this movie to some other actor.

The movie contract treats the two parties differently on this issue. Producer has the right to assign the contract, but he must stay secondarily liable on it. In other words, Producer can transfer to someone else the right to receive the benefits of the contract (that is, to make the movie with Artist), but he cannot transfer his obligations (to pay Artist). If the person who takes over the contract from him fails to pay Artist, then Producer is liable. Artist might be unhappy if another production company makes the movie, but he is still bound by the terms of the contract. At least he knows that Producer is ultimately liable for his paycheck.

However, the contract also provides that:

> It is expressly understood and agreed that the services to be rendered by Artist hereunder are of the essence of this Agreement and that such services shall not be delegated to any other person or entity, nor shall Artist assign the right to receive compensation hereunder.

It matters to Producer which actor shows up to do the filming. Artist cannot say, "I'm too busy—here's my cousin Jack." And Producer also wants to make sure that no one else cashes the checks. He worries that if Artist assigns the right to receive payment, he will feel less motivated to do his job well.

Arbitration.

Some contracts prohibit the parties from suing in court and require that disputes be settled by an arbitrator. Arbitration has its advantages—flexibility and savings of time and money—but it also has disadvantages. For example, most contracts between consumers and brokerage houses require arbitration. Consumer advocates argue that the arbitrators in these disputes are biased in favor of the brokerage houses—which engage in many arbitrations—over consumers who are likely to be one-time customers. And many believe that employees receive a less favorable result when they arbitrate, rather than litigate, disputes with their employer.

Attorney's Fees.

As a general rule, if parties to a contract end up in litigation, they must pay their own legal fees, no matter who is in the wrong. But contracts may override this general rule and provide that the losing party in a dispute pays the attorney's fees for both sides. Such a provision tends to discourage the poorer party from litigating with a rich opponent for fear of having to pay two sets of attorney's fees. The movie contract provides:

> Artist hereby agrees to indemnify Producer from and against any and all losses, costs (including, without limitation, reasonable attorneys' fees), liabilities, damages, and claims of any nature arising from or in connection with any breach by Artist of any agreement, representation, or warranty made by Artist under this Agreement.

There is no equivalent provision for breaches by Producer. What does that omission tell you about the relative bargaining power of the two parties?

---

[6]Nassau Beekman, LLC v. Ann/Nassau Reality, LLC960 N.Y.S.2d (S.Ct. NY 2013).

Integration. During contract negotiations, the parties may discuss many ideas that are not ultimately included in the final version. The point of an integration clause is to prevent either side from later claiming that the two parties had agreed to additional provisions. The movie contract states:

> This Agreement, along with the exhibits attached hereto, shall constitute a binding contract between the parties hereto and shall supersede any and all prior negotiations and communications, whether written or oral, with respect hereto.

Without this clause, even a detailed written contract can be amended by an undocumented conversation—a dangerous situation since the existence and terms of the amendment will depend on what a court *thinks* was said and intended, which may or may not be what actually happened.

EXAM Strategy

Question: Daniel and Annie signed a contract providing that Daniel would lend $50,000 to Annie's craft beer business at an interest rate of 8 percent. During negotiations, Daniel and Annie agreed that the interest rate would go down to 5 percent once she had sold 25,000 cases. This provision never made it into the contract. After the contract was signed, Daniel agreed to reduce the interest rate to 6 percent once volume exceeded 15,000 cases. The contract had an integration provision but no modification clause. What interest rate must Annie pay?

Strategy: If a contract has an integration provision, then side agreements made during negotiations are unenforceable unless included in the written contract. Without a modification provision, oral agreements made after the contract was signed may be enforceable.

Result: A court would not enforce the side agreement that reduced the interest rate to 5 percent. However, it is possible that a court would enforce the 6 percent agreement.

Severability. If, for whatever reason, some part of the contract turns out to be unenforceable, a severability provision asks the court simply to delete the offending clause and enforce the rest of the contract. For example, courts will not enforce unreasonable noncompete clauses. (California courts will not enforce any noncompetes, unless made in connection with the sale of a business.) In one case, a consultant signed an employment contract that prohibited him from engaging in his occupation "anyplace in the world." The court struck down this noncompete provision but ruled that the rest of the contract (which contained trade secret clauses) was valid.

The movie contract states:

> In the event that there is any conflict between any provision of this Agreement and any statute, law, or regulation, the latter shall prevail; provided, however, that in such event, the provision of this Agreement so affected shall be curtailed and limited only to the minimum extent necessary to permit compliance with the minimum requirement, and no other provision of this Agreement shall be affected thereby and all other provisions of this Agreement shall continue in full force and effect.

Force Majeure. A **force majeure event** is a disruptive, unexpected occurrence for which neither party is to blame and that prevents one or both parties from complying with the contract. Force majeure events typically include war, terrorist attack, fire, flood, or general acts of God. If, for example, a major terrorist event were to halt air travel,

Force majeure event
A disruptive, unexpected occurrence for which neither party is to blame that prevents one or both parties from complying with a contract

497

Artist might not be able to appear on set as scheduled. The movie contract defines force majeure events thus:

> fire, war, governmental action or proceeding, third-party breach of contract, injunction, or other material interference with the production or distribution of motion pictures by Producer, or any other unexpected or disruptive event sufficient to excuse performance of this Agreement as a matter of law or other similar causes beyond Producer's control or by reason of the death, illness, or incapacity of the producer, director, or a member of the principal cast or other production personnel.

Notices. After a contract is signed, there may be times when the parties want to send each other official notices—of a breach, an objection, or an approval, for example. In this section, the parties list the addresses where these notices may be sent. For Producer, it is company headquarters. For Artist, there are three addresses: his agent, his manager, and his lawyer. The notice provision also typically specifies when the notice is effective: When sent, when it would normally be expected to arrive, or when it actually does arrive.

Closing. To indicate that the parties have agreed to the terms of the contract, they must sign it. A simple signature is sufficient, but contracts often contain flourishes. The movie contract, for example, states:

> IN WITNESS WHEREOF, the parties hereto have executed this Agreement as of the date first written above.

With clauses like this, it is important to make sure that there is an (accurate) date on the first page. If not otherwise provided in the "Notices" section, it is a good idea to include the parties' addresses. The movie contract also listed Artist's social security number.

When a party to the contract is a corporation, the signature lines should read like this: Winterfield Productions, Inc.

By: _____
Name:
Title:

If an individual signs her own name without indicating that she is doing so in her role as an employee of Winterfield Productions, Inc., she would be personally liable.

In the end, both parties signed the contract and made the movie. According to Rotten Tomatoes, the online movie site, professional reviewers rated it 7.9 out of 10.

Chapter Conclusion

You will undoubtedly sign many contracts in your life. Their length and complexity can be daunting. (In the movie contract, one of the paragraphs is 1,000 words.) The goal of this chapter is to help you understand the structure and meaning of the most important provisions so that you can negotiate, read, and analyze contracts more effectively.

Exam Review

1. **AMBIGUITY** Any ambiguity in a contract is interpreted against the party who drafted the agreement.

2. **SCRIVENER'S ERROR** A scrivener's error is a typographical mistake. In the case of a scrivener's error, a court will reform a contract if there is clear and convincing evidence that the mistake does not reflect the true intent of the parties.

Question: Martha intended to transfer one piece of land to Paul. By mistake, she signed a contract transferring two parcels of land. Each piece was accurately described in the contract. Will the court reform this contract and transfer one piece of land back to her?

Strategy: Begin by asking if this was a scrivener's error. Then consider whether the court will correct the mistake.

3. **BEFORE SIGNING A CONTRACT** Before signing a contract, check carefully and thoughtfully the names of the parties, the dates, dollar amounts, and interest rates.

4. **MATERIAL BREACH** A material breach is important enough to defeat an essential purpose of the contract.

Question: Laurie's contract to sell her tortilla chip business to Hudson contained a provision that she had to continue to work at the business for five years. One year later, she quit. Hudson refused to pay her the amounts still owing under the contract. Laurie alleged that he was liable for the full amount because her breach was not material. Is Laurie correct?

Strategy: What was the essential purpose of the contract? Was Laurie's breach important enough to defeat it?

5. **SOLE DISCRETION** A party with sole discretion has the absolute right to make any decision on that issue.

Question: A tenant rented space from a landlord for a seafood restaurant. Under the terms of the lease, the tenant could assign the lease only if the landlord gave her consent, which she had the right to withhold "for any reason whatsoever, at her sole discretion." The tenant grew too ill to run the restaurant and asked permission to assign the lease. The landlord refused. In court, the tenant argued that the landlord could not unreasonably withhold her consent. Is the tenant correct?

Strategy: A sole discretion clause grants the absolute right to make a decision. Are there any exceptions?

6. **REASONABLY** Reasonably means ordinary or usual under the circumstances.

7. **GOOD FAITH** Good faith means an honest effort to meet both the spirit and letter of the contract.

8. STRUCTURE OF A CONTRACT The structure of a contract looks like this:

1. Title
2. Introductory Paragraph
3. Definitions
4. Covenants
   i. Covenants are the promises the parties make about what they will do in the future.
5. Breach
6. Conditions
7. Representations and Warranties
   i. Representations and warranties are statements of fact about the present or past—they are true when the contract is signed (or at some other specific, designated time).
8. Boilerplate
   i. Choice of Law and Forum
   ii. Modification
   iii. Assignment of Rights and Delegation of Duties
   iv. Arbitration
   v. Attorney's Fees
   vi. Integration
   vii. Severability
   viii. Force Majeure
   ix. Notices
   x. Closing

---

2. Result: The court ruled that it was not a scrivener's error because it was not a typo or clerical error. Therefore, the court did not reform the contract and the land was not transferred back to Martha.

4. Result: The purpose of the contract was for Hudson to build up the business and make a profit. Laurie's departure interfered with that goal. The court ruled that the breach was material and Hudson did not have to pay the sums still owing under the contract.

5. Result: The court ruled for the landlord. She had the absolute right to make any decision so long as the decision was legal. The moral: Sole discretion clauses are serious business. Do not enter into one lightly.

MULTIPLE-CHOICE QUESTIONS

1. Which of the following statements is true?
   (a) Vagueness occurs when the parties do not want the contract to be clear.
   (b) Ambiguity occurs when the parties do not want the contract to be clear.
   (c) Vagueness in a contract is often appropriate as a way to clinch a deal.
   (d) Ambiguity is an appropriate tactic, particularly by the party drafting the contract.

2. A contract provided, "On January 5, Purchaser shall provide Seller with a certified check in the amount of $100,000. Seller shall transfer a deed for the Property to Purchaser." What is wrong with this provision?

(a) It is not clear who Purchaser and Seller are.

(b) The number $100,000 should be written in words.

(c) The promises are reciprocal.

(d) The promises are conditional.

3. In the case of a scrivener's error, what happens?

(a) A court will not reform the contract. The parties must live with the document they signed.

(b) A court will reform the contract if there is clear and convincing evidence that the clause in question does not reflect the true intent of the parties.

(c) A court will reform the contract if a preponderance of the evidence indicates that that the clause in question does not reflect the true intent of the parties.

(d) A court will invalidate the contract in its entirety.

4. A contract states (1) that Buzz Co. legally exists and (2) will provide 2,000 pounds of wild salmon each week. Which of the following statements is true?

(a) Clause 1 is a covenant and Clause 2 is a representation.

(b) Clause 1 is a representation and Clause 2 is a covenant.

(c) Both clauses are representations.

(d) Both clauses are covenants.

5. Simon has signed a contract with Miley agreeing to provide her company with 1,000 frozen pizzas each week. The contract states: "This agreement can only be modified by a written instrument signed by the party to be charged with such amendment." But when Simon and Miley run into each other on the train, they agree that he will provide 750 pizzas instead. Which of the following statements is true?

(a) As long as they both agree, they can amend the contract orally. They do not have to sign anything.

(b) For the change to be valid, both parties must sign an amendment because both parties are affected by it.

(c) Only Miley has to sign the amendment because she is the one to be charged by it.

(d) Only Simon must sign the amendment because he is the one to be charged by it.

CASE QUESTIONS

1. List three types of contracts that should definitely be in writing, and one that probably does not need to be.

2. Zoe has been offered a job as CIO at Appsley Co, but first she has to negotiate a contract with the CEO, Phil. Do a role-play with another student in your class in which one of you takes the role of Zoe and the other is Phil. What terms do you each want? Draft the contract. Now compare your results with others in the class. Who has negotiated the best deal? Who has written the best contract?

3. List three provisions in a contract that would be material, and three that would not be.

4. Slimline and Distributor signed a contract providing that Distributor would use reasonable efforts to promote and sell Slimline's diet drink. Slimline was already being sold in Warehouse Club. After the contract was signed, Distributor stopped conducting in-store demos of Slimline. It did not repackage the product as Slimline Warehouse requested. Sales of Slimline continued to increase during the term of the contract. Slimline sued Distributor, alleging a violation of the agreement. Who should win?

5. *YOU BE THE JUDGE* **WRITING PROBLEM** Chip bought an insurance policy on his house from Insurance Co. The policy covered damage from fire but explicitly excluded coverage for harm caused "by or through an earthquake." When an earthquake struck, Chip's house suffered no fire damage, but the earthquake caused a building some blocks away to catch on fire. That fire ultimately spread to Chip's house, burning it down. Is Insurance Co. liable to Chip?

Argument for Insurance Co.: The policy could not have been clearer or more explicit. If there had been no earthquake, Chip's house would still be standing. The policy does not cover his loss. **Argument for Chip:** His house was not damaged by an earthquake; it burned down. The policy covered fire damage. If a contract is ambiguous, it must be interpreted against the drafter of the contract.

DISCUSSION QUESTIONS

1. In the movie contract, which side was the more successful negotiator? Can you think of any terms that either party left out? Are any of the provisions unreasonable?

2. What are the advantages and disadvantages of hiring a lawyer to draft or review a contract?

3. What are the penalties if Artist breaches the movie contract? Are these reasonable? Too heavy? Too light?

4. **ETHICS** Sophia negotiated a contract with Pete under which she would buy his company for $10 million plus the amount of the company's outstanding debt (approximately $1 million). But when Pete sent a draft of the contract, it stated that the purchase price would be $10 million *less* the company's debt. What is Sophia's ethical obligation to Pete? Should she tell him about the mistake? What Life Principles would you apply in this situation?

5. Blair Co.'s top officers asked an investment bank to find a buyer for the company. The bank sent an engagement letter to Blair with the following language:

> If, within 24 months after the termination of this agreement, Blair is bought by anyone with whom Bank has had substantial discussions about such a sale, Blair must pay Bank its full fee.

Is there any problem with the drafting of this provision? What could be done to clarify the language?

ANSWERS TO SELECTED END OF CHAPTER QUESTIONS

MULTIPLE-CHOICE QUESTIONS

Presented are the answers for the ODD-numbered multiple-choice questions in the end-of-chapter material.

1. D
3. B
5. D

CASE QUESTIONS

Presented are the answers for all of the ODD-numbered case questions in the end-of-chapter material.

1. **Answer:** Should be in writing: the sale of stock, a merger agreement, the sale of land, anything that falls under the statute of frauds. Need not be in writing: an agreement with friends in which not much money is involved —to chip in to buy a present together. It is with someone with whom you have an ongoing relationship and who has proved to be trustworthy in the past, and you can afford the loss—a routine supplier. You do not have time to do a proper written contract, and you would prefer to bear the risk of loss over the risk of not getting the deal done.

3. **Answer:** Material: payment, item to be sold or services to be rendered, term of the contract; not material: notices, choice of law, arbitration, attorney's fees.

5. **Answer:** Chip won. The court ruled that the provision was ambiguous and so should be interpreted against the drafter—in this case, Insurance Co.

Chapter 24

SECURED TRANSACTIONS

© Creative Travel Projects/Shutterstock.com

James is a secret agent. His mission? To capture the targets. His tactics? Fast and sneaky. His equipment? State-of-the-art digital technology. His victims? Both shaken and stirred.

But James is not working for the government—he is employed by a bank. James is a modern repo man, paid to recover vehicles from delinquent borrowers. Equipped with a digital camera, he drives up and down highways and city streets capturing images of every passing license plate. Instantaneously, his on-board computer matches these numbers to a database of "wanted" vehicles.

And a match means the chase is on. Armed with digital maps, he follows the target car. Once it is parked, he swoops in and takes it away. Does this sound wrong? Everything James does is legal. The moral of the story? He knows who you are and where you live. Pay your car loan on time.[1]

> He knows who you are and where you live. Pay your car loan on time.

---

[1]Based on Ken Belson, "The Wired Repo Man: He's Not 'As Seen on TV,'" *The New York Times*, February 26, 2010.

24-1 ARTICLE 9: TERMS AND SCOPE

We can sympathize with the delinquent borrowers that James stalks, but as we will see in this chapter, the bank is entitled to its money. The car buyers and their banks entered into secured transactions, meaning that one party gave credit to another, demanding in return an assurance of repayment. Whether a used-car lot sells a car on credit for $18,000 or a bank takes collateral for a $600 million corporate loan, the parties have created a secured transaction.

Article 9 of the Uniform Commercial Code (UCC) governs secured transactions in personal property. It is essential to understand the basics of this law because we live and work in a world economy based on credit. Gravity may cause the earth to spin, but it is secured transactions that keep the commercial world going 'round. The quantity of disputes tells us how important this law is: About *one-half* of all UCC lawsuits involve Article 9.

This part of the Code employs terms not used elsewhere, so we must lead off with some definitions.

24-1a Article 9 Vocabulary

- **Fixtures** are goods that have become attached to real estate. For example, elevators are *goods* when a company manufactures them and also when it sells them to a retailer. But when a contractor installs an elevator in a new building, it becomes a *fixture*.

- **Security interest** means an interest in personal property or fixtures that secures the performance of some obligation. If an automobile dealer sells you a new car on credit and retains a security interest in the car, it means it is keeping legal rights in your car, including the right to drive it away if you fall behind in your payments. Usually, your obligation is to pay money, such as the money due on the new car. Occasionally, the obligation is to perform some other action, but in this chapter, we concentrate on the payment of money because that is what security interests are generally designed to ensure.

- **Secured party** is the person or company that holds the security interest. The automobile dealer who sells you a car on credit is the secured party.

- **Collateral** is the property subject to a security interest. When a dealer sells you a new car and keeps a security interest, the vehicle is the collateral.

- **Debtor and obligor.** For our purposes, **debtor** refers to a person who has some original ownership interest in the collateral. Having a security interest in the collateral does not make one a debtor. If Alice borrows money from a bank and uses her Mercedes as collateral, she is the debtor because she owns the car. **Obligor** means a person who must repay money, or perform some other task.

Throughout this chapter, the obligor and debtor will generally be the same person, but not always. When Alice borrows money from a bank and uses her Mercedes as collateral, she is the obligor, because she must repay the loan; as we know, Alice is also the debtor. However, suppose that Toby borrows money from a bank and provides no collateral; Jake co-signs the loan as a favor to Toby, using his Steinway piano as collateral. Jake is the only debtor, because he owns the piano. Both parties are obligors, because both have agreed to repay the loan.

- **Security agreement** is the contract in which the debtor gives a security interest to the secured party. This agreement protects the secured party's rights in the collateral.

- **Default** occurs when the debtor fails to pay money that is due, for example, on a loan or for a purchase made on credit. Default also includes other failures by the debtor, such as failing to keep the collateral insured.

- **Repossession** occurs when the secured party takes back collateral because the debtor has defaulted. Typically, the secured party will demand that the debtor deliver the collateral; if the debtor fails to do so, the secured party may find the collateral and take it, as James did in the chapter opener.

- **Perfection** is a series of steps the secured party must take to protect its rights in the collateral against people other than the debtor. This is important because if the debtor cannot pay his debts, several creditors may attempt to seize the collateral, but only one may actually obtain it. To perfect its rights in the collateral, the secured party will typically file specific papers with a state agency.

- **Financing statement** is a document that the secured party files to give the general public notice that it has a secured interest in the collateral.

- **Record** refers to information written on paper or stored in an electronic or other medium.

- **Authenticate** means to sign a document or to use any symbol or encryption method that identifies the person and clearly indicates she is adopting the record as her own. You authenticate a security agreement when you sign papers at an auto dealership, for example. A corporation electronically authenticates a loan agreement by using the Internet to transmit an encrypted signature.

An Example

Here is an example using the terms just discussed. A medical equipment company manufactures a CAT scan machine and sells it to a clinic for $2 million, taking $500,000 cash and the clinic's promise to pay the rest over five years. The clinic simultaneously authenticates a security agreement, giving the manufacturer a security interest in the CAT scan. If the clinic fails to make its payments, the manufacturer can repossess the machine. The manufacturer then electronically files a financing statement with an appropriate state agency. This *perfects* the manufacturer's rights, meaning that its security interest in the CAT scanner is now valid against all the world. If the clinic goes bankrupt and many creditors try to seize its assets, the manufacturer has first claim to the CAT scan machine. Exhibit 24.1 illustrates this transaction.

The clinic's bankruptcy is of great importance. When a debtor has money to pay all of its debts, there are no concerns about security interests. But what if there is not enough money to go around? A creditor insists on a security interest to protect itself in the event the debtor cannot pay all of its debts. **The secured party intends (1) to give itself a legal interest in specific property of the debtor and (2) to establish a priority claim in that property, ahead of other creditors.** In this chapter, we look at a variety of issues that arise in secured transactions.

24-1b Scope of Article 9

Article 9 applies to any transaction intended to create a security interest in personal property or fixtures.

Types of Collateral

The personal property used as collateral may be goods, such as cars or jewelry, but it may also be a variety of other things:

- **Instruments.** Drafts, checks, certificates of deposit, and notes may all be used as collateral, as may stocks, bonds, and other securities.

- **Investment property**, which refers primarily to securities and related rights.

- **Documents of title.** These are papers used by an owner of goods who ships or stores them. The documents are the owner's proof that he owns goods no longer in his

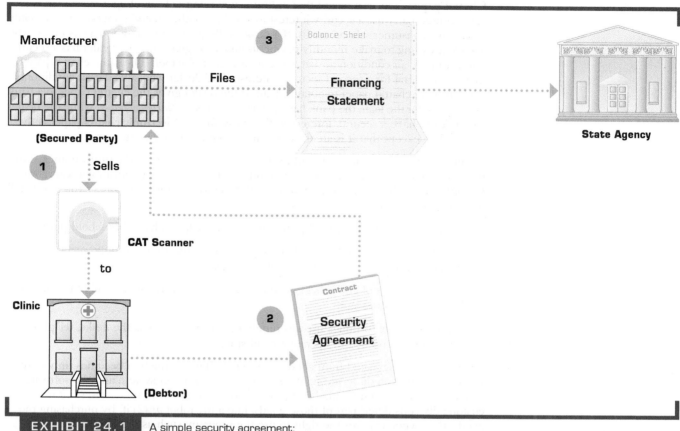

Manufacturer

(Secured Party)

1 Sells

Files

3 **Financing Statement**

Balance Sheet

State Agency

CAT Scanner

to

Clinic

(Debtor)

2 **Security Agreement**

Contract

EXHIBIT 24.1 A simple security agreement:
(1) The manufacturer sells a CAT scan machine to a clinic, taking $500,000 and the clinic's promise to pay the balance over five years.
(2) The clinic simultaneously authenticates a security agreement.
(3) The manufacturer perfects by electronically filing a financing statement.

possession. For example, an owner sending goods by truck will obtain a *bill of lading,* a receipt indicating where the goods will be shipped and who gets them when they arrive. Similarly, a *warehouse receipt* is the owner's receipt for goods stored at a warehouse. The owner may use these and other similar documents of title as collateral.

- **Account** means a right to receive payment for goods sold or leased. This includes, for example, accounts receivable, indicating various buyers owe a merchant money for goods they have already received. The category now includes health-insurance receivables.

- **Deposit accounts.** Article 9 also covers security interests in money held in bank accounts.

- **Commercial tort claims.** An organization that has filed a tort suit may use its claim as collateral. Personal injuries to *individuals* are not covered by this article.

- **General intangibles.** This is a catchall category, designed to include many kinds of collateral that do not appear elsewhere on the list, such as intellectual property rights, goodwill, the right to payment of some loans, and even liquor licenses.[2]

---

[2] Gibson v. Alaska Alcoholic Beverage Control Board, 377 F. Supp. 151 (D. Alaska 1974).

- **Chattel paper.** This is a record that indicates two things: (1) an obligor owes money and (2) a secured party has a security interest in specific goods. Chattel paper most commonly occurs in a consumer sale on credit. If a dealer sells an air conditioner to a customer, who agrees in writing to make monthly payments and also agrees that the dealer has a security interest in the air conditioner, that agreement is chattel paper. The same chattel paper may be collateral for a second security interest. The dealer who sells the air conditioner could use the chattel paper to obtain a loan. If the dealer gives the chattel paper to a bank as collateral for the loan, the bank has a security interest *in the chattel paper*, while the dealer continues to have a security interest *in the air conditioner*. **Electronic chattel paper** is the same thing, except that it is an electronic record rather than a written one.

- **Goods** are movable things, including fixtures, crops, and manufactured homes. For purposes of secured transactions, the Code divides goods into additional categories. In some cases, the rights of the parties will depend upon what category the goods fall into. These are the key categories:

  - *Consumer goods* are those used primarily for personal, family, or household purposes.

  - *Farm products* are crops, livestock, or supplies used directly in farming operations (as opposed to the business aspects of farming).

  - *Inventory* consists of goods held by someone for sale or lease, such as all of the beds and chairs in a furniture store.

  - *Equipment* refers to things used in running a business, such as the desks, telephones, and computers needed to operate a retail store.

- **Software** is distinguished from goods in Article 9. This distinction becomes important when competing creditors are fighting over both a computer system and the software inside it. A program embedded in a product counts as goods in two ways: (1) *if* it is customarily considered part of those goods, like a toy robot *or* (2) if, by purchasing the goods, the owner acquires the right to use the program, such as the operating system included in a personal computer purchase. A program that does *not* meet those criteria is termed *software*, and will be treated differently for some purposes.

Article 9 applies anytime the parties intended to create a security interest in any of the items just listed. But note that the nature of the item itself is not the only factor used in determining the type of collateral. Collateral may change classification depending on how it is used and by whom. The same laptop is inventory in the hands of a vendor, equipment in the hands of an entrepreneur using it for business, and a consumer good when a student uses it in daily life. Since different rules apply to each category, creditors must foresee the item's future uses to ensure that the financing statements reflect their intended collateral.

24-2 ATTACHMENT OF A SECURITY INTEREST

Attachment
A three-step process that creates an enforceable security interest

Attachment is a vital step in a secured transaction. This means that the secured party has taken all of the following steps to create an enforceable security interest:

- The two parties made a security agreement, and either the debtor has authenticated a security agreement describing the collateral *or* the secured party has obtained *possession* or *control;*

- The secured party has given value to obtain the security agreement; and

- The debtor has rights in the collateral.[3]

---

[3]UCC §9-203.

24-2a Agreement

Without an agreement, there can be no security interest. Generally, the agreement will be in writing and signed by the debtor or electronically recorded and authenticated by the debtor. The agreement must reasonably identify the collateral. A description of collateral by *type* is often acceptable. For example, a security agreement may properly describe the collateral as "all equipment in the store at 123 Periwinkle Street."[4] In a security agreement for consumer goods, however, a description by type is *not* sufficient, and more specificity is required.

A security agreement at a minimum might:

- State that Happy Homes, Inc., and Martha agree that Martha is buying an Arctic Co. refrigerator and identify the exact unit by its serial number;

- Give the price, the down payment, the monthly payments, and interest rate;

- State that because Happy Homes is selling Martha the refrigerator on credit, it has a security interest in the refrigerator; and

- Provide that if Martha defaults on her payments, Happy Homes is entitled to repossess the refrigerator.

An actual security agreement will add many details, such as Martha's obligation to keep the refrigerator in good condition and to deliver it to the store if she defaults; a precise definition of "default"; and how Happy Homes may go about repossessing if Martha defaults and fails to return the refrigerator.

24-2b Control and Possession

In many cases, the security agreement need not be in writing if the parties have an oral agreement and the secured party has either **control** or **possession**. For many kinds of collateral, it is safer for the secured party actually to take the item than to rely upon a security agreement. The rules follow.

Control

For deposit accounts, electronic chattel paper, and certain other collateral, the security interest attaches if the secured party has control. The UCC specifies exactly what the secured party must do to obtain control for each type of collateral. In a general sense, control means that the secured party has certain exclusive rights to dispose of the collateral.

- **Deposit account (in a bank).** The secured party has control if it is itself the bank holding the deposit or if the debtor has authorized the bank to dispose of funds according to the secured party's instructions.

- **Electronic chattel paper.** A secured party has control of electronic chattel paper when it possesses the only authoritative copy of it, and the record(s) designate the secured party as the assignee. This means that the parties have agreed on an electronic method to verify the uniqueness of the record, so that any copies of the electronic original are clearly recognizable as reproductions.

- **Investment property and letter-of-credit rights.** The Code specifies analogous methods of controlling investment properties and letter-of-credit rights.[5]

---

[4]A security agreement may not use a super-generic term such as "all of Smith's personal property." We will see later that, by contrast, such a super-generic description is legally adequate in a *financing statement*.

[5]*Control* is described in the following sections: 9-104 (deposit accounts), 9-105 (electronic chattel paper), 9-106 (investment property), and 9-107 (letter-of-credit rights).

Possession

For most other forms of collateral, including goods, securities, and most other items, a security interest attaches if the secured party has *possession*. For example, if you loan your neighbor $175,000 and he gives you a Winslow Homer watercolor as collateral, you have an attached security interest in the painting once it is in your possession. It would still be wise to put the agreement in writing, to be certain both parties understand all terms and can prove them if necessary, but the writing is not legally required.

EXAM Strategy

Question: Hector needs money to keep his business afloat. He asks his uncle for a $1 million loan. The uncle agrees, but he insists that his nephew grant him a security interest in Hector's splendid gold clarinet, worth over $2 million. Hector agrees. The uncle prepares a handwritten document summarizing the agreement and asks his nephew to sign it. Hector hands the clarinet to his uncle and receives his money, but he forgets to sign the document. Has a security agreement attached?

Strategy: Attachment occurs if the parties made a security agreement and there was authentication or possession; the secured party has given value; and the debtor had rights in the collateral.

Result: Hector agreed to give his uncle a security interest in the instrument. He never authenticated (signed) the agreement, but the uncle did take possession of the clarinet. The uncle gave Hector $1 million, and Hector owned the instrument. Yes, the security interest attached.

24-2c Value

For the security interest to attach, the secured party must give value. Usually, the value will be apparent. If a bank loans $400 million to an airline, that money is the value, and the bank, therefore, may obtain a security interest in the planes that the airline is buying. If a store sells a living room set to a customer for a small down payment and two years of monthly payments, the value given is the furniture.

Future Value

The parties may also agree that some of the value will be given in the future. For example, a finance company might extend a $5 million line of credit to a retail store, even though the store initially takes only $1 million of the money. The remaining credit is available whenever the store needs it to purchase inventory. The Uniform Commercial Code considers the entire $5 million line of credit to be value.[6]

24-2d Debtor Rights in the Collateral

The debtor can grant a security interest in goods only if he has some legal right to those goods himself. Typically, the debtor owns the goods. But a debtor may also give a security interest if he is leasing the goods or even if he is a bailee, meaning that he is lawfully holding them for someone else. Suppose Importer receives a shipment of scallops on behalf

---

[6]UCC §9-204(c).

of Seafood Wholesaler. Wholesaler asks Importer to hold the scallops for three days as a favor, and to keep a customer happy, Importer agrees. Importer then arranges a $150,000 loan from a bank, using the scallops as collateral. Although Importer has acted unethically, it does have *some right* in the collateral—the right to hold them for three days. That is enough to satisfy this rule.

By contrast, suppose Railroad is transporting 10 carloads of cattle on behalf of Walter, the owner. A devious Meat Dealer uses forged documents to trick Railroad into believing that Meat Dealer is entitled to the animals. Meat Dealer trucks the cattle away and uses them to obtain a bank loan, giving the bank a security interest in the animals. That "security interest" has never attached and is invalid because Dealer had *no* legal interest in the cattle. When Walter, the rightful owner, locates his cattle, he may take them back. The bank can only hope to find the deceitful Dealer, who in fact has probably disappeared.

Once the security interest has attached to the collateral, the secured party is protected against the debtor. If the debtor fails to pay, the secured party may repossess the collateral.

24-2e Attachment to Future Property

The security agreement may specify that the security interest attaches to personal property that the debtor does not yet possess but might obtain in the future.

After-Acquired Property

After-acquired property refers to items that the debtor obtains after the parties have made their security agreement. **The parties may agree that the security interest attaches to after-acquired property.**[7] Basil is starting a catering business, but owns only a beat-up car. He borrows $55,000 from the Pesto Bank, which takes a security interest in the car. But Pesto also insists on an after-acquired clause. When Basil purchases a commercial stove, cooking equipment, and freezer, Pesto's security interest attaches to each item as Basil acquires it.

> **After-acquired property**
> Items that the debtor obtains after the parties have made their security agreement

Proceeds

Proceeds are whatever is obtained by a debtor who sells the collateral or otherwise disposes of it. **The secured party *automatically* obtains a security interest in the *proceeds* of the collateral, unless the security agreement states otherwise.**[8] Suppose the Pesto Bank obtains a security interest in Basil's $4,000 freezer. Basil then decides he needs a larger model and sells the original freezer to his neighbor for $3,000. The $3,000 cash is proceeds, in which Pesto automatically obtains a security interest.

24-3 PERFECTION

24-3a Nothing less than Perfection

Once the security interest has attached to the collateral, the secured party is protected against *the debtor*, but it may not be protected against *anyone else*. Pesto Bank loaned money to Basil and has a security interest in all of his property. If Basil defaults on his loan, Pesto may insist he deliver the goods to the bank. If he fails to do that, the bank can seize the collateral. But Pesto's security interest is valid only against Basil; if a third person claims some interest in the goods, the bank may never get them. For example, Basil might have taken out *another* loan, from his friend Olive, and used the same property as collateral.

---

[7] UCC §9-204(a).
[8] UCC §9-203(f).

Olive knew nothing about the bank's original loan. To protect itself against Olive, and all other parties, the bank must *perfect* its interest.

There are several kinds of perfection:

- Perfection by filing
- Perfection by possession
- Perfection of consumer goods
- Perfection of movable collateral and fixtures

In some cases, the secured party will have a choice of which method to use; in other cases, only one method works.

24-3b Perfection by Filing

Financing statement
A statement that gives the names of all parties, describes the collateral, and outlines the security interest

The most common way to perfect an interest is by filing a financing statement with one or more state agencies. A **financing statement** gives the names of all parties, describes the collateral, and outlines the security interest, enabling any interested person to learn about it. Suppose the Pesto Bank obtains a security interest in Basil's catering equipment and then perfects by filing with the secretary of state. When Basil asks his friend Olive for a loan, she has the opportunity to check the records to see if anyone already has a security interest in the catering equipment. If Olive's search uncovers Basil's previous security agreement, she will realize it would be unwise to make the loan. If Basil were to default, the collateral would go straight to Pesto Bank, leaving Olive empty-handed. See Exhibit 24-2.

Article 9 prescribes one form to be used nationwide for financing statements.[9] The financing form is available online at many websites. Remember that the filing may be done on paper or electronically.

If the collateral is either *accounts* or *general intangibles*, filing is the *only* way to perfect. Suppose Nestor uses his copyright in a screenplay as collateral for a loan. The bank that gives him the loan may perfect *only* by filing.

The most common problems that arise in filing cases are (1) whether the financing statement contained enough information to put other people on notice of the security interest and (2) whether the secured party filed the papers in the right place.

Contents of the Financing Statement

A financing statement is sufficient if it provides the name of the debtor, the name of the secured party, and an indication of the collateral.[10]

The name of the debtor is critical because that is what an interested person will use to search among the millions of other financing statements on file. Faulty descriptions of the debtor's name have led to thousands of disputes and untold years of litigation, as subsequent creditors have failed to locate any record of an earlier claim on the debtor's property. In response, the UCC is very precise about what name must be used. If the debtor is a "registered organization," such as a corporation, limited partnership, or limited liability company, the official registered name of the company is the only one acceptable. If the debtor is a person or an unregistered organization (such as a club), then the *correct* name is required. Trade names are not sufficient.

Because misnamed debtors have created so much conflict, the Code now offers a straightforward test: A financing statement is effective if a computer search run under the debtor's correct name produces it. That is true even if the financing statement used the

---

[9]UCC §9-521.
[10]UCC §9-502(a).

EXHIBIT 24.2

The Pesto Bank:

(1) Loans money to Basil and

(2) Takes a security interest in his equipment.

Later, when Olive:

(1) Considers loaning Basil money, she will

(2) Check to see if any other creditors already have a security interest in his goods.

incorrect name. If the search does not reveal the document, then the financing statement is ineffective as a matter of law. The burden is on the secured party to file accurately, not on the searcher to seek out erroneous filings.[11]

The collateral must be described reasonably so that another party contemplating a loan to the debtor will understand which property is already secured. A financing statement could properly state that it applies to "all inventory in the debtor's Houston warehouse." If the debtor has given a security interest in everything he owns, then it is sufficient to state simply that the financing statement covers "all assets" or "all personal property."

The filing must be done by the debtor's last name. But which name is the last? The answer is not always entirely straightforward, as the following case indicates. Did the court get it right?

---

[11]UCC §9-506(c).

CORONA FRUITS & VEGGIES, INC. V. FROZSUN FOODS, INC.

143 Cal. App. 4th 319
California Court of Appeals, 2006

Facts: Corona Fruits & Veggies (Corona) leased farmland to a strawberry farmer named Armando Munoz Juarez. He signed the lease, "Armando Munoz." Corona advanced money for payroll and farm production expenses. The company filed a UCC-1 financing statement, claiming a security interest in the strawberry crop. The financing statement listed the debtor's name as "Armando Munoz." Six months later, Armando Munoz Juarez contracted with Frozsun Foods, Inc., to sell processed strawberries. Frozsun advanced money and filed a financing statement listing the debtor's name as "Armando Juarez."

By the next year, the strawberry farmer owed Corona $230,000 and Frozsun $19,600. When he was unable to make payments on Corona's loan, the company repossessed the farmland. And, while it may sound a bit … odd … it also repossessed the strawberries.

Both Corona and Frozsun claimed the proceeds of the crop. The trial court awarded the money to Frozsun, finding that Corona had filed its financing statement under the wrong last name and therefore had failed to perfect its security interest in the strawberry crop. Corona appealed.

Issue: *Did Corona correctly file its financing statement?*

Excerpts from Judge Yegan's Decision: Shakespeare asked, "What's in a name?" We supply an answer only for the Uniform Commercial Code lien priority statutes: Everything when the last name is true and nothing when the last name is false. When a creditor files a UCC-1 financing statement, the debtor's true last name is crucial because the financing statements are indexed by last names. A subsequent creditor who loans money to a debtor with the same name is put on notice that its lien is secondary.

Substantial evidence supports the finding that debtor's true last name was "Juarez" and not "Munoz." The pleadings state that debtor's last name is "Juarez," as do many of appellants' business records. Debtor provided appellants with a photo I.D. and Green Card bearing the name "Armando Munoz Juarez." The name appears on the sublease and other documents including the Farmer Agreement, a Crop Exhibit, a second sublease agreement (identifying debtor as "Juarez Farms, Armando Munoz Juarez"), a crop assignment, appellants' accounting records, receipts for advances, appellants' letters to debtor, and checks issued by appellants.

As a general rule, minor errors in a UCC financing statement do not affect the effectiveness of the financing statement unless the errors render the document seriously misleading to other creditors. If a search of the filing office's records under the debtor's correct name, using the filing office's standard search logic, would nevertheless disclose that financing statement, the name provided does not make the financing statement seriously misleading.

The record indicates that Frozsun's agent conducted a "Juarez" debtor name search and did not discover appellants' UCC-1 financing statement. No evidence was presented that the financing statement would have been discovered under debtor's true legal name, using the filing office's standard search logic. Absent such a showing, the trial court reasonably concluded that the "Armando Munoz" debtor name in appellants' financing statement was seriously misleading. The secured party, not the debtor or uninvolved third parties, has the duty of insuring proper filing and indexing of the notice.

Appellants contend that the debtor name requirement is governed by the naming convention of Latin American countries because debtor is from Mexico. We reject the argument because the strawberries were planted in and the debt obligation arose in Santa Barbara County, not Mexico. In most Latin American countries, the surname is formed by listing first the father's name, then the mother's name. This is exactly opposite Anglo-American tradition. Debtor's last name did not change when he crossed the border into the United States. The "naming convention" is legally irrelevant for UCC-1 purposes and, if accepted, would seriously undermine the concept of lien perfection.

Appellants knew that debtor's legal name was "Armando Juarez" or "Armando Munoz Juarez." Elodia Corona, appellants' account manager, prepared the UCC Financing Statements and testified: "I don't know why I didn't put his last name on the financing statement. I could have made a mistake." Ms. Corona was asked: "So the last name on all the Agreements is Juarez, but on the U.C.C. 1 Forms, you filed them as Munoz?" Ms. Corona answered, "Yes."

Appellants are [defeated by their own] pleadings, the contracts, business records, the checks for the cash advances, debtor's identification papers and tax papers, and the testimony of appellants' account manager. Appellants could have protected themselves by using both names on their financing statements. The trial court did not err in finding that the UCC-1 financing statement filed by Frozsun Foods perfected a security interest superior to appellants' liens.

The judgment is affirmed.

Article 9—2013 Amendments. In 2013, the authors of the UCC—The National Conference of Commissioners on Uniform State Laws (NCCUSL)—proposed a set of Amendments to Article 9. Remember that the NCCUSL has no power to make law. Once it creates a set of model rules, it is up to the states to decide whether or not to actually enact the proposals. Almost all states have now adopted the changes to Article 9.

While most of these changes are so technical as to be beyond the scope of this chapter, one of the amendments addresses the issue of what name must appear on a financing statement. Under the Amendments, most states now require that individuals use the same name on a financing statement that is on their driver's license or state ID card (for non-drivers).[12] For organizations, the correct name is the one on the "public organic record," defined as any record available for public inspection, including its charter or limited partnership agreement.[13]

Debtor's Signature. Notice one important item that is *not* required on a financing statement: the debtor's signature. The drafters of the UCC have greatly facilitated electronic filing by eliminating the old requirement that a debtor sign. Does this allow a secured party to create any financing statement it wishes? No. The debtor must have entered into a valid security agreement before the secured party is entitled to file any financing statement. Of course, there is the possibility of a fraudulent filing, but the drafters reasoned that the efficiency achieved far outweighs the danger of occasional fraud.

Place of Filing

The United States is a big country, and potential creditors do not want to stagger from one end of it to the other to learn whether particular collateral is already secured elsewhere. Article 9 specifies *where* a secured party must file. These provisions may vary from state to state, so it is essential to check local law because a misfiled record accomplishes nothing. The general rules are as follows.

A secured party must file in the state of the debtor's location. An individual is located at his principal residence. If Luigi, the debtor, lives in Maryland, works in Virginia, and has a vacation home in Florida, a secured party must file in Maryland. An organization that has only one place of business is located in that state. If the organization has more than one place of business, it is considered to be located at its chief executive office.[14]

Article 9 prescribes central filing within the state for most types of collateral. For goods, the central location will typically be the secretary of state's office, although a state may designate some other office if it wishes. For fixtures, the secured party generally has a choice between filing in the same central office that is used for goods (which, again, is usually the secretary of state's office), or filing in the local county office that would be used to file real estate mortgages.[15]

Duration of Filing

Once a financing statement has been filed, it is effective for five years.[16] After five years, the statement will expire and leave the secured party unprotected, unless she files a continuation statement within six months prior to expiration. The continuation

---

[12]UCC §9-503. If a person has neither kind of state ID card, then her surname and first personal name will be required to perfect by filing.

[13]UCC §102(a)(68).

[14]UCC §9-307.

[15]UCC §9-501.

[16]The exception to this is for a manufactured home, where it lasts 30 years.

statement is valid for an additional five years, and if necessary, a secured party may continue to file one periodically, forever.[17]

24-3c Perfection by Possession or Control

For most types of collateral, in addition to filing, a secured party generally may perfect by possession or control. So if the collateral is a diamond brooch or 1,000 shares of stock, a bank may perfect its security interest by holding the items until the loan is paid off. When the debtor gives collateral to the secured party, it is often called a **pledge**: The debtor pledges her goods to secure her performance, and the secured party (sometimes called the **pledgee**) takes the goods to perfect its interest.

Pledge
A secured transaction in which a debtor gives collateral to the secured party

Possession

When may a party use possession? Whenever the collateral is goods, negotiable documents, instruments, money, chattel paper that is tangible (as opposed to electronic), or most securities.[18]

Perfection by possession has some advantages. First, notice to other parties is very effective. No reasonable finance company assumes that it can obtain a security interest in a Super Bowl championship ring when another creditor already holds the ring. Second, possession enables the creditor to ensure that the collateral will not be damaged during the life of the security interest. A bank that loans money based on a rare painting may worry about the painting's condition, but it knows the painting is safe if it is locked up in the bank's vault. Third, if the debtor defaults, a secured party has no difficulties repossessing goods that it already holds.

Of course, for some collateral, possession is impractical. If a consumer buys a new yacht on credit, the seller can hardly expect to perfect its security interest by possession. The buyer would become edgy sailing the boat around the dealer's parking lot. In such a case, the secured party must perfect by filing.

© iStockphoto.com/PhilipCacka

A bank may wish to perfect its security interest by holding this valuable ring in its vault.

Mandatory Possession

A party *must* perfect a security interest in *money* by taking possession.[19] Money is easy to transfer, and one $100 bill is the same as another, so only possession will do. Suppose Ed's Real Estate claims that Jennifer, a former employee, has opened her own realty business in violation of their noncompete agreement. Jennifer promises to move her business to another city within 90 days, and Ed agrees not to sue. To secure Jennifer's promise to move, Ed takes a security interest in $50,000 cash. If she fails to move on time, he is entitled to the money. To perfect that interest, Ed must take possession of the money and hold it until Jennifer is out of town.

---

[17]UCC §9-515.
[18]UCC §9-313.
[19]UCC §9-312(b)(3).

Control

A security interest in investment property, deposit accounts, letter-of-credit rights, and electronic chattel paper may be perfected by control.[20] We described control in the section on attachment. **In general, control means that the secured party has certain exclusive rights to dispose of the collateral.** Recall, for example, that a secured party which is a bank has control of any deposit account located in that bank.

Mandatory Control. **Security interests in deposit accounts and letter-of-credit rights may be perfected *only* by control.**[21] Once again, filing would be ineffectual with forms of collateral so easily moved, and the UCC will grant perfection only to a secured party that has control.

Care of the Collateral

Possession and control give several advantages to the secured party, but also one important duty: **A secured party must use reasonable care in the custody and preservation of collateral in her possession or control.**[22] If the collateral is something tangible, such as a painting, the secured party must take reasonable steps to ensure that it is safe from harm.

What does "reasonable care" mean when the collateral is something as volatile as shares of stock?

LAYNE V. BANK ONE

395 F.3d 271
United States Court of Appeals for the Sixth Circuit, 2005

Facts: Charles E. Johnson was the founder and CEO of PurchasePro.com, Inc., and Geoff Layne was its marketing director. When their Internet stock went public, both officers suddenly owned shares worth millions of dollars. To increase his liquidity, Johnson took out a loan for $2.8 million from Bank One, and Layne borrowed $3.25 million. Each secured the loan with shares of Purchase Pro stock.

The loan agreement required a loan-to-value (LTV) ratio of 50 percent, meaning that the value of the shares had to be at least double the outstanding loan balance. If the value of the shares sank below the required level, the two men could either pay off some of the loan or offer additional security. If the two borrowers failed to remedy the problem, the bank was entitled (but not obligated) to sell the shares. Johnson secured his loan with $6.9 million worth of Purchase Pro stock.

In February, Internet stocks suddenly plummeted, and both loans immediately exceeded their LTV ratio.

Johnson and Layne spoke with the bank several times, stating that they would offer additional collateral. During March and April, more calls went back and forth, with the debtors occasionally suggesting that the collateral be sold, while at other times agreeing to provide more security. Finally, in July, over a four-day period, the bank sold Johnson's Purchase Pro shares for $524,757, less than 10 percent of its original worth.

Johnson and Layne both filed suit against the bank, claiming that it failed to exercise reasonable care of the collateral. The trial court gave judgment for the bank, and the plaintiffs appealed.

Issue: *Did the bank exercise reasonable care of the shares?*

Excerpts from Judge Moore's Decision: We first consider Johnson's argument that Bank One violated a duty under Kentucky law to preserve the value of the collateral held in its possession. With respect to the regulation of secured transactions, Kentucky has adopted

---

[20]UCC §9-314(a).
[21]UCC §9-312(b)(1).
[22]UCC §9-207.

the Uniform Commercial Code, which states that "a secured party shall use reasonable care in the custody and preservation of collateral in the secured party's possession. In the case of chattel paper or an instrument, reasonable care includes taking necessary steps to preserve rights against prior parties unless otherwise agreed."

The comment to §9-207 states that the provision "imposes a duty of care, similar to that imposed on a pledgee at common law, on a secured party in possession of collateral," and cites to [a different treatise that says,] "The pledgee is not liable *for a decline in the value* of pledged instruments, even if timely action could have prevented such decline." In the context of pledged stock, courts have used this language to hold that "a bank has no duty to its borrower to sell collateral stock of declining value."

As [another court] stated, "It is the borrower who makes the investment decision to purchase stock. A lender in these situations merely accepts the stock as collateral, and does not thereby itself invest in the issuing firm. Given the volatility of the stock market, a requirement that a secured party sell shares held as collateral, at a particular time, would be to shift the investment risk from the borrower to the lender."

We conclude that under Kentucky law a lender has no obligation to sell pledged stock held as collateral merely because of a market decline. If the borrower is concerned with the decline in the share value, it is his responsibility, rather than that of the lender, to take appropriate remedial steps, such as paying off the loan in return for the collateral, substituting the pledged stock with other equally valued assets, or selling the pledged stock himself and paying off the loan.

24-3d Perfection of Consumer Goods

The UCC gives special treatment to security interests in most consumer goods. Merchants sell a vast amount of consumer goods on credit. They cannot file a financing statement for every bed, television, and stereo for which a consumer owes money. Yet perfecting by possession is also impossible since the consumer expects to take the goods home. To understand the UCC's treatment of these transactions, we need to know two terms. The first is consumer goods, which as we saw earlier means goods used primarily for personal, family, or household purposes. The second term is purchase money security interest.

Purchase money security interest (PMSI)

An interest taken by the person who sells the collateral or advances money so the debtor can buy it

A **purchase money security interest (PMSI)** is one taken by the person who sells the collateral or by the person who advances money so the debtor can buy the collateral.[23] Assume the Gobroke Home Center sells Marion a $5,000 stereo system. The sales document requires a payment of $500 down and $50 per month for the next three centuries, and gives Gobroke a security interest in the system. Because the security interest was "taken by the seller," the document is a PMSI. It would also be a PMSI if a bank had loaned Marion the money to buy the system and the document gave the bank a security interest.

But aren't all security interests PMSIs? No, many are not. Suppose a bank loans a retail company $800,000 and takes a security interest in the store's present inventory. That is not a PMSI since the store did not use the $800,000 to purchase the collateral.

What must Gobroke Home Center do to perfect its security interest? Nothing. **A PMSI in *consumer goods* perfects *automatically*, without filing.**[24] Marion's new stereo is clearly consumer goods because she will use it only in her home. Gobroke's security interest is a PMSI, so the interest has perfected automatically. (See Exhibit 24.3.)

---

[23]UCC §9-103.
[24]UCC §9-309(1).

EXHIBIT 24.3   A purchase money security interest can arise in either of two ways. In the first example, a store sells a sound system to a consumer on credit; the consumer in turn signs a PMSI, giving the store a security interest in the stereo. In the second example, the consumer buys the stereo with money loaned from a bank; the consumer signs a PMSI giving the *bank* a security interest in the sound system.

EXAM Strategy

Question: Winona owns a tropical fish store. To buy a spectacular new aquarium, she borrows $25,000 from her sister, Pauline, and signs an agreement giving Pauline a security interest in the tank. Pauline never files the security agreement. Winona's business goes belly up, and both Pauline and other creditors angle to repossess the tank. Does Pauline have a perfected interest in the tank?

Strategy: Generally, a creditor obtains a perfected security interest by filing or possession. However, a PMSI in consumer goods perfects automatically, without filing. Was Pauline's security agreement a PMSI? Was the fish tank a consumer good?

Result: A PMSI is one taken by the person who sells the collateral or advances money for its purchase. Pauline advanced the money for Winona to buy the tank, so Pauline does have a PMSI, but she has a problem, because PMSIs perfect automatically only for *consumer goods*. Consumer goods are those used primarily for personal, family, or household purposes, and so this was not a consumer purchase. Pauline failed to perfect and is unprotected against other creditors.3pt?>

24-3e Perfection of Movable Collateral and Fixtures

The rules for perfection are slightly different for security interests in movable goods, such as cars and boats, and in fixtures. We look briefly at each.

Movable Goods Generally

Goods that are easily moved create problems for creditors. Suppose a bank in Colorado loans Dorothy money, takes a security interest in her Degas sculpture, and perfects its interest in the proper state offices in Colorado. But then Dorothy moves to Ohio and uses the same collateral for another loan. A lender in Ohio will never discover the security interest perfected in Colorado. If Dorothy defaults, who gets the sculpture?

For most collateral, when the debtor moves to a new state, a security interest from the old state remains perfected for four months; when the collateral is transferred to a new state, the security interest remains perfected for one year.[25] If the secured party re-perfects in the new state within the time limits mentioned, the security interest remains valid until it would normally expire. If the secured party fails to re-perfect in the new state, the security interest lapses. Suppose Dorothy takes her Degas into Ohio on February 10 and on March 5 uses it as collateral for a new loan. The original Colorado bank still has a valid security interest in the sculpture and may seize the art if Dorothy defaults. But if Dorothy applies for her new loan on October 10, and the Colorado bank has failed to re-perfect, the Colorado bank has lost its protection.

Motor Vehicles and the Like

The UCC's provisions about perfecting generally do not apply to motor vehicles, trailers, mobile homes, boats, or farm tractors.[26] Because all of these are so numerous and so mobile, filing may be ineffective and possession is impossible. As a result, almost all states have

---

[25]UCC §9-316(a).
[26]UCC §9-311(a)(2).

created special laws to deal with this problem. Anyone offering or taking a security interest in any of these goods must consult local law.

State title laws generally require that a security interest in an automobile be noted directly on the vehicle's certificate of title. A driver needs a certificate of title to obtain registration plates, so the law presumes that the certificate will stay with the car. By requiring that the security interest be noted on the certificate, the law gives the best possible notice to anyone thinking of buying the car or accepting it as collateral. Generally, if a buyer or lender examines the certificate and finds no security interest, he may accept the vehicle for sale, or as collateral, and take it free of any interest. In most states, the same requirement applies to boats.

Fixtures

Fixtures, you recall, are goods that have become attached to real estate. A security interest may be created in goods that *are* fixtures and may continue in goods that *become* fixtures; however, the UCC does not permit a security interest in ordinary building materials, such as lumber and concrete, once they become part of a construction project.

The primary disputes in these cases are between a creditor holding a security interest in a fixture, such as a furnace, and another creditor with rights in the real estate, such as a bank holding a mortgage on the house. The issues are complex, involving local real property law, and we cannot undertake here a thorough explanation of them. However, we can highlight the issues that arise so that you can anticipate the potential problems. Common disputes concern:

- The status of the personal property when the security interest was created (Was it still goods, or had it already been attached to real estate and become a fixture?);

- The status of the real estate (Does the debtor *also* have a legal interest in the *real property?*);

- The type of perfection (Which was recorded first, the security interest in the fixture or the real estate? Does the secured party hold a PMSI?); and

- The physical status of the fixture (Can it be removed without damaging the real estate?).[27]

Any creditor who considers accepting collateral that might become a fixture must anticipate these problems and clarify with the debtor exactly what she plans to do with the goods. Armed with that information, the creditor should consult local law on fixtures and make an appropriate security agreement (or just refuse to accept the fixture as collateral).

24-4 PROTECTION OF BUYERS

Generally, once a security interest is perfected, it remains effective regardless of whether the collateral is sold, exchanged, or transferred in some other way. Bubba's Bus Co. needs money to meet its payroll, so it borrows $150,000 from Francine's Finance Co., which takes a security interest in Bubba's 180 buses and perfects its interest. Bubba, still short of cash, sells 30 of his buses to Antelope Transit. But even that money is not enough to keep Bubba solvent: He defaults on his loan to Francine and goes into bankruptcy. Francine pounces on Bubba's buses. May she repossess the 30 that Antelope now operates? Yes. The security interest continued in the buses even after Antelope purchased them, and Francine can whisk them away. (Antelope has a valid claim against Bubba for the value of the buses, but the claim may prove fruitless, since Bubba is now bankrupt.)

---

[27]UCC §9-334.

There are some exceptions to this rule. The Code gives a few kinds of buyers special protection.

24-4a Buyers in Ordinary Course of Business

Buyer in ordinary course of business (BIOC)

Someone who buys goods in good faith from a seller who routinely deals in such goods

As we saw in Chapter 22, a **buyer in ordinary course of business (BIOC)** is someone who buys goods in good faith from a seller who routinely deals in such goods.[28] For example, Plato's Garden Supply purchases 500 hemlocks from Socrates' Farm, a grower. Plato is a BIOC: He is buying in good faith, and Socrates routinely deals in hemlocks. This is an important status because a BIOC is generally *not affected* by security interests in the goods. However, if Plato *actually realized* that the sale violated another party's rights in the goods, there would be no good faith. If Plato knew that Socrates was bankrupt and had agreed with a creditor not to sell any of his inventory, Plato would not achieve BIOC status.

A buyer in ordinary course of business takes the goods free of a security interest created by its seller even though the security interest is perfected.[29] Suppose that, a month before Plato made his purchase, Socrates borrowed $200,000 from the Athenian Bank. Athenian took a security interest in all of Socrates' trees and perfected by filing. Then Plato purchased his 500 hemlocks. If Socrates defaults on the loan, Athenian will have *no right* to repossess the 500 trees that are now at the Garden Supply. Plato took them free and clear. (Of course, Athenian can still attempt to repossess other trees from Socrates.)

The BIOC exception is designed to encourage ordinary commerce. A buyer making routine purchases should not be forced to perform a financing check before buying. But the rule, efficient though it may be, creates its own problems. A creditor may extend a large sum of money to a merchant based on collateral, such as inventory, only to discover that by the time the merchant defaults the collateral has been sold to BIOCs.

EXAM Strategy

Question: Troy owns an art gallery specializing in Greek artifacts. To modernize the gallery, Troy borrows $150,000 from the Sparta Bank, which takes a security interest in all of his inventory. Sparta promptly perfects. A month later, Troy sells Helen an Athenian warrior's helmet for $675,000. Helen does not bother to perform a financing check, and she is unaware of Sparta's security interest. Troy soon goes bankrupt, and Sparta attempts to seize all of the inventory, including the helmet. Sparta proves that a routine financing check would have revealed its interest. Who wins the helmet?

Strategy: A creditor perfects a security interest to ensure that it is protected against all the world. However, exceptions leave the secured party unprotected in certain cases, including those of consumers. Analyze this case using that exception.

Result: A BIOC takes the goods free of a security interest created by his seller. Helen acted in good faith, buying from a dealer who routinely dealt in such goods. And it was Troy, Helen's seller, who created the security interest. Helen takes the helmet free of the bank's security interest, despite the fact that it was perfected.

---

[28]UCC §1-201(9).

[29]UCC §9-320(a). In fact, the buyer takes free of the security interest *even if the buyer knew of it*. Yet a BIOC, by definition, must be acting in good faith. Is this a contradiction? No. Plato might know that a third party has a security interest in Socrates' crops yet not realize that his purchase violates the third party's rights. Generally, for example, a security interest will permit a retailer to sell consumer goods, the presumption being that part of the proceeds will go to the secured party. A BIOC cannot be expected to determine what a retailer plans to do with the money he is paid.

Because the BIOC exception undercuts the basic protection given to a secured party, the courts interpret it narrowly. BIOC status is available only if the *seller* created the security interest. Oftentimes, a buyer will purchase goods that have a security interest created by someone other than the seller. If that happens, the buyer is not a BIOC. However, should that rule be strictly enforced even when the results are harsh? You make the call.

You be the Judge

CONSECO FINANCE SERVICING CORP. v. LEE
2004 WL 1243417, 2004 Tex. App. LEXIS 5035
Court of Appeals of Texas, 2004

Facts: Lila Williams purchased a new Roadtrek 200 motor home from New World R.V., Inc. She paid about $14,000 down and financed $63,000, giving a security interest to New World. The RV company assigned its security interest to Conseco Finance, which perfected. Two years later, Williams returned the vehicle to New World (the record does not indicate why), and New World sold the RV to Robert and Ann Lee for $42,800. A year later, Williams defaulted on her payments to Conseco.

The Lees sued Conseco, claiming to be BIOCs and asking for a court declaration that they had sole title to the Roadtrek. Conseco counterclaimed, seeking title based on its perfected security interest. The trial court ruled that the Lees were BIOCs, with full rights to the vehicle. Conseco appealed.

You Be the Judge: *Were the Lees BIOCs?*

Argument for Conseco: Under UCC §9-319, a BIOC takes free of a security interest created by the buyer's seller. The buyers were the Lees. The seller was New World. New World did not create the security interest— Lila Williams did. There is no security interest created by New World. The security interest held by Conseco was created by someone else (Williams) and is not affected by the Lees' status as BIOC. The law is clear and Conseco is entitled to the Roadtrek.

Argument for the Lees: Conseco weaves a clever argument, but let's look at what they are really saying. Two honest buyers, acting in perfect good faith, can walk into an RV dealership, spend $42,000 for a used vehicle, and end up with —nothing. Conseco claims it is entitled to an RV that the Lees paid for because someone that the Lees have never dealt with, never even heard of, gave to this RV seller a security interest which the seller, years earlier, passed on to a finance company. Conseco's argument defies common sense and the goals of Article 9.

Rebuttal from Conseco: The best part of the Lees' argument is the emotional appeal; the worst part is that it does not reflect the law. Yes, $42,000 is a lot of money. That is why a reasonable buyer is careful to do business with conscientious, ethical sellers. New World, which knew that Williams financed the RV and knew who held the security interest, never bothered to check on the status of the payments. If the Lees have suffered wrongdoing, it is at the hands of an irresponsible seller—the company with which they chose to work, the company from which they must seek relief.

Rebuttal from the Lees: The purpose of the UCC is to make dealing fair and commerce work; one of its methods is to get away from obscure, technical arguments. Conseco's suggestion would demolish the used-car industry. What buyers will ever pay serious money—*any* money—for a used vehicle, knowing that thousands of dollars later, the car might be towed out of their driveway by a finance company they never heard of?

24-4b Buyers of Consumer Goods

Another exception exists to protect buyers of consumer goods who do not realize that the item they are buying has a security interest in it. This exception tends to apply to relatively casual purchases, such as those between friends. Typically, the pattern is that one purchaser buys consumer goods on credit and then resells. The original purchaser is considered a debtor-seller since she still owes money but is now selling to a second buyer. **In the case of consumer goods purchased from a debtor-seller, a buyer takes free of a security interest if he is not aware of the security interest, he pays value for the goods, he is buying for his own family or household use, and the second party has not yet filed a financing statement.**[30]

Here is how this exception works. Charles Lau used a Sears credit card to buy a 46-inch TV, a sleeper sofa, loveseat, entertainment center, diamond ring, gold chain, and microwave. He had the items delivered to the house of his girlfriend, Teresa Rierman, because he did not want his father to know he had been using the credit card (we can't imagine why). Lau later sold the items to Rierman's family and then (wait for it) defaulted on his payments to Sears and declared bankruptcy. Sears attempted to repossess its merchandise, but the Riermans claimed they were innocent buyers. The court ruled that if the Riermans could show that they knew nothing about Sears's security interest in the goods, they could keep the goods.[31]

This rule may be confusing because earlier, we discussed the automatic perfection of a security interest in consumer goods. When Sears sold the merchandise to Lau, it took a purchase money security interest in consumer goods. That interest perfected automatically (without filing) and was valid against *almost* everyone. Suppose Lau had used the furniture as collateral to obtain a bank loan. Sears would have retained its perfected security interest in the goods, and when Lau defaulted, Sears could have repossessed everything, leaving the bank with no collateral and no money.

The one person that Sears's perfect security interest could not defeat, however, was a buyer purchasing for personal use without knowledge of the security interest—in other words, the Riermans. Assuming the Riermans knew nothing of the security interest, they win. If Sears considers this type of loss important, it must, in the future, protect itself by filing a financing statement. Taking this extra step will leave Sears protected against everyone. Then, if a buyer defaults, Sears can pull the sofa out from under any purchaser.

24-4c Buyers of Chattel Paper, Instruments, and Documents

We have seen that debtors often use chattel paper, instruments, or documents as collateral. Because each of these is so easily transferred, Article 9 gives buyers special protection. **A buyer who purchases chattel paper or an instrument in the ordinary course of her business and then takes possession generally takes free of any security interest.**[32]

Suppose Tele-Maker sells 500 televisions to Retailer on credit, keeping a security interest in the televisions and the proceeds. The proceeds are any money or paper that Retailer earns from selling the sets. Retailer sells 300 of the sets to customers, most of whom pay on credit. The customers sign chattel paper, promising to pay for the sets over time (and giving Retailer a security interest in the sets). All of this chattel paper is proceeds, so Tele-Maker has a perfected security interest in it. The chattel paper is worth about $150,000 if all of the customers pay in full. But Retailer wants money now, so Retailer sells its chattel paper to Financer, who pays $120,000 cash for it. Next, Retailer defaults on its obligation to pay Tele-Maker for the sets. Tele-Maker cannot repossess the televisions because each customer was a BIOC (buyer in ordinary course of business) and took the goods free of any security interest. So Tele-Maker attempts to repossess the chattel paper. Will it succeed? No. The buyer of chattel paper takes it free of a perfected security interest. See Exhibit 24.4.

---

[30]UCC §9-320.
[31]In re Lau, 140 B.R. 172 (N.D. Ohio 1992).
[32]UCC §9-330(a)(b)(d).

EXHIBIT 24.4 The buyer of chattel paper takes it free of a perfected security interest. In this case, Tele-Maker (1) sells 500 units to Retailer on credit, keeping (2) a security interest in the televisions and the proceeds. Retailer (3) sells the sets to customers who (4) sign chattel paper. Retailer (5) sells the chattel paper to Financer and then defaults on its obligations to Tele-Maker.

Other Paper

Similar rules apply for holders in due course of instruments and for purchasers of securities and documents of title. Those parties obtain special rights, described in Articles 3, 7, and 8 of the UCC. The details of those rules are beyond the scope of this chapter, but once again, the lesson for any lender is simple: A security interest is safest when the collateral is in your vault. If you do not take possession of the paper, you may lose it to an innocent buyer.[33]

24-4d Liens

Law student Paul King got a costly lesson when his $28.09 check for an oil change bounced and the repo man snatched his prized Corvette. The bill for the car's return: $644. King was a third-year law student, working part time in a private firm in Houston. He had just walked in from lunch when coworkers told him his car was being towed.

---

[33]UCC §9-331.

611

"I thought they were joking," King said. They weren't. King saw a tow truck backing up to his car and hurried out to speak with the workers. They advised him that Texas law authorized them to pick up his car to satisfy a lien for work done to the car. King hurried inside to telephone the company that had performed the oil change. Unable to make a deal on the phone, he ran back outside and found—no car.

King phoned Harris County Repossession to see about getting his car back. That's easy, they told him. But you owe some fees: $28.09 for the oil change, $20 for the returned check, $25 for the legal notice in the newspapers, $21.24 per day for storage—plus, of course, the $550 repossession fee.[34]

Is that legal? Probably. The service station had a lien on the car. A **lien** is a security interest created by law (rather than by agreement). State and federal law both allow parties to assert a lien against a debtor under prescribed conditions. For example, a state may claim a lien based on unpaid taxes; the state is giving notice to the world that it may seize the debtor's property and sell it. A company may claim a lien based on work performed by the debtor.

To understand the difference between a lien and a security interest, assume that when Paul King bought his Corvette, he made a down payment and signed a security agreement to ensure future payments. His agreement gave the dealer a security interest in the sports car. Later, when he paid for an oil change, his check bounced. State law gave the service station a lien on the auto, meaning the right to hold the car if it is in the garage and to seize the auto if it is elsewhere.

Because automobile repossessions provide such a graphic view of secured transactions, we will return to the subject later in the chapter. In this case, the oil company had an **artisan's lien**, meaning a security interest in personal property created when a worker makes some improvement to the property. A car mechanic, a computer repairman, and a furniture restorer all create artisan's liens. A **mechanic's lien** is similar and is created when a worker improves real property. A carpenter who puts an addition on a kitchen and a painter who paints the kitchen's interior both have a mechanic's lien on the house. The owner of an apartment may obtain a **landlord's lien** in a tenant's personal property if the tenant fails to pay the rent. These security interests vary from state to state, so an affected person must consult local law.

Because liens are the creation of statutes rather than agreements, Article 9 generally does not apply to them. The one aspect of liens that Article 9 does govern is priority between lienholders and other secured parties, which we examine in the following section. In Paul King's case, the repair shop certainly had a valid lien on his car, even though the amount in question was small. The company's method of collecting on its lien is more debatable. King admitted that the company had telephoned him and given him a chance to pay for the bounced check. Some courts would hold that the repair shop had done all it was required to do, but others might rule that it should have shown more patience and avoided running up the bill.

24-5 PRIORITIES AMONG CREDITORS

What happens when two creditors have a security interest in the same collateral? The party who has **priority** in the collateral gets it. Typically, the debtor lacks assets to pay everyone, so all creditors struggle to be the first in line. After the first creditor has repossessed the collateral, sold it, and taken enough of the proceeds to pay off his debt, there may be nothing left for anyone else. Who gets priority? There are three principal rules.

---

[34]Rad Sallee and James T. Campbell, "Repo Men Hitch Up Big Fee to Car," *Houston Chronicle*, October 15, 1991, Section A, p. 21.

Lien
A security interest created by law, rather than by agreement

Artisan's lien
A security interest in personal property

Mechanic's lien
A security created when a worker improves real property

The first rule is easy: **A party with a perfected security interest takes priority over a party with an unperfected interest.**[35] This, of course, is the whole point of perfecting: to ensure that your security interest gets priority over everyone else's. On August 15, Meredith's Market, an antique store, borrows $100,000 from the Happy Bank, which takes a security interest in all of Meredith's inventory. Happy Bank does not perfect. On September 15, Meredith uses the same collateral to borrow $50,000 from the Suspicion Bank, which files a financing statement the same day. On October 15, as if on cue, Meredith files for bankruptcy and stops paying both creditors. Suspicion wins because it holds a perfected interest, whereas the Happy Bank holds merely an unperfected interest.

The second rule: **If neither secured party has perfected, the first interest to attach gets priority.**[36] Suppose that Suspicion Bank and Happy Bank had both failed to perfect. In that case, Happy Bank would have the first claim to Meredith's inventory since Happy's interest attached first.

And the third rule follows logically: **Between perfected security interests, the first to file or perfect wins.**[37] Diminishing Perspective, a railroad, borrows $75 million from the First Bank, which takes a security interest in Diminishing's railroad cars and immediately perfects by filing. Two months later, Diminishing borrows $100 million from Second Bank, which takes a security interest in the same collateral and also files. When Diminishing arrives, on schedule, in bankruptcy court, both banks will race to seize the rolling stock. First Bank gets the railcars because it perfected first.

March 1:	April 2:	May 3:	The Winner:
First Bank lends money and perfects its security interest by filing a financing statement.	Second Bank lends money and perfects its security interest by filing a financing statement.	Diminishing goes bankrupt, and both banks attempt to take the rolling stock.	First Bank, because it perfected first.

The general rules of priority are quite straightforward; however, you will not be surprised to learn that there are some exceptions.

24-5a Filing versus Control or Possession

Recall that a secured party may use either filing or control to perfect its security interest in deposit accounts, investment property, and letter-of-credit rights. Which method *should* the secured party use? Control. **For these three types of collateral, a secured party who has control wins over a party who merely filed.**[38] Early Bank obtains a security interest in Lionel's investment property and perfects by filing. Nine months later, Late Bank obtains a security interest in the same property and perfects by taking control. Late Bank wins.

Similarly, a secured party may perfect its interest in an instrument either by filing or possession. Once again, possession is the better idea: **Between competing secured parties, the one who possesses wins, even over one who filed earlier.**[39]

---

[35] UCC §9-322(a)(2).
[36] UCC §9-322(a)(3).
[37] UCC §9-322(a)(1).
[38] UCC §§9-327, 9-328, 9-329. If more than one creditor has control of the same collateral, the security interests rank according to the time of obtaining control.
[39] UCC §9-330(d).

24-5b Priority Involving a Purchase Money Security Interest

You may recall that a purchase money security interest (PMSI) is a security interest taken by the seller of the collateral or by a lender whose loan enables the debtor to buy the collateral. A PMSI can be created only in goods, fixtures, and software. On November 1, Manufacturer sells a specially built lathe to Tool Shop for $80,000 and takes a security interest in the lathe. The parties have created a PMSI. Parties holding a PMSI often take priority over other perfected security interests in the same goods, even if the other security interest was perfected first. How can the conflict arise? Suppose that on February 1, Tool Shop had borrowed $100,000 from the Gargoyle Bank, giving Gargoyle a security interest in after-acquired property. When the lathe arrives at the Tool Shop on November 1, Gargoyle's security interest attaches to it. But Manufacturer has a PMSI in the lathe, hence the conflict.

We need to examine PMSIs involving inventory and those involving noninventory. **Inventory** means goods that the seller is holding for sale or lease in the ordinary course of its business. The furniture in a furniture store is inventory; the store's computer, telephones, and filing cabinets are not.

Inventory
Goods that a seller is holding for sale or lease in the ordinary course of its business

PMSI in Inventory

A PMSI in inventory takes priority over a conflicting perfected security interest (even one perfected earlier), if two conditions are met:

- Before filing its PMSI, the secured party must check for earlier security interests and, if there are any, must notify the holder of that interest concerning the new PMSI; and

- The secured party must then perfect its PMSI (normally by filing) *before* the debtor receives the inventory.[40]

If the holder of the PMSI has met both of these conditions, its PMSI takes priority over any security interests filed earlier, as illustrated in the following chart.

1. February 1:	**2. March 2:**	**3. March 3:**	**4. March 4:**
Coltrane Bank loans Monk's Jazz Store $90,000, taking a security interest in all after-acquired property, including inventory.	Monk offers to buy 10 saxophones from Webster's Supply for $3,000 each.	Webster checks the financing records and learns that Coltrane Bank has a security interest in all of Monk's after-acquired property.	Webster notifies Coltrane Bank that he is selling 10 saxophones to Monk for $30,000 and is taking a PMSI in the instruments, which Webster carefully describes.
5. March 4:	**6. March 5:**	**7. September:**	**8. The Winner:**
Webster files a financing statement indicating a PMSI in the 10 saxophones.	Webster sells the 10 saxophones to Monk.	Monk goes bankrupt.	Webster. His PMSI in inventory takes priority over Coltrane's earlier interest.

---

[40]UCC §9-324(b)(c).

PMSI in Noninventory Collateral

PMSIs are often given for noninventory goods. When Tool Shop bought the lathe, in the example discussed, the company gave a PMSI to the seller. The bank simultaneously obtained a security interest in the same lathe, based on its after-acquired property interest. Who wins?

A PMSI in collateral other than inventory takes priority over a conflicting security interest if the PMSI is perfected at the time the debtor receives the collateral or within 20 days after he receives it.[41] As long as Computer Co. perfects (by filing) within 20 days of delivering the computer, its PMSI takes priority over the bank's earlier security interest. Manufacturer may repossess the machine, and the bank may never get a dime back.

Again, we must note that the PMSI exception undercuts the ability of a creditor to rely on its perfected security interest. As a result, courts insist that a party asserting the PMSI exception demonstrate that it has complied with every requirement. In the following case, the creditor just got in under the wire.

In Re Roser

613 F.3d 1240
United States Court of Appeals for the Tenth Circuit, 2010

Facts: Robert Roser obtained a loan from Sovereign Bank, which he promptly used to buy a car. Nineteen days later, Sovereign filed a lien with the state of Colorado. The bank expected that with a perfected interest, it would have priority over everyone else.

Unknown to Sovereign Bank, Roser had declared bankruptcy only 12 days after he purchased the car. Later, the bankruptcy trustee argued that he had priority over Sovereign because the bankruptcy filing happened before Sovereign perfected its security interest. When the court found for the trustee, Sovereign Bank appealed.

Issue: *Did Sovereign Bank, a PMSI holder, obtain priority over the bankruptcy trustee?*

Excerpts from Judge Hartz's Decision: The Bankruptcy Code gives the bankruptcy trustee the rights and powers of a person who acquired a judicial lien on the debtor's property at the time that the bankruptcy petition was filed. In general, the trustee can avoid liens that are unperfected when the petition for bankruptcy is filed. But in some circumstances, a lien that is perfected after the bankruptcy filing may nevertheless have priority.

The Bank presents a straightforward argument why its lien would have priority under Colorado law over a lien of a judgment creditor who obtained judgment at the time Roser filed for bankruptcy. Under the UCC:

If a person [1] files a financing statement [2] with respect to a purchase-money security interest [3] before or within twenty days after the debtor receives delivery of the collateral, the security interest takes priority over the rights of a buyer, lessee, or lien creditor which arise between the time the security interest attaches and the time of filing.

There is no doubt that the Bank satisfied the requirements of this section. The filing of a lien constitutes the filing of a financing statement. Nor is there any dispute that the Bank held a purchase-money security interest in Roser's vehicle. Thus, because the Bank filed its lien within 20 days of Roser's obtaining the vehicle, it contends that [the] UCC gives its lien a priority over any rights in the vehicle—including the Trustee's interest.

The Trustee's arguments to the contrary are not persuasive. The Trustee cannot avoid the Bank's lien. We reverse the judgment of the district court and remand for further proceedings consistent with this opinion.

---

[41]UCC §9-324(a).

24-6 DEFAULT AND TERMINATION

We have reached the end of the line. Either the debtor has defaulted or it has performed its obligations and may terminate the security agreement.

24-6a Default

The parties define "default" in their security agreement. **Generally, a debtor defaults when he fails to make payments due or enters bankruptcy proceedings.** The parties can agree that other acts will constitute default, such as the debtor's failure to maintain insurance on the collateral. When a debtor defaults, the secured party has two principal options: (1) It may take possession of the collateral, or (2) it may file suit against the debtor for the money owed. The secured party does not have to choose between these two remedies; it may try one remedy, such as repossession, and if that fails, attempt the other.[42]

Taking Possession of the Collateral

When the debtor defaults, the secured party may take possession of the collateral.[43] How does the secured party do so? In either of two ways: The secured party can file suit against the debtor to obtain a court order requiring the debtor to deliver the collateral. Otherwise, the secured party may act on its own, without any court order, and simply take the collateral, provided this can be done without a breach of the peace. A **breach of the peace** occurs when the repossession disturbs public tranquility, such as through violent, threatening, or harassing acts.

Breach of the peace
Any action that disturbs public tranquility and order

Secured parties often repossess automobiles without the debtor's cooperation. Typically, the security agreement will state that, in the event of default, the secured party has a right to take possession of the car and drive it away. As we saw earlier, the secured party could be the seller or it could be a mechanic with an artisan's lien on the car.

The following case discusses a repossession in which everything went wrong. It was a disaster, but was it a breach of the peace?

CHAPA v. TRACIERS & ASSOCIATES, INC.

267 S.W.3d 386
Texas Court of Appeals, 2008

Facts: Marissa Chapa defaulted on her car loan, so Ford Motor Credit Corp. hired Traciers & Associates to repossess her white Ford Expedition. Traciers assigned its field manager, Paul Chambers, to the task and gave him the vehicle's tag number and address. Chambers staked out the house, waiting for a chance to make his move.

One fateful morning, Chambers observed a woman drive the car out into the street and leave it running while she ran back into the house. Chambers seized the moment. It only took him thirty seconds to hook up his tow truck to the Ford and drive away. Chambers may have been quick but he was mistaken about two things. First, he took the wrong car: This white Expedition belonged to Marissa's brother Carlos and his wife Maria. It was not in default. Second, their two children were in the backseat of the towed vehicle.

When Maria emerged from the house and saw that the Expedition, with her children, was gone, she naturally panicked and hysterically called 911. Meanwhile, on an adjacent street, Chambers noticed that the Expedition's wheels were turning. When he stopped the tow truck to investigate, he discovered the two Chapa children. Within minutes, Chambers returned the kids and the car to a hysterical Maria.

Carlos and Maria Chapa sued Traciers, Chambers, and FMCC for breach of the peace. The trial court dismissed the case and the Chapas appealed.

---

[42]UCC §9-601(a)(b)(c).
[43]UCC §9-609.

Issue: *Did Chambers commit a breach of the peace in repossessing the car?*

Excerpts from Justice Guzman's Decision: After default, a secured party may take possession of the collateral without judicial process, if it proceeds without breach of the peace. The Chapas argue that the act of taking children from the possession of their mother which leaves her in a hysterical crying state, is clearly a breach of peace.

The expression "breach of the peace" as used in the Uniform Commercial Code connotes conduct that incites or is likely to incite immediate public turbulence, or that leads to or is likely to lead to an immediate loss of public order and tranquility. [The] secured creditor, in exercising its privilege to enter upon premises of another to repossess collateral, may not perpetrate any action manifesting force or violence, or naturally calculated to provide a breach of peace. Although actual violence is not required to find breach of the peace, disturbance or violence must be reasonably likely, and not merely a remote possibility. In addition, breach of the peace refers to conduct at, near, or incident to seizure of property. Even in attempted repossession of a chattel off a street, parking lot, or unenclosed space, if repossession is contested at actual time of and in immediate vicinity of attempted repossession, the secured party must desist and pursue his remedy in court.

Here, there is no evidence that Chambers proceeded with the attempted repossession over an objection communicated to him at, near, or incident to the seizure of the property. To the contrary, Chambers immediately desisted repossession efforts and peaceably returned the vehicle and the children when he learned of their presence. Moreover, Chambers actively avoided confrontation. By removing an apparently unoccupied vehicle from a public street when the driver was not present, he reduced the likelihood of violence or other public disturbance.

In sum, Chambers's conduct did not violate a duty imposed by section 9.609 of the Texas Business and Commerce Code.

Disposition of the Collateral

Once the secured party has obtained possession of the collateral, it has two choices. The secured party may (1) dispose of the collateral or (2) retain the collateral as full satisfaction of the debt.

Disposal of the Collateral. **A secured party may sell, lease, or otherwise dispose of the collateral in any commercially reasonable manner.**[44] Typically, the secured party will sell the collateral in either a private or a public sale. First, however, the debtor must receive reasonable notice of the time and place of the sale so that she may bid on the collateral. The higher the price that the secured party gets for the collateral, the lower the balance still owed by the debtor. Giving the debtor notice of the sale and a chance to bid ensures that the collateral will not be sold for an unreasonably low price.

Suppose Bank loans $65,000 to Farmer to purchase a tractor. While still owing $40,000, Farmer defaults. Bank takes possession of the tractor and then notifies Farmer that it intends to sell the tractor at an auction. Farmer has the right to attend and bid on the tractor.

When the secured party has sold the collateral, it applies the proceeds of the sale: first, to its expenses in repossessing and selling the collateral, and second, to the debt.[45] Assume Bank sold the tractor for $35,000 and that the process of repossessing and selling the tractor cost $5,000. Bank applies the remaining $30,000 to the debt.

Deficiency or Surplus. The sale of the tractor yielded $30,000 to be applied to the debt, which was $40,000. The disposition has left a **deficiency**; that is, insufficient funds to pay off the debt. **The debtor is liable for any deficiency.** So the bank will sue the farmer for

Deficiency

Having insufficient funds to pay off a debt

---

[44]UCC §9-610.
[45]UCC §9-615(a).

Surplus

A sum of money greater than the debt incurred

the remaining $10,000. On the other hand, sometimes the sale of the collateral yields a **surplus**; that is, a sum greater than the debt. In that case, the secured party must pay the surplus to the debtor.[46]

When a secured party disposes of collateral in a commercially unreasonable manner, then a deficiency or surplus claim may be adjusted based on the sum that should have been obtained.[47] Suppose that Seller, who is owed $300,000, repossesses 500 bedroom sets from a hotel and, without giving proper notice, quickly sells them for a net amount of $200,000. Seller sues for the $100,000 deficiency. If a court determines that a properly announced sale would have netted $250,000, Seller is only entitled to a deficiency judgment of $50,000. Similarly, if the collateral is sold to the secured party or someone related, and the price obtained is significantly below what would be expected, then any deficiency or surplus must be calculated on what the sale would normally have brought. This protects the debtor from a sale in which the secured party has followed all formalities but ended up owning the goods for a suspiciously low price.[48]

Acceptance

Retention of the collateral by a secured party as full or partial satisfaction of a debt

Acceptance of Collateral.   In many cases, the secured party has the option to satisfy the debt simply by keeping the collateral. **Acceptance** refers to a secured party's retention of the collateral as full or partial satisfaction of the debt. **Partial satisfaction** means that the debtor will still owe some deficiency to the secured party. This is how the system works.[49]

A secured party who wishes to accept the collateral must notify the debtor. If the debtor agrees in an authenticated record, then the secured party may keep the collateral as full *or* partial satisfaction of the debt. If the debtor does not respond within 20 days, the secured party may still accept the collateral as full satisfaction, but not as partial satisfaction. In other words, the debtor's silence does not give the secured party the right to keep the goods and still sue for more money.

Suppose the buyer of a $13 million yacht, Icarus, has defaulted, and the retailer has repossessed the boat. The firm may decide the boat is worth more than the debt, so it notifies the buyer that it plans to keep Icarus. If the buyer does not object, the retailer automatically owns the boat after 20 days.

If the buyer promptly objects to acceptance, the retailer must then dispose of Icarus as described earlier, typically by sale. Why would a debtor object? Because she believes the boat is worth more than the debt. The debtor anticipates that a sale will create a surplus.

Consumers receive additional protection. A secured party may not accept collateral that is consumer goods if the debtor has possession of the goods *or* if the debtor has paid 60 percent of the purchase price. If Maud has defaulted on an oven that is in her kitchen, the Gobroke retail store may be entitled to repossess the oven, but the company must then dispose of the goods (sell the oven) and apply the proceeds to Maud's debt. Similarly, if Ernest is paying for his $10,000 television set in a "layaway" plan, with Gobroke warehousing the goods until the full price is paid, the store may not accept the television once Ernest has paid $6,000. Finally, a secured party is never permitted to accept consumer goods in partial satisfaction.[50]

Redeem

To pay the full value of a debt to get the collateral back

Right of Redemption.   Up to the time the secured party disposes of the collateral, the debtor has the right to **redeem** it, that is, to pay the full value of the debt. If the debtor redeems, she obtains the collateral back. Sylvia borrows $25,000 from the bank and pledges

---

[46]UCC §9-615(d).
[47]UCC §9-626(a)(3).
[48]UCC §§9-615(f), 9-626(a)(5).
[49]UCC §9-620.
[50]UCC §9-620(a)(3), (e), (g).

a ruby necklace as collateral. She defaults, still owing $9,000, and the bank notifies her that it will sell the necklace. If Sylvia pays the full $9,000 before the sale occurs, plus any expenses the bank has incurred in arranging the sale, she receives her necklace back.[51]

Proceeding to Judgment

Occasionally, the secured party will prefer to ignore its rights in the collateral and simply sue the debtor. **A secured party may sue the debtor for the full debt.**[52] Why would a creditor, having gone to so much effort to perfect its security interest, ignore that interest and simply file a lawsuit? The collateral may have decreased in value and be insufficient to cover the debt. Suppose a bank loaned $300,000 to a debtor to buy a rare baseball cap worn by Babe Ruth in a World Series game. The debtor defaults, owing $190,000. The bank discovers that the cap is now worth only $110,000. It is true that the bank could sell the cap and sue for the deficiency. But the sale will take time, and the outcome is uncertain. Suppose the bank knows that the debtor has recently paid cash for a $2 million house. The bank may promptly file suit for the full $190,000. The bank will ask the court to freeze the debtor's bank account and legally hold the house until the suit is resolved. The bank expects to prove the debt quickly—the loan documents are clear, and the amount of debt is easily calculated. It will obtain its $190,000 without ever donning the cap. Of course, the bank has the option of doing both things simultaneously: It may slap on the cap and a lawsuit all at once.

24-6b Termination

Finally, we need to look at what happens when a debtor does not default, but pays the full debt. (You are forgiven if you have lost track of the fact that things sometimes work out smoothly.) Once that happens, the secured party must complete a **termination statement**, a document indicating that it no longer claims a security interest in the collateral.[53]

For a consumer debt, the secured party must file the termination statement in every place that it filed a financing statement. The secured party must do this within one month from the date the debt is fully paid, or within 20 days of a demand from the consumer, whichever comes first. For other transactions, the secured party must, within 20 days, either file the termination statement or send it to the secured party so that he may file it himself. In both cases, the goal is the same: to notify all interested parties that the debt is extinguished.

Termination statement
A document indicating that a secured party no longer claims a security interest in the collateral

Chapter Conclusion

Secured transactions are essential to modern commerce. Billions of dollars' worth of goods are sold on credit annually, and creditors normally demand an assurance of payment. A secured party that understands Article 9 and follows its provisions to the letter should be well protected. A company that operates in ignorance of Article 9 invites disaster because others may obtain superior rights in the goods, leaving the "secured" party with no money, no security—and no sympathy from the courts.

---

[51]UCC §9-623.
[52]UCC §9-601(a).
[53]UCC §9-513.

EXAM REVIEW

1. **ARTICLE 9** Article 9 applies to any transaction intended to create a security interest in personal property or fixtures.

2. **ATTACHMENT** Attachment means that (1) the two parties made a security agreement *and* either the debtor has *authenticated a security agreement* describing the collateral *or* the secured party has obtained *possession* or *control;* and (2) the secured party gave value in order to get the security agreement; and (3) the debtor has rights in the collateral.

3. **AFTER-ACQUIRED PROPERTY** A security interest may attach to after-acquired property.

4. **PERFECTION** Attachment protects against the debtor. Perfection of a security interest protects the secured party against parties other than the debtor.

5. **FILING** Filing is the most common way to perfect. For many forms of collateral, the secured party may also perfect by obtaining either possession or control.

6. **PMSI** A purchase money security interest (PMSI) is one taken by the person who sells the collateral or advances money so the debtor can buy the collateral.

7. **PMSI PERFECTION** A PMSI in consumer goods perfects automatically, without filing.

EXAM Strategy

Question: John and Clara Lockovich bought a 22-foot Chaparrel Villian II boat from Greene County Yacht Club for $32,500. They paid $6,000 cash and borrowed the rest of the purchase price from Gallatin National Bank, which took a security interest in the boat. Gallatin filed a financing statement in Greene County, Pennsylvania, where the bank was located. But Pennsylvania law requires financing statements to be filed in the county of the debtor's residence, and the Lockoviches lived in Allegheny County. The Lockoviches soon washed up in bankruptcy court. Other creditors demanded that the boat be sold, claiming that Gallatin's security interest had been filed in the wrong place. Who wins?

Strategy: Gallatin National Bank obtained a special kind of security interest in the boat. Identify that type of interest. What special rights does this give to the bank? (See the "Result" at the end of this section.)

8. **BIOC** A buyer in ordinary course of business (BIOC) takes the goods free of a security interest created by his seller even though the security interest is perfected.

9. **CHATTEL PAPER** A buyer who purchases chattel paper or an instrument in good faith in the ordinary course of his business and then obtains possession or control generally takes free of any security interest.

10. **PRIORITY** Priority among secured parties is generally as follows:

1. A party with a perfected security interest takes priority over a party with an unperfected interest.

2. If neither secured party has perfected, the first interest to attach gets priority.

3. Between perfected security interests, the first to file or perfect wins.

EXAM Strategy

Question: Barwell, Inc., sold McMann Golf Ball Co. a "preformer," a machine that makes golf balls, for $55,000. Barwell delivered the machine on February 20. McMann paid $3,000 down, the remainder to be paid over several years, and signed an agreement giving Barwell a security interest in the preformer. Barwell did not perfect its interest. On March 1, McMann borrowed $350,000 from First of America Bank, giving the bank a security interest in McMann's present and after-acquired property. First of America perfected by filing on March 2. McMann, of course, became insolvent, and both Barwell and the bank attempted to repossess the preformer. Who gets it?

Strategy: Two parties have a valid security interest in this machine. When that happens, there is a three-step process to determine which party gets priority. Apply it. (See the "Result" at the end of this section.)

11. **PMSI AND PRIORITY** A PMSI may take priority over a conflicting perfected security interest (even one perfected earlier) if the holder of the PMSI meets certain conditions.

12. **CONTROL OR POSSESSION** For deposit accounts, investment property, letter-of-credit rights, and instruments, a secured party who obtains control or possession takes priority over one who merely filed.

13. **DEFAULT** When the debtor defaults, the secured party may take possession of the collateral on its own, without a court order, if it can do so without a breach of the peace.

14. **DISPOSAL OF COLLATERAL** A secured party may sell, lease, or otherwise dispose of the collateral in any commercially reasonable way; in many cases, it may accept the collateral in full or partial satisfaction of the debt. The secured party may also ignore the collateral and sue the debtor for the full debt.

EXAM Strategy

Question: Jerry Payne owed the First State Bank of Pflugerville $342,000. The loan was secured by a 9.25-carat diamond ring. The bank claimed a default on the loan and, without notifying Payne, sold the ring. But the proceeds did not pay off the full debt, and the bank sued Payne for the deficiency. Is Payne liable for the deficiency?

> **Strategy:** A secured party may dispose of the collateral in any commercially reasonable way. What must the secured party do to ensure commercial reasonableness? (See the "Result" at the end of this section.)

15. **TERMINATION** When the debtor pays the full debt, the secured party must complete a termination statement, notifying the public that it no longer claims a security interest in the collateral.

---

7. Result: Gallatin advanced the money that the Lockoviches used to buy the boat, meaning the bank obtained a PMSI. A PMSI in consumer goods perfects automatically, without filing. The boat was a consumer good. Gallatin's security interest perfected without any filing at all, and so the bank wins.

10. Result: This question is resolved by the first of those three steps. A party with a perfected security interest takes priority over a party with an unperfected interest. The bank wins because its perfected security interest takes priority over Barwell's unperfected interest.

14. Result: The secured party must give the debtor notice of the time and place of the sale. This ensures that the debtor may bid on the collateral, preventing an unreasonably low sales price. The bank failed to give such notice, and so it lost its right to the deficiency.

MULTIPLE-CHOICE QUESTIONS

1. *CPA QUESTION* Under the UCC Article 9, which of the following actions will best perfect a security interest in a negotiable instrument against any other party?
   (a) Filing a security agreement
   (b) Taking possession of the instrument
   (c) Perfecting by attachment
   (d) Obtaining a duly executed financing statement

2. Jim's birth certificate lists him as "James Brown Smith"; his driver's license identifies him as "Jim Smith"; but his business card reads "J.B. Smith" and his friends call him Jimbo. How should the financing statement list this debtor's name?
   (a) James Smith
   (b) J.B. Smith
   (c) Jim Smith
   (d) James Brown Smith

3. *CPA QUESTION* Under the UCC Article 9, perfection of a security interest by a creditor provides added protection against other parties in the event the debtor does

not pay its debts. Which of the following parties is not affected by perfection of a security interest?

(a) Other prospective creditors of the debtor

(b) The trustee in a bankruptcy case

(c) A buyer in ordinary course of business

(d) A subsequent personal injury judgment creditor

4. *CPA QUESTION* Mars, Inc., manufactures and sells VCRs on credit directly to wholesalers, retailers, and consumers. Mars can perfect its security interest in the VCRs it sells without having to file a financing statement or take possession of the VCRs if the sale is made to which of the following?

(a) Retailers

(b) Wholesalers that sell to distributors for resale

(c) Consumers

(d) Wholesalers that sell to buyers in ordinary course of business

5. Alpha perfects its security interest by properly filing a financing statement on January 1, 2010. Alpha files a continuation statement on September 1, 2014. It files another continuation statement on September 1, 2018. When will Alpha's financing statement expire?

(a) January 1, 2015

(b) September 1, 2019

(c) September 1, 2023

(d) Never

CASE QUESTIONS

1. Eugene Ables ran an excavation company. He borrowed $500,000 from the Highland Park State Bank. Ables signed a note promising to repay the money and an agreement giving Highland a security interest in all of his equipment, including after-acquired equipment. Several years later, Ables agreed with Patricia Myers to purchase a Bantam Backhoe from her for $16,000, which he would repay at the rate of $100 per month, while he used the machine. Ables later defaulted on his note to Highland, and the bank attempted to take the backhoe. Myers and Ables contended that the bank had no right to take the backhoe. Was the backhoe covered by Highland's security interest? Did Ables have sufficient rights in the backhoe for the bank's security interest to attach?

2. The Copper King Inn, Inc., had money problems. It borrowed $62,500 from two of its officers, Noonan and Patterson, but that did not suffice to keep the inn going. So Noonan, on behalf of Copper King, arranged for the inn to borrow $100,000 from Northwest Capital, an investment company that worked closely with Noonan in other ventures. Copper King signed an agreement giving Patterson, Noonan, and Northwest a security interest in the inn's furniture and equipment. But the financing statement that the parties filed made no mention of Northwest. Copper King went bankrupt. Northwest attempted to seize assets, but other creditors objected. Is Northwest entitled to Copper King's furniture and equipment?

3. Sears sold a lawn tractor to Cosmo Fiscante for $1,481. Fiscante paid with his personal credit card. Sears kept a valid security interest in the lawnmower but did not perfect. Fiscante had the machine delivered to his business, Trackers Raceway Park, the only place he ever used the machine. When Fiscante was unable to meet his obligations, various creditors attempted to seize the lawnmower. Sears argued that because it had a purchase money security interest (PMSI) in the lawnmower, its interest had perfected automatically. Is Sears correct?

4. The state of Kentucky filed a tax lien against Panbowl Energy, claiming unpaid taxes. Six months later, Panbowl bought a powerful drill from Whayne Supply, making a down payment of $11,500 and signing a security agreement for the remaining debt of $220,000. Whayne perfected the next day. Panbowl defaulted. Whayne sold the drill for $58,000, leaving a deficiency of just over $100,000. The state filed suit, seeking the $58,000 proceeds. The trial court gave summary judgment to the state, and Whayne appealed. Who gets the $58,000?

5. *YOU BE THE JUDGE* WRITING PROBLEM   Dupont Feed bought and sold agricultural products. Dupont borrowed $300,000 from Wells Fargo Bank and gave Wells Fargo a security interest in all inventory, including after-acquired inventory. Wells Fargo perfected its interest by filing on June 17, 1982. Later, Dupont borrowed $150,000 from the Rushville National Bank and used the money to buy fertilizer. Dupont gave a PMSI to Rushville in the amount of $150,000. Rushville filed its financing statement in February 1984 at the County Recorder's office—the wrong place to file a financing statement for inventory. Then Dupont took possession of the fertilizer, and finally, in December 1984, Rushville filed correctly, with the Indiana Secretary of State. Dupont defaulted on both loans. Rushville seized the fertilizer, and Wells Fargo sued, claiming that it had perfected first. Rushville asserted that it had a PMSI, which took priority over an earlier-filed security interest. Does Rushville's PMSI take priority over Wells Fargo? (Go slowly, the rules are very technical.) **Argument for Rushville:** It is black-letter law that PMSIs take priority over virtually everything, including interests perfected earlier. We are not fools at Rushville: we would not loan $150,000 to buy inventory if our security interest in that inventory was instantly inferior to someone else's. **Argument for Wells Fargo:** A PMSI in inventory gets priority only if the secured party perfects before the debtor receives the collateral. When Dupont obtained the fertilizer, Rushville had not perfected because it had filed in the wrong office. It only perfected long after Dupont bought the inventory; thus, Rushville's PMSI does not get priority.

Discussion Questions

1. Collateral may change categories depending on its holder and how it is being used at the time of default. Classify a refrigerator in the following circumstances:

   (a) When sold by an appliance store;

   (b) When used by a restaurateur in his business; and

   (c) When installed in a homeowner's kitchen.

2. ETHICS   The Dannemans bought a Kodak copier worth over $40,000. Kodak arranged financing by GECC and assigned its rights to that company. Although the Dannemans thought they had purchased the copier on credit, the papers described the deal as a lease. The Dannemans had constant problems with the machine and stopped making payments. GECC repossessed the machine and, without notifying the Dannemans, sold it back to Kodak for $12,500, leaving a deficiency of $39,927. GECC sued the Dannemans for that amount. The Dannemans argued that the deal was not a lease, but a sale on credit. Why does it matter whether the parties had a sale or a lease? Is GECC entitled to its money? Finally, comment on the ethics. Why did the Dannemans not understand the papers they had signed? Who is responsible for that? Are you satisfied with the ethical conduct of the Dannemans? Kodak? GECC?

3. After a federal judge refused to dismiss criminal charges against him, Michael Reed took revenge by electronically filing a UCC financing statement listing the judge, the prosecuting attorney, and former Secretary of the Treasury Timothy Geithner as $3.4 million debtors. Reed himself was listed as the secured party. The lien became part of the public record. When Reed was later prosecuted for violating a statute intended to prevent harassment of public officials, he argued that he was innocent because the financing statement listed no real or personal property as collateral—and would never have succeeded in perfecting a claim. What should the judge rule?

4. After reading this chapter, will your behavior as a consumer change? Are there any types of transactions that you might be more inclined to avoid?

5. After reading this chapter, will your future behavior as a businessperson change? What specific steps will you be most careful to take to protect your interests?

ANSWERS TO SELECTED END OF CHAPTER QUESTIONS

MULTIPLE-CHOICE QUESTIONS

Presented are the answers for the ODD-numbered multiple-choice questions in the end-of-chapter material.

1. B
3. C
5. B

CASE QUESTIONS

Presented are the answers for all of the ODD-numbered case questions in the end-of-chapter material.

1. **Answer:** Yes to both questions. The bank had a valid security interest in all of Able's equipment, including after-acquired equipment. After-acquired clauses are valid. The only question is whether the bank's security interest could attach to the backhoe. Attachment requires that the debtor has rights in the collateral. But this does not mean that the debtor must own the goods. Here, Able had the lawful use and possession of the backhoe, based on his purchase agreement with Myers. He thus had rights in the backhoe, and as soon as he took possession of it, the bank's security interest attached. The bank gets the backhoe. *United States v. Allies*, 739 F. Supp. 1439, 1990 U.S. Dist. LEWIS 7064 (D. Kan. 1990).

3. **Answer:** No. A PMSI in consumer goods perfects automatically. A consumer good is one that is used primarily for personal, family, or household purposes. Many lawnmowers are consumer goods, but this one was not, and Sears's security interest was not perfected. *IN RE Cosmo Nick Fiscante*, 141 Bankr. 303, 1992 Bankr. LEXIS 907 (W.D. Pa. 1992).

5. **Answer:** Wells Fargo wins. The court ruled:

    The exception to the "first to file or perfect" rule for purchase money security interests in inventory is relevant in this case. Rushville claims that it had a valid purchase money security interest (PMSI) in the fertilizer. Under Indiana law, effective when these transactions transpired, a PMSI in inventory has priority over a conflicting security interest in the same collateral [if (1) the PMSI is perfected when the debtor receives possession of the collateral, and (2) the holder of the PMSI notifies the holder of the earlier interest that a PMSI will be filed, and (3) this notice arrives before the debtor obtains the collateral].

    In order to acquire priority, a purchase money secured creditor must satisfy each of these three requirements. Because Rushville filed its financing statement covering [the] inventory with the Rush County Recorder, its PMSI was not perfected when DuPont received the fertilizer. So, Rushville cannot be found to have a PMSI in the fertilizer. *IN RE Dupont Feed Mill Corp.*, 121 Bankr. 555, 1990 U.S. Dist. LEXIS 16554 United States District Court, So District of Indiana, 1990.

Chapter 28

AGENCY LAW

Lauren Brenner had a great idea for a new kind of fitness studio in New York. Called Pure Power Boot Camp, Brenner's gym was modeled on a U.S. Marine training facility, with an indoor obstacle course, camouflage colors, and a rubber floor designed to look like dirt. Brenner's special insight was that people would be more likely to stick to an exercise regime if they worked out together in a small group. So she limited classes to 16 people (called "recruits") who went through the training program (a "tour of duty") together. Brenner also hired retired Marines as "drill instructors."

© Tomas Tichy/Shutterstock.com

Ruben Belliard, a retired Marine, was Pure Power's head drill instructor. On his recommendation, Brenner also hired Alexander Fell. But, as Brenner began plans to franchise her concept, the two men went to war against her. They decided to start their own copycat gym, which was to be called Warrior Fitness Boot Camp. Meanwhile, Fell began dating Jennifer Lee, a Pure Power client, which was wrong for two reasons: (1) Pure Power's policies prohibited instructors from dating clients, and (2) she was a business school grad, who helped the two men develop their competing business plan. (Clearly, she had been dozing through her business law class.)

> **As Brenner began plans to franchise her concept, the two men went to war against her.**

While still employed by Brenner, Belliard and Fell rented a gym space near Pure Power. Belliard stole copies of Pure Power's confidential customer list, business plan, and operations manuals. The two men sent marketing emails about Warrior to Pure Power's clients and even invited them to a cocktail party to announce Warrior Fitness's launch. On another front, Lee spread false rumors about Brenner—that she had fired an employee because he was gay.

Then one day at Pure Power, Fell openly defied Brenner's instructions, screaming at her that he dared her to fire him. She had little choice but to do so. Belliard then convinced her to fire another drill inspector. Two weeks later, Belliard quit without giving notice, intentionally leaving Brenner with only one drill instructor. Two months later, Fell and Belliard opened Warrior Fitness.

Thus far, this book has primarily dealt with issues of *individual* responsibility: What happens if *you* knock someone down or *you* sign an agreement? But most businesses need more than one worker. Certainly Lauren Brenner could not operate her business by herself.

That is where agency law comes in. It is concerned with your responsibility for the actions of others and their obligations to you. What happens if your agent assaults someone or signs a contract in your name? Or tries to leave with all of your clients?

Hiring other people presents a significant trade-off: If you do everything yourself, you have control over the result. But the size and scope of your business (and your life) will be severely limited. Once you bring in other people, both your risks and your rewards can increase immensely.

The Pure Power case highlights a common agency issue: If your employees decide to leave for greener pastures, what obligation do they owe you in that period before they actually walk out the door? The court's opinion is later in the chapter.

28-1 CREATING AN AGENCY RELATIONSHIP

Let's begin with two important definitions:

- **Principal:** A person who has someone else acting for him.

- **Agent:** A person who acts for someone else.

Principals have substantial liability for the actions of their agents.[1] Therefore, disputes about whether an agency relationship exists are not mere legal quibbles but important issues with potentially profound financial consequences.

In an agency relationship, someone (the agent) agrees to perform a task for, and under the control of, someone else (the principal). **To create an agency relationship, there must be:**

- a **principal** and

- an **agent,**

- who mutually **consent** that the agent will act on behalf of the principal and

- be subject to the principal's **control**

- thereby creating a **fiduciary relationship**.

28-1a Consent

To establish consent, the principal must ask the agent to do something, and the agent must agree. In the most straightforward example, you ask a neighbor to walk your dog, and she agrees. Matters were more complicated, however, when Steven James met some friends one evening at a restaurant. During the two hours he was there, he drank four to six beers. (It is probably a bad sign that he cannot remember how many.) From then on, one misfortune piled upon another. After leaving the restaurant at about 7:00 p.m., James sped down a highway and crashed into a car that had stalled on the road, thereby killing the driver. James told the police at the scene that he had not seen the parked car (another bad sign). Evidently, James's lawyer was not as perceptive as the police in recognizing drunkenness. In a misguided attempt to help his client, James's lawyer took him to the local hospital for a blood test. Unfortunately, the test confirmed that James had indeed been drunk at the time of the accident.

Principal
In an agency relationship, the person for whom an agent is acting

Agent
In an agency relationship, the person who is acting on behalf of a principal

---

[1]The word *principal* is always used when referring to a person. It is not to be confused with the word *principle*, which refers to a fundamental idea.

The attorney knew that if this evidence was admitted at trial, his client would soon be receiving free room and board from the Massachusetts Department of Corrections. So at trial, the lawyer argued that the blood test was protected by the client–attorney privilege because the hospital had been his agent and therefore a member of the defense team. The court disagreed, however, holding that the hospital employees were not agents for the lawyer because they had not consented to act in that role.

The court upheld James's conviction of murder in the first degree by reason of extreme atrocity or cruelty.[2]

28-1b Control

Principals are liable for an agent's acts because they exercise control over that person. If principals direct their agents to commit an act, it seems fair to hold the principal liable when that act causes harm. How would you apply that rule to the following situation?

William Stanford was an employee of the Agency for International Development. While on his way home to Pakistan to spend the holidays with his family, his plane was hijacked and taken to Iran, where he was killed. Stanford had originally purchased a ticket on Northwest Airlines but had traded it for a seat on Kuwait Airways (KA). The airlines had an agreement permitting passengers to exchange tickets from one to the other. Stanford's widow sued Northwest on the theory that KA was Northwest's agent. The court found, however, that no agency relationship existed because Northwest had no control over KA.[3] Northwest did not tell KA how to fly planes or handle terrorists; therefore, it should not be liable when KA made fatal errors. Not only must an agent and principal consent to an agency relationship, but the principal also must have control over the agent.

28-1c Fiduciary Relationship

A **fiduciary relationship** is one of trust: A trustee acts for the benefit of the beneficiary, always putting the interests of the beneficiary before his own. The beneficiary places special confidence in the fiduciary who, in turn, is obligated to act in good faith and candor, doing what is best for the beneficiary. **Agents have a fiduciary duty to their principals.**

All three elements—consent, control, and a fiduciary duty—are necessary to create an agency relationship. In some relationships, for example, there might be a *fiduciary duty* but no *control*. A trustee of a trust must act for the benefit of the beneficiaries, but the beneficiaries have no right to control the trustee. Therefore, a trustee is not an agent of the beneficiaries. *Consent* is present in every contractual relationship, but that does not necessarily mean that the two parties are agent and principal. If Horace sells his car to Lily, they both expect to benefit under the contract, but neither has a *fiduciary duty* to the other and neither *controls* the other, so there is no agency relationship.

28-1d Elements Not Required for an Agency Relationship

Consent, control, and a fiduciary relationship are necessary to establish an agency relationship. **The following elements are *not* required for an agency relationship:**

- **Written Agreement.** In most cases, an agency agreement does not have to be in writing. An oral understanding is valid, except in one circumstance—the **equal dignities rule**. According to this rule, if an agent is empowered to enter into a contract that must be in writing, then the appointment of the agent must also be written. For

Equal dignities rule
If an agent is empowered to enter into a contract that must be in writing, then the appointment of the agent must also be written.

---

[2]Commonwealth v. James, 427 Mass. 312 (S.J.C. MA 1998).
[3]Stanford v. Kuwait Airways Corp., 648 F. Supp. 1158 (S.D.N.Y. 1986).

example, under the Statute of Frauds, a contract for the sale of land is unenforceable unless in writing, so the agency agreement to sell land must also be in writing.

- **Formal Agreement.** The principal and agent need not agree formally that they have an agency relationship. They do not even have to utter the word *agent*. So long as they act like an agent and a principal, the law will treat them as such.

- **Compensation.** An agency relationship need not meet all the standards of contract law. For example, a contract is not valid without consideration, but an agency agreement is valid *even if the agent is not paid*.

28-2 DUTIES OF AGENTS TO PRINCIPALS

Agents owe a fiduciary duty to their principals. There are four elements to this duty.

28-2a Duty of Loyalty

An agent has a fiduciary duty to act loyally for the principal's benefit in all matters connected with the agency relationship.[4] The agent has an obligation to put the principal first, to strive to accomplish the principal's goals.

The following case reveals the outcome of the opening scenario.

PURE POWER BOOT CAMP, INC. v. WARRIOR FITNESS BOOT CAMP, LLC

813 F. Supp. 2d 489
United States District Court for the Southern District of New York, 2011

Facts: Based on the facts in the opening scenario, Brenner filed suit against Belliard and Fell, alleging that they had violated their duty of loyalty to her company.

Issue: *Did Belliard and Fell violate their duty of loyalty to Pure Power?*

Excerpts from Judge Katz's Decision: An agent is obligated under New York law to be loyal to his employer and is prohibited from acting in any manner inconsistent with his agency or trust and is at all times bound to exercise the utmost good faith and loyalty in the performance of his duties. This duty is not dependent upon an express contractual relationship, but exists even where the employment relationship is at-will.

When an employee uses an employer's proprietary or confidential information when establishing a competing business, the employee breaches his or her fiduciary duty to the employer. Although an employee may, of course, make preparations to compete with his employer while still working for

the employer, he or she may not do so at the employer's expense, and may not use the employer's resources, time, facilities, or confidential information; specifically, whether or not the employee has signed an agreement not-to-compete, the employee, while still employed by the employer, may not solicit clients of his employer, may not copy his employer's business records for his own use, may not charge expenses to his employer, which were incurred while acting on behalf of his own interest, and may not actively divert the employer's business for his own personal benefit or the benefit of others. In addition, even in the absence of trade secret protection, employees are not permitted to copy their employer's client list, and such acts have been deemed to be an egregious breach of trust and confidence.

This ongoing and deliberate conduct, transpiring over the course of several months, constitutes a clear breach of the duty of loyalty owed by employees, Belliard and Fell, to their employer, Pure Power. [Belliard and Fell must pay Brenner $245,000.]

---

[4]Restatement (Third) of Agency §8.01.

The various components of the duty of loyalty follow.

Outside Benefits

An agent may not receive profits unless the principal knows and approves. Suppose that Hope is an employee of the agency Big Egos and Talents, Inc. (BEAT). She has been representing Robert Downey Jr. in his latest movie negotiations.[5] Downey often drives her to meetings in his new Aston Martin. He is so thrilled that she has arranged for him to star in the new movie *Little Men* that he buys her an Aston Martin. Can Hope keep this generous gift? Only with BEAT's permission. She must tell BEAT about the gift; the company may then take the vehicle itself or allow her to keep it.

Confidential Information

The ability to keep secrets is important in any relationship, but especially a fiduciary relationship. **Agents can neither disclose nor use for their own benefit any confidential information they acquire during their agency.** As the following case shows, this duty continues even after the agency relationship ends.

ABKCO MUSIC, INC. v. HARRISONGS MUSIC, LTD.

722 F.2d 988
United States Court of Appeals for the Second Circuit, 1983

Facts: Bright Tunes Music Corp. (Bright Tunes) owned the copyright to the song "He's So Fine," a chart-topping hit for the Chiffons. The company sued Beatle George Harrison alleging that his composition "My Sweet Lord" copied "He's So Fine." At the time the suit was filed, Allen B. Klein handled the business affairs of the Beatles.

Klein (representing Harrison) met with the president of Bright Tunes to discuss possible settlement of the copyright lawsuit. Klein suggested that Harrison might be interested in purchasing the copyright to "He's So Fine." Shortly thereafter, Klein's management contract with the Beatles expired. Without telling Harrison, Klein began negotiating with Bright Tunes to purchase the copyright to "He's So Fine" for himself. To advance these negotiations, Klein gave Bright Tunes information about royalty income for "My Sweet Lord"—information that he had gained as Harrison's agent.

The trial judge in the copyright case ultimately found that Harrison had infringed the copyright on "He's So Fine" and assessed damages of $1.6 million. After the trial, Klein purchased the "He's So Fine" copyright from Bright Tunes and with it, the right to recover from Harrison for his breach of copyright.

George Harrison, a few months after writing "My Sweet Lord."

Issue: *Did Klein violate his fiduciary duty to Harrison by using confidential information after the agency relationship terminated?*

Excerpts from Judge Pierce's Decision: There is no doubt that the relationship between Harrison and [Klein]

---

[5]Do not be confused by the fact that Hope works as an agent for movie stars. As an employee of BEAT, her duty is to the company. She is an agent of BEAT, and BEAT works for the celebrities.

prior to the termination of the management agreement was that of principal and agent, and that the relationship was fiduciary in nature. [A]n agent has a duty not to use confidential knowledge acquired in his employment in competition with his principal. This duty exists as well after the employment is terminated as during its continuance.

On the other hand, use of information based on general business knowledge or gleaned from general business experience is not covered by the rule, and the former agent is permitted to compete with his former principal in reliance on such general publicly available information. The evidence presented herein is not at all convincing that the information imparted to Bright Tunes by Klein was publicly available.

While the initial attempt to purchase [the copyright to "He's So Fine"] was several years removed from the eventual purchase on [Klein]'s own account, we are not of the view that such a fact rendered [Klein] unfettered in the later negotiations. Taking all of these circumstances together, we agree that [Klein's] conduct did not meet the standard required of him as a former fiduciary.

Ethics Both this case and *Pure Power* provide examples of agents who competed against their principal. You may well be in this situation at some point in your own life. As we saw in the Ethics chapter, rationalization is a common, and dangerous, trap. Imagine how Klein, Belliard, and Fell might have rationalized their wrong-doing. What steps can you take to ensure that you do not fall prey to this same ethics trap?

Competition with the Principal

Agents are not allowed to compete with their principal in any matter within the scope of the agency business. If Allen Klein had purchased the "He's So Fine" copyright while he was George Harrison's agent, he would have committed an additional sin against the agency relationship. Owning song rights was clearly part of the agency business, so Klein could not make such purchases without Harrison's consent. Once the agency relationship ends, however, so does the rule against competition. Klein was entitled to buy the "He's So Fine" copyright after the agency relationship ended (so long as he did not use confidential information).

Conflict of Interest between Two Principals

Unless otherwise agreed, an agent may not act for two principals whose interests conflict. Suppose Travis represents both director Steven Spielberg and actor Jennifer Lawrence. Spielberg is casting the title role in his new movie, *Nancy Drew: Girl Detective*, a role that Lawrence covets. Travis cannot represent these two clients when they are negotiating with each other unless they both know about the conflict and agree to ignore it. The following example illustrates the dangers of acting for two principals at once.

EXAM Strategy

Question: The Sisters of Charity was an order of nuns in New Jersey. Faced with growing healthcare and retirement costs, they decided to sell off a piece of property. The nuns soon found, however, that the world is not always a charitable place. They agreed to sell the land to Linpro for nearly $10 million. But before the deal closed, Linpro signed a contract to resell the property to Sammis for $34 million. So, you say, the sisters made a bad deal. There is no law against that. But it turned out that the nuns' law firm also represented Linpro. Their lawyer at the firm, Peter Berkley, never told the sisters about the deal between Linpro and Sammis. Was that the charitable—or legal—thing to do?

Strategy: Always begin by asking if there is an agency relationship. Was there consent, control, and a fiduciary relationship? *Consent:* Berkley had agreed to work for the nuns. *Control:* they told him what he was to do—sell the land. The purpose of a *fiduciary relationship* is for one person to benefit another. The point of the nuns' relationship with Berkley was for him to help them. Once you know there is an agency relationship, then ask if the agent has violated his duty of loyalty.

Result: You know that an agent is not permitted to act for two principals whose interests conflict. Here, Berkley was working for the nuns, who wanted the highest possible price for their land, and Linpro, who wanted the lowest price. Berkley has violated his duty of loyalty.

Secretly Dealing with the Principal

If a principal hires an agent to arrange a transaction, the agent may not become a party to the transaction without the principal's permission. Suppose Spielberg hires Trang to read new scripts for him. Unbeknownst to Spielberg, Trang has written her own script, which she thinks would be ideal for him. She may not sell it to him without revealing that she wrote it herself. Spielberg may be perfectly happy to buy Trang's script, but he has the right, as her principal, to know that she is the person selling it.

Appropriate Behavior

An agent may not engage in inappropriate behavior that reflects badly on the principal. This rule applies even to *off-duty* conduct. While off-duty (but still in uniform), a coed trio of flight attendants went wild at a hotel bar in London. They kissed and caressed each other, showed off their underwear, and poured alcohol down their trousers. The airline fired two of the employees and gave a warning letter to the third.

28-2b Other Duties of an Agent

Before Taylor left for a five-week trip to Antarctica, he hired Angie to rent out his vacation house. Angie neither listed his house on the Multiple Listing Service used by all the area brokers, nor posted it online, but when the Fords contacted her looking for rental housing, she did show them Taylor's place. They offered to rent it for $750 per month.

Angie emailed Taylor in Antarctica to tell him. He responded that he would not accept less than $850 a month, which Angie thought the Fords would be willing to pay. He told Angie to email him back if there was any problem. The Fords decided that they would go no higher than $800 a month. Although Taylor had told Angie that he had no cell phone service in Antarctica, she texted him the Fords' counteroffer. Taylor never received it, so he never responded. When the Fords pressed Angie for an answer, she said she could not get in touch with Taylor. Not until Taylor returned home did he learn that the Fords had rented another house. Did Angie violate any of the duties that agents owe to their principals?

Duty to Obey Instructions

An agent must obey her principal's instructions unless the principal directs her to behave illegally or unethically. Taylor instructed Angie to email him if the Fords rejected the offer. When Angie failed to do so, she violated her duty to obey instructions. If, however, Taylor had asked her to say that the house's basement was dry when in fact it looked like a swamp every spring, Angie would be under no obligation to follow those illegal instructions.

Duty of Care

An agent has a duty to act with reasonable care. In other words, an agent must act as a reasonable person would, under the circumstances. A reasonable person would not have texted Taylor while he was in Antarctica.

Under some circumstances, an agent is held to a higher—or lower—standard than usual. **An agent with special skills is held to a higher standard because she is expected to use those skills.** A trained real estate agent should know enough to post all listings online.

But suppose Taylor had asked his neighbor, Jed, to help him sell the house. Jed is not a trained real estate agent, and he is not being paid, which makes him a **gratuitous agent**. A gratuitous agent is held to a lower standard because he is doing his principal a favor and, as the old saying goes, you get what you pay for—up to a point. **Gratuitous agents are liable if they commit *gross* negligence, but not *ordinary* negligence.** If Jed, as a gratuitous agent, texted Taylor an important message because he forgot that Taylor could not receive these messages in Antarctica, he would not be liable for that ordinary negligence. But if Taylor had, just that day, sent Jed an email complaining that he could not get any text messages, Jed would be liable for gross negligence and a violation of his duty.

Gratuitous agent
Someone not paid for performing duties

Duty to Provide Information

An agent has a duty to provide the principal with all information in her possession that she has reason to believe the principal wants to know. She also has a duty to provide accurate information. Angie knew that the Fords had counteroffered for $800 a month. She had a duty to pass this information on to Taylor.

28-2c Principal's Remedies when the Agent Breaches a Duty

A principal has three potential remedies when an agent breaches her duty:

- **Damages**. The principal can recover from the agent any damages the breach has caused. Thus, if Taylor can rent his house for only $600 a month instead of the $800 the Fords offered, Angie would be liable for $2,400—$200 a month for one year.

- **Profits**. If an agent breaches the duty of loyalty, he must turn over to the principal any profits he has earned as a result of his wrongdoing. Thus, after Klein violated his duty of loyalty to Harrison, he forfeited profits he would have earned from the copyright of "He's So Fine." Some states also allow punitive damages against disloyal employees.

- **Rescission**. If the agent has violated her duty of loyalty, the principal may rescind the transaction. When Trang sold a script to her principal, Spielberg, without telling him that she was the author, she violated her duty of loyalty. Spielberg could rescind the contract to buy the script.[6]

---

[6]A principal can rescind his contract with an agent who has violated her duty but, as we shall see later in the chapter, the principal might not be able to rescind a contract that the agent has made with a third party.

28-3 DUTIES OF PRINCIPALS TO AGENTS

In a typical agency relationship, the agent agrees to perform tasks for the principal, and the principal agrees to pay the agent. The range of tasks undertaken by an agent is limited only by the imagination of the principal. Because the agent's job can be so varied, the law needs to define an agent's duties carefully. The role of the principal, on the other hand, is typically less complicated—often little more than paying the agent as required by the agreement. Thus, the law enumerates fewer duties for the principal. Primarily, the principal must reimburse the agent for reasonable expenses and cooperate with the agent in performing agency tasks. The respective duties of agents and principals can be summarized as follows:

Duties of Agents to Principals	Duty of Principals to Agents
Duty of loyalty	Duty to compensate as provided by the agreement
Duty to obey instructions	Duty to reimburse reasonable expenses
Duty of care	Duty to cooperate with the agent
Duty to provide information	

28-3a Duty to Indemnify

As a general rule, the principal must indemnify (i.e., reimburse) the agent for any expenses she has reasonably incurred. These reimbursable expenses fall into three categories:

- **A principal must indemnify an agent for any expenses or damages reasonably incurred in carrying out his agency responsibilities.** Peace Baptist Church of Birmingham, Alabama, asked its pastor to buy land for a new church. He paid part of the purchase price out of his own pocket, but the church refused to reimburse him. Although the pastor lost in church, he won in court.[7]

- **A principal must indemnify an agent for tort claims brought by a third party if the principal authorized the agent's behavior and the agent did not realize he was committing a tort.** Marisa owns all the apartment buildings on Elm Street, except one. She hires Rajiv to manage the units and tells him that, under the terms of the leases, she has the right to ask guests to leave if a party becomes too rowdy. But she forgets to tell Rajiv that she does not own one of the buildings, which happens to house a college sorority. One night, when the sorority is having a raucous party, Rajiv hustles over and starts ejecting the noisy guests. The sorority is furious and sues Rajiv for trespass. If the sorority wins its suit against Rajiv, Marisa would have to pay the judgment, plus Rajiv's attorney's fees, because she had told him to quell noisy parties and he did not realize he was trespassing.

- **The principal must indemnify the agent for any liability to third parties that she incurs as a result of entering into a contract on the principal's behalf, including attorney's fees and reasonable settlements.** An agent signed a contract to buy cucumbers for Vlasic Food Products Co. to use in making pickles. When the first shipment of

---

[7]Lauderdale v. Peace Baptist Church of Birmingham, 246 Ala. 178 (S. Ct. AL 1944).

cucumbers arrived, Vlasic inspectors found them unsuitable and directed the agent to refuse the shipment. The agent found himself in a pickle when the cucumber farmer sued. The agent notified Vlasic, but the company refused to defend him. He settled the claim himself and, in turn, sued Vlasic. The court ordered Vlasic to reimburse the agent because he had notified them of the suit and had acted reasonably and in good faith.[8]

28-3b Duty to Cooperate

Principals have a duty to cooperate with their agent:

- **The principal must furnish the agent with the opportunity to work.** If Lewis agrees to serve as Ida's real estate agent in selling her house, Ida must allow Lewis access to the house. It is unlikely that Lewis will be able to sell the house without taking anyone inside.

- **The principal cannot unreasonably interfere with the agent's ability to accomplish his task.** Ida allows Lewis to show the house, but she refuses to clean it and then makes disparaging comments to prospective purchasers. "I really get tired of living in such a dark, dreary house," she says. "And the neighborhood children are vicious thugs." This behavior would constitute unreasonable interference with an agent.

- **The principal must perform her part of the contract.** Once the agent has successfully completed the task, the principal must pay him, even if the principal has changed her mind and no longer wants the agent to perform. Ida is a 78-year-old widow who has lived alone for many years in a house that she loves. Her asking price is outrageously high because she does not really want to sell. She put her house on the market so that she could show it to all the nice young families who move to town. When Lewis actually finds a couple willing to pay Ida's price, she rejects the offer. But the contract had provided that Lewis would find a willing buyer at the asking price. Because he has done so, Ida must pay his real estate commission even if she refuses to sell her house.

28-4 TERMINATING AN AGENCY RELATIONSHIP

Either the agent or the principal can terminate the agency relationship at any time. In addition, the relationship terminates automatically if the principal or agent no longer can perform their required duties or a change in circumstances renders the agency relationship pointless.

28-4a Termination by Agent or Principal

The two parties—principal and agent—have these choices in terminating their relationship:

- **Term Agreement.** If the principal and agent agree in advance how long their relationship will last, they have a term agreement. For example:
  - ○ **Time.** Alexandra hires Boris to help her add to her collection of guitars previously owned by rock stars. If they agree that the relationship will last two years, they have a term agreement.

---

[8]Long v. Vlasic Food Products Co., 439 F.2d 229 (4th Cir. 1971).

- ○ **Achieving a Purpose.** The principal and agent can agree that the agency relationship will terminate when the principal's goals have been achieved. Alexandra and Boris might agree that their relationship will end when Alexandra has purchased 10 guitars.

- ○ **Mutual Agreement.** No matter what the principal and agent agree at the start, they can always change their minds later on, so long as the change is mutual. If Boris and Alexandra originally agree to a two-year term, but Boris decides he wants to go back to business school and Alexandra runs out of money after only one year, they can decide together to terminate the agency.

- **Agency at Will.** If they make no agreement in advance about the term of the agreement, either principal or agent can terminate at any time.

- **Wrongful Termination.** An agency relationship is a personal relationship. Hiring an agent is not like buying a book. You might not care which copy of the book you buy, but you do care which agent you hire. If an agency relationship is not working out, the courts will not force the agent and principal to stay together. **Either party always has the *power* to terminate. They may not, however, have the *right*.** If one party's departure from the agency relationship violates the agreement and causes harm to the other party, the wrongful party must pay damages. Nonetheless, he will be permitted to leave. If Boris has agreed to work for Alexandra for two years but he wants to leave after one, he can leave, provided he pays Alexandra the cost of hiring and training a replacement.

If the agent is a gratuitous agent (i.e., is not being paid), he has both the power and the right to quit any time he wants, regardless of the agency agreement. If Boris is doing this job for Alexandra as a favor, he will not owe her damages when he stops work.

28-4b Principal or Agent Can No Longer Perform Required Duties

If the principal or the agent is unable to perform the duties required under the agency agreement, the agreement terminates.

- **If either the agent or the principal fails to obtain (or keep) a license necessary to perform duties under the agency agreement, the agreement ends.** Caleb hires Allegra to represent him in a lawsuit. If she is disbarred, their agency agreement terminates because the agent is no longer allowed in court. Alternatively, if Emil hires Bess to work in his gun shop, their agency relationship terminates when he loses his license to sell firearms.

- **The bankruptcy of the agent or the principal terminates an agency relationship only if it affects their ability to perform.** Bankruptcy rarely interferes with an agent's responsibilities. After all, there is generally no reason why an agent cannot continue to act for the principal whether the agent is rich or poor. If Lewis, the real estate agent, becomes bankrupt, he can continue to represent Ida or anyone else who wants to sell a house. The bankruptcy of a principal is different, however, because after filing for bankruptcy, the principal loses control of his assets. A bankrupt principal may be unable to pay the agent or honor contracts that the agent enters into on his behalf. Therefore, the bankruptcy of a principal is more likely to terminate an agency relationship.

- **An agency relationship terminates upon the death or incapacity of either the principal or the agent.** Agency is a personal relationship, and when the principal dies, the agent cannot act on behalf of a nonexistent person.[9] Of course, a nonexistent person cannot act either, so the relationship also terminates when the agent dies. Incapacity has the same legal effect because either the principal or the agent is at least temporarily unable to act.

- **If the agent violates her duty of loyalty, the agency agreement automatically terminates.** Agents are appointed to represent the principal's interest; if they fail to do so, there is no point to the relationship. Thus, in the Pure Power case, Belliard's and Fell's agency relationship with Brenner automatically ended once they engaged in disloyal activities. She had the right to fire them on the spot, whether or not they had employment contracts.

28-4c Change in Circumstances

After the agency agreement is negotiated, circumstances may change. **If these changes are significant enough to undermine the purpose of the agreement, the relationship ends automatically.** Andrew hires Melissa to sell his country farm for $100,000. Shortly thereafter, the largest natural gas reserve in North America is discovered nearby. The farm is now worth 10 times Andrew's asking price. Melissa's authority terminates automatically.

Other changes in circumstance that affect an agency agreement are:

- **Change of law.** If the agent's responsibilities become illegal, the agency agreement terminates. Oscar has hired Marta to ship him succulent avocados from California's Imperial Valley. Before she sends the shipment, Mediterranean fruit flies are discovered, and all fruits and vegetables in California are quarantined. The agency agreement terminates because it is now illegal to ship the California avocados.

- **Loss or destruction of subject matter.** Andrew hired Damian to sell his Palm Beach condominium, but before Damian could even measure the living room, Andrew's creditors attached the condo. Damian is no longer authorized to sell the real estate because Andrew has "lost" the subject matter of his agency agreement with Damian.

28-4d Effect of Termination

Once an agency relationship ends, the agent no longer has the authority to act for the principal. If she continues to act, she is liable to the principal for any damages he incurs as a result. The Mediterranean fruit fly quarantine ended Marta's agency. If she sends Oscar the avocados anyway and he is fined for possession of a fruit fly, Marta must pay the fine.

The agent loses her authority to act, but some of the duties of both the principal and agent continue even after the relationship ends:

- **Principal's duty to indemnify agent.** Oscar must reimburse Marta for expenses she incurred before the agency ended. If Marta accumulated mileage on her car during her search for the perfect avocado, Oscar must pay her for gasoline and depreciation. But he owes her nothing for her expenses after the agency relationship ends.

- **Confidential information.** An agent is not entitled to use confidential information even after the agency relationship terminates. Remember the "He's So Fine" case earlier in the chapter? George Harrison's former agent was wrong to use confidential information to negotiate on his own behalf the purchase of the "He's So Fine" copyright.

---

[9]Restatement (Third) of Agency §§3.05, 3.06, 3.07, 3.08.

28-5 LIABILITY TO THIRD PARTIES

Thus far, this chapter has dealt with the relationship between principals and agents. Although an agent can dramatically increase his principal's ability to accomplish her goals, an agency relationship also dramatically increases the risk of legal liability to third parties. A principal may be liable in tort for any harm the agent causes and also liable in contract for agreements that the agent signs. Indeed, once a principal hires an agent, she may be liable to third parties for his acts, even if he *disobeys* instructions. Agents may also find themselves liable to third parties.

28-5a Principal's Liability for Contracts

Many agents are hired for the primary purpose of entering into contracts on behalf of their principals. Salespeople may do little other than sign on the dotted line. Most of the time, the principal is pleased to be liable on these contracts. But even if the principal is unhappy (because, say, the agent has disobeyed orders), the principal generally cannot rescind contracts entered into by the agent. After all, if someone is going to suffer, it should be the principal who hired the disobedient agent, not the innocent third party.

The principal is liable for the acts and statements of his agent if (1) the agent had authority, or (2) the principal ratified the acts of the agent. In other words, the principal is as responsible as if he had performed those acts himself. Thus, when a lawyer lied on an application for malpractice insurance, the insurance company was allowed to void the policy for the entire law firm. It was as if the firm had lied. In addition, the principal is deemed to know any information that the agent knows or should know.

Authority

A principal is bound by the acts of an agent if the agent had authority. There are three types of authority: express, implied, and apparent. Express and implied authority are categories of actual authority because the agent is truly authorized to act for the principal. In apparent authority, the principal is liable for the agent's actions even though the agent was *not* authorized.

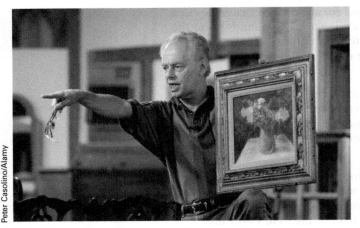

Peter Casolino/Alamy

Did Nell have the authority to hire this auctioneer?

Express Authority. **The principal grants express authority by words or conduct that, reasonably interpreted, cause the agent to believe the principal desires her to act on the principal's account.**[10] In other words, the principal asks the agent to do something and the agent does it. Craig calls his stockbroker, Alice, and asks her to buy 100 shares of Banshee Corp. for his account. She has *express authority* to carry out this transaction.

Implied Authority. **Unless otherwise agreed, authority to conduct a transaction includes authority to do acts that are reasonably necessary to accomplish it.**[11] The principal does not have to micromanage the agent. David has recently inherited a house from his

---

[10]Restatement (Third) of Agency §2.01.
[11]Restatement (Third) of Agency §2.02.

grandmother. He hires Nell to auction off the house and its contents. She hires an auction-eer, advertises the event, rents a tent, and generally does everything necessary to conduct a successful auction. After withholding her expenses, she sends the tidy balance to David. Totally outraged, he calls her on the phone, "How dare you hire an auctioneer and rent a tent? I never gave you permission! I absolutely *refuse* to pay these expenses!"

David is wrong. A principal almost never gives an agent absolutely complete instruc-tions. Unless some authority is implied, David would have had to say, "Open the car door, get in, put the key in the ignition, drive to the store, buy stickers, mark an auction number on each sticker, ..." and so forth. To solve this problem, the law assumes that the agent has authority to do anything that is reasonably necessary to accomplish her task.

Apparent Authority. **A principal can be liable for the acts of an agent who is not, in fact, acting with authority if the *principal's* conduct causes a third party reasonably to believe that the agent is authorized.**[12] In the case of *express* and *implied* authority, the principal has authorized the agent to act. Apparent authority is different: The principal has *not* authorized the agent, but has done something to make an innocent third party *believe* the agent is authorized. As a result, the principal is every bit as liable to the third party as if the agent had had authority.

Zbigniew Lambo and Scott Kennedy were brokers at Paulson Investment Co., a stock brokerage firm in Oregon. The two men violated securities laws by selling unregistered stock, which ultimately proved to be worthless. Kennedy and Lambo were liable, but they were unable to repay the money. Either Paulson or its customers would end up bearing the loss. What is the fair result? The law takes the view that the principal is liable, not the third party, if the principal, by word or deed, allowed the third party to believe that the agent was acting on the principal's behalf. In that case, the principal could have prevented the third party from losing money.

Although the two brokers did not have *express* or *implied* authority to sell the stock (Paulson had not authorized them to break the law), the company was nonetheless liable on the grounds that the brokers had *apparent* authority. Paulson had sent letters to its customers notifying them when it hired Kennedy. The two brokers made sales presentations at Paulson's offices. The company had never told customers that the two men were not authorized to sell this worthless stock.[13] Thus the agents *appeared* to have authority, even though they did not. Of course, Paulson had the right to recover from Kennedy and Lambo, in the unlikely event that they had assets.

Remember that the issue in apparent authority is always what the *principal* has done to make the *third party* believe that the *agent* has authority. Suppose that Kennedy and Lambo never worked for Paulson but, on their own, printed up Paulson stationery. The company would not be liable for the stock the two men sold because it had never done or said anything that would reasonably make a third party believe that the men were its agents.

Ratification

If a person accepts the benefit of an unauthorized transaction or fails to repudiate it, then he is as bound by the act as if he had originally authorized it. He has *ratified* the act.[14] Many of the cases in agency law involve instances in which one person acts *without* authority for another. But sometimes after the fact, the principal decides that he approves of what the agent has done even though it was not authorized at the time. The law would be perverse if it did not permit the principal, under those circumstances, to agree to the deal the agent has made. The law is not perverse, but it is careful. **Even if an agent**

---

[12]Restatement (Third) of Agency §2.03.
[13]Badger v. Paulson Investment Co., 311 Ore. 14 (S. Ct. OR 1991).
[14]Restatement (Third) of Agency §4.01.

acts without authority, the principal can decide later to be bound by her actions as long as these requirements are met:

- The "agent" indicates to the third party that she is acting for a principal.
- The "principal" knows all the material facts of the transaction.
- The "principal" accepts the benefit of the whole transaction, not just part.
- The third party does not withdraw from the contract before ratification.

A night clerk at the St. Regis Hotel in Detroit, Michigan, was brutally murdered in the course of a robbery. A few days later, the *Detroit News* reported that the St. Regis management had offered a $1,000 reward for any information leading to the arrest and conviction of the killer. Two days after the article appeared, Robert Jackson turned in the man who was subsequently convicted of the crime. But then it was Jackson's turn to be robbed—the hotel refused to pay the reward on the grounds that the manager who had made the offer had no authority. Jackson still had one weapon left: He convinced the court that the hotel had ratified the offer. One of the hotel's owners admitted he read the *Detroit News*. The court concluded that if someone reads a newspaper, he is sure to read any articles about a business he owns; therefore, the owner must have been aware of the offer. He accepted the benefit of the offer by failing to revoke it publicly by, say, announcing to the press that the reward was invalid. This failure to revoke constituted a ratification, and the hotel was liable.[15]

Subagents

Many of the examples in this chapter involve a single agent acting for a principal. Real life is often more complex. Daniel, the owner of a restaurant, hires Michaela to manage it. She in turn hires chefs, waiters, and dishwashers. Michaela is called an **intermediary agent**—someone who hires **subagents** for the principal. Daniel has never even met the restaurant help, yet they are his subagents.

As a general rule, an agent has no authority to delegate her tasks to another unless the principal authorizes her to do so. **But when an agent is authorized to hire a subagent, the principal is as liable for the acts of the subagent as he is for the acts of a regular agent.** After Daniel authorizes Michaela to hire a restaurant staff, she hires Lydia to serve as produce buyer. When Lydia buys food for the restaurant, Daniel must pay the bill.

Intermediary agent
Someone who hires subagents for the principal

Subagents
Someone appointed by an agent to perform the agent's duties

28-5b **Agent's Liability for Contracts**

The agent's liability on a contract depends upon how much the third party knows about the principal. Disclosure is the agent's best protection against liability.

Fully Disclosed Principal

An agent is not liable for any contracts she makes on behalf of a *fully* disclosed principal. A principal is fully disclosed if the third party knows of his *existence* and his *identity*. Augusta acts as agent for Parker when he buys Tracey's prize-winning show horse. Augusta and Tracey both grew up in posh Grosse Pointe, Michigan, where they attended the same elite schools. Tracey does not know Parker, but she figures any friend of Augusta's must be OK. She figures wrong—Parker is a charming deadbeat. He injures Tracey's horse, fails to pay the full contract price, and promptly disappears. Tracey angrily demands that Augusta make good on Parker's debt. Unfortunately for Tracey, Parker was a fully disclosed principal— Tracey knew of his *existence* and his *identity*. Although Tracey partly relied on Augusta's good

---

[15]Jackson v. Goodman, 69 Mich. App. 225 (Mich. Ct. App. 1976).

character when contracting with Parker, Augusta is not liable because Tracey knew who the principal was and could have (should have) investigated him. Augusta did not promise anything herself, and Tracey's only recourse is against the principal, Parker (wherever he may be).

To avoid liability when signing a contract on behalf of a principal, an agent must clearly state that she is an agent and also must identify the principal. Augusta should sign a contract on behalf of her principal, Parker, as follows: "Augusta, as agent for Parker" or "Parker, by Augusta, Agent."

Unidentified Principal

In the case of an *unidentified* principal, the third party can recover from either the agent or the principal. (An unidentified principal is also sometimes called a "partially disclosed principal.") A principal is unidentified if the third party knew of his *existence* but not his *identity*. Suppose that, when approaching Tracey about the horse, Augusta simply says, "I have a friend who is interested in buying your champion." Any friend of Augusta's is a friend of Tracey's—or so Tracey thinks. Parker is an unidentified principal because Tracey knows only that he exists, not who he is. She cannot investigate his creditworthiness because she does not know his name. Tracey relies solely on what she is able to learn from the agent, Augusta. Parker and Augusta are **jointly and severally liable** to Tracey. Thus, Tracey can recover from either or both of them. However, she cannot recover more than the total she is owed: If her damages are $100,000, she can recover that amount from either Parker or Augusta, or partial amounts from both, but in no event more than $100,000.

Undisclosed Principal

In the case of an *undisclosed* principal, the third party can recover from either the agent or the principal. A principal is undisclosed if the third party did not know of his existence. Suppose that Augusta simply asks to buy the horse herself, without mentioning that she is purchasing it for Parker. In this case, Parker is an undisclosed principal because Tracey does not know that Augusta is acting for someone else. Both Parker and Augusta are jointly and severally liable. As Exhibit 28.1 illustrates, the principal is always liable, but the agent is not unless the principal's identity is a mystery.

Jointly and severally liable
All members of a group are liable. They can be sued as a group, or any one of them can be sued individually for the full amount owed. But the plaintiff cannot recover more than the total she is owed.

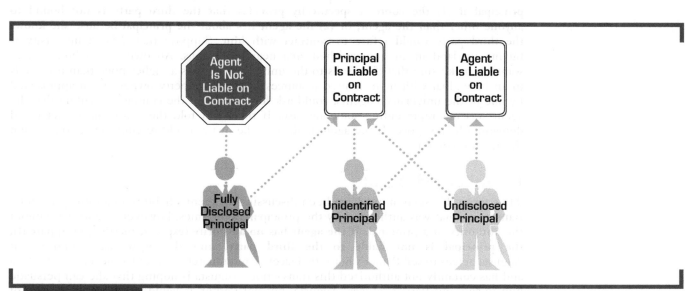

EXHIBIT 28.1

In some ways, the concept of an undisclosed principal violates principles of contract law. If Tracey does not even know that Parker exists, how can they have an agreement or a meeting of the minds? Is such an arrangement fair to Tracey? The following incident illustrates why this type of contract is permitted.

William Zeckendorf was a man with a plan. For years, he had been eyeing a six-block tract of land along New York's East River. It was a wasteland of slums and slaughterhouses, but he could see its potential. The meat packers had refused to sell to him, however, because they knew they would never be permitted to build slaughterhouses in Manhattan again. Finally, he got the phone call he had been waiting for. The companies were willing to sell—at more than three times the market price of surrounding land. Undeterred, Zeckendorf immediately put down a $1 million deposit. But to make his investment worthwhile, he needed to buy the neighboring property—once the slaughterhouses were gone, the other land would be much more valuable.

Zeckendorf was well known as a wealthy developer; he had begun his career managing the Astor family's real estate holdings. If sellers knew that he was involved in the deal, prices would skyrocket, and the project would become too costly. So he hired agents to purchase the land for him. To conceal his involvement further, he went to South America for a month. When he returned, his agents had completed 75 different purchases, and he owned 18 acres of Manhattan land.

> **Without the cooperation of agency law, the UN headquarters would not be in New York today.**

Shortly afterward, the United Nations (UN) began seeking a site for its headquarters. President Truman favored Boston, Philadelphia, or a location in the Midwest. The UN committee suggested Greenwich or Stamford, Connecticut. But John D. Rockefeller settled the question once and for all. He purchased Zeckendorf's land and donated it to the UN (netting Zeckendorf a 25 percent profit). Without the cooperation of agency law, the UN headquarters would not be in New York today.

Because of concerns about fair play, there are some exceptions to the rule on undisclosed principals. **A third party is not bound to the contract with an undisclosed principal if (1) the contract specifically provides that the third party is not bound to anyone other than the agent, or (2) the agent lies about the principal because she knows the third party would refuse to contract with him.** Suppose that a large university is buying up land in an impoverished area near its campus. An owner of a house there wants to make sure that if he sells to the university, he gets a higher price than if he sells to an individual with more limited resources. A cagey property owner, when approached by one of the university's agents, could ask for a clause in the contract providing that the agent was not representing someone else. If the agent told the truth, the owner could demand a higher price. If the agent lied, then the owner could rescind the contract when the truth emerged.

Unauthorized Agent

Thus far in this section, we have been discussing an agent's liability to a third party for a transaction that was authorized by the principal. Sometimes, however, agents act without the authority of a principal. **If the agent has no authority (express, implied, or apparent), the principal is not liable to the third party, and the agent is.** Suppose that Augusta agrees to sell Parker's horse to Tracey. Unfortunately, Parker has never met Augusta and has certainly not authorized this transaction. Augusta is hoping that she can persuade him to sell, but Parker refuses. Augusta, but not Parker, is liable to Tracey for breach of contract.

28-5c **Principal's Liability for Torts**

The general rule of tort liability is this: **An employer is liable for a** *physical* **tort committed by an employee acting within the scope of employment and a** *nonphysical* **tort of an employee acting with authority.**[16] This principle of liability is called *respondeat superior*, which is a Latin phrase meaning "let the master answer." Under the theory of *respondeat superior*, the employer (that is, the principal) is liable for misbehavior by the employee (that is, the agent) whether or not the employer was at fault. Indeed, the employer may be liable even if he *forbade* or tried to *prevent* the employee from misbehaving. Thus, a company could be liable for the damage an on-duty worker causes if speeding while driving, even if she is violating company policy at the time.

This rule sounds harsh. But the theory is that, because the principal controls the agent, he should be able to *prevent* misbehavior. If he cannot prevent it, at least he can *insure* against the risks. Furthermore, the principal may have deeper pockets than the agent or the injured third party and thus be better able to *afford* the cost of the agent's misbehavior.

To apply the principle of *respondeat superior*, it is important to understand these terms: employee, scope of employment, nonphysical tort, and acting with authority.

Employee

There are two kinds of agents: (1) employee and (2) independent contractor. **Generally, a principal** *is* **liable for the physical torts of an employee but is** *not* **liable for the physical torts of an independent contractor.** Because of this rule, the distinction between an employee and an independent contractor is important.

Employee or Independent Contractor? The more control the principal has over an agent, the more likely that the agent will be considered an employee. Therefore, **when determining if agents are employees or independent contractors, courts consider whether:**

- The principal supervises details of the work.
- The principal supplies the tools and place of work.
- The agents work full time for the principal.
- The agents receive a salary or hourly wages, not a fixed price for the job.
- The work is part of the regular business of the principal.
- The principal and agents believe they have an employer-employee relationship.
- The principal is in business.[17]

Suppose that Mutt and Jeff work 40 hours a week at Swansong Media preparing food for the company's onsite dining room. They earn a weekly salary. Swansong provides food, utensils, and a kitchen. This year, however, Swansong decides to go all out for its holiday party, so it hires FiFi LaBelle to cater the event. She buys the food, prepares it in her own kitchen, and delivers it to the company in time for the party. She is an independent contractor, while Mutt and Jeff are employees.

Respondeat superior
An employer is liable for a physical tort committed by an employee acting within the scope of employment and a nonphysical tort of an employee acting with authority.

---

[16]Restatement (Third) of Agency §7.07.
[17]Ibid.

Ethics For employers, the advantages of independent contractors extend beyond agency law. Contractors cost substantially less in payroll taxes and benefits, and require less paperwork. Also, companies with fewer than 50 employees are not required to provide health insurance under the Patient Protection and Affordable Care Act.

To increase tax revenue, the federal government is aggressively auditing employers to ensure that workers are being properly classified as employees. Microsoft paid almost $100 million to settle such a case. But even apart from the legal issues, employees who are inaccurately classified as independent contractors suffer from a large tear in their financial safety net, with unemployment, Social Security, and healthcare benefits at risk. What ethical obligation do employers have? What would Mill, Kant and Milton Friedman say?

Negligent Hiring. Although, as we have seen, principals are generally not liable for the physical torts of an independent contractor, there is one exception to this rule: **A principal is liable for the physical torts of an independent contractor *if* the principal has been negligent in hiring or supervising her.** Remember that, under *respondeat superior*, the principal is liable *without fault* for the torts of employees. The case of independent contractors is different: The principal is liable only if he was *at fault* by being careless in his hiring or supervising.

Exhibit 28.2 illustrates the difference in liability between an employee and an independent contractor.

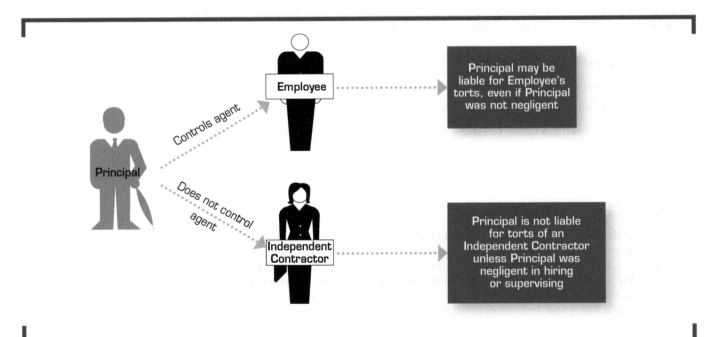

Principal

Controls agent

Employee

Principal may be liable for Employee's torts, even if Principal was not negligent

Does not control agent

Independent Contractor

Principal is not liable for torts of an Independent Contractor unless Principal was negligent in hiring or supervising

EXHIBIT 28.2

Scope of Employment

You remember that: An employer is liable for a physical tort committed by an employee acting within the scope of employment. **An employee is acting within the scope of employment if the act:**

- is one that employees are generally responsible for,
- takes place during hours that the employee is generally employed,
- is part of the principal's business,
- is similar to the one the principal authorized,
- is one for which the principal supplied the tools, and
- is not seriously criminal.

If an employee leaves a pool of water on the floor of a store and a customer slips and falls, the employer is liable. But if the same employee leaves water on his own kitchen floor and a friend falls, the employer is not liable because the employee is not acting within the scope of employment.

Scope of employment cases raise two major issues: authorization and abandonment.

Authorization.   In authorization cases, the agent is clearly working for the principal but commits an act that the principal has not authorized. Although Jane has often told the driver of her delivery van not to speed, Hank ignores her instructions and plows into Bernadette. At the time of the accident, he is working for Jane, delivering flowers for her shop, but his act is not authorized. **An act is within the scope of employment, even if expressly forbidden, if it is of the same general nature as that authorized or if it is incidental to the conduct authorized.** Hank was authorized to drive the van, but not to speed. However, his speeding was of the same general nature as the authorized act, so Jane is liable to Bernadette.

EXAM Strategy

Question: While on a business trip, Trevor went sightseeing on his day off. Although company policy forbade talking on a cell phone while driving, Trevor did answer his phone while in his car. Distracted, he crashed into Olivia's house, causing substantial damage. Was his employer liable for the damage?

Strategy: Whenever a case involves a company's liability for the acts of an employee, begin by asking if *respondeat superior* applies. Was he acting within the scope of employment? Does it matter that it was his day off and he was violating company policy?

Result: In a similar case, the court ruled that the employer was liable because it is foreseeable that travelling employees will go sightseeing and, therefore, companies should include this potential liability as a cost of doing business.[18] The fact that the employer's policy prohibits talking on a cell phone does not protect the company from liability if an employee violates that policy. The employer should not have hired such a disobedient worker.

---

[18]Potter v. Shaw, 60 Mass. App. Ct. 1112 (Mass. App. Ct. 2004).

Abandonment. This Exam Strategy also illustrates the second major issue in a scope of employment case: abandonment. **The principal is liable for the actions of the employee that occur while the employee is at work, but not for actions that occur after the employee has abandoned the principal's business.** Although the rule sounds straightforward, the difficulty lies in determining whether the employee has in fact abandoned the principal's business. The employer is liable if the employee is simply on a *detour* from company business, but the employer is not liable if the employee is off on a *frolic of his own*. Suppose that Hank, the delivery van driver, speeds during his afternoon commute home. An employee is generally not acting within the scope of his employment when he commutes to and from work, so his principal, Jane, is not liable. On the other hand, if Hank stops at the Burger Box drive-in window en route to making a delivery, Jane is liable when he crashes into Anna on the way out of the parking lot because this time, he is simply making a detour.

Was the employee in the following case acting within the scope of his employment while driving to work? You be the judge.

You be the Judge

Facts: Staff Sergeant William E. Dreyer was a recruiter for the United States Marine Corps, which provided Dreyer with a car to drive while on government business. He was not permitted to use this car while commuting to and from home unless he had specific authorization from his boss, Major Michael Sherman, but Sherman was lenient in giving authorization and even permitted his soldiers simply to leave a message on his voicemail. He had denied only about a dozen of such requests over a three-year period.

Each month, Dreyer was expected to meet specific quotas for the number of contracts signed and recruits shipped to basic training. However, despite working 16 to 18 hours every day of the week, Dreyer had not met his recruiting quotas for months. Sherman had formally reprimanded him and increased his target for the following month.

On the day before the accident, Dreyer left home at 6:30 a.m., driving his own car. At the office, he switched to a government car and worked until 10:45 p.m. He then discovered that his personal car would not start. He did not want to call Sherman that late, so he drove his government car home without permission. He believed that, had he called, Sherman would have said it was OK.

Dreyer arrived home at midnight. He was under orders to attend an early morning training session the next day. So he awoke early and left home at 6:35 a.m. At 6:40 a.m., his car struck and killed 12-year-old Justin Zankel. The child's parents sued the U.S. government, claiming that it was liable for Dreyer's actions because he had been

ZANKEL V. UNITED STATES OF AMERICA

2008 U.S. Dist. LEXIS 23655, 2008 WL 828032
United States District Court for the Western District of Pennsylvania, 2008

acting within the scope of his employment at the time of the accident.

You Be the Judge: *Was Dreyer within the scope of employment when he killed Zankel? Is the government liable?*

Argument for the Zankels: At the time of the accident, Dreyer was driving a government vehicle. Although he had not requested permission to drive the car, if he had done so, permission certainly would have been granted.

Moreover, even if Dreyer was not authorized to drive the Marine Corps car, the government is still liable because his activity was of the same general nature as that authorized and it was incidental to the conduct authorized. Driving the car was part of Dreyer's work. Indeed, he could not perform his job without it. In addition, Dreyer was on the road early so that he could attend a required training session. He was exhausted from trying to reach impossible goals. The Marine Corps must bear responsibility for this tragic accident.

Argument for the United States: The government had a clear policy stating that recruiters were not authorized to drive a government car without first requesting permission. Dreyer had not done so. Therefore, he was not authorized to drive the government car at the time of the accident.

Moreover, it is well established that an employee commuting to and from work is not within the scope of employment. If Dreyer had been driving from one recruiting effort to another, that would be a different story. But in this case, he had not yet started work for the Marine Corps, and therefore the government is not liable.

Intentional Torts

A principal is *not* liable for the *intentional* physical torts of an employee unless (1) the employee intended to serve some purpose of the employer, or (2) the employer was negligent in hiring or supervising this employee. Thieves have stolen a number of computers and purses from the desks of Compania employees. When Aubrey sees a stranger walking down the hallway carrying a computer, she tackles him from behind, breaking his nose. It turns out that he was an authorized computer repair person. Compania is liable for Aubrey's actions because she was motivated, at least in part, by a desire to help her employer. But if Aubrey attacks someone in the parking lot because he dented her car, Compania is *not* liable. Aubrey was acting out of personal revenge or frustration, not a desire to help her employer.

In the following case, a priest committed terrible crimes. Was the Church liable for his acts?

DOE v. LIBERATORE

478 F. Supp. 2d 742
United States District Court for the Middle District of Pennsylvania, 2007

Facts: A number of priests wrote to James Timlin, the Bishop of Scranton, warning him that Father Albert Liberatore was engaging in a sexual relationship with one of his adult male students at a seminary. Bishop Timlin transferred Liberatore from the seminary to the Sacred Heart church.

Fourteen year-old John Doe was a member of Liberatore's parish. Liberatore befriended Doe, taking him on outings and giving him expensive gifts. Doe routinely slept in Liberatore's bed. A number of priests told Bishop Timlin that they feared Liberatore was sexually abusing Doe. One witness reported that she had seen Doe put his hand down Liberatore's pants. Eventually, Doe himself told a priest that he was being sexually abused. The priest instructed Doe to forgive Liberatore and not to tell other people because it would ruin Doe's life and the lives of others.

Only after Liberatore pleaded guilty to multiple counts of sexual abuse did the Church dismiss him from the priesthood. Doe filed suit against the Church and Bishop Timlin, alleging that they were liable for the torts committed by Liberatore. The defendants filed a motion to dismiss.

Issues: *Was Liberatore acting within the scope of his employment? Was the Church liable for his criminal acts?*

Excerpts from Judge Caputo's Decision: Under Pennsylvania law, an employer is held liable for the negligent acts of his employee which cause injuries to a third party, provided that such acts were committed during the course of and within the scope of the employment.

The conduct of an employee is considered within the scope of employment if: (1) it is of a kind and nature that the employee is employed to perform; (2) it occurs substantially within the authorized time and space limits; (3) it is actuated, at least in part, by a purpose to serve the employer; and (4) if force is intentionally used by the employee against another, the use of force is not unexpected by the employer.[19]

Here, it is clear that Liberatore's sexual molestation of Plaintiff was not within the scope or nature of his employment as a priest. Indeed, the activity of which Plaintiff now complains is wholly inconsistent with the role of one who is received into the Holy Orders as an ordained priest of the Roman Catholic Church. Moreover, the acts of sexual abuse perpetrated by Liberatore were both outrageous and certainly not actuated by any purpose of serving the Diocese, Sacred Heart, or Bishop Timlin. Therefore, the Court will grant summary judgment in favor of the Diocese, Sacred Heart, and Bishop Timlin as to [this issue].

Plaintiff next claims that the Diocese, Sacred Heart, and Bishop Timlin are liable for negligence in their hiring, supervision, and retention of Liberatore as a Diocesan

---

[19]Note that Pennsylvania requires this fourth element but the Restatement (Third) of Agency does not.

priest. [A]n employer owes a duty to exercise reasonable care in selecting, supervising and controlling employees. In the instant case, the Diocese, Sacred Heart, and Bishop Timlin may be liable if they knew or should have known that Liberatore had a propensity for committing sexual abuse and his employment as Pastor at Sacred Heart might create a situation where his propensity would harm a third person, such as Plaintiff. [A] reasonable jury could

conclude that the Diocese, Sacred Heart, and Bishop Timlin were negligent or reckless in supervising and retaining Liberatore. However, the Court concludes that a reasonable jury could not find that the Diocese, Sacred Heart, and Bishop Timlin were negligent or reckless in hiring Liberatore because there is no evidence suggesting that Liberatore was or would become a child sex predator when he was hired.

Nonphysical Torts

Nonphysical tort
One that harms only reputation, feelings, or wallet

So far, we have seen the rules on *physical* torts. A **nonphysical tort** is one that harms only reputation, feelings, or wallet. **Nonphysical torts (whether intentional or unintentional) are treated like a contract claim: The principal is liable only if the employee acted with express, implied, or apparent authority.**[20] Suppose that Dwayne buys a house insurance policy from Andy, who is an agent of the Balls of Fire Insurance Company. Andy throws away Dwayne's policy and pockets his premiums. When Dwayne's house burns down, Balls of Fire is liable because Andy was acting with apparent authority.

EXAM Strategy

Question: Daisy was the founder of an Internet start-up company. Jay was her driver. One day, after he had dropped her at a board meeting, he went to the car wash. There, he told an attractive woman that he worked for a money management firm. She gave him money to invest. On the way out of the car wash, he was so excited that he hit another customer's expensive car. Who is liable for Jay's misdeeds?

Strategy: In determining a principal's liability, begin by figuring out whether the agent has committed a physical or nonphysical tort. Remember that the principal is liable for physical torts within the scope of employment, but for nonphysical torts, she is liable only if the employee acted with authority.

Result: In this case, Daisy is liable for the damage to the car because that was a physical tort within the scope of employment. But she is not liable for the investment money because Jay did not have authority (express, implied, or apparent) to take those funds.

28-5d Agent's Liability for Torts

The focus of the prior section was on the *principal's* liability for the agent's torts. But it is important to remember that **agents are always liable for their own torts.** Agents who commit torts are personally responsible, whether or not their principal is also liable. Even if the tort was committed to benefit the principal, the agent is still liable. So the sailor who got into a fistfight while rousing a shipmate from bed is liable even though he thought he was acting for the benefit of his principal.

[20]Restatement (Third) of Agency §7.08.

This rule makes obvious sense. If the agent was not liable, he would have little incentive to be careful. Imagine Hank driving his delivery van for Jane. If he was not personally liable for his own torts, he might think, "If I drive fast enough, I can make it through that light even though it just turned red. And if I don't, what the heck, it'll be Jane's problem, not mine." Agents, as a rule, may have fewer assets than their principal, but it is important that their personal assets be at risk in the event of their negligent behavior.

If the agent and principal are *both* liable, which does the injured third party sue? The principal and the agent are *jointly and severally liable*, which means, as we have seen, that the injured third party can sue either one or both, as she chooses. If she recovers from the principal, he can sue the agent.

Chapter Conclusion

When students enroll in a business law course, they fully expect to learn about torts and contracts, corporations, and antitrust. They probably do not think much about agency law; many of them have not even heard the term before. Yet it is an area of the law that affects us all because each of us has been and will continue to be both an agent and a principal many times in our lives.

EXAM REVIEW

1. **CREATING AN AGENCY RELATIONSHIP** A principal and an agent mutually consent that the agent will act on behalf of the principal and be subject to the principal's control, thereby creating a fiduciary relationship.

2. **ELEMENTS NOT REQUIRED** An agency relationship can exist without either a written agreement, a formal agreement, or compensation.

3. **AN AGENT'S DUTIES TO THE PRINCIPAL** An agent owes these duties to the principal: duty of loyalty, duty to obey instructions, duty of care, and duty to provide information.

4. **THE PRINCIPAL'S REMEDIES IN THE EVENT OF A BREACH** The principal has three potential remedies when the agent breaches her duty: recovery of damages the breach has caused, recovery of any profits earned by the agent from the breach, and rescission of any transaction with the agent.

EXAM Strategy

Question: Jonah tells his friend Derek that he would like to go parasailing. Derek suggests that they try an outfit called Wind Beneath Your Wings because he has heard good things about it. Derek offers to arrange everything. He makes a reservation, puts the $600 fee on his credit card, and picks Jonah up to drive him to the Wings location. What a friend! But the day does not turn out as Jonah had hoped. While he is soaring up in the air over the Pacific Ocean, his sail springs a leak, he goes plummeting into the sea and breaks both legs. During his recuperation in the hospital, he learns that Wings is unlicensed. He also sees an ad for Wings offering parasailing for only $350. And Derek is listed in the ad as one of the company's owners. Was Derek Jonah's agent? Has he violated his fiduciary responsibility?

Strategy: There are three issues to consider in answering this question: (1) Was there an agency relationship? This requires consent, control, and a fiduciary relationship. (2) Is anything missing—does it matter if the agent is unpaid or the contract is not in writing? (3) Has the agent fulfilled his duties? (See the "Result" at the end of this section.)

5. **THE PRINCIPAL'S DUTIES TO THE AGENT** The principal has three duties to the agent: to compensate as provided by the agreement, to reimburse legitimate expenses, and to cooperate with the agent.

6. **POWER AND RIGHT TO TERMINATE** Both the agent and the principal have the power to terminate an agency relationship, but they may not have the right. If the termination violates the agency agreement and causes harm to the other party, the wrongful party must pay damages.

7. **AUTOMATIC TERMINATION** An agency relationship automatically terminates if the principal or agent no longer can perform the required duties or if a change in circumstances renders the agency relationship pointless.

8. **A PRINCIPAL'S LIABILITY FOR CONTRACTS** A principal is liable for the contracts of the agent if the agent has express, implied, or apparent authority.

9. **EXPRESS AUTHORITY** The principal grants express authority by words or conduct that, reasonably interpreted, cause the agent to believe that the principal desires her to act on the principal's account.

10. **IMPLIED AUTHORITY** Implied authority includes authority to do acts that are incidental to a transaction, usually accompany it, or are reasonably necessary to accomplish it.

11. **APPARENT AUTHORITY** Apparent authority means that a principal is liable for the acts of an agent who is not, in fact, acting with authority if the principal's conduct causes a third party reasonably to believe that the agent is authorized.

EXAM Strategy

Question: Dr. James Leonard wrote Dr. Edward Jacobson to offer him the position of chief of audiology at Jefferson Medical College in Philadelphia. In the letter, Leonard stated that this appointment would have to be approved by the promotion and appointment committee. Jacobson believed that the appointment committee acted only as a rubber stamp, affirming whatever recommendation Leonard made. Jacobson accepted Leonard's offer and proceeded to sell his house and quit his job in Colorado. You can guess what happened next. Two weeks later, Leonard sent Jacobson another letter, rescinding his offer because of opposition from the appointment committee. Did Leonard have apparent authority?

Strategy: In cases of apparent authority, begin by asking what the principal did to make the third party believe that the agent was authorized. What did the Medical College do? (See the "Result" at the end of this section.)

12. **AN AGENT'S LIABILITY FOR A CONTRACT** An agent is not liable for any contract she makes on behalf of a fully disclosed principal. The principal is liable. In the case of an unidentified or undisclosed principal, both the agent and the principal are liable on the contract.

13. **A PRINCIPAL'S LIABILITY FOR TORTS** An employer is liable for a physical tort committed by an employee acting within the scope of employment and a nonphysical tort of an employee acting with authority.

Question: While drunk, the driver of a subway car plows into the back of the car ahead of him, killing a passenger. It was against the rules for the driver to be drunk. Is the subway authority liable for the negligence of its employee?

Strategy: With a tort case, always determine first if the agents are employees or independent contractors. This worker was an employee. Then ask if the employee was acting within the scope of employment. Yes, he was driving a subway car, which is what he was hired to do. Does it matter than he had violated subway rules? No, his violation of the rules does not eliminate his principal's liability because his actions are of the same general nature as those that are authorized. (See the "Result" at the end of this section.)

14. **INDEPENDENT CONTRACTOR** The principal is liable for the physical torts of an independent contractor only if the principal has been negligent in hiring or supervising him.

15. **INTENTIONAL TORTS** A principal is not liable for the intentional physical torts of an employee unless (1) the employee intended to serve some purpose of the employer; or (2) the employer was negligent in hiring or supervising this employee.

16. **NONPHYSICAL TORTS** A principal is liable for nonphysical torts of an employee (whether intentional or unintentional) only if the employee was acting with express, implied or apparent authority.

17. **AGENT'S LIABILITY FOR TORTS** Agents are always liable for their own torts.

> **4. Result:** There is an agency relationship: Derek had agreed to help Jonah; it was Jonah who set the goal for the relationship (parasailing); the purpose of this relationship was for one person to benefit another. It does not matter if Derek was not paid or the agreement not written. Derek has violated his duty to exercise due care. He should not have taken Jonah to an unlicensed company. He has also violated his duty to provide information: He should have told Jonah the true cost for the lessons and also revealed that he was a principal of the company. And he violated his duty of loyalty when he worked for two principals whose interests were in conflict.
>
> **11. Result:** No. Leonard had told Jacobson that he did not have authority. If Jacobson chose to believe otherwise, that was his problem.
>
> **13. Result:** The subway authority is liable.

MULTIPLE-CHOICE QUESTIONS

1. At Business University, semester enrollment begins at midnight on April 1. Jasper asked his roommate, Alonso, to register him for an important required course as a favor. Alonso agreed to do so but then overslept. As a result, Jasper could not enroll in the required course he needed to graduate and had to stay in school for an additional semester. Is Alonso liable to Jasper?

   (a) No, because an agency agreement is invalid unless the agent receives payment.

   (b) No, because Alonso was not grossly negligent.

   (c) No, because the cost of the extra semester is unreasonably high.

   (d) Yes, because Alonso disobeyed his instructions.

2. Finn learns that, despite his stellar record, he is being paid less than other salespeople at Barry Co., so he decides to start his own company. During his last month on the Barry payroll, he tells all of his clients about his new business. He also tells them that Barry is a great company, but his fees will be lower. After he opens the doors of his new business, most of his former clients move with him. Is Finn liable to Barry?

   (a) No, because he has not been disloyal to Barry—he praised the company.

   (b) No, because Barry was underpaying him.

   (c) No, because his clients have the right to hire whichever company they choose.

   (d) Yes, Finn has violated his duty of loyalty to Barry.

3. Kurt asked his car mechanic, Quinn, for help in buying a used car. Quinn recommends a Ford Focus that she has been taking care of its whole life. Quinn was working for the seller. Which of the following statements is true?

   (a) Quinn must pay Kurt the amount of money she received from the Ford's prior owner.

   (b) After buying the car, Kurt finds out that it needs $1,000 in repairs. He can recover that amount from Quinn, but only if Quinn knew about the needed repairs before Kurt bought the car.

   (c) Kurt cannot recover anything because Quinn had no obligation to reveal her relationship with the car's seller.

   (d) Kurt cannot recover anything because he had not paid Quinn for her help.

4. Figgins is the dean of a college. He appointed Sue as acting dean while he was out of the country and posted an announcement on the college website announcing that she was authorized to act in his place. He also told Sue privately that she did not have the right to make admissions decisions. While Figgins was gone, Sue overruled the admissions committee to admit the child of a wealthy alumnus. Does the child have the right to attend this college?

    (a) No, because Sue was not authorized to admit him.

    (b) No, because Figgins did not ratify Sue's decision.

    (c) Yes, because Figgins was a fully disclosed principal.

    (d) Yes, because Sue had apparent authority.

5. *CPA QUESTION* A principal will not be liable to a third party for a tort committed by an agent:

    (a) unless the principal instructed the agent to commit the tort.

    (b) unless the tort was committed within the scope of the agency relationship.

    (c) if the agency agreement limits the principal's liability for the agent's tort.

    (d) if the tort is also regarded as a criminal act.

6. *CPA QUESTION* Cox engaged Datz as her agent. It was mutually agreed that Datz would not disclose that he was acting as Cox's agent. Instead, he was to deal with prospective customers as if he were a principal acting on his own behalf. This he did and made several contracts for Cox. Assuming Cox, Datz, or the customer seeks to avoid liability on one of the contracts involved, which of the following statements is correct?

    (a) Cox must ratify the Datz contracts to be held liable.

    (b) Datz has no liability once he discloses that Cox was the real principal.

    (c) The third party can avoid liability because he believed he was dealing with Datz as a principal.

    (d) The third party may choose to hold either Datz or Cox liable.

CASE QUESTIONS

1. An elementary school custodian hit a child who wrote graffiti on the wall. Is the school district liable for this intentional tort by its employee?

2. What if the custodian hit one of the schoolchildren for calling him a name? Is the school district liable?

3. A soldier was drinking at a training seminar. Although he was told to leave his car at the seminar, he disobeyed orders and drove to a military club. On the way to the club, he was involved in an accident. Is the military liable for the damage he caused?

4. One afternoon while visiting friends, tennis star Vitas Gerulaitis fell asleep in their pool house. A mechanic had improperly installed the swimming pool heater, which leaked carbon monoxide fumes into the house where he slept, killing him. His mother filed suit against the owners of the estate. On what theory would they be liable?

5. *YOU BE THE JUDGE* **WRITING PROBLEM** Sarah went to an auction at Christie's to bid on a tapestry for her employer, Fine Arts Gallery. The good news is that she purchased a Dufy tapestry for $77,000. The bad news is that it was not the one her employer had told her to buy. In the excitement of the auction, she forgot her instructions. Fine Art refused to pay, and Christie's filed suit. Is Fine Arts liable for the unauthorized act of its agent? **Argument for Christie's:** Christie's cannot possibly ascertain in each case the exact nature of a bidder's authority. Whether or not Sarah had actual authority, she certainly had apparent authority, and Fine Arts is liable. **Argument for Fine Arts:** Sarah was not authorized to purchase the Dufy tapestry, and therefore Christie's must recover from her, not Fine Arts.

DISCUSSION QUESTIONS

1. **ETHICS** Mercedes has just begun work at Photobook.com. What a great place to work! Although the salary is not high, the company has fabulous perks. The dining room provides great food from 7 a.m. to midnight, five days a week. There is also a free laundry and dry-cleaning service. Mercedes's social life has never been better. She invites her friends over for Photobook meals and has their laundry done for free. And because her job requires her to be online all the time, she has plenty of opportunity to stay in touch with her friends by g-chatting, tweeting, and checking Facebook updates. She is, however, shocked that one of her colleagues takes paper home from the office for his children to use at home. Are these employees behaving ethically?

2. Kevin was the manager of a radio station, WABC. A competing station lured him away. In his last month on the job at WABC, he notified two key on-air personalities that if they were to leave the station, he would not hold them to their noncompete agreements. What can WABC do?

3. Jesse worked as a buyer for the Vegetable Co. Rachel offered to sell Jesse 10 tons of tomatoes for the account of Vegetable. Jesse accepted the offer. Later, Jesse discovered that Rachel was an agent for Sylvester Co. Who is liable on this contract?

4. The Pharmaceutical Association holds an annual convention. At the convention, Brittany, who was president of the association, told Luke that Research Corp. had a promising new cancer vaccine. Luke was so excited that he chartered a plane to fly to Research's headquarters. On the way, the plane crashed and Luke was killed. Is the Pharmaceutical Association liable for Luke's death?

5. Betsy has a two-year contract as a producer at Jackson Movie Studios. She produces a remake of the movie *Footloose*. Unfortunately, it bombs, and Jackson is so furious that he fires her on the weekend the movie opens. Does he have the power to do this?

ANSWERS TO SELECTED END OF CHAPTER QUESTIONS

MULTIPLE-CHOICE QUESTIONS

Presented are the answers for the ODD-numbered multiple-choice questions in the end-of-chapter material.

1. B
3. A
5. B

CASE QUESTIONS

Presented are the answers for all of the ODD-numbered case questions in the end-of-chapter material.

1. **Answer:**   Yes, because the custodian thought he was serving the purpose of his employer.
3. **Answer:**   No, he was not acting within the scope of employment.
5. **Answer:**   Sarah had apparent authority and Fine Arts is liable.

Chapter 29

Chatper 29

EMPLOYMENT AND LABOR LAW

"On the killing beds you were apt to be covered with blood, and it would freeze solid; if you leaned against a pillar, you would freeze to that, and if you put your hand upon the blade of your knife, you would run a chance of leaving your skin on it. The men would tie up their feet in newspapers and old sacks, and these would be soaked in blood and frozen, and then soaked again, and so on, until by nighttime a man would be walking on great lumps the size of the feet of an elephant. Now and then, when the bosses were not looking, you would see them plunging their feet and ankles into the steaming hot carcass of the steer.... The cruelest thing of all was that nearly all of them—all of those who used knives—were unable to wear gloves, and their arms would be white with frost and their hands would grow numb, and then of course there would be accidents."[1]

> … you would see them plunging their feet and ankles into the steaming hot carcass of the steer.

[1]From Upton Sinclair, *The Jungle* (New York: Bantam Books, 1981), p. 80, a 1906 novel about the meat-packing industry.

29-1 INTRODUCTION

For most of history, the concept of career planning was unknown. By and large, people were born into their jobs. Whatever their parents had been—landowner, soldier, farmer, servant, merchant, or beggar—they became, too. People not only knew their place, they also understood the rights and obligations inherent in each position. The landowner had the right to receive labor from his tenants, but he also cared for them if they fell ill. Certainly, there were abuses, but at a time when people held religious convictions about their position in life and workers had few expectations that their lives would be better than their parents', the role of law was limited.

The primary English law of employment simply established that, in the absence of a contract, an employee was hired for a year at a time. This rule was designed to prevent injustice in a farming society. If an employee worked through harvest time, the landowner could not fire him in the unproductive winter. Conversely, a worker could not stay the winter and then leave for greener pastures in the spring.

In the eighteenth and nineteenth centuries, the Industrial Revolution profoundly altered the employment relationship. Many workers left the farms and villages for large factories in the city. Bosses no longer knew their workers personally, so they felt little responsibility toward them. The old laws that had suited an agrarian economy with stable relationships did not fit the new employment conditions. Instead of duties and responsibilities, courts emphasized the freedom to contract. Since employees could quit their factory jobs whenever they wanted, it seemed only fair for employers to have the same freedom to fire a worker. That was indeed the rule adopted by the courts: Unless workers had an explicit employment contract, they were employees at will. **An *employee at will* could be fired for a good reason, a bad reason, or no reason at all.** For nearly a century, this was the basic common law rule of employment. A court explained the rule this way:

> Precisely as may the employee cease labor at his whim or pleasure, and, whatever be his reason, good, bad, or indifferent, leave no one a legal right to complain; so, upon the other hand, may the employer discharge, and, whatever be his reason, good, bad, or indifferent, no one has suffered a legal wrong.[2]

However evenhanded this common law rule of employment may have sounded in theory, in practice, it could lead to harsh results. As the opening scenario illustrates, the lives of factory workers were grim. It was not as if they could simply pack up and leave; conditions were no better elsewhere. Courts and legislatures gradually began to recognize that individual workers were generally unable to negotiate fair contracts with powerful employers. Since the beginning of the twentieth century, employment law has changed dramatically. Now, the employment relationship is more strictly regulated by statutes and by the common law.

Note well, though: **In the absence of a specific legal exception, the rule in the United States is *still* that an employee at will can be fired for any reason. But today there are several important exceptions to this rule.** Many of the statutes discussed in this chapter were passed by Congress and therefore apply *nationally*. The common law, however, comes from state courts and only applies *locally*. We will look at a sampling of cases that illustrates national trends, even though the law is not the same in every state.

This chapter covers five topics in employment law: (1) employment security, (2) workplace freedom, (3) workplace safety, (4) financial protection, and (5) collective bargaining. Chapter 30 covers employment discrimination.

---

[2]Union Labor Hospital Association v. Vance Redwood Lumber Company, 158 Cal. 551, 554 (Cal. 1910).

29-2 EMPLOYMENT SECURITY

29-2a Family and Medical Leave Act

The Family and Medical Leave Act (FMLA) guarantees both men and women up to 12 weeks of *unpaid* leave each year for childbirth, adoption, or a serious health condition of their own or in their immediate family. This statute defines an immediate family member as a spouse, child, or parent—but not a sibling, grandchild, or in-law. An employee who takes a leave must be allowed to return to the same or an equivalent job with the same pay and benefits. The FMLA applies only to companies with at least 50 workers and to employees who have been with the company full time for at least a year, which means that only about 60 percent of workers are covered by this statute.

Here are some examples of what counts as a "serious health condition" under this statute:

- Any health issue that requires hospitalization.

- A condition that requires more than one visit to a healthcare provider. The visits may be spread out over as long as a year.

- A condition that requires only one visit to a healthcare provider but that also requires a course of treatment such as physical therapy or prescription medication.

Thus, the FMLA would apply in the case of a heart attack, ongoing kidney dialysis, and an ear infection that required antibiotics. It would generally not cover food poisoning that did not require hospitalization, the common cold, or a sprained ankle.

In many FMLA lawsuits, a worker claims that he or she was fired in retaliation for taking leave, while the employer argues that the termination was for some other reason. The following case illustrates this dynamic.

PETERSON V. EXIDE TECHNOLOGIES

477 Fed. Appx. 474
United States Court of Appeals for the Tenth Circuit, 2012

Facts: Exide Technologies issued repeated warnings to Robert Peterson for driving forklifts too fast and violating other safety rules. After he was injured in a forklift crash, Exide granted him FMLA leave for 10 days while he recovered.

Peterson's manager fired him during the leave period for "flagrant violations of safety rules." Peterson sued, claiming that he was terminated in retaliation for exercising his right to take FMLA leave. The lower court granted summary judgment to Exide, and Peterson appealed.

Issue: *Was Peterson fired in retaliation for claiming FMLA leave?*

Excerpts from Judge Baldock's Decision: The FMLA makes it unlawful for any employer to interfere with, restrain, or deny the exercise of the rights provided by the FMLA, or to discriminate against any individual for opposing any practice prohibited by the FMLA.

[I]f Plaintiff makes out a prima facie retaliation case, the burden shifts to Defendant to demonstrate a legitimate, nonretaliatory reason for its termination decision. If Defendant meets this burden, the burden shifts back to Plaintiff to show that there is a genuine dispute of material fact as to whether Defendant's explanations are pretextual.

Defendant asserts it dismissed Plaintiff for the legitimate reason that he violated company safety policies. According to Defendant's Plant Manager:

Based on my own review of the photographs and the damage they depicted, Plaintiff was driving too fast at the time of the crash and was not operating his forklift in a safe manner. Such conduct on Plaintiff's part was a flagrant violation of company health and safety policy and posed a threat to the safety of Plaintiff and other Exide employees.

The Plant Manager also based his decision to fire Plaintiff on the "history of careless and unsafe conduct" reflected in Plaintiff s personnel file. Defendant has adequately demonstrated a nonretaliatory reason for Plaintiff's termination: his repeated safety violations. Thus, the burden shifts back to Plaintiff to show pretext.

Plaintiff argues Defendant's asserted justification is pretextual because the forklift accident was a "minor incident." Whether the accident was "minor" is questionable. But even if it was, we see nothing that prevents Defendant from firing employees for minor safety violations. Particularly where, as here, the employee has a record of unsafe work performance, even a minor infraction could be the last straw.

Plaintiff has produced no evidence to undermine Defendant's nonretaliatory explanation for the termination. Aside from the fact Plaintiff was on FMLA leave when he was fired, no evidence suggests a causal connection between Plaintiff's firing and his exercise of FMLA rights. Therefore, the district court properly granted summary judgment.

AFFIRMED.

Ethics Although the FMLA offers important protections, the time off it provides is unpaid. Some cities require employers to provide paid family leave, but currently, only 11 percent of private sector employees are eligible for this type of time off. The federal government provides none for its own employees, not even for childbirth. The United States is the only advanced country that does not require employers to provide paid maternity leave. Should Congress modify the FMLA to require some period of paid leave for new mothers? If so, for how long? A few weeks while they recuperate from childbirth? Or a few months to care for the newborn? What about paternity leave, which many countries require? And how about workers who take FMLA leave to deal with a serious illness? Should they be paid?

29-2b Common-Law Protections

Wrongful discharge
An employer may not fire a worker for a reason that violates basic social rights, duties, or responsibilities.

The employment-at-will doctrine was created by the courts. Because that rule sometimes led to grossly unfair results, the courts created a major exception: **wrongful discharge**.

Wrongful Discharge: Violating Public Policy

Olga Monge was a schoolteacher in her native Costa Rica. After moving to New Hampshire, she attended college in the evenings to earn U.S. teaching credentials. At night, she worked at the Beebe Rubber Co. During the day, she cared for her husband and three children. When she applied for a better job at her plant, the foreman offered to promote her if she would be "nice" and go out on a date with him. When she refused, he assigned her to a lower-wage job, took away her overtime, made her clean the washrooms, and generally ridiculed her. Finally, she collapsed at work, and he fired her.[3]

Imagine that you are one of the judges who decided this case. Olga Monge was an employee at will and therefore could be fired for any reason. But how can you let the foreman get away with this despicable behavior? The New Hampshire Supreme Court decided that even an employee at will has some rights:

> We hold that a termination by the employer of a contract of employment at will which is motivated by bad faith or malice or based on retaliation is not in the best interest of the economic system or the public good and constitutes a breach of the employment contract.[4]

---

[3]Monge v. Beebe, 114 N.H. 130 (NH 1974).
[4]Ibid at 133.

The *Monge* case illustrates the concept of **wrongful discharge, which prohibits an employer from firing a worker for certain particularly *bad reasons*.** A bad reason is one that violates public policy. Unfortunately, this public policy rule is easier to name than it is to define because its definition and application vary from state to state. **In essence, the public policy rule prohibits an employer from firing a worker for a reason that violates fundamental social rights, duties, or responsibilities.**

Almost every employee who has ever been fired feels that a horrible injustice has been done. The difficulty, from the courts' perspective, is to distinguish those cases of dismissal that are offensive enough to harm the community at large from those that injure only the employee. The courts have primarily applied the public policy rule when an employee refuses to violate the law, performs a legal duty, exercises a legal right, or supports fundamental societal values.

Refusing to Violate the Law.   Larry Downs went to Duke Hospital for surgery on his cleft palate. When he came out of the operating room, the doctor instructed a nurse, Marie Sides, to give Downs enough anesthetic to immobilize him. Sides refused because she thought the anesthetic was wrong for this patient. The doctor angrily administered the anesthetic himself. Shortly thereafter, Downs stopped breathing. Before the doctors could resuscitate him, he suffered permanent brain damage. When Downs's family sued the hospital, Sides was called to testify. A number of Duke doctors told her that she would be "in trouble" if she testified. She did testify, and after three months of harassment, she was fired. When she sued Duke University, the court held:

> It would be obnoxious to the interests of the state and contrary to public policy and sound morality to allow an employer to discharge any employee, whether the employment be for a designated or unspecified duration, on the ground that the employee declined to commit perjury, an act specifically enjoined by statute. To hold otherwise would be without reason and contrary to the spirit of the law.[5]

As a general rule, employees may not be discharged for refusing to break the law. Courts have protected employees who refused to participate in an illegal price-fixing scheme, falsify pollution control records required by state law, pollute navigable waters in violation of federal law, or assist a supervisor in stealing from customers.[6]

Performing a Legal Duty.   **Courts have consistently held that an employee may not be fired for serving on a jury.** Employers sometimes have difficulty replacing employees who are called up for jury duty and, therefore, prefer that their workers find some excuse for not serving. But jury duty is an important civic obligation that employers are not permitted to undermine.

Exercising a Legal Right.   **As a general rule, an employer may not discharge a worker for exercising a legal right if that right supports public policy.** Dorothy Frampton injured her arm while working at the Central Indiana Gas Co. Her employer (and its insurance company) paid her medical expenses and her salary during the four months she was unable to work. When she discovered that she also qualified for benefits under the state's workers' compensation plan, she filed a claim and received payment. One month later, the company fired her without giving a reason. When she sued, the court held that the gas company had violated public policy. If workers fear that making a claim for workers' comp will get them fired, then no one will file and the whole point of the statute will be undermined.[7]

---

[5]Sides v. Duke University, 74 N.C. App. 331 (N.C. Ct. App. 1985).
[6]Tameny v. Atlantic Richfield Co., 27 Cal. 3d 167 (Cal. 1980); Trombetta v. Detroit, T. & I. R., 81 Mich. App. 489 (Mich. Ct. App. 1978); Sabine Pilot Service, Inc. v. Hauck, 28 Tex. Sup. J. 339 (Tex. 1985); Vermillion v. AAA Pro Moving & Storage, 146 Ariz. 215 (Ariz. Ct. App. 1985).
[7]Frampton v. Central Indiana Gas Co., 260 Ind. 249 (Ind. 1973).

Supporting Societal Values. **Courts are sometimes willing to protect employees who do the right thing, even if they violate the boss's orders.** Kevin Gardner had just parked his armored truck in front of a bank in Spokane, Washington, when he saw a man with a knife chase the manager out of the bank. While running past the truck, the manager looked directly at Gardner and yelled, "Help me, help me." Gardner got out of his truck and locked the door. By then, the suspect had grabbed another woman, put his knife to her throat, and dragged her into the bank. Gardner followed them in, tackled the suspect, and disarmed him. The rescued woman hailed Gardner as a hero, but his employer fired him for violating a "fundamental" company rule that prohibited drivers from leaving their armored trucks unattended. However, the court held for Gardner on the grounds that, although he had no affirmative legal duty to intervene in such a situation, society values and encourages voluntary rescuers when a life is in danger.[8] This issue is, however, one on which the courts are divided. Not all judges would have made the same decision.

In the following case, an employee was fired for exercising her legal right to use medical marijuana. Did her employer violate public policy?

---

[8]Gardner v. Loomis Armored, Inc., 128 Wn.2d 931 (Wash. 1996).

You be the Judge

Facts: The voters of Washington state passed the Medical Use of Marijuana Act (MUMA), which stated that:

ROE V. TELETECH CUSTOMER CARE MGMT. (COLO.) LLC
171 Wn.2d 736
Washington Supreme Court, 2011

Humanitarian compassion necessitates that the decision to authorize the medical use of marijuana by patients with terminal or debilitating illnesses is a personal, individual decision, based upon their physician's professional medical judgment and discretion.

Qualifying patients and medical practitioners shall not be found guilty of a crime under state law for their possession and limited use of marijuana. This act is intended to provide clarification to law enforcement and to all participants in the judicial system.

Any person meeting the requirements appropriate to his or her status under this chapter shall not be penalized in any manner, or denied any right or privilege, for such actions.

Nothing in this chapter requires any accommodation of any on-site medical use of marijuana in any place of employment.

Jane Roe suffered from debilitating migraine headaches that caused chronic pain, nausea, blurred vision, and sensitivity to light. On a medical questionnaire, she described her average pain as an 8 on a scale of 1 to 10 where 10 represented "pain as bad as you can imagine." Because other medications were not effective, she obtained a prescription for medical marijuana. It alleviated her symptoms without side effects and allowed Roe to work and care for her children. She ingested marijuana only in her home.

TeleTech Customer Care Mgmt. offered Roe a position as a customer service representative but required that she first pass a drug test. She told the company about her medical marijuana use. On the day she started work, TeleTech received notice that Roe had failed the drug test. A week later, it fired her.

Roe sued TeleTech for wrongful discharge, alleging that her termination had violated public policy. (She filed suit under a pseudonym because medical marijuana use is illegal under federal law.) The trial court granted TeleTech's motion for summary judgment. The appeals court confirmed. The Washington Supreme Court agreed to hear the case.

You Be the Judge: *Did TeleTech violate public policy when it fired Roe? Was this discharge wrongful?*

Arguments for Roe: Roe is exactly the sort of person this statute is intended to protect. Medical marijuana changed her life—now she can hold a job and care for her family.

But, of course, she cannot hold a job if employers terminate her for using this legal medication. TeleTech is undermining the whole point of the statute and jeopardizing its clear policies. A ruling in favor of TeleTech would inhibit other people from using medication that citizens voted to make available.

Furthermore, the statute specifically states that, "No person ... shall be penalized in any manner, or denied any right or privilege, for such actions." Being fired is a substantial penalty.

No one is asking TeleTech to tolerate drug-impaired workers. Marijuana should be treated like any other medication—it cannot be used if it hurts job performance. But there is no evidence that it did so.

Arguments for TeleTech: Just because medical marijuana is legal in Washington does not mean that it is an important social right. Indeed, employers can fire workers for many *legal* behaviors, such as smoking, or being disagreeable.

The purpose of MUMA is to protect doctors and patients from criminal liability, not to create an unlimited right to use medical marijuana. The statute does not explicitly prevent employers from banning its use. And how can marijuana use be an important public policy when it is still illegal under federal law?

Contract Law

Traditionally, many employers (and employees) thought that only a formal, signed document qualified as an employment contract. Increasingly, however, courts have been willing to enforce an employer's more casual promises, whether written or verbal. Sometimes courts have also been willing to *imply* contract terms in the absence of an *express* agreement.

Truth in Hiring. **Verbal promises made during the hiring process are generally enforceable, even if not approved by the company's top executives.** When the Tanana Valley Medical-Surgical Group, Inc., hired James Eales as a physician's assistant, it promised him that, as long as he did his job, he could stay there until retirement age. Six years later, the company fired him without cause. The Alaska Supreme Court held that the clinic's promise was enforceable.[9]

Employee Handbooks. The employee handbook at Blue Cross & Blue Shield stated that employees could be fired only for just cause and then only after warnings, notice, a hearing, and other procedures. Charles Toussaint was fired summarily five years after he joined the company. Although this decision was ultimately reviewed by the personnel department, company president, and chairman of the board of trustees, Toussaint was not given the benefit of all of the procedures in the handbook. The court held that **an employee handbook creates a contract.**[10]

Some employers have responded to cases like this by including provisions in their handbooks stating that it is not a contract and can be modified at any time. Generally, these provisions have been enforced.[11] However, employers cannot have it both ways. If a handbook states that it is not a contract, then employers cannot enforce provisions favorable to them, such as required arbitration clauses.[12]

---

[9]Eales v. Tanana Valley Medical-Surgical Group, Inc., 663 P.2d 958 (Alaska 1983).
[10]Toussaint v. Blue Cross & Blue Shield, 408 Mich. 579 (Mich. 1980).
[11]See, for example, Federal Express Corp. v. Dutschmann, 36 Tex. Sup. J. 530 (Tex. 1993).
[12]See, for example, Sparks v. Vista Del Mar Child & Family Services, 207 Cal. App. 4th 1511 (Cal. App. 2d Dist. 2012).

Covenant of Good Faith and Fair Dealing.   As we saw in Chapter 20 on practical contracts, about half the states imply a covenant of good faith and fair dealing in contracts. This covenant requires both parties to behave reasonably, making an honest effort to meet both the spirit and letter of the contract.

In the employment context, these cases mostly arise in situations in which an employer fires a worker to avoid paying promised income or benefits. When Forrest Fleming went to work for Parametric Technology Corp., the company promised him valuable stock options if he met his sales goals. He would not be able to *exercise* the options (that is, purchase the stock), however, until several years after they were granted, and then only if he was still employed by the company. During his four years with Parametric, Fleming received options for about 18,000 shares at a price as low as 25 cents each. The shares ultimately traded in the market for as much as $50. Although Fleming exercised some options, the company fired him three months before he became eligible to purchase an additional 1,000 shares. The jury awarded him $1.6 million in damages. Although Parametric had not violated the explicit terms of the option agreement, the jury believed it had violated the covenant of good faith and fair dealing by firing Fleming to prevent him from exercising his remaining options.[13]

Tort Law

Workers have successfully sued their employers under the following tort theories.

Defamation.   **Employers may be liable for defamation when they give false references about an employee.** In his job as a bartender at the Capitol Grille restaurant, Christopher Kane often flirted with customers. After he was fired from his job, his ex-boss claimed that Kane had been "fired from every job he ever had for sexual misconduct." In fact, Kane had never been fired before. He recovered $300,000 in damages for this defamation.

More than half of the states, however, recognize a qualified privilege for employers who give references about former employees. A qualified privilege means that employers are liable only for false statements that they know to be false or that are primarily motivated by ill will. After Becky Chambers left her job at American Trans Air, Inc., she discovered that her former boss was telling anyone who called for a reference that Chambers "does not work good with other people," is a "troublemaker," and "would not be a good person to rehire." Chambers was unable, however, to present compelling evidence that her boss had been primarily motivated by ill will. Neither Trans Air nor the boss was held liable for these statements because they were protected by a qualified privilege.[14]

To reduce the likelihood of defamation suits, many companies refuse to provide references for former employees. They instruct their managers to reveal only a person's salary and dates of employment and not to offer an opinion on job performance.

What about risky workers? Do employers have any obligation to warn about them? **Generally, courts have held that employers do *not* have a legal obligation to disclose information about former employees. But, in the case of violence, courts are divided.** While Jeffrey St. Clair worked as a maintenance man at the St. Joseph Nursing Home, he was disciplined 24 times for actions ranging from extreme violence to drug and alcohol use. When he applied for a job with another firm, St. Joseph refused to give any information other than St. Clair's dates of employment. After he savagely murdered a security guard at his new job, the guard's family sued, but a Michigan court dismissed the case.[15]

A California court, however, reached the opposite decision in a school case. **Officials** from two junior high schools gave Robert Gadams glowing letters of recommendation without mentioning that he had been fired for inappropriate sexual conduct with students. While an assistant principal at a new school, he molested a 13-year-old. The court held that

Qualified privilege
Employers who give references are liable only for false statements that they know to be false or that are primarily motivated by ill will.

---

[13]Fleming v. Parametric Tech. Corp., 1999 U.S. App. LEXIS 14864 (9th Cir. 1999).
[14]Chambers v. American Trans Air, Inc., 577 N.E.2d 612 (Ind. Ct. App. 1991).
[15]Moore v. St. Joseph Nursing Home, Inc., 184 Mich. App. 766 (Mich. Ct. App. 1990).

the writer of a letter of recommendation owes to third parties (in this case, the student) "a duty not to misrepresent the facts in describing the qualifications and character of a former employee, if making these misrepresentations would present a substantial, foreseeable risk of physical injury to the third persons."[16]

To assist employers in giving references, Lehigh economist Robert Thornton has written *The Lexicon of Intentional Ambiguous Recommendations* (LIAR). For a candidate with interpersonal problems, he suggests saying, "I am pleased to say that this person is a former colleague of mine." For a candidate with drug or alcohol problems, there are several possibilities: "She was always high in my opinion," "We remember the hours she spent working with us as happy hours," or "I would say that her real talent is getting wasted at her current job."[17]

Intentional Infliction of Emotional Distress. **Employers who condone cruel treatment of their workers may face liability under the tort of intentional infliction of emotional distress.** Morris Shields, a supervisor at GTE, was continuously in a rage. He would yell and scream profanity at the top of his voice while pounding his fists. He would charge at employees, stopping uncomfortably close to their faces while screaming and yelling. He regularly threatened to fire the clerks he supervised. At least once a day, he would call one of the clerks into his office and have her stand in front of him, sometimes for as long as 30 minutes, while he stared at her, read papers, or talked on the phone. Once, when Shields discovered a spot on the carpet, he made a clerk get on her hands and knees to clean it while he stood over her yelling. The Supreme Court of Texas upheld a jury award of $100,000 for the workers.[18]

29-2c Whistleblowing

No one likes to be accused of wrongdoing even if (or, perhaps, especially if) the accusations are true. This is exactly what **whistleblowers** do: They are employees who disclose illegal behavior on the part of their employer. Not surprisingly, some companies, when faced with such an accusation, prefer to shoot the messenger. Rather than fixing the reported problem, they retaliate against the informer.

Whistleblower
Someone who discloses wrongdoing

For eight years, medical device maker C.R. Bard paid kickbacks to doctors and hospitals to get them to buy its radioactive seeds for treating prostate cancer. To cover the cost of the kickbacks, the company inflated its bills to Medicare. Bard paid the government $48 million to settle this case. Of this amount, $10 million went to Julie Darity, a former Bard employee who was fired after she blew the whistle on the company's wrongdoing.

The law on whistleblowers varies across the country. As a general rule, however, whistleblowers are protected in the following situations:

- **The False Claims Act.** Darity recovered under the federal False Claims Act, a statute that permits lawsuits against anyone who defrauds the government. The recovery is shared between the government and the whistleblower. This act prohibits employers from firing workers who file suit under the statute.

- **The Dodd-Frank Wall Street Reform and Consumer Protection Act.** Anyone who provides information to the government about violations of securities or commodities laws is entitled to a payout of from 10 to 30 percent of whatever

---

[16]Randi W. v. Muroc Joint Unified School District, 14 Cal. 4th 1066 (1997), modified, 14 Cal. 4th 1282c, 97 Cal. Daily Op. Service 1439.

[17]Robert J.Thornton, *Lexicon of Intentionally Ambiguous Recommendations*, Barnes and Noble Books, 2005.

[18]Gte Southwest v. Bruce, 42 Tex. Sup. J. 907 (Tex. 1999).

award the government receives, provided that the award tops $1 million. If a company retaliates against tipsters, they are entitled to reinstatement, double back pay, and attorney's fees.

This whistleblowing provision is intended to encourage tips to the government, but companies fear it may also discourage employees from reporting wrongdoing to corporate compliance offices—why report a problem to your own company for free when you could get paid a lot of money to report it to the government?

- **Sarbanes-Oxley Act of 2002.** This act protects employees of publicly traded companies who provide evidence of fraud to investigators (whether in or outside the company). A successful plaintiff is entitled to reinstatement, back pay, and attorney's fees.

- **Constitutional protection for government employees.** Employees of federal, state, and local governments have a right to free speech under the United States Constitution. Therefore, the government cannot retaliate against public employees who blow the whistle if the employee is speaking out on a matter of *public concern*. A New York City social worker complained on TV that the city child welfare agency was not adequately protecting children from horrible abuse. When the city suspended her, she sued. The court ruled that the government has the right to prohibit some employee speech, but if the employee speaks on matters of public concern, the government bears the burden of justifying any retaliation. In this case, the court held for the social worker.[19]

- **Statutory protection for federal employees.** The Civil Service Reform Act and the Whistleblower Protection Act prevent retaliation against federal employees who report wrongdoing. They also permit the award of back pay and attorney's fees to the whistleblower. This statute was used to prevent the National Park Service from disciplining two managers who wrote a report expressing concern over development in Yellowstone National Park.

- **State laws.** The good news is that all 50 states have laws that protect whistleblowers from retaliation by their employers. The bad news is that the scope of this protection varies greatly from state to state. Most courts, however, prohibit the discharge of employees who report illegal activity. A Connecticut court held a company liable when it fired a quality control director who reported to his boss that some products had failed quality tests.[20]

EXAM Strategy

Question: When Shiloh interviewed for a sales job at a medical supply company, the interviewer promised that she would only have to sell medical devices, not medications. Once she began work (as an employee at will), Shiloh discovered that the sales force was organized around regions, not products, so she had to sell both devices and drugs. When she complained to her boss over lunch in the employee lunchroom, he said in a loud voice, "You're a big girl now—it's time you learned that you don't always get what you want." That afternoon, she was fired. Does she have a valid claim against the company?

---

[19]Harman v. City of New York, 140 F.3d 111 (2d Cir. 1998).
[20]Smith v. Calgon Carbon Corp., 917 F.2d 1338 (3rd Cir. 1990).

Strategy: Shiloh is an employee at will. Does she have any protection under the law? Shiloh has had two key interactions with the company—being hired and being fired. The employer's promises made during the hiring process are enforceable. Here, the company is liable because the interviewer clearly made a promise that the company did not keep. What about the way in which Shiloh was fired? Is it intentional infliction of emotional distress? Was this treatment cruel? Probably not cruel enough to constitute intentional infliction of emotional distress.

Result: The company is liable to Shiloh for making false promises to her during the hiring process, but not for the manner in which she was fired.

29-3 WORKPLACE FREEDOM

The line between home and workplace often blurs. Employees respond to customer emails 24/7, while their behavior at home (say, drug use) can have an impact on their employer. This section deals with worker freedom: The right to personal lifestyle choices and to the public expression of opinions about the workplace.

29-3a Off-Duty Activities

In the absence of a specific law to the contrary, employers *do* have the right to fire workers for off-duty conduct. Employees have been fired or disciplined for such extracurricular activities as taking part in dangerous sports (such as skydiving), dating coworkers, smoking, or even having high cholesterol.

> **Employers *do* have the right to fire workers for off-duty conduct.**

Lifestyle Laws

A few states, such as California, have passed lifestyle laws that protect the right of employees to engage in *any* lawful activity or use any lawful product when off duty. Thus, if California residents skydive while smoking a cigarette, they may lose their lives, but not their jobs. Some laws also protect *particular* off-duty conduct.

Smoking

Smokers tend to take more sick days and have higher healthcare expenses than other employees. The federal government estimates that it costs an extra $3,400 a year to employ a worker who smokes. As a result, several thousand employers, including Union Pacific and Alaska Airlines, simply refuse to hire those who light up. **In roughly 60 percent of the states, however, employers cannot prohibit workers from smoking.**

Some workers have also claimed that nicotine addiction is a disability under the Americans with Disabilities Act (ADA; see Chapter 30 for more information about this statute), but so far, courts have been skeptical that Congress intended ADA coverage for the roughly 60 million Americans who smoke.[21] Several amendments to the ADA passed in 2008 could provide more protection for smokers, but the courts have not yet decided such a case.

---

[21]See Brashear v. Simms, 138 F.Supp.2d 693 (D.Md. 2001).

Alcohol and Drug Use

Private Employers.   Under *federal* law, *private* **employers are permitted to test job applicants and workers for alcohol and *illegal* drugs.** They may sanction workers who fail the test, even if the drug or alcohol use was off duty. *State* laws on drug testing vary widely.

Although employers were traditionally most concerned about illegal drugs, they now also worry about *legal* use of prescription drugs such as Xanax and oxycodone because these medications may cause impairment. In one study, workers drug-tested after accidents in the workplace were four times more likely to have opiates in their system than job applicants.

However, **the Equal Employment Opportunity Commission (EEOC), the federal agency charged with enforcing federal employment laws, prohibits testing for prescription drugs unless a worker seems impaired.** The EEOC filed suit against a company that randomly tested for legal use of prescription drugs, and a jury awarded substantial damages to the employees.[22]

Government Employers.   Governments are sometimes allowed to conduct drug and alcohol tests of their employees. Public safety workers, such as police and firefighters, can be randomly tested for illegal drugs, and they may also be required to report legal drug use that could compromise their ability to perform their jobs. If their drug use (legal or not) is a threat to public safety, they may be suspended or fired from their jobs. Other government employees, whose work does not involve public safety, can be tested only if they show signs of impairment.

29-3b Free Speech in the Workplace

The National Labor Relations Act (NLRA) is well known as pioneer legislation that protects employees' right to unionize. However, many people do not realize that **the NRLA protects *all employees* (1) who engage in collective activity (2) in connection with work conditions and (3) who are not supervisors.** Thus, the National Labor Relations Board (NLRB), which enforces this statute, has long held that even non-unionized workers cannot be fired for complaining about their jobs. When a hair salon fired two (non-unionized) hairdressers for violating the salon's "negativity policy" by complaining about work conditions, the NLRB ruled that this action was a violation of the statute.[23]

Recently, however, the NLRB has applied this principle online, ruling that company social media policies violate the NLRA if they unreasonably constrain employee speech about work conditions. In short, **workers (who are not supervisors) have the right to discuss work conditions, whether that discussion takes place in the lunchroom or in a chat room and whether or not the employee is engaged in union activities.** The following case illustrates the NLRB's views on this issue.

HISPANICS UNITED OF BUFFALO, INC. AND CARLOS ORTIZ BEFORE THE NLRB

359 NLRB No. 37
National Labor Relations Board, 2012

Facts: Lydia Cruz-Moore and Marianna Cole-Rivera worked at Hispanics United of Buffalo (the Agency), an organization that assisted victims of domestic violence. At work and at home, by phone and by text, Cruz-Moore routinely complained to Cole-Riviera that other employees provided poor service to their clients. At home one Saturday night, Cruz-Moore texted Cole-Riviera that she intended to tell the executive director, Lourdes Iglesias,

---

[22]Bates v. Dura Auto Sys Inc, 2011 U.S. Dist. LEXIS 97469 (M.D. Tenn 2011)
[23]Salon/Spa at Boro, 2010 NLRB LEXIS 533 (N.L.R.B. Dec. 30, 2010).

that these other employees had been performing poorly. Cole-Rivera then posted the following message on her Facebook page:

> Lydia Cruz, a coworker feels that we don't help our clients enough at [the Agency]. I about had it! My fellow coworkers how do u feel?

Four off-duty employees posted comments saying that they were upset with Cruz-Moore. She responded with a comment demanding that Cole-Rivera "stop with ur lies about me."

Cruz-Moore then complained to Iglesias that she felt defamed by the Facebook postings. After looking at them, Iglesias fired Cole-Rivera and the four coworkers on the grounds that their remarks violated the Agency's zero tolerance policy on bullying and harassment.

Issue: *Were these Facebook postings protected speech under the NLRA?*

Excerpts from the Decision of the NLRB:[24] [Two issues are] in dispute here: whether the employees' Facebook comments constituted concerted activity and, if so, whether that activity was protected by the Act.

The Board defined concerted activity as that which is engaged in with or on the authority of other employees, and not solely by and on behalf of the employee himself. Applying these principles, there should be no question that the activity engaged in by the five employees was concerted. As set forth in her initial Facebook post, Cole-Rivera alerted fellow employees of another employee's complaint that they "don't help our clients enough," stated that she "about had it" with the complaints, and solicited her coworkers' views about this criticism. By responding to this solicitation with comments of protest, Cole-Rivera's four coworkers made common cause with her, and, together, their actions were concerted because they were undertaken with other employees.

As to the [other] element of the violation, whether the employees' concerted activity was protected, we find that the Facebook comments here fall well within the Act's protection. The Board has long held that [the NLRA] protects employee discussions about their job performance, and the Facebook comments plainly centered on that subject. As discussed, the employees were directly responding to allegations they were providing substandard service to the Agency's clients. Given the negative impact such criticisms could have on their employment, the five employees were clearly engaged in protected activity in mutual aid of each other's defense to those criticisms.

According to the Agency, it was privileged to discharge the five employees because their comments constituted unprotected harassment and bullying of Cruz-Moore, in violation of its "zero tolerance" policy. [We] reject this argument. First, the Facebook comments cannot reasonably be construed as a form of harassment or bullying within the meaning of the Agency's policy. Second, legitimate managerial concerns to prevent harassment do not justify policies that discourage the free exercise of [NLRA] rights by subjecting employees to discipline on the basis of the subjective reactions of others to their protected activity. Here, the Agency applied its harassment policy to the discharged employees based solely on Cruz-Moore's subjective claim that she felt offended by the Facebook comments.

Note, however, that to be protected, the employee speech must be "concerted." The *Arizona Daily Star* fired a reporter for tweeting a series of comments, including:

> You stay homicidal, Tucson. See Star Net for the bloody deets.
> What?!?!? No overnight homicide? WTF? You're slacking Tucson.

The NLRB ruled that this tweets were not protected activity because the reporter had been acting alone, not in concert with other workers.[25]

29-3c Polygraph Tests

A polygraph exam is a type of lie detector test. **Under the Employee Polygraph Protection Act of 1988, employers may not require, or even *suggest*, that an employee or job candidate submit to a polygraph test** *except in the following cases*:

- an employee who is part of an "ongoing investigation" into crimes that have already occurred,

---

[24]For ease of reading, we have replaced "Respondent" with "Agency."
[25]NLRB Case No. 28-CA-23267.

- an applicant applying for a government job, or
- an applicant for a job in public transport, security services, banking, or at pharmaceutical firms that deal with controlled substances.

If an employer requires a polygraph test, it must give advance written notice of when the test will be given and advise workers that they are entitled to legal counsel. A private employer may not fire or discriminate against an employee who fails a polygraph exam unless it also finds supporting evidence that the worker has done something wrong.

29-3d Guns

Employers have the right to prohibit guns in the workplace but, in almost half the states, Bring Your Gun to Work Laws prevent companies from banning firearms in the parking lot. Advocates for gun rights argue that workers have the right to protect themselves during their commutes and that, ultimately, such laws improve employee safety. However, a study found that a workplace that permits guns is five times as likely to suffer a homicide as one in which they are banned.[26]

Some executives worry about the dangers of disciplining workers in states with Bring Your Gun to Work laws. An employment lawyer reported that he had attended termination meetings in which executives had sought protection from bulletproof vests or armed guards. In one case, a company held a termination meeting in an airport conference room so that participants would have to pass through security first.[27]

EXAM Strategy

Question: To ensure that its employees did not use illegal drugs in or outside the workplace, Marvel Grocery Store required all employees to take a polygraph exam. Moreover, managers began to check employees' Facebook pages for reference to drug use. Jagger was fired for refusing to take the polygraph test. Pete was dismissed after revealing on his Facebook page that he was using marijuana (illegally). Has the company acted in accordance with the law?

Strategy: First: As employees at will, are Jagger and Pete protected by a statute? The Employee Polygraph Protection Act permits employers to require a polygraph test as part of ongoing investigations into crimes that have occurred.

Second: What about Pete's marijuana use? No statutes protect a worker for *illegal* off-duty conduct. Can the company punish Pete for what he wrote on his Facebook page? Not if it relates to work conditions and involves concerted activity.

Result: Here, Marvel has no reason to believe that a crime occurred, so it cannot require a polygraph test. Pete's Facebook postings have nothing to do with work conditions and illegal activity is not protected. So the company is liable to Jagger for requiring him to take the polygraph exam, but not to Pete for firing him over illegal drug use.

---

[26]Dana Loomis, Stephen W. Marshall, and Myduc L. Ta, "Employer Policies Toward Guns and the Risk of Homicides in the Workplace," *Am J Public Health*. 2005 May; 95(5): 830–832.
[27]Sara Murray, "Guns in the Parking Lot: A Delicate Workplace Issue," *The Wall Street Journal*, Oct. 15, 2013.

29-4 WORKPLACE SAFETY

29-4a OSHA

In 1970, Congress passed the Occupational Safety and Health Act (OSHA) to ensure safe working conditions. **Under OSHA:**

- Employers must comply with specific health and safety standards. For example, healthcare personnel who work with blood are not permitted to eat or drink in areas where the blood is kept. Protective clothing—gloves, gowns, and laboratory coats—must be impermeable to blood.

- Employers are under a general obligation to keep their workplace "free from recognized hazards that are causing or are likely to cause death or serious physical harm" to employees.

- Employers must keep records of all workplace injuries and accidents.

- The Occupational Safety and Health Administration (which is also known as OSHA) may inspect workplaces to ensure that they are safe. OSHA may assess fines for violations and order employers to correct unsafe conditions.

29-4b **Workplace Bullying**

Rich was on the company's leadership council, where one of his responsibilities was to help new employees. But he seemed to misinterpret his responsibilities—instead of helping, he singled out Jonathan, to whom he sent texts and voicemails that were racist, mocking, and threatening. Rich also publicly called Jonathan "the Big Weirdo" and told others that he was the easiest one to scare. After a series of incidents in which other employees joined with Rich to publicly embarrass him, Jonathan quit.

Studies estimate that as many as 60 percent of employees are bullied at some point in their careers. A bullying atmosphere is bad for two reasons. One, it impairs worker productivity. In the example above, Rich Incognito and Jonathan Martin were offensive linemen on the Miami Dolphins football team. Players had a practice of hazing rookies, but Incognito took the harassment to a new level with Martin. If a 300-pound lineman could be so troubled by bullying, imagine how more vulnerable employees might feel.

Two, bullying may also subject employers to liability. Half of the states have introduced anti-bullying legislation, although none has passed it. And the Supreme Court of Indiana ruled that "workplace bullying" is an entirely appropriate term to be used in front of a jury and could be considered a form of intentional infliction of emotional distress.[28]

29-5 FINANCIAL PROTECTION

Congress and the states have enacted laws designed to provide employees with a measure of financial security. All of the laws in this section were created by statute, not by the courts.

---

[28]Raess v. Doescher, 883 N.E.2d 790 (Ind. 2008).

29-5a Fair Labor Standards Act: Minimum Wage, Overtime, and Child Labor

Passed in 1938, the Fair Labor Standards Act (FLSA) regulates wages and limits child labor nationally. It provides that hourly workers must be paid a minimum wage of $7.25 per hour, plus time and a half for any hours over 40 in one week. These wage provisions do not apply to salaried workers, such as managerial, administrative, or professional staff. More than half the states and even some cities set a higher minimum wage, so it is important to check state guidelines as well.

One significant issue that employers face under the FLSA is: "What counts as work, and how do you keep track of it?" What if a worker answers email during lunch or takes a phone call on the train ride home? Although these activities count as work, how can the employer keep track of them? Carla Bird, an assistant at Oprah Winfrey's production company, submitted timesheets showing 800 hours of overtime in 17 weeks. She said she had worked 12 or 13 hours a day, seven days a week, for four months. The company paid her $32,000 in overtime.[29] If employees work all the time, or even if they are just on call, they are entitled to be paid for those hours.

Another issue facing employers: Are unpaid internships covered by the FLSA? Eric Glatt and Alexander Footman were unpaid interns at Fox Searchlight Pictures Inc., where they worked on the movie *Black Swan*. A court ruled that they were actually employees who were entitled to wages under the FLSA. **To be unpaid, an internship must:**

- provide training similar to that given in school,

- be for the benefit of the intern,

- not displace regular employees, and

- not provide any immediate advantage to the employer.[30]

The FLSA also prohibits "oppressive child labor," which means that children under 14 may work only in agriculture, entertainment, a family business, babysitting, or newspaper delivery. Fourteen- and fifteen-year-olds are permitted to work *limited* hours after school in nonhazardous jobs, such as retail. Sixteen- and seventeen-year-olds may work *unlimited* hours in nonhazardous jobs.

29-5b Workers' Compensation

Workers' compensation statutes ensure that employees receive payment for injuries incurred at work. Before workers' comp, injured employees could recover damages only if they sued their employer. It was the brave worker who was willing to risk a suit against his boss. Lawsuits not only poisoned the atmosphere at work, but employers frequently won anyway by claiming that (1) the injured worker was contributorily negligent, (2) a fellow employee had caused the accident, or (3) the injured worker had assumed the risk of injury. As a result, seriously injured workers (or their families) often had no recourse against the employer.

Workers' comp statutes provide a fixed, certain recovery to the injured employee, no matter who was at fault for the accident. In return, employees are not permitted to sue their employers for negligence. The amounts allowed (for medical expenses and lost wages) under workers' comp statutes are often less than a worker might recover in court, but the injured employee trades the certainty of some recovery for the higher risk of rolling the dice at trial. Payments are approved by an administrative board that conducts an informal hearing into each claim.

---

[29]Lisa Belkin, "O.T. Isn't as Simple as Telling Time," *The New York Times*, September 20, 2007.
[30]Glatt v. Fox Searchlight Pictures Inc., 293 F.R.D. 516 (S.D.N.Y. 2013).

29-5c Health Insurance

Under the Patient Protection and Affordable Care Act, employers with 50 or more full-time employees must pay a penalty if they do not provide basic health insurance. In addition, company insurance policies must cover employees' children up to the age of 26.

Losing your job does not mean that you must also give up your health insurance—at least not immediately. Under the Consolidated Omnibus Budget Reconciliation Act (COBRA), **former employees must be allowed to continue their health coverage for 18 months after leaving their job.** But they must pay the cost themselves, plus as much as an additional 2 percent to cover administrative expenses. COBRA applies to any company with 20 or more workers.

29-5d Social Security

The federal social security system began in 1935, during the depths of the Great Depression, to provide a basic safety net for the elderly, ill, and unemployed. **The Social Security system pays benefits to workers who are retired, disabled, or temporarily unemployed, and to the spouses and children of disabled or deceased workers.** The social security program is financed through a tax on wages that is paid by employers, employees, and the self-employed.

Although the social security system has done much to reduce poverty among the elderly, many worry that it cannot survive in its current form. The system was designed to be "pay as you go"; that is, when workers pay taxes, the proceeds do not go into a savings account for their retirement, but instead are used to pay benefits to current retirees. In 1940, there were 40 workers for each retiree; currently, there are 3.3. As a result, the system now pays out more in benefits each year than it receives in tax revenues. To ensure long-term viability, some aspects of social security will have to change.

The Federal Unemployment Tax Act (FUTA) is the part of the social security system that provides support to the unemployed. FUTA establishes some national standards, but states are free to set their own benefit levels and payment schedules. **A worker who quits voluntarily or is fired for just cause is ineligible for unemployment benefits.** While receiving payments, she must make a good-faith effort to look for other employment.

Before social security, breadlines were often the only safety net available to the unemployed.

29-5e Pension Benefits

In 1974, Congress passed the Employee Retirement Income Security Act (ERISA) to protect workers covered by private pension plans. Under ERISA, employers are not required to establish pension plans, but if they do, they must follow these federal rules. The law was aimed, in particular, at protecting benefits of retired workers if their companies subsequently go bankrupt. The statute also prohibits risky investments by pension plans. In addition, the statute sets rules on the vesting of benefits. (An employer cannot cancel *vested* benefits; *nonvested* benefits are forfeited when the employee leaves.) Before ERISA, retirement benefits at some companies did not vest until the employee retired—if he quit or was fired before retirement, even after years of service, he lost his pension. Under current law, employee benefits normally must vest within five years of employment.

29-6 LABOR UNIONS

The opening scenario of this chapter provides a graphic example of how painful (literally) working conditions could be in the past. In a desire for better pay and improved working conditions, workers in the nineteenth and early twentieth centuries sought strength through collective bargaining. They began to join together in unions.

But American courts treated any coordinated effort by workers as a criminal conspiracy. They convicted workers merely for the *act* of joining together, even if no strike took place. A company could usually obtain an immediate injunction merely by alleging that a strike *might* cause harm. Courts were so quick to issue injunctions that most companies became immune to union efforts.

But with the economic collapse of 1929 and the vast suffering of the Great Depression, public sympathy shifted to the workers. Congress responded with two landmark statutes.

29-6a Key Pro-Union Statutes

In 1932, Congress passed **the Norris-LaGuardia Act, which prohibited federal court injunctions in nonviolent labor disputes.** No longer could management stop a strike merely by saying the word *strike*. By taking away the injunction remedy, Congress was declaring that workers should be permitted to organize unions and to use their collective power to achieve legitimate economic ends. The statute led to explosive growth in union membership.

In 1935, Congress passed the Wagner Act, generally known as the National Labor Relations Act (NLRA). This is the most important of all labor laws. **The NLRA ensures the right of workers to form unions and encourages management and unions to bargain collectively and productively.** With the enactment of the NLRA, Congress put an end to any notion that unions were inherently illegal.

Section 7 of the NLRA is the cornerstone of union power. **It guarantees employees the right to organize and join unions, bargain collectively through representatives of their own choosing, and engage in other concerted activities.** Note, however, that for the purposes of this statute, **"supervisors" are not employees and do not have the right to form a union.** A **supervisor** is anyone with the authority to make independent decisions on hiring, firing, disciplining, or promoting other workers.[31] For example, the Supreme Court ruled that university faculty were supervisors and, therefore, were not covered by the NLRA.[32]

Section 8 prohibits employers from engaging in the following unfair labor practices (ULPs):

- Interfering with union organizing efforts
- Dominating or interfering with any union
- Discriminating against a union member
- Refusing to bargain collectively with a union

Later, Section 8 was amended to prohibit unions from engaging in these ULPs:

- Interfering with employees who are exercising their labor rights
- Causing an employer to discriminate against workers as a means to strengthen the union
- Charging excessive dues

When a union tried to organize Starbucks workers, the company prohibited employees from discussing the union or their working conditions and posting union material on employee bulletin boards. It also punished pro-union employees with unfavorable work assignments. All of these actions were ULPs.[33]

The NLRA also established the National Labor Relations Board (NLRB) to administer and interpret the statute and to adjudicate labor cases. For example, when a union charges that an employer has committed a ULP—say, by refusing to bargain—the claim goes first to the NLRB.

Supervisor

Anyone with the authority to make independent decisions on hiring, firing, disciplining, or promoting other workers

---

[31]29 U.S.C. § 152(11).

[32]NLRB v. Yeshiva Univ., 444 U.S. 672 (U.S. 1980).

[33]NLRB v. Starbucks Corp., 679 F.3d 70 (2d Cir. 2012).

29-6b Labor Unions Today

Organized labor is in flux in the United States. In the 1950s, about 25 percent of workers belonged to a union. Today, only about 11 percent do. That is the lowest level since 1916. Even more remarkable, membership in private sector unions has declined from 35 percent in the 1950s to 6.6 percent now.

There are four major reasons for this decline. One: More states have passed right-to-work laws that permit employees in unionized workplaces to opt out of joining the union or paying dues. Two: Some large employers (such as Boeing) have relocated to states with little union presence. Three: Employment is increasing in industries, such as services, that have not traditionally been unionized. Four: Public employees (such as teachers and police officers) are much more likely to be unionized, but they are generally not covered by the NLRA. Instead, state labor laws apply, which tend to provide less protection than federal statutes.

This decline in strength reduces union bargaining power. Thus, the auto unions agreed to a two-tiered structure that pays new workers little more than half the wages of long-term employees. All of these factors have contributed to stagnation in pay for the bottom half of wage earners, even as their productivity has increased dramatically.

29-7 ORGANIZING A UNION

29-7a Exclusivity

Under §9 of the NLRA, a validly recognized union is the *exclusive* representative of the employees. This means that the union represents all of the designated employees, regardless of whether a particular worker *wants* to be included. The company may not bargain directly with any employee in the group, nor with any other organization representing the designated employees.

However, a union may not exercise power however it likes: Along with a union's exclusive bargaining power goes a duty of fair representation, which requires that a union treat all members fairly, impartially, and in good faith. A union may not favor some members over others, nor may a union discriminate against a member based on characteristics such as race or gender.

29-7b Organizing: Stages

A union organizing effort generally involves the following pattern:

Campaign

Union organizers talk—or attempt to talk—with employees and persuade them to form a union. The organizers may be employees of the company, who simply chat with fellow workers about unsatisfactory conditions; or a union may send nonemployees of the company to hand out union leaflets to workers as they arrive and depart from work.

Authorization Cards

Union organizers ask workers to sign authorization cards, which state that the particular worker requests the specified union to act as her sole bargaining representative.

If a union obtains authorization cards from a sizable percentage of workers, it seeks recognition as the exclusive representative for the bargaining unit. The union may ask the employer to recognize it as the bargaining representative, but most of the time, employers refuse to recognize the union voluntarily.

Petition

Assuming that the employer does not voluntarily recognize a union, the union generally petitions the NLRB for an election. It must submit to the NLRB regional office authorization cards signed by at least 30 percent of the workers. The regional office verifies whether there are enough valid cards to warrant an election and looks closely at the proposed bargaining unit to make sure that it is appropriate. If the regional office determines that the union has identified an appropriate bargaining unit and has enough valid cards, it orders an election.

Election

The NLRB closely supervises the election to ensure fairness. All members of the proposed bargaining unit vote on whether they want the union to represent them. If more than 50 percent of the workers vote for the union, the NLRB designates that union as the exclusive representative of all members of the bargaining unit. When unions hold representation elections, they win about 60 percent of the time.

29-7c Organizing: Actions

What Workers May Do

The NLRA guarantees employees the right (1) to talk among themselves about working conditions and forming a union, (2) to hand out literature, and ultimately, (3) to join a union.[34] Workers have the right to urge other employees to sign authorization cards and to push their cause vigorously. When employees hand out leaflets, the employer generally may not limit the content, as long as it is somewhat related to union activity.

There are, of course, limits to what union organizers may do. An employer may restrict organizing discussions if they interfere with business. A worker on a moving assembly line has no right to walk away from his task to talk with other employees about organizing a union; these discussions must be left until lunch or some other break time.[35] Likewise, management may prohibit union discussions in the presence of customers.

What Employers May Do

The employer may vigorously present anti-union views to its employees but may not use either threats or rewards to defeat a union drive.[36] A company may not fire a worker who favors a union; nor may it suddenly grant a significant pay raise in the midst of a union campaign.

EXAM Strategy

Question: The Teamsters Union is attempting to organize the drivers at We Haul trucking company. Workers who favor a union have been using the lunchroom to hand out petitions and urge other drivers to sign authorization cards. The company posts a notice in the lunchroom: "Many employees do not want unions discussed in the lunchroom. Out of respect for them, we are prohibiting further union efforts in this lunchroom." Is this sign legal?

Strategy: The NLRA guarantees employees the right to talk among themselves about forming a union and to hand out literature. Management has the right to present anti-union views.

---

[34]NLRA §7.
[35]NLRB v. Babcock & Wilcox Co, 351 U.S. 105 (S. Ct. 1956).
[36]NLRB v. Gissel Packing Co, 395 U.S. 575 (S. Ct. 1969).

Result: We Haul has violated the NLRA. The company has the right to urge employees not to join the union. However, it is not entitled to block the union from its organizing campaign. Even assuming the company is correct that some employees do not want unions discussed, it has no right to prohibit such advocacy.

29-8 COLLECTIVE BARGAINING

Once a union is formed, a company must then bargain with it toward the goal of creating a new contract, which is called a **collective bargaining agreement (CBA)**.

The NLRA *permits* the parties to bargain almost any subject they wish, but it only *requires* them to bargain certain issues. **Under the statute, mandatory subjects include wages, hours, and other terms and conditions of employment.** In addition, courts have interpreted the statute to include: benefits, order of layoffs and recalls, production quotas, work rules (such as safety practices), retirement benefits, and onsite food service and prices. An employer may not *unilaterally* make changes in conditions of employment without first bargaining with the union.

The union and the employer are *not* obligated to reach an agreement, but they are required to bargain in good faith. In other words, the two sides must meet with open minds and make a reasonable effort to reach a contract. In the following Landmark Case, a company violated this rule.

Collective bargaining agreement (CBA)
A contract between a union and management

Landmark Case

NLRB v. TRUITT MANUFACTURING CO.
351 U.S. 149
United States Supreme Court, 1956

Facts: A union representing workers at Truitt Manufacturing Company requested a raise of 10 cents per hour for all members. The company countered with an offer of 2.5 cents, arguing that a larger increase would bankrupt the company. The union demanded to examine Truitt's books, and when the company refused, the union complained to the NLRB.

The NLRB determined that the company had committed a ULP by failing to bargain in good faith and ordered it to allow union representatives to examine its finances. A court of appeals found no ULP and refused to enforce the Board's order. The Supreme Court granted *certiorari*.

Issue: *Did the company refuse to bargain in good faith?*

Excerpts from Justice Black's Decision: While Congress did not compel agreement between employers and bargaining representatives, it did require collective bargaining in the hope that agreements would result. [T]he Act admonishes both employers and employees to exert every reasonable effort to make and maintain agreements.

In their effort to reach an agreement here, both the union and the company treated the company's ability to pay increased wages as highly relevant. Claims for increased wages have sometimes been abandoned because of an employer's unsatisfactory business condition; employees have even voted to accept wage decreases because of such conditions.

Good-faith bargaining necessarily requires that claims made by either bargainer should be honest claims. This is true about an asserted inability to pay an increase in wages. If such an argument is important enough to present in the give and take of bargaining, it is important enough to require some sort of proof of its accuracy.

The Board concluded that under the facts and circumstances of this case, the respondent was guilty of an unfair labor practice in failing to bargain in good faith. We see no reason to disturb the findings of the Board.

Reversed.

29-9 CONCERTED ACTION

Concerted action
Tactics taken by union members to gain bargaining advantage

Concerted action refers to any tactics that union members take in unison to gain some bargaining advantage. It is this power that gives a union strength. **The NLRA guarantees the right of employees to engage in concerted action for mutual aid or protection.**[37] The most common forms of concerted action are strikes and picketing.

29-9a Strikes

The NLRA guarantees employees the right to strike, but with some limitations.[38] A union has a guaranteed right to call a strike if the parties are unable to reach a CBA. A union may also call a strike to protest a ULP, or to preserve work that the employer is considering sending elsewhere. Note that the right to strike can be waived. Management will generally insist that the CBA include a **no-strike clause**, which prohibits the union from striking while the CBA is in force. A strike is illegal in several other situations as well; here, we mention the most important.

No-strike clause
A clause in a CBA that prohibits the union from striking while the CBA is in force

Cooling-Off Period

Before striking to terminate or modify a CBA, a union must give management 60 days' notice. This cooling-off period is designed to give both sides a chance to reassess negotiations and to decide whether some additional compromise would be wiser than enduring a strike. Suppose a union contract expires July 1. The two sides attempt to bargain a new contract, but progress is slow. The union may strike as an economic weapon, but it must notify management of its intention to do so *and then must wait 60 days.*

Statutory Prohibition

Many states have outlawed strikes by public employees. The purpose of these statutes is to ensure that unions do not use public health or welfare as a weapon to secure an unfair bargaining advantage. However, even employees subject to such a rule may find other tactics to press their cause.

Sit-down strike
Members stop working but remain at their job posts, blocking replacement workers

Sit-down Strikes

In a **sitown strike**, members stop working but remain at their job posts, physically blocking replacement workers from taking their places. This type of strike is illegal.

Fast food workers are using strikes as a means to raise their standard of living.

Partial Strikes

A partial strike occurs when employees stop working temporarily, then resume, then stop again, and so forth. This tactic is particularly disruptive because management cannot bring in replacement workers. **A union may either walk off the job or stay on it, but it may not alternate.**

29-9b Replacement Workers

When employees go on strike, management has the right to use replacement workers to keep the business operating. What about after the strike ends? May the employer offer the replacement workers *permanent* jobs, or must the company give union members their jobs back? It depends on the type of strike.

---

[37]NLRA §7.
[38]NLRA §13.

An **economic strike** is one intended to gain wages or benefits. **During an economic strike, an employer may hire** *permanent* **replacement workers.** When the strike is over, the company has no obligation to lay off the replacement workers to make room for the strikers. However, if and when the company does hire more workers, it may not discriminate against the strikers.

After an unfair labor practices (ULP) strike, union members are entitled to their jobs back, even if that means the employer must lay off replacement workers. In the *Truitt* case, the Supreme Court ruled that the company had committed a ULP. If the union had gone out on strike, the company would have had to hire back all the union members once the strike was over, regardless of how many replacement workers it had hired.

29-9c Picketing

The goal of picketing is to discourage employees, replacement workers, and customers from doing business with the company. **Picketing the employer's workplace in support of a strike is generally lawful.** However, the picketers are not permitted to use physical force to *prevent* someone from crossing the line. The company may terminate violent picketers and permanently replace them, regardless of the nature of the strike.

Secondary boycotts are generally illegal. A **secondary boycott** is a picket line established not at the employer's premises but at a different workplace. If Union is on strike against Truck Co., it is free to picket Truck Co.'s office and terminal. But Union cannot set up a picket line at a supermarket where Truck Co. delivers in an effort to pressure Truck Co. by persuading shoppers and other workers to boycott the store.

29-9d Lockouts

The workers have bargained with management for weeks, and discussions have turned belligerent. It is 6:00 a.m., the start of another day at the factory. But as 150 employees arrive for work, they are surprised to find the company's gate locked and armed guards standing on the other side. This is a **lockout**: Management has prohibited workers from entering the premises and earning their paychecks. **Most lockouts are legal.**

Economic strike
One intended to gain wages or benefits

Secondary boycott
A picket line established not at the employer's premises but at a different workplace

Lockout
Management prohibits workers from entering the premises

Chapter Conclusion

Since the first time one person hired another, there has been tension in the workplace. The law attempts to balance the right of a boss to run a business with the right of a worker to fair treatment. Different countries balance these rights differently. The United States, for instance, guarantees its workers fewer rights than virtually any other industrialized nation. American bosses have great freedom to manage their employees. Alternatively, in Canada, France, Germany, Great Britain, and Japan, employers must show just cause before terminating workers. Which system is best? On the one hand, being mistreated at work can be a terrible, life-altering experience, but on the other, companies that cannot lay off unproductive employees are less likely to add to their workforce, which may be one reason that Europe tends to have a higher unemployment rate than the United States.

EXAM REVIEW

1. **TRADITIONAL COMMON LAW RULE** The traditional common law rule of employment provided that an employee at will could be fired for a good reason, a bad reason, or no reason at all. But modern law has created exceptions to this rule that prohibit firing an employee-at-will for a bad reason.

2. **FMLA** The Family and Medical Leave Act guarantees workers up to 12 weeks of unpaid leave each year for childbirth, adoption, or a serious health condition of their own or in their immediate family.

3. **WRONGFUL DISCHARGE AND PUBLIC POLICY** Generally, an employee may not be fired for refusing to violate the law, performing a legal duty, exercising a legal right, or supporting fundamental societal values.

EXAM Strategy

Question: When Theodore Staats went to his company's "Council of Honor Convention," he was accompanied by a woman who was not his wife, although he told everyone she was. The company fired him. Staats alleged that his termination violated public policy because it infringed upon his freedom of association. He also alleged that he had been fired because he was too successful—his commissions were so high, he out-earned even the highest-paid officer of the company. Has Staats's employer violated public policy?

Strategy: Is Staats protected by a statute? No. Is he being asked to break the law? No. Is he trying to perform a legal duty? No. Is he being denied a legal right? Is he supporting fundamental societal values? (See the "Result" at the end of this section.)

4. **PROMISES MADE DURING THE HIRING PROCESS** Promises made during the hiring process are generally enforceable, even if not approved by the company's top executives. An employee handbook also creates a contract.

EXAM Strategy

Question: When Phil McConkey interviewed for a job as an insurance agent with Alexander & Alexander, the company did not tell him that it was engaged in secret negotiations to merge with Aon. When the merger went through soon thereafter, Aon fired McConkey. Was Alexander liable for not telling McConkey about the possible merger?

Strategy: Was McConkey protected by a statute? No. Did the company make any promises to him during the hiring process? (See the "Result" at the end of this section.)

5. **COVENANT OF GOOD FAITH AND FAIR DEALING** About half the states imply a covenant of good faith and fair dealing in contracts. This covenant requires both parties to behave reasonably, making an honest effort to meet both the spirit and letter of the contract.

6. **DEFAMATION** Employers may be liable for defamation when they give false references about an employee.

7. **INTENTIONAL INFLICTION OF EMOTIONAL DISTRESS** Employers who condone cruel treatment of their workers may face liability under the tort of intentional infliction of emotional distress.

8. **WHISTLEBLOWERS** Whistleblowers receive some protection under both federal and state laws.

9. **OFF-DUTY ACTIVITIES** In the absence of a specific law to the contrary, employers have the right to fire workers for off-duty conduct.

10. **ALCOHOL AND DRUG USE** Under federal law, private employers are permitted to test job applicants and workers for alcohol and illegal drugs. The Equal Employment Opportunity Commission prohibits testing for prescription drugs unless a worker seems impaired.

11. **FREE SPEECH** Under the NLRA, workers (who are not supervisors) have the right to discuss work conditions, whether that discussion takes place in the lunchroom or in a chat room and whether or not the employee is engaged in union activities.

12. **GUNS** Employers have the right to ban guns from the workplace but, in almost half the states, laws prevent companies from banning firearms in the parking lot.

13. **OSHA** The goal of the Occupational Safety and Health Act is to ensure safe conditions in the workplace.

14. **WORKERS' COMPENSATION** Workers' compensation statutes ensure that employees receive payment for injuries incurred at work.

15. **HEALTH INSURANCE** Under the Patient Protection and Affordable Care Act, employers with 50 or more full-time employees must pay a penalty if they do not provide basic health insurance. In addition, former employees must be allowed to continue their health insurance for 18 months after being terminated from their job, but they must pay for it themselves.

16. **SOCIAL SECURITY** The Social Security system pays benefits to workers who are retired, disabled, or temporarily unemployed and to the spouses and children of disabled or deceased workers.

17. **UNEMPLOYMENT COMPENSATION** Workers are eligible for unemployment compensation unless they have quit their job voluntarily or were fired for just cause.

18. **ERISA** The Employee Retirement Income Security Act regulates private pension plans.

19. **RIGHT TO ORGANIZE** Section 7 of the NLRA guarantees employees the right to organize and join unions, bargain collectively, and engage in other concerted activities. Section 8 of the NLRA makes it a ULP for an employer to interfere with union organizing, discriminate against a union member, or refuse to bargain collectively. During a union organizing campaign, an employer may vigorously

present anti-union views to its employees, but it may not use threats or rewards to defeat the union effort.

20. **EXCLUSIVITY** Under §9 of the NLRA, a validly recognized union is the exclusive representative of the employees.

EXAM Strategy

Question: Power, Inc., which operated a coal mine, suffered financial losses and had to lay off employees. The United Mine Workers of America (UMWA) began an organizing drive. Power's general manager warned miners that if the company was unionized, it would be shut down. An office manager told one of the miners that the company would get rid of union supporters. Shortly before the election was to take place, Power laid off 13 employees, all of whom had signed union cards. A low-seniority employee who had not signed a union card was not laid off. The union claimed that Power had committed ULPs. Comment.

Strategy: The NLRA guarantees employees the right to organize. An employer may vigorously advocate against a union organizing campaign. However, it is a ULP to interfere with union organizing or discriminate against a union member. (See the "Result" at the end of this section.)

21. **BARGAINING** The employer and the union *must* bargain over wages, hours, and other terms and conditions of employment. They *may* bargain over other subjects, but neither side may insist on doing so. The union and the employer must bargain in good faith, but they are not obligated to reach an agreement.

22. **STRIKES** The NLRA guarantees employees the right to strike, with some limitations. After an *economic* strike, an employer is not obligated to lay off replacement workers to give strikers their jobs back, but it may not discriminate against strikers when filling job openings. After a ULP strike, the striking workers must get their jobs back.

23. **PICKETING** Picketing the employer's workplace in support of a strike is generally lawful. Secondary boycotts are generally illegal.

24. **LOCKOUTS** Most lockouts are legal.

3. Result: The court held that freedom of association is an important social right and should be protected. However, being fired for bringing a lover to an employer's convention is not a threat to public policy. Nor is discharge for being too successful.

4. Result: The court held that when Alexander hired him, it was making an implied promise that he would not be fired immediately. The company was liable for not having revealed the merger negotiations.

20. Result: Each of the acts described was a ULP. Threatening layoffs or company closure are classic examples of ULPs. Laying off those who had signed union cards, but not those who refused, was clear discrimination.

MULTIPLE-CHOICE QUESTIONS

1. When Brook went to work at an advertising agency, his employment contract stated that he was "at will and could be terminated at any time." After 28 months with the company, he was fired without explanation. Which of the following statements is true?

   (a) The company must give him an explanation for his termination.

   (b) Because he had a contract, he was not an employee at will.

   (c) He could only be fired for a good reason.

   (d) He could be fired for any reason.

   (e) He could be fired for any reason except a bad reason.

2. **CPA QUESTION** An unemployed CPA generally would receive unemployment compensation benefits if the CPA _____.

   (a) was fired as a result of the employer's business reversals

   (b) refused to accept a job as an accountant while receiving extended benefits

   (c) was fired for embezzling from a client

   (d) left work voluntarily without good cause

3. During a job interview with Venetia, Jack reveals that he and his wife are expecting twins. Venetia asks him if he is planning to take a leave once the babies are born. When Jack admits that he would like to take a month off work, he can see her face fall. She ultimately decides not to hire him because of the twins. Which of the following statements are true?

   (a) Venetia has violated the FMLA.

   (b) Venetia has violated COBRA.

   (c) Both (a) and (b)

   (d) None of the above

4. Which of the following statements is true?

   (a) In about half the states, employees have the right to bring guns into their workplace.

   (b) In about half the states, employees have the right to bring guns into their workplace parking lot.

   (c) Both (a) and (b) are true.

   (d) None of the above is true.

5. Alpha Company's workers go on strike. The company hires replacement workers so that it can continue to operate its business. When the strike ends, Alpha must rehire the original workers if the strike was over _____.

   (a) wages

   (b) a ULP

   (c) both (a) and (b)

   (d) None of the above

CASE QUESTIONS

1. When Walton Weiner interviewed for a job with McGraw-Hill, Inc., he was assured that the company would not terminate an employee without "just cause." Weiner also signed a contract specifying that his employment would be subject to the provisions of McGraw-Hill's handbook. The handbook said, "[The] company will resort to dismissal for just and sufficient cause only, and only after all practical steps toward rehabilitation or salvage of the employee have been taken and failed. However, if the welfare of the company indicates that dismissal is necessary, then that decision is arrived at and is carried out forthrightly." After eight years, Weiner was fired suddenly for "lack of application." Does Weiner have a valid claim against McGraw-Hill?

2. Hugo's sister posted a message on his Facebook page asking him how his evening as a bartender had gone. He responded with complaints that he had not had a raise in five years and that his tips "sucked." He also called his customers "rednecks" and stated that he hoped they choked on glass as they drove home drunk. Can Hugo's boss fire him for these comments?

3. *YOU BE THE JUDGE* **WRITING PROBLEM** Apex gave Marcie an employment handbook stating that (1) she was an at-will employee, (2) the handbook did not create any contractual rights, and (3) employees who were fired had the right to a termination hearing. The company fired Marcie, claiming that she had falsified delivery records. She said that Apex was retaliating against her because she had complained of sexual harassment. Apex refused her request for a termination hearing. Did the employee handbook create a contract guaranteeing Marcie a hearing? **Argument for Apex:** The handbook could not have been clearer—it did not create a contract. Marcie is an employee at will and is not entitled to a hearing. **Argument for Marcie:** Apex intended that employees would rely on the handbook. The company used promises of a hearing to attract and retain good employees. Marcie was entitled to a hearing.

4. Triec, Inc., is a small electrical contracting company in Springfield, Ohio, owned by its executives, Yeazell, Jones, and Heaton. Employees contacted the International Brotherhood of Electrical Workers, which began an organizing drive, and 6 of the 11 employees in the bargaining unit signed authorization cards. The company declined to recognize the union, which petitioned the NLRB to schedule an election. The company then granted several new benefits for all workers, including higher wages, paid vacations, and other measures. When the election was held, only 2 of the 11 bargaining unit members voted for the union. Did the company violate the NLRA?

5. Sally is sent home from school with the chicken pox. Her father takes her to a pediatrician who says that she will be fine in about a week and in the meantime just needs bed rest and plenty of fluids. Is Sally's father entitled to leave under the FMLA to care for Sally?

DISCUSSION QUESTIONS

1. Debra Agis worked as a waitress in a Ground Round restaurant. The manager informed the waitresses that "there was some stealing going on." Until he found out who was doing it, he intended to fire all the waitresses in alphabetical order, starting with the letter "A." Dionne then fired Agis. Does she have a valid claim against her employer?

2. **ETHICS** Should employers be allowed to fire smokers? Nicotine is highly addictive and many smokers begin as teenagers, when they may not fully understand the consequences of their decisions. As Mark Twain, who began smoking at 12, famously said, "Giving up smoking is the easiest thing in the world. I know because I've done it thousands of times."

3. Noelle was the principal of a charter school and an employee at will. The head administrator imposed a rule requiring cafeteria workers to stamp the hands of children who did not have sufficient funds in their lunch accounts. Some of these children were entitled to free lunches, others needed to ask their parents to replenish their accounts. Noelle directed the cafeteria workers to stop this humiliating practice. The administrator fired her. Does Noelle have a valid claim for wrongful termination?

4. **ETHICS** As the manager of BigBox Store, you are afraid that, if your workers unionize, you will not be able to compete against stores with a non-union workforce. You would very much like to fire Geraldo, the employee who is leading the unionization effort. Of course, you know this action would be a violation of the NLRA. But you also know that, if you were found to have violated the law (after years of litigation), you would simply be required to reinstate Geraldo, pay him some back wages, and post a notice promising never to do it again.[39] (After all that time, Geraldo probably would not even want his BigBox job back.) In the meantime, all the other employees would be so scared, they would not support the union. This strategy is the most cost effective, but is it the right thing to do? What would Mill and Kant say?

5. Despite its detailed dress code for employees, Starbucks stores permitted workers to wear multiple pins and buttons, some of which, but not all, were related to its employee-reward and product-promotion programs. When a union tried to organize employees, management prohibited workers from wearing more than one pro-union pin at a time. (One employee had tried to wear eight union buttons.) Is this rule a ULP?

6. Catherine Wagenseller was a nurse at Scottsdale Memorial Hospital and an employee at will. While on a camping trip with other nurses, Wagenseller refused to join in a parody of the song "Moon River," which concluded with members of the group "mooning" the audience. Her supervisor seemed upset by her refusal. Prior to the trip, Wagenseller had received consistently favorable performance evaluations. Six months after the outing, Wagenseller was fired. She contends it was because she had not mooned. Should the hospital be able to fire Wagenseller for this reason?

---

[39]House Report 110-023 Employee Free Choice Act of 2007.

7. *YOU BE THE JUDGE* **WRITING PROBLEM** Nationwide Insurance Co. circulated a memorandum asking all employees to lobby in favor of a bill that had been introduced in the Pennsylvania House of Representatives. By limiting the damages that an injured motorist could recover from a person who caused an accident, this bill promised to save Nationwide significant money. Not only did John Novosel refuse to lobby, but he privately criticized the bill for harming consumers. Nationwide was definitely not on his side—it fired him. Novosel filed suit, alleging that his discharge had violated public policy by infringing his right to free speech. Did Nationwide violate public policy by firing Novosel? **Argument for Novosel:** The United States Constitution and the Pennsylvania Constitution both guarantee the right to free speech. Nationwide has violated an important public policy by firing Novosel for expressing his opinions. **Argument for Nationwide:** For all the high-flown talk about the Constitution, what we have here is an employee who refused to carry out company policy. If the employee wins in this case, where will it all end? What if an employee for a tobacco company refuses to market cigarettes because he does not approve of smoking? How can businesses operate without loyalty from their employees?

8. **ETHICS** Edward Snowden was a contractor at the National Security Agency (NSA) who publicly released a huge number of highly classified documents. From these files, the world learned for the first time that the NSA had been collecting vast amounts of information about the email, mail, and telephone usage of millions of people, many of them American citizens. In releasing this data, Snowden had embarrassed U.S. officials and possibly damaged spy operations. However, the NSA's own auditor found that the NSA had exceeded its authority. Two federal judges ruled that the NSA had violated the Constitution. Because Snowden broke the law, he was not protected by whistleblower statutes. He sought asylum overseas because, if he returned to the United States, he faced life in prison. Does he deserve life in prison? Should he be offered amnesty? A reduced sentence? How important is it to encourage whistleblowing?

ANSWERS TO SELECTED END OF CHAPTER QUESTIONS

MULTIPLE-CHOICE QUESTIONS

Presented are the answers for the ODD-numbered multiple-choice questions in the end-of-chapter material.

1. E
3. A
5. B

CASE QUESTIONS

Presented are the answers for all of the ODD-numbered case questions in the end-of-chapter material.

1. **Answer:** The court held that the handbook had created a contract between Weiner and McGraw Hill and, therefore, Weiner could be fired only for "just cause." Also, McGraw Hill could not fire Weiner until it had tried to rehabilitate him. *Weiner v. McGraw Hill*, 443 N.E.2d 441 (N.Y. 1982).

3. **Answer:** The Supreme Court of Texas ruled that there was no implied contract. Marcie was not entitled to a hearing.

5. **Answer:** No, because treatment for Sally's illness only needed one visit to a health-care provider, without any course of treatment or prescription medication.

Chapter 36

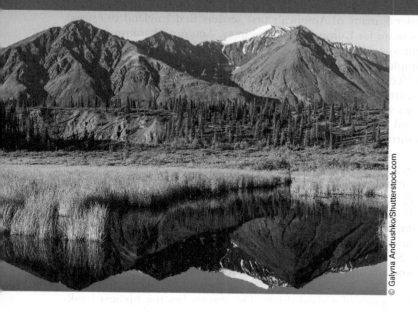

© Galyna Andrushko/Shutterstock.com

BANKRUPTCY

Three bankruptcy stories:

1. Tim's account: "First, there was Christmas. Was I really not going to buy my eight-year-old the Xbox he'd been begging for? Then my daughter's basketball team qualified for the nationals at Disney World. She's a talented player, and if she sticks with it, maybe she'll get a college scholarship. The kids had never been to Disney World. How could we say no? Then my car died. And I didn't get a bonus this year. Next thing you know, we had $27,000 in credit card debt. Then we had some uninsured medical bills. We were seriously underwater. There was just no way we could pay all that money back."

> **We were seriously underwater. There was just no way we could pay all that money back.**

2. Kristen was a talented gardener and had always loved flowers. Sometimes she did the flowers for friends' weddings. When the guy who owned the local flower shop wanted to retire, it seemed a great opportunity to buy the business. She had lots of good ideas for improving it. First, she renovated the space so that people could hold parties there. She hired staff to keep the shop open longer hours. Everything went really well. Then the recession hit, and people cut back on nonessentials like flowers. How could she pay her loans?

3. General Motors (GM), once a symbol of American business, filed for bankruptcy in 2009. At the time, its liabilities were $90 billion more than its assets. It also had 325,000 employees and even more stakeholders: Retired employees, car owners, suppliers, investors, and communities in which it operated and its employees lived and paid taxes. GM emerged from bankruptcy 40 days later with fewer brands, factories, and workers, but ready to do business. The next year, the company was profitable.

Bankruptcy law always has been and always will be controversial. Typically, in other countries, the goal of bankruptcy law is to protect creditors and punish debtors, even sending debtors to prison. Indeed, many of America's first settlers fled England to escape debtors' prison. As if to compensate for Europe's harsh regimes, American bankruptcy laws were traditionally more lenient toward debtors.[1]

The General Motors example illustrates the good news about American bankruptcy. It is efficient (40 days!) and effective at reviving ailing companies. Everyone—investors, employees, the country—benefited from GM's survival. And although Kristen's flower shop did not survive, bankruptcy laws will protect her so that she is not afraid to try entrepreneurship again.[2] New businesses fail more often than not, but they are nonetheless important engines of growth for our country. We all benefit from the jobs they create and the taxes they pay.

Tim represents the bad news in bankruptcy laws. Unfortunately, he is often the type of person who first comes to mind when people think about bankrupts. And people do not like Tim very much. They think: Why should he be rewarded for his irresponsibility, when I get stuck paying all my bills? But a more difficult bankruptcy process will probably not discourage Tim. He is the kind of guy who cares a lot about current pleasures and little about future pain. No matter what bankruptcy laws we have, he will not say no to Disney World. Should the laws become too onerous, businesses will fail, entrepreneurs will be discouraged, and the Tims of the world will continue to spend more than they should.

But maybe America has too much of a good thing. This nation has the highest bankruptcy rate in the world. In one recent year, there was one bankruptcy filing for every 200 Americans.[3] Clearly, bankruptcy laws play a vital role in our economy. They have the potential to resuscitate failing companies while encouraging entrepreneurship. At the same time, it is important not to enable irresponsible spendthrifts. Do American bankruptcy laws reach the right balance?

36-1 OVERVIEW OF THE BANKRUPTCY CODE

The federal Bankruptcy Code (the Code) is divided into eight chapters. All chapters except one have odd numbers. Chapters 1, 3, and 5 are administrative rules that generally apply to all types of bankruptcy proceedings. These chapters, for example, define terms and establish the rules of the bankruptcy court. Chapters 7, 9, 11, 12, and 13 are substantive rules for different types of bankruptcies. All of these substantive chapters have one of two objectives—rehabilitation or liquidation.

---

[1]Bankruptcy law was so important to the drafters of the Constitution that they specifically listed it as one of the subjects that Congress had the right to regulate (Article 1, Section 8).

[2]See, for example, Seung-Hyun Lee, Yasuhiro Yamakawa, Mike W. Peng, and Jay B. Barney, "How do bankruptcy laws affect entrepreneurship development around the world?" *Journal of Business Venturing*, 2011, vol. 26, issue 5, pages 505–520.

[3]Some of these filings are by businesses, although that percentage is small. In the last 15 years, more than 95 percent of all bankruptcy filings have been by consumers.

36-1a Rehabilitation

The objective of Chapters 11 and 13 is to rehabilitate the debtor. Many debtors can return to financial health provided they have the time and breathing space to work out their problems. These chapters hold creditors at bay while the debtor develops a payment plan. In return for retaining some of their assets, debtors typically promise to pay creditors a portion of their future earnings.

36-1b Liquidation

When debtors are unable to develop a feasible plan for rehabilitation under Chapter 11 or 13, **Chapter 7 provides for liquidation** (also known as a **straight bankruptcy**). Most of the debtor's assets are distributed to creditors, but the debtor has no obligation to share future earnings.

Straight bankruptcy
Also known as liquidation, this form of bankruptcy mandates that the bankrupt's assets be distributed to creditors, but the debtor has no obligation to share future earnings.

36-1c Chapter Description

The following options are available under the Bankruptcy Code:

Number	Topic	Description
Chapter 7	Liquidation	The bankrupt's assets are sold to pay creditors. If the debtor owns a business, it terminates. The creditors have no right to the debtor's future earnings.
Chapter 11	Reorganization	This chapter is designed for businesses and wealthy individuals. Businesses continue in operation, and creditors receive a portion of the debtor's current assets and future earnings.
Chapter 13	Consumer reorganization	Chapter 13 offers reorganization for the typical consumer. Creditors usually receive a portion of the individual's current assets and future earnings.

Debtors are sometimes eligible to file under more than one chapter. No choice is irrevocable because both debtors and creditors have the right to ask the court to convert a case from one chapter to another at any time during the proceedings. For example, if creditors have asked for liquidation under Chapter 7, a bankrupt consumer may request rehabilitation under Chapter 13.

36-1d Goals

The Bankruptcy Code has three primary goals:

- **To preserve as much of the debtor's property as possible.** In keeping with this goal, the Code requires debtors to disclose all of their assets and prohibits them from transferring assets immediately before a bankruptcy filing.

- **To divide the debtor's assets fairly between the debtor and creditors.** On the one hand, creditors are entitled to payment. On the other hand, debtors are often so deeply in debt that full payment is virtually impossible in any reasonable period of time. The Code tries to balance the creditors' right to be paid with the debtors' desire to get on with their lives, unburdened by prior debts.

- **To divide the creditors' share of the assets fairly among them.** Creditors rarely receive all they are owed, but at least they are treated fairly, according to established rules. Creditors do not benefit from simply being the first to file or from any other gamesmanship.

36-2 CHAPTER 7 LIQUIDATION

All bankruptcy cases proceed in a roughly similar pattern, regardless of chapter. We use Chapter 7 as a template to illustrate common features of all bankruptcy cases. Later on, the discussions of the other chapters will indicate how they differ from Chapter 7.

36-2a Filing a Petition

Any individual, partnership, corporation, or other business organization that lives, conducts business, or owns property in the United States can file under the Code. (Chapter 13, however, is available only to individuals.) The traditional term for someone who could not pay his debts was **bankrupt**, but the Code uses the term **debtor** instead. We use both terms interchangeably.

A case begins with the filing of a bankruptcy petition in federal district court. The district court typically refers bankruptcy cases to a specialized bankruptcy judge. Either party can appeal the decision of the bankruptcy judge back to the district court and, from there, to the federal appeals court.

Debtors may go willingly into the bankruptcy process by filing a **voluntary petition**, or they may be dragged into court by creditors who file an **involuntary petition**. Originally, when the goal of bankruptcy laws was to protect creditors, voluntary petitions did not exist; all petitions were involuntary. Because the bankruptcy process is now viewed as being favorable to debtors, the vast majority of bankruptcy filings in this country are voluntary petitions.

Voluntary petition
Filed by a debtor to initiate a bankruptcy case

Involuntary petition
Filed by creditors to initiate a bankruptcy case

Voluntary Petition

Any debtor (whether a business or an individual) has the right to file for bankruptcy. It is not necessary that the debtor's liabilities exceed assets. Debtors sometimes file a bankruptcy petition because cash flow is so tight they cannot pay their debts, even though they are not technically insolvent. **However,** *individuals* **must meet two requirements before filing:**

- Within 180 days before the filing, an individual debtor must undergo credit counseling with an approved agency.

- Individual debtors may only file under Chapter 7 if they earn less than the median income in their state *or* they cannot afford to pay back at least $7,475 over five years.[4] Generally, all other debtors must file under Chapter 11 or Chapter 13. (These Chapters require the bankrupt to repay some debt.)

---

[4]In some circumstances, debtors with income higher than these amounts may still be eligible to file under Chapter 7, but the formula is highly complex and more than most readers want to know. The formula is available at 11 USC Section 707(b)(2)(A). Also, you can Google "bapcpa means test" and then click on the Department of Justice website. The dollar amounts are updated every three years. You can find them by googling "federal register bankruptcy revision of dollar amounts."

The voluntary petition must include the following documents:

Document	Description
Petition	Begins the case. Easy to fill out, it requires checking a few boxes and typing in little more than name, address, and social security number.
List of Creditors	The names and addresses of all creditors
Schedule of Assets and Liabilities	A list of the debtor's assets and debts
Claim of Exemptions	A list of all assets that the debtor is entitled to keep
Schedule of Income and Expenditures	The debtor's job, income, and expenses
Statement of Financial Affairs	A summary of the debtor's financial history and current financial condition. In particular, the debtor must list any recent payments to creditors and any other property held by someone else for the debtor.

Involuntary Petition

Creditors may force a debtor into bankruptcy by filing an involuntary petition. The creditors' goal is to preserve as much of the debtor's assets as possible and to ensure that all creditors receive a fair share. Naturally, the Code sets strict limits—debtors cannot be forced into bankruptcy every time they miss a credit card payment. In the event that a debtor objects to an involuntary petition, the bankruptcy court must hold a trial to determine whether the creditors have met the Code's requirements.

An involuntary petition must meet all of the following requirements:

- The debtor must owe at least $15,325 in unsecured claims to the creditors who file.[5]

- If the debtor has at least 12 creditors, 3 or more must sign the petition. If the debtor has fewer than 12 creditors, any one of them may file a petition.

- The creditors must allege either that a custodian for the debtor's property has been appointed in the prior 120 days or that the debtor has generally not been paying debts that are due.

What does "a custodian for the debtor's property" mean? *State* laws sometimes permit the appointment of a custodian to protect a debtor's assets. The Code allows creditors to pull a case out from under state law and into federal bankruptcy court by filing an involuntary petition.

Once a voluntary petition is filed or an involuntary petition approved, the bankruptcy court issues an **order for relief**. This order is an official acknowledgment that the debtor is under the jurisdiction of the court, and it is, in a sense, the start of the whole bankruptcy process. An involuntary debtor must now make all the filings that accompany a voluntary petition.

Order for relief
An official acknowledgment that a debtor is under the jurisdiction of the bankruptcy court

---

[5]In Chapter 24, on secured transactions, we discuss the difference between secured and unsecured claims at some length. A secured claim is one in which the creditor has the right to foreclose on a specific piece of the debtor's property (known as "collateral") if the debtor fails to pay the debt when due. For example, if Lee borrows money from GMAC Finance to buy a car, the company has the right to repossess the car if Lee fails to repay the loan. GMAC's loan is "secured." An "unsecured" loan has no collateral. If the debtor fails to repay, the creditor can make a general claim against the debtor but has no right to foreclose on a particular item of the debtor's property.

36-2b Trustee

The trustee is responsible for gathering the bankrupt's assets and dividing them among creditors. This is a critical role in a bankruptcy case. Trustees are typically lawyers or CPAs, but any generally competent person can serve. Creditors have the right to elect the trustee, but often they do not bother. If the creditors do not elect a trustee, then the **U.S. Trustee** appoints one. Each region of the country has a U.S. Trustee selected by the U.S. attorney general. Besides appointing trustees as necessary, this U.S. Trustee oversees the administration of bankruptcy law in the region.

U.S. Trustee
Oversees the administration of bankruptcy law in a region

36-2c Creditors

After the court issues an order for relief, the U.S. Trustee calls a meeting of all of the creditors. At the meeting, the bankrupt must answer (under oath) any question the creditors pose about his financial situation. If the creditors want to elect a trustee, they do so at this meeting.

After the meeting of creditors, unsecured creditors must submit a **proof of claim**. This document is a simple form stating the name of the creditor and the amount of the claim. The trustee and the debtor also have the right to file on behalf of a creditor. But if a claim is not filed, the creditor loses any right to be paid. The trustee, debtor, or any creditor can object to a claim on the grounds that the debtor does not really owe that money. The court then holds a hearing to determine the validity of the claim.

Proof of claim
A form stating the name of an unsecured creditor and the amount of the claim against the debtor

Secured creditors do not file proofs of claim unless the claim exceeds the value of their collateral. In this case, they are unsecured creditors for the excess amount and must file a proof of claim for it. Suppose that Deborah borrows $750,000 from Morton in return for a mortgage on her house. If she does not repay the debt, he can foreclose. Unfortunately, property values plummet, and by the time Deborah files a voluntary petition in bankruptcy, the house is worth only $500,000. Morton is a secured creditor for $500,000 and need file no proof of claim for that amount. But he is an unsecured creditor for $250,000 and will lose his right to this excess amount unless he files a proof of claim for it.

36-2d Automatic Stay

A fox chased by hounds has no time to make rational long-term decisions. What that fox needs is a safe burrow. Similarly, it is difficult for debtors to make sound financial decisions when hounded night and day by creditors shouting, "Pay me! Pay me!" The Code is designed to give debtors enough breathing space to sort out their affairs sensibly. An automatic stay is a safe burrow for the bankrupt. It goes into effect as soon as the petition is filed. An **automatic stay** prohibits creditors from collecting debts that the bankrupt incurred before the petition was filed. **Creditors may not sue a bankrupt to obtain payment, nor may they take other steps, outside of court, to pressure the debtor for payment.** The following case illustrates how persistent creditors can be.

Automatic stay
Prohibits creditors from collecting debts that the bankrupt incurred before the petition was filed

JACKSON V. HOLIDAY FURNITURE

309 B.R. 33
United States Bankruptcy Court for the Western District of Missouri, 2004

Facts: In April, Cora and Frank Jackson purchased a recliner chair on credit from Dan Holiday Furniture. They made payments until November. That month, they filed for protection under the Bankruptcy Code. Dan Holiday received a notice of the bankruptcy. This notice stated that the store must stop all efforts to collect on the Jacksons' debt.

Despite this notice, a Dan Holiday collector telephoned the Jacksons' house 10 times between November 15 and December 1 and left a card in their door threatening repossession of the chair. On December 1, Frank (without Cora's knowledge) went to Dan Holiday to pay the $230 owed for November and December. He told the store owner about the bankruptcy filing but allegedly added that he and his wife wanted to continue making payments directly to Dan Holiday.

In early January, employees at Dan Holiday learned that Frank had died the month before. Nevertheless, after Cora failed to make the payment for the month of January, a collector telephoned her house 26 times between January 14 and February 19. The store owner's sister left the following message on Cora's answering machine:

Hello. This is Judy over at Dan Holiday Furniture. And this is the last time I am going to call you. If you do not call me, I will be at your house. And I expect you to call me today. If there is a problem, I need to speak to you about it. You need to call me. We need to get this thing going. You are a January and February payment behind. And if you think you are going to get away with it, you've got another thing coming.

When Cora returned home on February 18, she found seven bright yellow slips of paper in her doorjamb stating that a Dan Holiday truck had stopped by to repossess her furniture. She also received a letter from the store stating, "Repossession Will Be Made and Legal Action Will Be Taken."

These threats were merely a ruse to frighten Cora. Dan Holiday did not really want the recliner back; the owner just wanted to negotiate a payment plan with her.

That same day, Cora's bankruptcy attorney contacted Dan Holiday. Thereafter, all collection activity ceased.

Issues: *Did Dan Holiday violate the automatic stay provisions of the Bankruptcy Code? What is the penalty for a violation?*

Excerpts from Judge Venters's Decision:[6] The automatic stay prohibits the commencement or continuation of any action against the debtor that arose before the commencement of the bankruptcy case and forbids any act by a pre-petition creditor to obtain possession of property of the bankruptcy estate. An individual injured by a creditor's violation of the automatic stay shall recover actual damages, including costs and attorneys' fees, and in appropriate circumstances, may recover punitive damages.

In this case, there is no question that Dan Holiday repeatedly violated the automatic stay. [T]he Court finds that the Jacksons suffered financial damages in the amount of $230.00, which represents the coerced payments that Dan Holiday received from Frank Jackson on December 1.

The Court finds that punitive damages are warranted in this case based on Dan Holiday's egregious, intentional violations of the automatic stay. Dan Holiday's conduct was remarkably bad in that, after it had actual knowledge of the Jacksons' bankruptcy, and after coercing payments from the Jacksons covering the months of November and December, it made no less than twenty-six telephone calls to the Jacksons' household in January and February. Dan Holiday's continued collection efforts were in flagrant violation of the protections Congress afforded to debtors under the automatic stay.

In this matter, the Court is somewhat hampered in assessing punitive damages by the lack of evidence concerning the ability of Dan Holiday to pay. [An owner] testified that Dan Holiday was a family-owned business that has been in existence for 52 years, and the Court assumes that it is a relatively small business. Under the circumstances of this case, the Court believes that an appropriate penalty would be $100.00 for each illegal contact with the Jacksons after December 1, when it is crystal clear that Dan Holiday had actual knowledge of the Jacksons' bankruptcy filing, for a total of $2,800.00. The Court believes that this penalty will be sufficient to sting the pocketbook of Dan Holiday and impress upon Dan Holiday and its owners and employees the importance of debtor protections under the Bankruptcy Code, as well as to deter further transgressions.

The Court also will award the Jacksons their attorneys' fees and costs in the amount of $1,142.42, an amount the Court considers eminently fair and reasonable under the circumstances of this case.

36-2e Bankruptcy Estate

The filing of the bankruptcy petition creates a new legal entity separate from the debtor— the **bankruptcy estate**. All of the bankrupt's assets pass to the estate except exempt property and new property that the debtor acquires after the petition is filed.

Bankruptcy estate
The new legal entity created when a bankruptcy petition is filed. The debtor's existing assets pass into the estate.

---

[6]For readability's sake, we refer to the plaintiffs as "the Jacksons," not "debtors," as the court did.

Exempt Property

Unpaid creditors may be angry, but generally they do not want the debtor to starve to death. **The Code permits *individual* debtors (but not organizations) to keep some property for themselves.** This exempt property saves the debtor from destitution during the bankruptcy process and provides the foundation for a new life once the process is over.

In this one area of bankruptcy law, the Code defers to state law. Although the Code lists various types of exempt property, it permits states to opt out of the federal system and define a different set of exemptions. A majority of states have indeed opted out of the Code, and for their residents, the Code exemptions are irrelevant. Alternatively, some states allow the debtor to choose between state or federal exemptions.

Under the *federal* Code, a debtor is allowed to exempt only $22,975 of the value of her home. If the house is worth more than that, the trustee sells it and returns $22,975 of the proceeds to the debtor. Most *states* exempt items such as the debtor's home, household goods, cars, work tools, disability and pension benefits, alimony, and health aids. Some states set no limit on the value of exempt property. Both Florida and Texas, for example, permit debtors to keep homes of unlimited value and a certain amount of land. (Texas also allows debtors to hang on to two firearms; athletic and sporting equipment; 12 head of cattle, two horses, mules or donkeys and a saddle, blanket, and bridle for each; up to a total value of $60,000 per family.) Not surprisingly, these generous exemptions sometimes lead to abuses. Therefore, the Code provides that debtors can take advantage of state exemptions only if they have lived in that state for two years prior to the bankruptcy. And they can exempt only $155,675 of any house that was acquired during the 40 months before the bankruptcy.

Voidable Preferences

A major goal of the bankruptcy system is to divide the debtor's assets fairly among creditors. It would not be fair, or in keeping with this goal, if debtors were permitted to pay off some of their creditors immediately before filing a bankruptcy petition. These transfers are called **preferences** because they give unfair preferential treatment to some creditors. The trustee has the right to void such preferences.

Preferences

When a debtor unfairly pays creditors immediately before filing a bankruptcy petition

Preferences can take two forms: payments and liens. A *payment* simply means that the debtor gives a creditor cash that would otherwise end up in the bankruptcy estate. A *lien* means a security interest in the debtor's property. In bankruptcy proceedings, secured creditors are more likely to be paid than unsecured creditors. If the debtor grants a security interest in specific property, he vaults that creditor out of the great unwashed mass of unsecured creditors and into the elite company of secured creditors. If it happens immediately before the petition is filed, it is unfair to other unsecured creditors.

The trustee can void any transfer (whether payment or lien) that meets all of the following requirements:

- The transfer was to a creditor of the bankrupt.

- It was to pay an existing debt.

- The creditor received more from the transfer than she would have received during the bankruptcy process.

- The debtor's liabilities exceeded assets at the time of the transfer.

- The transfer took place in the 90-day period before the filing of the petition.

The debtor who hides assets from the approaching storm of bankruptcy is making a fraudulent transfer.

In addition, the trustee can void a transfer to an insider that occurs in the *year* preceding the filing of the petition. **Insiders** are family members of an individual, officers and directors of a corporation, or partners of a partnership.

Fraudulent Transfers

Suppose that a debtor sees bankruptcy approaching across the horizon like a tornado. He knows that, once the storm hits and he files a petition, everything he owns except a few items of exempt property will become part of the bankruptcy estate. Before that happens, he may be tempted to give some of his property to friends or family to shelter it from the tornado. If he succumbs to temptation, however, he is committing a **fraudulent transfer**.

A transfer is fraudulent if it is made within the year before a petition is filed and its purpose is to hinder, delay, or defraud creditors. The trustee can void any fraudulent transfer. The debtor has committed a crime and may be prosecuted.

Not all payments by a debtor prior to filing are considered voidable preferences or fraudulent transfers. **A trustee cannot void pre-petition payments made in the ordinary course.** In a business context, that means a trustee cannot void payments from, say, a grocery store to its regular fruit supplier. For consumers, the trustee cannot void payments below $650 or other routine payments, say, to the electric or water company. In these situations, the bankrupt is clearly not trying to cheat creditors. Even the insolvent are allowed to shower with the lights on.

Insider
Family members of an individual debtor, officers and directors of a corporation, or partners of a partnership.

Fraudulent transfer
A transfer is fraudulent if it is made within the year before a petition is filed and its purpose is to hinder, delay, or defraud creditors.

> Even the insolvent are allowed to shower with the lights on.

EXAM Strategy

Question: Eddie and Lola appeared to be happily married. But then Eddie's business failed, and he owed millions. Suddenly, Lola announced that she wanted a divorce. In what had to be the friendliest divorce settlement of all time, Eddie quickly agreed to transfer all of the couple's remaining assets to her. Are you suspicious? Is there a problem?

Strategy: Was this a voidable preference or a fraudulent transfer? What difference does it make?

Result: In a voidable preference, the debtor makes an unfair transfer to a creditor. In a fraudulent transfer, the bankrupt's goal is to hold on to assets himself. In a case similar to this one, the court ruled that the transfer was fraudulent because Eddie intended to shield his assets from all creditors.

36-2f Payment of Claims

Imagine a crowded delicatessen on a Saturday evening. People are pushing and shoving because they know there is not enough food for everyone; some customers will go home hungry. The delicatessen could simply serve whoever pushes to the front of the line, or it could establish a number system to ensure that the most deserving customers are served first—longtime patrons or those who called ahead. The Code has, in essence, adopted a number system to prevent a free-for-all fight over the bankrupt's assets. Indeed, one of the Code's primary goals is to ensure that creditors are paid in the proper order, not according to who pushes to the front of the line.

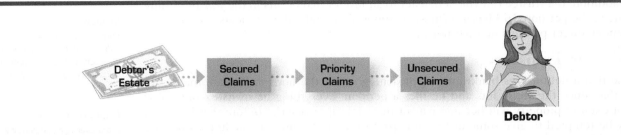

EXHIBIT 36.1 The order in which claims are paid

All claims are placed in one of three classes: (1) secured claims, (2) priority claims, and (3) unsecured claims. The second class—priority claims—has seven subcategories; the third class—unsecured claims—has three. **The trustee pays the bankruptcy estate to the various classes of claims in order of rank.** A higher class is paid in full before the next class receives any payment at all. In the case of *priority* claims, each *subcategory* is paid in order, with the higher subcategory receiving full payment before the next subcategory receives anything. If there are not enough funds to pay an entire subcategory, all claimants in that group receive a *pro rata* share.

The rule is different for unsecured claims. All categories of *unsecured* claims are treated the same, and if there are not enough funds to pay the *entire* class, everyone in the class shares *pro rata*. If, for example, there is only enough money to pay 10 percent of the claims owing to unsecured creditors, then each creditor receives 10 percent of her claim. In bankruptcy parlance, this is referred to as "getting 10 cents on the dollar." The debtor is entitled to any funds remaining after all claims have been paid. The payment order is shown in Exhibit 36.1.

Secured Claims

Creditors whose loans are secured by specific collateral are paid first. Secured claims are fundamentally different from all other claims because they are paid by selling a specific asset, not out of the general funds of the estate. Sometimes, however, collateral is not valuable enough to pay off the entire secured debt. In this case, the creditor must wait in line with the unsecured creditors for the balance. Deborah (whom we met earlier in the section entitled "Creditors") borrowed $750,000 from Morton, secured by a mortgage on her house. By the time she files a voluntary petition, the house is worth only $500,000. Morton is a secured creditor for $500,000 and is paid that amount as soon as the trustee sells the house. But Morton is an unsecured creditor for $250,000 and will only receive this amount if the estate has enough funds to pay the unsecured creditors.

Priority Claims

There are seven subcategories of priority claims. Each category is paid in order, with the first group receiving full payment before the next group receives anything.

- **Alimony and child support.** The trustee must first pay any claims for alimony and child support. However, if the trustee is administering assets that could pay these support claims, then the trustee's fees are paid first.

- **Administrative expenses.** These include fees to the trustee, lawyers, and accountants.

- **Gap expenses.** If creditors file an involuntary petition, the debtor will continue to operate her business until the order for relief. Any expenses she incurs in the ordinary course of her business during this so-called **gap period** are paid now.

Gap period
The period between the time that a creditor files an involuntary petition and the court issues the order for relief

- **Payments to employees.** The trustee now pays back wages to the debtor's employees for work performed during the 180 days prior to the date of the petition. The trustee, however, can pay no more than $12,475 to each employee. Any other wages become unsecured claims.

- **Employee benefit plans.** The trustee pays what the debtor owes to employee pension, health, or life insurance plans for work performed during the 180 days prior to the date of the petition. The total payment for wages and benefits under this and the prior paragraph cannot exceed $12,475 times the number of employees.

- **Consumer deposits.** Any individual who has put down a deposit with the bankrupt for consumer goods is entitled to a refund of up to $2,775. If Stewart puts down a $4,000 deposit on a Miata sports car, he is entitled to a refund of $2,775 when the Trustie Car Lot goes bankrupt.

- **Taxes.** The trustee pays the debtor's income taxes for the three years prior to filing and property taxes for one prior year.

- **DUI injuries.** The trustee next pays the claims of anyone injured by a bankrupt who was driving a vehicle under the influence.

Unsecured Claims

Last, and frequently very much least, the trustee pays unsecured claims. All three of these unsecured subcategories have an equal claim and must be paid together.

- **Secured claims that exceed the value of the available collateral.** If funds permit, the trustee pays Morton the $250,000 that his collateral did not cover.

- **Priority claims that exceed the priority limits.** The trustee now pays employees, Stewart, and the tax authorities who were not paid in full the first time around because their claims exceeded the priority limits.

- **All other unsecured claims.** Unsecured creditors have now reached the delicatessen counter. They can only hope that some goods remain.

36-2g Discharge

Filing a bankruptcy petition is embarrassing, time-consuming, and disruptive. It can affect the debtor's credit rating for years, making the simplest car loan a challenge. To encourage debtors to file for bankruptcy despite the pain involved, the Code offers a powerful incentive: the **fresh start**. Once a bankruptcy estate has been distributed to creditors, they cannot make a claim against the debtor for money owed before the filing, *whether or not they actually received any payment.* These pre-petition debts are **discharged**. All is forgiven, if not forgotten.

Discharge is an essential part of bankruptcy law. Without it, debtors would have little incentive to take part. To avoid abuses, however, the Code limits both the type of debts that can be discharged and the circumstances under which discharge can take place. In addition, a debtor must complete an approved course on financial management before receiving a discharge.

Debts That Cannot Be Discharged

The following debts are *never* discharged, and the debtor remains liable in full until they are paid:

- Income taxes for the three years prior to filing and property taxes for the prior year

- Money obtained fraudulently. Kenneth Smith ran a home repair business that fleeced senior citizens by making unnecessary repairs. Three months after he was found

Fresh start
After the termination of a bankruptcy case, creditors cannot make a claim against the debtor for money owed before the initial bankruptcy petition was filed.

Discharged
The debtor no longer has an obligation to pay a debt.

liable for fraud, he filed a voluntary petition in bankruptcy. The court held that his liability on the fraud claim could not be discharged.[7]

- Any loan of more than $650 that a consumer uses to purchase luxury goods within 90 days before the order for relief is granted

- Cash advances on a credit card totaling more than $925, that an individual debtor takes out within 70 days before the order for relief

- Debts omitted from the Schedule of Assets and Liabilities that the debtor filed with the petition, if the creditor did not know about the bankruptcy and therefore did not file a proof of claim

- Money that the debtor stole or obtained through a violation of fiduciary duty

- Money owed for alimony or child support

- Debts stemming from intentional and malicious injury

- Fines and penalties owed to the government

- Liability for injuries caused by the debtor while operating a vehicle under the influence of drugs or alcohol. (Yet another reason why friends don't let friends drive drunk.)

- Liability for breach of duty to a bank

- Debts stemming from a violation of securities laws

- Student loans. This topic requires more explanation.

Student loans. Many students leave school with a heavy burden of debt. Of the 38 million people who currently have student-loan debt, about 15 percent are in default—almost 6 million people. So for many, it is important to understand the legal landscape.

Prior to 2010, most student loans were made by for-profit lenders and guaranteed by the federal government. In these private student loans, both the amount of the principal and the interest rate were unregulated, and, as a result, the amount owed could easily grow to be overwhelming. Since 2010, the government has eliminated private lenders and makes student loans directly. Congress sets the interest rate.

What happens if these graduating students cannot pay their student loans?

Beginning in 2009, Congress introduced a so-called "income-based repayment" plan (IBR) for loans not already in default. If debtors are accepted into this plan (because they have a "partial financial hardship"), their monthly payments are based on their income, not the size of their debt. After 20 years, any outstanding balance is canceled. Many eligible debtors do not apply because they are unaware of this plan.

Debtors who are not eligible for the IBR and who are struggling to pay their debts may seek to discharge them through bankruptcy. But the discharge of a student loan debt cannot be done as a regular part of the bankruptcy process. Instead, the debtor must bring a separate suit against the creditor, asking the court to discharge the loan.[8] Unfortunately, this requirement imposes an additional expense on people without a lot of disposable income.

---

[7]In re Smith, 848 F.2d 813 (7th Cir. 1988).
[8]FED. R. BANKR. P. 7001(6).

Student loans cannot be discharged in bankruptcy unless repayment would cause undue hardship. The standard for what constitutes "undue hardship" is called the Brunner Test.[9] **Under the Brunner Test, a student loan will be discharged if:**

1. the debtor cannot maintain, based on current income and expenses, a minimal standard of living for herself and her dependents if forced to repay the loans;

2. this state of affairs is likely to persist for a significant portion of the repayment period of the student loans; and

3. the debtor has made good-faith efforts to repay the loans.

The second prong of the Brunner Test has been particularly controversial. It is referred to as the "hopelessness test" because it essentially asks the court to decide if there is any hope this debtor will ever have a better life. Courts do not like to be in the prediction business and debtors do not like to think their life is hopeless.

In the reported cases, plaintiffs who have been successful in obtaining discharge tend to be in dire circumstances, with serious illnesses. Carol Todd was 63 years old and autistic. She had been unemployed for a decade and was living on Social Security disability income payments. The court discharged her $340,000 in debt.[10] Janet Roth suffered numerous medical issues, including: diabetes, macular degeneration (which affects vision), and depression. She also had serious joint injuries that limited her mobility. After losing her job decorating cakes at Walmart, she applied for 280 different jobs, all without success. Despite this record, the bankruptcy court ruled that she did not meet the Brunner Test because she had not made a good-faith effort to pay her loans. The appellate court, however, overruled this decision and discharged her debts.[11]

In the following case, the debtors were not successful in obtaining discharge.

KELLY V. MICH. FIN. AUTH. (IN RE KELLY)

496 B.R. 230
United States Bankruptcy Court for the Middle District of Florida, 2013

Facts: Lisa Kelly had a B.S. in Elementary Education and a master's in Special Education. She worked at an elementary school in Florida. Her husband, Adam, had a B.A. in Fine Arts with a concentration in Digital Cinema. He worked remotely from their home for a television station in Michigan, so that he could provide care for one of their sons. Noah, who was 18 months old, had been born with spina bifida, in which the backbone and spinal canal do not close before birth. He also had hydrocephalus, a build-up of fluid inside the skull that leads to brain swelling. Noah had already undergone two surgeries and faced large ongoing medical expenses. Under their health insurance plan, the family had to pay 20 percent of the cost of their medical care.

The Kellys annual income totaled approximately $70,000; their combined educational loans exceeded $160,000. When the Kellys filed for bankruptcy, they asked the court to discharge these student loans.

Issue: *Would repayment of their student loans cause the Kellys undue hardship?*

Excerpts from Judge Jennemann's Decision:[12] Unless a debtor is able to meet all three prongs of the following

---

[9]It was established in a case by that name: Brunner v. New York State Higher Educ. Servs. Corp., 831 F.2d 395 (2d Cir. N.Y. 1987).

[10]Todd v. Access Group, Inc. (In re Todd), 473 B.R. 676 (Bankr. D. Md. 2012).

[11]Roth v. Educ. Credit Mgmt. Corp. (In re Roth), 490 B.R. 908 (B.A.P. 9th Cir. 2013).

[12]For readability, we have substituted the parties' names for "plaintiff."

Brunner Test, a debtor's student loan debt is not dischargeable:

1. The Debtor cannot maintain, based on current income and expenses, a minimal standard of living for herself and her dependents if forced to repay the loans;

2. Additional circumstances exist indicating that this state of affairs is likely to persist for a significant portion of the repayment period of the student loans; and

3. The Debtor has made good faith efforts to repay the loans.

If one of the elements of the test is not proven, the inquiry ends and the student loan cannot be discharged. A finding of undue hardship is an incredibly high hurdle to overcome. Debtors must prove more than just a garden variety of hardship.

Although the Kellys are not required to live in poverty, they have failed to adjust their lifestyle sufficiently to demonstrate undue hardship. By the Kellys' own estimates, [they] would need to reduce their expenses by only $374.88 per month to pay their student loans in full. The Kellys' discretionary spending is subject to reduction by at least $400 per month.

Here, the Kellys have recently traveled to Michigan over the holidays, to Miami twice in February, and to Clearwater in March to visit with family. Reducing these types of trips would help minimize their gas expenses and other travel-related costs. Given that Mr. Kelly works at home and that much of the Kellys' gas costs are associated with these trips, the Court finds gas costs of $200 per month is reasonable, as opposed to the $400 per month estimated by the Kellys.

The Kellys currently maintain two newer vehicles. If the Debtors truly need two vehicles, perhaps they can lease a less expensive model or buy an older car to further reduce payments. The Court specifically finds the Kellys could significantly reduce their vehicle expenses by at least $300 per month while still maintaining a minimal standard of living.

The Court also finds that the Kellys' $800 monthly food expense is high. The United States Department of Agriculture lists the average monthly cost of a thrifty meal plan for a family of four as approximately $550.65. One step up from the thrifty plan is the low-cost plan, which is commonly used by bankruptcy courts to determine a debtor's necessary food expenses. The average monthly cost of a low cost meal plan for a family of four is approximately $700. Both plans assume that all meals are purchased at grocery stores and prepared at home. The Kellys' reasonable food expenses should fall somewhere between those listed under the thrifty meal plan and those listed under the low cost meal plan. The Court estimates $625 per month (as opposed to $800 per month) for food costs, which allows for an extra $175 per month that can be used to pay their student loans.

After deducting [these sums], the Kellys have net disposable income enough to make their monthly student loan payment. Consequently, the Kellys have failed the first prong of the Brunner Test.

[The] second prong of the Brunner Test requires them to prove that their current financial situation is likely to persist for a significant portion of the repayment period of their student loans. The evidence shows that the Kellys' incomes are trending upward. Both of the Kellys are healthy, educated, and employed. Both Kellys have maintained employment within their chosen fields since obtaining their degrees.

Although the Court is cognizant of the financial uncertainty that necessarily stems from Noah's medical condition and is very sympathetic to the family's situation, courts do not discharge student loans because a debtor might have a precarious financial situation. The Kellys have failed to show their current financial problems would persist for the majority of repayment period.

[The] Kellys' student loans are not dischargeable.

How can debtors predict the outcome of a case if they do ask for a discharge of their student loan? Research indicates that the following factors affect the success of a discharge case:

- Ill health of the debtor or his family
- Whether the debtor actually got a degree
- His employment status
- His income the year before he filed

- Who the creditor is (The government typically wins.)
- Whether the case goes to trial (Settling is better for the debtor.)
- The judge who hears the case[13]

It is not clear that bankrupts even need to have a lawyer. One study found that debtors got a better result if their lawyer had at least 25 years of experience, while another found that debtors who represented themselves obtained as good a result as those who hired an attorney.[14] It seems that having an inexperienced lawyer is not helpful.

The research also indicates that more people could benefit from seeking discharge. Only 0.1 percent of debtors who file for bankruptcy ask for a discharge of their student loans.[15] Yet studies have shown that somewhere between one-third and almost two-thirds of student-loan debtors who ask for discharge receive at least some partial relief from their debts. And those who do receive a discharge are typically no worse off beforehand than those who never even apply.

In short, no one should enter into a student loan with the expectation that somehow they will not have to pay it back. The government makes it extremely difficult to avoid repayment. And the debtors who do escape repayment are in very unhappy situations. However, people who find themselves in desperate circumstances need to know: (1) about IBR, (2) how to apply for discharge, (3) that those who do apply have a reasonable success rate, and (4) only highly experienced lawyers are helpful. We hope you never have to use this knowledge, but now you know.

EXAM Strategy

Question: Someone stole a truck full of cigarettes. Zeke found the vehicle abandoned at a truck stop. Not being a thoughtful fellow, he took the truck and sold it with its cargo. Although Tobacco Company never found out who stole the truck originally, it did discover Zeke's role. A court ordered Zeke to pay Tobacco $50,000. He also owed his wife $25,000 in child support. Unfortunately, he only had $20,000 in assets. After he files for bankruptcy, who will get paid what?

Strategy: There are two issues: The order in which the debts are paid and whether they will be discharged.

Result: Child support is a priority claim, so that will be paid first. In a similar case, the court refused to discharge the claim over the theft of the truck, ruling that that was an intentional and malicious injury. Nor will a court discharge the child support claim. So Zeke will be on the hook for both debts, but the child support must be paid first.

---

[13]Pardo, Rafael I. and Lacey, Michelle R., "The Real Student-Loan Scandal: Undue Hardship Discharge Litigation," 79 Am. Bankr. L.J. 915 (2009) and Iuliano, Jason, "An Empirical Assessment of Student Loan Discharges and the Undue Hardship Standard," 86 Am. Bankr. L.J. 495 (2012).
[14]Pardo and Iuliano, ibid.
[15]Iuliano, supra.

Circumstances That Prevent Debts from Being Discharged

Apart from identifying the *kinds* of debts that cannot be discharged, **the Code also prohibits the discharge of debts under the following** *circumstances*:

- **Business organizations.** Under Chapter 7 (but *not* the other chapters), only the debts of individuals can be discharged, not those of business organizations. Once its assets have been distributed, the organization must cease operation. If it continues in business, it is responsible for all pre-petition debts. Shortly after E. G. Sprinkler Corp. entered into an agreement with its union employees, it filed for bankruptcy under Chapter 7. Its debts were discharged, and the company began operation again. A court ordered it to pay its obligations to the employees because, once the company resumed business, it was responsible for all of its pre-filing debts.[16]

- **Revocation.** A court can revoke a discharge within one year if it discovers the debtor engaged in fraud or concealment.

- **Dishonesty or bad faith behavior.** The court may deny discharge altogether if the debtor has, for example, made fraudulent transfers, hidden assets, falsified records, disobeyed court orders, refused to testify, or otherwise acted in bad faith. For instance, a court denied discharge under Chapter 7 to a couple who failed to list 15 pounds of marijuana on their Schedule of Assets and Liabilities. The court was unsympathetic to their arguments that a listing of this asset might have caused larger problems than merely being in debt.[17]

- **Repeated filings for bankruptcy.** Congress feared that some debtors, attracted by the lure of a fresh start, would make a habit of bankruptcy. Therefore, a debtor who has received a discharge under Chapter 7 or 11 cannot receive another discharge under Chapter 7 for at least eight years after the prior filing. And a debtor who has received a prior discharge under Chapter 13 cannot in most cases receive one under Chapter 7 for at least six years.

Ethics Banks and credit card companies lobbied Congress hard for the prohibition against repeated bankruptcy filings. They argued that irresponsible consumers run up debt and then blithely walk away. You might think that, if this were true, lenders would avoid customers with a history of bankruptcy. Research indicates, though, that lenders actually *target* those consumers, repeatedly sending them offers to borrow money. The reason is simple: These consumers are much more likely to take cash advances, which carry very high interest rates. And this is one audience that *must* repay its loans for the simple reason that these borrowers cannot declare bankruptcy again.[18] Is this strategy ethical?

Reaffirmation

Reaffirm

To promise to pay a debt even after it is discharged

Sometimes debtors are willing to **reaffirm** a debt, meaning they promise to pay even after discharge. They may want to reaffirm a secured debt to avoid losing the collateral. For example, a debtor who has taken out a loan secured by a car may reaffirm that debt so that

---

[16]In re Goodman, 873 F.2d 598 (2d Cir. 1989).

[17]In re Tripp, 224 B.R. 95 (1998). Possession of marijuana is legal in some states under some circumstances, but not under federal law.

[18]See Katherine M. Porter, "Bankrupt Profits: The Credit Industry's Business Model for Postbankruptcy Lending," 93 Iowa L. Rev. 1369 (2008).

the finance company will not repossess it. Sometimes debtors reaffirm because they feel guilty or want to maintain a good relationship with the creditor. They may have borrowed from a family member or an important supplier. Because discharge is a fundamental pillar of the bankruptcy process, creditors are not permitted to unfairly pressure the bankrupt. **To be valid, the reaffirmation must:**

- Not violate common law standards for fraud, duress, or unconscionability. If creditors force a bankrupt into reaffirming a debt, the reaffirmation is invalid.

- Have been filed in court before the discharge is granted

- Include the detailed disclosure statement required by the statute (§524)

- Be approved by the court if the debtor is not represented by an attorney or if, as a result of the reaffirmed debt, the bankrupt's expenses exceed his income

In the following case, the debtor sought to reaffirm the loan on his truck. He may have been afraid that if he did not, the lender would repossess it, leaving him stranded. It is hard to get around Dallas without a car. Should the court permit the reaffirmation?

In RE: Grisham

436 B.R. 896
United States Bankruptcy Court for the Northern District of Texas, 2010

Facts: Two months before filing for bankruptcy, William Grisham bought a Dodge truck (Nitro-V6 Utility 4D SLT 2WD). At the time of his bankruptcy filing, the vehicle was worth $16,000, but he owed $17,500 on it. The annual interest rate was 17.5 percent, the monthly payments were $400, and the payment schedule was almost 6 years. In addition, Grisham owed:

$29,000 to the IRS

$75,000 in alimony

$100,000 in student loans

$70,000 in unsecured debt

$274,000 total in addition to the truck

Grisham sought to reaffirm the truck loan. Should the court allow him to do so?

Issue: *Would reaffirmation of this debt create an undue hardship for the debtor?*

Excerpts from Judge Jernigan's Decision: [F]rom the outset, this court was concerned that the Debtor wished to reaffirm debt on personal property in which there is no equity. [T]he Debtor describes himself as "retired/unemployed." The Debtor's only source of income is $1,928 per month of social security income and $1,698 per month of unemployment benefits—the latter of which will soon expire. The Debtor owns no real property and

testified that he currently resides rent-free at a relative's home. The Debtor's monthly net income, after deducting his living expenses, is a negative $1,091.

While the monthly payments on the vehicle are not eye-popping, for this Debtor, in his current situation, it is unduly burdensome. In particular, this Debtor is burdened with several obligations that will likely survive his discharge in bankruptcy (large IRS debt; large alimony; and large student loan debt). Finally, the court heard no compelling testimony to justify why the Debtor purchased his vehicle right before filing bankruptcy (sometimes this may be defensible and sometimes not). In summary, the court will not stamp its seal of approval on the Debtor's reaffirmation of the debt. To do so would create a hardship on this Debtor and does not otherwise seem justified.

Bankruptcy is about "fresh starts" and new beginnings. It is about belt-tightening and shedding past bad habits. Too often, a reaffirmation agreement will reveal that someone just does not comprehend this and wants to go forward in a manner that will impair his fresh start and perpetuate bad habits from the past.

The court realizes that this is sometimes complicated. [T]here are probably situations in which a vehicle-lender will repossess the debtor's vehicle post-discharge, even when the debtor is making regular and timely contractual payments for the car post-discharge—for the simple reason that the debtor did not "reaffirm." Moreover, perhaps the debtor genuinely needs a car and worries that, absent an attempt at a reaffirmation agreement, he will surely lose the car post-discharge and may not be able to purchase (*i.e.*, obtain financing) for another vehicle in the near future.

Many reaffirmation agreements presented to the court are the farthest thing from a "fresh start" that one could ever imagine. Many times it is time to say "good riddance" to the car. And many times—maybe, just maybe—a car lender will see the wisdom of renegotiating a car loan if reaffirmation is denied.

Accordingly,

IT IS ORDERED that the Reaffirmation Agreement is disapproved.

36-3 CHAPTER 11 REORGANIZATION

For a business, the goal of a Chapter 7 bankruptcy is euthanasia—putting it out of its misery by shutting it down and distributing its assets to creditors. Chapter 11 has a much more complicated and ambitious goal—resuscitating a business so that it can ultimately emerge as a viable economic concern, as General Motors did. Keeping a business in operation benefits virtually all company stakeholders: employees, customers, creditors, shareholders, and the community.

Both individuals and businesses can use Chapter 11. Businesses usually prefer Chapter 11 over Chapter 7 because Chapter 11 does not require them to dissolve at the end, as Chapter 7 does. The threat of death creates a powerful incentive to try rehabilitation under Chapter 11. Individuals usually file under Chapter 7 if they can meet the income requirements because then they emerge from bankruptcy debt free (except for debts that are not dischargeable). Chapter 13 is specifically designed for individuals, but is only available to those whose debt does not exceed certain limits. For consumers with even modest income and high debt, Chapter 11 is the only option.

A Chapter 11 proceeding follows many of the same steps as Chapter 7: a petition (either voluntary or involuntary), order for relief, meeting of creditors, proofs of claim, and an automatic stay. There are, however, some significant differences.

36-3a Debtor in Possession

Debtor in possession

The debtor acts as trustee in a Chapter 11 bankruptcy

Chapter 11 does not require a trustee. The bankrupt is called the **debtor in possession** and, in essence, serves as trustee. The debtor in possession has two jobs: to operate the business and to develop a plan of reorganization. A trustee is chosen only if the debtor is incompetent or uncooperative. In that case, the creditors can elect the trustee, but if they do not choose to do so, the U.S. Trustee appoints one.

36-3b Creditors' Committee

In a Chapter 11 case, the creditors' committee is important because typically, there is no neutral trustee to watch over their interests. The committee generally protects the interests of its constituency and may play a role in developing the plan of reorganization. Moreover, the Bankruptcy Code requires the committee to communicate diligently with all creditors. The U.S. Trustee typically appoints the seven largest *un*secured creditors to the committee. However, the court may require the U.S. Trustee to appoint some small-business creditors as well. Secured creditors do not serve because their interests require less protection. If the debtor is a corporation, the U.S. Trustee may also appoint a committee of shareholders. The Code refers to the *claims* of creditors and the *interests* of shareholders.

36-3c Plan of Reorganization

Once the bankruptcy petition is filed, an automatic stay goes into effect to provide the debtor with temporary relief from creditors. The next stage is to develop a plan of reorganization that provides for the payment of debts and the continuation of the business. For the first 120 days (which the court can extend up to 18 months), the debtor has the exclusive right to propose a plan. If the debtor fails to file a plan, or if the court rejects it, then creditors and shareholders can develop their own plan. Congress established this 18-month limit in 2005. Some bankruptcy lawyers argue that it makes reorganization much more difficult because creditors no longer have to be patient, waiting years for payment. Instead, they can force liquidation at the end of the 18 months.

36-3d Confirmation of the Plan

Anyone who proposes a plan of reorganization must also prepare a **disclosure statement** to be mailed out with the plan. The purpose of this statement is to provide creditors and shareholders with enough information to make an informed judgment. The statement describes the company's business, explains the plan, calculates the company's liquidation value, and assesses the likelihood that the debtor can be rehabilitated. The court must approve a disclosure statement before it is sent to creditors and shareholders.

Disclosure statement
Provides creditors and shareholders with enough information to make an informed judgment about a proposed plan of reorganization

All the creditors and shareholders have the right to vote on the plan of reorganization. In preparation for the vote, each creditor and shareholder is assigned to a class. Everyone in a class has similar claims or interests. Chapter 11 classifies claims in the same way as Chapter 7: (1) secured claims, (2) priority claims, and (3) unsecured claims. Each secured claim is usually in its own class because each one is secured by different collateral. Shareholders are also divided into classes depending upon their interests. For example, holders of preferred stock are in a different class from common shareholders.

Creditors and shareholders receive a ballot with their disclosure statement to vote for or against the plan of reorganization. After the vote, the bankruptcy court holds a confirmation hearing to determine whether it should accept the plan. **The court will approve a plan if a majority of the debtors** *in each class* **votes in favor of it** *and* **if the "yes" votes hold at least two-thirds of the total debt in that class.**

As long as at least one class votes in favor of the plan, the court can still confirm it over the opposition of other classes in what is called a **cramdown** (as in "the plan is crammed down the creditors' throats"). The court will not impose a cramdown unless, in its view, the plan is feasible, fair, and in the best interests of the creditors. If the court rejects the plan of reorganization, the creditors must develop a new one. In the following case, the court did impose a cramdown.

Cramdown
When a court approves a plan of reorganization over the opposition of some creditors

In RE Fox

2000 Bankr. LEXIS 1713, 2000 WL 33287982
United States Bankruptcy Court, District of Kansas, 2000

Facts: Donald Fox founded Midland Fumigant, Inc., a company in the business of fumigating stored wheat, corn, and other grain. In a prior case, a competitor, United Phosphorus, Ltd., obtained a verdict of $2 million against Midland and Fox for fraud.

Unable to pay the judgment, Fox filed a voluntary petition under Chapter 11 of the Bankruptcy Code. His plan of reorganization envisioned that he would use revenues from Midland to pay off his creditors in full over five years, with interest. To ensure that the plan of reorganization was feasible, Fox hired CPA Kirk Wiesner to analyze Midland's financial statements and prepare projections of its income and expenses. Wiesner also reviewed Midland's operations, business, products, and the industry. He concluded that the plan's projections were conservative and could be met easily.

Midland had six classes of creditors. All of the classes accepted the plan except the two classes in which United was a member. The bankruptcy judge noted that United had an incentive to oppose Midland's reorganization because this business was highly competitive and, if Midland was to cease operations, United would be able to raise its prices substantially.

Issues: *Was Fox's plan of reorganization feasible and fair? Should the court impose a cramdown?*

Excerpts from Judge Robinson's Decision: Debtor has proposed a plan which pays all creditors in full, with interest. United, the only objecting creditor, will be paid in full [within 16 months]. Debtor's desire and intent to provide a mechanism for him to retain his business interests and assets is consistent with the purposes of the Bankruptcy Code. The plan may satisfy [the Code] even though the plan may not be one which the creditors would themselves design.

United contends that the Plan is not feasible because the projections of Midland's income and expenses are unreliable. The purpose [of the Bankruptcy Code] is to prevent confirmation of visionary schemes that promise creditors and equity security holders more than the debtor can possibly attain after confirmation.

Will the reorganized debtor emerge from bankruptcy solvent and with a reasonable prospect of success? Debtor's expert, Kirk Wiesner, analyzed Midland's financial statements, and determined that Midland would have sufficient income and cash flow during the life of Debtor's Plan, to make the anticipated distributions and loans that will fund Debtor's Plan. Based on Wiesner's Projections, which proved conservative in [the past], when Midland's actual income doubled the projected income, the Court concludes that Midland will have a continuing ability to distribute and loan funds to the Debtor as contemplated.

The Plan has a reasonable assurance of success and is not likely to be followed by liquidation, or the need for further financial reorganization. As such, the Debtor's Plan meets the feasibility requirement. The Court further notes that the United States Trustee has filed a statement in support of confirmation of the Plan.

[T]he Court finds that the Debtor's Plan is fair and equitable and, as a result, the fact that [two] Classes did not accept the Plan does not preclude confirmation.

The Debtor's Plan is confirmed over the objection of United and over the dissenting votes of [two] Classes for the reasons stated.

36-3e Discharge

A confirmed plan of reorganization is binding on the debtor, creditors, and shareholders. **The debtor now owns the assets in the bankrupt estate, free of all obligations except those listed in the plan.** Under a typical plan of reorganization, the debtor gives some current assets to creditors and also promises to pay them a portion of future earnings. In contrast, the Chapter 7 debtor typically relinquishes all assets (except exempt property) to creditors but then has no obligation to turn over future income (except for non-dischargeable debts). Exhibit 36.2 illustrates the steps in a Chapter 11 bankruptcy.

36-3f Small-Business Bankruptcy

To aid the creditors of small businesses, Congress added provisions that speed up the bankruptcy process for entities with less than $2,490,925 million in debt. After the order for relief, the bankrupt has the exclusive right to file a plan for 180 days. Both a plan and a disclosure statement must be filed within 300 days. The court must confirm or reject the plan within 45 days after its filing. If these deadlines are not met, the case can be converted to Chapter 7 or dismissed.

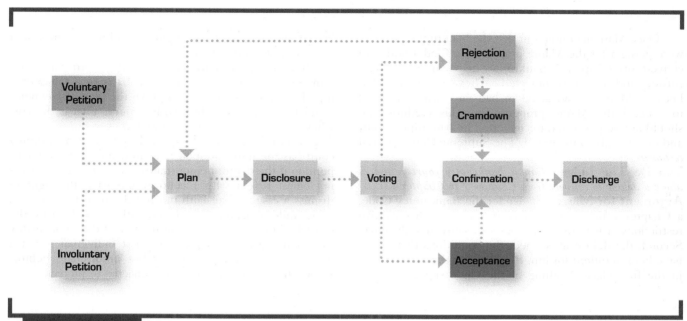

EXHIBIT 36.2   The steps in a Chapter 11 bankruptcy

36-4 CHAPTER 13 CONSUMER REORGANIZATIONS

The purpose of Chapter 13 is to rehabilitate an individual debtor. It is only available to individuals with less than $383,175 in unsecured debts or $1,149,525 in secured debts. Under Chapter 13, the bankrupt consumer typically keeps most of her assets in exchange for a promise to repay some of her debts using future income. Therefore, to be eligible, the debtor must have a regular source of income. Individuals who do not qualify for Chapter 7 usually choose this chapter because it is easier and cheaper than Chapter 11. Consequently, more money is retained for both creditors and debtor.

As you read at the beginning of the chapter, debtors can convert from one chapter to another as they wish. In the following case, the trustees objected to a conversion. The case went all the way to the Supreme Court, which split 5-4. How would you have voted?

You be the Judge

Facts: When Robert Marrama filed a voluntary petition under Chapter 7, he lied. Although he disclosed that he was the sole beneficiary of a trust that owned a house in Maine, he listed its value as zero. Marrama also denied that he had transferred any property during the prior year. Neither statement was true:

MARRAMA V. CITIZENS BANK OF MASSACHUSETTS
549 U.S. 365
United States Supreme Court, 2007

The Maine property was valuable (how many houses are worth zero?), and he had given it for free to the trust seven months prior to filing for bankruptcy protection. Marrama also lied when he claimed that he was not entitled to a tax refund. In fact, he knew that a check for $8,700 from the Internal Revenue Service was in the mail.

Once Marrama found out that the bankruptcy trustees were going after the Maine property, he filed a notice to convert his Chapter 7 bankruptcy to Chapter 13. The trustee and creditors objected. They contended that because Marrama had acted in bad faith when he tried to conceal the Maine property from his creditors, he should not be permitted to convert. The bankruptcy court and the appeals court agreed. The Supreme Court granted *certiorari*.

You Be The Judge: *Can a bankruptcy court refuse to allow a debtor to convert from Chapter 7 to Chapter 13?*

Argument for Marrama: Under the Bankruptcy Code, a Chapter 7 debtor may convert a case, with only two restrictions. First, the bankrupt can convert only once. Second, the debtor must meet the conditions that would have been required for him to file under the new chapter in the first place. Nothing in the Code suggests that a

bankruptcy judge has the right to prohibit a conversion because of the debtor's bad faith.

If a debtor acts in bad faith, the court has other remedies: It can convert the case back to a Chapter 7 liquidation; it can refuse to approve the plan of payment; or it can charge the debtor with perjury. That is the law, whether the trustee and creditors like it or not.

Argument for the Bankruptcy Trustee: A bankruptcy court has the unquestioned right to dismiss a Chapter 13 petition if the debtor demonstrates bad faith. There seems no logical reason why a court would have the right to dismiss a case for bad faith but not the right to prohibit a filing under Chapter 13 to begin with. In both cases, the court is simply saying that the individual does not qualify as a debtor under Chapter 13. That individual is not a member of the class of honest but unfortunate debtors whom the bankruptcy laws were enacted to protect.

EXAM Strategy

Question: Why did Marrama first file under Chapter 7 and then try to switch to Chapter 13 after he was caught lying?

Strategy: This question is a good test of your understanding of the advantages and disadvantages of the different chapters. For help in answering this question, you might want to look at the chart at the end of the chapter. Remember that Chapter 7 is a liquidation provision—it takes more of the bankrupt's money upfront but then discharges his debts and gives him a fresh start for the future. Chapter 13 does not take as many assets during the bankruptcy process but may attach all the debtor's disposable income for the next five years.

Result: Marrama filed under Chapter 7 in the hope that he could hold on to his house while all his debts were discharged. Once that plan failed, he tried to switch to Chapter 13 hoping that he could keep the house and give up his disposable income instead. This case illustrates the different emphases of Chapters 7 and 13.

A bankruptcy under Chapter 13 generally follows the same course as Chapter 11: The debtor files a petition, creditors submit proofs of claim, the court imposes an automatic stay, the debtor files a plan, and the court confirms the plan. But there are some differences.

36-4a Beginning a Chapter 13 Case

To initiate a Chapter 13 case, the debtor must file a voluntary petition. **Creditors cannot use an involuntary petition to force a debtor into Chapter 13.** In all Chapter 13 cases, the U.S. Trustee appoints a trustee to supervise the debtor, although the debtor remains in possession of the bankruptcy estate. The trustee also serves as a central clearinghouse for the debtor's payments to creditors. The debtor pays the trustee who, in turn, transmits these funds to creditors. For this service, the trustee is allowed up to 10 percent of the payments.

36-4b Plan of Payment

The debtor must file a plan of payment within 15 days after filing the voluntary petition. Only the debtor can file a plan; the creditors have no right to file their own version. **Under the plan, the debtor must** (1) commit some future earnings to pay off debts, (2) promise to pay all secured and priority claims in full, and (3) treat all remaining classes equally. If the plan does not provide for the debtor to pay off creditors in full, then all of the debtor's disposable income for the next five years must go to creditors.

Within 30 days after filing the plan of payment, the debtor must begin making payments to the trustee under the plan. The trustee holds these payments until the plan is confirmed and then transmits them to creditors. The debtor continues to make payments to the trustee until the plan has been fully implemented. If the plan is rejected, the trustee returns the payments to the debtor.

Only the bankruptcy court has the authority to confirm or reject a plan of payment. Creditors have no right to vote on it. However, **to confirm a plan, the court must ensure that:**

- the creditors have the opportunity to voice their objections at a hearing,

- all of the unsecured creditors receive at least as much as they would have if the bankruptcy estate had been liquidated under Chapter 7,

- the plan is feasible and the bankrupt will be able to make the promised payments,

- the plan does not extend beyond three years without good reason and in no event lasts longer than five years, and

- the debtor is acting in good faith, making a reasonable effort to pay obligations.

36-4c Discharge

Once confirmed, a plan is binding on all creditors whether they like it or not. **The debtor is washed clean of all pre-petition debts except those provided for in the plan, but, unlike Chapter 7, the debts are not *permanently* discharged.** If the debtor violates the plan, all of the debts are revived, and the court may either dismiss the case or convert it to a liquidation proceeding under Chapter 7. The debts become permanently discharged only when the bankrupt fully complies with the plan.

Note, however, that any debtor who has received a discharge under Chapter 7 or 11 within the prior four years, or under Chapter 13 within the prior two years, is not eligible under Chapter 13.

If the debtor's circumstances change, the debtor, the trustee, or unsecured creditors can ask the court to modify the plan. Most such requests come from debtors whose income has declined. However, if the debtor's income rises, the creditors or the trustee can ask that payments increase, too.

Chapter Conclusion

Whenever an individual or organization incurs more debts than it can pay in a timely fashion, everyone loses. The debtor loses control of his assets and the creditors lose money. Bankruptcy laws cannot create assets where there are none (or not enough), but they can ensure that the debtor's assets, however limited, are fairly divided between the debtor and creditors. Any bankruptcy system that accomplishes this goal must be deemed a success. Is the U.S. Bankruptcy Code fair?

EXAM REVIEW

This chart sets out the important elements of each bankruptcy chapter.

	Chapter 7	Chapter 11	Chapter 13
Objective	Liquidation	Reorganization	Consumer reorganization
Who May Use It	Individual or organization	Individual or organization	Individual
Type of Petition	Voluntary or involuntary	Voluntary or involuntary	Only voluntary
Administration of Bankruptcy Estate	Trustee	Debtor in possession (trustee selected only if debtor is unable to serve)	Trustee
Selection of Trustee	Creditors have right to elect trustee; otherwise, U.S. Trustee makes appointment	Usually no trustee	Appointed by U.S. Trustee
Participation in Formulation of Plan	No plan is filed.	Both creditors and debtor can propose plans.	Only debtor can propose a plan
Creditor Approval of Plan	Creditors do not vote on plan.	Creditors vote on the plan, but court may approve plan without the creditors' support.	Creditors do not vote on plan.
Impact on Debtor's Post-petition Income	Not affected; debtor keeps all future earnings	Must contribute toward payment of pre-petition debts	Must contribute toward payment of pre-petition debts

The following table sets out the waiting times before debtors can file a new bankruptcy petition:

Prior case	To file under Chapter 7, must wait:	To file under Chapter 13, must wait:
Chapter 7	8 years	4 years
Chapter 11	8 years	4 years
Chapter 13	6 years	2 years

EXAM Strategy

1. Question: Mark Milbank's custom furniture business was unsuccessful, so he repeatedly borrowed money from his wife and her father. He promised that the loans would enable him to spend more time with his family. Instead, he spent more time in bed with his next-door neighbor. After the divorce, his ex-wife and her father demanded repayment of the loans. Milbank filed for protection under Chapter 13. What could his ex-wife and her father do to help their chances of being repaid?

Strategy: First ask yourself what kind of creditor they are: secured or unsecured. Then think about what creditors can do to get special treatment. (See the "Result" at the end of this section.)

EXAM Strategy

2. Question: After a jury ordered actor Kim Basinger to pay $8 million for breaching a movie contract, she filed for bankruptcy protection, claiming $5 million in assets and $11 million in liabilities. Under which chapter should she file? Why?

Strategy: Look at the requirements for each chapter. Was Basinger eligible for Chapter 13? What would be the advantages and disadvantages of Chapters 7 and 11? (See the "Result" at the end of this section.)

1. Result: The father and the ex-wife were unsecured creditors who, as a class, come last on the priority list. The court granted their request not to discharge their loans on the grounds that Milbank had acted in bad faith.

2. Result: Basinger was not eligible to file under Chapter 13 because she had debts of $11 million. She first filed under Chapter 11 in a effort to retain some of her assets, but then her creditors would not approve her plan of reorganization, so she converted to liquidation under Chapter 7.

MULTIPLE-CHOICE QUESTIONS

1. *CPA QUESTION* A voluntary petition filed under the liquidation provisions of Chapter 7 of the federal Bankruptcy Code ——————— .

   (a) is not available to a corporation unless it has previously filed a petition under the reorganization provisions of Chapter 11 of the Code

   (b) automatically stays collection actions against the debtor except by secured creditors

   (c) will be dismissed unless the debtor has 12 or more unsecured creditors whose claims total at least $5,000

(d) does not require the debtor to show that the debtor's liabilities exceed the fair market value of assets

2. *CPA QUESTION* Decal Corp. incurred substantial operating losses for the past three years. Unable to meet its current obligations, Decal filed a petition of reorganization under Chapter 11 of the federal Bankruptcy Code. Which of the following statements is correct?

(a) A creditors' committee, if appointed, will consist of unsecured creditors.

(b) The court must appoint a trustee to manage Decal's affairs.

(c) Decal may continue in business only with the approval of a trustee.

(d) The creditors' committee must select a trustee to manage Decal's affairs.

3. *CPA QUESTION* Unger owes a total of $50,000 to eight unsecured creditors and one fully secured creditor. Quincy is one of the unsecured creditors and is owed $6,000. Quincy has filed a petition against Unger under the liquidation provisions of Chapter 7 of the federal Bankruptcy Code. Unger has been unable to pay debts as they become due. Unger's liabilities exceed Unger's assets. Unger has filed papers opposing the bankruptcy petition. Which of the following statements regarding Quincy's petition is correct?

(a) It will be dismissed because the secured creditor failed to join in the filing of the petition.

(b) It will be dismissed because three unsecured creditors must join in the filing of the petition.

(c) It will be granted because Unger's liabilities exceed Unger's assets.

(d) It will be granted because Unger is unable to pay Unger's debts as they become due.

4. Dale is in bankruptcy proceedings under Chapter 13. Which of the following statements is true?

(a) His debtors must have filed an involuntary petition.

(b) His unsecured creditors will be worse off than if he had filed under Chapter 7.

(c) All of his debts are discharged as soon as the court approves his plan.

(d) His creditors have an opportunity to voice objections to his plan.

5. Grass Co. is in bankruptcy proceedings under Chapter 11. _____ serves as trustee. In the case of _____ the court can approve a plan of reorganization over the objections of the creditors.

(a) The debtor in possession, a cramdown

(b) A person appointed by the U.S. Trustee, fraud

(c) The head of the creditors' committee, reaffirmation

(d) The U.S. Trustee, voidable preference

CASE QUESTIONS

1. James, the owner of an auto parts store, told his employee, Rickey, to clean and paint some tires in the basement. Highly flammable gasoline fumes accumulated in the poorly ventilated space. James threw a firecracker into the basement as a joke, intending only to startle Rickey. Sparks from the firecracker caused an explosion and fire that severely burned him. Rickey filed a personal injury suit against James for $1 million. Is this debt dischargeable under Chapter 7?

2. Mary Price went for a consultation about a surgical procedure to remove abdominal fat. When Robert Britton met with her, he wore a name tag that identified him as a doctor, and was addressed as "doctor" by the nurse. Britton then examined Price, touching her stomach and showing her where the incision would be made. Britton was not a doctor; he was the office manager. Although a doctor actually performed the surgery on Price, Britton was present. The doctor left a tube in Price's body at the site of the incision. The area became infected, requiring corrective surgery. A jury awarded Price $275,000 in damages in a suit against Britton. He subsequently filed a Chapter 7 bankruptcy petition. Is this judgment dischargeable in bankruptcy court?

3. *YOU BE THE JUDGE* **WRITING PROBLEM** Lydia D'Ettore received a degree in computer programming at the DeVry Institute of Technology, with a grade point average of 2.51. To finance her education, she borrowed $20,516.52 from a federal student loan program. After graduation, she could not find a job in her field, so she went to work as a clerk at an annual salary of $12,500. D'Ettore and her daughter lived with her parents free of charge. After setting aside $50 a month in savings and paying bills that included $233 for a new car and $50 for jewelry from Zales, her disposable income was $125 per month. D'Ettore asked the bankruptcy court to discharge the debts she owed DeVry for her education. Did the debts to the DeVry Institute impose an undue hardship on D'Ettore? **Argument for D'Ettore:** D'Ettore lives at home with her parents. Even so, her disposable income is a meager $125 a month. She would have to spend every single penny of her disposable income for nearly 15 years to pay back her $20,500 debt to DeVry. That would be an undue hardship. **Argument for the Creditors:** The U.S. government guaranteed D'Ettore's loan. Therefore, if the court discharges it, the American taxpayer will have to pay the bill. Why should taxpayers subsidize an irresponsible student? D'Ettore must also stop buying new cars and jewelry. And why should the government pay her debts while she saves money every month?

4. Dr. Ibrahim Khan caused an automobile accident in which a fellow physician, Dolly Yusufji, became a quadriplegic. Khan signed a contract for the lifetime support of Yusufji. When he refused to make payments under the contract, she sued him and obtained a judgment for $1,205,400. Khan filed a Chapter 11 petition. At the time of the bankruptcy hearing, five years after the accident, Khan had not paid Yusufji anything. She was dependent on a motorized wheelchair; he drove a Rolls-Royce. Is Khan's debt dischargeable under Chapter 11?

5. After filing for bankruptcy, Yvonne Brown sought permission of the court to reaffirm a $6,000 debt to her credit union. The debt was unsecured, and she was under no obligation to pay it. The credit union had published the following notice in its newsletter:

> If you are thinking about filing bankruptcy, THINK about the long-term implications. This action, filing bankruptcy, closes the door on TOMORROW. Having no credit means no ability to purchase cars, houses, credit cards. Look into the future—no loans for the education of your children.

Should the court approve Brown's reaffirmation?

Discussion Questions

1. **ETHICS** On November 5, Hawes, Inc., a small subcontractor, opened an account with Basic Corp., a supplier of construction materials. Hawes promised to pay its bills within 30 days of purchase. Although Hawes purchased a substantial quantity of goods on credit from Basic, it made few payments on the accounts until the following March, when it paid Basic over $21,000. On May 14, Hawes filed a voluntary petition under Chapter 7. Why did Hawes pay Basic in March? Does the bankruptcy trustee have a right to recover this payment? Is it fair to Hawes's other creditors if Basic is allowed to keep the $21,000 payment?

2. Look on the Internet for your state's rules on exempt property. Compared with other states and the federal government, is your state generous or stingy with exemptions? In considering a new bankruptcy statute, Congress struggled mightily over whether or not to permit state exemptions at all. Is it fair for exemptions to vary by state? Why should someone in one state fare better than his her neighbor across the state line? How much should the exemption be?

3. Some states permit debtors an unlimited exemption on their homes. Is it fair for bankrupts to be allowed to keep multimillion dollar homes while their creditors remain unpaid? But other states allow as little as $5,000. Should bankrupts be thrown out on the street? What amount is fair?

4. What about the rules regarding repeated bankruptcy filings? (See the chart in Exam Review.) Are these rules too onerous, too lenient, or just right?

5. A bankrupt who owns a house has the option of either paying the mortgage or losing his home. The court cannot reduce the amount owed; its choice is to discharge the entire debt or leave it whole. Congress considered a bill that would permit a bankruptcy judge to adjust the terms of mortgages to aid debtors in holding onto their houses. Proponents argued that this change in the law would reduce foreclosures and stabilize the national housing market. Opponents said that it was not fair to reward homeowners for being irresponsible. How would you have voted on this bill?

6. In the *Grisham* case, the debtor had virtually no income but owed about $200,000 in debts that could not be discharged. What kind of fresh start is that? Should limits be placed on the total debt that cannot be discharged? Is the list of non-dischargeable debts appropriate?

ANSWERS TO SELECTED END OF CHAPTER QUESTIONS

MULTIPLE-CHOICE QUESTIONS

Presented are the answers for the ODD-numbered multiple-choice questions in the end-of-chapter material.

1. D
3. D
5. A

CASE QUESTIONS

Presented are the answers for all of the ODD-numbered case questions in the end-of-chapter material.

1. **Answer:**   Injuries caused by a stupid accident are dischargeable, not those caused intentionally or maliciously. James's behavior was foolish, but his debt to Rickey was dischargeable because the injury was not intentional or malicious.

3. **Answer:**   The court refused to discharge D'Ettore's debts. It reasoned that anyone who can afford to buy jewelry and a new car, while saving money, can also afford to pay her educational loans. If there was hardship, it was clearly caused by her extravagant purchases. *IN RE D'Ettore*, 106 Bankr. 715 (Bankr. M.D. Fla. 1989).

5. **Answer:**   The court refused to approve the reaffirmation because the credit union's threats constituted duress. *IN RE Brown*, 95 Bankr. 35, 1989 Bankr. LEXIS 543 (Bankr. E.D. Va. 1989).

Chapter 42

REAL PROPERTY AND LANDLORD–TENANT LAW

© Iakov Filimonov/Shutterstock.com

Some men have staked claims to land for its oil, others for its gold. But Paul Termarco and Gene Murdoch are staking their claim to an island using … hot dogs. Their quest to market frankfurters in the New Jersey wilderness has made their children blush with embarrassment, their wives shrug in bewilderment, and strangers burst into laughter. But for three years, the two friends from West Milford have sold chili dogs, cheese dogs, and the ever traditional, hold-everything-but-the-mustard hot dogs from a tiny island in Greenwood Lake. Now it seems as though everyone knows about "Hot Dog Island."

> Paul Termarco and Gene Murdoch are staking their claim to an island using … hot dogs.

"People love it," said Termarco. "They say, 'Thank you for being here.' I always say, 'No. Thank *you*.'" The personalized service and the inexpensive prices (hot dogs cost $1.75; chili dogs, cheese dogs, and sauerkraut, $2) have cultivated a base of regulars. "I think it's great. It's better than going to a restaurant for two hours and spending a lot of money," said Joan Vaillant, who frequently jet skis to the island for hot dogs slathered in mustard.

At two-eighths of an acre, the island's craggy rocks, scrubby bushes, and ash trees are difficult to spot. Termarco doesn't mind. "Not everyone can say they own an island," he boasted. Termarco and Murdoch decided to claim the slip of land after chatting with a local restaurateur a few years ago. Termarco had just finished suggesting that the man expand his lakeside business to the island when Murdoch kicked his friend under the table.

"We left thinking, 'We can do this ourselves,'" said Murdoch, who rushed to the township offices the following day to see who owned the island.

Property records showed that the state owned the lake and lake floor, but nobody owned the island. An attorney told them about the law of adverse possession written in the 1820s. If Murdoch and Termarco could show that they used the island for five years, it would be theirs. As crazy as the scheme sounded, Murdoch figured it was worth trying.[1]

Can two friends acquire an island simply by *pretending* they own it? Yes. As we will see, the law of adverse possession permits people to obtain title to land by using it, if they meet certain stringent criteria. We examine the rules later in the chapter and decide how likely Murdoch and Termarco are to succeed. For now, the lesson is that real property law can provide surprises—and profit.

42-1 NATURE OF REAL PROPERTY

Property falls into three categories: real, personal, and intellectual. Real property, which is the focus of this chapter, consists of the following:

- **Land.** Land is the most common and important form of real property. In England, land was historically the greatest source of wealth and social status, far more important than industrial or commercial enterprises. As a result, the law of real property has been of paramount importance for nearly 1,000 years, developing very gradually to reflect changing conditions. Some real property terms sound medieval for the simple reason that they *are* medieval. By contrast, the common law of torts and contracts is comparatively new.

    Real property usually also includes anything underground (subsurface right), and some amount of airspace above land (air rights).

- **Buildings.** Buildings are real property. Houses, office buildings, apartment complexes, and factories all fall in this category.

- **Plant life.** Plant life growing on land is real property whether the plants are naturally occurring, such as trees, or cultivated crops. When a landowner sells his property, plant life is automatically included in the sale unless the parties agree otherwise. A landowner may also sell the plant life separately if he wishes. A sale of the plant life alone, without the land, is a sale of goods. (Goods, as you may recall, are movable things.) If Douglas agrees to sell all of the fir trees on his property, this sale of goods will be governed by the Uniform Commercial Code (UCC), regardless of whether Douglas or the buyer is obligated to cut the trees.[2]

- **Fixtures.** Fixtures are goods that have become attached to real property. A house (which is real property) contains many fixtures. The furnace and heating ducts were goods when they were manufactured and when they were sold to the builder because they were movable. But when the builder attached them to the house, the items became fixtures. By contrast, neither the refrigerator nor the grand piano is a fixture.

When an owner sells real property, the buyer normally obtains the fixtures unless the parties specify otherwise. Sometimes it is difficult to determine whether something is a

---

[1]Leslie Haggin, "Pair Stake Their Claim to Hot Dog Island," *The Record* (Bergen, NJ), Sep. 5, 1994, p. A12. Excerpted with permission of *The Record*, Hackensack, NJ.
[2]UCC §2-107(2).

fixture. The general rule is this: **An object is a fixture if a reasonable person would consider the item to be a permanent part of the property**, taking into account attachment, adaptation, and other objective manifestations of permanence:

- *Attachment.* If an object is attached to property in such a way that removing it would damage the property, it is probably a fixture. Heating ducts could be removed from a house, but only by ripping open walls and floors, so they are fixtures.

- *Adaptation.* Something that is made or adapted *especially for attachment* to the particular property is probably a fixture, such as custom-made bookshelves fitted in a library.

- *Other manifestations of permanence.* If the owner of the property clearly intends the item to remain permanently, it is probably a fixture. Suppose a homeowner constructs a large concrete platform in his backyard, then buys a heavy metal shed and bolts it to the platform. His preparatory work indicates that he expects the shed to remain permanently, and a court would likely declare it a fixture.

For many, beef is a dietary fixture. Is the cattle scale a fixture?

FREEMAN v. BARRS

237 S.W.3d 285
Missouri Court of Appeals, 2007

Facts: Mary Ann Barrs paid $3.5 million to Francis Freeman for 4,000 acres of ranch land, including a covered "pole-barn," which had open sides, a large cattle scale, and an enclosed veterinarian's office. The parties used a form contract, which stated that all fixtures were included with the sale. The document offered space for the parties to specify items that were included or excluded with the sale, but neither party listed the cattle scale as either in or out of the deal. After the agreement went through, Barrs and Freeman got into a beef over who owned the scale. The trial judge grilled numerous witnesses and ultimately weighed in on the side of Barrs, declaring the scale a fixture that belonged to the real estate. Broiling, Freeman appealed.

Issue: *Was the cattle scale a fixture?*

Excerpts from Judge Parrish's Decision: Steve McFadden, the president of Sooner Scale, Inc., the maker of the scale, testified that he had designed the present scale. The scale was designed to be portable, and 70 percent of the scales he sold were installed in the present manner. He further stated that he could move the present scales by cutting away a welded metal fence and lifting the scale with heavy machinery, [a] process he often performs. McFadden further stated that the removal of the fence would take approximately one hour with use of a cutting torch, and thereafter the scale could be moved within fifteen minutes.

Characterization of an item as a fixture depends upon the finding of three elements: annexation to the realty, adaptation to the use to which the realty is devoted, and intent of the annexor that the object become a permanent accession to the freehold. The latter two elements, adaptation and intent, are more important in determining whether a chattel became a fixture than the method by which the chattel is affixed to a freehold.

Annexation. The scale was purchased by plaintiff to "start selling cattle from the ranch and not sending them to the sale barn to keep the price up a little." The scale weighs approximately 6,500 pounds. A fence and gates within the structure had to be cut off in order to install the scale. A concrete slab was poured in the structure for placement of the scale. The scale was placed on pipes on the ground and pushed with a tractor across the pipes onto the slab. Concrete ramps were installed on two sides of the scale and fencing was constructed to direct cattle onto the scale. The metal posts for the fence were set in the concrete. The scale has remained in place since its installation.

Adaptation. Ray Stone had been ranch manager for plaintiff. At the time of trial he had an agreement with defendant that permitted him to run cattle on the property. He "just kind of saw after the place" for her. He told the court that the scale was integral to a cattle-working facility. The scale was used to weigh cattle for sale and to determine required dosages of medicine administered to cattle.

Intent. The manufacturer sold peripheral items that permitted the scale to be moved. This included a trailer and an inverter. Plaintiff did not buy that equipment. Ray Stone told the court that the scale was purchased "to be stationary whether it was portable or not."

This court concludes that the scale was a fixture; that, therefore, the sale of the real estate on which it was situate included the sale of the scale. A 6,500-pound scale placed on a specially sized concrete pad and surrounded by metal pole fencing set in the concrete is annexed to the real estate on which the concrete pad is poured. The permanency of the installation is emphasized by the fact the facility is covered and has a veterinary office in which the printer for the scale may be operated. The scale was put in place to facilitate the cattle operation on the premises. It had been used for that purpose since its purchase. Its adaptation for that purpose enhanced the operation of the cattle ranch.

Affirmed.

42-2 ESTATES IN REAL PROPERTY

Use and ownership of real estate can take many different legal forms. A person may own property outright, having the unrestricted use of the land and an unlimited right to sell it. Such a person owns a **fee simple absolute**. However, someone may also own a lesser interest in real property. The different rights that someone can hold in real property are known as **estates** or **interests**. Both terms simply indicate specified rights in property.

Fee simple absolute
Full ownership privileges in a property

42-2a Concurrent Estates

When two or more people own real property at the same time, they have **concurrent estates**. The most common forms of concurrent estates are tenancy in common, joint tenancy, and tenancy by the entirety.

Concurrent estates
Two or more people owning property at the same time

Tenancy in Common

The most common form of concurrent estate is **tenancy in common**. Suppose Patricia owns a house. Patricia agrees to sell her house to Quincy and Rebecca. When she **conveys** the deed—that is, transfers the deed—"to Quincy and Rebecca," those two now have a tenancy in common. This kind of estate can also be created in a will. If Patricia had died still owning the house, and left it in her will to "Sam and Tracy," then Sam and Tracy would have a tenancy in common. Tenancy in common is the "default setting" when multiple people acquire property. Co-owners are automatically considered tenants in common unless another type of interest (joint tenancy, tenancy by the entirety) is specified.

Tenancy in common
Two or more people holding equal interest in a property, but with no right of survivorship

A tenancy in common might have 2 owners, or 22, or any number. The tenants in common do not own a particular section of the property; they own an equal interest in the entire property. Quincy and Rebecca each own a 50 percent interest in the entire house.

Any co-tenant may convey her interest in the property to another person. Thus, if Rebecca moves 1,000 miles away, she may sell her 50 percent interest in the house to Sidney. Further, when a co-tenant dies, her interest in the property passes to her heirs, along with all of her other assets.

Partition. Since any tenant in common has the power to convey her interest, some people may find themselves sharing ownership with others they do not know or, worse, dislike. What to do? Partition, or division of the property among the co-tenants. Any co-tenant is entitled to demand partition of the property. If the various co-tenants cannot agree on a fair division, a co-tenant may request a court to do it. **All co-tenants have an absolute right to partition.**

A court will normally attempt a **partition by kind**, meaning that it actually divides the land equally among the co-tenants. If three co-tenants own a 300-acre farm and the

Partition by kind might be the best way to divide a piece of property like this vineyard.

Joint tenancy

Two or more people holding equal interest in a property, with the right of survivorship

court can divide the land so that the three sections are of roughly equal value, it will perform a partition in kind, even if one or two of the co-tenants oppose partition. If partition by kind is impossible because there is no fair way to divide the property, the court will order the real estate sold and the proceeds divided equally.

Joint Tenancy

Joint tenancy is similar to tenancy in common but is used less frequently. The parties, called joint tenants, again own a percentage of the entire property and also have the absolute right of partition. The primary difference is that a **joint tenancy** includes the right of survivorship. This means that when one joint tenant dies, his interest in the property passes to *the surviving joint tenants*. Recall that a tenant in common, by contrast, has the power to leave his interest in the real estate to his heirs. Because a joint tenant cannot leave the property to his heirs, courts do not favor this form of ownership. The law presumes that a concurrent estate is a tenancy in common; a court will interpret an estate as a joint tenancy only if the parties creating it clearly intended that result.

Joint tenancy has one other curious feature. Although joint tenants may not convey their interest by will, they may do so during their lifetime. If Frank and George own vacation property as joint tenants, Frank has the power to sell his interest to Harry. But as soon as he does so, the joint tenancy is **severed**: that is, broken. Harry and George are now tenants in common, and the right of survivorship is destroyed.

But when does a severance officially take place? The answer was of critical importance in the following case.

JACKSON v. ESTATE OF GREEN

771 N.W.2d 675
Supreme Court of Michigan, 2009

Facts: Green and Jackson owned land as joint tenants. Green filed a petition asking a court to partition the parcels, but he died while the partition was still pending.

The lower courts found that because the partition was not complete at the time of Green's death, the land reverted to Jackson.

Green's estate appealed.

Issue: *Does filing for the partition of a joint tenancy terminate survivorship rights?*

Excerpts from Justice Corrigan's Decision: We agree with the Court of Appeals that defendant's interest in the parcel of land automatically reverted to plaintiff when

defendant died. Thus, defendant's estate has no interest in the property, and even if defendant's partition action survived his death under Michigan's survival statute, nothing remains to partition.

The principal characteristic of the joint tenancy is the right of survivorship. Upon the death of one joint tenant, the surviving tenant or tenants take the whole estate. An ordinary joint tenancy may be severed, and the right of survivorship thereby destroyed, by an act of the parties, conveyance by either party, or levy and sale on an execution against one of the parties.

A party can sever a joint tenancy by compelling a partition. Until an order of partition has been entered, however, a partition has not been compelled and, thus, the joint tenancy has not been severed. It is not the filing of the partition action which terminates the joint tenancy, but only the judgment in such action which has that effect.

This rule is based on two related concepts: First, the theory of survivorship—that at the moment of death, ownership vests exclusively in the surviving joint tenant or tenants—and second, the doctrine that severance of the joint tenancy does not occur until the partition suit reaches final judgment.

Accordingly, we would hold that the filing of the partition action did not sever the joint tenancy because an order effectuating a partition had not entered at the time of defendant's death. Therefore, regardless whether defendant's partition action survived his death under the survival statute, his interest in the parcel of land did not.

Affirmed.

Exhibit 42.1 illustrates tenancy in common and joint tenancy.

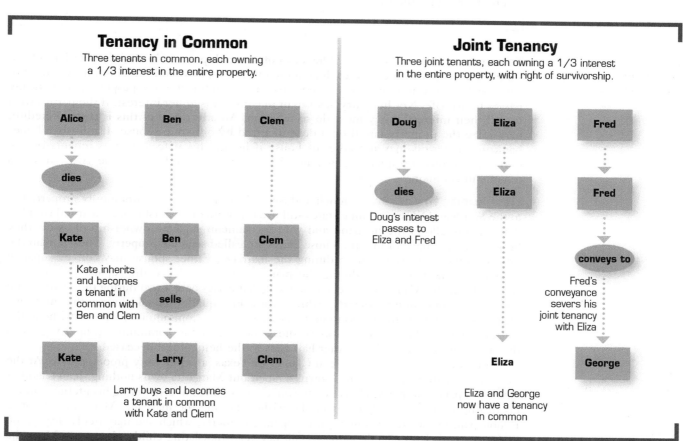

Tenancy in Common

Three tenants in common, each owning a 1/3 interest in the entire property.

Alice → dies → Kate → Kate

Ben → Ben → sells → Larry

Clem → Clem → Clem

Kate inherits and becomes a tenant in common with Ben and Clem

Larry buys and becomes a tenant in common with Kate and Clem

Joint Tenancy

Three joint tenants, each owning a 1/3 interest in the entire property, with right of survivorship.

Doug → dies

Eliza → Eliza → Eliza

Fred → Fred → conveys to → George

Doug's interest passes to Eliza and Fred

Fred's conveyance severs his joint tenancy with Eliza

Eliza and George now have a tenancy in common

EXHIBIT 42.1

EXAM Strategy

Question: Thomas, aged 80, has spent a lifetime accumulating unspoiled land in Oregon. He owns 16,000 acres, which he plans to leave to his five children. He is not so crazy about his grandchildren. Thomas cringes at the problems the grandchildren would cause if some of them inherited an interest in the land and became part-owners along with Thomas's own children. Should Thomas leave his land to his children as tenants in common or joint tenants?

Strategy: When a co-tenant dies, her interest in property passes to her heirs. When a joint tenant dies, his interest in the property passes to the surviving joint tenants.

Result: Thomas is better off leaving the land to his children as joint tenants. That way, when one of his children dies, that child's interest in the land will go to Thomas's surviving children, not to his grandchildren. (There are other approaches Thomas could take, such as creation of a trust, and they are discussed in Chapter 44, on planning for the future.)

Tenancy by the Entirety.   This form of ownership exists in slightly over half of the states. The husband and wife each own the entire property, and they both have a right of survivorship. So when the husband dies, his one-half interest in the property automatically passes to his wife. Neither party has a right to convey his or her interest. If the parties wish to sell their interests, they must do so together. An advantage of this is that no creditor may seize the property based on a debt incurred by only one spouse. If a husband goes bankrupt, creditors may not take his house if he and his wife own it as tenants by the entirety. Divorce terminates a tenancy by the entirety and leaves the two parties as tenants in common.

Community Property.   French and Spanish settlers brought **community property** law to the South and West, and nine states still use this form of ownership for a married couple.[3] This system allows the husband and wife to maintain separate ownership of assets they bring to the marriage or inherit. Those assets are called **separate property**. They remain the private property of each spouse during the marriage. Either spouse may convey separate property to another person during the marriage and may leave the separate property to anyone he or she wishes. But income or assets that either party *earns* during the marriage are considered **community property, which must be equally shared** during the marriage, regardless of who earns it. Neither party may convey community property without the consent of the other. When a spouse dies, one-half of the community property goes to the surviving spouse, and the other half goes to the heirs of the deceased.

Suppose Margarita marries Jean Claude in Texas, a community property state. At the time of the marriage, Jean Claude owns a ranch but Margarita owns nothing. Jean Claude's ranch is separate property. He is free to convey it to someone else during his lifetime, and at his death, he may leave it to anyone he wishes. During the marriage, Margarita inherits a Renoir painting worth $3 million; it is separate property, which she may freely dispose of. While married, Jean Claude earns $6,000 per year, translating children's poetry. Margarita earns $900,000 producing gory television shows. The income is community property, and each spouse is entitled to $453,000 per year.

---

[3]Arizona, California, Idaho, Louisiana, Nevada, New Mexico, Texas, and Washington all have a community property law, while Wisconsin's system is a variation of the same principle.

42-2b Future Interests

A property owner may convey less than all of his rights to another person. For example, if Andrew has a fee simple absolute in Serenity Farm, he may convey a **life estate** to Claire, meaning that Claire gets the property only for her life. The remaining rights in the land are called *future interests*.

We look at two future interests: reversion and remainder.

Reversion

If Andrew conveys Serenity Farm "to Claire for her life," Claire has a life estate in the property. Andrew has a **reversion**, meaning that upon Claire's death, the property automatically returns to him or to his heirs. The significance of a future interest is this: Even though Claire may live for 50 more years, Andrew may convey his reversion at any time. The right to own Serenity Farm upon Claire's death is a valuable right, and Andrew may sell the reversion. Once a sale is made, however, the buyer has to bide his time until Claire's death, but when she dies, the land is his.

Remainder

Suppose Andrew conveys Tranquility Farm "to Douglas for life, and then to Ernie." Douglas has a life estate and Ernie has a **remainder**. A remainder has exactly the same value as a reversion. The difference is that when the life tenant dies, the property goes to a named third person, not to the original owner.

Life estate
Ownership of property for the lifetime of a particular person

Reversion
The right of an owner (or her heirs) to property upon the death of a life tenant

Example: Andrew owns a fee simple absolute in property and ...	What was conveyed?	What future interest remains?
Conveys the property "to Betty."	Sale of the entire estate	None
Conveys the property "to Claire for her life."	Life estate	Andrew has a reversion. The property reverts to him or his heirs upon Claire's death.
Conveys the property "to Douglas for his life and then to Ernie."	Life estate	Ernie has a remainder and Andrew has nothing.

42-3 NONPOSSESSORY INTERESTS

All of the estates and interests that we have examined thus far focused on one thing: possession of the land. Now we look at interests that *never* involve possession. These interests may be very valuable, even though the holder never lives on the land.

42-3a Easements

The Alabama Power Co. drove a flatbed truck over land owned by Thomas Burgess, damaging the property. The power company did this to reach its power lines and wooden transmission poles. Burgess had never given Alabama Power permission to enter his land, and he sued for the damage that the heavy trucks caused. He recovered—nothing. Alabama Power had an *easement* to use Burgess's land.

Easement

The right to enter land belonging to another and make limited use of it

An **easement** gives one person the right to enter land belonging to another and make a limited use of it, without taking anything away. Burgess had bought his land from a man named Denton, who years earlier had sold an easement to Alabama Power. The easement gave the power company the right to construct several transmission poles on one section of Denton's land and to use reasonable means to reach the poles. Alabama Power owned that easement forever, and when Burgess bought the land, he took it subject to the easement. Alabama Power drove its trucks across a section of land where the power company had never gone before, and the easement did not explicitly give the company this right. But the court found that the company had no other way to reach its poles, and therefore, the easement allowed this use. Burgess is stuck with his uninvited guest as long as he owns the land.[4]

There are two kinds of easements. The first, an **easement appurtenant**, benefits its owner in the use of *another parcel of land*. Suppose Madeline buys vacation land that is near a lake but without waterfront access. Wade owns lakefront land, and he sells Madeline an easement, allowing her to cross his property, on foot or in a car, to reach the water. This is an easement appurtenant since it benefits its owner (Madeline) in the use of her land. Madeline's land is the **dominant tenement**; that is, the property that benefits from the easement. Wade's parcel is the **servient tenement**, the land that is burdened by the easement. Typically, the dominant tenement is adjacent to the servient, but it need not be.

An easement appurtenant *runs with the land*, meaning that if the owner of the dominant tenement sells her land, the buyer acquires the easement as well. However, the owner may *not* sell an easement by itself to someone else. If Madeline sells her property to Jason, he acquires the right to waltz across Wade's land. But Madeline has no right to sell only the easement to Jason while retaining her property.

The second kind of easement, an **easement in gross**, benefits its owner, but *not in the use of other land*. The Alabama Power Co. had an easement in gross in Burgess's land. The company had the right to install power lines across the property and use reasonable means to reach them. However, this right did not benefit any other property owned by the company, so it was an easement in gross. Most easements in gross *may* be sold. If Alabama Power no longer needed its power lines on Burgess's land, it could sell its easement to another company, for example, a cable television company.[5]

Creation of Easements

Grant or Reservation. Property owners normally create easements in one of two ways. A **grant** occurs when a landowner expressly intends to convey an easement to someone else. This is how Alabama Power acquired its easement. The company offered to buy the right to use the land, and Denton agreed to sell. The parties signed an agreement and *recorded* the easement, meaning they placed it on file in the land registry, so that interested parties were on notice. When Burgess bought the land from Denton, he knew (or should have known) about the easement.

A **reservation** occurs when an owner sells land but keeps some right to enter the property. A farmer might sell 40 acres to a developer but reserve an easement giving him the right to drive his equipment across a specified strip of the land.

Implication or Necessity. Easements are less frequently created in these two ways. An **easement by implication** arises when an owner subdivides land in a way that *clearly implies* the creation of an easement in favor of the new parcels. Suppose Jason owns

---

[4]Burgess v. Alabama Power Co., 658 So. 2d 435 (Ala. 1995).

[5]A related nonpossessory estate—and one that can benefit society and posterity—is a **conservation easement**, in which a property owner agrees to forbid certain development on her property, forever.

lakefront property with a boat ramp. He subdivides his land and sells several parcels that do not reach the lake, promising all purchasers use of the boat ramp. This subdivision clearly implies the right to cross Jason's land to use the boat ramp since there is no other access. The new owners have an easement by implication.

An **easement by necessity** arises when the dominant tenement *absolutely must* make use of other property. Yolanda leases a ninth-floor apartment to Darrin. Darrin has an easement by necessity to use the stairs and elevators since he has no other method of reaching his apartment, short of skydiving.

Prescription.   Joseph Leto bought undeveloped land in 1946 and used it on weekends for family gatherings, picnicking, and nature walks. He reached his property by using a jeep trail that crossed land he did not own, land eventually purchased by Digital Equipment Corp. (DEC). Leto continued to use the trail for nearly 30 years, until DEC sued to keep him off its property. Neither DEC nor the previous owner had ever given Leto permission to use the land. Did Leto have an easement? Yes, he had an **easement by prescription.**[6] An easement by prescription may arise when someone makes use of property belonging to another, if his use is:

- open and notorious,

- adverse to the owner, and

- continuous and uninterrupted for the number of years required by local statute.

The theory of easement by prescription is that landowners must take some initiative to protect their property rights. If they fail to do so, they may lose certain rights in their land (or, as we will see in the section on adverse possession later in this chapter, they may lose the land altogether). But someone seeking an easement by prescription must satisfy each element. His use of the property must be open and notorious, so that a reasonable landowner would be aware of what is happening and have a chance to stop it. The use must be adverse to the owner, meaning without the owner's permission. A landowner who *permits* another to cross his land nullifies any possibility of easement by implication. Finally, the use must continue without interruption for as long as required by the state statute, which is often seven years but may be more or less in a particular state. Joseph Leto continued his use of the trail for nearly 30 years, much longer than the local statute required. Once he acquired the easement by prescription, it was potentially his forever, and when DEC acquired the land, it did so subject to Leto's easement.

During the nineteenth century, many railroads obtained easements to lay down rails, and, by 1900, trains ran on over 300,000 miles of track throughout the country. Today, railroads use less than half that much track. What happens to the thousands of miles of unused land? Some state laws, and some contracts, require property to revert to the owner when an easement is abandoned. Yet federal, state, and local governments have turned many miles of unused track into trails for hiking and biking. Many environmentalists strongly support this "rails to trails" conversion. Some property owners believe that their reversionary rights are being violated and demand compensation. Local governments point out that they continue to shore up and maintain the original rail bank for possible future train use, and that the easements are therefore not abandoned.

42-3b Profit

A **profit** gives one person the right to enter land belonging to another and take something away. You own 100 acres of vacation property, and suddenly a mining company informs you that the land contains valuable nickel deposits. You may choose to sell a profit to the mining

Profit
The right to enter land belonging to another and take something from it

---

[6]Digital Equipment Corp. v. Leto, *Mass. Lawyers Weekly*, No. 14-008-94 (Mass. Land Court 1994).

company, allowing it to enter your land and take away the nickel. You receive cash up front, and the company earns money from the sale of the mineral. The rules about creating and transferring easements apply to profits as well.

42-3c License

License
The right to temporarily enter land belonging to another

A **license** gives the holder temporary permission to enter another's property. Unlike an easement or profit, a license is a *temporary* right. When you attend a basketball game by buying a ticket, the basketball team that sells you the ticket is the licensor and you are the licensee. You are entitled to enter the licensor's premises, namely the basketball arena, and to remain during the game, though the club can revoke the license if you behave unacceptably.

42-3d Mortgage

Mortgage
A security interest in real property

Mortgagor
An owner who gives a security interest in property in order to obtain a loan

Mortgagee
The party acquiring a security interest in property

Generally, in order to buy a house, a prospective owner must borrow money. The bank or other lender will require security before it hands over its money, and the most common form of security for a real estate loan is a mortgage. A **mortgage** is a security interest in real property. The homeowner who borrows money is the **mortgagor** because she is *giving* the mortgage to the lender. The lender, in turn, is the **mortgagee**, the party acquiring a security interest. The mortgagee in most cases obtains a **lien** on the house, meaning the right to foreclose on the property if the mortgagor fails to pay back the money borrowed. A mortgagee forecloses by taking legal possession of the property, auctioning it to the highest bidder, and using the proceeds to pay off the loan.

42-4 ADVERSE POSSESSION

You may recall Paul Termarco and Gene Murdoch, who opened this chapter by trying to sell you—and all the world—a hot dog from an island in the middle of a New Jersey lake. As we mentioned then, Termarco and Murdoch had their sights set on more than mustard and relish: They hoped that by using the island *as if* they owned it, they *would* own it. They were relying on the doctrine of adverse possession. This old rule of law is analogous to easement by prescription, which we analyzed earlier. Under certain conditions, easement by prescription permits a person who makes use of land continuously to establish an easement for that use. Adverse possession goes even further, allowing someone to take title to land if she meets certain tests.

In most states, to gain ownership of land by adverse possession, the user must prove:

- entry and exclusive possession,
- open and notorious possession,
- a claim adverse to the owner, and
- continuous possession for a statutory period.

42-4a Entry and Exclusive Possession

The user must take physical possession of the land and must be the only one to do so. If the owner is still occupying the land, or if other members of the public share its use, there can be no adverse possession.

42-4b Open and Notorious Possession

The user's presence must be visible and generally known in the area, so that the owner is on notice that his title is contested. This ensures that the owner can protect his property by ejecting the user. Someone making secret use of the land gives the owner no opportunity to do this, and hence acquires no rights in the land.

42-4c A Claim Adverse to the Owner

The user must clearly assert that the land is his. He does not need to register a deed or take other legal steps, but he must act as though he is the sole owner. If the user occupies the land with the owner's permission, there is no adverse claim and the user acquires no rights in the property. To succeed, the user must protect his possession of the land against all others the way any normal landowner would. This may mean erecting a home if the area is residential, or fencing property that is used to graze cattle, or posting "No Trespassing" signs in a wilderness area.

Must the user *believe* he has a title, or only act as though he does? The states are divided on this question. Many states focus only on the adverse *acts* of the user: It is sufficient if his conduct indicates he is the sole owner, regardless of what he thinks. This is the modern trend. But other states require a mistaken *belief* that the user has title to the land. For example, some states require that the user demonstrate "color of title," meaning that he has some document that *he believed* gave him good title to the land, although in reality it never did.

42-4d Continuous Possession for the Statutory Period

State statutes on adverse possession prescribe a period of years for continuous use of the land. Originally, most states required about 20 years to gain adverse possession, but the trend has been to shorten this period. Many states now demand 10 years, and a few require only five years' use. The reason for shortening the period is to reward those who *make use* of land. Even within a single state, statutes may prescribe various periods for different types of land. For example, adverse possession in a wilderness area may require more than 20 years' possession.

Regardless of the length of time required, the use must be continuous. In a residential area, the user would have to occupy the land year round for the prescribed period. In a wilderness area generally used only in the summer, a user could gain ownership by seasonal use.

A user may be able to meet the statutory period by **tacking**, which permits her to add on to her years of occupancy any years certain predecessors were in possession. The predecessors must have been in *privity* with the current user, meaning there was some legal relationship. Suppose that for 12 years, Martha adversely possesses land owned by Jake. Martha then moves, selling her interest in the land to Nancy, who occupies the land for 9 years. The total of 21 years is sufficient for adverse possession in any state, and Nancy now owns the land.

Sailing back to Hot Dog Island, how did Murdoch and Termarco fare? They certainly entered on the land and established themselves as the exclusive occupants. Their use has been open and notorious, allowing anyone who claimed ownership to take steps to eject them from the property. Their actions have been adverse to anyone else's claim. If the two hot dog entrepreneurs have grilled those dogs for the full statutory period, they should take title to the island.[7]

In the following case, the couple claiming adverse possession must do without friendly hot dog sellers because they have taken up residence in a ghost town.

---

[7]Unfortunately, there are no press accounts to inform us of the island's current status.

RAY v. BEACON HUDSON MOUNTAIN CORP.

88 N.Y.2d 154
Court of Appeals of New York, 1996

Facts: In 1931, Rose Ray purchased a cottage in a mountaintop resort town in the Adirondacks, at the same time agreeing to rent the land on which the structure stood. The long-term lease required her to pay the real estate taxes and provided that when the tenancy ended, the landlord would buy back the cottage at fair market value. In 1960, the landlord terminated the lease of everyone in the town, so Ray and all other residents packed up and left. She died in 1962, without ever getting a penny for the cottage. The next year, Mt. Beacon Incline Lands, Inc., bought all rights to the abandoned 156-acre resort.

Robert and Margaret Ray, the son and daughter-in-law of Rose Ray, reentered the cottage and began to use it one month per year, every summer from 1963 to 1988. They paid taxes, insured the property, installed utilities, and posted "No Trespassing" signs.

In 1978, Beacon Hudson bought the resort in a tax foreclosure sale. Finally, in 1988, the Rays filed suit, claiming title to the cottage by adverse possession. Beacon Hudson counterclaimed, seeking to eject the Rays. The trial court ruled for the couple. The appellate court reversed, stating that the Rays had been absent too frequently to achieve adverse possession. The Rays appealed to New York's highest court.

Issue: *Did the Rays acquire title by adverse possession?*

Excerpts from Judge Titone's Decision: The element of continuity will be defeated where the adverse possessor interrupts the period of possession by abandoning the premises. However, the hostile claimant's actual possession of the property need not be constant to satisfy the "continuity" element of the claim. Rather, the requirement of continuous possession is satisfied when the adverse claimant's acts of possessing the property are consistent with acts of possession that ordinary owners of like properties would undertake.

Here, defendant claims that plaintiffs' possession of the property was not continuous because they were physically present there for only one month out of the summer season. However, this argument fails to take into consideration plaintiffs' other acts of dominion and control over the premises that are indicative of their actual possession of an estate in land. Here, plaintiffs' installation of utilities and overall preservation of the cottage, a permanent and substantial structure, in a veritable ghost town, for the duration of the statutory period demonstrates continuous, actual occupation of land by improvement. Thus, plaintiffs' actual summertime use for a full month each season, coupled with their repeated acts of repelling trespassers, improving, posting, padlocking, and securing of the property in their absences throughout the statutory period, demonstrated their continuous dominion and control over, and thus possession of, the property.

Such seasonal presence, coupled with plaintiffs' preservation of the premises for the statutory period of 10 years—which was made more obvious by the fact that all neighboring structures had collapsed due to vandalism and abandonment—was sufficient to place the record owner on notice of their hostile and exclusive claim of ownership.

[The appellate court is reversed and the Rays obtain title by adverse possession.]

42-5 LAND USE REGULATION

42-5a Nuisance Law

A **nuisance** is an unprivileged interference with a person's use and enjoyment of her property. Offensive noise, odors, or smoke often give rise to nuisance claims. Courts typically balance the utility of the act that is causing the problem against the harm done to neighboring property owners. If a suburban homeowner begins to raise pigs in her backyard, the neighbors may find the bouquet offensive; a court will probably issue an **abatement**; that is, an order requiring the homeowner to eliminate the nuisance.

Community members can use the old doctrine of nuisance for more serious problems than pigs. An apartment building in Berkeley, California, became widely known as a drug house, and the neighbors suffered. Here is how two of the neighbors described their lives:

> I have been confronted by the drug dealers, drug customers, and prostitutes that frequent and work around and from 1615–1617 Russell Street. Weekly I have lost many hours of sleep from the cars that burn rubber after each drug buy in the middle of the night.
>
> Because of this illegal activity, my child is unable to use our front yard, and I even have to check the back yard since it has been intruded upon from time to time by people running from the police. He is learning to count by how many gunshots he hears and can't understand why he can't even enjoy our rose garden.

These were but two of the affidavits written by neighbors of a 36-unit building owned by Albert Lew. Month after month neighbors complained to Lew that his tenants were destroying the neighborhood. But Lew refused to evict the drug dealers or take any serious steps to limit the crime. So the neighbors used the law of nuisance to restore their community.

Sixty-six neighbors of the drug house each filed a small claims case against Lew, claiming that he was permitting a nuisance to exist on his property. The neighbors won their small claims cases, but Lew appealed, as he had a right to, for a new trial in Superior Court. A police sergeant testified that he had been to the building over 250 times during two years. Residents testified about how frightening life had become. The Superior Court awarded damages of $218,325 to the neighbors and the court of appeals affirmed the award, holding that neighbors injured by a nuisance may seek an abatement and damages. As Lew discovered, the law of nuisance can be a powerful weapon for creating a better neighborhood.[8]

42-5b Zoning

Zoning statutes are state laws that permit local communities to regulate building and land use. The local communities, whether cities, towns, or counties, then pass zoning ordinances that control many aspects of land development. For example, a town's zoning ordinance may divide the community into an industrial zone where factories may be built, a commercial zone in which stores of a certain size are allowed, and several residential zones in which only houses may be constructed. Within the residential zones, there may be further divisions, for example, permitting two-family houses in certain areas and requiring larger lots in others.

An owner prohibited by an ordinance from erecting a certain kind of building, or adding on to his present building, may seek a **variance** from the zoning board, meaning an exception granted for special reasons unique to the property. Whether a board will grant a variance generally depends upon the type of the proposed building, the nature of the community, the reason the owner claims he is harmed by the ordinance, and the reaction of neighbors.

Ethics Many people abhor "adult" businesses, such as strip clubs and pornography shops. Urban experts agree that the presence of these businesses in a neighborhood often causes crime to increase and property values to drop. Nonetheless, many people patronize such businesses, which can earn a good profit. Should a city have the right to restrict adult businesses? New York City officials determined that the number of sex

---

[8]Lew v. Superior Court, 20 Cal. App. 4th 866 (Cal. Ct. App. 1993).

shops had grown steadily for two decades and that their presence harmed various neighborhoods. With the support of community groups, the city passed a zoning ordinance that prohibited adult businesses from all residential neighborhoods, from some commercial districts, *and* from being within 500 feet of schools, houses of worship, day-care centers, or other sex shops (to avoid clustering). Owners and patrons of these shops protested, claiming that the city was unfairly denying the public access to a form of entertainment that it obviously desired. Is the New York City zoning ordinance reasonable?

42-5c Eminent Domain

Eminent domain
The power of the government to take private property for public use

Eminent domain is the power of the government to take private property for public use. A government may need land to construct a highway, airport, university, or public housing. All levels of government—federal, state, and local—have this power. But the Fifth Amendment of the United States Constitution states: "… nor shall private property be taken for public use, without just compensation." The Supreme Court has held that this clause, the Takings Clause, applies not only to the federal government but also to state and local governments. So, although all levels of government have the power to take property, they must pay the owner a fair price.

A "fair price" generally means the reasonable market value of the land. Generally, if the property owner refuses the government's offer, the government will file suit seeking **condemnation** of the land; that is, a court order specifying what compensation is just and awarding title to the government.

A related issue concerns local governments requiring property owners to *dedicate* some of their land to public use in exchange for zoning permission to build or expand on their own property. For example, if a store owner wishes to expand his store, a town might grant zoning permission only if the owner dedicates a different part of his property for use as a public bike path. The Supreme Court has recently diminished the power of local governments to require such dedication.[9]

42-6 LANDLORD–TENANT LAW

Apartments are certainly a type of real property, and many students are keenly interested in renters' rights. We now turn our attention to landlord–tenant law.

A freehold estate is the right to possess real property and use it in any lawful manner. What we think of as "owning" land is in fact a freehold estate. **When an owner of a freehold estate allows another person temporary, exclusive possession of the property, the parties have created a landlord–tenant relationship.** The freehold owner is the **landlord**, and the person allowed to possess the property is the **tenant**. The landlord has conveyed a **leasehold** interest to the tenant, meaning the right to temporary possession. Courts also use the word *tenancy* to describe the tenant's right to possession.

Landlord
The owner of a freehold estate who allows another person temporarily to live on his property

Tenant
A person given temporary possession of the landlord's property

A leasehold may be commercial or residential. In a commercial tenancy, the owner of a building may rent retail space to a merchant, offices to a business, or industrial space to a manufacturer. When someone rents an apartment or house, he has a residential leasehold.

---

[9]The Supreme Court's ruling came in Dolan v. City of Tigard, 512 U.S. 374 (1994).

42-6a Three Legal Areas Combined

Property law influences landlord–tenant cases because the landlord is conveying rights in real property to the tenant. She is also keeping a **reversionary interest** in the property, meaning the right to possess the property when the lease ends. Contract law plays a role because the basic agreement between the landlord and tenant is a contract. A **lease** is a contract that creates a landlord–tenant relationship. And negligence law increasingly determines the liability of landlord and tenant when there is an injury to a person or property. Many states have combined these three legal issues into landlord–tenant statutes.

Lease
An agreement in which an owner gives a tenant the right to use property

42-6b Lease

The statute of frauds generally requires that a lease be in writing. Some states will enforce an oral lease if it is for a short term, such as one year or less, but even when an oral lease is permitted, it is wiser for the parties to put their agreement in writing because a written lease avoids many misunderstandings. At a minimum, a lease must state the names of the parties, the premises being leased, the duration of the agreement, and the rent. But a well-drafted lease generally includes many provisions, called *covenants* and *conditions.* A **covenant** is simply a promise by either the landlord or the tenant to do something or refrain from doing something. For example, most leases include a covenant concerning the tenant's payment of a security deposit and the landlord's return of the deposit, a covenant describing how the tenant may use the premises, and several covenants about who must maintain and repair the property. Generally, tenants may be fined but not evicted for violating lease covenants. A **condition** is similar to a covenant, but it allows for a landlord to evict a tenant if there is a violation. In many states, conditions in leases must be clearly labeled as "conditions" or "evictable offenses."

42-7 TYPES OF TENANCY

There are four types of tenancy: a tenancy for years, a periodic tenancy, a tenancy at will, and a tenancy at sufferance. The most important feature distinguishing one from the other is how each tenancy terminates. In some cases, a tenancy terminates automatically, while in others, one party must take certain steps to end the agreement.

42-7a Tenancy for Years

Any lease for a stated, fixed period is a **tenancy for years**. If a landlord rents a summer apartment for the months of June, July, and August of next year, that is a tenancy for years. A company that rents retail space in a mall beginning January 1, 2015, and ending December 31, 2018, also has a tenancy for years. A tenancy for years terminates automatically when the agreed period ends.

Tenancy for years
A lease for a stated, fixed period

42-7b Periodic Tenancy

A **periodic tenancy** is created for a fixed period and then automatically continues for additional periods until either party notifies the other of termination. This is probably the most common variety of tenancy, and the parties may create one in either of two ways. Suppose a landlord agrees to rent you an apartment "from month to month, rent payable on the first." That is a periodic tenancy. The tenancy automatically renews itself every month unless either party gives adequate notice to the other that she wishes to terminate. A periodic tenancy could also be for one-year periods—in which case it automatically renews for an additional year if neither party terminates—or for any other period.

Periodic tenancy
A lease for a fixed period, automatically renewable unless terminated

The parties also create a periodic tenancy if, when a *tenancy for years* expires, the tenant continues to pay rent and the landlord accepts it. Ariadne agrees to rent property called Naxos for three years, with rent payable once per month. When the three years are up, the tenancy for years expires automatically. Ariadne continues to pay the monthly rent, however, and the landlord accepts her checks. The parties have created a periodic tenancy.

What is the period? If the tenant is renting *commercial property*, the new periodic tenancy is for the same period as the old tenancy for years, up to a maximum of one year. In other words, if Naxos is an office building, Ariadne's new periodic tenancy is for one year (since her original lease was for more than a year). Once the landlord accepts a single monthly rental check, both he and Ariadne are bound for the full year. In many states, if the property is *residential*, the new periodic tenancy is month to month. If Naxos is a vacation house, either party can end the lease with 30 days' notice. A landlord's notice terminating a tenancy is often called a **notice to quit**.

Notice to quit
A landlord's notice terminating a tenancy

42-7c Tenancy at Will

A **tenancy at will** has no fixed duration and may be terminated by either party at any time. Tenancies at will are unusual tenancies.[10] Typically, the agreement is vague, with no specified rental period and with payment, perhaps, to be made in kind. The parties might agree, for example, that a tenant farmer could use a portion of his crop as rent. Since either party can end the agreement at any time, it provides no security for either landlord or tenant.

Tenancy at will
A tenancy with no fixed duration, which may be terminated by either party at any time

42-7d Tenancy at Sufferance

A **tenancy at sufferance** occurs when a tenant remains on the premises, against the wishes of the landlord, after the expiration of a true tenancy. Thus, a tenancy at sufferance is not a true tenancy because the tenant is staying without the landlord's agreement. The landlord has the option of seeking to evict the tenant or of forcing the tenant to pay a *use and occupancy fee* for as long as she stays. These distinctions are technical but important.

In the following case, all parties acknowledged that the tenant refused to pay rent. But it was the landlord's failure to understand different types of tenancy that proved more important and led to a surprising result.

Tenancy at sufferance
A tenancy that exists without the permission of the landlord, after the expiration of a true tenancy

ELWELL V. MINOR

2006 WL 1920562, 2006 Conn. Super. LEXIS 1933
Connecticut Superior Court, 2006

Facts: Winfield Elwell orally agreed to rent an apartment in Vernon, Connecticut, to Lucille Minor on a month-to-month basis. The rent was $575. Four years later, Elwell increased the rent to $625, and the next year to $650, taking effect that September. Minor tendered $625 and included a letter explaining that she did not want to pay the increased rent for September or October but that she would pay the increase in later months. Elwell rejected the payment. Minor then tendered the check a second time, and Elwell again returned it.

---

[10]The courts of some states, annoyingly, use the term "tenancy at will" for what are, in reality, periodic tenancies. They do this to bewilder law students and even lawyers, a goal at which they are quite successful. This text uses tenancy at will in its more widely known sense, meaning a tenancy terminable at any time.

Elwell told Minor to pay $650 or vacate. She did neither, so Elwell began eviction proceedings (called "summary process") by serving on Minor a Notice to Quit for nonpayment of rent. After additional negotiations failed, Elwell served a second Notice to Quit. At trial, Minor argued that nonpayment of *rent* was an improper grounds for evicting a tenant at sufferance. She asked the court to dismiss the case.

Issue: *May a landlord evict a tenant at sufferance for nonpayment of rent?*

Excerpts from Judge White's Decision: During the month of September, Minor and Elwell corresponded extensively. In her letters, Minor refused to pay the increased rental amount which Elwell demanded. She gave reasons why she did not want to pay $650 instead of $625 and even attempted to negotiate postponing the rent increase until later months. Elwell rejected Minor's efforts by returning the checks that she tendered and continuing to insist on a $650 rental amount. These communications reveal a definite dispute between the parties which precludes the formation of a new one-month lease.

Because Minor remained in possession of the premises without a new monthly contract, she should be treated as a holdover occupying the apartment without the legal right to do so [in other words, as a tenant at sufferance]. In this case, the defendant was not a tenant at will, because such a tenancy exists only when the occupation of the property is with the landlord's consent, continuing during the tenancy. Elwell also served Minor with the first notice to quit for nonpayment of rent expressing his intention to terminate the lease. Once the lease terminated, Minor became a tenant at sufferance.

Nonpayment of rent is not a proper ground for the eviction of a tenant at sufferance because a tenant at sufferance is not required to pay rent, but only use and occupancy. When two parties enter into a month-to-month lease, they do not ordinarily designate a definite date when the lease, by its own terms, will expire. Instead the parties establish a tenancy at will which the tenant may terminate by moving out and the landlord may terminate by serving a notice to quit. Such a lease could never expire by lapse of time because there is no term defining the temporal existence of the lease. So, the law treats a month-to-month lease as a series of individual leases which expire at the end of the month and are ordinarily renewed each month by implication. Once the agreement expires by operation of law, the tenant's obligation to pay rent transforms into an obligation to pay a reasonable sum for the use and occupancy of the premises. Without an obligation to pay rent there can be no summary process for nonpayment of rent.

The proper statutory basis for pursuing summary process against a tenant who failed to pay a reasonable sum for use and occupancy would be that the tenant originally had the right or privilege to occupy the premises but such right or privilege has terminated. Elwell's second notice to quit cites improper grounds for the eviction of a tenant at sufferance. The notice to quit is defective and deprives this court of subject matter jurisdiction in this summary process action. This action is dismissed.

42-8 LANDLORD'S DUTIES

42-8a Duty to Deliver Possession

The landlord's first important duty is to deliver possession of the premises at the beginning of the tenancy; that is, to make the rented space available to the tenant. In most cases, this presents no problems and the new tenant moves in. But what happens if the previous tenant has refused to leave when the new tenancy begins?

The **"English rule"** obligates the landlord to remove the previous tenant in time for the new tenant to take possession. The majority of American states enforce this rule. If the old tenant is still in possession when the new tenant arrives, the landlord has breached the lease. The new tenant has two alternative remedies. She may terminate the lease and sue the landlord for costs she incurs obtaining other accommodations. Or she may affirm the lease, refuse to pay rent for the period in which she cannot take possession, sue for the cost of other accommodations, and then take possession when the old tenant is finally evicted.

The **"American rule"** is more favorable to the landlord. (Although called the American rule, this is in fact the minority rule in this country—anything to keep you off balance.) This rule holds that the landlord has no duty to deliver actual possession of the premises. If the previous tenant remains in possession, the landlord has not breached the lease. Under this rule, the new tenant generally has the power to act as a landlord toward the old tenant. The new tenant may evict the old tenant and recover damages caused by her delay in leaving. Alternatively, the new tenant may treat the holdover as a tenant at will for a new rental period and may charge the normal rent for that period.

42-8b Quiet Enjoyment

All tenants are entitled to quiet enjoyment of the premises, meaning the right to use the property without the interference of the landlord. Most leases expressly state this covenant of quiet enjoyment. And if a lease includes no such covenant, the law implies the right of quiet enjoyment anyway, so all tenants are protected. If a landlord interferes with the tenant's quiet enjoyment, he has breached the lease, entitling the tenant to damages.

Eviction
An act that forces a tenant to abandon the property

The most common interference with quiet enjoyment is an **eviction**, meaning some act that forces the tenant to abandon the premises. Of course, some evictions are legal, as when a tenant fails to pay the rent. But some evictions are illegal. There are two types of eviction: actual and constructive.

Actual Eviction

If a landlord prevents the tenant from possessing the premises, he has actually evicted her. Suppose a landlord decides that a group of students are "troublemakers." Without going through lawful eviction procedures in court, the landlord simply waits until the students are out of the apartment and changes all the locks. By denying the students access to the premises, the landlord has actually evicted them and has breached their right of quiet enjoyment. He is liable for all expenses they suffer, such as retrieving their possessions, the cost of alternate housing, and moving expenses. In some states, he may be liable for punitive damages for failing to go through proper eviction procedures.

Even a partial eviction is an interference with quiet enjoyment. Suppose Louise rents an apartment with a storage room. If the landlord places his own goods in the storage room, he has partially evicted Louise because a tenant is entitled to the *exclusive* possession of the premises. In all states, Louise would be allowed to deduct from her rent the value of the storage space, and in many states, she would not be obligated to pay any rent for the apartment as long as the landlord continued the partial eviction.

Constructive Eviction

If a landlord substantially interferes with the tenant's use and enjoyment of the premises, he has constructively evicted her. Courts construe certain behavior as the equivalent of an eviction. In these cases, the landlord has not actually prevented the tenant from *possessing* the premises but has instead interfered so greatly with her *use and enjoyment* that the law regards the landlord's actions as equivalent to an eviction. Suppose the heating system in an apartment house in Juneau, Alaska, fails during January. The landlord, an avid sled dog racer, tells the tenants he is too busy to fix the problem. If the tenants move out, the landlord has constructively evicted them and is liable for all expenses they suffer.

To claim a constructive eviction, the tenant must vacate the premises. The tenant must also prove that the interference was sufficiently serious and lasted long enough that she was forced to move out. A lack of hot water for two days is not fatal, but lack of any water for two weeks creates a constructive eviction.

Other Interference

A landlord's conduct may interfere with quiet enjoyment even when it is not so harmful as to force a constructive eviction. Suppose a landlord, living in the ground-floor unit, gives trumpet lessons in his apartment six nights a week until 1:00 a.m., producing such a cacophony that a group of students living upstairs can neither study nor sleep. If the students continue to live in the apartment because they cannot afford a better place, there has been no constructive eviction. But the landlord's conduct interferes with the tenants' quiet enjoyment, and the students are entitled to damages.

42-8c Duty to Maintain Premises

Historically, the common law placed no burden on the landlord to repair and maintain the premises. This made sense because rental property had traditionally been farmland. Buildings, such as a house or barn, were far less important than the land itself, and no one expected the landlord to fix a leaking roof. Today, the vast majority of rental property is used for housing or business purposes. Space in a building is frequently all that a tenant is renting, and the condition of the building is

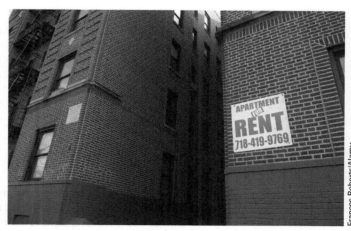

In most states, landlords have a duty to keep their properties in a habitable condition.

of paramount importance. Most states have changed the common law rule and placed various obligations on the landlord to maintain the property.

In most states, a landlord has a duty to deliver the premises in a habitable condition and a continuing duty to maintain the habitable condition. This duty overlaps with the quiet enjoyment obligation, but it is not identical. The tenant's right to quiet enjoyment focuses primarily on the tenant's *ability to use* the rented property. The landlord's duty to maintain the property focuses on whether the property *meets a particular legal standard*. The required standard may be stated in the lease, created by a state statute, or implied by law.

Lease

The lease itself generally obligates the landlord to maintain the exterior of any buildings and the common areas. If a lease does not do so, state law may imply the obligation.

Building Codes

Many state and local governments have passed building codes, which mandate minimum standards for commercial and/or residential property. The codes are likely to be stricter for residential property and may demand such things as minimum room size, sufficient hot water, secure locks, proper working kitchens and bathrooms, absence of insects and rodents, and other basics of decent housing. Generally, all rental property must comply with the building code, whether the lease mentions the code or not.

Implied Warranty of Habitability

Students Maria Ivanow, Thomas Tecza, and Kenneth Gearin rented a house from Les and Martha Vanlandingham. The monthly rent was $900. But the roommates failed to pay any rent for the final five months of the tenancy. After they moved out, the Vanlandinghams sued. How much did the landlords recover? Nothing. The landlords had breached the implied warranty of habitability.

The implied warranty of habitability requires that a landlord meet all standards set by the local building code, or that the premises be fit for human habitation. Most states, though not all, *imply* this warranty of habitability, meaning that the landlord must meet this standard whether the lease includes it or not. In some states, the implied warranty means that the premises must at least satisfy the local building code. Other states require property that is "fit for human habitation," which means that a landlord might comply with the building code, yet still fail the implied warranty of habitability if the rental property is unfit to live in.

> # The basement often flooded, and when it was dry, rats and opossums lived in it.

The Vanlandinghams breached the implied warranty. The students had complained repeatedly about a variety of problems. The washer and dryer, which were included in the lease, frequently failed. A severe roof leak caused water damage in one of the bedrooms. Defective pipes flooded the bathroom. The refrigerator frequently malfunctioned, and the roommates repaired it several times. The basement often flooded, and when it was dry, rats and opossums lived in it. The heat sometimes failed.

In warranty of habitability cases, a court normally considers the severity of the problems and their duration. If the defective conditions seriously interfere with the tenancy, the court declares the implied warranty breached and orders a **rent abatement**; that is, a reduction in the rent owed. The longer the defects continued and the greater their severity, the more the rent is abated. In the case of Maria Ivanow and friends, the court abated the rent 50 percent. The students had already paid more than the abated rent to the landlord, so they owed nothing for the last five months.[11]

Duty to Return Security Deposit

Most landlords require tenants to pay a security deposit, in case the tenant damages the premises. In many states, a landlord must either return the security deposit soon after the tenant has moved out or notify the tenant of the damage and the cost of the repairs. In addition, landlords are often obligated to credit tenants with interest earned on the deposit. Many states have statutes requiring a landlord who fails to return the deposit in a timely fashion to pay double or even triple damages to the tenant.

In a commercial lease, the tenant may have less statutory protection but more bargaining power. A financially sound company might negotiate a lease with no security deposit or perhaps offer a letter of credit for security instead of cash. The interest saved over several years could be substantial.

42-9 Tenant's Duties

42-9a Duty to Pay Rent

Rent

Compensation paid by a tenant to a landlord

Rent is the compensation the tenant pays the landlord for use of the premises, and paying the rent is the tenant's foremost obligation. The lease normally specifies the amount of rent and when it must be paid. Typically, the landlord requires that rent be paid at the beginning of each rental period, whether that is monthly, annually, or otherwise.

Escalator clause

A lease clause allowing the landlord to raise the rent for specified reasons

Both parties must be certain they understand whether the rent includes utilities such as heat and hot water. Some states mandate that the landlord pay certain utilities, such as water. Many leases include an **escalator clause**, permitting the landlord to raise the rent during the course of the lease if his expenses increase for specified reasons. For example, a tax escalator clause allows the landlord to raise the rent if his real estate taxes go up. Any escalator clause should state the percentage of the increase that the landlord may pass on to the tenant.

---

[11]Vanlandingham v. Ivanow, 246 Ill. App. 3d 348 (Ill. Ct. App. 1993).

Landlord's Remedies for Nonpayment of Rent

If the tenant fails to pay rent on time, the landlord has several remedies. She is entitled to apply the security deposit to the unpaid rent. She may also sue the tenant for nonpayment of rent, demanding the unpaid sums, cost of collection, and interest. Finally, the landlord may evict a tenant who has failed to pay rent.

State statutes prescribe the steps a landlord must take to evict a tenant for nonpayment. Typically, the landlord must serve a termination notice on the tenant and wait for a court hearing. At the hearing, the landlord must prove that the tenant has failed to pay rent on time. If the tenant has no excuse for the nonpayment, the court grants an order evicting him. The order authorizes a sheriff to remove the tenant's goods and place them in storage, at the tenant's expense. However, if the tenant was withholding rent because of unlivable conditions, the court may refuse to evict.

EXAM Strategy

Question: Leo rents an apartment from Donna for $900 per month, both parties signing a lease. After six months, Leo complains about defects, including bugs, inadequate heat, and window leaks. He asks Donna to fix the problems, but she responds that the heat is fine and that Leo caused the insects and leaks. Leo begins to send in only $700 for the monthly rent. Donna repeatedly phones Leo, asking for the remaining rent. When he refuses to pay, she waits until he leaves for the day, then has a moving company place his belongings in storage. She changes the locks, making it impossible for him to reenter. Leo sues. What is the likely outcome?

Strategy: A landlord is entitled to begin proper eviction proceedings against a tenant who has not paid rent. However, the landlord must follow specified steps, including a termination notice and a court hearing. Review the consequences for actual eviction, described in the section "Quiet Enjoyment."

Result: Donna has ignored the legal procedures for evicting a tenant. Instead, she engaged in *actual eviction*, which is quick, and in the short term, effective. However, by breaking the law, Donna has ensured that Leo will win his lawsuit. He is entitled to possession of the apartment, as well as damages for rent he may have been forced to pay elsewhere, injury to his possessions, and the cost of retrieving them. He may receive punitive damages as well. Bad strategy, Donna.

Duty to Mitigate

Pickwick & Perkins, Ltd., was a store in the Burlington Square Mall in Burlington, Vermont. Pickwick had a five-year lease but abandoned the space almost two years early and ceased paying rent. The landlord waited approximately eight months before renting the space to a new tenant and then sued, seeking the unpaid rent. Pickwick defended on the grounds that Burlington had failed to **mitigate damages**; that is, to keep its losses to a minimum by promptly seeking another tenant. Burlington argued that it had no legal obligation to mitigate. Burlington's position accurately reflected the common law rule, which permitted the landlord to let the property lie vacant and allow the damages to add up. But the common law evolves over time, and this time, the Vermont Supreme Court changed the rule. The judges pointed out that, historically, a lease was a conveyance of an estate, and property law had never required mitigation. However, the court asserted, a lease is now regarded as both a contract and a conveyance. Under contract law, the nonbreaching party must make a reasonable effort to minimize losses, and that same rule applies, said the court, to a landlord. Burlington lost. The Vermont ruling is typical of current decisions, although some courts still do not require mitigation.[12]

42-9b Duty to Use Premises for Proper Purpose

A lease normally lists what a tenant may do in the premises and prohibits other activities. For example, a residential lease allows the tenant to use the property for normal living purposes, but not for any retail, commercial, or industrial purpose. A commercial lease might allow a tenant to operate a retail clothing store but not a restaurant. A landlord may evict a tenant who violates the lease by using the premises for prohibited purposes.

A tenant may not use the premises for any illegal activity, such as gambling or selling drugs. The law itself implies this condition in every lease, so a tenant who engages in illegal acts on the leased property is subject to eviction, regardless of whether the lease mentions such conduct.

42-9c Duty Not to Damage Premises

A tenant is liable to the landlord for any significant damage he causes to the property. The tenant is not liable for normal wear and tear. If, however, he knocks a hole in a wall or damages the plumbing, the landlord may collect the cost of repairs, either by using the security deposit or by suing, if necessary. A landlord may also seek to evict a tenant for serious damage to the property.

A tenant is permitted to make reasonable changes in the leased property so that he can use it as intended. Someone leasing an apartment is permitted to hang pictures on the wall. But a tenant leasing commercial space should make certain that the lease specifies the alterations he can make and whether he is obligated to return the premises to their original condition at the end of the lease.

Recall that a **fixture** is an item of personal property that is permanently attached to real estate. A furnace is a fixture, as are custom cabinets installed in a kitchen. The common law rule held that all fixtures belonged to the landlord. The contemporary trend, though, is the opposite. In commercial leases, it is common for tenants to install expensive equipment as part of their business, for example, commercial ovens in a restaurant. These are called **trade fixtures**. Most states permit commercial tenants to remove trade fixtures, provided the tenant restores the property to its original condition. In residential leases, some states still prohibit the tenant from removing a fixture, but courts today are likelier to permit removal, provided the tenant does not harm the premises in the process.

42-9d Duty Not to Disturb Other Tenants

Most leases, commercial and residential, include a covenant that the tenant will not disturb other tenants in the building. A landlord may evict a tenant who unreasonably disturbs others. The test is *reasonableness*. A landlord does not have the right to evict a residential tenant for giving one loud party but may evict a tenant who repeatedly plays loud music late at night and disturbs the quiet enjoyment of other tenants.

---

[12]O'Brien v. Black, 162 Vt. 448 (1994).

42-10 INJURIES

You invite a friend to dinner in your rented home, but after the meal, she slips and falls, seriously injuring her back. Are you liable? Is the landlord?

42-10a Tenant's Liability

A tenant is generally liable for injuries occurring within the premises she is leasing, whether that is an apartment, a store, or otherwise. If a tenant permits grease to accumulate on a kitchen floor and a guest slips and falls, the tenant is liable. If a merchant negligently installs display shelving that tips onto a customer, the merchant pays for the harm. Generally, a tenant is not liable for injuries occurring in common areas over which she has no control, such as exterior walkways. If a tenant's dinner guest falls because the building's common stairway has loose steps, the landlord is probably liable.

42-10b Landlord's Liability

Common Law Rules

Historically, the common law held a landlord responsible for injuries on the premises only in a limited number of circumstances, which we will describe. In reading these common law rules, be aware that many states have changed them, dramatically increasing the landlord's liability.

Latent Defects.   If the landlord knows of a dangerous condition on the property and realizes the tenant will not notice it, the landlord is liable for any injuries. For example, if a landlord knows that a porch railing is weak and fails to inform the tenant, the landlord is responsible if the tenant plunges off the porch. But notice that, under the common law, if the landlord notifies the tenant of the latent defect, he is no longer liable.

Common Areas.   The landlord is usually responsible for maintaining the common areas, and along with this obligation may go liability for torts. As we saw earlier, if your guest falls downstairs in a common hallway because the stairs were defective, the landlord is probably liable.

Negligent Repairs.   Even in areas where the landlord has no duty to make repairs, if he volunteers to do so and does the work badly, he is responsible for resulting harm.

Public Use.   If the premises are to be used for a public purpose, such as a store or office, the landlord is generally obligated to repair any dangerous defects, although the tenant is probably liable as well. The purpose of this stricter rule is to ensure that the general public can safely visit commercial establishments. If a landlord realizes that the plate glass in a store's door is loose, he must promptly repair it or suffer liability for any injuries.

Modern Trend

Increasingly, state legislatures and courts are discarding the common law classifications previously described and holding landlords liable under the normal rules of negligence law. **In many states, a landlord must use reasonable care to maintain safe premises and is liable for foreseeable harm.** For example, the common law rule merely required a landlord to notify a tenant of a latent defect, such as a defective porch railing. Most states now have building codes that require a landlord to maintain structural elements such as railings in safe condition. States further imply a warranty of habitability, which mandates reasonably safe living conditions. So, in many states, a landlord is no longer saved from negligence suits merely by giving notice of defects—he has to fix them.

In the following case, the court held that a landlord was required to take reasonable steps to protect a tenant.

LINDSAY P. v. TOWNE PROPERTIES ASSET MANAGEMENT CO., LTD.

2013-Ohio-4124
Court of Appeals of Ohio, 2013

Facts: Lindsay[13] and her young daughter lived above Rhonda Schmidt, in an apartment complex operated by Towne Properties (TP). Schmidt's boyfriend, Courtney Haynes, often stayed in Schmidt's apartment, but was not on her lease. The couple blared rap music and fought loudly, often waking Lindsay's child.

Lindsay frequently complained to TP about the noise coming from Schmidt's apartment. In retaliation, Haynes banged on Lindsay's door with a fire extinguisher and confronted her menacingly. When Lindsay reported this intimidating behavior, TP representatives suggested she call the police. One TP agent even offered to sit with a terrified Lindsay so she would not be alone in her apartment.

Late one night, Haynes sent Lindsay a series of Facebook messages. He anonymously wrote, "leave all your worries and concerns and troubles behind and have fun with me, let things go beyond and experience excitement together like never before…. You will really like having a friend so close that can satisfy you in so many great ways." Haynes also included a link to a pornographic website. Lindsay knew it was Haynes.

Lindsay immediately reported the Facebook incident to TP managers. Fearing for her safety, she begged TP to let her out of her lease. TP refused, and offered instead to move her to an available first-floor unit. Although Lindsay was wary of living on the first floor, TP assured her it would be safe.

Meanwhile, TP advised Schmidt that since Haynes was not on the lease, he would have to leave. In response, Schmidt insisted on adding him to the lease and TP agreed to go forward with the paperwork. In the process, TP divulged that Lindsay was moving to another unit.

A few days later, Haynes broke into Lindsay's new apartment and raped her in her daughter's presence. He was ultimately sentenced to nine years in prison. Lindsay sued TP, alleging that it was negligent. The trial court found that TP had no duty to protect its tenant from the criminal acts of third parties and dismissed the case. Lindsay appealed.

Issue: *Was the landlord liable for the tenant's injuries?*

Excerpts from Judge Piper's Decision: Generally, landlords do not have a duty to protect their tenants from the criminal acts of third parties. However, such a duty exists when the landlord should have reasonably foreseen the criminal activity and failed to take reasonable precautions to prevent such activity.

This court is cognizant that the criminal acts of third parties are very difficult to predict. However, there are issues of fact regarding whether TP should have reasonably foreseen Haynes' criminal activity. The record demonstrates that TP was aware of how Haynes was acting toward Lindsay. The record also demonstrates that TP was aware of Haynes' dangerous propensities, as it knew that Lindsay felt threatened by Haynes to the point that an employee offered to sit with Lindsay even after business hours so that she would not be alone.

TP was also made aware of Haynes' Facebook communication with Lindsay and that he propositioned her sexually. TP told Lindsay that it was "taking care of it," and asked Lindsay to contact police so that such police records would allow TP "the means we need to take action on the matter." TP also told Lindsay that it would "keep an eye on" the relations between Haynes and Lindsay.

In addition to not letting Lindsay break her lease, expressly informing Haynes that Lindsay was moving, and then placing Lindsay in a first-floor apartment even though she expressed concern for her safety, TP also began the process of adding Haynes to Schmidt's lease. When various facts are put into context with one another, it creates a question of fact as to whether TP took reasonable steps to protect Lindsay.

Summary judgment is not proper in this case. Accordingly, we remand to the trial court for further proceedings.

---

[13]The court refers to Lindsay by her first name alone to protect her privacy.

Exculpatory Clauses

You have found an apartment you can afford, in the right neighborhood, and the landlord presents you with a lease to sign. You notice an **exculpatory clause**, which states that the landlord is *not* liable for any injuries that occur on the rented premises, whether to you or your guests, regardless of the cause. You feel uncomfortable about the clause because it seems to suggest that the landlord can ignore serious defects and still escape liability. Should you sign the lease?

Today, **exculpatory clauses are generally void in residential leases.** Courts dislike such clauses because the parties typically have unequal bargaining power, and the goal of the law is to encourage safe housing managed by responsible landlords. So courts in many states simply ignore exculpatory clauses and apply normal rules of negligence to determine whether or not a landlord is liable for an injury. However, this is not universally the case; in some states, a court may still enforce an exculpatory clause in a residential lease. A concerned tenant should learn the local law before signing such a lease.

Exculpatory clause
A lease clause that relieves a landlord of liability for injuries

Chapter Conclusion

Real property law is ancient but forceful. Although real property today is not the dominant source of wealth that it was in medieval England, it is still the greatest asset that most people will ever possess—and is worth understanding.

When property is rented, a special relationship exists between landlord and tenant. Each has numerous obligations to the other. The current trend is clearly for expanded landlord liability, but how far that will continue is impossible to divine.

EXAM REVIEW

EXAM Strategy

1. **REAL PROPERTY; FIXTURES**   Real property includes land, buildings, air and subsurface rights, plant life, and fixtures. A fixture is any good that has become attached to other real property, such as land.

   Question: Paul and Shelly Higgins had two wood stoves in their home. Each rested on, but was not attached to, a built-in brick platform. The downstairs wood stove was connected to the chimney flue and was used as part of the main heating system for the house. The upstairs stove, in the master bedroom, was purely decorative. It had no stovepipe connecting it to the chimney. The Higginses sold their house to Jack Everitt, and neither party said anything about the two stoves. Is Everitt entitled to either stove? Both stoves?

   Strategy: An object is a fixture if a reasonable person would consider the item to be a permanent part of the property, taking into account attachment, adaptation, and other objective manifestations of permanence. (See the "Result" at the end of this section.)

2. **CONCURRENT ESTATES**   When two or more people own real property at the same time, they have a concurrent estate. In both a tenancy in common and a joint tenancy, all owners have a share in the entire property. The primary difference is that joint tenants have the right of survivorship, meaning that when a joint tenant dies, his interest passes to the other joint tenants. A tenant in common has the power to leave her estate to her heirs.

EXAM Strategy

Question: Howard Geib, Walker McKinney, and John D. McKinney owned two vacation properties as joint tenants with right of survivorship. The parties were not getting along well, and Geib petitioned the court to partition the properties. The trial court ruled that the fairest way to do this was to sell both properties and divide the proceeds. The two McKinneys appealed, claiming that a partition by sale was improper because it would destroy their right of survivorship. Comment.

Strategy: Do joint tenants have a right to partition? Are there any limits on that right? (See the "Result" at the end of this section.)

3. **FUTURE INTERESTS**   Future interests are presently existing nonpossessory rights that may or may not develop later.

4. **ADVERSE POSSESSION**   Adverse possession permits the user of land to gain title if he can prove entry and exclusive possession, open and notorious possession, a claim adverse to the owner, and continuous possession for the required statutory period.

5. **GOVERNMENT REGULATION**   Nuisance law, zoning ordinances, and eminent domain all permit a government to regulate property and in some cases to take it for public use.

6. **LANDLORD–TENANT**   When an owner of a freehold estate allows another person temporary, exclusive possession of the property, the parties have created a landlord–tenant relationship.

7. **TENANCIES**   Any lease for a stated, fixed period is a tenancy for years. A periodic tenancy is created for a fixed period and then automatically continues for additional periods until either party notifies the other of termination. A tenancy at will has no fixed duration and may be terminated by either party at any time. A tenancy at sufferance occurs when a tenant remains, against the wishes of the landlord, after the expiration of a true tenancy.

8. **QUIET ENJOYMENT**   All tenants are entitled to the quiet enjoyment of the premises, without the interference of the landlord.

9. **SECURITY DEPOSITS**   Landlords may require tenants to post a deposit that can be used to pay for repairs if a tenant damages the property. But many landlords

fail to promptly return security deposits to tenants who leave no damage behind. In those cases, tenants are often able to sue for as much as three times their security deposit.

10. **RENT**   The tenant is obligated to pay the rent, and the landlord may evict the tenant for nonpayment. The modern trend is to require a landlord to mitigate damages caused by a tenant who abandons the premises before the lease expires.

EXAM Strategy

Question: Loren Andreo leased retail space in his shopping plaza to Tropical Isle Pet Shop for five years, at a monthly rent of $2,100. Tropical Isle vacated the premises 18 months early, turned in the key to Andreo, and acknowledged liability for the unpaid rent. Andreo placed a "for rent" sign in the store window and spoke to a commercial real estate broker about the space. But he did not enter into a formal listing agreement with the broker, or take any other steps to rent the space, for about nine months. With approximately nine months remaining on the unused part of Tropical's lease, Andreo hired a commercial broker to rent the space. He also sued Tropical for 18 months' rent. Comment.

Strategy: When a tenant abandons leased property early, the landlord is obligated to mitigate damages. Did Andreo? (See the "Result" at the end of this section.)

11. **DAMAGE**   A tenant is liable to the landlord for any significant damage he causes to the property.

12. **DISTURBANCES**   A tenant must not disturb other tenants.

EXAM Strategy

Question: Doris Rowley rented space from the city of Mobile, Alabama, to run the Back Porch Restaurant. Her lease prohibited assignment or subletting without the landlord's permission. Rowley's business became unprofitable, and she asked the city's real estate officer for permission to assign her lease. She told the officer that she had "someone who would accept if the lease was assigned." Rowley provided no other information about the assignee. The city refused permission. Rowley repeated her requests several times without success, and finally she sued. Rowley alleged that the city had unreasonably withheld permission to assign and had caused her serious financial losses as a result. Comment.

Strategy: A landlord may not unreasonably refuse permission to assign a lease. Was the city's refusal unreasonable? (See the "Result" at the end of this section.)

13. **PERSONAL INJURY**   At common law, a landlord had very limited liability for injuries on the premises, but today many courts require a landlord to use reasonable care and hold her liable for foreseeable harm.

> **1. Result:** A buyer normally takes all fixtures. The downstairs stove was permanently attached to the house and used as part of the heating system. The owner who installed it intended that it remain, and it was a fixture; Everitt got it. The upstairs stove was not permanently attached and was not a fixture; the sellers could take it with them.
>
> **2. Result:** The McKinneys lost. Any co-tenant (including a joint tenant) has an absolute right to partition. Difficulties in partitioning are irrelevant.
>
> **10. Result:** For about nine months, Andreo made no serious effort to lease the store. The court rejected his rent claim for that period, permitting him to recover unpaid money only for the period he made a genuine effort to lease the space.
>
> **12. Result:** A landlord is allowed to evaluate a prospective assignee, including its financial stability and intended use of the property. Mobile could not do that because Rowley provided no information about the proposed assignee. Mobile wins.

MULTIPLE-CHOICE QUESTIONS

1. Quick, Onyx, and Nash were deeded a piece of land as tenants in common. The deed provided that Quick owned one-half the property and Onyx and Nash owned one-quarter each. If Nash dies, the property will be owned as follows:
   (a) Quick 1/2, Onyx 1/2
   (b) Quick 5/8, Onyx 3/8
   (c) Quick 1/3, Onyx 1/3, Nash's heirs 1/3
   (d) Quick 1/2, Onyx 1/4, Nash's heirs 1/4

2. Which of the following forms of tenancy will be created if a tenant stays in possession of leased premises without the landlord's consent, after the tenant's one-year written lease expires?
   (a) Tenancy at will
   (b) Tenancy for years
   (c) Periodic tendency
   (d) Tenancy at sufferance

3. To be enforceable, a long-term residential real estate lease must _____ .
   (a) require the tenant to obtain liability insurance
   (b) define the tenant's duty to mitigate
   (c) be in writing
   (d) specify a due date for rent
   (e) All of the above

4. A tenant renting an apartment under a three-year written lease that does not contain any specific restrictions may be evicted for _____ .
   (a) counterfeiting money in the apartment
   (b) keeping a dog in the apartment

    (c)   failing to maintain a liability insurance policy on the apartment

    (d)   making structural repairs to the apartment

5. A tenant's personal property will become a fixture and belong to the landlord if its removal would _____ .

    (a)   increase the value of the personal property

    (b)   cause a material change to the personal property

    (c)   result in substantial harm to the landlord's property

    (d)   change the use of the landlord's property back to its prior use

CASE QUESTIONS

1. In 1944, W. E. Collins conveyed land to the Church of God of Prophecy. The deed said: "This deed is made with the full understanding that should the property fail to be used for the Church of God, it is to be null and void and property to revert to W. E. Collins or heirs." In the late 1980s, the church wished to move to another property and sought a judicial ruling that it had the right to sell the land. The trial court ruled that the church owned a fee simple absolute and had the right to sell the property. Comment.

2. Nome 2000, a partnership, owned a large tract of wilderness land in Alaska. The Fagerstrom family had used the property for camping and holidays since about 1944. In 1966, Charles and Peggy Fagerstrom marked off an area for a cabin and brought material to build the cabin, but never did so. In about 1970, they built a picnic area on the land, and in about 1974, they placed a camper trailer on the land, where it remained until the lawsuit. In 1987, Nome 2000 sued to eject the Fagerstroms from the land. The Fagerstroms had used the land only during the summer months. No one lived in the area during the winter months, when it was virtually uninhabitable. Has the family adversely possessed the land from Nome 2000?

3. *YOU BE THE JUDGE* **WRITING PROBLEM** Frank Deluca and his son David owned the Sportsman's Pub on Fountain Street in Providence, Rhode Island. The Delucas applied to the city for a license to employ topless dancers in the pub. Did the city have the power to deny the Delucas' request? **Argument for the Delucas:** Our pub is perfectly legal. Further, no law in Rhode Island prohibits topless dancing. We are morally and legally entitled to present this entertainment. The city should not use some phony moralizing to deny customers what they want. **Argument for Providence:** This section of Providence is zoned to prohibit topless dancing, just as it is zoned to bar manufacturing. There are other parts of town where the Delucas can open one of their sleazy clubs if they want to, but we are entitled to deny a permit in this area.

4. Kenmart Realty sued to evict Mr. and Ms. Alghalabio for nonpayment of rent and sought the unpaid monies, totaling several thousand dollars. In defense, the Alghalabios claimed that their apartment was infested with rats. They testified that there were numerous rat holes in the walls of the living room, bedroom, and kitchen, that there were rat droppings all over the apartment, and that on one occasion, they saw their toddler holding a live rat. They testified that the landlord had refused numerous requests to exterminate. Please rule on the landlord's suit.

5. Lisa Preece rented an apartment from Turman Realty, paying a $300 security deposit. Georgia law states: "Any landlord who fails to return any part of a security deposit which is required to be returned to a tenant pursuant to this article shall be liable to the tenant in the amount of three times the sum improperly withheld plus reasonable attorney's fees." When Preece moved out, Turman did not return her security deposit, and she sued for triple damages plus attorney's fees, totaling $1,800. Turman offered evidence that its failure to return the deposit was inadvertent and that it had procedures reasonably designed to avoid such errors. Is Preece entitled to triple damages? Attorney's fees?

Discussion Questions

1. The Estates is a suburb outside of Los Angeles. Local zoning ordinances require that lots be "at least 1 acre in size." Al owns a 1-acre lot in The Estates which has never been developed. He needs cash and wants to sell the property. Al finds a potential buyer who offers him $100,000 for the acre. But he also finds a pair of interested buyers who each offer him $75,000 for half of his acre. Al is furious that he cannot divide his acre and sell it to two buyers. "I need that extra $50,000," he rants. "It's my land, and I should be able to do what I want with it!" Do you sympathize with Al, or do you think the zoning restriction is reasonable?

2. Donny Delt and Sammy Sigma are students and roommates. They lease a house in a neighborhood near campus. Few students live on the block. The students do not have large parties, but they often have friends over at night. The friends sometimes play high-volume music in their cars and sometimes speak loudly when going to and from their cars. Also, departing late-night guests often leave beer cans and fast-food wrappers in the street. Neighbors complain about being awakened in the wee hours of the morning. They are considering filing a nuisance lawsuit against Donny and Sammy. Would such an action be reasonable? Do you think Donny and Sammy are creating a nuisance? If so, why? If not, where is the line—what amount of late-night noise does amount to a nuisance?

3. **ETHICS** During the Great Recession, home foreclosures hit an all-time high. In many instances, banks ended up as landlords and property managers, a job for which they were ill-prepared. As a result, many homes were abandoned for long periods. Some people who knew a little bit about adverse possession decided to take advantage of this ancient common law doctrine: They shamelessly occupied vacant homes, claiming them as their own, changing locks, and purchasing electricity. The new residents argued that they were not hurting anyone and acting within the bounds of the law. In response, some states lengthened the time period necessary for adverse possession. Examine the squatters' ethics. What do you think of their behavior? Does your opinion vary if the squatters were the home's former owners? What if the banks were ignoring the home? What would Kant and Mill say?

4. In 1966, Arketex Ceramic Corp. sold land in rural Indiana to Malcolm Aukerman. The deed described the southern boundary as the section line between sections 11 and 14 of the land. Farther south than this section line stood a dilapidated fence running east to west. Aukerman and Arketex both believed that this fence was the actual southern boundary of his new land, though in fact it lay on Arketex's property.

Aukerman installed a new electrified fence, cleared the land on "his" side of the new fence, and began to graze cattle there. In 1974, Harold Clark bought the land that bordered Aukerman's fence, assuming that the fence was the correct boundary. In 1989, Clark had his land surveyed and discovered that the true property line lay north of the electric fence. Aukerman filed suit, seeking a court order that he had acquired the disputed land by adverse possession. The statutory period in Indiana is 20 years. Who wins? Who *ought* to win? Does adverse possession make sense as a social policy? Why or why not?

5. Imagine that you sign a lease and that you are to move into your new apartment on August 15. When you arrive, the previous tenant has not moved out. In fact, he has no intention of moving out. Compare the English and the American rules. Should the landlord be in charge of getting rid of the old tenant, or should you have the obligation to evict him?

6. When landlords wrongfully withhold security deposits, they can often be sued for three times the amount of the security deposit. Is this reasonable? Should a landlord have to pay $3,000 for a $1,000 debt? What if you fail to pay a rent on time? Should you have to pay three times the amount of your normal rent? If your answers to these two questions are different, why?

ANSWERS TO SELECTED END OF CHAPTER QUESTIONS

MULTIPLE-CHOICE QUESTIONS

Presented are the answers for the ODD-numbered multiple-choice questions in the end-of-chapter material.

1. D
3. C
5. C

CASE QUESTIONS

Presented are the answers for all of the ODD-numbered case questions in the end-of-chapter material.

1. **Answer:** The trial court was wrong. The church held a fee simple defeasible. The moment the church ceased to use the property as a church, the land reverted automatically to Collins and his heirs. *Collins v. Church of God of Prophecy*, 304 Ark. 37, 800 S.W.2d 418, 1990 Ark. LEXIS 566 (1990).

3. **Answer:** Yes, the city could use its zoning powers to deny the license. Earlier zoning ordinances had allowed topless dancing in the section of the city where the pub was located, but the current ordinance prohibited such dancing in that section. The city had no obligation to grant a variance for the Delucas and denied the request. Jonathan Saltzman, "License Is Denied for Topless Dancing at Downtown Pub," *Providence Journal-Bulletin*, July 11, 1995, p. 2C.

5. **Answer:** The court held the defendant liable for $900 (treble damages) and an additional $900 in attorney's fees. The rationale for treble damages is that, historically, landlords often willfully refuse to refund security deposits, knowing that most tenants would not bother to sue. That was obviously unethical. By trebling the damages, state legislatures have given landlords a financial incentive to be fair. By permitting attorney's fees, such laws ensure that injured tenants have access to court and a remedy. *Preece v. Turman Realty Co., Inc.*, 228 Ga. App. 609, 492 S.E.2d 342, 1997 Ga. App. LEXIS 1216 (Ga. App. 1997).

Appendix A

THE CONSTITUTION OF THE UNITED STATES

Preamble

We the People of the United States, in Order to form a more perfect Union, establish Justice, insure domestic Tranquility, provide for the common defense, promote the general Welfare, and secure the Blessings of Liberty to ourselves and our Posterity, do ordain and establish this Constitution for the United States of America.

ARTICLE I

Section 1.

All legislative Powers herein granted shall be vested in a Congress of the United States, which shall consist of a Senate and House of Representatives.

Section 2.

The House of Representatives shall be composed of Members chosen every second Year by the People of the several States, and the Electors in each State shall have the Qualifications requisite for Electors of the most numerous Branch of the State Legislature.

No Person shall be a Representative who shall not have attained to the Age of twenty five Years, and been seven Years a Citizen of the United States, and who shall not, when elected, be an Inhabitant of that State in which he shall be chosen.

Representatives and direct Taxes shall be apportioned among the several States which may be included within this Union, according to their respective Numbers, which shall be determined by adding to the whole Number of free Persons, including those bound to Service for a Term of Years, and excluding Indians not taxed, three fifths of all other Persons. The actual Enumeration shall be made within three Years after the first Meeting of the Congress of the United States, and within every subsequent Term of ten Years, in such Manner as they shall by Law direct. The number of Representatives shall not exceed one for every thirty Thousand, but each State shall have at Least one Representative; and until such enumeration shall be made, the State of New Hampshire shall be entitled to chuse three, Massachusetts eight, Rhode Island and Providence Plantations one, Connecticut five, New-York six, New Jersey four, Pennsylvania eight, Delaware one, Maryland six, Virginia ten, North Carolina five, South Carolina five, and Georgia three.

When vacancies happen in the Representation from any State, the Executive Authority thereof shall issue Writs of Election to fill such vacancies.

The House of Representatives shall chuse their Speaker and other Officers; and shall have the sole Power of Impeachment.

Section 3.

The Senate of the United States shall be composed of two Senators from each State, chosen by the Legislature thereof, for six Years; and each Senator shall have one Vote.

Immediately after they shall be assembled in Consequence of the first Election, they shall be divided as equally as may be into three Classes. The Seats of the Senators of the first Class shall be vacated at the Expiration of the second Year, of the second Class at the Expiration of the fourth Year, and of the third Class at the Expiration of the sixth Year, so that one third may be chosen every second Year; and if Vacancies happen by Resignation or otherwise, during the Recess of the Legislature of any State, the Executive thereof may make temporary Appointments until the next Meeting of the Legislature, which shall then fill such Vacancies.

No Person shall be a Senator who shall not have attained to the Age of thirty Years, and been nine Years a Citizen of the United States, and who shall not, when elected, be an Inhabitant of that State for which he shall be chosen.

The Vice President of the United States shall be President of the Senate, but shall have no Vote, unless they be equally divided.

The Senate shall chuse their other Officers, and also a President pro tempore, in the Absence of the Vice President, or when he shall exercise the Office of President of the United States.

The Senate shall have the sole power to try all Impeachments. When sitting for that Purpose, they shall be an Oath or Affirmation. When the President of the United States is tried, the Chief Justice shall preside: And no Person shall be convicted without the Concurrence of two thirds of the Members present.

Judgment in Cases of Impeachment shall not extend further than to removal from Office, and disqualification to hold and enjoy any Office of honor, Trust or Profit under the United States: but the Party convicted shall nevertheless be liable and subject to Indictment, Trial, Judgment and Punishment, according to Law.

Section 4.

The Times, Places and Manner of holding Elections for Senators and Representatives, shall be prescribed in each State by the Legislature thereof: but the Congress may at any time by Law make or alter such Regulations, except as to the Places of chusing Senators.

The Congress shall assemble at least once in every Year, and such Meeting shall be on the first Monday in December, unless they shall by Law appoint a different Day.

Section 5.

Each House shall be the Judge of the Elections, Returns and Qualifications of its own Members, and a Majority of each shall constitute a Quorum to do Business; but a smaller Number may adjourn from day to day, and may be authorized to compel the Attendance of absent Members, in such Manner, and under such Penalties as each House may provide.

Each House may determine the Rules of its Proceedings, punish its Members for disorderly Behaviour, and, with the Concurrence of two thirds, expel a Member.

Each House shall keep a Journal of its Proceedings, and from time to time publish the same, excepting such Parts as may in their Judgment require Secrecy; and the Yeas and Nays of the Members of either House on any question shall, at the Desire of one fifth of those Present, be entered on the Journal.

Neither House, during the Session of Congress, shall, without the Consent of the other, adjourn for more than three days, nor to any other Place than that in which the two Houses shall be sitting.

Section 6.

The Senators and Representatives shall receive a Compensation for their Services, to be ascertained by Law, and paid out of the Treasury of the United States. They shall in all Cases, except Treason, Felony and Breach of the Peace, be privileged from Arrest during their Attendance at the Session of their respective Houses, and in going to and returning from the same; and for any Speech or Debate in either House, they shall not be questioned in any other Place.

No Senator or Representative shall, during the Time for which he was elected, be appointed to any civil Office under the Authority of the United States, which shall have been created, or the Emoluments whereof shall have been encreased during such time; and no Person holding any Office under the United States, shall be a Member of either House during his Continuance in Office.

Section 7.

All Bills for raising Revenue shall originate in the House of Representatives; but the Senate may propose or concur with Amendments as on other Bills.

Every Bill which shall have passed the House of Representatives and the Senate, shall, before it become a Law, be presented to the President of the United States; If he approve he shall sign it, but if not he shall return it, with his Objections to that House in which it shall have originated, who shall enter the Objections at large on their Journal, and proceed to reconsider it. If after such Reconsideration two thirds of that House shall agree to pass the Bill, it shall be sent, together with the Objections, to the other House, by which it shall likewise be reconsidered, and if approved by two thirds of that House, it shall become a Law. But in all such Cases the Votes of both Houses shall be determined by Yeas and Nays, and the Names of the Persons voting for and against the Bill shall be entered on the Journal of each House respectively. If any Bill shall not be returned by the President within ten Days (Sundays excepted) after it shall have been presented to him, the Same shall be a Law, in like Manner as if he had signed it, unless the Congress by their Adjournment prevent its Return, in which Case it shall not be a Law.

Every Order, Resolution, or Vote to which the Concurrence of the Senate and House of Representatives may be necessary (except on a question of Adjournment) shall be presented to the President of the United States; and before the Same shall take Effect, shall be approved by him, or being disapproved by him, shall be repassed by two thirds of the Senate and House of Representatives, according to the Rules and Limitations prescribed in the Case of a Bill.

Section 8.

The Congress shall have Power to lay and collect Taxes, Duties, Imposts and Excises, to pay the Debts and provide for the common Defence and general Welfare of the United States; but all Duties, Imposts and Excises shall be uniform throughout the United States;

To borrow Money on the credit of the United States;

To regulate Commerce with foreign Nations, and among the several States, and with the Indian Tribes;

To establish an uniform Rule of Naturalization, and uniform Laws on the subject of Bankruptcies throughout the United States;

To coin Money, regulate the Value thereof, and of foreign Coin, and fix the Standard of Weights and Measures;

To provide for the Punishment of counterfeiting the Securities and current Coin of the United States;

To establish Post Offices and post Roads;

To promote the Progress of Science and useful Arts, by securing for limited Times to Authors and Inventors the exclusive Right to their respective Writings and Discoveries;

To constitute Tribunals inferior to the Supreme Court;

To define and punish Piracies and Felonies committed on the high Seas, and Offenses against the Law of Nations;

To declare War, grant Letters of Marque and Reprisal, and make Rules concerning Captures on Land and Water;

To raise and support Armies, but no Appropriation of Money to that Use shall be for a longer Term than two Years;

To provide and maintain a Navy;

To make Rules for the Government and Regulation of the land and naval Forces;

To provide for calling forth the Militia to execute the Laws of the Union, suppress Insurrections and repel Invasions;

To provide for organizing, arming, and disciplining, the Militia, and for governing such Part of them as may be employed in the Service of the United States, reserving to the States respectively, the Appointment of the Officers, and the Authority of training the Militia according to the discipline described by Congress;

To exercise exclusive Legislation in all Cases whatsoever, over such District (not exceeding ten Miles square) as may, by Cession of particular States, and the Acceptance of Congress, become the Seat of the Government of the United States, and to exercise like Authority over all Places purchased by the Consent of the Legislature of the State in which the Same shall be, for the Erection of Forts, Magazines, Arsenals, dock-Yards, and other needful Buildings;—And

To make all Laws which shall be necessary and proper for carrying into Execution the foregoing Powers, and all other Powers vested by this Constitution in the Government of the United States, or in any Department or Officer thereof.

Section 9.

The Migration or Importation of such Persons as any of the States now existing shall think proper to admit, shall not be prohibited by the Congress prior to the Year one thousand eight hundred and eight, but a Tax or Duty may be imposed on such Importation, not exceeding ten dollars for each Person.

The Privilege of the Writ of Habeas Corpus shall not be suspended, unless when in Cases of Rebellion or Invasion the public Safety may require it.

No Bill of Attainder or ex post facto Law shall be passed.

No Capitation, or other direct, Tax shall be laid, unless in Proportion to the Census or Enumeration herein before directed to be taken.

No Tax or Duty shall be laid on Articles exported from any State.

No Preference shall be given by any Regulation of Commerce or Revenue to the Ports of one State over those of another; nor shall Vessels bound to, or from, one State, be obliged to enter, clear, or pay Duties in another.

No Money shall be drawn from the Treasury, but in Consequence of Appropriations made by Laws; and a regular Statement and Account of the Receipts and Expenditures of all public Money shall be published from time to time.

No Title of Nobility shall be granted by the United States: And no Person holding any Office of Profit or Trust under them, shall, without the Consent of the Congress, accept of any present, Emolument, Office, or Title, of any kind whatever, from any King, Prince, or foreign State.

Section 10.

No State shall enter into any Treaty, Alliance, or Confederation; grant Letters of Marque and Reprisal; coin Money; emit Bills of Credit; make any Thing but gold and silver Coin a Tender in Payment of Debts; pass any Bill of Attainder, ex post facto Law, or Law impairing the Obligation of Contracts, or grant any Title of Nobility.

No State shall, without the Consent of the Congress, lay any Imposts or Duties on Imports or Exports, except what may be absolutely necessary for executing its inspection Laws: and the net Produce of all Duties and Imposts, laid by any State on Imports or Exports, shall be for the Use of the Treasury of the United States; and all such Laws shall be subject to the Revision and Controul of the Congress.

No State shall, without the Consent of Congress, lay any Duty of Tonnage, keep Troops, or Ships of War in time of Peace, enter into any Agreement or Compact with another State, or with a foreign Power, or engage in War, unless actually invaded, or in such imminent Danger as will not admit of delay.

ARTICLE II

Section 1.

The executive Power shall be vested in a President of the United States of America. He shall hold his Office during the Term of four Years, and, together with the Vice President, chosen for the same Term, be elected, as follows:

Each State shall appoint, in such Manner as the Legislature thereof may direct, a Number of Electors, equal to the whole Number of Senators and Representatives to which the State may be entitled in the Congress: but no Senator or Representative, or Person holding an Office of Trust or Profit under the United States, shall be appointed an Elector.

The Electors shall meet in their respective States, and vote by Ballot for two Persons, of whom one at least shall not be an Inhabitant of the same State with themselves. And they shall make a list of all the Persons voted for, and of the Number of Votes for each; which List they shall sign and certify, and transmit sealed to the Seat of the Government of the United States, directed to the President of the Senate. The President of the Senate shall, in the presence of the Senate and House of Representatives, open all the Certificates, and the Votes shall be counted. The Person having the greatest Number of Votes shall be the President, if such Number be a Majority of the whole Number of Electors appointed; and if there be more than one who have such Majority, and have an equal Number of Votes, then the House of Representatives shall immediately chuse by Ballot one of them for President; and if no Person have a Majority, then from the five highest on the List the said House shall in like Manner chuse the President. But in chusing the President, the Votes shall be taken by States, the Representation from each State having one Vote; A quorum for this Purpose shall consist of a Member or Members from two thirds of the States, and a Majority of all the States shall be necessary to a Choice. In every Case, after the Choice of the President, the Person having the greatest Number of Votes of the Electors shall be the Vice President. But if there should remain two or more who have equal Votes, the Senate shall chuse from them by Ballot the Vice President.

The Congress may determine the Time of Chusing the Electors, and the Day on which they shall give their Votes; which Day shall be the same throughout the United States.

No Person except a natural born Citizen, or a Citizen of the United States, at the time of the Adoption of this Constitution, shall be eligible to the Office of President; neither shall any Person be eligible to that Office who shall not have attained to the Age of thirty five Years, and been fourteen Years a Resident within the United States.

In Case of the Removal of the President from Office, or of his Death, Resignation, or Inability to discharge the Powers and Duties of the said Office, the Same shall devolve on the Vice President, and the Congress may by Law provide for the Case of Removal, Death, Resignation or Inability, both of the President and Vice President, declaring what Officer shall then act as President, and such Officer shall act accordingly, until the Disability be removed, or a President shall be elected.

The President shall, at stated Times, receive for his Services, a Compensation, which shall neither be increased nor diminished during the Period for which he shall have been elected, and he shall not receive within that Period any other Emolument from the United States, or any of them.

Before he enter on the Execution of his Office, he shall take the following Oath or Affirmation:—"I do solemnly swear (or affirm) that I will faithfully execute the Office of President of the United States, and will to the best of my Ability, preserve, protect and defend the Constitution of the United States."

Section 2.

The President shall be Commander in Chief of the Army and Navy of the United States, and of the Militia of the several States, when called into the actual Service of the United States; he may require the Opinion, in writing, of the principal Officer in each of the executive Departments, upon any Subject relating to the Duties of their respective Offices, and he shall have Power to grant Reprieves and Pardons for Offenses against the United States, except in Cases of Impeachment.

He shall have Power, by and with the Advice and Consent of the Senate, to make Treaties, providing two thirds of the Senators present concur; and he shall nominate, and by and with the Advice and Consent of the Senate, shall appoint Ambassadors, other public Ministers and Consuls, Judges of the supreme Court, and all other Officers of the United States, whose Appointments are not herein otherwise provided for, and which shall be established by Law: but the Congress may by Law vest the Appointment of such inferior Officers, as they think proper, in the President alone, in the Courts of Law, or in the Heads of Departments.

The President shall have Power to fill up all Vacancies that may happen during the Recess of the Senate, by granting Commissions which shall expire at the End of their next Session.

Section 3.

He shall from time to time give to the Congress Information of the State of the Union, and recommend to their Consideration such Measures as he shall judge necessary and expedient; he may, on extraordinary Occasions, convene both Houses, or either of them, and in Case of Disagreement between them, with Respect to the Time of Adjournment, he may adjourn them to such Time as he shall think proper, he shall receive Ambassadors and other public Ministers; he shall take Care that the Laws be faithfully executed, and shall Commission all the Offices of the United States.

Section 4.

The President, Vice President and all civil Officers of the United States, shall be removed from Office on Impeachment for, and Conviction of, Treason, Bribery, or other high Crimes and Misdemeanors.

ARTICLE III

Section 1.

The judicial Power of the United States, shall be vested in one supreme Court, and in such inferior Courts as the Congress may from time to time ordain and establish. The Judges, both of the supreme and inferior Courts, shall hold their Offices during good Behaviour, and shall, at Times, receive for their Services, a Compensation, which shall not be diminished during their Continuance in Office.

Section 2.

The judicial Power shall extend to all Cases, in Law and Equity, arising under this Constitution, the Laws of the United States, and Treaties made, or which shall be made, under their Authority;—to all Cases affecting Ambassadors, other public Ministers and Consuls;—to all Cases of admiralty and maritime Jurisdiction;—to Controversies to which the United States shall be a Party;—to controversies between two or more States;—between a State and Citizens of another State;—between Citizens of different States;—between Citizens of the same State claiming Lands under Grants of different States; and between a State, or the Citizens thereof, and foreign States, Citizens or Subjects.

In all Cases affecting Ambassadors, other public Ministers and Consuls, and those in which a State shall be Party, the supreme Court shall have original Jurisdiction. In all the other Cases before mentioned, the supreme Court shall have appellate Jurisdiction, both as to Law and Fact, with such Exceptions, and under such Regulations as the Congress shall make.

The Trial of all Crimes, except in Cases of Impeachment, shall be by Jury; and such Trial shall be held in the State where the said Crimes shall have been committed; but when not committed within any State, the Trial shall be at such Place or Places as the Congress may by Law have directed.

Section 3.

Treason against the United States, shall consist only in levying War against them, or in adhering to their Enemies, giving them Aid and Comfort. No Person shall be convicted of Treason unless on the Testimony of two Witnesses to the same overt Act, or on Confession in open Court.

The Congress shall have Power to declare the Punishment of Treason, but no Attainder of Treason shall work Corruption of Blood, or Forfeiture except during the Life of the Person attainted.

ARTICLE IV

Section 1.

Full Faith and Credit shall be given in each State to the public Acts, Records, and judicial Proceedings of every other State. And the Congress may by general Laws prescribe the Manner in which such Acts, Records and Proceedings shall be proved, and the Effect thereof.

Section 2.

The Citizens of each State shall be entitled to all Privileges and Immunities of Citizens in the several States.

A Person charged in any State with Treason, Felony, or other Crime, who shall flee from Justice, and be found in another State, shall on Demand of the executive Authority of the State from which he fled, be delivered up, to be removed to the State having Jurisdiction of the Crime.

No Person held to Service or Labour in one State, under the Laws thereof, escaping into another, shall, in Consequence of any Law or Regulation therein, be discharged from such Service or Labour, but shall be delivered up on Claim of the Party to whom such Service or Labour may be due.

Section 3.

New States may be admitted by the Congress into this Union; but no new State shall be formed or erected within the Jurisdiction of any other State; nor any State be formed by the Junction of two or more States, or Parts of States, without the Consent of the Legislatures of the States concerned as well as the Congress.

The Congress shall have Power to dispose of and make all needful Rules and Regulations respecting the Territory or other Property belonging to the United States; and nothing in this Constitution shall be so construed as to Prejudice any Claims of the United States, or of any particular State.

Section 4.

The United States shall guarantee to every State in this Union a Republican Form of Government, and shall protect each of them against Invasion; and on Application of the Legislature, or of the Executive (when the Legislature cannot be convened) against domestic Violence.

ARTICLE V

The Congress, whenever two thirds of both Houses shall deem it necessary, shall propose Amendments to this Constitution, or, on the Application of the Legislatures of two thirds of the several States, shall call a Convention for proposing Amendments, which, in either Case, shall be valid to all Intents and Purposes, as Part of this Constitution, when ratified by the Legislatures of three fourths of the several States, or by Conventions in three fourths thereof, as the one or the other Mode of Ratification may be proposed by the Congress; Provided that no Amendment which may be made prior to the Year One thousand eight hundred and eight shall in any Manner affect the first and fourth Clauses in the Ninth Section of the first Article; and that no State, without its Consent, shall be deprived of its equal Suffrage in the Senate.

ARTICLE VI

All Debts contracted and Engagements entered into, before the Adoption of this Constitution, shall be as valid against the United States under this Constitution, as under the Confederation.

This Constitution, and the Laws of the United States which shall be made in Pursuance thereof; and all Treaties made, or which shall be made, under the Authority of the United States, shall be the supreme Law of the Land; and the Judges in every State shall be bound thereby, any Thing in the Constitution or Laws of any State to the Contrary notwithstanding.

The Senators and Representatives before mentioned, and the Members of the several State Legislatures, and all executive and judicial Officers, both of the United States and of the Several States, shall be bound by Oath or Affirmation, to support this Constitution; but no religious Test shall ever be required as a Qualification to any Office or public Trust under the United States.

ARTICLE VII

The Ratification of the Conventions of nine States, shall be sufficient for the Establishment of this Constitution between the States so ratifying the Same.

Amendment I [1791].

Congress shall make no law respecting an establishment of religion, or prohibiting the free exercise thereof; or abridging the freedom of speech, or the press; or the right of the people peaceably to assemble, and to petition the Government for a redress of grievances.

Amendment II [1791].

A well regulated Militia, being necessary to the security for a free State, the right of the people to keep and bear Arms, shall not be infringed.

Amendment III [1791].

No Soldier shall, in time of peace be quartered in any house, without the consent of the Owner, nor in time of war, but in a manner to be prescribed by law.

Amendment IV [1791].

The right of the people to be secure in their persons, houses, papers, and effects, against unreasonable searches and seizures, shall not be violated, and no Warrants shall issue, but upon probable cause, supported by Oath or Affirmation, and particularly describing the place to be searched, and the persons or things to be seized.

Amendment V [1791].

No person shall be held to answer for a capital, or otherwise infamous crime, unless on a presentment or indictment of a Grand Jury, except in cases arising in the land or naval forces, or in the Militia, when in actual service in time of War or public danger;

nor shall any person be subject for the same offense to be twice put in jeopardy of life or limb; nor shall be compelled in any criminal case to be a witness against himself, nor be deprived of life, liberty, or property, without due process of law; nor shall private property be taken for public use, without just compensation.

Amendment VI [1791].

In all criminal prosecutions, the accused shall enjoy the right to a speedy and public trial, by an impartial jury of the State and district wherein the crime shall have been committed, which district shall have been previously ascertained by law, and to be informed of the nature and cause of the accusation; to be confronted with the Witnesses against him; to have compulsory process for obtaining witnesses in his favor, and to have the Assistance of counsel for his defence.

Amendment VII [1791].

In suits at common law, where the value in controversy shall exceed twenty dollars, the right of trial by jury shall be preserved, and no fact tried by a jury, shall be otherwise re-examined in any Court of the United States, than according to the rules of the common law.

Amendment VIII [1791].

Excessive bail shall not be required, no excessive fines imposed, nor cruel and unusual punishments inflicted.

Amendment IX [1791].

The enumeration in the Constitution, of certain rights, shall not be construed to deny or disparage others retained by the people.

Amendment X [1791].

The powers not delegated to the United States by the Constitution, nor prohibited by it to the States, are reserved to the States respectively, or to the people.

Amendment XI [1798].

The judicial power of the United States shall not be construed to extend to any suit in law or equity, commenced or prosecuted against one of the United States by Citizens of another State, or by Citizens or Subjects of any Foreign State.

Amendment XII [1804].

The Electors shall meet in their respective states and vote by ballot for President and Vice-President, one of whom, at least, shall not be an inhabitant of the same state with themselves; they shall name in their ballots the person voted for as President, and in distinct ballots the person voted for as Vice-President, and they shall make distinct lists of all persons voted for as President, and of all persons voted for as Vice-President, and of the number of votes for each, which lists they shall sign and certify, and transmit sealed to the seat of the government of the United States, directed to the President of the Senate;—The President of the Senate shall, in the presence of the Senate and House of Representatives, open all the certificates and the votes shall then be counted;—The person having the greatest number of votes for President, shall be the President, if such number be a majority of the whole number of Electors appointed; and if no person have such majority, then from the persons having the highest numbers not exceeding three on the list of those voted for as President, the House of Representatives shall choose immediately, by ballot, the President. But in choosing the President, the votes shall be taken by states, the representation from each state having one vote; a quorum for this purpose shall consist of a member or members from two-thirds of the states, and a majority of all the states shall be necessary to a choice. And if the House of Representatives shall not choose a President whenever the right of choice shall devolve upon them, before the fourth day of March next following, then the Vice-President shall act as President, as in the case of the death or other constitutional disability of the President. The person having the greatest number of votes as Vice-President, shall be the Vice-President, if such number be a majority of the whole number of Electors appointed, and if no person have a majority, then from the two highest numbers on the list, the Senate shall choose the Vice-President; a quorum for the purpose shall consist of two-thirds of the whole number of Senators, and a majority of the whole number shall be necessary to a choice. But no person constitutionally ineligible to the office of President shall be eligible to that of the Vice-President of the United States.

Amendment XIII [1865].

Section 1. Neither slavery nor involuntary servitude, except as a punishment for crime whereof the party shall have been duly convicted, shall exist within the United States, or any place subject to their jurisdiction.

Section 2. Congress shall have power to enforce this article by appropriate legislation.

Amendment XIV [1868].

Section 1. All persons born or naturalized in the United States, and subject to the jurisdiction thereof, are citizens of the United States and of the State wherein they reside. No State shall make or enforce any law which shall abridge the privileges or immunities of citizens of the United States; nor shall any State deprive any person of life, liberty, or property, without due process of law; nor deny to any person within its jurisdiction the equal protection of the laws.

Section 2. Representatives shall be appointed among the several States according to their respective numbers, counting the whole number of persons in each State, excluding Indians not taxed. But when the right to vote at any election for the choice of electors for President and Vice President of the United States, Representatives in Congress, the Executive and Judicial officers of a State, or the members of the Legislature thereof, is denied to any of the male inhabitants of such State, being twenty-one years of age, and citizens of the United States, or in any way abridged, except for participation in rebellion, or other crime, the basis of representation therein shall be reduced in the proportion which the number of such male citizens shall bear the whole number of male citizens twenty-one years of age in such State.

Section 3. No person shall be a Senator or Representative in Congress, or elector of President and Vice President, or hold any office, civil or military, under the United States, or under any State, who, having previously taken an oath, as a member of Congress, or as an officer of the United States, or as a member of any State legislature, or as an executive or judicial officer of any State, to support the Constitution of the United States, shall have engaged in insurrection or rebellion against the same, or given aid or comfort to the enemies thereof. But Congress may by a vote of two-thirds of each House, remove such disability.

Section 4. The validity of the public debt of the United States, authorized by law, including debts incurred for payment of pensions and bounties for services in suppressing insurrection or rebellion, shall not be questioned. But neither the United States nor any State shall assume or pay any debt or obligation incurred in aid of insurrection of rebellion against the United States, or any claim for the loss or emancipation of any slave; but all such debts, obligations and claims shall be held illegal and void.

Section 5. The Congress shall have power to enforce, by appropriate legislation, the provisions of this article.

Amendment XV [1870].

Section 1. The right of citizens of the United States to vote shall not be denied or abridged by the United States or by any State on account of race, color, or previous condition of servitude.

Section 2. The Congress shall have power to enforce this article by appropriate legislation.

Amendment XVI [1913].

The Congress shall have power to lay and collect taxes on incomes, from whatever source derived, without apportionment among the several States, and without regard to any census or enumeration.

Amendment XVII [1913].

The Senate of the United States shall be composed of two Senators from each State, elected by the people thereof, for six years; and each Senator shall have one vote. The electors in each State shall have the qualifications requisite for electors of the most numerous branch of the State legislatures.

When vacancies happen in the representation of any State in the Senate, the executive authority of each State shall issue writs of election to fill such vacancies; *Provided,* That the legislature of any State may empower the executive thereof to make temporary appointments until the people fill the vacancies by election as the legislature may direct.

This amendment shall not be construed as to affect the election or term of any Senator chosen before it becomes valid as part of the Constitution.

Amendment XVIII [1919].

Section 1. After one year from the ratification of this article the manufacture, sale, or transportation of intoxicating liquors within, the importation thereof into, or the exportation thereof from the United States and all territory subject to the jurisdiction thereof for beverage purposes is hereby prohibited.

Section 2. The Congress and the several States shall have concurrent power to enforce this article by appropriate legislation.

Section 3. This article shall be inoperative unless it shall have been ratified as an amendment to the Constitution by the legislatures of the several States, as provided in the Constitution, within seven years from the date of the submission hereof to the States by the Congress.

Amendment XIX [1920].

The right of citizens of the United States to vote shall not be denied or abridged by the United States or by any State on account of sex.

Congress shall have power to enforce this article by appropriate legislation.

Amendment XX [1933].

Section 1. The terms of the President and Vice President shall end at noon on the 20th day of January, and the terms of Senators and Representatives at noon on the 3d day of January, of the years in which such terms would have ended if this article had not been ratified; and the terms of their successors shall then begin.

Section 2. The Congress shall assemble at least once in every year, and such meeting shall begin at noon on the 3d day of January, unless they shall by law appoint a different day.

Section 3. If, at the time fixed for the beginning of the term of the President, the President elect shall have died, the Vice President elect shall become President. If a President shall not have been chosen before the time fixed for the beginning of his term, or if the President elect shall have failed to qualify, then the Vice President elect shall act as President until a President shall have qualified; and the Congress may by law provide for the case wherein neither a President elect nor a Vice President elect shall have qualified, declaring who shall then act as President, or the manner in which one who is to act shall be selected, and such person shall act accordingly until a President or Vice President shall have qualified.

Section 4. The Congress may by law provide for the case of the death of any of the persons from whom the House of Representatives may choose a President whenever the right of choice shall have devolved upon them, and for the case of the death of any of the persons from whom the Senate may choose a Vice President whenever the right of choice shall have devolved upon them.

Section 5. Sections 1 and 2 shall take effect on the 15th day of October following the ratification of this article.

Section 6. This article shall be inoperative unless it shall have been ratified as an amendment to the Constitution by the legislatures of three-fourths of the several States within seven years from the date of its submission.

Amendment XXI [1933].

Section 1. The eighteenth article of amendment to the Constitution of the United States is hereby repealed.

Section 2. The transportation or importation into any State, Territory, or possession of the United States for delivery or use therein of intoxicating liquors, in violation of the laws thereof, is hereby prohibited.

Section 3. This article shall be inoperative unless it shall have been ratified as an amendment to the Constitution by conventions in the several States, as provided in the Constitution, within seven years from the date of the submission hereof to the States by the Congress.

Amendment XXII [1951].

Section 1. No person shall be elected to the office of the President more than twice, and no person who has held the office of President, or acted as President, for more than two years of a term to which some other person was elected President shall be elected to the office of the President more than once. But this Article shall not apply to any person holding the office of President when this Article was proposed by the Congress, and shall not prevent any person who may be holding the office of President, or acting as President, during the term within which this Article becomes operative from holding the office of President, or acting as President during the remainder of such term.

Section 2. This article shall be inoperative unless it shall have been ratified as an amendment to the Constitution by the legislatures of three-fourths of the several States within seven years from the date of its submission to the States by the Congress.

Amendment XXIII [1961].

Section 1. The District constituting the seat of Government of the United States shall appoint in such manner as the Congress may direct:

A number of electors of President and Vice President equal to the whole number of Senators and Representatives in Congress to which the District would be entitled if it were a State, but in no event more than the least populous State; they shall be in addition to those appointed by the States, but they shall be considered, for the purposes of the election of President and Vice President, to be electors appointed by a State; and they shall meet in the District and perform such duties as provided by the twelfth article of amendment.

Section 2. The Congress shall have power to enforce this article by appropriate legislation.

Amendment XXIV [1964].

Section 1. The right of citizens of the United States to vote in any primary or other election for President or Vice President, for electors for President or Vice President, or for Senator or Representative in Congress, shall not be denied or abridged by the United States or any State by reason of failure to pay any poll tax or other tax.

Section 2. The Congress shall have power to enforce this article by appropriate legislation.

Amendment XXV [1967].

Section 1. In case of the removal of the President from office or of his death or resignation, the Vice President shall become President.

Section 2. Whenever there is a vacancy in the office of the Vice President, the President shall nominate a Vice President who shall take office upon confirmation by a majority vote of both Houses of Congress.

Section 3. Whenever the President transmits to the President pro tempore of the Senate and the Speaker of the House of Representatives his written declaration that he is unable to discharge the powers and duties of his office, and until he transmits to them a written declaration to the contrary, such powers and duties shall be discharged by the Vice President as Acting President.

Section 4. Whenever the Vice President and a majority of either the principal officers of the executive departments or of such other body as Congress may by law provide, transmit to the President pro tempore of the Senate and the Speaker of the House of Representatives their written declaration that the President is unable to discharge the powers and duties of his office, the Vice President shall immediately assume the powers and duties of the office as Acting President.

Thereafter, when the President transmits to the President pro tempore of the Senate and the Speaker of the House of Representatives his written declaration that no inability exists, he shall resume the powers and duties of his office unless the Vice President and a majority of either the principal officers of the executive department or of such other body as Congress may by law provide, transmit within four days to the President pro tempore of the Senate and the Speaker of the House of Repre-sentatives their written declaration that the President is unable to discharge the powers and duties of his office. Thereupon Congress shall decide the issue, assem-bling within forty-eight hours for that purpose if not in session. If the Congress, within twenty-one days after receipt of the latter written declaration, or, if Congress is not in session, within twenty-one days after Congress is required to assemble, determines by two-thirds vote of both Houses that the President is unable to discharge the powers and duties of his office, the Vice President shall continue to discharge the same as Acting President; otherwise, the President shall resume the powers and duties of his office.

Amendment XXVI [1971].

Section 1. The right of citizens of the United States, who are eighteen years of age or older, to vote shall not be denied or abridged by the United States or by any State on account of age.

Section 2. The Congress shall have power to enforce this article by appropriate legislation.

Amendment XXVII [1992].

No law, varying the compensation for the services of the Senators and Representatives, shall take effect, until an election of Representatives shall have intervened.

Appendix B

UNIFORM COMMERCIAL CODE (SELECTED PROVISIONS)

The code consists of the following articles:

Art.

1. General provisions
2. Sales
2A. Leases
3. Negotiable instruments
4. Bank deposits and collections
4A. Fund transfers
5. Letters of credit

6. Repealer of Article 6—Bulk Transfers and [Revised] Article 6—Bulk sales
7. Warehouse Receipts, Bills of Lading and Other Documents of Title
8. Investment Securities
9. Secured Transactions
10. Effective Date and Repealer
11. Effective Date and Transmission provisions

ARTICLE I
GENERAL PROVISIONS

PART 1 Short Title, Construction, Application and Subject Matter of the Act

§ 1–101. Short Title.

This Act shall be known and may be cited as Uniform Commercial Code.

§ 1–102. Purposes; Rules of Construction; Variation by Agreement.

(1) This Act shall be liberally construed and applied to promote its underlying purposes and policies.

(2) Underlying purposes and policies of this Act are

    (a) to simplify, clarify and modernize the law governing commercial transactions;

    (b) to permit the continued expansion of commercial practices through custom, usage and agreement of the parties;

    (c) to make uniform the law among the various jurisdictions.

(3) The effect of provisions of this Act may be varied by agreement, except as otherwise provided in this Act and except that the obligations of good faith, diligence, reasonableness and care prescribed by this Act may not be disclaimed by agreement but the parties may by agreement determine the standards by which the performance of such obligations is to be measured if such standards are not manifestly unreasonable.

(4) The presence in certain provisions of this Act of the words "unless otherwise agreed" or words of similar import does not imply that the effect of other provisions may not be varied by agreement under subsection (3).

(5) In this Act unless the context otherwise requires

    (a) words in the singular number include the plural, and in the plural include the singular;

    (b) words of the masculine gender include the feminine and the neuter, and when the sense so indicates words of the neuter gender may refer to any gender.

§ 1–103. Supplementary General Principles of Law Applicable.

Unless displaced by the particular provisions of this Act, the principles of law and equity, including the law merchant and the law relative to capacity to contract, principal and agent, estoppel, fraud, misrepresentation, duress, coercion, mistake, bankruptcy, or other validating or invalidating cause shall supplement its provisions.

§ 1–104. Construction Against Implicit Repeal.

This Act being a general act intended as a unified coverage of its subject matter, no part of it shall be deemed to be impliedly repealed by subsequent legislation if such construction can reasonably be avoided.

§ 1–105. Territorial Application of the Act; Parties' Power to Choose Applicable Law.

(1) Except as provided hereafter in this section, when a transaction bears a reasonable relation to this state and also to another state or nation the parties may agree that the law either of this state or of such other state or nation shall govern their rights and duties. Failing such agreement this Act applies to transactions bearing an appropriate relation to this state.

(2) Where one of the following provisions of this Act specifies the applicable law, that provision governs and a contrary agreement is effective only to the extent permitted by the law (including the conflict of laws rules) so specified:

Rights of creditors against sold goods. Section 2–402.

Applicability of the Article on Leases. Sections 2A–105 and 2A–106.

Applicability of the Article on Bank Deposits and Collections. Section 4–102.

Governing law in the Article on Funds Transfers. Section 4A–507.

Letters of Credit, Section 5–116.

Bulk sales subject to the Article on Bulk Sales. Section 6–103.

Applicability of the Article on Investment Securities. Section 8–106.

Law governing perfection, the effect of perfection or nonperfection, and the priority of security interests and agricultural liens. Sections 9–301 through 9–307.

As amended in 1972, 1987, 1988, 1989, 1994, 1995, and 1999.

§ 1–106. Remedies to Be Liberally Administered.

(1) The remedies provided by this Act shall be liberally administered to the end that the aggrieved party may be put in as good a position as if the other party had fully performed but neither consequential or special nor penal damages may be had except as specifically provided in this Act or by other rule of law.

(2) Any right or obligation declared by this Act is enforceable by action unless the provision declaring it specifies a different and limited effect.

§ 1–107. Waiver or Renunciation of Claim or Right After Breach.

Any claim or right arising out of an alleged breach can be discharged in whole or in part without consideration by a written waiver or renunciation signed and delivered by the aggrieved party.

§ 1–108. Severability.

If any provision or clause of this Act or application thereof to any person or circumstances is held invalid, such invalidity shall not affect other provisions or applications of the Act which can be given effect without the invalid provision or application, and to this end the provisions of this Act are declared to be severable.

§ 1–109. Section Captions.

Section captions are parts of this Act.

PART 2 General Definitions and Principles of Interpretation

§ 1–201. General Definitions.

Subject to additional definitions contained in the subsequent Articles of this Act which are applicable to specific Articles or Parts thereof, and unless the context otherwise requires, in this Act:

(1) "Action" in the sense of a judicial proceeding includes recoupment, counterclaim, set-off, suit in equity and any other proceedings in which rights are determined.

(2) "Aggrieved party" means a party entitled to resort to a remedy.

(3) "Agreement" means the bargain of the parties in fact as found in their language or by implication from other circumstances including course of dealing or usage of trade or course of performance as provided in this Act (Sections 1–205 and 2–208). Whether an agreement has legal consequences is determined by the provisions of this Act, if applicable; otherwise by the law of contracts (Section 1–103). (Compare "Contract".)

(4) "Bank" means any person engaged in the business of banking.

(5) "Bearer" means the person in possession of an instrument, document of title, or certificated security payable to bearer or indorsed in blank.

(6) "Bill of lading" means a document evidencing the receipt of goods for shipment issued by a person engaged in the business of transporting or forwarding goods, and includes an airbill. "Airbill" means a document serving for air transportation as a bill of lading does for marine or rail transportation, and includes an air consignment note or air waybill.

(7) "Branch" includes a separately incorporated foreign branch of a bank.

(8) "Burden of establishing" a fact means the burden of persuading the triers of fact that the existence of the fact is more probable than its non-existence.

(9) "Buyer in ordinary course of business" means a person that buys goods in good faith, without knowledge that the sale violates the rights of another person in the goods, and in the ordinary course from a person, other than a pawnbroker, in the business of selling goods of that kind. A person buys goods in the ordinary course if the sale to the person comports with the usual or customary practices in the kind of business in which the seller is engaged or with the seller's own usual or customary practices. A person that sells oil, gas, or other minerals at the wellhead or minehead is a person in the business of selling goods of that kind. A buyer in ordinary course of business may buy for cash, by exchange of other property, or on secured or unsecured credit, and may acquire goods or documents of title under a pre-existing contract for sale. Only a buyer that takes possession of the goods or has a right to recover the goods from the seller under Article 2 may be a buyer in ordinary course of business. A person that acquires goods in a transfer in bulk or as security for or in total or partial satisfaction of a money debt is not a buyer in ordinary course of business.

(10) "Conspicuous": A term or clause is conspicuous when it is so written that a reasonable person against whom it is to operate ought to have noticed it. A printed heading in capitals (as: NON-NEGOTIABLE BILL OF LADING) is conspicuous. Language in the body of a form is "conspicuous" if it is in larger or other contrasting type or color. But in a telegram any stated term is "conspicuous". Whether a term or clause is "conspicuous" or not is for decision by the court.

(11) "Contract" means the total legal obligation which results from the parties' agreement as affected by this Act and any other applicable rules of law. (Compare "Agreement".)

(12) "Creditor" includes a general creditor, a secured creditor, a lien creditor and any representative of creditors, including an assignee for the benefit of creditors, a trustee in bankruptcy, a receiver in equity and an executor or administrator of an insolvent debtor's or assignor's estate.

(13) "Defendant" includes a person in the position of defendant in a cross-action or counterclaim.

(14) "Delivery" with respect to instruments, documents of title, chattel paper, or certificated securities means voluntary transfer of possession.

(15) "Document of title" includes bill of lading, dock warrant, dock receipt, warehouse receipt or order for the delivery of goods, and also any other document which in the regular course of business or financing is treated as adequately evidencing that the person in possession of it is entitled to receive, hold and dispose of the document and the goods it covers. To be a document of title a document must purport to be issued by or addressed to a bailee and purport to cover goods in the bailee's possession which are either identified or are fungible portions of an identified mass.

(16) "Fault" means wrongful act, omission or breach.

(17) "Fungible" with respect to goods or securities means goods or securities of which any unit is, by nature or usage of trade, the equivalent of any other like unit. Goods which are not fungible shall be deemed fungible for the purposes of this Act to the extent that under a particular agreement or document unlike units are treated as equivalents.

(18) "Genuine" means free of forgery or counterfeiting.

(19) "Good faith" means honesty in fact in the conduct or transaction concerned.

(20) "Holder" with respect to a negotiable instrument, means the person in possession if the instrument is payable to bearer or, in the cases of an instrument payable to an identified person, if the identified person is in possession. "Holder" with respect to a document of title means the person in possession if the goods are deliverable to bearer or to the order of the person in possession.

(21) To "honor" is to pay or to accept and pay, or where a credit so engages to purchase or discount a draft complying with the terms of the credit.

(22) "Insolvency proceedings" includes any assignment for the benefit of creditors or other proceedings intended to liquidate or rehabilitate the estate of the person involved.

(23) A person is "insolvent" who either has ceased to pay his debts in the ordinary course of business or cannot pay his debts as they become due or is insolvent within the meaning of the federal bankruptcy law.

(24) "Money" means a medium of exchange authorized or adopted by a domestic or foreign government and includes a monetary unit of account established by an intergovernmental organization or by agreement between two or more nations.

(25) A person has "notice" of a fact when

(a) he has actual knowledge of it; or

(b) he has received a notice or notification of it; or

(c) from all the facts and circumstances known to him at the time in question he has reason to know that it exists.

A person "knows" or has "knowledge" of a fact when he has actual knowledge of it. "Discover" or "learn" or a word or phrase of similar import refers to knowledge rather than to reason to know. The time and circumstances under which a notice or notification may cease to be effective are not determined by this Act.

(26) A person "notifies" or "gives" a notice or notification to another by taking such steps as may be reasonably required to inform the other in ordinary course whether or not such other actually comes to know of it. A person "receives" a notice or notification when

(a) it comes to his attention; or

(b) it is duly delivered at the place of business through which the contract was made or at any other place held out by him as the place for receipt of such communications.

(27) Notice, knowledge or a notice or notification received by an organization is effective for a particular transaction from the

time when it is brought to the attention of the individual conducting that transaction, and in any event from the time when it would have been brought to his attention if the organization had exercised due diligence. An organization exercises due diligence if it maintains reasonable routines for communicating significant information to the person conducting the transaction and there is reasonable compliance with the routines. Due diligence does not require an individual acting for the organization to communicate information unless such communication is part of his regular duties or unless he has reason to know of the transaction and that the transaction would be materially affected by the information.

(28) "Organization" includes a corporation, government or governmental subdivision or agency, business trust, estate, trust, partnership or association, two or more persons having a joint or common interest, or any other legal or commercial entity.

(29) "Party", as distinct from "third party", means a person who has engaged in a transaction or made an agreement within this Act.

(30) "Person" includes an individual or an organization (See Section 1–102).

(31) "Presumption" or "presumed" means that the trier of fact must find the existence of the fact presumed unless and until evidence is introduced which would support a finding of its non-existence.

(32) "Purchase" includes taking by sale, discount, negotiation, mortgage, pledge, lien, issue or re-issue, gift or any other voluntary transaction creating an interest in property.

(33) "Purchaser" means a person who takes by purchase.

(34) "Remedy" means any remedial right to which an aggrieved party is entitled with or without resort to a tribunal.

(35) "Representative" includes an agent, an officer of a corporation or association, and a trustee, executor or administrator of an estate, or any other person empowered to act for another.

(36) "Rights" includes remedies.

(37) "Security interest" means an interest in personal property or fixtures which secures payment or performance of an obligation. The term also includes any interest of a consignor and a buyer of accounts, chattel paper, a payment intangible, or a promissory note in a transaction that is subject to Article 9. The special property interest of a buyer of goods on identification of those goods to a contract for sale under Section 2–401 is not a "security interest", but a buyer may also acquire a "security interest" by complying with Article 9. Except as otherwise provided in Section 2–505, the right of a seller or lessor of goods under Article 2 or 2A to retain or acquire possession of the goods is not a "security interest", but a seller or lessor may also acquire a "security interest" by complying with Article 9. The retention or reservation of title by a seller of goods notwithstanding shipment or delivery to the buyer (Section 2–401) is limited in effect to a reservation of a "security interest".

Whether a transaction creates a lease or security interest is determined by the facts of each case; however, a transaction creates a security interest if the consideration the lessee is to pay the lessor for the right to possession and use of the goods is an obligation for the term of the lease not subject to termination by the lessee, and

(a) the original term of the lease is equal to or greater than the remaining economic life of the goods,

(b) the lessee is bound to renew the lease for the remaining economic life of the goods or is bound to become the owner of the goods,

(c) the lessee has an option to renew the lease for the remaining economic life of the goods for no additional consideration or nominal additional consideration upon compliance with the lease agreement, or

(d) the lessee has an option to become the owner of the goods for no additional consideration or nominal additional consideration upon compliance with the lease agreement.

A transaction does not create a security interest merely because it provides that

(a) the present value of the consideration the lessee is obligated to pay the lessor for the right to possession and use of the goods is substantially equal to or is greater than the fair market value of the goods at the time the lease is entered into,

(b) the lessee assumes risk of loss of the goods, or agrees to pay taxes, insurance, filing, recording, or registration fees, or service or maintenance costs with respect to the goods,

(c) the lessee has an option to renew the lease or to become the owner of the goods,

(d) the lessee has an option to renew the lease for a fixed rent that is equal to or greater than the reasonably predictable fair market rent for the use of the goods for the term of the renewal at the time the option is to be performed, or

(e) the lessee has an option to become the owner of the goods for a fixed price that is equal to or greater than the reasonably predictable fair market value of the goods at the time the option is to be performed.

For purposes of this subsection (37):

(x) Additional consideration is not nominal if (i) when the option to renew the lease is granted to the lessee the rent is stated to be the fair market rent for the use of the goods for the term of the renewal determined at the time the option is to be performed, or (ii) when the option to become the owner of the goods is granted to the lessee the price is stated to be the fair market value of the goods determined at the time the option is to be performed. Additional consideration is nominal if it is less than the lessee's reasonably predictable cost of performing under the lease agreement if the option is not exercised;

(y) "Reasonably predictable" and "remaining economic life of the goods" are to be determined with reference to the facts and circumstances at the time the transaction is entered into; and

(z) "Present value" means the amount as of a date certain of one or more sums payable in the future, discounted to the date certain. The discount is determined by the interest rate specified by the parties if the rate is not manifestly unreasonable at the time the transaction is entered into; otherwise, the discount is determined by a commercially reasonable rate that takes into account the facts and circumstances of each case at the time the transaction was entered into.

(38) "Send" in connection with any writing or notice means to deposit in the mail or deliver for transmission by any other usual means of communication with postage or cost of transmission provided for and properly addressed and in the case of an instrument to an address specified thereon or otherwise agreed, or if there be none to any address reasonable under the circumstances. The receipt of any writing or notice within the time at which it would have arrived if properly sent has the effect of a proper sending.

(39) "Signed" includes any symbol executed or adopted by a party with present intention to authenticate a writing.

(40) "Surety" includes guarantor.

(41) "Telegram" includes a message transmitted by radio, teletype, cable, any mechanical method of transmission, or the like.

(42) "Term" means that portion of an agreement which relates to a particular matter.

(43) "Unauthorized" signature means one made without actual, implied or apparent authority and includes a forgery.

(44) "Value". Except as otherwise provided with respect to negotiable instruments and bank collections (Sections 3–303, 4–210 and 4–211) a person gives "value" for rights if he acquires them

    (a) in return for a binding commitment to extend credit or for the extension of immediately available credit whether or not drawn upon and whether or not a chargeback is provided for in the event of difficulties in collection; or

    (b) as security for or in total or partial satisfaction of a pre-existing claim; or

    (c) by accepting delivery pursuant to a preexisting contract for purchase; or

    (d) generally, in return for any consideration sufficient to support a simple contract.

(45) "Warehouse receipt" means a receipt issued by a person engaged in the business of storing goods for hire.

(46) "Written" or "writing" includes printing, typewriting or any other intentional reduction to tangible form.

§ 1–202. Prima Facie Evidence by Third Party Documents.

A document in due form purporting to be a bill of lading, policy or certificate of insurance, official weigher's or inspector's certificate, consular invoice, or any other document authorized or required by the contract to be issued by a third party shall be prima facie evidence of its own authenticity and genuineness and of the facts stated in the document by the third party.

§ 1–203. Obligation of Good Faith.

Every contract or duty within this Act imposes an obligation of good faith in its performance or enforcement.

§ 1–204. Time; Reasonable Time; "Seasonably".

(1) Whenever this Act requires any action to be taken within a reasonable time, any time which is not manifestly unreasonable may be fixed by agreement.

(2) What is a reasonable time for taking any action depends on the nature, purpose and circumstances of such action.

(3) An action is taken "seasonably" when it is taken at or within the time agreed or if no time is agreed at or within a reasonable time.

§ 1–205. Course of Dealing and Usage of Trade.

(1) A course of dealing is a sequence of previous conduct between the parties to a particular transaction which is fairly to be regarded as establishing a common basis of understanding for interpreting their expressions and other conduct.

(2) A usage of trade is any practice or method of dealing having such regularity of observance in a place, vocation or trade as to justify an expectation that it will be observed with respect to the transaction in question. The existence and scope of such a usage are to be proved as facts. If it is established that such a usage is embodied in a written trade code or similar writing the interpretation of the writing is for the court.

(3) A course of dealing between parties and any usage of trade in the vocation or trade in which they are engaged or of which they are or should be aware give particular meaning to and supplement or qualify terms of an agreement.

(4) The express terms of an agreement and an applicable course of dealing or usage of trade shall be construed wherever reasonable as consistent with each other; but when such construction is unreasonable express terms control both course of dealing and usage of trade and course of dealing controls usage trade.

(5) An applicable usage of trade in the place where any part of performance is to occur shall be used in interpreting the agreement as to that part of the performance.

(6) Evidence of a relevant usage of trade offered by one party is not admissible unless and until he has given the other party such notice as the court finds sufficient to prevent unfair surprise to the latter.

§ 1–206. Statute of Frauds for Kinds of Personal Property Not Otherwise Covered.

(1) Except in the cases described in subsection (2) of this section a contract for the sale of personal property is not enforceable by way of action or defense beyond five thousand dollars in amount or value of remedy unless there is some writing which indicates that a contract for sale has been made between the parties at a defined or stated price, reasonably identifies the subject matter, and is signed by the party against whom enforcement is sought or by his authorized agent.

(2) Subsection (1) of this section does not apply to contracts for the sale of goods (Section 2–201) nor of securities (Section 8–113) nor to security agreements (Section 9–203).

As amended in 1994.

§ 1–207. Performance or Acceptance Under Reservation of Rights.

(1) A party who with explicit reservation of rights performs or promises performance or assents to performance in a manner demanded or offered by the other party does not thereby prejudice the rights reserved. Such words as "without prejudice", "under protest" or the like are sufficient.

(2) Subsection (1) does not apply to an accord and satisfaction.

As amended in 1990.

§ 1–208. Option to Accelerate at Will.

A term providing that one party or his successor in interest may accelerate payment or performance or require collateral or additional collateral "at will" or "when he deems himself insecure" or in words of similar import shall be construed to mean that he shall have power to do so only if he in good faith believes that the prospect of payment or performance is impaired. The burden of establishing lack of good faith is on the party against whom the power has been exercised.

§ 1–209. Subordinated Obligations.

An obligation may be issued as subordinated to payment of another obligation of the person obligated, or a creditor may subordinate his right to payment of an obligation by agreement with either the person obligated or another creditor of the person obligated. Such a subordination does not create a security interest as against either the common debtor or a subordinated creditor. This section shall be construed as declaring the law as it existed prior to the enactment of this section and not as modifying it. Added 1966.

Note: *This new section is proposed as an optional provision to make it clear that a subordination agreement does not create a security interest unless so intended.*

ARTICLE II
SALES

PART 1   Short Title, General Construction and Subject Matter

§ 2–101. Short Title.

This Article shall be known and may be cited as Uniform Commercial Code—Sales.

§ 2–102. Scope; Certain Security and Other Transactions Excluded From This Article.

Unless the context otherwise requires, this Article applies to transactions in goods; it does not apply to any transaction which although in the form of an unconditional contract to sell or present sale is intended to operate only as a security transaction nor does this Article impair or repeal any statute regulating sales to consumers, farmers or other specified classes of buyers.

§ 2–103. Definitions and Index of Definitions.

(1) In this Article unless the context otherwise requires

    (a) "Buyer" means a person who buys or contracts to buy goods.

    (b) "Good faith" in the case of a merchant means honesty in fact and the observance of reasonable commercial standards of fair dealing in the trade.

    (c) "Receipt" of goods means taking physical possession of them.

    (d) "Seller" means a person who sells or contracts to sell goods.

(2) Other definitions applying to this Article or to specified Parts thereof, and the sections in which they appear are:

    "Acceptance". Section 2–606.
    "Banker's credit". Section 2–325.
    "Between merchants". Section 2–104.
    "Cancellation". Section 2–106(4).
    "Commercial unit". Section 2–105.
    "Confirmed credit". Section 2–325.
    "Conforming to contract". Section 2–106.
    "Contract for sale". Section 2–106.
    "Cover". Section 2–712.
    "Entrusting". Section 2–403.
    "Financing agency". Section 2–104.
    "Future goods". Section 2–105.
    "Goods". Section 2–105.

"Identification". Section 2–501.
"Installment contract". Section 2–612.
"Letter of Credit". Section 2–325.
"Lot". Section 2–105
"Merchant". Section 2–104.
"Overseas". Section 2–323.
"Person in position of seller". Section 2–707.
"Present sale". Section 2–106.
"Sale". Section 2–106.
"Sale on approval". Section 2–326.
"Sale or return". Section 2–326.
"Termination". Section 2–106.

(3) The following definitions in other Articles apply to this Article:

"Check". Section 3–104.
"Consignee". Section 7–102.
"Consignor". Section 7–102.
"Consumer goods". Section 9–109.
"Dishonor". Section 3–507.
"Draft". Section 3–104.

(4) In addition Article 1 contains general definitions and principles of construction and interpretation applicable throughout this Article.

As amended in 1994 and 1999.

§ 2–104. Definitions: "Merchant"; "Between Merchants"; "Financing Agency".

(1) "Merchant" means a person who deals in goods of the kind or otherwise by his occupation holds himself out as having knowledge or skill peculiar to the practices or goods involved in the transaction or to whom such knowledge or skill may be attributed by his employment of an agent or broker or other intermediary who by his occupation holds himself out as having such knowledge or skill.

(2) "Financing agency" means a bank, finance company or other person who in the ordinary course of business makes advances against goods or documents of title or who by arrangement with either the seller or the buyer intervenes in ordinary course to make or collect payment due or claimed under the contract for sale, as by purchasing or paying the seller's draft or making advances against it or by merely taking it for collection whether or not documents of title accompany the draft. "Financing agency" includes also a bank or other person who similarly intervenes between persons who are in the position of seller and buyer in respect to the goods (Section 2–707).

(3) "Between merchants" means in any transaction with respect to which both parties are chargeable with the knowledge or skill of merchants.

§ 2–105. Definitions: Transferability; "Goods"; "Future" Goods; "Lot"; "Commercial Unit".

(1) "Goods" means all things (including specially manufactured goods) which are movable at the time of identification to the contract for sale other than the money in which the price is to be paid, investment securities (Article 8) and things in action. "Goods" also includes the unborn young of animals and growing crops and other identified things attached to realty as described in the section on goods to be severed from realty (Section 2–107).

(2) Goods must be both existing and identified before any interest in them can pass. Goods which are not both existing and identified are "future" goods. A purported present sale of future goods or of any interest therein operates as a contract to sell.

(3) There may be a sale of a part interest in existing identified goods.

(4) An undivided share in an identified bulk of fungible goods is sufficiently identified to be sold although the quantity of the bulk is not determined. Any agreed proportion of such a bulk or any quantity thereof agreed upon by number, weight or other measure may to the extent of the seller's interest in the bulk be sold to the buyer who then becomes an owner in common.

(5) "Lot" means a parcel or a single article which is the subject matter of a separate sale or delivery, whether or not it is sufficient to perform the contract.

(6) "Commercial unit" means such a unit of goods as by commercial usage is a single whole for purposes of sale and division of which materially impairs its character or value on the market or in use. A commercial unit may be a single article (as a machine) or a set of articles (as a suite of furniture or an assortment of sizes) or a quantity (as a bale, gross, or carload) or any other unit treated in use or in the relevant market as a single whole.

§ 2–106. Definitions: "Contract"; "Agreement"; "Contract for Sale"; "Sale"; "Present Sale"; "Conforming" to Contract; "Termination"; "Cancellation".

(1) In this Article unless the context otherwise requires "contract" and "agreement" are limited to those relating to the present or future sale of goods. "Contract for sale" includes both a present sale of goods and a contract to sell goods at a future time. A "sale" consists in the passing of title from the seller to the buyer for a price (Section 2–401). A "present sale" means a sale which is accomplished by the making of the contract.

(2) Goods or conduct including any part of a performance are "conforming" or conform to the contract when they are in accordance with the obligations under the contract.

(3) "Termination" occurs when either party pursuant to a power created by agreement or law puts an end to the contract otherwise than for its breach. On "termination" all obligations which are still executory on both sides are discharged but any right based on prior breach or performance survives.

(4) "Cancellation" occurs when either party puts an end to the contract for breach by the other and its effect is the same as that of "termination" except that the cancelling party also retains any remedy for breach of the whole contract or any unperformed balance.

§ 2–107. Goods to Be Severed From Realty: Recording.

(1) A contract for the sale of minerals or the like (including oil and gas) or a structure or its materials to be removed from realty is a contract for the sale of goods within this Article if they are to be severed by the seller but until severance a purported present sale thereof which is not effective as a transfer of an interest in land is effective only as a contract to sell.

(2) A contract for the sale apart from the land of growing crops or other things attached to realty and capable of severance without material harm thereto but not described in subsection (1) or of timber to be cut is a contract for the sale of goods within this Article whether the subject matter is to be severed by the buyer or by the seller even though it forms part of the realty at the time of contracting, and the parties can by identification effect a present sale before severance.

(3) The provisions of this section are subject to any third party rights provided by the law relating to realty records, and the contract for sale may be executed and recorded as a document transferring an interest in land and shall then constitute notice to third parties of the buyer's rights under the contract for sale.

As amended in 1972.

PART 2   Form, Formation and Readjustment of Contract

§ 2–201.   Formal Requirements; Statute of Frauds.

(1) Except as otherwise provided in this section a contract for the sale of goods for the price of $500 or more is not enforceable by way of action or defense unless there is some writing sufficient to indicate that a contract for sale has been made between the parties and signed by the party against whom enforcement is sought or by his authorized agent or broker. A writing is not insufficient because it omits or incorrectly states a term agreed upon but the contract is not enforceable under this paragraph beyond the quantity of goods shown in such writing.

(2) Between merchants if within a reasonable time a writing in confirmation of the contract and sufficient against the sender is received and the party receiving it has reason to know its contents, it satisfies the requirements of subsection (1) against such party unless written notice of objection to its contents is given within ten days after it is received.

(3) A contract which does not satisfy the requirements of subsection (1) but which is valid in other respects is enforceable

(a) if the goods are to be specially manufactured for the buyer and are not suitable for sale to others in the ordinary course of the seller's business and the seller, before notice of repudiation is received and under circumstances which reasonably indicate that the goods are for the buyer, has made either a substantial beginning of their manufacture or commitments for their procurement; or

(b) if the party against whom enforcement is sought admits in his pleading, testimony or otherwise in court that a contract for sale was made, but the contract is not enforceable under this provision beyond the quantity of goods admitted; or

(c) with respect to goods for which payment has been made and accepted or which have been received and accepted (Sec. 2–606).

§ 2–202.   Final Written Expression: Parol or Extrinsic Evidence.

Terms with respect to which the confirmatory memoranda of the parties agree or which are otherwise set forth in a writing intended by the parties as a final expression of their agreement with respect to such terms as are included therein may not be contradicted by evidence of any prior agreement or of a contemporaneous oral agreement but may be explained or supplemented

(a) by course of dealing or usage of trade (Section 1–205) or by course of performance (Section 2–208); and

(b) by evidence of consistent additional terms unless the court finds the writing to have been intended also as a complete and exclusive statement of the terms of the agreement.

§ 2–203.   Seals Inoperative.

The affixing of a seal to a writing evidencing a contract for sale or an offer to buy or sell goods does not constitute the writing a sealed instrument and the law with respect to sealed instruments does not apply to such a contract or offer.

§ 2–204.   Formation in General.

(1) A contract for sale of goods may be made in any manner sufficient to show agreement, including conduct by both parties which recognizes the existence of such a contract.

(2) An agreement sufficient to constitute a contract for sale may be found even though the moment of its making is undetermined.

(3) Even though one or more terms are left open a contract for sale does not fail for indefiniteness if the parties have intended to make a contract and there is a reasonably certain basis for giving an appropriate remedy.

§ 2–205. Firm Offers.

An offer by a merchant to buy or sell goods in a signed writing which by its terms gives assurance that it will be held open is not revocable, for lack of consideration, during the time stated or if no time is stated for a reasonable time, but in no event may such period of irrevocability exceed three months; but any such term of assurance on a form supplied by the offeree must be separately signed by the offeror.

§ 2–206. Offer and Acceptance in Formation of Contract.

(1) Unless other unambiguously indicated by the language or circumstances

(a) an offer to make a contract shall be construed as inviting acceptance in any manner and by any medium reasonable in the circumstances;

(b) an order or other offer to buy goods for prompt or current shipment shall be construed as inviting acceptance either by a prompt promise to ship or by the prompt or current shipment of conforming or nonconforming goods, but such a shipment of non-conforming goods does not constitute an acceptance if the seller seasonably notifies the buyer that the shipment is offered only as an accommodation to the buyer.

(2) Where the beginning of a requested performance is a reasonable mode of acceptance an offeror who is not notified of acceptance within a reasonable time may treat the offer as having lapsed before acceptance.

§ 2–207. Additional Terms in Acceptance or Confirmation.

(1) A definite and seasonable expression of acceptance or a written confirmation which is sent within a reasonable time operates as an acceptance even though it states terms additional to or different from those offered or agreed upon, unless acceptance is expressly made conditional on assent to the additional or different terms.

(2) The additional terms are to be construed as proposals for addition to the contract. Between merchants such terms become part of the contract unless:

(a) the offer expressly limits acceptance to the terms of the offer;

(b) they materially alter it; or

(c) notification of objection to them has already been given or is given within a reasonable time after notice of them is received.

(3) Conduct by both parties which recognizes the existence of a contract is sufficient to establish a contract for sale although the writings of the parties do not otherwise establish a contract. In such case the terms of the particular contract consist of those terms on which the writings of the parties agree, together with any supplementary terms incorporated under any other provisions of this Act.

§ 2–208. Course of Performance or Practical Construction.

(1) Where the contract for sale involves repeated occasions for performance by either party with knowledge of the nature of the performance and opportunity for objection to it by the other, any course of performance accepted or acquiesced in without objection shall be relevant to determine the meaning of the agreement.

(2) The express terms of the agreement and any such course of performance, as well as any course of dealing and usage of trade, shall be construed whenever reasonable as consistent with each other; but when such construction is unreasonable, express terms shall control course of performance and course of performance shall control both course of dealing and usage of trade (Section 1–205).

(3) Subject to the provisions of the next section on modification and waiver, such course of performance shall be relevant to show a waiver or modification of any term inconsistent with such course of performance.

§ 2–209. Modification, Rescission and Waiver.

(1) An agreement modifying a contract within this Article needs no consideration to be binding.

(2) A signed agreement which excludes modification or rescission except by a signed writing cannot be otherwise modified or rescinded, but except as between merchants such a requirement on a form supplied by the merchant must be separately signed by the other party.

(3) The requirements of the statute of frauds section of this Article (Section 2–201) must be satisfied if the contract as modified is within its provisions.

(4) Although an attempt at modification or rescission does not satisfy the requirements of subsection (2) or (3) it can operate as a waiver.

(5) A party who has made a waiver affecting an executory portion of the contract may retract the waiver by reasonable notification received by the other party that strict performance will be required of any term waived, unless the retraction would be unjust in view of a material change of position in reliance on the waiver.

§ 2–210. Delegation of Performance; Assignment of Rights.

(1) A party may perform his duty through a delegate unless otherwise agreed or unless the other party has a substantial interest in having his original promisor perform or control the acts required by the contract. No delegation of performance relieves the party delegating of any duty to perform or any liability for breach.

(2) Except as otherwise provided in Section 9–406, unless otherwise agreed, all rights of either seller or buyer can be assigned except where the assignment would materially change the duty of the other party, or increase materially the burden or risk imposed on him by his contract, or impair materially his chance of obtaining return performance. A right to damages for breach of the whole contract or a right arising out of the assignor's due performance of his entire obligation can be assigned despite agreement otherwise.

(3) The creation, attachment, perfection, or enforcement of a security interest in the seller's interest under a contract is not a transfer that materially changes the duty of or increases materially the burden or risk imposed on the buyer or impairs materially the buyer's chance of obtaining return performance within the purview of subsection (2) unless, and then only to the extent that, enforcement actually results in a delegation of material performance of the seller. Even in that event, the creation, attachment, perfection, and enforcement of the security interest remain effective, but (i) the seller is liable to the buyer for damages caused by the delegation to the extent that the damages could not reasonably by prevented by the buyer, and (ii) a court having jurisdiction may grant other appropriate relief, including cancellation of the contract for sale or an injunction against enforcement of the security interest or consummation of the enforcement.

(4) Unless the circumstances indicate the contrary a prohibition of assignment of "the contract" is to be construed as barring only the delegation to the assignee of the assignor's performance.

(5) An assignment of "the contract" or of "all my rights under the contract" or an assignment in similar general terms is an assignment of rights and unless the language or the circumstances (as in an assignment for security) indicate the contrary, it is a delegation of performance of the duties of the assignor and its acceptance by the assignee constitutes a promise by him to perform those duties. This promise is enforceable by either the assignor or the other party to the original contract.

(6) The other party may treat any assignment which delegates performance as creating reasonable grounds for insecurity and may without prejudice to his rights against the assignor demand assurances from the assignee (Section 2–609).

As amended in 1999.

PART 3   General Obligation and Construction of Contract

§ 2–301.   General Obligations of Parties.

The obligation of the seller is to transfer and deliver and that of the buyer is to accept and pay in accordance with the contract.

§ 2–302.   Unconscionable Contract or Clause.

(1) If the court as a matter of law finds the contract or any clause of the contract to have been unconscionable at the time it was made the court may refuse to enforce the contract, or it may enforce the remainder of the contract without the unconscionable clause, or it may so limit the application of any unconscionable clause as to avoid any unconscionable result.

(2) When it is claimed or appears to the court that the contract or any clause thereof may be unconscionable the parties shall be afforded a reasonable opportunity to present evidence as to its commercial setting, purpose and effect to aid the court in making the determination.

§ 2–303.   Allocations or Division of Risks.

Where this Article allocates a risk or a burden as between the parties "unless otherwise agreed", the agreement may not only shift the allocation but may also divide the risk or burden.

§ 2–304.   Price Payable in Money, Goods, Realty, or Otherwise.

(1) The price can be made payable in money or otherwise. If it is payable in whole or in part in goods each party is a seller of the goods which he is to transfer.

(2) Even though all or part of the price is payable in an interest in realty the transfer of the goods and the seller's obligations with reference to them are subject to this Article, but not the transfer of the interest in realty or the transferor's obligations in connection therewith.

§ 2–305.   Open Price Term.

(1) The parties if they so intend can conclude a contract for sale even though the price is not settled. In such a case the price is a reasonable price at the time for delivery if

    (a) nothing is said as to price; or

    (b) the price is left to be agreed by the parties and they fail to agree; or

    (c) the price is to be fixed in terms of some agreed market or other standard as set or recorded by a third person or agency and it is not so set or recorded.

(2) A price to be fixed by the seller or by the buyer means a price for him to fix in good faith.

(3) When a price left to be fixed otherwise than by agreement of the parties fails to be fixed through fault of one party the other may at his option treat the contract as cancelled or himself fix a reasonable price.

(4) Where, however, the parties intend not to be bound unless the price be fixed or agreed and it is not fixed or

agreed there is no contract. In such a case the buyer must return any goods already received or if unable so to do must pay their reasonable value at the time of delivery and the seller must return any portion of the price paid on account.

§ 2–306. Output, Requirements and Exclusive Dealings.

(1) A term which measures the quantity by the output of the seller or the requirements of the buyer means such actual output or requirements as may occur in good faith, except that no quantity unreasonably disproportionate to any stated estimate or in the absence of a stated estimate to any normal or otherwise comparable prior output or requirements may be tendered or demanded.

(2) A lawful agreement by either the seller or the buyer for exclusive dealing in the kind of goods concerned imposes unless otherwise agreed an obligation by the seller to use best efforts to supply the goods and by the buyer to use best efforts to promote their sale.

§ 2–307. Delivery in Single Lot or Several Lots.

Unless otherwise agreed all goods called for by a contract for sale must be tendered in a single delivery and payment is due only on such tender but where the circumstances give either party the right to make or demand delivery in lots the price if it can be apportioned may be demanded for each lot.

§ 2–308. Absence of Specified Place for Delivery.

Unless otherwise agreed

  (a) the place for delivery of goods is the seller's place of business or if he has none his residence; but

  (b) in a contract for sale of identified goods which to the knowledge of the parties at the time of contracting are in some other place, that place is the place for their delivery; and

  (c) documents of title may be delivered through customary banking channels.

§ 2–309. Absence of Specific Time Provisions; Notice of Termination.

(1) The time for shipment or delivery or any other action under a contract if not provided in this Article or agreed upon shall be a reasonable time.

(2) Where the contract provides for successive performances but is indefinite in duration it is valid for a reasonable time but unless otherwise agreed may be terminated at any time by either party.

(3) Termination of a contract by one party except on the happening of an agreed event requires that reasonable notification be received by the other party and an agreement dispensing with notification is invalid if its operation would be unconscionable.

§ 2–310. Open Time for Payment or Running of Credit; Authority to Ship Under Reservation.

Unless otherwise agreed

  (a) payment is due at the time and place at which the buyer is to receive the goods even though the place of shipment is the place of delivery; and

  (b) if the seller is authorized to send the goods he may ship them under reservation, and may tender the documents of title, but the buyer may inspect the goods after their arrival before payment is due unless such inspection is inconsistent with the terms of the contract (Section 2–513); and

  (c) if delivery is authorized and made by way of documents of title otherwise than by subsection (b) then payment is due at the time and place at which the buyer is to receive the documents regardless of where the goods are to be received; and

  (d) where the seller is required or authorized to ship the goods on credit the credit period runs from the time of shipment but post-dating the invoice or delaying its dispatch will correspondingly delay the starting of the credit period.

§ 2–311. Options and Cooperation Respecting Performance.

(1) An agreement for sale which is otherwise sufficiently definite (subsection (3) of Section 2–204) to be a contract is not made invalid by the fact that it leaves particulars of performance to be specified by one of the parties. Any such specification must be made in good faith and within limits set by commercial reasonableness.

(2) Unless otherwise agreed specifications relating to assortment of the goods are at the buyer's option and except as otherwise provided in subsections (1)(c) and (3) of Section 2–319 specifications or arrangements relating to shipment are at the seller's option.

(3) Where such specification would materially affect the other party's performance but is not seasonably made or where one party's cooperation is necessary to the agreed performance of the other but is not seasonably forthcoming, the other party in addition to all other remedies

  (a) is excused for any resulting delay in his own performance; and

  (b) may also either proceed to perform in any reasonable manner or after the time for a material part of his own performance treat the failure to specify or to cooperate as a breach by failure to deliver or accept the goods.

§ 2–312. Warranty of Title and Against Infringement; Buyer's Obligation Against Infringement.

(1) Subject to subsection (2) there is in a contract for sale a warranty by the seller that

(a) the title conveyed shall be good, and its transfer rightful; and

(b) the goods shall be delivered free from any security interest or other lien or encumbrance of which the buyer at the time of contracting has no knowledge.

(2) A warranty under subsection (1) will be excluded or modified only by specific language or by circumstances which give the buyer reason to know that the person selling does not claim title in himself or that he is purporting to sell only such right or title as he or a third person may have.

(3) Unless otherwise agreed a seller who is a merchant regularly dealing in goods of the kind warrants that the goods shall be delivered free of the rightful claim of any third person by way of infringement or the like but a buyer who furnishes specifications to the seller must hold the seller harmless against any such claim which arises out of compliance with the specifications.

§ 2–313. Express Warranties by Affirmation, Promise, Description, Sample.

(1) Express warranties by the seller are created as follows:

(a) Any affirmation of fact or promise made by the seller to the buyer which relates to the goods and becomes part of the basis of the bargain creates an express warranty that the goods shall conform to the affirmation or promise.

(b) Any description of the goods which is made part of the basis of the bargain creates an express warranty that the goods shall conform to the description.

(c) Any sample or model which is made part of the basis of the bargain creates an express warranty that the whole of the goods shall conform to the sample or model.

(2) It is not necessary to the creation of an express warranty that the seller use formal words such as "warrant" or "guarantee" or that he have a specific intention to make a warranty, but an affirmation merely of the value of the goods or a statement purporting to be merely the seller's opinion or commendation of the goods does not create a warranty.

§ 2–314. Implied Warranty: Merchantability; Usage of Trade.

(1) Unless excluded or modified (Section 2–316), a warranty that the goods shall be merchantable is implied in a contract for their sale if the seller is a merchant with respect to goods of that kind. Under this section the serving for value of food or drink to be consumed either on the premises or elsewhere is a sale.

(2) Goods to be merchantable must be at least such as

(a) pass without objection in the trade under the contract description; and

(b) in the case of fungible goods, are of fair average quality within the description; and

(c) are fit for the ordinary purposes for which such goods are used; and

(d) run, within the variations permitted by the agreement, of even kind, quality and quantity within each unit and among all units involved; and

(e) are adequately contained, packaged, and labeled as the agreement may require; and

(f) conform to the promises or affirmations of fact made on the container or label if any.

(3) Unless excluded or modified (Section 2–316) other implied warranties may arise from course of dealing or usage of trade.

§ 2–315. Implied Warranty: Fitness for Particular Purpose.

Where the seller at the time of contracting has reason to know any particular purpose for which the goods are required and that the buyer is relying on the seller's skill or judgment to select or furnish suitable goods, there is unless excluded or modified under the next section an implied warranty that the goods shall be fit for such purpose.

§ 2–316. Exclusion or Modification of Warranties.

(1) Words or conduct relevant to the creation of an express warranty and words or conduct tending to negate or limit warranty shall be construed wherever reasonable as consistent with each other; but subject to the provisions of this Article on parol or extrinsic evidence (Section 2–202) negation or limitation is inoperative to the extent that such construction is unreasonable.

(2) Subject to subsection (3), to exclude or modify the implied warranty of merchantability or any part of it the language must mention merchantability and in case of a writing must be conspicuous, and to exclude or modify any implied warranty of fitness the exclusion must be by a writing and conspicuous. Language to exclude all implied warranties of fitness is sufficient if it states, for example, that "There are no warranties which extend beyond the description on the face hereof."

(3) Notwithstanding subsection (2)

(a) unless the circumstances indicate otherwise, all implied warranties are excluded by expressions like "as is", "with all faults" or other language which in common understanding calls the buyer's attention to the exclusion of warranties and makes plain that there is no implied warranty; and

(b) when the buyer before entering into the contract has examined the goods or the sample or model as fully as he desired or has refused to examine the goods there is no implied warranty with regard to defects which an examination ought in the circumstances to have revealed to him; and

(c) an implied warranty can also be excluded or modified by course of dealing or course of performance or usage of trade.

(4) Remedies for breach of warranty can be limited in accordance with the provisions of this Article on liquidation or limitation of damages and on contractual modification of remedy (Sections 2–718 and 2–719).

§ 2–317. Cumulation and Conflict of Warranties Express or Implied.

Warranties whether express or implied shall be construed as consistent with each other and as cumulative, but if such construction is unreasonable the intention of the parties shall determine which warranty is dominant. In ascertaining that intention the following rules apply:

(a) Exact or technical specifications displace an inconsistent sample or model or general language of description.

(b) A sample from an existing bulk displaces inconsistent general language of description.

(c) Express warranties displace inconsistent implied warranties other than an implied warranty of fitness for a particular purpose.

§ 2–318. Third Party Beneficiaries of Warranties Express or Implied.

Note: If this Act is introduced in the Congress of the United States this section should be omitted. (States to select one alternative.)

Alternative A A seller's warranty whether express or implied extends to any natural person who is in the family or household of his buyer or who is a guest in his home if it is reasonable to expect that such person may use, consume or be affected by the goods and who is injured in person by breach of the warranty. A seller may not exclude or limit the operation of this section.

Alternative B A seller's warranty whether express or implied extends to any natural person who may reasonably be expected to use, consume or be affected by the goods and who is injured in person by breach of the warranty. A seller may not exclude or limit the operation of this section.

Alternative C A seller's warranty whether express or implied extends to any person who may reasonably be expected to use, consume or be affected by the goods and who is injured by breach of the warranty. A seller may not exclude or limit the operation of this section with respect to injury to the person of an individual to whom the warranty extends.

As amended 1966.

§ 2–319. F.O.B. and F.A.S. Terms.

(1) Unless otherwise agreed the term F.O.B. (which means "free on board") at a named place, even though used only in connection with the stated price, is a delivery term under which

(a) when the term is F.O.B. the place of shipment, the seller must at that place ship the goods in the manner provided in this Article (Section 2–504) and bear the expense and risk of putting them into the possession of the carrier; or

(b) when the term is F.O.B. the place of destination, the seller must at his own expense and risk transport the goods to that place and there tender delivery of them in the manner provided in this Article (Section 2–503);

(c) when under either (a) or (b) the term is also F.O.B. vessel, car or other vehicle, the seller must in addition at his own expense and risk load the goods on board. If the term is F.O.B. vessel the buyer must name the vessel and in an appropriate case the seller must comply with the provisions of this Article on the form of bill of lading (Section 2–323).

(2) Unless otherwise agreed the term F.A.S. vessel (which means "free alongside") at a named port, even though used only in connection with the stated price, is a delivery term under which the seller must

(a) at his own expense and risk deliver the goods alongside the vessel in the manner usual in that port or on a dock designated and provided by the buyer; and

(b) obtain and tender a receipt for the goods in exchange for which the carrier is under a duty to issue a bill of lading.

(3) Unless otherwise agreed in any case falling within subsection (1)(a) or (c) or subsection (2) the buyer must seasonably give any needed instructions for making delivery, including when the term is F.A.S. or F.O.B. the loading berth of the vessel and in an appropriate case its name and sailing date. The seller may treat the failure of needed instructions as a failure of cooperation under this Article (Section 2–311). He may also at his option move the goods in any reasonable manner preparatory to delivery or shipment.

(4) Under the term F.O.B. vessel or F.A.S. unless otherwise agreed the buyer must make payment against tender of the required documents and the seller may not tender nor the buyer demand delivery of the goods in substitution for the documents.

§ 2–320. C.I.F. and C. & F. Terms.

(1) The term C.I.F. means that the price includes in a lump sum the cost of the goods and the insurance and freight to the named destination. The term C. & F. or C.F. means that the price so includes cost and freight to the named destination.

(2) Unless otherwise agreed and even though used only in connection with the stated price and destination, the term C.I.F. destination or its equivalent requires the seller at his own expense and risk to

(a) put the goods into the possession of a carrier at the port for shipment and obtain a negotiable bill or bills of lading covering the entire transportation to the named destination; and

(b) load the goods and obtain a receipt from the carrier (which may be contained in the bill of lading) showing that the freight has been paid or provided for; and

(c) obtain a policy or certificate of insurance, including any war risk insurance, of a kind and on terms then current at the port of shipment in the usual amount, in the currency of the contract, shown to cover the same goods covered by the bill of lading and providing for payment of loss to the order of the buyer or for the account of whom it may concern; but the seller may add to the price the amount of the premium for any such war risk insurance; and

(d) prepare an invoice of the goods and procure any other documents required to effect shipment or to comply with the contract; and

(e) forward and tender with commercial promptness all the documents in due form and with any indorsement necessary to perfect the buyer's rights.

(3) Unless otherwise agreed the term C. & F. or its equivalent has the same effect and imposes upon the seller the same obligations and risks as a C.I.F. term except the obligation as to insurance.

(4) Under the term C.I.F. or C. & F. unless otherwise agreed the buyer must make payment against tender of the required documents and the seller may not tender nor the buyer demand delivery of the goods in substitution for the documents.

§ 2–321. C.I.F. or C. & F.: "Net Landed Weights"; "Payment on Arrival"; Warranty of Condition on Arrival.

Under a contract containing a term C.I.F. or C. & F.

(1) Where the price is based on or is to be adjusted according to "net landed weights", "delivered weights", "out turn" quantity or quality or the like, unless otherwise agreed the seller must reasonably estimate the price. The payment due on tender of the documents called for by the contract is the amount so estimated, but after final adjustment of the price a settlement must be made with commercial promptness.

(2) An agreement described in subsection (1) or any warranty of quality or condition of the goods on arrival places upon the seller the risk of ordinary deterioration, shrinkage and the like in transportation but has no effect on the place or time of identification to the contract for sale or delivery or on the passing of the risk of loss.

(3) Unless otherwise agreed where the contract provides for payment on or after arrival of the goods the seller must before payment allow such preliminary inspection as is feasible; but if the goods are lost delivery of the documents and payment are due when the goods should have arrived.

§ 2–322. Delivery "Ex-Ship".

(1) Unless otherwise agreed a term for delivery of goods "ex-ship" (which means from the carrying vessel) or in equivalent language is not restricted to a particular ship and requires delivery from a ship which has reached a place at the named port of destination where goods of the kind are usually discharged.

(2) Under such a term unless otherwise agreed

(a) the seller must discharge all liens arising out of the carriage and furnish the buyer with a direction which puts the carrier under a duty to deliver the goods; and

(b) the risk of loss does not pass to the buyer until the goods leave the ship's tackle or are otherwise properly unloaded.

§ 2–323. Form of Bill of Lading Required in Overseas Shipment; "Overseas".

(1) Where the contract contemplates overseas shipment and contains a term C.I.F. or C. & F. or F.O.B. vessel, the seller unless otherwise agreed must obtain a negotiable bill of lading stating that the goods have been loaded on board or, in the case of a term C.I.F. or C. & F., received for shipment.

(2) Where in a case within subsection (1) a bill of lading has been issued in a set of parts, unless otherwise agreed if the documents are not to be sent from abroad the buyer may demand tender of the full set; otherwise only one part of the bill of lading need be tendered. Even if the agreement expressly requires a full set

(a) due tender of a single part is acceptable within the provisions of this Article on cure of improper delivery (subsection (1) of Section 2–508); and

(b) even though the full set is demanded, if the documents are sent from abroad the person tendering an incomplete set may nevertheless require payment upon furnishing an indemnity which the buyer in good faith deems adequate.

(3) A shipment by water or by air or a contract contemplating such shipment is "overseas" insofar as by usage of trade or agreement it is subject to the commercial, financing or shipping practices characteristic of international deep water commerce.

§ 2–324. "No Arrival, No Sale" Term.

Under a term "no arrival, no sale" or terms of like meaning, unless otherwise agreed,

(a) the seller must properly ship conforming goods and if they arrive by any means he must tender them on arrival but he assumes no obligation that the goods will arrive unless he has caused the non-arrival; and

(b) where without fault of the seller the goods are in part lost or have so deteriorated as no longer to conform to the contract or arrive after the contract time, the buyer may proceed as if there had been casualty to identified goods (Section 2–613).

§ 2–325. "Letter of Credit" Term; "Confirmed Credit".

(1) Failure of the buyer seasonably to furnish an agreed letter of credit is a breach of the contract for sale.

(2) The delivery to seller of a proper letter of credit suspends the buyer's obligation to pay. If the letter of credit is dishonored, the seller may on seasonable notification to the buyer require payment directly from him.

(3) Unless otherwise agreed the term "letter of credit" or "banker's credit" in a contract for sale means an irrevocable credit issued by a financing agency of good repute and, where the shipment is overseas, of good international repute. The term "confirmed credit" means that the credit must also carry the direct obligation of such an agency which does business in the seller's financial market.

§ 2–326. Sale on Approval and Sale or Return; Rights of Creditors.

(1) Unless otherwise agreed, if delivered goods may be returned by the buyer even though they conform to the contract, the transaction is

(a) a "sale on approval" if the goods are delivered primarily for use, and

(b) a "sale or return" if the goods are delivered primarily for resale.

(2) Goods held on approval are not subject to the claims of the buyer's creditors until acceptance; goods held on sale or return are subject to such claims while in the buyer's possession.

(3) Any "or return" term of a contract for sale is to be treated as a separate contract for sale within the statute of frauds section of this Article (Section 2–201) and as contradicting the sale aspect of the contract within the provisions of this Article or on parol or extrinsic evidence (Section 2–202).

As amended in 1999.

§ 2–327. Special Incidents of Sale on Approval and Sale or Return.

(1) Under a sale on approval unless otherwise agreed

(a) although the goods are identified to the contract the risk of loss and the title do not pass to the buyer until acceptance; and

(b) use of the goods consistent with the purpose of trial is not acceptance but failure seasonably to notify the seller of election to return the goods is acceptance, and if the goods conform to the contract acceptance of any part is acceptance of the whole; and

(c) after due notification of election to return, the return is at the seller's risk and expense but a merchant buyer must follow any reasonable instructions.

(2) Under a sale or return unless otherwise agreed

(a) the option to return extends to the whole or any commercial unit of the goods while in substantially their original condition, but must be exercised seasonably; and

(b) the return is at the buyer's risk and expense.

§ 2–328. Sale by Auction.

(1) In a sale by auction if goods are put up in lots each lot is the subject of a separate sale.

(2) A sale by auction is complete when the auctioneer so announces by the fall of the hammer or in other customary manner. Where a bid is made while the hammer is falling in acceptance of a prior bid the auctioneer may in his discretion reopen the bidding or declare the goods sold under the bid on which the hammer was falling.

(3) Such a sale is with reserve unless the goods are in explicit terms put up without reserve. In an auction with reserve the auctioneer may withdraw the goods at any time until he announces completion of the sale. In an auction without reserve, after the auctioneer calls for bids on an article or lot, that article or lot cannot be withdrawn unless no bid is made within a reasonable time. In either case a bidder may retract his bid until the auctioneer's announcement of completion of the sale, but a bidder's retraction does not revive any previous bid.

(4) If the auctioneer knowingly receives a bid on the seller's behalf or the seller makes or procures such as bid, and notice has not been given that liberty for such bidding is reserved, the buyer may at his option avoid the sale or take the goods at the price of the last good faith bid prior to the completion of the sale. This subsection shall not apply to any bid at a forced sale.

PART 4   Title, Creditors and Good Faith Purchasers

§ 2–401. Passing of Title; Reservation for Security; Limited Application of This Section.

Each provision of this Article with regard to the rights, obligations and remedies of the seller, the buyer, purchasers or other third parties applies irrespective of title to the goods except where the provision refers to such title. Insofar as situations are not covered by the other provisions of this Article and matters concerning title became material the following rules apply:

(1) Title to goods cannot pass under a contract for sale prior to their identification to the contract (Section 2–501), and unless otherwise explicitly agreed the buyer acquires by their identification a special property as limited by this Act. Any retention or reservation by the seller of the title (property) in

goods shipped or delivered to the buyer is limited in effect to a reservation of a security interest. Subject to these provisions and to the provisions of the Article on Secured Transactions (Article 9), title to goods passes from the seller to the buyer in any manner and on any conditions explicitly agreed on by the parties.

(2) Unless otherwise explicitly agreed title passes to the buyer at the time and place at which the seller completes his performance with reference to the physical delivery of the goods, despite any reservation of a security interest and even though a document of title is to be delivered at a different time or place; and in particular and despite any reservation of a security interest by the bill of lading

(a) if the contract requires or authorizes the seller to send the goods to the buyer but does not require him to deliver them at destination, title passes to the buyer at the time and place of shipment; but

(b) if the contract requires delivery at destination, title passes on tender there.

(3) Unless otherwise explicitly agreed where delivery is to be made without moving the goods,

(a) if the seller is to deliver a document of title, title passes at the time when and the place where he delivers such documents; or

(b) if the goods are at the time of contracting already identified and no documents are to be delivered, title passes at the time and place of contracting.

(4) A rejection or other refusal by the buyer to receive or retain the goods, whether or not justified, or a justified revocation of acceptance revests title to the goods in the seller. Such revesting occurs by operation of law and is not a "sale".

§ 2–402. Rights of Seller's Creditors Against Sold Goods.

(1) Except as provided in subsections (2) and (3), rights of unsecured creditors of the seller with respect to goods which have been identified to a contract for sale are subject to the buyer's rights to recover the goods under this Article (Sections 2–502 and 2–716).

(2) A creditor of the seller may treat a sale or an identification of goods to a contract for sale as void if as against him a retention of possession by the seller is fraudulent under any rule of law of the state where the goods are situated, except that retention of possession in good faith and current course of trade by a merchant-seller for a commercially reasonable time after a sale or identification is not fraudulent.

(3) Nothing in this Article shall be deemed to impair the rights of creditors of the seller

(a) under the provisions of the Article on Secured Transactions (Article 9); or

(b) where identification to the contract or delivery is made not in current course of trade but in satisfaction of or as

security for a pre-existing claim for money, security or the like and is made under circumstances which under any rule of law of the state where the goods are situated would apart from this Article constitute the transaction a fraudulent transfer or voidable preference.

§ 2–403. Power to Transfer; Good Faith Purchase of Goods; "Entrusting".

(1) A purchaser of goods acquires all title which his transferor had or had power to transfer except that a purchaser of a limited interest acquires rights only to the extent of the interest purchased. A person with voidable title has power to transfer a good title to a good faith purchaser for value. When goods have been delivered under a transaction of purchase the purchaser has such power even though

(a) the transferor was deceived as to the identity of the purchaser, or

(b) the delivery was in exchange for a check which is later dishonored, or

(c) it was agreed that the transaction was to be a "cash sale", or

(d) the delivery was procured through fraud punishable as larcenous under the criminal law.

(2) Any entrusting of possession of goods to a merchant who deals in goods of that kind gives him power to transfer all rights of the entruster to a buyer in ordinary course of business.

(3) "Entrusting" includes any delivery and any acquiescence in retention of possession regardless of any condition expressed between the parties to the delivery or acquiescence and regardless of whether the procurement of the entrusting or the possessor's disposition of the goods have been such as to be larcenous under the criminal law.

(4) The rights of other purchasers of goods and of lien creditors are governed by the Articles on Secured Transactions (Article 9), Bulk Transfers (Article 6) and Documents of Title (Article 7).

As amended in 1988.

PART 5   Performance

§ 2–501. Insurable Interest in Goods; Manner of Identification of Goods.

(1) The buyer obtains a special property and an insurable interest in goods by identification of existing goods as goods to which the contract refers even though the goods so identified are non-conforming and he has an option to return or reject them. Such identification can be made at any time and in any manner explicitly agreed to by the parties. In the absence of explicit agreement identification occurs

(a) when the contract is made if it is for the sale of goods already existing and identified;

(b) if the contract is for the sale of future goods other than those described in paragraph (c), when goods are shipped, marked or otherwise designated by the seller as goods to which the contract refers;

(c) when the crops are planted or otherwise become growing crops or the young are conceived if the contract is for the sale of unborn young to be born within twelve months after contracting or for the sale of crops to be harvested within twelve months or the next normal harvest season after contracting whichever is longer.

(2) The seller retains an insurable interest in goods so long as title to or any security interest in the goods remains in him and where the identification is by the seller alone he may until default or insolvency or notification to the buyer that the identification is final substitute other goods for those identified.

(3) Nothing in this section impairs any insurable interest recognized under any other statute or rule of law.

§ 2–502. Buyer's Right to Goods on Seller's Insolvency.

(1) Subject to subsections (2) and (3) and even though the goods have not been shipped a buyer who has paid a part or all of the price of goods in which he has a special property under the provisions of the immediately preceding section may on making and keeping good a tender of any unpaid portion of their price recover them from the seller if:

(a) in the case of goods bought for personal, family, or household purposes, the seller repudiates or fails to deliver as required by the contract; or

(b) in all cases, the seller becomes insolvent within ten days after receipt of the first installment on their price.

(2) The buyer's right to recover the goods under subsection (1)(a) vests upon acquisition of a special property, even if the seller had not then repudiated or failed to deliver.

(3) If the identification creating his special property has been made by the buyer he acquires the right to recover the goods only if they conform to the contract for sale.

As amended in 1999.

§ 2–503. Manner of Seller's Tender of Delivery.

(1) Tender of delivery requires that the seller put and hold conforming goods at the buyer's disposition and give the buyer any notification reasonably necessary to enable him to take delivery. The manner, time and place for tender are determined by the agreement and this Article, and in particular

(a) tender must be at a reasonable hour, and if it is of goods they must be kept available for the period reasonably necessary to enable the buyer to take possession; but

(b) unless otherwise agreed the buyer must furnish facilities reasonably suited to the receipt of the goods.

(2) Where the case is within the next section respecting shipment tender requires that the seller comply with its provisions.

(3) Where the seller is required to deliver at a particular destination tender requires that he comply with subsection (1) and also in any appropriate case tender documents as described in subsections (4) and (5) of this section.

(4) Where goods are in the possession of a bailee and are to be delivered without being moved

(a) tender requires that the seller either tender a negotiable document of title covering such goods or procure acknowledgment by the bailee of the buyer's right to possession of the goods; but

(b) tender to the buyer of a non-negotiable document of title or of a written direction to the bailee to deliver is sufficient tender unless the buyer seasonably objects, and receipt by the bailee of notification of the buyer's rights fixes those rights as against the bailee and all third persons; but risk of loss of the goods and of any failure by the bailee to honor the non-negotiable document of title or to obey the direction remains on the seller until the buyer has had a reasonable time to present the document or direction, and a refusal by the bailee to honor the document or to obey the direction defeats the tender.

(5) Where the contract requires the seller to deliver documents

(a) he must tender all such documents in correct form, except as provided in this Article with respect to bills of lading in a set (subsection (2) of Section 2–323); and

(b) tender through customary banking channels is sufficient and dishonor of a draft accompanying the documents constitutes non-acceptance or rejection.

§ 2–504. Shipment by Seller.

Where the seller is required or authorized to send the goods to the buyer and the contract does not require him to deliver them at a particular destination, then unless otherwise agreed he must

(a) put the goods in the possession of such a carrier and make such a contract for their transportation as may be reasonable having regard to the nature of the goods and other circumstances of the case; and

(b) obtain and promptly deliver or tender in due form any document necessary to enable the buyer to obtain possession of the goods or otherwise required by the agreement or by usage of trade; and

(c) promptly notify the buyer of the shipment.

Failure to notify the buyer under paragraph (c) or to make a proper contract under paragraph (a) is a ground for rejection only if material delay or loss ensues.

§ 2–505. Seller's Shipment under Reservation.

(1) Where the seller has identified goods to the contract by or before shipment:

(a) his procurement of a negotiable bill of lading to his own order or otherwise reserves in him a security interest in the goods. His procurement of the bill to the order of a financing agency or of the buyer indicates in addition only the seller's expectation of transferring that interest to the person named.

(b) a non-negotiable bill of lading to himself or his nominee reserves possession of the goods as security but except in a case of conditional delivery (subsection (2) of Section 2–507) a non-negotiable bill of lading naming the buyer as consignee reserves no security interest even though the seller retains possession of the bill of lading.

(2) When shipment by the seller with reservation of a security interest is in violation of the contract for sale it constitutes an improper contract for transportation within the preceding section but impairs neither the rights given to the buyer by shipment and identification of the goods to the contract nor the seller's powers as a holder of a negotiable document.

§ 2–506. Rights of Financing Agency.

(1) A financing agency by paying or purchasing for value a draft which relates to a shipment of goods acquires to the extent of the payment or purchase and in addition to its own rights under the draft and any document of title securing it any rights of the shipper in the goods including the right to stop delivery and the shipper's right to have the draft honored by the buyer.

(2) The right to reimbursement of a financing agency which has in good faith honored or purchased the draft under commitment to or authority from the buyer is not impaired by subsequent discovery of defects with reference to any relevant document which was apparently regular on its face.

§ 2–507. Effect of Seller's Tender; Delivery on Condition.

(1) Tender of delivery is a condition to the buyer's duty to accept the goods and, unless otherwise agreed, to his duty to pay for them. Tender entitles the seller to acceptance of the goods and to payment according to the contract.

(2) Where payment is due and demanded on the delivery to the buyer of goods or documents of title, his right as against the seller to retain or dispose of them is conditional upon his making the payment due.

§ 2–508. Cure by Seller of Improper Tender or Delivery; Replacement.

(1) Where any tender or delivery by the seller is rejected because non-conforming and the time for performance has not yet expired, the seller may seasonably notify the buyer of his intention to cure and may then within the contract time make a conforming delivery.

(2) Where the buyer rejects a non-conforming tender which the seller had reasonable grounds to believe would be acceptable with or without money allowance the seller may if he seasonably notifies the buyer have a further reasonable time to substitute a conforming tender.

§ 2–509. Risk of Loss in the Absence of Breach.

(1) Where the contract requires or authorizes the seller to ship the goods by carrier

(a) if it does not require him to deliver them at a particular destination, the risk of loss passes to the buyer when the goods are duly delivered to the carrier even though the shipment is under reservation (Section 2–505); but

(b) if it does require him to deliver them at a particular destination and the goods are there duly tendered while in the possession of the carrier, the risk of loss passes to the buyer when the goods are there duly so tendered as to enable the buyer to take delivery.

(2) Where the goods are held by a bailee to be delivered without being moved, the risk of loss passes to the buyer

(a) on his receipt of a negotiable document of title covering the goods; or

(b) on acknowledgment by the bailee of the buyer's right to possession of the goods; or

(c) after his receipt of a non-negotiable document of title or other written direction to deliver, as provided in subsection (4)(b) of Section 2–503.

(3) In any case not within subsection (1) or (2), the risk of loss passes to the buyer on his receipt of the goods if the seller is a merchant; otherwise the risk passes to the buyer on tender of delivery.

(4) The provisions of this section are subject to contrary agreement of the parties and to the provisions of this Article on sale on approval (Section 2–327) and on effect of breach on risk of loss (Section 2–510).

§ 2–510. Effect of Breach on Risk of Loss.

(1) Where a tender or delivery of goods so fails to conform to the contract as to give a right of rejection the risk of their loss remains on the seller until cure or acceptance.

(2) Where the buyer rightfully revokes acceptance he may to the extent of any deficiency in his effective insurance

coverage treat the risk of loss as having rested on the seller from the beginning.

(3) Where the buyer as to conforming goods already identified to the contract for sale repudiates or is otherwise in breach before risk of their loss has passed to him, the seller may to the extent of any deficiency in his effective insurance coverage treat the risk of loss as resting on the buyer for a commercially reasonable time.

§ 2–511. Tender of Payment by Buyer; Payment by Check.

(1) Unless otherwise agreed tender of payment is a condition to the seller's duty to tender and complete any delivery.

(2) Tender of payment is sufficient when made by any means or in any manner current in the ordinary course of business unless the seller demands payment in legal tender and gives any extension of time reasonably necessary to procure it.

(3) Subject to the provisions of this Act on the effect of an instrument on an obligation (Section 3–310), payment by check is conditional and is defeated as between the parties by dishonor of the check on due presentment.

As amended in 1994.

§ 2–512. Payment by Buyer Before Inspection.

(1) Where the contract requires payment before inspection non-conformity of the goods does not excuse the buyer from so making payment unless

    (a) the non-conformity appears without inspection; or

    (b) despite tender of the required documents the circumstances would justify injunction against honor under this Act (Section 5–109(b)).

(2) Payment pursuant to subsection (1) does not constitute an acceptance of goods or impair the buyer's right to inspect or any of his remedies.

As amended in 1995.

§ 2–513. Buyer's Right to Inspection of Goods.

(1) Unless otherwise agreed and subject to subsection (3), where goods are tendered or delivered or identified to the contract for sale, the buyer has a right before payment or acceptance to inspect them at any reasonable place and time and in any reasonable manner. When the seller is required or authorized to send the goods to the buyer, the inspection may be after their arrival.

(2) Expenses of inspection must be borne by the buyer but may be recovered from the seller if the goods do not conform and are rejected.

(3) Unless otherwise agreed and subject to the provisions of this Article on C.I.F. contracts (subsection (3) of Section 2–321), the buyer is not entitled to inspect the goods before payment of the price when the contract provides

    (a) for delivery "C.O.D." or on other like terms; or

    (b) for payment against documents of title, except where such payment is due only after the goods are to become available for inspection.

(4) A place or method of inspection fixed by the parties is presumed to be exclusive but unless otherwise expressly agreed it does not postpone identification or shift the place for delivery or for passing the risk of loss. If compliance becomes impossible, inspection shall be as provided in this section unless the place or method fixed was clearly intended as an indispensable condition failure of which avoids the contract.

§ 2–514. When Documents Deliverable on Acceptance; When on Payment.

Unless otherwise agreed documents against which a draft is drawn are to be delivered to the drawee on acceptance of the draft if it is payable more than three days after presentment; otherwise, only on payment.

§ 2–515. Preserving Evidence of Goods in Dispute.

In furtherance of the adjustment of any claim or dispute

    (a) either party on reasonable notification to the other and for the purpose of ascertaining the facts and preserving evidence has the right to inspect, test and sample the goods including such of them as may be in the possession or control of the other; and

    (b) the parties may agree to a third party inspection or survey to determine the conformity or condition of the goods and may agree that the findings shall be binding upon them in any subsequent litigation or adjustment.

PART 6 Breach, Repudiation and Excuse

§ 2–601. Buyer's Rights on Improper Delivery.

Subject to the provisions of this Article on breach in installment contracts (Section 2–612) and unless otherwise agreed under the sections on contractual limitations of remedy (Sections 2–718 and 2–719), if the goods or the tender of delivery fail in any respect to conform to the contract, the buyer may

    (a) reject the whole; or

    (b) accept the whole; or

    (c) accept any commercial unit or units and reject the rest.

§ 2–602. Manner and Effect of Rightful Rejection.

(1) Rejection of goods must be within a reasonable time after their delivery or tender. It is ineffective unless the buyer seasonably notifies the seller.

(2) Subject to the provisions of the two following sections on rejected goods (Sections 2–603 and 2–604),

(a) after rejection any exercise of ownership by the buyer with respect to any commercial unit is wrongful as against the seller; and

(b) if the buyer has before rejection taken physical possession of goods in which he does not have a security interest under the provisions of this Article (subsection (3) of Section 2–711), he is under a duty after rejection to hold them with reasonable care at the seller's disposition for a time sufficient to permit the seller to remove them; but

(c) the buyer has no further obligations with regard to goods rightfully rejected.

(3) The seller's rights with respect to goods wrongfully rejected are governed by the provisions of this Article on Seller's remedies in general (Section 2–703).

§ 2–603. Merchant Buyer's Duties as to Rightfully Rejected Goods.

(1) Subject to any security interest in the buyer (subsection (3) of Section 2–711), when the seller has no agent or place of business at the market of rejection a merchant buyer is under a duty after rejection of goods in his possession or control to follow any reasonable instructions received from the seller with respect to the goods and in the absence of such instructions to make reasonable efforts to sell them for the seller's account if they are perishable or threaten to decline in value speedily. Instructions are not reasonable if on demand indemnity for expenses is not forthcoming.

(2) When the buyer sells goods under subsection (1), he is entitled to reimbursement from the seller or out of the proceeds for reasonable expenses of caring for and selling them, and if the expenses include no selling commission then to such commission as is usual in the trade or if there is none to a reasonable sum not exceeding ten percent on the gross proceeds.

(3) In complying with this section the buyer is held only to good faith and good faith conduct hereunder is neither acceptance nor conversion nor the basis of an action for damages.

§ 2–604. Buyer's Options as to Salvage of Rightfully Rejected Goods.

Subject to the provisions of the immediately preceding section on perishables if the seller gives no instructions within a reasonable time after notification of rejection the buyer may store the rejected goods for the seller's account or reship them to him or resell them for the seller's account with reimbursement as provided in the preceding section. Such action is not acceptance or conversion.

§ 2–605. Waiver of Buyer's Objections by Failure to Particularize.

(1) The buyer's failure to state in connection with rejection a particular defect which is ascertainable by reasonable inspection precludes him from relying on the unstated defect to justify rejection or to establish breach

(a) where the seller could have cured it if stated seasonably; or

(b) between merchants when the seller has after rejection made a request in writing for a full and final written statement of all defects on which the buyer proposes to rely.

(2) Payment against documents made without reservation of rights precludes recovery of the payment for defects apparent on the face of the documents.

§ 2–606. What Constitutes Acceptance of Goods.

(1) Acceptance of goods occurs when the buyer

(a) after a reasonable opportunity to inspect the goods signifies to the seller that the goods are conforming or that he will take or retain them in spite of their nonconformity; or

(b) fails to make an effective rejection (subsection (1) of Section 2–602), but such acceptance does not occur until the buyer has had a reasonable opportunity to inspect them; or

(c) does any act inconsistent with the seller's ownership; but if such act is wrongful as against the seller it is an acceptance only if ratified by him.

(2) Acceptance of a part of any commercial unit is acceptance of that entire unit.

§ 2–607. Effect of Acceptance; Notice of Breach; Burden of Establishing Breach After Acceptance; Notice of Claim or Litigation to Person Answerable Over.

(1) The buyer must pay at the contract rate for any goods accepted.

(2) Acceptance of goods by the buyer precludes rejection of the goods accepted and if made with knowledge of a non-conformity cannot be revoked because of it unless the acceptance was on the reasonable assumption that the non-conformity would be seasonably cured but acceptance does not of itself impair any other remedy provided by this Article for non-conformity.

(3) Where a tender has been accepted

(a) the buyer must within a reasonable time after he discovers or should have discovered any breach notify the seller of breach or be barred from any remedy; and

(b) if the claim is one for infringement or the like (subsection (3) of Section 2–312) and the buyer is sued as a result of such a breach he must so notify the seller within a reasonable time after he receives notice of the litigation or be barred from any remedy over for liability established by the litigation.

(4) The burden is on the buyer to establish any breach with respect to the goods accepted.

(5) Where the buyer is sued for breach of a warranty or other obligation for which his seller is answerable over

(a) he may give his seller written notice of the litigation. If the notice states that the seller may come in and defend and that if the seller does not do so he will be bound in any action against him by his buyer by any determination of fact common to the two litigations, then unless the seller after seasonable receipt of the notice does come in and defend he is so bound.

(b) if the claim is one for infringement or the like (subsection (3) of Section 2–312) the original seller may demand in writing that his buyer turn over to him control of the litigation including settlement or else be barred from any remedy over and if he also agrees to bear all expense and to satisfy any adverse judgment, then unless the buyer after seasonable receipt of the demand does turn over control the buyer is so barred.

(6) The provisions of subsections (3), (4) and (5) apply to any obligation of a buyer to hold the seller harmless against infringement or the like (subsection (3) of Section 2–312).

§ 2–608. Revocation of Acceptance in Whole or in Part.

(1) The buyer may revoke his acceptance of a lot or commercial unit whose non-conformity substantially impairs its value to him if he has accepted it

(a) on the reasonable assumption that its nonconformity would be cured and it has not been seasonably cured; or

(b) without discovery of such non-conformity if his acceptance was reasonably induced either by the difficulty of discovery before acceptance or by the seller's assurances.

(2) Revocation of acceptance must occur within a reasonable time after the buyer discovers or should have discovered the ground for it and before any substantial change in condition of the goods which is not caused by their own defects. It is not effective until the buyer notifies the seller of it.

(3) A buyer who so revokes has the same rights and duties with regard to the goods involved as if he had rejected them.

§ 2–609. Right to Adequate Assurance of Performance.

(1) A contract for sale imposes an obligation on each party that the other's expectation of receiving due performance will not be impaired. When reasonable grounds for insecurity arise with respect to the performance of either party the other may in writing demand adequate assurance of due performance and until he receives such assurance may if commercially reasonable suspend any performance for which he has not already received the agreed return.

(2) Between merchants the reasonableness of grounds for insecurity and the adequacy of any assurance offered shall be determined according to commercial standards.

(3) Acceptance of any improper delivery or payment does not prejudice the party's right to demand adequate assurance of future performance.

(4) After receipt of a justified demand failure to provide within a reasonable time not exceeding thirty days such assurance of due performance as is adequate under the circumstances of the particular case is a repudiation of the contract.

§ 2–610. Anticipatory Repudiation.

When either party repudiates the contract with respect to a performance not yet due the loss of which will substantially impair the value of the contract to the other, the aggrieved party may

(a) for a commercially reasonable time await performance by the repudiating party; or

(b) resort to any remedy for breach (Section 2–703 or Sec-tion 2–711), even though he has notified the repudiating party that he would await the latter's performance and has urged retraction; and

(c) in either case suspend his own performance or proceed in accordance with the provisions of this Article on the seller's right to identify goods to the contract notwithstanding breach or to salvage unfinished goods (Section 2–704).

§ 2–611. Retraction of Anticipatory Repudiation.

(1) Until the repudiating party's next performance is due he can retract his repudiation unless the aggrieved party has since the repudiation cancelled or materially changed his position or otherwise indicated that he considers the repudiation final.

(2) Retraction may be by any method which clearly indicates to the aggrieved party that the repudiating party intends to perform, but must include any assurance justifiably demanded under the provisions of this Article (Section 2–609).

(3) Retraction reinstates the repudiating party's rights under the contract with due excuse and allowance to the aggrieved party for any delay occasioned by the repudiation.

§ 2–612. "Installment Contract"; Breach.

(1) An "installment contract" is one which requires or authorizes the delivery of goods in separate lots to be separately accepted, even though the contract contains a clause "each delivery is a separate contract" or its equivalent.

(2) The buyer may reject any installment which is non-conforming if the non-conformity substantially impairs the value of that installment and cannot be cured or if the non-conformity is a defect in the required documents; but if the non-conformity does not fall within subsection (3) and the seller gives adequate assurance of its cure the buyer must accept that installment.

(3) Whenever non-conformity or default with respect to one or more installments substantially impairs the value of the whole contract there is a breach of the whole. But the aggrieved party reinstates the contract if he accepts a non-conforming installment without seasonably notifying of cancellation or if he brings an action with respect only to past installments or demands performance as to future installments.

§ 2–613. Casualty to Identified Goods.

Where the contract requires for its performance goods identified when the contract is made, and the goods suffer casualty without fault of either party before the risk of loss passes to the buyer, or in a proper case under a "no arrival, no sale" term (Section 2–324) then

(a) if the loss is total the contract is avoided; and

(b) if the loss is partial or the goods have so deteriorated as no longer to conform to the contract the buyer may nevertheless demand inspection and at his option either treat the contract as voided or accept the goods with due allowance from the contract price for the deterioration or the deficiency in quantity but without further right against the seller.

§ 2–614. Substituted Performance.

(1) Where without fault of either party the agreed berthing, loading, or unloading facilities fail or an agreed type of carrier becomes unavailable or the agreed manner of delivery otherwise becomes commercially impracticable but a commercially reasonable substitute is available, such substitute performance must be tendered and accepted.

(2) If the agreed means or manner of payment fails because of domestic or foreign governmental regulation, the seller may withhold or stop delivery unless the buyer provides a means or manner of payment which is commercially a substantial equivalent. If delivery has already been taken, payment by the means or in the manner provided by the regulation discharges the buyer's obligation unless the regulation is discriminatory, oppressive or predatory.

§ 2–615. Excuse by Failure of Presupposed Conditions.

Except so far as a seller may have assumed a greater obligation and subject to the preceding section on substituted performance:

(a) Delay in delivery or non-delivery in whole or in part by a seller who complies with paragraphs (b) and (c) is not a breach of his duty under a contract for sale if performance as agreed has been made impracticable by the occurrence of a contingency the nonoccurrence of which was a basic assumption on which the contract was made or by compliance in good faith with any applicable foreign or domestic governmental regulation or order whether or not it later proves to be invalid.

(b) Where the causes mentioned in paragraph (a) affect only a part of the seller's capacity to perform, he must allocate production and deliveries among his customers but may at his option include regular customers not then under contract as well as his own requirements for further manufacture. He may so allocate in any manner which is fair and reasonable.

(c) The seller must notify the buyer seasonably that there will be delay or non-delivery and, when allocation is required under paragraph (b), of the estimated quota thus made available for the buyer.

§ 2–616. Procedure on Notice Claiming Excuse.

(1) Where the buyer receives notification of a material or indefinite delay or an allocation justified under the preceding section he may by written notification to the seller as to any delivery concerned, and where the prospective deficiency substantially impairs the value of the whole contract under the provisions of this Article relating to breach of installment contracts (Section 2–612), then also as to the whole,

(a) terminate and thereby discharge any unexecuted portion of the contract; or

(b) modify the contract by agreeing to take his available quota in substitution.

(2) If after receipt of such notification from the seller the buyer fails so to modify the contract within a reasonable time not exceeding thirty days the contract lapses with respect to any deliveries affected.

(3) The provisions of this section may not be negated by agreement except in so far as the seller has assumed a greater obligation under the preceding section.

PART 7   Remedies

§ 2–701. Remedies for Breach of Collateral Contracts Not Impaired.

Remedies for breach of any obligation or promise collateral or ancillary to a contract for sale are not impaired by the provisions of this Article.

§ 2–702. Seller's Remedies on Discovery of Buyer's Insolvency.

(1) Where the seller discovers the buyer to be insolvent he may refuse delivery except for cash including payment for all goods theretofore delivered under the contract, and stop delivery under this Article (Section 2–705).

(2) Where the seller discovers that the buyer has received goods on credit while insolvent he may reclaim the goods upon demand made within ten days after the receipt, but if misrepresentation of solvency has been made to the particular seller in writing within three months before delivery the ten day limitation does not apply. Except as provided in this subsection the seller may not base a right to reclaim goods on the buyer's fraudulent or innocent misrepresentation of solvency or of intent to pay.

(3) The seller's right to reclaim under subsection (2) is subject to the rights of a buyer in ordinary course or other good faith purchaser under this Article (Section 2–403). Successful reclamation of goods excludes all other remedies with respect to them.

§ 2–703. Seller's Remedies in General.

Where the buyer wrongfully rejects or revokes acceptance of goods or fails to make a payment due on or before delivery or repudiates with respect to a part or the whole, then with respect to any goods directly affected and, if the breach is of the whole contract (Section 2–612), then also with respect to the whole undelivered balance, the aggrieved seller may

(a) withhold delivery of such goods;

(b) stop delivery by any bailee as hereafter provided (Section 2–705);

(c) proceed under the next section respecting goods still unidentified to the contract;

(d) resell and recover damages as hereafter provided (Section 2–706);

(e) recover damages for non-acceptance (Section 2–708) or in a proper case the price (Section 2–709);

(f) cancel.

§ 2–704. Seller's Right to Identify Goods to the Contract Notwithstanding Breach or to Salvage Unfinished Goods.

(1) An aggrieved seller under the preceding section may

(a) identify to the contract conforming goods not already identified if at the time he learned of the breach they are in his possession or control;

(b) treat as the subject of resale goods which have demonstrably been intended for the particular contract even though those goods are unfinished.

(2) Where the goods are unfinished an aggrieved seller may in the exercise of reasonable commercial judgment for the purposes of avoiding loss and of effective realization either complete the manufacture and wholly identify the goods to the contract or cease manufacture and resell for scrap or salvage value or proceed in any other reasonable manner.

§ 2–705. Seller's Stoppage of Delivery in Transit or Otherwise.

(1) The seller may stop delivery of goods in the possession of a carrier or other bailee when he discovers the buyer to be insolvent (Section 2–702) and may stop delivery of carload, truckload, planeload or larger shipments of express or freight when the buyer repudiates or fails to make a payment due before delivery or if for any other reason the seller has a right to withhold or reclaim the goods.

(2) As against such buyer the seller may stop delivery until

(a) receipt of the goods by the buyer; or

(b) acknowledgment to the buyer by any bailee of the goods except a carrier that the bailee holds the goods for the buyer; or

(c) such acknowledgment to the buyer by a carrier by reshipment or as warehouseman; or

(d) negotiation to the buyer of any negotiable document of title covering the goods.

(3) (a) To stop delivery the seller must so notify as to enable the bailee by reasonable diligence to prevent delivery of the goods.

(b) After such notification the bailee must hold and deliver the goods according to the directions of the seller but the seller is liable to the bailee for any ensuing charges or damages.

(c) If a negotiable document of title has been issued for goods the bailee is not obliged to obey a notification to stop until surrender of the document.

(d) A carrier who has issued a non-negotiable bill of lading is not obliged to obey a notification to stop received from a person other than the consignor.

§ 2–706. Seller's Resale Including Contract for Resale.

(1) Under the conditions stated in Section 2–703 on seller's remedies, the seller may resell the goods concerned or the undelivered balance thereof. Where the resale is made in good faith and in a commercially reasonable manner the seller may recover the difference between the resale price and the contract price together with any incidental damages allowed under the provisions of this Article (Section 2–710), but less expenses saved in consequence of the buyer's breach.

(2) Except as otherwise provided in subsection (3) or unless otherwise agreed resale may be at public or private sale

including sale by way of one or more contracts to sell or of identification to an existing contract of the seller. Sale may be as a unit or in parcels and at any time and place and on any terms but every aspect of the sale including the method, manner, time, place and terms must be commercially reasonable. The resale must be reasonably identified as referring to the broken contract, but it is not necessary that the goods be in existence or that any or all of them have been identified to the contract before the breach.

(3) Where the resale is at private sale the seller must give the buyer reasonable notification of his intention to resell.

(4) Where the resale is at public sale

(a) only identified goods can be sold except where there is a recognized market for a public sale of futures in goods of the kind; and

(b) it must be made at a usual place or market for public sale if one is reasonably available and except in the case of goods which are perishable or threaten to decline in value speedily the seller must give the buyer reasonable notice of the time and place of the resale; and

(c) if the goods are not to be within the view of those attending the sale the notification of sale must state the place where the goods are located and provide for their reasonable inspection by prospective bidders; and

(d) the seller may buy.

(5) A purchaser who buys in good faith at a resale takes the goods free of any rights of the original buyer even though the seller fails to comply with one or more of the requirements of this section.

(6) The seller is not accountable to the buyer for any profit made on any resale. A person in the position of a seller (Section 2–707) or a buyer who has rightfully rejected or justifiably revoked acceptance must account for any excess over the amount of his security interest, as hereinafter defined (subsection (3) of Section 2–711).

§ 2–707.   "Person in the Position of a Seller".

(1) A "person in the position of a seller" includes as against a principal an agent who has paid or become responsible for the price of goods on behalf of his principal or anyone who otherwise holds a security interest or other right in goods similar to that of a seller.

(2) A person in the position of a seller may as provided in this Article withhold or stop delivery (Section 2–705) and resell (Section 2–706) and recover incidental damages (Section 2–710).

§ 2–708.   Seller's Damages for Non-Acceptance or Repudiation.

(1) Subject to subsection (2) and to the provisions of this Article with respect to proof of market price (Section 2–723),

the measure of damages for non-acceptance or repudiation by the buyer is the difference between the market price at the time and place for tender and the unpaid contract price together with any incidental damages provided in this Article (Section 2–710), but less expenses saved in consequence of the buyer's breach.

(2) If the measure of damages provided in subsection (1) is inadequate to put the seller in as good a position as performance would have done then the measure of damages is the profit (including reasonable overhead) which the seller would have made from full performance by the buyer, together with any incidental damages provided in this Article (Section 2–710), due allowance for costs reasonably incurred and due credit for payments or proceeds of resale.

§ 2–709.   Action for the Price.

(1) When the buyer fails to pay the price as it becomes due the seller may recover, together with any incidental damages under the next section, the price

(a) of goods accepted or of conforming goods lost or damaged within a commercially reasonable time after risk of their loss has passed to the buyer; and

(b) of goods identified to the contract if the seller is unable after reasonable effort to resell them at a reasonable price or the circumstances reasonably indicate that such effort will be unavailing.

(2) Where the seller sues for the price he must hold for the buyer any goods which have been identified to the contract and are still in his control except that if resale becomes possible he may resell them at any time prior to the collection of the judgment. The net proceeds of any such resale must be credited to the buyer and payment of the judgment entitles him to any goods not resold.

(3) After the buyer has wrongfully rejected or revoked acceptance of the goods or has failed to make a payment due or has repudiated (Section 2–610), a seller who is held not entitled to the price under this section shall nevertheless be awarded damages for non-acceptance under the preceding section.

§ 2–710.   Seller's Incidental Damages.

Incidental damages to an aggrieved seller include any commercially reasonable charges, expenses or commissions incurred in stopping delivery, in the transportation, care and custody of goods after the buyer's breach, in connection with return or resale of the goods or otherwise resulting from the breach.

§ 2–711.   Buyer's Remedies in General; Buyer's Security Interest in Rejected Goods.

(1) Where the seller fails to make delivery or repudiates or the buyer rightfully rejects or justifiably revokes acceptance then with respect to any goods involved, and with respect to

the whole if the breach goes to the whole contract (Section 2–612), the buyer may cancel and whether or not he has done so may in addition to recovering so much of the price as has been paid

(a) "cover" and have damages under the next section as to all the goods affected whether or not they have been identified to the contract; or

(b) recover damages for non-delivery as provided in this Article (Section 2–713).

(2) Where the seller fails to deliver or repudiates the buyer may also

(a) if the goods have been identified recover them as provided in this Article (Section 2–502); or

(b) in a proper case obtain specific performance or replevy the goods as provided in this Article (Section 2–716).

(3) On rightful rejection or justifiable revocation of acceptance a buyer has a security interest in goods in his possession or control for any payments made on their price and any expenses reasonably incurred in their inspection, receipt, transportation, care and custody and may hold such goods and resell them in like manner as an aggrieved seller (Section 2–706).

§ 2–712. "Cover"; Buyer's Procurement of Substitute Goods.

(1) After a breach within the preceding section the buyer may "cover" by making in good faith and without unreasonable delay any reasonable purchase of or contract to purchase goods in substitution for those due from the seller.

(2) The buyer may recover from the seller as damages the difference between the cost of cover and the contract price together with any incidental or consequential damages as hereinafter defined (Section 2–715), but less expenses saved in consequence of the seller's breach.

(3) Failure of the buyer to effect cover within this section does not bar him from any other remedy.

§ 2–713. Buyer's Damages for Non-Delivery or Repudiation.

(1) Subject to the provisions of this Article with respect to proof of market price (Section 2–723), the measure of damages for non-delivery or repudiation by the seller is the difference between the market price at the time when the buyer learned of the breach and the contract price together with any incidental and consequential damages provided in this Article (Section 2–715), but less expenses saved in consequence of the seller's breach.

(2) Market price is to be determined as of the place for tender or, in cases of rejection after arrival or revocation of acceptance, as of the place of arrival.

§ 2–714. Buyer's Damages for Breach in Regard to Accepted Goods.

(1) Where the buyer has accepted goods and given notification (subsection (3) of Section 2–607) he may recover as damages for any non-conformity of tender the loss resulting in the ordinary course of events from the seller's breach as determined in any manner which is reasonable.

(2) The measure of damages for breach of warranty is the difference at the time and place of acceptance between the value of the goods accepted and the value they would have had if they had been as warranted, unless special circumstances show proximate damages of a different amount.

(3) In a proper case any incidental and consequential damages under the next section may also be recovered.

§ 2–715. Buyer's Incidental and Consequential Damages.

(1) Incidental damages resulting from the seller's breach include expenses reasonably incurred in inspection, receipt, transportation and care and custody of goods rightfully rejected, any commercially reasonable charges, expenses or commissions in connection with effecting cover and any other reasonable expense incident to the delay or other breach.

(2) Consequential damages resulting from the seller's breach include

(a) any loss resulting from general or particular requirements and needs of which the seller at the time of contracting had reason to know and which could not reasonably be prevented by cover or otherwise; and

(b) injury to person or property proximately resulting from any breach of warranty.

§ 2–716. Buyer's Right to Specific Performance or Replevin.

(1) Specific performance may be decreed where the goods are unique or in other proper circumstances.

(2) The decree for specific performance may include such terms and conditions as to payment of the price, damages, or other relief as the court may deem just.

(3) The buyer has a right of replevin for goods identified to the contract if after reasonable effort he is unable to effect cover for such goods or the circumstances reasonably indicate that such effort will be unavailing or if the goods have been shipped under reservation and satisfaction of the security interest in them has been made or tendered. In the case of goods bought for personal, family, or household purposes, the buyer's right of replevin vests upon acquisition of a special property, even if the seller had not then repudiated or failed to deliver.

As amended in 1999.

§ 2–717. Deduction of Damages From the Price.

The buyer on notifying the seller of his intention to do so may deduct all or any part of the damages resulting from any breach of the contract from any part of the price still due under the same contract.

§ 2–718. Liquidation or Limitation of Damages; Deposits.

(1) Damages for breach by either party may be liquidated in the agreement but only at an amount which is reasonable in the light of the anticipated or actual harm caused by the breach, the difficulties of proof of loss, and the inconvenience or nonfeasibility of otherwise obtaining an adequate remedy. A term fixing unreasonably large liquidated damages is void as a penalty.

(2) Where the seller justifiably withholds delivery of goods because of the buyer's breach, the buyer is entitled to restitution of any amount by which the sum of his payments exceeds

(a) the amount to which the seller is entitled by virtue of terms liquidating the seller's damages in accordance with subsection (1), or

(b) in the absence of such terms, twenty percent of the value of the total performance for which the buyer is obligated under the contract or $500, whichever is smaller.

(3) The buyer's right to restitution under subsection (2) is subject to offset to the extent that the seller establishes

(a) a right to recover damages under the provisions of this Article other than subsection (1), and

(b) the amount or value of any benefits received by the buyer directly or indirectly by reason of the contract.

(4) Where a seller has received payment in goods their reasonable value or the proceeds of their resale shall be treated as payments for the purposes of subsection (2); but if the seller has notice of the buyer's breach before reselling goods received in part performance, his resale is subject to the conditions laid down in this Article on resale by an aggrieved seller (Section 2–706).

§ 2–719. Contractual Modification or Limitation of Remedy.

(1) Subject to the provisions of subsections (2) and (3) of this section and of the preceding section on liquidation and limitation of damages,

(a) the agreement may provide for remedies in addition to or in substitution for those provided in this Article and may limit or alter the measure of damages recoverable under this Article, as by limiting the buyer's remedies to return of the goods and repayment of the price or to repair and replacement of nonconforming goods or parts; and

(b) resort to a remedy as provided is optional unless the remedy is expressly agreed to be exclusive, in which case it is the sole remedy.

(2) Where circumstances cause an exclusive or limited remedy to fail of its essential purpose, remedy may be had as provided in this Act.

(3) Consequential damages may be limited or excluded unless the limitation or exclusion is unconscionable. Limitation of consequential damages for injury to the person in the case of consumer goods is prima facie unconscionable but limitation of damages where the loss is commercial is not.

§ 2–720. Effect of "Cancellation" or "Rescission" on Claims for Antecedent Breach.

Unless the contrary intention clearly appears, expressions of "cancellation" or "rescission" of the contract or the like shall not be construed as a renunciation or discharge of any claim in damages for an antecedent breach.

§ 2–721. Remedies for Fraud.

Remedies for material misrepresentation or fraud include all remedies available under this Article for non-fraudulent breach. Neither rescission or a claim for rescission of the contract for sale nor rejection or return of the goods shall bar or be deemed inconsistent with a claim for damages or other remedy.

§ 2–722. Who Can Sue Third Parties for Injury to Goods.

Where a third party so deals with goods which have been identified to a contract for sale as to cause actionable injury to a party to that contract

(a) a right of action against the third party is in either party to the contract for sale who has title to or a security interest or a special property or an insurable interest in the goods; and if the goods have been destroyed or converted a right of action is also in the party who either bore the risk of loss under the contract for sale or has since the injury assumed that risk as against the other;

(b) if at the time of the injury the party plaintiff did not bear the risk of loss as against the other party to the contract for sale and there is no arrangement between them for disposition of the recovery, his suit or settlement is, subject to his own interest, as a fiduciary for the other party to the contract;

(c) either party may with the consent of the other sue for the benefit of whom it may concern.

§ 2–723. Proof of Market Price: Time and Place.

(1) If an action based on anticipatory repudiation comes to trial before the time for performance with respect to some or

all of the goods, any damages based on market price (Section 2–708 or Section 2–713) shall be determined according to the price of such goods prevailing at the time when the aggrieved party learned of the repudiation.

(2) If evidence of a price prevailing at the times or places described in this Article is not readily available the price prevailing within any reasonable time before or after the time described or at any other place which in commercial judgment or under usage of trade would serve as a reasonable substitute for the one described may be used, making any proper allowance for the cost of transporting the goods to or from such other place.

(3) Evidence of a relevant price prevailing at a time or place other than the one described in this Article offered by one party is not admissible unless and until he has given the other party such notice as the court finds sufficient to prevent unfair surprise.

§ 2–724. Admissibility of Market Quotations.

Whenever the prevailing price or value of any goods regularly bought and sold in any established commodity market is in issue, reports in official publications or trade journals or in newspapers or periodicals of general circulation published as the reports of such market shall be admissible in evidence. The circumstances of the preparation of such a report may be shown to affect its weight but not its admissibility.

§ 2–725. Statute of Limitations in Contracts for Sale.

(1) An action for breach of any contract for sale must be commenced within four years after the cause of action has accrued. By the original agreement the parties may reduce the period of limitation to not less than one year but may not extend it.

(2) A cause of action accrues when the breach occurs, regardless of the aggrieved party's lack of knowledge of the breach. A breach of warranty occurs when tender of delivery is made, except that where a warranty explicitly extends to future performance of the goods and discovery of the breach must await the time of such performance the cause of action accrues when the breach is or should have been discovered.

(3) Where an action commenced within the time limited by subsection (1) is so terminated as to leave available a remedy by another action for the same breach such other action may be commenced after the expiration of the time limited and within six months after the termination of the first action unless the termination resulted from voluntary discontinuance or from dismissal for failure or neglect to prosecute.

(4) This section does not alter the law on tolling of the statute of limitations nor does it apply to causes of action which have accrued before this Act becomes effective.

ARTICLE II
AMENDMENTS (EXCERPTS)[1]

PART 1 Short Title, General Construction and Subject Matter

§ 2–103. Definitions and Index of Definitions.

* * * *

(1) In this article unless the context otherwise requires
* * * *

(b) "Conspicuous", with reference to a term, means so written, displayed, or presented that a reasonable person against which it is to operate ought to have noticed it. A term in an electronic record intended to evoke a response by an electronic agent is conspicuous if it is presented in a form that would enable a reasonably configured electronic agent to take it into account or react to it without review of the record by an individual. Whether a term is "conspicuous" or not is a decision for the court. Conspicuous terms include the following:

  (i) for a person:

    (A) a heading in capitals equal to or greater in size than the surrounding text, or in contrasting type, font, or color to the surrounding text of the same or lesser size;

    (B) language in the body of a record or display in larger type than the surrounding text, or in contrasting type, font, or color to the surrounding text of the same size, or set off from surrounding text of the same size by symbols or other marks that call attention to the language; and

  (ii) for a person or an electronic agent, a term that is so placed in a record or display that the person or electronic agent cannot proceed without taking action with respect to the particular term.

(c) "Consumer" means an individual who buys or contracts to buy goods that, at the time of contracting, are intended by the individual to be used primarily for personal, family, or household purposes.

(d) "Consumer contract" means a contract between a merchant seller and a consumer.
* * * *

(j) "Good faith" means honesty in fact and the observance of reasonable commercial standards of fair dealing.

(k) "Goods" means all things that are movable at the time of identification to a contract for sale. The term includes future goods, specially manufactured goods, the unborn young of animals, growing crops, and other identified things attached to realty as described in Section 2–107. The term does not include information, the money in which the price is to be paid, investment securities under Article 8, the subject matter of foreign exchange transactions, and choses in action.

* * * *

(m) "Record" means information that is inscribed on a tangible medium or that is stored in an electronic or other medium and is retrievable in perceivable form.

(n) "Remedial promise" means a promise by the seller to repair or replace the goods or to refund all or part of the price upon the happening of a specified event.

* * * *

(p) "Sign" means, with present intent to authenticate or adopt a record,

(i) to execute or adopt a tangible symbol; or

(ii) to attach to or logically associate with the record an electronic sound, symbol, or process.

* * * *

PART 2 Form, Formation, Terms and Readjustment of Contract; Electronic Contracting

§ 2–201. Formal Requirements; Statute of Frauds.

(1) A contract for the sale of goods for the price of $5,000 or more is not enforceable by way of action or defense unless there is some record sufficient to indicate that a contract for sale has been made between the parties and signed by the party against whom which enforcement is sought or by the party's authorized agent or broker. A record is not insufficient because it omits or incorrectly states a term agreed upon but the contract is not enforceable under this subsection beyond the quantity of goods shown in the record.

(2) Between merchants if within a reasonable time a record in confirmation of the contract and sufficient against the sender is received and the party receiving it has reason to know its contents, it satisfies the requirements of subsection (1) against such party the recipient unless notice of objection to its contents is given in a record within 10 days after it is received.

(3) A contract which does not satisfy the requirements of subsection (1) but which is valid in other respects is enforceable

(a) if the goods are to be specially manufactured for the buyer and are not suitable for sale to others in the ordinary course of the seller's business and the seller, before notice of repudiation is received and under circumstances which reasonably indicate that the goods are for the buyer, has made either a substantial beginning of their manufacture or commitments for their procurement; or

(b) if the party against whom which enforcement is sought admits in the party's pleading, or in the party's

testimony or otherwise under oath that a contract for sale was made, but the contract is not enforceable under this paragraph beyond the quantity of goods admitted; or

(c) with respect to goods for which payment has been made and accepted or which have been received and accepted (Sec. 2–606).

(4) A contract that is enforceable under this section is not rendered unenforceable merely because it is not capable of being performed within one year or any other applicable period after its making.

* * * *

§ 2–207. Terms of Contract; Effect of Confirmation.

If (i) conduct by both parties recognizes the existence of a contract although their records do not otherwise establish a contract, (ii) a contract is formed by an offer and acceptance, or (iii) a contract formed in any manner is confirmed by a record that contains terms additional to or different from those in the contract being confirmed, the terms of the contract, subject to Section 2–202, are:

(a) terms that appear in the records of both parties;

(b) terms, whether in a record or not, to which both parties agree; and

(c) terms supplied or incorporated under any provision of this Act.

* * * *

PART 3 General Obligation and Construction of Contract

* * * *

§ 2–312. Warranty of Title and Against Infringement; Buyer's Obligation Against Infringement.

(1) Subject to subsection (2) there is in a contract for sale a warranty by the seller that

(a) the title conveyed shall be good, good and its transfer rightful and shall not, because of any colorable claim to or interest in the goods, unreasonably expose the buyer to litigation; and

(b) the goods shall be delivered free from any security interest or other lien or encumbrance of which the buyer at the time of contracting has no knowledge.

(2) Unless otherwise agreed a seller that is a merchant regularly dealing in goods of the kind warrants that the goods shall be delivered free of the rightful claim of any third person by way of infringement or the like but a buyer that furnishes specifications to the seller must hold the seller harmless against any such claim that arises out of compliance with the specifications.

(3) A warranty under this section may be disclaimed or modified only by specific language or by circumstances that give the buyer reason to know that the seller does not claim title, that the seller is purporting to sell only the right or title as the seller or a third person may have, or that the seller is selling subject to any claims of infringement or the like.

§ 2–313. Express Warranties by Affirmation, Promise, Description, Sample; Remedial Promise.

(1) In this section, "immediate buyer" means a buyer that enters into a contract with the seller.

* * * *

(4) Any remedial promise made by the seller to the immediate buyer creates an obligation that the promise will be performed upon the happening of the specified event.

§ 2–313A. Obligation to Remote Purchaser Created by Record Packaged with or Accompanying Goods.

(1) This section applies only to new goods and goods sold or leased as new goods in a transaction of purchase in the normal chain of distribution. In this section:

(a) "Immediate buyer" means a buyer that enters into a contract with the seller.

(b) "Remote purchaser" means a person that buys or leases goods from an immediate buyer or other person in the normal chain of distribution.

(2) If a seller in a record packaged with or accompanying the goods makes an affirmation of fact or promise that relates to the goods, provides a description that relates to the goods, or makes a remedial promise, and the seller reasonably expects the record to be, and the record is, furnished to the remote purchaser, the seller has an obligation to the remote purchaser that:

(a) the goods will conform to the affirmation of fact, promise or description unless a reasonable person in the position of the remote purchaser would not believe that the affirmation of fact, promise or description created an obligation; and

(b) the seller will perform the remedial promise.

(3) It is not necessary to the creation of an obligation under this section that the seller use formal words such as "warrant" or "guarantee" or that the seller have a specific intention to undertake an obligation, but an affirmation merely of the value of the goods or a statement purporting to be merely the seller's opinion or commendation of the goods does not create an obligation.

(4) The following rules apply to the remedies for breach of an obligation created under this section:

(a) The seller may modify or limit the remedies available to the remote purchaser if the modification or limitation is furnished to the remote purchaser no later than the time of purchase or if the modification or limitation is contained in the record that contains the affirmation of fact, promise or description.

(b) Subject to a modification or limitation of remedy, a seller in breach is liable for incidental or consequential damages under Section 2–715, but the seller is not liable for lost profits.

(c) The remote purchaser may recover as damages for breach of a seller's obligation arising under subsection (2) the loss resulting in the ordinary course of events as determined in any manner that is reasonable.

(5) An obligation that is not a remedial promise is breached if the goods did not conform to the affirmation of fact, promise or description creating the obligation when the goods left the seller's control.

§ 2–313B. Obligation to Remote Purchaser Created by Communication to the Public.

(1) This section applies only to new goods and goods sold or leased as new goods in a transaction of purchase in the normal chain of distribution. In this section:

(a) "Immediate buyer" means a buyer that enters into a contract with the seller.

(b) "Remote purchaser" means a person that buys or leases goods from an immediate buyer or other person in the normal chain of distribution.

(2) If a seller in advertising or a similar communication to the public makes an affirmation of fact or promise that relates to the goods, provides a description that relates to the goods, or makes a remedial promise, and the remote purchaser enters into a transaction of purchase with knowledge of and with the expectation that the goods will conform to the affirmation of fact, promise, or description, or that the seller will perform the remedial promise, the seller has an obligation to the remote purchaser that:

(a) the goods will conform to the affirmation of fact, promise or description unless a reasonable person in the position of the remote purchaser would not believe that the affirmation of fact, promise or description created an obligation; and

(b) the seller will perform the remedial promise.

(3) It is not necessary to the creation of an obligation under this section that the seller use formal words such as "warrant" or "guarantee" or that the seller have a specific intention to undertake an obligation, but an affirmation merely of the value of the goods or a statement purporting to be merely the seller's opinion or commendation of the goods does not create an obligation.

(4) The following rules apply to the remedies for breach of an obligation created under this section:

(a) The seller may modify or limit the remedies available to the remote purchaser if the modification or limitation is furnished to the remote purchaser no later than the time of purchase. The modification or limitation may be furnished as part of the communication that contains the affirmation of fact, promise or description.

(b) Subject to a modification or limitation of remedy, a seller in breach is liable for incidental or consequential damages under Section 2–715, but the seller is not liable for lost profits.

(c) The remote purchaser may recover as damages for breach of a seller's obligation arising under subsection (2) the loss resulting in the ordinary course of events as determined in any manner that is reasonable.

(5) An obligation that is not a remedial promise is breached if the goods did not conform to the affirmation of fact, promise or description creating the obligation when the goods left the seller's control.

* * * *

§ 2–316. Exclusion or Modification of Warranties.

* * * *

(2) Subject to subsection (3), to exclude or modify the implied warranty of merchantability or any part of it in a consumer contract the language must be in a record, be conspicuous and state "The seller undertakes no responsibility for the quality of the goods except as otherwise provided in this contract," and in any other contract the language must mention merchantability and in case of a record must be conspicuous. Subject to subsection (3), to exclude or modify the implied warranty of fitness the exclusion must be in a record and be conspicuous. Language to exclude all implied warranties of fitness in a consumer contract must state "The seller assumes no responsibility that the goods will be fit for any particular purpose for which you may be buying these goods, except as otherwise provided in the contract," and in any other contract the language is sufficient if it states, for example, that "There are no warranties which extend beyond the description on the face hereof." Language that satisfies the requirements of this subsection for the exclusion and modification of a warranty in a consumer contract also satisfies the requirements for any other contract.

(3) Notwithstanding subsection (2):

(a) unless the circumstances indicate otherwise, all implied warranties are excluded by expressions like "as is", "with all faults" or other language which in common understanding calls the buyer's attention to the exclusion of warranties, makes plain that there is no implied warranty, and in a consumer contract evidenced by a record is set forth conspicuously in the record; and

(b) when the buyer before entering into the contract has examined the goods or the sample or model as fully as desired or has refused to examine the goods after a demand by the seller there is no implied warranty with regard to defects which an examination ought in the circumstances to have revealed to the buyer; and

(c) an implied warranty can also be excluded or modified by course of dealing or course of performance or usage of trade.

* * * *

§ 2–318. Third Party Beneficiaries of Warranties Express or Implied.

(1) In this section:

(a) "Immediate buyer" means a buyer that enters into a contract with the seller.

(b) "Remote purchaser" means a person that buys or leases goods from an immediate buyer or other person in the normal chain of distribution.

Alternative A to subsection (2) (2) A seller's warranty whether express or implied to an immediate buyer, a seller's remedial promise to an immediate buyer, or a seller's obligation to a remote purchaser under Section 2–313A or 2–313B extends to any natural person who is in the family or household of the immediate buyer or the remote purchaser or who is a guest in the home of either if it is reasonable to expect that the person may use, consume or be affected by the goods and who is injured in person by breach of the warranty, remedial promise or obligation. A seller may not exclude or limit the operation of this section.

Alternative B to subsection (2) (2) A seller's warranty whether express or implied to an immediate buyer, a seller's remedial promise to an immediate buyer, or a seller's obligation to a remote purchaser under Section 2–313A or 2–313B extends to any natural person who may reasonably be expected to use, consume or be affected by the goods and who is injured in person by breach of the warranty, remedial promise or obligation. A seller may not exclude or limit the operation of this section.

Alternative C to subsection (2) (2) A seller's warranty whether express or implied to an immediate buyer, a seller's remedial promise to an immediate buyer, or a seller's obligation to a remote purchaser under Section 2–313A or 2–313B extends to any person that may reasonably be expected to use, consume or be affected by the goods and that is injured by breach of the warranty, remedial promise or obligation. A seller may not exclude or limit the operation of this section with respect to injury to the person of an individual to whom the warranty, remedial promise or obligation extends.

* * * *

PART 5   Performance
* * * *

§ 2–502. Buyer's Right to Goods on Seller's Insolvency.

(1) Subject to subsections (2) and (3) and even though the goods have not been shipped a buyer who that has paid a part

or all of the price of goods in which the buyer has a special property under the provisions of the immediately preceding section may on making and keeping good a tender of any unpaid portion of their price recover them from the seller if:

(a) in the case of goods bought by a consumer, the seller repudiates or fails to deliver as required by the contract; or

(b) in all cases, the seller becomes insolvent within ten days after receipt of the first installment on their price.

(2) The buyer's right to recover the goods under subsection (1) vests upon acquisition of a special property, even if the seller had not then repudiated or failed to deliver.

(3) If the identification creating the special property has been made by the buyer, the buyer acquires the right to recover the goods only if they conform to the contract for sale.
* * * *

§ 2–508. Cure by Seller of Improper Tender or Delivery; Replacement.

(1) Where the buyer rejects goods or a tender of delivery under Section 2–601 or 2–612 or except in a consumer contract justifiably revokes acceptance under Section 2–608 (1)(b) and the agreed time for performance has not expired, a seller that has performed in good faith, upon seasonable notice to the buyer and at the seller's own expense, may cure the breach of contract by making a conforming tender of delivery within the agreed time. The seller shall compensate the buyer for all of the buyer's reasonable expenses caused by the seller's breach of contract and subsequent cure.

(2) Where the buyer rejects goods or a tender of delivery under Section 2–601 or 2–612 or except in a consumer contract justifiably revokes acceptance under Section 2–608 (1)(b) and the agreed time for performance has expired, a seller that has performed in good faith, upon seasonable notice to the buyer and at the seller's own expense, may cure the breach of contract, if the cure is appropriate and timely under the circumstances, by making a tender of conforming goods. The seller shall compensate the buyer for all of the buyer's reasonable expenses caused by the seller's breach of contract and subsequent cure.

§ 2–509. Risk of Loss in the Absence of Breach.

(1) Where the contract requires or authorizes the seller to ship the goods by carrier

(a) if it does not require the seller to deliver them at a particular destination, the risk of loss passes to the buyer when the goods are delivered to the carrier even though the shipment is under reservation (Section 2–505); but

(b) if it does require the seller to deliver them at a particular destination and the goods are there tendered while in the possession of the carrier, the risk of loss passes to the buyer when the goods are there so tendered as to enable the buyer to take delivery.

(2) Where the goods are held by a bailee to be delivered without being moved, the risk of loss passes to the buyer

(a) on the buyer's receipt of a negotiable document of title covering the goods; or

(b) on acknowledgment by the bailee to the buyer of the buyer's right to possession of the goods; or

(c) after the buyer's receipt of a non-negotiable document of title or other direction to deliver in a record, as provided in subsection (4)(b) of Section 2–503.

(3) In any case not within subsection (1) or (2), the risk of loss passes to the buyer on the buyer's receipt of the goods.
* * * *

§ 2–513. Buyer's Right to Inspection of Goods.
* * * *

(3) Unless otherwise agreed, the buyer is not entitled to inspect the goods before payment of the price when the contract provides

(a) for delivery on terms that under applicable course of performance, course of dealing, or usage of trade are interpreted to preclude inspection before payment; or

(b) for payment against documents of title, except where such payment is due only after the goods are to become available for inspection.
* * * *

PART 6   Breach, Repudiation and Excuse
* * * *

§ 2–605. Waiver of Buyer's Objections by Failure to Particularize.

(1) The buyer's failure to state in connection with rejection a particular defect or in connection with revocation of acceptance a defect that justifies revocation precludes the buyer from relying on the unstated defect to justify rejection or revocation of acceptance if the defect is ascertainable by reasonable inspection

(a) where the seller had a right to cure the defect and could have cured it if stated seasonably; or

(b) between merchants when the seller has after rejection made a request in a record for a full and final statement in record form of all defects on which the buyer proposes to rely.

(2) A buyer's payment against documents tendered to the buyer made without reservation of rights precludes recovery of the payment for defects apparent on the face of the documents.
* * * *

§ 2–607. Effect of Acceptance; Notice of Breach; Burden of Establishing Breach After Acceptance; Notice of Claim or Litigation to Person Answerable Over.

(3) Where a tender has been accepted

(a) the buyer must within a reasonable time after the buyer discovers or should have discovered any breach notify the seller; however, failure to give timely notice bars the buyer from a remedy only to the extent that the seller is prejudiced by the failure and

(b) if the claim is one for infringement or the like (subsection (3) of Section 2–312) and the buyer is sued as a result of such a breach the buyer must so notify the seller within a reasonable time after the buyer receives notice of the litigation or be barred from any remedy over for liability established by the litigation.

* * * *

§ 2–608. Revocation of Acceptance in Whole or in Part.

* * * *

(4) If a buyer uses the goods after a rightful rejection or justifiable revocation of acceptance, the following rules apply:

(a) Any use by the buyer that is unreasonable under the circumstances is wrongful as against the seller and is an acceptance only if ratified by the seller.

(b) Any use of the goods that is reasonable under the circumstances is not wrongful as against the seller and is not an acceptance, but in an appropriate case the buyer shall be obligated to the seller for the value of the use to the buyer.

* * * *

§ 2–612. "Installment Contract"; Breach.
* * * *

(2) The buyer may reject any installment which is non-conforming if the non-conformity substantially impairs the value of that installment to the buyer or if the non-conformity is a defect in the required documents; but if the non-conformity does not fall within subsection (3) and the seller gives adequate assurance of its cure the buyer must accept that installment.

(3) Whenever non-conformity or default with respect to one or more installments substantially impairs the value of the whole contract there is a breach of the whole. But the aggrieved party reinstates the contract if the party accepts a non-conforming installment without seasonably notifying of cancellation or if the party brings an action with respect only to past installments or demands performance as to future installments.

* * * *

PART 7 Remedies

§ 2–702. Seller's Remedies on Discovery of Buyer's Insolvency.
* * * *

(2) Where the seller discovers that the buyer has received goods on credit while insolvent the seller may reclaim the goods upon demand made within a reasonable time after the buyer's receipt of the goods. Except as provided in this subsection the seller may not base a right to reclaim goods on the buyer's fraudulent or innocent misrepresentation of solvency or of intent to pay.
* * * *

§ 2–705. Seller's Stoppage of Delivery in Transit or Otherwise.

(1) The seller may stop delivery of goods in the possession of a carrier or other bailee when the seller discovers the buyer to be insolvent (Section 2–702) or when the buyer repudiates or fails to make a payment due before delivery or if for any other reason the seller has a right to withhold or reclaim the goods.
* * * *

§ 2–706. Seller's Resale Including Contract for Resale.

(1) In an appropriate case involving breach by the buyer, the seller may resell the goods concerned or the undelivered balance thereof. Where the resale is made in good faith and in a commercially reasonable manner the seller may recover the difference between the contract price and the resale price together with any incidental or consequential damages allowed under the provisions of this Article (Section 2–710), but less expenses saved in consequence of the buyer's breach.
* * * *

§ 2–708. Seller's Damages for Non-Acceptance or Repudiation.

(1) Subject to subsection (2) and to the provisions of this Article with respect to proof of market price (Section 2–723)

(a) the measure of damages for non-acceptance by the buyer is the difference between the contract price and the market price at the time and place for tender together with any incidental or consequential damages provided in this Article (Section 2–710), but less expenses saved in consequence of the buyer's breach; and

(b) the measure of damages for repudiation by the buyer is the difference between the contract price and the market price at the place for tender at the expiration of a commercially reasonable time after the seller learned of the repudiation, but no later than the time stated in paragraph (a), together with any incidental or consequential damages provided in this Article (Section 2–710), but less expenses saved in consequence of the buyer's breach.

(2) If the measure of damages provided in subsection (1) or in Section 2–706 is inadequate to put the seller in as good a position as performance would have done then the measure of damages is the profit (including reasonable overhead) which the seller would have made from full performance by the buyer, together with any incidental or consequential damages provided in this Article (Section 2–710).

§ 2–709. Action for the Price.

(1) When the buyer fails to pay the price as it becomes due the seller may recover, together with any incidental or consequential damages under the next section, the price

(a) of goods accepted or of conforming goods lost or damaged within a commercially reasonable time after risk of their loss has passed to the buyer; and

(b) of goods identified to the contract if the seller is unable after reasonable effort to resell them at a reasonable price or the circumstances reasonably indicate that such effort will be unavailing.

* * * *

* * * *

* * * *

§ 2–710. Seller's Incidental and Consequential Damages.

(1) Incidental damages to an aggrieved seller include any commercially reasonable charges, expenses or commissions incurred in stopping delivery, in the transportation, care and custody of goods after the buyer's breach, in connection with return or resale of the goods or otherwise resulting from the breach.

(2) Consequential damages resulting from the buyer's breach include any loss resulting from general or particular requirements and needs of which the buyer at the time of contracting had reason to know and which could not reasonably be prevented by resale or otherwise.

(3) In a consumer contract, a seller may not recover consequential damages from a consumer.

* * * *

§ 2–713. Buyer's Damages for Non-Delivery or Repudiation.

(1) Subject to the provisions of this Article with respect to proof of market price (Section 2–723), if the seller wrongfully fails to deliver or repudiates or the buyer rightfully rejects or justifiably revokes acceptance

(a) the measure of damages in the case of wrongful failure to deliver by the seller or rightful rejection or justifiable revocation of acceptance by the buyer is the

difference between the market price at the time for tender under the contract and the contract price together with any incidental or consequential damages provided in this Article (Section 2–715), but less expenses saved in consequence of the seller's breach; and

(b) the measure of damages for repudiation by the seller is the difference between the market price at the expiration of a commercially reasonable time after the buyer learned of the repudiation, but no later than the time stated in paragraph (a), and the contract price together with any incidental or consequential damages provided in this Article (Section 2–715), but less expenses saved in consequence of the seller's breach.

* * * *

§ 2–725. Statute of Limitations in Contracts for Sale.

(1) Except as otherwise provided in this section, an action for breach of any contract for sale must be commenced within the later of four years after the right of action has accrued under subsection (2) or (3) or one year after the breach was or should have been discovered, but no longer than five years after the right of action accrued. By the original agreement the parties may reduce the period of limitation to not less than one year but may not extend it; however, in a consumer contract, the period of limitation may not be reduced.

(2) Except as otherwise provided in subsection (3), the following rules apply:

(a) Except as otherwise provided in this subsection, a right of action for breach of a contract accrues when the breach occurs, even if the aggrieved party did not have knowledge of the breach.

(b) For breach of a contract by repudiation, a right of action accrues at the earlier of when the aggrieved party elects to treat the repudiation as a breach or when a commercially reasonable time for awaiting performance has expired.

(c) For breach of a remedial promise, a right of action accrues when the remedial promise is not performed when due.

(d) In an action by a buyer against a person that is answerable over to the buyer for a claim asserted against the buyer, the buyer's right of action against the person answerable over accrues at the time the claim was originally asserted against the buyer.

(3) If a breach of a warranty arising under Section 2–312, 2–313(2), 2–314, or 2–315, or a breach of an obligation other than a remedial promise arising under Section 2–313A or 2–313B, is claimed the following rules apply:

(a) Except as otherwise provided in paragraph (c), a right of action for breach of a warranty arising under Section 2–313 (2), 2–314 or 2–315 accrues when the seller has tendered delivery to the immediate buyer, as defined in Section 2–313, and has completed performance of any agreed installation or assembly of the goods.

(b) Except as otherwise provided in paragraph (c), a right of action for breach of an obligation other than a remedial promise arising under Section 2–313A or 2–313B accrues when the remote purchaser, as defined in sections 2–313A and 2–313B, receives the goods.

(c) Where a warranty arising under Section 2–313(2) or an obligation other than a remedial promise arising under 2–313A or 2–313B explicitly extends to future performance of the goods and discovery of the breach must await the time for performance the right of action accrues when the immediate buyer as defined in Section 2–313 or the remote purchaser as defined in Sections 2–313A and 2–313B discovers or should have discovered the breach.

(d) A right of action for breach of warranty arising under Section 2–312 accrues when the aggrieved party discovers or should have discovered the breach. However, an action for breach of the warranty of non-infringement may not be commenced more than six years after tender of delivery of the goods to the aggrieved party.

* * * *

ARTICLE IIA
LEASES

PART 1   General Provisions

§ 2A–101. Short Title.

This Article shall be known and may be cited as the Uniform Commercial Code—Leases.

§ 2A–102. Scope.

This Article applies to any transaction, regardless of form, that creates a lease.

§ 2A–103. Definitions and Index of Definitions.

(1) In this Article unless the context otherwise requires:

(a) "Buyer in ordinary course of business" means a person who in good faith and without knowledge that the sale to him [or her] is in violation of the ownership rights or security interest or leasehold interest of a third party in the goods buys in ordinary course from a person in the business of selling goods of that kind but does not include a pawnbroker. "Buying" may be for cash or by exchange of other property or on secured or unsecured credit and includes receiving goods or documents of title under a pre-existing contract for sale but does not include a transfer in bulk or as security for or in total or partial satisfaction of a money debt.

(b) "Cancellation" occurs when either party puts an end to the lease contract for default by the other party.

(c) "Commercial unit" means such a unit of goods as by commercial usage is a single whole for purposes of lease and

division of which materially impairs its character or value on the market or in use. A commercial unit may be a single article, as a machine, or a set of articles, as a suite of furniture or a line of machinery, or a quantity, as a gross or carload, or any other unit treated in use or in the relevant market as a single whole.

(d) "Conforming" goods or performance under a lease contract means goods or performance that are in accordance with the obligations under the lease contract.

(e) "Consumer lease" means a lease that a lessor regularly engaged in the business of leasing or selling makes to a lessee who is an individual and who takes under the lease primarily for a personal, family, or household purpose [, if the total payments to be made under the lease contract, excluding payments for options to renew or buy, do not exceed $_____].

(f) "Fault" means wrongful act, omission, breach, or default.

(g) "Finance lease" means a lease with respect to which:

(i) the lessor does not select, manufacture or supply the goods;

(ii) the lessor acquires the goods or the right to possession and use of the goods in connection with the lease; and

(iii) one of the following occurs:

(A) the lessee receives a copy of the contract by which the lessor acquired the goods or the right to possession and use of the goods before signing the lease contract;

(B) the lessee's approval of the contract by which the lessor acquired the goods or the right to possession and use of the goods is a condition to effectiveness of the lease contract;

(C) the lessee, before signing the lease contract, receives an accurate and complete statement designating the promises and warranties, and any disclaimers of warranties, limitations or modifications of remedies, or liquidated damages, including those of a third party, such as the manufacturer of the goods, provided to the lessor by the person supplying the goods in connection with or as part of the contract by which the lessor acquired the goods or the right to possession and use of the goods; or

(D) if the lease is not a consumer lease, the lessor, before the lessee signs the lease contract, informs the lessee in writing (a) of the identity of the person supplying the goods to the lessor, unless the lessee has selected that person and directed the lessor to acquire the goods or the right to possession and use of the goods from that person, (b) that the lessee is entitled under this Article to any promises and warranties, including those of any third party, provided to the lessor by the person supplying the goods in connection with or as part of the contract by which the lessor acquired the goods or the right to possession and use of the goods, and (c) that the lessee may communicate with the person supplying the goods to the lessor and receive an accurate and complete statement of those promises and warranties, including any disclaimers and limitations of them or of remedies.

(h) "Goods" means all things that are movable at the time of identification to the lease contract, or are fixtures (Section 2A–309), but the term does not include money, documents, instruments, accounts, chattel paper, general intangibles, or minerals or the like, including oil and gas, before extraction. The term also includes the unborn young of animals.

(i) "Installment lease contract" means a lease contract that authorizes or requires the delivery of goods in separate lots to be separately accepted, even though the lease contract contains a clause "each delivery is a separate lease" or its equivalent.

(j) "Lease" means a transfer of the right to possession and use of goods for a term in return for consideration, but a sale, including a sale on approval or a sale or return, or retention or creation of a security interest is not a lease. Unless the context clearly indicates otherwise, the term includes a sublease.

(k) "Lease agreement" means the bargain, with respect to the lease, of the lessor and the lessee in fact as found in their language or by implication from other circumstances including course of dealing or usage of trade or course of performance as provided in this Article. Unless the context clearly indicates otherwise, the term includes a sublease agreement.

(l) "Lease contract" means the total legal obligation that results from the lease agreement as affected by this Article and any other applicable rules of law. Unless the context clearly indicates otherwise, the term includes a sublease contract.

(m) "Leasehold interest" means the interest of the lessor or the lessee under a lease contract.

(n) "Lessee" means a person who acquires the right to possession and use of goods under a lease. Unless the context clearly indicates otherwise, the term includes a sublessee.

(o) "Lessee in ordinary course of business" means a person who in good faith and without knowledge that the lease to him [or her] is in violation of the ownership rights or security interest or leasehold interest of a third party in the goods, leases in ordinary course from a person in the business of selling or leasing goods of that kind but does not include a pawnbroker. "Leasing" may be for cash or by exchange of other property or on secured or unsecured credit and includes receiving goods or documents of title under a pre-existing lease contract but does not include a transfer in bulk or as security for or in total or partial satisfaction of a money debt.

(p) "Lessor" means a person who transfers the right to possession and use of goods under a lease. Unless the context clearly indicates otherwise, the term includes a sublessor.

(q) "Lessor's residual interest" means the lessor's interest in the goods after expiration, termination, or cancellation of the lease contract.

(r) "Lien" means a charge against or interest in goods to secure payment of a debt or performance of an obligation, but the term does not include a security interest.

(s) "Lot" means a parcel or a single article that is the subject matter of a separate lease or delivery, whether or not it is sufficient to perform the lease contract.

(t) "Merchant lessee" means a lessee that is a merchant with respect to goods of the kind subject to the lease.

(u) "Present value" means the amount as of a date certain of one or more sums payable in the future, discounted to the date certain. The discount is determined by the interest rate specified by the parties if the rate was not manifestly unreasonable at the time the transaction was entered into; otherwise, the discount is determined by a commercially reasonable rate that takes into account the facts and circumstances of each case at the time the transaction was entered into.

(v) "Purchase" includes taking by sale, lease, mortgage, security interest, pledge, gift, or any other voluntary transaction creating an interest in goods.

(w) "Sublease" means a lease of goods the right to possession and use of which was acquired by the lessor as a lessee under an existing lease.

(x) "Supplier" means a person from whom a lessor buys or leases goods to be leased under a finance lease.

(y) "Supply contract" means a contract under which a lessor buys or leases goods to be leased.

(z) "Termination" occurs when either party pursuant to a power created by agreement or law puts an end to the lease contract otherwise than for default.

(2) Other definitions applying to this Article and the sections in which they appear are:

"Accessions". Section 2A–310(1).
"Construction mortgage". Section 2A–309(1)(d).
"Encumbrance". Section 2A–309(1)(e).
"Fixtures". Section 2A–309(1)(a).
"Fixture filing". Section 2A–309(1)(b).
"Purchase money lease". Section 2A–309(1)(c).

(3) The following definitions in other Articles apply to this Article:

"Accounts". Section 9–106.
"Between merchants". Section 2–104(3).
"Buyer". Section 2–103(1)(a).
"Chattel paper". Section 9–105(1)(b).
"Consumer goods". Section 9–109(1).
"Document". Section 9–105(1)(f).
"Entrusting". Section 2–403(3).
"General intangibles". Section 9–106.
"Good faith". Section 2–103(1)(b).
"Instrument". Section 9–105(1)(i).
"Merchant". Section 2–104(1).
"Mortgage". Section 9–105(1)(j).
"Pursuant to commitment". Section 9–105(1)(k).
"Receipt". Section 2–103(1)(c).
"Sale". Section 2–106(1).
"Sale on approval". Section 2–326.

"Sale or return". Section 2–326.

"Seller". Section 2–103(1)(d).

(4) In addition Article 1 contains general definitions and principles of construction and interpretation applicable throughout this Article.

As amended in 1990 and 1999.

§ 2A–104. Leases Subject to Other Law.

(1) A lease, although subject to this Article, is also subject to any applicable:

(a) certificate of title statute of this State: (list any certificate of title statutes covering automobiles, trailers, mobile homes, boats, farm tractors, and the like);

(b) certificate of title statute of another jurisdiction (Section 2A–105); or

(c) consumer protection statute of this State, or final consumer protection decision of a court of this State existing on the effective date of this Article.

(2) In case of conflict between this Article, other than Sections 2A–105, 2A–304(3), and 2A–305(3), and a statute or decision referred to in subsection (1), the statute or decision controls.

(3) Failure to comply with an applicable law has only the effect specified therein.

As amended in 1990.

§ 2A–105. Territorial Application of Article to Goods Covered by Certificate of Title.

Subject to the provisions of Sections 2A–304(3) and 2A–305(3), with respect to goods covered by a certificate of title issued under a statute of this State or of another jurisdiction, compliance and the effect of compliance or noncompliance with a certificate of title statute are governed by the law (including the conflict of laws rules) of the jurisdiction issuing the certificate until the earlier of (a) surrender of the certificate, or (b) four months after the goods are removed from that jurisdiction and thereafter until a new certificate of title is issued by another jurisdiction.

§ 2A–106. Limitation on Power of Parties to Consumer Lease to Choose Applicable Law and Judicial Forum.

(1) If the law chosen by the parties to a consumer lease is that of a jurisdiction other than a jurisdiction in which the lessee resides at the time the lease agreement becomes enforceable or within 30 days thereafter or in which the goods are to be used, the choice is not enforceable.

(2) If the judicial forum chosen by the parties to a consumer lease is a forum that would not otherwise have jurisdiction over the lessee, the choice is not enforceable.

§ 2A–107. Waiver or Renunciation of Claim or Right After Default.

Any claim or right arising out of an alleged default or breach of warranty may be discharged in whole or in part without consideration by a written waiver or renunciation signed and delivered by the aggrieved party.

§ 2A–108. Unconscionability.

(1) If the court as a matter of law finds a lease contract or any clause of a lease contract to have been unconscionable at the time it was made the court may refuse to enforce the lease contract, or it may enforce the remainder of the lease contract without the unconscionable clause, or it may so limit the application of any unconscionable clause as to avoid any unconscionable result.

(2) With respect to a consumer lease, if the court as a matter of law finds that a lease contract or any clause of a lease contract has been induced by unconscionable conduct or that unconscionable conduct has occurred in the collection of a claim arising from a lease contract, the court may grant appropriate relief.

(3) Before making a finding of unconscionability under subsection (1) or (2), the court, on its own motion or that of a party, shall afford the parties a reasonable opportunity to present evidence as to the setting, purpose, and effect of the lease contract or clause thereof, or of the conduct.

(4) In an action in which the lessee claims unconscionability with respect to a consumer lease:

(a) If the court finds unconscionability under subsection (1) or (2), the court shall award reasonable attorney's fees to the lessee.

(b) If the court does not find unconscionability and the lessee claiming unconscionability has brought or maintained an action he [or she] knew to be groundless, the court shall award reasonable attorney's fees to the party against whom the claim is made.

(c) In determining attorney's fees, the amount of the recovery on behalf of the claimant under subsections (1) and (2) is not controlling.

§ 2A–109. Option to Accelerate at Will.

(1) A term providing that one party or his [or her] successor in interest may accelerate payment or performance or require collateral or additional collateral "at will" or "when he [or she] deems himself [or herself] insecure" or in words of similar import must be construed to mean that he [or she] has

power to do so only if he [or she] in good faith believes that the prospect of payment or performance is impaired.

(2) With respect to a consumer lease, the burden of establishing good faith under subsection (1) is on the party who exercised the power; otherwise the burden of establishing lack of good faith is on the party against whom the power has been exercised.

PART 2 Formation and Construction of Lease Contract

§ 2A–201. Statute of Frauds.

(1) A lease contract is not enforceable by way of action or defense unless:

(a) the total payments to be made under the lease contract, excluding payments for options to renew or buy, are less than $1,000; or

(b) there is a writing, signed by the party against whom enforcement is sought or by that party's authorized agent, sufficient to indicate that a lease contract has been made between the parties and to describe the goods leased and the lease term.

(2) Any description of leased goods or of the lease term is sufficient and satisfies subsection (1)(b), whether or not it is specific, if it reasonably identifies what is described.

(3) A writing is not insufficient because it omits or incorrectly states a term agreed upon, but the lease contract is not enforceable under subsection (1)(b) beyond the lease term and the quantity of goods shown in the writing.

(4) A lease contract that does not satisfy the requirements of subsection (1), but which is valid in other respects, is enforceable:

(a) if the goods are to be specially manufactured or obtained for the lessee and are not suitable for lease or sale to others in the ordinary course of the lessor's business, and the lessor, before notice of repudiation is received and under circumstances that reasonably indicate that the goods are for the lessee, has made either a substantial beginning of their manufacture or commitments for their procurement;

(b) if the party against whom enforcement is sought admits in that party's pleading, testimony or otherwise in court that a lease contract was made, but the lease contract is not enforceable under this provision beyond the quantity of goods admitted; or

(c) with respect to goods that have been received and accepted by the lessee.

(5) The lease term under a lease contract referred to in subsection (4) is:

(a) if there is a writing signed by the party against whom enforcement is sought or by that party's authorized agent specifying the lease term, the term so specified;

(b) if the party against whom enforcement is sought admits in that party's pleading, testimony, or otherwise in court a lease term, the term so admitted; or

(c) a reasonable lease term.

§ 2A–202. Final Written Expression: Parol or Extrinsic Evidence.

Terms with respect to which the confirmatory memoranda of the parties agree or which are otherwise set forth in a writing intended by the parties as a final expression of their agreement with respect to such terms as are included therein may not be contradicted by evidence of any prior agreement or of a contemporaneous oral agreement but may be explained or supplemented:

(a) by course of dealing or usage of trade or by course of performance; and

(b) by evidence of consistent additional terms unless the court finds the writing to have been intended also as a complete and exclusive statement of the terms of the agreement.

§ 2A–203. Seals Inoperative.

The affixing of a seal to a writing evidencing a lease contract or an offer to enter into a lease contract does not render the writing a sealed instrument and the law with respect to sealed instruments does not apply to the lease contract or offer.

§ 2A–204. Formation in General.

(1) A lease contract may be made in any manner sufficient to show agreement, including conduct by both parties which recognizes the existence of a lease contract.

(2) An agreement sufficient to constitute a lease contract may be found although the moment of its making is undetermined.

(3) Although one or more terms are left open, a lease contract does not fail for indefiniteness if the parties have intended to make a lease contract and there is a reasonably certain basis for giving an appropriate remedy.

§ 2A–205. Firm Offers.

An offer by a merchant to lease goods to or from another person in a signed writing that by its terms gives assurance it will be held open is not revocable, for lack of consideration, during the time stated or, if no time is stated, for a reasonable time, but in no event may the period of irrevocability exceed 3 months. Any such term of assurance on a form supplied by the offeree must be separately signed by the offeror.

§ 2A–206. Offer and Acceptance in Formation of Lease Contract.

(1) Unless otherwise unambiguously indicated by the language or circumstances, an offer to make a lease contract

must be construed as inviting acceptance in any manner and by any medium reasonable in the circumstances.

(2) If the beginning of a requested performance is a reasonable mode of acceptance, an offeror who is not notified of acceptance within a reasonable time may treat the offer as having lapsed before acceptance.

§ 2A–207. Course of Performance or Practical Construction.

(1) If a lease contract involves repeated occasions for performance by either party with knowledge of the nature of the performance and opportunity for objection to it by the other, any course of performance accepted or acquiesced in without objection is relevant to determine the meaning of the lease agreement.

(2) The express terms of a lease agreement and any course of performance, as well as any course of dealing and usage of trade, must be construed whenever reasonable as consistent with each other; but if that construction is unreasonable, express terms control course of performance, course of performance controls both course of dealing and usage of trade, and course of dealing controls usage of trade.

(3) Subject to the provisions of Section 2A–208 on modification and waiver, course of performance is relevant to show a waiver or modification of any term inconsistent with the course of performance.

§ 2A–208. Modification, Rescission and Waiver.

(1) An agreement modifying a lease contract needs no consideration to be binding.

(2) A signed lease agreement that excludes modification or rescission except by a signed writing may not be otherwise modified or rescinded, but, except as between merchants, such a requirement on a form supplied by a merchant must be separately signed by the other party.

(3) Although an attempt at modification or rescission does not satisfy the requirements of subsection (2), it may operate as a waiver.

(4) A party who has made a waiver affecting an executory portion of a lease contract may retract the waiver by reasonable notification received by the other party that strict performance will be required of any term waived, unless the retraction would be unjust in view of a material change of position in reliance on the waiver.

§ 2A–209. Lessee Under Finance Lease as Beneficiary of Supply Contract.

(1) The benefit of the supplier's promises to the lessor under the supply contract and of all warranties, whether express or implied, including those of any third party provided in connection with or as part of the supply contract, extends to the lessee to the extent of the lessee's leasehold interest under a finance lease related to the supply contract, but is subject to the terms warranty and of the supply contract and all defenses or claims arising therefrom.

(2) The extension of the benefit of supplier's promises and of warranties to the lessee (Section 2A–209(1)) does not: (i) modify the rights and obligations of the parties to the supply contract, whether arising therefrom or otherwise, or (ii) impose any duty or liability under the supply contract on the lessee.

(3) Any modification or rescission of the supply contract by the supplier and the lessor is effective between the supplier and the lessee unless, before the modification or rescission, the supplier has received notice that the lessee has entered into a finance lease related to the supply contract. If the modification or rescission is effective between the supplier and the lessee, the lessor is deemed to have assumed, in addition to the obligations of the lessor to the lessee under the lease contract, promises of the supplier to the lessor and warranties that were so modified or rescinded as they existed and were available to the lessee before modification or rescission.

(4) In addition to the extension of the benefit of the supplier's promises and of warranties to the lessee under subsection (1), the lessee retains all rights that the lessee may have against the supplier which arise from an agreement between the lessee and the supplier or under other law.

As amended in 1990.

§ 2A–210. Express Warranties.

(1) Express warranties by the lessor are created as follows:

(a) Any affirmation of fact or promise made by the lessor to the lessee which relates to the goods and becomes part of the basis of the bargain creates an express warranty that the goods will conform to the affirmation or promise.

(b) Any description of the goods which is made part of the basis of the bargain creates an express warranty that the goods will conform to the description.

(c) Any sample or model that is made part of the basis of the bargain creates an express warranty that the whole of the goods will conform to the sample or model.

(2) It is not necessary to the creation of an express warranty that the lessor use formal words, such as "warrant" or "guarantee," or that the lessor have a specific intention to make a warranty, but an affirmation merely of the value of the goods or a statement purporting to be merely the lessor's opinion or commendation of the goods does not create a warranty.

§ 2A–211. Warranties Against Interference and Against Infringement; Lessee's Obligation Against Infringement.

(1) There is in a lease contract a warranty that for the lease term no person holds a claim to or interest in the goods that arose from an act or omission of the lessor, other than a claim by way of infringement or the like, which will interfere with the lessee's enjoyment of its leasehold interest.

(2) Except in a finance lease there is in a lease contract by a lessor who is a merchant regularly dealing in goods of the kind a warranty that the goods are delivered free of the rightful claim of any person by way of infringement or the like.

(3) A lessee who furnishes specifications to a lessor or a supplier shall hold the lessor and the supplier harmless against any claim by way of infringement or the like that arises out of compliance with the specifications.

§ 2A–212. Implied Warranty of Merchantability.

(1) Except in a finance lease, a warranty that the goods will be merchantable is implied in a lease contract if the lessor is a merchant with respect to goods of that kind.

(2) Goods to be merchantable must be at least such as

(a) pass without objection in the trade under the description in the lease agreement;

(b) in the case of fungible goods, are of fair average quality within the description;

(c) are fit for the ordinary purposes for which goods of that type are used;

(d) run, within the variation permitted by the lease agreement, of even kind, quality, and quantity within each unit and among all units involved;

(e) are adequately contained, packaged, and labeled as the lease agreement may require; and

(f) conform to any promises or affirmations of fact made on the container or label.

(3) Other implied warranties may arise from course of dealing or usage of trade.

§ 2A–213. Implied Warranty of Fitness for Particular Purpose.

Except in a finance of lease, if the lessor at the time the lease contract is made has reason to know of any particular purpose for which the goods are required and that the lessee is relying on the lessor's skill or judgment to select or furnish suitable goods, there is in the lease contract an implied warranty that the goods will be fit for that purpose.

§ 2A–214. Exclusion or Modification of Warranties.

(1) Words or conduct relevant to the creation of an express warranty and words or conduct tending to negate or limit a warranty must be construed wherever reasonable as consistent with each other; but, subject to the provisions of Section 2A–202 on parol or extrinsic evidence, negation or limitation is inoperative to the extent that the construction is unreasonable.

(2) Subject to subsection (3), to exclude or modify the implied warranty of merchantability or any part of it the language must mention "merchantability", be by a writing, and be conspicuous. Subject to subsection (3), to exclude or modify any implied warranty of fitness the exclusion must be by a writing and be conspicuous. Language to exclude all implied warranties of fitness is sufficient if it is in writing, is conspicuous and states, for example, "There is no warranty that the goods will be fit for a particular purpose".

(3) Notwithstanding subsection (2), but subject to subsection (4),

(a) unless the circumstances indicate otherwise, all implied warranties are excluded by expressions like "as is" or "with all faults" or by other language that in common understanding calls the lessee's attention to the exclusion of warranties and makes plain that there is no implied warranty, if in writing and conspicuous;

(b) if the lessee before entering into the lease contract has examined the goods or the sample or model as fully as desired or has refused to examine the goods, there is no implied warranty with regard to defects that an examination ought in the circumstances to have revealed; and

(c) an implied warranty may also be excluded or modified by course of dealing, course of performance, or usage of trade.

(4) To exclude or modify a warranty against interference or against infringement (Section 2A–211) or any part of it, the language must be specific, be by a writing, and be conspicuous, unless the circumstances, including course of performance, course of dealing, or usage of trade, give the lessee reason to know that the goods are being leased subject to a claim or interest of any person.

§ 2A–215. Cumulation and Conflict of Warranties Express or Implied.

Warranties, whether express or implied, must be construed as consistent with each other and as cumulative, but if that construction is unreasonable, the intention of the parties determines which warranty is dominant. In ascertaining that intention the following rules apply:

(a) Exact or technical specifications displace an inconsistent sample or model or general language of description.

(b) A sample from an existing bulk displaces inconsistent general language of description.

(c) Express warranties displace inconsistent implied warranties other than an implied warranty of fitness for a particular purpose.

§ 2A–216. Third-Party Beneficiaries of Express and Implied Warranties.

Alternative A A warranty to or for the benefit of a lessee under this Article, whether express or implied, extends to any natural person who is in the family or household of the lessee or who is a guest in the lessee's home if it is reasonable to expect that such person may use, consume, or be affected by the goods and who is injured in person by breach of the warranty. This section does not displace principles of law and equity that extend a warranty to or for the benefit of a lessee to other persons. The operation of this section may not be excluded, modified, or limited, but an exclusion, modification, or limitation of the warranty, including any with respect to rights and remedies, effective against the lessee is also effective against any beneficiary designated under this section.

Alternative B A warranty to or for the benefit of a lessee under this Article, whether express or implied, extends to any natural person who may reasonably be expected to use, consume, or be affected by the goods and who is injured in person by breach of the warranty. This section does not displace principles of law and equity that extend a warranty to or for the benefit of a lessee to other persons. The operation of this section may not be excluded, modified, or limited, but an exclusion, modification, or limitation of the warranty, including any with respect to rights and remedies, effective against the lessee is also effective against the beneficiary designated under this section.

Alternative C A warranty to or for the benefit of a lessee under this Article, whether express or implied, extends to any person who may reasonably be expected to use, consume, or be affected by the goods and who is injured by breach of the warranty. The operation of this section may not be excluded, modified, or limited with respect to injury to the person of an individual to whom the warranty extends, but an exclusion, modification, or limitation of the warranty, including any with respect to rights and remedies, effective against the lessee is also effective against the beneficiary designated under this section.

§ 2A–217. Identification.

Identification of goods as goods to which a lease contract refers may be made at any time and in any manner explicitly agreed to by the parties. In the absence of explicit agreement, identification occurs:

(a) when the lease contract is made if the lease contract is for a lease of goods that are existing and identified;

(b) when the goods are shipped, marked, or otherwise designated by the lessor as goods to which the lease contract refers, if the lease contract is for a lease of goods that are not existing and identified; or

(c) when the young are conceived, if the lease contract is for a lease of unborn young of animals.

§ 2A–218. Insurance and Proceeds.

(1) A lessee obtains an insurable interest when existing goods are identified to the lease contract even though the goods identified are nonconforming and the lessee has an option to reject them.

(2) If a lessee has an insurable interest only by reason of the lessor's identification of the goods, the lessor, until default or insolvency or notification to the lessee that identification is final, may substitute other goods for those identified.

(3) Notwithstanding a lessee's insurable interest under subsections (1) and (2), the lessor retains an insurable interest until an option to buy has been exercised by the lessee and risk of loss has passed to the lessee.

(4) Nothing in this section impairs any insurable interest recognized under any other statute or rule of law.

(5) The parties by agreement may determine that one or more parties have an obligation to obtain and pay for insurance covering the goods and by agreement may determine the beneficiary of the proceeds of the insurance.

§ 2A–219. Risk of Loss.

(1) Except in the case of a finance lease, risk of loss is retained by the lessor and does not pass to the lessee. In the case of a finance lease, risk of loss passes to the lessee.

(2) Subject to the provisions of this Article on the effect of default on risk of loss (Section 2A–220), if risk of loss is to pass to the lessee and the time of passage is not stated, the following rules apply:

(a) If the lease contract requires or authorizes the goods to be shipped by carrier

(i) and it does not require delivery at a particular destination, the risk of loss passes to the lessee when the goods are duly delivered to the carrier; but

(ii) if it does require delivery at a particular destination and the goods are there duly tendered while in the possession of the carrier, the risk of loss passes to the lessee when the goods are there duly so tendered as to enable the lessee to take delivery.

(b) If the goods are held by a bailee to be delivered without being moved, the risk of loss passes to the lessee on acknowledgment by the bailee of the lessee's right to possession of the goods.

(c) In any case not within subsection (a) or (b), the risk of loss passes to the lessee on the lessee's receipt of the goods if the lessor, or, in the case of a finance lease, the supplier, is a merchant; otherwise the risk passes to the lessee on tender of delivery.

§ 2A–220. Effect of Default on Risk of Loss.

(1) Where risk of loss is to pass to the lessee and the time of passage is not stated:

(a) If a tender or delivery of goods so fails to conform to the lease contract as to give a right of rejection, the risk of their loss remains with the lessor, or, in the case of a finance lease, the supplier, until cure or acceptance.

(b) If the lessee rightfully revokes acceptance, he [or she], to the extent of any deficiency in his [or her] effective insurance coverage, may treat the risk of loss as having remained with the lessor from the beginning.

(2) Whether or not risk of loss is to pass to the lessee, if the lessee as to conforming goods already identified to a lease contract repudiates or is otherwise in default under the lease contract, the lessor, or, in the case of a finance lease, the supplier, to the extent of any deficiency in his [or her] effective insurance coverage may treat the risk of loss as resting on the lessee for a commercially reasonable time.

§ 2A–221. Casualty to Identified Goods.

If a lease contract requires goods identified when the lease contract is made, and the goods suffer casualty without fault of the lessee, the lessor or the supplier before delivery, or the goods suffer casualty before risk of loss passes to the lessee pursuant to the lease agreement or Section 2A–219, then:

(a) if the loss is total, the lease contract is avoided; and

(b) if the loss is partial or the goods have so deteriorated as to no longer conform to the lease contract, the lessee may nevertheless demand inspection and at his [or her] option either treat the lease contract as avoided or, except in a finance lease that is not a consumer lease, accept the goods with due allowance from the rent payable for the balance of the lease term for the deterioration or the deficiency in quantity but without further right against the lessor.

PART 3   Effect of Lease Contract

§ 2A–301. Enforceability of Lease Contract.

Except as otherwise provided in this Article, a lease contract is effective and enforceable according to its terms between the parties, against purchasers of the goods and against creditors of the parties.

§ 2A–302. Title to and Possession of Goods.

Except as otherwise provided in this Article, each provision of this Article applies whether the lessor or a third party has title to the goods, and whether the lessor, the lessee, or a third party has possession of the goods, notwithstanding any statute or rule of law that possession or the absence of possession is fraudulent.

§ 2A–303. Alienability of Party's Interest Under Lease Contract or of Lessor's Residual Interest in Goods; Delegation of Performance; Transfer of Rights.

(1) As used in this section, "creation of a security interest" includes the sale of a lease contract that is subject to Article 9, Secured Transactions, by reason of Section 9–109(a)(3).

(2) Except as provided in subsections (3) and Section 9–407, a provision in a lease agreement which (i) prohibits the voluntary or involuntary transfer, including a transfer by sale, sublease, creation or enforcement of a security interest, or attachment, levy, or other judicial process, of an interest of a party under the lease contract or of the lessor's residual interest in the goods, or (ii) makes such a transfer an event of default, gives rise to the rights and remedies provided in subsection (4), but a transfer that is prohibited or is an event of default under the lease agreement is otherwise effective.

(3) A provision in a lease agreement which (i) prohibits a transfer of a right to damages for default with respect to the whole lease contract or of a right to payment arising out of the transferor's due performance of the transferor's entire obligation, or (ii) makes such a transfer an event of default, is not enforceable, and such a transfer is not a transfer that materially impairs the prospect of obtaining return performance by, materially changes the duty of, or materially increases the burden or risk imposed on, the other party to the lease contract within the purview of subsection (4).

(4) Subject to subsection (3) and Section 9–407:

(a) if a transfer is made which is made an event of default under a lease agreement, the party to the lease contract not making the transfer, unless that party waives the default or otherwise agrees, has the rights and remedies described in Section 2A–501(2);

(b) if paragraph (a) is not applicable and if a transfer is made that (i) is prohibited under a lease agreement or (ii) materially impairs the prospect of obtaining return performance by, materially changes the duty of, or materially increases the burden or risk imposed on, the other party to the lease contract, unless the party not making the transfer agrees at any time to the transfer in the lease contract or otherwise, then, except as limited by contract, (i) the transferor is liable to the party not making the transfer for damages caused by the transfer to the extent that the damages could not reasonably be prevented by the party not making the transfer and (ii) a court having jurisdiction may grant other appropriate relief, including cancellation of the lease contract or an injunction against the transfer.

(5) A transfer of "the lease" or of "all my rights under the lease", or a transfer in similar general terms, is a transfer of rights and, unless the language or the circumstances, as in a transfer for security, indicate the contrary, the transfer is a delegation of duties by the transferor to the transferee. Acceptance by the transferee constitutes a promise by the transferee to perform those duties. The promise is enforceable by either the transferor or the other party to the lease contract.

(6) Unless otherwise agreed by the lessor and the lessee, a delegation of performance does not relieve the transferor as against the other party of any duty to perform or of any liability for default.

(7) In a consumer lease, to prohibit the transfer of an interest of a party under the lease contract or to make a transfer an event of default, the language must be specific, by a writing, and conspicuous.

As amended in 1990 and 1999.

§ 2A–304. Subsequent Lease of Goods by Lessor.

(1) Subject to Section 2A–303, a subsequent lessee from a lessor of goods under an existing lease contract obtains, to the extent of the leasehold interest transferred, the leasehold interest in the goods that the lessor had or had power to transfer, and except as provided in subsection (2) and Section 2A–527(4), takes subject to the existing lease contract. A lessor with voidable title has power to transfer a good leasehold interest to a good faith subsequent lessee for value, but only to the extent set forth in the preceding sentence. If goods have been delivered under a transaction of purchase the lessor has that power even though:

   (a) the lessor's transferor was deceived as to the identity of the lessor;

   (b) the delivery was in exchange for a check which is later dishonored;

   (c) it was agreed that the transaction was to be a "cash sale"; or

   (d) the delivery was procured through fraud punishable as larcenous under the criminal law.

(2) A subsequent lessee in the ordinary course of business from a lessor who is a merchant dealing in goods of that kind to whom the goods were entrusted by the existing lessee of that lessor before the interest of the subsequent lessee became enforceable against that lessor obtains, to the extent of the leasehold interest transferred, all of that lessor's and

the existing lessee's rights to the goods, and takes free of the existing lease contract.

(3) A subsequent lessee from the lessor of goods that are subject to an existing lease contract and are covered by a certificate of title issued under a statute of this State or of another jurisdiction takes no greater rights than those provided both by this section and by the certificate of title statute.

As amended in 1990.

§ 2A–305. Sale or Sublease of Goods by Lessee.

(1) Subject to the provisions of Section 2A–303, a buyer or sublessee from the lessee of goods under an existing lease contract obtains, to the extent of the interest transferred, the leasehold interest in the goods that the lessee had or had power to transfer, and except as provided in subsection (2) and Section 2A–511(4), takes subject to the existing lease contract. A lessee with a voidable leasehold interest has power to transfer a good leasehold interest to a good faith buyer for value or a good faith sublessee for value, but only to the extent set forth in the preceding sentence. When goods have been delivered under a transaction of lease the lessee has that power even though:

   (a) the lessor was deceived as to the identity of the lessee;

   (b) the delivery was in exchange for a check which is later dishonored; or

   (c) the delivery was procured through fraud punishable as larcenous under the criminal law.

(2) A buyer in the ordinary course of business or a sublessee in the ordinary course of business from a lessee who is a merchant dealing in goods of that kind to whom the goods were entrusted by the lessor obtains, to the extent of the interest transferred, all of the lessor's and lessee's rights to the goods, and takes free of the existing lease contract.

(3) A buyer or sublessee from the lessee of goods that are subject to an existing lease contract and are covered by a certificate of title issued under a statute of this State or of another jurisdiction takes no greater rights than those provided both by this section and by the certificate of title statute.

§ 2A–306. Priority of Certain Liens Arising by Operation of Law.

If a person in the ordinary course of his [or her] business furnishes services or materials with respect to goods subject to a lease contract, a lien upon those goods in the possession of that person given by statute or rule of law for those materials or services takes priority over any interest of the lessor or lessee under the lease contract or this Article unless the lien is created by statute and the statute provides otherwise or unless the lien is created by rule of law and the rule of law provides otherwise.

§ 2A–307. Priority of Liens Arising by Attachment or Levy on, Security Interests in, and Other Claims to Goods.

(1) Except as otherwise provided in Section 2A–306, a creditor of a lessee takes subject to the lease contract.

(2) Except as otherwise provided in subsection (3) and in Sections 2A–306 and 2A–308, a creditor of a lessor takes subject to the lease contract unless the creditor holds a lien that attached to the goods before the lease contract became enforceable.

(3) Except as otherwise provided in Sections 9–317, 9–321, and 9–323, a lessee takes a leasehold interest subject to a security interest held by a creditor of the lessor.

As amended in 1990 and 1999.

§ 2A–308. Special Rights of Creditors.

(1) A creditor of a lessor in possession of goods subject to a lease contract may treat the lease contract as void if as against the creditor retention of possession by the lessor is fraudulent under any statute or rule of law, but retention of possession in good faith and current course of trade by the lessor for a commercially reasonable time after the lease contract becomes enforceable is not fraudulent.

(2) Nothing in this Article impairs the rights of creditors of a lessor if the lease contract (a) becomes enforceable, not in current course of trade but in satisfaction of or as security for a pre-existing claim for money, security, or the like, and (b) is made under circumstances which under any statute or rule of law apart from this Article would constitute the transaction a fraudulent transfer or voidable preference.

(3) A creditor of a seller may treat a sale or an identification of goods to a contract for sale as void if as against the creditor retention of possession by the seller is fraudulent under any statute or rule of law, but retention of possession of the goods pursuant to a lease contract entered into by the seller as lessee and the buyer as lessor in connection with the sale or identification of the goods is not fraudulent if the buyer bought for value and in good faith.

§ 2A–309. Lessor's and Lessee's Rights When Goods Become Fixtures.

(1) In this section:

(a) goods are "fixtures" when they become so related to particular real estate that an interest in them arises under real estate law;

(b) a "fixture filing" is the filing, in the office where a mortgage on the real estate would be filed or recorded, of a financing statement covering goods that are or are to become fixtures and conforming to the requirements of Section 9–502 (a) and (b);

(c) a lease is a "purchase money lease" unless the lessee has possession or use of the goods or the right to possession or use of the goods before the lease agreement is enforceable;

(d) a mortgage is a "construction mortgage" to the extent it secures an obligation incurred for the construction of an improvement on land including the acquisition cost of the land, if the recorded writing so indicates; and

(e) "encumbrance" includes real estate mortgages and other liens on real estate and all other rights in real estate that are not ownership interests.

(2) Under this Article a lease may be of goods that are fixtures or may continue in goods that become fixtures, but no lease exists under this Article of ordinary building materials incorporated into an improvement on land.

(3) This Article does not prevent creation of a lease of fixtures pursuant to real estate law.

(4) The perfected interest of a lessor of fixtures has priority over a conflicting interest of an encumbrancer or owner of the real estate if:

(a) the lease is a purchase money lease, the conflicting interest of the encumbrancer or owner arises before the goods become fixtures, the interest of the lessor is perfected by a fixture filing before the goods become fixtures or within ten days thereafter, and the lessee has an interest of record in the real estate or is in possession of the real estate; or

(b) the interest of the lessor is perfected by a fixture filing before the interest of the encumbrancer or owner is of record, the lessor's interest has priority over any conflicting interest of a predecessor in title of the encumbrancer or owner, and the lessee has an interest of record in the real estate or is in possession of the real estate.

(5) The interest of a lessor of fixtures, whether or not perfected, has priority over the conflicting interest of an encumbrancer or owner of the real estate if:

(a) the fixtures are readily removable factory or office machines, readily removable equipment that is not primarily used or leased for use in the operation of the real estate, or readily removable replacements of domestic appliances that are goods subject to a consumer lease, and before the goods become fixtures the lease contract is enforceable; or

(b) the conflicting interest is a lien on the real estate obtained by legal or equitable proceedings after the lease contract is enforceable; or

(c) the encumbrancer or owner has consented in writing to the lease or has disclaimed an interest in the goods as fixtures; or

(d) the lessee has a right to remove the goods as against the encumbrancer or owner. If the lessee's right to remove terminates, the priority of the interest of the lessor continues for a reasonable time.

(6) Notwithstanding paragraph (4)(a) but otherwise subject to subsections (4) and (5), the interest of a lessor of fixtures, including the lessor's residual interest, is subordinate to the conflicting interest of an encumbrancer of the real estate under a construction mortgage recorded before the goods become fixtures if the goods become fixtures before the completion of the construction. To the extent given to refinance a construction mortgage, the conflicting interest of an encumbrancer of the real estate under a mortgage has this priority to the same extent as the encumbrancer of the real estate under the construction mortgage.

(7) In cases not within the preceding subsections, priority between the interest of a lessor of fixtures, including the lessor's residual interest, and the conflicting interest of an encumbrancer or owner of the real estate who is not the lessee is determined by the priority rules governing conflicting interests in real estate.

(8) If the interest of a lessor of fixtures, including the lessor's residual interest, has priority over all conflicting interests of all owners and encumbrancers of the real estate, the lessor or the lessee may (i) on default, expiration, termination, or cancellation of the lease agreement but subject to the agreement and this Article, or (ii) if necessary to enforce other rights and remedies of the lessor or lessee under this Article, remove the goods from the real estate, free and clear of all conflicting interests of all owners and encumbrancers of the real estate, but the lessor or lessee must reimburse any encumbrancer or owner of the real estate who is not the lessee and who has not otherwise agreed for the cost of repair of any physical injury, but not for any diminution in value of the real estate caused by the absence of the goods removed or by any necessity of replacing them. A person entitled to reimbursement may refuse permission to remove until the party seeking removal gives adequate security for the performance of this obligation.

(9) Even though the lease agreement does not create a security interest, the interest of a lessor of fixtures, including the lessor's residual interest, is perfected by filing a financing statement as a fixture filing for leased goods that are or are to become fixtures in accordance with the relevant provisions of the Article on Secured Transactions (Article 9).

As amended in 1990 and 1999.

§ 2A–310. Lessor's and Lessee's Rights When Goods Become Accessions.

(1) Goods are "accessions" when they are installed in or affixed to other goods.

(2) The interest of a lessor or a lessee under a lease contract entered into before the goods became accessions is superior to all interests in the whole except as stated in subsection (4).

(3) The interest of a lessor or a lessee under a lease contract entered into at the time or after the goods became accessions is superior to all subsequently acquired interests in the whole except as stated in subsection (4) but is subordinate to interests in the whole existing at the time the lease contract was made unless the holders of such interests in the whole have in writing consented to the lease or disclaimed an interest in the goods as part of the whole.

(4) The interest of a lessor or a lessee under a lease contract described in subsection (2) or (3) is subordinate to the interest of

(a) a buyer in the ordinary course of business or a lessee in the ordinary course of business of any interest in the whole acquired after the goods became accessions; or

(b) a creditor with a security interest in the whole perfected before the lease contract was made to the extent that the creditor makes subsequent advances without knowledge of the lease contract.

(5) When under subsections (2) or (3) and (4) a lessor or a lessee of accessions holds an interest that is superior to all interests in the whole, the lessor or the lessee may (a) on default, expiration, termination, or cancellation of the lease contract by the other party but subject to the provisions of the lease contract and this Article, or (b) if necessary to enforce his [or her] other rights and remedies under this Article, remove the goods from the whole, free and clear of all interests in the whole, but he [or she] must reimburse any holder of an interest in the whole who is not the lessee and who has not otherwise agreed for the cost of repair of any physical injury but not for any diminution in value of the whole caused by the absence of the goods removed or by any necessity for replacing them. A person entitled to reimbursement may refuse permission to remove until the party seeking removal gives adequate security for the performance of this obligation.

§ 2A–311. Priority Subject to Subordination.

Nothing in this Article prevents subordination by agreement by any person entitled to priority.

As added in 1990.

PART 4   Performance of Lease Contract: Repudiated, Substituted and Excused

§ 2A–401. Insecurity: Adequate Assurance of Performance.

(1) A lease contract imposes an obligation on each party that the other's expectation of receiving due performance will not be impaired.

(2) If reasonable grounds for insecurity arise with respect to the performance of either party, the insecure party may demand in writing adequate assurance of due performance. Until the

insecure party receives that assurance, if commercially reasonable the insecure party may suspend any performance for which he [or she] has not already received the agreed return.

(3) A repudiation of the lease contract occurs if assurance of due performance adequate under the circumstances of the particular case is not provided to the insecure party within a reasonable time, not to exceed 30 days after receipt of a demand by the other party.

(4) Between merchants, the reasonableness of grounds for insecurity and the adequacy of any assurance offered must be determined according to commercial standards.

(5) Acceptance of any nonconforming delivery or payment does not prejudice the aggrieved party's right to demand adequate assurance of future performance.

§ 2A–402. Anticipatory Repudiation.

If either party repudiates a lease contract with respect to a performance not yet due under the lease contract, the loss of which performance will substantially impair the value of the lease contract to the other, the aggrieved party may:

(a) for a commercially reasonable time, await retraction of repudiation and performance by the repudiating party;

(b) make demand pursuant to Section 2A–401 and await assurance of future performance adequate under the circumstances of the particular case; or

(c) resort to any right or remedy upon default under the lease contract or this Article, even though the aggrieved party has notified the repudiating party that the aggrieved party would await the repudiating party's performance and assurance and has urged retraction. In addition, whether or not the aggrieved party is pursuing one of the foregoing remedies, the aggrieved party may suspend performance or, if the aggrieved party is the lessor, proceed in accordance with the provisions of this Article on the lessor's right to identify goods to the lease contract notwithstanding default or to salvage unfinished goods (Section 2A–524).

§ 2A–403. Retraction of Anticipatory Repudiation.

(1) Until the repudiating party's next performance is due, the repudiating party can retract the repudiation unless, since the repudiation, the aggrieved party has cancelled the lease contract or materially changed the aggrieved party's position or otherwise indicated that the aggrieved party considers the repudiation final.

(2) Retraction may be by any method that clearly indicates to the aggrieved party that the repudiating party intends to perform under the lease contract and includes any assurance demanded under Section 2A–401.

(3) Retraction reinstates a repudiating party's rights under a lease contract with due excuse and allowance to the aggrieved party for any delay occasioned by the repudiation.

§ 2A–404. Substituted Performance.

(1) If without fault of the lessee, the lessor and the supplier, the agreed berthing, loading, or unloading facilities fail or the agreed type of carrier becomes unavailable or the agreed manner of delivery otherwise becomes commercially impracticable, but a commercially reasonable substitute is available, the substitute performance must be tendered and accepted.

(2) If the agreed means or manner of payment fails because of domestic or foreign governmental regulation:

(a) the lessor may withhold or stop delivery or cause the supplier to withhold or stop delivery unless the lessee provides a means or manner of payment that is commercially a substantial equivalent; and

(b) if delivery has already been taken, payment by the means or in the manner provided by the regulation discharges the lessee's obligation unless the regulation is discriminatory, oppressive, or predatory.

§ 2A–405. Excused Performance.

Subject to Section 2A–404 on substituted performance, the following rules apply:

(a) Delay in delivery or nondelivery in whole or in part by a lessor or a supplier who complies with paragraphs (b) and (c) is not a default under the lease contract if performance as agreed has been made impracticable by the occurrence of a contingency the nonoccurrence of which was a basic assumption on which the lease contract was made or by compliance in good faith with any applicable foreign or domestic governmental regulation or order, whether or not the regulation or order later proves to be invalid.

(b) If the causes mentioned in paragraph (a) affect only part of the lessor's or the supplier's capacity to perform, he [or she] shall allocate production and deliveries among his [or her] customers but at his [or her] option may include regular customers not then under contract for sale or lease as well as his [or her] own requirements for further manufacture. He [or she] may so allocate in any manner that is fair and reasonable.

(c) The lessor seasonally shall notify the lessee and in the case of a finance lease the supplier seasonally shall notify the lessor and the lessee, if known, that there will be delay or nondelivery and, if allocation is required under paragraph (b), of the estimated quota thus made available for the lessee.

§ 2A–406. Procedure on Excused Performance.

(1) If the lessee receives notification of a material or indefinite delay or an allocation justified under Section 2A–405, the lessee may by written notification to the lessor as to any goods involved, and with respect to all of the goods

if under an installment lease contract the value of the whole lease contract is substantially impaired (Section 2A–510):

(a) terminate the lease contract (Section 2A–505(2)); or

(b) except in a finance lease that is not a consumer lease, modify the lease contract by accepting the available quota in substitution, with due allowance from the rent payable for the balance of the lease term for the deficiency but without further right against the lessor.

(2) If, after receipt of a notification from the lessor under Section 2A–405, the lessee fails so to modify the lease agreement within a reasonable time not exceeding 30 days, the lease contract lapses with respect to any deliveries affected.

§ 2A–407. Irrevocable Promises: Finance Leases.

(1) In the case of a finance lease that is not a consumer lease the lessee's promises under the lease contract become irrevocable and independent upon the lessee's acceptance of the goods.

(2) A promise that has become irrevocable and independent under subsection (1):

(a) is effective and enforceable between the parties, and by or against third parties including assignees of the parties, and

(b) is not subject to cancellation, termination, modification, repudiation, excuse, or substitution without the consent of the party to whom the promise runs.

(3) This section does not affect the validity under any other law of a covenant in any lease contract making the lessee's promises irrevocable and independent upon the lessee's acceptance of the goods.

As amended in 1990.

PART 5 Default

A. In General

§ 2A–501. Default: Procedure.

(1) Whether the lessor or the lessee is in default under a lease contract is determined by the lease agreement and this Article.

(2) If the lessor or the lessee is in default under the lease contract, the party seeking enforcement has rights and remedies as provided in this Article and, except as limited by this Article, as provided in the lease agreement.

(3) If the lessor or the lessee is in default under the lease contract, the party seeking enforcement may reduce the party's claim to judgment, or otherwise enforce the lease contract by self-help or any available judicial procedure or nonjudicial procedure, including administrative proceeding, arbitration, or the like, in accordance with this Article.

(4) Except as otherwise provided in Section 1–106(1) or this Article or the lease agreement, the rights and remedies referred to in subsections (2) and (3) are cumulative.

(5) If the lease agreement covers both real property and goods, the party seeking enforcement may proceed under this Part as to the goods, or under other applicable law as to both the real property and the goods in accordance with that party's rights and remedies in respect of the real property, in which case this Part does not apply.

As amended in 1990.

§ 2A–502. Notice After Default.

Except as otherwise provided in this Article or the lease agreement, the lessor or lessee in default under the lease contract is not entitled to notice of default or notice of enforcement from the other party to the lease agreement.

§ 2A–503. Modification or Impairment of Rights and Remedies.

(1) Except as otherwise provided in this Article, the lease agreement may include rights and remedies for default in addition to or in substitution for those provided in this Article and may limit or alter the measure of damages recoverable under this Article.

(2) Resort to a remedy provided under this Article or in the lease agreement is optional unless the remedy is expressly agreed to be exclusive. If circumstances cause an exclusive or limited remedy to fail of its essential purpose, or provision for an exclusive remedy is unconscionable, remedy may be had as provided in this Article.

(3) Consequential damages may be liquidated under Section 2A–504, or may otherwise be limited, altered, or excluded unless the limitation, alteration, or exclusion is unconscionable. Limitation, alteration, or exclusion of consequential damages for injury to the person in the case of consumer goods is prima facie unconscionable but limitation, alteration, or exclusion of damages where the loss is commercial is not prima facie unconscionable.

(4) Rights and remedies on default by the lessor or the lessee with respect to any obligation or promise collateral or ancillary to the lease contract are not impaired by this Article.

As amended in 1990.

§ 2A–504. Liquidation of Damages.

(1) Damages payable by either party for default, or any other act or omission, including indemnity for loss or

diminution of anticipated tax benefits or loss or damage to lessor's residual interest, may be liquidated in the lease agreement but only at an amount or by a formula that is reasonable in light of the then anticipated harm caused by the default or other act or omission.

(2) If the lease agreement provides for liquidation of damages, and such provision does not comply with subsection (1), or such provision is an exclusive or limited remedy that circumstances cause to fail of its essential purpose, remedy may be had as provided in this Article.

(3) If the lessor justifiably withholds or stops delivery of goods because of the lessee's default or insolvency (Section 2A–525 or 2A–526), the lessee is entitled to restitution of any amount by which the sum of his [or her] payments exceeds:

(a) the amount to which the lessor is entitled by virtue of terms liquidating the lessor's damages in accordance with subsection (1); or

(b) in the absence of those terms, 20 percent of the then present value of the total rent the lessee was obligated to pay for the balance of the lease term, or, in the case of a consumer lease, the lesser of such amount or $500.

(4) A lessee's right to restitution under subsection (3) is subject to offset to the extent the lessor establishes:

(a) a right to recover damages under the provisions of this Article other than subsection (1); and

(b) the amount or value of any benefits received by the lessee directly or indirectly by reason of the lease contract.

§ 2A–505. Cancellation and Termination and Effect of Cancellation, Termination, Rescission, or Fraud on Rights and Remedies.

(1) On cancellation of the lease contract, all obligations that are still executory on both sides are discharged, but any right based on prior default or performance survives, and the cancelling party also retains any remedy for default of the whole lease contract or any unperformed balance.

(2) On termination of the lease contract, all obligations that are still executory on both sides are discharged but any right based on prior default or performance survives.

(3) Unless the contrary intention clearly appears, expressions of "cancellation," "rescission," or the like of the lease contract may not be construed as a renunciation or discharge of any claim in damages for an antecedent default.

(4) Rights and remedies for material misrepresentation or fraud include all rights and remedies available under this Article for default.

(5) Neither rescission nor a claim for rescission of the lease contract nor rejection or return of the goods may bar or be deemed inconsistent with a claim for damages or other right or remedy.

§ 2A–506. Statute of Limitations.

(1) An action for default under a lease contract, including breach of warranty or indemnity, must be commenced within 4 years after the cause of action accrued. By the original lease contract the parties may reduce the period of limitation to not less than one year.

(2) A cause of action for default accrues when the act or omission on which the default or breach of warranty is based is or should have been discovered by the aggrieved party, or when the default occurs, whichever is later. A cause of action for indemnity accrues when the act or omission on which the claim for indemnity is based is or should have been discovered by the indemnified party, whichever is later.

(3) If an action commenced within the time limited by subsection (1) is so terminated as to leave available a remedy by another action for the same default or breach of warranty or indemnity, the other action may be commenced after the expiration of the time limited and within 6 months after the termination of the first action unless the termination resulted from voluntary discontinuance or from dismissal for failure or neglect to prosecute.

(4) This section does not alter the law on tolling of the statute of limitations nor does it apply to causes of action that have accrued before this Article becomes effective.

§ 2A–507. Proof of Market Rent: Time and Place.

(1) Damages based on market rent (Section 2A–519 or 2A–528) are determined according to the rent for the use of the goods concerned for a lease term identical to the remaining lease term of the original lease agreement and prevailing at the times specified in Sections 2A–519 and 2A–528.

(2) If evidence of rent for the use of the goods concerned for a lease term identical to the remaining lease term of the original lease agreement and prevailing at the times or places described in this Article is not readily available, the rent prevailing within any reasonable time before or after the time described or at any other place or for a different lease term which in commercial judgment or under usage of trade would serve as a reasonable substitute for the one described may be used, making any proper allowance for the difference, including the cost of transporting the goods to or from the other place.

(3) Evidence of a relevant rent prevailing at a time or place or for a lease term other than the one described in this Article offered by one party is not admissible unless and until he

[or she] has given the other party notice the court finds sufficient to prevent unfair surprise.

(4) If the prevailing rent or value of any goods regularly leased in any established market is in issue, reports in official publications or trade journals or in newspapers or periodicals of general circulation published as the reports of that market are admissible in evidence. The circumstances of the preparation of the report may be shown to affect its weight but not its admissibility.

As amended in 1990.

B. Default by Lessor

§ 2A–508. Lessee's Remedies.

(1) If a lessor fails to deliver the goods in conformity to the lease contract (Section 2A–509) or repudiates the lease contract (Section 2A–402), or a lessee rightfully rejects the goods (Section 2A–509) or justifiably revokes acceptance of the goods (Section 2A–517), then with respect to any goods involved, and with respect to all of the goods if under an installment lease contract the value of the whole lease contract is substantially impaired (Section 2A–510), the lessor is in default under the lease contract and the lessee may:

(a) cancel the lease contract (Section 2A–505(1));

(b) recover so much of the rent and security as has been paid and is just under the circumstances;

(c) cover and recover damages as to all goods affected whether or not they have been identified to the lease contract (Sections 2A–518 and 2A–520), or recover damages for nondelivery (Sections 2A–519 and 2A–520);

(d) exercise any other rights or pursue any other remedies provided in the lease contract.

(2) If a lessor fails to deliver the goods in conformity to the lease contract or repudiates the lease contract, the lessee may also:

(a) if the goods have been identified, recover them (Section 2A–522); or

(b) in a proper case, obtain specific performance or replevy the goods (Section 2A–521).

(3) If a lessor is otherwise in default under a lease contract, the lessee may exercise the rights and pursue the remedies provided in the lease contract, which may include a right to cancel the lease, and in Section 2A–519(3).

(4) If a lessor has breached a warranty, whether express or implied, the lessee may recover damages (Section 2A–519(4)).

(5) On rightful rejection or justifiable revocation of acceptance, a lessee has a security interest in goods in the lessee's possession or control for any rent and security that has been paid and any expenses reasonably incurred in their

inspection, receipt, transportation, and care and custody and may hold those goods and dispose of them in good faith and in a commercially reasonable manner, subject to Section 2A–527(5).

(6) Subject to the provisions of Section 2A–407, a lessee, on notifying the lessor of the lessee's intention to do so, may deduct all or any part of the damages resulting from any default under the lease contract from any part of the rent still due under the same lease contract.

As amended in 1990.

§ 2A–509. Lessee's Rights on Improper Delivery; Rightful Rejection.

(1) Subject to the provisions of Section 2A–510 on default in installment lease contracts, if the goods or the tender or delivery fail in any respect to conform to the lease contract, the lessee may reject or accept the goods or accept any commercial unit or units and reject the rest of the goods.

(2) Rejection of goods is ineffective unless it is within a reasonable time after tender or delivery of the goods and the lessee seasonably notifies the lessor.

§ 2A–510. Installment Lease Contracts: Rejection and Default.

(1) Under an installment lease contract a lessee may reject any delivery that is nonconforming if the nonconformity substantially impairs the value of that delivery and cannot be cured or the nonconformity is a defect in the required documents; but if the nonconformity does not fall within subsection (2) and the lessor or the supplier gives adequate assurance of its cure, the lessee must accept that delivery.

(2) Whenever nonconformity or default with respect to one or more deliveries substantially impairs the value of the installment lease contract as a whole there is a default with respect to the whole. But, the aggrieved party reinstates the installment lease contract as a whole if the aggrieved party accepts a nonconforming delivery without seasonably notifying of cancellation or brings an action with respect only to past deliveries or demands performance as to future deliveries.

§ 2A–511. Merchant Lessee's Duties as to Rightfully Rejected Goods.

(1) Subject to any security interest of a lessee (Section 2A–508 (5)), if a lessor or a supplier has no agent or place of business at the market of rejection, a merchant lessee, after rejection of goods in his [or her] possession or control, shall follow any reasonable instructions received from the lessor or the supplier with respect to the goods. In the absence of those instructions, a merchant lessee shall make reasonable

efforts to sell, lease, or otherwise dispose of the goods for the lessor's account if they threaten to decline in value speedily. Instructions are not reasonable if on demand indemnity for expenses is not forthcoming.

(2) If a merchant lessee (subsection (1)) or any other lessee (Section 2A–512) disposes of goods, he [or she] is entitled to reimbursement either from the lessor or the supplier or out of the proceeds for reasonable expenses of caring for and disposing of the goods and, if the expenses include no disposition commission, to such commission as is usual in the trade, or if there is none, to a reasonable sum not exceeding 10 percent of the gross proceeds.

(3) In complying with this section or Section 2A–512, the lessee is held only to good faith. Good faith conduct hereunder is neither acceptance or conversion nor the basis of an action for damages.

(4) A purchaser who purchases in good faith from a lessee pursuant to this section or Section 2A–512 takes the goods free of any rights of the lessor and the supplier even though the lessee fails to comply with one or more of the requirements of this Article.

§ 2A–512. Lessee's Duties as to Rightfully Rejected Goods.

(1) Except as otherwise provided with respect to goods that threaten to decline in value speedily (Section 2A–511) and subject to any security interest of a lessee (Section 2A–508(5)):

(a) the lessee, after rejection of goods in the lessee's possession, shall hold them with reasonable care at the lessor's or the supplier's disposition for a reasonable time after the lessee's seasonable notification of rejection;

(b) if the lessor or the supplier gives no instructions within a reasonable time after notification of rejection, the lessee may store the rejected goods for the lessor's or the supplier's account or ship them to the lessor or the supplier or dispose of them for the lessor's or the supplier's account with reimbursement in the manner provided in Section 2A–511; but

(c) the lessee has no further obligations with regard to goods rightfully rejected.

(2) Action by the lessee pursuant to subsection (1) is not acceptance or conversion.

§ 2A–513. Cure by Lessor of Improper Tender or Delivery; Replacement.

(1) If any tender or delivery by the lessor or the supplier is rejected because nonconforming and the time for performance has not yet expired, the lessor or the supplier

may seasonably notify the lessee of the lessor's or the supplier's intention to cure and may then make a conforming delivery within the time provided in the lease contract.

(2) If the lessee rejects a nonconforming tender that the lessor or the supplier had reasonable grounds to believe would be acceptable with or without money allowance, the lessor or the supplier may have a further reasonable time to substitute a conforming tender if he [or she] seasonably notifies the lessee.

§ 2A–514. Waiver of Lessee's Objections.

(1) In rejecting goods, a lessee's failure to state a particular defect that is ascertainable by reasonable inspection precludes the lessee from relying on the defect to justify rejection or to establish default:

(a) if, stated seasonably, the lessor or the supplier could have cured it (Section 2A–513); or

(b) between merchants if the lessor or the supplier after rejection has made a request in writing for a full and final written statement of all defects on which the lessee proposes to rely.

(2) A lessee's failure to reserve rights when paying rent or other consideration against documents precludes recovery of the payment for defects apparent on the face of the documents.

§ 2A–515. Acceptance of Goods.

(1) Acceptance of goods occurs after the lessee has had a reasonable opportunity to inspect the goods and

(a) the lessee signifies or acts with respect to the goods in a manner that signifies to the lessor or the supplier that the goods are conforming or that the lessee will take or retain them in spite of their nonconformity; or

(b) the lessee fails to make an effective rejection of the goods (Section 2A–509(2)).

(2) Acceptance of a part of any commercial unit is acceptance of that entire unit.

§ 2A–516. Effect of Acceptance of Goods; Notice of Default; Burden of Establishing Default After Acceptance; Notice of Claim or Litigation to Person Answerable Over.

(1) A lessee must pay rent for any goods accepted in accordance with the lease contract, with due allowance for goods rightfully rejected or not delivered.

(2) A lessee's acceptance of goods precludes rejection of the goods accepted. In the case of a finance lease, if made with knowledge of a nonconformity, acceptance cannot be revoked because of it. In any other case, if made with

knowledge of a nonconformity, acceptance cannot be revoked because of it unless the acceptance was on the reasonable assumption that the nonconformity would be seasonably cured. Acceptance does not of itself impair any other remedy provided by this Article or the lease agreement for nonconformity.

(3) If a tender has been accepted:

(a) within a reasonable time after the lessee discovers or should have discovered any default, the lessee shall notify the lessor and the supplier, if any, or be barred from any remedy against the party notified;

(b) except in the case of a consumer lease, within a reasonable time after the lessee receives notice of litigation for infringement or the like (Section 2A–211) the lessee shall notify the lessor or be barred from any remedy over for liability established by the litigation; and

(c) the burden is on the lessee to establish any default.

(4) If a lessee is sued for breach of a warranty or other obligation for which a lessor or a supplier is answerable over the following apply:

(a) The lessee may give the lessor or the supplier, or both, written notice of the litigation. If the notice states that the person notified may come in and defend and that if the person notified does not do so that person will be bound in any action against that person by the lessee by any determination of fact common to the two litigations, then unless the person notified after seasonable receipt of the notice does come in and defend that person is so bound.

(b) The lessor or the supplier may demand in writing that the lessee turn over control of the litigation including settlement if the claim is one for infringement or the like (Section 2A–211) or else be barred from any remedy over. If the demand states that the lessor or the supplier agrees to bear all expense and to satisfy any adverse judgment, then unless the lessee after seasonable receipt of the demand does turn over control the lessee is so barred.

(5) Subsections (3) and (4) apply to any obligation of a lessee to hold the lessor or the supplier harmless against infringement or the like (Section 2A–211).

As amended in 1990.

§ 2A–517. Revocation of Acceptance of Goods.

(1) A lessee may revoke acceptance of a lot or commercial unit whose nonconformity substantially impairs its value to the lessee if the lessee has accepted it:

(a) except in the case of a finance lease, on the reasonable assumption that its nonconformity would be cured and it has not been seasonably cured; or

(b) without discovery of the nonconformity if the lessee's acceptance was reasonably induced either by the lessor's assurances or, except in the case of a finance lease, by the difficulty of discovery before acceptance.

(2) Except in the case of a finance lease that is not a consumer lease, a lessee may revoke acceptance of a lot or commercial unit if the lessor defaults under the lease contract and the default substantially impairs the value of that lot or commercial unit to the lessee.

(3) If the lease agreement so provides, the lessee may revoke acceptance of a lot or commercial unit because of other defaults by the lessor.

(4) Revocation of acceptance must occur within a reasonable time after the lessee discovers or should have discovered the ground for it and before any substantial change in condition of the goods which is not caused by the nonconformity. Revocation is not effective until the lessee notifies the lessor.

(5) A lessee who so revokes has the same rights and duties with regard to the goods involved as if the lessee had rejected them.

As amended in 1990.

§ 2A–518. Cover; Substitute Goods.

(1) After a default by a lessor under the lease contract of the type described in Section 2A–508(1), or, if agreed, after other default by the lessor, the lessee may cover by making any purchase or lease of or contract to purchase or lease goods in substitution for those due from the lessor.

(2) Except as otherwise provided with respect to damages liquidated in the lease agreement (Section 2A–504) or otherwise determined pursuant to agreement of the parties (Sections 1–102(3) and 2A–503), if a lessee's cover is by lease agreement substantially similar to the original lease agreement and the new lease agreement is made in good faith and in a commercially reasonable manner, the lessee may recover from the lessor as damages (i) the present value, as of the date of the commencement of the term of the new lease agreement, of the rent under the new lease agreement applicable to that period of the new lease term which is comparable to the then remaining term of the original lease agreement minus the present value as of the same date of the total rent for the then remaining lease term of the original lease agreement, and (ii) any incidental or consequential damages, less expenses saved in consequence of the lessor's default.

(3) If a lessee's cover is by lease agreement that for any reason does not qualify for treatment under subsection (2), or is by purchase or otherwise, the lessee may recover from the lessor as if the lessee had elected not to cover and Section 2A–519 governs.

As amended in 1990.

§ 2A–519. Lessee's Damages for Non-Delivery, Repudiation, Default, and Breach of Warranty in Regard to Accepted Goods.

(1) Except as otherwise provided with respect to damages liquidated in the lease agreement (Section 2A–504) or otherwise determined pursuant to agreement of the parties (Sections 1–102(3) and 2A–503), if a lessee elects not to cover or a lessee elects to cover and the cover is by lease agreement that for any reason does not qualify for treatment under Section 2A–518(2), or is by purchase or otherwise, the measure of damages for non-delivery or repudiation by the lessor or for rejection or revocation of acceptance by the lessee is the present value, as of the date of the default, of the then market rent minus the present value as of the same date of the original rent, computed for the remaining lease term of the original lease agreement, together with incidental and consequential damages, less expenses saved in consequence of the lessor's default.

(2) Market rent is to be determined as of the place for tender or, in cases of rejection after arrival or revocation of acceptance, as of the place of arrival.

(3) Except as otherwise agreed, if the lessee has accepted goods and given notification (Section 2A–516(3)), the measure of damages for non-conforming tender or delivery or other default by a lessor is the loss resulting in the ordinary course of events from the lessor's default as determined in any manner that is reasonable together with incidental and consequential damages, less expenses saved in consequence of the lessor's default.

(4) Except as otherwise agreed, the measure of damages for breach of warranty is the present value at the time and place of acceptance of the difference between the value of the use of the goods accepted and the value if they had been as warranted for the lease term, unless special circumstances show proximate damages of a different amount, together with incidental and consequential damages, less expenses saved in consequence of the lessor's default or breach of warranty.

As amended in 1990.

§ 2A–520. Lessee's Incidental and Consequential Damages.

(1) Incidental damages resulting from a lessor's default include expenses reasonably incurred in inspection, receipt, transportation, and care and custody of goods rightfully rejected or goods the acceptance of which is justifiably revoked, any commercially reasonable charges, expenses or commissions in connection with effecting cover, and any other reasonable expense incident to the default.

(2) Consequential damages resulting from a lessor's default include:

(a) any loss resulting from general or particular requirements and needs of which the lessor at the time of contracting had reason to know and which could not reasonably be prevented by cover or otherwise; and

(b) injury to person or property proximately resulting from any breach of warranty.

§ 2A–521. Lessee's Right to Specific Performance or Replevin.

(1) Specific performance may be decreed if the goods are unique or in other proper circumstances.

(2) A decree for specific performance may include any terms and conditions as to payment of the rent, damages, or other relief that the court deems just.

(3) A lessee has a right of replevin, detinue, sequestration, claim and delivery, or the like for goods identified to the lease contract if after reasonable effort the lessee is unable to effect cover for those goods or the circumstances reasonably indicate that the effort will be unavailing.

§ 2A–522. Lessee's Right to Goods on Lessor's Insolvency.

(1) Subject to subsection (2) and even though the goods have not been shipped, a lessee who has paid a part or all of the rent and security for goods identified to a lease contract (Section 2A–217) on making and keeping good a tender of any unpaid portion of the rent and security due under the lease contract may recover the goods identified from the lessor if the lessor becomes insolvent within 10 days after receipt of the first installment of rent and security.

(2) A lessee acquires the right to recover goods identified to a lease contract only if they conform to the lease contract.

C. Default by Lessee

§ 2A–523. Lessor's Remedies.

(1) If a lessee wrongfully rejects or revokes acceptance of goods or fails to make a payment when due or repudiates with respect to a part or the whole, then, with respect to any goods involved, and with respect to all of the goods if under an installment lease contract the value of the whole lease contract is substantially impaired (Section 2A–510), the lessee is in default under the lease contract and the lessor may:

(a) cancel the lease contract (Section 2A–505(1));

(b) proceed respecting goods not identified to the lease contract (Section 2A–524);

(c) withhold delivery of the goods and take possession of goods previously delivered (Section 2A–525);

(d) stop delivery of the goods by any bailee (Section 2A–526);

(e) dispose of the goods and recover damages (Section 2A–527), or retain the goods and recover damages (Section 2A–528), or in a proper case recover rent (Section 2A–529) or

(f) exercise any other rights or pursue any other remedies provided in the lease contract.

(2) If a lessor does not fully exercise a right or obtain a remedy to which the lessor is entitled under subsection (1), the lessor may recover the loss resulting in the ordinary course of events from the lessee's default as determined in any reasonable manner, together with incidental damages, less expenses saved in consequence of the lessee's default.

(3) If a lessee is otherwise in default under a lease contract, the lessor may exercise the rights and pursue the remedies provided in the lease contract, which may include a right to cancel the lease. In addition, unless otherwise provided in the lease contract:

(a) if the default substantially impairs the value of the lease contract to the lessor, the lessor may exercise the rights and pursue the remedies provided in subsections (1) or (2); or

(b) if the default does not substantially impair the value of the lease contract to the lessor, the lessor may recover as provided in subsection (2).

As amended in 1990.

§ 2A–524. Lessor's Right to Identify Goods to Lease Contract.

(1) After default by the lessee under the lease contract of the type described in Section 2A–523(1) or 2A–523(3)(a) or, if agreed, after other default by the lessee, the lessor may:

(a) identify to the lease contract conforming goods not already identified if at the time the lessor learned of the default they were in the lessor's or the supplier's possession or control; and

(b) dispose of goods (Section 2A–527(1)) that demonstrably have been intended for the particular lease contract even though those goods are unfinished.

(2) If the goods are unfinished, in the exercise of reasonable commercial judgment for the purposes of avoiding loss and of effective realization, an aggrieved lessor or the supplier may either complete manufacture and wholly identify the goods to the lease contract or cease manufacture and lease, sell, or otherwise dispose of the goods for scrap or salvage value or proceed in any other reasonable manner.

As amended in 1990.

§ 2A–525. Lessor's Right to Possession of Goods.

(1) If a lessor discovers the lessee to be insolvent, the lessor may refuse to deliver the goods.

(2) After a default by the lessee under the lease contract of the type described in Section 2A–523(1) or 2A–523(3) (a) or, if agreed, after other default by the lessee, the lessor has the right to take possession of the goods. If the lease contract so provides, the lessor may require the lessee to assemble the goods and make them available to the lessor at a place to be designated by the lessor which is reasonably convenient to both parties. Without removal, the lessor may render unusable any goods employed in trade or business, and may dispose of goods on the lessee's premises (Section 2A–527).

(3) The lessor may proceed under subsection (2) without judicial process if that can be done without breach of the peace or the lessor may proceed by action.

As amended in 1990.

§ 2A–526. Lessor's Stoppage of Delivery in Transit or Otherwise.

(1) A lessor may stop delivery of goods in the possession of a carrier or other bailee if the lessor discovers the lessee to be insolvent and may stop delivery of carload, truckload, planeload, or larger shipments of express or freight if the lessee repudiates or fails to make a payment due before delivery, whether for rent, security or otherwise under the lease contract, or for any other reason the lessor has a right to withhold or take possession of the goods.

(2) In pursuing its remedies under subsection (1), the lessor may stop delivery until

(a) receipt of the goods by the lessee;

(b) acknowledgment to the lessee by any bailee of the goods, except a carrier, that the bailee holds the goods for the lessee; or

(c) such an acknowledgment to the lessee by a carrier via reshipment or as warehouseman.

(3) (a) To stop delivery, a lessor shall so notify as to enable the bailee by reasonable diligence to prevent delivery of the goods.

(b) After notification, the bailee shall hold and deliver the goods according to the directions of the lessor, but the lessor is liable to the bailee for any ensuing charges or damages.

(c) A carrier who has issued a nonnegotiable bill of lading is not obliged to obey a notification to stop received from a person other than the consignor.

§ 2A–527. Lessor's Rights to Dispose of Goods.

(1) After a default by a lessee under the lease contract of the type described in Section 2A–523(1) or 2A–523(3)(a) or after the lessor refuses to deliver or takes possession of goods (Section 2A–525 or 2A–526), or, if agreed, after other default by a lessee, the lessor may dispose of the goods concerned or the undelivered balance thereof by lease, sale, or otherwise.

(2) Except as otherwise provided with respect to damages liquidated in the lease agreement (Section 2A–504) or otherwise determined pursuant to agreement of the parties (Sections 1–102(3) and 2A–503), if the disposition is by lease agreement substantially similar to the original lease agreement and the new lease agreement is made in good faith and in a commercially reasonable manner, the lessor may recover from the lessee as damages (i) accrued and unpaid rent as of the date of the commencement of the term of the new lease agreement, (ii) the present value, as of the same date, of the total rent for the then remaining lease term of the original lease agreement minus the present value, as of the same date, of the rent under the new lease agreement applicable to that period of the new lease term which is comparable to the then remaining term of the original lease agreement, and (iii) any incidental damages allowed under Section 2A–530, less expenses saved in consequence of the lessee's default.

(3) If the lessor's disposition is by lease agreement that for any reason does not qualify for treatment under subsection (2), or is by sale or otherwise, the lessor may recover from the lessee as if the lessor had elected not to dispose of the goods and Section 2A–528 governs.

(4) A subsequent buyer or lessee who buys or leases from the lessor in good faith for value as a result of a disposition under this section takes the goods free of the original lease contract and any rights of the original lessee even though the lessor fails to comply with one or more of the requirements of this Article.

(5) The lessor is not accountable to the lessee for any profit made on any disposition. A lessee who has rightfully rejected or justifiably revoked acceptance shall account to the lessor for any excess over the amount of the lessee's security interest (Section 2A–508(5)).

As amended in 1990.

§ 2A–528. Lessor's Damages for Non-acceptance, Failure to Pay, Repudiation, or Other Default.

(1) Except as otherwise provided with respect to damages liquidated in the lease agreement (Section 2A–504) or otherwise determined pursuant to agreement of the parties (Section 1–102(3) and 2A–503), if a lessor elects to retain the goods or a lessor elects to dispose of the goods and the disposition is by lease agreement that for any reason does not qualify for treatment under Section 2A–527(2), or is by sale or otherwise, the lessor may recover from the lessee as damages for a default of the type described in Section 2A–523(1) or 2A–523(3)(a), or if agreed, for other default of the lessee, (i) accrued and unpaid rent as of the date of the default if the lessee has never taken possession of the goods, or, if the lessee has taken possession of the goods, as of the date the lessor repossesses the goods or an earlier date on which the lessee makes a tender of the goods to the lessor, (ii) the present value as of the date determined under clause (i) of the total rent for the then remaining lease term of the original lease agreement minus the present value as of the same date of the market rent as the place where the goods are located computed for the same lease term, and (iii) any incidental damages allowed under Section 2A–530, less expenses saved in consequence of the lessee's default.

(2) If the measure of damages provided in subsection (1) is inadequate to put a lessor in as good a position as performance would have, the measure of damages is the present value of the profit, including reasonable overhead, the lessor would have made from full performance by the lessee, together with any incidental damages allowed under Section 2A–530, due allowance for costs reasonably incurred and due credit for payments or proceeds of disposition.

As amended in 1990.

§ 2A–529. Lessor's Action for the Rent.

(1) After default by the lessee under the lease contract of the type described in Section 2A–523(1) or 2A–523(3)(a) or, if agreed, after other default by the lessee, if the lessor complies with subsection (2), the lessor may recover from the lessee as damages:

(a) for goods accepted by the lessee and not repossessed by or tendered to the lessor, and for conforming goods lost or damaged within a commercially reasonable time after risk of loss passes to the lessee (Section 2A–219), (i) accrued and unpaid rent as of the date of entry of judgment in favor of the lessor (ii) the present value as of the same date of the rent for the then remaining lease term of the lease agreement, and (iii) any incidental damages allowed under Section 2A–530, less expenses saved in consequence of the lessee's default; and

(b) for goods identified to the lease contract if the lessor is unable after reasonable effort to dispose of them at a reasonable price or the circumstances reasonably indicate that effort will be unavailing, (i) accrued and unpaid rent as of the date of entry of judgment in favor of the lessor, (ii) the present value as of the same date of the rent for the then remaining lease term of the lease agreement, and (iii) any incidental damages allowed under Section 2A–530, less expenses saved in consequence of the lessee's default.

(2) Except as provided in subsection (3), the lessor shall hold for the lessee for the remaining lease term of the lease agreement any goods that have been identified to the lease contract and are in the lessor's control.

(3) The lessor may dispose of the goods at any time before collection of the judgment for damages obtained pursuant to subsection (1). If the disposition is before the end of the remaining lease term of the lease agreement, the lessor's recovery against the lessee for damages is governed by Section 2A–527 or Section 2A–528, and the lessor will cause an appropriate credit to be provided against a judgment for damages to the extent that the amount of the judgment exceeds the recovery available pursuant to Section 2A–527 or 2A–528.

(4) Payment of the judgment for damages obtained pursuant to subsection (1) entitles the lessee to the use and possession of the goods not then disposed of for the remaining lease term of and in accordance with the lease agreement.

(5) After default by the lessee under the lease contract of the type described in Section 2A–523(1) or Section 2A–523 (3)(a) or, if agreed, after other default by the lessee, a lessor who is held not entitled to rent under this section must nevertheless be awarded damages for non-acceptance under Sections 2A–527 and 2A–528.

As amended in 1990.

§ 2A–530. Lessor's Incidental Damages.

Incidental damages to an aggrieved lessor include any commercially reasonable charges, expenses, or commissions incurred in stopping delivery, in the transportation, care and custody of goods after the lessee's default, in connection with return or disposition of the goods, or otherwise resulting from the default.

§ 2A–531. Standing to Sue Third Parties for Injury to Goods.

(1) If a third party so deals with goods that have been identified to a lease contract as to cause actionable injury to a party to the lease contract (a) the lessor has a right of action against the third party, and (b) the lessee also has a right of action against the third party if the lessee:

(i) has a security interest in the goods;

(ii) has an insurable interest in the goods; or

(iii) bears the risk of loss under the lease contract or has since the injury assumed that risk as against the lessor and the goods have been converted or destroyed.

(2) If at the time of the injury the party plaintiff did not bear the risk of loss as against the other party to the lease contract and there is no arrangement between them for disposition of the recovery, his [or her] suit or settlement, subject to his [or her] own interest, is as a fiduciary for the other party to the lease contract.

(3) Either party with the consent of the other may sue for the benefit of whom it may concern.

§ 2A–532. Lessor's Rights to Residual Interest.

In addition to any other recovery permitted by this Article or other law, the lessor may recover from the lessee an amount that will fully compensate the lessor for any loss of or damage to the lessor's residual interest in the goods caused by the default of the lessee.

As added in 1990.

REVISED ARTICLE III NEGOTIABLE INSTRUMENTS

PART 1   General Provisions and Definitions

§ 3–101. Short Title.

This Article may be cited as Uniform Commercial Code–Negotiable Instruments.

§ 3–102. Subject Matter.

(a) This Article applies to negotiable instruments. It does not apply to money, to payment orders governed by Article 4A, or to securities governed by Article 8.

(b) If there is conflict between this Article and Article 4 or 9, Articles 4 and 9 govern.

(c) Regulations of the Board of Governors of the Federal Reserve System and operating circulars of the Federal Reserve Banks supersede any inconsistent provision of this Article to the extent of the inconsistency.

§ 3–103. Definitions.

(a) In this Article:

(1) "Acceptor" means a drawee who has accepted a draft.

(2) "Drawee" means a person ordered in a draft to make payment.

(3) "Drawer" means a person who signs or is identified in a draft as a person ordering payment.

(4) "Good faith" means honesty in fact and the observance of reasonable commercial standards of fair dealing.

(5) "Maker" means a person who signs or is identified in a note as a person undertaking to pay.

(6) "Order" means a written instruction to pay money signed by the person giving the instruction. The instruction may be addressed to any person, including the person giving the instruction, or to one or more persons jointly or in the alternative but not in succession. An authorization to pay is not an order unless the person authorized to pay is also instructed to pay.

(7) "Ordinary care" in the case of a person engaged in business means observance of reasonable commercial standards, prevailing in the area in which the person is located, with respect to the business in which the person is engaged. In the case of a bank that takes an instrument for processing for collection or payment by automated means, reasonable commercial standards do not require the bank to examine the instrument if the failure to examine does not violate the bank's prescribed procedures and the bank's procedures do not vary unreasonably from general banking usage not disapproved by this Article or Article 4.

(8) "Party" means a party to an instrument.

(9) "Promise" means a written undertaking to pay money signed by the person undertaking to pay. An acknowledgment of an obligation by the obligor is not a promise unless the obligor also undertakes to pay the obligation.

(10) "Prove" with respect to a fact means to meet the burden of establishing the fact (Section 1–201(8)).

(11) "Remitter" means a person who purchases an instrument from its issuer if the instrument is payable to an identified person other than the purchaser.

(b) [Other definitions' section references deleted.]

(c) [Other definitions' section references deleted.]

(d) In addition, Article 1 contains general definitions and principles of construction and interpretation applicable throughout this Article.

§ 3–104. Negotiable Instrument.

(a) Except as provided in subsections (c) and (d), "negotiable instrument" means an unconditional promise or order to pay a fixed amount of money, with or without interest or other charges described in the promise or order, if it:

(1) is payable to bearer or to order at the time it is issued or first comes into possession of a holder;

(2) is payable on demand or at a definite time; and

(3) does not state any other undertaking or instruction by the person promising or ordering payment to do any act in addition to the payment of money, but the promise or order may contain (i) an undertaking or power to give, maintain, or protect collateral to secure payment, (ii) an authorization or power to the holder to confess judgment or realize on or dispose of collateral, or (iii) a waiver of the benefit of any law intended for the advantage or protection of an obligor.

(b) "Instrument" means a negotiable instrument.

(c) An order that meets all of the requirements of subsection (a), except paragraph (1), and otherwise falls within the definition of "check" in subsection (f) is a negotiable instrument and a check.

(d) A promise or order other than a check is not an instrument if, at the time it is issued or first comes into possession of a holder, it contains a conspicuous statement, however expressed, to the effect that the promise or order is not negotiable or is not an instrument governed by this Article.

(e) An instrument is a "note" if it is a promise and is a "draft" if it is an order. If an instrument falls within the definition of both "note" and "draft," a person entitled to enforce the instrument may treat it as either.

(f) "Check" means (i) a draft, other than a documentary draft, payable on demand and drawn on a bank or (ii) a cashier's check or teller's check. An instrument may be a check even though it is described on its face by another term, such as "money order."

(g) "Cashier's check" means a draft with respect to which the drawer and drawee are the same bank or branches of the same bank.

(h) "Teller's check" means a draft drawn by a bank (i) on another bank, or (ii) payable at or through a bank.

(i) "Traveler's check" means an instrument that (i) is payable on demand, (ii) is drawn on or payable at or through a bank, (iii) is designated by the term "traveler's check" or by a substantially similar term, and (iv) requires, as a condition to payment, a countersignature by a person whose specimen signature appears on the instrument.

(j) "Certificate of deposit" means an instrument containing an acknowledgment by a bank that a sum of money has been received by the bank and a promise by the bank to repay the sum of money. A certificate of deposit is a note of the bank.

§ 3–105. Issue of Instrument.

(a) "Issue" means the first delivery of an instrument by the maker or drawer, whether to a holder or nonholder, for the purpose of giving rights on the instrument to any person.

(b) An unissued instrument, or an unissued incomplete instrument that is completed, is binding on the maker or drawer, but nonissuance is a defense. An instrument that is conditionally issued or is issued for a special purpose is binding on the maker or drawer, but failure of the condition or special purpose to be fulfilled is a defense.

(c) "Issuer" applies to issued and unissued instruments and means a maker or drawer of an instrument.

§ 3–106. Unconditional Promise or Order.

(a) Except as provided in this section, for the purposes of Section 3–104(a), a promise or order is unconditional unless it states (i) an express condition to payment, (ii) that the promise or order is subject to or governed by another writing, or (iii) that rights or obligations with respect to the promise or order are stated in another writing. A reference to another writing does not of itself make the promise or order conditional.

(b) A promise or order is not made conditional (i) by a reference to another writing for a statement of rights with respect to collateral, prepayment, or acceleration, or (ii) because payment is limited to resort to a particular fund or source.

(c) If a promise or order requires, as a condition to payment, a countersignature by a person whose specimen signature appears on the promise or order, the condition does not make the promise or order conditional for the purposes of Section 3–104(a). If the person whose specimen signature appears on an instrument fails to countersign the instrument, the failure to countersign is a defense to the obligation of the issuer, but the failure does not prevent a transferee of the instrument from becoming a holder of the instrument.

(d) If a promise or order at the time it is issued or first comes into possession of a holder contains a statement, required by applicable statutory or administrative law, to the effect that the rights of a holder or transferee are subject to claims or defenses that the issuer could assert against the original payee, the promise or order is not thereby made conditional for the purposes of Section 3–104(a); but if the promise or order is an instrument, there cannot be a holder in due course of the instrument.

§ 3–107. Instrument Payable in Foreign Money.

Unless the instrument otherwise provides, an instrument that states the amount payable in foreign money may be paid in the foreign money or in an equivalent amount in dollars calculated by using the current bank-offered spot rate at the place of payment for the purchase of dollars on the day on which the instrument is paid.

§ 3–108. Payable on Demand or at Definite Time.

(a) A promise or order is "payable on demand" if it (i) states that it is payable on demand or at sight, or otherwise indicates that it is payable at the will of the holder, or (ii) does not state any time of payment.

(b) A promise or order is "payable at a definite time" if it is payable on elapse of a definite period of time after sight or acceptance or at a fixed date or dates or at a time or times readily ascertainable at the time the promise or order is issued, subject to rights of (i) prepayment, (ii) acceleration, (iii) extension at the option of the holder, or (iv) extension to a further definite time at the option of the maker or acceptor or automatically upon or after a specified act or event.

(c) If an instrument, payable at a fixed date, is also payable upon demand made before the fixed date, the instrument is payable on demand until the fixed date and, if demand for payment is not made before that date, becomes payable at a definite time on the fixed date.

§ 3–109. Payable to Bearer or to Order.

(a) A promise or order is payable to bearer if it:

(1) states that it is payable to bearer or to the order of bearer or otherwise indicates that the person in possession of the promise or order is entitled to payment;

(2) does not state a payee; or

(3) states that it is payable to or to the order of cash or otherwise indicates that it is not payable to an identified person.

(b) A promise or order that is not payable to bearer is payable to order if it is payable (i) to the order of an identified person or (ii) to an identified person or order. A promise or order that is payable to order is payable to the identified person.

(c) An instrument payable to bearer may become payable to an identified person if it is specially indorsed pursuant to Section 3–205(a). An instrument payable to an identified person may become payable to bearer if it is indorsed in blank pursuant to Section 3–205(b).

§ 3–110. Identification of Person to Whom Instrument Is Payable.

(a) The person to whom an instrument is initially payable is determined by the intent of the person, whether or not authorized, signing as, or in the name or behalf of, the issuer of the instrument. The instrument is payable to the person intended by the signer even if that person is identified in the instrument by a name or other identification that is not that of the intended person. If more than one person signs in the name or behalf of the issuer of an instrument and all the signers do not intend the same person as payee, the instrument is payable to any person intended by one or more of the signers.

(b) If the signature of the issuer of an instrument is made by automated means, such as a check-writing machine, the payee of the instrument is determined by the intent of the person who supplied the name or identification of the payee, whether or not authorized to do so.

(c) A person to whom an instrument is payable may be identified in any way, including by name, identifying number, office, or account number. For the purpose of determining the holder of an instrument, the following rules apply:

(1) If an instrument is payable to an account and the account is identified only by number, the instrument is payable to the person to whom the account is payable. If an instrument is payable to an account identified by number and by the name of a person, the instrument is payable to the named person, whether or not that person is the owner of the account identified by number.

(2) If an instrument is payable to:

(i) a trust, an estate, or a person described as trustee or representative of a trust or estate, the instrument is payable to the trustee, the representative, or a successor of either, whether or not the beneficiary or estate is also named;

(ii) a person described as agent or similar representative of a named or identified person, the instrument is payable to the represented person, the representative, or a successor of the representative;

(iii) a fund or organization that is not a legal entity, the instrument is payable to a representative of the members of the fund or organization; or

(iv) an office or to a person described as holding an office, the instrument is payable to the named person, the incumbent of the office, or a successor to the incumbent.

(d) If an instrument is payable to two or more persons alternatively, it is payable to any of them and may be negotiated, discharged, or enforced by any or all of them in possession of the instrument. If an instrument is payable to two or more persons not alternatively, it is payable to all of them and may be negotiated, discharged, or enforced only by all of them. If an instrument payable to two or more persons is ambiguous as to whether it is payable to the persons alternatively, the instrument is payable to the persons alternatively.

§ 3–111. Place of Payment.

Except as otherwise provided for items in Article 4, an instrument is payable at the place of payment stated in the instrument. If no place of payment is stated, an instrument is payable at the address of the drawee or maker stated in the instrument. If no address is stated, the place of payment is the place of business of the drawee or maker. If a drawee or maker has more than one place of business, the place of payment is any place of business of the drawee or maker chosen by the person entitled to enforce the instrument. If the drawee or maker has no place of business, the place of payment is the residence of the drawee or maker.

§ 3–112. Interest.

(a) Unless otherwise provided in the instrument, (i) an instrument is not payable with interest, and (ii) interest on an interest-bearing instrument is payable from the date of the instrument.

(b) Interest may be stated in an instrument as a fixed or variable amount of money or it may be expressed as a fixed or variable rate or rates. The amount or rate of interest may be stated or described in the instrument in any manner and may require reference to information not contained in the instrument. If an instrument provides for interest, but the amount of interest payable cannot be ascertained from the description, interest is payable at the judgment rate in effect at the place of payment of the instrument and at the time interest first accrues.

§ 3–113. Date of Instrument.

(a) An instrument may be antedated or postdated. The date stated determines the time of payment if the instrument is payable at a fixed period after date. Except as provided in Section 4–401(c), an instrument payable on demand is not payable before the date of the instrument.

(b) If an instrument is undated, its date is the date of its issue or, in the case of an unissued instrument, the date it first comes into possession of a holder.

§ 3–114. Contradictory Terms of Instrument.

If an instrument contains contradictory terms, typewritten terms prevail over printed terms, handwritten terms prevail over both, and words prevail over numbers.

§ 3–115. Incomplete Instrument.

(a) "Incomplete instrument" means a signed writing, whether or not issued by the signer, the contents of which show at the time of signing that it is incomplete but that the signer intended it to be completed by the addition of words or numbers.

(b) Subject to subsection (c), if an incomplete instrument is an instrument under Section 3–104, it may be enforced according to its terms if it is not completed, or according to its terms as augmented by completion. If an incomplete instrument is not an instrument under Section 3–104, but, after completion, the requirements of Section 3–104 are met, the instrument may be enforced according to its terms as augmented by completion.

(c) If words or numbers are added to an incomplete instrument without authority of the signer, there is an alteration of the incomplete instrument under Section 3–407.

(d) The burden of establishing that words or numbers were added to an incomplete instrument without authority of the signer is on the person asserting the lack of authority.

§ 3–116. Joint and Several Liability; Contribution.

(a) Except as otherwise provided in the instrument, two or more persons who have the same liability on an instrument as makers, drawers, acceptors, indorsers who indorse as joint payees, or anomalous indorsers are jointly and severally liable in the capacity in which they sign.

(b) Except as provided in Section 3–419(e) or by agreement of the affected parties, a party having joint and several liability who pays the instrument is entitled to receive from any party having the same joint and several liability contribution in accordance with applicable law.

(c) Discharge of one party having joint and several liability by a person entitled to enforce the instrument does not affect the right under subsection (b) of a party having the same joint and several liability to receive contribution from the party discharged.

§ 3–117. Other Agreements Affecting Instrument.

Subject to applicable law regarding exclusion of proof of contemporaneous or previous agreements, the obligation of a party to an instrument to pay the instrument may be modified, supplemented, or nullified by a separate agreement of the obligor and a person entitled to enforce the instrument, if the instrument is issued or the obligation is incurred in reliance on the agreement or as part of the same transaction giving rise to the agreement. To the extent an obligation is modified, supplemented, or nullified by an agreement under this section, the agreement is a defense to the obligation.

§ 3–118. Statute of Limitations.

(a) Except as provided in subsection (e), an action to enforce the obligation of a party to pay a note payable at a definite time must be commenced within six years after the due date or dates stated in the note or, if a due date is accelerated, within six years after the accelerated due date.

(b) Except as provided in subsection (d) or (e), if demand for payment is made to the maker of a note payable on demand, an action to enforce the obligation of a party to pay the note must be commenced within six years after the demand. If no demand for payment is made to the maker, an action to enforce the note is barred if neither principal nor interest on the note has been paid for a continuous period of 10 years.

(c) Except as provided in subsection (d), an action to enforce the obligation of a party to an unaccepted draft to pay the draft must be commenced within three years after dishonor of the draft or 10 years after the date of the draft, whichever period expires first.

(d) An action to enforce the obligation of the acceptor of a certified check or the issuer of a teller's check, cashier's check, or traveler's check must be commenced within three years after demand for payment is made to the acceptor or issuer, as the case may be.

(e) An action to enforce the obligation of a party to a certificate of deposit to pay the instrument must be commenced within six years after demand for payment is made to the maker, but if the instrument states a due date and the maker is not required to pay before that date, the six-year period begins when a demand for payment is in effect and the due date has passed.

(f) An action to enforce the obligation of a party to pay an accepted draft, other than a certified check, must be commenced (i) within six years after the due date or dates stated in the draft or acceptance if the obligation of the acceptor is payable at a definite time, or (ii) within six years after the date of the acceptance if the obligation of the acceptor is payable on demand.

(g) Unless governed by other law regarding claims for indemnity or contribution, an action (i) for conversion of an instrument, for money had and received, or like action based on conversion, (ii) for breach of warranty, or (iii) to enforce an obligation, duty, or right arising under this Article and not governed by this section must be commenced within three years after the [cause of action] accrues.

§ 3–119. Notice of Right to Defend Action.

In an action for breach of an obligation for which a third person is answerable over pursuant to this Article or Article 4, the defendant may give the third person written notice of the litigation, and the person notified may then give similar notice to any other person who is answerable over. If the notice states (i) that the person notified may come in and defend and (ii) that failure to do so will bind the person notified in an action later brought by the person giving the notice as to any determination of fact common to the two litigations, the person notified is so bound unless after seasonable receipt of the notice the person notified does come in and defend.

PART 2 Negotiation, Transfer, and Indorsement

§ 3–201. Negotiation.

(a) "Negotiation" means a transfer of possession, whether voluntary or involuntary, of an instrument by a person other than the issuer to a person who thereby becomes its holder.

(b) Except for negotiation by a remitter, if an instrument is payable to an identified person, negotiation requires transfer of possession of the instrument and its indorsement by the holder. If an instrument is payable to bearer, it may be negotiated by transfer of possession alone.

§ 3–202. Negotiation Subject to Rescission.

(a) Negotiation is effective even if obtained (i) from an infant, a corporation exceeding its powers, or a person without capacity, (ii) by fraud, duress, or mistake, or (iii) in breach of duty or as part of an illegal transaction.

(b) To the extent permitted by other law, negotiation may be rescinded or may be subject to other remedies, but those remedies may not be asserted against a subsequent holder in due course or a person paying the instrument in good faith and without knowledge of facts that are a basis for rescission or other remedy.

§ 3–203. Transfer of Instrument; Rights Acquired by Transfer.

(a) An instrument is transferred when it is delivered by a person other than its issuer for the purpose of giving to the person receiving delivery the right to enforce the instrument.

(b) Transfer of an instrument, whether or not the transfer is a negotiation, vests in the transferee any right of the transferor to enforce the instrument, including any right as a holder in due course, but the transferee cannot acquire rights of a holder in due course by a transfer, directly or indirectly, from a holder in due course if the transferee engaged in fraud or illegality affecting the instrument.

(c) Unless otherwise agreed, if an instrument is transferred for value and the transferee does not become a holder because of lack of indorsement by the transferor, the transferee has a specifically enforceable right to the unqualified indorsement of the transferor, but negotiation of the instrument does not occur until the indorsement is made.

(d) If a transferor purports to transfer less than the entire instrument, negotiation of the instrument does not occur. The transferee obtains no rights under this Article and has only the rights of a partial assignee.

§ 3–204. Indorsement.

(a) "Indorsement" means a signature, other than that of a signer as maker, drawer, or acceptor, that alone or accompanied by other words is made on an instrument for the purpose of (i) negotiating the instrument, (ii) restricting payment of the instrument, or (iii) incurring indorser's liability on the instrument, but regardless of the intent of the signer, a signature and its accompanying words is an indorsement unless the accompanying words, terms of the instrument, place of the signature, or other circumstances unambiguously indicate that the signature was made for a purpose other than indorsement. For the purpose of determining whether a signature is made on an instrument, a paper affixed to the instrument is a part of the instrument.

(b) "Indorser" means a person who makes an indorsement.

(c) For the purpose of determining whether the transferee of an instrument is a holder, an indorsement that transfers a security interest in the instrument is effective as an unqualified indorsement of the instrument.

(d) If an instrument is payable to a holder under a name that is not the name of the holder, indorsement may be made by the holder in the name stated in the instrument or in the holder's name or both, but signature in both names may be required by a person paying or taking the instrument for value or collection.

§ 3–205. Special Indorsement; Blank Indorsement; Anomalous Indorsement.

(a) If an indorsement is made by the holder of an instrument, whether payable to an identified person or payable to bearer, and the indorsement identifies a person to whom it makes the instrument payable, it is a "special indorsement." When specially indorsed, an instrument becomes payable to the identified person and may be negotiated only by the indorsement of that person. The principles stated in Section 3–110 apply to special indorsements.

(b) If an indorsement is made by the holder of an instrument and it is not a special indorsement, it is a "blank indorsement." When indorsed in blank, an instrument becomes payable to bearer and may be negotiated by transfer of possession alone until specially indorsed.

(c) The holder may convert a blank indorsement that consists only of a signature into a special indorsement by writing, above the signature of the indorser, words identifying the person to whom the instrument is made payable.

(d) "Anomalous indorsement" means an indorsement made by a person who is not the holder of the instrument. An anomalous indorsement does not affect the manner in which the instrument may be negotiated.

§ 3–206. Restrictive Indorsement.

(a) An indorsement limiting payment to a particular person or otherwise prohibiting further transfer or negotiation of the instrument is not effective to prevent further transfer or negotiation of the instrument.

(b) An indorsement stating a condition to the right of the indorsee to receive payment does not affect the right of the indorsee to enforce the instrument. A person paying the instrument or taking it for value or collection may disregard the condition, and the rights and liabilities of that person are not affected by whether the condition has been fulfilled.

(c) If an instrument bears an indorsement (i) described in Section 4–201(b), or (ii) in blank or to a particular bank using the words "for deposit," "for collection," or other words indicating a purpose of having the instrument collected by a bank for the indorser or for a particular account, the following rules apply:

(1) A person, other than a bank, who purchases the instrument when so indorsed converts the instrument unless the amount paid for the instrument is received by the indorser or applied consistently with the indorsement.

(2) A depositary bank that purchases the instrument or takes it for collection when so indorsed converts the instrument unless the amount paid by the bank with respect to the instrument is received by the indorser or applied consistently with the indorsement.

(3) A payor bank that is also the depositary bank or that takes the instrument for immediate payment over the counter from a person other than a collecting bank converts the instrument unless the proceeds of the instrument are received by the indorser or applied consistently with the indorsement.

(4) Except as otherwise provided in paragraph (3), a payor bank or intermediary bank may disregard the indorsement and is not liable if the proceeds of the instrument are not received by the indorser or applied consistently with the indorsement.

(d) Except for an indorsement covered by subsection (c), if an instrument bears an indorsement using words to the effect that payment is to be made to the indorsee as agent, trustee, or other fiduciary for the benefit of the indorser or another person, the following rules apply:

(1) Unless there is notice of breach of fiduciary duty as provided in Section 3–307, a person who purchases the instrument from the indorsee or takes the instrument from the indorsee for collection or payment may pay the proceeds of payment or the value given for the instrument to the indorsee without regard to whether the indorsee violates a fiduciary duty to the indorser.

(2) A subsequent transferee of the instrument or person who pays the instrument is neither given notice nor otherwise affected by the restriction in the indorsement unless the transferee or payor knows that the fiduciary dealt with the instrument or its proceeds in breach of fiduciary duty.

(e) The presence on an instrument of an indorsement to which this section applies does not prevent a purchaser of the instrument from becoming a holder in due course of the instrument unless the purchaser is a converter under subsection (c) or has notice or knowledge of breach of fiduciary duty as stated in subsection (d).

(f) In an action to enforce the obligation of a party to pay the instrument, the obligor has a defense if payment would violate an indorsement to which this section applies and the payment is not permitted by this section.

§ 3–207. Reacquisition.

Reacquisition of an instrument occurs if it is transferred to a former holder, by negotiation or otherwise. A former holder who reacquires the instrument may cancel indorsements made after the reacquirer first became a holder of the instrument. If the cancellation causes the instrument to be payable to the reacquirer or to bearer, the reacquirer may negotiate the instrument. An indorser whose indorsement is canceled is discharged, and the discharge is effective against any subsequent holder.

PART 3   Enforcement of Instruments

§ 3–301. Person Entitled to Enforce Instrument.

"Person entitled to enforce" an instrument means (i) the holder of the instrument, (ii) a nonholder in possession of the instrument who has the rights of a holder, or (iii) a person not in possession of the instrument who is entitled to enforce the instrument pursuant to Section 3–309 or 3–418(d). A person may be a person entitled to enforce the instrument even though the person is not the owner of the instrument or is in wrongful possession of the instrument.

§ 3–302. Holder in Due Course.

(a) Subject to subsection (c) and Section 3–106(d), "holder in due course" means the holder of an instrument if:

(1) the instrument when issued or negotiated to the holder does not bear such apparent evidence of forgery or alteration

or is not otherwise so irregular or incomplete as to call into question its authenticity; and

(2) the holder took the instrument (i) for value, (ii) in good faith, (iii) without notice that the instrument is overdue or has been dishonored or that there is an uncured default with respect to payment of another instrument issued as part of the same series, (iv) without notice that the instrument contains an unauthorized signature or has been altered, (v) without notice of any claim to the instrument described in Section 3–306, and (vi) without notice that any party has a defense or claim in recoupment described in Section 3–305(a).

(b) Notice of discharge of a party, other than discharge in an insolvency proceeding, is not notice of a defense under subsection (a), but discharge is effective against a person who became a holder in due course with notice of the discharge. Public filing or recording of a document does not of itself constitute notice of a defense, claim in recoupment, or claim to the instrument.

(c) Except to the extent a transferor or predecessor in interest has rights as a holder in due course, a person does not acquire rights of a holder in due course of an instrument taken (i) by legal process or by purchase in an execution, bankruptcy, or creditor's sale or similar proceeding, (ii) by purchase as part of a bulk transaction not in ordinary course of business of the transferor, or (iii) as the successor in interest to an estate or other organization.

(d) If, under Section 3–303(a)(1), the promise of performance that is the consideration for an instrument has been partially performed, the holder may assert rights as a holder in due course of the instrument only to the fraction of the amount payable under the instrument equal to the value of the partial performance divided by the value of the promised performance.

(e) If (i) the person entitled to enforce an instrument has only a security interest in the instrument and (ii) the person obliged to pay the instrument has a defense, claim in recoupment, or claim to the instrument that may be asserted against the person who granted the security interest, the person entitled to enforce the instrument may assert rights as a holder in due course only to an amount payable under the instrument which, at the time of enforcement of the instrument, does not exceed the amount of the unpaid obligation secured.

(f) To be effective, notice must be received at a time and in a manner that gives a reasonable opportunity to act on it.

(g) This section is subject to any law limiting status as a holder in due course in particular classes of transactions.

§ 3–303. Value and Consideration.

(a) An instrument is issued or transferred for value if:

(1) the instrument is issued or transferred for a promise of performance, to the extent the promise has been performed;

(2) the transferee acquires a security interest or other lien in the instrument other than a lien obtained by judicial proceeding;

(3) the instrument is issued or transferred as payment of, or as security for, an antecedent claim against any person, whether or not the claim is due;

(4) the instrument is issued or transferred in exchange for a negotiable instrument; or

(5) the instrument is issued or transferred in exchange for the incurring of an irrevocable obligation to a third party by the person taking the instrument.

(b) "Consideration" means any consideration sufficient to support a simple contract. The drawer or maker of an instrument has a defense if the instrument is issued without consideration. If an instrument is issued for a promise of performance, the issuer has a defense to the extent performance of the promise is due and the promise has not been performed. If an instrument is issued for value as stated in subsection (a), the instrument is also issued for consideration.

§ 3–304. Overdue Instrument.

(a) An instrument payable on demand becomes overdue at the earliest of the following times:

(1) on the day after the day demand for payment is duly made;

(2) if the instrument is a check, 90 days after its date; or

(3) if the instrument is not a check, when the instrument has been outstanding for a period of time after its date which is unreasonably long under the circumstances of the particular case in light of the nature of the instrument and usage of the trade.

(b) With respect to an instrument payable at a definite time the following rules apply:

(1) If the principal is payable in installments and a due date has not been accelerated, the instrument becomes overdue upon default under the instrument for nonpayment of an installment, and the instrument remains overdue until the default is cured.

(2) If the principal is not payable in installments and the due date has not been accelerated, the instrument becomes overdue on the day after the due date.

(3) If a due date with respect to principal has been accelerated, the instrument becomes overdue on the day after the accelerated due date.

(c) Unless the due date of principal has been accelerated, an instrument does not become overdue if there is default in payment of interest but no default in payment of principal.

§ 3–305. Defenses and Claims in Recoupment.

(a) Except as stated in subsection (b), the right to enforce the obligation of a party to pay an instrument is subject to the following:

(1) a defense of the obligor based on (i) infancy of the obligor to the extent it is a defense to a simple contract, (ii) duress, lack of legal capacity, or illegality of the transaction which, under other law, nullifies the obligation of the obligor, (iii) fraud that induced the obligor to sign the instrument with neither knowledge nor reasonable opportunity to learn of its character or its essential terms, or (iv) discharge of the obligor in insolvency proceedings;

(2) a defense of the obligor stated in another section of this Article or a defense of the obligor that would be available if the person entitled to enforce the instrument were enforcing a right to payment under a simple contract; and

(3) a claim in recoupment of the obligor against the original payee of the instrument if the claim arose from the transaction that gave rise to the instrument; but the claim of the obligor may be asserted against a transferee of the instrument only to reduce the amount owing on the instrument at the time the action is brought.

(b) The right of a holder in due course to enforce the obligation of a party to pay the instrument is subject to defenses of the obligor stated in subsection (a)(1), but is not subject to defenses of the obligor stated in subsection (a)(2) or claims in recoupment stated in subsection (a)(3) against a person other than the holder.

(c) Except as stated in subsection (d), in an action to enforce the obligation of a party to pay the instrument, the obligor may not assert against the person entitled to enforce the instrument a defense, claim in recoupment, or claim to the instrument (Section 3–306) of another person, but the other person's claim to the instrument may be asserted by the obligor if the other person is joined in the action and personally asserts the claim against the person entitled to enforce the instrument. An obligor is not obliged to pay the instrument if the person seeking enforcement of the instrument does not have rights of a holder in due course and the obligor proves that the instrument is a lost or stolen instrument.

(d) In an action to enforce the obligation of an accommodation party to pay an instrument, the accommodation party may assert against the person entitled to enforce the instrument any defense or claim in recoupment under subsection (a) that the accommodated party could assert against the person entitled to enforce the instrument, except the defenses of discharge in insolvency proceedings, infancy, and lack of legal capacity.

§ 3–306. Claims to an Instrument.

A person taking an instrument, other than a person having rights of a holder in due course, is subject to a claim of a property or possessory right in the instrument or its proceeds, including a claim to rescind a negotiation and to recover the instrument or its proceeds. A person having rights of a holder in due course takes free of the claim to the instrument.

§ 3–307. Notice of Breach of Fiduciary Duty.

(a) In this section:

(1) "Fiduciary" means an agent, trustee, partner, corporate officer or director, or other representative owing a fiduciary duty with respect to an instrument.

(2) "Represented person" means the principal, beneficiary, partnership, corporation, or other person to whom the duty stated in paragraph (1) is owed.

(b) If (i) an instrument is taken from a fiduciary for payment or collection or for value, (ii) the taker has knowledge of the fiduciary status of the fiduciary, and (iii) the represented person makes a claim to the instrument or its proceeds on the basis that the transaction of the fiduciary is a breach of fiduciary duty, the following rules apply:

(1) Notice of breach of fiduciary duty by the fiduciary is notice of the claim of the represented person.

(2) In the case of an instrument payable to the represented person or the fiduciary as such, the taker has notice of the breach of fiduciary duty if the instrument is (i) taken in payment of or as security for a debt known by the taker to be the personal debt of the fiduciary, (ii) taken in a transaction known by the taker to be for the personal benefit of the fiduciary, or (iii) deposited to an account other than an account of the fiduciary, as such, or an account of the represented person.

(3) If an instrument is issued by the represented person or the fiduciary as such, and made payable to the fiduciary personally, the taker does not have notice of the breach of fiduciary duty unless the taker knows of the breach of fiduciary duty.

(4) If an instrument is issued by the represented person or the fiduciary as such, to the taker as payee, the taker has notice of the breach of fiduciary duty if the instrument is (i) taken in payment of or as security for a debt known by the taker to be the personal debt of the fiduciary, (ii) taken in a transaction known by the taker to be for the personal benefit of the fiduciary, or (iii) deposited to an account other than an account of the fiduciary, as such, or an account of the represented person.

§ 3–308. Proof of Signatures and Status as Holder in Due Course.

(a) In an action with respect to an instrument, the authenticity of, and authority to make, each signature on the instrument is admitted unless specifically denied in the pleadings. If the validity of a signature is denied in the pleadings, the burden of establishing validity is on the person claiming validity, but the signature is presumed to be authentic and authorized unless the action is to enforce the liability of the purported signer and the signer is dead or incompetent at the time of trial of the issue of validity of the signature. If an action to enforce the instrument is brought against a person as the undisclosed principal of a person who signed the instrument as a party to the instrument, the plaintiff has the burden of establishing that the defendant is liable on the instrument as a represented person under Section 3–402(a).

(b) If the validity of signatures is admitted or proved and there is compliance with subsection (a), a plaintiff producing the instrument is entitled to payment if the plaintiff proves entitlement to enforce the instrument under Section 3–301, unless the defendant proves a defense or claim in recoupment. If a defense or claim in recoupment is proved, the right to payment of the plaintiff is subject to the defense or claim, except to the extent the plaintiff proves that the plaintiff has rights of a holder in due course which are not subject to the defense or claim.

§ 3–309. Enforcement of Lost, Destroyed, or Stolen Instrument.

(a) A person not in possession of an instrument is entitled to enforce the instrument if (i) the person was in possession of the instrument and entitled to enforce it when loss of possession occurred, (ii) the loss of possession was not the result of a transfer by the person or a lawful seizure, and (iii) the person cannot reasonably obtain possession of the instrument because the instrument was destroyed, its whereabouts cannot be determined, or it is in the wrongful possession of an unknown person or a person that cannot be found or is not amenable to service of process.

(b) A person seeking enforcement of an instrument under subsection (a) must prove the terms of the instrument and the person's right to enforce the instrument. If that proof is made, Section 3–308 applies to the case as if the person seeking enforcement had produced the instrument. The court may not enter judgment in favor of the person seeking enforcement unless it finds that the person required to pay the instrument is adequately protected against loss that might occur by reason of a claim by another person to enforce the instrument. Adequate protection may be provided by any reasonable means.

§ 3–310. Effect of Instrument on Obligation for Which Taken.

(a) Unless otherwise agreed, if a certified check, cashier's check, or teller's check is taken for an obligation, the obligation is discharged to the same extent discharge would result if an amount of money equal to the amount of the instrument were taken in payment of the obligation. Discharge of the obligation does not affect any liability that the obligor may have as an indorser of the instrument.

(b) Unless otherwise agreed and except as provided in subsection (a), if a note or an uncertified check is taken for an obligation, the obligation is suspended to the same extent the obligation would be discharged if an amount of money equal to the amount of the instrument were taken, and the following rules apply:

(1) In the case of an uncertified check, suspension of the obligation continues until dishonor of the check or until it is paid or certified. Payment or certification of the check results in discharge of the obligation to the extent of the amount of the check.

(2) In the case of a note, suspension of the obligation continues until dishonor of the note or until it is paid. Payment of the note results in discharge of the obligation to the extent of the payment.

(3) Except as provided in paragraph (4), if the check or note is dishonored and the obligee of the obligation for which the instrument was taken is the person entitled to enforce the instrument, the obligee may enforce either the instrument or the obligation. In the case of an instrument of a third person which is negotiated to the obligee by the obligor, discharge of the obligor on the instrument also discharges the obligation.

(4) If the person entitled to enforce the instrument taken for an obligation is a person other than the obligee, the obligee may not enforce the obligation to the extent the obligation is suspended. If the obligee is the person entitled to enforce the instrument but no longer has possession of it because it was lost, stolen, or destroyed, the obligation may not be enforced to the extent of the amount payable on the instrument, and to that extent the obligee's rights against the obligor are limited to enforcement of the instrument.

(c) If an instrument other than one described in subsection (a) or (b) is taken for an obligation, the effect is (i) that stated in subsection (a) if the instrument is one on which a bank is liable as maker or acceptor, or (ii) that stated in subsection (b) in any other case.

§ 3–311. Accord and Satisfaction by Use of Instrument.

(a) If a person against whom a claim is asserted proves that (i) that person in good faith tendered an instrument to the claimant as full satisfaction of the claim, (ii) the amount of the claim was unliquidated or subject to a bona fide dispute, and (iii) the claimant obtained payment of the instrument, the following subsections apply.

(b) Unless subsection (c) applies, the claim is discharged if the person against whom the claim is asserted proves that the instrument or an accompanying written communication contained a conspicuous statement to the effect that the instrument was tendered as full satisfaction of the claim.

(c) Subject to subsection (d), a claim is not discharged under subsection (b) if either of the following applies:

(1) The claimant, if an organization, proves that (i) within a reasonable time before the tender, the claimant sent a conspicuous statement to the person against whom the claim is asserted that communications concerning disputed debts, including an instrument tendered as full satisfaction of a debt, are to be sent to a designated person, office, or place, and (ii) the instrument or accompanying communication was not received by that designated person, office, or place.

(2) The claimant, whether or not an organization, proves that within 90 days after payment of the instrument, the claimant tendered repayment of the amount of the instrument to the person against whom the claim is asserted. This paragraph does not apply if the claimant is an organization that sent a statement complying with paragraph (1)(i).

(d) A claim is discharged if the person against whom the claim is asserted proves that within a reasonable time before collection of the instrument was initiated, the claimant, or an agent of the claimant having direct responsibility with respect to the disputed obligation, knew that the instrument was tendered in full satisfaction of the claim.

§ 3–312. Lost, Destroyed, or Stolen Cashier's Check, Teller's Check, or Certified Check.*

(a) In this section:

(1) "Check" means a cashier's check, teller's check, or certified check.

(2) "Claimant" means a person who claims the right to receive the amount of a cashier's check, teller's check, or certified check that was lost, destroyed, or stolen.

(3) "Declaration of loss" means a written statement, made under penalty of perjury, to the effect that (i) the declarer lost possession of a check, (ii) the declarer is the drawer or payee of the check, in the case of a certified check, or the remitter or payee of the check, in the case of a cashier's check or teller's check, (iii) the loss of possession was not the result of a transfer by the declarer or a lawful seizure, and (iv) the declarer cannot reasonably obtain possession of the check because the check was destroyed, its whereabouts cannot be determined, or it is in the wrongful possession of an unknown person or a person that cannot be found or is not amenable to service of process.

(4) "Obligated bank" means the issuer of a cashier's check or teller's check or the acceptor of a certified check.

(b) A claimant may assert a claim to the amount of a check by a communication to the obligated bank describing the check with reasonable certainty and requesting payment of the amount of the check, if (i) the claimant is the drawer or payee of a certified check or the remitter or payee of a cashier's check or teller's check, (ii) the communication contains or is accompanied by a declaration of loss of the claimant with respect to the check, (iii) the communication is received at a time and in a manner affording the bank a reasonable time to act on it before the check is paid, and (iv) the claimant provides reasonable identification if requested by the obligated bank. Delivery of a declaration of loss is a warranty of the truth of the statements made in the declaration. If a claim is asserted in compliance with this subsection, the following rules apply:

(1) The claim becomes enforceable at the later of (i) the time the claim is asserted, or (ii) the 90th day following the date of the check, in the case of a cashier's check or teller's check, or the 90th day following the date of the acceptance, in the case of a certified check.

(2) Until the claim becomes enforceable, it has no legal effect and the obligated bank may pay the check or, in the case of a teller's check, may permit the drawee to pay the check. Payment to a person entitled to enforce the check discharges all liability of the obligated bank with respect to the check.

(3) If the claim becomes enforceable before the check is presented for payment, the obligated bank is not obliged to pay the check.

(4) When the claim becomes enforceable, the obligated bank becomes obliged to pay the amount of the check to the claimant if payment of the check has not been made to a person entitled to enforce the check. Subject to Section 4–302(a)(1), payment to the claimant discharges all liability of the obligated bank with respect to the check.

(c) If the obligated bank pays the amount of a check to a claimant under subsection (b)(4) and the check is presented for payment by a person having rights of a holder in due course, the claimant is obliged to (i) refund the payment to the obligated bank if the check is paid, or (ii) pay the amount of the check to the person having rights of a holder in due course if the check is dishonored.

(d) If a claimant has the right to assert a claim under subsection (b) and is also a person entitled to enforce a cashier's check, teller's check, or certified check which is lost, destroyed, or stolen, the claimant may assert rights with respect to the check either under this section or Section 3–309.

Added in 1991.

PART 4 Liability of Parties

§ 3–401. Signature.

(a) A person is not liable on an instrument unless (i) the person signed the instrument, or (ii) the person is represented by an agent or representative who signed the instrument and the signature is binding on the represented person under Section 3–402.

(b) A signature may be made (i) manually or by means of a device or machine, and (ii) by the use of any name, including a trade or assumed name, or by a word, mark, or symbol executed or adopted by a person with present intention to authenticate a writing.

§ 3–402. Signature by Representative.

(a) If a person acting, or purporting to act, as a representative signs an instrument by signing either the name of the represented person or the name of the signer, the represented person is bound by the signature to the same extent the represented person would be bound if the signature were on a simple contract. If the represented person is bound, the signature of the representative is the "authorized signature of the represented person" and the represented person is liable on the instrument, whether or not identified in the instrument.

(b) If a representative signs the name of the representative to an instrument and the signature is an authorized signature of the represented person, the following rules apply:

(1) If the form of the signature shows unambiguously that the signature is made on behalf of the represented person who is identified in the instrument, the representative is not liable on the instrument.

(2) Subject to subsection (c), if (i) the form of the signature does not show unambiguously that the signature is made in a representative capacity or (ii) the represented person is not identified in the instrument, the representative is liable on the instrument to a holder in due course that took the instrument without notice that the representative was not intended to be liable on the instrument. With respect to any other person, the representative is liable on the instrument unless the representative proves that the original parties did not intend the representative to be liable on the instrument.

(c) If a representative signs the name of the representative as drawer of a check without indication of the representative status and the check is payable from an account of the represented person who is identified on the check, the signer is not liable on the check if the signature is an authorized signature of the represented person.

§ 3–403. Unauthorized Signature.

(a) Unless otherwise provided in this Article or Article 4, an unauthorized signature is ineffective except as the signature of the unauthorized signer in favor of a person who in good faith pays the instrument or takes it for value. An unauthorized signature may be ratified for all purposes of this Article.

(b) If the signature of more than one person is required to constitute the authorized signature of an organization, the signature of the organization is unauthorized if one of the required signatures is lacking.

(c) The civil or criminal liability of a person who makes an unauthorized signature is not affected by any provision of this Article which makes the unauthorized signature effective for the purposes of this Article.

§ 3–404. Impostors; Fictitious Payees.

(a) If an impostor, by use of the mails or otherwise, induces the issuer of an instrument to issue the instrument to the impostor, or to a person acting in concert with the impostor, by impersonating the payee of the instrument or a person authorized to act for the payee, an indorsement of the instrument by any person in the name of the payee is effective as the indorsement of the payee in favor of a person who, in good faith, pays the instrument or takes it for value or for collection.

(b) If (i) a person whose intent determines to whom an instrument is payable (Section 3–110(a) or (b)) does not intend the person identified as payee to have any interest in the instrument, or (ii) the person identified as payee of an instrument is a fictitious person, the following rules apply until the instrument is negotiated by special indorsement:

(1) Any person in possession of the instrument is its holder.

(2) An indorsement by any person in the name of the payee stated in the instrument is effective as the indorsement of the payee in favor of a person who, in good faith, pays the instrument or takes it for value or for collection.

(c) Under subsection (a) or (b), an indorsement is made in the name of a payee if (i) it is made in a name substantially similar to that of the payee or (ii) the instrument, whether or not indorsed, is deposited in a depositary bank to an account in a name substantially similar to that of the payee.

(d) With respect to an instrument to which subsection (a) or (b) applies, if a person paying the instrument or taking it for value or for collection fails to exercise ordinary care in paying or taking the instrument and that failure substantially contributes to loss resulting from payment of the instrument, the person bearing the loss may recover from the person failing to exercise ordinary care to the extent the failure to exercise ordinary care contributed to the loss.

§ 3–405. Employer's Responsibility for Fraudulent Indorsement by Employee.

(a) In this section:

(1) "Employee" includes an independent contractor and employee of an independent contractor retained by the employer.

(2) "Fraudulent indorsement" means (i) in the case of an instrument payable to the employer, a forged indorsement purporting to be that of the employer, or (ii) in the case of an instrument with respect to which the employer is the issuer, a forged indorsement purporting to be that of the person identified as payee.

(3) "Responsibility" with respect to instruments means authority (i) to sign or indorse instruments on behalf of the employer, (ii) to process instruments received by the employer for bookkeeping purposes, for deposit to an account, or for other disposition, (iii) to prepare or process instruments for issue in the name of the employer, (iv) to supply information determining the names or addresses of payees of instruments to be issued in the name of the employer, (v) to control the disposition of instruments to be issued in the name of the employer, or (vi) to act otherwise with respect to instruments in a responsible capacity. "Responsibility" does not include authority that merely allows an employee to have access to instruments or blank or incomplete instrument forms that are being stored or transported or are part of incoming or outgoing mail, or similar access.

(b) For the purpose of determining the rights and liabilities of a person who, in good faith, pays an instrument or takes it for value or for collection, if an employer entrusted an employee with responsibility with respect to the instrument and the employee or a person acting in concert with the employee makes a fraudulent indorsement of the instrument, the indorsement is effective as the indorsement of the person to whom the instrument is payable if it is made in the name of that person. If the person paying the instrument or taking it for value or for collection fails to exercise ordinary care in paying or taking the instrument and that failure substantially contributes to loss resulting from the fraud, the person bearing the loss may recover from the person failing to exercise ordinary care to the extent the failure to exercise ordinary care contributed to the loss.

(c) Under subsection (b), an indorsement is made in the name of the person to whom an instrument is payable if (i) it is made in a name substantially similar to the name of that person or (ii) the instrument, whether or not indorsed, is deposited in a depositary bank to an account in a name substantially similar to the name of that person.

§ 3–406. Negligence Contributing to Forged Signature or Alteration of Instrument.

(a) A person whose failure to exercise ordinary care substantially contributes to an alteration of an instrument or to the making of a forged signature on an instrument is precluded from asserting the alteration or the forgery against a person who, in good faith, pays the instrument or takes it for value or for collection.

(b) Under subsection (a), if the person asserting the preclusion fails to exercise ordinary care in paying or taking the instrument and that failure substantially contributes to loss, the loss is allocated between the person precluded and the person asserting the preclusion according to the extent to which the failure of each to exercise ordinary care contributed to the loss.

(c) Under subsection (a), the burden of proving failure to exercise ordinary care is on the person asserting the preclusion. Under subsection (b), the burden of proving failure to exercise ordinary care is on the person precluded.

§ 3–407. Alteration.

(a) "Alteration" means (i) an unauthorized change in an instrument that purports to modify in any respect the obligation of a party, or (ii) an unauthorized addition of words or numbers or other change to an incomplete instrument relating to the obligation of a party.

(b) Except as provided in subsection (c), an alteration fraudulently made discharges a party whose obligation is affected by the alteration unless that party assents or is precluded from asserting the alteration. No other alteration discharges a party, and the instrument may be enforced according to its original terms.

(c) A payor bank or drawee paying a fraudulently altered instrument or a person taking it for value, in good faith and without notice of the alteration, may enforce rights with respect to the instrument (i) according to its original terms, or (ii) in the case of an incomplete instrument altered by unauthorized completion, according to its terms as completed.

§ 3–408. Drawee Not Liable on Unaccepted Draft.

A check or other draft does not of itself operate as an assignment of funds in the hands of the drawee available for its payment, and the drawee is not liable on the instrument until the drawee accepts it.

§ 3–409. Acceptance of Draft; Certified Check.

(a) "Acceptance" means the drawee's signed agreement to pay a draft as presented. It must be written on the draft and may consist of the drawee's signature alone. Acceptance may be made at any time and becomes effective when notification pursuant to instructions is given or the accepted draft is delivered for the purpose of giving rights on the acceptance to any person.

(b) A draft may be accepted although it has not been signed by the drawer, is otherwise incomplete, is overdue, or has been dishonored.

(c) If a draft is payable at a fixed period after sight and the acceptor fails to date the acceptance, the holder may complete the acceptance by supplying a date in good faith.

(d) "Certified check" means a check accepted by the bank on which it is drawn. Acceptance may be made as stated in subsection (a) or by a writing on the check which indicates that the check is certified. The drawee of a check has no obligation to certify the check, and refusal to certify is not dishonor of the check.

§ 3–410. Acceptance Varying Draft.

(a) If the terms of a drawee's acceptance vary from the terms of the draft as presented, the holder may refuse the acceptance and treat the draft as dishonored. In that case, the drawee may cancel the acceptance.

(b) The terms of a draft are not varied by an acceptance to pay at a particular bank or place in the United States, unless the acceptance states that the draft is to be paid only at that bank or place.

(c) If the holder assents to an acceptance varying the terms of a draft, the obligation of each drawer and indorser that does not expressly assent to the acceptance is discharged.

§ 3–411. Refusal to Pay Cashier's Checks, Teller's Checks, and Certified Checks.

(a) In this section, "obligated bank" means the acceptor of a certified check or the issuer of a cashier's check or teller's check bought from the issuer.

(b) If the obligated bank wrongfully (i) refuses to pay a cashier's check or certified check, (ii) stops payment of a teller's check, or (iii) refuses to pay a dishonored teller's check, the person asserting the right to enforce the check is entitled to compensation for expenses and loss of interest resulting from the nonpayment and may recover consequential damages if the obligated bank refuses to pay after receiving notice of particular circumstances giving rise to the damages.

(c) Expenses or consequential damages under subsection (b) are not recoverable if the refusal of the obligated bank to pay occurs because (i) the bank suspends payments, (ii) the obligated bank asserts a claim or defense of the bank that it has reasonable grounds to believe is available against the person entitled to enforce the instrument, (iii) the obligated bank has a reasonable doubt whether the person demanding payment is the person entitled to enforce the instrument, or (iv) payment is prohibited by law.

§ 3–412. Obligation of Issuer of Note or Cashier's Check.

The issuer of a note or cashier's check or other draft drawn on the drawer is obliged to pay the instrument (i) according to its terms at the time it was issued or, if not issued, at the time it first came into possession of a holder, or (ii) if the issuer signed an incomplete instrument, according to its terms when completed, to the extent stated in Sections 3–115 and 3–407. The obligation is owed to a person entitled to enforce the instrument or to an indorser who paid the instrument under Section 3–415.

§ 3–413. Obligation of Acceptor.

(a) The acceptor of a draft is obliged to pay the draft (i) according to its terms at the time it was accepted, even though the acceptance states that the draft is payable "as originally drawn" or equivalent terms, (ii) if the acceptance varies the terms of the draft, according to the terms of the draft as varied, or (iii) if the acceptance is of a draft that is an incomplete instrument, according to its terms when completed, to the extent stated in Sections 3–115 and 3–407. The obligation is owed to a person entitled to enforce the draft or to the drawer or an indorser who paid the draft under Section 3–414 or 3–415.

(b) If the certification of a check or other acceptance of a draft states the amount certified or accepted, the obligation of the acceptor is that amount. If (i) the certification or acceptance does not state an amount, (ii) the amount of the instrument is subsequently raised, and (iii) the instrument is then negotiated to a holder in due course, the obligation of the acceptor is the amount of the instrument at the time it was taken by the holder in due course.

§ 3–414. Obligation of Drawer.

(a) This section does not apply to cashier's checks or other drafts drawn on the drawer.

(b) If an unaccepted draft is dishonored, the drawer is obliged to pay the draft (i) according to its terms at the time it was issued or, if not issued, at the time it first came into possession of a holder, or (ii) if the drawer signed an incomplete instrument, according to its terms when completed, to the extent stated in Sections 3–115 and 3–407. The obligation is owed to a person entitled to enforce the draft or to an indorser who paid the draft under Section 3–415.

(c) If a draft is accepted by a bank, the drawer is discharged, regardless of when or by whom acceptance was obtained.

(d) If a draft is accepted and the acceptor is not a bank, the obligation of the drawer to pay the draft if the draft is dishonored by the acceptor is the same as the obligation of an indorser under Section 3–415(a) and (c).

(e) If a draft states that it is drawn "without recourse" or otherwise disclaims liability of the drawer to pay the draft, the drawer is not liable under subsection (b) to pay the draft if the draft is not a check. A disclaimer of the liability stated in subsection (b) is not effective if the draft is a check.

(f) If (i) a check is not presented for payment or given to a depositary bank for collection within 30 days after its date, (ii) the drawee suspends payments after expiration of the 30-day period without paying the check, and (iii) because of the suspension of payments, the drawer is deprived of funds maintained with the drawee to cover payment of the check, the drawer to the extent deprived of funds may discharge its obligation to pay the check by assigning to the person entitled to enforce the check the rights of the drawer against the drawee with respect to the funds.

§ 3–415. Obligation of Indorser.

(a) Subject to subsections (b), (c), and (d) and to Section 3–419(d), if an instrument is dishonored, an indorser is obliged to pay the amount due on the instrument (i) according to the terms of the instrument at the time it was indorsed, or (ii) if the indorser indorsed an incomplete instrument, according to its terms when completed, to the extent stated in Sections 3–115 and 3–407. The obligation of the indorser is owed to a person entitled to enforce the instrument or to a subsequent indorser who paid the instrument under this section.

(b) If an indorsement states that it is made "without recourse" or otherwise disclaims liability of the indorser, the indorser is not liable under subsection (a) to pay the instrument.

(c) If notice of dishonor of an instrument is required by Section 3–503 and notice of dishonor complying with that section is not given to an indorser, the liability of the indorser under subsection (a) is discharged.

(d) If a draft is accepted by a bank after an indorsement is made, the liability of the indorser under subsection (a) is discharged.

(e) If an indorser of a check is liable under subsection (a) and the check is not presented for payment, or given to a depositary bank for collection, within 30 days after the day the indorsement was made, the liability of the indorser under subsection (a) is discharged.

As amended in 1993.

§ 3–416. Transfer Warranties.

(a) A person who transfers an instrument for consideration warrants to the transferee and, if the transfer is by indorsement, to any subsequent transferee that:

(1) the warrantor is a person entitled to enforce the instrument;
(2) all signatures on the instrument are authentic and authorized;
(3) the instrument has not been altered;
(4) the instrument is not subject to a defense or claim in recoupment of any party which can be asserted against the warrantor; and
(5) the warrantor has no knowledge of any insolvency proceeding commenced with respect to the maker or acceptor or, in the case of an unaccepted draft, the drawer.

(b) A person to whom the warranties under subsection (a) are made and who took the instrument in good faith may recover from the warrantor as damages for breach of warranty an amount equal to the loss suffered as a result of the breach, but not more than the amount of the instrument plus expenses and loss of interest incurred as a result of the breach.

(c) The warranties stated in subsection (a) cannot be disclaimed with respect to checks. Unless notice of a claim for breach of warranty is given to the warrantor within 30 days after the claimant has reason to know of the breach and the identity of the warrantor, the liability of the warrantor under subsection (b) is discharged to the extent of any loss caused by the delay in giving notice of the claim.

(d) A [cause of action] for breach of warranty under this section accrues when the claimant has reason to know of the breach.

§ 3–417. Presentment Warranties.

(a) If an unaccepted draft is presented to the drawee for payment or acceptance and the drawee pays or accepts the draft, (i) the person obtaining payment or acceptance, at the time of presentment, and (ii) a previous transferor of the draft, at the time of transfer, warrant to the drawee making payment or accepting the draft in good faith that:

(1) the warrantor is, or was, at the time the warrantor transferred the draft, a person entitled to enforce the draft or authorized to obtain payment or acceptance of the draft on behalf of a person entitled to enforce the draft;

(2) the draft has not been altered; and

(3) the warrantor has no knowledge that the signature of the drawer of the draft is unauthorized.

(b) A drawee making payment may recover from any warrantor damages for breach of warranty equal to the amount paid by the drawee less the amount the drawee received or is entitled to receive from the drawer because of the payment. In addition, the drawee is entitled to compensation for expenses and loss of interest resulting from the breach. The right of the drawee to recover damages under this subsection is not affected by any failure of the drawee to exercise ordinary care in making payment. If the drawee accepts the draft, breach of warranty is a defense to the obligation of the acceptor. If the acceptor makes payment with respect to the draft, the acceptor is entitled to recover from any warrantor for breach of warranty the amounts stated in this subsection.

(c) If a drawee asserts a claim for breach of warranty under subsection (a) based on an unauthorized indorsement of the draft or an alteration of the draft, the warrantor may defend by proving that the indorsement is effective under Section 3–404 or 3–405 or the drawer is precluded under Section 3–406 or 4–406 from asserting against the drawee the unauthorized indorsement or alteration.

(d) If (i) a dishonored draft is presented for payment to the drawer or an indorser or (ii) any other instrument is presented for payment to a party obliged to pay the instrument, and (iii) payment is received, the following rules apply:

(1) The person obtaining payment and a prior transferor of the instrument warrant to the person making payment in good faith that the warrantor is, or was, at the time the warrantor transferred the instrument, a person entitled to enforce the instrument or authorized to obtain payment on behalf of a person entitled to enforce the instrument.

(2) The person making payment may recover from any warrantor for breach of warranty an amount equal to the amount paid plus expenses and loss of interest resulting from the breach.

(e) The warranties stated in subsections (a) and (d) cannot be disclaimed with respect to checks. Unless notice of a claim for breach of warranty is given to the warrantor within 30 days after the claimant has reason to know of the breach and the identity of the warrantor, the liability of the warrantor under subsection (b) or (d) is discharged to the extent of any loss caused by the delay in giving notice of the claim.

(f) A [cause of action] for breach of warranty under this section accrues when the claimant has reason to know of the breach.

§ 3–418. Payment or Acceptance by Mistake.

(a) Except as provided in subsection (c), if the drawee of a draft pays or accepts the draft and the drawee acted on the mistaken belief that (i) payment of the draft had not been

stopped pursuant to Section 4–403 or (ii) the signature of the drawer of the draft was authorized, the drawee may recover the amount of the draft from the person to whom or for whose benefit payment was made or, in the case of acceptance, may revoke the acceptance. Rights of the drawee under this subsection are not affected by failure of the drawee to exercise ordinary care in paying or accepting the draft.

(b) Except as provided in subsection (c), if an instrument has been paid or accepted by mistake and the case is not covered by subsection (a), the person paying or accepting may, to the extent permitted by the law governing mistake and restitution, (i) recover the payment from the person to whom or for whose benefit payment was made or (ii) in the case of acceptance, may revoke the acceptance.

(c) The remedies provided by subsection (a) or (b) may not be asserted against a person who took the instrument in good faith and for value or who in good faith changed position in reliance on the payment or acceptance. This subsection does not limit remedies provided by Section 3–417 or 4–407.

(d) Notwithstanding Section 4–215, if an instrument is paid or accepted by mistake and the payor or acceptor recovers payment or revokes acceptance under subsection (a) or (b), the instrument is deemed not to have been paid or accepted and is treated as dishonored, and the person from whom payment is recovered has rights as a person entitled to enforce the dishonored instrument.

§ 3–419. Instruments Signed for Accommodation.

(a) If an instrument is issued for value given for the benefit of a party to the instrument ("accommodated party") and another party to the instrument ("accommodation party") signs the instrument for the purpose of incurring liability on the instrument without being a direct beneficiary of the value given for the instrument, the instrument is signed by the accommodation party "for accommodation."

(b) An accommodation party may sign the instrument as maker, drawer, acceptor, or indorser and, subject to subsection (d), is obliged to pay the instrument in the capacity in which the accommodation party signs. The obligation of an accommodation party may be enforced notwithstanding any statute of frauds and whether or not the accommodation party receives consideration for the accommodation.

(c) A person signing an instrument is presumed to be an accommodation party and there is notice that the instrument is signed for accommodation if the signature is an anomalous indorsement or is accompanied by words indicating that the signer is acting as surety or guarantor with respect to the obligation of another party to the instrument. Except as provided in Section 3–605, the obligation of an accommodation party to pay the instrument is not affected by the fact that the person enforcing the obligation had notice when the instrument was taken by that person that the accommodation party signed the instrument for accommodation.

(d) If the signature of a party to an instrument is accompanied by words indicating unambiguously that the party is guaranteeing collection rather than payment of the obligation of another party to the instrument, the signer is obliged to pay the amount due on the instrument to a person entitled to enforce the instrument only if (i) execution of judgment against the other party has been returned unsatisfied, (ii) the other party is insolvent or in an insolvency proceeding, (iii) the other party cannot be served with process, or (iv) it is otherwise apparent that payment cannot be obtained from the other party.

(e) An accommodation party who pays the instrument is entitled to reimbursement from the accommodated party and is entitled to enforce the instrument against the accommodated party. An accommodated party who pays the instrument has no right of recourse against, and is not entitled to contribution from, an accommodation party.

§ 3–420. Conversion of Instrument.

(a) The law applicable to conversion of personal property applies to instruments. An instrument is also converted if it is taken by transfer, other than a negotiation, from a person not entitled to enforce the instrument or a bank makes or obtains payment with respect to the instrument for a person not entitled to enforce the instrument or receive payment. An action for conversion of an instrument may not be brought by (i) the issuer or acceptor of the instrument or (ii) a payee or indorsee who did not receive delivery of the instrument either directly or through delivery to an agent or a co-payee.

(b) In an action under subsection (a), the measure of liability is presumed to be the amount payable on the instrument, but recovery may not exceed the amount of the plaintiff's interest in the instrument.

(c) A representative, other than a depositary bank, who has in good faith dealt with an instrument or its proceeds on behalf of one who was not the person entitled to enforce the instrument is not liable in conversion to that person beyond the amount of any proceeds that it has not paid out.

PART 5 Dishonor

§ 3–501. Presentment.

(a) "Presentment" means a demand made by or on behalf of a person entitled to enforce an instrument (i) to pay the instrument made to the drawee or a party obliged to pay the instrument or, in the case of a note or accepted draft payable at a bank, to the bank, or (ii) to accept a draft made to the drawee.

(b) The following rules are subject to Article 4, agreement of the parties, and clearing-house rules and the like:

(1) Presentment may be made at the place of payment of the instrument and must be made at the place of payment if the instrument is payable at a bank in the United States; may be made by any commercially reasonable means, including an oral, written, or electronic communication; is effective when the demand for payment or acceptance is received by the person to whom presentment is made; and is effective if made to any one of two or more makers, acceptors, drawees, or other payors.

(2) Upon demand of the person to whom presentment is made, the person making presentment must (i) exhibit the instrument, (ii) give reasonable identification and, if presentment is made on behalf of another person, reasonable evidence of authority to do so, and (...) sign a receipt on the instrument for any payment made or surrender the instrument if full payment is made.

(3) Without dishonoring the instrument, the party to whom presentment is made may (i) return the instrument for lack of a necessary indorsement, or (ii) refuse payment or acceptance for failure of the presentment to comply with the terms of the instrument, an agreement of the parties, or other applicable law or rule.

(4) The party to whom presentment is made may treat presentment as occurring on the next business day after the day of presentment if the party to whom presentment is made has established a cut-off hour not earlier than 2 P.M. for the receipt and processing of instruments presented for payment or acceptance and presentment is made after the cut-off hour.

§ 3–502. Dishonor.

(a) Dishonor of a note is governed by the following rules:

(1) If the note is payable on demand, the note is dishonored if presentment is duly made to the maker and the note is not paid on the day of presentment.

(2) If the note is not payable on demand and is payable at or through a bank or the terms of the note require presentment, the note is dishonored if presentment is duly made and the note is not paid on the day it becomes payable or the day of presentment, whichever is later.

(3) If the note is not payable on demand and paragraph (2) does not apply, the note is dishonored if it is not paid on the day it becomes payable.

(b) Dishonor of an unaccepted draft other than a documentary draft is governed by the following rules:

(1) If a check is duly presented for payment to the payor bank otherwise than for immediate payment over the

counter, the check is dishonored if the payor bank makes timely return of the check or sends timely notice of dishonor or nonpayment under Section 4–301 or 4–302, or becomes accountable for the amount of the check under Section 4–302.

(2) If a draft is payable on demand and paragraph (1) does not apply, the draft is dishonored if presentment for payment is duly made to the drawee and the draft is not paid on the day of presentment.

(3) If a draft is payable on a date stated in the draft, the draft is dishonored if (i) presentment for payment is duly made to the drawee and payment is not made on the day the draft becomes payable or the day of presentment, whichever is later, or (ii) presentment for acceptance is duly made before the day the draft becomes payable and the draft is not accepted on the day of presentment.

(4) If a draft is payable on elapse of a period of time after sight or acceptance, the draft is dishonored if presentment for acceptance is duly made and the draft is not accepted on the day of presentment.

(c) Dishonor of an unaccepted documentary draft occurs according to the rules stated in subsection (b)(2), (3), and (4), except that payment or acceptance may be delayed without dishonor until no later than the close of the third business day of the drawee following the day on which payment or acceptance is required by those paragraphs.

(d) Dishonor of an accepted draft is governed by the following rules:

(1) If the draft is payable on demand, the draft is dishonored if presentment for payment is duly made to the acceptor and the draft is not paid on the day of presentment.

(2) If the draft is not payable on demand, the draft is dishonored if presentment for payment is duly made to the acceptor and payment is not made on the day it becomes payable or the day of presentment, whichever is later.

(e) In any case in which presentment is otherwise required for dishonor under this section and presentment is excused under Section 3–504, dishonor occurs without presentment if the instrument is not duly accepted or paid.

(f) If a draft is dishonored because timely acceptance of the draft was not made and the person entitled to demand acceptance consents to a late acceptance, from the time of acceptance the draft is treated as never having been dishonored.

§ 3–503. Notice of Dishonor.

(a) The obligation of an indorser stated in Section 3–415 (a) and the obligation of a drawer stated in Section 3–414(d) may not be enforced unless (i) the indorser or drawer is given notice of dishonor of the instrument complying with this section or (ii) notice of dishonor is excused under Section 3–504(b).

(b) Notice of dishonor may be given by any person; may be given by any commercially reasonable means, including an oral, written, or electronic communication; and is sufficient if it reasonably identifies the instrument and indicates that the instrument has been dishonored or has not been paid or accepted. Return of an instrument given to a bank for collection is sufficient notice of dishonor.

(c) Subject to Section 3–504(c), with respect to an instrument taken for collection by a collecting bank, notice of dishonor must be given (i) by the bank before midnight of the next banking day following the banking day on which the bank receives notice of dishonor of the instrument, or (ii) by any other person within 30 days following the day on which the person receives notice of dishonor. With respect to any other instrument, notice of dishonor must be given within 30 days following the day on which dishonor occurs.

§ 3–504. Excused Presentment and Notice of Dishonor.

(a) Presentment for payment or acceptance of an instrument is excused if (i) the person entitled to present the instrument cannot with reasonable diligence make presentment, (ii) the maker or acceptor has repudiated an obligation to pay the instrument or is dead or in insolvency proceedings, (iii) by the terms of the instrument presentment is not necessary to enforce the obligation of indorsers or the drawer, (iv) the drawer or indorser whose obligation is being enforced has waived presentment or otherwise has no reason to expect or right to require that the instrument be paid or accepted, or (v) the drawer instructed the drawee not to pay or accept the draft or the drawee was not obligated to the drawer to pay the draft.

(b) Notice of dishonor is excused if (i) by the terms of the instrument notice of dishonor is not necessary to enforce the obligation of a party to pay the instrument, or (ii) the party whose obligation is being enforced waived notice of dishonor. A waiver of presentment is also a waiver of notice of dishonor.

(c) Delay in giving notice of dishonor is excused if the delay was caused by circumstances beyond the control of the person giving the notice and the person giving the notice exercised reasonable diligence after the cause of the delay ceased to operate.

§ 3–505. Evidence of Dishonor.

(a) The following are admissible as evidence and create a presumption of dishonor and of any notice of dishonor stated:

(1) a document regular in form as provided in subsection (b) which purports to be a protest;

(2) a purported stamp or writing of the drawee, payor bank, or presenting bank on or accompanying the instrument stating that acceptance or payment has been refused unless reasons for the refusal are stated and the reasons are not consistent with dishonor;

(3) a book or record of the drawee, payor bank, or collecting bank, kept in the usual course of business which shows dishonor, even if there is no evidence of who made the entry.

(b) A protest is a certificate of dishonor made by a United States consul or vice consul, or a notary public or other person authorized to administer oaths by the law of the place where dishonor occurs. It may be made upon information satisfactory to that person. The protest must identify the instrument and certify either that presentment has been made or, if not made, the reason why it was not made, and that the instrument has been dishonored by nonacceptance or nonpayment. The protest may also certify that notice of dishonor has been given to some or all parties.

PART 6   Discharge and Payment

§ 3–601.   Discharge and Effect of Discharge.

(a) The obligation of a party to pay the instrument is discharged as stated in this Article or by an act or agreement with the party which would discharge an obligation to pay money under a simple contract.

(b) Discharge of the obligation of a party is not effective against a person acquiring rights of a holder in due course of the instrument without notice of the discharge.

§ 3–602.   Payment.

(a) Subject to subsection (b), an instrument is paid to the extent payment is made (i) by or on behalf of a party obliged to pay the instrument, and (ii) to a person entitled to enforce the instrument. To the extent of the payment, the obligation of the party obliged to pay the instrument is discharged even though payment is made with knowledge of a claim to the instrument under Section 3–306 by another person.

(b) The obligation of a party to pay the instrument is not discharged under subsection (a) if:

(1) a claim to the instrument under Section 3–306 is enforceable against the party receiving payment and (i) payment is made with knowledge by the payor that payment is prohibited by injunction or similar process of a court of competent jurisdiction, or (ii) in the case of an instrument

other than a cashier's check, teller's check, or certified check, the party making payment accepted, from the person having a claim to the instrument, indemnity against loss resulting from refusal to pay the person entitled to enforce the instrument; or

(2) the person making payment knows that the instrument is a stolen instrument and pays a person it knows is in wrongful possession of the instrument.

§ 3–603.   Tender of Payment.

(a) If tender of payment of an obligation to pay an instrument is made to a person entitled to enforce the instrument, the effect of tender is governed by principles of law applicable to tender of payment under a simple contract.

(b) If tender of payment of an obligation to pay an instrument is made to a person entitled to enforce the instrument and the tender is refused, there is discharge, to the extent of the amount of the tender, of the obligation of an indorser or accommodation party having a right of recourse with respect to the obligation to which the tender relates.

(c) If tender of payment of an amount due on an instrument is made to a person entitled to enforce the instrument, the obligation of the obligor to pay interest after the due date on the amount tendered is discharged. If presentment is required with respect to an instrument and the obligor is able and ready to pay on the due date at every place of payment stated in the instrument, the obligor is deemed to have made tender of payment on the due date to the person entitled to enforce the instrument.

§ 3–604.   Discharge by Cancellation or Renunciation.

(a) A person entitled to enforce an instrument, with or without consideration, may discharge the obligation of a party to pay the instrument (i) by an intentional voluntary act, such as surrender of the instrument to the party, destruction, mutilation, or cancellation of the instrument, cancellation or striking out of the party's signature, or the addition of words to the instrument indicating discharge, or (ii) by agreeing not to sue or otherwise renouncing rights against the party by a signed writing.

(b) Cancellation or striking out of an indorsement pursuant to subsection (a) does not affect the status and rights of a party derived from the indorsement.

§ 3–605.   Discharge of Indorsers and Accommodation Parties.

(a) In this section, the term "indorser" includes a drawer having the obligation described in Section 3–414(d).

(b) Discharge, under Section 3–604, of the obligation of a party to pay an instrument does not discharge the obligation of an indorser or accommodation party having a right of recourse against the discharged party.

(c) If a person entitled to enforce an instrument agrees, with or without consideration, to an extension of the due date of the obligation of a party to pay the instrument, the extension discharges an indorser or accommodation party having a right of recourse against the party whose obligation is extended to the extent the indorser or accommodation party proves that the extension caused loss to the indorser or accommodation party with respect to the right of recourse.

(d) If a person entitled to enforce an instrument agrees, with or without consideration, to a material modification of the obligation of a party other than an extension of the due date, the modification discharges the obligation of an indorser or accommodation party having a right of recourse against the person whose obligation is modified to the extent the modification causes loss to the indorser or accommodation party with respect to the right of recourse. The loss suffered by the indorser or accommodation party as a result of the modification is equal to the amount of the right of recourse unless the person enforcing the instrument proves that no loss was caused by the modification or that the loss caused by the modification was an amount less than the amount of the right of recourse.

(e) If the obligation of a party to pay an instrument is secured by an interest in collateral and a person entitled to enforce the instrument impairs the value of the interest in collateral, the obligation of an indorser or accommodation party having a right of recourse against the obligor is discharged to the extent of the impairment. The value of an interest in collateral is impaired to the extent (i) the value of the interest is reduced to an amount less than the amount of the right of recourse of the party asserting discharge, or (ii) the reduction in value of the interest causes an increase in the amount by which the amount of the right of recourse exceeds the value of the interest. The burden of proving impairment is on the party asserting discharge.

(f) If the obligation of a party is secured by an interest in collateral not provided by an accommodation party and a person entitled to enforce the instrument impairs the value of the interest in collateral, the obligation of any party who is jointly and severally liable with respect to the secured obligation is discharged to the extent the impairment causes the party asserting discharge to pay more than that party would have been obliged to pay, taking into account rights of contribution, if impairment had not occurred. If the party asserting discharge is an accommodation party not entitled to discharge under subsection (e), the party is deemed to have a right to contribution based on joint and several liability rather than a right to reimbursement. The burden of proving impairment is on the party asserting discharge.

(g) Under subsection (e) or (f), impairing value of an interest in collateral includes (i) failure to obtain or maintain perfection or recordation of the interest in collateral, (ii) release of collateral without substitution of collateral of equal value, (iii) failure to perform a duty to preserve the value of collateral owed, under Article 9 or other law, to a debtor or surety or other person secondarily liable, or (iv) failure to comply with applicable law in disposing of collateral.

(h) An accommodation party is not discharged under subsection (c), (d), or (e) unless the person entitled to enforce the instrument knows of the accommodation or has notice under Section 3–419(c) that the instrument was signed for accommodation.

(i) A party is not discharged under this section if (i) the party asserting discharge consents to the event or conduct that is the basis of the discharge, or (ii) the instrument or a separate agreement of the party provides for waiver of discharge under this section either specifically or by general language indicating that parties waive defenses based on suretyship or impairment of collateral.

ADDENDUM TO REVISED ARTICLE III

Notes to Legislative Counsel

1. If revised Article 3 is adopted in your state, the reference in Section 2–511 to Section 3–802 should be changed to Section 3–310.

2. If revised Article 3 is adopted in your state and the Uniform Fiduciaries Act is also in effect in your state, you may want to consider amending Uniform Fiduciaries Act § 9 to conform to Section 3–307(b)(2)(iii) and (4)(iii). See Official Comment 3 to Section 3–307.

A

Absolute privilege A witness testifying in a court or legislature may never be sued for defamation.

Acceptance Retention of the collateral by a secured party as full or partial satisfaction of a debt.

Accepts To sign a draft.

Accession Occurs when one person uses labor, materials, or both to add value to personal property belonging to another person.

Accommodated party Someone who receives a benefit from an accommodation party.

Accommodation party Someone other than an issuer, acceptor, or indorser, who adds her signature to an instrument for the purpose of being liable on it.

Accord and satisfaction A completed agreement to settle a debt for less than the sum claimed.

Accredited investors Institutions (such as banks and insurance companies) or wealthy individuals. To qualify, individuals must have a net worth (not counting their home) of more than $1 million or an annual income of more than $200,000.

Act Any action that a party was not legally required to take in the first place.

Activist investor A shareholder with a large block of stock whose goal is to influence management decisions and strategic direction.

Additional terms Terms that raise issues not covered in the offer.

Adhesion contracts Standard form contracts prepared by one party and presented to the other on a "take it or leave it" basis.

Adjudicate To hold a formal hearing about an issue and then decide it.

Administrative law judge An agency employee who acts as an impartial decision maker.

Adoption When a corporation accepts legal responsibility for a contract.

Affirm To allow the decision to stand.

Affirmed Permitted to stand.

After-acquired property Items that the debtor obtains after the parties have made their security agreement.

Agent In an agency relationship, the person who is acting on behalf of a principal.

Agreement on Trade Related Aspects of Intellectual Property (TRIPs) A treaty on intellectual property.

Alternative dispute resolution Any other formal or informal process used to settle disputes without resorting to a trial.

Ambiguity When a provision in a contract is unclear by accident.

Annual report A document that the SEC requires public companies to provide to their shareholders each year.

Annuities Provide payment to a beneficiary during his lifetime.

Antitakeover devices Defensive measures to protect against a hostile takeover.

Appeals courts Higher courts that review the trial record to see if the court made errors of law.

Appellant The party filing the appeal.

Appellee The party opposing the appeal.

Approved intermediary A broker or website that is registered with the SEC.

Arbitration A binding process of resolving legal disputes by submitting them to a neutral third party.

Arson The malicious use of fire or explosives to damage or destroy real estate or personal property.

Artisan's lien A security interest in personal property.

Assault An act that makes a person reasonably fear an imminent battery.

Assignment Transferring contract *rights*.

Assignment of rights A transfer of benefits under a contract to another person.

Attachment A three-step process that creates an enforceable security interest.

Authorized and issued Stock has been authorized and sold; another word for it is *outstanding*.

Authorized and unissued Stock that has been authorized, but not yet sold.

Automatic stay Prohibits creditors from collecting debts that the bankrupt incurred before the petition was filed.

B

BACT Best available control technology.

Bailee The one with temporary possession of another's goods.

Bailment The rightful possession of goods by one who is not the owner, usually by mutual agreement between the bailor and bailee

Bailor The one who owns goods legally held by another.

Bait-and-switch A practice whereby sellers advertise products that are not generally available but are being used to draw interested parties in so that they will buy other products.

Bankruptcy estate The new legal entity created when a bankruptcy petition is filed. The debtor's existing assets pass into the estate.

Bargained for When something is sought by the promisor and given by the promise in exchange for their promises.

Battery An intentional touching of another person in a way that is harmful or offensive.

Bearer paper A note is bearer paper if it is made out to "bearer" or it is not made out to any specific person. It can be redeemed by any holder in due course.

Behavioral marketing, or behavioral targeting The practice of aiming certain advertisements at consumers based on their online behavior.

Bench trial There is no jury; the judge reaches a verdict.

Best efforts underwriting The underwriter does not buy the stock from the issuer but instead acts as the issuer's agent in selling the securities.

Beyond a reasonable doubt The very high burden of proof in a criminal trial, demanding much more certainty than required in a civil trial.

Bilateral contract A promise made in exchange for another promise.

Bill A proposed statute, submitted to Congress or a state legislature.

Binder A short document acknowledging receipt of an application and premium for an insurance policy.

Blue sky laws State securities statutes.

Bona fide occupational qualification (BFOQ) An employer is permitted to establish discriminatory job requirements if they are essential to the position in question.

Breach of the peace Any action that disturbs public tranquility and order.

Briefs Written arguments on the case.

But-for causation The retaliatory action would not have occurred if it were not for the defendants's discriminatory intent.

Buyer in ordinary course of business (BIOC) Someone who buys goods in good faith from a seller who routinely deals in such goods.

Buyer in the ordinary course of business (BIOC) One who acts in good faith, without knowing that the sale violates the owner's rights.

Bylaws A document that specifies the organizational rules of a corporation or other organization, such as the date of the annual meeting and the required number of directors.

C

Cap and Trade A market-based system for reducing emissions.

Cashier's check A check drawn on the bank itself. It is a promise that the bank will pay out of its own funds.

Certificate of deposit A note that is made by a bank (also known as a CD).

Certified check A check that the issuer's bank has signed, indicating its acceptance of the check.

Challenges for cause A claim that a juror has demonstrated probable bias.

Charging order A court order granting a third party the right to receive a share of partnership profits.

Check The most common form of a draft, it is an order telling a bank to pay money.

Check cards Another name for a debit card.

Check kiting Moving funds between bank accounts to take advantage of the float.

Choice of forum Determine the state in which any litigation would take place.

Choice of law provisions Determine which state's laws will be used to interpret the contract.

Civil law Civil law regulates the rights and duties between parties.

Claim in recoupment The issuer subtracts (i.e., "sets off") any other claims he has against the initial payee from the amount he owes on the instrument.

Class action One plaintiff represents the entire group of plaintiffs, including those who are unaware of the lawsuit or even unaware they were harmed.

Close corporation A corporation with a small number of shareholders whose stock is not publicly traded and whose shareholders play an active role in management—it is entitled to special treatment under state law.

Codicil An amendment to a will.

Collective bargaining agreement (CBA) A contract between a union and management.

Comment letter A letter from the SEC to an issuer with a list of changes that must be made to the registration statement.

Commerce Clause The part of Article I, Section 8, that gives Congress the power to regulate commerce with foreign nations and among states.

Commercial impracticability The UCC may excuse contract performance when an unforeseen, external event disrupts the contract relationship.

Commercial speech Communication, such as advertisements, that has the dominant theme of proposing a business transaction.

Common carrier A company that transports goods and makes its services regularly available to the general public.

Common law Judge-made law.

Communications Decency Act of 1996 (CDA) Provides ISPs immunity from liability when information was provided by an end user.

Compensatory damages Money intended to restore a plaintiff to the position he was in before the injury.

Complaint A short, plain statement of the facts alleged and the legal claims made.

Compliance program A plan to prevent and detect improper conduct at all levels of the company.

Concerted action Tactics taken by union members to gain bargaining advantage.

Concurrent estates Two or more people owning property at the same time.

Condition An event that must occur before a party becomes obligated under a contract.

Conditional Promises that a party agrees to perform only if the other side has first done what it promised.

Conditional promises Promises that a party agrees to perform only if the other side has first done what it promised.

Conscious parallelism When competitors who do not have an explicit agreement nonetheless all make the same competitive decisions.

Consequential damages Contract damages resulting as an indirect consequence of the breach.

Consideration The inducement, price, or promise that causes a person to enter into a contract and forms the basis for the parties' exchange.

Consumer credit contract A contract in which a consumer borrows money from a lender to purchase goods and services from a seller who is affiliated with the lender.

Consumer protection statute Laws protecting consumers from fraud.

Consumer report Any communication about a consumer's creditworthiness, character, general reputation, or lifestyle that is considered as a factor in establishing credit.

Consumer reporting agencies Businesses that supply consumer reports to third parties.

Contract A legally enforceable agreement.

Contract carrier A company that transports goods for particular customers.

Control security Stock held by any shareholder who owns more than 10 percent of a class of stock or by any officer or director of the company.

Conversion Taking or using someone's personal property without consent.

Conversion (1) Someone has stolen an instrument or (2) a bank has paid a check that has a forged indorsement.

Corporate social responsibility An organization's obligation to contribute positively to the world around it.

Corporation by estoppel If a party enters into a contract *believing* in good faith that the corporation exists, he cannot later take advantage of the fact that it does not.

Counterclaim A second lawsuit by the defendant against the plaintiff.

Counteroffer A different proposal made in response to an original offer.

Covenant A promise in a contract.

Cover To make a good faith purchase of goods similar to those in the contract.

Cramdown When a court approves a plan of reorganization over the opposition of some creditors.

Criminal law Criminal law prohibits certain behavior for the benefit of society.

Criminal law Prohibits and punishes conduct that threatens public safety and welfare.

Criminal procedure The process by which criminals are investigated, accused, tried, and sentenced.

Cross-elasticity of demand How high can your prices rise before buyers switch to a different product?

Cross-examine To ask questions of an opposing witness.

Customary international law International rules that have become binding through a pattern of consistent, longstanding behavior.

D

De facto A Latin phrase meaning, "in fact".

De facto **corporation** The promoter has made a good-faith effort to incorporate and has actually used the corporation to conduct business.

De jure A Latin phrase meaning "by law".

De jure **corporation** A promoter has substantially complied with the requirements for incorporation but has made some minor error.

Debtor in possession The debtor acts as trustee in a Chapter 11 bankruptcy.

Default judgment A decision that the plaintiff wins without trial because the defendant failed to answer in time.

Default rules Rules that govern a partnership unless the partners agree otherwise.

Defendant The party being sued.

Deficiency Having insufficient funds to pay off a debt.

Delegation Transferring contract *duties*.

Delegation of duties A transfer of obligations under a contract.

Deontological From the Greek word for *obligation*. The duty to do the right thing, regardless of the result.

Deponent The person being questioned in a deposition.

Difference principle Rawls's suggestion that society should reward behavior that provides the most benefit to the community as a whole.

Directed verdict A ruling that the plaintiff has entirely failed to prove some aspect of her case.

Disability insurance Replaces the insured's income if he becomes unable to work because of illness or injury.

Discharge A party is discharged when she has no more duties under the contract.

Discharged The debtor no longer has an obligation to pay a debt.

Disclaimer A statement that a particular warranty does not apply.

Disclosure statement Provides creditors and shareholders with enough information to make an informed judgment about a proposed plan of reorganization.

Dishonor An obligor refuses to pay an instrument that is due.

Dissenters' rights If a private corporation decides to undertake a fundamental change, the company must buy back at fair value the stock of any shareholders who object.

Dissociation When a partner leaves a partnership.

Diversity jurisdiction Applies when (1) the plaintiff and defendant are citizens of different states and (2) the amount in dispute exceeds $75,000.

Domestic corporation A corporation operating in the state in which it was incorporated.

Donee A person who receives a gift of property.

Donor A person who gives property away.

Double jeopardy A criminal defendant may be prosecuted only once for a particular criminal offense.

Draft An instrument ordering someone else to pay money.

Drawee The bank on which a check is drawn.

Drawer The issuer of a draft.

Due diligence An investigation of the registration statement by someone who signs it.

Due Process Requires fundamental fairness at all stages of the case.

Duress An improper threat made to force another party to enter into a contract.

Duty of care The requirement that a manager act with care and in the best interests of the corporation.

Duty of loyalty The obligation of a manager to act without a conflict of interest.

E

Easement The right to enter land belonging to another and make limited use of it.

Economic strike One intended to gain wages or benefits.

Embezzlement The fraudulent conversion of property already in the defendant's possession.

Emerging growth company (EGC) An issuer with annual gross revenues of less than $1 billion.

Eminent domain The power of the government to take private property for public use.

Engagement letter A written contract by which a client hires an accountant.

Equal dignities rule If an agent is empowered to enter into a contract that must be in writing, then the appointment of the agent must also be written.

Equal Protection Clause A clause in the Fourteenth Amendment that generally requires the government to treat people equally.

Error of law Because of this, the appeals court may require a new trial.

Escalator clause A lease clause allowing the landlord to raise the rent for specified reasons.

Ethics How people should behave.

Ethics decision Any choice about how a person should behave that is based on a sense of right and wrong.

Eviction An act that forces a tenant to abandon the property. The basement often flooded, and when it was dry, rats and opossums lived in it.

Exclusionary rule Evidence obtained illegally may not be used at trial.

Exclusive dealing contract A contract in which a distributor or retailer agrees with a supplier not to carry the products of any other supplier.

Exculpatory clause A contract provision that attempts to release one party from liability in the event the other is injured.

Executed contract An agreement in which all parties have fulfilled their obligations.

Executory contract An agreement in which one or more parties has not yet fulfilled its obligations.

Expectation damages The money required to put one party in the position she would have been in had the other side performed the contract.

Express contract An agreement with all the important terms explicitly stated.

Express warranty One that the seller creates with his words or actions.

Externality When people do not bear the full cost of their decisions.

Extraterritoriality The power of one country's laws to reach activities outside of its borders.

F

Fair use doctrine Permits limited use of copyrighted material without permission of the author for purposes such as criticism, comment, news reporting, scholarship, or research.

False imprisonment The intentional restraint of another person without reasonable cause and without consent.

Federal question A case in which the claim is based on the United States Constitution, a federal statute, or a federal treaty.

Federal Sentencing Guidelines The detailed rules that judges must follow when sentencing defendants convicted of crimes in federal court.

Fee simple absolute Full ownership privileges in a property.

Felony A serious crime, for which a defendant can be sentenced to one year or more in prison.

Fiduciary relationship One party has an obligation (1) to act in a trustworthy fashion for the benefit of the other person and (2) to put that person's interests first.

Financing statement A statement that gives the names of all parties, describes the collateral, and outlines the security interest.

Finding statutes Laws that govern found property. Also known as estray statutes.

Firm commitment underwriting The underwriter buys stock from the issuer and sells it to the public.

Flow-through tax entity An organization that does not pay income tax on its profits but passes them through to its owners who pay the tax at their individual rates.

Forbearance Refraining from doing something that one has a legal right to do.

Force majeure event A disruptive, unexpected occurrence for which neither party is to blame that prevents one or both parties from complying with a contract.

Forced share or statutory share The percentage of a decedent's estate that a spouse is entitled to claim, regardless of the will's content.

Foreign corporation A corporation operating in a state in which it was not incorporated.

Foreign enforcement Means that the court system of a country will assist in enforcing or collecting on the verdict awarded by a foreign court.

Foreign recognition Means that a foreign judgment has legal validity in another country.

Foreign Sovereign Immunities Act A U.S. statute that provides that American courts generally cannot entertain suits against foreign governments.

Franchise Disclosure Document A disclosure document that a franchisor must deliver to a potential purchaser.

Fraud Deception for the purpose of obtaining money or property. Injuring another person by deliberate deception.

Fraudulent transfer A transfer is fraudulent if it is made within the year before a petition is filed and its purpose is to hinder, delay, or defraud creditors.

Fresh start After the termination of a bankruptcy case, creditors cannot make a claim against the debtor for money owed before the initial bankruptcy petition was filed.

Fundamental rights Rights so basic that any governmental interference with them is suspect and likely to be unconstitutional.

G

GAAP "Generally accepted accounting principles," these are the rules for preparing financial statements.

GAAS "Generally accepted auditing standards," these are the rules for conducting audits.

Gap period The period between the time that a creditor files an involuntary petition and the court issues the order for relief.

Gap-filler provisions UCC rules for supplying missing terms.

General Agreement on Trade in Services, or GATS A treaty on transnational services.

General partner One of the owners of a general partnership.

Geographic market Areas where the same purchase can be made.

Gharar The Islamic prohibition on risk and deception.

Gift A voluntary transfer of property from one person to another, without consideration.

Gift *Causa mortis* A gift made in contemplation of approaching death.

Go effective The SEC authorizes a company to begin the public sale of its stock.

Going dark When a company deregisters under the 1934 Act.

Good faith An honest effort to meet both the spirit and letter of the contract. The UCC requires that contracting parties perform and enforce their deals honestly.

Goods Are things that are movable, other than money and investment securities.

Grand jury A group of ordinary citizens who decides whether there is probable cause the defendant committed the crime with which she is charged.

Gratuitous agent Someone not paid for performing duties.

Gratuitous assignment One made as a gift, for no consideration.

Guilty A judge or jury's finding that a defendant has committed a crime.

H

Hacking Gaining unauthorized access to a computer system.

Harmless error A mistake by the trial judge that was too minor to affect the outcome.

Holder For order paper, anyone in possession of the instrument if it is payable to or indorsed to her. For bearer paper, anyone in possession.

Holder in due course Someone who has given value for an instrument, in good faith, without notice of outstanding claims or other defenses.

Holographic will A will that is handwritten and signed by the testator, but not witnessed.

Horizontal agreement An agreement among competitors.

Hostile takeovers An attempt by an outside to acquire a company in the face of opposition from the target corporation's board of directors.

I

IFRS "International financial reporting standards," a set of international standards being proposed for U.S. companies to follow.

Ijtihad The process of Islamic legal and religious reasoning.

Incidental beneficiary Someone who might have benefited from a contract between two others but has no right to enforce that agreement.

Incidental damages Relatively minor costs that the injured party suffers when responding to the breach.

Incorporator The person who signs the charter and files it with the secretary of state.

Incoterms A series of three-letter codes used in international contracts for the sale of goods.

Indemnification Requires a company to pay the legal fees of directors who are sued for actions taken on behalf of the company.

Independent directors Members of the board of directors who are not employees of the company. Also known as outside directors.

Indictment The government's formal charge that the defendant has committed a crime and must stand trial.

Indorsement The signature of a payee.

Indorser Anyone, other than an issuer or acceptor, who signs an instrument.

Injunction A court order that requires someone to do something or refrain from doing something.

Inside directors Members of the board of directors who are also employees of the corporation.

Insiders Family members of an individual debtor, officers and directors of a corporation, or partners of a partnership.

Installment contract Agreement in which performance is to be made in a series of separate payments or deliveries.

Integrated contract A writing that the parties intend as the final, complete expression of their agreement.

Intended beneficiary Someone who may enforce a contract made between two other parties.

Intentional infliction of emotional distress An intentional tort in which the harm results from extreme and outrageous conduct that causes serious emotional harm.

Intentional torts Harm caused by a deliberate action.

Inter vivos gift A gift made during the donor's life, with no fear of impending death.

Interest A legal right in something.

Intermediary agent Someone who hires subagents for the principal.

International Court of Arbitration (ICA) A forum for international dispute resolution, run by the ICC.

International Court of Justice The judicial branch of the United Nations.

Internet service providers (ISPs) Companies that connect users to the Internet.

Inventory Goods that a seller is holding for sale or lease in the ordinary course of its business.

Investigative reports Discuss character, reputation, or lifestyle. They become obsolete in three months.

Invitee A person who has a right to enter another's property because it is a public place or a business open to the public.

Involuntary petition Filed by creditors to initiate a bankruptcy case.

Involuntary, bailment A bailment that occurs without an agreement between the bailor and bailee.

Issuer The maker of a promissory note or the drawer of a draft.

Issuer A company that sells its own stock.

J

Joint and several All members of a group are liable. They can be sued as a group, or any of them can be sued individually for the full amount owing. But the plaintiff may not recover more than 100 percent of her damages.

Joint and several liability The partnership and the partners are all individually liable for the full amount of the debt, but the creditor cannot collect more than the total amount he is owed.

Joint tenancy Two or more people holding equal interest in a property, with the right of survivorship.

Joint venture A partnership for a limited purpose.

Jointly and severally liable All members of a group are liable. They can be sued as a group, or any one of them can be sued individually for the full amount owed. But the plaintiff cannot recover more than the total she is owed.

Judgment *non obstante veredicto* A judgment notwithstanding the jury's verdict.

Judgment rate The interest rate that courts use on court-ordered judgments.

Judicial activism A court's willingness to decide issues on constitutional grounds.

Judicial restraint A court's attitude that it should leave lawmaking to legislators.

Jurisdiction A court's power to hear a case.

Jurisprudence The philosophy of law.

Jus cogens When rule of customary international law becomes a fundamental legal principle across all nations, it cannot be changed by custom or practice.

K

Kantian Evasion or a palter A truthful statement that is nonetheless misleading.

Key person life insurance Companies buy insurance on their officers as compensation were they to die.

L

Landlord The owner of a freehold estate who allows another person temporarily to live on his property.

Larceny The trespassory taking of personal property with the intent to steal it.

Lease An agreement in which an owner gives a tenant the right to use property.

Letter of intent A letter that summarizes negotiating progress.

Liability insurance Reimburses the insured for any liability she incurs by accidentally harming someone else.

Libel Written defamation.

Libel per se When written statements relate to criminal or sexual conduct, contagious diseases, or professional abilities, they are assumed to be harmful to the subject's reputation.

License The right to enter land belonging to another temporarily.

Licensee A person on another's land for her own purposes but with the owner's permission.

Lien A security interest created by law, rather than by agreement.

Life estate Ownership of property for the lifetime of a particular person.

Life insurance Provides for payments to a beneficiary upon the death of the insured.

Life Principles The rules by which you live your life.

Life prospects The opportunities one has at birth, based on one's natural attributes and initial place in society.

Limitation of remedy clause Contract clause allowing parties to limit or exclude applicable UCC remedies.

Liquidated damages clause A provision in the contract that declares in advance what one party will receive if the other side breaches.

Liquidated debt A debt in which there is no dispute about the amount owed.

Litigation The process of filing claims in court and ultimately going to trial.

Lockout Management prohibits workers from entering the premises.

Long-arm statute A statute that gives a court jurisdiction over someone who commits a tort, signs a contract, or conducts "regular business activities" in the state.

M

MACT Maximum achievable control technology.

Mailbox rule Acceptance is generally effective upon dispatch. Terminations are effective when received.

Majority voting Directors must resign if fewer than half of the shares vote for them.

Maker The issuer of a promissory note.

Managing partner A partner in charge of running a partnership.

Material Important to the insurer's decision to issue a policy or set a premium amount.

Material breach A violation of a contract that defeats an essential purpose of the agreement.

Mechanic's lien A security created when a worker improves real property.

Merchant Generally, someone who routinely deals in the particular goods involved.

Merchantable The goods are fit for the ordinary purpose for which they are used.

Minute book A book that contains a summary of a corporation's official actions.

Mirror image rule Requires that acceptance be on precisely the same terms as the offer.

Misdemeanor A less serious crime, often punishable by less than a year in a county jail.

Mitigate To keep damages as low as reasonable.

Modify To affirm the outcome but with changes.

Money laundering Using the proceeds of criminal acts either to promote crime or conceal the source of the money.

Moral relativism A belief that a decision may be right even if it is not in keeping with our own ethical standards.

Moral universalism A belief that some acts are always right or always wrong.

Mortgage A security interest in real property.

Mortgagee The party acquiring a security interest in property.

Mortgagor An owner who gives a security interest in property in order to obtain a loan.

Most favored nation WTO/GATT requires that favors offered to one country must be given to all member nations.

Motion A formal request to the court that it take some step or issue some order.

Motion for a protective order Request that the court limit discovery.

Motion to dismiss A request that the court terminate a case without permitting it to go further.

N

NAAQS National ambient air quality standards.

National Treatment The principle of nondiscrimination between foreigners and locals.

Negotiation An instrument has been transferred to the holder by someone other than the issuer.

NESHAPS National Emission Standards for Hazardous Air Pollutants.

Net neutrality The principle that all information flows on the Internet must receive equal treatment.

New York Convention Widely accepted treaty on the court enforcement of arbitral awards.

Nominal damages A token sum, such as one dollar, given to a plaintiff who demonstrates a breach but no serious injury.

Noncompetition agreement A contract in which one party agrees not to compete with another.

Nonconforming goods Merchandise that differs from that specified in the contract.

Nonphysical tort One that harms only reputation, feelings, or wallet.

Nonpoint source Pollutants that have no single source, such as water runoff from city streets.

North American Free Trade Agreement (NAFTA) A treaty that reduced trade barriers among Canada, the United States, and Mexico.

No-strike clause A clause in a CBA that prohibits the union from striking while the CBA is in force.

Notice to quit A landlord's notice terminating a tenancy.

Novation A three-way agreement in which the obligor transfers all rights and duties to a third party.

Novation A new contract.

O

Obligor The party obligated to do something.

Offer An act or statement that proposes definite terms and permits the other party to create a contract by accepting those terms.

Offeree The person to whom an offer is made.

Offeror The person who makes an offer.

Open Internet Order An FCC regulation prohibiting broadband ISPs from (1) blocking lawful content and services and (2) giving preferential treatment to certain Internet content or traffic.

Order for relief An official acknowledgment that a debtor is under the jurisdiction of the bankruptcy court.

Order paper An instrument that includes the words "pay to the order of" or their equivalent.

Output contract Contract in which the seller guarantees to sell all of its output to one buyer, and the buyer agrees to accept the entire quantity.

P

Partnership An unincorporated association of two or more co-owners who operate a business for profit.

Partnership at will A partnership with no fixed duration. Any of the partners may leave at any time, for any reason.

Partnership by estoppel Two parties incur the liability of a partnership without actually being partners.

Patent A grant by the government permitting the inventor exclusive use of an invention for a specified period.

Payable on demand The maker must pay whenever he is asked.

Payday loans A high-interest loan that is supposed to be paid off when the borrower receives her next paycheck.

Payee Someone who is owed money under the terms of an instrument.

Per capita Each heir receives the same amount.

Per se violation An automatic breach of antitrust laws.

Per stirpes Each branch of the family receives an equal share.

Peremptory challenges The right to excuse a juror for virtually any reason.

Perfect Tender Rule Under the UCC, tendered goods must be exactly as described in the contract.

Periodic tenancy A lease for a fixed period, automatically renewable unless terminated.

Personal jurisdiction A court's authority to bind the defendant to its decisions.

Personal property All tangible property other than real property.

Personal satisfaction contract Permit the promisee to make subjective evaluations of the promisor's performance.

Pierce the corporate veil A court holds shareholders personally liable for the debts of the corporation.

Piercing the company veil A court holds members of an LLC personally liable for the debts of the organization.

Plaintiff The party who is suing.

Plea bargain An agreement in which the defendant pleads guilty to a reduced charge, and the prosecution recommends to the judge a relatively lenient sentence.

Pleadings The documents that begin a lawsuit, consisting of the complaint, the answer, and sometimes a reply.

Pledge A secured transaction in which a debtor gives collateral to the secured party.

Plurality voting To be elected, a candidate only needs to receive more votes than his opponent, not a majority of the votes cast.

Point source Discharges from a single producer.

Preauthorized transfer An electronic fund transfer authorized in advance to recur at regular intervals.

Precedent The tendency to decide current cases based on previous rulings.

Precedent An earlier case that decided the issue.

Precedent Earlier decisions by the state appellate courts on similar or identical issues.

Preferences When a debtor unfairly pays creditors immediately before filing a bankruptcy petition.

Preferred stock The owners of preferred stock have preference on dividends and also, typically, in liquidation.

Preponderance of the evidence The plaintiff's burden of proof in a civil lawsuit.

Presentment A holder of an instrument demands payment from someone who is obligated to pay it.

Pretermitted child A child who is left nothing under the parent's will.

Prima facie From the Latin, meaning "from its first appearance," something that appears to be true upon a first look.

Principal In an agency relationship, the person for whom an agent is acting.

Private international law International rules and standards applying to cross-border commerce.

Private offering A sale of securities that involves a small number of investors or takes in a relatively modest amount of money.

Probable cause It is likely that evidence of crime will be found in the place to be searched.

Procedural due process The doctrine that ensures that before the government takes liberty or property, the affected person has a fair chance to oppose the action.

Procedural unconscionability One party uses its superior power to force a contract on the weaker party.

Product market Items that compete against each other for purchase.

Profit The right to enter land belonging to another and take something from it.

Promisee The contract party *to whom* a promise is made.

Promisor Makes the promise that a third party seeks to enforce.

Promissory estoppel A *possible* remedy for an injured plaintiff in a case with no valid contract, when the plaintiff can show a promise, reasonable reliance, and injustice.

Promissory note A written promise to pay money.

Proof of claim A form stating the name of an unsecured creditor and the amount of the claim against the debtor.

Proper purpose One that aids a shareholder in managing and protecting her investment.

Prospectus A document that provides potential investors with information about a security.

Protected categories Race, color, religion, sex, or national origin.

Proxy The person whom a shareholder appoints to vote for her at a meeting of the corporation. Also, the document a shareholder signs appointing this substitute voter.

Proxy advisory firms Companies that advise shareholders on how to vote in corporate elections.

Proxy statement A company provides information to shareholders to aid them in voting their stock.

Public Company Accounting Oversight Board The PCAOB regulates public accounting firms.

Public international law Rules and norms governing relationships among states and international organizations.

Punitive damages Damages that are intended to punish the defendant for conduct that is extreme and outrageous.

Purchase money security interest (PMSI) An interest taken by the person who sells the collateral or advances money so the debtor can buy it.

Purchaser representative Someone who has enough knowledge and experience in financial matters to evaluate the merits and risks of an investment.

Q

Qualified mortgage A mortgage that, according to the CFPB, complies with TILA.

Qualified privilege Employers who give references are liable only for false statements that they know to be false or that are primarily motivated by ill will.

Quantum meruit "As much as he deserves"—the damages awarded in a quasi-contract case.

Quasi-contract A *possible* remedy for an injured plaintiff in a case with no valid contract, when the plaintiff can show benefit to the defendant, reasonable expectation of payment, and unjust enrichment.

Quorum The percentage of stock that must be represented for a meeting to count. The percentage of voters who must be present for a meeting to count.

R

Racketeer Influenced and Corrupt Organizations Act (RICO) A powerful federal statute, originally aimed at organized crime, now used in many criminal prosecutions and civil lawsuits.

Racketeering acts Any of a long list of specified crimes, such as embezzlement, arson, mail fraud, wire fraud, and so forth.

Ratification Words or actions indicating an intention to be bound by a contract.

Reaffirm To promise to pay a debt even after it is discharged.

Reasonably Ordinary or usual under the circumstances.

Reciprocal promises Promises that are each enforceable independently.

Record date Everyone who owns stock on this date is entitled to vote at the shareholders meeting.

Redeem To pay the full value of a debt to get the collateral back.

Reformation A court may partially rewrite a contract to fix a mistake or cure an unenforceable provision.

Regional trade agreements (RTAs) Treaties that reduce trade restrictions and promote common policies among member nations.

Registration statement The document that an issuer files with the SEC to initiate a public offering of securities.

Reliance interest Puts the injured party in the position he would have been in had the parties never entered into a contract.

Remedy A court's compensation to the injured party.

Rent Compensation paid by a tenant to a landlord.

Reply An answer to a counterclaim.

Reporting companies Companies registered under the 1934 Act.

Representations and warranties Statements of fact about the past or present.

Requirements contract Obligates a buyer to obtain all of his needed goods from the seller.

Res ipsa loquitur The facts *imply* that the defendant's negligence caused the accident.

Resale price maintenance (RPM) A manufacturer sets minimum prices that retailers may charge.

Rescind To terminate a contract by mutual agreement.

Rescission To "undo" a contract and put the parties where they were before they made the agreement.

Respondeat superior An employer is liable for a physical tort committed by an employee acting within the scope of employment and a nonphysical tort of an employee acting with authority.

Restitution A court order that a guilty defendant reimburse the victim for the harm suffered.

Restitution interest Designed to return to the injured party a benefit he has conferred on the other party.

Restricted security Stock purchased in a private offering.

Restricted stock Securities purchased strictly for investment purposes.

Reverse and remand To nullify the lower decision and return the case for reconsideration or retrial.

Reversed Nullified.

Reversion The right of an owner (or her heirs) to property upon the death of a life tenant.

Revocable A trust that can be terminated or changed at any time.

Rider An amendment or addition to a contract.

Right to cure The UCC gives the seller the opportunity to fix the problem of nonconforming goods.

Road show As part of the sales process, company executives and investment bankers make presentations to potential investors.

Rule of reason violation An action that breaches antitrust laws only if it has an anticompetitive impact.

S

Safe harbor A set of requirements that, if met, provide *automatic* protection under the law.

Scienter Acting with the intent to deceive or with deliberate recklessness.

Scrivener's error A typo.

Secondary boycott A picket line established not at the employer's premises but at a different workplace.

Secondary offering Any public sale of securities by a company after the initial public offering.

Security Any transaction in which the buyer invests money in a common enterprise and expects to earn a profit predominantly from the efforts of others.

Security interests Rights in personal property that assure payment or the performance of some obligation.

Shari'a Islamic law.

Shark repellents Defensive measures to protect against a hostile takeover.

Sight draft Payable on demand.

Signature liability The liability of someone who signs an instrument.

Single recovery principle Requires a court to settle the matter once and for all by awarding a lump sum for past and future expenses.

Sit-down strike Members stop working but remain at their job posts, blocking replacement workers.

Slander Oral defamation.

Slander per se When oral statements relate to criminal or sexual conduct, contagious diseases, or professional abilities, they are assumed to be harmful to the subject's reputation.

Social enterprises These organizations pledge to behave in a socially responsible manner even as they pursue profits.

Sole discretion The *absolute* right to make any decision on an issue.

Sole proprietorship An unincorporated business owned by one person.

Sophisticated investors People who are able to assess the risk of an offering.

Sovereign The recognized political power, whom citizens obey.

Spam Unsolicited commercial email.

Special committee Independent board members form a committee to review a self-dealing transaction and determine if it is entirely fair to the corporation.

Specific performance A court order requiring the seller to perform as promised.

Stakeholders Anyone who is affected by the activities of a corporation, such as employees, customers, creditors, suppliers, shareholders, and the communities in which they operate.

Stare decisis The principle that legal conclusions must be reached after an analysis of past judgments.

Stationary source Any building or facility that emits pollution.

Statute of limitations A statutory time limit within which an injured party must file suit.

Statute A law created by a legislature.

Straight bankruptcy Also known as liquidation, this form of bankruptcy mandates that the bankrupt's assets be distributed to creditors, but the debtor has no obligation to share future earnings.

Strict liability A branch of tort law that imposes a much higher level of liability when harm results from ultrahazardous acts or defective products.

Strict performance Requires one party to perform its obligations precisely, with no deviation from the contract terms.

Subagents Someone appointed by an agent to perform the agent's duties.

Subject matter jurisdiction A court's authority to hear a particular type of case.

Subpoena An order to appear at a particular place and time. A subpoena *Duces tecum* requires a person to produce certain documents or things.

Substantially performce Occurs when one party fulfills enough of its contract obligations to warrant payment.

Substantive due process A form of due process that holds that certain rights are so fundamental that the government may not eliminate them.

Substantive unconscionability A contract with extremely one-sided and unfair terms.

Summary judgment A ruling by the court that no trial is necessary because there are no essential facts in dispute.

Summons The court's written notice that a lawsuit has been filed against the defendant.

Supervisor Anyone with the authority to make independent decisions on hiring, firing, disciplining, or promoting other workers.

Surplus A sum of money greater than the debt incurred.

T

Takings Clause A clause in the Fifth Amendment that ensures that when any governmental unit takes private property for public use, it must compensate the owner.

Tenancy at sufferance A tenancy that exists without the permission of the landlord, after the expiration of a true tenancy.

Tenancy at will A tenancy with no fixed duration, which may be terminated by either party at any time.

Tenancy for years A lease for a stated, fixed period.

Tenancy in common Two or more people holding equal interest in a property, but with no right of survivorship.

Tenant A person given temporary possession of the landlord's property.

Tender offer A public offer to buy a block of stock directly from shareholders.

Term partnership A partnership in which the partners agree in advance how long it will last.

Termination statement A document indicating that a secured party no longer claims a security interest in the collateral.

Testamentary trust A trust that goes into effect when a grantor dies.

The Supremacy Clause Makes the Constitution, and federal statutes and treaties, the supreme law of the land.

Tied product In a tying arrangement, the product that a buyer must purchase as the condition for being allowed to buy another product.

Time draft Payable in the future.

Time is of the essence clause Generally make contract dates strictly enforceable.

Tort A violation of a duty imposed by the civil law.

Tortious interference with a contract An intentional tort in which the defendant improperly induced a third party to breach a contract with the plaintiff.

Tortious interference with a prospective advantage Malicious interference with a developing economic relationship.

Tracing An auditor takes an item of original data and tracks it forward to ensure that it has been properly recorded throughout the bookkeeping process.

Tracking tool A computer program that tracks information about Internet users.

Trade acceptance A draft drawn by a seller of goods on the buyer and payable to the seller or some third party.

Trade secret A formula, device, process, method, or compilation of information that, when used in business, gives the owner an advantage over competitors.

Trademark Any combination of words and symbols that a business uses to identify its products or services and distinguish them from others.

Treasury stock Stock that a company has sold, but later bought back.

Treaty An agreement between two or more states that is governed by international law.

Trespass Intentionally entering land that belongs to someone else or remaining on the land after being asked to leave.

Trespasser A person on another's property without consent.

Trial courts Determine the facts of a particular dispute and apply to those facts the law given by earlier appellate court decisions.

Trust An entity that separates the legal and beneficial ownership of assets.

Tying arrangement An agreement to sell a product on the condition that a buyer also purchases another, usually less desirable, product.

Tying product In a tying arrangement, the product offered for sale on the condition that another product be purchased as well.

U

U.S. Trustee Oversees the administration of bankruptcy law in a region.

***Ultra vires* doctrine** A corporation cannot undertake any transaction unless its charter permits it.

Unconscionable A contract that is shockingly one-sided and fundamentally unfair.

Unilateral mistake Occurs when only one party enters a contract under a mistaken assumption.

Unliquidated A debt that is disputed because the parties disagree over its existence or amount.

User-generated content Any content created and made publicly available by end users.

Utter To pass on an instrument that one knows to be forged.

V

Vagueness When a provision in a contract is deliberately left unclear.

Value The holder has *already* done something in exchange for the instrument.

Veil of ignorance The rules for society that we would propose if we did not know how lucky we would be in life's lottery.

Vertical agreement An agreement among participants operating at different stages of the production process.

Veto The power of the president to reject legislation passed by Congress.

Void agreement A contract that neither party can enforce, because the bargain is illegal or one of the parties had no legal authority to make it.

Voidable contract An agreement that may be terminated by one of the parties.

Voidable title Limited rights in goods, inferior to those of the owner.

Voir dire The process of selecting a jury.

Voluntary petition Filed by a debtor to initiate a bankruptcy case.

Vouching An auditor chooses a transaction listed in a company's books and checks backwards for original data to support it.

W

Warrant Written permission from a neutral officer to conduct a search.

Warranty A contractual assurance that goods will meet certain standards.

Warranty liability The liability of someone who receives payment on an instrument.

Whistleblower Someone who discloses wrongdoing.

Will A legal document that disposes of the testator's property after death.

World Trade Organization (WTO) An international organization whose mandate is to lower trade barriers.

Writ of *Certiorari* A petition asking the Supreme Court to hear a case.

Written consent A signed document that takes the place of a shareholders' or directors' meeting.

Wrongful discharge An employer may not fire a worker for a reason that violates basic social rights, duties, or responsibilities.

V

Vagueness When a provision in a contract is neither clearly... left uncertain.

Value The holder has already done something in exchange for the instrument.

Veil of ignorance The rule: the society that we would propose if we did not know how lucky we so and for in life's lottery.

Vertical agreement An agreement among parties operating at different stages of the production process.

Veto The power of the president to reject legislation passed by Congress.

Void agreement A contract that neither party can enforce, because the bargain is illegal or one of the parties had no legal authority to make it.

Voidable contract An agreement that may be terminated by one of the parties.

Voidable title Limited rights in goods, inferior to those of the owner.

Voir dire The process of selecting a jury.

Voluntary petition Filed by a debtor to initiate a bankruptcy case.

Vouching An audit... a transaction listed in a company's books and checks backwards for original data to support it.

W

Warrant Written permission from a neutral officer to conduct a search.

Warranty A contractual assurance that goods will meet certain standards.

Warranty liability The liability of someone who... reuses or... on an instrument.

Whistleblower Someone who discloses wrongdoing.

Will A legal document that disposes of the testator's property after death.

World Trade Organization (WTO) An international organization whose mandate is to lower trade barriers.

Writ of Certiorari A petition asking the Supreme Court to hear a case.

Written contract A signed document that reflects the place of a manifestation of... assent, meaning...

Wrongful discharge An employer may not fire a worker... for a reason... violates... public policy... rights... or recognized...

TABLE OF CASES